OPERATING SYSTEMS DESIGN AND IMPLEMENTATION

Third Edition

OPERATING SYSTEMS DESIGN AND IMPLEMENTATION

Third Edition

ANDREW S. TANENBAUM
Vrije Universiteit
Amsterdam, The Netherlands

ALBERT S. WOODHULL
Amherst, Massachusetts

PEARSON
Prentice
Hall

Upper Saddle River, New Jersey 07458

Library of Congress Cataloging in Publication Data
Tanenbaum, Andrew S.
    Operating Systems: Design and Implementation / Andrew S. Tanenbaum, Albert S. Woodhull. -- 3rd ed.
    ISBN: 0-13-142938-8
    1. Operating systems (Computers) I. Woodhull, Albert S. II. Title

QA76.76.O63T36 2006
005.4'3--dc22

Vice President and Editorial Director, ECS: *Marcia J. Horton*
Executive Editor: *Tracy Dunkelberger*
Editorial Assistant: *Christianna Lee*
Executive Managing Editor: *Vince O'Brien*
Managing Editor: *Camille Trentacoste*
Director of Creative Services: *Paul Belfanti*
Art Director and Cover Manager: *Heather Scott*
Cover Design and Illutsration: *Tamara Newnam*
Managing Editor, AV Management and Production: *Patricia Burns*
Art Editor: *Gregory Dulles*
Manufacturing Manager, ESM: *Alexis Heydt-Long*
Manufacturing Buyer: *Lisa McDowell*
Executive Marketing Manager: *Robin O'Brien*
Marketing Assistant: *Barrie Reinhold*

 © 2006, 1997, 1987 by Pearson Education, Inc.
Pearson Prentice Hall
Pearson Education, Inc.
Upper Saddle River, NJ 07458

Pearson Prentice Hall® is a trademark of Pearson Education, Inc.

The authors and publisher of this book have used their best efforts in preparing this book. These efforts include the development, research, and testing of the theories and programs to determine their effectiveness. The authors and publisher make no warranty of any kind, expressed or implied, with regard to these programs or to the documentation contained in this book. The authors and publisher shall not be liable in any event for incidental or consequential damages in connection with, or arising out of, the furnishing, performance, or use of these programs.

10 9 8 7 6 5 4 3 2 1

ISBN 0-13-0-13-142938-8

Pearson Education Ltd., London
Pearson Education Australia Pty. Ltd., Sydney
Pearson Education Singapore, Pte. Ltd.
Pearson Education North Asia Ltd., Hong Kong
Pearson Education Canada, Inc., Toronto
Pearson Educación de Mexico, S.A. de C.V.
Pearson Education-Japan, Tokyo
Pearson Education Malaysia, Pte. Ltd.
Pearson Education, Inc., Upper Saddle River, New Jersey

To Suzanne, Barbara, Marvin, and the memory of Sweetie π and Bram
- AST

To Barbara and Gordon
- ASW

The MINIX 3 Mascot

Other operating systems have an animal mascot, so we felt MINIX 3 ought to have one too. We chose the raccoon because raccoons are small, cute, clever, agile, eat bugs, and are user-friendly—at least if you keep your garbage can well locked.

CONTENTS

2   PROCESSES   55

5   FILE SYSTEMS   481

APPENDICES

PREFACE

Most books on operating systems are strong on theory and weak on practice. This one aims to provide a better balance between the two. It covers all the fundamental principles in great detail, including processes, interprocess communication, semaphores, monitors, message passing, scheduling algorithms, input/output, deadlocks, device drivers, memory management, paging algorithms, file system design, security, and protection mechanisms. But it also discusses one particular system—MINIX 3—a UNIX-compatible operating system in detail, and even provides a source code listing for study. This arrangement allows the reader not only to learn the principles, but also to see how they are applied in a real operating system.

When the first edition of this book appeared in 1987, it caused something of a small revolution in the way operating systems courses were taught. Until then, most courses just covered theory. With the appearance of MINIX, many schools began to have laboratory courses in which students examined a real operating system to see how it worked inside. We consider this trend highly desirable and hope it continues.

It its first 10 years, MINIX underwent many changes. The original code was designed for a 256K 8088-based IBM PC with two diskette drives and no hard disk. It was also based on UNIX Version 7 As time went on, MINIX evolved in many ways: it supported 32-bit protected mode machines with large memories and hard disks. It also changed from being based on Version 7, to being based on the international POSIX standard (IEEE 1003.1 and ISO 9945-1). Finally, many new features were added, perhaps too many in our view, but too few in the view of some other people, which led to the creation of Linux. In addition, MINIX was ported to many other platforms, including the Macintosh, Amiga, Atari, and SPARC. A second edition of the book, covering this system, was published in 1997 and was widely used at universities.

The popularity of MINIX has continued, as can be observed by examining the number of hits for MINIX found by Google.

This third edition of the book has many changes throughout. Nearly all of the material on principles has been revised, and considerable new material has been added. However, the main change is the discussion of the new version of the system, called MINIX 3. and the inclusion of the new code in this book. Although loosely based on MINIX 2, MINIX 3 is fundamentally different in many key ways.

The design of MINIX 3 was inspired by the observation that operating systems are becoming bloated, slow, and unreliable. They crash far more often than other electronic devices such as televisions, cell phones, and DVD players and have so many features and options that practically nobody can understand them fully or manage them well. And of course, computer viruses, worms, spyware, spam, and other forms of malware have become epidemic.

To a large extent, many of these problems are caused by a fundamental design flaw in current operating systems: their lack of modularity. The entire operatng system is typically millions of lines of C/C++ code compiled into a single massive executable program run in kernel mode. A bug in any one of those millions of lines of code can cause the system to malfunction. Getting all this code correct is impossible, especially when about 70% consists of device drivers, written by third parties, and outside the purview of the people maintaining the operating system.

With MINIX 3, we demonstrate that this monolithic design is not the only possibility. The MINIX 3 kernel is only about 4000 lines of executable code, not the millions found in Windows, Linux, Mac OS X, or FreeBSD. The rest of the system, including all the device drivers (except the clock driver), is a collection of small, modular, user-mode processes, each of which is tightly restricted in what it can do and with which other processes it may communicate.

While MINIX 3 is a work in progress, we believe that this model of building an operating system as a collection of highly-encapsulated user-mode processes holds promise for building more reliable systems in the future. MINIX 3 is especially focused on smaller PCs (such as those commonly found in Third-World countries and on embedded systems, which are always resource constrained). In any event, this design makes it much easier for students to learn how an operating system works than attempting to study a huge monolithic system.

The CD-ROM that is included in this book is a live CD. You can put it in your CD-ROM drive, reboot the computer, and MINIX 3 will give a login prompt within a few seconds. You can log in as *root* and give the system a try without first having to install it on your hard disk. Of course, it can also be installed on the hard disk. Detailed installation instructions are given in Appendix A.

As suggested above, MINIX 3 is rapidly evolving, with new versions being issued frequently. To download the current CD-ROM image file for burning, please go to the official Website: *www.minix3.org*. This site also contains a large amount of new software, documentation, and news about MINIX 3 development. For discussions about MINIX 3, or to ask questions, there is a USENET news-group: *comp.os.minix*. People without newsreaders can follow discussions on the Web at *http://groups.google.com/group/comp.os.minix*.

As an alternative to installing MINIX 3 on your hard disk, it is possible to run it on any one of several PC simulators now available. Some of these are listed on the main page of the Website.

Instructors who are using the book as the text for a university course can get the problem solutions from their local Prentice Hall representative. The book has its own Website. It can be found by going to *www.prenhall.com/tanenbaum* and selecting this title.

We have been extremely fortunate in having the help of many people during the course of this project. First and foremost, Ben Gras and Jorrit Herder have done most of the programming of the new version. They did a great job under tight time constraints, including responding to e-mail well after midnight on many occasions. They also read the manuscript and made many useful comments. Our deepest appreciation to both of them.

Kees Bot also helped greatly with previous versions, giving us a good base to work with. Kees wrote large chunks of code for versions up to 2.0.4, repaired bugs, and answered numerous questions. Philip Homburg wrote most of the net-working code as well as helping out in numerous other useful ways, especially providing detailed feedback on the manuscript.

People too numerous to list contributed code to the very early versions, help-ing to get MINIX off the ground in the first place. There were so many of them and their contributions have been so varied that we cannot even begin to list them all here, so the best we can do is a generic thank you to all of them.

Several people read parts of the manuscript and made suggestions. We would like to give our special thanks to Gojko Babic, Michael Crowley, Joseph M. Kizza, Sam Kohn Alexander Manov, and Du Zhang for their help.

Finally, we would like to thank our families. Suzanne has been through this 16 times now. Barbara has been through it 15 times now. Marvin has been through it 14 times now. It's kind of getting to be routine, but the love and sup-port is still much appreciated. (AST)

Al's Barbara has been through this twice now. Her support, patience, and good humor were essential. Gordon has been a patient listener. It is still a delight to have a son who understands and cares about the things that fascinate me. Finally, step-grandson Zain's first birthday coincides with the release of MINIX 3. Some day he will appreciate this. (ASW)

Andrew S. Tanenbaum
Albert S. Woodhull

1

INTRODUCTION

Without its software, a computer is basically a useless lump of metal. With its software, a computer can store, process, and retrieve information; play music and videos; send e-mail, search the Internet; and engage in many other valuable activities to earn its keep. Computer software can be divided roughly into two kinds: system programs, which manage the operation of the computer itself, and application programs, which perform the actual work the user wants. The most fundamental system program is the **operating system**, whose job is to control all the computer's resources and provide a base upon which the application programs can be written. Operating systems are the topic of this book. In particular, an operating system called MINIX 3 is used as a model, to illustrate design principles and the realities of implementing a design.

A modern computer system consists of one or more processors, some main memory, disks, printers, a keyboard, a display, network interfaces, and other input/output devices. All in all, a complex system. Writing programs that keep track of all these components and use them correctly, let alone optimally, is an extremely difficult job. If every programmer had to be concerned with how disk drives work, and with all the dozens of things that could go wrong when reading a disk block, it is unlikely that many programs could be written at all.

Many years ago it became abundantly clear that some way had to be found to shield programmers from the complexity of the hardware. The way that has evolved gradually is to put a layer of software on top of the bare hardware, to manage all parts of the system, and present the user with an interface or **virtual**

1

machine that is easier to understand and program. This layer of software is the operating system.

The placement of the operating system is shown in Fig. 1-1. At the bottom is the hardware, which, in many cases, is itself composed of two or more levels (or layers). The lowest level contains physical devices, consisting of integrated circuit chips, wires, power supplies, cathode ray tubes, and similar physical devices. How these are constructed and how they work is the province of the electrical engineer.

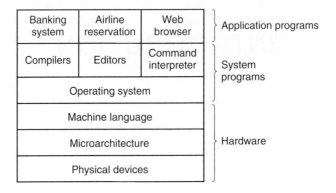

Figure 1-1. A computer system consists of hardware, system programs, and application programs.

Next comes the **microarchitecture level**, in which the physical devices are grouped together to form functional units. Typically this level contains some registers internal to the CPU (Central Processing Unit) and a data path containing an arithmetic logic unit. In each clock cycle, one or two operands are fetched from the registers and combined in the arithmetic logic unit (for example, by addition or Boolean AND). The result is stored in one or more registers. On some machines, the operation of the data path is controlled by software, called the **microprogram**. On other machines, it is controlled directly by hardware circuits.

The purpose of the data path is to execute some set of instructions. Some of these can be carried out in one data path cycle; others may require multiple data path cycles. These instructions may use registers or other hardware facilities. Together, the hardware and instructions visible to an assembly language programmer form the **ISA** (**Instruction Set Architecture**) This level is often called **machine language**.

The machine language typically has between 50 and 300 instructions, mostly for moving data around the machine, doing arithmetic, and comparing values. In this level, the input/output devices are controlled by loading values into special **device registers**. For example, a disk can be commanded to read by loading the values of the disk address, main memory address, byte count, and direction (read or write) into its registers. In practice, many more parameters are needed, and the status returned by the drive after an operation may be complex. Furthermore, for many I/O (Input/Output) devices, timing plays an important role in the programming.

A major function of the operating system is to hide all this complexity and give the programmer a more convenient set of instructions to work with. For example, read block from file is conceptually much simpler than having to worry about the details of moving disk heads, waiting for them to settle down, and so on.

On top of the operating system is the rest of the system software. Here we find the command interpreter (shell), window systems, compilers, editors, and similar application-independent programs. It is important to realize that these programs are definitely not part of the operating system, even though they are typically supplied preinstalled by the computer manufacturer, or in a package with the operating system if it is installed after purchase. This is a crucial, but subtle, point. The operating system is (usually) that portion of the software that runs in **kernel mode** or **supervisor mode**. It is protected from user tampering by the hardware (ignoring for the moment some older or low-end microprocessors that do not have hardware protection at all). Compilers and editors run in **user mode**. If a user does not like a particular compiler, he† is free to write his own if he so chooses; he is not free to write his own clock interrupt handler, which is part of the operating system and is normally protected by hardware against attempts by users to modify it.

This distinction, however, is sometimes blurred in embedded systems (which may not have kernel mode) or interpreted systems (such as Java-based systems that use interpretation, not hardware, to separate the components). Still, for traditional computers, the operating system is what runs in kernel mode.

That said, in many systems there are programs that run in user mode but which help the operating system or perform privileged functions. For example, there is often a program that allows users to change their passwords. This program is not part of the operating system and does not run in kernel mode, but it clearly carries out a sensitive function and has to be protected in a special way.

In some systems, including MINIX 3, this idea is carried to an extreme form, and pieces of what is traditionally considered to be the operating system (such as the file system) run in user space. In such systems, it is difficult to draw a clear boundary. Everything running in kernel mode is clearly part of the operating system, but some programs running outside it are arguably also part of it, or at least closely associated with it. For example, in MINIX 3, the file system is simply a big C program running in user-mode.

Finally, above the system programs come the application programs. These programs are purchased (or written by) the users to solve their particular problems, such as word processing, spreadsheets, engineering calculations, or storing information in a database.

---

† "He" should be read as "he or she" throughout the book.

1.1 WHAT IS AN OPERATING SYSTEM?

Most computer users have had some experience with an operating system, but it is difficult to pin down precisely what an operating system is. Part of the problem is that operating systems perform two basically unrelated functions, extending the machine and managing resources, and depending on who is doing the talking, you hear mostly about one function or the other. Let us now look at both.

1.1.1 The Operating System as an Extended Machine

As mentioned earlier, the **architecture** (instruction set, memory organization, I/O, and bus structure) of most computers at the machine language level is primitive and awkward to program, especially for input/output. To make this point more concrete, let us briefly look at how floppy disk I/O is done using the NEC PD765 compatible controller chips used on many Intel-based personal computers. (Throughout this book we will use the terms "floppy disk" and "diskette" interchangeably.) The PD765 has 16 commands, each specified by loading between 1 and 9 bytes into a device register. These commands are for reading and writing data, moving the disk arm, and formatting tracks, as well as initializing, sensing, resetting, and recalibrating the controller and the drives.

The most basic commands are read and write, each of which requires 13 parameters, packed into 9 bytes. These parameters specify such items as the address of the disk block to be read, the number of sectors per track, the recording mode used on the physical medium, the intersector gap spacing, and what to do with a deleted-data-address-mark. If you do not understand this mumbo jumbo, do not worry; that is precisely the point—it is rather esoteric. When the operation is completed, the controller chip returns 23 status and error fields packed into 7 bytes. As if this were not enough, the floppy disk programmer must also be constantly aware of whether the motor is on or off. If the motor is off, it must be turned on (with a long startup delay) before data can be read or written. The motor cannot be left on too long, however, or the floppy disk will wear out. The programmer is thus forced to deal with the trade-off between long startup delays versus wearing out floppy disks (and losing the data on them).

Without going into the *real* details, it should be clear that the average programmer probably does not want to get too intimately involved with the programming of floppy disks (or hard disks, which are just as complex and quite different). Instead, what the programmer wants is a simple, high-level abstraction to deal with. In the case of disks, a typical abstraction would be that the disk contains a collection of named files. Each file can be opened for reading or writing, then read or written, and finally closed. Details such as whether or not recording should use modified frequency modulation and what the current state of the motor is should not appear in the abstraction presented to the user.

The program that hides the truth about the hardware from the programmer and presents a nice, simple view of named files that can be read and written is, of course, the operating system. Just as the operating system shields the programmer from the disk hardware and presents a simple file-oriented interface, it also conceals a lot of unpleasant business concerning interrupts, timers, memory management, and other low-level features. In each case, the abstraction offered by the operating system is simpler and easier to use than that offered by the underlying hardware.

In this view, the function of the operating system is to present the user with the equivalent of an **extended machine** or **virtual machine** that is easier to program than the underlying hardware. How the operating system achieves this goal is a long story, which we will study in detail throughout this book. To summarize it in a nutshell, the operating system provides a variety of services that programs can obtain using special instructions called system calls. We will examine some of the more common system calls later in this chapter.

1.1.2 The Operating System as a Resource Manager

The concept of the operating system as primarily providing its users with a convenient interface is a top-down view. An alternative, bottom-up, view holds that the operating system is there to manage all the pieces of a complex system. Modern computers consist of processors, memories, timers, disks, mice, network interfaces, printers, and a wide variety of other devices. In the alternative view, the job of the operating system is to provide for an orderly and controlled allocation of the processors, memories, and I/O devices among the various programs competing for them.

Imagine what would happen if three programs running on some computer all tried to print their output simultaneously on the same printer. The first few lines of printout might be from program 1, the next few from program 2, then some from program 3, and so forth. The result would be chaos. The operating system can bring order to the potential chaos by buffering all the output destined for the printer on the disk. When one program is finished, the operating system can then copy its output from the disk file where it has been stored to the printer, while at the same time the other program can continue generating more output, oblivious to the fact that the output is not really going to the printer (yet).

When a computer (or network) has multiple users, the need for managing and protecting the memory, I/O devices, and other resources is even greater, since the users might otherwise interfere with one another. In addition, users often need to share not only hardware, but information (files, databases, etc.) as well. In short, this view of the operating system holds that its primary task is to keep track of who is using which resource, to grant resource requests, to account for usage, and to mediate conflicting requests from different programs and users.

Resource management includes multiplexing (sharing) resources in two ways: in time and in space. When a resource is time multiplexed, different programs or users take turns using it. First one of them gets to use the resource, then another, and so on. For example, with only one CPU and multiple programs that want to run on it, the operating system first allocates the CPU to one program, then after it has run long enough, another one gets to use the CPU, then another, and then eventually the first one again. Determining how the resource is time multiplexed—who goes next and for how long—is the task of the operating system. Another example of time multiplexing is sharing the printer. When multiple print jobs are queued up for printing on a single printer, a decision has to be made about which one is to be printed next.

The other kind of multiplexing is space multiplexing. Instead of the customers taking turns, each one gets part of the resource. For example, main memory is normally divided up among several running programs, so each one can be resident at the same time (for example, in order to take turns using the CPU). Assuming there is enough memory to hold multiple programs, it is more efficient to hold several programs in memory at once rather than give one of them all of it, especially if it only needs a small fraction of the total. Of course, this raises issues of fairness, protection, and so on, and it is up to the operating system to solve them. Another resource that is space multiplexed is the (hard) disk. In many systems a single disk can hold files from many users at the same time. Allocating disk space and keeping track of who is using which disk blocks is a typical operating system resource management task.

1.2 HISTORY OF OPERATING SYSTEMS

Operating systems have been evolving through the years. In the following sections we will briefly look at a few of the highlights. Since operating systems have historically been closely tied to the architecture of the computers on which they run, we will look at successive generations of computers to see what their operating systems were like. This mapping of operating system generations to computer generations is crude, but it does provide some structure where there would otherwise be none.

The first true digital computer was designed by the English mathematician Charles Babbage (1792–1871). Although Babbage spent most of his life and fortune trying to build his "analytical engine," he never got it working properly because it was purely mechanical, and the technology of his day could not produce the required wheels, gears, and cogs to the high precision that he needed. Needless to say, the analytical engine did not have an operating system.

As an interesting historical aside, Babbage realized that he would need software for his analytical engine, so he hired a young woman named Ada Lovelace, who was the daughter of the famed British poet Lord Byron, as the world's first programmer. The programming language Ada® was named after her.

1.2.1 The First Generation (1945–55) Vacuum Tubes and Plugboards

After Babbage's unsuccessful efforts, little progress was made in constructing digital computers until World War II. Around the mid-1940s, Howard Aiken at Harvard University, John von Neumann at the Institute for Advanced Study in Princeton, J. Presper Eckert and John Mauchley at the University of Pennsylvania, and Konrad Zuse in Germany, among others, all succeeded in building calculating engines. The first ones used mechanical relays but were very slow, with cycle times measured in seconds. Relays were later replaced by vacuum tubes. These machines were enormous, filling up entire rooms with tens of thousands of vacuum tubes, but they were still millions of times slower than even the cheapest personal computers available today.

In these early days, a single group of people designed, built, programmed, operated, and maintained each machine. All programming was done in absolute machine language, often by wiring up plugboards to control the machine's basic functions. Programming languages were unknown (even assembly language was unknown). Operating systems were unheard of. The usual mode of operation was for the programmer to sign up for a block of time on the signup sheet on the wall, then come down to the machine room, insert his or her plugboard into the computer, and spend the next few hours hoping that none of the 20,000 or so vacuum tubes would burn out during the run. Virtually all the problems were straightforward numerical calculations, such as grinding out tables of sines, cosines, and logarithms.

By the early 1950s, the routine had improved somewhat with the introduction of punched cards. It was now possible to write programs on cards and read them in instead of using plugboards; otherwise, the procedure was the same.

1.2.2 The Second Generation (1955–65) Transistors and Batch Systems

The introduction of the transistor in the mid-1950s changed the picture radically. Computers became reliable enough that they could be manufactured and sold to paying customers with the expectation that they would continue to function long enough to get some useful work done. For the first time, there was a clear separation between designers, builders, operators, programmers, and maintenance personnel.

These machines, now called **mainframes**, were locked away in specially air-conditioned computer rooms, with staffs of specially-trained professional operators to run them. Only big corporations or major government agencies or universities could afford their multimillion dollar price tags. To run a **job** (i.e., a program or set of programs), a programmer would first write the program on paper (in FORTRAN or possibly even in assembly language), then punch it on cards. He would then bring the card deck down to the input room and hand it to one of the operators and go drink coffee until the output was ready.

When the computer finished whatever job it was currently running, an operator would go over to the printer and tear off the output and carry it over to the output room, so that the programmer could collect it later. Then he would take one of the card decks that had been brought from the input room and read it in. If the FORTRAN compiler was needed, the operator would have to get it from a file cabinet and read it in. Much computer time was wasted while operators were walking around the machine room.

Given the high cost of the equipment, it is not surprising that people quickly looked for ways to reduce the wasted time. The solution generally adopted was the **batch system**. The idea behind it was to collect a tray full of jobs in the input room and then read them onto a magnetic tape using a small (relatively) inexpensive computer, such as the IBM 1401, which was very good at reading cards, copying tapes, and printing output, but not at all good at numerical calculations. Other, much more expensive machines, such as the IBM 7094, were used for the real computing. This situation is shown in Fig. 1-2.

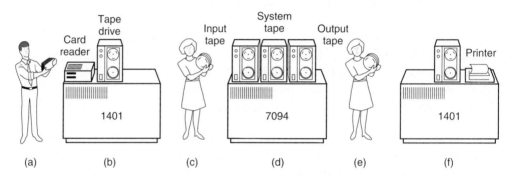

Figure 1-2. An early batch system. (a) Programmers bring cards to 1401. (b) 1401 reads batch of jobs onto tape. (c) Operator carries input tape to 7094. (d) 7094 does computing. (e) Operator carries output tape to 1401. (f) 1401 prints output.

After about an hour of collecting a batch of jobs, the tape was rewound and brought into the machine room, where it was mounted on a tape drive. The operator then loaded a special program (the ancestor of today's operating system), which read the first job from tape and ran it. The output was written onto a second tape, instead of being printed. After each job finished, the operating system automatically read the next job from the tape and began running it. When the whole batch was done, the operator removed the input and output tapes, replaced the input tape with the next batch, and brought the output tape to a 1401 for printing **off line** (i.e., not connected to the main computer).

The structure of a typical input job is shown in Fig. 1-3. It started out with a $JOB card, specifying the maximum run time in minutes, the account number to be charged, and the programmer's name. Then came a $FORTRAN card, telling the operating system to load the FORTRAN compiler from the system tape. It was followed by the program to be compiled, and then a $LOAD card, directing the operating system to load the object program just compiled. (Compiled programs were often written on scratch tapes and had to be loaded explicitly.) Next came the $RUN card, telling the operating system to run the program with the data following it. Finally, the $END card marked the end of the job. These primitive control cards were the forerunners of modern job control languages and command interpreters.

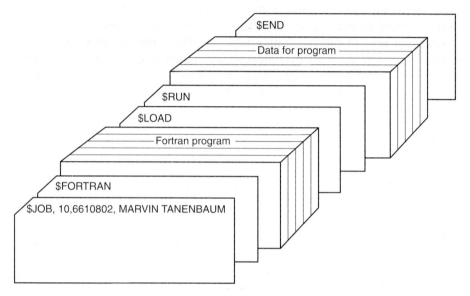

Figure 1-3. Structure of a typical FMS job.

Large second-generation computers were used mostly for scientific and engineering calculations, such as solving the partial differential equations that often occur in physics and engineering. They were largely programmed in FORTRAN and assembly language. Typical operating systems were FMS (the Fortran Monitor System) and IBSYS, IBM's operating system for the 7094.

1.2.3 The Third Generation (1965–1980) ICs and Multiprogramming

By the early 1960s, most computer manufacturers had two distinct, and totally incompatible, product lines. On the one hand there were the word-oriented, large-scale scientific computers, such as the 7094, which were used for numerical calculations in science and engineering. On the other hand, there were the character-oriented, commercial computers, such as the 1401, which were widely used for tape sorting and printing by banks and insurance companies.

Developing, maintaining, and marketing two completely different product lines was an expensive proposition for the computer manufacturers. In addition, many new computer customers initially needed a small machine but later outgrew it and wanted a bigger machine that had the same architectures as their current one so it could run all their old programs, but faster.

IBM attempted to solve both of these problems at a single stroke by introducing the System/360. The 360 was a series of software-compatible machines ranging from 1401-sized to much more powerful than the 7094. The machines differed only in price and performance (maximum memory, processor speed, number of I/O devices permitted, and so forth). Since all the machines had the same architecture and instruction set, programs written for one machine could run on all the others, at least in theory. Furthermore, the 360 was designed to handle both scientific (i.e., numerical) and commercial computing. Thus a single family of machines could satisfy the needs of all customers. In subsequent years, IBM has come out with compatible successors to the 360 line, using more modern technology, known as the 370, 4300, 3080, 3090, and Z series.

The 360 was the first major computer line to use (small-scale) Integrated Circuits (ICs), thus providing a major price/performance advantage over the second-generation machines, which were built up from individual transistors. It was an immediate success, and the idea of a family of compatible computers was soon adopted by all the other major manufacturers. The descendants of these machines are still in use at computer centers today. Nowadays they are often used for managing huge databases (e.g., for airline reservation systems) or as servers for World Wide Web sites that must process thousands of requests per second.

The greatest strength of the "one family" idea was simultaneously its greatest weakness. The intention was that all software, including the operating system, **OS/360**, had to work on all models. It had to run on small systems, which often just replaced 1401s for copying cards to tape, and on very large systems, which often replaced 7094s for doing weather forecasting and other heavy computing. It had to be good on systems with few peripherals and on systems with many peripherals. It had to work in commercial environments and in scientific environments. Above all, it had to be efficient for all of these different uses.

There was no way that IBM (or anybody else) could write a piece of software to meet all those conflicting requirements. The result was an enormous and extraordinarily complex operating system, probably two to three orders of magnitude larger than FMS. It consisted of millions of lines of assembly language written by thousands of programmers, and contained thousands upon thousands of bugs, which necessitated a continuous stream of new releases in an attempt to correct them. Each new release fixed some bugs and introduced new ones, so the number of bugs probably remained constant in time.

One of the designers of OS/360, Fred Brooks, subsequently wrote a witty and incisive book describing his experiences with OS/360 (Brooks, 1995). While it would be impossible to summarize the book here, suffice it to say that the cover shows a herd of prehistoric beasts stuck in a tar pit. The cover of Silberschatz et al. (2004) makes a similar point about operating systems being dinosaurs.

Despite its enormous size and problems, OS/360 and the similar third-generation operating systems produced by other computer manufacturers actually satisfied most of their customers reasonably well. They also popularized several key techniques absent in second-generation operating systems. Probably the most important of these was **multiprogramming**. On the 7094, when the current job paused to wait for a tape or other I/O operation to complete, the CPU simply sat idle until the I/O finished. With heavily CPU-bound scientific calculations, I/O is infrequent, so this wasted time is not significant. With commercial data processing, the I/O wait time can often be 80 or 90 percent of the total time, so something had to be done to avoid having the (expensive) CPU be idle so much.

The solution that evolved was to partition memory into several pieces, with a different job in each partition, as shown in Fig. 1-4. While one job was waiting for I/O to complete, another job could be using the CPU. If enough jobs could be held in main memory at once, the CPU could be kept busy nearly 100 percent of the time. Having multiple jobs safely in memory at once requires special hardware to protect each job against snooping and mischief by the other ones, but the 360 and other third-generation systems were equipped with this hardware.

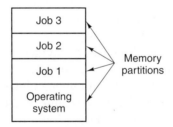

Figure 1-4. A multiprogramming system with three jobs in memory.

Another major feature present in third-generation operating systems was the ability to read jobs from cards onto the disk as soon as they were brought to the computer room. Then, whenever a running job finished, the operating system could load a new job from the disk into the now-empty partition and run it. This technique is called **spooling** (from Simultaneous Peripheral Operation On Line) and was also used for output. With spooling, the 1401s were no longer needed, and much carrying of tapes disappeared.

Although third-generation operating systems were well suited for big scientific calculations and massive commercial data processing runs, they were still basically batch systems. Many programmers pined for the first-generation days when they had the machine all to themselves for a few hours, so they could debug their programs quickly. With third-generation systems, the time between submitting a job and getting back the output was often hours, so a single misplaced comma could cause a compilation to fail, and the programmer to waste half a day.

This desire for quick response time paved the way for **timesharing**, a variant of multiprogramming, in which each user has an online terminal. In a timesharing system, if 20 users are logged in and 17 of them are thinking or talking or drinking coffee, the CPU can be allocated in turn to the three jobs that want service. Since people debugging programs usually issue short commands (e.g., compile a five-page procedure†) rather than long ones (e.g., sort a million-record file), the computer can provide fast, interactive service to a number of users and perhaps also work on big batch jobs in the background when the CPU is otherwise idle. The first serious timesharing system, **CTSS** (Compatible Time Sharing System), was developed at M.I.T. on a specially modified 7094 (Corbató et al., 1962). However, timesharing did not really become popular until the necessary protection hardware became widespread during the third generation.

After the success of the CTSS system, MIT, Bell Labs, and General Electric (then a major computer manufacturer) decided to embark on the development of a "computer utility," a machine that would support hundreds of simultaneous timesharing users. Their model was the electricity distribution system—when you need electric power, you just stick a plug in the wall, and within reason, as much power as you need will be there. The designers of this system, known as **MULTICS** (MULTiplexed Information and Computing Service), envisioned one huge machine providing computing power for everyone in the Boston area. The idea that machines far more powerful than their GE-645 mainframe would be sold for under a thousand dollars by the millions only 30 years later was pure science fiction, like the idea of supersonic trans-Atlantic undersea trains would be now.

MULTICS was a mixed success. It was designed to support hundreds of users on a machine only slightly more powerful than an Intel 80386-based PC, although it had much more I/O capacity. This is not quite as crazy as it sounds, since people knew how to write small, efficient programs in those days, a skill that has subsequently been lost. There were many reasons that MULTICS did not take over the world, not the least of which is that it was written in PL/I, and the PL/I compiler was years late and barely worked at all when it finally arrived. In addition, MULTICS was enormously ambitious for its time, much like Charles Babbage's analytical engine in the nineteenth century.

MULTICS introduced many seminal ideas into the computer literature, but turning it into a serious product and a commercial success was a lot harder than anyone had expected. Bell Labs dropped out of the project, and General Electric quit the computer business altogether. However, M.I.T. persisted and eventually got MULTICS working. It was ultimately sold as a commercial product by the company that bought GE's computer business (Honeywell) and installed by about 80 major companies and universities worldwide. While their numbers were small, MULTICS users were fiercely loyal. General Motors, Ford, and the U.S. National Security Agency, for example, only shut down their MULTICS systems in the late 1990s. The last MULTICS running, at the Canadian Department of National Defence, shut down in October 2000. Despite its lack of commercial success,

---

† We will use the terms "procedure," "subroutine," and "function" interchangeably in this book.

MULTICS had a huge influence on subsequent operating systems. A great deal of information about it exists (Corbató et al., 1972; Corbató and Vyssotsky, 1965; Daley and Dennis, 1968; Organick, 1972; and Saltzer, 1974). It also has a still-active Web site, *www.multicians.org*, with a great deal of information about the system, its designers, and its users.

The phrase "computer utility" is no longer heard, but the idea has gained new life in recent years. In its simplest form, PCs or **workstations** (high-end PCs) in a business or a classroom may be connected via a **LAN** (**Local Area Network**) to a **file server** on which all programs and data are stored. An administrator then has to install and protect only one set of programs and data, and can easily reinstall local software on a malfunctioning PC or workstation without worrying about retrieving or preserving local data. In more heterogeneous environments, a class of software called **middleware** has evolved to bridge the gap between local users and the files, programs, and databases they use on remote servers. Middleware makes networked computers look local to individual users' PCs or workstations and presents a consistent user interface even though there may be a wide variety of different servers, PCs, and workstations in use. The World Wide Web is an example. A web browser presents documents to a user in a uniform way, and a document as seen on a user's browser can consist of text from one server and graphics from another server, presented in a format determined by a style sheet on yet another server. Businesses and universities commonly use a web interface to access databases and run programs on a computer in another building or even another city. Middleware appears to be the operating system of a **distributed system**, but it is not really an operating system at all, and is beyond the scope of this book. For more on distributed systems see Tanenbaum and Van Steen (2002).

Another major development during the third generation was the phenomenal growth of minicomputers, starting with the Digital Equipment Company (DEC) PDP-1 in 1961. The PDP-1 had only 4K of 18-bit words, but at $120,000 per machine (less than 5 percent of the price of a 7094), it sold like hotcakes. For certain kinds of nonnumerical work, it was almost as fast as the 7094 and gave birth to a whole new industry. It was quickly followed by a series of other PDPs (unlike IBM's family, all incompatible) culminating in the PDP-11.

One of the computer scientists at Bell Labs who had worked on the MULTICS project, Ken Thompson, subsequently found a small PDP-7 minicomputer that no one was using and set out to write a stripped-down, one-user version of MULTICS. This work later developed into the **UNIX** operating system, which became popular in the academic world, with government agencies, and with many companies.

The history of UNIX has been told elsewhere (e.g., Salus, 1994). Because the source code was widely available, various organizations developed their own (incompatible) versions, which led to chaos. Two major versions developed, **System V**, from AT&T, and **BSD**, (Berkeley Software Distribution) from the University of California at Berkeley. These had minor variants as well, now including FreeBSD, OpenBSD, and NetBSD. To make it possible to write programs that could run on any UNIX system, IEEE developed a standard for UNIX, called **POSIX**, that most versions of UNIX now support. POSIX defines a minimal system call interface that conformant UNIX systems must support. In fact, some other operating systems now also support the POSIX interface. The information needed to write POSIX-compliant software is available in books (IEEE, 1990; Lewine, 1991), and online as the Open Group's "Single UNIX Specification" at *www.unix.org*. Later in this chapter, when we refer to UNIX, we mean all of these systems as well, unless stated otherwise. While they differ internally, all of them support the POSIX standard, so to the programmer they are quite similar.

1.2.4 The Fourth Generation (1980–Present) Personal Computers

With the development of LSI (Large Scale Integration) circuits, chips containing thousands of transistors on a square centimeter of silicon, the age of the **microprocessor**-based personal computer dawned. In terms of architecture, personal computers (initially called **microcomputers**) were not all that different from minicomputers of the PDP-11 class, but in terms of price they certainly were different. The minicomputer made it possible for a department in a company or university to have its own computer. The microcomputer made it possible for an individual to have his or her own computer.

There were several families of microcomputers. Intel came out with the 8080, the first general-purpose 8-bit microprocessor, in 1974. A number of companies produced complete systems using the 8080 (or the compatible Zilog Z80) and the **CP/M** (Control Program for Microcomputers) operating system from a company called Digital Research was widely used with these. Many application programs were written to run on CP/M, and it dominated the personal computing world for about 5 years.

Motorola also produced an 8-bit microprocessor, the 6800. A group of Motorola engineers left to form MOS Technology and manufacture the 6502 CPU after Motorola rejected their suggested improvements to the 6800. The 6502 was the CPU of several early systems. One of these, the Apple II, became a major competitor for CP/M systems in the home and educational markets. But CP/M was so popular that many owners of Apple II computers purchased Z-80 coprocessor add-on cards to run CP/M, since the 6502 CPU was not compatible with CP/M. The CP/M cards were sold by a little company called Microsoft, which also had a market niche supplying BASIC interpreters used by a number of microcomputers running CP/M.

The next generation of microprocessors were 16-bit systems. Intel came out with the 8086, and in the early 1980s, IBM designed the IBM PC around Intel's 8088 (an 8086 on the inside, with an 8 bit external data path). Microsoft offered IBM a package which included Microsoft's BASIC and an operating system, **DOS** (Disk Operating System) originally developed by another company—Microsoft bought the product and hired the original author to improve it. The revised system was renamed **MS-DOS** (MicroSoft Disk Operating System) and quickly came to dominate the IBM PC market.

CP/M, MS-DOS, and the Apple DOS were all command-line systems: users typed commands at the keyboard. Years earlier, Doug Engelbart at Stanford Research Institute had invented the **GUI (Graphical User Interface)**, pronounced "gooey," complete with windows, icons, menus, and mouse. Apple's Steve Jobs saw the possibility of a truly **user-friendly** personal computer (for users who knew nothing about computers and did not want to learn), and the Apple Macintosh was announced in early 1984. It used Motorola's 16-bit 68000 CPU, and had 64 KB of **ROM (Read Only Memory)**, to support the GUI. The Macintosh has evolved over the years. Subsequent Motorola CPUs were true 32-bit systems, and later still Apple moved to IBM PowerPC CPUs, with RISC 32-bit (and later, 64-bit) architecture. In 2001 Apple made a major operating system change, releasing **Mac OS X**, with a new version of the Macintosh GUI on top of Berkeley UNIX. And in 2005 Apple announced that it would be switching to Intel processors.

To compete with the Macintosh, Microsoft invented Windows. Originally Windows was just a graphical environment on top of 16-bit MS-DOS (i.e., it was more like a shell than a true operating system). However, current versions of Windows are descendants of Windows NT, a full 32-bit system, rewritten from scratch.

The other major contender in the personal computer world is UNIX (and its various derivatives). UNIX is strongest on workstations and other high-end computers, such as network servers. It is especially popular on machines powered by high-performance RISC chips. On Pentium-based computers, Linux is becoming a popular alternative to Windows for students and increasingly many corporate users. (Throughout this book we will use the term "Pentium" to mean the entire Pentium family, including the low-end Celeron, the high end Xeon, and compatible AMD microprocessors).

Although many UNIX users, especially experienced programmers, prefer a command-based interface to a GUI, nearly all UNIX systems support a windowing system called the **X Window** system developed at M.I.T. This system handles the basic window management, allowing users to create, delete, move, and resize windows using a mouse. Often a complete GUI, such as **Motif**, is available to run on top of the X Window system giving UNIX a look and feel something like the Macintosh or Microsoft Windows for those UNIX users who want such a thing.

An interesting development that began taking place during the mid-1980s is the growth of networks of personal computers running **network operating systems** and **distributed operating systems** (Tanenbaum and Van Steen, 2002). In a network operating system, the users are aware of the existence of multiple computers and can log in to remote machines and copy files from one machine to another. Each machine runs its own local operating system and has its own local user (or users). Basically, the machines are independent of one another.

Network operating systems are not fundamentally different from single-processor operating systems. They obviously need a network interface controller and some low-level software to drive it, as well as programs to achieve remote login and remote file access, but these additions do not change the essential structure of the operating system.

A distributed operating system, in contrast, is one that appears to its users as a traditional uniprocessor system, even though it is actually composed of multiple processors. The users should not be aware of where their programs are being run or where their files are located; that should all be handled automatically and efficiently by the operating system.

True distributed operating systems require more than just adding a little code to a uniprocessor operating system, because distributed and centralized systems differ in critical ways. Distributed systems, for example, often allow applications to run on several processors at the same time, thus requiring more complex processor scheduling algorithms in order to optimize the amount of parallelism.

Communication delays within the network often mean that these (and other) algorithms must run with incomplete, outdated, or even incorrect information. This situation is radically different from a single-processor system in which the operating system has complete information about the system state.

1.2.5 History of MINIX 3

When UNIX was young (Version 6), the source code was widely available, under AT&T license, and frequently studied. John Lions, of the University of New South Wales in Australia, even wrote a little booklet describing its operation, line by line (Lions, 1996). This booklet was used (with permission of AT&T) as a text in many university operating system courses.

When AT&T released Version 7, it dimly began to realize that UNIX was a valuable commercial product, so it issued Version 7 with a license that prohibited the source code from being studied in courses, in order to avoid endangering its status as a trade secret. Many universities complied by simply dropping the study of UNIX and teaching only theory.

Unfortunately, teaching only theory leaves the student with a lopsided view of what an operating system is really like. The theoretical topics that are usually covered in great detail in courses and books on operating systems, such as scheduling algorithms, are in practice not really that important. Subjects that really are important, such as I/O and file systems, are generally neglected because there is little theory about them.

To remedy this situation, one of the authors of this book (Tanenbaum) decided to write a new operating system from scratch that would be compatible with UNIX from the user's point of view, but completely different on the inside. By not using even one line of AT&T code, this system avoided the licensing restrictions, so it could be used for class or individual study. In this manner, readers could dissect a real operating system to see what is inside, just as biology students dissect frogs. It was called **MINIX** and was released in 1987 with its complete source code for anyone to study or modify. The name MINIX stands for mini-UNIX because it is small enough that even a nonguru can understand how it works.

In addition to the advantage of eliminating the legal problems, MINIX had another advantage over UNIX. It was written a decade after UNIX and was structured in a more modular way. For instance, from the very first release of MINIX the file system and the memory manager were not part of the operating system at all but ran as user programs. In the current release (MINIX 3) this modularization has been extended to the I/O device drivers, which (with the exception of the clock driver) all run as user programs. Another difference is that UNIX was designed to be efficient; MINIX was designed to be readable (inasmuch as one can speak of any program hundreds of pages long as being readable). The MINIX code, for example, has thousands of comments in it.

MINIX was originally designed for compatibility with Version 7 (V7) UNIX. Version 7 was used as the model because of its simplicity and elegance. It is sometimes said that Version 7 was an improvement not only over all its predecessors, but also over all its successors. With the advent of POSIX, MINIX began evolving toward the new standard, while maintaining backward compatibility with existing programs. This kind of evolution is common in the computer industry, as no vendor wants to introduce a new system that none of its existing customers can use without great upheaval. The version of MINIX described in this book, MINIX 3, is based on the POSIX standard.

Like UNIX, MINIX was written in the C programming language and was intended to be easy to port to various computers. The initial implementation was for the IBM PC. MINIX was subsequently ported to several other platforms. In keeping with the "Small is Beautiful" philosophy, MINIX originally did not even require a hard disk to run (in the mid-1980s hard disks were still an expensive novelty). As MINIX grew in functionality and size, it eventually got to the point that a hard disk was needed for PCs, but in keeping with the MINIX philosophy, a 200-MB partition is sufficient (for embedded applications, no hard disk is required though). In contrast, even small Linux systems require 500-MB of disk space, and several GB will be needed to install common applications.

To the average user sitting at an IBM PC, running MINIX is similar to running UNIX. All of the basic programs, such as *cat*, *grep*, *ls*, *make*, and the shell are present and perform the same functions as their UNIX counterparts. Like the operating system itself, all these utility programs have been rewritten completely from scratch by the author, his students, and some other dedicated people, with no AT&T or other proprietary code. Many other freely-distributable programs now exist, and in many cases these have been successfully ported (recompiled) on MINIX.

MINIX continued to develop for a decade and MINIX 2 was released in 1997, together with the second edition of this book, which described the new release.

The changes between versions 1 and 2 were substantial (e.g., from 16-bit real mode on an 8088 using floppy disks to 32-bit protected mode on a 386 using a hard disk) but evolutionary.

Development continued slowly but systematically until 2004, when Tanenbaum became convinced that software was getting too bloated and unreliable and decided to pick up the slightly-dormant MINIX thread again. Together with his students and programmers at the Vrije Universiteit in Amsterdam, he produced MINIX 3, a major redesign of the system, greatly restructuring the kernel, reducing its size, and emphasizing modularity and reliability. The new version was intended both for PCs and embedded systems, where compactness, modularity, and reliability are crucial. While some people in the group called for a completely new name, it was eventually decided to call it MINIX 3 since the name MINIX was already well known. By way of analogy, when Apple abandoned it own operating system, Mac OS 9 and replaced it with a variant of Berkeley UNIX, the name chosen was Mac OS X rather than APPLIX or something like that. Similar fundamental changes have happened in the Windows family while retaining the Windows name.

The MINIX 3 kernel is well under 4000 lines of executable code, compared to millions of executable lines of code for Windows, Linux, FreeBSD, and other operating systems. Small kernel size is important because kernel bugs are far more devastating than bugs in user-mode programs and more code means more bugs. One careful study has shown that the number of *detected* bugs per 1000 executable lines of code varies from 6 to 16 (Basili and Perricone, 1984). The actual number of bugs is probably much higher since the researchers could only count reported bugs, not unreported bugs. Yet another study (Ostrand et al., 2004) showed that even after more than a dozen releases, on the average 6% of all files contained bugs that were later reported and after a certain point the bug level tends to stabilize rather than go asymptotically to zero. This result is supported by the fact that when a very simple, automated, model-checker was let loose on stable versions of Linux and OpenBSD, it found hundreds of kernel bugs, overwhelmingly in device drivers (Chou et al., 2001; and Engler et al., 2001). This is the reason the device drivers were moved out of the kernel in MINIX 3; they can do less damage in user mode.

Throughout this book MINIX 3 will be used as an example. Most of the comments about the MINIX 3 system calls, however (as opposed to comments about the actual code), also apply to other UNIX systems. This remark should be kept in mind when reading the text.

A few words about Linux and its relationship to MINIX may possibly be of interest to some readers. Shortly after MINIX was released, a USENET newsgroup, *comp.os.minix*, was formed to discuss it. Within weeks, it had 40,000 subscribers, most of whom wanted to add vast numbers of new features to MINIX to make it bigger and better (well, at least bigger). Every day, several hundred of them offered suggestions, ideas, and frequently snippets of source code. The author of

MINIX was able to successfully resist this onslaught for several years, in order to keep MINIX clean enough for students to understand and small enough that it could run on computers that students could afford. For people who thought little of MS-DOS, the existence of MINIX (with source code) as an alternative was even a reason to finally go out and buy a PC.

One of these people was a Finnish student named Linus Torvalds. Torvalds installed MINIX on his new PC and studied the source code carefully. Torvalds wanted to read USENET newsgroups (such as *comp.os.minix*) on his own PC rather than at his university, but some features he needed were lacking in MINIX, so he wrote a program to do that, but soon discovered he needed a different terminal driver, so he wrote that too. Then he wanted to download and save postings, so he wrote a disk driver, and then a file system. By Aug. 1991 he had produced a primitive kernel. On Aug. 25, 1991, he announced it on *comp.os.minix*. This announcement attracted other people to help him, and on March 13, 1994 Linux 1.0 was released. Thus was Linux born.

Linux has become one of the notable successes of the **open source** movement (which MINIX helped start). Linux is challenging UNIX (and Windows) in many environments, partly because commodity PCs which support Linux are now available with performance that rivals the proprietary RISC systems required by some UNIX implementations. Other open source software, notably the Apache web server and the MySQL database, work well with Linux in the commercial world. Linux, Apache, MySQL, and the open source Perl and PHP programming languages are often used together on web servers and are sometimes referred to by the acronym **LAMP**. For more on the history of Linux and open source software see DiBona et al. (1999), Moody (2001), and Naughton (2000).

1.3 OPERATING SYSTEM CONCEPTS

The interface between the operating system and the user programs is defined by the set of "extended instructions" that the operating system provides. These extended instructions have been traditionally known as **system calls**, although they can be implemented in several ways. To really understand what operating systems do, we must examine this interface closely. The calls available in the interface vary from operating system to operating system (although the underlying concepts tend to be similar).

We are thus forced to make a choice between (1) vague generalities ("operating systems have system calls for reading files") and (2) some specific system ("MINIX 3 has a read system call with three parameters: one to specify the file, one to tell where the data are to be put, and one to tell how many bytes to read").

We have chosen the latter approach. It's more work that way, but it gives more insight into what operating systems really do. In Sec. 1.4 we will look closely at the basic system calls present in UNIX (including the various versions of BSD), Linux, and MINIX 3. For simplicity's sake, we will refer only to MINIX 3, but the corresponding UNIX and Linux system calls are based on POSIX in most cases. Before we look at the actual system calls, however, it is worth taking a bird's-eye view of MINIX 3, to get a general feel for what an operating system is all about. This overview applies equally well to UNIX and Linux, as mentioned above.

The MINIX 3 system calls fall roughly in two broad categories: those dealing with processes and those dealing with the file system. We will now examine each of these in turn.

1.3.1 Processes

A key concept in MINIX 3, and in all operating systems, is the **process**. A process is basically a program in execution. Associated with each process is its **address space**, a list of memory locations from some minimum (usually 0) to some maximum, which the process can read and write. The address space contains the executable program, the program's data, and its stack. Also associated with each process is some set of registers, including the program counter, stack pointer, and other hardware registers, and all the other information needed to run the program.

We will come back to the process concept in much more detail in Chap. 2, but for the time being, the easiest way to get a good intuitive feel for a process is to think about multiprogramming systems. Periodically, the operating system decides to stop running one process and start running another, for example, because the first one has had more than its share of CPU time in the past second.

When a process is suspended temporarily like this, it must later be restarted in exactly the same state it had when it was stopped. This means that all information about the process must be explicitly saved somewhere during the suspension. For example, the process may have several files open for reading at once. Associated with each of these files is a pointer giving the current position (i.e., the number of the byte or record to be read next). When a process is temporarily suspended, all these pointers must be saved so that a read call executed after the process is restarted will read the proper data. In many operating systems, all the information about each process, other than the contents of its own address space, is stored in an operating system table called the **process table**, which is an array (or linked list) of structures, one for each process currently in existence.

Thus, a (suspended) process consists of its address space, usually called the **core image** (in honor of the magnetic core memories used in days of yore), and its process table entry, which contains its registers, among other things.

The key process management system calls are those dealing with the creation and termination of processes. Consider a typical example. A process called the **command interpreter** or **shell** reads commands from a terminal. The user has just typed a command requesting that a program be compiled. The shell must now create a new process that will run the compiler. When that process has finished the compilation, it executes a system call to terminate itself.

On Windows and other operating systems that have a GUI, (double) clicking on a desktop icon launches a program in much the same way as typing its name at the command prompt. Although we will not discuss GUIs much, they are really simple command interpreters.

If a process can create one or more other processes (usually referred to as **child processes**) and these processes in turn can create child processes, we quickly arrive at the process tree structure of Fig. 1-5. Related processes that are cooperating to get some job done often need to communicate with one another and synchronize their activities. This communication is called **interprocess communication**, and will be addressed in detail in Chap. 2.

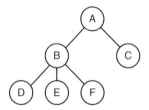

Figure 1-5. A process tree. Process *A* created two child processes, *B* and *C*. Process *B* created three child processes, *D*, *E*, and *F*.

Other process system calls are available to request more memory (or release unused memory), wait for a child process to terminate, and overlay its program with a different one.

Occasionally, there is a need to convey information to a running process that is not sitting around waiting for it. For example, a process that is communicating with another process on a different computer does so by sending messages to the remote process over a network. To guard against the possibility that a message or its reply is lost, the sender may request that its own operating system notify it after a specified number of seconds, so that it can retransmit the message if no acknowledgement has been received yet. After setting this timer, the program may continue doing other work.

When the specified number of seconds has elapsed, the operating system sends an **alarm signal** to the process. The signal causes the process to temporarily suspend whatever it was doing, save its registers on the stack, and start running a special signal handling procedure, for example, to retransmit a presumably lost message. When the signal handler is done, the running process is restarted in the state it was in just before the signal. Signals are the software analog of hardware interrupts. They are generated by a variety of causes in addition to timers expiring. Many traps detected by hardware, such as executing an illegal instruction or using an invalid address, are also converted into signals to the guilty process.

Each person authorized to use a MINIX 3 system is assigned a **UID** (User IDentification) by the system administrator. Every process started has the UID of the person who started it. A child process has the same UID as its parent. Users can be members of groups, each of which has a **GID** (Group IDentification).

One UID, called the **superuser** (in UNIX), has special power and may violate many of the protection rules. In large installations, only the system administrator knows the password needed to become superuser, but many of the ordinary users (especially students) devote considerable effort to trying to find flaws in the system that allow them to become superuser without the password.

We will study processes, interprocess communication, and related issues in Chap. 2.

1.3.2 Files

The other broad category of system calls relates to the file system. As noted before, a major function of the operating system is to hide the peculiarities of the disks and other I/O devices and present the programmer with a nice, clean abstract model of device-independent files. System calls are obviously needed to create files, remove files, read files, and write files. Before a file can be read, it must be opened, and after it has been read it should be closed, so calls are provided to do these things.

To provide a place to keep files, MINIX 3 has the concept of a **directory** as a way of grouping files together. A student, for example, might have one directory for each course he is taking (for the programs needed for that course), another directory for his electronic mail, and still another directory for his World Wide Web home page. System calls are then needed to create and remove directories. Calls are also provided to put an existing file into a directory, and to remove a file from a directory. Directory entries may be either files or other directories. This model also gives rise to a hierarchy—the file system—as shown in Fig. 1-6.

The process and file hierarchies both are organized as trees, but the similarity stops there. Process hierarchies usually are not very deep (more than three levels is unusual), whereas file hierarchies are commonly four, five, or even more levels deep. Process hierarchies are typically short-lived, generally a few minutes at most, whereas the directory hierarchy may exist for years. Ownership and protection also differ for processes and files. Typically, only a parent process may control or even access a child process, but mechanisms nearly always exist to allow files and directories to be read by a wider group than just the owner.

Every file within the directory hierarchy can be specified by giving its **path name** from the top of the directory hierarchy, the **root directory**. Such absolute path names consist of the list of directories that must be traversed from the root directory to get to the file, with slashes separating the components. In Fig. 1-6, the path for file *CS101* is */Faculty/Prof.Brown/Courses/CS101*. The leading slash indicates that the path is absolute, that is, starting at the root directory. As an

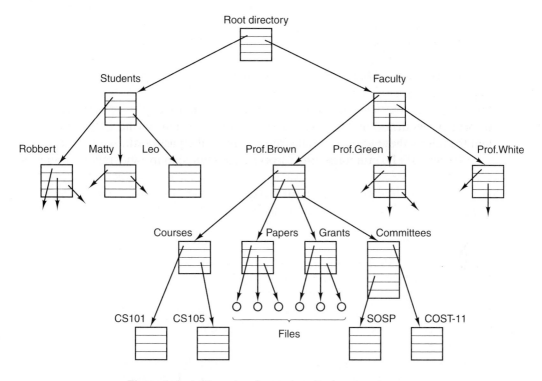

Figure 1-6. A file system for a university department.

aside, in Windows, the backslash (\) character is used as the separator instead of the slash (/) character, so the file path given above would be written as *Faculty\Prof.Brown\Courses\CS101*. Throughout this book we will use the UNIX convention for paths.

At every instant, each process has a current **working directory**, in which path names not beginning with a slash are looked for. As an example, in Fig. 1-6, if */Faculty/Prof.Brown* were the working directory, then use of the path name *Courses/CS101* would yield the same file as the absolute path name given above. Processes can change their working directory by issuing a system call specifying the new working directory.

Files and directories in MINIX 3 are protected by assigning each one an 11-bit binary protection code. The protection code consists of three 3-bit fields: one for the owner, one for other members of the owner's group (users are divided into groups by the system administrator), one for everyone else, and 2 bits we will discuss later. Each field has a bit for read access, a bit for write access, and a bit for execute access. These 3 bits are known as the **rwx bits**. For example, the protection code *rwxr-x--x* means that the owner can read, write, or execute the file, other group members can read or execute (but not write) the file, and everyone else can execute (but not read or write) the file. For a directory (as opposed to a file), *x* indicates search permission. A dash means that the corresponding permission is absent (the bit is zero).

Before a file can be read or written, it must be opened, at which time the permissions are checked. If access is permitted, the system returns a small integer called a **file descriptor** to use in subsequent operations. If the access is prohibited, an error code (-1) is returned.

Another important concept in MINIX 3 is the mounted file system. Nearly all personal computers have one or more CD-ROM drives into which CD-ROMs can be inserted and removed. To provide a clean way to deal with removable media (CD-ROMs, DVDs, floppies, Zip drives, etc.), MINIX 3 allows the file system on a CD-ROM to be attached to the main tree. Consider the situation of Fig. 1-7(a). Before the mount call, the **root file system**, on the hard disk, and a second file system, on a CD-ROM, are separate and unrelated.

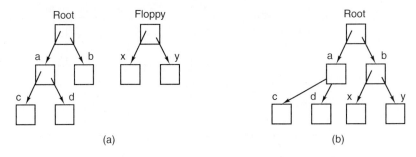

Figure 1-7. (a) Before mounting, the files on drive 0 are not accessible. (b) After mounting, they are part of the file hierarchy.

However, the file system on the CD-ROM cannot be used, because there is no way to specify path names on it. MINIX 3 does not allow path names to be prefixed by a drive name or number; that is precisely the kind of device dependence that operating systems ought to eliminate. Instead, the mount system call allows the file system on the CD-ROM to be attached to the root file system wherever the program wants it to be. In Fig. 1-7(b) the file system on drive 0 has been mounted on directory *b*, thus allowing access to files */b/x* and */b/y*. If directory *b* had originally contained any files they would not be accessible while the CD-ROM was mounted, since */b* would refer to the root directory of drive 0. (Not being able to access these files is not as serious as it at first seems: file systems are nearly always mounted on empty directories.) If a system contains multiple hard disks, they can all be mounted into a single tree as well.

Another important concept in MINIX 3 is the **special file**. Special files are provided in order to make I/O devices look like files. That way, they can be read and written using the same system calls as are used for reading and writing files. Two kinds of special files exist: **block special files** and **character special files**. Block special files are normally used to model devices that consist of a collection of randomly addressable blocks, such as disks. By opening a block special file and reading, say, block 4, a program can directly access the fourth block on the device, without regard to the structure of the file system contained on it. Similarly, character special files are used to model printers, modems, and other devices that accept or output a character stream. By convention, the special files are kept in the */dev* directory. For example, */dev/lp* might be the line printer.

The last feature we will discuss in this overview is one that relates to both processes and files: pipes. A **pipe** is a sort of pseudofile that can be used to connect two processes, as shown in Fig. 1-8. If processes *A* and *B* wish to talk using a pipe, they must set it up in advance. When process *A* wants to send data to process *B*, it writes on the pipe as though it were an output file. Process *B* can read the data by reading from the pipe as though it were an input file. Thus, communication between processes in MINIX 3 looks very much like ordinary file reads and writes. Stronger yet, the only way a process can discover that the output file it is writing on is not really a file, but a pipe, is by making a special system call.

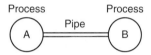

Figure 1-8. Two processes connected by a pipe.

1.3.3 The Shell

The operating system is the code that carries out the system calls. Editors, compilers, assemblers, linkers, and command interpreters definitely are not part of the operating system, even though they are important and useful. At the risk of confusing things somewhat, in this section we will look briefly at the MINIX 3 command interpreter, called the **shell**. Although it is not part of the operating system, it makes heavy use of many operating system features and thus serves as a good example of how the system calls can be used. It is also the primary interface between a user sitting at his terminal and the operating system, unless the user is using a graphical user interface. Many shells exist, including *csh*, *ksh*, *zsh*, and *bash*. All of them support the functionality described below, which derives from the original shell (*sh*).

When any user logs in, a shell is started up. The shell has the terminal as standard input and standard output. It starts out by typing the **prompt**, a character such as a dollar sign, which tells the user that the shell is waiting to accept a command. If the user now types

    date

for example, the shell creates a child process and runs the *date* program as the child. While the child process is running, the shell waits for it to terminate. When the child finishes, the shell types the prompt again and tries to read the next input line.

The user can specify that standard output be redirected to a file, for example,

```
date >file
```

Similarly, standard input can be redirected, as in

```
sort <file1 >file2
```

which invokes the sort program with input taken from *file1* and output sent to *file2*.

The output of one program can be used as the input for another program by connecting them with a pipe. Thus

```
cat file1 file2 file3 | sort >/dev/lp
```

invokes the *cat* program to concatenate three files and send the output to *sort* to arrange all the lines in alphabetical order. The output of *sort* is redirected to the file */dev/lp*, typically the printer.

If a user puts an ampersand after a command, the shell does not wait for it to complete. Instead it just gives a prompt immediately. Consequently,

```
cat file1 file2 file3 | sort >/dev/lp &
```

starts up the sort as a background job, allowing the user to continue working normally while the sort is going on. The shell has a number of other interesting features, which we do not have space to discuss here. Most books for UNIX beginners are useful for MINIX 3 users who want to learn more about using the system. Examples are Ray and Ray (2003) and Herborth (2005).

1.4 SYSTEM CALLS

Armed with our general knowledge of how MINIX 3 deals with processes and files, we can now begin to look at the interface between the operating system and its application programs, that is, the set of system calls. Although this discussion specifically refers to POSIX (International Standard 9945-1), hence also to MINIX 3, UNIX, and Linux, most other modern operating systems have system calls that perform the same functions, even if the details differ. Since the actual mechanics of issuing a system call are highly machine dependent, and often must be expressed in assembly code, a procedure library is provided to make it possible to make system calls from C programs.

It is useful to keep the following in mind: any single-CPU computer can execute only one instruction at a time. If a process is running a user program in user mode and needs a system service, such as reading data from a file, it has to execute a trap or system call instruction to transfer control to the operating system. The operating system then figures out what the calling process wants by inspecting the parameters. Then it carries out the system call and returns control to the instruction following the system call. In a sense, making a system call is like making a special kind of procedure call, only system calls enter the kernel or other privileged operating system components and procedure calls do not.

To make the system call mechanism clearer, let us take a quick look at read. It has three parameters: the first one specifying the file, the second one specifying the buffer, and the third one specifying the number of bytes to read. A call to read from a C program might look like this:

```
count = read(fd, buffer, nbytes);
```

The system call (and the library procedure) return the number of bytes actually read in *count*. This value is normally the same as *nbytes*, but may be smaller, if, for example, end-of-file is encountered while reading.

If the system call cannot be carried out, either due to an invalid parameter or a disk error, *count* is set to −1, and the error number is put in a global variable, *errno*. Programs should always check the results of a system call to see if an error occurred.

MINIX 3 has a total of 53 main system calls. These are listed in Fig. 1-9, grouped for convenience in six categories. A few other calls exist, but they have very specialized uses so we will omit them here. In the following sections we will briefly examine each of the calls of Fig. 1-9 to see what it does. To a large extent, the services offered by these calls determine most of what the operating system has to do, since the resource management on personal computers is minimal (at least compared to big machines with many users).

This is a good place to point out that the mapping of POSIX procedure calls onto system calls is not necessarily one-to-one. The POSIX standard specifies a number of procedures that a conformant system must supply, but it does not specify whether they are system calls, library calls, or something else. In some cases, the POSIX procedures are supported as library routines in MINIX 3. In others, several required procedures are only minor variations of one another, and one system call handles all of them.

1.4.1 System Calls for Process Management

The first group of calls in Fig. 1-9 deals with process management. Fork is a good place to start the discussion. Fork is the only way to create a new process in MINIX 3. It creates an exact duplicate of the original process, including all the file descriptors, registers—everything. After the fork, the original process and the copy (the parent and child) go their separate ways. All the variables have identical values at the time of the fork, but since the parent's data are copied to create

Process management	pid = **fork**()	Create a child process identical to the parent
	pid = **waitpid**(pid, &statloc, opts)	Wait for a child to terminate
	s = **wait**(&status)	Old version of waitpid
	s = **execve**(name, argv, envp)	Replace a process core image
	exit(status)	Terminate process execution and return status
	size = **brk**(addr)	Set the size of the data segment
	pid = **getpid**()	Return the caller's process id
	pid = **getpgrp**()	Return the id of the caller's process group
	pid = **setsid**()	Create a new session and return its proc. group id
	l = **ptrace**(req, pid, addr, data)	Used for debugging
Signals	s = **sigaction**(sig, &act, &oldact)	Define action to take on signals
	s = **sigreturn**(&context)	Return from a signal
	s = **sigprocmask**(how, &set, &old)	Examine or change the signal mask
	s = **sigpending**(set)	Get the set of blocked signals
	s = **sigsuspend**(sigmask)	Replace the signal mask and suspend the process
	s = **kill**(pid, sig)	Send a signal to a process
	residual = **alarm**(seconds)	Set the alarm clock
	s = **pause**()	Suspend the caller until the next signal
File Management	fd = **creat**(name, mode)	Obsolete way to create a new file
	fd = **mknod**(name, mode, addr)	Create a regular, special, or directory i-node
	fd = **open**(file, how, ...)	Open a file for reading, writing or both
	s = **close**(fd)	Close an open file
	n = **read**(fd, buffer, nbytes)	Read data from a file into a buffer
	n = **write**(fd, buffer, nbytes)	Write data from a buffer into a file
	pos = **lseek**(fd, offset, whence)	Move the file pointer
	s = **stat**(name, &buf)	Get a file's status information
	s = **fstat**(fd, &buf)	Get a file's status information
	fd = **dup**(fd)	Allocate a new file descriptor for an open file
	s = **pipe**(&fd[0])	Create a pipe
	s = **ioctl**(fd, request, argp)	Perform special operations on a file
	s = **access**(name, amode)	Check a file's accessibility
	s = **rename**(old, new)	Give a file a new name
	s = **fcntl**(fd, cmd, ...)	File locking and other operations
Dir. & File System Mgt.	s = **mkdir**(name, mode)	Create a new directory
	s = **rmdir**(name)	Remove an empty directory
	s = **link**(name1, name2)	Create a new entry, name2, pointing to name1
	s = **unlink**(name)	Remove a directory entry
	s = **mount**(special, name, flag)	Mount a file system
	s = **umount**(special)	Unmount a file system
	s = **sync**()	Flush all cached blocks to the disk
	s = **chdir**(dirname)	Change the working directory
	s = **chroot**(dirname)	Change the root directory
Protection	s = **chmod**(name, mode)	Change a file's protection bits
	uid = **getuid**()	Get the caller's uid
	gid = **getgid**()	Get the caller's gid
	s = **setuid**(uid)	Set the caller's uid
	s = **setgid**(gid)	Set the caller's gid
	s = **chown**(name, owner, group)	Change a file's owner and group
	oldmask = **umask**(complmode)	Change the mode mask
Time Management	seconds = **time**(&seconds)	Get the elapsed time since Jan. 1, 1970
	s = **stime**(tp)	Set the elapsed time since Jan. 1, 1970
	s = **utime**(file, timep)	Set a file's "last access" time
	s = **times**(buffer)	Get the user and system times used so far

Figure 1-9. The main MINIX system calls. *fd* is a file descriptor; *n* is a byte count.

the child, subsequent changes in one of them do not affect the other one. (The program text, which is unchangeable, is shared between parent and child.) The fork call returns a value, which is zero in the child and equal to the child's process identifier or **PID** in the parent. Using the returned PID, the two processes can see which one is the parent process and which one is the child process.

In most cases, after a fork, the child will need to execute different code from the parent. Consider the shell. It reads a command from the terminal, forks off a child process, waits for the child to execute the command, and then reads the next command when the child terminates. To wait for the child to finish, the parent executes a waitpid system call, which just waits until the child terminates (any child if more than one exists). Waitpid can wait for a specific child, or for any old child by setting the first parameter to −1. When waitpid completes, the address pointed to by the second parameter, *statloc*, will be set to the child's exit status (normal or abnormal termination and exit value). Various options are also provided, specified by the third parameter. The waitpid call replaces the previous wait call, which is now obsolete but is provided for reasons of backward compatibility.

Now consider how fork is used by the shell. When a command is typed, the shell forks off a new process. This child process must execute the user command. It does this by using the execve system call, which causes its entire core image to be replaced by the file named in its first parameter. (Actually, the system call itself is exec, but several different library procedures call it with different parameters and slightly different names. We will treat these as system calls here.) A highly simplified shell illustrating the use of fork, waitpid, and execve is shown in Fig. 1-10.

```
#define TRUE 1

while (TRUE) {                              /* repeat forever */
     type_prompt( );                        /* display prompt on the screen */
     read_command(command, parameters);     /* read input from terminal */

     if (fork( ) != 0) {                     /* fork off child process */
          /* Parent code. */
          waitpid(-1, &status, 0);           /* wait for child to exit */
     } else {
          /* Child code. */
          execve(command, parameters, 0);    /* execute command */
     }
}
```

Figure 1-10. A stripped-down shell. Throughout this book, *TRUE* is assumed to be defined as 1.

In the most general case, execve has three parameters: the name of the file to be executed, a pointer to the argument array, and a pointer to the environment array. These will be described shortly. Various library routines, including *execl*, *execv*, *execle*, and *execve*, are provided to allow the parameters to be omitted or specified in various ways. Throughout this book we will use the name exec to represent the system call invoked by all of these.

Let us consider the case of a command such as

cp file1 file2

used to copy *file1* to *file2*. After the shell has forked, the child process locates and executes the file *cp* and passes to it the names of the source and target files.

The main program of *cp* (and main program of most other C programs) contains the declaration

main(argc, argv, envp)

where *argc* is a count of the number of items on the command line, including the program name. For the example above, *argc* is 3.

The second parameter, *argv*, is a pointer to an array. Element *i* of that array is a pointer to the *i*-th string on the command line. In our example, *argv*[0] would point to the string "cp", *argv*[1] would point to the string "file1", and *argv*[2] would point to the string "file2".

The third parameter of *main*, *envp*, is a pointer to the environment, an array of strings containing assignments of the form *name=value* used to pass information such as the terminal type and home directory name to a program. In Fig. 1-10, no environment is passed to the child, so the third parameter of *execve* is a zero.

If exec seems complicated, do not despair; it is (semantically) the most complex of all the POSIX system calls. All the other ones are much simpler. As an example of a simple one, consider exit, which processes should use when they are finished executing. It has one parameter, the exit status (0 to 255), which is returned to the parent via *statloc* in the waitpid system call. The low-order byte of *status* contains the termination status, with 0 being normal termination and the other values being various error conditions. The high-order byte contains the child's exit status (0 to 255). For example, if a parent process executes the statement

n = waitpid(−1, &statloc, options);

it will be suspended until some child process terminates. If the child exits with, say, 4 as the parameter to *exit*, the parent will be awakened with *n* set to the child's PID and *statloc* set to 0x0400 (the C convention of prefixing hexadecimal constants with 0x will be used throughout this book).

Processes in MINIX 3 have their memory divided up into three segments: the **text segment** (i.e., the program code), the **data segment** (i.e., the variables), and the **stack segment**. The data segment grows upward and the stack grows downward, as shown in Fig. 1-11. Between them is a gap of unused address space. The stack grows into the gap automatically, as needed, but expansion of the data segment is done explicitly by using a system call, brk, which specifies the new address where the data segment is to end. This address may be more than the current value (data segment is growing) or less than the current value (data segment is shrinking). The parameter must, of course, be less than the stack pointer or the data and stack segments would overlap, which is forbidden.

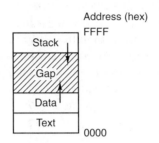

Figure 1-11. Processes have three segments: text, data, and stack. In this example, all three are in one address space, but separate instruction and data space is also supported.

As a convenience for programmers, a library routine *sbrk* is provided that also changes the size of the data segment, only its parameter is the number of bytes to add to the data segment (negative parameters make the data segment smaller). It works by keeping track of the current size of the data segment, which is the value returned by brk, computing the new size, and making a call asking for that number of bytes. The brk and sbrk calls, however, are not defined by the POSIX standard. Programmers are encouraged to use the *malloc* library procedure for dynamically allocating storage, and the underlying implementation of *malloc* was not thought to be a suitable subject for standardization since few programmers use it directly.

The next process system call is also the simplest, getpid. It just returns the caller's PID. Remember that in fork, only the parent was given the child's PID. If the child wants to find out its own PID, it must use getpid. The getpgrp call returns the PID of the caller's process group. setsid creates a new session and sets the process group's PID to the caller's. Sessions are related to an optional feature of POSIX, **job control**, which is not supported by MINIX 3 and which will not concern us further.

The last process management system call, ptrace, is used by debugging programs to control the program being debugged. It allows the debugger to read and write the controlled process' memory and manage it in other ways.

1.4.2 System Calls for Signaling

Although most forms of interprocess communication are planned, situations exist in which unexpected communication is needed. For example, if a user accidently tells a text editor to list the entire contents of a very long file, and then realizes the error, some way is needed to interrupt the editor. In MINIX 3, the user can hit the CTRL-C key on the keyboard, which sends a **signal** to the editor. The editor catches the signal and stops the print-out. Signals can also be used to report certain traps detected by the hardware, such as illegal instruction or floating point overflow. Timeouts are also implemented as signals.

When a signal is sent to a process that has not announced its willingness to accept that signal, the process is simply killed without further ado. To avoid this fate, a process can use the sigaction system call to announce that it is prepared to accept some signal type, and to provide the address of the signal handling procedure and a place to store the address of the current one. After a sigaction call, if a signal of the relevant type is generated (e.g., by pressing CTRL-C), the state of the process is pushed onto its own stack, and then the signal handler is called. It may run for as long as it wants to and perform any system calls it wants to. In practice, though, signal handlers are usually fairly short. When the signal handling procedure is done, it calls sigreturn to continue where it left off before the signal. The sigaction call replaces the older signal call, which is now provided as a library procedure, however, for backward compatibility.

Signals can be blocked in MINIX 3. A blocked signal is held pending until it is unblocked. It is not delivered, but also not lost. The sigprocmask call allows a process to define the set of blocked signals by presenting the kernel with a bitmap. It is also possible for a process to ask for the set of signals currently pending but not allowed to be delivered due to their being blocked. The sigpending call returns this set as a bitmap. Finally, the sigsuspend call allows a process to atomically set the bitmap of blocked signals and suspend itself.

Instead of providing a function to catch a signal, the program may also specify the constant SIG_IGN to have all subsequent signals of the specified type ignored, or SIG_DFL to restore the default action of the signal when it occurs. The default action is either to kill the process or ignore the signal, depending upon the signal. As an example of how SIG_IGN is used, consider what happens when the shell forks off a background process as a result of

    command &

It would be undesirable for a SIGINT signal (generated by pressing CTRL-C) to affect the background process, so after the fork but before the exec, the shell does

    sigaction(SIGINT, SIG_IGN, NULL);

and

    sigaction(SIGQUIT, SIG_IGN, NULL);

to disable the SIGINT and SIGQUIT signals. (SIGQUIT is generated by CTRL-\; it is the same as SIGINT generated by CTRL-C except that if it is not caught or ignored it makes a core dump of the process killed.) For foreground processes (no ampersand), these signals are not ignored.

Hitting CTRL-C is not the only way to send a signal. The kill system call allows a process to signal another process (provided they have the same UID— unrelated processes cannot signal each other). Getting back to the example of background processes used above, suppose a background process is started up, but later it is decided that the process should be terminated. SIGINT and SIGQUIT have been disabled, so something else is needed. The solution is to use the *kill* program, which uses the kill system call to send a signal to any process. By sending signal 9 (SIGKILL), to a background process, that process can be killed. SIG-KILL cannot be caught or ignored.

For many real-time applications, a process needs to be interrupted after a specific time interval to do something, such as to retransmit a potentially lost packet over an unreliable communication line. To handle this situation, the alarm system call has been provided. The parameter specifies an interval, in seconds, after which a SIGALRM signal is sent to the process. A process may only have one alarm outstanding at any instant. If an alarm call is made with a parameter of 10 seconds, and then 3 seconds later another alarm call is made with a parameter of 20 seconds, only one signal will be generated, 20 seconds after the second call. The first signal is canceled by the second call to alarm. If the parameter to alarm is zero, any pending alarm signal is canceled. If an alarm signal is not caught, the default action is taken and the signaled process is killed.

It sometimes occurs that a process has nothing to do until a signal arrives. For example, consider a computer-aided-instruction program that is testing reading speed and comprehension. It displays some text on the screen and then calls alarm to signal it after 30 seconds. While the student is reading the text, the program has nothing to do. It could sit in a tight loop doing nothing, but that would waste CPU time that another process or user might need. A better idea is to use pause, which tells MINIX 3 to suspend the process until the next signal.

1.4.3 System Calls for File Management

Many system calls relate to the file system. In this section we will look at calls that operate on individual files; in the next one we will examine those that involve directories or the file system as a whole. To create a new file, the creat call is used (why the call is creat and not create has been lost in the mists of time). Its parameters provide the name of the file and the protection mode. Thus

```
fd = creat("abc", 0751);
```

creates a file called *abc* with mode 0751 octal (in C, a leading zero means that a constant is in octal). The low-order 9 bits of 0751 specify the *rwx* bits for the owner (7 means read-write-execute permission), his group (5 means read-execute), and others (1 means execute only).

Creat not only creates a new file but also opens it for writing, regardless of the file's mode. The file descriptor returned, *fd*, can be used to write the file. If a creat is done on an existing file, that file is truncated to length 0, provided, of course, that the permissions are all right. The creat call is obsolete, as open can now create new files, but it has been included for backward compatibility.

Special files are created using mknod rather than creat. A typical call is

fd = mknod("/dev/ttyc2", 020744, 0x0402);

which creates a file named */dev/ttyc2* (the usual name for console 2) and gives it mode 020744 octal (a character special file with protection bits *rwxr--r--*). The third parameter contains the major device (4) in the high-order byte and the minor device (2) in the low-order byte. The major device could have been anything, but a file named */dev/ttyc2* ought to be minor device 2. Calls to mknod fail unless the caller is the superuser.

To read or write an existing file, the file must first be opened using open. This call specifies the file name to be opened, either as an absolute path name or relative to the working directory, and a code of *O_RDONLY*, *O_WRONLY*, or *O_RDWR*, meaning open for reading, writing, or both. The file descriptor returned can then be used for reading or writing. Afterward, the file can be closed by close, which makes the file descriptor available for reuse on a subsequent creat or open.

The most heavily used calls are undoubtedly read and write. We saw read earlier; write has the same parameters.

Although most programs read and write files sequentially, for some applications programs need to be able to access any part of a file at random. Associated with each file is a pointer that indicates the current position in the file. When reading (writing) sequentially, it normally points to the next byte to be read (written). The lseek call changes the value of the position pointer, so that subsequent calls to read or write can begin anywhere in the file, or even beyond the end.

lseek has three parameters: the first is the file descriptor for the file, the second is a file position, and the third tells whether the file position is relative to the beginning of the file, the current position, or the end of the file. The value returned by lseek is the absolute position in the file after changing the pointer.

For each file, MINIX 3 keeps track of the file mode (regular file, special file, directory, and so on), size, time of last modification, and other information. Programs can ask to see this information via the stat and fstat system calls. These differ only in that the former specifies the file by name, whereas the latter takes a file descriptor, making it useful for open files, especially standard input and standard output, whose names may not be known. Both calls provide as the second parameter a pointer to a structure where the information is to be put. The structure is shown in Fig. 1-12.

When manipulating file descriptors, the dup call is occasionally helpful. Consider, for example, a program that needs to close standard output (file descriptor 1), substitute another file as standard output, call a function that writes some output onto standard output, and then restore the original situation. Just closing file

```
struct stat {
    short st_dev;                  /* device where i-node belongs */
    unsigned short st_ino;         /* i-node number */
    unsigned short st_mode;        /* mode word */
    short st_nlink;                /* number of links */
    short st_uid;                  /* user id */
    short st_gid;                  /* group id */
    short st_rdev;                 /* major/minor device for special files */
    long st_size;                  /* file size */
    long st_atime;                 /* time of last access */
    long st_mtime;                 /* time of last modification */
    long st_ctime;                 /* time of last change to i-node */
};
```

Figure 1-12. The structure used to return information for the stat and fstat system calls. In the actual code, symbolic names are used for some of the types.

descriptor 1 and then opening a new file will make the new file standard output (assuming standard input, file descriptor 0, is in use), but it will be impossible to restore the original situation later.

The solution is first to execute the statement

    fd = dup(1);

which uses the dup system call to allocate a new file descriptor, *fd*, and arrange for it to correspond to the same file as standard output. Then standard output can be closed and a new file opened and used. When it is time to restore the original situation, file descriptor 1 can be closed, and then

    n = dup(fd);

executed to assign the lowest file descriptor, namely, 1, to the same file as *fd*. Finally, *fd* can be closed and we are back where we started.

The dup call has a variant that allows an arbitrary unassigned file descriptor to be made to refer to a given open file. It is called by

    dup2(fd, fd2);

where *fd* refers to an open file and *fd2* is the unassigned file descriptor that is to be made to refer to the same file as *fd*. Thus if *fd* refers to standard input (file descriptor 0) and *fd2* is 4, after the call, file descriptors 0 and 4 will both refer to standard input.

Interprocess communication in MINIX 3 uses pipes, as described earlier. When a user types

    cat file1 file2 | sort

the shell creates a pipe and arranges for standard output of the first process to write to the pipe, so standard input of the second process can read from it. The pipe system call creates a pipe and returns two file descriptors, one for writing and one for reading. The call is

```
pipe(&fd[0]);
```

where *fd* is an array of two integers and *fd*[0] is the file descriptor for reading and *fd*[1] is the one for writing. Typically, a fork comes next, and the parent closes the file descriptor for reading and the child closes the file descriptor for writing (or vice versa), so when they are done, one process can read the pipe and the other can write on it.

Figure 1-13 depicts a skeleton procedure that creates two processes, with the output of the first one piped into the second one. (A more realistic example would do error checking and handle arguments.) First a pipe is created, and then the procedure forks, with the parent eventually becoming the first process in the pipeline and the child process becoming the second one. Since the files to be executed, *process1* and *process2*, do not know that they are part of a pipeline, it is essential that the file descriptors be manipulated so that the first process' standard output be the pipe and the second one's standard input be the pipe. The parent first closes off the file descriptor for reading from the pipe. Then it closes standard output and does a DUP call that allows file descriptor 1 to write on the pipe. It is important to realize that dup always returns the lowest available file descriptor, in this case, 1. Then the program closes the other pipe file descriptor.

After the exec call, the process started will have file descriptors 0 and 2 be unchanged, and file descriptor 1 for writing on the pipe. The child code is analogous. The parameter to *execl* is repeated because the first one is the file to be executed and the second one is the first parameter, which most programs expect to be the file name.

The next system call, ioctl, is potentially applicable to all special files. It is, for instance, used by block device drivers like the SCSI driver to control tape and CD-ROM devices. Its main use, however, is with special character files, primarily terminals. POSIX defines a number of functions which the library translates into ioctl calls. The *tcgetattr* and *tcsetattr* library functions use ioctl to change the characters used for correcting typing errors on the terminal, changing the **terminal mode**, and so forth.

Traditionally, there are three terminal modes, cooked, raw, and cbreak. **Cooked mode** is the normal terminal mode, in which the erase and kill characters work normally, CTRL-S and CTRL-Q can be used for stopping and starting terminal output, CTRL-D means end of file, CTRL-C generates an interrupt signal, and CTRL-\ generates a quit signal to force a core dump.

In **raw mode**, all of these functions are disabled; consequently, every character is passed directly to the program with no special processing. Furthermore, in raw mode, a read from the terminal will give the program any characters that have been typed, even a partial line, rather than waiting for a complete line to be typed, as in cooked mode. Screen editors often use this mode.

```
#define STD_INPUT 0              /* file descriptor for standard input */
#define STD_OUTPUT 1             /* file descriptor for standard output */
pipeline(process1, process2)
char *process1, *process2;       /* pointers to program names */
{
  int fd[2];

  pipe(&fd[0]);                  /* create a pipe */
  if (fork() != 0) {
      /* The parent process executes these statements. */
      close(fd[0]);              /* process 1 does not need to read from pipe */
      close(STD_OUTPUT);         /* prepare for new standard output */
      dup(fd[1]);                /* set standard output to fd[1] */
      close(fd[1]);              /* this file descriptor not needed any more */
      execl(process1, process1, 0);
  } else {
      /* The child process executes these statements. */
      close(fd[1]);              /* process 2 does not need to write to pipe */
      close(STD_INPUT);          /* prepare for new standard input */
      dup(fd[0]);                /* set standard input to fd[0] */
      close(fd[0]);              /* this file descriptor not needed any more */
      execl(process2, process2, 0);
  }
}
```

Figure 1-13. A skeleton for setting up a two-process pipeline.

Cbreak mode is in between. The erase and kill characters for editing are disabled, as is CTRL-D, but CTRL-S, CTRL-Q, CTRL-C, and CTRL-\ are enabled. Like raw mode, partial lines can be returned to programs (if intraline editing is turned off there is no need to wait until a whole line has been received—the user cannot change his mind and delete it, as he can in cooked mode).

POSIX does not use the terms cooked, raw, and cbreak. In POSIX terminology **canonical mode** corresponds to cooked mode. In this mode there are eleven special characters defined, and input is by lines. In **noncanonical mode** a minimum number of characters to accept and a time, specified in units of 1/10th of a second, determine how a read will be satisfied. Under POSIX there is a great deal of flexibility, and various flags can be set to make noncanonical mode behave like either cbreak or raw mode. The older terms are more descriptive, and we will continue to use them informally.

Ioctl has three parameters, for example a call to *tcsetattr* to set terminal parameters will result in

    ioctl(fd, TCSETS, &termios);

The first parameter specifies a file, the second one specifies an operation, and the third one is the address of the POSIX structure that contains flags and the array of control characters. Other operation codes instruct the system to postpone the changes until all output has been sent, cause unread input to be discarded, and return the current values.

The access system call is used to determine whether a certain file access is permitted by the protection system. It is needed because some programs can run using a different user's UID. This SETUID mechanism will be described later.

The rename system call is used to give a file a new name. The parameters specify the old and new names.

Finally, the fcntl call is used to control files, somewhat analogous to ioctl (i.e., both of them are horrible hacks). It has several options, the most important of which is for advisory file locking. Using fcntl, it is possible for a process to lock and unlock parts of files and test part of a file to see if it is locked. The call does not enforce any lock semantics. Programs must do this themselves.

1.4.4 System Calls for Directory Management

In this section we will look at some system calls that relate more to directories or the file system as a whole, rather than just to one specific file as in the previous section. The first two calls, mkdir and rmdir, create and remove empty directories, respectively. The next call is link. Its purpose is to allow the same file to appear under two or more names, often in different directories. A typical use is to allow several members of the same programming team to share a common file, with each of them having the file appear in his own directory, possibly under different names. Sharing a file is not the same as giving every team member a private copy, because having a shared file means that changes that any member of the team makes are instantly visible to the other members—there is only one file. When copies are made of a file, subsequent changes made to one copy do not affect the other ones.

To see how link works, consider the situation of Fig. 1-14(a). Here are two users, *ast* and *jim*, each having their own directories with some files. If *ast* now executes a program containing the system call

```
link("/usr/jim/memo", "/usr/ast/note");
```

the file *memo* in *jim*'s directory is now entered into *ast*'s directory under the name *note*. Thereafter, */usr/jim/memo* and */usr/ast/note* refer to the same file.

Understanding how link works will probably make it clearer what it does. Every file in UNIX has a unique number, its i-number, that identifies it. This i-number is an index into a table of **i-nodes**, one per file, telling who owns the file, where its disk blocks are, and so on. A directory is simply a file containing a set of (i-number, ASCII name) pairs. In the first versions of UNIX, each directory entry was 16 bytes—2 bytes for the i-number and 14 bytes for the name. A more complicated structure is needed to support long file names, but conceptually a directory is still a set of (i-number, ASCII name) pairs. In Fig. 1-14, *mail* has i-number 16, and so on. What link does is simply create a new directory entry with

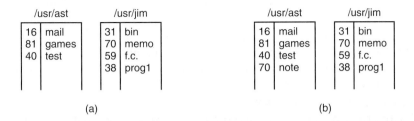

Figure 1-14. (a) Two directories before linking */usr/jim/memo* to ast's directory. (b) The same directories after linking.

a (possibly new) name, using the i-number of an existing file. In Fig. 1-14(b), two entries have the same i-number (70) and thus refer to the same file. If either one is later removed, using the unlink system call, the other one remains. If both are removed, UNIX sees that no entries to the file exist (a field in the i-node keeps track of the number of directory entries pointing to the file), so the file is removed from the disk.

As we have mentioned earlier, the mount system call allows two file systems to be merged into one. A common situation is to have the root file system containing the binary (executable) versions of the common commands and other heavily used files, on a hard disk. The user can then insert a CD-ROM with files to be read into the CD-ROM drive.

By executing the mount system call, the CD-ROM file system can be attached to the root file system, as shown in Fig. 1-15. A typical statement in C to perform the mount is

    mount("/dev/cdrom0", "/mnt", 0);

where the first parameter is the name of a block special file for CD-ROM drive 0, the second parameter is the place in the tree where it is to be mounted, and the third one tells whether the file system is to be mounted read-write or read-only.

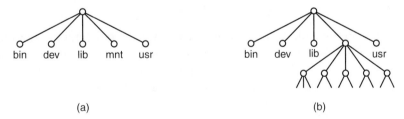

Figure 1-15. (a) File system before the mount. (b) File system after the mount.

After the mount call, a file on CD-ROM drive 0 can be accessed by just using its path from the root directory or the working directory, without regard to which drive it is on. In fact, second, third, and fourth drives can also be mounted anywhere in the tree. The mount call makes it possible to integrate removable media into a single integrated file hierarchy, without having to worry about which device a file is on. Although this example involves CD-ROMs, hard disks or portions of hard disks (often called **partitions** or **minor devices**) can also be mounted this way. When a file system is no longer needed, it can be unmounted with the umount system call.

MINIX 3 maintains a **block cache** cache of recently used blocks in main memory to avoid having to read them from the disk if they are used again quickly. If a block in the cache is modified (by a write on a file) and the system crashes before the modified block is written out to disk, the file system will be damaged. To limit the potential damage, it is important to flush the cache periodically, so that the amount of data lost by a crash will be small. The system call sync tells MINIX 3 to write out all the cache blocks that have been modified since being read in. When MINIX 3 is started up, a program called *update* is started as a background process to do a sync every 30 seconds, to keep flushing the cache.

Two other calls that relate to directories are chdir and chroot. The former changes the working directory and the latter changes the root directory. After the call

    chdir("/usr/ast/test");

an open on the file *xyz* will open */usr/ast/test/xyz*. chroot works in an analogous way. Once a process has told the system to change its root directory, all absolute path names (path names beginning with a "/") will start at the new root. Why would you want to do that? For security—server programs for protocols such as **FTP** (File Transfer Protocol) and **HTTP** (HyperText Transfer Protocol) do this so remote users of these services can access only the portions of a file system below the new root. Only superusers may execute chroot, and even superusers do not do it very often.

1.4.5 System Calls for Protection

In MINIX 3 every file has an 11-bit mode used for protection. Nine of these bits are the read-write-execute bits for the owner, group, and others. The chmod system call makes it possible to change the mode of a file. For example, to make a file read-only by everyone except the owner, one could execute

    chmod("file", 0644);

The other two protection bits, 02000 and 04000, are the SETGID (set-group-id) and SETUID (set-user-id) bits, respectively. When any user executes a program with the SETUID bit on, for the duration of that process the user's effective UID is changed to that of the file's owner. This feature is heavily used to allow users to execute programs that perform superuser only functions, such as creating directories. Creating a directory uses mknod, which is for the superuser only. By arranging for the *mkdir* program to be owned by the superuser and have mode 04755, ordinary users can be given the power to execute mknod but in a highly restricted way.

When a process executes a file that has the SETUID or SETGID bit on in its mode, it acquires an effective UID or GID different from its real UID or GID. It is sometimes important for a process to find out what its real and effective UID or GID is. The system calls getuid and getgid have been provided to supply this information. Each call returns both the real and effective UID or GID, so four library routines are needed to extract the proper information: *getuid*, *getgid*, *geteuid*, and *getegid*. The first two get the real UID/GID, and the last two the effective ones.

Ordinary users cannot change their UID, except by executing programs with the SETUID bit on, but the superuser has another possibility: the setuid system call, which sets both the effective and real UIDs. setgid sets both GIDs. The superuser can also change the owner of a file with the chown system call. In short, the superuser has plenty of opportunity for violating all the protection rules, which explains why so many students devote so much of their time to trying to become superuser.

The last two system calls in this category can be executed by ordinary user processes. The first one, umask, sets an internal bit mask within the system, which is used to mask off mode bits when a file is created. After the call

    umask(022);

the mode supplied by creat and mknod will have the 022 bits masked off before being used. Thus the call

    creat("file", 0777);

will set the mode to 0755 rather than 0777. Since the bit mask is inherited by child processes, if the shell does a umask just after login, none of the user's processes in that session will accidently create files that other people can write on.

When a program owned by the root has the SETUID bit on, it can access any file, because its effective UID is the superuser. Frequently it is useful for the program to know if the person who called the program has permission to access a given file. If the program just tries the access, it will always succeed, and thus learn nothing.

What is needed is a way to see if the access is permitted for the real UID. The access system call provides a way to find out. The *mode* parameter is 4 to check for read access, 2 for write access, and 1 for execute access. Combinations of these values are also allowed. For example, with *mode* equal to 6, the call returns 0 if both read and write access are allowed for the real ID; otherwise −1 is returned. With *mode* equal to 0, a check is made to see if the file exists and the directories leading up to it can be searched.

Although the protection mechanisms of all UNIX-like operating systems are generally similar, there are some differences and inconsistencies that lead to security vulnerabilities. See Chen et al. (2002) for a discussion.

1.4.6 System Calls for Time Management

MINIX 3 has four system calls that involve the time-of-day clock. Time just returns the current time in seconds, with 0 corresponding to Jan. 1, 1970 at midnight (just as the day was starting, not ending). Of course, the system clock must be set at some point in order to allow it to be read later, so stime has been provided to let the clock be set (by the superuser). The third time call is utime, which allows the owner of a file (or the superuser) to change the time stored in a file's i-node. Application of this system call is fairly limited, but a few programs need it, for example, *touch*, which sets the file's time to the current time.

Finally, we have times, which returns the accounting information to a process, so it can see how much CPU time it has used directly, and how much CPU time the system itself has expended on its behalf (handling its system calls). The total user and system times used by all of its children combined are also returned.

1.5 OPERATING SYSTEM STRUCTURE

Now that we have seen what operating systems look like on the outside (i.e, the programmer's interface), it is time to take a look inside. In the following sections, we will examine five different structures that have been tried, in order to get some idea of the spectrum of possibilities. These are by no means exhaustive, but they give an idea of some designs that have been tried in practice. The five designs are monolithic systems, layered systems, virtual machines, exokernels, and client-server systems.

1.5.1 Monolithic Systems

By far the most common organization, this approach might well be subtitled "The Big Mess." The structure is that there is no structure. The operating system is written as a collection of procedures, each of which can call any of the other ones whenever it needs to. When this technique is used, each procedure in the system has a well-defined interface in terms of parameters and results, and each one is free to call any other one, if the latter provides some useful computation that the former needs.

To construct the actual object program of the operating system when this approach is used, one first compiles all the individual procedures, or files containing the procedures, and then binds them all together into a single object file using the system linker. In terms of information hiding, there is essentially none—every procedure is visible to every other procedure (as opposed to a structure containing modules or packages, in which much of the information is hidden away inside modules, and only the officially designated entry points can be called from out-side the module).

Even in monolithic systems, however, it is possible to have at least a little structure. The services (system calls) provided by the operating system are requested by putting the parameters in well-defined places, such as in registers or on the stack, and then executing a special trap instruction known as a **kernel call** or **supervisor call**.

This instruction switches the machine from user mode to kernel mode and transfers control to the operating system. (Most CPUs have two modes: kernel mode, for the operating system, in which all instructions are allowed; and user mode, for user programs, in which I/O and certain other instructions are not allowed.)

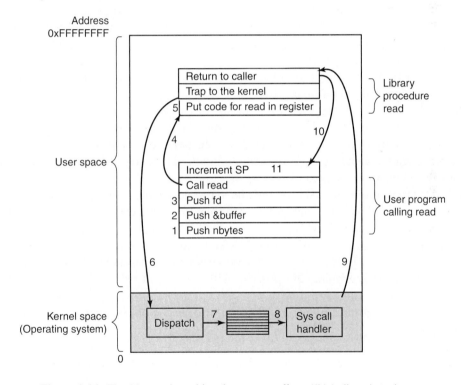

Figure 1-16. The 11 steps in making the system call read(fd, buffer, nbytes).

This is a good time to look at how system calls are performed. Recall that the read call is used like this:

```
count = read(fd, buffer, nbytes);
```

In preparation for calling the *read* library procedure, which actually makes the read system call, the calling program first pushes the parameters onto the stack, as shown in steps 1–3 in Fig. 1-16. C and C++ compilers push the parameters onto the stack in reverse order for historical reasons (having to do with making the first parameter to *printf*, the format string, appear on top of the stack). The first and third parameters are called by value, but the second parameter is passed by reference, meaning that the address of the buffer (indicated by &) is passed, not the contents of the buffer. Then comes the actual call to the library procedure (step 4). This instruction is the normal procedure call instruction used to call all procedures.

The library procedure, possibly written in assembly language, typically puts the system call number in a place where the operating system expects it, such as a register (step 5). Then it executes a TRAP instruction to switch from user mode to kernel mode and start execution at a fixed address within the kernel (step 6). The kernel code that starts examines the system call number and then dispatches to the correct system call handler, usually via a table of pointers to system call handlers indexed on system call number (step 7). At that point the system call handler runs (step 8). Once the system call handler has completed its work, control may be returned to the user-space library procedure at the instruction following the TRAP instruction (step 9). This procedure then returns to the user program in the usual way procedure calls return (step 10).

To finish the job, the user program has to clean up the stack, as it does after any procedure call (step 11). Assuming the stack grows downward, as it often does, the compiled code increments the stack pointer exactly enough to remove the parameters pushed before the call to *read*. The program is now free to do whatever it wants to do next.

In step 9 above, we said "may be returned to the user-space library procedure" for good reason. The system call may block the caller, preventing it from continuing. For example, if it is trying to read from the keyboard and nothing has been typed yet, the caller has to be blocked. In this case, the operating system will look around to see if some other process can be run next. Later, when the desired input is available, this process will get the attention of the system and steps 9–11 will occur.

This organization suggests a basic structure for the operating system:

1. A main program that invokes the requested service procedure.

2. A set of service procedures that carry out the system calls.

3. A set of utility procedures that help the service procedures.

In this model, for each system call there is one service procedure that takes care of it. The utility procedures do things that are needed by several service procedures, such as fetching data from user programs. This division of the procedures into three layers is shown in Fig. 1-17.

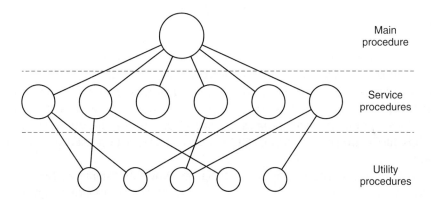

Figure 1-17. A simple structuring model for a monolithic system.

1.5.2 Layered Systems

A generalization of the approach of Fig. 1-17 is to organize the operating system as a hierarchy of layers, each one constructed upon the one below it. The first system constructed in this way was the THE system built at the Technische Hogeschool Eindhoven in the Netherlands by E. W. Dijkstra (1968) and his students. The THE system was a simple batch system for a Dutch computer, the Electrologica X8, which had 32K of 27-bit words (bits were expensive back then).

The system had 6 layers, as shown in Fig. 1-18. Layer 0 dealt with allocation of the processor, switching between processes when interrupts occurred or timers expired. Above layer 0, the system consisted of sequential processes, each of which could be programmed without having to worry about the fact that multiple processes were running on a single processor. In other words, layer 0 provided the basic multiprogramming of the CPU.

Layer	Function
5	The operator
4	User programs
3	Input/output management
2	Operator-process communication
1	Memory and drum management
0	Processor allocation and multiprogramming

Figure 1-18. Structure of the THE operating system.

Layer 1 did the memory management. It allocated space for processes in main memory and on a 512K word drum used for holding parts of processes (pages) for which there was no room in main memory. Above layer 1, processes did not have to worry about whether they were in memory or on the drum; the layer 1 software took care of making sure pages were brought into memory whenever they were needed.

Layer 2 handled communication between each process and the operator console. Above this layer each process effectively had its own operator console. Layer 3 took care of managing the I/O devices and buffering the information streams to and from them. Above layer 3 each process could deal with abstract I/O devices with nice properties, instead of real devices with many peculiarities. Layer 4 was where the user programs were found. They did not have to worry about process, memory, console, or I/O management. The system operator process was located in layer 5.

A further generalization of the layering concept was present in the MULTICS system. Instead of layers, MULTICS was organized as a series of concentric rings, with the inner ones being more privileged than the outer ones. When a procedure in an outer ring wanted to call a procedure in an inner ring, it had to make the equivalent of a system call, that is, a TRAP instruction whose parameters were carefully checked for validity before allowing the call to proceed. Although the entire operating system was part of the address space of each user process in MULTICS, the hardware made it possible to designate individual procedures (memory segments, actually) as protected against reading, writing, or executing.

Whereas the THE layering scheme was really only a design aid, because all the parts of the system were ultimately linked together into a single object program, in MULTICS, the ring mechanism was very much present at run time and enforced by the hardware. The advantage of the ring mechanism is that it can easily be extended to structure user subsystems. For example, a professor could write a program to test and grade student programs and run this program in ring n, with the student programs running in ring $n + 1$ so that they could not change their grades. The Pentium hardware supports the MULTICS ring structure, but no major operating system uses it at present.

1.5.3 Virtual Machines

The initial releases of OS/360 were strictly batch systems. Nevertheless, many 360 users wanted to have timesharing, so various groups, both inside and outside IBM decided to write timesharing systems for it. The official IBM timesharing system, TSS/360, was delivered late, and when it finally arrived it was so big and slow that few sites converted over to it. It was eventually abandoned after its development had consumed some $50 million (Graham, 1970). But a group at IBM's Scientific Center in Cambridge, Massachusetts, produced a radically different system that IBM eventually accepted as a product, and which is now widely used on its mainframes.

This system, originally called CP/CMS and later renamed VM/370 (Seawright and MacKinnon, 1979), was based on a very astute observation: a timesharing system provides (1) multiprogramming and (2) an extended machine with a more convenient interface than the bare hardware. The essence of VM/370 is to completely separate these two functions.

The heart of the system, known as the **virtual machine monitor**, runs on the bare hardware and does the multiprogramming, providing not one, but several virtual machines to the next layer up, as shown in Fig. 1-19. However, unlike all other operating systems, these virtual machines are not extended machines, with files and other nice features. Instead, they are *exact* copies of the bare hardware, including kernel/user mode, I/O, interrupts, and everything else the real machine has.

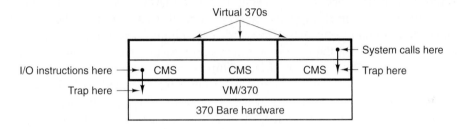

Figure 1-19. The structure of VM/370 with CMS.

Because each virtual machine is identical to the true hardware, each one can run any operating system that will run directly on the bare hardware. Different virtual machines can, and frequently do, run different operating systems. Some run one of the descendants of OS/360 for batch or transaction processing, while others run a single-user, interactive system called **CMS** (Conversational Monitor System) for timesharing users.

When a CMS program executes a system call, the call is trapped to the operating system in its own virtual machine, not to VM/370, just as it would if it were running on a real machine instead of a virtual one. CMS then issues the normal hardware I/O instructions for reading its virtual disk or whatever is needed to carry out the call. These I/O instructions are trapped by VM/370, which then performs them as part of its simulation of the real hardware. By making a complete separation of the functions of multiprogramming and providing an extended machine, each of the pieces can be much simpler, more flexible, and easier to maintain.

The idea of a virtual machine is used nowadays in a different context: running old MS-DOS programs on a Pentium. When designing the Pentium and its software, both Intel and Microsoft realized that there would be a big demand for running old software on new hardware. For this reason, Intel provided a virtual 8086 mode on the Pentium. In this mode, the machine acts like an 8086 (which is identical to an 8088 from a software point of view), including 16-bit addressing with a 1-MB limit.

This mode is used by Windows, and other operating systems for running old MS-DOS programs. These programs are started up in virtual 8086 mode. As long as they execute normal instructions, they run on the bare hardware. However, when a program tries to trap to the operating system to make a system call, or tries to do protected I/O directly, a trap to the virtual machine monitor occurs.

Two variants on this design are possible. In the first one, MS-DOS itself is loaded into the virtual 8086's address space, so the virtual machine monitor just reflects the trap back to MS-DOS, just as would happen on a real 8086. When MS-DOS later tries to do the I/O itself, that operation is caught and carried out by the virtual machine monitor.

In the other variant, the virtual machine monitor just catches the first trap and does the I/O itself, since it knows what all the MS-DOS system calls are and thus knows what each trap is supposed to do. This variant is less pure than the first one, since it emulates only MS-DOS correctly, and not other operating systems, as the first one does. On the other hand, it is much faster, since it saves the trouble of starting up MS-DOS to do the I/O. A further disadvantage of actually running MS-DOS in virtual 8086 mode is that MS-DOS fiddles around with the interrupt enable/disable bit quite a lot, all of which must be emulated at considerable cost.

It is worth noting that neither of these approaches are really the same as VM/370, since the machine being emulated is not a full Pentium, but only an 8086. With the VM/370 system, it is possible to run VM/370, itself, in the virtual machine. Even the earliest versions of Windows require at least a 286 and cannot be run on a virtual 8086.

Several virtual machine implementations are marketed commercially. For companies that provide web-hosting services, it can be more economical to run multiple virtual machines on a single fast server (perhaps one with multiple CPUs) than to run many small computers, each hosting a single Web site. VMWare and Microsoft's Virtual PC are marketed for such installations. These programs use large files on a host system as simulated disks for their guest systems. To achieve efficiency they analyze guest system program binaries and allow safe code to run directly on the host hardware, trapping instructions that make operating system calls. Such systems are also useful in education. For instance, students working on MINIX 3 lab assignments can work using MINIX 3 as a guest operating system on VMWare on a Windows, Linux or UNIX host with no risk of damaging other software installed on the same PC. Most professors teaching other subjects would be very nervous about sharing laboratory computers with an operating systems course where student mistakes could corrupt or erase disk data.

Another area where virtual machines are used, but in a somewhat different way, is for running Java programs. When Sun Microsystems invented the Java programming language, it also invented a virtual machine (i.e., a computer architecture) called the **JVM** (**Java Virtual Machine**). The Java compiler produces code for JVM, which then typically is executed by a software JVM interpreter. The advantage of this approach is that the JVM code can be shipped over the Internet to any computer that has a JVM interpreter and run there. If the compiler had produced SPARC or Pentium binary programs, for example, they could not have been shipped and run anywhere as easily. (Of course, Sun could have produced a compiler that produced SPARC binaries and then distributed a SPARC interpreter, but JVM is a much simpler architecture to interpret.) Another advantage of using JVM is that if the interpreter is implemented properly, which is not completely trivial, incoming JVM programs can be checked for safety and then executed in a protected environment so they cannot steal data or do any damage.

1.5.4 Exokernels

With VM/370, each user process gets an exact copy of the actual computer. With virtual 8086 mode on the Pentium, each user process gets an exact copy of a different computer. Going one step further, researchers at M.I.T. built a system that gives each user a clone of the actual computer, but with a subset of the resources (Engler et al., 1995; and Leschke, 2004). Thus one virtual machine might get disk blocks 0 to 1023, the next one might get blocks 1024 to 2047, and so on.

At the bottom layer, running in kernel mode, is a program called the **exokernel**. Its job is to allocate resources to virtual machines and then check attempts to use them to make sure no machine is trying to use somebody else's resources. Each user-level virtual machine can run its own operating system, as on VM/370 and the Pentium virtual 8086s, except that each one is restricted to using only the resources it has asked for and been allocated.

The advantage of the exokernel scheme is that it saves a layer of mapping. In the other designs, each virtual machine thinks it has its own disk, with blocks running from 0 to some maximum, so the virtual machine monitor must maintain tables to remap disk addresses (and all other resources). With the exokernel, this remapping is not needed. The exokernel need only keep track of which virtual machine has been assigned which resource. This method still has the advantage of separating the multiprogramming (in the exokernel) from the user operating system code (in user space), but with less overhead, since all the exokernel has to do is keep the virtual machines out of each other's hair.

1.5.5 Client-Server Model

VM/370 gains much in simplicity by moving a large part of the traditional operating system code (implementing the extended machine) into a higher layer, CMS. Nevertheless, VM/370 itself is still a complex program because simulating a number of virtual 370s is not *that* simple (especially if you want to do it reasonably efficiently).

A trend in modern operating systems is to take this idea of moving code up into higher layers even further and remove as much as possible from the operating system, leaving a minimal **kernel**. The usual approach is to implement most of the operating system functions in user processes. To request a service, such as reading a block of a file, a user process (now known as the **client process**) sends the request to a **server process**, which then does the work and sends back the answer.

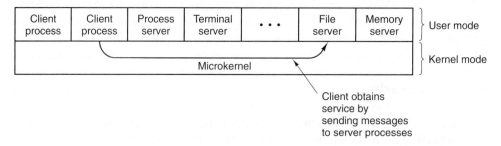

Figure 1-20. The client-server model.

In this model, shown in Fig. 1-20, all the kernel does is handle the communication between clients and servers. By splitting the operating system up into parts, each of which only handles one facet of the system, such as file service, process service, terminal service, or memory service, each part becomes small and manageable. Furthermore, because all the servers run as user-mode processes, and not in kernel mode, they do not have direct access to the hardware. As a consequence, if a bug in the file server is triggered, the file service may crash, but this will not usually bring the whole machine down.

Another advantage of the client-server model is its adaptability to use in distributed systems (see Fig. 1-21). If a client communicates with a server by sending it messages, the client need not know whether the message is handled locally in its own machine, or whether it was sent across a network to a server on a remote machine. As far as the client is concerned, the same thing happens in both cases: a request was sent and a reply came back.

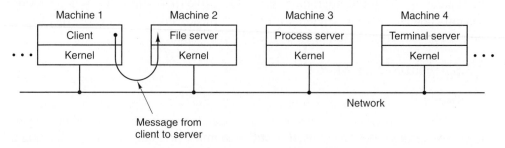

Figure 1-21. The client-server model in a distributed system.

The picture painted above of a kernel that handles only the transport of messages from clients to servers and back is not completely realistic. Some operating system functions (such as loading commands into the physical I/O device registers) are difficult, if not impossible, to do from user-space programs. There are two ways of dealing with this problem. One way is to have some critical server processes (e.g., I/O device drivers) actually run in kernel mode, with complete access to all the hardware, but still communicate with other processes using the normal message mechanism. A variant of this mechanism was used in earlier versions of MINIX where drivers were compiled into the kernel but ran as separate processes.

The other way is to build a minimal amount of **mechanism** into the kernel but leave the **policy** decisions up to servers in user space. For example, the kernel might recognize that a message sent to a certain special address means to take the contents of that message and load it into the I/O device registers for some disk, to start a disk read. In this example, the kernel would not even inspect the bytes in the message to see if they were valid or meaningful; it would just blindly copy them into the disk's device registers. (Obviously, some scheme for limiting such messages to authorized processes only must be used.) This is how MINIX 3 works, drivers are in user space and use special kernel calls to request reads and writes of I/O registers or to access kernel information. The split between mechanism and policy is an important concept; it occurs again and again in operating systems in various contexts.

1.6 OUTLINE OF THE REST OF THIS BOOK

Operating systems typically have four major components: process management, I/O device management, memory management, and file management. MINIX 3 is also divided into these four parts. The next four chapters deal with these four topics, one topic per chapter. Chapter 6 is a list of suggested readings and a bibliography.

The chapters on processes, I/O, memory management, and file systems have the same general structure. First the general principles of the subject are laid out. Then comes an overview of the corresponding area of MINIX 3 (which also applies to UNIX). Finally, the MINIX 3 implementation is discussed in detail. The implementation section may be skimmed or skipped without loss of continuity by readers just interested in the principles of operating systems and not interested in the MINIX 3 code. Readers who *are* interested in finding out how a real operating system (MINIX 3) works should read all the sections.

1.7 SUMMARY

Operating systems can be viewed from two viewpoints: resource managers and extended machines. In the resource manager view, the operating system's job is to efficiently manage the different parts of the system. In the extended machine view, the job of the system is to provide the users with a virtual machine that is more convenient to use than the actual machine.

Operating systems have a long history, starting from the days when they replaced the operator, to modern multiprogramming systems.

The heart of any operating system is the set of system calls that it can handle. These tell what the operating system really does. For MINIX 3, these calls can be divided into six groups. The first group of system calls relates to process creation and termination. The second group handles signals. The third group is for reading and writing files. A fourth group is for directory management. The fifth group protects information, and the sixth group is about keeping track of time.

Operating systems can be structured in several ways. The most common ones are as a monolithic system, as a hierarchy of layers, as a virtual machine system, using an exokernel, and using the client-server model.

PROBLEMS

1. What are the two main functions of an operating system?

2. What is the difference between kernel mode and user mode? Why is the difference important to an operating system?

3. What is multiprogramming?

4. What is spooling? Do you think that advanced personal computers will have spooling as a standard feature in the future?

5. On early computers, every byte of data read or written was directly handled by the CPU (i.e., there was no DMA—Direct Memory Access). What implications does this organization have for multiprogramming?

6. Why was timesharing not widespread on second-generation computers?

7. Which of the following instructions should be allowed only in kernel mode?

   (a) Disable all interrupts.
   (b) Read the time-of-day clock.
   (c) Set the time-of-day clock.
   (d) Change the memory map.

8. List some differences between personal computer operating systems and mainframe operating systems.

9. Give one reason why a closed-source proprietary operating system like Windows should have better quality than an open-source operating system like Linux. Now give one reason why an open-source operating system like Linux should have better quality than a closed-source proprietary operating system like Windows.

10. A MINIX file whose owner has UID = 12 and GID = 1 has mode *rwxr-x---*. Another user with UID = 6, GID = 1 tries to execute the file. What will happen?

11. In view of the fact that the mere existence of a superuser can lead to all kinds of security problems, why does such a concept exist?

12. All versions of UNIX support file naming using both absolute paths (relative to the root) and relative paths (relative to the working directory). Would it be possible to dispose of one of these and just use the other? If so, which would you suggest keeping?

13. Why is the process table needed in a timesharing system? Is it also needed in personal computer systems in which only one process exists, that process taking over the entire machine until it is finished?

14. What is the essential difference between a block special file and a character special file?

15. In MINIX 3 if user 2 links to a file owned by user 1, then user 1 removes the file, what happens when user 2 tries to read the file?

16. Are pipes an essential facility? Would major functionality be lost if they were not available?

17. Modern consumer appliances such as stereos and digital cameras often have a display where commands can be entered and the results of entering those commands can be viewed. These devices often have a primitive operating system inside. To what part of a personal computer software is the command processing via the stereo or camera's display similar to?

18. Windows does not have a fork system call, yet it is able to create new processes. Make an educated guess about the semantics of the system call Windows uses to create new processes.

19. Why is the chroot system call limited to the superuser? (*Hint*: Think about protection problems.)

20. Examine the list of system calls in Fig. 1-9. Which call do you think is likely to execute most quickly. Explain your answer.

21. Suppose that a computer can execute 1 billion instructions/sec and that a system call takes 1000 instructions, including the trap and all the context switching. How many system calls can the computer execute per second and still have half the CPU capacity for running application code?

22. There is a mknod system call in Fig. 1-16 but there is no rmnod call. Does this mean that you have to be very, very careful about making nodes this way because there is no way to every remove them?

23. Why does MINIX 3 have the program *update* running in the background all the time?

24. Does it ever make any sense to ignore the SIGALRM signal?

25. The client-server model is popular in distributed systems. Can it also be used in a single-computer system?

26. The initial versions of the Pentium could not support a virtual machine monitor. What essential characteristic is needed to allow a machine to be virtualizable?

27. Write a program (or series of programs) to test all the MINIX 3 system calls. For each call, try various sets of parameters, including some incorrect ones, to see if they are detected.

28. Write a shell that is similar to Fig. 1-10 but contains enough code that it actually works so you can test it. You might also add some features such as redirection of input and output, pipes, and background jobs.

2

PROCESSES

We are now about to embark on a detailed study of how operating systems, in general, and MINIX 3, in particular, are designed and constructed. The most central concept in any operating system is the *process*: an abstraction of a running program. Everything else hinges on this concept, and it is important that the operating system designer (and student) understand this concept well.

2.1 INTRODUCTION TO PROCESSES

All modern computers can do several things at the same time. While running a user program, a computer can also be reading from a disk and outputting text to a screen or printer. In a multiprogramming system, the CPU also switches from program to program, running each for tens or hundreds of milliseconds. While, strictly speaking, at any instant of time, the CPU is running only one program, in the course of 1 second, it may work on several programs, thus giving the users the illusion of parallelism. Sometimes people speak of **pseudoparallelism** in this context, to contrast it with the true hardware parallelism of **multiprocessor** systems (which have two or more CPUs sharing the same physical memory). Keeping track of multiple, parallel activities is hard for people to do. Therefore, operating system designers over the years have evolved a conceptual model (sequential processes) that makes parallelism easier to deal with. That model, its uses, and some of its consequences form the subject of this chapter.

2.1.1 The Process Model

In this model, all the runnable software on the computer, sometimes including the operating system, is organized into a number of **sequential processes**, or just **processes** for short. A process is just an executing program, including the current values of the program counter, registers, and variables. Conceptually, each process has its own virtual CPU. In reality, of course, the real CPU switches back and forth from process to process, but to understand the system, it is much easier to think about a collection of processes running in (pseudo) parallel, than to try to keep track of how the CPU switches from program to program. This rapid switching back and forth is called **multiprogramming**, as we saw in Chap. 1.

In Fig. 2-1(a) we see a computer multiprogramming four programs in memory. In Fig. 2-1(b) we see four processes, each with its own flow of control (i.e., its own program counter), and each one running independently of the other ones. Of course, there is only one physical program counter, so when each process runs, its logical program counter is loaded into the real program counter. When it is finished for the time being, the physical program counter is saved in the process' logical program counter in memory. In Fig. 2-1(c) we see that viewed over a long enough time interval, all the processes have made progress, but at any given instant only one process is actually running.

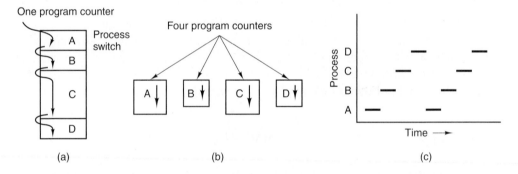

Figure 2-1. (a) Multiprogramming of four programs. (b) Conceptual model of four independent, sequential processes. (c) Only one program is active at any instant.

With the CPU switching back and forth among the processes, the rate at which a process performs its computation will not be uniform, and probably not even reproducible if the same processes are run again. Thus, processes must not be programmed with built-in assumptions about timing. Consider, for example, an I/O process that starts a streamer tape to restore backed up files, executes an idle loop 10,000 times to let it get up to speed, and then issues a command to read the first record. If the CPU decides to switch to another process during the idle loop, the tape process might not run again until after the first record was already past the read head. When a process has critical real-time requirements like this, that is, particular events *must* occur within a specified number of milliseconds, special measures must be taken to ensure that they do occur. Normally, however, most processes are not affected by the underlying multiprogramming of the CPU or the relative speeds of different processes.

The difference between a process and a program is subtle, but crucial. An analogy may help make this point clearer. Consider a culinary-minded computer scientist who is baking a birthday cake for his daughter. He has a birthday cake recipe and a kitchen well stocked with the necessary input: flour, eggs, sugar, extract of vanilla, and so on. In this analogy, the recipe is the program (i.e., an algorithm expressed in some suitable notation), the computer scientist is the processor (CPU), and the cake ingredients are the input data. The process is the activity consisting of our baker reading the recipe, fetching the ingredients, and baking the cake.

Now imagine that the computer scientist's son comes running in crying, saying that he has been stung by a bee. The computer scientist records where he was in the recipe (the state of the current process is saved), gets out a first aid book, and begins following the directions in it. Here we see the processor being switched from one process (baking) to a higher priority process (administering medical care), each having a different program (recipe vs. first aid book). When the bee sting has been taken care of, the computer scientist goes back to his cake, continuing at the point where he left off.

The key idea here is that a process is an activity of some kind. It has a program, input, output, and a state. A single processor may be shared among several processes, with some scheduling algorithm being used to determine when to stop work on one process and service a different one.

2.1.2 Process Creation

Operating systems need some way to make sure all the necessary processes exist. In very simple systems, or in systems designed for running only a single application (e.g., controlling a device in real time), it may be possible to have all the processes that will ever be needed be present when the system comes up. In general-purpose systems, however, some way is needed to create and terminate processes as needed during operation. We will now look at some of the issues.

There are four principal events that cause processes to be created:

1. System initialization.

2. Execution of a process creation system call by a running process.

3. A user request to create a new process.

4. Initiation of a batch job.

When an operating system is booted, often several processes are created. Some of these are foreground processes, that is, processes that interact with (human) users and perform work for them. Others are background processes, which are not associated with particular users, but instead have some specific function. For example, a background process may be designed to accept incoming requests for web pages hosted on that machine, waking up when a request arrives to service the request. Processes that stay in the background to handle some activity such as web pages, printing, and so on are called **daemons**. Large systems commonly have dozens of them. In MINIX 3, the *ps* program can be used to list the running processes.

In addition to the processes created at boot time, new processes can be created afterward as well. Often a running process will issue system calls to create one or more new processes to help it do its job. Creating new processes is particularly useful when the work to be done can easily be formulated in terms of several related, but otherwise independent interacting processes. For example, when compiling a large program, the *make* program invokes the C compiler to convert source files to object code, and then it invokes the *install* program to copy the program to its destination, set ownership and permissions, etc. In MINIX 3, the C compiler itself is actually several different programs, which work together. These include a preprocessor, a C language parser, an assembly language code generator, an assembler, and a linker.

In interactive systems, users can start a program by typing a command. In MINIX 3, virtual consoles allow a user to start a program, say a compiler, and then switch to an alternate console and start another program, perhaps to edit documentation while the compiler is running.

The last situation in which processes are created applies only to the batch systems found on large mainframes. Here users can submit batch jobs to the system (possibly remotely). When the operating system decides that it has the resources to run another job, it creates a new process and runs the next job from the input queue in it.

Technically, in all these cases, a new process is created by having an existing process execute a process creation system call. That process may be a running user process, a system process invoked from the keyboard or mouse, or a batch manager process. What that process does is execute a system call to create the new process. This system call tells the operating system to create a new process and indicates, directly or indirectly, which program to run in it.

In MINIX 3, there is only one system call to create a new process: fork. This call creates an exact clone of the calling process. After the fork, the two processes, the parent and the child, have the same memory image, the same environment strings, and the same open files. That is all there is. Usually, the child process then executes execve or a similar system call to change its memory image and run a new program. For example, when a user types a command, say, *sort*, to the shell, the shell forks off a child process and the child executes *sort*. The reason for this two-step process is to allow the child to manipulate its file descriptors after the fork but before the execve to accomplish redirection of standard input, standard output, and standard error.

In both MINIX 3 and UNIX, after a process is created both the parent and child have their own distinct address spaces. If either process changes a word in its address space, the change is not visible to the other process. The child's initial address space is a *copy* of the parent's, but there are two distinct address spaces involved; no writable memory is shared (like some UNIX implementations, MINIX 3 can share the program text between the two since that cannot be modified). It is, however, possible for a newly created process to share some of its creator's other resources, such as open files.

2.1.3 Process Termination

After a process has been created, it starts running and does whatever its job is. However, nothing lasts forever, not even processes. Sooner or later the new process will terminate, usually due to one of the following conditions:

1. Normal exit (voluntary).

2. Error exit (voluntary).

3. Fatal error (involuntary).

4. Killed by another process (involuntary).

Most processes terminate because they have done their work. When a compiler has compiled the program given to it, the compiler executes a system call to tell the operating system that it is finished. This call is exit in MINIX 3. Screen-oriented programs also support voluntary termination. For instance, editors always have a key combination that the user can invoke to tell the process to save the working file, remove any temporary files that are open and terminate.

The second reason for termination is that the process discovers a fatal error. For example, if a user types the command

    cc foo.c

to compile the program *foo.c* and no such file exists, the compiler simply exits.

The third reason for termination is an error caused by the process, perhaps due to a program bug. Examples include executing an illegal instruction, referencing nonexistent memory, or dividing by zero. In MINIX 3, a process can tell the operating system that it wishes to handle certain errors itself, in which case the process is signaled (interrupted) instead of terminated when one of the errors occurs.

The fourth reason a process might terminate is that one process executes a system call telling the operating system to kill some other process. In MINIX 3, this call is kill. Of course, the killer must have the necessary authorization to do in the killee. In some systems, when a process terminates, either voluntarily or otherwise, all processes it created are immediately killed as well. MINIX 3 does not work this way, however.

2.1.4 Process Hierarchies

In some systems, when a process creates another process, the parent and child continue to be associated in certain ways. The child can itself create more processes, forming a process hierarchy. Unlike plants and animals that use sexual reproduction, a process has only one parent (but zero, one, two, or more children).

In MINIX 3, a process, its children, and further descendants together may form a process group. When a user sends a signal from the keyboard, the signal may be delivered to all members of the process group currently associated with the keyboard (usually all processes that were created in the current window). This is signal-dependent. If a signal is sent to a group, each process can catch the signal, ignore the signal, or take the default action, which is to be killed by the signal.

As a simple example of how process trees are used, let us look at how MINIX 3 initializes itself. Two special processes, the **reincarnation server** and **init** are present in the boot image. The reincarnation server's job is to (re)start drivers and servers. It begins by blocking, waiting for a message telling it what to create.

In contrast, *init* executes the */etc/rc* script that causes it to issue commands to the reincarnation server to start the drivers and servers not present in the boot image. This procedure makes the drivers and servers so started children of the reincarnation server, so if any of them ever terminate, the reincarnation server will be informed and can restart (i.e., reincarnate) them again. This mechanism is intended to allow MINIX 3 to tolerate a driver or server crash because a new one will be started automatically. In practice, replacing a driver is much easier than replacing a server, however, since there fewer repercussions elsewhere in the system. (And, we do not say this always works perfectly; it is still work in progress.)

When *init* has finished this, it reads a configuration file */etc/ttytab*) to see which terminals and virtual terminals exist. *Init* forks a *getty* process for each one, displays a login prompt on it, and then waits for input. When a name is typed, *getty* execs a *login* process with the name as its argument. If the user succeeds in logging in, *login* will exec the user's shell. So the shell is a child of *init*. User commands create children of the shell, which are grandchildren of *init*. This sequence of events is an example of how process trees are used. As an aside, the code for the reincarnation server and *init* is not listed in this book; neither is the shell. The line had to be drawn somewhere. But now you have the basic idea.

2.1.5 Process States

Although each process is an independent entity, with its own program counter registers, stack, open files, alarms, and other internal state, processes often need to interact, communicate, and synchronize with other processes. One process may generate some output that another process uses as input, for example. In that case, the data needs to be moved between processes. In the shell command

     cat chapter1 chapter2 chapter3 | grep tree

the first process, running *cat*, concatenates and outputs three files. The second process, running *grep*, selects all lines containing the word "tree." Depending on the relative speeds of the two processes (which depends on both the relative complexity of the programs and how much CPU time each one has had), it may happen that *grep* is ready to run, but there is no input waiting for it. It must then **block** until some input is available.

When a process blocks, it does so because logically it cannot continue, typically because it is waiting for input that is not yet available. It is also possible for a process that is conceptually ready and able to run to be stopped because the operating system has decided to allocate the CPU to another process for a while. These two conditions are completely different. In the first case, the suspension is inherent in the problem (you cannot process the user's command line until it has been typed). In the second case, it is a technicality of the system (not enough CPUs to give each process its own private processor). In Fig. 2-2 we see a state diagram showing the three states a process may be in:

1. Running (actually using the CPU at that instant).

2. Ready (runnable; temporarily stopped to let another process run).

3. Blocked (unable to run until some external event happens).

Logically, the first two states are similar. In both cases the process is willing to run, only in the second one, there is temporarily no CPU available for it. The third state is different from the first two in that the process cannot run, even if the CPU has nothing else to do.

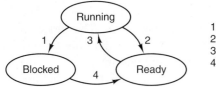

1. Process blocks for input
2. Scheduler picks another process
3. Scheduler picks this process
4. Input becomes available

Figure 2-2. A process can be in running, blocked, or ready state. Transitions between these states are as shown.

Four transitions are possible among these three states, as shown. Transition 1 occurs when a process discovers that it cannot continue. In some systems the process must execute a system call, **block** or **pause** to get into blocked state. In other systems, including MINIX 3, when a process reads from a pipe or special file (e.g., a terminal) and there is no input available, the process is automatically moved from the running state to the blocked state.

Transitions 2 and 3 are caused by the process scheduler, a part of the operating system, without the process even knowing about them. Transition 2 occurs when the scheduler decides that the running process has run long enough, and it is time to let another process have some CPU time. Transition 3 occurs when all the other processes have had their fair share and it is time for the first process to get the CPU to run again. The subject of scheduling—deciding which process should run when and for how long—is an important one. Many algorithms have been devised to try to balance the competing demands of efficiency for the system as a whole and fairness to individual processes. We will look at scheduling and study some of these algorithms later in this chapter.

Transition 4 occurs when the external event for which a process was waiting (e.g., the arrival of some input) happens. If no other process is running then, transition 3 will be triggered immediately, and the process will start running. Otherwise it may have to wait in *ready* state for a little while until the CPU is available.

Using the process model, it becomes much easier to think about what is going on inside the system. Some of the processes run programs that carry out commands typed in by a user. Other processes are part of the system and handle tasks such as carrying out requests for file services or managing the details of running a disk or a tape drive. When a disk interrupt occurs, the system may make a decision to stop running the current process and run the disk process, which was blocked waiting for that interrupt. We say "may" because it depends upon relative priorities of the running process and the disk driver process. But the point is that instead of thinking about interrupts, we can think about user processes, disk processes, terminal processes, and so on, which block when they are waiting for something to happen. When the disk block has been read or the character typed, the process waiting for it is unblocked and is eligible to run again.

This view gives rise to the model shown in Fig. 2-3. Here the lowest level of the operating system is the scheduler, with a variety of processes on top of it. All the interrupt handling and details of actually starting and stopping processes are hidden away in the scheduler, which is actually quite small. The rest of the operating system is nicely structured in process form. The model of Fig. 2-3 is used in MINIX 3. Of course, the "scheduler" is not the only thing in the lowest layer, there is also support for interrupt handling and interprocess communication. Nevertheless, to a first approximation, it does show the basic structure.

2.1.6 Implementation of Processes

To implement the process model, the operating system maintains a table (an array of structures), called the **process table**, with one entry per process. (Some authors call these entries **process control blocks**.) This entry contains information about the process' state, its program counter, stack pointer, memory allocation, the status of its open files, its accounting and scheduling information, alarms and other signals, and everything else about the process that must be saved when

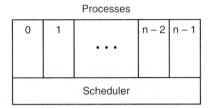

Processes

Figure 2-3. The lowest layer of a process-structured operating system handles interrupts and scheduling. Above that layer are sequential processes.

the process is switched from *running* to *ready* state so that it can be restarted later as if it had never been stopped.

In MINIX 3, interprocess communication, memory management, and file management are each handled by separate modules within the system, so the process table is partitioned, with each module maintaining the fields that it needs. Figure 2-4 shows some of the more important fields. The fields in the first column are the only ones relevant to this chapter. The other two columns are provided just to give an idea of what information is needed elsewhere in the system.

Kernel	Process management	File management
Registers	Pointer to text segment	UMASK mask
Program counter	Pointer to data segment	Root directory
Program status word	Pointer to bss segment	Working directory
Stack pointer	Exit status	File descriptors
Process state	Signal status	Real id
Current scheduling priority	Process ID	Effective UID
Maximum scheduling priority	Parent process	Real GID
Scheduling ticks left	Process group	Effective GID
Quantum size	Children's CPU time	Controlling tty
CPU time used	Real UID	Save area for read/write
Message queue pointers	Effective UID	System call parameters
Pending signal bits	Real GID	Various flag bits
Various flag bits	Effective GID	
Process name	File info for sharing text	
	Bitmaps for signals	
	Various flag bits	
	Process name	

Figure 2-4. Some of the fields of the MINIX 3 process table. The fields are distributed over the kernel, the process manager, and the file system.

Now that we have looked at the process table, it is possible to explain a little more about how the illusion of multiple sequential processes is maintained on a machine with one CPU and many I/O devices. What follows is technically a description of how the "scheduler" of Fig. 2-3 works in MINIX 3 but most modern operating systems work essentially the same way. Associated with each I/O device class (e.g., floppy disks, hard disks, timers, terminals) is a data structure in a table called the **interrupt descriptor table**. The most important part of each entry in this table is called the **interrupt vector**. It contains the address of the interrupt service procedure. Suppose that user process 23 is running when a disk interrupt occurs. The program counter, program status word, and possibly one or more registers are pushed onto the (current) stack by the interrupt hardware. The computer then jumps to the address specified in the disk interrupt vector. That is all the hardware does. From here on, it is up to the software.

The interrupt service procedure starts out by saving all the registers in the process table entry for the current process. The current process number and a pointer to its entry are kept in global variables so they can be found quickly. Then the information deposited by the interrupt is removed from the stack, and the stack pointer is set to a temporary stack used by the process handler. Actions such as saving the registers and setting the stack pointer cannot even be expressed in high-level languages such as C, so they are performed by a small assembly language routine. When this routine is finished, it calls a C procedure to do the rest of the work for this specific interrupt type.

Interprocess communication in MINIX 3 is via messages, so the next step is to build a message to be sent to the disk process, which will be blocked waiting for it. The message says that an interrupt occurred, to distinguish it from messages from user processes requesting disk blocks to be read and things like that. The state of the disk process is now changed from *blocked* to *ready* and the scheduler is called. In MINIX 3, different processes have different priorities, to give better service to I/O device handlers than to user processes, for example. If the disk process is now the highest priority runnable process, it will be scheduled to run. If the process that was interrupted is just as important or more so, then it will be scheduled to run again, and the disk process will have to wait a little while.

Either way, the C procedure called by the assembly language interrupt code now returns, and the assembly language code loads up the registers and memory map for the now-current process and starts it running. Interrupt handling and scheduling are summarized in Fig. 2-5. It is worth noting that the details vary slightly from system to system.

2.1.7 Threads

In traditional operating systems, each process has an address space and a single thread of control. In fact, that is almost the definition of a process. Nevertheless, there are often situations in which it is desirable to have multiple threads of

1. Hardware stacks program counter, etc.
2. Hardware loads new program counter from interrupt vector.
3. Assembly language procedure saves registers.
4. Assembly language procedure sets up new stack.
5. C interrupt service constructs and sends message.
6. Message passing code marks waiting message recipient ready.
7. Scheduler decides which process is to run next.
8. C procedure returns to the assembly code.
9. Assembly language procedure starts up new current process.

Figure 2-5. Skeleton of what the lowest level of the operating system does when an interrupt occurs.

control in the same address space running in quasi-parallel, as though they were separate processes (except for the shared address space). These threads of control are usually just called **threads**, although some people call them **lightweight processes**.

One way of looking at a process is that it is a way to group related resources together. A process has an address space containing program text and data, as well as other resources. These resources may include open files, child processes, pending alarms, signal handlers, accounting information, and more. By putting them together in the form of a process, they can be managed more easily.

The other concept a process has is a thread of execution, usually shortened to just **thread**. The thread has a program counter that keeps track of which instruction to execute next. It has registers, which hold its current working variables. It has a stack, which contains the execution history, with one frame for each procedure called but not yet returned from. Although a thread must execute in some process, the thread and its process are different concepts and can be treated separately. Processes are used to group resources together; threads are the entities scheduled for execution on the CPU.

What threads add to the process model is to allow multiple executions to take place in the same process environment, to a large degree independent of one another. In Fig. 2-6(a) we see three traditional processes. Each process has its own address space and a single thread of control. In contrast, in Fig. 2-6(b) we see a single process with three threads of control. Although in both cases we have three threads, in Fig. 2-6(a) each of them operates in a different address space, whereas in Fig. 2-6(b) all three of them share the same address space.

As an example of where multiple threads might be used, consider a web browser process. Many web pages contain multiple small images. For each image on a web page, the browser must set up a separate connection to the page's home site and request the image. A great deal of time is spent establishing and releasing all these connections. By having multiple threads within the browser, many images can be requested at the same time, greatly speeding up performance

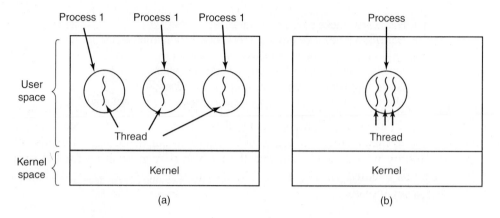

Figure 2-6. (a) Three processes each with one thread. (b) One process with three threads.

in most cases since with small images, the set-up time is the limiting factor, not the speed of the transmission line.

When multiple threads are present in the same address space, a few of the fields of Fig. 2-4 are not per process, but per thread, so a separate thread table is needed, with one entry per thread. Among the per-thread items are the program counter, registers, and state. The program counter is needed because threads, like processes, can be suspended and resumed. The registers are needed because when threads are suspended, their registers must be saved. Finally, threads, like processes, can be in *running*, *ready*, or *blocked* state. Fig. 2-7 lists some per-process and per-thread items.

Per process items	Per thread items
Address space	Program counter
Global variables	Registers
Open files	Stack
Child processes	State
Pending alarms	
Signals and signal handlers	
Accounting information	

Figure 2-7. The first column lists some items shared by all threads in a process. The second one lists some items private to each thread.

In some systems, the operating system is not aware of the threads. In other words, they are managed entirely in user space. When a thread is about to block, for example, it chooses and starts its successor before stopping. Several user-level threads packages are in common use, including the POSIX **P-threads** and Mach **C-threads** packages.

In other systems, the operating system is aware of the existence of multiple threads per process, so when a thread blocks, the operating system chooses the next one to run, either from the same process or a different one. To do scheduling, the kernel must have a thread table that lists all the threads in the system, analogous to the process table.

Although these two alternatives may seem equivalent, they differ considerably in performance. Switching threads is much faster when thread management is done in user space than when a system call is needed. This fact argues strongly for doing thread management in user space. On the other hand, when threads are managed entirely in user space and one thread blocks (e.g., waiting for I/O or a page fault to be handled), the kernel blocks the entire process, since it is not even aware that other threads exist. This fact as well as others argue for doing thread management in the kernel (Boehm, 2005). As a consequence, both systems are in use, and various hybrid schemes have been proposed as well (Anderson et al., 1992).

No matter whether threads are managed by the kernel or in user space, they introduce a raft of problems that must be solved and which change the programming model appreciably. To start with, consider the effects of the fork system call. If the parent process has multiple threads, should the child also have them? If not, the process may not function properly, since all of them may be essential.

However, if the child process gets as many threads as the parent, what happens if a thread was blocked on a read call, say, from the keyboard? Are two threads now blocked on the keyboard? When a line is typed, do both threads get a copy of it? Only the parent? Only the child? The same problem exists with open network connections.

Another class of problems is related to the fact that threads share many data structures. What happens if one thread closes a file while another one is still reading from it? Suppose that one thread notices that there is too little memory and starts allocating more memory. Then, part way through, a thread switch occurs, and the new thread also notices that there is too little memory and also starts allocating more memory. Does the allocation happen once or twice? In nearly all systems that were not designed with threads in mind, the libraries (such as the memory allocation procedure) are not reentrant, and will crash if a second call is made while the first one is still active.

Another problem relates to error reporting. In UNIX, after a system call, the status of the call is put into a global variable, *errno*. What happens if a thread makes a system call, and before it is able to read *errno*, another thread makes a system call, wiping out the original value?

Next, consider signals. Some signals are logically thread specific; others are not. For example, if a thread calls alarm, it makes sense for the resulting signal to go to the thread that made the call. When the kernel is aware of threads, it can usually make sure the right thread gets the signal. When the kernel is not aware of threads, the threads package must keep track of alarms by itself. An additional complication for user-level threads exists when (as in UNIX) a process may only have one alarm at a time pending and several threads call alarm independently.

Other signals, such as a keyboard-initiated *SIGINT*, are not thread specific. Who should catch them? One designated thread? All the threads? A newly created thread? Each of these solutions has problems. Furthermore, what happens if one thread changes the signal handlers without telling other threads?

One last problem introduced by threads is stack management. In many systems, when stack overflow occurs, the kernel just provides more stack, automatically. When a process has multiple threads, it must also have multiple stacks. If the kernel is not aware of all these stacks, it cannot grow them automatically upon stack fault. In fact, it may not even realize that a memory fault is related to stack growth.

These problems are certainly not insurmountable, but they do show that just introducing threads into an existing system without a fairly substantial system redesign is not going to work at all. The semantics of system calls have to be redefined and libraries have to be rewritten, at the very least. And all of these things must be done in such a way as to remain backward compatible with existing programs for the limiting case of a process with only one thread. For additional information about threads, see Hauser et al. (1993) and Marsh et al. (1991).

2.2 INTERPROCESS COMMUNICATION

Processes frequently need to communicate with other processes. For example, in a shell pipeline, the output of the first process must be passed to the second process, and so on down the line. Thus there is a need for communication between processes, preferably in a well-structured way not using interrupts. In the following sections we will look at some of the issues related to this **InterProcess Communication** or **IPC**.

There are three issues here. The first was alluded to above: how one process can pass information to another. The second has to do with making sure two or more processes do not get into each other's way when engaging in critical activities (suppose two processes each try to grab the last 1 MB of memory). The third concerns proper sequencing when dependencies are present: if process *A* produces data and process *B* prints it, *B* has to wait until *A* has produced some data before starting to print. We will examine all three of these issues in some detail in this section.

It is also important to mention that two of these issues apply equally well to threads. The first one—passing information—is easy for threads since they share a common address space (threads in different address spaces that need to communicate fall under the heading of communicating processes). However, the other two—keeping out of each other's hair and proper sequencing—apply as well to threads. The same problems exist and the same solutions apply. Below we will discuss the problem in the context of processes, but please keep in mind that the same problems and solutions also apply to threads.

2.2.1 Race Conditions

In some operating systems, processes that are working together may share some common storage that each one can read and write. The shared storage may be in main memory (possibly in a kernel data structure) or it may be a shared file; the location of the shared memory does not change the nature of the communication or the problems that arise. To see how interprocess communication works in practice, let us consider a simple but common example, a print spooler. When a process wants to print a file, it enters the file name in a special **spooler directory**. Another process, the **printer daemon**, periodically checks to see if so are any files to be printed, and if so removes their names from the directory.

Imagine that our spooler directory has a large number of slots, numbered 0, 1, 2, ..., each one capable of holding a file name. Also imagine that there are two shared variables, *out*, which points to the next file to be printed, and *in*, which points to the next free slot in the directory. These two variables might well be kept in a two-word file available to all processes. At a certain instant, slots 0 to 3 are empty (the files have already been printed) and slots 4 to 6 are full (with the names of files to be printed). More or less simultaneously, processes *A* and *B* decide they want to queue a file for printing. This situation is shown in Fig. 2-8.

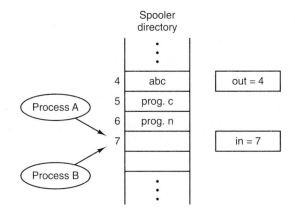

Figure 2-8. Two processes want to access shared memory at the same time.

In jurisdictions where Murphy's law† is applicable, the following might well happen. Process *A* reads *in* and stores the value, 7, in a local variable called *next_free_slot*. Just then a clock interrupt occurs and the CPU decides that

----
† If something can go wrong, it will.

process *A* has run long enough, so it switches to process *B*. Process *B* also reads *in*, and also gets a 7, so it stores the name of its file in slot 7 and updates *in* to be an 8. Then it goes off and does other things.

Eventually, process *A* runs again, starting from the place it left off last time. It looks at *next_free_slot*, finds a 7 there, and writes its file name in slot 7, erasing the name that process *B* just put there. Then it computes *next_free_slot* + 1, which is 8, and sets *in* to 8. The spooler directory is now internally consistent, so the printer daemon will not notice anything wrong, but process *B* will never receive any output. User *B* will hang around the printer room for years, wistfully hoping for output that never comes. Situations like this, where two or more processes are reading or writing some shared data and the final result depends on who runs precisely when, are called **race conditions**. Debugging programs containing race conditions is no fun at all. The results of most test runs are fine, but once in a blue moon something weird and unexplained happens.

2.2.2 Critical Sections

How do we avoid race conditions? The key to preventing trouble here and in many other situations involving shared memory, shared files, and shared everything else is to find some way to prohibit more than one process from reading and writing the shared data at the same time. Put in other words, what we need is **mutual exclusion** —some way of making sure that if one process is using a shared variable or file, the other processes will be excluded from doing the same thing. The difficulty above occurred because process *B* started using one of the shared variables before process *A* was finished with it. The choice of appropriate primitive operations for achieving mutual exclusion is a major design issue in any operating system, and a subject that we will now examine in great detail.

The problem of avoiding race conditions can also be formulated in an abstract way. Part of the time, a process is busy doing internal computations and other things that do not lead to race conditions. However, sometimes a process may be accessing shared memory or files. That part of the program where the shared memory is accessed is called the **critical region** or **critical section**. If we could arrange matters such that no two processes were ever in their critical regions at the same time, we could avoid race conditions.

Although this requirement avoids race conditions, this is not sufficient for having parallel processes cooperate correctly and efficiently using shared data. We need four conditions to hold to have a good solution:

1. No two processes may be simultaneously inside their critical regions.

2. No assumptions may be made about speeds or the number of CPUs.

3. No process running outside its critical region may block other processes.

4. No process should have to wait forever to enter its critical region.

The behavior that we want is shown in Fig. 2-9. Here process A enters its critical region at time T_1. A little later, at time T_2 process B attempts to enter its critical region but fails because another process is already in its critical region and we allow only one at a time. Consequently, B is temporarily suspended until time T_3 when A leaves its critical region, allowing B to enter immediately. Eventually B leaves (at T_4) and we are back to the original situation with no processes in their critical regions.

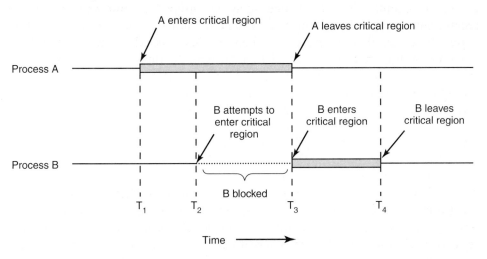

Figure 2-9. Mutual exclusion using critical regions.

2.2.3 Mutual Exclusion with Busy Waiting

In this section we will examine various proposals for achieving mutual exclusion, so that while one process is busy updating shared memory in its critical region, no other process will enter *its* critical region and cause trouble.

Disabling Interrupts

The simplest solution is to have each process disable all interrupts just after entering its critical region and reenable them just before leaving it. With interrupts disabled, no clock interrupts can occur. The CPU is only switched from process to process as a result of clock or other interrupts, after all, and with interrupts turned off the CPU will not be switched to another process. Thus, once a process has disabled interrupts, it can examine and update the shared memory without fear that any other process will intervene.

This approach is generally unattractive because it is unwise to give user processes the power to turn off interrupts. Suppose that one of them did, and then never turned them on again? That could be the end of the system. Furthermore, if the system is a multiprocessor, with two or more CPUs, disabling interrupts affects only the CPU that executed the disable instruction. The other ones will continue running and can access the shared memory.

On the other hand, it is frequently convenient for the kernel itself to disable interrupts for a few instructions while it is updating variables or lists. If an interrupt occurred while the list of ready processes, for example, was in an inconsistent state, race conditions could occur. The conclusion is: disabling interrupts is often a useful technique within the operating system itself but is not appropriate as a general mutual exclusion mechanism for user processes.

Lock Variables

As a second attempt, let us look for a software solution. Consider having a single, shared, (lock) variable, initially 0. When a process wants to enter its critical region, it first tests the lock. If the lock is 0, the process sets it to 1 and enters the critical region. If the lock is already 1, the process just waits until it becomes 0. Thus, a 0 means that no process is in its critical region, and a 1 means that some process is in its critical region.

Unfortunately, this idea contains exactly the same fatal flaw that we saw in the spooler directory. Suppose that one process reads the lock and sees that it is 0. Before it can set the lock to 1, another process is scheduled, runs, and sets the lock to 1. When the first process runs again, it will also set the lock to 1, and two processes will be in their critical regions at the same time.

Now you might think that we could get around this problem by first reading out the lock value, then checking it again just before storing into it, but that really does not help. The race now occurs if the second process modifies the lock just after the first process has finished its second check.

Strict Alternation

A third approach to the mutual exclusion problem is shown in Fig. 2-10. This program fragment, like most others in this book, is written in C. C was chosen here because real operating systems are commonly written in C (or occasionally C++), but hardly ever in languages like Java. C is powerful, efficient, and predictable, characteristics critical for writing operating systems. Java, for example, is not predictable because it might run out of storage at a critical moment and need to invoke the garbage collector at a most inopportune time. This cannot happen in C because there is no garbage collection in C. A quantitative comparison of C, C++, Java, and four other languages is given by Prechelt (2000).

In Fig. 2-10, the integer variable *turn*, initially 0, keeps track of whose turn it is to enter the critical region and examine or update the shared memory. Initially, process 0 inspects *turn*, finds it to be 0, and enters its critical region. Process 1 also finds it to be 0 and therefore sits in a tight loop continually testing *turn* to see

```
while (TRUE) {                              while (TRUE) {
    while (turn != 0)    /* loop */ ;          while (turn != 1)      /* loop */ ;
    critical_region( );                        critical_region( );
    turn = 1;                                  turn = 0;
    noncritical_region( );                     noncritical_region( );
}                                          }
```

              (a)   (b)

Figure 2-10. A proposed solution to the critical region problem. (a) Process 0.
(b) Process 1. In both cases, be sure to note the semicolons terminating the while
statements.

when it becomes 1. Continuously testing a variable until some value appears is
called **busy waiting**. It should usually be avoided, since it wastes CPU time.
Only when there is a reasonable expectation that the wait will be short is busy
waiting used. A lock that uses busy waiting is called a **spin lock**.

When process 0 leaves the critical region, it sets *turn* to 1, to allow process 1
to enter its critical region. Suppose that process 1 finishes its critical region
quickly, so both processes are in their noncritical regions, with *turn* set to 0. Now
process 0 executes its whole loop quickly, exiting its critical region and setting
turn to 1. At this point *turn* is 1 and both processes are executing in their noncritical regions.

Suddenly, process 0 finishes its noncritical region and goes back to the top of
its loop. Unfortunately, it is not permitted to enter its critical region now, because
turn is 1 and process 1 is busy with its noncritical region. It hangs in its while
loop until process 1 sets *turn* to 0. Put differently, taking turns is not a good idea
when one of the processes is much slower than the other.

This situation violates condition 3 set out above: process 0 is being blocked by
a process not in its critical region. Going back to the spooler directory discussed
above, if we now associate the critical region with reading and writing the spooler
directory, process 0 would not be allowed to print another file because process 1
was doing something else.

In fact, this solution requires that the two processes strictly alternate in entering their critical regions, for example, in spooling files. Neither one would be
permitted to spool two in a row. While this algorithm does avoid all races, it is
not really a serious candidate as a solution because it violates condition 3.

Peterson's Solution

By combining the idea of taking turns with the idea of lock variables and
warning variables, a Dutch mathematician, T. Dekker, was the first one to devise
a software solution to the mutual exclusion problem that does not require strict
alternation. For a discussion of Dekker's algorithm, see Dijkstra (1965).

In 1981, G.L. Peterson discovered a much simpler way to achieve mutual exclusion, thus rendering Dekker's solution obsolete. Peterson's algorithm is shown in Fig. 2-11. This algorithm consists of two procedures written in ANSI C, which means that function prototypes should be supplied for all the functions defined and used. However, to save space, we will not show the prototypes in this or subsequent examples.

```
#define FALSE  0
#define TRUE   1
#define N       2                      /* number of processes */

int turn;                              /* whose turn is it? */
int interested[N];                     /* all values initially 0 (FALSE) */

void enter_region(int process)         /* process is 0 or 1 */
{
        int other;                     /* number of the other process */

        other = 1 – process;           /* the opposite of process */
        interested[process] = TRUE;    /* show that you are interested */
        turn = process;                /* set flag */
        while (turn == process && interested[other] == TRUE) /* null statement */ ;
}

void leave_region(int process)         /* process: who is leaving */
{
        interested[process] = FALSE;   /* indicate departure from critical region */
}
```

Figure 2-11. Peterson's solution for achieving mutual exclusion.

Before using the shared variables (i.e., before entering its critical region), each process calls *enter_region* with its own process number, 0 or 1, as the parameter. This call will cause it to wait, if need be, until it is safe to enter. After it has finished with the shared variables, the process calls *leave_region* to indicate that it is done and to allow the other process to enter, if it so desires.

Let us see how this solution works. Initially, neither process is in its critical region. Now process 0 calls *enter_region*. It indicates its interest by setting its array element and sets *turn* to 0. Since process 1 is not interested, *enter_region* returns immediately. If process 1 now calls *enter_region*, it will hang there until *interested*[0] goes to *FALSE*, an event that only happens when process 0 calls *leave_region* to exit the critical region.

Now consider the case that both processes call *enter_region* almost simultaneously. Both will store their process number in *turn*. Whichever store is done last is the one that counts; the first one is lost. Suppose that process 1 stores last, so *turn* is 1. When both processes come to the while statement, process 0 executes it zero times and enters its critical region. Process 1 loops and does not enter its critical region.

The TSL Instruction

Now let us look at a proposal that requires a little help from the hardware. Many computers, especially those designed with multiple processors in mind, have an instruction

    TSL RX,LOCK

(Test and Set Lock) that works as follows: it reads the contents of the memory word *LOCK* into register RX and then stores a nonzero value at the memory address *LOCK*. The operations of reading the word and storing into it are guaranteed to be indivisible—no other processor can access the memory word until the instruction is finished. The CPU executing the TSL instruction locks the memory bus to prohibit other CPUs from accessing memory until it is done.

To use the TSL instruction, we will use a shared variable, *LOCK*, to coordinate access to shared memory. When *LOCK* is 0, any process may set it to 1 using the TSL instruction and then read or write the shared memory. When it is done, the process sets *LOCK* back to 0 using an ordinary move instruction.

How can this instruction be used to prevent two processes from simultaneously entering their critical regions? The solution is given in Fig. 2-12. There a four-instruction subroutine in a fictitious (but typical) assembly language is shown. The first instruction copies the old value of *LOCK* to the register and then sets *LOCK* to 1. Then the old value is compared with 0. If it is nonzero, the lock was already set, so the program just goes back to the beginning and tests it again. Sooner or later it will become 0 (when the process currently in its critical region is done with its critical region), and the subroutine returns, with the lock set. Clearing the lock is simple. The program just stores a 0 in *LOCK*. No special instructions are needed.

```
enter_region:
        TSL REGISTER,LOCK       | copy LOCK to register and set LOCK to 1
        CMP REGISTER,#0         | was LOCK zero?
        JNE ENTER_REGION        | if it was non zero, LOCK was set, so loop
        RET                     | return to caller; critical region entered


leave_region:
        MOVE LOCK,#0            | store a 0 in LOCK
        RET                     | return to caller
```

Figure 2-12. Entering and leaving a critical region using the TSL instruction.

One solution to the critical region problem is now straightforward. Before entering its critical region, a process calls *enter_region*, which does busy waiting until the lock is free; then it acquires the lock and returns. After the critical region the process calls *leave_region*, which stores a 0 in *LOCK*. As with all solutions based on critical regions, the processes must call *enter_region* and *leave_region* at the correct times for the method to work. If a process cheats, the mutual exclusion will fail.

2.2.4 Sleep and Wakeup

Both Peterson's solution and the solution using TSL are correct, but both have the defect of requiring busy waiting. In essence, what these solutions do is this: when a process wants to enter its critical region, it checks to see if the entry is allowed. If it is not, the process just sits in a tight loop waiting until it is.

Not only does this approach waste CPU time, but it can also have unexpected effects. Consider a computer with two processes, *H*, with high priority and *L*, with low priority, which share a critical region. The scheduling rules are such that *H* is run whenever it is in ready state. At a certain moment, with *L* in its critical region, *H* becomes ready to run (e.g., an I/O operation completes). *H* now begins busy waiting, but since *L* is never scheduled while *H* is running, *L* never gets the chance to leave its critical region, so *H* loops forever. This situation is sometimes referred to as the **priority inversion problem**.

Now let us look at some interprocess communication primitives that block instead of wasting CPU time when they are not allowed to enter their critical regions. One of the simplest is the pair sleep and wakeup. sleep is a system call that causes the caller to block, that is, be suspended until another process wakes it up. The wakeup call has one parameter, the process to be awakened. Alternatively, both sleep and wakeup each have one parameter, a memory address used to match up sleeps with wakeups.

The Producer-Consumer Problem

As an example of how these primitives can be used in practice, let us consider the **producer-consumer** problem (also known as the **bounded buffer** problem). Two processes share a common, fixed-size buffer. One of them, the producer, puts information into the buffer, and the other one, the consumer, takes it out. (It is also possible to generalize the problem to have *m* producers and *n* consumers, but we will only consider the case of one producer and one consumer because this assumption simplifies the solutions).

Trouble arises when the producer wants to put a new item in the buffer, but it is already full. The solution is for the producer to go to sleep, to be awakened when the consumer has removed one or more items. Similarly, if the consumer wants to remove an item from the buffer and sees that the buffer is empty, it goes to sleep until the producer puts something in the buffer and wakes it up.

This approach sounds simple enough, but it leads to the same kinds of race conditions we saw earlier with the spooler directory. To keep track of the number of items in the buffer, we will need a variable, *count*. If the maximum number of items the buffer can hold is *N*, the producer's code will first test to see if *count* is *N*. If it is, the producer will go to sleep; if it is not, the producer will add an item and increment *count*.

The consumer's code is similar: first test *count* to see if it is 0. If it is, go to sleep; if it is nonzero, remove an item and decrement the counter. Each of the processes also tests to see if the other should be sleeping, and if not, wakes it up. The code for both producer and consumer is shown in Fig. 2-13.

```
#define N 100                              /* number of slots in the buffer */
int count = 0;                             /* number of items in the buffer */

void producer(void)
{
    int item;

    while (TRUE) {                         /* repeat forever */
        item = produce_item( );            /* generate next item */
        if (count == N) sleep( );          /* if buffer is full, go to sleep */
        insert_item(item);                 /* put item in buffer */
        count = count + 1;                 /* increment count of items in buffer */
        if (count == 1) wakeup(consumer);  /* was buffer empty? */
    }
}


void consumer(void)
{
    int item;

    while (TRUE) {                         /* repeat forever */
        if (count == 0) sleep( );          /* if buffer is empty, got to sleep */
        item = remove_item( );             /* take item out of buffer */
        count = count - 1;                 /* decrement count of items in buffer */
        if (count == N - 1) wakeup(producer); /* was buffer full? */
        consume_item(item);                /* print item */
    }
}
```

Figure 2-13. The producer-consumer problem with a fatal race condition.

To express system calls such as sleep and wakeup in C, we will show them as calls to library routines. They are not part of the standard C library but presumably would be available on any system that actually had these system calls. The procedures *enter_item* and *remove_item*, which are not shown, handle the book-keeping of putting items into the buffer and taking items out of the buffer.

Now let us get back to the race condition. It can occur because access to *count* is unconstrained. The following situation could possibly occur. The buffer is empty and the consumer has just read *count* to see if it is 0. At that instant, the scheduler decides to stop running the consumer temporarily and start running the producer. The producer enters an item in the buffer, increments *count*, and notices that it is now 1. Reasoning that *count* was just 0, and thus the consumer must be sleeping, the producer calls *wakeup* to wake the consumer up.

Unfortunately, the consumer is not yet logically asleep, so the wakeup signal is lost. When the consumer next runs, it will test the value of *count* it previously read, find it to be 0, and go to sleep. Sooner or later the producer will fill up the buffer and also go to sleep. Both will sleep forever.

The essence of the problem here is that a wakeup sent to a process that is not (yet) sleeping is lost. If it were not lost, everything would work. A quick fix is to modify the rules to add a **wakeup waiting bit** to the picture. When a wakeup is sent to a process that is still awake, this bit is set. Later, when the process tries to go to sleep, if the wakeup waiting bit is on, it will be turned off, but the process will stay awake. The wakeup waiting bit is a piggy bank for wakeup signals.

While the wakeup waiting bit saves the day in this simple example, it is easy to construct examples with three or more processes in which one wakeup waiting bit is insufficient. We could make another patch, and add a second wakeup waiting bit, or maybe 8 or 32 of them, but in principle the problem is still there.

2.2.5 Semaphores

This was the situation until E. W. Dijkstra (1965) suggested using an integer variable to count the number of wakeups saved for future use. In his proposal, a new variable type, called a **semaphore**, was introduced. A semaphore could have the value 0, indicating that no wakeups were saved, or some positive value if one or more wakeups were pending.

Dijkstra proposed having two operations, **down** and **up** (which are generalizations of **sleep** and **wakeup**, respectively). The **down** operation on a semaphore checks to see if the value is greater than 0. If so, it decrements the value (i.e., uses up one stored wakeup) and just continues. If the value is 0, the process is put to sleep without completing the **down** for the moment. Checking the value, changing it, and possibly going to sleep is all done as a single, indivisible, **atomic action**. It is guaranteed that once a semaphore operation has started, no other process can access the semaphore until the operation has completed or blocked. This atomicity is absolutely essential to solving synchronization problems and avoiding race conditions.

The **up** operation increments the value of the semaphore addressed. If one or more processes were sleeping on that semaphore, unable to complete an earlier down operation, one of them is chosen by the system (e.g., at random) and is allowed to complete its down. Thus, after an up on a semaphore with processes sleeping on it, the semaphore will still be 0, but there will be one fewer process sleeping on it. The operation of incrementing the semaphore and waking up one process is also indivisible. No process ever blocks doing an up, just as no process ever blocks doing a wakeup in the earlier model.

As an aside, in Dijkstra's original paper, he used the names p and v instead of down and up, respectively, but since these have no mnemonic significance to people who do not speak Dutch (and only marginal significance to those who do), we will use the terms down and up instead. These were first introduced in Algol 68.

Solving the Producer-Consumer Problem using Semaphores

Semaphores solve the lost-wakeup problem, as shown in Fig. 2-14. It is essential that they be implemented in an indivisible way. The normal way is to implement up and down as system calls, with the operating system briefly disabling all interrupts while it is testing the semaphore, updating it, and putting the process to sleep, if necessary. As all of these actions take only a few instructions, no harm is done in disabling interrupts. If multiple CPUs are being used, each semaphore should be protected by a lock variable, with the TSL instruction used to make sure that only one CPU at a time examines the semaphore. Be sure you understand that using TSL to prevent several CPUs from accessing the semaphore at the same time is quite different from busy waiting by the producer or consumer waiting for the other to empty or fill the buffer. The semaphore operation will only take a few microseconds, whereas the producer or consumer might take arbitrarily long.

This solution uses three semaphores: one called *full* for counting the number of slots that are full, one called *empty* for counting the number of slots that are empty, and one called *mutex* to make sure the producer and consumer do not access the buffer at the same time. *Full* is initially 0, *empty* is initially equal to the number of slots in the buffer, and *mutex* is initially 1. Semaphores that are initialized to 1 and used by two or more processes to ensure that only one of them can enter its critical region at the same time are called **binary semaphores**. If each process does a down just before entering its critical region and an up just after leaving it, mutual exclusion is guaranteed.

Now that we have a good interprocess communication primitive at our disposal, let us go back and look at the interrupt sequence of Fig. 2-5 again. In a system using semaphores, the natural way to hide interrupts is to have a semaphore, initially set to 0, associated with each I/O device. Just after starting an I/O device, the managing process does a down on the associated semaphore, thus blocking immediately. When the interrupt comes in, the interrupt handler then does an up on the associated semaphore, which makes the relevant process ready to run again. In this model, step 6 in Fig. 2-5 consists of doing an up on the device's

```
#define N 100                      /* number of slots in the buffer */
typedef int semaphore;            /* semaphores are a special kind of int */
semaphore mutex = 1;              /* controls access to critical region */
semaphore empty = N;              /* counts empty buffer slots */
semaphore full = 0;               /* counts full buffer slots */

void producer(void)
{
    int item;

    while (TRUE) {                /* TRUE is the constant 1 */
        item = produce_item( );  /* generate something to put in buffer */
        down(&empty);            /* decrement empty count */
        down(&mutex);            /* enter critical region */
        insert_item(item);       /* put new item in buffer */
        up(&mutex);              /* leave critical region */
        up(&full);               /* increment count of full slots */
    }
}


void consumer(void)
{
    int item;

    while (TRUE) {                /* infinite loop */
        down(&full);            /* decrement full count */
        down(&mutex);           /* enter critical region */
        item = remove_item( );  /* take item from buffer */
        up(&mutex);             /* leave critical region */
        up(&empty);             /* increment count of empty slots */
        consume_item(item);     /* do something with the item */
    }
}
```

Figure 2-14. The producer-consumer problem using semaphores.

semaphore, so that in step 7 the scheduler will be able to run the device manager. Of course, if several processes are now ready, the scheduler may choose to run an even more important process next. We will look at how scheduling is done later in this chapter.

In the example of Fig. 2-14, we have actually used semaphores in two different ways. This difference is important enough to make explicit. The *mutex* semaphore is used for mutual exclusion. It is designed to guarantee that only one process at a time will be reading or writing the buffer and the associated variables.

This mutual exclusion is required to prevent chaos. We will study mutual exclusion and how to achieve it more in the next section.

The other use of semaphores is for **synchronization**. The *full* and *empty* semaphores are needed to guarantee that certain event sequences do or do not occur. In this case, they ensure that the producer stops running when the buffer is full, and the consumer stops running when it is empty. This use is different from mutual exclusion.

2.2.6 Mutexes

When the semaphore's ability to count is not needed, a simplified version of the semaphore, called a mutex, is sometimes used. Mutexes are good only for managing mutual exclusion to some shared resource or piece of code. They are easy and efficient to implement, which makes them especially useful in thread packages that are implemented entirely in user space.

A **mutex** is a variable that can be in one of two states: unlocked or locked. Consequently, only 1 bit is required to represent it, but in practice an integer often is used, with 0 meaning unlocked and all other values meaning locked. Two procedures are used with mutexes. When a process (or thread) needs access to a critical region, it calls *mutex_lock*. If the mutex is currently unlocked (meaning that the critical region is available), the call succeeds and the calling thread is free to enter the critical region.

On the other hand, if the mutex is already locked, the caller is blocked until the process in the critical region is finished and calls *mutex_unlock*. If multiple processes are blocked on the mutex, one of them is chosen at random and allowed to acquire the lock.

2.2.7 Monitors

With semaphores interprocess communication looks easy, right? Forget it. Look closely at the order of the downs before entering or removing items from the buffer in Fig. 2-14. Suppose that the two downs in the producer's code were reversed in order, so *mutex* was decremented before *empty* instead of after it. If the buffer were completely full, the producer would block, with *mutex* set to 0. Consequently, the next time the consumer tried to access the buffer, it would do a down on *mutex*, now 0, and block too. Both processes would stay blocked forever and no more work would ever be done. This unfortunate situation is called a **deadlock**. We will study deadlocks in detail in Chap. 3.

This problem is pointed out to show how careful you must be when using semaphores. One subtle error and everything comes to a grinding halt. It is like programming in assembly language, only worse, because the errors are race conditions, deadlocks, and other forms of unpredictable and irreproducible behavior.

To make it easier to write correct programs, Brinch Hansen (1973) and Hoare (1974) proposed a higher level synchronization primitive called a **monitor**. Their proposals differed slightly, as described below. A monitor is a collection of procedures, variables, and data structures that are all grouped together in a special kind of module or package. Processes may call the procedures in a monitor whenever they want to, but they cannot directly access the monitor's internal data structures from procedures declared outside the monitor. This rule, which is common in modern object-oriented languages such as Java, was relatively unusual for its time, although objects can be traced back to Simula 67. Figure 2-15 illustrates a monitor written in an imaginary language, Pidgin Pascal.

```
monitor example
  integer i;
  condition c;

  procedure producer(x);
  .
  .
  .
  end;

  procedure consumer(x);
  .
  .
  .
  end;
end monitor;
```

Figure 2-15. A monitor.

Monitors have a key property that makes them useful for achieving mutual exclusion: only one process can be active in a monitor at any instant. Monitors are a programming language construct, so the compiler knows they are special and can handle calls to monitor procedures differently from other procedure calls. Typically, when a process calls a monitor procedure, the first few instructions of the procedure will check to see if any other process is currently active within the monitor. If so, the calling process will be suspended until the other process has left the monitor. If no other process is using the monitor, the calling process may enter.

It is up to the compiler to implement the mutual exclusion on monitor entries, but a common way is to use a mutex or binary semaphore. Because the compiler, not the programmer, arranges for the mutual exclusion, it is much less likely that something will go wrong. In any event, the person writing the monitor does not have to be aware of how the compiler arranges for mutual exclusion. It is sufficient to know that by turning all the critical regions into monitor procedures, no two processes will ever execute their critical regions at the same time.

Although monitors provide an easy way to achieve mutual exclusion, as we have seen above, that is not enough. We also need a way for processes to block when they cannot proceed. In the producer-consumer problem, it is easy enough to put all the tests for buffer-full and buffer-empty in monitor procedures, but how should the producer block when it finds the buffer full?

The solution lies in the introduction of **condition variables**, along with two operations on them, wait and signal. When a monitor procedure discovers that it cannot continue (e.g., the producer finds the buffer full), it does a wait on some condition variable, say, *full*. This action causes the calling process to block. It also allows another process that had been previously prohibited from entering the monitor to enter now.

This other process, for example, the consumer, can wake up its sleeping partner by doing a signal on the condition variable that its partner is waiting on. To avoid having two active processes in the monitor at the same time, we need a rule telling what happens after a signal. Hoare proposed letting the newly awakened process run, suspending the other one. Brinch Hansen proposed finessing the problem by requiring that a process doing a signal *must* exit the monitor immediately. In other words, a signal statement may appear only as the final statement in a monitor procedure. We will use Brinch Hansen's proposal because it is conceptually simpler and is also easier to implement. If a signal is done on a condition variable on which several processes are waiting, only one of them, determined by the system scheduler, is revived.

There is also a third solution, not proposed by either Hoare or Brinch Hansen. This is to let the signaler continue to run and allow the waiting process to start running only after the signaler has exited the monitor.

Condition variables are not counters. They do not accumulate signals for later use the way semaphores do. Thus if a condition variable is signaled with no one waiting on it, the signal is lost. In other words, the wait must come before the signal. This rule makes the implementation much simpler. In practice it is not a problem because it is easy to keep track of the state of each process with variables, if need be. A process that might otherwise do a signal can see that this operation is not necessary by looking at the variables.

A skeleton of the producer-consumer problem with monitors is given in Fig. 2-16 in Pidgin Pascal. The advantage of using Pidgin Pascal here is that it is pure and simple and follows the Hoare/Brinch Hansen model exactly.

You may be thinking that the operations wait and signal look similar to sleep and wakeup, which we saw earlier had fatal race conditions. They *are* very similar, but with one crucial difference: sleep and wakeup failed because while one process was trying to go to sleep, the other one was trying to wake it up. With monitors, that cannot happen. The automatic mutual exclusion on monitor procedures guarantees that if, say, the producer inside a monitor procedure discovers that the buffer is full, it will be able to complete the wait operation without having to worry about the possibility that the scheduler may switch to the consumer just

```
monitor ProducerConsumer
      condition full, empty;
      integer count;

      procedure insert(item: integer);
      begin
            if count = N then wait(full);
            insert_item(item);
            count := count + 1;
            if count = 1 then signal(empty)
      end;

      function remove: integer;
      begin
            if count = 0 then wait(empty);
            remove = remove_item;
            count := count − 1;
            if count = N − 1 then signal(full)
      end;

      count := 0;
end monitor;


procedure producer;
begin
      while true do
      begin
            item = produce_item;
            ProducerConsumer.insert(item)
      end
end;

procedure consumer;
begin
      while true do
      begin
            item = ProducerConsumer.remove;
            consume_item(item)
      end
end;
```

Figure 2-16. An outline of the producer-consumer problem with monitors. Only one monitor procedure at a time is active. The buffer has *N* slots.

before the wait completes. The consumer will not even be let into the monitor at all until the wait is finished and the producer is marked as no longer runnable.

Although Pidgin Pascal is an imaginary language, some real programming languages also support monitors, although not always in the form designed by

Hoare and Brinch Hansen. One such language is Java. Java is an object-oriented language that supports user-level threads and also allows methods (procedures) to be grouped together into classes. By adding the keyword synchronized to a method declaration, Java guarantees that once any thread has started executing that method, no other thread will be allowed to start executing any other synchronized method in that class.

Synchronized methods in Java differ from classical monitors in an essential way: Java does not have condition variables. Instead, it offers two procedures, *wait* and *notify* that are the equivalent of *sleep* and *wakeup* except that when they are used inside synchronized methods, they are not subject to race conditions.

By making the mutual exclusion of critical regions automatic, monitors make parallel programming much less error-prone than with semaphores. Still, they too have some drawbacks. It is not for nothing that Fig. 2-16 is written in Pidgin Pascal rather than in C, as are the other examples in this book. As we said earlier, monitors are a programming language concept. The compiler must recognize them and arrange for the mutual exclusion somehow. C, Pascal, and most other languages do not have monitors, so it is unreasonable to expect their compilers to enforce any mutual exclusion rules. In fact, how could the compiler even know which procedures were in monitors and which were not?

These same languages do not have semaphores either, but adding semaphores is easy: all you need to do is add two short assembly code routines to the library to issue the up and down system calls. The compilers do not even have to know that they exist. Of course, the operating systems have to know about the semaphores, but at least if you have a semaphore-based operating system, you can still write the user programs for it in C or C++ (or even FORTRAN if you are masochistic enough). With monitors, you need a language that has them built in.

Another problem with monitors, and also with semaphores, is that they were designed for solving the mutual exclusion problem on one or more CPUs that all have access to a common memory. By putting the semaphores in the shared memory and protecting them with TSL instructions, we can avoid races. When we go to a distributed system consisting of multiple CPUs, each with its own private memory, connected by a local area network, these primitives become inapplicable. The conclusion is that semaphores are too low level and monitors are not usable except in a few programming languages. Also, none of the primitives provide for information exchange between machines. Something else is needed.

2.2.8 Message Passing

That something else is **message passing**. This method of interprocess communication uses two primitives, send and receive, which, like semaphores and unlike monitors, are system calls rather than language constructs. As such, they can easily be put into library procedures, such as

```
send(destination, &message);
```

and

```
receive(source, &message);
```

The former call sends a message to a given destination and the latter one receives a message from a given source (or from *ANY*, if the receiver does not care). If no message is available, the receiver could block until one arrives. Alternatively, it could return immediately with an error code.

Design Issues for Message Passing Systems

Message passing systems have many challenging problems and design issues that do not arise with semaphores or monitors, especially if the communicating processes are on different machines connected by a network. For example, messages can be lost by the network. To guard against lost messages, the sender and receiver can agree that as soon as a message has been received, the receiver will send back a special **acknowledgement** message. If the sender has not received the acknowledgement within a certain time interval, it retransmits the message.

Now consider what happens if the message itself is received correctly, but the acknowledgement is lost. The sender will retransmit the message, so the receiver will get it twice. It is essential that the receiver can distinguish a new message from the retransmission of an old one. Usually, this problem is solved by putting consecutive sequence numbers in each original message. If the receiver gets a message bearing the same sequence number as the previous message, it knows that the message is a duplicate that can be ignored.

Message systems also have to deal with the question of how processes are named, so that the process specified in a send or receive call is unambiguous. **Authentication** is also an issue in message systems: how can the client tell that he is communicating with the real file server, and not with an imposter?

At the other end of the spectrum, there are also design issues that are important when the sender and receiver are on the same machine. One of these is performance. Copying messages from one process to another is always slower than doing a semaphore operation or entering a monitor. Much work has gone into making message passing efficient. Cheriton (1984), for example, has suggested limiting message size to what will fit in the machine's registers, and then doing message passing using the registers.

The Producer-Consumer Problem with Message Passing

Now let us see how the producer-consumer problem can be solved with message passing and no shared memory. A solution is given in Fig. 2-17. We assume that all messages are the same size and that messages sent but not yet received are buffered automatically by the operating system. In this solution, a total of *N* messages is used, analogous to the *N* slots in a shared memory buffer. The consumer starts out by sending *N* empty messages to the producer. Whenever the producer has an item to give to the consumer, it takes an empty message and sends back a full one. In this way, the total number of messages in the system remains constant in time, so they can be stored in a given amount of memory known in advance.

If the producer works faster than the consumer, all the messages will end up full, waiting for the consumer; the producer will be blocked, waiting for an empty to come back. If the consumer works faster, then the reverse happens: all the messages will be empties waiting for the producer to fill them up; the consumer will be blocked, waiting for a full message.

```
#define N 100                          /* number of slots in the buffer */

void producer(void)
{
     int item;
     message m;                        /* message buffer */

     while (TRUE) {
          item = produce_item( );      /* generate something to put in buffer */
          receive(consumer, &m);       /* wait for an empty to arrive */
          build_message(&m, item);     /* construct a message to send */
          send(consumer, &m);          /* send item to consumer */
     }
}

void consumer(void)
{
     int item, i;
     message m;

     for (i = 0; i < N; i++) send(producer, &m);  /* send N empties */
     while (TRUE) {
          receive(producer, &m);       /* get message containing item */
          item = extract_item(&m);     /* extract item from message */
          send(producer, &m);          /* send back empty reply */
          consume_item(item);          /* do some1thing with the item */
     }
}
```

Figure 2-17. The producer-consumer problem with *N* messages.

Many variants are possible with message passing. For starters, let us look at how messages are addressed. One way is to assign each process a unique address and have messages be addressed to processes. A different way is to invent a new data structure, called a **mailbox**. A mailbox is a place to buffer a certain number of messages, typically specified when the mailbox is created. When mailboxes are used, the address parameters in the send and receive calls are mailboxes, not processes. When a process tries to send to a mailbox that is full, it is suspended until a message is removed from that mailbox, making room for a new one.

For the producer-consumer problem, both the producer and consumer would create mailboxes large enough to hold N messages. The producer would send messages containing data to the consumer's mailbox, and the consumer would send empty messages to the producer's mailbox. When mailboxes are used, the buffering mechanism is clear: the destination mailbox holds messages that have been sent to the destination process but have not yet been accepted.

The other extreme from having mailboxes is to eliminate all buffering. When this approach is followed, if the send is done before the receive, the sending process is blocked until the receive happens, at which time the message can be copied directly from the sender to the receiver, with no intermediate buffering. Similarly, if the receive is done first, the receiver is blocked until a send happens. This strategy is often known as a **rendezvous**. It is easier to implement than a buffered message scheme but is less flexible since the sender and receiver are forced to run in lockstep.

The processes that make up the MINIX 3 operating system itself use the rendezvous method with fixed size messages for communication among themselves. User processes also use this method to communicate with operating system components, although a programmer does not see this, since library routines mediate systems calls. Interprocess communication between user processes in MINIX 3 (and UNIX) is via pipes, which are effectively mailboxes. The only real difference between a message system with mailboxes and the pipe mechanism is that pipes do not preserve message boundaries. In other words, if one process writes 10 messages of 100 bytes to a pipe and another process reads 1000 bytes from that pipe, the reader will get all 10 messages at once. With a true message system, each read should return only one message. Of course, if the processes agree always to read and write fixed-size messages from the pipe, or to end each message with a special character (e.g., linefeed), no problems arise.

Message passing is commonly used in parallel programming systems. One well-known message-passing system, for example, is **MPI** (**Message-Passing Interface**). It is widely used for scientific computing. For more information about it, see for example Gropp et al. (1994) and Snir et al. (1996).

2.3 CLASSICAL IPC PROBLEMS

The operating systems literature is full of interprocess communication problems that have been widely discussed using a variety of synchronization methods. In the following sections we will examine two of the better-known problems.

2.3.1 The Dining Philosophers Problem

In 1965, Dijkstra posed and solved a synchronization problem he called the **dining philosophers problem**. Since that time, everyone inventing yet another synchronization primitive has felt obligated to demonstrate how wonderful the new primitive is by showing how elegantly it solves the dining philosophers problem. The problem can be stated quite simply as follows. Five philosophers are seated around a circular table. Each philosopher has a plate of spaghetti. The spaghetti is so slippery that a philosopher needs two forks to eat it. Between each pair of plates is one fork. The layout of the table is illustrated in Fig. 2-18.

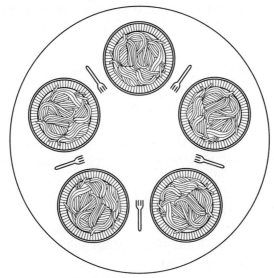

Figure 2-18. Lunch time in the Philosophy Department.

The life of a philosopher consists of alternate periods of eating and thinking. (This is something of an abstraction, even for philosophers, but the other activities are irrelevant here.) When a philosopher gets hungry, she tries to acquire her left and right fork, one at a time, in either order. If successful in acquiring two forks, she eats for a while, then puts down the forks and continues to think. The key question is: can you write a program for each philosopher that does what it is supposed to do and never gets stuck? (It has been pointed out that the two-fork requirement is somewhat artificial; perhaps we should switch from Italian to Chinese food, substituting rice for spaghetti and chopsticks for forks.)

Figure 2-19 shows the obvious solution. The procedure *take_fork* waits until the specified fork is available and then seizes it. Unfortunately, the obvious solution is wrong. Suppose that all five philosophers take their left forks simultaneously. None will be able to take their right forks, and there will be a deadlock.

We could modify the program so that after taking the left fork, the program checks to see if the right fork is available. If it is not, the philosopher puts down

```
#define N 5                          /* number of philosophers */

void philosopher(int i)             /* i: philosopher number, from 0 to 4 */
{
    while (TRUE) {
        think( );                   /* philosopher is thinking */
        take_fork(i);               /* take left fork */
        take_fork((i+1) % N);       /* take right fork; % is modulo operator */
        eat( );                     /* yum-yum, spaghetti */
        put_fork(i);                /* put left fork back on the table */
        put_fork((i+1) % N);        /* put right fork back on the table */
    }
}
```

Figure 2-19. A nonsolution to the dining philosophers problem.

the left one, waits for some time, and then repeats the whole process. This proposal too, fails, although for a different reason. With a little bit of bad luck, all the philosophers could start the algorithm simultaneously, picking up their left forks, seeing that their right forks were not available, putting down their left forks, waiting, picking up their left forks again simultaneously, and so on, forever. A situation like this, in which all the programs continue to run indefinitely but fail to make any progress is called **starvation**. (It is called starvation even when the problem does not occur in an Italian or a Chinese restaurant.)

Now you might think, "If the philosophers would just wait a random time instead of the same time after failing to acquire the right-hand fork, the chance that everything would continue in lockstep for even an hour is very small." This observation is true, and in nearly all applications trying again later is not a problem. For example, in a local area network using Ethernet, a computer sends a packet only when it detects no other computer is sending one. However, because of transmission delays, two computers separated by a length of cable may send packets that overlap—a collision. When a collision of packets is detected each computer waits a random time and tries again; in practice this solution works fine. However, in some applications one would prefer a solution that always works and cannot fail due to an unlikely series of random numbers. Think about safety control in a nuclear power plant.

One improvement to Fig. 2-19 that has no deadlock and no starvation is to protect the five statements following the call to *think* by a binary semaphore. Before starting to acquire forks, a philosopher would do a down on *mutex*. After replacing the forks, she would do an up on *mutex*. From a theoretical viewpoint, this solution is adequate. From a practical one, it has a performance bug: only one philosopher can be eating at any instant. With five forks available, we should be able to allow two philosophers to eat at the same time.

```
#define N            5              /* number of philosophers */
#define LEFT         (i+N−1)%N      /* number of i's left neighbor */
#define RIGHT        (i+1)%N        /* number of i's right neighbor */
#define THINKING     0              /* philosopher is thinking */
#define HUNGRY       1              /* philosopher is trying to get forks */
#define EATING       2              /* philosopher is eating */
typedef int semaphore;             /* semaphores are a special kind of int */
int state[N];                      /* array to keep track of everyone's state */
semaphore mutex = 1;               /* mutual exclusion for critical regions */
semaphore s[N];                    /* one semaphore per philosopher */

void philosopher(int i)            /* i: philosopher number, from 0 to N−1 */
{
     while (TRUE) {                /* repeat forever */
          think( );                /* philosopher is thinking */
          take_forks(i);           /* acquire two forks or block */
          eat( );                  /* yum-yum, spaghetti */
          put_forks(i);            /* put both forks back on table */
     }
}

void take_forks(int i)             /* i: philosopher number, from 0 to N−1 */
{
     down(&mutex);                 /* enter critical region */
     state[i] = HUNGRY;            /* record fact that philosopher i is hungry */
     test(i);                      /* try to acquire 2 forks */
     up(&mutex);                   /* exit critical region */
     down(&s[i]);                  /* block if forks were not acquired */
}

void put_forks(i)                  /* i: philosopher number, from 0 to N−1 */
{
     down(&mutex);                 /* enter critical region */
     state[i] = THINKING;          /* philosopher has finished eating */
     test(LEFT);                   /* see if left neighbor can now eat */
     test(RIGHT);                  /* see if right neighbor can now eat */
     up(&mutex);                   /* exit critical region */
}

void test(i)                       /* i: philosopher number, from 0 to N−1 */
{
     if (state[i] == HUNGRY && state[LEFT] != EATING && state[RIGHT] != EATING) {
          state[i] = EATING;
          up(&s[i]);
     }
}
```

Figure 2-20. A solution to the dining philosophers problem.

The solution presented in Fig. 2-20 is deadlock-free and allows the maximum parallelism for an arbitrary number of philosophers. It uses an array, *state*, to keep track of whether a philosopher is eating, thinking, or hungry (trying to acquire forks). A philosopher may move into eating state only if neither neighbor is eating. Philosopher *i*'s neighbors are defined by the macros *LEFT* and *RIGHT*. In other words, if *i* is 2, *LEFT* is 1 and *RIGHT* is 3.

The program uses an array of semaphores, one per philosopher, so hungry philosophers can block if the needed forks are busy. Note that each process runs the procedure *philosopher* as its main code, but the other procedures, *take_forks*, *put_forks*, and *test* are ordinary procedures and not separate processes.

2.3.2 The Readers and Writers Problem

The dining philosophers problem is useful for modeling processes that are competing for exclusive access to a limited number of resources, such as I/O devices. Another famous problem is the readers and writers problem which models access to a database (Courtois et al., 1971). Imagine, for example, an airline reservation system, with many competing processes wishing to read and write it. It is acceptable to have multiple processes reading the database at the same time, but if one process is updating (writing) the database, no other process may have access to the database, not even a reader. The question is how do you program the readers and the writers? One solution is shown in Fig. 2-21.

In this solution, the first reader to get access to the data base does a down on the semaphore *db*. Subsequent readers merely have to increment a counter, *rc*. As readers leave, they decrement the counter and the last one out does an up on the semaphore, allowing a blocked writer, if there is one, to get in.

The solution presented here implicitly contains a subtle decision that is worth commenting on. Suppose that while a reader is using the data base, another reader comes along. Since having two readers at the same time is not a problem, the second reader is admitted. A third and subsequent readers can also be admitted if they come along.

Now suppose that a writer comes along. The writer cannot be admitted to the data base, since writers must have exclusive access, so the writer is suspended. Later, additional readers show up. As long as at least one reader is still active, subsequent readers are admitted. As a consequence of this strategy, as long as there is a steady supply of readers, they will all get in as soon as they arrive. The writer will be kept suspended until no reader is present. If a new reader arrives, say, every 2 seconds, and each reader takes 5 seconds to do its work, the writer will never get in.

To prevent this situation, the program could be written slightly differently: When a reader arrives and a writer is waiting, the reader is suspended behind the writer instead of being admitted immediately. In this way, a writer has to wait for readers that were active when it arrived to finish but does not have to wait for

```
typedef int semaphore;          /* use your imagination */
semaphore mutex = 1;            /* controls access to 'rc' */
semaphore db = 1;              /* controls access to the database */
int rc = 0;                 /* # of processes reading or wanting to */

void reader(void)
{
    while (TRUE) {               /* repeat forever */
        down(&mutex);             /* get exclusive access to 'rc' */
        rc = rc + 1;             /* one reader more now */
        if (rc == 1) down(&db);       /* if this is the first reader ... */
        up(&mutex);              /* release exclusive access to 'rc' */
        read_data_base( );          /* access the data */
        down(&mutex);             /* get exclusive access to 'rc' */
        rc = rc - 1;             /* one reader fewer now */
        if (rc == 0) up(&db);        /* if this is the last reader ... */
        up(&mutex);              /* release exclusive access to 'rc' */
        use_data_read( );          /* noncritical region */
    }
}


void writer(void)
{
    while (TRUE) {               /* repeat forever */
        think_up_data( );          /* noncritical region */
        down(&db);              /* get exclusive access */
        write_data_base( );         /* update the data */
        up(&db);               /* release exclusive access */
    }
}
```

Figure 2-21. A solution to the readers and writers problem.

readers that came along after it. The disadvantage of this solution is that it achieves less concurrency and thus lower performance. Courtois et al. present a solution that gives priority to writers. For details, we refer you to the paper.

2.4 SCHEDULING

In the examples of the previous sections, we have often had situations in which two or more processes (e.g., producer and consumer) were logically runnable. When a computer is multiprogrammed, it frequently has multiple processes competing for the CPU at the same time. When more than one process is in the ready state and there is only one CPU available, the operating system must decide which process to run first. The part of the operating system that makes the choice is called the **scheduler**; the algorithm it uses is called the **scheduling algorithm**.

Many scheduling issues apply both to processes and threads. Initially, we will focus on process scheduling, but later we will take a brief look at some issues specific to thread scheduling.

2.4.1 Introduction to Scheduling

Back in the old days of batch systems with input in the form of card images on a magnetic tape, the scheduling algorithm was simple: just run the next job on the tape. With timesharing systems, the scheduling algorithm became more complex, because there were generally multiple users waiting for service. There may be one or more batch streams as well (e.g., at an insurance company, for processing claims). On a personal computer you might think there would be only one active process. After all, a user entering a document on a word processor is unlikely to be simultaneously compiling a program in the background. However, there are often background jobs, such as electronic mail daemons sending or receiving e-mail. You might also think that computers have gotten so much faster over the years that the CPU is rarely a scarce resource any more. However, new applications tend to demand more resources. Processing digital photographs or watching real time video are examples.

Process Behavior

Nearly all processes alternate bursts of computing with (disk) I/O requests, as shown in Fig. 2-22. Typically the CPU runs for a while without stopping, then a system call is made to read from a file or write to a file. When the system call completes, the CPU computes again until it needs more data or has to write more data, and so on. Note that some I/O activities count as computing. For example, when the CPU copies bits to a video RAM to update the screen, it is computing, not doing I/O, because the CPU is in use. I/O in this sense is when a process enters the blocked state waiting for an external device to complete its work.

The important thing to notice about Fig. 2-22 is that some processes, such as the one in Fig. 2-22(a), spend most of their time computing, while others, such as the one in Fig. 2-22(b), spend most of their time waiting for I/O. The former are called **compute-bound**; the latter are called **I/O-bound**. Compute-bound processes typically have long CPU bursts and thus infrequent I/O waits, whereas I/O-bound processes have short CPU bursts and thus frequent I/O waits. Note that the key factor is the length of the CPU burst, not the length of the I/O burst. I/O-bound processes are I/O bound because they do not compute much between I/O requests, not because they have especially long I/O requests. It takes the same

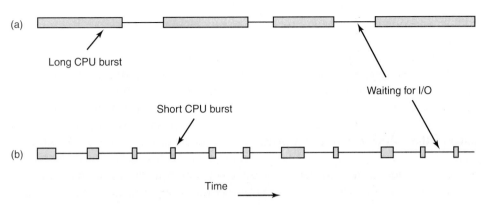

Figure 2-22. Bursts of CPU usage alternate with periods of waiting for I/O. (a) A CPU-bound process. (b) An I/O-bound process.

time to read a disk block no matter how much or how little time it takes to process the data after they arrive.

It is worth noting that as CPUs get faster, processes tend to get more I/O-bound. This effect occurs because CPUs are improving much faster than disks. As a consequence, the scheduling of I/O-bound processes is likely to become a more important subject in the future. The basic idea here is that if an I/O-bound process wants to run, it should get a chance quickly so it can issue its disk request and keep the disk busy.

When to Schedule

There are a variety of situations in which scheduling may occur. First, scheduling is absolutely required on two occasions:

1. When a process exits.

2. When a process blocks on I/O, or a semaphore.

In each of these cases the process that had most recently been running becomes unready, so another must be chosen to run next.

There are three other occasions when scheduling is usually done, although logically it is not absolutely necessary at these times:

1. When a new process is created.

2. When an I/O interrupt occurs.

3. When a clock interrupt occurs.

In the case of a new process, it makes sense to reevaluate priorities at this time. In some cases the parent may be able to request a different priority for its child.

In the case of an I/O interrupt, this usually means that an I/O device has now completed its work. So some process that was blocked waiting for I/O may now be ready to run.

In the case of a clock interrupt, this is an opportunity to decide whether the currently running process has run too long. Scheduling algorithms can be divided into two categories with respect to how they deal with clock interrupts. A **non-preemptive** scheduling algorithm picks a process to run and then just lets it run until it blocks (either on I/O or waiting for another process) or until it voluntarily releases the CPU. In contrast, a **preemptive** scheduling algorithm picks a process and lets it run for a maximum of some fixed time. If it is still running at the end of the time interval, it is suspended and the scheduler picks another process to run (if one is available). Doing preemptive scheduling requires having a clock interrupt occur at the end of the time interval to give control of the CPU back to the scheduler. If no clock is available, nonpreemptive scheduling is the only option.

Categories of Scheduling Algorithms

Not surprisingly, in different environments different scheduling algorithms are needed. This situation arises because different application areas (and different kinds of operating systems) have different goals. In other words, what the scheduler should optimize for is not the same in all systems. Three environments worth distinguishing are

1. Batch.

2. Interactive.

3. Real time.

In batch systems, there are no users impatiently waiting at their terminals for a quick response. Consequently, nonpreemptive algorithms, or preemptive algorithms with long time periods for each process are often acceptable. This approach reduces process switches and thus improves performance.

In an environment with interactive users, preemption is essential to keep one process from hogging the CPU and denying service to the others. Even if no process intentionally ran forever, due to a program bug, one process might shut out all the others indefinitely. Preemption is needed to prevent this behavior.

In systems with real-time constraints, preemption is, oddly enough, sometimes not needed because the processes know that they may not run for long periods of time and usually do their work and block quickly. The difference with interactive systems is that real-time systems run only programs that are intended to further the application at hand. Interactive systems are general purpose and may run arbitrary programs that are not cooperative or even malicious.

Scheduling Algorithm Goals

In order to design a scheduling algorithm, it is necessary to have some idea of what a good algorithm should do. Some goals depend on the environment (batch, interactive, or real time), but there are also some that are desirable in all cases. Some goals are listed in Fig. 2-23. We will discuss these in turn below.

All systems
        Fairness — giving each process a fair share of the CPU
        Policy enforcement — seeing that stated policy is carried out
        Balance — keeping all parts of the system busy

Batch systems
        Throughput — maximize jobs per hour
        Turnaround time — minimize time between submission and termination
        CPU utilization — keep the CPU busy all the time

Interactive systems
        Response time — respond to requests quickly
        Proportionality — meet users' expectations

Real—time systems
        Meeting deadlines — avoid losing data
        Predictability — avoid quality degradation in multimedia systems

Figure 2-23. Some goals of the scheduling algorithm under different circumstances.

Under all circumstances, fairness is important. Comparable processes should get comparable service. Giving one process much more CPU time than an equivalent one is not fair. Of course, different categories of processes may be treated differently. Think of safety control and doing the payroll at a nuclear reactor's computer center.

Somewhat related to fairness is enforcing the system's policies. If the local policy is that safety control processes get to run whenever they want to, even if it means the payroll is 30 sec late, the scheduler has to make sure this policy is enforced.

Another general goal is keeping all parts of the system busy when possible. If the CPU and all the I/O devices can be kept running all the time, more work gets done per second than if some of the components are idle. In a batch system, for example, the scheduler has control of which jobs are brought into memory to run. Having some CPU-bound processes and some I/O-bound processes in memory together is a better idea than first loading and running all the CPU-bound jobs and then, when they are finished, loading and running all the I/O-bound jobs. If the latter strategy is used, when the CPU-bound processes are running, they will fight for the CPU and the disk will be idle. Later, when the I/O-bound jobs come in, they will fight for the disk and the CPU will be idle. Better to keep the whole system running at once by a careful mix of processes.

The managers of corporate computer centers that run many batch jobs (e.g., processing insurance claims) typically look at three metrics to see how well their systems are performing: **throughput, turnaround time**, and **CPU utilization**. Throughput is the number of jobs per second that the system completes. All things considered, finishing 50 jobs per second is better than finishing 40 jobs per second. Turnaround time is the average time from the moment that a batch job is submitted until the moment it is completed. It measures how long the average user has to wait for the output. Here the rule is: Small is Beautiful.

A scheduling algorithm that maximizes throughput may not necessarily minimize turnaround time. For example, given a mix of short jobs and long jobs, a scheduler that always ran short jobs and never ran long jobs might achieve an excellent throughput (many short jobs per second) but at the expense of a terrible turnaround time for the long jobs. If short jobs kept arriving at a steady rate, the long jobs might never run, making the mean turnaround time infinite while achieving a high throughput.

CPU utilization is also an issue with batch systems because on the big mainframes where batch systems run, the CPU is still a major expense. Thus computer center managers feel guilty when it is not running all the time. Actually though, this is not such a good metric. What really matters is how many jobs per second come out of the system (throughput) and how long it takes to get a job back (turnaround time). Using CPU utilization as a metric is like rating cars based on how many times per second the engine turns over.

For interactive systems, especially timesharing systems and servers, different goals apply. The most important one is to minimize **response time**, that is the time between issuing a command and getting the result. On a personal computer where a background process is running (for example, reading and storing email from the network), a user request to start a program or open a file should take precedence over the background work. Having all interactive requests go first will be perceived as good service.

A somewhat related issue is what might be called **proportionality**. Users have an inherent (but often incorrect) idea of how long things should take. When a request that is perceived as complex takes a long time, users accept that, but when a request that is perceived as simple takes a long time, users get irritated. For example, if clicking on a icon that calls up an Internet provider using an analog modem takes 45 seconds to establish a connection, the user will probably accept that as a fact of life. On the other hand, if clicking on an icon that breaks the connection takes 45 seconds, the user will probably be swearing a blue streak by the 30-sec mark and frothing at the mouth by 45 sec. This behavior is due to the common user perception that placing a phone call and getting a connection is *supposed* to take a lot longer than just hanging up. In some cases (such as this one), the scheduler cannot do anything about the response time, but in other cases it can, especially when the delay is due to a poor choice of process order.

Real-time systems have different properties than interactive systems, and thus different scheduling goals. They are characterized by having deadlines that must or at least should be met. For example, if a computer is controlling a device that produces data at a regular rate, failure to run the data-collection process on time may result in lost data. Thus the foremost need in a real-time system is meeting all (or most) deadlines.

In some real-time systems, especially those involving multimedia, predictability is important. Missing an occasional deadline is not fatal, but if the audio process runs too erratically, the sound quality will deteriorate rapidly. Video is also an issue, but the ear is much more sensitive to jitter than the eye. To avoid this problem, process scheduling must be highly predictable and regular.

2.4.2 Scheduling in Batch Systems

It is now time to turn from general scheduling issues to specific scheduling algorithms. In this section we will look at algorithms used in batch systems. In the following ones we will examine interactive and real-time systems. It is worth pointing out that some algorithms are used in both batch and interactive systems. We will study these later. Here we will focus on algorithms that are only suitable in batch systems.

First-Come First-Served

Probably the simplest of all scheduling algorithms is nonpreemptive **first-come first-served**. With this algorithm, processes are assigned the CPU in the order they request it. Basically, there is a single queue of ready processes. When the first job enters the system from the outside in the morning, it is started immediately and allowed to run as long as it wants to. As other jobs come in, they are put onto the end of the queue. When the running process blocks, the first process on the queue is run next. When a blocked process becomes ready, like a newly arrived job, it is put on the end of the queue.

The great strength of this algorithm is that it is easy to understand and equally easy to program. It is also fair in the same sense that allocating scarce sports or concert tickets to people who are willing to stand on line starting at 2 A.M. is fair. With this algorithm, a single linked list keeps track of all ready processes. Picking a process to run just requires removing one from the front of the queue. Adding a new job or unblocked process just requires attaching it to the end of the queue. What could be simpler?

Unfortunately, first-come first-served also has a powerful disadvantage. Suppose that there is one compute-bound process that runs for 1 sec at a time and many I/O-bound processes that use little CPU time but each have to perform 1000 disk reads in order to complete. The compute-bound process runs for 1 sec, then it reads a disk block. All the I/O processes now run and start disk reads. When the compute-bound process gets its disk block, it runs for another 1 sec, followed by all the I/O-bound processes in quick succession.

The net result is that each I/O-bound process gets to read 1 block per second and will take 1000 sec to finish. With a scheduling algorithm that preempted the compute-bound process every 10 msec, the I/O-bound processes would finish in 10 sec instead of 1000 sec, and without slowing down the compute-bound process very much.

Shortest Job First

Now let us look at another nonpreemptive batch algorithm that assumes the run times are known in advance. In an insurance company, for example, people can predict quite accurately how long it will take to run a batch of 1000 claims, since similar work is done every day. When several equally important jobs are sitting in the input queue waiting to be started, the scheduler picks the **shortest job first**. Look at Fig. 2-24. Here we find four jobs *A*, *B*, *C*, and *D* with run times of 8, 4, 4, and 4 minutes, respectively. By running them in that order, the turn-around time for *A* is 8 minutes, for *B* is 12 minutes, for *C* is 16 minutes, and for *D* is 20 minutes for an average of 14 minutes.

Figure 2-24. An example of shortest job first scheduling. (a) Running four jobs in the original order. (b) Running them in shortest job first order.

Now let us consider running these four jobs using shortest job first, as shown in Fig. 2-24(b). The turnaround times are now 4, 8, 12, and 20 minutes for an average of 11 minutes. Shortest job first is provably optimal. Consider the case of four jobs, with run times of *a*, *b*, *c*, and *d*, respectively. The first job finishes at time *a*, the second finishes at time $a + b$, and so on. The mean turnaround time is $(4a + 3b + 2c + d)/4$. It is clear that *a* contributes more to the average than the other times, so it should be the shortest job, with *b* next, then *c*, and finally *d* as the longest as it affects only its own turnaround time. The same argument applies equally well to any number of jobs.

It is worth pointing out that shortest job first is only optimal when all the jobs are available simultaneously. As a counterexample, consider five jobs, *A* through *E*, with run times of 2, 4, 1, 1, and 1, respectively. Their arrival times are 0, 0, 3, 3, and 3. Initially, only *A* or *B* can be chosen, since the other three jobs have not arrived yet. Using shortest job first we will run the jobs in the order A, B, C, D, E, for an average wait of 4.6. However, running them in the order B, C, D, E, A has an average wait of 4.4.

Shortest Remaining Time Next

A preemptive version of shortest job first is **shortest remaining time next**. With this algorithm, the scheduler always chooses the process whose remaining run time is the shortest. Again here, the run time has to be known in advance. When a new job arrives, its total time is compared to the current process' remaining time. If the new job needs less time to finish than the current process, the current process is suspended and the new job started. This scheme allows new short jobs to get good service.

Three-Level Scheduling

From a certain perspective, batch systems allow scheduling at three different levels, as illustrated in Fig. 2-25. As jobs arrive at the system, they are initially placed in an input queue stored on the disk. The **admission scheduler** decides which jobs to admit to the system. The others are kept in the input queue until they are selected. A typical algorithm for admission control might be to look for a mix of compute-bound jobs and I/O-bound jobs. Alternatively, short jobs could be admitted quickly whereas longer jobs would have to wait. The admission scheduler is free to hold some jobs in the input queue and admit jobs that arrive later if it so chooses.

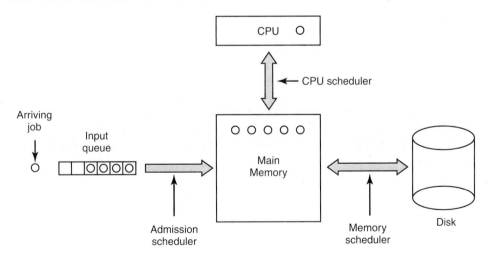

Figure 2-25. Three-level scheduling.

Once a job has been admitted to the system, a process can be created for it and it can contend for the CPU. However, it might well happen that the number of processes is so large that there is not enough room for all of them in memory. In that case, some of the processes have to be swapped out to disk. The second level of scheduling is deciding which processes should be kept in memory and which ones should be kept on disk. We will call this scheduler the **memory scheduler**, since it determines which processes are kept in memory and which on the disk.

This decision has to be reviewed frequently to allow the processes on disk to get some service. However, since bringing a process in from disk is expensive, the review probably should not happen more often than once per second, maybe less often. If the contents of main memory are shuffled too often, a large amount of disk bandwidth will be wasted, slowing down file I/O.

To optimize system performance as a whole, the memory scheduler might well want to carefully decide how many processes it wants in memory, called the **degree of multiprogramming**, and what kind of processes. If it has information about which processes are compute bound and which are I/O bound, it can try to keep a mix of these process types in memory. As a very crude approximation, if a certain class of process computes about 20% of the time, keeping five of them around is roughly the right number to keep the CPU busy.

To make its decisions, the memory scheduler periodically reviews each process on disk to decide whether or not to bring it into memory. Among the criteria that it can use to make its decision are the following ones:

1. How long has it been since the process was swapped in or out?

2. How much CPU time has the process had recently?

3. How big is the process? (Small ones do not get in the way.)

4. How important is the process?

The third level of scheduling is actually picking one of the ready processes in main memory to run next. Often this is called the **CPU scheduler** and is the one people usually mean when they talk about the "scheduler." Any suitable algorithm can be used here, either preemptive or nonpreemptive. These include the ones described above as well as a number of algorithms to be described in the next section.

2.4.3 Scheduling in Interactive Systems

We will now look at some algorithms that can be used in interactive systems. All of these can also be used as the CPU scheduler in batch systems as well. While three-level scheduling is not possible here, two-level scheduling (memory scheduler and CPU scheduler) is possible and common. Below we will focus on the CPU scheduler and some common scheduling algorithms.

Round-Robin Scheduling

Now let us look at some specific scheduling algorithms. One of the oldest, simplest, fairest, and most widely used algorithms is **round robin**. Each process is assigned a time interval, called its **quantum**, which it is allowed to run. If the process is still running at the end of the quantum, the CPU is preempted and given to another process. If the process has blocked or finished before the quantum has elapsed, the CPU switching is done when the process blocks, of course. Round robin is easy to implement. All the scheduler needs to do is maintain a list of runnable processes, as shown in Fig. 2-26(a). When the process uses up its quantum, it is put on the end of the list, as shown in Fig. 2-26(b).

Figure 2-26. Round-robin scheduling. (a) The list of runnable processes. (b) The list of runnable processes after *B* uses up its quantum.

The only interesting issue with round robin is the length of the quantum. Switching from one process to another requires a certain amount of time for doing the administration—saving and loading registers and memory maps, updating various tables and lists, flushing and reloading the memory cache, etc. Suppose that this **process switch** or **context switch**, as it is sometimes called, takes 1 msec, including switching memory maps, flushing and reloading the cache, etc. Also suppose that the quantum is set at 4 msec. With these parameters, after doing 4 msec of useful work, the CPU will have to spend 1 msec on process switching. Twenty percent of the CPU time will be wasted on administrative overhead. Clearly, this is too much.

To improve the CPU efficiency, we could set the quantum to, say, 100 msec. Now the wasted time is only 1 percent. But consider what happens on a timesharing system if ten interactive users hit the carriage return key at roughly the same time. Ten processes will be put on the list of runnable processes. If the CPU is idle, the first one will start immediately, the second one may not start until 100 msec later, and so on. The unlucky last one may have to wait 1 sec before getting a chance, assuming all the others use their full quanta. Most users will perceive a 1-sec response to a short command as sluggish.

Another factor is that if the quantum is set longer than the mean CPU burst, preemption will rarely happen. Instead, most processes will perform a blocking operation before the quantum runs out, causing a process switch. Eliminating preemption improves performance because process switches then only happen when they are logically necessary, that is, when a process blocks and cannot continue because it is logically waiting for something.

The conclusion can be formulated as follows: setting the quantum too short causes too many process switches and lowers the CPU efficiency, but setting it too long may cause poor response to short interactive requests. A quantum of around 20–50 msec is often a reasonable compromise.

Priority Scheduling

Round-robin scheduling makes the implicit assumption that all processes are equally important. Frequently, the people who own and operate multiuser computers have different ideas on that subject. At a university, the pecking order may be deans first, then professors, secretaries, janitors, and finally students. The need to take external factors into account leads to **priority scheduling**. The basic idea is straightforward: Each process is assigned a priority, and the runnable process with the highest priority is allowed to run.

Even on a PC with a single owner, there may be multiple processes, some more important than others. For example, a daemon process sending electronic mail in the background should be assigned a lower priority than a process displaying a video film on the screen in real time.

To prevent high-priority processes from running indefinitely, the scheduler may decrease the priority of the currently running process at each clock tick (i.e., at each clock interrupt). If this action causes its priority to drop below that of the next highest process, a process switch occurs. Alternatively, each process may be assigned a maximum time quantum that it is allowed to run. When this quantum is used up, the next highest priority process is given a chance to run.

Priorities can be assigned to processes statically or dynamically. On a military computer, processes started by generals might begin at priority 100, processes started by colonels at 90, majors at 80, captains at 70, lieutenants at 60, and so on. Alternatively, at a commercial computer center, high-priority jobs might cost 100 dollars an hour, medium priority 75 dollars an hour, and low priority 50 dollars an hour. The UNIX system has a command, *nice*, which allows a user to voluntarily reduce the priority of his process, in order to be nice to the other users. Nobody ever uses it.

Priorities can also be assigned dynamically by the system to achieve certain system goals. For example, some processes are highly I/O bound and spend most of their time waiting for I/O to complete. Whenever such a process wants the CPU, it should be given the CPU immediately, to let it start its next I/O request, which can then proceed in parallel with another process actually computing. Making the I/O-bound process wait a long time for the CPU will just mean having it around occupying memory for an unnecessarily long time. A simple algorithm for giving good service to I/O-bound processes is to set the priority to $1/f$, where f is the fraction of the last quantum that a process used. A process that used only 1 msec of its 50 msec quantum would get priority 50, while a process that ran 25 msec before blocking would get priority 2, and a process that used the whole quantum would get priority 1.

It is often convenient to group processes into priority classes and use priority scheduling among the classes but round-robin scheduling within each class. Figure 2-27 shows a system with four priority classes. The scheduling algorithm is as follows: as long as there are runnable processes in priority class 4, just run each one for one quantum, round-robin fashion, and never bother with lower priority classes. If priority class 4 is empty, then run the class 3 processes round robin. If classes 4 and 3 are both empty, then run class 2 round robin, and so on. If priorities are not adjusted occasionally, lower priority classes may all starve to death.

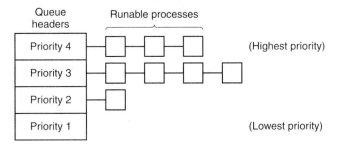

Figure 2-27. A scheduling algorithm with four priority classes.

MINIX 3 uses a similar system to Fig. 2-27, although there are sixteen priority classes in the default configuration. In MINIX 3, components of the operating system run as processes. MINIX 3 puts tasks (I/O drivers) and servers (memory manager, file system, and network) in the highest priority classes. The initial priority of each task or service is defined at compile time; I/O from a slow device may be given lower priority than I/O from a fast device or even a server. User processes generally have lower priority than system components, but all priorities can change during execution.

Multiple Queues

One of the earliest priority schedulers was in CTSS (Corbató et al., 1962). CTSS had the problem that process switching was very slow because the 7094 could hold only one process in memory. Each switch meant swapping the current process to disk and reading in a new one from disk. The CTSS designers quickly realized that it was more efficient to give CPU-bound processes a large quantum once in a while, rather than giving them small quanta frequently (to reduce swapping). On the other hand, giving all processes a large quantum would mean poor response time, as we have already observed. Their solution was to set up priority classes. Processes in the highest class were run for one quantum. Processes in the next highest class were run for two quanta. Processes in the next class were run for four quanta, and so on. Whenever a process used up all the quanta allocated to it, it was moved down one class.

As an example, consider a process that needed to compute continuously for 100 quanta. It would initially be given one quantum, then swapped out. Next time it would get two quanta before being swapped out. On succeeding runs it would get 4, 8, 16, 32, and 64 quanta, although it would have used only 37 of the final 64 quanta to complete its work. Only 7 swaps would be needed (including the initial load) instead of 100 with a pure round-robin algorithm. Furthermore, as the process sank deeper and deeper into the priority queues, it would be run less and less frequently, saving the CPU for short, interactive processes.

The following policy was adopted to prevent a process that needed to run for a long time when it first started but became interactive later, from being punished forever. Whenever a carriage return was typed at a terminal, the process belonging to that terminal was moved to the highest priority class, on the assumption that it was about to become interactive. One fine day, some user with a heavily CPU-bound process discovered that just sitting at the terminal and typing carriage returns at random every few seconds did wonders for his response time. He told all his friends. Moral of the story: getting it right in practice is much harder than getting it right in principle.

Many other algorithms have been used for assigning processes to priority classes. For example, the influential XDS 940 system (Lampson, 1968), built at Berkeley, had four priority classes, called terminal, I/O, short quantum, and long quantum. When a process that was waiting for terminal input was finally awakened, it went into the highest priority class (terminal). When a process waiting for a disk block became ready, it went into the second class. When a process was still running when its quantum ran out, it was initially placed in the third class. However, if a process used up its quantum too many times in a row without blocking for terminal or other I/O, it was moved down to the bottom queue. Many other systems use something similar to favor interactive users and processes over background ones.

Shortest Process Next

Because shortest job first always produces the minimum average response time for batch systems, it would be nice if it could be used for interactive processes as well. To a certain extent, it can be. Interactive processes generally follow the pattern of wait for command, execute command, wait for command, execute command, and so on. If we regard the execution of each command as a separate "job," then we could minimize overall response time by running the shortest one first. The only problem is figuring out which of the currently runnable processes is the shortest one.

One approach is to make estimates based on past behavior and run the process with the shortest estimated running time. Suppose that the estimated time per command for some terminal is T_0. Now suppose its next run is measured to be T_1. We could update our estimate by taking a weighted sum of these two numbers, that is, $aT_0 + (1 - a)T_1$. Through the choice of a we can decide to have the estimation process forget old runs quickly, or remember them for a long time. With $a = 1/2$, we get successive estimates of

$$T_0, \quad T_0/2 + T_1/2, \quad T_0/4 + T_1/4 + T_2/2, \quad T_0/8 + T_1/8 + T_2/4 + T_3/2$$

After three new runs, the weight of T_0 in the new estimate has dropped to 1/8.

The technique of estimating the next value in a series by taking the weighted average of the current measured value and the previous estimate is sometimes called **aging**. It is applicable to many situations where a prediction must be made based on previous values. Aging is especially easy to implement when $a = 1/2$. All that is needed is to add the new value to the current estimate and divide the sum by 2 (by shifting it right 1 bit).

Guaranteed Scheduling

A completely different approach to scheduling is to make real promises to the users about performance and then live up to them. One promise that is realistic to make and easy to live up to is this: If there are n users logged in while you are working, you will receive about $1/n$ of the CPU power. Similarly, on a single-user system with n processes running, all things being equal, each one should get $1/n$ of the CPU cycles.

To make good on this promise, the system must keep track of how much CPU each process has had since its creation. It then computes the amount of CPU each one is entitled to, namely the time since creation divided by n. Since the amount of CPU time each process has actually had is also known, it is straightforward to compute the ratio of actual CPU time consumed to CPU time entitled. A ratio of 0.5 means that a process has only had half of what it should have had, and a ratio of 2.0 means that a process has had twice as much as it was entitled to. The algorithm is then to run the process with the lowest ratio until its ratio has moved above its closest competitor.

Lottery Scheduling

While making promises to the users and then living up to them is a fine idea, it is difficult to implement. However, another algorithm can be used to give similarly predictable results with a much simpler implementation. It is called **lottery scheduling** (Waldspurger and Weihl, 1994).

The basic idea is to give processes lottery tickets for various system resources, such as CPU time. Whenever a scheduling decision has to be made, a lottery ticket is chosen at random, and the process holding that ticket gets the resource. When applied to CPU scheduling, the system might hold a lottery 50 times a second, with each winner getting 20 msec of CPU time as a prize.

To paraphrase George Orwell: "All processes are equal, but some processes are more equal." More important processes can be given extra tickets, to increase their odds of winning. If there are 100 tickets outstanding, and one process holds 20 of them, it will have a 20 percent chance of winning each lottery. In the long run, it will get about 20 percent of the CPU. In contrast to a priority scheduler, where it is very hard to state what having a priority of 40 actually means, here the rule is clear: a process holding a fraction f of the tickets will get about a fraction f of the resource in question.

Lottery scheduling has several interesting properties. For example, if a new process shows up and is granted some tickets, at the very next lottery it will have a chance of winning in proportion to the number of tickets it holds. In other words, lottery scheduling is highly responsive.

Cooperating processes may exchange tickets if they wish. For example, when a client process sends a message to a server process and then blocks, it may give all of its tickets to the server, to increase the chance of the server running next. When the server is finished, it returns the tickets so the client can run again. In fact, in the absence of clients, servers need no tickets at all.

Lottery scheduling can be used to solve problems that are difficult to handle with other methods. One example is a video server in which several processes are feeding video streams to their clients, but at different frame rates. Suppose that the processes need frames at 10, 20, and 25 frames/sec. By allocating these processes 10, 20, and 25 tickets, respectively, they will automatically divide the CPU in approximately the correct proportion, that is, 10 : 20 : 25.

Fair-Share Scheduling

So far we have assumed that each process is scheduled on its own, without regard to who its owner is. As a result, if user 1 starts up 9 processes and user 2 starts up 1 process, with round robin or equal priorities, user 1 will get 90% of the CPU and user 2 will get only 10% of it.

To prevent this situation, some systems take into account who owns a process before scheduling it. In this model, each user is allocated some fraction of the CPU and the scheduler picks processes in such a way as to enforce it. Thus if two users have each been promised 50% of the CPU, they will each get that, no matter how many processes they have in existence.

As an example, consider a system with two users, each of which has been promised 50% of the CPU. User 1 has four processes, A, B, C, and D, and user 2 has only 1 process, E. If round-robin scheduling is used, a possible scheduling sequence that meets all the constraints is this one:

A E B E C E D E A E B E C E D E ...

On the other hand, if user 1 is entitled to twice as much CPU time as user 2, we might get

ABECDEABECDE...

Numerous other possibilities exist, of course, and can be exploited, depending on what the notion of fairness is.

2.4.4 Scheduling in Real-Time Systems

A **real-time** system is one in which time plays an essential role. Typically, one or more physical devices external to the computer generate stimuli, and the computer must react appropriately to them within a fixed amount of time. For example, the computer in a compact disc player gets the bits as they come off the drive and must convert them into music within a very tight time interval. If the calculation takes too long, the music will sound peculiar. Other real-time systems are patient monitoring in a hospital intensive-care unit, the autopilot in an aircraft, and robot control in an automated factory. In all these cases, having the right answer but having it too late is often just as bad as not having it at all.

Real-time systems are generally categorized as **hard real time**, meaning there are absolute deadlines that must be met, or else, and **soft real time**, meaning that missing an occasional deadline is undesirable, but nevertheless tolerable. In both cases, real-time behavior is achieved by dividing the program into a number of processes, each of whose behavior is predictable and known in advance. These processes are generally short lived and can run to completion in well under a second. When an external event is detected, it is the job of the scheduler to schedule the processes in such a way that all deadlines are met.

The events that a real-time system may have to respond to can be further categorized as **periodic** (occurring at regular intervals) or **aperiodic** (occurring unpredictably). A system may have to respond to multiple periodic event streams. Depending on how much time each event requires for processing, it may not even be possible to handle them all. For example, if there are m periodic events and event i occurs with period P_i and requires C_i seconds of CPU time to handle each event, then the load can only be handled if

$$\sum_{i=1}^{m} \frac{C_i}{P_i} \leq 1$$

A real-time system that meets this criteria is said to be **schedulable**.

As an example, consider a soft real-time system with three periodic events, with periods of 100, 200, and 500 msec, respectively. If these events require 50, 30, and 100 msec of CPU time per event, respectively, the system is schedulable because $0.5 + 0.15 + 0.2 < 1$. If a fourth event with a period of 1 sec is added, the system will remain schedulable as long as this event does not need more than 150 msec of CPU time per event. Implicit in this calculation is the assumption that the context-switching overhead is so small that it can be ignored.

Real-time scheduling algorithms can be static or dynamic. The former make their scheduling decisions before the system starts running. The latter make their scheduling decisions at run time. Static scheduling only works when there is perfect information available in advance about the work needed to be done and the deadlines that have to be met. Dynamic scheduling algorithms do not have these restrictions.

2.4.5 Policy versus Mechanism

Up until now, we have tacitly assumed that all the processes in the system belong to different users and are thus competing for the CPU. While this is often true, sometimes it happens that one process has many children running under its control. For example, a database management system process may have many children. Each child might be working on a different request, or each one might have some specific function to perform (query parsing, disk access, etc.). It is entirely possible that the main process has an excellent idea of which of its children are the most important (or the most time critical) and which the least. Unfortunately, none of the schedulers discussed above accept any input from user processes about scheduling decisions. As a result, the scheduler rarely makes the best choice.

The solution to this problem is to separate the **scheduling mechanism** from the **scheduling policy**. What this means is that the scheduling algorithm is parameterized in some way, but the parameters can be filled in by user processes. Let us consider the database example once again. Suppose that the kernel uses a priority scheduling algorithm but provides a system call by which a process can set (and change) the priorities of its children. In this way the parent can control in detail how its children are scheduled, even though it does not do the scheduling itself. Here the mechanism is in the kernel but policy is set by a user process.

2.4.6 Thread Scheduling

When several processes each have multiple threads, we have two levels of parallelism present: processes and threads. Scheduling in such systems differs substantially depending on whether user-level threads or kernel-level threads (or both) are supported.

Let us consider user-level threads first. Since the kernel is not aware of the existence of threads, it operates as it always does, picking a process, say, A, and giving A control for its quantum. The thread scheduler inside A decides which thread to run, say A1. Since there are no clock interrupts to multiprogram threads, this thread may continue running as long as it wants to. If it uses up the process' entire quantum, the kernel will select another process to run.

When the process *A* finally runs again, thread *A1* will resume running. It will continue to consume all of *A*'s time until it is finished. However, its antisocial behavior will not affect other processes. They will get whatever the scheduler considers their appropriate share, no matter what is going on inside process *A*.

Now consider the case that *A*'s threads have relatively little work to do per CPU burst, for example, 5 msec of work within a 50-msec quantum. Consequently, each one runs for a little while, then yields the CPU back to the thread scheduler. This might lead to the sequence *A1, A2, A3, A1, A2, A3, A1, A2, A3, A1*, before the kernel switches to process *B*. This situation is illustrated in Fig. 2-28(a).

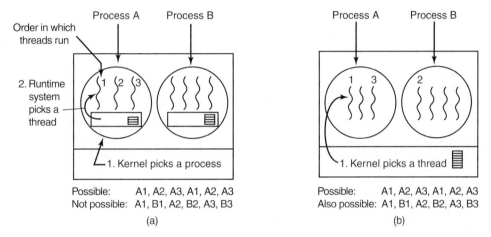

Figure 2-28. (a) Possible scheduling of user-level threads with a 50-msec process quantum and threads that run 5 msec per CPU burst. (b) Possible scheduling of kernel-level threads with the same characteristics as (a).

The scheduling algorithm used by the run-time system can be any of the ones described above. In practice, round-robin scheduling and priority scheduling are most common. The only constraint is the absence of a clock to interrupt a thread that has run too long.

Now consider the situation with kernel-level threads. Here the kernel picks a particular thread to run. It does not have to take into account which process the thread belongs to, but it can if it wants to. The thread is given a quantum and is forceably suspended if it exceeds the quantum. With a 50-msec quantum but threads that block after 5 msec, the thread order for some period of 30 msec might be *A1, B1, A2, B2, A3, B3*, something not possible with these parameters and user-level threads. This situation is partially depicted in Fig. 2-28(b).

A major difference between user-level threads and kernel-level threads is the performance. Doing a thread switch with user-level threads takes a handful of machine instructions. With kernel-level threads it requires a full context switch, changing the memory map, and invalidating the cache, which is several orders of magnitude slower. On the other hand, with kernel-level threads, having a thread block on I/O does not suspend the entire process as it does with user-level threads.

Since the kernel knows that switching from a thread in process A to a thread in process B is more expensive that running a second thread in process A (due to having to change the memory map and having the memory cache spoiled), it can take this information into account when making a decision. For example, given two threads that are otherwise equally important, with one of them belonging to the same process as a thread that just blocked and one belonging to a different process, preference could be given to the former.

Another important factor to consider is that user-level threads can employ an application-specific thread scheduler. For example, consider a web server which has a dispatcher thread to accept and distribute incoming requests to worker threads. Suppose that a worker thread has just blocked and the dispatcher thread and two worker threads are ready. Who should run next? The run-time system, knowing what all the threads do, can easily pick the dispatcher to run next, so it can start another worker running. This strategy maximizes the amount of parallelism in an environment where workers frequently block on disk I/O. With kernel-level threads, the kernel would never know what each thread did (although they could be assigned different priorities). In general, however, application-specific thread schedulers can tune an application better than the kernel can.

2.5 OVERVIEW OF PROCESSES IN MINIX 3

Having completed our study of the principles of process management, interprocess communication, and scheduling, we can now take a look at how they are applied in MINIX 3. Unlike UNIX, whose kernel is a monolithic program not split up into modules, MINIX 3 itself is a collection of processes that communicate with each other and also with user processes, using a single interprocess communication primitive—message passing. This design gives a more modular and flexible structure, making it easy, for example, to replace the entire file system by a completely different one, without having even to recompile the kernel.

2.5.1 The Internal Structure of MINIX 3

Let us begin our study of MINIX 3 by taking a bird's-eye view of the system. MINIX 3 is structured in four layers, with each layer performing a well-defined function. The four layers are illustrated in Fig. 2-29.

The **kernel** in the bottom layer schedules processes and manages the transitions between the ready, running, and blocked states of Fig. 2-2. The kernel also handles all messages between processes. Message handling requires checking for legal destinations, locating the send and receive buffers in physical memory, and

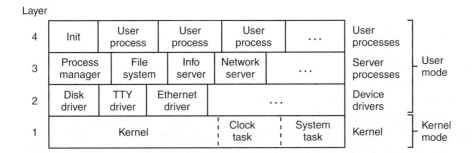

Figure 2-29. MINIX 3 is structured in four layers. Only processes in the bottom layer may use privileged (kernel mode) instructions.

copying bytes from sender to receiver. Also part of the kernel is support for access to I/O ports and interrupts, which on modern processors require use of privileged **kernel mode** instructions not available to ordinary processes.

In addition to the kernel itself, this layer contains two modules that function similarly to device drivers. The **clock task** is an I/O device driver in the sense that it interacts with the hardware that generates timing signals, but it is not user-accessible like a disk or communications line driver—it interfaces only with the kernel.

One of the main functions of layer 1 is to provide a set of privileged **kernel calls** to the drivers and servers above it. These include reading and writing I/O ports, copying data between address spaces, and so on. Implementation of these calls is done by the **system task**. Although the system task and the clock task are compiled into the kernel's address space, they are scheduled as separate processes and have their own call stacks.

Most of the kernel and all of the clock and system tasks are written in C. However, a small amount of the kernel is written in assembly language. The assembly language parts deal with interrupt handling, the low-level mechanics of managing context switches between processes (saving and restoring registers and the like), and low-level parts of manipulating the MMU hardware. By and large, the assembly-language code handles those parts of the kernel that deal directly with the hardware at a very low level and which cannot be expressed in C. These parts have to be rewritten when MINIX 3 is ported to a new architecture.

The three layers above the kernel could be considered to be a single layer because the kernel fundamentally treats them all of them the same way. Each one is limited to **user mode** instructions, and each is scheduled to run by the kernel. None of them can access I/O ports directly. Furthermore, none of them can access memory outside the segments allotted to it.

However, processes potentially have special privileges (such as the ability to make kernel calls). This is the real difference between processes in layers 2, 3, and 4. The processes in layer 2 have the most privileges, those in layer 3 have some privileges, and those in layer 4 have no special privileges. For example, processes in layer 2, called **device drivers**, are allowed to request that the system task read data from or write data to I/O ports on their behalf. A driver is needed for each device type, including disks, printers, terminals, and network interfaces. If other I/O devices are present, a driver is needed for each one of those, as well. Device drivers may also make other kernel calls, such as requesting that newly-read data be copied to the address space of a different process.

The third layer contains **servers**, processes that provide useful services to the user processes. Two servers are essential. The **process manager** (**PM**) carries out all the MINIX 3 system calls that involve starting or stopping process execution, such as fork, exec, and exit, as well as system calls related to signals, such as alarm and kill, which can alter the execution state of a process. The process manager also is responsible for managing memory, for instance, with the brk system call. The **file system** (**FS**) carries out all the file system calls, such as read, mount, and chdir.

It is important to understand the difference between kernel calls and POSIX system calls. Kernel calls are low-level functions provided by the system task to allow the drivers and servers to do their work. Reading a hardware I/O port is a typical kernel call. In contrast, the POSIX system calls such as read, fork, and unlink are high-level calls defined by the POSIX standard, and are available to user programs in layer 4. User programs contain many POSIX calls but no kernel calls. Occasionally when we are not being careful with our language we may call a kernel call a system call. The mechanisms used to make these calls are similar, and kernel calls can be considered a special subset of system calls.

In addition to the PM and FS, other servers exist in layer 3. They perform functions that are specific to MINIX 3. It is safe to say that the functionality of the process manager and the file system will be found in any operating system. The **information server** (**IS**) handles jobs such as providing debugging and status information about other drivers and servers, something that is more necessary in a system like MINIX 3, designed for experimentation, than would be the case for a commercial operating system which users cannot alter. The **reincarnation server** (**RS**) starts, and if necessary restarts, device drivers that are not loaded into memory at the same time as the kernel. In particular, if a driver fails during operation, the reincarnation server detects this failure, kills the driver if it is not already dead, and starts a fresh copy of the driver, making the system highly fault tolerant. This functionality is absent from most operating systems. On a networked system the optional **network server** (**inet**) is also in level 3. Servers cannot do I/O directly, but they can communicate with drivers to request I/O. Servers can also communicate with the kernel via the system task.

As we noted at the start of Chap. 1, operating systems do two things: manage resources and provide an extended machine by implementing system calls. In MINIX 3 the resource management is largely done by the drivers in layer 2, with help from the kernel layer when privileged access to I/O ports or the interrupt system is required. System call interpretation is done by the process manager and file system servers in layer 3. The file system has been carefully designed as a file "server" and could be moved to a remote machine with few changes.

The system does not need to be recompiled to include additional servers. The process manager and the file system can be supplemented with the network server and other servers by attaching additional servers as required when MINIX 3 starts up or later. Device drivers, although typically started when the system is started, can also be started later. Both device drivers and servers are compiled and stored on disk as ordinary executable files, but when properly started up they are granted access to the special privileges needed. A user program called **service** provides an interface to the reincarnation server which manages this. Although the drivers and servers are independent processes, they differ from user processes in that normally they never terminate while the system is active.

We will often refer to the drivers and servers in layers 2 and 3 as **system processes**. Arguably, system processes are part of the operating system. They do not belong to any user, and many if not all of them will be activated before the first user logs on. Another difference between system processes and user processes is that system processes have higher execution priority than user processes. In fact, normally drivers have higher execution priority than servers, but this is not automatic. Execution priority is assigned on a case-by-case basis in MINIX 3; it is possible for a driver that services a slow device to be given lower priority than a server that must respond quickly.

Finally, layer 4 contains all the user processes—shells, editors, compilers, and user-written *a.out* programs. Many user processes come and go as users log in, do work, and log out. A running system normally has some user processes that are started when the system is booted and which run forever. One of these is *init*, which we will describe in the next section. Also, several daemons are likely to be running. A **daemon** is a background process that executes periodically or always waits for some event, such as the arrival of a packet from the network. In a sense a daemon is a server that is started independently and runs as a user process. Like true servers installed at startup time, it is possible to configure a daemon to have a higher priority than ordinary user processes.

A note about the terms **task** and **device driver** is needed. In older versions of MINIX all device drivers were compiled together with the kernel, which gave them access to data structures belonging to the kernel and each other. They also could all access I/O ports directly. They were referred to as "tasks" to distinguish them from pure independent user-space processes. In MINIX 3, device drivers have been implemented completely in user-space. The only exception is the clock task, which is arguably not a device driver in the same sense as drivers that can be accessed through device files by user processes. Within the text we have taken pains to use the term "task" only when referring to the clock task or the system task, both of which are compiled into the kernel to function. We have been careful to replace the word "task" with "device driver" where we refer to user-space device drivers. However, function names, variable names, and comments in the source code have not been as carefully updated. Thus, as you look at source code during your study of MINIX 3 you may find the word "task" where "device driver" is meant.

2.5.2 Process Management in MINIX 3

Processes in MINIX 3 follow the general process model described at length earlier in this chapter. Processes can create subprocesses, which in turn can create more subprocesses, yielding a tree of processes. In fact, all the user processes in the whole system are part of a single tree with *init* (see Fig. 2-29) at the root. Servers and drivers are a special case, of course, since some of them must be started before any user process, including *init*.

MINIX 3 Startup

How does an operating system start up? We will summarize the MINIX 3 startup sequence in the next few pages. For a look at how some other operating systems do this, see Dodge et al. (2005).

On most computers with disk devices, there is a **boot disk** hierarchy. Typically, if a floppy disk is in the first floppy disk drive, it will be the boot disk. If no floppy disk is present and a CD-ROM is present in the first CD-ROM drive, it becomes the boot disk. If there is neither a floppy disk nor a CD-ROM present, the first hard drive becomes the boot disk. The order of this hierarchy may be configurable by entering the BIOS immediately after powering the computer up. Additional devices, especially other removable storage devices, may be supported as well.

When the computer is turned on, if the boot device is a diskette, the hardware reads the first sector of the first track of the boot disk into memory and executes the code it finds there. On a diskette this sector contains the **bootstrap** program. It is very small, since it has to fit in one sector (512 bytes). The MINIX 3 bootstrap loads a larger program, *boot*, which then loads the operating system itself.

In contrast, hard disks require an intermediate step. A hard disk is divided into **partitions**, and the first sector of a hard disk contains a small program and the disk's **partition table**. Collectively these two pieces are called the **master boot record**. The program part is executed to read the partition table and to select the **active partition**. The active partition has a bootstrap on its first sector, which is then loaded and executed to find and start a copy of *boot* in the partition, exactly as is done when booting from a diskette.

CD-ROMs came along later in the history of computers than floppy disks and hard disks, and when support for booting from a CD-ROM is present it is capable of more than just loading one sector. A computer that supports booting from a CD-ROM can load a large block of data into memory immediately. Typically what is loaded from the CD-ROM is an exact copy of a bootable floppy disk, which is placed in memory and used as a **RAM disk**. After this first step control is transferred to the RAM disk and booting continues exactly as if a physical floppy disk were the boot device. On an older computer which has a CD-ROM drive but does not support booting from a CD-ROM, the bootable floppy disk image can be copied to a floppy disk which can then be used to start the system. The CD-ROM must be in the CD-ROM drive, of course, since the bootable floppy disk image expects that.

In any case, the MINIX 3 *boot* program looks for a specific multipart file on the diskette or partition and loads the individual parts into memory at the proper locations. This is the **boot image**. The most important parts are the kernel (which include the clock task and the system task), the process manager, and the file system. Additionally, at least one disk driver must be loaded as part of the boot image. There are several other programs loaded in the boot image. These include the reincarnation server, the RAM disk, console, and log drivers, and *init*.

It should be strongly emphasized that all parts of the boot image are separate programs. After the essential kernel, process manager and file system have been loaded many other parts could be loaded separately. An exception is the reincarnation server. It must be part of the boot image. It gives ordinary processes loaded after initialization the special priorities and privileges which make them into system processes, It can also restart a crashed driver, which explains its name. As mentioned above, at least one disk driver is essential. If the root file system is to be copied to a RAM disk, the memory driver is also required, otherwise it could be loaded later. The *tty* and *log* drivers are optional in the boot image. They are loaded early just because it is useful to be able to display messages on the console and save information to a log early in the startup process. *Init* could certainly be loaded later, but it controls initial configuration of the system, and it was easiest just to include it in the boot image file.

Startup is not a trivial operation. Operations that are in the realms of the disk driver and the file system must be performed by *boot* before these parts of the system are active. In a later section we will detail how MINIX 3 is started. For now, suffice it to say that once the loading operation is complete the kernel starts running.

During its initialization phase the kernel starts the system and clock tasks, and then the process manager and the file system. The process manager and the file system then cooperate in starting other servers and drivers that are part of the boot image. When all these have run and initialized themselves, they will block, waiting for something to do. MINIX 3 scheduling prioritizes processes. Only when all tasks, drivers, and servers loaded in the boot image have blocked will *init*, the first user process, be executed. System components loaded with the boot image or during initialization are shown in Fig. 2-30.

Component	Description	Loaded by
kernel	Kernel + clock and system tasks	(in boot image)
pm	Process manager	(in boot image)
fs	File system	(in boot image)
rs	(Re)starts servers and drivers	(in boot image)
memory	RAM disk driver	(in boot image)
log	Buffers log output	(in boot image)
tty	Console and keyboard driver	(in boot image)
driver	Disk (at, bios, or floppy) driver	(in boot image)
init	parent of all user processes	(in boot image)
floppy	Floppy driver (if booted from hard disk)	/etc/rc
is	Information server (for debug dumps)	/etc/rc
cmos	Reads CMOS clock to set time	/etc/rc
random	Random number generator	/etc/rc
printer	Printer driver	/etc/rc

Figure 2-30. Some important MINIX 3 system components. Others such as an Ethernet driver and the inet server may also be present.

Initialization of the Process Tree

Init is the first user process, and also the last process loaded as part of the boot image. You might think building of a process tree such as that of Fig. 1-5 begins once *init* starts running. Well, not exactly. That would be true in a conventional operating system, but MINIX 3 is different. First, there are already quite a few system processes running by the time *init* gets to run. The tasks *CLOCK* and *SYSTEM* that run within the kernel are unique processes that are not visible outside of the kernel. They receive no PIDs and are not considered part of any tree of processes. The process manager is the first process to run in user space; it is given PID 0 and is neither a child nor a parent of any other process. The reincarnation server is made the parent of all the other processes started from the boot image (e.g., the drivers and servers). The logic of this is that the reincarnation server is the process that should be informed if any of these should need to be restarted.

As we will see, even after *init* starts running there are differences between the way a process tree is built in MINIX 3 and the conventional concept. *Init* in a UNIX-like system is given PID 1, and even though *init* is not the first process to run, the traditional PID 1 is reserved for it in MINIX 3. Like all the user space processes in the boot image (except the process manager), *init* is made one of the children of the reincarnation server. As in a standard UNIX-like system, *init* first executes the **/etc/rc** shell script. This script starts additional drivers and servers that are not part of the boot image. Any program started by the *rc* script will be a child of *init*. One of the first programs run is a utility called *service*. Service itself runs as a child of *init*, as would be expected. But now things once again vary from the conventional.

Service is the user interface to the reincarnation server. The reincarnation server starts an ordinary program and converts it into a system process. It starts *floppy* (if it was not used in booting the system), *cmos* (which is needed to read the real-time clock), and *is*, the information server which manages the debug dumps that are produced by pressing function keys (F1, F2, etc.) on the console keyboard. One of the actions of the reincarnation server is to adopt all system processes except the process manager as its own children.

After the *cmos* device driver has been started the *rc* script can initialize the real-time clock. Up to this point all files needed must be found on the root device. The servers and drivers needed initially are in the */sbin* directory; other commands needed for startup are in */bin*. Once the initial startup steps have been completed other file systems such as */usr* are mounted. An important function of the *rc* script is to check for file system problems that might have resulted from a previous system crash. The test is simple—when the system is shutdown correctly by executing the *shutdown* command an entry is written to the login history file, */usr/adm/wtmp*. The command shutdown –C checks whether the last entry in *wtmp* is a shutdown entry. If not, it is assumed an abnormal shutdown occurred, and the *fsck* utility is run to check all file systems. The final job of */etc/rc* is to start daemons. This may be done by subsidiary scripts. If you look at the output of a ps axl command, which shows both PIDs and parent PIDs (PPIDs), you will see that daemons such as *update* and *usyslogd* will normally be the among the first persistent processes which are children of *init*.

Finally *init* reads the file */etc/ttytab*, which lists all potential terminal devices. Those devices that can be used as login terminals (in the standard distribution, just the main console and up to three virtual consoles, but serial lines and network pseudo terminals can be added) have an entry in the *getty* field of */etc/ttytab*, and *init* forks off a child process for each such terminal. Normally, each child executes */usr/bin/getty* which prints a message, then waits for a name to be typed. If a particular terminal requires special treatment (e.g., a dial-up line) */etc/ttytab* can specify a command (such as */usr/bin/stty*) to be executed to initialize the line before running *getty*.

When a user types a name to log in, */usr/bin/login* is called with the name as its argument. *Login* determines if a password is required, and if so prompts for and verifies the password. After a successful login, *login* executes the user's shell (by default */bin/sh*, but another shell may be specified in the */etc/passwd* file). The shell waits for commands to be typed and then forks off a new process for each command. In this way, the shells are the children of *init*, the user processes are the grandchildren of *init*, and all the user processes in the system are part of a single tree. In fact, except for the tasks compiled into the kernel and the process manager, all processes, both system processes and user processes, form a tree. But unlike the process tree of a conventional UNIX system, *init* is not at the root of the tree, and the structure of the tree does not allow one to determine the order in which system processes were started.

The two principal MINIX 3 system calls for process management are fork and exec. Fork is the only way to create a new process. Exec allows a process to execute a specified program. When a program is executed, it is allocated a portion of memory whose size is specified in the program file's header. It keeps this amount of memory throughout its execution, although the distribution among data segment, stack segment, and unused can vary as the process runs.

All the information about a process is kept in the process table, which is divided up among the kernel, process manager, and file system, with each one having those fields that it needs. When a new process comes into existence (by fork), or an old process terminates (by exit or a signal), the process manager first updates its part of the process table and then sends messages to the file system and kernel telling them to do likewise.

2.5.3 Interprocess Communication in MINIX 3

Three primitives are provided for sending and receiving messages. They are called by the C library procedures

    send(dest, &message);

to send a message to process *dest*,

    receive(source, &message);

to receive a message from process *source* (or *ANY*), and

    sendrec(src_dst, &message);

to send a message and wait for a reply from the same process. The second parameter in each call is the local address of the message data. The message passing mechanism in the kernel copies the message from the sender to the receiver. The reply (for sendrec) overwrites the original message. In principle this kernel mechanism could be replaced by a function which copies messages over a network to a corresponding function on another machine, to implement a distributed system. In practice this would be complicated somewhat by the fact that message contents sometimes include pointers to large data structures, and a distributed system would have to provide for copying the data itself over the network.

Each task, driver or server process is allowed to exchange messages only with certain other processes. Details of how this is enforced will be described later. The usual flow of messages is downward in the layers of Fig 2-29, and messages can be between processes in the same layer or between processes in adjacent layers. User processes cannot send messages to each other. User processes in layer 4 can initiate messages to servers in layer 3, servers in layer 3 can initiate messages to drivers in layer 2.

When a process sends a message to a process that is not currently waiting for a message, the sender blocks until the destination does a receive. In other words, MINIX 3 uses the rendezvous method to avoid the problems of buffering sent, but not yet received, messages. The advantage of this approach is that it is simple and eliminates the need for buffer management (including the possibility of running out of buffers). In addition, because all messages are of fixed length determined at compile time, buffer overrun errors, a common source of bugs, are structurally prevented.

The basic purpose of the restrictions on exchanges of messages is that if process *A* is allowed to generate a send or sendrec directed to process *B*, then process *B* can be allowed to call receive with *A* designated as the sender, but *B* should not be allowed to send to *A*. Obviously, if *A* tries to send to *B* and blocks, and *B* tries to send to *A* and blocks we have a deadlock. The "resource" that each would need to complete the operations is not a physical resource like an I/O device, it is a call to receive by the target of the message. We will have more to say about deadlocks in Chap. 3.

Occasionally something different from a blocking message is needed. There exists another important message-passing primitive. It is called by the C library procedure

```
notify(dest);
```

and is used when a process needs to make another process aware that something important has happened. A notify is nonblocking, which means the sender continues to execute whether or not the recipient is waiting. Because it does not block, a notification avoids the possibility of a message deadlock.

The message mechanism is used to deliver a notification, but the information conveyed is limited. In the general case the message contains only the identity of the sender and a timestamp added by the kernel. Sometimes this is all that is necessary. For instance, the keyboard uses a notify call when one of the function keys (F1 to F12 and shifted F1 to F12) is pressed. In MINIX 3, function keys are used to trigger debugging dumps. The Ethernet driver is an example of a process that generates only one kind of debug dump and never needs to get any other communication from the console driver. Thus a notification to the Ethernet driver from the keyboard driver when the dump-Ethernet-stats key is pressed is unambiguous. In other cases a notification is not sufficient, but upon receiving a notification the target process can send a message to the originator of the notification to request more information.

There is a reason notification messages are so simple. Because a notify call does not block, it can be made when the recipient has not yet done a receive. But the simplicity of the message means that a notification that cannot be received is easily stored so the recipient can be informed of it the next time the recipient calls receive. In fact, a single bit suffices. Notifications are meant for use between system processes, of which there can be only a relatively small number. Every system process has a bitmap for pending notifications, with a distinct bit for every system process. So if process *A* needs to send a notification to process *B* at a time when process *B* is not blocked on a receive, the message-passing mechanism sets a bit which corresponds to *A* in *B*'s bitmap of pending notifications. When *B* finally does a receive, the first step is to check its pending notifications bitmap. It can learn of attempted notifications from multiple sources this way. The single bit is enough to regenerate the information content of the notification. It tells the identity of the sender, and the message passing code in the kernel adds the timestamp when it is delivered. Timestamps are used primarily to see if timers have expired, so it does not matter that the timestamp may be for a time later than the time when the sender first tried to send the notification.

There is a further refinement to the notification mechanism. In certain cases an additional field of the notification message is used. When the notification is generated to inform a recipient of an interrupt, a bitmap of all possible sources of interrupts is included in the message. And when the notification is from the system task a bitmap of all pending signals for the recipient is part of the message. The natural question at this point is, how can this additional information be stored when the notification must be sent to a process that is not trying to receive a message? The answer is that these bitmaps are in kernel data structures. They do not need to be copied to be preserved. If a notification must be deferred and reduced to setting a single bit, when the recipient eventually does a receive and the notification message is regenerated, knowing the origin of the notification is enough to specify which additional information needs to be included in the message. And for the recipient, the origin of the notification also tells whether or not the message contains additional information, and, if so, how it is to be interpreted,

A few other primitives related to interprocess communication exist. They will be mentioned in a later section. They are less important than send, receive, sendrec, and notify.

2.5.4 Process Scheduling in MINIX 3

The interrupt system is what keeps a multiprogramming operating system going. Processes block when they make requests for input, allowing other processes to execute. When input becomes available, the current running process is interrupted by the disk, keyboard, or other hardware. The clock also generates interrupts that are used to make sure a running user process that has not requested input eventually relinquishes the CPU, to give other processes their chance to run. It is the job of the lowest layer of MINIX 3 to hide these interrupts by turning them into messages. As far as processes are concerned, when an I/O device completes an operation it sends a message to some process, waking it up and making it eligible to run.

Interrupts are also generated by software, in which case they are often called **traps**. The send and receive operations that we described above are translated by the system library into **software interrupt** instructions which have exactly the same effect as hardware-generated interrupts—the process that executes a software interrupt is immediately blocked and the kernel is activated to process the interrupt. User programs do not refer to send or receive directly, but any time one of the system calls listed in Fig. 1-9 is invoked, either directly or by a library routine, sendrec is used internally and a software interrupt is generated.

Each time a process is interrupted (whether by a conventional I/O device or by the clock) or due to execution of a software interrupt instruction, there is an opportunity to redetermine which process is most deserving of an opportunity to run. Of course, this must be done whenever a process terminates, as well, but in a system like MINIX 3 interruptions due to I/O operations or the clock or message passing occur more frequently than process termination.

The MINIX 3 scheduler uses a multilevel queueing system. Sixteen queues are defined, although recompiling to use more or fewer queues is easy. The lowest priority queue is used only by the *IDLE* process which runs when there is nothing else to do. User processes start by default in a queue several levels higher than the lowest one.

Servers are normally scheduled in queues with priorities higher than allowed for user processes, drivers in queues with priorities higher than those of servers, and the clock and system tasks are scheduled in the highest priority queue. Not all of the sixteen available queues are likely to be in use at any time. Processes are started in only a few of them. A process may be moved to a different priority queue by the system or (within certain limits) by a user who invokes the *nice* command. The extra levels are available for experimentation, and as additional drivers are added to MINIX 3 the default settings can be adjusted for best performance. For instance, if it were desired to add a server to stream digital audio or video to a network, such a server might be assigned a higher starting priority than current servers, or the initial priority of a current server or driver might be reduced in order for the new server to achieve better performance.

In addition to the priority determined by the queue on which a process is placed, another mechanism is used to give some processes an edge over others. The quantum, the time interval allowed before a process is preempted, is not the same for all processes. User processes have a relatively low quantum. Drivers and servers normally should run until they block. However, as a hedge against malfunction they are made preemptable, but are given a large quantum. They are allowed to run for a large but finite number of clock ticks, but if they use their entire quantum they are preempted in order not to hang the system. In such a case the timed-out process will be considered ready, and can be put on the end of its queue. However, if a process that has used up its entire quantum is found to have been the process that ran last, this is taken as a sign it may be stuck in a loop and preventing other processes with lower priority from running. In this case its priority is lowered by putting it on the end of a lower priority queue. If the process times out again and another process still has not been able to run, its priority will again be lowered. Eventually, something else should get a chance to run.

A process that has been demoted in priority can earn its way back to a higher priority queue. If a process uses all of its quantum but is not preventing other processes from running it will be promoted to a higher priority queue, up to the maximum priority permitted for it. Such a process apparently needs its quantum, but is not being inconsiderate of others.

Otherwise, processes are scheduled using a slightly modified round robin. If a process has not used its entire quantum when it becomes unready, this is taken to mean that it blocked waiting for I/O, and when it becomes ready again it is put on the head of the queue, but with only the left-over part of its previous quantum. This is intended to give user processes quick response to I/O. A process that became unready because it used its entire quantum is placed at the end of the queue in pure round robin fashion.

With tasks normally having the highest priority, drivers next, servers below drivers, and user processes last, a user process will not run unless all system processes have nothing to do, and a system process cannot be prevented from running by a user process.

When picking a process to run, the scheduler checks to see if any processes are queued in the highest priority queue. If one or more are ready, the one at the head of the queue is run. If none is ready the next lower priority queue is similarly tested, and so on. Since drivers respond to requests from servers and servers respond to requests from user processes, eventually all high priority processes should complete whatever work was requested of them. They will then block with nothing to do until user processes get a turn to run and make more requests. If no process is ready, the *IDLE* process is chosen. This puts the CPU in a low-power mode until the next interrupt occurs.

At each clock tick, a check is made to see if the current process has run for more than its allotted quantum. If it has, the scheduler moves it to the end of its queue (which may require doing nothing if it is alone on the queue). Then the next process to run is picked, as described above. Only if there are no processes on higher-priority queues and if the previous process is alone on its queue will it get to run again immediately. Otherwise the process at the head of the highest priority nonempty queue will run next. Essential drivers and servers are given such large quanta that normally they are normally never preempted by the clock. But if something goes wrong their priority can be temporarily lowered to prevent the system from coming to a total standstill. Probably nothing useful can be done if this happens to an essential server, but it may be possible to shut the system down gracefully, preventing data loss and possibly collecting information that can help in debugging the problem.

2.6 IMPLEMENTATION OF PROCESSES IN MINIX 3

We are now moving closer to looking at the actual code, so a few words about the notation we will use are perhaps in order. The terms "procedure," "function," and "routine" will be used interchangeably. Names of variables, procedures, and files will be written in italics, as in *rw_flag*. When a variable, procedure, or file name starts a sentence, it will be capitalized, but the actual names begin with lower case letters. There are a few exceptions, the tasks which are compiled into the kernel are identified by upper case names, such as *CLOCK*, *SYSTEM*, and *IDLE*. System calls will be in lower case Helvetica, for example, read.

The book and the software, both of which are continuously evolving, did not "go to press" on the same day, so there may be minor discrepancies between the references to the code, the printed listing, and the CD-ROM version. Such differences generally only affect a line or two, however. The source code printed in the book has been simplified by omitting code used to compile options that are not discussed in the book. The complete version is on the CD-ROM. The MINIX 3 Web site (*www.minix3.org*) has the current version, which has new features and additional software and documentation.

2.6.1 Organization of the MINIX 3 Source Code

The implementation of MINIX 3 as described in this book is for an IBM PC-type machine with an advanced processor chip (e.g., 80386, 80486, Pentium, Pentium Pro, II, III, 4, M, or D) that uses 32-bit words. We will refer to all of these as Intel 32-bit processors. The full path to the C language source code on a standard Intel-based platform is */usr/src/* (a trailing "/" in a path name indicates that it refers to a directory). The source directory tree for other platforms may be in a different location. Throughout the book, MINIX 3 source code files will be referred to using a path starting with the top *src/* directory. An important subdirectory of the source tree is *src/include/*, where the master copy of the C header files are located. We will refer to this directory as *include/*.

Each directory in the source tree contains a file named **Makefile** which directs the operation of the UNIX-standard *make* utility. The *Makefile* controls compilation of files in its directory and may also direct compilation of files in one or more subdirectories. The operation of *make* is complex and a full description is beyond the scope of this section, but it can be summarized by saying that *make* manages efficient compilation of programs involving multiple source files. *Make* assures that all necessary files are compiled. It tests previously compiled modules to see if they are up to date and recompiles any whose source files have been modified since the previous compilation. This saves time by avoiding recompilation of files that do not need to be recompiled. Finally, *make* directs the combination of separately compiled modules into an executable program and may also manage installation of the completed program.

All or part of the *src/* tree can be relocated, since the *Makefile* in each source directory uses a relative path to C source directories. For instance, you may want to make a source directory on the root filesystem, */src/*, for speedy compilation if the root device is a RAM disk. If you are developing a special version you can make a copy of *src/* under another name.

The path to the C header files is a special case. During compilation every *Makefile* expects to find header files in */usr/include/* (or the equivalent path on a non-Intel platform). However, *src/tools/Makefile*, used to recompile the system, expects to find a master copy of the headers in */usr/src/include* (on an Intel system). Before recompiling the system, however, the entire */usr/include/* directory tree is deleted and */usr/src/include/* is copied to */usr/include/*. This was done to make it possible to keep all files needed in the development of MINIX 3 in one place. This also makes it easy to maintain multiple copies of the entire source and headers tree for experimenting with different configurations of the MINIX 3 system. However, if you want to edit a header file as part of such an experiment, you must be sure to edit the copy in the *src/include* directory and not the one in */usr/include/*.

This is a good place to point out for newcomers to the C language how file names are quoted in a #include statement. Every C compiler has a default header directory where it looks for include files. Frequently, this is */usr/include/*. When the name of a file to include is quoted between less-than and greater-than symbols ("< ... >") the compiler searches for the file in the default header directory or a specified subdirectory, for example,

    #include <*filename*>

includes a file from */usr/include/*.

Many programs also require definitions in local header files that are not meant to be shared system-wide. Such a header may have the same name as and be meant to replace or supplement a standard header. When the name is quoted between ordinary quote characters (" *"* ... *"*") the file is searched for first in the same directory as the source file (or a specified subdirectory) and then, if not found there, in the default directory. Thus

    #include "*filename*"

reads a local file.

The *include/* directory contains a number of POSIX standard header files. In addition, it has three subdirectories:

sys/ – additional POSIX headers.

minix/ – header files used by the MINIX 3 operating system.

ibm/ – header files with IBM PC-specific definitions.

To support extensions to MINIX 3 and programs that run in the MINIX 3 environment, other files and subdirectories are also present in *include/* as provided on the

CD-ROM and also on the MINIX 3 Web site. For instance, *include/arpa/* and the *include/net/* directory and its subdirectory *include/net/gen/* support network extensions. These are not necessary for compiling the basic MINIX 3 system, and files in these directories are not listed in Appendix B.

In addition to *src/include/*, the *src/* directory contains three other important subdirectories with operating system source code:

kernel/   – layer 1 (scheduling, messages, clock and system tasks).

drivers/   – layer 2 (device drivers for disk, console, printer, etc.).

servers/   –layer 3 (process manager, file system, other servers).

Three other source code directories are not printed or discussed in the text, but are essential to producing a working system:

src/lib/   – source code for library procedures (e.g., open, read).

src/tools/   – Makefile and scripts for building the MINIX 3 system.

src/boot/   – the code for booting and installing MINIX 3.

The standard distribution of MINIX 3 includes many additional source files not discussed in this text. In addition to the process manager and file system source code, the system source directory *src/servers/* contains source code for the *init* program and the reincarnation server, *rs*, both of which are essential parts of a running MINIX 3 system. The network server source code is in *src/servers/inet/*. *Src/drivers/* has source code for device drivers not discussed in this text, including alternative disk drivers, sound cards, and network adapters. Since MINIX 3 is an experimental operating system, meant to be modified, there is a *src/test/* directory with programs designed to test thoroughly a newly compiled MINIX 3 system. An operating system exists, of course, to support commands (programs) that will run on it, so there is a large *src/commands/* directory with source code for the utility programs (e.g., *cat*, *cp*, *date*, *ls*, *pwd* and more than 200 others). Source code for some major open source applications originally developed by the GNU and BSD projects is here, too.

The "book" version of MINIX 3 is configured with many of the optional parts omitted (trust us: we cannot fit everything into one book or into your head in a semester-long course). The "book" version is compiled using modified *Makefiles* that do not refer to unnecessary files. (A standard *Makefile* requires that files for optional components be present, even if not to be compiled.) Omitting these files and the conditional statements that select them makes reading the code easier.

For convenience we will usually refer to simple file names when it it is clear from the context what the complete path is. However, be aware that some file names appear in more than one directory. For instance, there are several files named *const.h*. *Src/kernel/const.h* defines constants used in the kernel, while *src/servers/pm/const.h* defines constants used by the process manager, etc.

The files in a particular directory will be discussed together, so there should not be any confusion. The files are listed in Appendix B in the order they are discussed in the text, to make it easier to follow along. Acquisition of a couple of bookmarks might be of use at this point, so you can go back and forth between the text and the listing. To keep the size of the listing reasonable, code for every file is not printed. In general, those functions that are described in detail in the text are listed in Appendix B; those that are just mentioned in passing are not listed, but the complete source is on the CD-ROM and Web site, both of which also provide an index to functions, definitions, and global variables in the source code.

Appendix C contains an alphabetical list of all files described in Appendix B, divided into sections for headers, drivers, kernel, file system, and process manager. This appendix and the Web site and CD-ROM indices reference the listed objects by line number in the source code.

The code for layer 1 is contained in the directory *src/kernel/*. Files in this directory support process control, the lowest layer of the MINIX 3 structure we saw in Fig. 2-29. This layer includes functions which handle system initialization, interrupts, message passing and process scheduling. Intimately connected with these are two modules compiled into the same binary, but which run as independent processes. These are the system task which provides an interface between kernel services and processes in higher layers, and the clock task which provides timing signals to the kernel. In Chap. 3, we will look at files in several of the subdirectories of *src/drivers*, which support various device drivers, the second layer in Fig. 2-29. Then in Chap. 4, we will look at the process manager files in *src/servers/pm/*. Finally, in Chap. 5, we will study the file system, whose source files are located in *src/servers/fs/*.

2.6.2 Compiling and Running MINIX 3

To compile MINIX 3, run make in *src/tools/*. There are several options, for installing MINIX 3 in different ways. To see the possibilities run make with no argument. The simplest method is make image.

When make image is executed, a fresh copy of the header files in *src/include/* is copied to */usr/include/*. Then source code files in *src/kernel/* and several subdirectories of *src/servers/* and *src/drivers/* are compiled to object files. All the object files in *src/kernel/* are linked to form a single executable program, *kernel*. The object files in *src/servers/pm/* are also linked together to form a single executable program, *pm*, and all the object files in *src/servers/fs/* are linked to form *fs*. The additional programs listed as part of the boot image in Fig. 2-30 are also compiled and linked in their own directories. These include *rs* and *init* in subdirectories of *src/servers/* and *memory/*, *log/*, and *tty/* in subdirectories of *src/drivers/*. The component designated "driver" in Fig. 2-30 can be one of several disk drivers; we discuss here a MINIX 3 system configured to boot from the hard disk using the standard *at_wini* driver, which will be compiled in *src/drivers/at_wini/*.   Other drivers can be added, but most drivers need not be compiled into the boot image. The same is true for networking support; compilation of the basic MINIX 3 system is the same whether or not networking will be used.

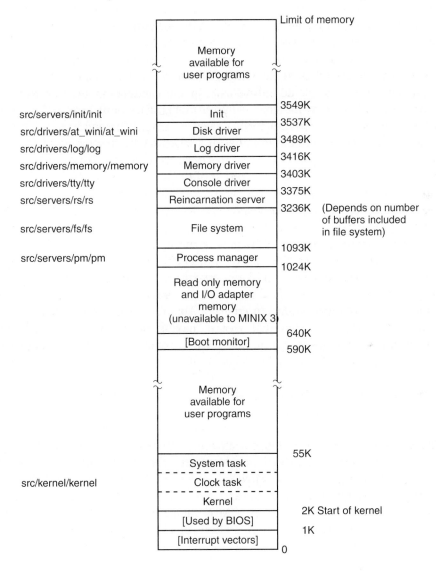

Figure 2-31. Memory layout after MINIX 3 has been loaded from the disk into memory. The kernel, servers, and drivers are independently compiled and linked programs, listed on the left. Sizes are approximate and not to scale.

To install a working MINIX 3 system capable of being booted, a program called *installboot* (whose source is in *src/boot/*) adds names to *kernel, pm, fs, init,* and the other components of the boot image, pads each one out so that its length is a multiple of the disk sector size (to make it easier to load the parts independently), and concatenates them onto a single file. This new file is the boot image and can be copied into the */boot/* directory or the */boot/image/* directory of a floppy disk or a hard disk partition. Later, the boot monitor program can load the boot image and transfer control to the operating system.

Figure 2-31 shows the layout of memory after the concatenated programs are separated and loaded. The kernel is loaded in low memory, all the other parts of the boot image are loaded above 1 MB. When user programs are run, the available memory above the kernel will be used first. When a new program will not fit there, it will be loaded in the high memory range, above *init*. Details, of course, depend upon the system configuration. For instance, the example in the figure is for a MINIX 3 file system configured with a block cache that can hold 512 4-KB disk blocks. This is a modest amount; more is recommended if adequate memory is available. On the other hand, if the size of the block cache were reduced drastically it would be possible to make the entire system fit into less than 640K of memory, with room for a few user processes as well.

It is important to realize that MINIX 3 consists of several totally independent programs that communicate only by passing messages. A procedure called *panic* in the directory *src/servers/fs/* does not conflict with a procedure called *panic* in *src/servers/pm/* because they ultimately are linked into different executable files. The only procedures that the three pieces of the operating system have in common are a few of the library routines in *src/lib/*. This modular structure makes it very easy to modify, say, the file system, without having these changes affect the process manager. It also makes it straightforward to remove the file system altogether and to put it on a different machine as a file server, communicating with user machines by sending messages over a network.

As another example of the modularity of MINIX 3, adding network support makes absolutely no difference to the process manager, the file system, or the kernel. Both an Ethernet driver and the *inet* server can be activated after the boot image is loaded; they would appear in Fig. 2-30 with the processes started by */etc/rc*, and they would be loaded into one of the "Memory available for user programs" regions of Fig. 2-31. A MINIX 3 system with networking enabled can be used as a remote terminal or an ftp and web server. Only if you want to allow incoming logins to the MINIX 3 system over the network would any part of MINIX 3 as described in the text need modification: this is *tty*, the console driver, which would need to be recompiled with pseudo terminals configured to allow remote logins.

2.6.3 The Common Header Files

The *include/* directory and its subdirectories contain a collection of files defining constants, macros, and types. The POSIX standard requires many of these definitions and specifies in which files of the main *include/* directory and its subdirectory *include/sys/* each required definition is to be found. The files in these directories are **header** or **include** files, identified by the suffix *.h*, and used by means of #include statements in C source files. These statements are a built-in feature of the C language. Include files make maintenance of a large system easier.

Headers likely to be needed for compiling user programs are mainly found in *include/* whereas *include/sys/* traditionally is used for files that are used primarily for compiling system programs and utilities. The distinction is not terribly important, and a typical compilation, whether of a user program or part of the operating system, will include files from both of these directories. We will discuss here the files that are needed to compile the standard MINIX 3 system, first treating those in *include/* and then those in *include/sys/*. In the next section we will discuss files in the *include/minix/* and *include/ibm/* directories, which, as the directory names indicate, are unique to MINIX 3 and its implementation on IBM-type (really, Intel-type) computers.

The first headers to be considered are truly general purpose ones, so much so that they are not referenced directly by any of the C language source files for the MINIX 3 system. Rather, they are themselves included in other header files. Each major component of MINIX 3 has a master header file, such as *src/kernel/kernel.h*, *src/servers/pm/pm.h*, and *src/servers/fs/fs.h*. These are included in every compilation of these components. Source code for each of the device drivers includes a somewhat similar file, *src/drivers/drivers.h*. Each master header is tailored to the needs of the corresponding part of the MINIX 3 system, but each one starts with a section like the one shown in Fig. 2-32 and includes most of the files shown there. The master headers will be discussed again in other sections of the book. This preview is to emphasize that headers from several directories are used together. In this section and the next one we will mention each of the files referenced in Fig. 2-32.

```
#include <minix/config.h>        /* MUST be first */
#include <ansi.h>                /* MUST be second */
#include <limits.h>
#include <errno.h>
#include <sys/types.h>
#include <minix/const.h>
#include <minix/type.h>
#include <minix/syslib.h>
#include "const.h"
```

Figure 2-32. Part of a master header which ensures inclusion of header files needed by all C source files. Note that two *const.h* files, one from the *include/* tree and one from the local directory, are referenced.

Let us start with the first header in *include/*, *ansi.h* (line 0000). This is the second header that is processed whenever any part of the MINIX 3 system is compiled; only *include/minix/config.h* is processed earlier. The purpose of *ansi.h* is to test whether the compiler meets the requirements of Standard C, as defined by the International Organization for Standards. Standard C is also often referred to as ANSI C, since the standard was originally developed by the American National Standards Institute before gaining international recognition. A Standard C compiler defines several macros that can then be tested in programs being compiled. *__STDC__* is such a macro, and it is defined by a standard compiler to have a value of 1, just as if the C preprocessor had read a line like

        #define __STDC__ 1

The compiler distributed with current versions of MINIX 3 conforms to Standard C, but older versions of MINIX were developed before the adoption of the standard, and it is still possible to compile MINIX 3 with a classic (Kernighan & Ritchie) C compiler. It is intended that MINIX 3 should be easy to port to new machines, and allowing older compilers is part of this. At lines 0023 to 0025 the statement

        #define _ANSI

is processed if a Standard C compiler is in use. *Ansi.h* defines several macros in different ways, depending upon whether the *_ANSI* macro is defined. This is an example of a **feature test macro**.

Another feature test macro defined here is *_POSIX_SOURCE* (line 0065). This is required by POSIX. Here we ensure it is defined if other macros that imply POSIX conformance are defined.

When compiling a C program the data types of the arguments and the returned values of functions must be known before code that references such data can be generated. In a complex system ordering of function definitions to meet this requirement is difficult, so C allows use of **function prototypes** to **declare** the arguments and return value types of a function before it is **defined**. The most important macro in *ansi.h* is *_PROTOTYPE*. This macro allows us to write function prototypes in the form

        _PROTOTYPE (return-type function-name, (argument-type argument, ...))

and have this transformed by the C preprocessor into

        return-type function-name(argument-type, argument, ...)

if the compiler is an ANSI Standard C compiler, or

        return-type function-name()

if the compiler is an old-fashioned (i.e., Kernighan & Ritchie) compiler.

Before we leave *ansi.h* let us mention one additional feature. The entire file (except for initial comments) is enclosed between lines that read

```
#ifndef _ANSI_H
```

and

```
#endif /* _ANSI_H */
```

On the line immediately following the #ifndef _ANSI_H itself is defined. A header file should be included only once in a compilation; this construction ensures that the contents of the file will be ignored if it is included multiple times. We will see this technique used in all the header files in the *include/* directory.

Two points about this deserve mention. First, in all of the #ifndef ... #define sequences for files in the master header directories, the filename is preceded by an underscore. Another header with the same name may exist within the C source code directories, and the same mechanism will be used there, but underscores will not be used. Thus inclusion of a file from the master header directory will not prevent processing of another header file with the same name in a local directory. Second, note that the comment /* _ANSI_H */ after the #ifndef is not required. Such comments can be helpful in keeping track of nested #ifndef ... #endif and #ifdef ... #endif sections. However, care is needed in writing such comments: if incorrect they are worse than no comment at all.

The second file in *include/* that is indirectly included in most MINIX 3 source files is the *limits.h* header (line 0100). This file defines many basic sizes, both language types such as the number of bits in an integer, as well as operating system limits such as the length of a file name.

Note that for convenience, the line numbering in Appendix B is ratcheted up to the next multiple of 100 when a new file is listed. Thus do not expect *ansi.h* to contain 100 lines (00000 through 00099). In this way, small changes to one file will (probably) not affect subsequent files in a revised listing. Also note that when a new file is encountered in the listing, a special three-line header consisting of a row of + signs, the file name, and another row of + signs is present (without line numbering). An example of this header is shown between lines 00068 and 00100.

Errno.h (line 0200), is also included by most of the master headers. It contains the error numbers that are returned to user programs in the global variable *errno* when a system call fails. *Errno* is also used to identify some internal errors, such as trying to send a message to a nonexistent task. Internally, it would be inefficient to examine a global variable after a call to a function that might generate an error, but functions must often return other integers, for instance, the number of bytes transferred during an I/O operation. The MINIX 3 solution is to return error numbers as negative values to mark them as error codes within the system, and then to convert them to positive values before being returned to user programs. The trick that is used is that each error code is defined in a line like

```
#define EPERM   (_SIGN 1)
```

(line 0236). The master header file for each part of the operating system defines the _SYSTEM macro, but _SYSTEM is never defined when a user program is compiled. If _SYSTEM_ is defined, then _SIGN_ is defined as "−"; otherwise it is given a null definition.

The next group of files to be considered are not included in all the master headers, but are nevertheless used in many source files in all parts of the MINIX 3 system. The most important is *unistd.h* (line 0400). This header defines many constants, most of which are required by POSIX. In addition, it includes proto-types for many C functions, including all those used to access MINIX 3 system calls. Another widely used file is *string.h* (line 0600), which provides prototypes for many C functions used for string manipulation. The header *signal.h* (line 0700) defines the standard signal names. Several MINIX 3-specific signals for operating system use are defined, as well. The fact that operating systems functions are handled by independent processes rather than within a monolithic kernel requires some special signal-like communication between the system components. *Signal.h* also contains prototypes for some signal-related functions. As we will see later, signal handling involves all parts of MINIX 3.

Fcntl.h (line 0900) symbolically defines many parameters used in file control operations. For instance, it allows one to use the macro *O_RDONLY* instead of the numeric value 0 as a parameter to a *open* call. Although this file is referenced mostly by the file system, its definitions are also needed in a number of places in the kernel and the process manager.

As we will see when we look at the device driver layer in Chap. 3, the console and terminal interface of an operating system is complex, because many different types of hardware have to interact with the operating system and user programs in a standardized way. *Termios.h* (line 1000) defines constants, macros, and func-tion prototypes used for control of terminal-type I/O devices. The most important structure is the *termios* structure. It contains flags to signal various modes of op-eration, variables to set input and output transmission speeds, and an array to hold special characters (e.g., the *INTR* and *KILL* characters). This structure is required by POSIX, as are many of the macros and function prototypes defined in this file.

However, as all-encompassing as the POSIX standard is meant to be, it does not provide everything one might want, and the last part of the file, from line 1140 onward, provides extensions to POSIX. Some of these are of obvious value, such as extensions to define standard baud rates of 57,600 baud and higher, and support for terminal display screen windows. The POSIX standard does not forbid exten-sions, as no reasonable standard can ever be all-inclusive. But when writing a program in the MINIX 3 environment which is intended to be portable to other environments, some caution is required to avoid the use of definitions specific to MINIX 3. This is fairly easy to do. In this file and other files that define MINIX 3-specific extensions the use of the extensions is controlled by the

```
#ifdef _MINIX
```

statement. If the macro _MINIX_ is not defined, the compiler will not even see the MINIX 3 extensions; they will all be completely ignored.

Watchdog timers are supported by *timers.h* (line 1300), which is included in the kernel's master header. It defines a *struct timer*, as well as prototypes of functions used to operate on lists of timers. On line 1321 appears a *typedef* for *tmr_func_t*. This data type is a pointer to a function. At line 1332 its use is seen: within a *timer* structure, used as an element in a list of timers, one element is a *tmr_func_t* to specify a function to be called when the timer expires.

We will mention four more files in the *include/* directory that are not listed in Appendix B. *Stdlib.h* defines types, macros, and function prototypes that are likely to be needed in the compilation of all but the most simple of C programs. It is one of the most frequently used headers in compiling user programs, although within the MINIX 3 system source it is referenced by only a few files in the kernel. *Stdio.h* is familiar to everyone who has started to learn programming in C by writing the famous "Hello World!" program. It is hardly used at all in system files, although, like *stdlib.h*, it is used in almost every user program. *A.out.h* defines the format of the files in which executable programs are stored on disk. An *exec* structure is defined here, and the information in this structure is used by the process manager to load a new program image when an **exec** call is made. Finally, *stddef.h* defines a few commonly used macros.

Now let us go on to the subdirectory *include/sys/*. As shown in Fig. 2-32, the master headers for the main parts of the MINIX 3 system all cause *sys/types.h* (line 1400) to be read immediately after reading *ansi.h*. *Sys/types.h* defines many data types used by MINIX 3. Errors that could arise from misunderstanding which fundamental data types are used in a particular situation can be avoided by using the definitions provided here. Fig. 2-33 shows the way the sizes, in bits, of a few types defined in this file differ when compiled for 16-bit or 32-bit processors. Note that all type names end with "_t". This is not just a convention; it is a requirement of the POSIX standard. This is an example of a **reserved suffix**, and "_t" should not be used as a suffix of any name which is *not* a type name.

Type	16-Bit MINIX	32-Bit MINIX
gid_t	8	8
dev_t	16	16
pid_t	16	32
ino_t	16	32

Figure 2-33. The size, in bits, of some types on 16-bit and 32-bit systems.

MINIX 3 currently runs natively on 32-bit microprocessors, but 64-bit processors will be increasingly important in the future. A type that is not provided by the hardware can be synthesized if necessary. On line 1471 the *u64_t* type is defined as struct {u32_t[2]}. This type is not needed very often in the current implementation, but it can be useful—for instance, all disk and partition data (offsets and sizes) is stored as 64 bit numbers, allowing for very large disks.

MINIX 3 uses many type definitions that ultimately are interpreted by the compiler as a relatively small number of common types. This is intended to help make the code more readable; for instance, a variable declared as the type *dev_t* is recognizable as a variable meant to hold the major and minor device numbers that identify an I/O device. For the compiler, declaring such a variable as a *short* would work equally well. Another thing to note is that many of the types defined here are matched by corresponding types with the first letter capitalized, for instance, *dev_t* and *Dev_t*. The capitalized variants are all equivalent to type *int* to the compiler; these are provided to be used in function prototypes which must use types compatible with the *int* type to support K&R compilers. The comments in *types.h* explain this in more detail.

One other item worth mention is the section of conditional code that starts with

```
#if _EM_WSIZE == 2
```

(lines 1502 to 1516). As noted earlier, most conditional code has been removed from the source as discussed in the text. This example was retained so we could point out one way that conditional definitions can be used. The macro used, *_EM_WSIZE*, is another example of a compiler-defined feature test macro. It tells the word size for the target system in bytes. The #if ... #else ... #endif sequence is a way of getting some definitions right once and for all, to make subsequent code compile correctly whether a 16-bit or 32-bit system is in use.

Several other files in *include/sys/* are widely used in the MINIX 3 system. The file *sys/sigcontext.h* (line 1600) defines structures used to preserve and restore normal system operation before and after execution of a signal handling routine and is used both in the kernel and the process manager. *Sys/stat.h* (line 1700) defines the structure which we saw in Fig. 1-12, returned by the stat and fstat system calls, as well as the prototypes of the functions *stat* and *fstat* and other functions used to manipulate file properties. It is referenced in several parts of the file system and the process manager.

Other files we will discuss in this section are not as widely referenced as the ones discussed above. *Sys/dir.h* (line 1800) defines the structure of a MINIX 3 directory entry. It is only referenced directly once, but this reference includes it in another header that is widely used in the file system. It is important because, among other things, it tells how many characters a file name may contain (60). The *sys/wait.h* (line 1900) header defines macros used by the wait and waitpid system calls, which are implemented in the process manager.

Several other files in *include/sys/* should be mentioned, although they are not listed in Appendix B. MINIX 3 supports tracing executables and analyzing core dumps with a debugger program, and *sys/ptrace.h* defines the various operations possible with the ptrace system call. *Sys/svrctl.h* defines data structures and macros used by svrctl, which is not really a system call, but is used like one. Svrctl is used to coordinate server-level processes as the system starts up. The select sys-

tem call permits waiting for input on multiple channels—for instance, pseudo terminals waiting for network connections. Definitions needed by this call are in
sys/select.h.

We have deliberately left discussion of *sys/ioctl.h* and related files until last,
because they cannot be fully understood without also looking at a file in the next
directory, *minix/ioctl.h*. The ioctl system call is used for device control operations. The number of devices which can be interfaced with a modern computer
system is ever increasing. All need various kinds of control. Indeed, the main
difference between MINIX 3 as described in this book and other versions is that
for purposes of the book we describe MINIX 3 with relatively few input/output
devices. Many others, such as network interfaces, SCSI controllers, and sound
cards, can be added.

To make things more manageable, a number of small files, each containing
one group of definitions, are used. They are all included by *sys/ioctl.h* (line
2000), which functions similarly to the master header of Fig. 2-32. We have
listed only one of these included files, *sys/ioc_disk.h* (line 2100), in Appendix B.
This and the other files included by *sys_ioctl.h* are located in the *include/sys/*
directory because they are considered part of the "published interface," meaning
a programmer can use them in writing any program to be run in the MINIX 3
environment. However, they all depend upon additional macro definitions provided in *minix/ioctl.h* (line 2200), which is included by each. *Minix/ioctl.h* should
not be used by itself in writing programs, which is why it is in *include/minix/*
rather than *include/sys/*.

The macros defined together by these files define how the various elements
needed for each possible function are packed into a 32 bit integer to be passed to
ioctl. For instance, disk devices need five types of operations, as can be seen in
sys/ioc_disk.h at lines 2110 to 2114. The alphabetic 'd' parameter tells ioctl that
the operation is for a disk device, an integer from 3 through 7 codes for the operation, and the third parameter for a write or read operation tells the size of the
structure in which data is to be passed. In *minix/ioctl.h* lines 2225 to 2231 show
that 8 bits of the alphabetic code are shifted 8 bits to the left, the 13 least significant bits of the size of the structure are shifted 16 bits to the left, and these are
then logically ANDed with the small integer operation code. Another code in the
most significant 3 bits of a 32-bit number encodes the type of return value.

Although this looks like a lot of work, this work is done at compile time and
makes for a much more efficient interface to the system call at run time, since the
parameter actually passed is the most natural data type for the host machine CPU.
It does, however, bring to mind a famous comment Ken Thompson put into the
source code of an early version of UNIX:

/* You are not expected to understand this */

Minix/ioctl.h also contains the prototype for the ioctl system call at line 2241.
This call is not directly invoked by programmers in many cases, since the POSIX-

defined functions prototyped in *include/termios.h* have replaced many uses of the old *ioctl* library function for dealing with terminals, consoles, and similar devices. Nevertheless, it is still necessary. In fact, the POSIX functions for control of terminal devices are converted into ioctl system calls by the library.

2.6.4 The MINIX 3 Header Files

The subdirectories *include/minix/* and *include/ibm/* contain header files specific to MINIX 3. Files in *include/minix/* are needed for an implementation of MINIX 3 on any platform, although there are platform-specific alternative definitions within some of them. We have already discussed one file here, *ioctl.h*. The files in *include/ibm/* define structures and macros that are specific to MINIX 3 as implemented on IBM-type machines.

We will start with the *minix/* directory. In the previous section, it was noted that *config.h* (line 2300) is included in the master headers for all parts of the MINIX 3 system, and is thus the first file actually processed by the compiler. On many occasions, when differences in hardware or the way the operating system is intended to be used require changes in the configuration of MINIX 3, editing this file and recompiling the system is all that must be done. We suggest that if you modify this file you should also modify the comment on line 2303 to help identify the purpose of the modifications.

The user-settable parameters are all in the first part of the file, but some of these parameters are not intended to be edited here. On line 2326 another header file, *minix/sys_config.h* is included, and definitions of some parameters are inherited from this file. The programmers thought this was a good idea because a few files in the system need the basic definitions in *sys_config.h* without the rest of those in *config.h*. In fact, there are many names in *config.h* which do not begin with an underscore that are likely to conflict with names in common usage, such as *CHIP* or *INTEL* that would be likely to be found in software ported to MINIX 3 from another operating system. All of the names in *sys_config.h* begin with underscores, and conflicts are less likely.

MACHINE is actually configured as *_MACHINE_IBM_PC* in *sys_config.h*; lines 2330 to 2334 lists short alternatives for all possible values for *MACHINE*. Earlier versions of MINIX were ported to Sun, Atari, and MacIntosh platforms, and the full source code contains alternatives for alternative hardware. Most of the MINIX 3 source code is independent of the type of machine, but an operating system always has some system-dependent code. Also, it should be noted that, because MINIX 3 is so new, as of this writing additional work is needed to complete porting MINIX 3 to non-Intel platforms.

Other definitions in *config.h* allow customization for other needs in a particular installation. For instance, the number of buffers used by the file system for the disk cache should generally be as large as possible, but a large number of buffers requires lots of memory. Caching 128 blocks, as configured on line 2345, is considered minimal and satisfactory only for a MINIX 3 installation on a system with less than 16 MB of RAM; for systems with ample memory a much larger number can be put here. If it is desired to use a modem or log in over a network connection the *NR_RS_LINES* and *NR_PTYS* definitions (lines 2379 and 2380) should be increased and the system recompiled. The last part of *config.h* contains definitions that are necessary, but which should not be changed. Many definitions here just define alternate names for constants defined in *sys_config.h*.

Sys_config.h (line 2500) contains definitions that are likely to be needed by a system programmer, for instance someone writing a new device driver. You are not likely to need to change very much in this file, with the possible exception of *_NR_PROCS* (line 2522). This controls the size of the process table. If you want to use a MINIX 3 system as a network server with many remote users or many server processes running simultaneously, you might need to increase this constant.

The next file is *const.h* (line 2600), which illustrates another common use of header files. Here we find a variety of constant definitions that are not likely to be changed when compiling a new kernel but that are used in a number of places. Defining them here helps to prevent errors that could be hard to track down if inconsistent definitions were made in multiple places. Other files named *const.h* can be found elsewhere in the MINIX 3 source tree, but they are for more limited use. Similarly, definitions that are used only in the kernel are included in *src/kernel/const.h*. Definitions that are used only in the file system are included in *src/servers/fs/const.h*. The process manager uses *src/servers/pm/const.h* for its local definitions. Only those definitions that are used in more than one part of the MINIX 3 system are included in *include/minix/const.h*.

A few of the definitions in *const.h* are noteworthy. *EXTERN* is defined as a macro expanding into *extern* (line 2608). Global variables that are declared in header files and included in two or more files are declared *EXTERN*, as in

    EXTERN int who;

If the variable were declared just as

    int who;

and included in two or more files, some linkers would complain about a multiply defined variable. Furthermore, the C reference manual explicitly forbids this construction (Kernighan and Ritchie, 1988).

To avoid this problem, it is necessary to have the declaration read

    extern int who;

in all places but one. Using *EXTERN* prevents this problem by having it expand into *extern* everywhere that *const.h* is included, except following an explicit redefinition of *EXTERN* as the null string. This is done in each part of MINIX 3 by putting global definitions in a special file called *glo.h*, for instance, *src/kernel/glo.h*, which is indirectly included in every compilation. Within each *glo.h* there is a sequence

```
#ifdef _TABLE
#undef EXTERN
#define EXTERN
#endif
```

and in the *table.c* files of each part of MINIX 3 there is a line

```
#define _TABLE
```

preceding the #include section. Thus when the header files are included and expanded as part of the compilation of *table.c*, *extern* is not inserted anywhere (because *EXTERN* is defined as the null string within *table.c*) and storage for the global variables is reserved only in one place, in the object file *table.o*.

If you are new to C programming and do not quite understand what is going on here, fear not; the details are really not important. This is a polite way of rephrasing Ken Thompson's famous comment cited earlier. Multiple inclusion of header files can cause problems for some linkers because it can lead to multiple declarations for included variables. The *EXTERN* business is simply a way to make MINIX 3 more portable so it can be linked on machines whose linkers do not accept multiply defined variables.

PRIVATE is defined as a synonym for *static*. Procedures and data that are not referenced outside the file in which they are declared are always declared as *PRIVATE* to prevent their names from being visible outside the file in which they are declared. As a general rule, all variables and procedures should be declared with a local scope, if possible. *PUBLIC* is defined as the null string. An example from *kernel/proc.c* may help make this clear. The declaration

```
PUBLIC void lock_dequeue(rp)
```

comes out of the C preprocessor as

```
void lock_dequeue(rp)
```

which, according to the C language scope rules, means that the function name *lock_dequeue* is exported from the file and the function can be called from anywhere in any file linked into the same binary, in this case, anywhere in the kernel. Another function declared in the same file is

```
PRIVATE void dequeue(rp)
```

which is preprocessed to become

```
static void dequeue(rp)
```

This function can only be called from code in the same source file. *PRIVATE* and *PUBLIC* are not necessary in any sense but are attempts to undo the damage caused by the C scope rules (the default is that names are exported outside the file; it should be just the reverse).

The rest of *const.h* defines numerical constants used throughout the system. A section of *const.h* is devoted to machine or configuration-dependent definitions. For instance, throughout the source code the basic unit of memory allocation is the **click**. Different values for the click size may be chosen for different processor architectures. For Intel platforms it is 1024 bytes. Alternatives for Intel, Motorola 68000, and Sun SPARC architectures are defined on lines 2673 to 2681. This file also contains the macros *MAX* and *MIN*, so we can say

    z = MAX(x, y);

to assign the larger of x and y to z.

Type.h (line 2800) is another file that is included in every compilation by means of the master headers. It contains a number of key type definitions, along with related numerical values.

The first two structs define two different types of memory map, one for local memory regions (within the data space of a process) and one for remote memory areas, such as a RAM disk (lines 2828 to 2840). This is a good place to mention the concepts used in referring to memory. As we just mentioned, the click is the basic unit of measurement of memory; in MINIX 3 for Intel processors a click is 1024 bytes. Memory is measured as **phys_clicks**, which can be used by the kernel to access any memory element anywhere in the system, or as **vir_clicks**, used by processes other than the kernel. A *vir_clicks* memory reference is always with respect to the base of a segment of memory assigned to a particular process, and the kernel often has to make translations between virtual (i.e. process-based) and physical (RAM-based) addresses. The inconvenience of this is offset by the fact that a process can do all its own memory references in *vir_clicks*.

One might suppose that the same unit could be used to specify the size of either type of memory, but there is an advantage to using *vir_clicks* to specify the size of a unit of memory allocated to a process, since when this unit is used a check is done to be sure that no memory is accessed outside of what has been specifically assigned to the current process. This is a major feature of the **protected mode** of modern Intel processors, such as the Pentium family. Its absence in the early 8086 and 8088 processors caused some headaches in the design of earlier versions of MINIX.

Another important structure defined here is *sigmsg* (lines 2866 to 2872). When a signal is caught the kernel has to arrange that the next time the signaled process gets to run it will run the signal handler, rather than continuing execution where it was interrupted. The process manager does most of the work of managing signals; it passes a structure like this to the kernel when a signal is caught.

The *kinfo* structure (lines 2875 to 2893) is used to convey information about the kernel to other parts of the system. The process manager uses this information when it sets up its part of the process table.

Data structures and function prototypes for **interprocess communication** are defined in *ipc.h* (line 3000). The most important definition in this file is *message* on lines 3020 to 3032. While we could have defined *message* to be an array of some number of bytes, it is better programming practice to have it be a structure containing a union of the various message types that are possible. Seven message formats, *mess_1* through *mess_8*, are defined (type *mess_6* is obsolete). A message is a structure containing a field *m_source*, telling who sent the message, a field *m_type*, telling what the message type is (e.g., *SYS_EXEC* to the system task) and the data fields.

The seven message types are shown in Fig. 2-34. In the figure four message types, the first two and the last two, seem identical. Just in terms of size of the data elements they are identical, but many of the data types are different. It happens that on an Intel CPU with a 32-bit word size the *int*, *long*, and pointer data types are all 32-bit types, but this would not necessarily be the case on another kind of hardware. Defining seven distinct formats makes it easier to recompile MINIX 3 for a different architecture.

When it is necessary to send a message containing, say, three integers and three pointers (or three integers and two pointers), then the first format in Fig. 2-34 is the one to use. The same applies to the other formats. How does one assign a value to the first integer in the first format? Suppose that the message is called *x*. Then *x.m_u* refers to the union portion of the message struct. To refer to the first of the six alternatives in the union, we use *x.m_u.m_m1*. Finally, to get at the first integer in this struct we say *x.m_u.m_m1.m1i1*. This is quite a mouthful, so somewhat shorter field names are defined as macros after the definition of message itself. Thus *x.m1_i1* can be used instead of *x.m_u.m_m1.m1i1*. The short names all have the form of the letter m, the format number, an underscore, one or two letters indicating whether the field is an integer, pointer, long, character, character array, or function, and a sequence number to distinguish multiple instances of the same type within a message.

While discussing message formats, this is a good place to note that an operating system and its compiler often have an "understanding" about things like the layout of structures, and this can make the implementer's life easier. In MINIX 3, the *int* fields in messages are sometimes used to hold *unsigned* data types. In some cases this could cause overflow, but the code was written using the knowledge that the MINIX 3 compiler copies *unsigned* types to *ints* and *vice versa* without changing the data or generating code to detect overflow. A more compulsive approach would be to replace each *int* field with a *union* of an *int* and an *unsigned*. The same applies to the *long* fields in the messages; some of them may be used to pass *unsigned long* data. Are we cheating here? Perhaps a little bit, one might say, but if you wish to port MINIX 3 to a new platform, quite clearly the exact format of the messages is something to which you must pay a great deal of attention, and now you have been alerted that the behavior of the compiler is another factor that needs attention.

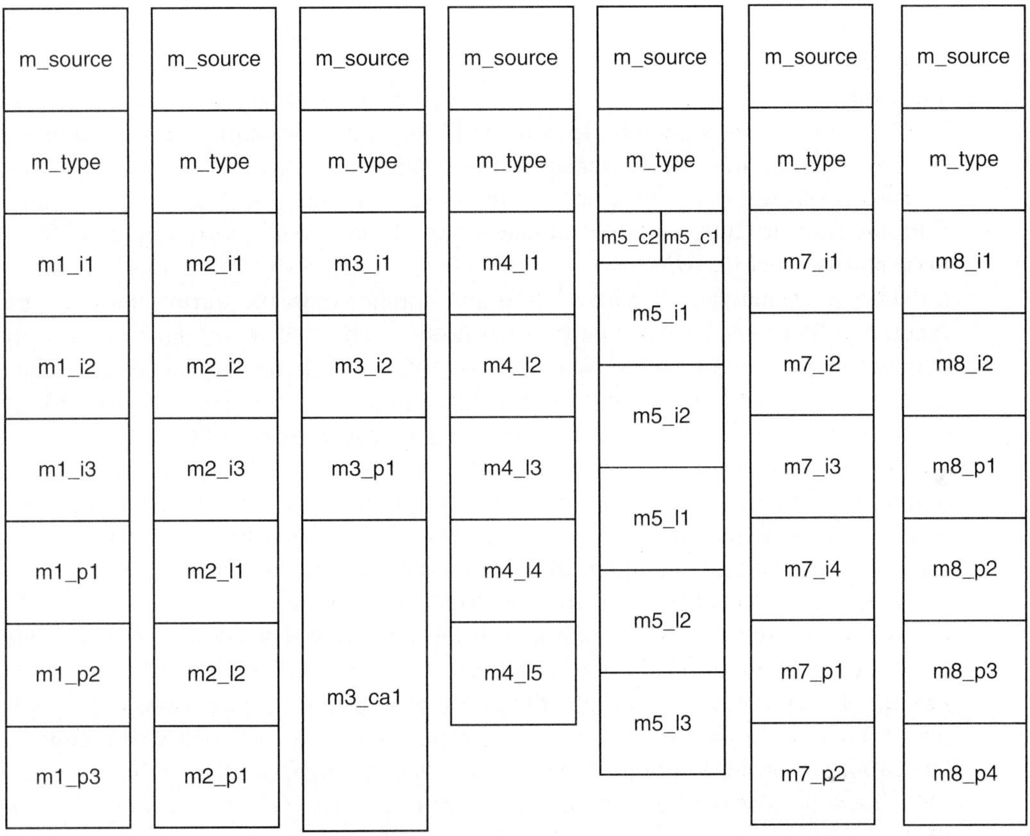

m_source	m_source	m_source	m_source	m_source	m_source	m_source
m_type	m_type	m_type	m_type	m_type	m_type	m_type
m1_i1	m2_i1	m3_i1	m4_l1	m5_c2 / m5_c1	m7_i1	m8_i1
m1_i2	m2_i2	m3_i2	m4_l2	m5_i1	m7_i2	m8_i2
m1_i3	m2_i3	m3_p1	m4_l3	m5_i2	m7_i3	m8_p1
m1_p1	m2_l1		m4_l4	m5_l1	m7_i4	m8_p2
m1_p2	m2_l2	m3_ca1	m4_l5	m5_l2	m7_p1	m8_p3
m1_p3	m2_p1			m5_l3	m7_p2	m8_p4

Figure 2-34. The seven message types used in MINIX 3. The sizes of message elements will vary, depending upon the architecture of the machine; this diagram illustrates sizes on CPUs with 32-bit pointers, such as those of Pentium family members.

Also defined in *ipc.h* are prototypes for the message passing primitives described earlier (lines 3095 to 3101). In addition to the important send, receive, sendrec, and notify primitives, several others are defined. None of these are much used; in fact one could say that they are relics of earlier stages of development of MINIX 3. Old computer programs make good archaeological digs. They might disappear in a future release. Nevertheless, if we do not explain them now some readers undoubtedly will worry about them. The nonblocking nb_send and nb_receive calls have mostly been replaced by notify, which was implemented later and considered a better solution to the problem of sending or checking for a message without blocking. The prototype for echo has no source or destination field. This primitive serves no useful purpose in production code, but was useful during development to test the time it took to send and receive a message.

One other file in *include/minix/*, *syslib.h* (line 3200), is almost universally used by means of inclusion in the master headers of all of the user-space components of MINIX 3. This file not included in the kernel's master header file, *src/kernel/kernel.h*, because the kernel does not need library functions to access itself. *Syslib.h* contains prototypes for C library functions called from within the operating system to access other operating system services.

We do not describe details of C libraries in this text, but many library functions are standard and will be available for any C compiler. However, the C functions referenced by *syslib.h* are of course quite specific to MINIX 3 and a port of MINIX 3 to a new system with a different compiler requires porting these library functions. Fortunately this is not difficult, since most of these functions simply extract the parameters of the function call and insert them into a message structure, then send the message and extract the results from the reply message. Many of these library functions are defined in a dozen or fewer lines of C code.

Noteworthy in this file are four macros for accessing I/O ports for input or output using byte or word data types and the prototype of the *sys_sdevio* function to which all four macros refer (lines 3241 to 3250). Providing a way for device drivers to request reading and writing of I/O ports by the kernel is an essential part of the MINIX 3 project to move all such drivers to user space.

A few functions which could have been defined in *syslib.h* are in a separate file, *sysutil.h* (line 3400), because their object code is compiled into a separate library. Two functions prototyped here need a little more explanation. The first is *printf* (line 3442). If you have experience programming in C you will recognize that *printf* is a standard library function, referenced in almost all programs.

This is not the *printf* function you think it is, however. The version of *printf* in the standard library cannot be used within system components. Among other things, the standard *printf* is intended to write to standard output, and must be able to format floating point numbers. Using standard output would require going through the file system, but for printing messages when there is a problem and a system component needs to display an error message, it is desirable to be able to do this without the assistance of any other system components. Also, support for the full range of format specifications usable with the standard *printf* would bloat the code for no useful purpose. So a simplified version of *printf* that does only what is needed by operating system components is compiled into the system utilities library. This is found by the compiler in a place that will depend upon the platform; for 32-bit Intel systems it is */usr/lib/i386/libsysutil.a*. When the file system, the process manager, or another part of the operating system is linked to library functions this version is found before the standard library is searched.

On the next line is a prototype for *kputc*. This is called by the system version of *printf* to do the work of displaying characters on the console. However, more tricky business is involved here. *Kputc* is defined in several places. There is a copy in the system utilities library, which will be the one used by default. But several parts of the system define their own versions. We will see one when we study the console interface in the next chapter. The log driver (which is not described in detail here) also defines its own version. There is even a definition of *kputc* in the kernel itself, but this is a special case. The kernel does not use *printf*. A special printing function, *kprintf*, is defined as part of the kernel and is used when the kernel needs to print.

When a process needs to execute a MINIX 3 system call, it sends a message to the process manager (PM for short) or the file system (FS for short). Each message contains the number of the system call desired. These numbers are defined in the next file, *callnr.h* (line 3500). Some numbers are not used, these are reserved for calls not yet implemented or represent calls implemented in other versions which are now handled by library functions. Near the end of the file some call numbers are defined that do not correspond to calls shown in Fig 1-9. Svrctl (mentioned earlier), ksig, unpause, revive, and task_reply are used only within the operating system itself. The system call mechanism is a convenient way to implement these. In fact, because they will not be used by external programs, these "system calls," may be modified in new versions of MINIX 3 without fear of breaking user programs.

The next file is *com.h* (line 3600). One interpretation of the file name is that is stands for common, another is that it stands for communication. This file provides common definitions used for communication between servers and device drivers. On lines 3623 to 3626 task numbers are defined. To distinguish them from process numbers, task numbers are negative. On lines 3633 to 3640 process numbers are defined for the processes that are loaded in the boot image. Note these are slot numbers in the process table; they should not be confused with process id (PID) numbers.

The next section of *com.h* defines how messages are constructed to carry out a notify operation. The process numbers are used in generating the value that is passed in the *m_type* field of the message. The message types for notifications and other messages defined in this file are built by combining a base value that signifies a type category with a small number that indicates the specific type. The rest of this file is a compendium of macros that translate meaningful identifiers into the cryptic numbers that identify message types and field names.

A few other files in *include/minix/* are listed in Appendix B. *Devio.h* (line 4100) defines types and constants that support user-space access to I/O ports, as well as some macros that make it easier to write code that specifies ports and values. *Dmap.h* (line 4200) defines a struct and an array of that struct, both named *dmap*. This table is used to relate major device numbers to the functions that support them. Major and minor device numbers for the *memory* device driver and major device numbers for other important device drivers are also defined.

Include/minix/ contains several additional specialized headers that are not listed in Appendix B, but which must be present to compile the system. One is *u64.h* which provides support for 64-bit integer arithmetic operations, necessary to manipulate disk addresses on high capacity disk drives. These were not even dreamed of when UNIX, the C language, Pentium-class processors, and MINIX were first conceived. A future version of MINIX 3 may be written in a language that has built-in support for 64-bit integers on CPUs with 64-bit registers; until then, the definitions in *u64.h* provide a work-around.

Three files remain to be mentioned. *Keymap.h* defines the structures used to implement specialized keyboard layouts for the character sets needed for different languages. It is also needed by programs which generate and load these tables. *Bitmap.h* provides a few macros to make operations like setting, resetting, and testing bits easier. Finally, *partition.h* defines the information needed by MINIX 3 to define a disk partition, either by its absolute byte offset and size on the disk, or by a cylinder, head, sector address. The *u64_t* type is used for the offset and size, to allow use of large disks. This file does not describe the layout of a partition table on a disk, the file that does that is in the next directory.

The last specialized header directory we will consider, *include/ibm/*, contains several files which provide definitions related to the IBM PC family of computers. Since the C language knows only memory addresses, and has no provision for accessing I/O port addresses, the library contains routines written in assembly language to read and write from ports. The various routines available are declared in *ibm/portio.h* (line 4300). All possible input and output routines for byte, integer, and long data types, singly or as strings, are available, from *inb* (input one byte) to *outsl* (output a string of longs). Low-level routines in the kernel may also need to disable or reenable CPU interrupts, which are also actions that C cannot handle. The library provides assembly code to do this, and *intr_disable* and *intr_enable* are declared on lines 4325 and 4326.

The next file in this directory is *interrupt.h* (line 4400), which defines port address and memory locations used by the interrupt controller chip and the BIOS of PC-compatible systems. Finally, more I/O ports are defined in *ports.h* (line 4500). This file provides addresses needed to access the keyboard interface and the timer chip used by the clock chip.

Several additional files in *include/ibm/* with IBM-specific data are not listed in Appendix B, but are essential and should be mentioned. *Bios.h*, *memory.h*, and *partition.h* are copiously commented and are worth reading if you would like to know more about memory use or disk partition tables. *Cmos.h*, *cpu.h*, and *int86.h* provide additional information on ports, CPU flag bits, and calling BIOS and DOS services in 16-bit mode. Finally, *diskparm.h* defines a data structure needed for formatting a floppy disk.

2.6.5 Process Data Structures and Header Files

Now let us dive in and see what the code in *src/kernel/* looks like. In the previous two sections we structured our discussion around an excerpt from a typical master header; we will look first at the real master header for the kernel, *kernel.h* (line 4600). It begins by defining three macros. The first, *_POSIX_SOURCE*, is a **feature test macro** defined by the POSIX standard itself. All such macros are required to begin with the underscore character, "_". The effect of defining the _POSIX_SOURCE macro is to ensure that all symbols required by the standard and any that are explicitly permitted, but not required, will be visible, while hiding any additional symbols that are unofficial extensions to POSIX. We have already mentioned the next two definitions: the _MINIX macro overrides the effect of _POSIX_SOURCE for extensions defined by MINIX 3, and _SYSTEM can be tested wherever it is important to do something differently when compiling system code, as opposed to user code, such as changing the sign of error codes. Kernel.h then includes other header files from include/ and its subdirectories include/sys/ include/minix/, and include/ibm/ including all those referred to in Fig. 2-32. We have discussed all of these files in the previous two sections. Finally, six additional headers from the local directory, src/kernel/, are included, their names included in quote characters.

Kernel.h makes it possible to guarantee that all source files share a large number of important definitions by writing the single line

        #include "kernel.h"

in each of the other kernel source files. Since the order of inclusion of header files is sometimes important, kernel.h also ensures that this ordering is done correctly, once and forever. This carries to a higher level the "get it right once, then forget the details" technique embodied in the header file concept. Similar master headers are provided in source directories for other system components, such as the file system and the process manager.

Now let us proceed to look at the local header files included in kernel.h. First we have yet another file named config.h, which, analogous to the system-wide file include/minix/config.h, must be included before any of the other local include files. Just as we have files const.h and type.h in the common header directory include/minix/, we also have files const.h. and type.h in the kernel source directory, src/kernel/. The files in include/minix/ are placed there because they are needed by many parts of the system, including programs that run under the control of the system. The files in src/kernel/ provide definitions needed only for compilation of the kernel. The FS, PM, and other system source directories also contain const.h and type.h files to define constants and types needed only for those parts of the system. Two of the other files included in the master header, proto.h glo.h, have no counterparts in the main include/ directories, but we will find that they, too, have counterparts used in compiling the file system and the process manager. The last local header included in kernel.h is another ipc.h.

Since this is the first time it has come up in our discussion, note at the beginning of kernel/config.h there is a #ifndef ... #define sequence to prevent trouble if the file is included multiple times. We have seen the general idea before. But note here that the macro defined here is CONFIG_H without an underscore. Thus it is distinct from the macro _CONFIG_H defined in include/minix/config.h.

The kernel's version of *config.h* gathers in one place a number of definitions that are unlikely to need changes if your interest in MINIX 3 is studying how an operating system works, or using this operating system in a conventional general-purpose computer. However, suppose you want to make a really tiny version of MINIX 3 for controlling a scientific instrument or a home-made cellular telephone. The definitions on lines 4717 to 4743 allow selective disabling of kernel calls. Eliminating unneeded functionality also reduces memory requirements because the code needed to handle each kernel call is conditionally compiled using the definitions on lines 4717 to 4743. If some function is disabled, the code needed to execute it is omitted from the system binary. For example, a cellular telephone might not need to fork off new processes, so the code for doing so could be omitted from the executable file, resulting in a smaller memory footprint. Most other constants defined in this file control basic parameters. For instance, while handling interrupts a special stack of size *K_STACK_BYTES* is used. This value is set on line 4772. The space for this stack is reserved within *mpx386.s*, an assembly language file.

In *const.h* (line 4800) a macro for converting virtual addresses relative to the base of the kernel's memory space to physical addresses is defined on line 4814. A C function, *umap_local*, is defined elsewhere in the kernel code so the kernel can do this conversion on behalf of other components of the system, but for use within the kernel the macro is more efficient. Several other useful macros are defined here, including several for manipulating bitmaps. An important security mechanism built into the Intel hardware is activated by two macro definition lines here. The **processor status word** (**PSW**) is a CPU register, and **I/O Protection Level** (**IOPL**) bits within it define whether access to the interrupt system and I/O ports is allowed or denied. On lines 4850 and 4851 different PSW values are defined that determine this access for ordinary and privileged processes. These values are put on the stack as part of putting a new process in execution.

In the next file we will consider, *type.h* (line 4900), the *memory* structure (lines 4925 to 4928) uses two quantities, base address and size, to uniquely specify an area of memory.

Type.h defines several other prototypes and structures used in any implementation of MINIX 3. For instance, two structures, *kmessages*, used for diagnostic messages from the kernel, and *randomness*, used by the random number generator, are defined. *Type.h* also contains several machine-dependent type definitions. To make the code shorter and more readable we have removed conditional code and definitions for other CPU types. But you should recognize that definitions like the *stackframe_s* structure (lines 4955 to 4974), which defines how machine registers are saved on the stack, is specific to Intel 32-bit processors. For another platform the *stackframe_s* structure would be defined in terms of the register structure of the CPU to be used. Another example is the *segdesc_s* structure (lines 4976 to 4983), which is part of the protection mechanism that keeps processes from accessing memory regions outside those assigned to them. For another

CPU the *segdesc_s* structure might not exist at all, depending upon the mechanism used to implement memory protection.

Another point to make about structures like these is that making sure all the required data is present is necessary, but possibly not sufficient for optimal performance. The *stackframe_s* must be manipulated by assembly language code. Defining it in a form that can be efficiently read or written by assembly language code reduces the time required for a context switch.

The next file, *proto.h* (line 5100), provides prototypes of all functions that must be known outside of the file in which they are defined. All are written using the *_PROTOTYPE* macro discussed in the previous section, and thus the MINIX 3 kernel can be compiled either with a classic C (Kernighan and Ritchie) compiler, such as the original MINIX 3 C compiler, or a modern ANSI Standard C compiler, such as the one which is part of the MINIX 3 distribution. A number of these prototypes are system-dependent, including interrupt and exception handlers and functions that are written in assembly language.

In *glo.h* (line 5300) we find the kernel's global variables. The purpose of the macro *EXTERN* was described in the discussion of *include/minix/const.h*. It normally expands into *extern*. Note that many definitions in *glo.h* are preceded by this macro. The symbol *EXTERN* is forced to be undefined when this file is included in *table.c*, where the macro *_TABLE* is defined. Thus the actual storage space for the variables defined this way is reserved when *glo.h* is included in the compilation of *table.c*. Including *glo.h* in other C source files makes the variables in *table.c* known to the other modules in the kernel.

Some of the kernel information structures here are used at startup. *Aout* (line 5321) will hold the address of an array of the headers of all of the MINIX 3 system image components. Note that these are **physical addresses**, that is, addresses relative to the entire address space of the processor. As we will see later, the physical address of *aout* will be passed from the boot monitor to the kernel when MINIX 3 starts up, so the startup routines of the kernel can get the addresses of all MINIX 3 components from the monitor's memory space. *Kinfo* (line 5322) is also an important piece of information. Recall that the structure was defined in *include/minix/type.h*. Just as the boot monitor uses *aout* to pass information about all processes in the boot image to the kernel, the kernel fills in the fields of *kinfo* with information about itself that other components of the system may need to know about.

The next section of *glo.h* contains variables related to control of process and kernel execution. *Prev_ptr*, *proc_ptr*, and *next_ptr* point to the process table entries of the previous, current, and next processes to run. *Bill_ptr* also points to a process table entry; it shows which process is currently being billed for clock ticks used. When a user process calls the file system, and the file system is running, *proc_ptr* points to the file system process. However, *bill_ptr* will point to the user making the call, since CPU time used by the file system is charged as system time to the caller. We have not actually heard of a MINIX system whose owner charges others for their use of CPU time, but it could be done. The next variable, *k_reenter*, is used to count nested executions of kernel code, such as when an interrupt occurs when the kernel itself, rather than a user process, is running. This is important, because switching context from a user process to the kernel or vice versa is different (and more costly) than reentering the kernel. When an interrupt service complete it is important for it to determine whether control should remain with the kernel or if a user-space process should be restarted. This variable is also tested by some functions which disable and reenable interrupts, such as *lock_enqueue*. If such a function is executed when interrupts are disabled already, the interrupts should not be reenabled when reenabling is not wanted. Finally, in this section there is a counter for lost clock ticks. How a clock tick can be lost and what is done about it will be discussed when we discuss the clock task.

The last few variables defined in *glo.h*, are declared here because they must be known throughout the kernel code, but they are declared as *extern* rather than as *EXTERN* because they are **initialized variables**, a feature of the C language. The use of the *EXTERN* macro is not compatible with C-style initialization, since a variable can only be initialized once.

Tasks that run in kernel space, currently just the clock task and the system task, have their own stacks within *t_stack*. During interrupt handling, the kernel uses a separate stack, but it is not declared here, since it is only accessed by the assembly language level routine that handles interrupt processing, and does not need to be known globally. The last file included in *kernel.h*, and thus used in every compilation, is *ipc.h* (line 5400). It defines various constants used in interprocess communication. We will discuss these later when we get to the file where they are used, *kernel/proc.c*.

Several more kernel header files are widely used, although not so much that they are included in *kernel.h*. The first of these is *proc.h* (line 5500), which defines the kernel's process table. The complete state of a process is defined by the process' data in memory, plus the information in its process table slot. The contents of the CPU registers are stored here when a process is not executing and then are restored when execution resumes. This is what makes possible the illusion that multiple processes are executing simultaneously and interacting, although at any instant a single CPU can be executing instructions of only one process. The time spent by the kernel saving and restoring the process state during each **context switch** is necessary, but obviously this is time during which the work of the processes themselves is suspended. For this reason these structures are designed for efficiency. As noted in the comment at the beginning of *proc.h*, many routines written in assembly language also access these structures, and another header, *sconst.h*, defines offsets to fields in the process table for use by the assembly code. Thus changing a definition in *proc.h* may necessitate a change in *sconst.h*.

Before going further we should mention that, because of MINIX 3's microkernel structure, the process table we will discuss is here is paralleled by tables in PM and FS which contain per-process entries relevant to the function of these parts of MINIX 3. Together, all three of these tables are equivalent to the process table of an operating system with a monolithic structure, but for the moment when we speak of the process table we will be talking about only the kernel's process table. The others will be discussed in later chapters.

Each slot in the process table is defined as a struct *proc* (lines 5516 to 5545). Each entry contains storage for the process' registers, stack pointer, state, memory map, stack limit, process id, accounting, alarm time, and message info. The first part of each process table entry is a *stackframe_s* structure. A process that is already in memory is put into execution by loading its stack pointer with the address of its process table entry and popping all the CPU registers from this struct.

There is more to the state of a process than just the CPU registers and the data in memory, however. In MINIX 3, each process has a pointer to a *priv* structure in its process table slot (line 5522). This structure defines allowed sources and destinations of messages for the process and many other privileges. We will look at details later. For the moment, note that each system process has a pointer to a unique copy of this structure, but user privileges are all equal—the pointers of all user processes point to the same copy of the structure. There is also a byte-sized field for a set of bit flags, *p_rts_flags* (line 5523). The meanings of the bits will be described below. Setting any bit to 1 means a process is not runnable, so a zero in this field indicates a process is ready.

Each slot in the process table provides space for information that may be needed by the kernel. For instance, the *p_max_priority* field (line 5526), tells which scheduling queue the process should be queued on when it is ready to run for the first time. Because the priority of a process may be reduced if it prevents other processes from running, there is also a *p_priority* field which is initially set equal to *p_max_priority*. *P_priority* is the field that actually determines the queue used each time the process is ready.

The time used by each process is recorded in the two *clock_t* variables at lines 5532 and 5533. This information must be accessed by the kernel and it would be inefficient to store this in a process' own memory space, although logically that could be done. *P_nextready* (line 5535), is used to link processes together on the scheduler queues.

The next few fields hold information related to messages between processes. When a process cannot complete a send because the destination is not waiting, the sender is put onto a queue pointed to by the destination's *p_caller_q* pointer (line 5536). That way, when the destination finally does a receive, it is easy to find all the processes wanting to send to it. The *p_q_link* field (line 5537) is used to link the members of the queue together.

The rendezvous method of passing messages is made possible by the storage space reserved at lines 5538 to 5540. When a process does a receive and there is no message waiting for it, it blocks and the number of the process it wants to receive from is stored in *p_getfrom*. Similarly, *p_sendto* holds the process number of the destination when a process does a send and the recipient is not waiting. The address of the message buffer is stored in *p_messbuf*. The penultimate field in each process table slot is *p_pending* (line 5542), a bitmap used to keep track of signals that have not yet been passed to the process manager (because the process manager is not waiting for a message).

Finally, the last field in a process table entry is a character array, *p_name*, for holding the name of the process. This field is not needed for process management by the kernel. MINIX 3 provides various **debug dumps** triggered by pressing a special key on the console keyboard. Some of these allow viewing information about all processes, with the name of each process printed along with other data. Having a meaningful name associated with each process makes understanding and debugging kernel operation easier.

Following the definition of a process table slot come definitions of various constants used in its elements. The various flag bits that can be set in *p_rts_flags* are defined and described on lines 5548 to 5555. If the slot is not in use, *SLOT_FREE* is set. After a fork, *NO_MAP* is set to prevent the child process from running until its memory map has been set up. *SENDING* and *RECEIVING* indicate that the process is blocked trying to send or receive a message. *SIGNALED* and *SIG_PENDING* indicate that signals have been received, and *P_STOP* provides support for tracing. *NO_PRIV* is used to temporarily prevent a new system process from executing until its setup is complete.

The number of scheduling queues and allowable values for the *p_priority* field are defined next (lines 5562 to 5567). In the current version of this file user processes are allowed to be given access to the highest priority queue; this is probably a carry-over from the early days of testing drivers in user space and *MAX_USER_Q* should probably adjusted to a lower priority (larger number).

Next come several macros that allow addresses of important parts of the process table to be defined as constants at compilation time, to provide faster access at run time, and then more macros for run time calculations and tests. The macro *proc_addr* (line 5577) is provided because it is not possible to have negative subscripts in C. Logically, the array *proc* should go from *−NR_TASKS* to *+NR_PROCS*. Unfortunately, in C it must start at 0, so *proc*[0] refers to the most negative task, and so forth. To make it easier to keep track of which slot goes with which process, we can write

    rp = proc_addr(n);

to assign to *rp* the address of the process slot for process n, either positive or negative.

The process table itself is defined here as an array of *proc* structures, *proc*[*NR_TASKS* + *NR_PROCS*] (line 5593). Note that *NR_TASKS* is defined in *include/minix/com.h* (line 3630) and the constant *NR_PROCS* is defined in *include/minix/config.h* (line 2522). Together these set the size of the kernel's process table. *NR_PROCS* can be changed to create a system capable of handling a larger number of processes, if that is necessary (e.g., on a large server).

Finally, several macros are defined to speed access. The process table is accessed frequently, and calculating an address in an array requires slow multiplication operations, so an array of pointers to the process table elements, *pproc_addr* (line 5594), is provided. The two arrays *rdy_head* and *rdy_tail* are used to maintain the scheduling queues. For example, the first process on the default user queue is pointed to by *rdy_head*[*USER_Q*].

As we mentioned at the beginning of the discussion of *proc.h* there is another file *sconst.h* (line 5600), which must be synchronized with *proc.h* if there are changes in the structure of the process table. *Sconst.h* defines constants used by assembler code, expressed in a form usable by the assembler. All of these are offsets into the *stackframe_s* structure portion of a process table entry. Since assembler code is not processed by the C compiler, it is simpler to have such definitions in a separate file. Also, since these definitions are all machine dependent, isolating them here simplifies the process of porting MINIX 3 to another processor which will need a different version of *sconst.h*. Note that many offsets are expressed as the previous value plus *W*, which is set equal to the word size at line 5601. This allows the same file to serve for compiling a 16-bit or 32-bit version of MINIX 3.

Duplicate definitions create a potential problem. Header files are supposed to allow one to provide a single correct set of definitions and then proceed to use them in many places without devoting a lot of further attention to the details. Obviously, duplicate definitions, like those in *proc.h* and *sconst.h*, violate that principle. This is a special case, of course, but as such, special attention is required if changes are made to either of these files to ensure the two files remain consistent.

The system privileges structure, *priv*, that was mentioned briefly in the discussion of the process table is fully defined in *priv.h*, on lines 5718 to 5735. First there is a set of flag bits, *s_flags*, and then come the *s_trap_mask*, *s_ipc_from*, *s_ipc_to*, and *s_call_mask* fields which define which system calls may be initiated, which processes messages may be received from or sent to, and which kernel calls are allowed.

The *priv* structure is not part of the process table, rather each process table slot has a pointer to an instance of it. Only system processes have private copies; user processes all point to the same copy. Thus, for a user process the remaining fields of the structure are not relevant, as sharing them does not make sense. These fields are bitmaps of pending notifications, hardware interrupts, and signals, and a timer. It makes sense to provide these here for system processes, however. User processes have notifications, signals, and timers managed on their behalf by the process manager.

The organization of *priv.h* is similar to that of *proc.h*. After the definition of the *priv* structure come macros definitions for the flag bits, some important addresses known at compile time, and some macros for address calculations at run time. Then the table of *priv* structures, *priv[NR_SYS_PROCS]*, is defined, followed by an array of pointers, *ppriv_addr[NR_SYS_PROCS]* (lines 5762 and 5763). The pointer array provides fast access, analogous to the array of pointers that provides fast access to process table slots. The value of *STACK_GUARD* defined on line 5738 is a pattern that is easily recognizable. Its use will be seen later; the reader is invited to search the Internet to learn about the history of this value.

The last item in *priv.h* is a test to make sure that *NR_SYS_PROCS* has been defined to be larger than the number of processes in the boot image. The #error line will print a message if the test condition tests true. Although behavior may be different with other C compilers, with the standard MINIX 3 compiler this will also abort the compilation.

The F4 key triggers a debug dump that shows some of the information in the privilege table. Figure 2-35 shows a few lines of this table for some representative processes. The flags entries mean P: preemptable, B: billable, S: system. The traps mean E: echo, S: send, R: receive, B: both, N: notification. The bitmap has a bit for each of the *NR_SYS_PROCS* (32) system processes allowed, the order corresponds to the id field. (In the figure only 16 bits are shown, to make it fit the page better.) All user processes share id 0, which is the left-most bit position. The bitmap shows that user processes such as *init* can send messages only to the process manager, file system, and reincarnation server, and must use sendrec. The servers and drivers shown in the figure can use any of the ipc primitives and all but *memory* can send to any other process.

--nr-	-id-	-name-	-flags-	-traps-	-ipc_to mask------
(-4)	(01)	IDLE	P-BS-	-----	00000000 00001111
[-3]	(02)	CLOCK	---S-	--R--	00000000 00001111
[-2]	(03)	SYSTEM	---S-	--R--	00000000 00001111
[-1]	(04)	KERNEL	---S-	-----	00000000 00001111
0	(05)	pm	P--S-	ESRBN	11111111 11111111
1	(06)	fs	P--S-	ESRBN	11111111 11111111
2	(07)	rs	P--S-	ESRBN	11111111 11111111
3	(09)	memory	P--S-	ESRBN	00110111 01101111
4	(10)	log	P--S-	ESRBN	11111111 11111111
5	(08)	tty	P--S-	ESRBN	11111111 11111111
6	(11)	driver	P--S-	ESRBN	11111111 11111111
7	(00)	init	P-B--	E--B-	00000111 00000000

Figure 2-35. Part of a debug dump of the privilege table. The clock task, file server, tty, and init processes privileges are typical of tasks, servers, device drivers, and user processes, respectively. The bitmap is truncated to 16 bits.

Another header that is included in a number of different source files is *protect.h* (line 5800). Almost everything in this file deals with architecture details of the Intel processors that support protected mode (the 80286, 80386, 80486, and the Pentium series). A detailed description of these chips is beyond the scope of this book. Suffice it to say that they contain internal registers that point to **descriptor tables** in memory. Descriptor tables define how system resources are used and prevent processes from accessing memory assigned to other processes.

The architecture of 32-bit Intel processors also provides for four **privilege levels**, of which MINIX 3 takes advantage of three. These are defined symbolically on lines 5843 to 5845. The most central parts of the kernel, the parts that run during interrupts and that manage context switches, always run with *INTR_PRIVILEGE*. Every address in the memory and every register in the CPU can be accessed by a process with this privilege level. The tasks run at *TASK_PRIVILEGE* level, which allows them to access I/O but not to use instructions that modify special registers, like those that point to descriptor tables. Servers and user processes run at *USER_PRIVILEGE* level. Processes executing at this level are unable to execute certain instructions, for instance those that access I/O ports, change memory assignments, or change privilege levels themselves.

The concept of privilege levels will be familiar to those who are familiar with the architecture of modern CPUs, but those who have learned computer architecture through study of the assembly language of low-end microprocessors may not have encountered such features.

One header file in *kernel/* has not yet been described: *system.h*, and we will postpone discussing it until later in this chapter when we describe the system task, which runs as an independent process, although it is compiled with the kernel. For now we are through with header files and are ready to dig into the **.c* C language source files. The first of these that we will look at is *table.c* (line 6000). Compilation of this produces no executable code, but the compiled object file *table.o* will contain all the kernel data structures. We have already seen many of these data structures defined, in *glo.h* and other headers. On line 6028 the macro *_TABLE* is defined, immediately before the #include statements. As explained earlier, this definition causes *EXTERN* to become defined as the null string, and storage space to be allocated for all the data declarations preceded by *EXTERN*.

In addition to the variables declared in header files there are two other places where global data storage is allocated. Some definitions are made directly in *table.c*. On lines 6037 to 6041 the stack space needed by kernel components is defined, and the total amount of stack space for tasks is reserved as the array *t_stack[TOT_STACK_SPACE]* on line 6045.

The rest of *table.c* defines many constants related to properties of processes, such as the combinations of flag bits, call traps, and masks that define to whom messages and notifications can be sent that we saw in Fig. 2-35 (lines 6048 to 6071). Following this are masks to define the kernel calls allowed for various processes. The process manager and file server are all allowed unique combinations. The reincarnation server is allowed access to all kernel calls, not for its own use, but because as the parent of other system processes it can only pass to its children subsets of its own privileges. Drivers are given a common set of kernel call masks, except for the RAM disk driver which needs unusual access to memory. (Note that the comment on line 6075 that mentions the "system services manager" should say "reincarnation server"—the name was changed during development and some comments still refer to the old name.)

Finally, on lines 6095 to 6109, the *image* table is defined. It has been put here rather than in a header file because the trick with *EXTERN* used to prevent multiple declarations does not work with initialized variables; that is, you may not say

    extern int x = 3;

anywhere. The *image* table provides details needed to initialize all of the processes that are loaded from the boot image. It will be used by the system at startup. As an example of the information contained here, consider the field labeled "qs" in the comment on line 6096. This shows the size of the quantum assigned to each process. Ordinary user processes, as children of init, get to run for 8 clock ticks. The CLOCK and SYSTEM tasks are allowed to run for 64 clock ticks if necessary. They are not really expected to run that long before blocking, but unlike user-space servers and drivers they cannot be demoted to a lower-priority queue if they prevent other processes from getting a chance to run.

If a new process is to be added to the boot image, a new row must be provided in the *image* table. An error in matching the size of *image* to other constants is intolerable and cannot be permitted. At the end of *table.c* tests are made for errors, using a little trick. The array *dummy* is declared here twice. In each declaration the size of *dummy* will be impossible and will trigger a compiler error if a mistake has been made. Since *dummy* is declared as *extern*, no space is allocated for it here (or anywhere). Since it is not referenced anywhere else in the code, this will not bother the compiler.

Additional global storage is allocated at the end of the assembly language file *mpx386.s*. Although it will require skipping ahead several pages in the listing to see this, it is appropriate to discuss this now, since we are on the subject of global variables. On line 6822 the assembler directive .sect .rom is used to put a **magic number** (to identify a valid MINIX 3 kernel) at the very beginning of the kernel's data segment. A .sect bss assembler directive and the .space pseudoinstruction are also used here to reserve space for the kernel's stack. The .comm pseudoinstruction labels several words at the top of the stack so they may be manipulated directly. We will come back to *mpx386.s* in a few pages, after we have discussed bootstrapping MINIX 3.

2.6.6 Bootstrapping MINIX 3

It is almost time to start looking at the executable code—but not quite. Before we do that, let us take a few moments to understand how MINIX 3 is loaded into memory. It is, of course, loaded from a disk, but the process is not completely trivial and the exact sequence of events depends on the kind of disk. In particular, it depends on whether the disk is partitioned or not. Figure 2-36 shows how diskettes and partitioned disks are laid out.

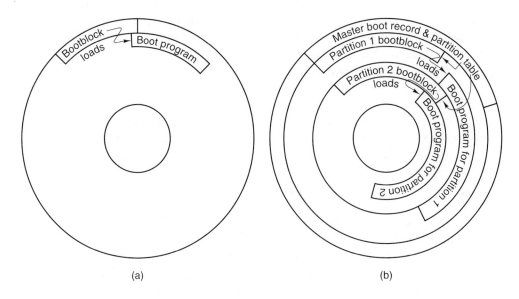

Figure 2-36. Disk structures used for bootstrapping. (a) Unpartitioned disk. The first sector is the bootblock. (b) Partitioned disk. The first sector is the master boot record, also called **masterboot**.

When the system is started, the hardware (actually, a program in ROM) reads the first sector of the boot disk, copies it to a fixed location in memory, and executes the code found there. On an unpartitioned MINIX 3 diskette, the first sector is a bootblock which loads the boot program, as in Fig. 2-36(a). Hard disks are partitioned, and the program on the first sector (called masterboot on MINIX systems) first relocates itself to a different memory region, then reads the partition table, loaded with it from the first sector. Then it loads and executes the first sector of the active partition, as shown in Fig. 2-36(b). (Normally one and only one partition is marked active). A MINIX 3 partition has the same structure as an unpartitioned MINIX 3 diskette, with a bootblock that loads the boot program. The bootblock code is the same for an unpartitioned or a partitioned disk. Since the masterboot program relocates itself the bootblock code can be written to run at the same memory address where masterboot is originally loaded.

The actual situation can be a little more complicated than the figure shows, because a partition may contain subpartitions. In this case the first sector of the partition will be another master boot record containing the partition table for the subpartitions. Eventually, however, control will be passed to a boot sector, the first sector on a device that is not further subdivided. On a diskette the first sector is always a boot sector. MINIX 3 does allow a form of partitioning of a diskette, but only the first partition may be booted; there is no separate master boot record, and subpartitions are not possible. This makes it possible for partitioned and non-partitioned diskettes to be mounted in exactly the same way. The main use for a partitioned floppy disk is that it provides a convenient way to divide an installation disk into a root image to be copied to a RAM disk and a mounted portion that can be dismounted when no longer needed, in order to free the diskette drive for continuing the installation process.

The MINIX 3 boot sector is modified at the time it is written to the disk by a special program called *installboot* which writes the boot sector and patches into it the disk address of a file named *boot* on its partition or subpartition. In MINIX 3, the standard location for the *boot* program is in a directory of the same name, that is, */boot/boot*. But it could be anywhere—the patching of the boot sector just mentioned locates the disk sectors from which it is to be loaded. This is necessary because previous to loading *boot* there is no way to use directory and file names to find a file.

Boot is the secondary loader for MINIX 3. It can do more than just load the operating system however, as it is a **monitor program** that allows the user to change, set, and save various parameters. *Boot* looks in the second sector of its partition to find a set of parameters to use. MINIX 3, like standard UNIX, reserves the first 1K block of every disk device as a **bootblock**, but only one 512-byte sector is loaded by the ROM boot loader or the master boot sector, so 512 bytes are available for saving settings. These control the boot operation, and are also passed to the operating system itself. The default settings present a menu with one choice, to start MINIX 3, but the settings can be modified to present a more complex menu allowing other operating systems to be started (by loading and executing boot sectors from other partitions), or to start MINIX 3 with various options. The default settings can also be modified to bypass the menu and start MINIX 3 immediately.

Boot is not a part of the operating system, but it is smart enough to use the file system data structures to find the actual operating system image. *Boot* looks for a file with the name specified in the *image=* boot parameter, which by default is */boot/image*. If there is an ordinary file with this name it is loaded, but if this is the name of a directory the newest file within it is loaded. Many operating systems have a predefined file name for the boot image. But MINIX 3 users are encouraged to modify it and to create new versions. It is useful to be able to select from multiple versions, in order to return to an older version if an experiment is unsuccessful.

We do not have space here to go into more detail about the boot monitor. It is a sophisticated program, almost a miniature operating system in itself. It works together with MINIX 3, and when MINIX 3 is properly shut down, the boot monitor regains control. If you would like to know more, the MINIX 3 Web site provides a link to a detailed description of the boot monitor source code.

The MINIX 3 **boot image** (also called **system image**) is a concatenation of several program files: the kernel, process manager, file system, reincarnation server, several device drivers, and *init*, as shown in Fig 2-30. Note that MINIX 3 as described here is configured with just one disk driver in the boot image, but several may be present, with the active one selected by a label. Like all binary programs, each file in the boot image includes a header that tells how much space to reserve for uninitialized data and stack after loading the executable code and initialized data, so the next program can be loaded at the proper address.

The memory regions available for loading the boot monitor and the component programs of MINIX 3 will depend upon the hardware. Also, some architectures may require adjustment of internal addresses within executable code to correct them for the actual address where a program is loaded. The segmented architecture of Intel processors makes this unnecessary.

Details of the loading process differ with machine type. The important thing is that by one means or another the operating system is loaded into memory. Following this, a small amount of preparation is required before MINIX 3 can be started. First, while loading the image, *boot* reads a few bytes from the image that tell boot some of its properties, most importantly whether it was compiled to run in 16-bit or 32-bit mode. Then some additional information needed to start the system is made available to the kernel. The *a.out* headers of the components of the MINIX 3 image are extracted into an array within *boot*'s memory space, and the base address of this array is passed to the kernel. MINIX 3 can return control to the boot monitor when it terminates, so the location where execution should resume in the monitor is also passed on. These items are passed on the stack, as we shall see later.

Several other pieces of information, the **boot parameters**, must be communicated from the boot monitor to the operating system. Some are needed by the kernel and some are not needed but are passed along for information, for instance, the name of the boot image that was loaded. These items can all be represented as *string=value* pairs, and the address of a table of these pairs is passed on the stack. Fig. 2-37 shows a typical set of boot parameters as displayed by the sysenv command from the MINIX 3 command line.

In this example, an important item we will see again soon is the *memory* parameter; in this case it indicates that the boot monitor has determined that there are two segments of memory available for MINIX 3 to use. One begins at hexadecimal address 800 (decimal 2048) and has a size of hexadecimal 0x92540 (decimal 599,360) bytes; the other begins at 100000 (1,048,576) and contains 0x3df00000 (64,946,176) bytes. This is typical of all but the most elderly PC-compatible computers. The design of the original IBM PC placed read-only memory at the top of the usable range of memory, which is limited to 1 MB on an 8088 CPU. Modern PC-compatible machines always have more memory than the original PC, but for compatibility they still have read-only memory at the same addresses as the older machines. Thus, the read-write memory is discontinuous,

```
rootdev=904
ramimagedev=904
ramsize=0
processor=686
bus=at
video=vga
chrome=color
memory=800:92540,100000:3DF0000
label=AT
controller=c0
image=boot/image
```

Figure 2-37. Boot parameters passed to the kernel at boot time in a typical MINIX 3 system.

with a block of ROM between the lower 640 KB and the upper range above 1 MB. The boot monitor loads the kernel into the low memory range and the servers, drivers, and *init* into the memory range above the ROM if possible. This is primarily for the benefit of the file system, so a large block cache can be used without bumping into the read-only memory.

We should also mention here that operating systems are not universally loaded from local disks. **Diskless workstations** may load their operating systems from a remote disk, over a network connection. This requires network software in ROM, of course. Although details vary from what we have described here, the elements of the process are likely to be similar. The ROM code must be just smart enough to get an executable file over the net that can then obtain the complete operating system. If MINIX 3 were loaded this way, very little would need to be changed in the initialization process that occurs once the operating system code is loaded into memory. It would, of course, need a network server and a modified file system that could access files via the network.

2.6.7 System Initialization

Earlier versions of MINIX could be compiled in 16-bit mode if compatibility with older processor chips were required, and MINIX 3 retains some source code for 16-bit mode. However, the version described here and distributed on the CD-ROM is usable only on 32-bit machines with 80386 or better processors. It does not work in 16-bit mode, and creation of a 16-bit version may require removing some features. Among other things, 32-bit binaries are larger than 16-bit ones, and independent user-space drivers cannot share code the way it could be done when drivers were compiled into a single binary. Nevertheless, a common base of C source code is used and the compiler generates the appropriate output depending upon whether the compiler itself is the 16-bit or 32-bit version of the compiler.

A macro defined by the compiler itself determines the definition of the _WORD_SIZE macro in the file *include/minix/sys_config.h*.

The first part of MINIX 3 to execute is written in assembly language, and different source code files must be used for the 16-bit or 32-bit compiler. The 32-bit version of the initialization code is in *mpx386.s*. The alternative, for 16-bit systems, is in *mpx88.s*. Both of these also include assembly language support for other low-level kernel operations. The selection is made automatically in *mpx.s*. This file is so short that the entire file can be presented in Fig. 2-38.

```
#include <minix/config.h>
#if _WORD_SIZE == 2
#include "mpx88.s"
#else
#include "mpx386.s"
#endif
```

Figure 2-38. How alternative assembly language source files are selected.

Mpx.s shows an unusual use of the C preprocessor #include statement. Customarily the #include preprocessor directive is used to include header files, but it can also be used to select an alternate section of source code. Using #if statements to do this would require putting all the code in both of the large files *mpx88.s* and *mpx386.s* into a single file. Not only would this be unwieldy; it would also be wasteful of disk space, since in a particular installation it is likely that one or the other of these two files will not be used at all and can be archived or deleted. In the following discussion we will use the 32-bit *mpx386.s*.

Since this is almost our first look at executable code, let us start with a few words about how we will do this throughout the book. The multiple source files used in compiling a large C program can be hard to follow. In general, we will keep discussions confined to a single file at a time. The order of inclusion of the files in Appendix B is the order in which we discuss them in the text. We will start with the entry point for each part of the MINIX 3 system, and we will follow the main line of execution. When a call to a supporting function is encountered, we will say a few words about the purpose of the call, but normally we will not go into a detailed description of the internals of the function at that point, leaving that until we arrive at the definition of the called function. Important subordinate functions are usually defined in the same file in which they are called, following the higher-level calling functions, but small or general-purpose functions are sometimes collected in separate files. We do not attempt to discuss the internals of every function, and files that contain such functions may not be listed in Appendix B.

To facilitate portability to other platforms, separate files are frequently used for machine-dependent and machine-independent code. To make code easier to understand and reduce the overall size of the listings, most conditional code for platforms other than Intel 32-bit systems has been stripped from the printed files in Appendix B. Complete versions of all files are in the source directories on the CD-ROM and are also available on the MINIX 3 Web site.

A substantial amount of effort has been made to make the code readable by humans. But a large program has many branches, and sometimes understanding a main function requires reading the functions it calls, so having a few slips of paper to use as bookmarks and deviating from our order of discussion to look at things in a different order may be helpful at times.

Having laid out our intended way of organizing the discussion of the code, we start by an exception. Startup of MINIX 3 involves several transfers of control between the assembly language routines in *mpx386.s* and C language routines in the files *start.c* and *main.c*. We will describe these routines in the order that they are executed, even though that involves jumping from one file to another.

Once the bootstrap process has loaded the operating system into memory, control is transferred to the label *MINIX* (in *mpx386.s*, line 6420). The first instruction is a jump over a few bytes of data; this includes the boot monitor flags (line 6423) mentioned earlier. At this point the flags have already served their purpose; they were read by the monitor when it loaded the kernel into memory. They are located here because it is an easily specified address. They are used by the boot monitor to identify various characteristics of the kernel, most importantly, whether it is a 16-bit or 32-bit system. The boot monitor always starts in 16-bit mode, but switches the CPU to 32-bit mode if necessary. This happens before control passes to the label *MINIX*.

Understanding the state of the stack at this point will help make sense of the following code. The monitor passes several parameters to MINIX 3, by putting them on the stack. First the monitor pushes the address of the variable *aout*, which holds the address of an array of the header information of the component programs of the boot image. Next it pushes the size and then the address of the boot parameters. These are all 32-bit quantities. Next come the monitor's code segment address and the location to return to within the monitor when MINIX 3 terminates. These are both 16-bit quantities, since the monitor operates in 16-bit protected mode. The first few instructions in *mpx386.s* convert the 16-bit stack pointer used by the monitor into a 32-bit value for use in protected mode. Then the instruction

```
mov     ebp, esp
```

(line 6436) copies the stack pointer value to the ebp register, so it can be used with offsets to retrieve from the stack the values placed there by the monitor, as is done at lines 6464 to 6467. Note that because the stack grows downward with Intel processors, 8(ebp) refers to a value pushed subsequent to pushing the value located at 12(ebp).

The assembly language code must do a substantial amount of work, setting up a stack frame to provide the proper environment for code compiled by the C compiler, copying tables used by the processor to define memory segments, and setting up various processor registers. As soon as this work is complete, the initialization process continues by calling (at line 6481) the C function *cstart* (in *start.c*, which we will consider next). Note that it is referred to as _*cstart* in the assembly language code. This is because all functions compiled by the C compiler have an underscore prepended to their names in the symbol tables, and the linker looks for such names when separately compiled modules are linked. Since the assembler does not add underscores, the writer of an assembly language program must explicitly add one in order for the linker to be able to find a corresponding name in the object file compiled by the C compiler.

Cstart calls another routine to initialize the **Global Descriptor Table**, the central data structure used by Intel 32-bit processors to oversee memory protection, and the **Interrupt Descriptor Table**, used to select the code to be executed for each possible interrupt type. Upon returning from *cstart* the lgdt and lidt instructions (lines 6487 and 6488) make these tables effective by loading the dedicated registers by which they are addressed. The instruction

jmpf   CS_SELECTOR:csinit

looks at first glance like a no-operation, since it transfers control to exactly where control would be if there were a series of nop instructions in its place. But this is an important part of the initialization process. This jump forces use of the structures just initialized. After some more manipulation of the processor registers, *MINIX* terminates with a jump (not a call) at line 6503 to the kernel's *main* entry point (in *main.c*). At this point the initialization code in *mpx386.s* is complete. The rest of the file contains code to start or restart a task or process, interrupt handlers, and other support routines that had to be written in assembly language for efficiency. We will return to these in the next section.

We will now look at the top-level C initialization functions. The general strategy is to do as much as possible using high-level C code. As we have seen, there are already two versions of the *mpx* code. One chunk of C code can eliminate two chunks of assembler code. Almost the first thing done by *cstart* (in *start.c*, line 6920) is to set up the CPU's protection mechanisms and the interrupt tables, by calling *prot_init*. Then it copies the boot parameters to the kernel's memory, and it scans them, using the function *get_value* (line 6997) to search for parameter names and return corresponding value strings. This process determines the type of video display, processor type, bus type, and, if in 16-bit mode, the processor operating mode (real or protected). All this information is stored in global variables, for access when needed by any part of the kernel code.

Main (in *main.c*, line 7130), completes initialization and then starts normal execution of the system. It configures the interrupt control hardware by calling *intr_init*. This is done here because it cannot be done until the machine type is known. (Because *intr_init* is very dependent upon the hardware the procedure is in a separate file which we will describe later.) The parameter (1) in the call tells *intr_init* that it is initializing for MINIX 3. With a parameter (0) it can be called to reinitialize the hardware to the original state when MINIX 3 terminates and returns control to the boot monitor. *Intr_init* ensures that any interrupts that occur before initialization is complete have no effect. How this is done will be described later.

The largest part of *main*'s code is devoted to setup of the process table and the privilege table, so that when the first tasks and processes are scheduled, their memory maps, registers, and privilege information will be set correctly. All slots in the process table are marked as free and the *pproc_addr* array that speeds access to the process table is initialized by the loop on lines 7150 to 7154. The loop on lines 7155 to 7159 clears the privilege table and the *ppriv_addr* array similarly to the process table and its access array. For both the process and privilege tables, putting a specific value in one field is adequate to mark the slot as not in use. But for each table every slot, whether in use or not, needs to be initialized with an index number.

An aside on a minor characteristic of the C language: the code on line 7153

```
(pproc_addr + NR_TASKS)[i] = rp;
```

could just as well have been written as

```
pproc_addr[i + NR_TASKS] = rp;
```

In the C language $a[i]$ is just another way of writing $*(a+i)$. So it does not make much difference if you add a constant to a or to i. Some C compilers generate slightly better code if you add a constant to the array instead of the index. Whether it really makes a difference here, we cannot say.

Now we come to the long loop on lines 7172 to 7242, which initializes the process table with the necessary information to run all of the processes in the boot image. (Note that there is another outdated comment on line 7161 which mentions only tasks and servers.) All of these processes must be present at startup time and none of them will terminate during normal operation. At the start of the loop, *ip* is assigned the address of an entry in the *image* table created in *table.c* (line 7173). Since *ip* is a pointer to a structure, the elements of the structure can be accessed using notation like *ip−>proc_nr*, as is done on line 7174. This notation is used extensively in the MINIX 3 source code. In a similar way, *rp* is a pointer to a slot of the process table, and *priv(rp)* points to a slot of the privilege table. Much of the initialization of the process and privilege tables in the long loop consists of reading a value from the image table and storing it in the process table or the privilege table.

On line 7185 a test is made for processes that are part of the kernel, and if this is true the special *STACK_GUARD* pattern is stored in the base of the task's stack area. This can be checked later on to be sure the stack has not overflowed. Then the initial stack pointer for each task is set up. Each task needs its own private stack pointer. Since the stack grows toward lower addresses in memory, the initial stack pointer is calculated by adding the size of the task's stack to the current base address (lines 7190 and 7191). There is one exception: the *KERNEL* process (also identified as *HARDWARE* in some places) is never considered ready, never runs as an ordinary process, and thus has no need of a stack pointer.

The binaries of boot image components are compiled like any other MINIX 3 programs, and the compiler creates a header, as defined in *include/a.out.h*, at the beginning of each of the files. The boot loader copies each of these headers into its own memory space before MINIX 3 starts, and when the monitor transfers control to the *MINIX:* entry point in *mpx386.s* the physical address of the header area is passed to the assembly code in the stack, as we have seen. At line 7202, one of these headers is copied to a local *exec* structure, *ehdr*, using *hdrindex* as the index into the array of headers. Then the data and text segment addresses are converted to clicks and entered into the memory map for this process (lines 7205 to 7214).

Before continuing, we should mention a few points. First, for kernel processes *hdrindex* is always assigned a value of zero at line 7178. These processes are all compiled into the same file as the kernel, and the information about their stack requirements is in the *image* table. Since a task compiled into the kernel can call code and access data located anywhere in the kernel's space, the size of an individual task is not meaningful. Thus the same element of the array at *aout* is accessed for the kernel and for each task, and the size fields for a task is filled with the sizes for the kernel itself. The tasks get their stack information from the *image* table, initialized during compilation of *table.c*. After all kernel processes have been processed, *hdrindex* is incremented on each pass through the loop (line 7196), so all the user-space system processes get the proper data from their own headers.

Another point to mention here is that functions that copy data are not necessarily consistent in the order in which the source and destination are specified. In reading this loop, beware of potential confusion. The arguments to *strncpy*, a function from the standard C library, are ordered such that the destination comes first: strncpy(to, from, count). This is analogous to an assignment operation, in which the left hand side specifies the variable being assigned to and the right hand side is the expression specifying the value to be assigned. This function is used at line 7179 to copy a process name into each process table slot for debugging and other purposes. In contrast, the *phys_copy* function uses an opposite convention, phys_copy(from, to, quantity). *Phys_copy* is used at line 7202 to copy program headers of user-space processes.

Continuing our discussion of the initialization of the process table, at lines 7220 and 7221 the initial value of the program counter and the processor status word are set. The processor status word for the tasks is different from that for device drivers and servers, because tasks have a higher privilege level that allows them to access I/O ports. Following this, if the process is a user-space one, its stack pointer is initialized.

One entry in the process table does not need to be (and cannot be) scheduled. The *HARDWARE* process exists only for bookkeeping purposes—it is credited with the time used while servicing an interrupt. All other processes are put on the appropriate queues by the code in lines 7234 and 7235. The function called *lock_enqueue* disables interrupts before modifying the queues and then reenables them when the queue has been modified. This is not required at this point when nothing is running yet, but it is the standard method, and there is no point in creating extra code to be used just once.

The last step in initializing each slot in the process table is to call the function *alloc_segments* at line 7241. This machine-dependent routine sets into the proper fields the locations, sizes, and permission levels for the memory segments used by each process. For older Intel processors that do not support protected mode, it defines only the segment locations. It would have to be rewritten to handle a processor type with a different method of allocating memory.

Once the process table has been initialized for all the tasks, the servers, and *init*, the system is almost ready to roll. The variable *bill_ptr* tells which process gets billed for processor time; it needs to have an initial value set at line 7250, and *IDLE* is clearly an appropriate choice. Now the kernel is ready to begin its normal work of controlling and scheduling the execution of processes, as illustrated in Fig. 2-2.

Not all of the other parts of the system are ready for normal operation yet, but all of these other parts run as independent processes and have been marked ready and queued to run. They will initialize themselves when they run. All that is left is for the kernel to call *announce* to announce it is ready and then to call *restart* (lines 7251 and 7252). In many C programs *main* is a loop, but in the MINIX 3 kernel its job is done once the initialization is complete. The call to *restart* on line 7252 starts the first queued process. Control never returns to *main*.

_Restart is an assembly language routine in *mpx386.s*. In fact, *_restart* is not a complete function; it is an intermediate entry point in a larger procedure. We will discuss it in detail in the next section; for now we will just say that *_restart* causes a context switch, so the process pointed to by *proc_ptr* will run. When *_restart* has executed for the first time we can say that MINIX 3 is running—it is executing a process. *_Restart* is executed again and again as tasks, servers, and user processes are given their opportunities to run and then are suspended, either to wait for input or to give other processes their turns.

Of course, the first time *_restart* is executed, initialization is only complete for the kernel. Recall that there are three parts to the MINIX 3 process table. You might ask how can any processes run when major parts of the process table have not been set up yet. The full answer to this will be seen in later chapters. The short answer is that the instruction pointers of all processes in the boot image initially point to initialization code for each process, and all will block fairly soon. Eventually, the process manager and the file system will get to run their initialization code, and their parts of the process table will be completed. Eventually *init* will fork off a *getty* process for each terminal. These processes will block until input is typed at some terminal, at which point the first user can log in.

We have now traced the startup of MINIX 3 through three files, two written in C and one in assembly language. The assembly language file, *mpx386.s*, contains additional code used in handling interrupts, which we will look at in the next section. However, before we go on let us wrap up with a brief description of the remaining routines in the two C files. The remaining function in *start.c* is *get_value* (line 6997). It is used to find entries in the kernel environment, which is a copy of the boot parameters. It is a simplified version of a standard library function which is rewritten here in order to keep the kernel simple.

There are three additional procedures in *main.c*. *Announce* displays a copyright notice and tells whether MINIX 3 is running in real mode or 16-bit or 32-bit protected mode, like this:

MINIX 3.1 Copyright 2006 Vrije Universiteit, Amsterdam, The Netherlands
Executing in 32-bit protected mode

When you see this message you know initialization of the kernel is complete. *Prepare_shutdown* (line 7272) signals all system processes with a *SIGKSTOP* signal (system processes cannot be signaled in the same way as user processes). Then it sets a timer to allow all the system process time to clean up before it calls the final procedure here, *shutdown*. *Shutdown* will normally return control to the MINIX 3 boot monitor. To do so the interrupt controllers are restored to the BIOS settings by the *intr_init(0)* call on line 7338.

2.6.8 Interrupt Handling in MINIX

Details of interrupt hardware are system dependent, but any system must have elements functionally equivalent to those to be described for systems with 32-bit Intel CPUs. Interrupts generated by hardware devices are electrical signals and are handled in the first place by an interrupt controller, an integrated circuit that can sense a number of such signals and for each one generate a unique data pattern on the processor's data bus. This is necessary because the processor itself has only one input for sensing all these devices, and thus cannot differentiate which device needs service. PCs using Intel 32-bit processors are normally equipped with two such controller chips. Each can handle eight inputs, but one is a slave which feeds its output to one of the inputs of the master, so fifteen distinct external devices can be sensed by the combination, as shown in Fig. 2-39. Some of the fifteen inputs are dedicated; the clock input, IRQ 0, for instance, does not have a connection to any socket into which a new adapter can be plugged. Others are connected to sockets and can be used for whatever device is plugged in.

In the figure, interrupt signals arrive on the various *IRQ n* lines shown at the right. The connection to the CPU's INT pin tells the processor that an interrupt has occurred. The INTA (interrupt acknowledge) signal from the CPU causes the controller responsible for the interrupt to put data on the system data bus telling the processor which service routine to execute. The interrupt controller chips are

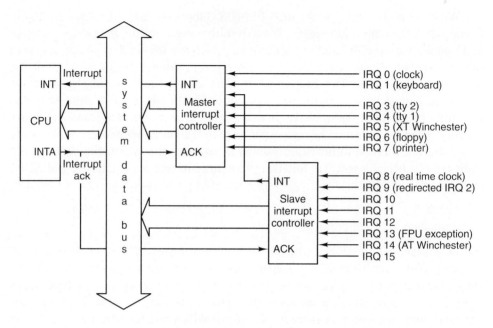

Figure 2-39. Interrupt processing hardware on a 32-bit Intel PC.

programmed during system initialization, when *main* calls *intr_init*. The programming determines the output sent to the CPU for a signal received on each of the input lines, as well as various other parameters of the controller's operation. The data put on the bus is an 8-bit number, used to index into a table of up to 256 elements. The MINIX 3 table has 56 elements. Of these, 35 are actually used; the others are reserved for use with future Intel processors or for future enhancements to MINIX 3. On 32-bit Intel processors this table contains interrupt gate descriptors, each of which is an 8-byte structure with several fields.

Several modes of response to interrupts are possible; in the one used by MINIX 3, the fields of most concern to us in each of the interrupt gate descriptors point to the service routine's executable code segment and the starting address within it. The CPU executes the code pointed to by the selected descriptor. The result is exactly the same as execution of an

    int   <nnn>

assembly language instruction. The only difference is that in the case of a hardware interrupt the <nnn> originates from a register in the interrupt controller chip, rather than from an instruction in program memory.

The task-switching mechanism of a 32-bit Intel processor that is called into play in response to an interrupt is complex, and changing the program counter to execute another function is only a part of it. When the CPU receives an interrupt while running a process it sets up a new stack for use during the interrupt service.

The location of this stack is determined by an entry in the **Task State Segment** (TSS). One such structure exists for the entire system, initialized by *cstart*'s call to *prot_init*, and modified as each process is started. The effect is that the new stack created by an interrupt always starts at the end of the *stackframe_s* structure within the process table entry of the interrupted process. The CPU automatically pushes several key registers onto this new stack, including those necessary to reinstate the interrupted process' own stack and restore its program counter. When the interrupt handler code starts running, it uses this area in the process table as its stack, and much of the information needed to return to the interrupted process will have already been stored. The interrupt handler pushes the contents of additional registers, filling the stackframe, and then switches to a stack provided by the kernel while it does whatever must be done to service the interrupt.

Termination of an interrupt service routine is done by switching the stack from the kernel stack back to a stackframe in the process table (but not necessarily the same one that was created by the last interrupt), explicitly popping the additional registers, and executing an iretd (return from interrupt) instruction. Iretd restores the state that existed before an interrupt, restoring the registers that were pushed by the hardware and switching back to a stack that was in use before an interrupt. Thus an interrupt stops a process, and completion of the interrupt service restarts a process, possibly a different one from the one that was most recently stopped. Unlike the simpler interrupt mechanisms that are the usual subject of assembly language programming texts, nothing is stored on the interrupted process' working stack when a user process is interrupted. Furthermore, because the stack is created anew in a known location (determined by the TSS) after an interrupt, control of multiple processes is simplified. To start a different process all that is necessary is to point the stack pointer to the stackframe of another process, pop the registers that were explicitly pushed, and execute an iretd instruction.

The CPU disables all interrupts when it receives an interrupt. This guarantees that nothing can occur to cause the stackframe within a process table entry to overflow. This is automatic, but assembly-level instructions exist to disable and enable interrupts, as well. Interrupts remain disabled while the kernel stack, located outside the process table, is in use. A mechanism exists to allow an exception handler (a response to an error detected by the CPU) to run when the kernel stack is in use. An exception is similar to an interrupt and exceptions cannot be disabled. Thus, for the sake of exceptions there must be a way to deal with what are essentially nested interrupts. In this case a new stack is not created. Instead, the CPU pushes the essential registers needed for resumption of the interrupted code onto the existing stack. An exception is not supposed to occur while the kernel is running, however, and will result in a panic.

When an iretd is encountered while executing kernel code, a the return mechanism is simpler than the one used when a user process is interrupted. The processor can determine how to handle the iretd by examining the code segment selector that is popped from the stack as part of the iretd's action.

The privilege levels mentioned earlier control the different responses to interrupts received while a process is running and while kernel code (including interrupt service routines) is executing. The simpler mechanism is used when the privilege level of the interrupted code is the same as the privilege level of the code to be executed in response to the interrupt. The usual case, however, is that the interrupted code is less privileged than the interrupt service code, and in this case the more elaborate mechanism, using the TSS and a new stack, is employed. The privilege level of a code segment is recorded in the code segment selector, and as this is one of the items stacked during an interrupt, it can be examined upon return from the interrupt to determine what the iretd instruction must do.

Another service is provided by the hardware when a new stack is created to use while servicing an interrupt. The hardware checks to make sure the new stack is big enough for at least the minimum quantity of information that must be placed on it. This protects the more privileged kernel code from being accidentally (or maliciously) crashed by a user process making a system call with an inadequate stack. These mechanisms are built into the processor specifically for use in the implementation of operating systems that support multiple processes.

This behavior may be confusing if you are unfamiliar with the internal working of 32-bit Intel CPUs. Ordinarily we try to avoid describing such details, but understanding what happens when an interrupt occurs and when an iretd instruction is executed is essential to understanding how the kernel controls the transitions to and from the "running" state of Fig. 2-2. The fact that the hardware handles much of the work makes life much easier for the programmer, and presumably makes the resulting system more efficient. All this help from the hardware does, however, make it hard to understand what is happening just by reading the software.

Having now described the interrupt mechanism, we will return to *mpx386.s* and look at the tiny part of the MINIX 3 kernel that actually sees hardware interrupts. An entry point exists for each interrupt. The source code at each entry point, *_hwint00* to *_hwint07*, (lines 6531 to 6560) looks like a call to *hwint_master* (line 6515), and the entry points *_hwint08* to *_hwint15* (lines 6583 to 6612) look like calls to *hwint_slave* (line 6566). Each entry point appears to pass a parameter in the call, indicating which device needs service. In fact, these are really not calls, but macros, and eight separate copies of the code defined by the macro definition of *hwint_master* are assembled, with only the *irq* parameter different. Similarly, eight copies of the *hwint_slave* macro are assembled. This may seem extravagant, but assembled code is very compact. The object code for each expanded macro occupies fewer than 40 bytes. In servicing an interrupt, speed is important, and doing it this way eliminates the overhead of executing code to load a parameter, call a subroutine, and retrieve the parameter.

We will continue the discussion of *hwint_master* as if it really were a single function, rather than a macro that is expanded in eight different places. Recall that before *hwint_master* begins to execute, the CPU has created a new stack in the *stackframe_s* of the interrupted process, within its process table slot. Several key registers have already been saved there, and all interrupts are disabled. The first action of *hwint_master* is to call *save* (line 6516). This subroutine pushes all the other registers necessary to restart the interrupted process. *Save* could have been written inline as part of the macro to increase speed, but this would have more than doubled the size of the macro, and in any case *save* is needed for calls by other functions. As we shall see, *save* plays tricks with the stack. Upon returning to *hwint_master*, the kernel stack, not a stackframe in the process table, is in use.

Two tables declared in *glo.h* are now used. *_Irq_handlers* contains the hook information, including addresses of handler routines. The number of the interrupt being serviced is converted to an address within *_irq_handlers*. This address is then pushed onto the stack as the argument to *_intr_handle*, and *_intr_handle* is called, We will look at the code of *_intr_handle* later. For the moment, we will just say that not only does it call the service routine for the interrupt that was called, it sets or resets a flag in the *_irq_actids* array to indicate whether this attempt to service the interrupt succeeded, and it gives other entries on the queue another chance to run and be removed from the list. Depending upon exactly what was required of the handler, the IRQ may or may not be available to receive another interrupt upon the return from the call to *_intr_handle*. This is determined by checking the corresponding entry in *_irq_actids*.

A nonzero value in *_irq_actids* shows that interrupt service for this IRQ is not complete. If so, the interrupt controller is manipulated to prevent it from responding to another interrupt from the same IRQ line. (lines 6722 to 6724). This operation masks the ability of the controller chip to respond to a particular input; the CPU's ability to respond to all interrupts is inhibited internally when it first receives the interrupt signal and has not yet been restored at this point.

A few words about the assembly language code used may be helpful to readers unfamiliar with assembly language programming. The instruction

```
jz 0f
```

on line 6521 does not specify a number of bytes to jump over. The 0f is not a hexadecimal number, nor is it a normal label. Ordinary label names are not permitted to begin with numeric characters. This is the way the MINIX 3 assembler specifies a **local label**; the 0f means a jump **forward** to the next numeric label 0, on line 6525. The byte written on line 6526 allows the interrupt controller to resume normal operation, possibly with the line for the current interrupt disabled.

An interesting and possibly confusing point is that the 0: label on line 6525 occurs elsewhere in the same file, on line 6576 in *hwint_slave*. The situation is even more complicated than it looks at first glance since these labels are within macros and the macros are expanded before the assembler sees this code. Thus there are actually sixteen 0: labels in the code seen by the assembler. The possible proliferation of labels declared within macros is the reason why the assembly language provides local labels; when resolving a local label, the assembler uses the nearest one that matches in the specified direction, and additional occurrences of a local label are ignored.

_Intr_handle_ is hardware dependent, and details of its code will be discussed when we get to the file *i8259.c*. However, a few word about how it functions are in order now. _Intr_handle_ scans a linked list of structures that hold, among other things, addresses of functions to be called to handle an interrupt for a device, and the process numbers of the device drivers. It is a linked list because a single IRQ line may be shared with several devices. The handler for each device is supposed to test whether its device actually needs service. Of course, this step is not necessary for an IRQ such as the clock interrupt, IRQ 0, which is hard wired to the chip that generates clock signals with no possibility of any other device triggering this IRQ.

The handler code is intended to be written so it can return quickly. If there is no work to be done or the interrupt service is completed immediately, the handler returns *TRUE*. A handler may perform an operation like reading data from an input device and transferring the data to a buffer where it can be accessed when the corresponding driver has its next chance to run. The handler may then cause a message to be sent to its device driver, which in turn causes the device driver to be scheduled to run as a normal process. If the work is not complete, the handler returns *FALSE*. An element of the _irq_act_ids_ array is a bitmap that records the results for all the handlers on the list in such a way that the result will be zero if and only if every one of the handlers returned *TRUE*. If that is not the case, the code on lines 6522 to 6524 disables the IRQ before the interrupt controller as a whole is reenabled on line 6536.

This mechanism ensures that none of the handlers on the chain belonging to an IRQ will be activated until all of the device drivers to which these handlers belong have completed their work. Obviously, there needs to be another way to reenable an IRQ. That is provided in a function *enable_irq* which we will see later. Suffice it to say, each device driver must be sure that *enable_irq* is called when its work is done. It also is obvious that *enable_irq* first should reset its own bit in the element of _irq_act_ids_ that corresponds to the IRQ of the driver, and then should test whether all bits have been reset. Only then should the IRQ be reenabled on the interrupt controller chip.

What we have just described applies in its simplest form only to the clock driver, because the clock is the only interrupt-driven device that is compiled into the kernel binary. The address of an interrupt handler in another process is not meaningful in the context of the kernel, and the *enable_irq* function in the kernel cannot be called by a separate process in its own memory space. For user-space device drivers, which means all device drivers that respond to hardware-initiated interrupts except for the clock driver, the address of a common handler, *generic_handler*, is stored in the linked list of hooks. The source code for this function is in the system task files, but since the system task is compiled together with the kernel and since this code is executed in response to an interrupt it cannot really be considered part of the system task. The other information in each element of the list of hooks includes the process number of the associated device driver. When *generic_handler* is called it sends a message to the correct device driver which causes the specific handler functions of the driver to run. The system task supports the other end of the chain of events described above as well. When a user-space device driver completes its work it makes a sys_irqctl kernel call, which causes the system task to call *enable_irq* on behalf of that driver to prepare for the next interrupt.

Returning our attention to *hwint_master*, note that it terminates with a ret instruction (line 6527). It is not obvious that something tricky happens here. If a process has been interrupted, the stack in use at this point is the kernel stack, and not the stack within a process table that was set up by the hardware before *hwint_master* was started. In this case, manipulation of the stack by *save* will have left the address of *_restart* on the kernel stack. This results in a task, driver, server, or user process once again executing. It may not be, and in fact very likely is not, the same process as was executing when the interrupt occurred. This depends upon whether the processing of the message created by the device-specific interrupt service routine caused a change in the process scheduling queues. In the case of a hardware interrupt this will almost always be the case. Interrupt handlers usually result in messages to device drivers, and device drivers generally are queued on higher priority queues than user processes. This, then, is the heart of the mechanism which creates the illusion of multiple processes executing simultaneously.

To be complete, let us mention that if an interrupt could occur while kernel code were executing, the kernel stack would already be in use, and *save* would leave the address of *restart1* on the kernel stack. In this case, whatever the kernel was doing previously would continue after the ret at the end of *hwint_master*. This is a description of handling of nested interrupts, and these are not allowed to occur in MINIX 3— interrupts are not enabled while kernel code is running. However, as mentioned previously, the mechanism is necessary in order to handle exceptions. When all the kernel routines involved in responding to an exception are complete *_restart* will finally execute. In response to an exception while executing kernel code it will almost certainly be true that a process different from the one that was interrupted last will be put into execution. The response to an exception in the kernel is a panic, and what happens will be an attempt to shut down the system with as little damage as possible.

Hwint_slave (line 6566) is similar to *hwint_master*, except that it must reenable both the master and slave controllers, since both of them are disabled by receipt of an interrupt by the slave.

Now let us move on to look at *save* (line 6622), which we have already mentioned. Its name describes one of its functions, which is to save the context of the interrupted process on the stack provided by the CPU, which is a stackframe within the process table. *Save* uses the variable *_k_reenter* to count and determine the level of nesting of interrupts. If a process was executing when the current interrupt occurred, the

```
mov    esp, k_stktop
```

instruction on line 6635 switches to the kernel stack, and the following instruction pushes the address of *_restart*. If an interrupt could occur while the kernel stack were already in use the address of *restart1* would be pushed instead (line 6642). Of course, an interrupt is not allowed here, but the mechanism is here to handle exceptions. In either case, with a possibly different stack in use from the one that was in effect upon entry, and with the return address in the routine that called it buried beneath the registers that have just been pushed, an ordinary return instruction is not adequate for returning to the caller. The

```
jmp    RETADR-P_STACKBASE(eax)
```

instructions that terminate the two exit points of *save*, at line 6638 and line 6643 use the address that was pushed when *save* was called.

Reentrancy in the kernel causes many problems, and eliminating it resulted in simplification of code in several places. In MINIX 3 the *_k_reenter* variable still has a purpose—although ordinary interrupts cannot occur while kernel code is executing exceptions are still possible. For now, the thing to keep in mind is that the jump on line 6634 will never occur in normal operation. It is, however, necessary for dealing with exceptions.

As an aside, we must admit that the elimination of reentrancy is a case where programming got ahead of documentation in the development of MINIX 3. In some ways documentation is harder than programming—the compiler or the program will eventually reveal errors in a program. There is no such mechanism to correct comments in source code. There is a rather long comment at the start of *mpx386.s* which is, unfortunately, incorrect. The part of the comment on lines 6310 to 6315 should say that a kernel reentry can occur only when an exception is detected.

The next procedure in *mpx386.s* is *_s_call*, which begins on line 6649. Before looking at its internal details, look at how it ends. It does not end with a ret or jmp instruction. In fact, execution continues at *_restart* (line 6681). *_S_call* is the system call counterpart of the interrupt-handling mechanism. Control arrives at *_s_call* following a software interrupt, that is, execution of an int <nnn> instruction. Software interrupts are treated like hardware interrupts, except of course the index into the Interrupt Descriptor Table is encoded into the nnn part of an int <nnn> instruction, rather than being supplied by an interrupt controller chip. Thus, when *_s_call* is entered, the CPU has already switched to a stack inside the process table (supplied by the Task State Segment), and several registers have already been pushed onto this stack. By falling through to *_restart*, the call to *_s_call* ultimately terminates with an iretd instruction, and, just as with a hardware interrupt, this instruction will start whatever process is pointed to by *proc_ptr* at that point. Figure 2-40 compares the handling of a hardware interrupt and a system call using the software interrupt mechanism.

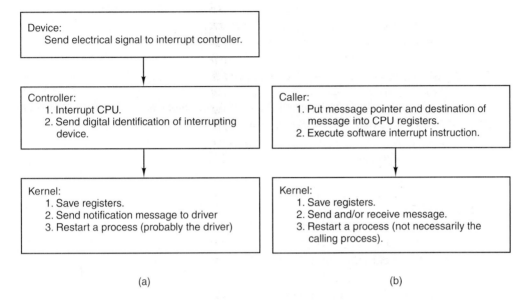

Figure 2-40. (a) How a hardware interrupt is processed. (b) How a system call is made.

Let us now look at some details of _s_call. The alternate label, _p_s_call, is a vestige of the 16-bit version of MINIX 3, which has separate routines for protected mode and real mode operation. In the 32-bit version all calls to either label end up here. A programmer invoking a MINIX 3 system call writes a function call in C that looks like any other function call, whether to a locally defined function or to a routine in the C library. The library code supporting a system call sets up a message, loads the address of the message and the process id of the destination into CPU registers, and then invokes an int SYS386_VECTOR instruction. As described above, the result is that control passes to the start of _s_call, and several registers have already been pushed onto a stack inside the process table. All interrupts are disabled, too, as with a hardware interrupt.

The first part of the _s_call code resembles an inline expansion of *save* and saves the additional registers that must be preserved. Just as in *save*, a

```
mov    esp, k_stktop
```

instruction then switches to the kernel stack. (The similarity of a software interrupt to a hardware interrupt extends to both disabling all interrupts). Following this comes a call to _sys_call (line 6672), which we will discuss in the next section. For now we just say that it causes a message to be delivered, and that this in

turn causes the scheduler to run. Thus, when _sys_call_ returns, it is probable that
_proc_ptr_ will be pointing to a different process from the one that initiated the system call. Then execution falls through to _restart_.

We have seen that _restart_ (line 6681) is reached in several ways:

1. By a call from _main_ when the system starts.

2. By a jump from _hwint_master_ or _hwint_slave_ after a hardware interrupt.

3. By falling through from _s_call_ after a system call.

Fig. 2-41 is a simplified summary of how control passes back and forth between
processes and the kernel via _restart_.

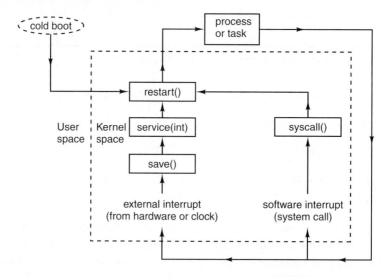

Figure 2-41. _Restart_ is the common point reached after system startup, interrupts, or system calls. The most deserving process (which may be and often is a
different process from the last one interrupted) runs next. Not shown in this diagram are interrupts that occur while the kernel itself is running.

In every case interrupts are disabled when _restart_ is reached. By line 6690
the next process to run has been definitively chosen, and with interrupts disabled
it cannot be changed. The process table was carefully constructed so it begins
with a stack frame, and the instruction on this line,

```
mov  esp, (_proc_ptr)
```

points the CPU's stack pointer register at the stack frame. The

```
lldt   P_LDT_SEL(esp)
```

instruction then loads the processor's local descriptor table register from the stack
frame. This prepares the processor to use the memory segments belonging to the

next process to be run. The following instruction sets the address in the next process' process table entry to that where the stack for the next interrupt will be set up, and the following instruction stores this address into the TSS.

The first part of _restart would not be necessary if an interrupt occured when kernel code (including interrupt service code) were executing, since the kernel stack would be in use and termination of the interrupt service would allow the kernel code to continue. But, in fact, the kernel is not reentrant in MINIX 3, and ordinary interrupts cannot occur this way. However, disabling interrupts does not disable the ability of the processor to detect exceptions. The label *restart1* (line 6694) marks the point where execution resumes if an exception occurs while executing kernel code (something we hope will never happen). At this point k_reenter is decremented to record that one level of possibly nested interrupts has been disposed of, and the remaining instructions restore the processor to the state it was in when the next process executed last. The penultimate instruction modifies the stack pointer so the return address that was pushed when *save* was called is ignored. If the last interrupt occurred when a process was executing, the final instruction, iretd, completes the return to execution of whatever process is being allowed to run next, restoring its remaining registers, including its stack segment and stack pointer. If, however, this encounter with the iretd came via *restart1*, the kernel stack in use is not a stackframe, but the kernel stack, and this is not a return to an interrupted process, but the completion of handling an exception that occurred while kernel code was executing. The CPU detects this when the code segment descriptor is popped from the stack during execution of the iretd, and the complete action of the iretd in this case is to retain the kernel stack in use.

Now it is time to say something more about exceptions. An exception is caused by various error conditions internal to the CPU. Exceptions are not always bad. They can be used to stimulate the operating system to provide a service, such as providing more memory for a process to use, or swapping in a currently swapped-out memory page, although such services are not implemented in MINIX 3. They also can be caused by programming errors. Within the kernel an exception is very serious, and grounds to panic. When an exception occurs in a user program the program may need to be terminated, but the operating system should be able to continue. Exceptions are handled by the same mechanism as interrupts, using descriptors in the interrupt descriptor table. These entries in the table point to the sixteen exception handler entry points, beginning with _divide_error and ending with _copr_error, found near the end of *mpx386.s*, on lines 6707 to 6769. These all jump to *exception* (line 6774) or *errexception* (line 6785) depending upon whether the condition pushes an error code onto the stack or not. The handling here in the assembly code is similar to what we have already seen, registers are pushed and the C routine _exception (note the underscore) is called to handle the event. The consequences of exceptions vary. Some are ignored, some cause panics, and some result in sending signals to processes. We will examine _exception in a later section.

One other entry point is handled like an interrupt: _level0_call (line 6714). It is used when code must be run with privilege level 0, the most privileged level. The entry point is here in *mpx386.s* with the interrupt and exception entry points because it too is invoked by execution of an int <nnn> instruction. Like the exception routines, it calls *save*, and thus the code that is jumped to eventually will terminate with a ret that leads to _restart. Its usage will be described in a later section, when we encounter some code that needs privileges normally not available, even to the kernel.

Finally, some data storage space is reserved at the end of the assembly language file. Two different data segments are defined here. The

.sect .rom

declaration at line 6822 ensures that this storage space is allocated at the very beginning of the kernel's data segment and that it is the start of a read-only section of memory. The compiler puts a magic number here so *boot* can verify that the file it loads is a valid kernel image. When compiling the complete system various string constants will be stored following this. The other data storage area defined at the

.sect .bss

(line 6825) declaration reserves space in the kernel's normal uninitialized variable area for the kernel stack, and above that some space is reserved for variables used by the exception handlers. Servers and ordinary processes have stack space reserved when an executable file is linked and depend upon the kernel to properly set the stack segment descriptor and the stack pointer when they are executed. The kernel has to do this for itself.

2.6.9 Interprocess Communication in MINIX 3

Processes in MINIX 3 communicate by messages, using the rendezvous principle. When a process does a send, the lowest layer of the kernel checks to see if the destination is waiting for a message from the sender (or from ANY sender). If so, the message is copied from the sender's buffer to the receiver's buffer, and both processes are marked as runnable. If the destination is not waiting for a message from the sender, the sender is marked as blocked and put onto a queue of processes waiting to send to the receiver.

When a process does a receive, the kernel checks to see if any process is queued trying to send to it. If so, the message is copied from the blocked sender to the receiver, and both are marked as runnable. If no process is queued trying to send to it, the receiver blocks until a message arrives.

In MINIX 3, with components of the operating system running as totally separate processes, sometimes the rendezvous method is not quite good enough. The notify primitive is provided for precisely these occasions. A notify sends a bare-bones message. The sender is not blocked if the destination is not waiting for a message. The notify is not lost, however. The next time the destination does a receive pending notifications are delivered before ordinary messages. Notifications can be used in situations where using ordinary messages could cause deadlocks. Earlier we pointed out that a situation where process *A* blocks sending a message to process *B* and process *B* blocks sending a message to process *A* must be avoided. But if one of the messages is a nonblocking notification there is no problem.

In most cases a notification informs the recipient of its origin, and little more. Sometimes that is all that is needed, but there are two special cases where a notification conveys some additional information. In any case, the destination process can send a message to the source of the notification to request more information.

The high-level code for interprocess communication is found in *proc.c*. The kernel's job is to translate either a hardware interrupt or a software interrupt into a message. The former are generated by hardware and the latter are the way a request for system services, that is, a system call, is communicated to the kernel. These cases are similar enough that they could have been handled by a single function, but it was more efficient to create specialized functions.

One comment and two macro definitions near the beginning of this file deserve mention. For manipulating lists, pointers to pointers are used extensively, and a comment on lines 7420 to 7436 explains their advantages and use. Two useful macros are defined. *BuildMess* (lines 7458 to 7471), although its name implies more generality, is used only for constructing the messages used by notify. The only function call is to *get_uptime*, which reads a variable maintained by the clock task so the notification can include a timestamp. The apparent calls to a function named *priv* are expansions of another macro, defined in *priv.h*,

```
#define priv(rp)      ((rp)->p_priv)
```

The other macro, *CopyMess*, is a programmer-friendly interface to the assembly language routine *cp_mess* in *klib386.s*.

More should be said about *BuildMess*. The *priv* macro is used for two special cases. If the origin of a notification is *HARDWARE*, it carries a payload, a copy of the destination process' bitmap of pending interrupts. If the origin is *SYSTEM*, the payload is the bitmap of pending signals. Because these bitmaps are available in the *priv* table slot of the destination process, they can be accessed at any time. Notifications can be delivered later if the destination process is not blocked waiting for them at the time they are sent. For ordinary messages this would require some kind of buffer in which an undelivered message could be stored. To store a notification all that is required is a bitmap in which each bit corresponds to a process that can send a notification. When a notification cannot be sent the bit corresponding to the sender is set in the recipient's bitmap. When a receive is done the bitmap is checked and if a bit is found to have been set the message is regenerated. The bit tells the origin of the message, and if the origin is *HARDWARE* or

SYSTEM, the additional content is added. The only other item needed is the time-stamp, which is added when the message is regenerated. For the purposes for which they are used, timestamps do not need to show when a notification was first attempted, the time of delivery is sufficient.

The first function in *proc.c* is *sys_call* (line 7480). It converts a software interrupt (the int SYS386_VECTOR instruction by which a system call is initiated) into a message. There are a wide range of possible sources and destinations, and the call may require either sending or receiving or both sending and receiving a message. A number of tests must be made. On lines 7480 and 7481 the function code *SEND*), *RECEIVE*, etc.,) and the flags are extracted from the first argument of the call. The first test is to see if the calling process is allowed to make the call. *Iskerneln*, used on line 7501, is a macro defined in proc.h (line 5584). The next test is to see that the specified source or destination is a valid process. Then a check is made that the message pointer points to a valid area of memory. MINIX 3 privileges define which other processes any given process is allowed to send to, and this is tested next (lines 7537 to 7541). Finally, a test is made to verify that the destination process is running and has not initiated a shutdown (lines 7543 to 7547). After all the tests have been passed one of the functions *mini_send*, *mini_receive*, or *mini_notify* is called to do the real work. If the function was *ECHO* the *CopyMess* macro is used, with identical source and destination. *ECHO* is meant only for testing, as mentioned earlier.

The errors tested for in *sys_call* are unlikely, but the tests are easily done, as ultimately they compile into code to perform comparisons of small integers. At this most basic level of the operating system testing for even the most unlikely errors is advisable. This code is likely to be executed many times each second during every second that the computer system on which it runs is active.

The functions *mini_send*, *mini_rec*, and *mini_notify* are the heart of the normal message passing mechanism of MINIX 3 and deserve careful study.

Mini_send (line 7591) has three parameters: the caller, the process to be sent to, and a pointer to the buffer where the message is. After all the tests performed by *sys_call*, only one more is necessary, which is to detect a send deadlock. The test on lines 7606 to 7610 verifies that the caller and destination are not trying to send to each other. The key test in *mini_send* is on lines 7615 and 7616. Here a check is made to see if the destination is blocked on a receive, as shown by the *RECEIVING* bit in the *p_rts_flags* field of its process table entry. If it is waiting, then the next question is: "Who is it waiting for?" If it is waiting for the sender, or for ANY, the *CopyMess* macro is used to copy the message and the receiver is unblocked by resetting its *RECEIVING* bit. Then *enqueue* is called to give the receiver an opportunity to run (line 7620).

If, on the other hand, the receiver is not blocked, or is blocked but waiting for a message from someone else, the code on lines 7623 to 7632 is executed to block and dequeue the sender. All processes wanting to send to a given destination are strung together on a linked list, with the destination's *p_callerq* field pointing to the process table entry of the process at the head of the queue. The example of Fig. 2-42(a) shows what happens when process 3 is unable to send to process 0. If process 4 is subsequently also unable to send to process 0, we get the situation of Fig. 2-42(b).

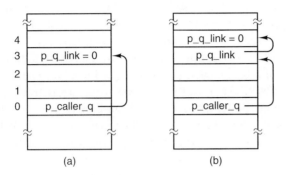

(a)   (b)

Figure 2-42. Queueing of processes trying to send to process 0.

Mini_receive (line 7642) is called by *sys_call* when its *function* parameter is *RECEIVE* or *BOTH*. As we mentioned earlier, notifications have a higher priority than ordinary messages. However, a notification will never be the right reply to a send, so the bitmaps are checked to see if there are pending notifications only if the *SENDREC_BUSY* flag is not set. If a notification is found it is marked as no longer pending and delivered (lines 7670 to 7685). Delivery uses both the *Build-Mess* and *CopyMess* macros defined near the top of *proc.c*.

One might have thought that, because a timestamp is part of a notify message, it would convey useful information, for instance, if the recipient had been unable to do a receive for a while the timestamp would tell how long it had been undelivered. But the notification message is generated (and timestamped) at the time it is delivered, not at the time it was sent. There is a purpose behind constructing the notification messages at the time of delivery, however. The code is unnecessary to save notification messages that cannot be delivered immediately. All that is necessary is to set a bit to remember that a notification should be generated when delivery becomes possible. You cannot get more economical storage than that: one bit per pending notification.

It is also the case that the current time is usually what is needed. For instance, notification is used to deliver a *SYN_ALARM* message to the process manager, and if the timestamp were not generated when the message was delivered the PM would need to ask the kernel for the correct time before checking its timer queue.

Note that only one notification is delivered at a time, *mini_send* returns on line 7684 after delivery of a notification. But the caller is not blocked, so it is free to do another receive immediately after getting the notification. If there are no notifications, the caller queues are checked to see if a message of any other type is pending (lines 7690 to 7699. If such a message is found it is delivered by the

CopyMess macro and the originator of the message is then unblocked by the call to *enqueue* on line 7694. The caller is not blocked in this case.

If no notifications or other messages were available, the caller will be blocked by the call to *dequeue* on line 7708.

Mini_notify (line 7719) is used to effectuate a notification. It is similar to *mini_send*, and can be discussed quickly. If the recipient of a message is blocked and waiting to receive, the notification is generated by *BuildMess* and delivered. The recipient's *RECEIVING* flag is turned off and it is then *enqueue*-ed (lines 7738 to 7743). If the recipient is not waiting a bit is set in its *s_notify_pending* map, which indicates that a notification is pending and identifies the sender. The sender then continues its own work, and if another notification to the same recipient is needed before an earlier one has been received, the bit in the recipient's bitmap is overwritten—effectively, multiple notifications from the same sender are merged into a single notification message. This design eliminates the need for buffer management while offering asynchronous message passing.

When *mini_notify* is called because of a software interrupt and a subsequent call to *sys_call*, interrupts will be disabled at the time. But the clock or system task, or some other task that might be added to MINIX 3 in the future might need to send a notification at a time when interrupts are not disabled. *Lock_notify* (line 7758) is a safe gateway to *mini_notify*. It checks *k_reenter* to see if interrupts are already disabled, and if they are, it just calls *mini_notify* right away. If interrupts are enabled they are disabled by a call to *lock*, *mini_notify* is called, and then interrupts are reenabled by a call to *unlock*.

2.6.10 Scheduling in MINIX 3

MINIX 3 uses a multilevel scheduling algorithm. Processes are given initial priorities that are related to the structure shown in Fig. 2-29, but there are more layers and the priority of a process may change during its execution. The clock and system tasks in layer 1 of Fig. 2-29 receive the highest priority. The device drivers of layer 2 get lower priority, but they are not all equal. Server processes in layer 3 get lower priorities than drivers, but some less than others. User processes start with less priority than any of the system processes, and initially are all equal, but the *nice* command can raise or lower the priority of a user process.

The scheduler maintains 16 queues of runnable processes, although not all of them may be used at a particular moment. Fig. 2-43 shows the queues and the processes that are in place at the instant the kernel completes initialization and begins to run, that is, at the call to *restart* at line 7252 in *main.c*. The array *rdy_head* has one entry for each queue, with that entry pointing to the process at the head of the queue. Similarly, *rdy_tail* is an array whose entries point to the last process on each queue. Both of these arrays are defined with the *EXTERN* macro in *proc.h* (lines 5595 and 5596). The initial queueing of processes during system startup is determined by the *image* table in *table.c* (lines 6095 to 6109).

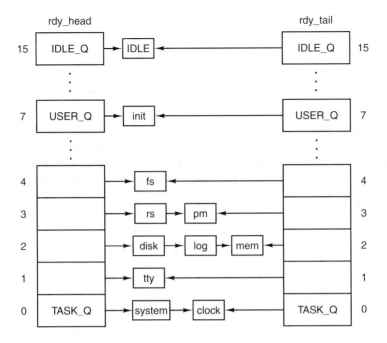

Figure 2-43. The scheduler maintains sixteen queues, one per priority level. Shown here is the initial queuing of processes as MINIX 3 starts up.

Scheduling is round robin in each queue. If a running process uses up its quantum it is moved to the tail of its queue and given a new quantum. However, when a blocked process is awakened, it is put at the head of its queue if it had any part of its quantum left when it blocked. It is not given a complete new quantum, however; it gets only what it had left when it blocked. The existence of the array *rdy_tail* makes adding a process to the end of a queue efficient. Whenever a running process becomes blocked, or a runnable process is killed by a signal, that process is removed from the scheduler's queues. Only runnable processes are queued.

Given the queue structures just described, the scheduling algorithm is simple: find the highest priority queue that is not empty and pick the process at the head of that queue. The *IDLE* process is always ready, and is in the lowest priority queue. If all the higher priority queues are empty, *IDLE* is run.

We saw a number of references to *enqueue* and *dequeue* in the last section. Now let us look at them. *Enqueue* is called with a pointer to a process table entry as its argument (line 7787). It calls another function, *sched*, with pointers to variables that determine which queue the process should be on and whether it is to be added to the head or the tail of that queue. Now there are three possibilities. These are classic data structures examples. If the chosen queue is empty, both *rdy_head* and *rdy_tail* are made to point to the process being added, and the link field, *p_nextready*, gets the special pointer value that indicates nothing follows, *NIL_PROC*. If the process is being added to the head of a queue, its *p_nextready* gets the current value of *rdy_head*, and then *rdy_head* is pointed to the new process. If the process is being added to the tail of a queue, the *p_nextready* of the current occupant of the tail is pointed to the new process, as is *rdy_tail*. The *p_nextready* of the newly-ready process then is pointed to *NIL_PROC*. Finally, *pick_proc* is called to determine which process will run next.

When a process must be made unready *dequeue* line 7823 is called. A process must be running in order to block, so the process to be removed is likely to be at the head of its queue. However, a signal could have been sent to a process that was not running. So the queue is traversed to find the victim, with a high likelihood it will be found at the head. When it is found all pointers are adjusted appropriately to take it out of the chain. If it was running, *pick_proc* must also be called.

One other point of interest is found in this function. Because tasks that run in the kernel share a common hardware-defined stack area, it is a good idea to check the integrity of their stack areas occasionally. At the beginning of *dequeue* a test is made to see if the process being removed from the queue is one that operates in kernel space. If it is, a check is made to see that the distinctive pattern written at the end of its stack area has not been overwritten (lines 7835 to 7838).

Now we come to *sched*, which picks which queue to put a newly-ready process on, and whether to put it on the head or the tail of that queue. Recorded in the process table for each process are its quantum, the time left on its quantum, its priority, and the maximum priority it is allowed. On lines 7880 to 7885 a check is made to see if the entire quantum was used. If not, it will be restarted with whatever it had left from its last turn. If the quantum was used up, then a check is made to see if the process had two turns in a row, with no other process having run. This is taken as a sign of a possible infinite, or at least, excessively long, loop, and a penalty of +1 is assigned. However, if the entire quantum was used but other processes have had a chance to run, the penalty value becomes −1. Of course, this does not help if two or more processes are executing in a loop together. How to detect that is an open problem.

Next the queue to use is determined. Queue 0 is highest priority; queue 15 is lowest. One could argue it should be the other way around, but this way is consistent with the traditional "nice" values used by UNIX, where a positive "nice" means a process runs with lower priority. Kernel processes (the clock and system tasks) are immune, but all other processes may have their priority reduced, that is, be moved to a higher-numbered queue, by adding a positive penalty. All processes start with their maximum priority, so a negative penalty does not change anything until positive penalties have been assigned. There is also a lower bound on priority, ordinary processes never can be put on the same queue as *IDLE*.

Now we come to *pick_proc* (line 7910). This function's major job is to set *next_ptr*. Any change to the queues that might affect the choice of which process to run next requires *pick_proc* to be called again. Whenever the current process blocks, *pick_proc* is called to reschedule the CPU. In essence, *pick_proc* is the scheduler.

Pick_proc is simple. Each queue is tested. *TASK_Q* is tested first, and if a process on this queue is ready, *pick_proc* sets *proc_ptr* and returns immediately. Otherwise, the next lower priority queue is tested, all the way down to *IDLE_Q*. The pointer *bill_ptr* is changed to charge the user process for the CPU time it is about to be given (line 7694). This assures that the last user process to run is charged for work done on its behalf by the system.

The remaining procedures in *proc.c* are *lock_send*, *lock_enqueue*, and *lock_dequeue*. These all provide access to their basic functions using *lock* and *unlock*, in the same way we discussed for *lock_notify*.

In summary, the scheduling algorithm maintains multiple priority queues. The first process on the highest priority queue is always run next. The clock task monitors the time used by all processes. If a user process uses up its quantum, it is put at the end of its queue, thus achieving a simple round-robin scheduling among the competing user processes. Tasks, drivers, and servers are expected to run until they block, and are given large quanta, but if they run too long they may also be preempted. This is not expected to happen very often, but it is a mechanism to prevent a high-priority process with a problem from locking up the system. A process that prevents other processes from running may also be moved to a lower priority queue temporarily.

2.6.11 Hardware-Dependent Kernel Support

Several functions written in C are nevertheless hardware specific. To facilitate porting MINIX 3 to other systems these functions are segregated in the files to be discussed in this section, *exception.c*, *i8259.c*, and *protect.c*, rather than being included in the same files with the higher-level code they support.

Exception.c contains the exception handler, *exception* (line 8012), which is called (as *_exception*) by the assembly language part of the exception handling code in *mpx386.s*. Exceptions that originate from user processes are converted to signals. Users are expected to make mistakes in their own programs, but an exception originating in the operating system indicates something is seriously wrong and causes a panic. The array *ex_data* (lines 8022 to 8040) determines the error message to be printed in case of panic, or the signal to be sent to a user process for each exception. Earlier Intel processors do not generate all the exceptions, and the third field in each entry indicates the minimum processor model that is capable of generating each one. This array provides an interesting summary of the evolution of the Intel family of processors upon which MINIX 3 has been implemented. On line 8065 an alternate message is printed if a panic results from an interrupt that would not be expected from the processor in use.

Hardware-Dependent Interrupt Support

The three functions in *i8259.c* are used during system initialization to initialize the Intel 8259 interrupt controller chips. The macro on line 8119 defines a dummy function (the real one is needed only when MINIX 3 is compiled for a 16-bit Intel platform). *Intr_init* (line 8124) initializes the controllers. Two steps ensure that no interrupts will occur before all the initialization is complete. First *intr_disable* is called at line 8134. This is a C language call to an assembly language function in the library that executes a single instruction, cli, which disables the CPU's response to interrupts. Then a sequence of bytes is written to registers on each interrupt controller, the effect of which is to inhibit response of the controllers to external input. The byte written at line 8145 is all ones, except for a zero at the bit that controls the cascade input from the slave controller to the master controller (see Fig. 2-39). A zero enables an input, a one disables. The byte written to the secondary controller at line 8151 is all ones.

A table stored in the i8259 interrupt controller chip generates an 8-bit index that the CPU uses to find the correct interrupt gate descriptor for each possible interrupt input (the signals on the right-hand side of Fig. 2-39). This is initialized by the BIOS when the computer starts up, and these values can almost all be left in place. As drivers that need interrupts start up, changes can be made where necessary. Each driver can then request that a bit be reset in the interrupt controller chip to enable its own interrupt input. The argument *mine* to *intr_init* is used to determine whether MINIX 3 is starting up or shutting down. This function can be used both to initialize at startup and to restore the BIOS settings when MINIX 3 shuts down.

After initialization of the hardware is complete, the last step in *intr_init* is to copy the BIOS interrupt vectors to the MINIX 3 vector table.

The second function in *8259.c* is *put_irq_handler* (line 8162). At initialization *put_irq_handler* is called for each process that must respond to an interrupt. This puts the address of the handler routine into the interrupt table, *irq_handlers*, defined as *EXTERN* in *glo.h*. With modern computers 15 interrupt lines is not always enough (because there may be more than 15 I/O devices) so two I/O devices may need to share an interrupt line. This will not occur with any of the basic devices supported by MINIX 3 as described in this text, but when network interfaces, sound cards, or more esoteric I/O devices must be supported they may need to share interrupt lines. To allow for this, the interrupt table is not just a table of addresses. *Irq_handlers[NR_IRQ_VECTORS]* is an array of pointers to *irq_hook* structs, a type defined in *kernel/type.h*. These structures contain a field which is a pointer to another structure of the same type, so a linked list can be built, starting with one of the elements of *irq_handlers*. *Put_irq_handler* adds an entry to one of these lists. The most important element of such an entry is a pointer to an **interrupt handler**, the function to be executed when an interrupt is generated, for example, when requested I/O has completed.

Some details of *put_irq_handler* deserve mention. Note the variable *id* which is set to 1 just before the beginning of the while loop that scans through the linked list (lines 8176 to 8180). Each time through the loop *id* is shifted left 1 bit. The test on line 8181 limits the length of the chain to the size of *id*, or 32 handlers for a 32-bit system. In the normal case the scan will result in finding the end of the chain, where a new handler can be linked. When this is done, *id* is also stored in the field of the same name in the new item on the chain. *Put_irq_handler* also sets a bit in the global variable *irq_use*, to record that a handler exists for this IRQ.

If you fully understand the MINIX 3 design goal of putting device drivers in user-space, the preceding discussion of how interrupt handlers are called will have left you slightly confused. The interrupt handler addresses stored in the hook structures cannot be useful unless they point to functions within the kernel's address space. The only interrupt-driven device in the kernel's address space is the clock. What about device drivers that have their own address spaces?

The answer is, the system task handles it. Indeed, that is the answer to most questions regarding communication between the kernel and processes in user-space. A user space device driver that is to be interrupt driven makes a sys_irqctl call to the system task when it needs to register as an interrupt handler. The system task then calls *put_irq_handler*, but instead of the address of an interrupt handler in the driver's address space, the address of *generic_handler*, part of the system task, is stored in the interrupt handler field. The process number field in the hook structure is used by *generic_handler* to locate the *priv* table entry for the driver, and the bit in the driver's pending interrupts bitmap corresponding to the interrupt is set. Then *generic_handler* sends a notification to the driver. The notification is identified as being from *HARDWARE*, and the pending interrupts bitmap for the driver is included in the message. Thus, if a driver must respond to interrupts from more than one source, it can learn which one is responsible for the current notification. In fact, since the bitmap is sent, one notification provides information on all pending interrupts for the driver. Another field in the hook structure is a policy field, which determines whether the interrupt is to be reenabled immediately, or whether it should remain disabled. In the latter case, it will be up to the driver to make a sys_irqenable kernel call when service of the current interrupt is complete.

One of the goals of MINIX 3 design is to support run-time reconfiguration of I/O devices. The next function, *rm_irq_handler*, removes a handler, a necessary step if a device driver is to be removed and possibly replaced by another. Its action is just the opposite of *put_irq_handler*.

The last function in this file, *intr_handle* (line 8221), is called from the *hwint_master* and *hwint_slave* macros we saw in *mpx386.s*. The element of the array of bitmaps *irq_actids* which corresponds the interrupt being serviced is used to keep track of the current status of each handler in a list. For each function in the list, *intr_handle* sets the corresponding bit in *irq_actids*, and calls the handler.

If a handler has nothing to do or if it completes its work immediately, it returns "true" and the corresponding bit in *irq_actids* is cleared. The entire bitmap for an interrupt, considered as an integer, is tested near the end of the *hwint_master* and *hwint_slave* macros to determine if that interrupt can be reenabled before another process is restarted.

Intel Protected Mode Support

Protect.c contains routines related to protected mode operation of Intel processors. The **Global Descriptor Table** (GDT), **Local Descriptor Tables** (LDTs), and the **Interrupt Descriptor Table**, all located in memory, provide protected access to system resources. The **GDT** and **IDT** are pointed to by special registers within the CPU, and GDT entries point to **LDT**s. The GDT is available to all processes and holds segment descriptors for memory regions used by the operating system. Normally, there is one LDT for each process, holding segment descriptors for the memory regions used by the process. Descriptors are 8-byte structures with a number of components, but the most important parts of a segment descriptor are the fields that describe the base address and the limit of a memory region. The IDT is also composed of 8-byte descriptors, with the most important part being the address of the code to be executed when the corresponding interrupt is activated.

Cstart in *start.c* calls *prot_init* (line 8368), which sets up the GDT on lines 8421 to 8438. The IBM PC BIOS requires that it be ordered in a certain way, and all the indices into it are defined in *protect.h*. Space for an LDT for each process is allocated in the process table. Each contains two descriptors, for a code segment and a data segment—recall we are discussing here segments as defined by the hardware; these are not the same as the segments managed by the operating system, which considers the hardware-defined data segment to be further divided into data and stack segments. On lines 8444 to 8450 descriptors for each LDT are built in the GDT. The functions *init_dataseg* and *init_codeseg* build these descriptors. The entries in the LDTs themselves are initialized when a process' memory map is changed (i.e., when an exec system call is made).

Another processor data structure that needs initialization is the **Task State Segment** (TSS). The structure is defined at the start of this file (lines 8325 to 8354) and provides space for storage of processor registers and other information that must be saved when a task switch is made. MINIX 3 uses only the fields that define where a new stack is to be built when an interrupt occurs. The call to *init_dataseg* on line 8460 ensures that it can be located using the GDT.

To understand how MINIX 3 works at the lowest level, perhaps the most important thing is to understand how exceptions, hardware interrupts, or int <nnn> instructions lead to the execution of the various pieces of code that has been written to service them. These events are processed by means of the interrupt gate descriptor table. The array *gate_table* (lines 8383 to 8418), is initialized by the compiler with the addresses of the routines that handle exceptions and hardware interrupts and then is used in the loop at lines 8464 to 8468 to initialize this table, using calls to the *int_gate* function.

There are good reasons for the way the data are structured in the descriptors, based on details of the hardware and the need to maintain compatibility between advanced processors and the 16-bit 286 processor. Fortunately, we can usually leave these details to Intel's processor designers. For the most part, the C language allows us to avoid the details. However, in implementing a real operating system the details must be faced at some point. Figure 2-44 shows the internal structure of one kind of segment descriptor. Note that the base address, which C programs can refer to as a simple 32-bit unsigned integer, is split into three parts, two of which are separated by a number of 1-, 2-, and 4-bit quantities. The limit is a 20-bit quantity stored as separate 16-bit and 4-bit chunks. The limit is interpreted as either a number of bytes or a number of 4096-byte pages, based on the value of the *G* (granularity) bit. Other descriptors, such as those used to specify how interrupts are handled, have different, but equally complex structures. We discuss these structures in more detail in Chap. 4.

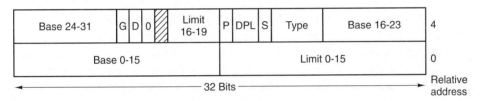

Figure 2-44. The format of an Intel segment descriptor.

Most of the other functions defined in *protect.c* are devoted to converting between variables used in C programs and the rather ugly forms these data take in the machine readable descriptors such as the one in Fig. 2-44. *Init_codeseg* (line 8477) and *init_dataseg* (line 8493) are similar in operation and are used to convert the parameters passed to them into segment descriptors. They each, in turn, call the next function, *sdesc* (line 8508), to complete the job. This is where the messy details of the structure shown in Fig. 2-44 are dealt with. *Init_codeseg* and *init_data_seg* are not used just at system initialization. They are also called by the system task whenever a new process is started up, in order to allocate the proper memory segments for the process to use. *Seg2phys* (line 8533), called only from *start.c*, performs an operation which is the inverse of that of *sdesc*, extracting the base address of a segment from a segment descriptor. *Phys2seg* (line 8556), is no longer needed, the sys_segctl kernel call now handles access to remote memory segments, for instance, memory in the PC's reserved area between 640K and 1M. *Int_gate* (line 8571) performs a similar function to *init_codeseg* and *init_dataseg* in building entries for the interrupt descriptor table.

Now we come to a function in *protect.c*, *enable_iop* (line 8589), that can perform a dirty trick. It changes the privilege level for I/O operations, allowing the current process to execute instructions which read and write I/O ports. The description of the purpose of the function is more complicated than the function itself, which just sets two bits in the word in the stack frame entry of the calling process that will be loaded into the CPU status register when the process is next executed. A function to undo this is not needed, as it will apply only to the calling process. This function is not currently used and no method is provided for a user space function to activate it.

The final function in *protect.c* is *alloc_segments* (line 8603). It is called by *do_newmap*. It is also called by the *main* routine of the kernel during initialization. This definition is very hardware dependent. It takes the segment assignments that are recorded in a process table entry and manipulates the registers and descriptors the Pentium processor uses to support protected segments at the hardware level. Multiple assignments like those on lines 8629 to 8633 are a feature of the C language.

2.6.12 Utilities and the Kernel Library

Finally, the kernel has a library of support functions written in assembly language that are included by compiling *klib.s* and a few utility programs, written in C, in the file *misc.c*. Let us first look at the assembly language files. *Klib.s* (line 8700) is a short file similar to *mpx.s*, which selects the appropriate machine-specific version based upon the definition of *WORD_SIZE*. The code we will discuss is in *klib386.s* (line 8800). This contains about two dozen utility routines that are in assembly code, either for efficiency or because they cannot be written in C at all.

_Monitor (line 8844) makes it possible to return to the boot monitor. From the point of view of the boot monitor, all of MINIX 3 is just a subroutine, and when MINIX 3 is started, a return address to the monitor is left on the monitor's stack. *_Monitor* just has to restore the various segment selectors and the stack pointer that was saved when MINIX 3 was started, and then return as from any other subroutine.

Int86 (line 8864) supports BIOS calls. The BIOS is used to provide alternative disk drivers which are not described here. *Int86* transfers control to the boot monitor, which manages a transfer from protected mode to real mode to execute a BIOS call, then back to protected mode for the return to 32-bit MINIX 3. The boot monitor also returns the number of clock ticks counted during the BIOS call. How this is used will be seen in the discussion of the clock task.

Although *_phys_copy* (see below) could have been used for copying messages, *_cp_mess* (line 8952), a faster specialized procedure, has been provided for that purpose. It is called by

```
cp_mess(source, src_clicks, src_offset, dest_clicks, dest_offset);
```

where *source* is the sender's process number, which is copied into the *m_source* field of the receiver's buffer. Both the source and destination addresses are specified by giving a click number, typically the base of the segment containing the buffer, and an offset from that click. This form of specifying the source and destination is more efficient than the 32-bit addresses used by *_phys_copy*.

_Exit, *__exit,* and *___exit* (lines 9006 to 9008) are defined because some library routines that might be used in compiling MINIX 3 make calls to the standard C function *exit.* An exit from the kernel is not a meaningful concept; there is nowhere to go. Consequently, the standard *exit* cannot be used here. The solution here is to enable interrupts and enter an endless loop. Eventually, an I/O operation or the clock will cause an interrupt and normal system operation will resume. The entry point for *___main* (line 9012) is another attempt to deal with a compiler action which, while it might make sense while compiling a user program, does not have any purpose in the kernel. It points to an assembly language ret (return from subroutine) instruction.

_Phys_insw (line 9022), *_phys_insb* (line 9047), *_phys_outsw* (line 9072), and *_phys_outsb* (line 9098), provide access to I/O ports, which on Intel hardware occupy a separate address space from memory and use different instructions from memory reads and writes. The I/O instructions used here, ins, insb, outs, and outsb, are designed to work efficiently with arrays (strings), and either 16-bit words or 8-bit bytes. The additional instructions in each function set up all the parameters needed to move a given number of bytes or words between a buffer, addressed physically, and a port. This method provides the speed needed to service disks, which must be serviced more rapidly than could be done with simpler byte- or word-at-a-time I/O operations.

A single machine instruction can enable or disable the CPU's response to all interrupts. *_Enable_irq* (line 9126) and *_disable_irq* (line 9162) are more complicated. They work at the level of the interrupt controller chips to enable and disable individual hardware interrupts.

_Phys_copy (line 9204) is called in C by

phys_copy(source_address, destination_address, bytes);

and copies a block of data from anywhere in physical memory to anywhere else. Both addresses are absolute, that is, address 0 really means the first byte in the entire address space, and all three parameters are unsigned longs.

For security, all memory to be used by a program should be wiped clean of any data remaining from a program that previously occupied that memory. This is done by the MINIX 3 exec call, ultimately using the next function in *klib386.s*, *phys_memset* (line 9248).

The next two short functions are specific to Intel processors. *_Mem_rdw* (line 9291) returns a 16-bit word from anywhere in memory. The result is zero-extended into the 32-bit *eax* register. The *_reset* function (line 9307) resets the processor. It does this by loading the processor's interrupt descriptor table register with a null pointer and then executing a software interrupt. This has the same effect as a hardware reset.

The *idle_task* (line 9318) is called when there is nothing else to do. It is written as an endless loop, but it is not just a busy loop (which could have been used to have the same effect). *Idle_task* takes advantage of the availability of a hlt instruction, which puts the processor into a power-conserving mode until an interrupt is received. However, hlt is a privileged instruction and executing hlt when the current privilege level is not 0 will cause an exception. So *idle_task* pushes the address of a subroutine containing a hlt and then calls *level0* (line 9322). This function retrieves the address of the *halt* subroutine, and copies it to a reserved storage area (declared in *glo.h* and actually reserved in *table.c*).

_Level0 treats whatever address is preloaded to this area as the functional part of an interrupt service routine to be run with the most privileged permission level, level zero.

The last two functions are *read_tsc* and *read_flags*. The former reads a CPU register which executes an assembly language instruction known as rdtsc, read time stamp counter. This counts CPU cycles and is intended for benchmarking or debugging. This instruction is not supported by the MINIX 3 assembler, and is generated by coding the opcode in hexadecimal. Finally, *read_flags* reads the processor flags and returns them as a C variable. The programmer was tired and the comment about the purpose of this function is incorrect.

The last file we will consider in this chapter is *utility.c* which provides three important functions. When something goes really, really wrong in the kernel, *panic* (line 9429) is invoked. It prints a message and calls *prepare_shutdown*. When the kernel needs to print a message it cannot use the standard library *printf*, so a special *kprintf* is defined here (line 9450). The full range of formatting options available in the library version are not needed here, but much of the functionality is available. Because the kernel cannot use the file system to access a file or a device, it passes each character to another function, *kputc* (line 9525), which appends each character to a buffer. Later, when *kputc* receives the *END_OF_KMESS* code it informs the process which handles such messages. This is defined in *include/minix/config.h*, and can be either the log driver or the console driver. If it is the log driver the message will be passed on to the console as well.

2.7 THE SYSTEM TASK IN MINIX 3

A consequence of making major system components independent processes outside the kernel is that they are forbidden from doing actual I/O, manipulating kernel tables and doing other things operating system functions normally do. For example, the fork system call is handled by the process manager. When a new process is created, the kernel must know about it, in order to schedule it. How can the process manager tell the kernel?

The solution to this problem is to have a kernel offer a set of services to the drivers and servers. These services, which are not available to ordinary user processes, allow the drivers and servers to do actual I/O, access kernel tables, and do other things they need to, all without being inside the kernel.

These special services are handled by the **system task**, which is shown in layer 1 in Fig. 2-29. Although it is compiled into the kernel binary program, it is really a separate process and is scheduled as such. The job of the system task is to accept all the requests for special kernel services from the drivers and servers and carry them out. Since the system task is part of the kernel's address space, it makes sense to study it here.

Earlier in this chapter we saw an example of a service provided by the system task. In the discussion of interrupt handling we described how a user-space device driver uses sys_irqctl to send a message to the system task to ask for installation of an interrupt handler. A user-space driver cannot access the kernel data structure where addresses of interrupt service routines are placed, but the system task is able to do this. Furthermore, since the interrupt service routine must also be in the kernel's address space, the address stored is the address of a function provided by the system task, *generic_handler*. This function responds to an interrupt by sending a notification message to the device driver.

This is a good place to clarify some terminology. In a conventional operating system with a monolithic kernel, the term **system call** is used to refer to all calls for services provided by the kernel. In a modern UNIX-like operating system the POSIX standard describes the system calls available to processes. There may be some nonstandard extensions to POSIX, of course, and a programmer taking advantage of a system call will generally reference a function defined in the C libraries, which may provide an easy-to-use programming interface. Also, sometimes separate library functions that appear to the programmer to be distinct "system calls" actually use the same access to the kernel.

In MINIX 3 the landscape is different; components of the operating system run in user space, although they have special privileges as system processes. We will still use the name "system call" for any of the POSIX-defined system calls (and a few MINIX extensions) listed in Fig. 1-9, but user processes do not request services directly of the kernel. In MINIX 3 system calls by user processes are transformed into messages to server processes. Server processes communicate with each other, with device drivers, and with the kernel by messages. The subject of this section, the system task, receives all requests for kernel services. Loosely speaking, we could call these requests system calls, but to be more exact we will refer to them as **kernel calls**. Kernel calls cannot be made by user processes. In many cases a system call that originates with a user process results in a kernel call with a similar name being made by a server. This is always because some part of the service being requested can only be dealt with by the kernel. For instance a fork system call by a user process goes to the process manager, which does some of the work. But a fork requires changes in the kernel part of the process table, and to complete the action the process manager makes a sys_fork call to the system task, which can manipulate data in kernel space. Not all kernel calls have such a clear connection to a single system call. For instance, there is a sys_devio kernel call to read or write I/O ports. This kernel call comes from a device driver. More than half of all the system calls listed in Fig. 1-9 could result in a device driver being activated and making one or more sys_devio calls.

Technically speaking, a third category of calls (besides system calls and kernel calls) should be distinguished. The **message primitives** used for interprocess communication such as send, receive, and notify can be thought of as system-call-like. We have probably called them that in various places in this book—after all, they do call the system. But they should properly be called something different from both system calls and kernel calls. Other terms may be used. **IPC primitive** is sometimes used, as well as **trap**, and both of these may be found in some comments in the source code. You can think of a message primitive as being like the carrier wave in a radio communications system. Modulation is usually needed to make a radio wave useful; the message type and other components of a message structure allow the message call to convey information. In a few cases an unmodulated radio wave is useful; for instance, a radio beacon to guide airplanes to an airport. This is analogous to the notify message primitive, which conveys little information other than its origin.

2.7.1 Overview of the System Task

The system task accepts 28 kinds of messages, shown in Fig. 2-45. Each of these can be considered a kernel call, although, as we shall see, in some cases there are multiple macros defined with different names that all result in just one of the message types shown in the figure. And in some other cases more than one of the message types in the figure are handled by a single procedure that does the work.

The main program of the system task is structured like other tasks. After doing necessary initialization it runs in a loop. It gets a message, dispatches to the appropriate service procedure, and then sends a reply. A few general support functions are found in the main file, *system.c*, but the main loop dispatches to a procedure in a separate file in the *kernel/system/* directory to process each kernel call. We will see how this works and the reason for this organization when we discuss the implementation of the system task.

First we will briefly describe the function of each kernel call. The message types in Fig. 2-45 fall into several categories. The first few are involved with process management. Sys_fork, sys_exec, sys_exit, and sys_trace are obviously closely related to standard POSIX system calls. Although *nice* is not a POSIX-required system call, the command ultimately results in a sys_nice kernel call to

Message type	From	Meaning
sys_fork	PM	A process has forked
sys_exec	PM	Set stack pointer after EXEC call
sys_exit	PM	A process has exited
sys_nice	PM	Set scheduling priority
sys_privctl	RS	Set or change privileges
sys_trace	PM	Carry out an operation of the PTRACE call
sys_kill	PM,FS, TTY	Send signal to a process after KILL call
sys_getksig	PM	PM is checking for pending signals
sys_endksig	PM	PM has finished processing signal
sys_sigsend	PM	Send a signal to a process
sys_sigreturn	PM	Cleanup after completion of a signal
sys_irqctl	Drivers	Enable, disable, or configure interrupt
sys_devio	Drivers	Read from or write to an I/O port
sys_sdevio	Drivers	Read or write string from/to I/O port
sys_vdevio	Drivers	Carry out a vector of I/O requests
sys_int86	Drivers	Do a real-mode BIOS call
sys_newmap	PM	Set up a process memory map
sys_segctl	Drivers	Add segment and get selector (far data access)
sys_memset	PM	Write char to memory area
sys_umap	Drivers	Convert virtual address to physical address
sys_vircopy	FS, Drivers	Copy using pure virtual addressing
sys_physcopy	Drivers	Copy using physical addressing
sys_virvcopy	Any	Vector of VCOPY requests
sys_physvcopy	Any	Vector of PHYSCOPY requests
sys_times	PM	Get uptime and process times
sys_setalarm	PM, FS, Drivers	Schedule a synchronous alarm
sys_abort	PM, TTY	Panic: MINIX is unable to continue
sys_getinfo	Any	Request system information

Figure 2-45. The message types accepted by the system task. "Any" means any system process; user processes cannot call the system task directly.

change the priority of a process. The only one of this group that is likely to be unfamiliar is sys_privctl. It is used by the reincarnation server (RS), the MINIX 3 component responsible for converting processes started as ordinary user processes into system processes. Sys_privctl changes the privileges of a process, for instance, to allow it to make kernel calls. Sys_privctl is used when drivers and servers that are not part of the boot image are started by the */etc/rc* script. MINIX

3 drivers also can be started (or restarted) at any time; privilege changes are needed whenever this is done.

The next group of kernel calls are related to signals. Sys_kill is related to the user-accessible (and misnamed) system call kill. The others in this group, sys_getksig, sys_endksig, sys_sigsend, and sys_sigreturn are all used by the process manager to get the kernel's help in handling signals.

The sys_irqctl, sys_devio, sys_sdevio, and sys_vdevio kernel calls are unique to MINIX 3. These provide the support needed for user-space device drivers. We mentioned sys_irqctl at the start of this section. One of its functions is to set a hardware interrupt handler and enable interrupts on behalf of a user-space driver. Sys_devio allows a user-space driver to ask the system task to read or write from an I/O port. This is obviously essential; it also should be obvious that it involves more overhead than would be the case if the driver were running in kernel space. The next two kernel calls offer a higher level of I/O device support. Sys_sdevio can be used when a sequence of bytes or words, i.e., a string, is to be read from or written to a single I/O address, as might be the case when accessing a serial port. Sys_vdevio is used to send a vector of I/O requests to the system task. By a vector is meant a series of (port, value) pairs. Earlier in this chapter, we described the *intr_init* function that initializes the Intel i8259 interrupt controllers. On lines 8140 to 8152 a series of instructions writes a series of byte values. For each of the two i8259 chips, there is a control port that sets the mode and another port that receives a sequence of four bytes in the initialization sequence. Of course, this code executes in the kernel, so no support from the system task is needed. But if this were being done by a user-space process a single message passing the address to a buffer containing 10 (port, value) pairs would be much more efficient than 10 messages each passing one port address and a value to be written.

The next three kernel calls shown in Fig. 2-45 involve memory in distinct ways. The first, sys_newmap, is called by the process manager when the memory used by a process changes, so the kernel's part of the process table can be updated. Sys_segctl and sys_memset provide a safe way to provide a process with access to memory outside its own data space. The memory area from 0xa0000 to 0xfffff is reserved for I/O devices, as we mentioned in the discussion of startup of the MINIX 3 system. Some devices use part of this memory region for I/O—for instance, video display cards expect to have data to be displayed written into memory on the card which is mapped here. Sys_segctl is used by a device driver to obtain a segment selector that will allow it to address memory in this range. The other call, sys_memset, is used when a server wants to write data into an area of memory that does not belong to it. It is used by the process manager to zero out memory when a new process is started, to prevent the new process from reading data left by another process.

The next group of kernel calls is for copying memory. Sys_umap converts virtual addresses to physical addresses. Sys_vircopy and sys_physcopy copy regions of memory, using either virtual or physical addresses. The next two calls, sys_virvcopy and sys_physvcopy are vector versions of the previous two. As with vectored I/O requests, these allow making a request to the system task for a series of memory copy operations.

Sys_times obviously has to do with time, and corresponds to the POSIX times system call. Sys_setalarm is related to the POSIX alarm system call, but the relation is a distant one. The POSIX call is mostly handled by the process manager, which maintains a queue of timers on behalf of user processes. The process manager uses a sys_setalarm kernel call when it needs to have a timer set on its behalf in the kernel. This is done only when there is a change at the head of the queue managed by the PM, and does not necessarily follow every alarm call from a user process.

The final two kernel calls listed in Fig. 2-45 are for system control. Sys_abort can originate in the process manager, after a normal request to shutdown the system or after a panic. It can also originate from the tty device driver, in response to a user pressing the Ctrl-Alt-Del key combination.

Finally, sys_getinfo is a catch-all that handles a diverse range of requests for information from the kernel. If you search through the MINIX 3 C source files you will, in fact, find very few references to this call by its own name. But if you extend your search to the header directories you will find no less than 13 macros in *include/minix/syslib.h* that give another name to Sys_getinfo. An example is

sys_getkinfo(dst)   sys_getinfo(GET_KINFO, dst, 0,0,0)

which is used to return the *kinfo* structure (defined in *include/minix/type.h* on lines 2875 to 2893) to the process manager for use during system startup. The same information may be needed at other times. For instance, the user command *ps* needs to know the location of the kernel's part of the process table to display information about the status of all processes. It asks the PM, which in turn uses the *sys_getkinfo* variant of sys_getinfo to get the information.

Before we leave this overview of kernel call types, we should mention that sys_getinfo is not the only kernel call that is invoked by a number of different names defined as macros in *include/minix/syslib.h*. For example, the sys_sdevio call is usually invoked by one of the macros sys_insb, sys_insw, sys_outsb, or sys_outsw. The names were devised to make it easy to see whether the operation is input or output, with data types byte or word. Similarly, the sys_irqctl call is usually invoked by a macro like sys_irqenable, sys_irqdisable, or one of several others. Such macros make the meaning clearer to a person reading the code. They also help the programmer by automatically generating constant arguments.

2.7.2 Implementation of the System Task

The system task is compiled from a header, *system.h*, and a C source file, *system.c*, in the main *kernel/* directory. In addition there is a specialized library built from source files in a subdirectory, *kernel/system/*. There is a reason for this organization. Although MINIX 3 as we describe it here is a general-purpose operating system, it is also potentially useful for special purposes, such as embedded support in a portable device. In such cases a stripped-down version of the operating system might be adequate. For instance, a device without a disk might not need a file system. We saw in *kernel/config.h* that compilation of kernel calls can be selectively enabled and disabled. Having the code that supports each kernel call linked from the library as the last stage of compilation makes it easier to build a customized system.

Putting support for each kernel call in a separate file simplifies maintenance of the software. But there is some redundancy between these files, and listing all of them would add 40 pages to the length of this book. Thus we will list in Appendix B and describe in the text only a few of the files in the *kernel/system/* directory. However, all the files are on the CD-ROM and the MINIX 3 Web site.

We will begin by looking at the header file, *kernel/system.h* (line 9600). It provides prototypes for functions corresponding to most of the kernel calls listed in Fig. 2-45. In addition there is a prototype for *do_unused*, the function that is invoked if an unsupported kernel call is made. Some of the message types in Fig. 2-45 correspond to macros defined here. These are on lines 9625 to 9630. These are cases where one function can handle more than one call.

Before looking at the code in *system.c*, note the declaration of the call vector *call_vec*, and the definition of the macro *map* on lines 9745 to 9749. *Call_vec* is an array of pointers to functions, which provides a mechanism for dispatching to the function needed to service a particular message by using the message type, expressed as a number, as an index into the array. This is a technique we will see used elsewhere in MINIX 3. The *map* macro is a convenient way to initialize such an array. The macro is defined in such a way that trying to expand it with an invalid argument will result in declaring an array with a negative size, which is, of course, impossible, and will cause a compiler error.

The top level of the system task is the procedure *sys_task*. After a call to initialize an array of pointers to functions, *sys_task* runs in a loop. It waits for a message, makes a few tests to validate the message, dispatches to the function that handles the call that corresponds to the message type, possibly generating a reply message, and repeats the cycle as long as MINIX 3 is running (lines 9768 to 9796). The tests consists of a check of the *priv* table entry for the caller to determine that it is allowed to make this type of call and making sure that this type of call is valid. The dispatch to the function that does the work is done on line 9783. The index into the *call_vec* array is the call number, the function called is the one whose address is in that cell of the array, the argument to the function is a pointer to the message, and the return value is a status code. A function may return a *EDONTREPLY* status, meaning no reply message is required, otherwise a reply message is sent at line 9792.

As you may have noticed in Fig. 2-43, when MINIX 3 starts up the system task is at the head of the highest priority queue, so it makes sense that the system task's *initialize* function initializes the array of interrupt hooks and the list of alarm timers (lines 9808 to 9815). In any case, as we noted earlier, the system task is used to enable interrupts on behalf of user-space drivers that need to respond to interrupts, so it makes sense to have it prepare the table. The system task is used to set up timers when synchronous alarms are requested by other system processes, so initializing the timer lists is also appropriate here.

Continuing with initialization, on lines 9822 to 9824 all slots in the *call_vec* array are filled with the address of the procedure *do_unused*, called if an unsupported kernel call is made. Then the rest of the file lines 9827 to 9867, consists of multiple expansions of the *map* macro, each one of which installs the address of a function into the proper slot in *call_vec*.

The rest of *system.c* consists of functions that are declared *PUBLIC* and that may be used by more than one of the routines that service kernel calls, or by other parts of the kernel. For instance, the first such function, *get_priv* (line 9872), is used by *do_privctl*, which supports the sys_privctl kernel call. It is also called by the kernel itself while constructing process table entries for processes in the boot image. The name is a perhaps a bit misleading. *Get_priv* does not retrieve information about privileges already assigned, it finds an available *priv* structure and assigns it to the caller. There are two cases—system processes each get their own entry in the *priv* table. If one is not available then the process cannot become a system process. User processes all share the same entry in the table.

Get_randomness (line 9899) is used to get seed numbers for the random number generator, which is a implemented as a character device in MINIX 3. The newest Pentium-class processors include an internal cycle counter and provide an assembly language instruction that can read it. This is used if available, otherwise a function is called which reads a register in the clock chip.

Send_sig generates a notification to a system process after setting a bit in the *s_sig_pending* bitmap of the process to be signaled. The bit is set on line 9942. Note that because the *s_sig_pending* bitmap is part of a *priv* structure, this mechanism can only be used to notify system processes. All user processes share a common *priv* table entry, and therefore fields like the *s_sig_pending* bitmap cannot be shared and are not used by user processes. Verification that the target is a system process is made before *send_sig* is called. The call comes either as a result of a *sys_kill* kernel call, or from the kernel when *kprintf* is sending a string of characters. In the former case the caller determines whether or not the target is a system process. In the latter case the kernel only prints to the configured output process, which is either the console driver or the log driver, both of which are system processes.

The next function, *cause_sig* (line 9949), is called to send a signal to a user process. It is used when a *sys_kill* kernel call targets a user process. It is here in *system.c* because it also may be called directly by the kernel in response to an exception triggered by the user process. As with *send_sig* a bit must be set in the recipient's bitmap for pending signals, but for user processes this is not in the *priv* table, it is in the process table. The target process must also be made not ready by a call to *lock_dequeue*, and its flags (also in the process table) updated to indicate it is going to be signaled. Then a message is sent—but not to the target process. The message is sent to the process manager, which takes care of all of the aspects of signaling a process that can be dealt with by a user-space system process.

Next come three functions which all support the sys_umap kernel call. Processes normally deal with virtual addresses, relative to the base of a particular segment. But sometimes they need to know the absolute (physical) address of a region of memory, for instance, if a request is going to be made for copying between memory regions belonging to two different segments. There are three ways a virtual memory address might be specified. The normal one for a process is relative to one of the memory segments, text, data, or stack, assigned to a process and recorded in its process table slot. Requesting conversion of virtual to physical memory in this case is done by a call to *umap_local* (line 9983).

The second kind of memory reference is to a region of memory that is outside the text, data, or stack areas allocated to a process, but for which the process has some responsibility. Examples of this are a video driver or an Ethernet driver, where the video or Ethernet card might have a region of memory mapped in the region from 0xa0000 to 0xfffff which is reserved for I/O devices. Another example is the memory driver, which manages the ramdisk and also can provide access to any part of the memory through the devices */dev/mem* and */dev/kmem*. Requests for conversion of such memory references from virtual to physical are handled by *umap_remote* (line 10025).

Finally, a memory reference may be to memory that is used by the BIOS. This is considered to include both the lowest 2 KB of memory, below where MINIX 3 is loaded, and the region from 0x90000 to 0xfffff, which includes some RAM above where MINIX 3 is loaded plus the region reserved for I/O devices. This could also be handled by *umap_remote*, but using the third function, *umap_bios* (line 10047), ensures that a check will be made that the memory being referenced is really in this region.

The last function defined in *system.c* is *virtual_copy* (line 10071). Most of this function is a C switch which uses one of the three *umap_* functions just described to convert virtual addresses to physical addresses. This is done for both the source and destination addresses. The actual copying is done (on line 10121) by a call to the assembly language routine *phys_copy* in *klib386.s*.

2.7.3 Implementation of the System Library

Each of the functions with a name of the form *do_xyz* has its source code in a file in a subdirectory, *kernel/system/do_xyz.c*. In the *kernel/* directory the *Makefile* contains a line

```
cd system && $(MAKE) −$(MAKEFLAGS) $@
```

which causes all of the files in *kernel/system/* to be compiled into a library, *system.a* in the main *kernel/* directory. When control returns to the main kernel directory another line in the *Makefile* cause this local library to be searched first when the kernel object files are linked.

We have listed two files from the *kernel/system/* directory in Appendix B. These were chosen because they represent two general classes of support that the system task provides. One category of support is access to kernel data structures on behalf of any user-space system process that needs such support. We will describe *system/do_setalarm.c* as an example of this category. The other general category is support for specific system calls that are mostly managed by user-space processes, but which need to carry out some actions in kernel space. We have chosen *system/do_exec.c* as our example.

The sys_setalarm kernel call is somewhat similar to sys_irqenable, which we mentioned in the discussion of interrupt handling in the kernel. Sys_irqenable sets up an address to an interrupt handler to be called when an IRQ is activated. The handler is a function within the system task, *generic_handler*. It generates a notify message to the device driver process that should respond to the interrupt. *System/do_setalarm.c* (line 10200) contains code to manage timers in a way similar to how interrupts are managed. A sys_setalarm kernel call initializes a timer for a user-space system process that needs to receive a synchronous alarm, and it provides a function to be called to notify the user-space process when the timer expires. It can also ask for cancellation of a previously scheduled alarm by passing zero in the expiration time field of its request message. The operation is simple—on lines 10230 to 10232 information from the message is extracted. The most important items are the time when the timer should go off and the process that needs to know about it. Every system process has its own timer structure in the *priv* table. On lines 10237 to 10239 the timer structure is located and the process number and the address of a function, *cause_alarm*, to be executed when the timer expires, are entered.

If the timer was already active, sys_setalarm returns the time remaining in its reply message. A return value of zero means the timer is not active. There are several possibilities to be considered. The timer might previously have been deactivated—a timer is marked inactive by storing a special value, *TMR_NEVER* in its *exp_time* field . As far as the C code is concerned this is just a large integer, so an explicit test for this value is made as part of checking whether the expiration time has passed. The timer might indicate a time that has already passed. This is unlikley to happen, but it is easy to check. The timer might also indicate a time in the future. In either of the first two cases the reply value is zero, otherwise the time remaining is returned (lines 10242 to 10247).

Finally, the timer is reset or set. At this level this is done putting the desired expiration time into the correct field of the timer structure and calling another function to do the work. Of course, resetting the timer does not require storing a value. We will see the functions *reset* and *set* soon, their code is in the source file for the clock task. But since the system task and the clock task are both compiled into the kernel image all functions declared *PUBLIC* are accessible.

There is one other function defined in *do_setalarm.c*. This is *cause_alarm*, the watchdog function whose address is stored in each timer, so it can be called when the timer expires. It is simplicity itself—it generates a notify message to the process whose process number is also stored in the timer structure. Thus the synchronous alarm within the kernel is converted into a message to the system process that asked for an alarm.

As an aside, note that when we talked about the initialization of timers a few pages back (and in this section as well) we referred to synchronous alarms requested by system processes. If that did not make complete sense at this point, and if you are wondering what is a synchronous alarm or what about timers for nonsystem processes, these questions will be dealt with in the next section, when we discuss the clock task. There are so many interconnected parts in an operating system that it is almost impossible to order all topics in a way that does not occasionally require a reference to a part that has not been already been explained. This is particularly true when discussing implementation. If we were not dealing with a real operating system we could probably avoid bringing up messy details like this. For that matter, a totally theoretical discussion of operating system principles would probably never mention a system task. In a theory book we could just wave our arms and ignore the problems of giving operating system components in user space limited and controlled access to privileged resources like interrupts and I/O ports.

The last file in the *kernel/system/* directory which we will discuss in detail is *do_exec.c* (line 10300). Most of the work of the exec system call is done within the process manager. The process manager sets up a stack for a new program that contains the arguments and the environment. Then it passes the resulting stack pointer to the kernel using sys_exec, which is handled by *do_exec* (line 10618). The stack pointer is set in the kernel part of the process table, and if the process being exec-ed is using an extra segment the assembly language *phys_memset* function defined in *klib386.s* is called to erase any data that might be left over from previous use of that memory region (line 10330).

An exec call causes a slight anomaly. The process invoking the call sends a message to the process manager and blocks. With other system calls, the resulting reply would unblock it. With exec there is no reply, because the newly loaded core image is not expecting a reply. Therefore, *do_exec* unblocks the process itself on line 10333 The next line makes the new image ready to run, using the *lock_enqueue* function that protects against a possible race condition. Finally, the command string is saved so the process can be identified when the user invokes the *ps* command or presses a function key to display data from the process table.

To finish our discussion of the system task, we will look at its role in handling a typical operating service, providing data in response to a read system call. When a user does a read call, the file system checks its cache to see if it has the block needed. If not, it sends a message to the appropriate disk driver to load it into the cache. Then the file system sends a message to the system task telling it to copy the block to the user process. In the worst case, eleven messages are needed to read a block; in the best case, four messages are needed. Both cases are shown in Fig. 2-46. In Fig. 2-46 (a), message 3 asks the system task to execute I/O instructions; 4 is the ACK. When a hardware interrupt occurs the system task tells the waiting driver about this event with message 5. Messages 6 and 7 are a request to copy the data to the FS cache and the reply, message 8 tells the FS the data is ready, and messages 9 and 10 are a request to copy the data from the cache to the user, and the reply. Finally message 11 is the reply to the user. In Fig. 2-46 (b), the data is already in the cache, messages 2 and 3 are the request to copy it to the user and the reply. These messages are a source of overhead in MINIX 3 and are the price paid for the highly modular design.

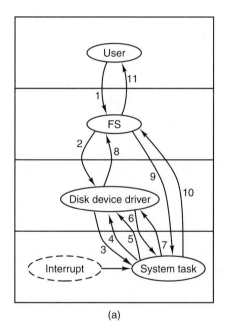
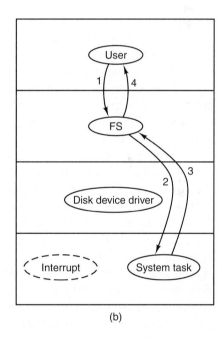

(a)   (b)

Figure 2-46. (a) Worst case for reading a block requires eleven messages.
(b) Best case for reading a block requires four messages.

Kernel calls to request copying of data are probably the most heavily used ones in MINIX 3. We have already seen the part of the system task that ultimately does the work, the function *virtual_copy*. One way to deal with some of the inefficiency of the message passing mechanism is to pack multiple requests into a message. The *sys_virvcopy* and *sys_physvcopy* kernel calls do this. The content of a message that invokes one of these call is a pointer to a vector specifying multiple blocks to be copied between memory locations. Both are supported by *do_vcopy*, which executes a loop, extracting source and destination addresses and block lengths and calling *phys_copy* repeatedly until all the copies are complete. We will see in the next chapter that disk devices have a similar ability to handle multiple transfers based on a single request.

2.8 THE CLOCK TASK IN MINIX 3

Clocks (also called **timers**) are essential to the operation of any timesharing system for a variety of reasons. For example, they maintain the time of day and prevent one process from monopolizing the CPU. The MINIX 3 clock task has some resemblance to a device driver, in that it is driven by interrupts generated by a hardware device. However, the clock is neither a block device, like a disk, nor a character device, like a terminal. In fact, in MINIX 3 an interface to the clock is not provided by a file in the */dev/* directory. Furthermore, the clock task executes in kernel space and cannot be accessed directly by user-space processes. It has access to all kernel functions and data, but user-space processes can only access it via the system task. In this section we will first a look at clock hardware and software in general, and then we will see how these ideas are applied in MINIX 3.

2.8.1 Clock Hardware

Two types of clocks are used in computers, and both are quite different from the clocks and watches used by people. The simpler clocks are tied to the 110- or 220-volt power line, and cause an interrupt on every voltage cycle, at 50 or 60 Hz. These are essentially extinct in modern PCs.

The other kind of clock is built out of three components: a crystal oscillator, a counter, and a holding register, as shown in Fig. 2-47. When a piece of quartz crystal is properly cut and mounted under tension, it can be made to generate a periodic signal of very high accuracy, typically in the range of 5 to 200 MHz, depending on the crystal chosen. At least one such circuit is usually found in any computer, providing a synchronizing signal to the computer's various circuits. This signal is fed into the counter to make it count down to zero. When the counter gets to zero, it causes a CPU interrupt. Computers whose advertised clock rate is higher than 200 MHz normally use a slower clock and a clock multiplier circuit.

Programmable clocks typically have several modes of operation. In **one-shot mode**, when the clock is started, it copies the value of the holding register into the counter and then decrements the counter at each pulse from the crystal. When the counter gets to zero, it causes an interrupt and stops until it is explicitly started again by the software. In **square-wave mode**, after getting to zero and causing the

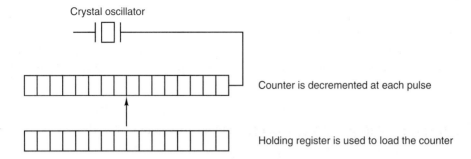

Figure 2-47. A programmable clock.

interrupt, the holding register is automatically copied into the counter, and the whole process is repeated again indefinitely. These periodic interrupts are called **clock ticks**.

The advantage of the programmable clock is that its interrupt frequency can be controlled by software. If a 1-MHz crystal is used, then the counter is pulsed every microsecond. With 16-bit registers, interrupts can be programmed to occur at intervals from 1 microsecond to 65.536 milliseconds. Programmable clock chips usually contain two or three independently programmable clocks and have many other options as well (e.g., counting up instead of down, interrupts disabled, and more).

To prevent the current time from being lost when the computer's power is turned off, most computers have a battery-powered backup clock, implemented with the kind of low-power circuitry used in digital watches. The battery clock can be read at startup. If the backup clock is not present, the software may ask the user for the current date and time. There is also a standard protocol for a networked system to get the current time from a remote host. In any case the time is then translated into the number of seconds since 12 A.M. **Universal Coordinated Time (UTC)** (formerly known as Greenwich Mean Time) on Jan. 1, 1970, as UNIX and MINIX 3 do, or since some other benchmark. Clock ticks are counted by the running system, and every time a full second has passed the real time is incremented by one count. MINIX 3 (and most UNIX systems) do not take into account leap seconds, of which there have been 23 since 1970. This is not considered a serious flaw. Usually, utility programs are provided to manually set the system clock and the backup clock and to synchronize the two clocks.

We should mention here that all but the earliest IBM-compatible computers have a separate clock circuit that provides timing signals for the CPU, internal data busses, and other components. This is the clock that is meant when people speak of CPU clock speeds, measured in Megahertz on the earliest personal computers, and in Gigahertz on modern systems. The basic circuitry of quartz crystals, oscillators and counters is the same, but the requirements are so different that modern computers have independent clocks for CPU control and timekeeping.

2.8.2 Clock Software

All the clock hardware does is generate interrupts at known intervals. Everything else involving time must be done by the software, the clock driver. The exact duties of the clock driver vary among operating systems, but usually include most of the following:

1. Maintaining the time of day.

2. Preventing processes from running longer than they are allowed to.

3. Accounting for CPU usage.

4. Handling the alarm system call made by user processes.

5. Providing watchdog timers for parts of the system itself.

6. Doing profiling, monitoring, and statistics gathering.

The first clock function, maintaining the time of day (also called the **real time**) is not difficult. It just requires incrementing a counter at each clock tick, as mentioned before. The only thing to watch out for is the number of bits in the time-of-day counter. With a clock rate of 60 Hz, a 32-bit counter will overflow in just over 2 years. Clearly the system cannot store the real time as the number of ticks since Jan. 1, 1970 in 32 bits.

Three approaches can be taken to solve this problem. The first way is to use a 64-bit counter, although doing so makes maintaining the counter more expensive since it has to be done many times a second. The second way is to maintain the time of day in seconds, rather than in ticks, using a subsidiary counter to count ticks until a whole second has been accumulated. Because 2^{32} seconds is more than 136 years, this method will work until well into the twenty-second century.

The third approach is to count ticks, but to do that relative to the time the system was booted, rather than relative to a fixed external moment. When the backup clock is read or the user types in the real time, the system boot time is calculated from the current time-of-day value and stored in memory in any convenient form. When the time of day is requested, the stored time of day is added to the counter to get the current time of day. All three approaches are shown in Fig. 2-48.

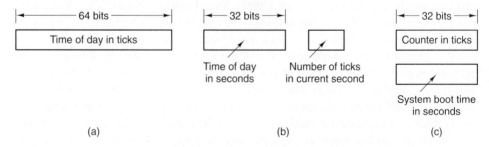

Figure 2-48. Three ways to maintain the time of day.

The second clock function is preventing processes from running too long. Whenever a process is started, the scheduler should initialize a counter to the value of that process' quantum in clock ticks. At every clock interrupt, the clock driver decrements the quantum counter by 1. When it gets to zero, the clock driver calls the scheduler to set up another process.

The third clock function is doing CPU accounting. The most accurate way to do it is to start a second timer, distinct from the main system timer, whenever a process is started. When that process is stopped, the timer can be read out to tell how long the process has run. To do things right, the second timer should be saved when an interrupt occurs and restored afterward.

A less accurate, but much simpler, way to do accounting is to maintain a pointer to the process table entry for the currently running process in a global variable. At every clock tick, a field in the current process' entry is incremented. In this way, every clock tick is "charged" to the process running at the time of the tick. A minor problem with this strategy is that if many interrupts occur during a process' run, it is still charged for a full tick, even though it did not get much work done. Properly accounting for the CPU during interrupts is too expensive and is rarely done.

In MINIX 3 and many other systems, a process can request that the operating system give it a warning after a certain interval. The warning is usually a signal, interrupt, message, or something similar. One application requiring such warnings is networking, in which a packet not acknowledged within a certain time interval must be retransmitted. Another application is computer-aided instruction, where a student not providing a response within a certain time is told the answer.

If the clock driver had enough clocks, it could set a separate clock for each request. This not being the case, it must simulate multiple virtual clocks with a single physical clock. One way is to maintain a table in which the signal time for all pending timers is kept, as well as a variable giving the time of the next one. Whenever the time of day is updated, the driver checks to see if the closest signal has occurred. If it has, the table is searched for the next one to occur.

If many signals are expected, it is more efficient to simulate multiple clocks by chaining all the pending clock requests together, sorted on time, in a linked list, as shown in Fig. 2-49. Each entry on the list tells how many clock ticks following the previous one to wait before causing a signal. In this example, signals are pending for 4203, 4207, 4213, 4215, and 4216.

In Fig. 2-49, a timer has just expired. The next interrupt occurs in 3 ticks, and 3 has just been loaded. On each tick, *Next signal* is decremented. When it gets to 0, the signal corresponding to the first item on the list is caused, and that item is removed from the list. Then *Next signal* is set to the value in the entry now at the head of the list, in this example, 4. Using absolute times rather than relative times is more convenient in many cases, and that is the approach used by MINIX 3.

Note that during a clock interrupt, the clock driver has several things to do. These things include incrementing the real time, decrementing the quantum and

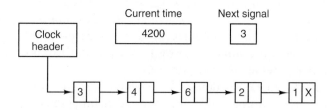

Figure 2-49. Simulating multiple timers with a single clock.

checking for 0, doing CPU accounting, and decrementing the alarm counter. However, each of these operations has been carefully arranged to be very fast because they have to be repeated many times a second.

Parts of the operating system also need to set timers. These are called **watchdog timers**. When we study the hard disk driver, we will see that a wakeup call is scheduled each time the disk controller is sent a command, so an attempt at recovery can be made if the command fails completely. Floppy disk drivers use timers to wait for the disk motor to get up to speed and to shut down the motor if no activity occurs for a while. Some printers with a movable print head can print at 120 characters/sec (8.3 msec/character) but cannot return the print head to the left margin in 8.3 msec, so the terminal driver must delay after typing a carriage return.

The mechanism used by the clock driver to handle watchdog timers is the same as for user signals. The only difference is that when a timer goes off, instead of causing a signal, the clock driver calls a procedure supplied by the caller. The procedure is part of the caller's code. This presented a problem in the design of MINIX 3, since one of the goals was to remove drivers from the kernel's address space. The short answer is that the system task, which is in kernel space, can set alarms on behalf of some user-space processes, and then notify them when a timer goes off. We will elaborate on this mechanism further on.

The last thing in our list is profiling. Some operating systems provide a mechanism by which a user program can have the system build up a histogram of its program counter, so it can see where it is spending its time. When profiling is a possibility, at every tick the driver checks to see if the current process is being profiled, and if so, computes the bin number (a range of addresses) corresponding to the current program counter. It then increments that bin by one. This mechanism can also be used to profile the system itself.

2.8.3 Overview of the Clock Driver in MINIX 3

The MINIX 3 clock driver is contained in the file *kernel/clock.c*. It can be considered to have three functional parts. First, like the device drivers that we will see in the next chapter, there is a task mechanism which runs in a loop, waiting for messages and dispatching to subroutines that perform the action requested in each message. However, this structure is almost vestigial in the clock task. The message mechanism is expensive, requiring all the overhead of a context switch. So for the clock this is used only when there is a substantial amount of work to be done. Only one kind of message is received, there is only one subroutine to service the message, and a reply message is not sent when the job is done.

The second major part of the clock software is the interrupt handler that is activated 60 times each second. It does basic timekeeping, updating a variable that counts clock ticks since the system was booted. It compares this with the time for the next timer expiration. It also updates counters that register how much of the quantum of the current process has been used and how much total time the current process has used. If the interrupt handler detects that a process has used its quantum or that a timer has expired it generates the message that goes to the main task loop. Otherwise no message is sent. The strategy here is that for each clock tick the handler does as little as necessary, as fast as possible. The costly main task is activated only when there is substantial work to do.

The third general part of the clock software is a collection of subroutines that provide general support, but which are not called in response to clock interrupts, either by the interrupt handler or by the main task loop. One of these subroutines is coded as *PRIVATE*, and is called before the main task loop is entered. It initializes the clock, which entails writing data to the clock chip to cause it to generate interrupts at the desired intervals. The initialization routine also puts the address of the interrupt handler in the right place to be found when the clock chip triggers the IRQ 8 input to the interrupt controller chip, and then enables that input to respond.

The rest of the subroutines in *clock.c* are declared *PUBLIC*, and can be called from anywhere in the kernel binary. In fact none of them are called from *clock.c* itself. They are mostly called by the system task in order to service system calls related to time. These subroutines do such things as reading the time-since-boot counter, for timing with clock-tick resolution, or reading a register in the clock chip itself, for timing that requires microsecond resolution. Other subroutines are used to set and reset timers. Finally, a subroutine is provided to be called when MINIX 3 shuts down. This one resets the hardware timer parameters to those expected by the BIOS.

The Clock Task

The main loop of the clock task accepts only a single kind of message, *HARD_INT*, which comes from the interrupt handler. Anything else is an error. Furthermore, it does not receive this message for every clock tick interrupt, although the subroutine called each time a message is received is named *do_clocktick*. A message is received, and *do_clocktick* is called only if process scheduling is needed or a timer has expired.

The Clock Interrupt Handler

The interrupt handler runs every time the counter in the clock chip reaches zero and generates an interrupt. This is where the basic timekeeping work is done. In MINIX 3 the time is kept using the method of Fig. 2-48(c). However, in *clock.c* only the counter for ticks since boot is maintained; records of the boot time are kept elsewhere. The clock software supplies only the current tick count to aid a system call for the real time. Further processing is done by one of the servers. This is consistent with the MINIX 3 strategy of moving functionality to processes that run in user space.

In the interrupt handler the local counter is updated for each interrupt received. When interrupts are disabled ticks are lost. In some cases it is possible to correct for this effect. A global variable is available for counting lost ticks, and it is added to the main counter and then reset to zero each time the handler is activated. In the implementation section we will see an example of how this is used.

The handler also affects variables in the process table, for billing and process control purposes. A message is sent to the clock task only if the current time has passed the expiration time of the next scheduled timer or if the quantum of the running process has been decremented to zero. Everything done in the interrupt service is a simple integer operation—arithmetic, comparison, logical AND/OR, or assignment—which a C compiler can translate easily into basic machine operations. At worst there are five additions or subtractions and six comparisons, plus a few logical operations and assignments in completing the interrupt service. In particular there is no subroutine call overhead.

Watchdog Timers

A few pages back we left hanging the question of how user-space processes can be provided with watchdog timers, which ordinarily are thought of as user-supplied procedures that are part of the user's code and are executed when a timer expires. Clearly, this can not be done in MINIX 3. But we can use a **synchronous alarm** to bridge the gap from the kernel to user space.

This is a good time to explain what is meant by a synchronous alarm. A signal may arrive or a conventional watchdog may be activated without any relation to what part of a process is currently executing, so these mechanisms are **asynchronous**. A synchronous alarm is delivered as a message, and thus can be received only when the recipient has executed receive. So we say it is synchronous because it will be received only when the receiver expects it. If the notify method is used to inform a recipient of an alarm, the sender does not have to block, and the recipient does not have to be concerned with missing the alarm. Messages from notify are saved if the recipient is not waiting. A bitmap is used, with each bit representing a possible source of a notification.

Watchdog timers take advantage of the *timer_t* type *s_alarm_timer* field that exists in each element of the *priv* table. Each system process has a slot in the *priv* table. To set a timer, a system process in user space makes a sys_setalarm call, which is handled by the system task. The system task is compiled in kernel space, and thus can initialize a timer on behalf of the calling process. Initialization entails putting the address of a procedure to execute when the timer expires into the correct field, and then inserting the timer into a list of timers, as in Fig. 2-49.

The procedure to execute has to be in kernel space too, of course. No problem. The system task contains a watchdog function, *cause_alarm*, which generates a notify when it goes off, causing a synchronous alarm for the user. This alarm can invoke the user-space watchdog function. Within the kernel binary this is a true watchdog, but for the process that requested the timer, it is a synchronous alarm. It is not the same as having the timer execute a procedure in the target's address space. There is a bit more overhead, but it is simpler than an interrupt.

What we wrote above was qualified: we said that the system task can set alarms on behalf of *some* user-space processes. The mechanism just described works only for system processes. Each system process has a copy of the *priv* structure, but a single copy is shared by all non-system (user) processes. The parts of the *priv* table that cannot be shared, such as the bitmap of pending notifications and the timer, are not usable by user processes. The solution is this: the process manager manages timers on behalf of user processes in a way similar to the way the system task manages timers for system processes. Every process has a *timer_t* field of its own in the process manager's part of the process table.

When a user process makes an alarm system call to ask for an alarm to be set, it is handled by the process manager, which sets up the timer and inserts it into its list of timers. The process manager asks the system task to send it a notification when the first timer in the PM's list of timers is scheduled to expire. The process manager only has to ask for help when the head of its chain of timers changes, either because the first timer has expired or has been cancelled, or because a new request has been received that must go on the chain before the current head. This is used to support the POSIX-standard alarm system call. The procedure to execute is within the address space of the process manager. When executed, the user process that requested the alarm is sent a signal, rather than a notification.

Millisecond Timing

A procedure is provided in *clock.c* that provides microsecond resolution timing. Delays as short as a few microseconds may be needed by various I/O devices. There is no practical way to do this using alarms and the message passing interface. The counter that is used for generating the clock interrupts can be read directly. It is decremented approximately every 0.8 microseconds, and reaches zero 60 times a second, or every 16.67 milliseconds. To be useful for I/O timing it would have to be polled by a procedure running in kernel-space, but much work has gone into moving drivers out of kernel-space. Currently this function is used only as a source of randomness for the random number generator. More use might be made of it on a very fast system, but this is a future project

Summary of Clock Services

Figure 2-50 summarizes the various services provided directly or indirectly by *clock.c*. There are several functions declared *PUBLIC* that can be called from the kernel or the system task. All other services are available only indirectly, by system calls ultimately handled by the system task. Other system processes can ask the system task directly, but user processes must ask the process manager, which also relies on the system task.

Service	Access	Response	Clients
get_uptime	Function call	Ticks	Kernel or system task
set_timer	Function call	None	Kernel or system task
reset_timer	Function call	None	Kernel or system task
read_clock	Function call	Count	Kernel or system task
clock_stop	Function call	None	Kernel or system task
Synchronous alarm	System call	Notification	Server or driver, via system task
POSIX alarm	System call	Signal	User process, via PM
Time	System call	Message	Any process, via PM

Figure 2-50. The time-related services supported by the clock driver.

The kernel or the system task can get the current uptime, or set or reset a timer without the overhead of a message. The kernel or the system task can also call *read_clock*, which reads the counter in the timer chip, to get time in units of approximately 0.8 microseconds. The *clock_stop* function is intended to be called only when MINIX 3 shuts down. It restores the BIOS clock rate. A system process, either a driver or a server, can request a synchronous alarm, which causes activation of a watchdog function in kernel space and a notification to the requesting process. A POSIX-alarm is requested by a user process by asking the process manager, which then asks the system task to activate a watchdog. When the timer expires, the system task notifies the process manager, and the process manager delivers a signal to the user process.

2.8.4 Implementation of the Clock Driver in MINIX 3

The clock task uses no major data structures, but several variables are used to keep track of time. The variable *realtime* (line 10462) is basic—it counts all clockticks. A global variable, *lost_ticks*, is defined in *glo.h* (line 5333). This variable is provided for the use of any function that executes in kernel space that might disable interrupts long enough that one or more clock ticks could be lost. It currently is used by the *int86* function in *klib386.s*. *Int86* uses the boot monitor to manage the transfer of control to the BIOS, and the monitor returns the number of clock ticks counted while the BIOS call was busy in the ecx register just before the return to the kernel. This works because, although the clock chip is not triggering the MINIX 3 clock interrupt handler when the BIOS request is handled, the boot monitor can keep track of the time with the help of the BIOS.

The clock driver accesses several other global variables. It uses *proc_ptr*, *prev_ptr*, and *bill_ptr* to reference the process table entry for the currently running process, the process that ran previously, and the process that gets charged for time. Within these process table entries it accesses various fields, including *p_user_time* and *p_sys_time* for accounting and *p_ticks_left* for counting down the quantum of a process.

When MINIX 3 starts up, all the drivers are called. Most of them do some initialization then try to get a message and block. The clock driver, *clock_task* (line 10468), does that too. First it calls *init_clock* to initialize the programmable clock frequency to 60 Hz. When a message is received, it calls *do_clocktick* if the message was a *HARD_INT* (line 10486). Any other kind of message is unexpected and treated as an error.

Do_clocktick (line 10497) is not called on each tick of the clock, so its name is not an exact description of its function. It is called when the interrupt handler has determined there might be something important to do. One of the conditions that results in running *do_clocktick* is the current process using up all of its quantum. If the process is preemptable (the system and clock tasks are not) a call to *lock_dequeue* followed immediately by a call to *lock_enqueue* (lines 10510 to 10512) removes the process from its queue, then makes it ready again and reschedules it. The other thing that activates *do_clocktick* is expiration of a watchdog timer. Timers and linked lists of timers are used so much in MINIX 3 that a library of functions to support them was created. The library function *tmrs_exptimers* called on line 10517 runs the watchdog functions for all expired timers and deactivates them.

Init_clock (line 10529) is called only once, when the clock task is started. There are several places one could point to and say, "This is where MINIX 3 starts running." This is a candidate; the clock is essential to a preemptive multitasking system. *Init_clock* writes three bytes to the clock chip that set its mode and set the proper count into the master register. Then it registers its process number, IRQ, and handler address so interrupts will be directed properly. Finally, it enables the interrupt controller chip to accept clock interrupts.

The next function, *clock_stop*, undoes the initialization of the clock chip. It is declared *PUBLIC* and is not called from anywhere in *clock.c*. It is placed here because of the obvious similarity to *init_clock*. It is only called by the system task when MINIX 3 is shut down and control is to be returned to the boot monitor.

As soon as (or, more accurately, 16.67 milliseconds after) *init_clock* runs, the first clock interrupt occurs, and clock interrupts repeat 60 times a second as long as MINIX 3 runs. The code in *clock_handler* (line 10556) probably runs more frequently than any other part of the MINIX 3 system. Consequently, *clock_handler* was built for speed. The only subroutine calls are on line 10586; they are only needed if running on an obsolete IBM PS/2 system. The update of the current time (in ticks) is done on lines 10589 to 10591. Then user and accounting times are updated.

Decisions were made in the design of the handler that might be questioned. Two tests are done on line 10610 and if either condition is true the clock task is notified. The *do_clocktick* function called by the clock task repeats both tests to decide what needs to be done. This is necessary because the notify call used by the handler cannot pass any information to distinguish different conditions. We leave it to the reader to consider alternatives and how they might be evaluated.

The rest of *clock.c* contains utility functions we have already mentioned. *Get_uptime* (line 10620) just returns the value of *realtime*, which is visible only to functions in *clock.c*. *Set_timer* and *reset_timer* use other functions from the timer library that take care of all the details of manipulating a chain of timers. Finally, *read_clock* reads and returns the current count in the clock chip's countdown register.

2.9 SUMMARY

To hide the effects of interrupts, operating systems provide a conceptual model consisting of sequential processes running in parallel. Processes can communicate with each other using interprocess communication primitives, such as semaphores, monitors, or messages. These primitives are used to ensure that no two processes are ever in their critical sections at the same time. A process can be running, runnable, or blocked and can change state when it or another process executes one of the interprocess communication primitives.

Interprocess communication primitives can be used to solve such problems as the producer-consumer, dining philosophers, and reader-writer. Even with these primitives, care has to be taken to avoid errors and deadlocks. Many scheduling algorithms are known, including round-robin, priority scheduling, multilevel queues, and policy-driven schedulers.

MINIX 3 supports the process concept and provides messages for interprocess communication. Messages are not buffered, so a send succeeds only when the receiver is waiting for it. Similarly, a receive succeeds only when a message is already available. If either operation does not succeed, the caller is blocked. MINIX 3 also provides a nonblocking supplement to messages with a notify primitive. An attempt to send a notify to a receiver that is not waiting results in a bit being set, which triggers notification when a receive is done later.

As an example of the message flow, consider a user doing a read. The user process sends a message to the FS requesting it. If the data are not in the FS' cache, the FS asks the driver to read it from the disk. Then the FS blocks waiting for the data. When the disk interrupt happens, the system task is notified, allowing it to reply to the disk driver, which then replies to the FS. At this point, the FS asks the system task to copy the data from its cache, where the newly requested block has been placed, to the user. These steps are illustrated in Fig. 2-46.

Process switching may follow an interrupt. When a process is interrupted, a stack is created within the process table entry of the process, and all the information needed to restart it is put on the new stack. Any process can be restarted by setting the stack pointer to point to its process table entry and initiating a sequence of instructions to restore the CPU registers, culminating with an iretd instruction. The scheduler decides which process table entry to put into the stack pointer.

Interrupts cannot occur when the kernel itself is running. If an exception occurs when the kernel is running, the kernel stack, rather than a stack within the process table, is used. When an interrupt has been serviced, a process is restarted.

The MINIX 3 scheduling algorithm uses multiple priority queues. System processes normally run in the highest priority queues and user processes in lower priority queues, but priorities are assigned on a process-by-process basis. A process stuck in a loop may have its priority temporarily reduced; the priority can be restored when other processes have had a chance to run. The *nice* command can be used to change the priority of a process within defined limits. Processes are run round robin for a quantum that can vary per process. However, after a process has blocked and becomes ready again it will be put on the head of its queue with just the unused part of its quantum. This is intended to give faster response to processes doing I/O. Device drivers and servers are allowed a large quantum, as they are expected to run until they block. However, even system processes can be preempted if they run too long.

The kernel image includes a system task which facilitates communication of user-space processes with the kernel. It supports the servers and device drivers by performing privileged operations on their behalf. In MINIX 3, the clock task is also compiled with the kernel. It is not a device driver in the ordinary sense. User-space processes cannot access the clock as a device.

PROBLEMS

1. Why is multiprogramming central to the operation of a modern operating system?

2. What are the three main states that a process can be in? Describe the meaning of each one briefly.

3. Suppose that you were to design an advanced computer architecture that did process switching in hardware, instead of having interrupts. What information would the CPU need? Describe how the hardware process switching might work.

4. On all current computers, at least part of the interrupt handlers are written in assembly language. Why?

5. Redraw Fig. 2-2 adding two new states: New and Terminated. When a process is created, it is initially in the New state. When it exits, it is in the Terminated state.

6. In the text it was stated that the model of Fig. 2-6(a) was not suited to a file server using a cache in memory. Why not? Could each process have its own cache?

7. What is the fundamental difference between a process and a thread?

8. In a system with threads, is there normally one stack per thread or one stack per process? Explain.

9. What is a race condition?

10. Give an example of a race condition that could possibly occur when buying airplane tickets for two people to go on a trip together.

11. Write a shell script that produces a file of sequential numbers by reading the last number in the file, adding 1 to it, and then appending to the file. Run one instance of the script in the background and one in the foreground, each accessing the same file. How long does it take before a race condition manifests itself? What is the critical section? Modify the script to prevent the race (*Hint*: use

    ln file file.lock

    to lock the data file).

12. Is a statement like

    ln file file.lock

    an effective locking mechanism for a user program like the scripts used in the previous problem? Why (or why not)?

13. Does the busy waiting solution using the *turn* variable (Fig. 2-10) work when the two processes are running on a shared-memory multiprocessor, that is, two CPUs, sharing a common memory?

14. Consider a computer that does not have a TEST AND SET LOCK instruction but does have an instruction to swap the contents of a register and a memory word in a single indivisible action. Can that be used to write a routine *enter_region* such as the one found in Fig. 2-12?

15. Give a sketch of how an operating system that can disable interrupts could implement semaphores.

16. Show how counting semaphores (i.e., semaphores that can hold an arbitrarily large value) can be implemented using only binary semaphores and ordinary machine instructions.

17. In Sec. 2.2.4, a situation with a high-priority process, H, and a low-priority process, L, was described, which led to H looping forever. Does the same problem occur if round-robin scheduling is used instead of priority scheduling? Discuss.

18. Synchronization within monitors uses condition variables and two special operations, WAIT and SIGNAL. A more general form of synchronization would be to have a single primitive, WAITUNTIL, that had an arbitrary Boolean predicate as parameter. Thus, one could say, for example,

WAITUNTIL $x < 0$ **or** $y + z < n$

The SIGNAL primitive would no longer be needed. This scheme is clearly more general than that of Hoare or Brinch Hansen, but it is not used. Why not? (*Hint*: think about the implementation.)

19. A fast food restaurant has four kinds of employees: (1) order takers, who take customer's orders; (2) cooks, who prepare the food; (3) packaging specialists, who stuff the food into bags; and (4) cashiers, who give the bags to customers and take their money. Each employee can be regarded as a communicating sequential process. What form of interprocess communication do they use? Relate this model to processes in MINIX 3.

20. Suppose that we have a message-passing system using mailboxes. When sending to a full mailbox or trying to receive from an empty one, a process does not block. Instead, it gets an error code back. The process responds to the error code by just trying again, over and over, until it succeeds. Does this scheme lead to race conditions?

21. In the solution to the dining philosophers problem (Fig. 2-20), why is the state variable set to *HUNGRY* in the procedure *take_forks*?

22. Consider the procedure *put_forks* in Fig. 2-20. Suppose that the variable *state*[*i*] was set to *THINKING after* the two calls to *test*, rather than *before*. How would this change affect the solution for the case of 3 philosophers? For 100 philosophers?

23. The readers and writers problem can be formulated in several ways with regard to which category of processes can be started when. Carefully describe three different variations of the problem, each one favoring (or not favoring) some category of processes. For each variation, specify what happens when a reader or a writer becomes ready to access the data base, and what happens when a process is finished using the data base.

24. The CDC 6600 computers could handle up to 10 I/O processes simultaneously using an interesting form of round-robin scheduling called **processor sharing**. A process switch occurred after each instruction, so instruction 1 came from process 1, instruction 2 came from process 2, etc. The process switching was done by special hardware, and the overhead was zero. If a process needed T sec to complete in the absence of competition, how much time would it need if processor sharing was used with n processes?

25. Round-robin schedulers normally maintain a list of all runnable processes, with each process occurring exactly once in the list. What would happen if a process occurred twice in the list? Can you think of any reason for allowing this?

26. Measurements of a certain system have shown that the average process runs for a time T before blocking on I/O. A process switch requires a time S, which is effectively wasted (overhead). For round-robin scheduling with quantum Q, give a formula for the CPU efficiency for each of the following:

(a) $Q = \infty$
(b) $Q > T$
(c) $S < Q < T$
(d) $Q = S$
(e) Q nearly 0

27. Five jobs are waiting to be run. Their expected run times are 9, 6, 3, 5, and X. In what order should they be run to minimize average response time? (Your answer will depend on X.)

28. Five batch jobs A through E, arrive at a computer center at almost the same time. They have estimated running times of 10, 6, 2, 4, and 8 minutes. Their (externally determined) priorities are 3, 5, 2, 1, and 4, respectively, with 5 being the highest priority. For each of the following scheduling algorithms, determine the mean process turnaround time. Ignore process switching overhead.

(a) Round robin.
(b) Priority scheduling.
(c) First-come, first-served (run in order 10, 6, 2, 4, 8).
(d) Shortest job first.

For (a), assume that the system is multiprogrammed, and that each job gets its fair share of the CPU. For (b) through (d) assume that only one job at a time runs, until it finishes. All jobs are completely CPU bound.

29. A process running on CTSS needs 30 quanta to complete. How many times must it be swapped in, including the very first time (before it has run at all)?

30. The aging algorithm with $a = 1/2$ is being used to predict run times. The previous four runs, from oldest to most recent, are 40, 20, 40, and 15 msec. What is the prediction of the next time?

31. In Fig. 2-25 we saw how three-level scheduling works in a batch system. Could this idea be applied to an interactive system without newly-arriving jobs? How?

32. Suppose that the threads of Fig. 2-28(a) are run in the order: one from A, one from B, one from A, one from B, etc. How many possible thread sequences are there for the first four times scheduling is done?

33. A soft real-time system has four periodic events with periods of 50, 100, 200, and 250 msec each. Suppose that the four events require 35, 20, 10, and x msec of CPU time, respectively. What is the largest value of x for which the system is schedulable?

34. During execution, MINIX 3 maintains a variable *proc_ptr* that points to the process table entry for the current process. Why?

35. MINIX 3 does not buffer messages. Explain how this design decision causes problems with clock and keyboard interrupts.

36. When a message is sent to a sleeping process in MINIX 3, the procedure *ready* is called to put that process on the proper scheduling queue. This procedure starts out by disabling interrupts. Explain.

37. The MINIX 3 procedure *mini_rec* contains a loop. Explain what it is for.

38. MINIX 3 essentially uses the scheduling method in Fig. 2-43, with different priorities for classes. The lowest class (user processes) has round-robin scheduling, but the tasks and servers always are allowed to run until they block. Is it possible for processes in the lowest class to starve? Why (or why not)?

39. Is MINIX 3 suitable for real-time applications, such as data logging? If not, what could be done to make it so?

40. Assume that you have an operating system that provides semaphores. Implement a message system. Write the procedures for sending and receiving messages.

41. A student majoring in anthropology and minoring in computer science has embarked on a research project to see if African baboons can be taught about deadlocks. He locates a deep canyon and fastens a rope across it, so the baboons can cross hand-over-hand. Several baboons can cross at the same time, provided that they are all going in the same direction. If eastward moving and westward moving baboons ever get onto the rope at the same time, a deadlock will result (the baboons will get stuck in the middle) because it is impossible for one baboon to climb over another one while suspended over the canyon. If a baboon wants to cross the canyon, he must check to see that no other baboon is currently crossing in the opposite direction. Write a program using semaphores that avoids deadlock. Do not worry about a series of eastward moving baboons holding up the westward moving baboons indefinitely.

42. Repeat the previous problem, but now avoid starvation. When a baboon that wants to cross to the east arrives at the rope and finds baboons crossing to the west, he waits until the rope is empty, but no more westward moving baboons are allowed to start until at least one baboon has crossed the other way.

43. Solve the dining philosophers problem using monitors instead of semaphores.

44. Add code to the MINIX 3 kernel to keep track of the number of messages sent from process (or task) *i* to process (or task) *j*. Print this matrix when the F4 key is hit.

45. Modify the MINIX 3 scheduler to keep track of how much CPU time each user process has had recently. When no task or server wants to run, pick the user process that has had the smallest share of the CPU.

46. Modify MINIX 3 so that each process can explicitly set the scheduling priority of its children using a new system call setpriority with parameters *pid* and *priority*.

47. Modify the *hwint_master* and *hwint_slave* macros in *mpx386.s* so the operations now performed by the *save* function are performed inline. What is the cost in code size? Can you measure an increase in performance?

48. Explain all of the items displayed by the MINIX 3 *sysenv* command on your MINIX 3 system. If you do not have access to a running MINIX 3 system, explain the items in Fig. 2-37.

49. In the discussion of initialization of the process table we mentioned that some C compilers may generate slightly better code if you add a constant to the array instead of the index. Write a pair of short C programs to test this hypothesis.

50. Modify MINIX 3 to collect statistics about messages sent by whom to whom and write a program to collect and print these statistics in a useful way.

3

INPUT/OUTPUT

One of the main functions of an operating system is to control all the computer's I/O (Input/Output) devices. It must issue commands to the devices, catch interrupts, and handle errors. It should also provide an interface between the devices and the rest of the system that is simple and easy to use. To the extent possible, the interface should be the same for all devices (device independence). The I/O code represents a significant fraction of the total operating system. Thus to really understand what an operating system does, you have to understand how I/O works. How the operating system manages I/O is the main subject of this chapter.

This chapter is organized as follows. First we will look at some of the principles of how I/O hardware is organized. Then we will look at I/O software in general. I/O software can be structured in layers, with each layer having a well-defined task to perform. We will look at these layers to see what they do and how they fit together.

After that comes a section on deadlocks. We will define deadlocks precisely, show how they are caused, give two models for analyzing them, and discuss some algorithms for preventing their occurrence.

Then we will move on to look at MINIX 3 We will start with a bird's-eye view of I/O in MINIX 3, including interrupts, device drivers, device-dependent I/O and device-independent I/O. Following that introduction, we will look at several I/O devices in detail: disks, keyboards, and displays. For each device we will look at its hardware and software.

3.1 PRINCIPLES OF I/O HARDWARE

Different people look at I/O hardware in different ways. Electrical engineers look at it in terms of chips, wires, power supplies, motors, and all the other physical components that make up the hardware. Programmers look at the interface presented to the software—the commands the hardware accepts, the functions it carries out, and the errors that can be reported back. In this book we are concerned with programming I/O devices, not designing, building, or maintaining them, so our interest will be restricted to how the hardware is programmed, not how it works inside. Nevertheless, the programming of many I/O devices is often intimately connected with their internal operation. In the next three subsections we will provide a little general background on I/O hardware as it relates to programming.

3.1.1 I/O Devices

I/O devices can be roughly divided into two categories: **block devices** and **character devices**. A block device is one that stores information in fixed-size blocks, each one with its own address. Common block sizes range from 512 bytes to 32,768 bytes. The essential property of a block device is that it is possible to read or write each block independently of all the other ones. Disks are the most common block devices.

If you look closely, the boundary between devices that are block addressable and those that are not is not well defined. Everyone agrees that a disk is a block addressable device because no matter where the arm currently is, it is always possible to seek to another cylinder and then wait for the required block to rotate under the head. Now consider a tape drive used for making disk backups. Tapes contain a sequence of blocks. If the tape drive is given a command to read block N, it can always rewind the tape and go forward until it comes to block N. This operation is analogous to a disk doing a seek, except that it takes much longer. Also, it may or may not be possible to rewrite one block in the middle of a tape. Even if it were possible to use tapes as random access block devices, that is stretching the point somewhat: they are not normally used that way.

The other type of I/O device is the character device. A character device delivers or accepts a stream of characters, without regard to any block structure. It is not addressable and does not have any seek operation. Printers, network interfaces, mice (for pointing), rats (for psychology lab experiments), and most other devices that are not disk-like can be seen as character devices.

This classification scheme is not perfect. Some devices just do not fit in. Clocks, for example, are not block addressable. Nor do they generate or accept character streams. All they do is cause interrupts at well-defined intervals. Still, the model of block and character devices is general enough that it can be used as a basis for making some of the operating system software dealing with I/O device independent. The file system, for example, deals only with abstract block devices and leaves the device-dependent part to lower-level software called **device drivers**.

I/O devices cover a huge range in speeds, which puts considerable pressure on the software to perform well over many orders of magnitude in data rates. Fig. 3-1 shows the data rates of some common devices. Most of these devices tend to get faster as time goes on.

Device	Data rate
Keyboard	10 bytes/sec
Mouse	100 bytes/sec
56K modem	7 KB/sec
Scanner	400 KB/sec
Digital camcorder	4 MB/sec
52x CD-ROM	8 MB/sec
FireWire (IEEE 1394)	50 MB/sec
USB 2.0	60 MB/sec
XGA Monitor	60 MB/sec
SONET OC-12 network	78 MB/sec
Gigabit Ethernet	125 MB/sec
Serial ATA disk	200 MB/sec
SCSI Ultrawide 4 disk	320 MB/sec
PCI bus	528 MB/sec

Figure 3-1. Some typical device, network, and bus data rates.

3.1.2 Device Controllers

I/O units typically consist of a mechanical component and an electronic component. It is often possible to separate the two portions to provide a more modular and general design. The electronic component is called the **device controller** or **adapter**. On personal computers, it often takes the form of a printed circuit card that can be inserted into an expansion slot. The mechanical component is the device itself. This arrangement is shown in Fig. 3-2

The controller card usually has a connector on it, into which a cable leading to the device itself can be plugged. Many controllers can handle two, four, or even eight identical devices. If the interface between the controller and device is a standard interface, either an official ANSI, IEEE, or ISO standard or a de facto one, then companies can make controllers or devices that fit that interface. Many companies, for example, make disk drives that match the IDE (Integrated Drive Electronics) and SCSI (Small Computer System Interface) interfaces.

We mention this distinction between controller and device because the operating system nearly always deals with the controller, not the device. Most personal computers and servers use the bus model of Fig. 3-2 for communication between the CPU and the controllers. Large mainframes often use a different model, with specialized I/O computers called **I/O channels** taking some of the load off the main CPU.

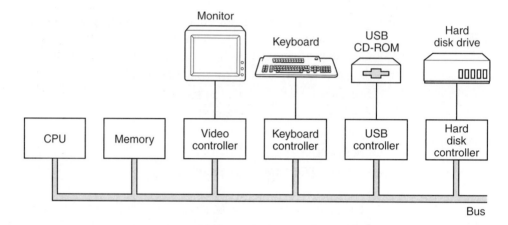

Figure 3-2. A model for connecting the CPU, memory, controllers, and I/O devices.

The interface between the controller and the device is often low-level. A disk, for example, might be formatted with 1024 sectors of 512 bytes per track. What actually comes off the drive, however, is a serial bit stream, starting with a **preamble**, then the 4096 bits in a sector, and finally a checksum, also called an **Error-Correcting Code** (**ECC**). The preamble is written when the disk is formatted and contains the cylinder and sector number, the sector size, and similar data.

The controller's job is to convert the serial bit stream into a block of bytes and perform any error correction necessary. The block of bytes is typically first assembled, bit by bit, in a buffer inside the controller. After its checksum has been verified and the block declared to be free of errors, it can then be copied to main memory.

The controller for a monitor also works as a bit serial device at an equally low level. It reads bytes containing the characters to be displayed from memory and generates the signals used to modulate the CRT beam. The controller also generates the signals for making a CRT beam do a horizontal retrace after it has finished a scan line, as well as the signals for making it do a vertical retrace after the entire screen has been scanned. On an LCD screen these signals select individual pixels and control their brightness, simulating the effect of the electron beam in a CRT. If it were not for the video controller, the operating system programmer would have to program the scanning explicitly. With the controller, the operating system initializes the controller with a few parameters, such as the number of characters or pixels per line and number of lines per screen, and lets the controller take care of actually driving the display.

Controllers for some devices, especially disks, are becoming extremely sophisticated. For example, modern disk controllers often have many megabytes of memory inside the controller. As a result, when a read is being processed, as soon as the arm gets to the correct cylinder, the controller begins reading and storing data, even if it has not yet reached the sector it needs. This cached data may come in handy for satisfying subsequent requests. Furthermore, even after the requested data has been obtained, the controller may continue to cache data from subsequent sectors, since they are likely to be needed later. In this manner, many disk reads can be handled without any disk activity at all.

3.1.3 Memory-Mapped I/O

Each controller has a few registers that are used for communicating with the CPU. By writing into these registers, the operating system can command the device to deliver data, accept data, switch itself on or off, or otherwise perform some action. By reading from these registers, the operating system can learn what the device's state is, whether it is prepared to accept a new command, and so on.

In addition to the control registers, many devices have a data buffer that the operating system can read and write. For example, a common way for computers to display pixels on the screen is to have a video RAM, which is basically just a data buffer, available for programs or the operating system to write into.

The issue thus arises of how the CPU communicates with the control registers and the device data buffers. Two alternatives exist. In the first approach, each control register is assigned an **I/O port** number, an 8- or 16-bit integer. Using a special I/O instruction such as

    IN REG,PORT

the CPU can read in control register PORT and store the result in CPU register REG. Similarly, using

    OUT PORT,REG

the CPU can write the contents of REG to a control register. Most early computers, including nearly all mainframes, such as the IBM 360 and all of its successors, worked this way.

In this scheme, the address spaces for memory and I/O are different, as shown in Fig. 3-3(a).

On other computers, I/O registers are part of the regular memory address space, as shown in Fig. 3-3(b). This scheme is called **memory-mapped I/O**, and was introduced with the PDP-11 minicomputer. Each control register is assigned a

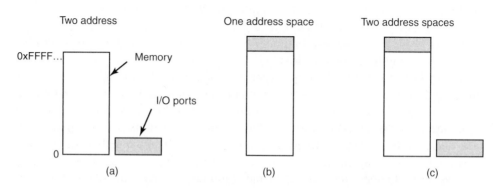

Figure 3-3. (a) Separate I/O and memory space. (b) Memory-mapped I/O.
(c) Hybrid.

unique memory address to which no memory is assigned. Usually, the assigned addresses are at the top of the address space. A hybrid scheme, with memory-mapped I/O data buffers and separate I/O ports for the control registers is shown in Fig. 3-3(c). The Pentium uses this architecture, with addresses 640K to 1M being reserved for device data buffers in IBM PC compatibles, in addition to I/O ports 0 through 64K.

How do these schemes work? In all cases, when the CPU wants to read a word, either from memory or from an I/O port, it puts the address it needs on the address lines of the bus and then asserts a READ signal on a bus control line. A second signal line is used to tell whether I/O space or memory space is needed. If it is memory space, the memory responds to the request. If it is I/O space, the I/O device responds to the request. If there is only memory space [as in Fig. 3-3(b)], every memory module and every I/O device compares the address lines to the range of addresses that it services. If the address falls in its range, it responds to the request. Since no address is ever assigned to both memory and an I/O device, there is no ambiguity and no conflict.

3.1.4 Interrupts

Usually, controller registers have one or more **status bits** that can be tested to determine if an output operation is complete or if new data is available from an input device. A CPU can execute a loop, testing a status bit each time until a device is ready to accept or provide new data. This is called **polling** or **busy waiting**. We saw this concept in Sec. 2.2.3 as a possible method to deal with critical sections, and in that context it was dismissed as something to be avoided in most circumstances. In the realm of I/O, where you might have to wait a very long time for the outside world to accept or produce data, polling is not acceptable except for very small dedicated systems not running multiple processes.

In addition to status bits, many controllers use interrupts to tell the CPU when they are ready to have their registers read or written. We saw how interrupts are handled by the CPU in Sec. 2.1.6. In the context of I/O, all you need to know is that most interface devices provide an output which is logically the same as the "operation complete" or "data ready" status bit of a register, but which is meant to be used to drive one of the IRQ (Interrupt ReQuest) lines of the system bus. Thus when an interrupt-enabled operation completes, it interrupts the CPU and starts the interrupt handler running. This piece of code informs the operating system that I/O is complete. The operating system may then check the status bits to verify that all went well, and either harvest the resulting data or initiate a retry.

The number of inputs to the interrupt controller may be limited; Pentium-class PCs have only 15 available for I/O devices. Some controllers are hard-wired onto the system parentboard, for example, the disk and keyboard controllers of an IBM PC. On older systems, the IRQ used by the device was set by a switch or jumper associated with the controller. If a user bought a new plug-in board, he had to manually set the IRQ to avoid conflicts with existing IRQs. Few users could do this correctly, which led the industry to develop **Plug 'n Play**, in which the BIOS can automatically assign IRQs to devices at boot time to avoid conflicts.

3.1.5 Direct Memory Access (DMA)

Whether or not a system has memory-mapped I/O, its CPU needs to address the device controllers to exchange data with them. The CPU can request data from an I/O controller one byte at a time but doing so for a device like a disk that produces a large block of data wastes the CPU's time, so a different scheme, called **DMA (Direct Memory Access)** is often used. The operating system can only use DMA if the hardware has a DMA controller, which most systems do. Sometimes this controller is integrated into disk controllers and other controllers, but such a design requires a separate DMA controller for each device. More commonly, a single DMA controller is available (e.g., on the parentboard) for regulating transfers to multiple devices, often concurrently.

No matter where it is physically located, the DMA controller has access to the system bus independent of the CPU, as shown in Fig. 3-4. It contains several registers that can be written and read by the CPU. These include a memory address register, a byte count register, and one or more control registers. The control registers specify the I/O port to use, the direction of the transfer (reading from the I/O device or writing to the I/O device), the transfer unit (byte at a time or word at a time), and the number of bytes to transfer in one burst.

To explain how DMA works, let us first look at how disk reads occur when DMA is not used. First the controller reads the block (one or more sectors) from the drive serially, bit by bit, until the entire block is in the controller's internal buffer. Next, it computes the checksum to verify that no read errors have occurred. Then the controller causes an interrupt. When the operating system starts

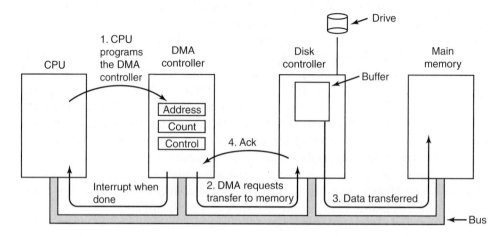

Figure 3-4. Operation of a DMA transfer.

running, it can read the disk block from the controller's buffer a byte or a word at a time by executing a loop, with each iteration reading one byte or word from a controller device register, storing it in main memory, incrementing the memory address, and decrementing the count of items to be read until it reaches zero.

When DMA is used, the procedure is different. First the CPU programs the DMA controller by setting its registers so it knows what to transfer where (step 1 in Fig. 3-4). It also issues a command to the disk controller telling it to read data from the disk into its internal buffer and verify the checksum. When valid data are in the disk controller's buffer, DMA can begin.

The DMA controller initiates the transfer by issuing a read request over the bus to the disk controller (step 2). This read request looks like any other read request, and the disk controller does not know or care whether it came from the CPU or from a DMA controller. Typically, the memory address to write to is on the address lines of the bus so when the disk controller fetches the next word from its internal buffer, it knows where to write it. The write to memory is another standard bus cycle (step 3). When the write is complete, the disk controller sends an acknowledgement signal to the disk controller, also over the bus (step 4). The DMA controller then increments the memory address to use and decrements the byte count. If the byte count is still greater than 0, steps 2 through 4 are repeated until the count reaches 0. At this point the controller causes an interrupt. When the operating system starts up, it does not have to copy the block to memory; it is already there.

You may be wondering why the controller does not just store the bytes in main memory as soon as it gets them from the disk. In other words, why does it need an internal buffer? There are two reasons. First, by doing internal buffering, the disk controller can verify the checksum before starting a transfer. If the checksum is incorrect, an error is signaled and no transfer to memory is done.

The second reason is that once a disk transfer has started, the bits keep arriving from the disk at a constant rate, whether the controller is ready for them or not. If the controller tried to write data directly to memory, it would have to go over the system bus for each word transferred. If the bus were busy due to some other device using it, the controller would have to wait. If the next disk word arrived before the previous one had been stored, the controller would have to store it somewhere. If the bus were very busy, the controller might end up storing quite a few words and having a lot of administration to do as well. When the block is buffered internally, the bus is not needed until the DMA begins, so the design of the controller is much simpler because the DMA transfer to memory is not time critical.

Not all computers use DMA. The argument against it is that the main CPU is often far faster than the DMA controller and can do the job much faster (when the limiting factor is not the speed of the I/O device). If there is no other work for it to do, having the (fast) CPU wait for the (slow) DMA controller to finish is pointless. Also, getting rid of the DMA controller and having the CPU do all the work in software saves money, important on low-end (embedded) computers.

3.2 PRINCIPLES OF I/O SOFTWARE

Let us now turn away from the I/O hardware and look at the I/O software. First we will look at the goals of the I/O software and then at the different ways I/O can be done from the point of view of the operating system.

3.2.1 Goals of the I/O Software

A key concept in the design of I/O software is **device independence**. What this means is that it should be possible to write programs that can access any I/O device without having to specify the device in advance. For example, a program that reads a file as input should be able to read a file on a floppy disk, on a hard disk, or on a CD-ROM, without having to modify the program for each different device. Similarly, one should be able to type a command such as

        sort <input >output

and have it work with input coming from a floppy disk, an IDE disk, a SCSI disk, or the keyboard, and the output going to any kind of disk or the screen. It is up to the operating system to take care of the problems caused by the fact that these devices really are different and require very different command sequences to read or write.

Closely related to device independence is the goal of **uniform naming**. The name of a file or a device should simply be a string or an integer and not depend on the device in any way. In UNIX and MINIX 3, all disks can be integrated into the file system hierarchy in arbitrary ways so the user need not be aware of which name corresponds to which device. For example, a floppy disk can be **mounted** on top of the directory */usr/ast/backup* so that copying a file to that directory copies the file to the diskette. In this way, all files and devices are addressed the same way: by a path name.

Another important issue for I/O software is **error handling**. In general, errors should be handled as close to the hardware as possible. If the controller discovers a read error, it should try to correct the error itself if it can. If it cannot, then the device driver should handle it, perhaps by just trying to read the block again. Many errors are transient, such as read errors caused by specks of dust on the read head, and will go away if the operation is repeated. Only if the lower layers are not able to deal with the problem should the upper layers be told about it. In many cases, error recovery can be done transparently at a low level without the upper levels even knowing about the error.

Still another key issue is **synchronous** (blocking) versus **asynchronous** (interrupt-driven) transfers. Most physical I/O is asynchronous—the CPU starts the transfer and goes off to do something else until the interrupt arrives. User programs are much easier to write if the I/O operations are blocking—after a receive system call the program is automatically suspended until the data are available in the buffer. It is up to the operating system to make operations that are actually interrupt-driven look blocking to the user programs.

Another issue for the I/O software is **buffering**. Often data that come off a device cannot be stored directly in its final destination. For example, when a packet comes in off the network, the operating system does not know where to put it until it has stored the packet somewhere and examined it. Also, some devices have severe real-time constraints (for example, digital audio devices), so the data must be put into an output buffer in advance to decouple the rate at which the buffer is filled from the rate at which it is emptied, in order to avoid buffer underruns. Buffering involves considerable copying and often has a major impact on I/O performance.

The final concept that we will mention here is sharable versus dedicated devices. Some I/O devices, such as disks, can be used by many users at the same time. No problems are caused by multiple users having open files on the same disk at the same time. Other devices, such as tape drives, have to be dedicated to a single user until that user is finished. Then another user can have the tape drive. Having two or more users writing blocks intermixed at random to the same tape will definitely not work. Introducing dedicated (unshared) devices also introduces a variety of problems, such as deadlocks. Again, the operating system must be able to handle both shared and dedicated devices in a way that avoids problems.

I/O software is often organized in four layers, as shown in Fig. 3-5. In the following subsections we will look at each in turn, starting at the bottom. The emphasis in this chapter is on the device drivers (layer 2), but we will summarize the rest of the I/O software to show how the pieces of the I/O system fit together.

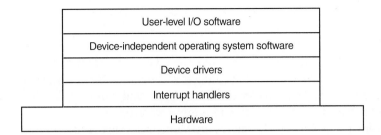

Figure 3-5. Layers of the I/O software system.

3.2.2 Interrupt Handlers

Interrupts are an unpleasant fact of life; although they cannot be avoided, they should be hidden away, deep in the bowels of the operating system, so that as little of the operating system as possible knows about them. The best way to hide them is to have the driver starting an I/O operation block until the I/O has completed and the interrupt occurs. The driver can block itself by doing a **down** on a semaphore, a **wait** on a condition variable, a **receive** on a message, or something similar, for example.

When the interrupt happens, the interrupt procedure does whatever it has to in order to handle the interrupt. Then it can unblock the driver that started it. In some cases it will just complete **up** on a semaphore. In others it will do a **signal** on a condition variable in a monitor. In still others, it will send a message to the blocked driver. In all cases the net effect of the interrupt will be that a driver that was previously blocked will now be able to run. This model works best if drivers are structured as independent processes, with their own states, stacks, and program counters.

3.2.3 Device Drivers

Earlier in this chapter we saw that each device controller has registers used to give it commands or to read out its status or both. The number of registers and the nature of the commands vary radically from device to device. For example, a mouse driver has to accept information from the mouse telling how far it has moved and which buttons are currently depressed. In contrast, a disk driver has to know about sectors, tracks, cylinders, heads, arm motion, motor drives, head settling times, and all the other mechanics of making the disk work properly. Obviously, these drivers will be very different.

Thus, each I/O device attached to a computer needs some device-specific code for controlling it. This code, called the **device driver**, is generally written by the device's manufacturer and delivered along with the device on a CD-ROM.

Since each operating system needs its own drivers, device manufacturers commonly supply drivers for several popular operating systems.

Each device driver normally handles one device type, or one class of closely related devices. For example, it would probably be a good idea to have a single mouse driver, even if the system supports several different brands of mice. As another example, a disk driver can usually handle multiple disks of different sizes and different speeds, and perhaps a CD-ROM as well. On the other hand, a mouse and a disk are so different that different drivers are necessary.

In order to access the device's hardware, meaning the controller's registers, the device driver traditionally has been part of the system kernel. This approach gives the best performance and the worst reliability since a bug in any device driver can crash the entire system. MINIX 3 departs from this model in order to enhance reliability. As we shall see, in MINIX 3 each device driver is now a separate user-mode process.

As we mentioned earlier, operating systems usually classify drivers as **block devices**, such as disks, or **character devices**, such as keyboards and printers. Most operating systems define a standard interface that all block drivers must support and a second standard interface that all character drivers must support. These interfaces consist of a number of procedures that the rest of the operating system can call to get the driver to do work for it.

In general terms, the job of a device driver is to accept abstract requests from the device-independent software above it and see to it that the request is executed. A typical request to a disk driver is to read block n. If the driver is idle at the time a request comes in, it starts carrying out the request immediately. If, however, it is already busy with a request, it will normally enter the new request into a queue of pending requests to be dealt with as soon as possible.

The first step in actually carrying out an I/O request is to check that the input parameters are valid and to return an error if they are not. If the request is valid the next step is to translate it from abstract to concrete terms. For a disk driver, this means figuring out where on the disk the requested block actually is, checking to see if the drive's motor is running, determining if the arm is positioned on the proper cylinder, and so on. In short, the driver must decide which controller operations are required and in what sequence.

Once the driver has determined which commands to issue to the controller, it starts issuing them by writing into the controller's device registers. Simple controllers can handle only one command at a time. More sophisticated controllers are willing to accept a linked list of commands, which they then carry out by themselves without further help from the operating system.

After the command or commands have been issued, one of two situations will apply. In many cases the device driver must wait until the controller does some work for it, so it blocks itself until the interrupt comes in to unblock it. In other cases, however, the operation finishes without delay, so the driver need not block. As an example of the latter situation, scrolling the screen on some graphics cards requires just writing a few bytes into the controller's registers. No mechanical motion is needed, so the entire operation can be completed in a few microseconds.

In the former case, the blocked driver will be awakened by the interrupt. In the latter case, it will never go to sleep. Either way, after the operation has been completed, it must check for errors. If everything is all right, the driver may have data to pass to the device-independent software (e.g., a block just read). Finally, it returns some status information for error reporting back to its caller. If any other requests are queued, one of them can now be selected and started. If nothing is queued, the driver blocks waiting for the next request.

Dealing with requests for reading and writing is the main function of a driver, but there may be other requirements. For instance, the driver may need to initialize a device at system startup or the first time it is used. Also, there may be a need to manage power requirements, handle Plug 'n Play, or log events.

3.2.4 Device-Independent I/O Software

Although some of the I/O software is device specific, a large fraction of it is device independent. The exact boundary between the drivers and the device-independent software is system dependent, because some functions that could be done in a device-independent way may actually be done in the drivers, for efficiency or other reasons. The functions shown in Fig. 3-6 are typically done in the device-independent software. In MINIX 3, most of the device-independent software is part of the file system. Although we will study the file system in Chap. 5, we will take a quick look at the device-independent software here, to provide some perspective on I/O and show better where the drivers fit in.

Uniform interfacing for device drivers
Buffering
Error reporting
Allocating and releasing dedicated devices
Providing a device-independent block size

Figure 3-6. Functions of the device-independent I/O software.

The basic function of the device-independent software is to perform the I/O functions that are common to all devices and to provide a uniform interface to the user-level software. Below we will look at the above issues in more detail.

Uniform Interfacing for Device Drivers

A major issue in an operating system is how to make all I/O devices and drivers look more-or-less the same. If disks, printers, monitors, keyboards, etc., are all interfaced in different ways, every time a new peripheral device comes along, the operating system must be modified for the new device. In Fig. 3-7(a) we illustrate symbolically a situation in which each device driver has a different interface to the operating system. In contrast, in Fig. 3-7(b), we show a different design in which all drivers have the same interface.

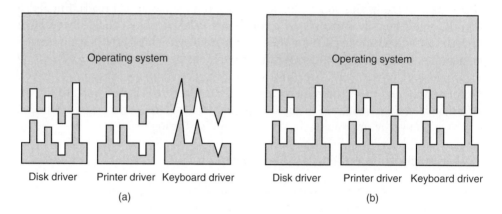

Figure 3-7. (a) Without a standard driver interface. (b) With a standard driver interface.

With a standard interface it is much easier to plug in a new driver, providing it conforms to the driver interface. It also means that driver writers know what is expected of them (e.g., what functions they must provide and what kernel functions they may call). In practice, not all devices are absolutely identical, but usually there are only a small number of device types and even these are generally almost the same. For example, even block and character devices have many functions in common.

Another aspect of having a uniform interface is how I/O devices are named. The device-independent software takes care of mapping symbolic device names onto the proper driver. For example, in UNIX and MINIX 3 a device name, such as */dev/disk0*, uniquely specifies the i-node for a special file, and this i-node contains the **major device number**, which is used to locate the appropriate driver. The i-node also contains the **minor device number**, which is passed as a parameter to the driver in order to specify the unit to be read or written. All devices have major and minor numbers, and all drivers are accessed by using the major device number to select the driver.

Closely related to naming is protection. How does the system prevent users from accessing devices that they are not entitled to access? In UNIX, MINIX 3, and also in later Windows versions such as Windows 2000 and Windows XP, devices appear in the file system as named objects, which means that the usual protection rules for files also apply to I/O devices. The system administrator can then set the proper permissions (i.e., in UNIX the *rwx* bits) for each device.

Buffering

Buffering is also an issue for both block and character devices. For block devices, the hardware generally insists upon reading and writing entire blocks at once, but user processes are free to read and write in arbitrary units. If a user process writes half a block, the operating system will normally keep the data around internally until the rest of the data are written, at which time the block can go out to the disk. For character devices, users can write data to the system faster than it can be output, necessitating buffering. Keyboard input that arrives before it is needed also requires buffering.

Error Reporting

Errors are far more common in the context of I/O than in any other context. When they occur, the operating system must handle them as best it can. Many errors are device-specific, so only the driver knows what to do (e.g., retry, ignore, or panic). A typical error is caused by a disk block that has been damaged and cannot be read any more. After the driver has tried to read the block a certain number of times, it gives up and informs the device-independent software. How the error is treated from here on is device independent. If the error occurred while reading a user file, it may be sufficient to report the error back to the caller. However, if it occurred while reading a critical system data structure, such as the block containing the bitmap showing which blocks are free, the operating system may have to display an error message and terminate.

Allocating and Releasing Dedicated Devices

Some devices, such as CD-ROM recorders, can be used only by a single process at any given moment. It is up to the operating system to examine requests for device usage and accept or reject them, depending on whether the requested device is available or not. A simple way to handle these requests is to require processes to perform opens on the special files for devices directly. If the device is unavailable, the open fails. Closing such a dedicated device then releases it.

Device-Independent Block Size

Not all disks have the same sector size. It is up to the device-independent software to hide this fact and provide a uniform block size to higher layers, for example, by treating several sectors as a single logical block. In this way, the higher layers only deal with abstract devices that all use the same logical block size, independent of the physical sector size. Similarly, some character devices deliver their data one byte at a time (e.g., modems), while others deliver theirs in larger units (e.g., network interfaces). These differences may also be hidden.

3.2.5 User-Space I/O Software

Although most of the I/O software is within the operating system, a small portion of it consists of libraries linked together with user programs, and even whole programs running outside the kernel. System calls, including the I/O system calls, are normally made by library procedures. When a C program contains the call

```
count = write(fd, buffer, nbytes);
```

the library procedure *write* will be linked with the program and contained in the binary program present in memory at run time. The collection of all these library procedures is clearly part of the I/O system.

While these procedures do little more than put their parameters in the appropriate place for the system call, there are other I/O procedures that actually do real work. In particular, formatting of input and output is done by library procedures. One example from C is *printf*, which takes a format string and possibly some variables as input, builds an ASCII string, and then calls write to output the string. As an example of *printf*, consider the statement

```
printf("The square of %3d is  %6d\n", i, i*i);
```

It formats a string consisting of the 14-character string "The square of " followed by the value i as a 3-character string, then the 4-character string " is ", then i^2 as six characters, and finally a line feed.

An example of a similar procedure for input is *scanf* which reads input and stores it into variables described in a format string using the same syntax as *printf*. The standard I/O library contains a number of procedures that involve I/O and all run as part of user programs.

Not all user-level I/O software consists of library procedures. Another important category is the spooling system. **Spooling** is a way of dealing with dedicated I/O devices in a multiprogramming system. Consider a typical spooled device: a printer. Although it would be technically simple to let any user process open the character special file for the printer, suppose a process opened it and then did nothing for hours? No other process could print anything.

Instead what is done is to create a special process, called a **daemon**, and a special directory, called a **spooling directory**. To print a file, a process first generates the entire file to be printed and puts it in the spooling directory. It is up to the daemon, which is the only process having permission to use the printer's special file, to print the files in the directory. By protecting the special file against direct use by users, the problem of having someone keeping it open unnecessarily long is eliminated.

Spooling is used not only for printers, but also in various other situations. For example, electronic mail usually uses a daemon. When a message is submitted it is put in a mail spool directory. Later on the mail daemon tries to send it. At any given instant of time a particular destination may be temporarily unreachable, so the daemon leaves the message in the spool with status information indicating it should be tried again in a while. The daemon may also send a message back to the sender saying delivery is delayed, or, after a delay of hours or days, saying the message cannot be delivered. All of this is outside the operating system.

Figure 3-8 summarizes the I/O system, showing the layers and principal functions of each layer. Starting at the bottom, the layers are the hardware, interrupt handlers, device drivers, device-independent software, and the user processes.

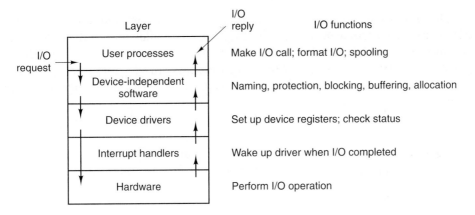

Figure 3-8. Layers of the I/O system and the main functions of each layer.

The arrows in Fig. 3-8 show the flow of control. When a user program tries to read a block from a file, for example, the operating system is invoked to carry out the call. The device-independent software looks for it in the buffer cache, for example. If the needed block is not there, it calls the device driver to issue the request to the hardware to go get it from the disk. The process is then blocked until the disk operation has been completed.

When the disk is finished, the hardware generates an interrupt. The interrupt handler is run to discover what has happened, that is, which device wants attention right now. It then extracts the status from the device and wakes up the sleeping process to finish off the I/O request and let the user process continue.

3.3 DEADLOCKS

Computer systems are full of resources that can only be used by one process at a time. Common examples include printers, tape drives, and slots in the system's internal tables. Having two processes simultaneously writing to the printer leads to gibberish. Having two processes using the same file system table slot will invariably lead to a corrupted file system. Consequently, all operating systems have the ability to (temporarily) grant a process exclusive access to certain resources, both hardware and software.

For many applications, a process needs exclusive access to not one resource, but several. Suppose, for example, two processes each want to record a scanned document on a CD. Process *A* requests permission to use the scanner and is granted it. Process *B* is programmed differently and requests the CD recorder first and is also granted it. Now *A* asks for the CD recorder, but the request is denied until *B* releases it. Unfortunately, instead of releasing the CD recorder *B* asks for the scanner. At this point both processes are blocked and will remain so forever. This situation is called a **deadlock**.

Deadlocks can occur in a variety of situations besides requesting dedicated I/O devices. In a database system, for example, a program may have to lock several records it is using, to avoid race conditions. If process *A* locks record *R1* and process *B* locks record *R2*, and then each process tries to lock the other one's record, we also have a deadlock. Thus deadlocks can occur on hardware resources or on software resources.

In this section, we will look at deadlocks more closely, see how they arise, and study some ways of preventing or avoiding them. Although this material is about deadlocks in the context of operating systems, they also occur in database systems and many other contexts in computer science, so this material is actually applicable to a wide variety of multiprocess systems.

3.3.1 Resources

Deadlocks can occur when processes have been granted exclusive access to devices, files, and so forth. To make the discussion of deadlocks as general as possible, we will refer to the objects granted as **resources**. A resource can be a hardware device (e.g., a tape drive) or a piece of information (e.g., a locked record in a database). A computer will normally have many different resources that can be acquired. For some resources, several identical instances may be available, such as three tape drives. When interchangeable copies of a resource are available, called **fungible resources**†, any one of them can be used to satisfy any request for the resource. In short, a resource is anything that can be used by only a single process at any instant of time.

Resources come in two types: preemptable and nonpreemptable. A **preemptable resource** is one that can be taken away from the process owning it with no ill effects. Memory is an example of a preemptable resource. Consider, for example, a system with 64 MB of user memory, one printer, and two 64-MB processes that each want to print something. Process *A* requests and gets the printer, then starts to compute the values to print. Before it has finished with the computation, it exceeds its time quantum and is swapped or paged out.

Process *B* now runs and tries, unsuccessfully, to acquire the printer. Potentially, we now have a deadlock situation, because *A* has the printer and *B* has the

†This is a legal and financial term. Gold is fungible: one gram of gold is as good as any other.

memory, and neither can proceed without the resource held by the other. Fortunately, it is possible to preempt (take away) the memory from B by swapping it out and swapping A in. Now A can run, do its printing, and then release the printer. No deadlock occurs.

A **nonpreemptable resource**, in contrast, is one that cannot be taken away from its current owner without causing the computation to fail. If a process has begun to burn a CD-ROM, suddenly taking the CD recorder away from it and giving it to another process will result in a garbled CD. CD recorders are not preemptable at an arbitrary moment.

In general, deadlocks involve nonpreemptable resources. Potential deadlocks that involve preemptable resources can usually be resolved by reallocating resources from one process to another. Thus our treatment will focus on nonpreemptable resources.

The sequence of events required to use a resource is given below in an abstract form.

1. Request the resource.

2. Use the resource.

3. Release the resource.

If the resource is not available when it is requested, the requesting process is forced to wait. In some operating systems, the process is automatically blocked when a resource request fails, and awakened when it becomes available. In other systems, the request fails with an error code, and it is up to the calling process to wait a little while and try again.

3.3.2 Principles of Deadlock

Deadlock can be defined formally as follows:

A set of processes is deadlocked if each process in the set is waiting for an event that only another process in the set can cause.

Because all the processes are waiting, none of them will ever cause any of the events that could wake up any of the other members of the set, and all the processes continue to wait forever. For this model, we assume that processes have only a single thread and that there are no interrupts possible to wake up a blocked process. The no-interrupts condition is needed to prevent an otherwise deadlocked process from being awakened by, say, an alarm, and then causing events that release other processes in the set.

In most cases, the event that each process is waiting for is the release of some resource currently possessed by another member of the set. In other words, each member of the set of deadlocked processes is waiting for a resource that is owned by a deadlocked process. None of the processes can run, none of them can release any resources, and none of them can be awakened. The number of processes and the number and kind of resources possessed and requested are unimportant. This result holds for any kind of resource, including both hardware and software.

Conditions for Deadlock

Coffman et al. (1971) showed that four conditions must hold for there to be a deadlock:

1. Mutual exclusion condition. Each resource is either currently assigned to exactly one process or is available.

2. Hold and wait condition. Processes currently holding resources that were granted earlier can request new resources.

3. No preemption condition. Resources previously granted cannot be forcibly taken away from a process. They must be explicitly released by the process holding them.

4. Circular wait condition. There must be a circular chain of two or more processes, each of which is waiting for a resource held by the next member of the chain.

All four of these conditions must be present for a deadlock to occur. If one of them is absent, no deadlock is possible.

In a series of papers, Levine (2003a, 2003b, 2005) points out there are various situations called deadlock in the literature, and that Coffman et al.'s conditions apply only to what should properly be called **resource deadlock**. The literature contains examples of "deadlock" that do not really meet all of these conditions. For instance, if four vehicles arrive simultaneously at a crossroad and try to obey the rule that each should yield to the vehicle on the right, none can proceed, but this is not a case where one process already has possession of a unique resource. Rather, this problem is a "scheduling deadlock" which can be resolved by a decision about priorities imposed from outside by a policeman.

It is worth noting that each condition relates to a policy that a system can have or not have. Can a given resource be assigned to more than one process at once? Can a process hold a resource and ask for another? Can resources be preempted? Can circular waits exist? Later on we will see how deadlocks can be attacked by trying to negate some of these conditions.

Deadlock Modeling

Holt (1972) showed how these four conditions can be modeled using directed graphs. The graphs have two kinds of nodes: processes, shown as circles, and resources, shown as squares. An arc from a resource node (square) to a process node (circle) means that the resource has previously been requested by, granted to, and is currently held by that process. In Fig. 3-9(a), resource *R* is currently assigned to process *A*.

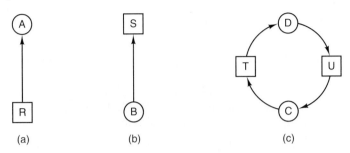

Figure 3-9. Resource allocation graphs. (a) Holding a resource. (b) Requesting a resource. (c) Deadlock.

An arc from a process to a resource means that the process is currently blocked waiting for that resource. In Fig. 3-9(b), process *B* is waiting for resource *S*. In Fig. 3-9(c) we see a deadlock: process *C* is waiting for resource *T*, which is currently held by process *D*. Process *D* is not about to release resource *T* because it is waiting for resource *U*, held by *C*. Both processes will wait forever. A cycle in the graph means that there is a deadlock involving the processes and resources in the cycle (assuming that there is one resource of each kind). In this example, the cycle is *C−T−D−U−C*.

Now let us see how resource graphs can be used. Imagine that we have three processes, *A*, *B*, and *C*, and three resources, *R*, *S*, and *T*. The requests and releases of the three processes are given in Fig. 3-10(a)-(c). The operating system is free to run any unblocked process at any instant, so it could decide to run *A* until *A* finished all its work, then run *B* to completion, and finally run *C*.

This ordering does not lead to any deadlocks (because there is no competition for resources) but it also has no parallelism at all. In addition to requesting and releasing resources, processes compute and do I/O. When the processes are run sequentially, there is no possibility that while one process is waiting for I/O, another can use the CPU. Thus running the processes strictly sequentially may not be optimal. On the other hand, if none of the processes do any I/O at all, shortest job first is better than round robin, so under some circumstances running all processes sequentially may be the best way.

Let us now suppose that the processes do both I/O and computing, so that round robin is a reasonable scheduling algorithm. The resource requests might occur in the order of Fig. 3-10(d). If these six requests are carried out in that order, the six resulting resource graphs are shown in Fig. 3-10(e)-(j). After request 4 has been made, *A* blocks waiting for *S*, as shown in Fig. 3-10(h). In the next two steps *B* and *C* also block, ultimately leading to a cycle and the deadlock of Fig. 3-10(j). From this point on, the system is frozen.

However, as we have already mentioned, the operating system is not required to run the processes in any special order. In particular, if granting a particular request might lead to deadlock, the operating system can simply suspend the process without granting the request (i.e., just not schedule the process) until it is safe. In Fig. 3-10, if the operating system knew about the impending deadlock, it could suspend *B* instead of granting it *S*. By running only *A* and *C*, we would get the requests and releases of Fig. 3-10(k) instead of Fig. 3-10(d). This sequence leads to the resource graphs of Fig. 3-10(l)-(q), which do not lead to deadlock.

After step (q), process *B* can be granted *S* because *A* is finished and *C* has everything it needs. Even if *B* should eventually block when requesting *T*, no deadlock can occur. *B* will just wait until *C* is finished.

Later in this chapter we will study a detailed algorithm for making allocation decisions that do not lead to deadlock. For the moment, the point to understand is that resource graphs are a tool that let us see if a given request/release sequence leads to deadlock. We just carry out the requests and releases step by step, and after every step check the graph to see if it contains any cycles. If so, we have a deadlock; if not, there is no deadlock. Although our treatment of resource graphs has been for the case of a single resource of each type, resource graphs can also be generalized to handle multiple resources of the same type (Holt, 1972). However, Levine (2003a, 2003b) points out that with fungible resources this can get very complicated indeed. If even one branch of the graph is not part of a cycle, that is, if one process which is not deadlocked holds a copy of one of the resources, then deadlock may not occur.

In general, four strategies are used for dealing with deadlocks.

1. Just ignore the problem altogether. Maybe if you ignore it, it will ignore you.

2. Detection and recovery. Let deadlocks occur, detect them, and take action.

3. Dynamic avoidance by careful resource allocation.

4. Prevention, by structurally negating one of the four conditions necessary to cause a deadlock.

We will examine each of these methods in turn in the next four sections.

3.3.3 The Ostrich Algorithm

The simplest approach is the ostrich algorithm: stick your head in the sand and pretend there is no problem at all.† Different people react to this strategy in

---

†Actually, this bit of folklore is nonsense. Ostriches can run at 60 km/hour and their kick is powerful enough to kill any lion with visions of a big chicken dinner.

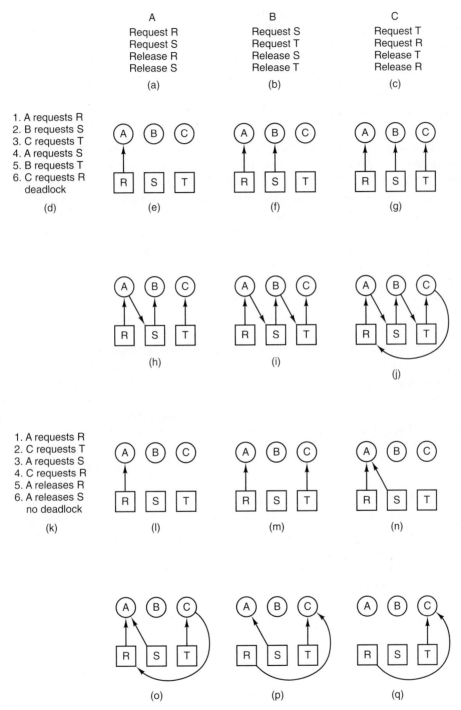

Figure 3-10. An example of how deadlock occurs and how it can be avoided.

very different ways. Mathematicians find it completely unacceptable and say that
deadlocks must be prevented at all costs. Engineers ask how often the problem is
expected, how often the system crashes for other reasons, and how serious a
deadlock is. If deadlocks occur on the average once every five years, but system
crashes due to hardware failures, compiler errors, and operating system bugs
occur once a week, most engineers would not be willing to pay a large penalty in
performance or convenience to eliminate deadlocks.

To make this contrast more specific, UNIX (and MINIX 3) potentially suffer
from deadlocks that are not even detected, let alone automatically broken. The
total number of processes in a system is determined by the number of entries in
the process table. Thus process table slots are finite resources. If a fork fails because the table is full, a reasonable approach for the program doing the fork is to
wait a random time and try again.

Now suppose that a MINIX 3 system has 100 process slots. Ten programs are
running, each of which needs to create 12 (sub)processes. After each process has
created 9 processes, the 10 original processes and the 90 new processes have
exhausted the table. Each of the 10 original processes now sits in an endless loop
forking and failing—a deadlock. The probability of this happening is minuscule,
but it *could* happen. Should we abandon processes and the fork call to eliminate
the problem?

The maximum number of open files is similarly restricted by the size of the i-
node table, so a similar problem occurs when it fills up. Swap space on the disk is
another limited resource. In fact, almost every table in the operating system
represents a finite resource. Should we abolish all of these because it might happen that a collection of n processes might each claim $1/n$ of the total, and then
each try to claim another one?

Most operating systems, including UNIX, MINIX 3, and Windows, just ignore
the problem on the assumption that most users would prefer an occasional deadlock to a rule restricting all users to one process, one open file, and one of everything. If deadlocks could be eliminated for free, there would not be much discussion. The problem is that the price is high, mostly in terms of putting inconvenient
restrictions on processes, as we will see shortly. Thus we are faced with an
unpleasant trade-off between convenience and correctness, and a great deal of discussion about which is more important, and to whom. Under these conditions,
general solutions are hard to find.

3.3.4 Detection and Recovery

A second technique is detection and recovery. When this technique is used,
the system does not do anything except monitor the requests and releases of
resources. Every time a resource is requested or released, the resource graph is
updated, and a check is made to see if any cycles exist. If a cycle exists, one of the

processes in the cycle is killed. If this does not break the deadlock, another process is killed, and so on until the cycle is broken.

A somewhat cruder method is not even to maintain the resource graph but instead periodically to check to see if there are any processes that have been continuously blocked for more than say, 1 hour. Such processes are then killed.

Detection and recovery is the strategy often used on large mainframe computers, especially batch systems in which killing a process and then restarting it is usually acceptable. Care must be taken to restore any modified files to their original state, however, and undo any other side effects that may have occurred.

3.3.5 Deadlock Prevention

The third deadlock strategy is to impose suitable restrictions on processes so that deadlocks are structurally impossible. The four conditions stated by Coffman et al. (1971) provide a clue to some possible solutions.

First let us attack the mutual exclusion condition. If no resource were ever assigned exclusively to a single process, we would never have deadlocks. However, it is equally clear that allowing two processes to write on the printer at the same time will lead to chaos. By spooling printer output, several processes can generate output at the same time. In this model, the only process that actually requests the physical printer is the printer daemon. Since the daemon never requests any other resources, we can eliminate deadlock for the printer.

Unfortunately, not all devices can be spooled (the process table does not lend itself well to being spooled). Furthermore, competition for disk space for spooling can itself lead to deadlock. What would happen if two processes each filled up half of the available spooling space with output and neither was finished producing output? If the daemon was programmed to begin printing even before all the output was spooled, the printer might lie idle if an output process decided to wait several hours after the first burst of output. For this reason, daemons are normally programmed to print only after the complete output file is available. In this case we have two processes that have each finished part, but not all, of their output, and cannot continue. Neither process will ever finish, so we have a deadlock on the disk.

The second of the conditions stated by Coffman et al. looks slightly more promising. If we can prevent processes that hold resources from waiting for more resources, we can eliminate deadlocks. One way to achieve this goal is to require all processes to request all their resources before starting execution. If everything is available, the process will be allocated whatever it needs and can run to completion. If one or more resources are busy, nothing will be allocated and the process would just wait.

An immediate problem with this approach is that many processes do not know how many resources they will need until after they have started running. Another problem is that resources will not be used optimally with this approach. Take, as an example, a process that reads data from an input tape, analyzes it for an hour, and then writes an output tape as well as plotting the results. If all resources must be requested in advance, the process will tie up the output tape drive and the plotter for an hour.

A slightly different way to break the hold-and-wait condition is to require a process requesting a resource to first temporarily release all the resources it currently holds. Then it tries to get everything it needs all at once.

Attacking the third condition (no preemption) is even less promising than attacking the second one. If a process has been assigned the printer and is in the middle of printing its output, forcibly taking away the printer because a needed plotter is not available is tricky at best and impossible at worst.

Only one condition is left. The circular wait can be eliminated in several ways. One way is simply to have a rule saying that a process is entitled only to a single resource at any moment. If it needs a second one, it must release the first one. For a process that needs to copy a huge file from a tape to a printer, this restriction is unacceptable.

Another way to avoid the circular wait is to provide a global numbering of all the resources, as shown in Fig. 3-11(a). Now the rule is this: processes can request resources whenever they want to, but all requests must be made in numerical order. A process may request first a scanner and then a tape drive, but it may not request first a plotter and then a scanner.

1. Imagesetter
2. Scanner
3. Plotter
4. Tape drive
5. CD Rom drive

(a)   (b)

Figure 3-11. (a) Numerically ordered resources. (b) A resource graph.

With this rule, the resource allocation graph can never have cycles. Let us see why this is true for the case of two processes, in Fig. 3-11(b). We can get a deadlock only if A requests resource j and B requests resource i. Assuming i and j are distinct resources, they will have different numbers. If $i > j$, then A is not allowed to request j because that is lower than what it already has. If $i < j$, then B is not allowed to request i because that is lower than what it already has. Either way, deadlock is impossible.

With multiple processes, the same logic holds. At every instant, one of the assigned resources will be highest. The process holding that resource will never ask for a resource already assigned. It will either finish, or at worst, request even higher numbered resources, all of which are available. Eventually, it will finish and free its resources. At this point, some other process will hold the highest resource and can also finish. In short, there exists a scenario in which all processes finish, so no deadlock is present.

A minor variation of this algorithm is to drop the requirement that resources be acquired in strictly increasing sequence and merely insist that no process request a resource lower than what it is already holding. If a process initially requests 9 and 10, and then releases both of them, it is effectively starting all over, so there is no reason to prohibit it from now requesting resource 1.

Although numerically ordering the resources eliminates the problem of deadlocks, it may be impossible to find an ordering that satisfies everyone. When the resources include process table slots, disk spooler space, locked database records, and other abstract resources, the number of potential resources and different uses may be so large that no ordering could possibly work. Also, as Levine (2005) points out, ordering resources negates fungibility—a perfectly good and available copy of a resource could be inaccessible with such a rule.

The various approaches to deadlock prevention are summarized in Fig. 3-12.

Condition	Approach
Mutual exclusion	Spool everything
Hold and wait	Request all resources initially
No preemption	Take resources away
Circular wait	Order resources numerically

Figure 3-12. Summary of approaches to deadlock prevention.

3.3.6 Deadlock Avoidance

In Fig. 3-10 we saw that deadlock was avoided not by imposing arbitrary rules on processes but by carefully analyzing each resource request to see if it could be safely granted. The question arises: is there an algorithm that can always avoid deadlock by making the right choice all the time? The answer is a qualified yes—we can avoid deadlocks, but only if certain information is available in advance. In this section we examine ways to avoid deadlock by careful resource allocation.

The Banker's Algorithm for a Single Resource

A scheduling algorithm that can avoid deadlocks is due to Dijkstra (1965) and is known as the **banker's algorithm**. It is modeled on the way a small-town banker might deal with a group of customers to whom he has granted lines of credit. The banker does not necessarily have enough cash on hand to lend every customer the full amount of each one's line of credit at the same time. In Fig. 3-13(a) we see four customers, *A*, *B*, *C*, and *D*, each of whom has been granted a certain number of credit units (e.g., 1 unit is 1K dollars). The banker knows that not all customers will need their maximum credit immediately, so he has reserved only 10 units rather than 22 to service them. He also trusts every customer to be able to repay his loan soon after receiving his total line of credit (it is a small town), so he knows eventually he can service all the requests. (In this analogy, customers are processes, units are, say, tape drives, and the banker is the operating system.)

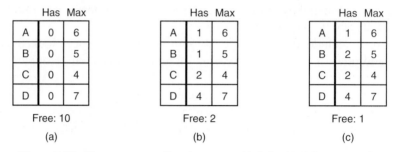

Figure 3-13. Three resource allocation states: (a) Safe. (b) Safe. (c) Unsafe.

Each part of the figure shows a **state** of the system with respect to resource allocation, that is, a list of customers showing the money already loaned (tape drives already assigned) and the maximum credit available (maximum number of tape drives needed at once later). A state is **safe** if there exists a sequence of other states that leads to all customers getting loans up to their credit limits (all processes getting all their resources and terminating).

The customers go about their respective businesses, making loan requests from time to time (i.e., asking for resources). At a certain moment, the situation is as shown in Fig. 3-13(b). This state is safe because with two units left, the banker can delay any requests except *C*'s, thus letting *C* finish and release all four of his resources. With four units in hand, the banker can let either *D* or *B* have the necessary units, and so on.

Consider what would happen if a request from *B* for one more unit were granted in Fig. 3-13(b). We would have situation Fig. 3-13(c), which is unsafe. If all the customers suddenly asked for their maximum loans, the banker could not satisfy any of them, and we would have a deadlock. An unsafe state does not *have* to lead to deadlock, since a customer might not need the entire credit line available, but the banker cannot count on this behavior.

The banker's algorithm considers each request as it occurs, and sees if granting it leads to a safe state. If it does, the request is granted; otherwise, it is postponed until later. To see if a state is safe, the banker checks to see if he has enough resources to satisfy some customer. If so, those loans are assumed to be repaid, and the customer now closest to the limit is checked, and so on. If all loans can eventually be repaid, the state is safe and the initial request can be granted.

Resource Trajectories

The above algorithm was described in terms of a single resource class (e.g., only tape drives or only printers, but not some of each). In Fig. 3-14 we see a model for dealing with two processes and two resources, for example, a printer and a plotter. The horizontal axis represents the number of instructions executed by process A. The vertical axis represents the number of instructions executed by process B. At I_1 A requests a printer; at I_2 it needs a plotter. The printer and plotter are released at I_3 and I_4, respectively. Process B needs the plotter from I_5 to I_7 and the printer from I_6 to I_8.

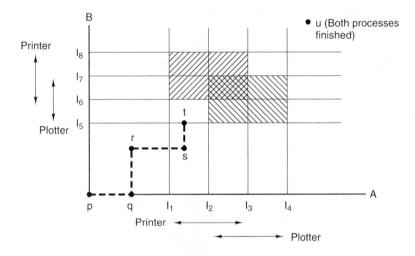

Figure 3-14. Two process resource trajectories.

Every point in the diagram represents a joint state of the two processes. Initially, the state is at p, with neither process having executed any instructions. If the scheduler chooses to run A first, we get to the point q, in which A has executed some number of instructions, but B has executed none. At point q the trajectory becomes vertical, indicating that the scheduler has chosen to run B. With a single processor, all paths must be horizontal or vertical, never diagonal. Furthermore, motion is always to the north or east, never to the south or west (processes cannot run backward).

When A crosses the I_1 line on the path from r to s, it requests and is granted the printer. When B reaches point t, it requests the plotter.

The regions that are shaded are especially interesting. The region with lines slanting from southwest to northeast represents both processes having the printer. The mutual exclusion rule makes it impossible to enter this region. Similarly, the region shaded the other way represents both processes having the plotter, and is equally impossible. Under no conditions can the system enter the shaded regions.

If the system ever enters the box bounded by I_1 and I_2 on the sides and I_5 and I_6 top and bottom, it will eventually deadlock when it gets to the intersection of I_2 and I_6. At this point, A is requesting the plotter and B is requesting the printer, and both are already assigned. The entire box is unsafe and must not be entered. At point t the only safe thing to do is run process A until it gets to I_4. Beyond that, any trajectory to u will do.

The important thing to see here is at point t B is requesting a resource. The system must decide whether to grant it or not. If the grant is made, the system will enter an unsafe region and eventually deadlock. To avoid the deadlock, B should be suspended until A has requested and released the plotter.

The Banker's Algorithm for Multiple Resources

This graphical model is difficult to apply to the general case of an arbitrary number of processes and an arbitrary number of resource classes, each with multiple instances (e.g., two plotters, three tape drives). However, the banker's algorithm can be generalized to do the job. Figure 3-15 shows how it works.

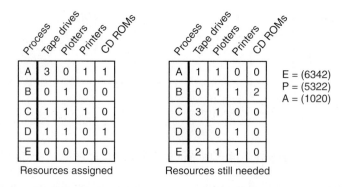

Figure 3-15. The banker's algorithm with multiple resources.

In Fig. 3-15 we see two matrices. The one on the left shows how many of each resource are currently assigned to each of the five processes. The matrix on the right shows how many resources each process still needs in order to complete. As in the single resource case, processes must state their total resource needs before executing, so that the system can compute the right-hand matrix at each instant.

The three vectors at the right of the figure show the existing resources, E, the possessed resources, P, and the available resources, A, respectively. From E we see that the system has six tape drives, three plotters, four printers, and two CD-ROM drives. Of these, five tape drives, three plotters, two printers, and two CD-ROM drives are currently assigned. This fact can be seen by adding up the four resource columns in the left-hand matrix. The available resource vector is simply the difference between what the system has and what is currently in use.

The algorithm for checking to see if a state is safe can now be stated.

1. Look for a row, *R*, whose unmet resource needs are all smaller than or equal to *A*. If no such row exists, the system will eventually deadlock since no process can run to completion.

2. Assume the process of the row chosen requests all the resources it needs (which is guaranteed to be possible) and finishes. Mark that process as terminated and add all its resources to the *A* vector.

3. Repeat steps 1 and 2 until either all processes are marked terminated, in which case the initial state was safe, or until a deadlock occurs, in which case it was not.

If several processes are eligible to be chosen in step 1, it does not matter which one is selected: the pool of available resources either gets larger or stays the same.

Now let us get back to the example of Fig. 3-15. The current state is safe. Suppose that process *B* now requests a printer. This request can be granted because the resulting state is still safe (process *D* can finish, and then processes *A* or *E*, followed by the rest).

Now imagine that after giving *B* one of the two remaining printers, *E* wants the last printer. Granting that request would reduce the vector of available resources to (1 0 0 0), which leads to deadlock. Clearly *E*'s request must be deferred for a while.

The banker's algorithm was first published by Dijkstra in 1965. Since that time, nearly every book on operating systems has described it in detail. Innumerable papers have been written about various aspects of it. Unfortunately, few authors have had the audacity to point out that although in theory the algorithm is wonderful, in practice it is essentially useless because processes rarely know in advance what their maximum resource needs will be. In addition, the number of processes is not fixed, but dynamically varying as new users log in and out. Furthermore, resources that were thought to be available can suddenly vanish (tape drives can break). Thus in practice, few, if any, existing systems use the banker's algorithm for avoiding deadlocks.

In summary, the schemes described earlier under the name "prevention" are overly restrictive, and the algorithm described here as "avoidance" requires information that is usually not available. If you can think of a general-purpose algorithm that does the job in practice as well as in theory, write it up and send it to your local computer science journal.

Although both avoidance and prevention are not terribly promising in the general case, for specific applications, many excellent special-purpose algorithms are known. As an example, in many database systems, an operation that occurs frequently is requesting locks on several records and then updating all the locked records. When multiple processes are running at the same time, there is a real danger of deadlock. To eliminate this problem, special techniques are used.

The approach most often used is called **two-phase locking**. In the first phase, the process tries to lock all the records it needs, one at a time. If it succeeds, it begins the second phase, performing its updates and releasing the locks. No real work is done in the first phase.

If during the first phase, some record is needed that is already locked, the process just releases all its locks and starts the first phase all over. In a certain sense, this approach is similar to requesting all the resources needed in advance, or at least before anything irreversible is done. In some versions of two-phase locking, there is no release and restart if a lock is encountered during the first phase. In these versions, deadlock can occur.

However, this strategy is not applicable in general. In real-time systems and process control systems, for example, it is not acceptable to just terminate a process partway through because a resource is not available and start all over again. Neither is it acceptable to start over if the process has read or written messages to the network, updated files, or anything else that cannot be safely repeated. The algorithm works only in those situations where the programmer has very carefully arranged things so that the program can be stopped at any point during the first phase and restarted. Many applications cannot be structured this way.

3.4 OVERVIEW OF I/O IN MINIX 3

MINIX 3 I/O is structured as shown in Fig. 3-8. The top four layers of that figure correspond to the four-layered structure of MINIX 3 shown in Fig. 2-29. In the following sections we will look briefly at each of the layers, with an emphasis on the device drivers. Interrupt handling was covered in Chap. 2 and the device-independent I/O will be discussed when we come to the file system, in Chap. 5.

3.4.1 Interrupt Handlers and I/O Access in MINIX 3

Many device drivers start some I/O device and then block, waiting for a message to arrive. That message is usually generated by the interrupt handler for the device. Other device drivers do not start any physical I/O (e.g., reading from RAM disk and writing to a memory-mapped display), do not use interrupts, and do not wait for a message from an I/O device. In the previous chapter the mechanisms in the kernel by which interrupts generate messages and cause task switches has been presented in great detail, and we will say no more about it here. Here we will discuss in a general way interrupts and I/O in device drivers. We will return to the details when we look at the code for various devices.

For disk devices, input and output is generally a matter of commanding a device to perform its operation, and then waiting until the operation is complete. The disk controller does most of the work, and very little is required of the interrupt handler. Life would be simple if all interrupts could be handled so easily.

However, there is sometimes more for the low-level handler to do. The message passing mechanism has a cost. When an interrupt may occur frequently but the amount of I/O handled per interrupt is small, it may pay to make the handler itself do somewhat more work and to postpone sending a message to the driver until a subsequent interrupt, when there is more for the driver to do. In MINIX 3 this is not possible for most I/O, because the low level handler in the kernel is a general purpose routine used for almost all devices.

In the last chapter we saw that the clock is an exception. Because it is compiled with the kernel the clock can have its own handler that does extra work. On many clock ticks there is very little to be done, except for maintaining the time. This is done without sending a message to the clock task itself. The clock's interrupt handler increments a variable, appropriately named *realtime*, possibly adding a correction for ticks counted during a BIOS call. The handler does some additional very simple arithmetic—it increments counters for user time and billing time, decrements the *ticks_left* counter for the current process, and tests to see if a timer has expired. A message is sent to the clock task only if the current process has used up its quantum or a timer has expired.

The clock interrupt handler is unique in MINIX 3, because the clock is the only interrupt driven device that runs in kernel space. The clock hardware is integral to the PC—in fact, the clock interrupt line does not connect to any pin on the sockets where add-on I/O controllers can be plugged in—so it is impossible to install a clock upgrade package with replacement clock hardware and a driver provided by the manufacturer. It is reasonable, then, for the clock driver to be compiled into the kernel and have access to any variable in kernel space. But a key design goal of MINIX 3 is to make it unnecessary for any other device driver to have that kind of access.

Device drivers that run in user space cannot directly access kernel memory or I/O ports. Although possible, it would also violate the design principles of MINIX 3 to allow an interrupt service routine to make a far call to execute a service routine within the text segment of a user process. This would be even more dangerous than letting a user space process call a function within kernel space. In that case we would at least be sure the function was written by a competent, security-aware operating system designer, possibly one who had read this book. But the kernel should not trust code provided by a user program.

There are several different levels of I/O access that might be needed by a user-space device driver.

1. A driver might need access to memory outside its normal data space. The memory driver, which manages the RAM disk, is an example of a driver which needs only this kind of access.

2. A driver may need to read and write to I/O ports. The machine-level instructions for these operations are available only in kernel mode. As we will soon see, the hard disk driver needs this kind of access.

3. A driver may need to respond to predictable interrupts. For example, the hard disk driver writes commands to the disk controller, which causes an interrupt to occur when the desired operation is complete.

4. A driver may need to respond to unpredictable interrupts. The keyboard driver is in this category. This could be considered a subclass of the preceding item, but unpredictability complicates things.

All of these cases are supported by kernel calls handled by the system task.

The first case, access to extra memory segments, takes advantage of the hardware segmentation support provided by Intel processors. Although a normal process has access only to its own text, data, and stack segments, the system task allows other segments to be defined and accessed by user-space processes. Thus the memory driver can access a memory region reserved for use as a RAM disk, as well as other regions designated for special access. The console driver accesses memory on a video display adapter in the same way.

For the second case, MINIX 3 provides kernel calls to use I/O instructions. The system task does the actual I/O on behalf of a less-privileged process. Later in this chapter we will see how the hard disk driver uses this service. We will present a preview here. The disk driver may have to write to a single output port to select a disk, then read from another port in order to verify the device is ready. If response is normally expected to be very quick, polling can be done. There are kernel calls to specify a port and data to be written or a location for receipt of data read. This requires that a call to read a port be nonblocking, and in fact, kernel calls do not block.

Some insurance against device failure is useful. A polling loop could include a counter that terminates the loop if the device does not become ready after a certain number of iterations. This is not a good idea in general because the loop execution time will depend upon the CPU speed. One way around this is to start the counter with a value that is related to CPU time, possibly using a global variable initialized when the system starts. A better way is provided by the MINIX 3 system library, which provides a *getuptime* function. This uses a kernel call to retrieve a counter of clock ticks since system startup maintained by the clock task. The cost of using this information to keep track of time spent in a loop is the overhead of an additional kernel call on each iteration. Another possibility is to ask the system task to set a watchdog timer. But to receive a notification from a timer a receive operation, which will block, is required. This is not a good solution if a fast response is expected.

The hard disk also makes use of variants of the kernel calls for I/O that make it possible to send a list of ports and data to write or variables to be altered to the system task. This is very useful—the hard disk driver we will examine requires writing a sequence of byte values to seven output ports to initiate an operation. The last byte in the sequence is a command, and the disk controller generates an interrupt when it completes a command. All this can be accomplished with a single kernel call, greatly reducing the number of messages needed.

This brings us to the third item in the list: responding to an expected interrupt. As noted in the discussion of the system task, when an interrupt is initialized on behalf of a user space program (using a sys_irqctl kernel call), the handler routine for the interrupt is always *generic_handler*, a function defined as part of the system task. This routine converts the interrupt into a notification message to the process on whose behalf the interrupt was set. The device driver therefore must initiate a receive operation after the kernel call that issues the command to the controller. When the notification is received the device driver can proceed to do what must be done to service the interrupt.

Although in this case an interrupt is expected, it is prudent to hedge against the possibility that something might go wrong sometime. To prepare for the possibility that the interrupt might fail to be triggered, a process can request the system task to set up a watchdog timer. Watchdog timers also generate notification messages, and thus the receive operation could get a notification either because an interrupt occurred or because a timer expired. This is not a problem because, although a notification does not convey much information, the notification message indicates its origin. Although both notifications are generated by the system task, notification of an interrupt will appear to come from *HARDWARE*, and notification of a timer expiring will appear to come from *CLOCK*.

There is another problem. If an interrupt is received in a timely way and a watchdog timer has been set, expiration of the timer at some future time will be detected by another receive operation, possibly in the main loop of the driver. One solution is to make a kernel call to disable the timer when the notification from *HARDWARE* is received. Alternatively, if it is likely that the next receive operation will be one where a message from *CLOCK* is not expected, such a message could be ignored and receive called again. Although less likely, it is conceivable that a disk operation could occur after an unexpectedly long delay, generating the interrupt only after the watchdog has timed out. The same solutions apply here. When a timeout occurs a kernel call can be made to disable an interrupt, or a receive operation that does not expect an interrupt could ignore any message from *HARDWARE*.

This is a good time to mention that when an interrupt is first enabled, a kernel call can be made to set a "policy" for the interrupt. The policy is simply a flag that determines whether the interrupt should be automatically reenabled or whether it should remain disabled until the device driver it serves makes a kernel call to reenable it. For the disk driver there may be a substantial amount of work to be done after an interrupt, and thus it may be best to leave the interrupt disabled until all data has been copied.

The fourth item in our list is the most problematic. Keyboard support is part of the tty driver, which provides output as well as input. Furthermore, multiple devices may be supported. So input may come from a local keyboard, but it can also come from a remote user connected by a serial line or a network connection. And several processes may be running, each producing output for a different local or remote terminal. When you do not know when, if ever, an interrupt might occur, you cannot just make a blocking receive call to accept input from a single source if the same process may need to respond to other input and output sources.

MINIX 3 uses several techniques to deal with this problem. The principal technique used by the terminal driver for dealing with keyboard input is to make the interrupt response as fast as possible, so characters will not be lost. The minimum possible amount of work is done to get characters from the keyboard hardware to a buffer. Additionally, when data has been fetched from the keyboard in response to an interrupt, as soon as the data is buffered the keyboard is read again before returning from the interrupt. Interrupts generate notification messages, which do not block the sender; this helps to prevent loss of input. A nonblocking receive operation is available, too, although it is only used to handle messages during a system crash. Watchdog timers are also used to activate the routine that checks the keyboard.

3.4.2 Device Drivers in MINIX 3

For each class of I/O device present in a MINIX 3 system, a separate I/O device driver is present. These drivers are full-fledged processes, each one with its own state, registers, stack, and so on. Device drivers communicate with the file system using the standard message passing mechanism used by all MINIX 3 processes. A simple device driver may be written as a single source file. For the RAM disk, hard disk, and floppy disk there is a source file to support each type of device, as well as a set of common routines in *driver.c* and *drvlib.c* to support all blcok device types. This separation of the hardware-dependent and hardware-independent parts of the software makes for easy adaptation to a variety of different hardware configurations. Although some common source code is used, the driver for each disk type runs as a separate process, in order to support rapid data transfers and isolate drivers from each other.

The terminal driver source code is organized in a similar way, with the hardware-independent code in *tty.c* and source code to support different devices, such as memory-mapped consoles, the keyboard, serial lines, and pseudo terminals in separate files. In this case, however, a single process supports all of the different device types.

For groups of devices such as disk devices and terminals, for which there are several source files, there are also header files. *Driver.h* supports all the block device drivers. *Tty.h* provides common definitions for all the terminal devices.

The MINIX 3 design principle of running components of the operating system as completely separate processes in user space is highly modular and moderately efficient. It is also one of the few places where MINIX 3 differs from UNIX in an essential way. In MINIX 3 a process reads a file by sending a message to the file system process. The file system, in turn, may send a message to the disk driver asking it to read the needed block. The disk driver uses kernel calls to ask the system task to do the actual I/O and to copy data between processes. This sequence (slightly simplified from reality) is shown in Fig. 3-16(a). By making these interactions via the message mechanism, we force various parts of the system to interface in standard ways with other parts.

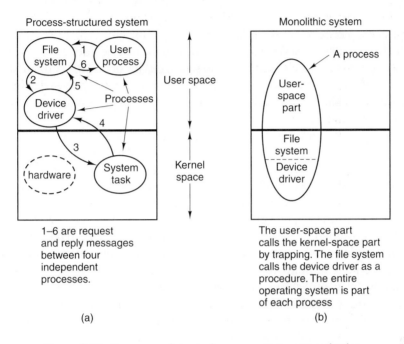

Figure 3-16. Two ways of structuring user-system communication.

In UNIX all processes have two parts: a user-space part and a kernel-space part, as shown in Fig. 3-16(b). When a system call is made, the operating system switches from the user-space part to the kernel-space part in a somewhat magical way. This structure is a remnant of the MULTICS design, in which the switch was just an ordinary procedure call, rather than a trap followed by saving the state of the user-part, as it is in UNIX.

Device drivers in UNIX are simply kernel procedures that are called by the kernel-space part of the process. When a driver needs to wait for an interrupt, it calls a kernel procedure that puts it to sleep until some interrupt handler wakes it up. Note that it is the user process itself that is being put to sleep here, because the kernel and user parts are really different parts of the same process.

Among operating system designers, arguments about the merits of monolithic systems, as in UNIX, versus process-structured systems, as in MINIX 3, are endless. The MINIX 3 approach is better structured (more modular), has cleaner interfaces between the pieces, and extends easily to distributed systems in which the various processes run on different computers. The UNIX approach is more efficient, because procedure calls are much faster than sending messages. MINIX 3 was split into many processes because we believe that with increasingly powerful personal computers available, cleaner software structure was worth making the system slightly slower. The performance loss due to having most of the operating system run in user space is typically in the range of 5–10%. Be warned that some operating system designers do not share the belief that it is worth sacrificing a little speed for a more modular and more reliable system.

In this chapter, drivers for RAM disk, hard disk, clock, and terminal are discussed. The standard MINIX 3 configuration also includes drivers for the floppy disk and the printer, which are not discussed in detail. The MINIX 3 software distribution contains source code for additional drivers for RS-232 serial lines, CD-ROMs, various Ethernet adapter, and sound cards. These may be compiled separately and started on the fly at any time.

All of these drivers interface with other parts of the MINIX 3 system in the same way: request messages are sent to the drivers. The messages contain a variety of fields used to hold the operation code (e.g., *READ* or *WRITE*) and its parameters. A driver attempts to fulfill a request and returns a reply message.

For block devices, the fields of the request and reply messages are shown in Fig. 3-17. The request message includes the address of a buffer area containing data to be transmitted or in which received data are expected. The reply includes status information so the requesting process can verify that its request was properly carried out. The fields for the character devices are basically similar but can vary slightly from driver to driver. Messages to the terminal driver can contain the address of a data structure which specifies all of the many configurable aspects of a terminal, such as the characters to use for the intraline editing functions erase-character and kill-line.

The function of each driver is to accept requests from other processes, normally the file system, and carry them out. All the block device drivers have been written to get a message, carry it out, and send a reply. Among other things, this decision means that these drivers are strictly sequential and do not contain any internal multiprogramming, to keep them simple. When a hardware request has been issued, the driver does a receive operation specifying that it is interested only in accepting interrupt messages, not new requests for work. Any new request messages are just kept waiting until the current work has been done (rendezvous principle). The terminal driver is slightly different, since a single driver services several devices. Thus, it is possible to accept a new request for input from the keyboard while a request to read from a serial line is still being fulfilled. Nevertheless, for each device a request must be completed before beginning a new one.

The main program for each block device driver is structurally the same and is outlined in Fig. 3-18. When the system first comes up, each one of the drivers is started up in turn to give each a chance to initialize internal tables and similar

Requests		
Field	**Type**	**Meaning**
m.m_type	int	Operation requested
m.DEVICE	int	Minor device to use
m.PROC_NR	int	Process requesting the I/O
m.COUNT	int	Byte count or ioctl code
m.POSITION	long	Position on device
m.ADDRESS	char*	Address within requesting process

Replies		
Field	**Type**	**Meaning**
m.m_type	int	Always DRIVER_REPLY
m.REP_PROC_NR	int	Same as PROC_NR in request
m.REP_STATUS	int	Bytes transferred or error number

Figure 3-17. Fields of the messages sent by the file system to the block device drivers and fields of the replies sent back.

things. Then each device driver blocks by trying to get a message. When a message comes in, the identity of the caller is saved, and a procedure is called to carry out the work, with a different procedure invoked for each operation available. After the work has been finished, a reply is sent back to the caller, and the driver then goes back to the top of the loop to wait for the next request.

Each of the *dev_XXX* procedures handles one of the operations of which the driver is capable. It returns a status code telling what happened. The status code, which is included in the reply message as the field *REP_STATUS*, is the count of bytes transferred (zero or positive) if all went well, or the error number (negative) if something went wrong. This count may differ from the number of bytes requested. When the end of a file is reached, the number of bytes available may be less than number requested. On terminals at most one line is returned (except in raw mode), even if the count requested is larger.

3.4.3 Device-Independent I/O Software in MINIX 3

In MINIX 3 the file system process contains all the device-independent I/O code. The I/O system is so closely related to the file system that they were merged into one process. The functions performed by the file system are those shown in Fig. 3-6, except for requesting and releasing dedicated devices, which do not exist in MINIX 3 as it is presently configured. They could, however, easily be added to the relevant device drivers should the need arise in the future.

```
message mess;                            /* message buffer */

void io_driver() {
    initialize();                        /* only done once, during system init. */
    while (TRUE) {
        receive(ANY, &mess);             /* wait for a request for work */
        caller = mess.source;            /* process from whom message came */
        switch(mess.type) {
            case READ:      rcode = dev_read(&mess); break;
            case WRITE:     rcode = dev_write(&mess); break;
            /* Other cases go here, including OPEN, CLOSE, and IOCTL */
             default:        rcode = ERROR;
        }
        mess.type = DRIVER_REPLY;
        mess.status = rcode;             /* result code */
        send(caller, &mess);             /* send reply message back to caller */
    }
}
```

Figure 3-18. Outline of the main procedure of an I/O device driver.

In addition to handling the interface with the drivers, buffering, and block allocation, the file system also handles protection and the management of i-nodes, directories, and mounted file systems. This will be covered in detail in Chap. 5.

3.4.4 User-Level I/O Software in MINIX 3

The general model outlined earlier in this chapter also applies here. Library procedures are available for making system calls and for all the C functions required by the POSIX standard, such as the formatted input and output functions *printf* and *scanf*. The standard MINIX 3 configuration contains one spooler daemon, lpd, which spools and prints files passed to it by the lp command. The standard MINIX 3 software distribution also provides a number of daemons that support various network functions. The MINIX 3 configuration described in this book supports most network operations, all that is needed is to enable the network server and drivers for ethernet adapters at startup time. Recompiling the terminal driver with pseudo terminals and serial line support will add support for logins from remote terminals and networking over serial lines (including modems). The network server runs at the same priority as the memory manager and the file system, and like them, it runs as a user process.

3.4.5 Deadlock Handling in MINIX 3

True to its heritage, MINIX 3 follows the same path as UNIX with respect to deadlocks of the types described earlier in this chapter: it just ignores the problem. Normally, MINIX 3 does not contain any dedicated I/O devices, although if someone wanted to hang an industry standard DAT tape drive on a PC, making the software for it would not pose any special problems. In short, the only place deadlocks can occur are with the implicit shared resources, such as process table slots, i-node table slots, and so on. None of the known deadlock algorithms can deal with resources like these that are not requested explicitly.

Actually, the above is not strictly true. Accepting the risk that user processes could deadlock is one thing, but within the operating system itself a few places do exist where considerable care has been taken to avoid problems. The main one is the message-passing interaction between processes. For instance, user processes are only allowed to use the sendrec messaging method, so a user process should never lock up because it did a receive when there was no process with an interest in sending to it. Servers only use send or sendrec to communicate with device drivers, and device drivers only use send or sendrec to communicate with the system task in the kernel layer. In the rare case where servers must communicate between themselves, such as exchanges between the process manager and the file system as they initialize their parts of the process table, the order of communication is very carefully designed to avoid deadlock. Also, at the very lowest level of the message passing system there is a check to make sure that when a process is about to do a send that the destination process is not trying to the same thing.

In addition to the above restrictions, in MINIX 3 the new notify message primitive is provided to handle those situations in which a message must be sent in the "upstream" direction. Notify is nonblocking, and notifications are stored when a recipient is not immediately available. As we examine the implementation of MINIX 3 device drivers in this chapter we will see that notify is used extensively.

Locks are another mechanism that can prevent deadlocks. It is possible to lock devices and files even without operating system support. A file name can serve as a truly global variable, whose presence or absence can be noted by all other processes. A special directory, */usr/spool/locks/*, is usually present on MINIX 3 systems, as on most UNIX-like systems, where processes can create **lock files**, to mark any resources they are using. The MINIX 3 file system also supports POSIX-style advisory file locking. But neither of these mechanisms is enforceable. They depend upon the good behavior of processes, and there is nothing to prevent a program from trying to use a resource that is locked by another process. This is not exactly the same thing as preemption of the resource, because it does not prevent the first process from attempting to continue its use of the resource. In other words, there is no mutual exclusion. The result of such an action by an ill-behaved process is likely to be a mess, but no deadlock results.

3.5 BLOCK DEVICES IN MINIX 3

MINIX 3 supports several different block devices, so we will begin by discussing common aspects of all block devices. Then we will discuss the RAM disk, the hard disk, and the floppy disk. Each of these is interesting for a different reason.

The RAM disk is a good example to study because it has all the properties of block devices in general except the actual I/O—because the "disk" is actually just a portion of memory. This simplicity makes it a good place to start. The hard disk shows what a real disk driver looks like. One might expect the floppy disk to be easier to support than the hard disk, but, in fact, it is not. We will not discuss all the details of the floppy disk, but we will point out several of the complications to be found in the floppy disk driver.

Looking ahead, after the discussion of block drivers, we will discuss the terminal (keyboard + display) driver, which is important on all systems, and, furthermore is a good example of a character device driver.

Each of these sections describes the relevant hardware, the software principles behind the driver, an overview of the implementation, and the code itself. This structure may make the sections useful reading even for readers who are not interested in the details of the code itself.

3.5.1 Overview of Block Device Drivers in MINIX 3

We mentioned earlier that the main procedures of all I/O drivers have a similar structure. MINIX 3 always has at least two block device drivers compiled into the system: the RAM disk driver, and either one of several possible hard disk drivers or a floppy disk driver. Usually, there are three block devices—both the floppy disk driver and an **IDE** (Integrated Drive Electronics) hard disk driver are present. The driver for each block device driver is compiled independently, but a common library of source code is shared by all of them.

In older versions of MINIX a separate CD-ROM driver was sometimes present, and could be added if necessary. Separate CD-ROM drivers are now obsolete. They used to be necessary to support the proprietary interfaces of different drive manufacturers, but modern CD-ROM drives are usually connected to the IDE controller, although on notebook computers some CD-ROMs are USB. The full version of the MINIX 3 hard disk device driver includes CD-ROM support, but we have taken the CD-ROM support out of the driver as described in this text and listed in Appendix B.

Each block device driver has to do some initialization, of course. The RAM disk driver has to reserve some memory, the hard disk driver has to determine the parameters of the hard disk hardware, and so on. All of the disk drivers are called individually for hardware-specific initialization. After doing whatever may be necessary, each driver then calls the function containing its main loop. This loop is executed forever; there is no return to the caller. Within the main loop a message is received, a function to perform the operation needed by each message is called, and then a reply message is generated.

The common main loop called by each disk driver process is compiled when *drivers/libdriver/driver.c* and the other files in its directory are compiled, and then a copy of the object file *driver.o* is linked into each disk driver's executable file.

The technique used is to have each driver pass to the main loop a parameter consisting of a pointer to a table of the addresses of the functions that driver will use for each operation and then to call these functions indirectly.

If the drivers were compiled together in a single executable file only one copy of the main loop would be needed. This code was, in fact, first written for an earlier version of MINIX in which all the drivers were compiled together. The emphasis in MINIX 3 is on making individual operating system components as independent as possible, but using common source code for separate programs is still a good way to increase reliability. Assuming you get it right once, it will be right for all the drivers. Or, a bug found in one use might very well exist unnoticed in other uses. Thus, shared source code gets tested more thoroughly.

A number of other functions potentially useful to multiple disk drivers are defined in *drivers/libdriver/drvlib.c*, and linking *drvlib.o* makes these available. All of the functionality could have been provided in a single file, but not all of it is needed by every disk driver. For instance, the *memory* driver, which is simpler than other drivers, links in only *driver.o*. The *at_wini* driver links in both *driver.o* and *drvlib.o*.

Figure 3-19 shows an outline of the main loop, in a form similar to that of Fig. 3-18. Statements like

```
code = (*entry_points->dev_read)(&mess);
```

are indirect function calls. A different *dev_read* function is called by each driver, even though each driver is executing a main loop compiled from the same source file. But some other operations, for example close, are simple enough that more than one device can call the same function.

There are six possible operations that can be requested of any device driver. These correspond to the possible values that can be found in the m.m_type field of the message of Fig. 3-17. They are:

1. OPEN

2. CLOSE

3. READ

4. WRITE

5. IOCTL

6. SCATTERED_IO

Many of these operations are most likely familiar to readers with programming experience. At the device driver level most operations are related to system calls with the same name. For instance, the meanings of *READ* and *WRITE* should be fairly clear. For each of these operations, a block of data is transferred from the device to the memory of the process that initiated the call, or vice versa. A *READ*

```
message mess;                        /* message buffer */

void shared_io_driver(struct driver_table *entry_points) {
/* initialization is done by each driver before calling this */
  while (TRUE) {
      receive(ANY, &mess);
      caller = mess.source;
      switch(mess.type) {
          case READ:     rcode = (*entry_points->dev_read)(&mess); break;
          case WRITE:    rcode = (*entry_points->dev_write)(&mess); break;
          /* Other cases go here, including OPEN, CLOSE, and IOCTL */
          default:       rcode = ERROR;
      }
      mess.type = DRIVER_REPLY;
      mess.status = rcode;               /* result code */
      send(caller, &mess);
  }
}
```

Figure 3-19. An I/O driver main procedure using indirect calls.

operation normally does not result in a return to the caller until the data transfer is complete, but an operating system may buffer data transferred during a *WRITE* for actual transfer to the destination at a later time, and return to the caller immediately. That is fine as far as the caller is concerned; it is then free to reuse the buffer from which the operating system has copied the data to write. *OPEN* and *CLOSE* for a device have similar meanings to the way the open and close system calls apply to operations on files: an *OPEN* operation should verify that the device is accessible, or return an error message if not, and a *CLOSE* should guarantee that any buffered data that were written by the caller are completely transferred to their final destination on the device.

The *IOCTL* operation may not be so familiar. Many I/O devices have operational parameters which occasionally must be examined and perhaps changed. *IOCTL* operations do this. A familiar example is changing the speed of transmission or the parity of a communications line. For block devices, *IOCTL* operations are less common. Examining or changing the way a disk device is partitioned is done using an *IOCTL* operation in MINIX 3 (although it could just as well have been done by reading and writing a block of data).

The *SCATTERED_IO* operation is no doubt the least familiar of these. Except with exceedingly fast disk devices (for example, the RAM disk), satisfactory disk I/O performance is difficult to obtain if all disk requests are for individual blocks, one at a time. A *SCATTERED_IO* request allows the file system to make a request to read or write multiple blocks. In the case of a *READ* operation, the additional blocks may not have been requested by the process on whose behalf the call is made; the operating system attempts to anticipate future requests for data. In such a request not all the transfers requested are necessarily honored by the device driver. The request for each block may be modified by a flag bit that tells the device driver that the request is optional. In effect the file system can say: "It would be nice to have all these data, but I do not really need them all right now." The device can do what is best for it. The floppy disk driver, for instance, will return all the data blocks it can read from a single track, effectively saying, "I will give you these, but it takes too long to move to another track; ask me again later for the rest."

When data must be written, there is no question of its being optional; every write is mandatory. Nevertheless, the operating system may buffer a number of write requests in the hope that writing multiple blocks can be done more efficiently than handling each request as it comes in. In a *SCATTERED_IO* request, whether for reading or writing, the list of blocks requested is sorted, and this makes the operation more efficient than handling the requests randomly. In addition, making only one call to the driver to transfer multiple blocks reduces the number of messages sent within MINIX 3.

3.5.2 Common Block Device Driver Software

Definitions that are needed by all of the block device drivers are located in *drivers/libdriver/driver.h*. The most important thing in this file is the *driver* structure, on lines 10829 to 10845, which is used by each driver to pass a list of the addresses of the functions it will use to perform each part of its job. Also defined here is the *device* structure (lines 10856 to 10859) which holds the most important information about partitions, the base address, and the size, in byte units. This format was chosen so no conversions are necessary when working with memory-based devices, maximizing speed of response. With real disks there are so many other factors delaying access that converting to sectors is not a significant inconvenience.

The source of the main loop and common functions of all the block device drivers are in *driver.c*. After doing whatever hardware-specific initialization may be necessary, each driver calls *driver_task*, passing a *driver* structure as the argument to the call. After obtaining the address of a buffer to use for DMA operations the main loop (lines 11071 to 11120) is entered.

In the switch statement in the main loop, the first five message types, *DEV_OPEN*, *DEV_CLOSE*, *DEV_IOCTL*, *DEV_CANCEL*, and *DEV_SELECT* result in indirect calls using addresses passed in the *driver* structure. The *DEV_READ* and *DEV_WRITE* messages both result in direct calls to *do_rdwt*; *DEV_GATHER* and *DEV_SCATTER* messages both result in direct calls to *do_vrdwt*. The *driver* structure is passed as an argument by all the calls from within the switch, whether direct or indirect, so all called functions can make further use of it as needed. *Do_rdwt* and *do_vrdwt* do some preliminary processing, but then they too make indirect calls to device-specific routines.

The other cases, *HARD_INT*, *SYS_SIG*, and *SYN_ALARM*, respond to notifications. These also result in indirect calls, but upon completion each of these executes a continue statement. This causes control to return to the top of the loop, bypassing the cleanup and reply message steps.

After doing whatever is requested in the message, some sort of cleanup may be necessary, depending upon the nature of the device. For a floppy disk, for instance, this might involve starting a timer to turn off the disk drive motor if another request does not arrive soon. An indirect call is used for this as well. Following the cleanup, a reply message is constructed and sent to the caller (lines 11113 to 11119). It is possible for a routine that services one of the message types to return a *EDONTREPLY* value to suppress the reply message, but none of the current drivers use this option.

The first thing each driver does after entering the main loop is to make a call to *init_buffer* (line 11126), which assigns a buffer for use in DMA operations. That this initialization is even necessary at all is due to a quirk of the hardware of the original IBM PC, which requires that the DMA buffer not cross a 64K boundary. That is, a 1-KB DMA buffer may begin at 64510, but not at 64514, because a buffer starting at the latter address extends just beyond the 64K boundary at 65536.

This annoying rule occurs because the IBM PC used an old DMA chip, the Intel 8237A, which contains a 16-bit counter. A bigger counter is needed because DMA uses absolute addresses, not addresses relative to a segment register. On older machines that can address only 1M of memory, the low-order 16 bits of the DMA address are loaded into the 8237A, and the high-order 4 bits are loaded into a 4-bit latch. Newer machines use an 8-bit latch and can address 16M. When the 8237A goes from 0xFFFF to 0x0000, it does not generate a carry into the latch, so the DMA address suddenly jumps down by 64K in memory.

A portable C program cannot specify an absolute memory location for a data structure, so there is no way to prevent the compiler from placing the buffer in an unusable location. The solution is to allocate an array of bytes twice as large as necessary at *buffer* (line 11044) and to reserve a pointer *tmp_buf* (line 11045) to use for actually accessing this array. *Init_buffer* makes a trial setting of *tmp_buf* pointing to the beginning of *buffer*, then tests to see if that allows enough space before a 64K boundary is hit. If the trial setting does not provide enough space, *tmp_buf* is incremented by the number of bytes actually required. Thus some space is always wasted at one end or the other of the space allocated in *buffer*, but there is never a failure due to the buffer falling on a 64K boundary.

Newer computers of the IBM PC family have better DMA controllers, and this code could be simplified, and a small amount of memory reclaimed, if one could be sure that one's machine were immune to this problem. If you are considering this, however, consider how the bug will manifest itself if you are wrong. If a 1K DMA buffer is desired, the chance is 1 in 64 that there will be a problem on a machine with the old DMA chip. Every time the kernel source code is modified in a way that changes the size of the compiled kernel, there is the same probability that the problem will manifest itself. Most likely, when the failure occurs next month or next year, it will be attributed to the code that was last modified. Unexpected hardware "features" like this can cause weeks of time spent looking for exceedingly obscure bugs (all the more so when, like this one, the technical reference manual says nary a word about them).

Do_rdwt (line 11148) is the next function in *driver.c*. It, in turn calls two device-dependent functions pointed to by the *dr_prepare* and *dr_transfer* fields in the *driver* structure. Here and in what follows we will use the C language-like notation *(*function_pointer)* to indicate we are talking about the function pointed to by *function_pointer*.

After checking to see that the byte count in the request is positive, *do_rdwt* calls *(*dr_prepare)*. This operation fills in the base and size of the disk, partition, or subpartition being accessed in a *device* structure. For the memory driver, which does not support partitions, it just checks that the minor device number is valid. For the hard disk it uses the minor device number to get the size of the partition or subpartition indicated by the minor device number. This should succeed, since *(*dr_prepare)* can fail only if an invalid device is specified in an open operation. Next, an *iovec_t* structure (which is defined on lines 2856 to 2859 in *include/minix/type.h*), *iovec1*, is filled in. This structure specifies the virtual address and size of the local buffer to or from which data will be copied by the system task. This is the same structure that is used as an element of an array of requests when the call is for multiple blocks. The address of a variable and the address of the first element of an array of the same type of variable can be handled exactly the same way. Then comes another indirect call, this time to *(*dr_transfer)*, which performs the data copy and I/O operations required. The routines that handle transfers all expect to receive an array of requests. In *do_rdwt* the last argument to the call is 1, specifying an array of one element.

As we will see in the discussion of disk hardware in the next section, responding to disk requests in the order they are received can be inefficient, and this routine allows a particular device to handle requests in the way that is best for the device. The indirection here masks much possible variation in the way individual devices perform. For the RAM disk, *dr_transfer* points to a routine that makes a kernel call to ask the system task to copy data from one part of physical memory to another, if the minor device being accessed is */dev/ram*, */dev/mem*, */dev/kmem*, */dev/boot*, or */dev/zero*. (No copying is required to access */dev/null*, of course.) For a real disk, the code pointed to by *dr_transfer* also has to ask the system task for a data transfer. But before the copy operation (for a read) or after it (for a write) a kernel call must also be made to ask the system task to do actual I/O, writing bytes to registers that are part of the disk controller to select the location on the disk and the size and direction of the transfer.

In the transfer routine the *iov_size* count in the *iovec1* structure is modified, returning an error code (a negative number) if there was an error or a positive number indicating the number of bytes transferred. It is not necessarily an error if no bytes are transferred; this indicates that the end of the device has been reached. Upon returning to the main loop, the error code or the byte count is returned in the *REP_STATUS* field in the reply message from *driver_task*.

The next function, *do_vrdwt* (line 11182), handles scattered I/O requests. A message that requests a scattered I/O request uses the *ADDRESS* field to point to an array of *iovec_t* structures, each of which specifies the address of a buffer and the number of bytes to transfer. In MINIX 3 such a request can be made only for contiguous blocks on the disk; the initial offset on the device and whether the operation is a read or a write are in the message. So all the operations in one request will be for either reading or writing, and they will be sorted into block order on the device. On line 11198 a check is done to see if this call is being done on behalf of a kernel-space I/O task; this is a vestige of an early phase of the development of MINIX 3 before all the disk drivers had been rewritten to run in user space.

Fundamentally, the code for this operation is very similar to that for the simple read or write performed by *do_rdwt*. The same indirect calls to the device-dependent *(*dr_prepare)* and *(*dr_transfer)* routines are made. The looping in order to handle multiple requests is all done internal to the function pointed to by *(*dr_transfer)*. The last argument in this case is not 1, it is the size of the array of *iovec_t* elements. After termination of the loop the array of requests is copied back where it came from. The *io_size* field of each element in the array will show the number of bytes transferred for that request, and although the total is not passed back directly in the reply message that *driver_task* constructs, the caller can extract the total from this array.

The next few routines in *driver.c* are for general support of the above operations. A *(*dr_name)* call can be used to return the name of a device. For a device with no specific name the *no_name* function returns the string "noname". Some devices may not require a particular service, for instance, a RAM disk does not require that anything special be done upon a *DEV_CLOSE* request. The *do_nop* function fills in here, returning various codes depending upon the kind of request made. Additional functions, *nop_signal*, *nop_alarm*, *nop_prepare*, *nop_cleanup*, and *nop_cancel*, are similar dummy routines for devices that do not need these services.

Finally, *do_diocntl* (line 11216) carries out *DEV_IOCTL* requests for a block device. It is an error if any *DEV_IOCTL* operation other than reading *(DIOCGETP)* or writing *(DIOCSETP)* partition information is requested. *Do_diocntl* calls the device's *(*dr_prepare)* function to verify the device is valid and to get a pointer to the *device* structure that describes the partition base and size in byte units. On a request to read, it calls the device's *(*dr_geometry)* function to get the last cylinder, head, and sector information about the partition. In each case a sys_datacopy kernel call is made to request that the system task copy the data between the memory spaces of the driver and the requesting process.

3.5.3 The Driver Library

The files *drvlib.h* and *drvlib.c* contain system-dependent code that supports disk partitions on IBM PC compatible computers.

Partitioning allows a single storage device to be divided up into subdevices. It is most commonly used with hard disks, but MINIX 3 provides support for partitioning floppy disks, as well. Some reasons to partition a disk device are:

1. Disk capacity is cheaper per unit in large disks. If two or more operating systems with different file systems are used, it is more economical to partition a single large disk than to install multiple smaller disks for each operating system.

2. Operating systems may have limits to the device size they can handle. The version of MINIX 3 discussed here can handle a 4-GB file system, but older versions are limited to 256 MB. Any disk space beyond that is wasted.

3. Two or more different file systems may be used by an operating system. For example, a standard file system may be used for ordinary files and a differently structured file system may be used for virtual memory swap space.

4. It may be convenient to put a portion of a system's files on a separate logical device. Putting the MINIX 3 root file system on a small device makes it easy to back up and facilitates copying it to a RAM disk at boot time.

Support for disk partitions is platform specific. This specificity is not related to the hardware. Partition support is device independent. But if more than one operating system is to run on a particular set of hardware, all must agree on a format for the partition table. On IBM PCs the standard is set by the MS-DOS *fdisk* command, and other OSs, such as MINIX 3, Windows, and Linux, use this format so they can coexist with MS-DOS. When MINIX 3 is ported to another machine type, it makes sense to use a partition table format compatible with other operating systems used on the new hardware. Thus the MINIX 3 source code to support partitions on IBM computers is put in *drvlib.c*, rather than being included in *driver.c*, for two reasons. First, not all disk types support partitions. As noted earlier, the memory driver links to *driver.o* but does not use the functions compiled into *drvlib.o*. Second, this makes it easier to port MINIX 3 to different hardware. It is easier to replace one small file than to edit a large one with many sections to be conditionally compiled for different environments.

The basic data structure inherited from the firmware designers is defined in *include/ibm/partition.h*, which is included by a #include statement in *drvlib.h* (line 10900). This includes information on the cylinder-head-sector geometry of each partition, as well as codes identifying the type of file system on the partition and an active flag indicating if it is bootable. Most of this information is not needed by MINIX 3 once the file system is verified.

The *partition* function (in *drvlib.c*, line 11426) is called the first time a block device is opened. Its arguments include a *driver* structure, so it can call device-specific functions, an initial minor device number, and a parameter indicating whether the partitioning style is floppy disk, primary partition, or subpartition. It calls the device-specific *(*dr_prepare)* function to verify the device is valid and to get the base address and the size into a *device* structure of the type mentioned in the previous section. Then it calls *get_part_table* to determine if a partition table is present and, if so, to read it. If there is no partition table, the work is done. Otherwise the minor device number of the first partition is computed, using the rules for numbering minor devices that apply to the style of partitioning specified in the original call. In the case of primary partitions the partition table is sorted so the order of the partitions is consistent with that used by other operating systems.

At this point another call is made to *(*dr_prepare)*, this time using the newly calculated device number of the first partition. If the subdevice is valid, then a loop is made over all the entries in the table, checking that the values read from the table on the device are not out of the range obtained earlier for the base and size of the entire device. If there is a discrepancy, the table in memory is adjusted to conform. This may seem paranoid, but since partition tables may be written by different operating systems, a programmer using another system may have cleverly tried to use the partition table for something unexpected or there could be garbage in the table on disk for some other reason. We put the most trust in the numbers we calculate using MINIX 3. Better safe than sorry.

Still within the loop, for all partitions on the device, if the partition is identified as a MINIX 3 partition, *partition* is called recursively to gather subpartition information. If a partition is identified as an extended partition, the next function, *extpartition*, is called instead.

Extpartition (line 11501) has nothing to do with MINIX 3 itself, so we will not discuss details. Some other operating systems (e.g., Windows) use **extended partitions**. These use linked lists rather than fixed-size arrays to support subpartitions. For simplicity MINIX 3 uses the same mechanism for subpartitions as for primary partitions. However, minimal support for extended partitions is provided to support MINIX 3 commands to read and write files and directories of other operating systems. These operations are easy; providing full support for mounting and otherwise using extended partitions in the same way as primary partitions would be much more complicated.

Get_part_table (line 11549) calls *do_rdwt* to get the sector on a device (or subdevice) where a partition table is located. The offset argument is zero if it is called to get a primary partition or nonzero for a subpartition. It checks for the magic number (0xaa55) and returns true or false status to indicate whether a valid partition table was found. If a table is found, it copies it to the table address that was passed as an argument.

Finally, *sort* (line 11582) sorts the entries in a partition table by lowest sector. Entries that are marked as having no partition are excluded from the sort, so they come at the end, even though they may have a zero value in their low sector field. The sort is a simple bubble sort; there is no need to use a fancy algorithm to sort a list of four items.

3.6 RAM DISKS

Now we will get back to the individual block device drivers and study several of them in detail. The first one we will look at is the memory driver. It can be used to provide access to any part of memory. Its primary use is to allow a part of memory to be reserved for use like an ordinary disk, and we will also refer to it as the RAM disk driver. A RAM disk does not provide permanent storage, but once files have been copied to this area they can be accessed extremely quickly.

A RAM disk is also useful for initial installation of an operating system on a computer with only one removable storage device, whether a floppy disk, CD-ROM, or some other device. By putting the root device on the RAM disk, removable storage devices can be mounted and unmounted as needed to transfer data to the hard disk. Putting the root device on a floppy disk would make it impossible to save files on floppies, since the root device (the only floppy) cannot be unmounted. RAM disks also are used with "live" CD-ROMs that allow one to run an operating system for tests and demonstrations, without copying any files onto the hard disk. Having the root device on the RAM disk makes the system highly flexible: any combination of floppy disks or hard disks can be mounted on it. MINIX 3 and many other operating systems are distributed on live CD-ROMs.

As we shall see, the memory driver supports several other functions in addition to a RAM disk. It supports straightforward random access to any part of memory, byte by byte or in chunks of any size. Used this way it acts as a character device rather than as a block device. Other character devices supported by the memory driver are */dev/zero*, and */dev/null*, otherwise known as the great bit bucket in the sky.

3.6.1 RAM Disk Hardware and Software

The idea behind a RAM disk is simple. A block device is a storage medium with two commands: write a block and read a block. Normally, these blocks are stored on rotating memories, such as floppy disks or hard disks. A RAM disk is simpler. It just uses a preallocated portion of main memory for storing the blocks. A RAM disk has the advantage of having instant access (no seek or rotational delay), making it suitable for storing programs or data that are frequently accessed.

As an aside, it is worth briefly pointing out a difference between systems that support mounted file systems and those that do not (e.g., MS-DOS and Windows). With mounted file systems, the root device is always present and in a fixed location, and removable file systems (i.e., disks) can be mounted in the file tree to form an integrated file system. Once everything has been mounted, the user need not worry at all about which device a file is on.

In contrast, with systems like MS-DOS, the user must specify the location of each file, either explicitly as in *B:\DIR\FILE* or by using certain defaults (current device, current directory, and so on). With only one or two floppy disks, this burden is manageable, but on a large computer system, with dozens of disks, having to keep track of devices all the time would be unbearable. Remember that UNIX-like operating systems run on hardware ranging from small home and office machines to supercomputers such as the IBM Blue Gene/L supercomputer, the world's fastest computer as of this writing; MS-DOS runs only on small systems.

Figure 3-20 shows the idea behind a RAM disk. The RAM disk is split up into *n* blocks, depending on how much memory has been allocated for it. Each block is the same size as the block size used on the real disks. When the driver receives a message to read or write a block, it just computes where in the RAM disk memory the requested block lies and reads from it or writes to it, instead of from or to a floppy or hard disk. Ultimately the system task is called to carry out the transfer. This is done by *phys_copy*, an assembly language procedure in the kernel that copies to or from the user program at the maximum speed of which the hardware is capable.

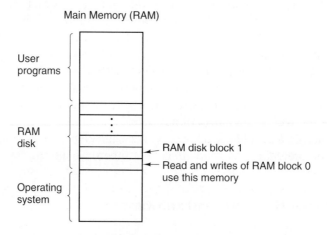

Figure 3-20. A RAM disk.

A RAM disk driver may support several areas of memory used as RAM disk, each distinguished by a different minor device number. Usually, these areas are distinct, but in some fairly specific situations it may be convenient to have them overlap, as we shall see in the next section.

3.6.2 Overview of the RAM Disk Driver in MINIX 3

The MINIX 3 RAM disk driver is actually six closely related drivers in one. Each message to it specifies a minor device as follows:

0: /dev/ram	2: /dev/kmem	4: /dev/boot
1: /dev/mem	3: /dev/null	5: /dev/zero

The first special file listed above, */dev/ram*, is a true RAM disk. Neither its size nor its origin is built into the driver. They are determined by the file system when MINIX 3 is booted. If the boot parameters specify that the root file system is to be on the RAM disk but the RAM disk size is not specified, a RAM disk of the same size as the root file system image device is created. A boot parameter can be used to specify a RAM disk larger than the root file system, or if the root is not to be copied to the RAM, the specified size may be any value that fits in memory and leaves enough memory for system operation. Once the size is known, a block of memory big enough is found and removed from the memory pool by the process manager during its initialization. This strategy makes it possible to increase or reduce the amount of RAM disk present without having to recompile the operating system.

The next two minor devices are used to read and write physical memory and kernel memory, respectively. When */dev/mem* is opened and read, it yields the contents of physical memory locations starting at absolute address zero (the real-mode interrupt vectors). Ordinary user programs never do this, but a system program concerned with debugging the system might possibly need this facility. Opening */dev/mem* and writing on it will change the interrupt vectors. Needless to say, this should only be done with the greatest of caution by an experienced user who knows exactly what he is doing.

The special file */dev/kmem* is like */dev/mem*, except that byte 0 of this file is byte 0 of the kernel's data memory, a location whose absolute address varies, depending on the size of the MINIX 3 kernel text segment. It too is used mostly for debugging and very special programs. Note that the RAM disk areas covered by these two minor devices overlap. If you know exactly how the kernel is placed in memory, you can open */dev/mem*, seek to the beginning of the kernel's data area, and see exactly the same thing as reading from the beginning of */dev/kmem*. But, if you recompile the kernel, changing its size, or if in a subsequent version of MINIX 3 the kernel is moved somewhere else in memory, you will have to seek a different amount in */dev/mem* to see the same thing you now see at the start of */dev/kmem*. Both of these special files should be protected to prevent everyone except the superuser from using them.

The next file in this group, */dev/null*, is a special file that accepts data and throws them away. It is commonly used in shell commands when the program being called generates output that is not needed. For example,

```
a.out >/dev/null
```

runs the program *a.out* but discards its output. The RAM disk driver effectively treats this minor device as having zero size, so no data are ever copied to or from it. If you read from it you will get an immediate EOF (End of File).

If you have looked at the directory entries for these files in */dev/* you may have noticed that, of those mentioned so far, only */dev/ram* is a block special file. All the others are character devices. There is one more block device supported by the memory driver. This is */dev/boot*. From the point of view of the device driver it is another block device implemented in RAM, just like */dev/ram*. However, it is meant to be initialized by copying a file appended to the boot image after *init* into memory, rather than starting with an empty block of memory, as is done for */dev/ram*. Support for this device is provided for future use and it is not used in MINIX 3 as described in this text.

Finally, the last device supported by the memory driver is another character special file, */dev/zero*. It is sometimes convenient to have a source of zeros. Writing to */dev/zero* is like writing to */dev/null*; it throws data away. But reading */dev/zero* gives you zeros, in any quantity you want, whether a single character or a disk full.

At the driver level, the code for handling */dev/ram*, */dev/mem*, */dev/kmem*, and */dev/boot* is identical. The only difference among them is that each one corresponds to a different region of memory, indicated by the arrays *ram_origin* and *ram_limit*, each indexed by minor device number. The file system manages devices at a higher level. The file system interprets devices as character or block devices, and thus can mount */dev/ram* and */dev/boot* and manage directories and files on these devices. For the devices defined as character devices the file system can only read and write streams of data (although a stream read from */dev/null* gets only EOF).

3.6.3 Implementation of the RAM Disk Driver in MINIX 3

As with other disk drivers, the main loop of the RAM disk driver is in the file *driver.c*. The device-specific support for memory devices is in *memory.c* (line 10800). When the memory driver is compiled, a copy of the object file called *drivers/libdriver/driver.o*, produced by compiling *drivers/libdriver/driver.c*, is linked with the object file *drivers/memory/memory.o*, the product of compiling *drivers/memory/memory.c*.

It may be worth taking a moment to consider how the main loop is compiled. The declaration of the *driver* structure in *driver.h* (lines 10829 to 10845) defines a data structure, but does not create one. The declaration of *m_dtab* on lines 11645 to 11660 creates an instance of this with each part of the structure filled in with a pointer to a function. Some of these functions are generic code compiled when *driver.c* is compiled, for instance, all of the *nop* functions. Others are code compiled when *memory.c* is compiled, for instance, *m_do_open*. Note that for the memory driver seven of the entries are do-little or do-nothing routines and the last two are defined as *NULL* (which means these functions will never be called, there is no need even for a *do_nop*). All this is a sure clue that the operation of a RAM disk is not terribly complicated.

The memory device does not require definition of a large number of data structures, either. The array *m_geom[NR_DEVS]* (line 11627) holds the base and size of each of the six memory devices in bytes, as 64 bit unsigned integers, so there is no immediate danger of MINIX 3 not being able to have a big enough RAM disk. The next line defines an interesting structure that will not be seen in other drivers. *M_seg[NR_DEVS]* is apparently just an aray of integers, but these integers are indices that allow segment descriptors to be found. The memory device driver is unusual among user-space processes in having the ability to access regions of memory outside of the ordinary text, data, and stack segments every process owns. This array holds the information that allows access to the designated additional memory regions. The variable *m_device* just holds the index into these arrays of the currently active minor device.

To use */dev/ram* as the root device the memory driver must be initialized very early during startup of MINIX 3. The *kinfo* and *machine* structures that are defined next will hold data retrieved from the kernel during startup that is necessary for initializing the memory driver.

One other data structure is defined before the executable code begins. This is *dev_zero*, an array of 1024 bytes, used to supply data when a read call is made to */dev/zero*.

The main procedure *main* (line 11672) calls one function to do some local initialization. After that, it calls the main loop, which gets messages, dispatches to the appropriate procedures, and sends the replies. There is no return to *main* upon completion.

The next function, *m_name*, is trivial. It returns the string "memory" when called.

On a read or write operation, the main loop makes three calls: one to prepare a device, one to do the actual data transfer, and one to do cleanup. For a memory device, a call to *m_prepare* is the first of these. It checks that a valid minor device has been requested and then returns the address of the structure that holds the base address and size of the requested RAM area. The second call is for *m_transfer* (line 11706). This does all the work. As we saw in *driver.c*, all calls to read or write data are transformed into calls to read or write multiple contiguous blocks of data—if only one block is needed the request is passed on as a request for multiple blocks with a count of one. So only two kinds of transfer requests are passed on to the driver, *DEV_GATHER*, requesting a read of one or more blocks, and *DEV_SCATTER*, a request to write one or more blocks. Thus, after getting the minor device number, *m_transfer* enters a loop, repeated for the number of transfers requested. Within the loop there is a switch on the device type.

The first case is for */dev/null*, and the action is to return immediately on a *DEV_GATHER* request or on a *DEV_SCATTER* request to fall through to the end of the switch. This is so the number of bytes transferred (although this number is zero for */dev/null*) can be returned, as would be done for any write operation.

For all of the device types that refer to real locations in memory the action is similar. The requested offset is checked against the size of the device to determine that the request is within the bounds of the memory allocated to the device. Then a kernel call is made to copy data either to or from the memory of the caller. There are two chunks of code that do this, however. For */dev/ram*, */dev/kmem*, and */dev/boot* virtual addresses are used, which requires retrieving the segment address of the memory region to be accessed from the *m_seg* array, and then making a sys_vircopy kernel call (lines 11640 to 11652). For */dev/mem* a physical address is used and the call is to sys_physcopy.

The remaining operation is a read or write to */dev/zero*. For reading the data is taken from the *dev_zero* array mentioned earlier. You might ask, why not just generate zero values as needed, rather than copying from a buffer full of them? Since the copying of the data to its destination has to be done by a kernel call, such a method would require either an inefficient copying of single bytes from the memory driver to the system task, or building code to generate zeros into the system task. The latter approach would increase the complexity of kernel-space code, something that we would like to avoid in MINIX 3.

A memory device does not need a third step to finish a read or write operation, and the corresponding slot in *m_dtab* is a call to *nop_finish*.

Opening a memory device is done by *m_do_open* (line 11801). The job is done by calling *m_prepare* to check that a valid device is being referenced. More interesting than the code that exists is a comment about code that was found here in older versions of MINIX. Previously a trick was hidden here. A call by a user process to open */dev/mem* or */dev/kmem* would also magically confer upon the caller the ability to execute instructions which access I/O ports. Pentium-class CPUs implement four privilege levels, and user processes normally run at the least-privileged level. The CPU generates a general protection exception when an process tries to execute an instruction not allowed at its privilege level. Providing a way to get around this was considered safe because the memory devices could only be accessed by a user with root privileges. In any case, this possibly risky "feature" is absent from MINIX 3 because kernel calls that allow I/O access via the system task are now available. The comment remains, to point out that if MINIX 3 is ported to hardware that uses memory-mapped I/O such a feature might need to be reintroduced. The function to do this, *enable_iop*, remains in the kernel code to show how this can be done, although it is now an orphan.

The next function, *m_init* (line 11817), is called only once, when *mem_task* is called for the first time. This routine uses a number of kernel calls, and is worth study to see how MINIX 3 drivers interact with kernel space by using system task services. First a sys_getkinfo kernel call is made to get a copy of the kernel's *kinfo* data. From this data it copies the base address and size of */dev/kmem* into the corresponding fields of the *m_geom* data structure. A different kernel call, sys_segctl, converts the physical address and size of */dev/kmem* into the segment descriptor information needed to treat the kernel memory as a virtual memory space. If an image of a boot device has been compiled into the system boot image, the field for the base address of */dev/boot* will be non-zero. If this is so, then information to access the memory region for this device is set up in exactly the same way it was done for */dev/kmem*. Next the array used to supply data when */dev/zero* is accessed is explicitly filled with zeros. This is probably unnecessary; C compilers are supposed to initialize newly created static variables to all zeros.

Finally, *m_init* uses a sys_getmachine kernel call to get another set of data from the kernel, the *machine* structure which flags various possible hardware alternatives. In this case the information needed is whether or not the CPU is capable of protected mode operation. Based on this information the size of */dev/mem* is set to either 1 MB, or 4 GB − 1, depending upon whether MINIX 3 is running in 8088 or 80386 mode. These sizes are the maximum sizes supported by MINIX 3 and do not have anything to do with how much RAM is installed in the machine. Only the size of the device is set; the compiler is trusted to set the base address correctly to zero. Also, since */dev/mem* is accessed as physical (not virtual) memory there is no need to make a sys_segctl kernel call to set up a segment descriptor.

Before we leave *m_init* we should mention another kernel call used here, although it is not obvious in the code. Many of the actions taken during initialization of the memory driver are essential to proper functioning of MINIX 3, and thus several tests are made and *panic* is called if a test fails. In this case *panic* is a library routine which ultimately results in a sys_exit kernel call. The kernel and (as we shall see) the process manager and the file system have their own *panic* routines. The library routine is provided for device drivers and other small system components.

Surprisingly, the function we just examined, *m_init*, does not initialize the quintessential memory device, */dev/ram*. This is taken care of in the next function, *m_ioctl* (line 11863). In fact, there is only one ioctl operation defined for the RAM disk; this is *MIOCRAMSIZE*, which is used by the file system to set the RAM disk size. Much of the job is done without requiring any services from the kernel. The call to allocmem on line 11887 is a system call, but not a kernel call. It is handled by the process manager, which maintains all of the information necessary to find an available region of memory. However, at the end one kernel call is needed. At line 11894 a sys_segctl call is made to convert the physical address and size returned by allocmem into the segment information needed for further access.

The last function defined in *memory.c* is *m_geometry*. This is a fake. Obviously, cylinders, heads, and sectors are irrelevant in addressing semiconductor memory, but if a request is made for such information for a memory device this function pretends it has 64 heads and 32 sectors per track, and calculates from the size how many cylinders there are.

3.7 DISKS

All modern computers except embedded ones have disk drives. For that reason, we will now study them, starting with the hardware, then moving on to say some general things about disk software. After that we will delve into the way MINIX 3 controls its disks.

3.7.1 Disk Hardware

All real disks are organized into cylinders, each one containing as many tracks as there are heads stacked vertically. The tracks are divided into sectors, with the number of sectors around the circumference typically being 8 to 32 on floppy disks, and up to several hundred on some hard disks. The simplest designs have the same number of sectors on each track. All sectors contain the same number of bytes, although a little thought will make it clear that sectors close to the outer rim of the disk will be physically longer than those close to the hub. The time to read or write each sector will be same, however. The data density is obviously higher on the innermost cylinders, and some disk designs require a change in the drive current to the read-write heads for the inner tracks. This is handled by the disk controller hardware and is not visible to the user (or the implementer of an operating system).

The difference in data density between inner and outer tracks means a sacrifice in capacity, and more sophisticated systems exist. Floppy disk designs that rotate at higher speeds when the heads are over the outer tracks have been tried. This allows more sectors on those tracks, increasing disk capacity. Such disks are not supported by any system for which MINIX 3 is currently available, however. Modern large hard drives also have more sectors per track on outer tracks than on inner tracks. These are **IDE (Integrated Drive Electronics)** drives, and the sophisticated processing done by the drive's built-in electronics masks the details. To the operating system they appear to have a simple geometry with the same number of sectors on each track.

The drive and controller electronics are as important as the mechanical hardware. The main element of the disk controller is a specialized integrated circuit, really a small microcomputer. Once this would have been on a card plugged into the computer's backplane, but on modern systems, the disk controller is on the parentboard. For a modern hard disk this disk controller circuitry may be simpler than for a floppy disk, since a hard drive has a powerful electronic controller integrated into the drive itself.

A device feature that has important implications for the disk driver is the possibility of a controller doing seeks on two or more drives at the same time. These are known as **overlapped seeks**. While the controller and software are waiting for a seek to complete on one drive, the controller can initiate a seek on another drive. Many controllers can also read or write on one drive while seeking on one or more other drives, but a floppy disk controller cannot read or write on two drives at the same time. (Reading or writing requires the controller to move bits on a microsecond time scale, so one transfer uses up most of its computing power.) The situation is different for hard disks with integrated controllers, and in a system with more than one of these hard drives they can operate simultaneously, at least to the extent of transferring between the disk and the controller's buffer memory. Only one transfer between the controller and the system memory is possible at once, however. The ability to perform two or more operations at the same time can reduce the average access time considerably.

One thing to be aware of in looking at the specifications of modern hard disks is that the geometry specified, and used by the driver software, is almost always different from the physical format. In fact, if you look up the "recommended setup parameters" for a large hard disk, you are likely to find it specified as 16383 cylinders, 16 heads, and 63 sectors per track, no matter what the size of the disk. These numbers correspond to a disk size of 8 GB, but are used for all disks this size or larger. The designers of the original IBM PC ROM BIOS allotted a 6-bit field for the sector count, 4 bits to specify the head, and 14 bits to select a cylinder. With 512 byte sectors this comes out to 8 GB. So if you try to install a large hard drive into a very old computer you may find you can access only 8 GB, even though you have a much bigger disk. The usual way around this limitation is to use **logical block addressing** in which disk sectors are just numbered consecutively starting at zero, without regard to the disk geometry.

The geometry of a modern disk is a fiction, anyway. On a modern disk the surface is divided into 20 or more zones. Zones closer to the center of the disk have fewer sectors per track than zones nearer the periphery. Thus sectors have approximately the same physical length no matter where they are located on the disk, making more efficient use of the disk surface. Internally, the integrated controller addresses the disk by calculating the zone, cylinder, head, and sector. But this is never visible to the user, and the details are rarely found in published specifications. The bottom line is, there is no point to using cylinder, head, sector addressing of a disk unless you are working with a very old computer that does not support logical block addressing. Also, it does not make sense to buy a new 400 GB drive for the PC-XT you bought in 1983; you will get no more than 8 GB use out of it.

This is a good place to mention a confusing point about disk capacity specifications. Computer professionals are accustomed to using powers of 2—a Kilobyte (KB) is 2^{10} = 1024 bytes, a Megabyte (MB) is 2^{20} = 1024^2 bytes, etc., to express the size of memory devices. A Gigabyte (GB), then, should be 1024^3, or 2^{30} bytes. However, disk manufacturers have adopted the habit of using the term "Gigabyte" to mean 10^9, which (on paper) instantly increases the size of their products. Thus the 8 GB limit mentioned above is an 8.4 GB disk in the language of the disk salesman. Recently there has been a move toward using the term Gibibyte (GiB) to mean 2^{30}. However, in this text the authors, being set in their ways and in protest of the hijacking of tradition for advertising purposes, will continue to use terms like Megabyte and Gigabyte to mean what they have always meant.

3.7.2 RAID

Although modern disks are much faster than older ones, improvements in CPU performance have far exceeded improvements in disk performance. It has occurred to various people over the years that parallel disk I/O might be helpful. Thus has come about a new class of I/O device called a **RAID**, an acronym for **Redundant Array of Independent Disks**. Actually, the designers of RAID (at Berkeley) originally used the acronym RAID to stand for "Redundant Array of Inexpensive Disks" to contrast this design with a **SLED (Single Large Expensive Disk)**. However, when RAID became commercially popular, disk manufacturers changed the meaning of the acronym because it was tough to sell an expensive product whose name stood for "inexpensive." The basic idea behind a RAID is to install a box full of disks next to the computer, typically a large server, replace the disk controller card with a RAID controller, copy the data over to the RAID, and then continue normal operation.

The independent disks can be used together in a variety of ways. We do not have space for an exhaustive description of all of these, and MINIX 3 does not (yet) support RAID, but an introduction to operating systems should at least mention some of the possibilities. RAID can be used both to speed disk access and to make data more secure.

For example, consider a very simple RAID of two drives. When multiple sectors of data are to be written to the "disk" the RAID controller sends sectors 0, 2, 4, etc., to the first drive, and sectors 1, 3, 5, etc., to the second drive. The controller divides up the data and the two disks are written simultaneously, doubling the writing speed. When reading, both drives are read simultaneously, but the controller reassembles the data in the proper order, and to the rest of the system it just looks like the reading speed is twice as fast. This technique is called **striping**. This is a simple example of RAID level 0. In practice four or more drives would be used. This works best when data are usually read or written in large blocks. Obviously, nothing is gained if a typical disk request is for a single sector at a time.

The previous example shows how multiple drives can increase speed. What about reliability? RAID level 1 works like RAID level 0, except the data is duplicated. Again, a very simple array of two drives could be used, and all of the data could be written to both of them. This provides no speedup, but there is 100% redundancy. If an error is detected during reading there is no need for a retry if the other drive reads the data correctly. The controller just has to make sure the correct data is passed on to the system. It probably would not be a good idea to skip retries if errors are detected while writing, however. And if errors occur frequently enough that skipping retries actually makes reading noticeably faster it is probably time to decide complete failure is imminent. Typically the drives used for RAIDs are hot-swappable, meaning they can be replaced without powering down the system.

More complex arrays of multiple disks can increase both speed and reliability. Consider, for instance, an array of 7 disks. Bytes could be split into 4-bit nybbles, with each bit being recorded on one of four drives and with the other three drives being used to record a three bit error-correcting code. If a drive goes bad and needs to be hot-swapped for a new one, a missing drive is equivalent to one bad bit, so the system can keep running while maintenance is done. For the cost of seven drives you get reliable performance that is four times as fast as one drive, and no downtime.

3.7.3 Disk Software

In this section we will look at some issues related to disk drivers in general. First, consider how long it takes to read or write a disk block. The time required is determined by three factors:

1. The seek time (the time to move the arm to the proper cylinder).

2. The rotational delay (the time for the proper sector to rotate under the head).

3. The actual data transfer time.

For most disks, the seek time dominates the other two times, so reducing the mean seek time can improve system performance substantially.

Disk devices are prone to errors. Some kind of error check, a checksum or a cyclic redundancy check, is always recorded along with the data in each sector on a disk. Even the sector addresses recorded when the disk is formatted have check data. Floppy disk controller hardware can usually report when an error is detected, but the software must then decide what to do about it. Hard disk controllers often take on much of this burden.

Particularly with hard disks, the transfer time for consecutive sectors within a track can be very fast. Thus reading more data than requested and caching it in memory can be very effective in speeding disk access.

Disk Arm Scheduling Algorithms

If the disk driver accepts requests one at a time and carries them out in that order, that is, First-Come, First-Served (FCFS), little can be done to optimize seek time. However, another strategy is possible when the disk is heavily loaded. It is likely that while the arm is seeking on behalf of one request, other disk requests may be generated by other processes. Many disk drivers maintain a table, indexed by cylinder number, with all pending requests for each cylinder chained together in a linked list headed by the table entries.

Given this kind of data structure, we can improve upon the first-come, first-served scheduling algorithm. To see how, consider a disk with 40 cylinders. A request comes in to read a block on cylinder 11. While the seek to cylinder 11 is in progress, new requests come in for cylinders 1, 36, 16, 34, 9, and 12, in that order. They are entered into the table of pending requests, with a separate linked list for each cylinder. The requests are shown in Fig. 3-21.

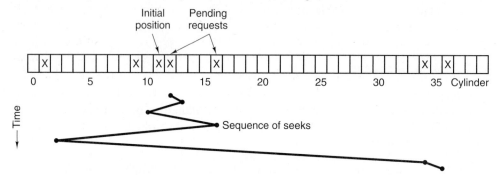

Figure 3-21. Shortest Seek First (SSF) disk scheduling algorithm.

When the current request (for cylinder 11) is finished, the disk driver has a choice of which request to handle next. Using FCFS, it would go next to cylinder 1, then to 36, and so on. This algorithm would require arm motions of 10, 35, 20, 18, 25, and 3, respectively, for a total of 111 cylinders.

Alternatively, it could always handle the closest request next, to minimize seek time. Given the requests of Fig. 3-21, the sequence is 12, 9, 16, 1, 34, and 36, as shown as the jagged line at the bottom of Fig. 3-21. With this sequence, the arm motions are 1, 3, 7, 15, 33, and 2, for a total of 61 cylinders. This algorithm, **Shortest Seek First** (SSF), cuts the total arm motion almost in half compared to FCFS.

Unfortunately, SSF has a problem. Suppose that more requests keep coming in while the requests of Fig. 3-21 are being processed. For example, if, after going to cylinder 16, a new request for cylinder 8 is present, that request will have priority over cylinder 1. If a request for cylinder 13 then comes in, the arm will next go to 13, instead of 1. With a heavily loaded disk, the arm will tend to stay in the middle of the disk most of the time, so requests at either extreme will have to wait until a statistical fluctuation in the load causes there to be no requests near the middle. Requests far from the middle may get poor service. The goals of minimal response time and fairness are in conflict here.

Tall buildings also have to deal with this trade-off. The problem of scheduling an elevator in a tall building is similar to that of scheduling a disk arm. Requests come in continuously calling the elevator to floors (cylinders) at random.

The microprocessor running the elevator could easily keep track of the sequence in which customers pushed the call button and service them using FCFS. It could also use SSF.

However, most elevators use a different algorithm to reconcile the conflicting goals of efficiency and fairness. They keep moving in the same direction until there are no more outstanding requests in that direction, then they switch directions. This algorithm, known both in the disk world and the elevator world as the **elevator algorithm**, requires the software to maintain 1 bit: the current direction bit, *UP* or *DOWN*. When a request finishes, the disk or elevator driver checks the bit. If it is *UP*, the arm or cabin is moved to the next highest pending request. If no requests are pending at higher positions, the direction bit is reversed. When the bit is set to *DOWN*, the move is to the next lowest requested position, if any.

Figure 3-22 shows the elevator algorithm using the same seven requests as Fig. 3-21, assuming the direction bit was initially *UP*. The order in which the cylinders are serviced is 12, 16, 34, 36, 9, and 1, which yields arm motions of 1, 4, 18, 2, 27, and 8, for a total of 60 cylinders. In this case the elevator algorithm is slightly better than SSF, although it is usually worse. One nice property that the elevator algorithm has is that given any collection of requests, the upper bound on the total motion is fixed: it is just twice the number of cylinders.

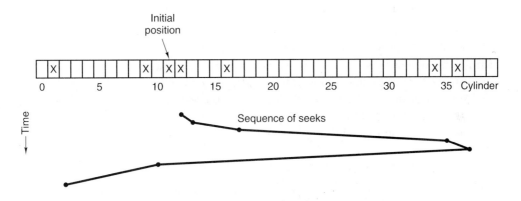

Figure 3-22. The elevator algorithm for scheduling disk requests.

A slight modification of this algorithm that has a smaller variance in response times is to always scan in the same direction (Teory, 1972). When the highest numbered cylinder with a pending request has been serviced, the arm goes to the lowest-numbered cylinder with a pending request and then continues moving in an upward direction. In effect, the lowest-numbered cylinder is thought of as being just above the highest-numbered cylinder.

Some disk controllers provide a way for the software to inspect the current sector number under the head. With such a controller, another optimization is possible. If two or more requests for the same cylinder are pending, the driver can issue a request for the sector that will pass under the head next. Note that when multiple tracks are present in a cylinder, consecutive requests can be for different tracks with no penalty. The controller can select any of its heads instantaneously, because head selection involves neither arm motion nor rotational delay.

With a modern hard disk, the data transfer rate is so much faster than that of a floppy disk that some kind of automatic caching is necessary. Typically any request to read a sector will cause that sector and up to the rest of the current track to be read, depending upon how much space is available in the controller's cache memory. Current caches are often 8 MB or more.

When several drives are present, a pending request table should be kept for each drive separately. Whenever any drive is idle, a seek should be issued to move its arm to the cylinder where it will be needed next (assuming the controller allows overlapped seeks). When the current transfer finishes, a check can be made to see if any drives are positioned on the correct cylinder. If one or more are, the next transfer can be started on a drive that is already on the right cylinder. If none of the arms is in the right place, the driver should issue a new seek on the drive that just completed a transfer and wait until the next interrupt to see which arm gets to its destination first.

Error Handling

RAM disks do not have to worry about seek or rotational optimization: at any instant all blocks can be read or written without any physical motion. Another area in which RAM disks are simpler than real disks is error handling. RAM disks always work; real ones do not always work. They are subject to a wide variety of errors. Some of the more common ones are:

1. Programming error (e.g., request for nonexistent sector).

2. Transient checksum error (e.g., caused by dust on the head).

3. Permanent checksum error (e.g., disk block physically damaged).

4. Seek error (e.g., the arm was sent to cylinder 6 but it went to 7).

5. Controller error (e.g., controller refuses to accept commands).

It is up to the disk driver to handle each of these as best it can.

Programming errors occur when the driver tells the controller to seek to a nonexistent cylinder, read from a nonexistent sector, use a nonexistent head, or transfer to or from nonexistent memory. Most controllers check the parameters given to them and complain if they are invalid. In theory, these errors should never occur, but what should the driver do if the controller indicates that one has happened? For a home-grown system, the best thing to do is stop and print a message like "Call the programmer" so the error can be tracked down and fixed. For a commercial software product in use at thousands of sites around the world, this approach is less attractive. Probably the only thing to do is terminate the current disk request with an error and hope it will not recur too often.

Transient checksum errors are caused by specks of dust in the air that get between the head and the disk surface. Most of the time they can be eliminated by just repeating the operation a few times. If the error persists, the block has to be marked as a **bad block** and avoided.

One way to avoid bad blocks is to write a very special program that takes a list of bad blocks as input and carefully hand crafts a file containing all the bad blocks. Once this file has been made, the disk allocator will think these blocks are occupied and never allocate them. As long as no one ever tries to read the bad block file, no problems will occur.

Not reading the bad block file is easier said than done. Many disks are backed up by copying their contents a track at a time to a backup tape or disk drive. If this procedure is followed, the bad blocks will cause trouble. Backing up the disk one file at a time is slower but will solve the problem, provided that the backup program knows the name of the bad block file and refrains from copying it.

Another problem that cannot be solved with a bad block file is the problem of a bad block in a file system data structure that must be in a fixed location. Almost every file system has at least one data structure whose location is fixed, so it can be found easily. On a partitioned file system it may be possible to repartition and work around a bad track, but a permanent error in the first few sectors of either a floppy or hard disk generally means the disk is unusable.

"Intelligent" controllers reserve a few tracks not normally available to user programs. When a disk drive is formatted, the controller determines which blocks are bad and automatically substitutes one of the spare tracks for the bad one. The table that maps bad tracks to spare tracks is kept in the controller's internal memory and on the disk. This substitution is transparent (invisible) to the driver, except that its carefully worked out elevator algorithm may perform poorly if the controller is secretly using cylinder 800 whenever cylinder 3 is requested. The technology of manufacturing disk recording surfaces is better than it used to be, but it is still not perfect. However, the technology of hiding the imperfections from the user has also improved. Many controllers also manage new errors that may develop with use, permanently assigning substitute blocks when they determine that an error is unrecoverable. With such disks the driver software rarely sees any indication that there any bad blocks.

Seek errors are caused by mechanical problems in the arm. The controller keeps track of the arm position internally. To perform a seek, it issues a series of pulses to the arm motor, one pulse per cylinder, to move the arm to the new cylinder. When the arm gets to its destination, the controller reads the actual cylinder number (written when the drive was formatted). If the arm is in the wrong place, a seek error has occurred and some corrective action is required.

Most hard disk controllers correct seek errors automatically, but many floppy controllers (including the IBM PCs) just set an error bit and leave the rest to the driver. The driver handles this error by issuing a recalibrate command, to move the arm as far out as it will go and reset the controller's internal idea of the current cylinder to 0. Usually, this solves the problem. If it does not, the drive must be repaired.

As we have seen, the controller is really a specialized little computer, complete with software, variables, buffers, and occasionally, bugs. Sometimes an unusual sequence of events such as an interrupt on one drive occurring simultaneously with a recalibrate command for another drive will trigger a bug and cause the controller to go into a loop or lose track of what it was doing. Controller designers usually plan for the worst and provide a pin on the chip which, when asserted, forces the controller to forget whatever it was doing and reset itself. If all else fails, the disk driver can set a bit to invoke this signal and reset the controller. If that does not help, all the driver can do is print a message and give up.

Track-at-a-Time Caching

The time required to seek to a new cylinder is usually much more than the rotational delay, and always vastly more than the transfer time to read or write one sector. In other words, once the driver has gone to the trouble of moving the arm somewhere, it hardly matters whether it reads one sector or a whole track. This effect is especially true if the controller provides rotational sensing, so the driver can see which sector is currently under the head and issue a request for the next sector, thereby making it possible to read an entire disk track in a single rotation time. (Normally it takes half a rotation plus one sector time just to read a single sector, on the average.)

Some disk drivers take advantage of these timing properties by maintaining a secret track-at-a-time cache, unknown to the device-independent software. If a sector that is in the cache is needed, no disk transfer is required. A disadvantage of track-at-a-time caching (in addition to the software complexity and buffer space needed) is that transfers from the cache to the calling program will have to be done by the CPU using a programmed loop, rather than letting the DMA hardware do the job.

Some controllers take this process a step further, and do track-at-a-time caching in their own internal memory, transparent to the driver, so that transfer between the controller and memory can use DMA. If the controller works this way, there is little point in having the disk driver do it as well. Note that both the controller and the driver are in a good position to read and write entire tracks in one command, but that the device-independent software cannot, because it regards a disk as a linear sequence of blocks, without regard to how they are divided up into tracks and cylinders. Only the controller knows the true geometry for sure.

3.7.4 Overview of the Hard Disk Driver in MINIX 3

The hard disk driver is the first part of MINIX 3 we have looked at that has to deal with a range of different types of hardware. Before we discuss the driver, we will briefly consider some of the problems hardware differences can cause.

The "PC" is really a family of different computers. Not only are different processors used in different members of the family, there are also some major differences in the basic hardware. MINIX 3 has been developed on and for newer systems with Pentium-class CPUs, but even among these there are differences. For instance, the oldest Pentium systems use the 16-bit AT bus originally designed for the 80286 processor. A feature of the AT bus is that it was cleverly designed so older 8-bit peripherals could still be used. Later systems added a 32-bit PCI bus for peripherals, while still providing AT bus slots. The newest designs have dropped AT-bus support, providing only a PCI bus. But it is reasonable to expect that users with computers of a certain age may want to be able to use MINIX 3 with a mix of 8-bit, 16-bit, and 32-bit peripherals.

For every bus there is a different family of **I/O adapters**. On older systems these are separate circuit boards which plug into the system parentboard. On newer systems many standard adapters, especially disk controllers, are integrated parts of the parentboard chipset. In itself this is not a problem for the programmer, as integrated adapters usually have a software interface identical to that of removable devices. Also, integrated controllers can usually be disabled. This allows use of a more advanced add-on device, such as a SCSI controller, in place of a built-in device. To take advantage of this flexibility the operating system should not be restricted to using just one kind of adapter.

In the IBM PC family, as in most other computer systems, each bus design also comes with firmware in the Basic I/O System Read-Only Memory (the BIOS ROM) which is designed to bridge the gap between the operating system and the peculiarities of the hardware. Some peripheral devices may even provide extensions to the BIOS in ROM chips on the peripheral cards themselves. The difficulty faced by an operating system implementer is that the BIOS in IBM-type computers (certainly the early ones) was designed for an operating system, MS-DOS, that does not support multiprogramming and that runs in 16-bit real mode, the lowest common denominator of the various modes of operation available from the 80x86 family of CPUs.

The implementer of a new operating system for the IBM PC is thus faced with several choices. One is whether to use the driver support for peripherals in the BIOS or to write new drivers from scratch. This was not a hard choice in the design of early versions of MINIX, since the BIOS was in many ways not suitable to its needs. Of course, to start MINIX 3 the boot monitor uses the BIOS to do the initial loading of the system, whether from hard disk, CD-ROM, or floppy disk— there is no practical alternative to doing it this way. Once we have loaded the system, including our own I/O drivers, we can do better than the BIOS.

The second choice then must be faced: without the BIOS support how are we going to make our drivers adapt to the varied kinds of hardware on different systems? To make the discussion concrete, consider that there are two fundamentally different types of hard disk controller usable on the modern 32-bit Pentium systems for which MINIX 3 has been designed: the integrated IDE controller and add-on SCSI controllers for the PCI bus. If you would like to take advantage of older hardware and adapt MINIX 3 to work on the hardware targeted by earlier versions of MINIX, there are four hard disk controller types to consider: the original 8-bit XT-type controller, the 16-bit AT-type controller, and two different controllers for two different types of IBM PS/2 series computers. There are several possible ways to deal with all these alternatives:

1. Recompile a unique version of the operating system for each type of hard disk controller we need to accommodate.

2. Compile several different hard disk drivers into the boot image and have the system automatically determine at startup time which one to use.

3. Compile several different hard disk drivers into the boot image and provide a way for the user to determine which one to use.

As we shall see, these are not mutually exclusive.

The first way is really the best way in the long run. For use on a particular installation there is no need to use up disk and memory space with code for alternative drivers that will never be used. However, it is a nightmare for the distributor of the software. Supplying four different startup disks and advising users on how to use them is expensive and difficult. Thus, another method is advisable, at least for the initial installation.

The second method is to have the operating system probe the peripherals, by reading the ROM on each card or writing and reading I/O ports to identify each card. This is possible (and works better on newer IBM-type systems than on older ones), but it does not accommodate nonstandard I/O devices. Also, probing I/O ports to identify one device sometimes can activate another device which seizes control and disables the system. This method complicates the startup code for each device, and yet still does not work very well. Operating systems that do use this method generally have to provide some kind of override, typically a mechanism such as we use with MINIX 3.

The third method, used in MINIX 3, is to allow inclusion of several drivers in the boot image. The MINIX 3 boot monitor allows various **boot parameters** to be read at startup time. These can be entered by hand, or stored permanently on the disk. At startup time, if a boot parameter of the form

    label = AT

is found, this forces the IDE disk controller (at_wini) to be used when MINIX 3 is started. This depends upon the at_wini driver being assigned this label. Labels are assigned when the boot image is compiled.

There are two other things MINIX 3 does to try to minimize problems with multiple hard disk drivers. One is that there is, after all, a driver that interfaces between MINIX 3 and the ROM BIOS hard disk support. This driver is almost guaranteed to work on any system and can be selected by use of a

label=BIOS

boot parameter. Generally, this should be a last resort, however. MINIX 3 as described here runs only in protected mode on systems with an 80386 or better processor, but the BIOS code always runs in real (8086) mode. Switching out of protected mode and back again whenever a routine in the BIOS is called is very slow.

The other strategy MINIX 3 uses in dealing with drivers is to postpone initialization until the last possible moment. Thus, if on some hardware configuration none of the hard disk drivers work, we can still start MINIX 3 from a floppy disk and do some useful work. MINIX 3 will have no problems as long as no attempt is made to access the hard disk. This may not seem like a major breakthrough in user friendliness, but consider this: if all the drivers try to initialize immediately on system startup, the system can be totally paralyzed by improper configuration of some device we do not need anyway. By postponing initialization of each driver until it is needed, the system can continue with whatever does work, while the user tries to resolve the problems.

We learned this lesson the hard way: earlier versions of MINIX tried to initialize the hard disk as soon as the system was booted. If no hard disk was present, the system hung. This behavior was especially unfortunate because MINIX would run quite happily on a system without a hard disk, albeit with restricted storage capacity and reduced performance.

In the discussion in this section and the next, we will take as our model the AT-style hard disk driver, which is the default driver in the standard MINIX 3 distribution. This is a versatile driver that handles hard disk controllers from the ones used in the earliest 80286 systems to modern **EIDE (Extended Integrated Drive Electronics)** controllers that handle gigabyte capacity hard disks. Modern EIDE controllers also support standard CD-ROM drives. However, in order to simplify our discussion the extensions that support CD-ROMs have been taken out of the code listed in Appendix B. The general aspects of hard disk operation we discuss in this section apply to the other supported drivers as well.

The main loop of the hard disk driver is the same common code we have already discussed, and supports the standard nine kinds of requests that can be made. A *DEV_OPEN* request can entail a substantial amount of work, as there are always partitions and may be subpartitions on a hard disk. These must be read when a device is opened, (i.e., when it is first accessed). When CD-ROMs are supported, on a *DEV_OPEN* the presence of the medium must be verified, since it is removable. On a CD-ROM a *DEV_CLOSE* operation also has meaning: it requires that the door be unlocked and the CD-ROM ejected. There are other complications of removable media that are more applicable to floppy drives, so we will discuss these in a later section. For CD-ROMs a *DEV_IOCTL* operation is used to set a flag to mark that the medium should be ejected from the drive upon a *DEV_CLOSE*. A *DEV_IOCTL* operation is also used to read and write partition tables.

DEV_READ, *DEV_WRITE*, *DEV_GATHER* and *DEV_SCATTER* requests are each handled in two phases, prepare and transfer, as we saw previously. For the hard disk *DEV_CANCEL* and *DEV_SELECT* calls are ignored.

No scheduling is done by the hard disk device driver at all, that is done by the file system, which assembles the vector requests for gather/scatter I/O. Requests come from the file system cache as *DEV__GATHER* or *DEV_SCATTER* requests for multiples of blocks (4-KB in the default configuration of MINIX 3), but the hard disk driver is able to handle requests for any multiple of a sector (512 bytes). In any case, as we have seen, the main loop of all disk drivers transforms requests for single blocks of data into one element vector requests.

Requests for reading and writing are not mixed in a vector of requests, nor can requests be marked as optional. The elements of a request vector are for contiguous disk sectors, and the vector is sorted by the file system before being passed to the device driver, so it suffices to specify just the starting position on the disk for an entire array of requests.

The driver is expected to succeed in reading or writing at least the first request in a request vector, and to return when a request fails. It is up to the file system to decide what to do; the file system will try to complete a write operation but will return to the calling process only as much data as it can get on a read.

The file system itself, by using scattered I/O, can implement something similar to Teory's version of the elevator algorithm—recall that in a scattered I/O request the list of requests is sorted on the block number. The second step in scheduling takes place in the controller of a modern hard disk. Such controllers are "smart" and can buffer large quantities of data, using internally programmed algorithms to retrieve data in the most efficient order, irrespective of the order of receipt of the requests.

3.7.5 Implementation of the Hard Disk Driver in MINIX 3

Small hard disks used on microcomputers are sometimes called "winchester" disks. The term was IBM's code name for the project that developed the disk technology in which the read/write heads fly on a thin cushion of air and land on the recording medium when the disk stops spinning. The explanation of the name is that an early model had two data modules, a 30-Mbyte fixed and a 30-Mbyte removable one. Supposedly this reminded the developers of the Winchester 30-30 firearm which figures in many tales of the United States' western frontier. Whatever the origin of the name, the basic technology remains the same, although today's typical PC disk is much smaller and the capacity is much larger than the 14-inch disks that were typical of the early 1970s when the winchester technology was developed.

The MINIX 3 AT-style hard disk driver is in *at_wini.c* (line 12100). This is a complicated driver for a sophisticated device, and there are several pages of macro definitions specifying controller registers, status bits and commands, data structures, and prototypes. As with other block device drivers, a *driver* structure, *w_dtab* (lines 12316 to 12331), is initialized with pointers to the functions that actually do the work. Most of them are defined in *at_wini.c*, but as the hard disk requires no special cleanup operation, its *dr_cleanup* entry points to the common *nop_cleanup* in *driver.c*, shared with other drivers that have no special cleanup requirement. Several other possible functions are also irrelevant for this driver and also are initialized to point to *nop_* functions. The entry function, called *at_winchester_task* (line 12336), calls a procedure that does hardware-specific initialization and then calls the main loop in *driver.c*, passing the address of *w_dtab*. The main loop, *driver_task* in *libdriver/driver.c*, runs forever, dispatching calls to the various functions pointed to by the *driver* table.

Since we are now dealing with real electromechanical storage devices, there is a substantial amount of work to be done by *init_params* (line 12347) to initialize the hard disk driver. Various parameters about the hard disks are kept in the *wini* table defined on lines 12254 to 12276, which has an element for each of the *MAX_DRIVES* (8) drives supported, up to four conventional IDE drives, and up to four drives on the PCI bus, either plug-in IDE controllers or **SATA** (**Serial AT Attachment**) controllers.

Following the policy of postponing initialization steps that could fail until the first time they are truly necessary, *init_params* does not do anything that requires accessing the disk devices themselves. The main thing it does is to copy information about the hard disk logical configuration into the *wini* array. The ROM BIOS on a Pentium-class computer retrieves basic configuration information from the CMOS memory used to preserve basic configuration data. The BIOS does this when the computer is first turned on, before the first part of the MINIX 3 loading process begins. On lines 12366 to 12392 the information is copied from the BIOS. Many of the constants used here, such as *NR_HD_DRIVES_ADDR* are defined in *include/ibm/bios.h*, a file which is not listed in Appendix B but which can be found on the MINIX 3 CD-ROM. It is not necessarily fatal if this information cannot be retrieved. If the disk is a modern one, the information can be retrieved directly from the disk when it is accessed for the first time. Following the entry of data obtained from the BIOS, additional disk information is filled in for each drive using a call to the next function, *init_drive*.

On older systems with IDE controllers, the disk functions as if it were an AT-style peripheral card, even though it may be integrated on the parentboard. Modern drive controllers usually function as PCI devices, with a 32-bit data path to the CPU, rather than the 16-bit AT bus. Fortunately for us, once initialization is complete, the interface to both generations of disk controller appears the same to the programmer. To make this work, *init_params_pci* (line 12437) is called if necessary to get the parameters of the PCI devices. We will not describe the details of this routine, but a few points should be mentioned. First, the boot parameter *ata_instance* is used on line 12361 to set the value of the variable *w_instance*. If the boot parameter is not explicitly set the value will be zero. If it is set and greater than zero the test on line 12365 causes querying the BIOS and initialization of standard IDE drives to be skipped. In this case only drives found on the PCI bus will be registered.

The second point is that a controller found on the PCI bus will be identified as controlling devices *c0d4* through *c0d7*. If *w_instance* is non-zero the drive identifiers *c0d0* through *c0d3* will be skipped, unless a PCI bus controller identifies itself as "compatible." Drives handled by a compatible PCI bus controller will be designated *c0d0* through *c0d3*. For most MINIX 3 users all of these complications can probably be ignored. A computer with less than four drives (including the CD-ROM drive), will most likely appear to the user to have the classical configuration, with drives designated *c0d0* to *c0d3*, whether they are connected to IDE or PCI controllers, and whether or not they use the classic 40-pin parallel connectors or the newer serial connectors. But the programming required to create this illusion is complicated.

After the call to the common main loop, nothing may happen for a while until the first attempt is made to access the hard disk. When the first attempt to access a disk is made a message requesting a *DEV_OPEN* operation will be received by the main loop and *w_do_open* (line 12521) will be indirectly called. In turn, *w_do_open* calls *w_prepare* to determine if the device requested is valid, and then *w_identify* to identify the type of device and initialize some more parameters in the *wini* array. Finally, a counter in the *wini* array is used to test whether this is first time the device has been opened since MINIX 3 was started. After being examined, the counter is incremented. If it is the first *DEV_OPEN* operation, the *partition* function (in *drvlib.c*) is called.

The next function, *w_prepare* (line 12577), accepts an integer argument, *device*, which is the minor device number of the drive or partition to be used, and returns a pointer to the *device* structure that indicates the base address and size of the device. In the C language, the use of an identifier to name a structure does not preclude use of the same identifier to name a variable. Whether a device is a drive, a partition, or a subpartition can be determined from the minor device number. Once *w_prepare* has completed its job, none of the other functions used to read or write the disk need to concern themselves with partitioning. As we have seen, *w_prepare* is called when a *DEV_OPEN* request is made; it is also one phase of the prepare/transfer cycle used by all data transfer requests.

Software-compatible AT-style disks have been in use for quite a while, and *w_identify* (line 12603) has to distinguish between a number of different designs that have been introduced over the years. The first step is to see that a readable and writeable I/O port exists where one should exist on all disk controllers in this family. This is the first example we have seen of I/O port access by a user-space driver, and the operation merits a description. For a disk device I/O is done using a *command* structure, defined on lines 12201 to 12208, which is filled in with a series of byte values. We will describe this in a bit more detail later; for the moment note that two bytes of this structure are filled in, one with a value *ATA_IDENTIFY*, interpreted as a command that asks an **ATA** (**AT Attached**) drive to identify itself, and another with a bit pattern that selects the drive. Then *com_simple* is called.

This function hides all the work of constructing a vector of seven I/O port addresses and bytes to be written to them, sending this information to the system task, waiting for an interrupt, and checking the status returned. This tests that the drive is alive and allows a string of 16-bit values to be read by the sys_insw kernel call on line 12629. Decoding this information is a messy process, and we will not describe it in detail. Suffice it to say that a considerable amount of information is retrieved, including a string that identifies the model of the disk, and the preferred physical cylinder, head, and sector parameters for the device. (Note that the "physical" configuration reported may not be the true physical configuration, but we have no alternative to accepting what the disk drive claims.) The disk information also indicates whether or not the disk is capable of **Logical Block Addressing** (**LBA**). If it is, the driver can ignore the cylinder, head, and sector parameters and can address the disk using absolute sector numbers, which is much simpler.

As we mentioned earlier, it is possible that *init_params* may not recover the logical disk configuration information from the BIOS tables. If that happens, the code at lines 12666 to 12674 tries to create an appropriate set of parameters based on what it reads from the drive itself. The idea is that the maximum cylinder, head, and sector numbers can be 1023, 255, and 63 respectively, due to the number of bits allowed for these fields in the original BIOS data structures.

If the *ATA_IDENTIFY* command fails, it may simply mean that the disk is an older model that does not support the command. In this case the logical configuration values previously read by *init_params* are all we have. If they are valid, they are copied to the physical parameter fields of *wini*; otherwise an error is returned and the disk is not usable.

Finally, MINIX 3 uses a *u32_t* variable to count addresses in bytes. This limits the size of a partition to 4 GB. However, the *device* structure used to record the base and size of a partition (defined in *drivers/libdriver/driver.h* on lines 10856 to 10858) uses *u64_t* numbers, and a 64 bit multiplication operation is used to calculate the size of the drive on (line 12688), and the base and size of the whole drive are then entered into the *wini* array, and *w_specify* is called, twice if necessary, to pass the parameters to be used back to the disk controller (line 12691). Finally, more kernel calls are made: a sys_irqsetpolicy call (line 12699) ensures that when a disk controller interrupt occurs and is serviced the interrupt will be automatically reenabled in preparation for the next one. Following that, a sys_irqenablecall actually enables the interrupt.

W_name (line 12711) returns a pointer to a string containing the device name, which will be either "AT-D0," "AT-D1" "AT-D2," or "AT-D3." When an error message must be generated this function tells which drive produced it.

It is possible that a drive will turn out to be incompatible with MINIX 3 for some reason. The function *w_io_test* (line 12723) is provided to test each drive the first time an attempt is made to open it. This routine tries to read the first block on the drive, with shorter timeout values than are used in normal operation. If the test fails the drive is permanently marked as unavailable.

W_specify (line 12775), in addition to passing the parameters to the controller, also recalibrates the drive (if it is an older model), by doing a seek to cylinder zero.

Do_transfer (line 12814) does what its name implies, it assembles a *command* structure with all the byte values needed to request transfer of a chunk of data (possibly as many as 255 disk sectors), and then it calls *com_out*, which sends the command to the disk controller. The data must be formatted differently depending upon how the disk is to be addressed, that is, whether by cylinder, head, and sector or by LBA. Internally MINIX 3 addresses disk blocks linearly, so if LBA is supported the first three byte-wide fields are filled in by shifting the sector count an appropriate number of bits to the right and then masking to get 8-bit values. The sector count is a 28 bit number, so the last masking operation uses a 4-bit mask (line 12830). If the disk does not support LBA then cylinder, head, and sector values are calculated, based on the parameters of the disk in use (lines 12833 to 12835).

The code contains a hint of a future enhancement. LBA addressing with a 28-bit sector count limits MINIX 3 to fully utilizing disks of 128 GB or smaller size. (You can use a bigger disk, but MINIX 3 can only access the first 128 GB). The programmers have been thinking about, but have not yet implemented, use of the newer **LBA48** method, which uses 48 bits to address disk blocks. On line 12824 a test is made for whether this is enabled. The test will always fail with the version of MINIX 3 described here. This is good, because no code is provided to be executed if the test succeeds. Keep in mind if you decide to modify MINIX 3 yourself to use LBA48 that you need to do more than just add some code here. You will have to make changes in many places to handle the 48-bit addresses. You might find it easier to wait until MINIX 3 has been ported to a 64-bit processor, too. But if a 128 GB disk is not big enough for you, LBA48 will give you access to 128 PB (Petabytes).

Now we will briefly look at how a data transfer takes place at a higher level. *W_prepare*, which we have already discussed, is called first. If the transfer operation requested was for multiple blocks (that is, a *DEV_GATHER* or *DEV_SCATTER* request), *w_transfer* line 12848 is called immediately afterward. If the transfer is for a single block (a *DEV_READ* or *DEV_WRITE* request), a one element scatter/gather vector is created, and then *w_transfer* is called. Accordingly, *w_transfer* is written to expect a vector of *iovec_t* requests. Each element of the request vector consists of a buffer address and the size of the buffer, constrained that the size must be a multiple of the size of a disk sector. All other information needed is passed as an argument to the call, and applies to the entire request vector.

The first thing done is a simple test to see if the disk address requested for the start of the transfer is aligned on a sector boundary (line 12863). Then the outer loop of the function is entered. This loop repeats for each element of the request vector. Within the loop, as we have seen many times before, a number of tests are made before the real work of the function is done. First the total number of bytes remaining in the request is calculated by summing the *iov_size* fields of each element of the request vector. This result is checked to be sure it is an exact multiple of the size of a sector. Other tests check that the starting position is not at or beyond the end of the device, and if the request would end past the end of the device the size of the request is truncated. All calculations so far have been in bytes, but on line 12876 a calculation is made of the block position on the disk, using 64 bit arithmetic. Note that although the variable used is named *block*, this is a number of disk blocks, that is, 512 byte sectors, not the "block" used internally by MINIX 3, normally 4096 bytes. After this one more adjustment is made. Every drive has a maximum number of bytes that can be requested at one time, and the request is scaled back to this quantity if necessary. After verifying that the disk has been initialized, and doing so again if necessary, a request for a chunk of data is made by calling *do_transfer* (line 12887).

After a transfer request has been made the inner loop is entered, which repeats for each sector. For a read or write operation an interrupt will be generated for each sector. On a read the interrupt signifies data is ready and can be transferred. The *sys_insw* kernel call on line 12913 asks the system task to read the specified I/O port repeatedly, transferring the data to a virtual address in the data space of the specified process. For a write operation the order is reversed. The *sys_outsw* call a few lines further down writes a string of data to the controller, and the interrupt comes from the disk controller when the transfer to the disk is complete. In the case of either a read or a write, *at_intr_wait* is called to receive the interrupt, for example, on line 12920 following the write operation. Although the interrupt is expected, this function provides a way to abort the wait if a malfunction occurs and the interrupt never arrives. *At_intr_wait* also reads the disk controller's status register and returns various codes. This is tested on line 12933. On an error when either reading or writing, there is a break which skips over the section where results are recorded and poiners and counters adjusted for the next sector, so the next time through the inner loop will be a retry of the same sector, if another try is allowed. If the disk controller reports a bad sector *w_transfer* terminates immediately. For other errors a counter is incremented and the function is allowed to continue if *max_errors* has not been reached.

The next function we will discuss is *com_out*, which sends the command to the disk controller, but before we look at its code let us first look at the controller as it is seen by the software. The disk controller is controlled through a set of registers, which could be memory mapped on some systems, but on an IBM compatible appear as I/O ports. We will look at these registers and discuss a few aspects of how they (and I/O control registers in general) are used. In MINIX 3 there is the added complication that drivers run in user space and cannot execute the instructions that read or write registers. This will provide an opportunity to look at how kernel calls are used to work around this restriction.

The registers used by a standard IBM-AT class hard disk controller are shown in Fig. 3-23.

Register	Read Function	Write Function
0	Data	Data
1	Error	Write Precompensation
2	Sector Count	Sector Count
3	Sector Number (0-7)	Sector Number (0-7)
4	Cylinder Low (8-15)	Cylinder Low (8-15)
5	Cylinder High (16-23)	Cylinder High (16-23)
6	Select Drive/Head (24-27)	Select Drive/Head (24-27)
7	Status	Command

(a)

7	6	5	4	3	2	1	0
1	LBA	1	D	HS3	HS2	HS1	HS0

LBA: 0 = Cylinder/Head/Sector Mode
       1 = Logical Block Addressing Mode
D: 0 = master drive
       1 = slave drive
HSn: CHS mode: Head select in CHS mode
       LBA mode: Block select bits 24 - 27

(b)

Figure 3-23. (a) The control registers of an IDE hard disk controller. The numbers in parentheses are the bits of the logical block address selected by each register in LBA mode. (b) The fields of the Select Drive/Head register.

We have mentioned several times reading and writing to I/O ports, but we tacitly treated them just like memory addresses. In fact, I/O ports often behave differently from memory addresses. For one thing, input and output registers that happen to have the same I/O port address are not the same register. Thus, the data written to a particular address cannot necessarily be retrieved by a subsequent read operation. For example, the last register address shown in Fig. 3-23 shows the status of the disk controller when read and is used to issue commands to the controller when written to. It is also common that the very act of reading or writing an I/O device register causes an action to occur, independently of the details of the data transferred. This is true of the command register on the AT disk controller. In use, data are written to the lower-numbered registers to select the disk address to be read from or written to, and then the command register is written last with an operation code. The data written to the command register determines what the operation will be. The act of writing the operation code into the command register starts the operation.

It is also the case that the use of some registers or fields in the registers may vary with different modes of operation. In the example given in the figure, writing a 0 or a 1 to the LBA bit, bit 6 of register 6, selects whether CHS (Cylinder-Head-Sector) or LBA (Logical Block Addressing) mode is used. The data written to or read from registers 3, 4, and 5, and the low four bits of register 6 are interpreted differently according to the setting of the LBA bit.

Now let us take a look at how a command is sent to the controller by calling *com_out* (line 12947). This function is called after setting up a *cmd* structure (with *do_transfer*, which we saw earlier). Before changing any registers, the status register is read to determine that the controller is not busy. This is done by testing the *STATUS_BSY* bit. Speed is important here, and normally the disk controller is ready or will be ready in a short time, so busy waiting is used. On line 12960 *w_waitfor* is called to test *STATUS_BSY*. *W_waitfor* uses a kernel call to ask the system task to read an I/O port so *w_waitfor* can test a bit in the status register. It loops until the bit is ready or until there is a timeout. The loop is programmed for a quick return when the disk is ready. Thus the returned value will be true with the minimum possible delay if the controller is ready, true after a delay if it is temporarily unavailable, or false if it is not ready after the timeout period. We will have more to say about the timeout when we discuss *w_waitfor* itself.

A controller can handle more than one drive, so once it is determined that the controller is ready, a byte is written to select the drive, head, and mode of operation (line 12966) and *w_waitfor* is called again. A disk drive sometimes fails to carry out a command or to properly return an error code—it is, after all, a mechanical device that can stick, jam, or break internally—and as insurance a sys_setalarm kernel call is made to have the system task schedule a call to a wakeup routine. Following this, the command is issued by first writing all the parameters to the various registers and finally writing the command code itself to the command register. This is done with a sys_voutb kernel call, which sends a vector of (*value*, *address*) pairs to the system task. The system task writes each *value* to the I/O port specified by the *address* in order. The vector of data for the sys_voutb call is constructed by use of a macro, *pv_set*, which is defined in *include/minix/devio.h*. The act of writing the operation code to the command register makes the operation begin. When it is complete, an interrupt is generated and a notification message is sent. If the command times out the alarm will expire and a synchronous alarm notification will wake up the disk driver.

The next several functions are short. *W_need_reset* (line 12999) is called when timeouts occur while waiting for the disk to interrupt or become ready. The action of *w_need_reset* is just to mark the *state* variable for every drive in the *wini* array to force initialization on the next access.

W_do_close (line 13016) has very little to do for a conventional hard disk. Additional code is needed to support CD-ROMs.

Com_simple is called to issue controller commands that terminate immediately without a data transfer phase. Commands that fall into this category include those that retrieve the disk identification, setting of some parameters, and recalibration. We saw an example of its use in *w_identify*. Before it is called the *command* structure must be correctly initialized. Note that immediately after the call to *com_out* a call to *at_intr_wait* is made. This eventually does a receive which blocks until a notification arrives signifying that an interrupt has occurred.

We noted that *com_out* does a sys_setalarm kernel call before asking the system task to write the registers which set up and execute a command. As we mentioned in the overview section, the next receive operation normally should receive a notification indicating an interrupt. If an alarm has been set and no interrupt occurs, the next message will be a *SYN_ALARM*. In this case *w_timeout* line 13046 is called. What needs to be done depends on the current command in *w_command*. The timeout might have been left over from a previous operation, and *w_command* may have the value *CMD_IDLE*, meaning the disk completed its operation. In that case there is nothing to do. If the command does not complete and the operation is a read or write, it may help to reduce the size of I/O requests. This is done in two steps, first reducing the maximum number of sectors that can be requested to 8, and then to 1. For all timeouts a message is printed and *w_need_reset* is called to force re-initialization of all drives on the next attempted access.

When a reset is required, *w_reset* (line 13076) is called. This function makes use of a library function, *tickdelay*, that sets a watchdog timer and then waits for it to expire. After an initial delay to give the drive time to recover from previous operations, a bit in the disk controller's control register is **strobed**—that is, set to a logical 1 level for a definite period, then returned to the logical 0 level. Following this operation, *w_waitfor* is called to give the drive a reasonable period to signal it is ready. In case the reset does not succeed, a message is printed and an error status returned.

Commands to the disk that involve data transfer normally terminate by generating an interrupt, which sends a message back to the disk driver. In fact, an interrupt is generated for each sector read or written. The function *w_intr_wait* (line 13123) calls *receive* in a loop, and if a *SYN_ALARM* message is received *w_timeout* is called. The only other message type this function should see is *HARD_INT*. When this is received the status register is read and *ack_args* is called to reinitialize the interrupt.

W_intr_wait is not called directly; when an interrupt is expected the function called is the next one, *at_intr_wait* (line 13152). After an interrupt is received by *at_intr_wait* a quick check is made of the drive status bits. All is OK if the bits corresponding to busy, write fault, and error are all clear. Otherwise a closer look is taken. If the register could not be read at all, it is panic time. If the problem was a bad sector a specific error is returned, any other problem results in a general error code. In all cases the *STATUS_ADMBSY* bit is set, to be reset later by the caller.

We have seen several places where *w_waitfor* (line 13177) is called to do busy waiting on a bit in the disk controller status register. This is used in situations where it is expected the bit might be clear on the first test, and a quick test is desirable. For the sake of speed, a macro that read the I/O port directly was used in earlier versions of MINIX—this is, of course, not allowable for a user-space driver in MINIX 3. The solution here is to use a do ... while loop with a minimum of overhead before the first test is made. If the bit being tested is clear there is an immediate return from within the loop. To deal with the possibility of failure a timeout is implemented within the loop by keeping track of clock ticks. If a timeout does occur *w_need_reset* is called.

The *timeout* parameter that is used by the *w_waitfor* function is defined by *DEF_TIMEOUT_TICKS* on line 12228 as 300 ticks, or 5 seconds. A similar parameter, *WAKEUP* (line 12216), used to schedule wakeups from the clock task, is set to 31 seconds. These are very long periods of time to spend busy waiting, when you consider that an ordinary process only gets 100 msec to run before it will be evicted. But, these numbers are based upon the published standard for interfacing disk devices to AT-class computers, which states that up to 31 seconds must be allowed for a disk to "spin up" to speed. The fact is, of course, that this is a worst-case specification, and that on most systems spin up will only occur at power-on time, or possibly after long periods of inactivity, at least for hard disks. For CD-ROMs or other devices which must spin up frequently this may be a more important issue.

There are a few more functions in *at_wini.c*. *W_geometry* returns the logical maximum cylinder, head, and sector values of the selected hard disk device. In this case the numbers are real ones, not made up as they were for the RAM disk driver. *W_other* is a catch-all for unrecognized commands and ioctls. In fact, it is not used in the current release of MINIX 3, and we should probably have removed it from the Appendix B listing. *W_hw_int* is called when a hardware interrupt is received when it is not expected. In the overview we mentioned that this can happen when a timeout expires before an expected interrupt occurs. This will satisfy a *receive* operation that was blocked waiting for the interrupt, but the interrupt notification may then be found by a subsequent receive. The only thing to be done is to reenable the interrupt, which is done by calling the next function, *ack_irqs* (line 13297). It cycles through all the known drives and uses the sys_irqenable kernel call to ensure all interrupts are enabled. Finally, at the end of *at_wini.c* two strange little functions are found, *strstatus* and *strerr*. These use macros defined just ahead of them on lines 13313 and 13314 to concatenate error codes into strings. These functions are not used in MINIX 3 as described here.

3.7.6 Floppy Disk Handling

The floppy disk driver is longer and more complicated than the hard disk driver. This may seem paradoxical, since floppy disk mechanisms are simpler than those of hard disks, but the simpler mechanism has a more primitive controller that requires more attention from the operating system. Also, the fact that the medium is removable adds complications. In this section we will describe some of the things an implementer must consider in dealing with floppy disks. However, we will not go into the details of the MINIX 3 floppy disk driver code. In fact, we have not listed the floppy disk driver in Appendix B. The most important parts are similar to those for the hard disk.

One of the things we do not have to worry about with the floppy driver is the multiple types of controller to support that we had to deal with in the case of the hard disk driver. Although the high-density floppy disks currently used were not supported in the design of the original IBM PC, the floppy disk controllers of all computers in the IBM PC family are supported by a single software driver. The contrast with the hard disk situation is probably due to lack of motivation to increase floppy disk performance. Floppy disks are rarely used as working storage during operation of a computer system; their speed and data capacity are too limited compared to those of hard disks. Floppy disks at one time were important for distribution of new software and for backup, but as networks and larger-capacity removable storage devices have become common, PCs rarely come standard with a floppy disk drives any more.

The floppy disk driver does not use the SSF or the elevator algorithm. It is strictly sequential, accepting a request and carrying it out before even accepting another request. In the original design of MINIX it was felt that, since MINIX was intended for use on personal computers, most of the time there would be only one process active. Thus the chance of a disk request arriving while another was being carried out was small. There would be little to gain from the considerable increase in software complexity that would be required for queueing requests. Complexity is even less worthwhile now, since floppy disks are rarely used for anything but transferring data into or out of a system with a hard disk.

That said, the floppy driver, like any other block driver, can handle a request for scattered I/O. However, in the case of the floppy driver the array of requests is smaller than for the hard disk, limited to the maximum number of sectors per track on a floppy diskette.

The simplicity of the floppy disk hardware is responsible for some of the complications in floppy disk driver software. Cheap, slow, low-capacity floppy drives do not justify the sophisticated integrated controllers that are part of modern hard drives, so the driver software has to deal explicitly with aspects of disk operation that are hidden in the operation of a hard drive. As an example of a complication caused by the simplicity of floppy drives, consider positioning the read/write head to a particular track during a *SEEK* operation. No hard disk has ever required the driver software to explicitly call for a *SEEK*. For a hard disk the cylinder, head, and sector geometry visible to the programmer often do not correspond to the physical geometry. In fact, the physical geometry may be quite complicated. Typically there are multiple zones (groups of cylinders) with more sectors per track on outer zones than on inner ones. This is not visible to the user, however. Modern hard disks accept Logical Block Addressing (LBA), addressing by the absolute sector number on the disk, as an alternative to cylinder, head, and sector addressing. Even if addressing is done by cylinder, head, and sector, any geometry that does not address nonexistent sectors may be used, since the integrated controller on the disk calculates where to move the read/write heads and does a seek operation when required.

For a floppy disk, however, explicit programming of *SEEK* operations is needed. In case a *SEEK* fails, it is necessary to provide a routine to perform a *RECALIBRATE* operation, which forces the heads to cylinder 0. This makes it possible for the controller to advance them to a desired track position by stepping the heads a known number of times. Similar operations are necessary for the hard drive, of course, but the controller handles them without detailed guidance from the device driver software.

Some characteristics of a floppy disk drive that complicate its driver are:

1. Removable media.

2. Multiple disk formats.

3. Motor control.

Some hard disk controllers provide for removable media, for instance, on a CD-ROM drive, but the drive controller is generally able to handle any complications without support in the device driver software. With a floppy disk, however, the built-in support is not there, and yet it is needed more. Some of the most common uses for floppy disks—installing new software or backing up files—are likely to require switching of disks in and out of the drives. It will cause grief if data intended for one diskette are written onto another. The device driver should do what it can to prevent this. This is not always possible, as not all floppy drive hardware allows determination of whether the drive door has been opened since the last access. Another problem that can be caused by removable media is that a system can become hung up if an attempt is made to access a floppy drive that currently has no diskette inserted. This can be solved if an open door can be detected, but since this is not always possible some provision must be made for a timeout and an error return if an operation on a floppy disk does not terminate in a reasonable time.

Removable media can be replaced with other media, and in the case of floppy disks there are many different possible formats. IBM compatible hardware supports both 3.5-inch and 5.25-inch disk drives and the diskettes can be formatted in a variety of ways to hold from 360 KB up to 1.2 MB (on a 5.25-inch diskette) or 1.44 MB (on a 3.5-inch diskette).

MINIX 3 supports seven different floppy disk formats. Two possible solutions are possible for the problem this causes. One way is to refer to each possible format as a distinct drive and provide multiple minor devices. Older versions of MINIX did this. Fourteen different devices were defined, ranging from */dev/pc0*, a 360 KB 5.25-inch diskette in the first drive, to */dev/PS1*, a 1.44 MB 3.5-inch diskette in the second drive. This was a cumbersome solution. MINIX 3 uses another method: when the first floppy disk drive is addressed as */dev/fd0*, or the second as */dev/fd1*, the floppy disk driver tests the diskette currently in the drive when it is accessed, in order to determine the format. Some formats have more cylinders, and others have more sectors per track than other formats. Determination of the format of a diskette is done by attempting to read the higher numbered sectors and tracks. By a process of elimination the format can be determined. This takes time, but on modern computers only 1.44 MB 3.5-inch diskettes are likely to be found, and this format is probed first. Another possible problem is that a disk with bad sectors could be misidentified. A utility program is available for testing disks; doing so automatically in the operating system would be too slow.

The final complication of the floppy disk driver is motor control. Diskettes cannot be read or written unless they are revolving. Hard disks are designed to run for thousands of hours on end without wearing out, but leaving the motors on all the time causes a floppy drive and diskette to wear out quickly. If the motor is not already on when a drive is accessed, it is necessary to issue a command to start the drive and then to wait about a half second before attempting to read or write data. Turning the motors on or off is slow, so MINIX 3 leaves a drive motor on for a few seconds after a drive is used. If the drive is used again within this interval, the timer is extended for another few seconds. If the drive is not used in this interval, the motor is turned off.

3.8 TERMINALS

For decades, users have communicated with computers using devices consisting of a keyboard for user input and a display for computer output. For many years, these were combined into free-standing devices called **terminals**, which were connected to the computer by a wire. Large mainframes used in the financial and travel industries sometimes still use these terminals, typically connected to the mainframe via a modem, especially when they are far from the mainframe. However, with the emergence of the personal computer, the keyboard and display have become separate peripherals rather than a single device, but they are so closely interrelated that we will discuss them together here under the combined name of "terminal."

Historically, terminals have come in a variety of forms. It is up to the terminal driver to hide all these differences, so that the device-independent part of the operating system and the user programs do not have to be rewritten for each kind of terminal. In the following sections we will follow our now-standard approach of first discussing terminal hardware and software in general, and then discussing the MINIX 3 software.

3.8.1 Terminal Hardware

From the operating system's point of view, terminals can be divided into three broad categories based on how the operating system communicates with them as well as their actual hardware characteristics. The first category consists of memory-mapped terminals, which consist of a keyboard and a display, both of which are hardwired to the computer. This model is used in all personal computers for the keyboard and the monitor. The second category consists of terminals that interface via a serial communication line using the RS-232 standard, most frequently over a modem. This model is still used on some mainframes, but PCs also have serial line interfaces. The third category consists of terminals that are connected to the computer via a network. This taxonomy is shown in Fig. 3-24.

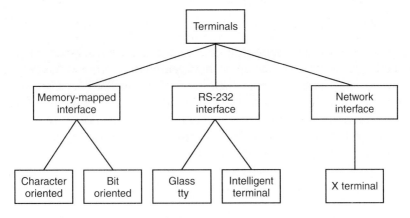

Figure 3-24. Terminal types.

Memory-Mapped Terminals

The first broad category of terminals named in Fig. 3-24 consists of memory-mapped terminals. These are an integral part of the computers themselves, especially personal computers. They consist of a display and a keyboard. Memory-mapped displays are interfaced via a special memory called a **video RAM**, which forms part of the computer's address space and is addressed by the CPU the same way as the rest of memory (see Fig. 3-25).

Also on the video RAM card is a chip called a **video controller**. This chip pulls bytes out of the video RAM and generates the video signal used to drive the display. Displays are usually one of two types: CRT monitors or flat panel displays. A **CRT monitor** generates a beam of electrons that scans horizontally across the screen, painting lines on it. Typically the screen has 480 to 1200 lines from top to bottom, with 640 to 1920 points per line. These points are called **pixels**. The video controller signal modulates the intensity of the electron beam, determining whether a given pixel will be light or dark. Color monitors have three beams, for red, green, and blue, which are modulated independently.

A **flat panel display** works very differently internally, but a CRT-compatible flat-panel display accepts the same synchronization and video signals as a CRT and uses these to control a liquid crystal element at each pixel position.

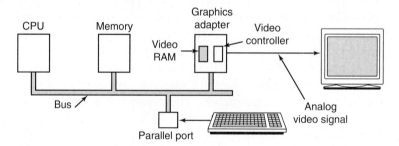

Figure 3-25. Memory-mapped terminals write directly into video RAM.

A simple monochrome display might fit each character in a box 9 pixels wide by 14 pixels high (including the space between characters), and have 25 lines of 80 characters. The display would then have 350 scan lines of 720 pixels each. Each of these frames is redrawn 45 to 70 times a second. The video controller could be designed to fetch the first 80 characters from the video RAM, generate 14 scan lines, fetch the next 80 characters from the video RAM, generate the following 14 scan lines, and so on. In fact, most fetch each character once per scan line to eliminate the need for buffering in the controller. The 9-by-14 bit patterns for the characters are kept in a ROM used by the video controller. (RAM may also be used to support custom fonts.) The ROM is addressed by a 12-bit address, 8 bits from the character code and 4 bits to specify a scan line. The 8 bits in each byte of the ROM control 8 pixels; the 9th pixel between characters is always blank. Thus $14 \times 80 = 1120$ memory references to the video RAM are needed per line of text on the screen. The same number of references are made to the character generator ROM.

The original IBM PC had several modes for the screen. In the simplest one, it used a character-mapped display for the console. In Fig. 3-26(a) we see a portion of the video RAM. Each character on the screen of Fig. 3-26(b) occupied two characters in the RAM. The low-order character was the ASCII code for the character to be displayed. The high-order character was the attribute byte, which was used to specify the color, reverse video, blinking, and so on. The full screen of 25 by 80 characters required 4000 bytes of video RAM in this mode. All modern displays still support this mode of operation.

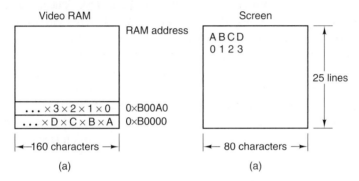

Figure 3-26. (a) A video RAM image for the IBM monochrome display. The ×s are attribute bytes. (b) The corresponding screen.

Contemporary bitmap displays use the same principle, except that each pixel on the screen is individually controlled. In the simplest configuration, for a monochrome display, each pixel has a corresponding bit in the video RAM. At the other extreme, each pixel is represented by a 24-bit number, with 8 bits each for red, green, and blue. A 768×1024 color display with 24 bits per pixel requires 2 MB of RAM to hold the image.

With a memory-mapped display, the keyboard is completely decoupled from the screen. It may be interfaced via a serial or parallel port. On every key action the CPU is interrupted, and the keyboard driver extracts the character typed by reading an I/O port.

On a PC, the keyboard contains an embedded microprocessor which communicates through a specialized serial port with a controller chip on the main board. An interrupt is generated whenever a key is struck and also when one is released. Furthermore, all that the keyboard hardware provides is the key number, not the ASCII code. When the A key is struck, the key code (30) is put in an I/O register. It is up to the driver to determine whether it is lower case, upper case, CTRL-A, ALT-A, CTRL-ALT-A, or some other combination. Since the driver can tell which keys have been depressed but not yet released (e.g., shift), it has enough information to do the job. Although this keyboard interface puts the full burden on the software, it is extremely flexible. For example, user programs may be interested in whether a digit just typed came from the top row of keys or the numeric key pad on the side. In principle, the driver can provide this information.

RS-232 Terminals

RS-232 terminals are devices containing a keyboard and a display that communicate using a serial interface, one bit at a time (see Fig. 3-27). These terminals use a 9-pin or 25-pin connector, of which one pin is used for transmitting data, one pin is for receiving data, and one pin is ground. The other pins are for various control functions, most of which are not used. To send a character to an RS-232 terminal, the computer must transmit it 1 bit at a time, prefixed by a start bit, and followed by 1 or 2 stop bits to delimit the character. A parity bit which provides rudimentary error detection may also be inserted preceding the stop bits, although this is commonly required only for communication with mainframe systems. Common transmission rates are 14,400 and 56,000 bits/sec, the former being for fax and the latter for data. RS-232 terminals are commonly used to communicate with a remote computer using a modem and a telephone line.

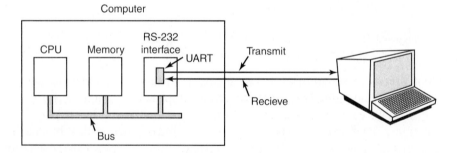

Figure 3-27. An RS-232 terminal communicates with a computer over a communication line, one bit at a time. The computer and the terminal are completely independent.

Since both computers and terminals work internally with whole characters but must communicate over a serial line a bit at a time, chips have been developed to do the character-to-serial and serial-to-character conversions. They are called **UARTs** (Universal Asynchronous Receiver Transmitters). UARTs are attached to the computer by plugging RS-232 interface cards into the bus as illustrated in Fig. 3-27. On modern computers the UART and RS-232 interface is frequently part of the parentboard chipset. It may be possible disable the on-board UART to allow use of a modem interface card plugged into the bus or two of them may be able to coexist. A modem also provides a UART (although it may be integrated with other functions in a multi-purpose chip), and the communication channel is a telephone line rather than a serial cable. However, to the computer the UART looks the same whether the medium is a dedicated serial cable or a telephone line.

RS-232 terminals are gradually dying off, being replaced by PCs, but they are still encountered on older mainframe systems, especially in banking, airline reservation, and similar applications. Terminal programs that allow a remote computer to simulate a terminal are still widely used, however.

To print a character, the terminal driver writes the character to the interface card, where it is buffered and then shifted out over the serial line one bit at a time by the UART. Even at 56,000 bps, it takes just over 140 microsec to send a character. As a result of this slow transmission rate, the driver generally outputs a character to the RS-232 card and blocks, waiting for the interrupt generated by the interface when the character has been transmitted and the UART is able to accept another character. The UART can simultaneously send and receive characters, as its name implies. An interrupt is also generated when a character is received, and usually a small number of input characters can be buffered. The terminal driver must check a register when an interrupt is received to determine the cause of the interrupt. Some interface cards have a CPU and memory and can handle multiple lines, taking over much of the I/O load from the main CPU.

RS-232 terminals can be subdivided into categories, as mentioned above. The simplest ones were hardcopy (printing) terminals. Characters typed on the keyboard were transmitted to the computer. Characters sent by the computer were typed on the paper. These terminals are obsolete and rarely seen any more.

Dumb CRT terminals work the same way, only with a screen instead of paper. These are frequently called "glass ttys" because they are functionally the same as hardcopy ttys. (The term "tty" is an abbreviation for Teletype, [®] a former company that pioneered in the computer terminal business; "tty" has come to mean any terminal.) Glass ttys are also obsolete.

Intelligent CRT terminals are in fact miniature, specialized computers. They have a CPU and memory and contain software, usually in ROM. From the operating system's viewpoint, the main difference between a glass tty and an intelligent terminal is that the latter understands certain escape sequences. For example, by sending the ASCII ESC character (033), followed by various other characters, it may be possible to move the cursor to any position on the screen, insert text in the middle of the screen, and so forth.

3.8.2 Terminal Software

The keyboard and display are almost independent devices, so we will treat them separately here. (They are not quite independent, since typed characters must be displayed on the screen.) In MINIX 3 the keyboard and screen drivers are part of the same process; in other systems they may be split into distinct drivers.

Input Software

The basic job of the keyboard driver is to collect input from the keyboard and pass it to user programs when they read from the terminal. Two possible philosophies can be adopted for the driver. In the first one, the driver's job is just to accept input and pass it upward unmodified. A program reading from the terminal gets a raw sequence of ASCII codes. (Giving user programs the key numbers is too primitive, as well as being highly machine dependent.)

This philosophy is well suited to the needs of sophisticated screen editors such as *emacs*, which allow the user to bind an arbitrary action to any character or sequence of characters. It does, however, mean that if the user types *dste* instead of *date* and then corrects the error by typing three backspaces and *ate*, followed by a carriage return, the user program will be given all 11 ASCII codes typed.

Most programs do not want this much detail. They just want the corrected input, not the exact sequence of how it was produced. This observation leads to the second philosophy: the driver handles all the intraline editing, and just delivers corrected lines to the user programs. The first philosophy is character-oriented; the second one is line-oriented. Originally they were referred to as **raw mode** and **cooked mode**, respectively. The POSIX standard uses the less-picturesque term **canonical mode** to describe line-oriented mode. On most systems canonical mode refers to a well-defined configuration. **Noncanonical mode** is equivalent to raw mode, although many details of terminal behavior can be changed. POSIX-compatible systems provide several library functions that support selecting either mode and changing many aspects of terminal configuration. In MINIX 3 the ioctl system call supports these functions.

The first task of the keyboard driver is to collect characters. If every keystroke causes an interrupt, the driver can acquire the character during the interrupt. If interrupts are turned into messages by the low-level software, it is possible to put the newly acquired character in the message. Alternatively, it can be put in a small buffer in memory and the message used to tell the driver that something has arrived. The latter approach is actually safer if a message can be sent only to a waiting process and there is some chance that the keyboard driver might still be busy with the previous character.

Once the driver has received the character, it must begin processing it. If the keyboard delivers key numbers rather than the character codes used by application software, then the driver must convert between the codes by using a table. Not all IBM "compatibles" use standard key numbering, so if the driver wants to support these machines, it must map different keyboards with different tables. A simple approach is to compile a table that maps between the codes provided by the keyboard and ASCII (American Standard Code for Information Interchange) codes into the keyboard driver, but this is unsatisfactory for users of languages other than English. Keyboards are arranged differently in different countries, and the ASCII character set is not adequate even for the majority of people in the Western

Hemisphere, where speakers of Spanish, Portuguese, and French need accented characters and punctuation marks not used in English. To respond to the need for flexibility of keyboard layouts to provide for different languages, many operating systems provide for loadable **keymaps** or **code pages**, which make it possible to choose the mapping between keyboard codes and codes delivered to the application, either when the system is booted or later.

If the terminal is in canonical (i.e., cooked) mode, characters must be stored until an entire line has been accumulated, because the user may subsequently decide to erase part of it. Even if the terminal is in raw mode, the program may not yet have requested input, so the characters must be buffered to allow type ahead. (System designers who do not allow users to type far ahead ought to be tarred and feathered, or worse yet, be forced to use their own system.)

Two approaches to character buffering are common. In the first one, the driver contains a central pool of buffers, each buffer holding perhaps 10 characters. Associated with each terminal is a data structure, which contains, among other items, a pointer to the chain of buffers for input collected from that terminal. As more characters are typed, more buffers are acquired and hung on the chain. When the characters are passed to a user program, the buffers are removed and put back in the central pool.

The other approach is to do the buffering directly in the terminal data structure itself, with no central pool of buffers. Since it is common for users to type a command that will take a little while (say, a compilation) and then type a few lines ahead, to be safe the driver should allocate something like 200 characters per terminal. In a large-scale timesharing system with 100 terminals, allocating 20K all the time for type ahead is clearly overkill, so a central buffer pool with space for perhaps 5K is probably enough. On the other hand, a dedicated buffer per terminal makes the driver simpler (no linked list management) and is to be preferred on personal computers with only one or two terminals. Figure 3-28 shows the difference between these two methods.

Although the keyboard and display are logically separate devices, many users have grown accustomed to seeing the characters they have just typed appear on the screen. Some (older) terminals oblige by automatically displaying (in hardware) whatever has just been typed, which is not only a nuisance when passwords are being entered but greatly limits the flexibility of sophisticated editors and other programs. Fortunately, PC keyboards display nothing when keys are struck. It is therefore up to the software to display the input. This process is called **echoing**.

Echoing is complicated by the fact that a program may be writing to the screen while the user is typing. At the very least, the keyboard driver has to figure out where to put the new input without it being overwritten by program output.

Echoing also gets complicated when more than 80 characters are typed on a terminal with 80-character lines. Depending on the application, wrapping around

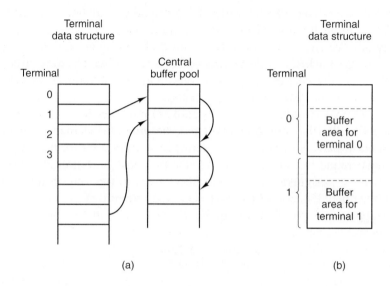

Figure 3-28. (a) Central buffer pool. (b) Dedicated buffer for each terminal.

to the next line may be appropriate. Some drivers just truncate lines to 80 characters by throwing away all characters beyond column 80.

Another problem is tab handling. All keyboards have a tab key, but displays can handle tab on output. It is up to the driver to compute where the cursor is currently located, taking into account both output from programs and output from echoing, and compute the proper number of spaces to be echoed.

Now we come to the problem of device equivalence. Logically, at the end of a line of text, one wants a carriage return, to move the cursor back to column 1, and a linefeed, to advance to the next line. Requiring users to type both at the end of each line would not sell well (although some old terminals had a key which generated both, with a 50 percent chance of doing so in the order that the software wanted them). It was (and still is) up to the driver to convert whatever comes in to the standard internal format used by the operating system.

If the standard form is just to store a linefeed (the convention in UNIX and all its descendants), carriage returns should be turned into linefeeds. If the internal format is to store both, then the driver should generate a linefeed when it gets a carriage return and a carriage return when it gets a linefeed. No matter what the internal convention, the terminal may require both a linefeed and a carriage return to be echoed in order to get the screen updated properly. Since a large computer may well have a wide variety of different terminals connected to it, it is up to the keyboard driver to get all the different carriage return/linefeed combinations converted to the internal system standard and arrange for all echoing to be done right.

A related problem is the timing of carriage return and linefeeds. On some terminals, it may take longer to display a carriage return or linefeed than a letter or number. If the microprocessor inside the terminal actually has to copy a large block of text to achieve scrolling, then linefeeds may be slow. If a mechanical print head has to be returned to the left margin of the paper, carriage returns may be slow. In both cases it is up to the driver to insert **filler characters** (dummy null characters) into the output stream or just stop outputting long enough for the terminal to catch up. The amount of time to delay is often related to the terminal speed; for example, at 4800 bps or slower, no delays may be needed, but at 9600 bps or higher one filler character might be required. Terminals with hardware tabs, especially hardcopy ones, may also require a delay after a tab.

When operating in canonical mode, a number of input characters have special meanings. Figure 3-29 shows all of the special characters required by POSIX and the additional ones recognized by MINIX 3. The defaults are all control characters that should not conflict with text input or codes used by programs, but all except the last two can be changed using the *stty* command, if desired. Older versions of UNIX used different defaults for many of these.

Character	POSIX name	Comment
CTRL-D	EOF	End of file
	EOL	End of line (undefined)
CTRL-H	ERASE	Backspace one character
CTRL-C	INTR	Interrupt process (SIGINT)
CTRL-U	KILL	Erase entire line being typed
CTRL-\	QUIT	Force core dump (SIGQUIT)
CTRL-Z	SUSP	Suspend (ignored by MINIX)
CTRL-Q	START	Start output
CTRL-S	STOP	Stop output
CTRL-R	REPRINT	Redisplay input (MINIX extension)
CTRL-V	LNEXT	Literal next (MINIX extension)
CTRL-O	DISCARD	Discard output (MINIX extension)
CTRL-M	CR	Carriage return (unchangeable)
CTRL-J	NL	Linefeed (unchangeable)

Figure 3-29. Characters that are handled specially in canonical mode.

The *ERASE* character allows the user to rub out the character just typed. In MINIX 3 it is the backspace (CTRL-H). It is not added to the character queue but instead removes the previous character from the queue. It should be echoed as a sequence of three characters, backspace, space, and backspace, in order to remove the previous character from the screen. If the previous character was a tab, erasing it requires keeping track of where the cursor was prior to the tab. In most systems, backspacing will only erase characters on the current line. It will not erase a carriage return and back up into the previous line.

When the user notices an error at the start of the line being typed in, it is often convenient to erase the entire line and start again. The *KILL* character (in MINIX 3 CTRL-U) erases the entire line. MINIX 3 makes the erased line vanish from the screen, but some systems echo it plus a carriage return and linefeed because some users like to see the old line. Consequently, how to echo *KILL* is a matter of taste. As with *ERASE* it is usually not possible to go further back than the current line. When a block of characters is killed, it may or may not be worth the trouble for the driver to return buffers to the pool, if one is used.

Sometimes the *ERASE* or *KILL* characters must be entered as ordinary data. The *LNEXT* character serves as an **escape character**. In MINIX 3 CTRL-V is the default. As an example, older UNIX systems normally used the @ sign for *KILL*, but the Internet mail system uses addresses of the form *linda@cs.washington.edu*. Someone who feels more comfortable with older conventions might redefine *KILL* as @, but then need to enter an @ sign literally to address e-mail. This can be done by typing CTRL-V @. The CTRL-V itself can be entered literally by typing CTRL-V CTRL-V. After seeing a CTRL-V, the driver sets a flag saying that the next character is exempt from special processing. The *LNEXT* character itself is not entered in the character queue.

To allow users to stop a screen image from scrolling out of view, control codes are provided to freeze the screen and restart it later. In MINIX 3 these are *STOP* (CTRL-S) and *START* (CTRL-Q), respectively. They are not stored but are used to set and clear a flag in the terminal data structure. Whenever output is attempted, the flag is inspected. If it is set, no output occurs. Usually, echoing is also suppressed along with program output.

It is often necessary to kill a runaway program being debugged. The *INTR* (CTRL-C) and *QUIT* (CTRL-\) characters can be used for this purpose. In MINIX 3, CTRL-C sends the SIGINT signal to all the processes started up from the terminal. Implementing CTRL-C can be quite tricky. The hard part is getting the information from the driver to the part of the system that handles signals, which, after all, has not asked for this information. CTRL-\ is similar to CTRL-C, except that it sends the SIGQUIT signal, which forces a core dump if not caught or ignored.

When either of these keys is struck, the driver should echo a carriage return and linefeed and discard all accumulated input to allow for a fresh start. Historically, DEL was commonly used as the default value for *INTR* on many UNIX systems. Since many programs use DEL interchangeably with the backspace for editing, CTRL-C is now preferred.

Another special character is *EOF* (CTRL-D), which in MINIX 3 causes any pending read requests for the terminal to be satisfied with whatever is available in the buffer, even if the buffer is empty. Typing CTRL-D at the start of a line causes the program to get a read of 0 bytes, which is conventionally interpreted as end-of-file and causes most programs to act the same way as they would upon seeing end-of-file on an input file.

Some terminal drivers allow much fancier intraline editing than we have sketched here. They have special control characters to erase a word, skip backward or forward characters or words, go to the beginning or end of the line being typed, and so forth. Adding all these functions to the terminal driver makes it much larger and, furthermore, is wasted when using fancy screen editors that work in raw mode anyway.

To allow programs to control terminal parameters, POSIX requires that several functions be available in the standard library, of which the most important are *tcgetattr* and *tcsetattr*. *Tcgetattr* retrieves a copy of the structure shown in Fig. 3-30, the *termios* structure, which contains all the information needed to change special characters, set modes, and modify other characteristics of a terminal. A program can examine the current settings and modify them as desired. *Tcsetattr* then writes the structure back to the terminal driver.

```
struct termios {
  tcflag_t c_iflag;                    /* input modes */
  tcflag_t c_oflag;                    /* output modes */
  tcflag_t c_cflag;                    /* control modes */
  tcflag_t c_lflag;                    /* local modes */
  speed_t  c_ispeed;                   /* input speed */
  speed_t  c_ospeed;                   /* output speed */
  cc_t c_cc[NCCS];                     /* control characters */
};
```

Figure 3-30. The termios structure. In MINIX 3 tc_flag_t is a short, speed_t is an int, and cc_t is a char.

The POSIX standard does not specify whether its requirements should be implemented through library functions or system calls. MINIX 3 provides a system call, ioctl, called by

```
ioctl(file_descriptor, request, argp);
```

that is used to examine and modify the configurations of many I/O devices. This call is used to implement the *tcgetattr* and *tcsetattr* functions. The variable *request* specifies whether the *termios* structure is to be read or written, and in the latter case, whether the request is to take effect immediately or should be deferred until all currently queued output is complete. The variable *argp* is a pointer to a *termios* structure in the calling program. This particular choice of communication between program and driver was chosen for its UNIX compatibility, rather than for its inherent beauty.

A few notes about the termios structure are in order. The four flag words provide a great deal of flexibility. The individual bits in *c_iflag* control various ways input is handled. For instance, the *ICRNL* bit causes *CR* characters to be converted into *NL* on input. This flag is set by default in MINIX 3. The *c_oflag* holds bits that affect output processing. For instance, the *OPOST* bit enables output processing. It and the *ONLCR* bit, which causes *NL* characters in the output to be converted into a *CR NL* sequence, are also set by default in MINIX 3. The *c_cflag* is the control flags word. The default settings for MINIX 3 enable a line to receive 8-bit characters and cause a modem to hang up if a user logs out on the line. The *c_lflag* is the *local mode* flags field. One bit, *ECHO*, enables echoing (this can be turned off during a login to provide security for entering a password). Its most important bit is the *ICANON* bit, which enables canonical mode. With *ICANON* off, several possibilities exist. If all other settings are left at their defaults, a mode identical to the traditional **cbreak mode** is entered. In this mode, characters are passed to the program without waiting for a full line, but the *INTR*, *QUIT*, *START*, and *STOP* characters retain their effects. All of these can be disabled by resetting bits in the flags, however, to produce the equivalent of traditional raw mode.

The various special characters that can be changed, including those which are MINIX 3 extensions, are held in the *c_cc* array. This array also holds two parameters which are used in noncanonical mode. The quantity *MIN*, stored in *c_cc[VMIN]*, specifies the minimum number of characters that must be received to satisfy a read call. The quantity *TIME* in *c_cc[VTIME]* sets a time limit for such calls. *MIN* and *TIME* interact as shown in Fig. 3-31. A call that asks for *N* bytes is illustrated. With *TIME* = 0 and *MIN* = 1, the behavior is similar to the traditional raw mode.

	TIME = 0	**TIME > 0**
MIN = 0	Return immediately with whatever is available, 0 to N bytes	Timer starts immediately. Return with first byte entered or with 0 bytes after timeout
MIN > 0	Return with at least MIN and up to N bytes. Possible indefinite block	Interbyte timer starts after first byte. Return N bytes if received by timeout, or at least 1 byte at timeout. Possible indefinite block

Figure 3-31. *MIN* and *TIME* determine when a call to read returns in noncanonical mode. *N* is the number of bytes requested.

Output Software

Output is simpler than input, but drivers for RS-232 terminals are radically different from drivers for memory-mapped terminals. The method that is commonly used for RS-232 terminals is to have output buffers associated with each terminal. The buffers can come from the same pool as the input buffers, or be dedicated, as with input. When programs write to the terminal, the output is first copied to the buffers. Similarly, output from echoing is also copied to the buffers. After all the output has been copied to the buffers (or the buffers are full), the first character is output, and the driver goes to sleep. When the interrupt comes in, the next character is output, and so on.

With memory-mapped terminals, a simpler scheme is possible. Characters to be printed are extracted one at a time from user space and put directly in the video RAM. With RS-232 terminals, each character to be output is just put on the line to the terminal. With memory mapping, some characters require special treatment, among them, backspace, carriage return, linefeed, and the audible bell (CTRL-G). A driver for a memory-mapped terminal must keep track in software of the current position in the video RAM, so that printable characters can be put there and the current position advanced. Backspace, carriage return, and linefeed all require this position to be updated appropriately. Tabs also require special processing.

In particular, when a linefeed is output on the bottom line of the screen, the screen must be scrolled. To see how scrolling works, look at Fig. 3-26. If the video controller always began reading the RAM at 0xB0000, the only way to scroll the screen when in character mode would be to copy 24×80 characters (each character requiring 2 bytes) from 0xB00A0 to 0xB0000, a time-consuming proposition. In bitmap mode, it would be even worse.

Fortunately, the hardware usually provides some help here. Most video controllers contain a register that determines where in the video RAM to begin fetching bytes for the top line on the screen. By setting this register to point to 0xB00A0 instead of 0xB0000, the line that was previously number two moves to the top, and the whole screen scrolls up one line. The only other thing the driver must do is copy whatever is needed to the new bottom line. When the video controller gets to the top of the RAM, it just wraps around and continues merrily fetching bytes starting at the lowest address. Similar hardware assistance is provided in bitmap mode.

Another issue that the driver must deal with on a memory-mapped terminal is cursor positioning. Again, the hardware usually provides some assistance in the form of a register that tells where the cursor is to go. Finally, there is the problem of the bell. It is sounded by outputting a sine or square wave to the loudspeaker, a part of the computer quite separate from the video RAM.

Screen editors and many other sophisticated programs need to be able to update the screen in more complex ways than just scrolling text onto the bottom of the display. To accommodate them, many terminal drivers support a variety of escape sequences. Although some terminals support idiosyncratic escape se-sequence sets, it is advantageous to have a standard to facilitate adapting software from one system to another. The American National Standards Institute (ANSI) has defined a set of standard escape sequences, and MINIX 3 supports a subset of the ANSI sequences, shown in Fig. 3-32, that is adequate for many common operations. When the driver sees the character that starts the escape sequences, it sets a flag and waits until the rest of the escape sequence comes in. When everything has arrived, the driver must carry it out in software. Inserting and deleting text require moving blocks of characters around the video RAM. The hardware is of no help with anything except scrolling and displaying the cursor.

Escape sequence	Meaning
ESC [*n* A	Move up *n* lines
ESC [*n* B	Move down *n* lines
ESC [*n* C	Move right *n* spaces
ESC [*n* D	Move left *n* spaces
ESC [*m* ; *n* H	Move cursor to (y = *m*, x = *n*)
ESC [*s* J	Clear screen from cursor (0 to end, 1 from start, 2 all)
ESC [*s* K	Clear line from cursor (0 to end, 1 from start, 2 all)
ESC [*n* L	Insert *n* lines at cursor
ESC [*n* M	Delete *n* lines at cursor
ESC [*n* P	Delete *n* chars at cursor
ESC [*n* @	Insert *n* chars at cursor
ESC [*n* m	Enable rendition *n* (0=normal, 4=bold, 5=blinking, 7=reverse)
ESC M	Scroll the screen backward if the cursor is on the top line

Figure 3-32. The ANSI escape sequences accepted by the terminal driver on output. ESC denotes the ASCII escape character (0x1B), and *n*, *m*, and *s* are optional numeric parameters.

3.8.3 Overview of the Terminal Driver in MINIX 3

The terminal driver is contained in four C files (six if RS-232 and pseudo terminal support are enabled) and together they far and away constitute the largest driver in MINIX 3. The size of the terminal driver is partly explained by the observation that the driver handles both the keyboard and the display, each of which is a complicated device in its own right, as well as two other optional types of terminals. Still, it comes as a surprise to most people to learn that terminal I/O requires thirty times as much code as the scheduler. (This feeling is reinforced by looking at the numerous books on operating systems that devote thirty times as much space to scheduling as to all I/O combined.)

The terminal driver accepts more than a dozen message types. The most important are:

1. Read from the terminal (from FS on behalf of a user process).

2. Write to the terminal (from FS on behalf of a user process).

3. Set terminal parameters for ioctl (from FS on behalf of a user process).

4. A keyboard interrupt has occurred (key pressed or released).

5. Cancel previous request (from FS when a signal occurs).

6. Open a device.

7. Close a device.

Other message types are used for special purposes such as generating diagnostic displays when function keys are pressed or triggering panic dumps.

The messages used for reading and writing have the same format as shown in Fig. 3-17, except that no *POSITION* field is needed. With a disk, the program has to specify which block it wants to read. With a keyboard, there is no choice: the program always gets the next character typed in. Keyboards do not support seeks.

The POSIX functions *tcgetattr* and *tcgetattr*, used to examine and modify terminal attributes (properties), are supported by the ioctl system call. Good programming practice is to use these functions and others in *include/termios.h* and leave it to the C library to convert library calls to ioctl system calls. There are, however, some control operations needed by MINIX 3 that are not provided for in POSIX, for example, loading an alternate keymap, and for these the programmer must use ioctl explicitly.

The message sent to the driver by an ioctl system call contains a function request code and a pointer. For the *tcsetattr* function, an ioctl call is made with a *TCSETS*, *TCSETSW*, or *TCSETSF* request type, and a pointer to a *termios* structure like the one shown in Fig. 3-30. All such calls replace the current set of attributes with a new set, the differences being that a *TCSETS* request takes effect immediately, a *TCSETSW* request does not take effect until all output has been transmitted, and a *TCSETSF* waits for output to finish and discards all input that has not yet been read. *Tcgetattr* is translated into an ioctl call with a *TCGETS* request type and returns a filled in *termios* structure to the caller, so the current state of a device can be examined. Ioctl calls that do not correspond to functions defined by POSIX, like the *KIOCSMAP* request used to load a new keymap, pass pointers to other kinds of structures, in this case to a *keymap_t* which is a 1536-byte structure (16-bit codes for 128 keys × 6 modifiers). Figure 3-39 summarizes how standard POSIX calls are converted into ioctl system calls.

The terminal driver uses one main data structure, *tty_table*, which is an array of *tty* structures, one per terminal. A standard PC has only one keyboard and display, but MINIX 3 can support up to eight virtual terminals, depending upon the amount of memory on the display adapter card. This permits the person at the console to log on multiple times, switching the display output and keyboard input from one "user" to another. With two virtual consoles, pressing ALT-F2 selects the second one and ALT-F1 returns to the first. ALT plus the arrow keys also can be used. In addition, serial lines can support two users at remote locations, connected by RS-232 cable or modem, and **pseudo terminals** can support users connected through a network. The driver has been written to make it easy to add additional terminals. The standard configuration illustrated in the source code in this text has two virtual consoles, with serial lines and pseudo terminals disabled.

Each *tty* structure in *tty_table* keeps track of both input and output. For input, it holds a queue of all characters that have been typed but not yet read by the program, information about requests to read characters that have not yet been received, and timeout information, so input can be requested without the driver blocking permanently if no character is typed. For output, it holds the parameters of write requests that are not yet finished. Other fields hold various general variables, such as the *termios* structure discussed above, which affects many properties of both input and output. There is also a field in the *tty* structure to point to information which is needed for a particular class of devices but is not needed in the *tty_table* entry for every device. For instance, the hardware-dependent part of the console driver needs the current position on the screen and in the video RAM, and the current attribute byte for the display, but this information is not needed to support an RS-232 line. The private data structures for each device type are also where the buffers that receive input from the interrupt service routines are located. Slow devices, such as the keyboard, do not need buffers as large as those needed by fast devices.

Terminal Input

To better understand how the driver works, let us first look at how characters typed in on the keyboard work their way through the system to the program that wants them. Although this section is intended as an overview we will use line number references to help the reader find each function used. You may find this a wild ride, getting input exercises code in *tty.c*, *keyboard.c*, and *console.c*, all of which are large files,

When a user logs in on the system console, a shell is created for him with */dev/console* as standard input, standard output, and standard error. The shell starts up and tries to read from standard input by calling the library procedure *read*. This procedure sends a message that contains the file descriptor, buffer address, and count to the file system. This message is shown as (1) in Fig. 3-33. After sending the message, the shell blocks, waiting for the reply. (User processes execute only the sendrec primitive, which combines a send with a receive from the process sent to.)

The file system gets the message and locates the i-node corresponding to the specified file descriptor. This i-node is for the character special file */dev/console* and contains the major and minor device numbers for the terminal. The major device type for terminals is 4; for the console the minor device number is 0.

The file system indexes into its device map, *dmap*, to find the number of the terminal driver, TTY. Then it sends a message to TTY, shown as (2) in Fig. 3-33. Normally, the user will not have typed anything yet, so the terminal driver will be unable to satisfy the request. It sends a reply back immediately to unblock the file system and report that no characters are available, shown as (3). The file system records the fact that a process is waiting for terminal (i.e., keyboard) input in the console's structure in *tty_table* and then goes off to get the next request for work. The user's shell remains blocked until the requested characters arrive, of course.

When a character is finally typed on the keyboard, it causes two interrupts, one when the key is depressed and one when it is released. An important point is

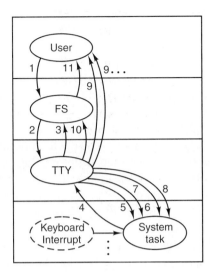

Figure 3-33. Read request from the keyboard when no characters are pending. FS is the file system. TTY is the terminal driver. The TTY receives a message for every keypress and queues scan codes as they are entered. Later these are interpreted and assembled into a buffer of ASCII codes which is copied to the user process.

that a PC keyboard does not generate ASCII codes; each key generates a **scan code** when pressed, and a different code when released. The lower 7 bits of the "press" and "release" codes are identical. The difference is the most significant bit, which is a 0 when the key is pressed and a 1 when it is released. This also applies to modifier keys such as CTRL and SHIFT. Although ultimately these keys do not cause ASCII codes to be returned to the user process, they generate scan codes indicating which key was pressed (the driver can distinguish between the left and right shift keys if desired), and they still cause two interrupts per key.

The keyboard interrupt is IRQ 1. This interrupt line is not accessible on the system bus, and can not be shared by any other I/O adapter. When *_hwint01* (line 6535) calls *intr_handle* (line 8221) there will not be a long list of hooks to traverse to find that the TTY should be notified. In Fig. 3-33 we show the system task originating the notification message (4) because it is generated by *generic_handler* in *system/do_irqctl.c* (not listed), but this routine is called directly by the low-level interrupt processing routines. The system task process is not activated. Upon receiving a *HARD_INT* message *tty_task* (line 13740) dispatches to *kbd_interrupt* (line 15335) which in turn calls *scan_keyboard* (line 15800). *Scan_keyboard* makes three kernel calls (5, 6, 7) to cause the system task to read from and write to several I/O ports, which ultimately returns the scan code, then is added to a circular buffer. A *tty_events* flag is then set to indicate this buffer contains characters and is not empty.

No message is needed as of this point. Every time the main loop of *tty_task* starts another cycle it inspects the *tty_events* flag for each terminal device, and, for each device which has the flag set, calls *handle_events* (line 14358). The *tty_events* flag can signal various kinds of activity (although input is the most likely), so *handle_events* always calls the device-specific functions for both input and output. For input from the keyboard this results in a call to *kb_read* (line 15360), which keeps track of keyboard codes that indicate pressing or releasing of the CTRL, SHIFT, and ALT keys and converts scan codes into ASCII codes. *Kb_read* in turn calls *in_process* (line 14486), which processes the ASCII codes, taking into account special characters and different flags that may be set, including whether or not canonical mode is in effect. The effect is normally to add characters to the console's input queue in *tty_table*, although some codes, for instance BACKSPACE, have other effects. Normally, also, *in_process* initiates echoing of the ASCII codes to the display.

When enough characters have come in, the terminal driver makes another kernel call (8) to ask the system task to copy the data to the address requested by the shell. The copying of the data is not message passing and for that reason is shown by dashed lines (9) in Fig. 3-33. More than one such line is shown because there may be more than one such operation before the user's request has been completely fulfilled. When the operation is finally complete, the terminal driver sends a message to the file system telling it that the work has been done (10), and the file system reacts to this message by sending a message back to the shell to unblock it (11).

The definition of when enough characters have come in depends upon the terminal mode. In canonical mode a request is complete when a linefeed, end-of-line, or end-of-file code is received, and, in order for proper input processing to be done, a line of input cannot exceed the size of the input queue. In noncanonical mode a read can request a much larger number of characters, and *in_process* may have to transfer characters more than once before a message is returned to the file system to indicate the operation is complete.

Note that the system task copies the actual characters directly from the TTY's address space to that of the shell. They do not go through the file system. With block I/O, data pass through the file system to allow it to maintain a buffer cache of the most recently used blocks. If a requested block happens to be in the cache, the request can be satisfied directly by the file system, without doing any actual disk I/O.

For keyboard I/O, a cache makes no sense. Furthermore, a request from the file system to a disk driver can always be satisfied in at most a few hundred milliseconds, so there is no harm in having the file system wait. Keyboard I/O may take hours to complete, or may never be complete (in canonical mode the terminal driver waits for a complete line, and it may also wait a long time in noncanonical mode, depending upon the settings of *MIN* and *TIME*). Thus, it is unacceptable to have the file system block until a terminal input request is satisfied.

Later on, it may happen that the user has typed ahead, and that characters are available before they have been requested, from previous interrupts and event 4. In that case, events 1, 2, and 5 through 11 all happen in quick succession after the read request; 3 does not occur at all.

Readers who are familiar with earlier versions of MINIX may remember that in these versions the TTY driver (and all other drivers) were compiled together with the kernel. Each driver had its own interrupt handler in kernel space. In the case of the keyboard driver, the interrupt handler itself could buffer a certain number of scan codes, and also do some preliminary processing (scan codes for most key releases could be dropped, only for modifier keys like the shift key is it necessary to buffer the release codes). The interrupt handler itself did not send messages to the TTY driver, because the probability was high that the TTY would not be blocked on a receive and able to receive a message at any given time. Instead, the clock interrupt handler awakened the TTY driver periodically. These techniques were adopted to avoid losing keyboard input.

Earlier we made something of a point of the differences between handling expected interrupts, such as those generated by a disk controller, and handling unpredictable interrupts like those from a keyboard. But in MINIX 3 nothing special seems to have been done to deal with the problems of unpredictable interrupts. How is this possible? One thing to keep in mind is the enormous difference in performance between the computers for which the earliest versions of MINIX were written and current designs. CPU clock speeds have increased, and the number of clock cycles needed to execute an instruction has decreased. The minimum processor recommended for use with MINIX 3 is an 80386. A slow 80386 will execute instructions approximately 20 times as fast as the original IBM PC. A 100 MHz Pentium will execute perhaps 25 times as fast as the slow 80386. So perhaps CPU speed is enough.

Another thing to keep in mind is that keyboard input is very slow by computer standards. At 100 words per minute a typist enters fewer than 10 characters per second. Even with a fast typist the terminal driver will probably be sent an interrupt message for each character typed at the keyboard. However, in the case of other input devices higher data rates are probable—rates 1000 or more times faster than those of a typist are possible from a serial port connected to a 56,000-bps modem. At that speed approximately 120 characters may be received by the modem between clock ticks, but to allow for data compression on the modem link the serial port connected to the modem must be able to handle at least twice as many.

One thing to consider with a serial port, however, is that characters, not scan codes, are transmitted, so even with an old UART that does no buffering, there will be only one interrupt per keypress instead of two. And newer PCs are equipped with UARTs that typically buffer at least 16, and perhaps as many 128 characters. So one interrupt per character is not required. For instance, a UART with a 16-character buffer might be configured to interrupt when 14 characters are in the buffer. Ethernet-based networks can deliver characters at a rate much faster than a serial line, but ethernet adapters buffer entire packets, and only one interrupt is necessary per packet.

We will complete our overview of terminal input by summarizing the events that occur when the terminal driver is first activated by a read request and when it is reactivated after receipt of keyboard input (see Fig. 3-34). In the first case, when a message comes in to the terminal driver requesting characters from the keyboard, the main procedure, *tty_task* (line 13740) calls *do_read* (line 13953) to handle the request. *Do_read* stores the parameters of the call in the keyboard's entry in *tty_table*, in case there are insufficient characters buffered to satisfy the request.

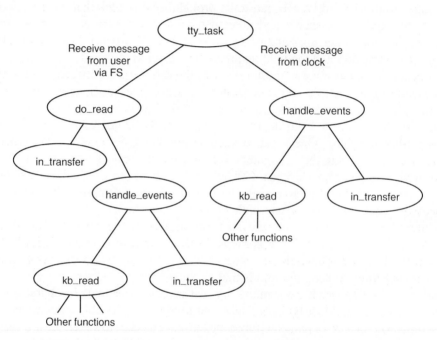

Figure 3-34. Input handling in the terminal driver. The left branch of the tree is taken to process a request to read characters. The right branch is taken when a keyboard message is sent to the driver before a user has requested input. [figure 3-X to be revised]

Then it calls *in_transfer* (line 14416) to get any input already waiting, and then *handle_events* (line 14358) which in turn calls (via the function pointer (*tp->tty_devread*)) *kb_read* (line 15360) and then *in_transfer* once again, in order to try to milk the input stream for a few more characters. *Kb_read* calls several other procedures not shown in Fig. 3-34 to accomplish its work. The result is that whatever is immediately available is copied to the user. If nothing is available then, nothing is copied. If the read is completed by *in_transfer* or by *handle_events*, a message is sent to the file system when all characters have been transferred, so the file system can unblock the caller. If the read was not completed (no characters, or not enough characters) *do_read* reports back to the file system, telling it whether it should suspend the original caller, or, if a nonblocking read was requested, cancel the read.

The right side of Fig. 3-34 summarizes the events that occur when the terminal driver is awakened subsequent to an interrupt from the keyboard. When a character is typed, the interrupt "handler" *kbd_interrupt* (line 15335) calls *scan_keyboard* which calls the system task to do the I/O. (We put "handler" in quotes because it is not a real handler called when an interrupt occurs, it is activated by a message sent to *tty_task* from *generic_handler* in the system task.) Then *kbd_interrupt* puts the scan code into the keyboard buffer, *ibuf*, and sets a flag to identify that the console device has experienced an event. When *kbd_interrupt* returns control to *tty_task* a continue statement results in starting another iteration of the main loop. The event flags of all terminal devices are checked and *handle_events* is called for each device with a raised flag. In the case of the keyboard, *handle_events* calls *kb_read* and *in_transfer*, just as was done on receipt of the original read request. The events shown on the right side of the figure may occur several times, until enough characters are received to fulfill the request accepted by *do_read* after the first message from the FS. If the FS tries to initiate a request for more characters from the same device before the first request is complete, an error is returned. Of course, each device is independent; a read request on behalf of a user at a remote terminal is processed separately from one for a user at the console.

The functions not shown in Fig. 3-34 that are called by *kb_read* include *map_key*, (line 15303) which converts the key codes (scan codes) generated by the hardware into ASCII codes, *make_break*, (line 15431) which keeps track of the state of modifier keys such as the SHIFT key, and *in_process*, (line 14486) which handles complications such as attempts by the user to backspace over input entered by mistake, other special characters, and options available in different input modes. *In_process* also calls *tty_echo* (line 14647), so the typed characters will be displayed on the screen.

Terminal Output

In general, console output is simpler than terminal input, because the operating system is in control and does not need to be concerned with requests for output arriving at inconvenient times. Also, because the MINIX 3 console is a memory-mapped display, output to the console is particularly simple. No interrupts are needed; the basic operation is to copy data from one memory region to another. On the other hand, all the details of managing the display, including handling escape sequences, must be handled by the driver software. As we did with keyboard input in the previous section, we will trace through the steps involved in sending characters to the console display. We will assume in this example that the active display is being written; minor complications caused by virtual consoles will be discussed later.

When a process wants to print something, it generally calls *printf. Printf* calls write to send a message to the file system. The message contains a pointer to the characters that are to be printed (not the characters themselves). The file system then sends a message to the terminal driver, which fetches them and copies them to the video RAM. Figure 3-35 shows the main procedures involved in output.

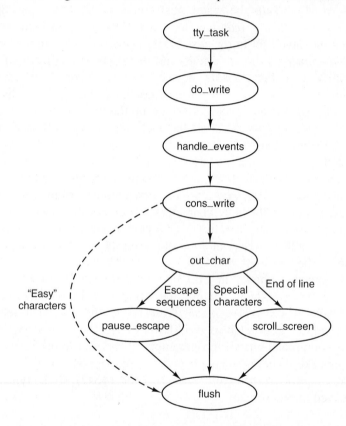

Figure 3-35. Major procedures used in terminal output. The dashed line indicates characters copied directly to *ramqueue* by *cons_write*.

When a message comes in to the terminal driver requesting it to write on the screen, *do_write* (line 14029) is called to store the parameters in the console's *tty* struct in the *tty_table*. Then *handle_events* (the same function called whenever the *tty_events* flag is found set) is called. On every call this function calls both the input and output routines for the device selected in its argument. In the case of the console display this means that any keyboard input that is waiting is processed first. If there is input waiting, characters to be echoed are added to whatever characters are already awaiting output. Then a call is made to *cons_write* (line 16036), the output procedure for memory-mapped displays. This procedure uses *phys_copy* to copy blocks of characters from the user process to a local buffer, possibly repeating this and the following steps a number of times, since the local buffer holds only 64 bytes. When the local buffer is full, each 8-bit byte is transferred to another buffer, *ramqueue*. This is an array of 16-bit words. Alternate bytes are filled in with the current value of the screen attribute byte, which determines foreground and background colors and other attributes. When possible, characters are transferred directly into *ramqueue*, but certain characters, such as control characters or characters that are parts of escape sequences, need special handling. Special handling is also required when a character's screen position would exceed the width of the screen, or when *ramqueue* becomes full. In these cases *out_char* (line 16119) is called to transfer the characters and take whatever additional action is called for. For instance, *scroll_screen* (line 16205) is called when a linefeed character is received while addressing the last line of the screen, and *parse_escape* handles characters during an escape sequence. Usually *out_char* calls *flush* (line 16259) which copies the contents of *ramqueue* to the video display memory, using the assembly language routine *mem_vid_copy*. *Flush* is also called after the last character is transferred into *ramqueue* to be sure all output is displayed. The final result of *flush* is to command the 6845 video controller chip to display the cursor in the correct position.

Logically, the bytes fetched from the user process could be written into the video RAM one per loop iteration. However, accumulating the characters in *ramqueue* and then copying the block with a call to *mem_vid_copy* are more efficient in the protected memory environment of Pentium-class processors. Interestingly, this technique was introduced in early versions of MINIX 3 that ran on older processors without protected memory. The precursor of *mem_vid_copy* dealt with a timing problem—with older video displays the copy into the video memory had to be done when the screen was blanked during vertical retrace of the CRT beam to avoid generating visual garbage all over the screen. MINIX 3 no longer provides this support for obsolete equipment as the performance penalty is too great. However, the modern version of MINIX 3 benefits in other ways from copying *ramqueue* as a block.

The video RAM available to a console is delimited in the *console* structure by the fields *c_start* and *c_limit*. The current cursor position is stored in the *c_column* and *c_row* fields. The coordinate (0, 0) is in the upper left corner of the screen, which is where the hardware starts to fill the screen. Each video scan begins at the address given by *c_org* and continues for 80×25 characters (4000 bytes). In other words, the 6845 chip pulls the word at offset *c_org* from the video RAM and displays the character byte in the upper left-hand corner, using the attribute byte to control color, blinking, and so forth. Then it fetches the next word and displays the character at (1, 0). This process continues until it gets to (79, 0), at which time it begins the second line on the screen, at coordinate (0, 1).

When the computer is first started, the screen is cleared, output is written into the video RAM starting at location c_start, and c_org is assigned the same value as c_start. Thus the first line appears on the top line of the screen. When output must go to a new line, either because the first line is full or because a newline character is detected by out_char, output is written into the location given by c_start plus 80. Eventually, all 25 lines are filled, and **scrolling** of the screen is required. Some programs, editors, for example, require scrolling in the downward direction too, when the cursor is on the top line and further movement upward within the text is required.

There are two ways scrolling the screen can be managed. In **software scrolling**, the character to be displayed at position $(0, 0)$ is always in the first location in video memory, word 0 relative to the position pointed to by c_start, and the video controller chip is commanded to display this location first by keeping the same address in c_org. When the screen is to be scrolled, the contents of relative location 80 in the video RAM, the beginning of the second line on the screen, is copied to relative location 0, word 81 is copied to relative location 1, and so on. The scan sequence is unchanged, putting the data at location 0 in the memory at screen position $(0, 0)$ and the image on the screen appears to have moved up one line. The cost is that the CPU has moved $80 \times 24 = 1920$ words. In **hardware scrolling**, the data are not moved in the memory; instead the video controller chip is instructed to start the display at a different point, for instance, with the data at word 80. The bookkeeping is done by adding 80 to the contents of c_org, saving it for future reference, and writing this value into the correct register of the video controller chip. This requires either that the controller be smart enough to wrap around the video RAM, taking data from the beginning of the RAM (the address in c_start) when it reaches the end (the address in c_limit), or that the video RAM have more capacity than just the 80×2000 words necessary to store a single screen of display.

Older display adapters generally have smaller memory but are able to wrap around and do hardware scrolling. Newer adapters generally have much more memory than needed to display a single screen of text, but the controllers are not able to wrap. Thus an adapter with 32,768 bytes of display memory can hold 204 complete lines of 160 bytes each, and can do hardware scrolling 179 times before the inability to wrap becomes a problem. But, eventually a memory copy operation will be needed to move the data for the last 24 lines back to location 0 in the video memory. Whichever method is used, a row of blanks is copied to the video RAM to ensure that the new line at the bottom of the screen is empty.

When virtual consoles are enabled, the available memory within a video adapter is divided equally between the number of consoles desired by properly initializing the c_start and c_limit fields for each console. This has an effect on scrolling. On any adapter large enough to support virtual consoles, software scrolling takes place every so often, even though hardware scrolling is nominally in effect. The smaller the amount of memory available to each console display, the more frequently software scrolling must be used. The limit is reached when the maximum possible number of consoles is configured. Then every scroll operation will be a software scroll operation.

The position of the cursor relative to the start of the video RAM can be derived from c_column and c_row, but it is faster to store it explicitly (in c_cur). When a character is to be printed, it is put into the video RAM at location c_cur, which is then updated, as is c_column. Figure 3-36 summarizes the fields of the *console* structure that affect the current position and the display origin.

Field	Meaning
c_start	Start of video memory for this console
c_limit	Limit of video memory for this console
c_column	Current column (0-79) with 0 at left
c_row	Current row (0-24) with 0 at top
c_cur	Offset into video RAM for cursor
c_org	Location in RAM pointed to by 6845 base register

Figure 3-36. Fields of the console structure that relate to the current screen position.

The characters that affect the cursor position (e.g., linefeed, backspace) are handled by adjusting the values of c_column, c_row, and c_cur. This work is done at the end of *flush* by a call to *set_6845* which sets the registers in the video controller chip.

The terminal driver supports escape sequences to allow screen editors and other interactive programs to update the screen in a flexible way. The sequences supported are a subset of an ANSI standard and should be adequate to allow many programs written for other hardware and other operating systems to be easily ported to MINIX 3. There are two categories of escape sequences: those that never contain a variable parameter, and those that may contain parameters. In the first category the only representative supported by MINIX 3 is ESC M, which reverse indexes the screen, moving the cursor up one line and scrolling the screen downward if the cursor is already on the first line. The other category can have one or two numeric parameters. Sequences in this group all begin with ESC [. The "[" is the **control sequence introducer**. A table of escape sequences defined by the ANSI standard and recognized by MINIX 3 was shown in Fig. 3-32.

Parsing escape sequences is not trivial. Valid escape sequences in MINIX 3 can be as short as two characters, as in ESC M, or up to 8 characters long in the case of a sequence that accepts two numeric parameters that each can have a two-digit values as in ESC [20;60H, which moves the cursor to line 20, column 60. In a sequence that accepts a parameter, the parameter may be omitted, and in a sequence that accepts two parameters either or both of them may be omitted.

When a parameter is omitted or one that is outside the valid range is used, a default is substituted. The default is the lowest valid value.

Consider the following ways a program could construct a sequence to move to the upper-left corner of the screen:

1. ESC [H is acceptable, because if no parameters are entered the lowest valid parameters are assumed.

2. ESC [1;1H will correctly send the cursor to row 1 and column 1 (with ANSI, the row and column numbers start at 1).

3. Both ESC [1;H and ESC [;1H have an omitted parameter, which defaults to 1 as in the first example.

4. ESC [0;0H will do the same, since each parameter is less than the minimum valid value the minimum is substituted.

These examples are presented not to suggest one should deliberately use invalid parameters but to show that the code that parses such sequences is nontrivial.

MINIX 3 implements a finite state automaton to do this parsing. The variable *c_esc_state* in the console structure normally has a value of 0. When *out_char* detects an ESC character, it changes *c_esc_state* to 1, and subsequent characters are processed by *parse_escape* (line 16293). If the next character is the control sequence introducer, state 2 is entered; otherwise the sequence is considered complete, and *do_escape* (line 16352) is called. In state 2, as long as incoming characters are numeric, a parameter is calculated by multiplying the previous value of the parameter (initially 0) by 10 and adding the numeric value of the current character. The parameter values are kept in an array and when a semicolon is detected the processing shifts to the next cell in the array. (The array in MINIX 3 has only two elements, but the principle is the same). When a nonnumeric character that is not a semicolon is encountered the sequence is considered complete, and again *do_escape* is called. The current character on entry to *do_escape* then is used to select exactly what action to take and how to interpret the parameters, either the defaults or those entered in the character stream. This is illustrated in Fig. 3-44.

Loadable Keymaps

The IBM PC keyboard does not generate ASCII codes directly. The keys are each identified with a number, starting with the keys that are located in the upper left of the original PC keyboard—1 for the "ESC" key, 2 for the "1", and so on. Each key is assigned a number, including modifier keys like the left SHIFT and right SHIFT keys, numbers 42 and 54. When a key is pressed, MINIX 3 receives the key number as a scan code. A scan code is also generated when a key is released, but the code generated upon release has the most significant bit set (equivalent to adding 128 to the key number). Thus a key press and a key release can be distinguished. By keeping track of which modifier keys have been pressed and not yet released, a large number of combinations are possible. For ordinary purposes, of course, two-finger combinations, such as SHIFT-A or CTRL-D, are most manageable for two-handed typists, but for special occasions three-key (or more) combinations are possible, for instance, CTRL-SHIFT-A, or the well-known CTRL-ALT-DEL combination that PC users recognize as the way to reset and reboot the system.

The complexity of the PC keyboard allows for a great deal of flexibility in how it used. A standard keyboard has 47 ordinary character keys defined (26 alphabetic, 10 numeric, and 11 punctuation). If we are willing to use three-fingered modifier key combinations, such as CTRL-ALT-SHIFT, we can support a character set of 376 (8×47) members. This is by no means the limit of what is possible, but for now let us assume we do not want to distinguish between the left- and right-hand modifier keys, or use any of the numeric keypad or function keys. Indeed, we are not limited to using just the CTRL, ALT, and SHIFT keys as modifiers; we could retire some keys from the set of ordinary keys and use them as modifiers if we desired to write a driver that supported such a system.

Operating systems that use such keyboards use a **keymap** to determine what character code to pass to a program based upon the key being pressed and the modifiers in effect. The MINIX 3 keymap logically is an array of 128 rows, representing possible scan code values (this size was chosen to accommodate Japanese keyboards; U.S. and European keyboards do not have this many keys) and 6 columns. The columns represent no modifier, the SHIFT key, the Control key, the left ALT key, the right ALT key, and a combination of either ALT key plus the SHIFT key. There are thus 720 ($(128 - 6) \times 6$) character codes that can be generated by this scheme, given an adequate keyboard. This requires that each entry in the table be a 16-bit quantity. For U.S. keyboards the ALT and ALT2 columns are identical. ALT2 is named ALTGR on keyboards for other languages, and many of these keymaps support keys with three symbols by using this key as a modifier.

A standard keymap (determined by the line

```
#include keymaps/us-std.src
```

in *keyboard.c*) is compiled into the MINIX 3 kernel at compilation time, but an

```
ioctl(0, KIOCSMAP, keymap)
```

call can be used to load a different map into the kernel at address *keymap*. A full keymap occupies 1536 bytes ($128 \times 6 \times 2$). Extra keymaps are stored in compressed form. A program called *genmap* is used to make a new compressed keymap. When compiled, *genmap* includes the *keymap.src* code for a particular keymap, so the map is compiled within *genmap*. Normally, *genmap* is executed immediately after being compiled, at which time it outputs the compressed version to a file, and then the *genmap* binary is deleted. The command *loadkeys* reads a compressed keymap, expands it internally, and then calls ioctl to transfer the keymap into the kernel memory. MINIX 3 can execute *loadkeys* automatically upon starting, and the program can also be invoked by the user at any time.

Scan code	Character	Regular	SHIFT	ALT1	ALT2	ALT+SHIFT	CTRL
00	none	0	0	0	0	0	0
01	ESC	C('[')	C('[')	CA('[')	CA('[')	CA('[')	C('[')
02	'1'	'1'	'!'	A('1')	A('1')	A('!')	C('A')
13	'='	'='	'+'	A('=')	A('=')	A('+')	C('@')
16	'q'	L('q')	'Q'	A('q')	A('q')	A('Q')	C('Q')
28	CR/LF	C('M')	C('M')	CA('M')	CA('M')	CA('M')	C('J')
29	CTRL	CTRL	CTRL	CTRL	CTRL	CTRL	CTRL
59	F1	F1	SF1	AF1	AF1	ASF1	CF1
127	???	0	0	0	0	0	0

Figure 3-37. A few entries from a keymap source file.

The source code for a keymap defines a large initialized array, and in the interest of saving space a keymap file is not printed in Appendix B. Figure 3-37 shows in tabular form the contents of a few lines of *src/kernel/keymaps/us-std.src* which illustrate several aspects of keymaps. There is no key on the IBM-PC keyboard that generates a scan code of 0. The entry for code 1, the ESC key, shows that the value returned is unchanged when the SHIFT key or CTRL key are pressed, but that a different code is returned when an ALT key is pressed simultaneously with the ESC key. The values compiled into the various columns are determined by macros defined in *include/minix/keymap.h*:

```
#define C(c)    ((c) & 0x1F)      /* Map to control code */
#define A(c)    ((c) | 0x80)      /* Set eight bit (ALT) */
#define CA(c)   A(C(c))           /* CTRL-ALT */
#define L(c)    ((c) | HASCAPS)   /* Add "Caps Lock has effect" attribute */
```

The first three of these macros manipulate bits in the code for the quoted character to produce the necessary code to be returned to the application. The last one sets the HASCAPS bit in the high byte of the 16-bit value. This is a flag that indicates that the state of the capslock variable has to be checked and the code possibly modified before being returned. In the figure, the entries for scan codes 2, 13, and 16 show how typical numeric, punctuation, and alphabetic keys are handled. For code 28 a special feature is seen—normally the ENTER key produces a CR (0x0D) code, represented here as C('M'). Because the newline character in UNIX files is the LF (0x0A) code, and it is sometimes necessary to enter this directly, this keyboard map provides for a CTRL-ENTER combination, which produces this code, C('J').

Scan code 29 is one of the modifier codes and must be recognized no matter what other key is pressed, so the CTRL value is returned regardless of any other key that may be pressed. The function keys do not return ordinary ASCII values, and the row for scan code 59 shows symbolically the values (defined in *include/minix/keymap.h*) that are returned for the F1 key in combination with other modifiers. These values are F1: 0x0110, SF1: 0x1010, AF1: 0x0810, ASF1: 0x0C10, and CF1: 0x0210. The last entry shown in the figure, for scan code 127, is typical of many entries near the end of the array. For many keyboards, certainly most of those used in Europe and the Americas, there are not enough keys to generate all the possible codes, and these entries in the table are filled with zeroes.

Loadable Fonts

Early PCs had the patterns for generating characters on a video screen stored only in ROM, but the displays used on modern systems provide RAM on the video display adapters into which custom character generator patterns can be loaded. This is supported by MINIX 3 with a

```
ioctl(0, TIOCSFON, font)
```

ioctl operation. MINIX 3 supports an 80 lines × 25 rows video mode, and font files contain 4096 bytes. Each byte represents a line of 8 pixels that are illuminated if the bit value is 1, and 16 such lines are needed to map each character. However the video display adapter uses 32 bytes to map each character, to provide higher resolution in modes not currently supported by MINIX 3. The *loadfont* command is provided to convert these files into the 8192-byte *font* structure referenced by the ioctl call and to use that call to load the font. As with the keymaps, a font can be loaded at startup time, or at any time during normal operation. However, every video adapter has a standard font built into its ROM that is available by default. There is no need to compile a font into MINIX 3 itself, and the only font support necessary in the kernel is the code to carry out the *TIOCSFON* ioctl operation.

3.8.4 Implementation of the Device-Independent Terminal Driver

In this section we will begin to look at the source code of the terminal driver in detail. We saw when we studied the block devices that multiple drivers supporting several different devices could share a common base of software. The case with the terminal devices is similar, but with the difference that there is one terminal driver that supports several different kinds of terminal device. Here we will start with the device-independent code. In later sections we will look at the device-dependent code for the keyboard and the memory-mapped console display.

Terminal Driver Data Structures

The file *tty.h* contains definitions used by the C files which implement the terminal drivers. Since this driver supports many different devices, the minor device numbers must be used to distinguish which device is being supported on a particular call, and they are defined on lines 13405 to 13409.

Within *tty.h*, the definitions of the *O_NOCTTY* and *O_NONBLOCK* flags (which are optional arguments to the open call) are duplicates of definitions in *include/fcntl.h* but they are repeated here so as not to require including another file. The *devfun_t* and *devfunarg_t* types (lines 13423 and 13424) are used to define pointers to functions, in order to provide for indirect calls using a mechanism similar to what we saw in the code for the main loop of the disk drivers.

Many variables declared in this file are identified by the prefix *tty_*. The most important definition in *tty.h* is the *tty* structure (lines 13426 to 13488). There is one such structure for each terminal device (the console display and keyboard together count as a single terminal). The first variable in the *tty* structure, *tty_events*, is the flag that is set when an interrupt causes a change that requires the terminal driver to attend to the device.

The rest of the *tty* structure is organized to group together variables that deal with input, output, status, and information about incomplete operations. In the input section, *tty_inhead* and *tty_intail* define the queue where received characters are buffered. *Tty_incount* counts the number of characters in this queue, and *tty_eotct* counts lines or characters, as explained below. All device-specific calls are done indirectly, with the exception of the routines that initialize the terminals, which are called to set up the pointers used for the indirect calls. The *tty_devread* and *tty_icancel* fields hold pointers to device-specific code to perform the read and input cancel operations. *Tty_min* is used in comparisons with *tty_eotct*. When the latter becomes equal to the former, a read operation is complete. During canonical input, *tty_min* is set to 1 and *tty_eotct* counts lines entered. During noncanonical input, *tty_eotct* counts characters and *tty_min* is set from the *MIN* field of the *termios* structure. The comparison of the two variables thus tells when a line is ready or when the minimum character count is reached, depending upon the mode. *Tty_tmr* is a timer for this tty, used for the *TIME* field of *termios*.

Since queueing of output is handled by the device-specific code, the output section of *tty* declares no variables and consists entirely of pointers to device-specific functions that write, echo, send a break signal, and cancel output. In the status section the flags *tty_reprint*, *tty_escaped*, and *tty_inhibited* indicate that the last character seen has a special meaning; for instance, when a CTRL-V (LNEXT) character is seen, *tty_escaped* is set to 1 to indicate that any special meaning of the next character is to be ignored.

The next part of the structure holds data about *DEV_READ*, *DEV_WRITE*, and *DEV_IOCTL* operations in progress. There are two processes involved in each of these operations. The server managing the system call (normally FS) is identified in *tty_incaller* (line 13458). The server calls the tty driver on behalf of another process that needs to do an I/O operation, and this client is identified in *tty_inproc* (line 13459). As described in Fig. 3-33, during a read, characters are transferred directly from the terminal driver to a buffer within the memory space of the original caller. *Tty_inproc* and *tty_in_vir* locate this buffer. The next two variables, *tty_inleft* and *tty_incum*, count the characters still needed and those already transferred. Similar sets of variables are needed for a write system call. For ioctl there may be an immediate transfer of data between the requesting process and the driver, so a virtual address is needed, but there is no need for variables to mark the progress of an operation. An ioctl request may be postponed, for instance, until current output is complete, but when the time is right the request is carried out in a single operation.

Finally, the *tty* structure includes some variables that fall into no other category, including pointers to the functions to handle the *DEV_IOCTL* and *DEV_CLOSE* operations at the device level, a POSIX-style *termios* structure, and a *winsize* structure that provides support for window-oriented screen displays. The last part of the structure provides storage for the input queue itself in the array *tty_inbuf*. Note that this is an array of *u16_t*, not of 8-bit *char* characters. Although applications and devices use 8-bit codes for characters, the C language requires the input function *getchar* to work with a larger data type so it can return a symbolic *EOF* value in addition to all 256 possible byte values.

The *tty_table*, an array of *tty* structures, is declared as *extern* on line 13491. There is one array element for each terminal enabled by the *NR_CONS*, *NR_RS_LINES*, and *NR_PTYS* definitions in *include/minix/config.h*. For the configuration discussed in this book, two consoles are enabled, but MINIX 3 may be recompiled to add additional virtual consoles, one or two 2 serial lines, and up to 64 pseudo terminals.

There is one other *extern* definition in *tty.h*. *Tty_timers* (line 13516) is a pointer used by the timer to hold the head of a linked list of *timer_t* fields. The *tty.h* header file is included in many files and storage for *tty_table* and *tty_timers* is allocated during compilation of *tty.c*.

Two macros, *buflen* and *bufend*, are defined on lines 13520 and 13521. These are used frequently in the terminal driver code, which does much copying of data into and out of buffers.

The Device-Independent Terminal Driver

The main terminal driver and the device-independent supporting functions are all in *tty.c*. Following this there are a number of macro definitions. If a device is not initialized, the pointers to that device's device-specific functions will contain zeroes put there by the C compiler. This makes it possible to define the *tty_active* macro (line 13687) which returns *FALSE* if a null pointer is found. Of course, the initialization code for a device cannot be accessed indirectly if part of its job is to initialize the pointers that make indirect access possible. On lines 13690 to 13696 are conditional macro definitions to equate initialization calls for RS-232 or pseudo terminal devices to calls to a null function when these devices are not configured. *Do_pty* may be similarly disabled in this section. This makes it possible to omit the code for these devices entirely if it is not needed.

Since there are so many configurable parameters for each terminal, and there may be quite a few terminals on a networked system, a *termios_defaults* structure is declared and initialized with default values (all of which are defined in *include/termios.h*) on lines 13720 to 13727. This structure is copied into the *tty_table* entry for a terminal whenever it is necessary to initialize or reinitialize it. The defaults for the special characters were shown in Fig. 3-29. Figure 3-38 shows the default values for the various flags used. On the following line the *winsize_defaults* structure is similarly declared. It is left to be initialized to all zeroes by the C compiler. This is the proper default action; it means "window size is unknown, use */etc/termcap*."

The final set of definitions before executable code begins are the PUBLIC declarations of global variables previously declared as extern in *tty.h* (lines 13731 to 13735).

Field	Default values
c_iflag	BRKINT ICRNL IXON IXANY
c_oflag	OPOST ONLCR
c_cflag	CREAD CS8 HUPCL
c_lflag	ISIG IEXTEN ICANON ECHO ECHOE

Figure 3-38. Default termios flag values.

The entry point for the terminal driver is *tty_task* (line 13740). Before entering the main loop, a call is made to *tty_init* (line 13752). Information about the host machine that will be needed to initialize the keyboard and the console is obtained by a sys_getmachine kernel call, and then the keyboard hardware is initialized. The routine called for this is *kb_init_once*. It is so named to distinguish it from another initialization routine which is called as part of initialization of each virtual console later on. Finally, a single 0 is printed to exercise the output system and kick anything that does not get initialized until first use. The source code shows a call to *printf*, but this is not the same *printf* used by user programs, it is a special version that calls a local function in the console driver called *putk*.

The main loop on lines 13764 to 13876 is, in principle, like the main loop of any driver—it receives a message, executes a switch on the message type to call the appropriate function, and then generates a return message. However, there are some complications. The first one is that since the last interrupt additional characters may have been read or characters to be written to an output device may be ready. Before attempting to receive a message, the main loop always checks the *tp->tty_events* flags for all terminals and *handle_events* is called as necessary to take care of unfinished business. Only when nothing demands immediate attention is a call made to receive.

The diagram showing message types in the comments near the beginning of *tty.c* shows the most often used types. A number of message types requesting specialized services from the terminal driver are not shown. These are not specific to any one device. The *tty_task* main loop checks for these and handles them before checking for device-specific messages. First a check is made for a *SYN_ALARM* message, and, if this is the message type a call is made to *expire_timers* to cause a watchdog routine to execute. Then comes a continue statement. In fact all of the next few cases we will look at are followed by continue. We will say more about this soon.

The next message type tested for is *HARD_INT*. This is most likely the result of a key being pressed or released on the local keyboard. It could also mean bytes have been received by a serial port, if serial ports are enabled—in the configuration we are studying they are not, but we left conditional code in the file here to illustrate how serial port input would be handled. A bit field in the message is used to determine the source of the interrupt.

Next a check is made for *SYS_SIG*. System processes (drivers and servers) are expected to block waiting for messages. Ordinary signals are received only by active processes, so the standard UNIX signaling method does not work with system processes. A *SYS_SIG* message is used to signal a system process. A signal to the terminal driver can mean the kernel is shutting down (*SIGKSTOP*), the terminal driver is being shut down (*SIGTERM*), or the kernel needs to print a message to the console (*SIGKMESS*), and appropriate routines are called for these cases.

The last group of non-device-specific messages are *PANIC_DUMPS*, *DIAGNOSTICS*, and *FKEY_CONTROL*. We will say more about these when we get to the functions that service them.

Now, about the continue statements: in the C language, a continue statement short-circuits a loop, and returns control to the top of the loop. So if any one of the message types mentioned so far is detected, as soon as it is serviced control returns to the top of the main loop, at line 13764, the check for events is repeated, and receive is called again to await a new message. Particularly in the case of input it is important to be ready to respond again as quickly as possible. Also, if any of the message-type tests in the first part of the loop succeeded there is no point in making any of the tests that come after the first switch.

Above we mentioned complications that the terminal driver must deal with. The second complication is that this driver services several devices. If the interrupt is not a hardware interrupt the *TTY_LINE* field in the message is used to determine which device should respond to the message. The minor device number is decoded by a series of comparisons, by means of which *tp* is pointed to the correct entry in the *tty_table* (lines 13834 to 13847). If the device is a pseudo terminal, *do_pty* (in *pty.c*) is called and the main loop is restarted. In this case *do_pty* generates the reply message. Of course, if pseudo terminals are not enabled, the call to *do_pty* uses the dummy macro defined earlier. One would hope that attempts to access nonexistent devices would not occur, but it is always easier to add another check than to verify that there are no errors elsewhere in the system. In case the device does not exist or is not configured, a reply message with an *ENXIO* error message is generated and, again, control returns to the top of the loop.

The rest of this driver resembles what we have seen in the main loop of other drivers, a switch on the message type (lines 13862 to 13875). The appropriate function for the type of request, *do_read*, *do_write*, and so on, is called. In each case the called function generates the reply message, rather than pass the information needed to construct the message back to the main loop. A reply message is generated at the end of the main loop only if a valid message type was not received, in which case an *EINVAL* error message is sent. Because reply messages are sent from many different places within the terminal driver a common routine, *tty_reply*, is called to handle the details of constructing reply messages.

If the message received by *tty_task* is a valid message type, not the result of an interrupt, and does not come from a pseudo terminal, the switch at the end of the main loop will dispatch to one of the functions *do_read*, *do_write*, *do_ioctl*, *do_open*, *do_close*, *do_select*, or *do_cancel*. The arguments to each of these calls are *tp*, a pointer to a *tty* structure, and the address of the message. Before looking at each of them in detail, we will mention a few general considerations. Since *tty_task* may service multiple terminal devices, these functions must return quickly so the main loop can continue.

However, *do_read*, *do_write*, and *do_ioctl* may not be able to complete all the requested work immediately. In order to allow FS to service other calls, an immediate reply is required. If the request cannot be completed immediately, the *SUSPEND* code is returned in the status field of the reply message. This corresponds to the message marked (3) in Fig. 3-33 and suspends the process that initiated the call, while unblocking the FS. Messages corresponding to (10) and (11) in the figure will be sent later when the operation can be completed. If the request can be fully satisfied, or an error occurs, either the count of bytes transferred or the error code is returned in the status field of the return message to the FS. In this case a message will be sent immediately from the FS back to the process that made the original call, to wake it up.

Reading from a terminal is fundamentally different from reading from a disk device. The disk driver issues a command to the disk hardware and eventually data will be returned, barring a mechanical or electrical failure. The computer can display a prompt upon the screen, but there is no way for it to force a person sitting at the keyboard to start typing. For that matter, there is no guarantee that anybody will be sitting there at all. In order to make the speedy return that is required, *do_read* (line 13953) starts by storing information that will enable the request to be completed later, when and if input arrives. There are a few error checks to be made first. It is an error if the device is still expecting input to fulfill a previous request, or if the parameters in the message are invalid (lines 13964 to 13972). If these tests are passed, information about the request is copied into the proper fields in the device's *tp−>tty_table* entry on lines 13975 to 13979. The last step, setting *tp−>tty_inleft* to the number of characters requested, is important. This variable is used to determine when the read request is satisfied. In canonical mode *tp−>tty_inleft* is decremented by one for each character returned, until an end of line is received, at which point it is suddenly reduced to zero. In noncanonical mode it is handled differently, but in any case it is reset to zero whenever the call is satisfied, whether by a timeout or by receiving at least the minimum number of bytes requested. When *tp−>tty_inleft* reaches zero, a reply message is sent. As we will see, reply messages can be generated in several places. It is sometimes necessary to check whether a reading process still expects a reply; a nonzero value of *tp−>tty_inleft* serves as a flag for that purpose.

In canonical mode a terminal device waits for input until either the number of characters asked for in the call has been received, or the end of a line or the end of the file is reached. The *ICANON* bit in the *termios* structure is tested on line 13981 to see if canonical mode is in effect for the terminal. If it is not set, the *termios MIN* and *TIME* values are checked to determine what action to take.

In Fig. 3-31 we saw how *MIN* and *TIME* interact to provide different ways a read call can behave. *TIME* is tested on line 13983. A value of zero corresponds to the left-hand column in Fig. 3-31, and in this case no further tests are needed at this point. If *TIME* is nonzero, then *MIN* is tested. If it is zero, *settimer* is called to start the timer that will terminate the *DEV_READ* request after a delay, even if no bytes have been received. *Tp−>tty_min* is set to 1 here, so the call will terminate immediately if one or more bytes are received before the timeout. At this point no check for possible input has yet been made, so more than one character may already be waiting to satisfy the request. In that case, as many characters as are ready, up to the number specified in the read call, will be returned as soon as the input is found. If both *TIME* and *MIN* are nonzero, the timer has a different meaning. The timer is used as an inter-character timer in this case. It is started only after the first character is received and is restarted after each successive character. *Tp−>tty_eotct* counts characters in noncanonical mode, and if it is zero at line 13993, no characters have been received yet and the inter-byte timer is inhibited.

In any case, at line 14001, *in_transfer* is called to transfer any bytes already in the input queue directly to the reading process. Next there is a call to *handle_events*, which may put more data into the input queue and which calls *in_transfer* again. This apparent duplication of calls requires some explanation. Although the discussion so far has been in terms of keyboard input, *do_read* is in the device-independent part of the code and also services input from remote terminals connected by serial lines. It is possible that previous input has filled the

RS-232 input buffer to the point where input has been inhibited. The first call to *in_transfer* does not start the flow again, but the call to *handle_events* can have this effect. The fact that it then causes a second call to *in_transfer* is just a bonus. The important thing is to be sure the remote terminal is allowed to send again. Either of these calls may result in satisfaction of the request and sending of the reply message to the FS. *Tp->tty_inleft* is used as a flag to see if the reply has been sent; if it is still nonzero at line 14004, *do_read* generates and sends the reply message itself. This is done on lines 14013 to 14021. (We assume here that no use has been made of the select system call, and therefore there will be no call to *select_retry* on line 14006).

If the original request specified a nonblocking read, the FS is told to pass an *EAGAIN* error code back to original caller. If the call is an ordinary blocking read, the FS receives a *SUSPEND* code, unblocking it but telling it to leave the original caller blocked. In this case the terminal's *tp->tty_inrepcode* field is set to *REVIVE*. When and if the read is later satisfied, this code will be placed in the reply message to the FS to indicate that the original caller was put to sleep and needs to be revived.

Do_write (line 14029) is similar to *do_read*, but simpler, because there are fewer options to be concerned about in handling a write system call. Checks similar to those made by *do_read* are made to see that a previous write is not still in progress and that the message parameters are valid, and then the parameters of the request are copied into the *tty* structure. *Handle_events* is then called, and *tp->tty_outleft* is checked to see if the work was done (lines 14058 to 14060). If so, a reply message already has been sent by *handle_events* and there is nothing left to do. If not, a reply message is generated. with the message parameters depending upon whether or not the original write call was called in nonblocking mode.

The next function, *do_ioctl* (line 14079), is a long one, but not difficult to understand. The body of *do_ioctl* is two switch statements. The first determines the size of the parameter pointed to by the pointer in the request message (lines 14094 to 14125). If the size is not zero, the parameter's validity is tested. The contents cannot be tested here, but what can be tested is whether a structure of the required size beginning at the specified address fits within the segment it is specified to be in. The rest of the function is another switch on the type of ioctl operation requested (lines 14128 to 14225).

Unfortunately, supporting the POSIX-required operations with the ioctl call meant that names for ioctl operations had to be invented that suggest, but do not duplicate, names required by POSIX. Figure 3-39 shows the relationship between the POSIX request names and the names used by the MINIX 3 ioctl call. A *TCGETS* operation services a *tcgetattr* call by the user and simply returns a copy of the terminal device's *tp->tty_termios* structure. The next four request types share code. The *TCSETSW*, *TCSETSF*, and *TCSETS* request types correspond to user calls to the POSIX-defined function *tcsetattr*, and all have the basic action of

POSIX function	POSIX operation	IOCTL type	IOCTL parameter
tcdrain	(none)	TCDRAIN	(none)
tcflow	TCOOFF	TCFLOW	int=TCOOFF
tcflow	TCOON	TCFLOW	int=TCOON
tcflow	TCIOFF	TCFLOW	int=TCIOFF
tcflow	TCION	TCFLOW	int=TCION
tcflush	TCIFLUSH	TCFLSH	int=TCIFLUSH
tcflush	TCOFLUSH	TCFLSH	int=TCOFLUSH
tcflush	TCIOFLUSH	TCFLSH	int=TCIOFLUSH
tcgetattr	(none)	TCGETS	termios
tcsetattr	TCSANOW	TCSETS	termios
tcsetattr	TCSADRAIN	TCSETSW	termios
tcsetattr	TCSAFLUSH	TCSETSF	termios
tcsendbreak	(none)	TCSBRK	int=duration

Figure 3-39. POSIX calls and IOCTL operations.

copying a new *termios* structure into a terminal's *tty* structure. The copying is done immediately for *TCSETS* calls and may be done for *TCSETSW* and *TCSETSF* calls if output is complete, by a *sys_vircopy* kernel call to get the data from the user, followed by a call to *setattr*, on lines 14153 to 14156. If *tcsetattr* was called with a modifier requesting postponement of the action until completion of current output, the parameters for the request are placed in the terminal's *tty* structure for later processing if the test of *tp->tty_outleft* on line 14139 reveals output is not complete. *Tcdrain* suspends a program until output is complete and is translated into an ioctl call of type *TCDRAIN*. If output is already complete, it has nothing more to do. If output is not complete, it also must leave information in the *tty* structure.

The POSIX *tcflush* function discards unread input and/or unsent output data, according to its argument, and the ioctl translation is straightforward, consisting of a call to the *tty_icancel* function that services all terminals, and/or the device-specific function pointed to by *tp->tty_ocancel* (lines 14159 to 14167). *Tcflow* is similarly translated in a straightforward way into an ioctl call. To suspend or restart output, it sets a *TRUE* or *FALSE* value into *tp->tty_inhibited* and then sets the *tp->tty_events* flag. To suspend or restart input, it sends the appropriate *STOP* (normally CTRL-S) or *START* (CTRL-Q) code to the remote terminal, using the device-specific echo routine pointed to by *tp->tty_echo* (lines 14181 to 14186).

Most of the rest of the operations handled by *do_ioctl* are handled in one line of code, by calling an appropriate function. In the cases of the *KIOCSMAP* (load keymap) and *TIOCSFON* (load font) operations, a test is made to be sure the device really is a console, since these operations do not apply to other terminals. If virtual terminals are in use the same keymap and font apply to all consoles, the hardware does not permit any easy way of doing otherwise. The window size operations copy a *winsize* structure between the user process and the terminal driver. Note, however, the comment under the code for the *TIOCSWINSZ* operation. When a process changes its window size, the kernel is expected to send a *SIGWINCH* signal to the process group under some versions of UNIX. The signal is not required by the POSIX standard and is not implemented in MINIX 3. However, anyone thinking of using these structures should consider adding code here to initiate this signal.

The last two cases in *do_ioctl* support the POSIX required *tcgetpgrp* and *tcsetpgrp* functions. There is no action associated with these cases, and they always return an error. There is nothing wrong with this. These functions support **job control**, the ability to suspend and restart a process from the keyboard. Job control is not required by POSIX and is not supported by MINIX 3. However, POSIX requires these functions, even when job control is not supported, to ensure portability of programs.

Do_open (line 14234) has a simple basic action to perform—it increments the variable *tp->tty_openct* for the device so it can be verified that it is open. However, there are some tests to be done first. POSIX specifies that for ordinary terminals the first process to open a terminal is the **session leader**, and when a session leader dies, access to the terminal is revoked from other processes in its group. Daemons need to be able to write error messages, and if their error output is not redirected to a file, it should go to a display that cannot be closed.

For this purpose a device called */dev/log* exists in MINIX 3. Physically it is the same device as */dev/console*, but it is addressed by a separate minor device number and is treated differently. It is a write-only device, and thus *do_open* returns an *EACCESS* error if an attempt is made to open it for reading (line 14246). The other test done by *do_open* is to test the *O_NOCTTY* flag. If it is not set and the device is not */dev/log*, the terminal becomes the controlling terminal for a process group. This is done by putting the process number of the caller into the *tp->tty_pgrp* field of the *tty_table* entry. Following this, the *tp->tty_openct* variable is incremented and the reply message is sent.

A terminal device may be opened more than once, and the next function, *do_close* (line 14260), has nothing to do except decrement *tp->tty_openct*. The test on line 14266 foils an attempt to close the device if it happens to be */dev/log*. If this operation is the last close, input is canceled by calling *tp->tty_icancel*. Device-specific routines pointed to by *tp->tty_ocancel* and *tp->tty_close* are also called. Then various fields in the *tty* structure for the device are set back to their default values and the reply message is sent.

The last message type handler we will consider is *do_cancel* (line 14281). This is invoked when a signal is received for a process that is blocked trying to read or write. There are three states that must be checked:

1. The process may have been reading when killed.

2. The process may have been writing when killed.

3. The process may have been suspended by *tcdrain* until its output was complete.

A test is made for each case, and the general *tp->tty_icancel*, or the device-specific routine pointed to by *tp->tty_ocancel*, is called as necessary. In the last case the only action required is to reset the flag *tp->tty_ioreq*, to indicate the ioctl operation is now complete. Finally, the *tp->tty_events* flag is set and a reply message is sent.

Terminal Driver Support Code

Now that we have looked at the top-level functions called in the main loop of *tty_task*, it is time to look at the code that supports them. We will start with *handle_events* (line 14358). As mentioned earlier, on each pass through the main loop of the terminal driver, the *tp->tty_events* flag for each terminal device is checked and *handle_events* is called if it shows that attention is required for a particular terminal. *Do_read* and *do_write* also call *handle_events*. This routine must work fast. It resets the *tp->tty_events* flag and then calls device-specific routines to read and write, using the pointers to the functions *tp->tty_devread* and *tp->ttydevwrite* (lines 14382 to 14385).

These functions are called unconditionally, because there is no way to test whether a read or a write caused the raising of the flag—a design choice was made here, that checking two flags for each device would be more expensive than making two calls each time a device was active. Also, most of the time a character received from a terminal must be echoed, so both calls will be necessary. As noted in the discussion of the handling of *tcsetattr* calls by *do_ioctl*, POSIX may postpone control operations on devices until current output is complete, so immediately after calling the device-specific *tty_devwrite* function is a good time take care of ioctl operations. This is done on line 14388, where *dev_ioctl* is called if there is a pending control request.

Since the *tp->tty_events* flag is raised by interrupts, and characters may arrive in a rapid stream from a fast device, there is a chance that by the time the calls to the device-specific read and write routines and *dev_ioctl* are completed, another interrupt will have raised the flag again. A high priority is placed on getting input moved along from the buffer where the interrupt routine places it initially. Thus *handle_events* repeats the calls to the device-specific routines as long as the *tp->tty_events* flag is found raised at the end of the loop (line 14389). When the flow of input stops (it also could be output, but input is more likely to make such repeated demands), *in_transfer* is called to transfer characters from the input queue to the buffer within the process that called for the read operation.

In_transfer itself sends a reply message if the transfer completes the request, either by transferring the maximum number of characters requested or by reaching the end of a line (in canonical mode). If it does so, *tp−>tty_left* will be zero upon the return to *handle_events*. Here a further test is made and a reply message is sent if the number of characters transferred has reached the minimum number requested. Testing *tp−>tty_inleft* prevents sending a duplicate message.

Next we will look at *in_transfer* (line 14416), which is responsible for moving data from the input queue in the driver's memory space to the buffer of the user process that requested the input. However, a straightforward block copy is not possible here. The input queue is a circular buffer and characters have to be checked to see that the end of the file has not been reached, or, if canonical mode is in effect, that the transfer only continues up through the end of a line. Also, the input queue is a queue of 16-bit quantities, but the recipient's buffer is an array of 8-bit characters. Thus an intermediate local buffer is used. Characters are checked one by one as they are placed in the local buffer, and when it fills up or when the input queue has been emptied, *sys_vircopy* is called to move the contents of the local buffer to the receiving process' buffer (lines 14432 to 14459).

Three variables in the *tty* structure, *tp−>tty_inleft*, *tp−>tty_eotct*, and *tp−>tty_min*, are used to decide whether *in_transfer* has any work to do, and the first two of these control its main loop. As mentioned earlier, *tp−>tty_inleft* is set initially to the number of characters requested by a read call. Normally, it is decremented by one whenever a character is transferred but it may be abruptly decreased to zero when a condition signaling the end of input is reached. Whenever it becomes zero, a reply message to the reader is generated, so it also serves as a flag to indicate whether or not a message has been sent. Thus in the test on line 14429, finding that *tp−>tty_inleft* is already zero is a sufficient reason to abort execution of *in_transfer* without sending a reply.

In the next part of the test, *tp−>tty_eotct* and *tp−>tty_min* are compared. In canonical mode both of these variables refer to complete lines of input, and in noncanonical mode they refer to characters. *Tp−>tty_eotct* is incremented whenever a "line break" or a byte is placed in the input queue and is decremented by *in_transfer* whenever a line or byte is removed from the queue. In other words, it counts the number of lines or bytes that have been received by the terminal driver but not yet passed on to a reader. *Tp−>tty_min* indicates the minimum number of lines (in canonical mode) or characters (in noncanonical mode) that must be transferred to complete a read request. Its value is always 1 in canonical mode and may be any value from 0 up to *MAX_INPUT* (255 in MINIX 3) in noncanonical mode. The second half of the test on line 14429 causes *in_transfer* to return immediately in canonical mode if a full line has not yet been received. The transfer is not done until a line is complete so the queue contents can be modified if, for instance, an ERASE or KILL character is subsequently typed in by the user before the ENTER key is pressed. In noncanonical mode an immediate return occurs if the minimum number of characters is not yet available.

A few lines later, *tp->tty_inleft* and *tp->tty_eotct* are used to control the main loop of *in_transfer*. In canonical mode the transfer continues until there is no longer a complete line left in the queue. In noncanonical mode *tp->tty_eotct* is a count of pending characters. *Tp->tty_min* controls whether the loop is entered but is not used in determining when to stop. Once the loop is entered, either all available characters or the number of characters requested in the original call will be transferred, whichever is smaller.

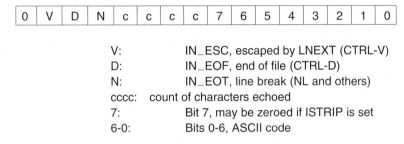

| 0 | V | D | N | c | c | c | c | 7 | 6 | 5 | 4 | 3 | 2 | 1 | 0 |

V:	IN_ESC, escaped by LNEXT (CTRL-V)
D:	IN_EOF, end of file (CTRL-D)
N:	IN_EOT, line break (NL and others)
cccc:	count of characters echoed
7:	Bit 7, may be zeroed if ISTRIP is set
6-0:	Bits 0-6, ASCII code

Figure 3-40. The fields in a character code as it is placed into the input queue.

Characters are 16-bit quantities in the input queue. The actual character code to be transferred to the user process is in the low 8 bits. Fig. 3-40 shows how the high bits are used. Three are used to flag whether the character is being escaped (by CTRL-V), whether it signifies end-of-file, or whether it represents one of several codes that signify a line is complete. Four bits are used for a count to show how much screen space is used when the character is echoed. The test on line 14435 checks whether the *IN_EOF* bit (*D* in the figure) is set. This is tested at the top of the inner loop because an end-of-file (CTRL-D) is not itself transferred to a reader, nor is it counted in the character count. As each character is transferred, a mask is applied to zero the upper 8 bits, and only the ASCII value in the low 8 bits is transferred into the local buffer (line 14437).

There is more than one way to signal the end of input, but the device-specific input routine is expected to determine whether a character received is a linefeed, CTRL-D, or other such character and to mark each such character. *In_transfer* only needs to test for this mark, the *IN_EOT* bit (*N* in Fig. 3-40), on line 14454. If this is detected, *tp->tty_eotct* is decremented. In noncanonical mode every character is counted this way as it is put into the input queue, and every character is also marked with the *IN_EOT* bit at that time, so *tp->tty_eotct* counts characters not yet removed from the queue. The only difference in the operation of the main loop of *in_transfer* in the two different modes is found on line 14457. Here *tp->tty_inleft* is zeroed in response to finding a character marked as a line break, but only if canonical mode is in effect. Thus when control returns to the top of the loop, the loop terminates properly after a line break in canonical mode, but in noncanonical line breaks are ignored.

When the loop terminates there is usually a partially full local buffer to be transferred (lines 14461 to 14468). Then a reply message is sent if *tp−>tty_inleft* has reached zero. This is always the case in canonical mode, but if noncanonical mode is in effect and the number of characters transferred is less than the full request, the reply is not sent. This may be puzzling if you have a good enough memory for details to remember that where we have seen calls to *in_transfer* (in *do_read* and *handle_events*), the code following the call to *in_transfer* sends a reply message if *in_transfer* returns having transferred more than the amount specified in *tp−>tty_min*, which will certainly be the case here. The reason why a reply is not made unconditionally from *in_transfer* will be seen when we discuss the next function, which calls *in_transfer* under a different set of circumstances.

That next function is *in_process* (line 14486). It is called from the device-specific software to handle the common processing that must be done on all input. Its parameters are a pointer to the *tty* structure for the source device, a pointer to the array of 8-bit characters to be processed, and a count. The count is returned to the caller. *In_process* is a long function, but its actions are not complicated. It adds 16-bit characters to the input queue that is later processed by *in_transfer*.

There are several categories of treatment provided by *in_transfer*.

1. Normal characters are added to the input queue, extended to 16 bits.

2. Characters which affect later processing modify flags to signal the effect but are not placed in the queue.

3. Characters which control echoing are acted upon immediately without being placed in the queue.

4. Characters with special significance have codes such as the *EOT* bit added to their high byte as they are placed in the input queue.

Let us look first at a completely normal situation: an ordinary character, such as "x" (ASCII code 0x78), typed in the middle of a short line, with no escape sequence in effect, on a terminal that is set up with the standard MINIX 3 default properties. As received from the input device this character occupies bits 0 through 7 in Fig. 3-40. On line 14504 it would have its most significant bit, bit 7, reset to zero if the *ISTRIP* bit were set, but the default in MINIX 3 is not to strip the bit, allowing full 8-bit codes to be entered. This would not affect our "x" anyway. The MINIX 3 default is to allow extended processing of input, so the test of the *IEXTEN* bit in *tp−>tty_termios.c_lflag* (line 14507) passes, but the succeeding tests fail under the conditions we postulate: no character escape is in effect (line 14510), this input is not itself the character escape character (line 14517), and this input is not the *REPRINT* character (line 14524).

Tests on the next several lines find that the input character is not the special *_POSIX_VDISABLE* character, nor is it a *CR* or an *NL*. Finally, a positive result:

canonical mode is in effect, this is the normal default (line 14324). However our "x" is not the *ERASE* character, nor is it any of the *KILL*, *EOF* (CTRL-D), *NL*, or *EOL* characters, so by line 14576 still nothing will have happened to it. Here it is found that the *IXON* bit is set, by default, allowing use of the *STOP* (CTRL-S) and *START* (CTRL-Q) characters, but in the ensuing tests for these no match is found. On line 14597 it is found that the *ISIG* bit, enabling the use of the *INTR* and *QUIT* characters, is set by default, but again no match is found.

In fact, the first interesting thing that might happen to an ordinary character occurs on line 14610, where a test is made to see if the input queue is already full. If this were the case, the character would be discarded at this point, since canonical mode is in effect, and the user would not see it echoed on the screen. (The continue statement discards the character, since it causes the outer loop to restart). However, since we postulate completely normal conditions for this illustration, let us assume the buffer is not full yet. The next test, to see if special noncanonical mode processing is needed (line 14616), fails, causing a jump forward to line 14629. Here *echo* is called to display the character to the user, since the *ECHO* bit in *tp−>tty_termios.c_lflag* is set by default.

Finally, on lines 14632 to 14636 the character is disposed of by being put into the input queue. At this time *tp−>tty_incount* is incremented, but since this is an ordinary character, not marked by the *EOT* bit, *tp−>tty_eotct* is not changed.

The last line in the loop calls *in_transfer* if the character just transferred into the queue fills it. However, under the ordinary conditions we postulate for this example, *in_transfer* would do nothing, even if called, since (assuming the queue has been serviced normally and previous input was accepted when the previous line of input was complete) *tp−>tty_eotct* is zero, *tp−>tty_min* is one, and the test at the start of *in_transfer* (line 14429) causes an immediate return.

Having passed through *in_process* with an ordinary character under ordinary conditions, let us now go back to the start of *in_process* and look at what happens in less ordinary circumstances. First, we will look at the character escape, which allows a character which ordinarily has a special effect to be passed on to the user process. If a character escape is in effect, the *tp−>tty_escaped* flag is set, and when this is detected (on line 14510) the flag is reset immediately and the *IN_ESC* bit, bit V in Fig. 3-40, is added to the current character. This causes special processing when the character is echoed—escaped control characters are displayed as "^" plus the character to make them visible. The *IN_ESC* bit also prevents the character from being recognized by tests for special characters.

The next few lines process the escape character itself, the *LNEXT* character (CTRL-V by default). When the *LNEXT* code is detected the *tp−>tty_escaped* flag is set, and *rawecho* is called twice to output a "^" followed by a backspace. This reminds the user at the keyboard that an escape is in effect, and when the following character is echoed, it overwrites the "^". The *LNEXT* character is an example of one that affects later characters (in this case, only the very next character). It is not placed in the queue, and the loop restarts after the two calls to *rawecho*. The order of these two tests is important, making it possible to enter the *LNEXT* character itself twice in a row, in order to pass the second copy on to a process as actual data.

The next special character processed by *in_process* is the *REPRINT* character (CTRL-R). When it is found a call to *reprint* ensues (line 14525), causing the current echoed output to be redisplayed. The *REPRINT* itself is then discarded with no effect upon the input queue.

Going into detail on the handling of every special character would be tedious, and the source code of *in_process* is straightforward. We will mention just a few more points. One is that the use of special bits in the high byte of the 16-bit value placed in the input queue makes it easy to identify a class of characters that have similar effects. Thus, *EOT* (CTRL-D), *LF*, and the alternate *EOL* character (undefined by default) are all marked by the *EOT* bit, bit D in Fig. 3-40 (lines 14566 to 14573), making later recognition easy.

Finally, we will justify the peculiar behavior of *in_transfer* noted earlier. A reply is not generated each time it terminates, although in the calls to *in_transfer* we have seen previously, it seemed that a reply would always be generated upon return. Recall that the call to *in_transfer* made by *in_process* when the input queue is full (line 14639) has no effect when canonical mode is in effect. But if noncanonical processing is desired, every character is marked with the *EOT* bit on line 14618, and thus every character is counted by *tp->tty_eotct* on line 14636. In turn, this causes entry into the main loop of *in_transfer* when it is called because of a full input queue in noncanonical mode. On such occasions no message should be sent at the termination of *in_transfer*, because there are likely to be more characters read after returning to *in_process*. Indeed, although in canonical mode input to a single read is limited by the size of the input queue (255 characters in MINIX 3), in noncanonical mode a read call must be able to deliver the POSIX-required constant *_POSIX_SSIZE_MAX* number of characters. Its value in MINIX 3 is 32767.

The next few functions in *tty.c* support character input. *Tty_echo* (line 14647) treats a few characters in a special way, but most just get displayed on the output side of the same device being used for input. Output from a process may be going to a device at the same time input is being echoed, which makes things messy if the user at the keyboard tries to backspace. To deal with this, the *tp->tty_reprint* flag is always set to *TRUE* by the device-specific output routines when normal output is produced, so the function called to handle a backspace can tell that mixed output has been produced. Since *tty_echo* also uses the device-output routines, the current value of *tp->tty_reprint* is preserved while echoing, using the local variable *rp* (lines 14668 to 14701). However, if a new line of input has just begun, *rp* is set to *FALSE* instead of taking on the old value, thus assuring that *tp->tty_reprint* will be reset when *echo* terminates.

You may have noticed that *tty_echo* returns a value, for instance, in the call on line 14629 in *in_process*:

ch = tty_echo(tp, ch)

The value returned by *echo* contains the number of spaces used on the screen for the echo display, which may be up to eight if the character is a *TAB*. This count is placed in the *cccc* field in Fig. 3-40. Ordinary characters occupy one space on the screen, but if a control character (other than *TAB*, *NL*, or *CR* or a *DEL* (0x7F) is echoed, it is displayed as a "^" plus a printable ASCII character and occupies two positions on the screen. On the other hand an *NL* or *CR* occupies zero spaces. The actual echoing must be done by a device-specific routine, of course, and whenever a character must be passed to the device, an indirect call is made using *tp->tty_echo*, as, for instance, on line 14696, for ordinary characters.

The next function, *rawecho*, is used to bypass the special handling done by *echo*. It checks to see if the *ECHO* flag is set, and if it is, sends the character along to the device-specific *tp->tty_echo* routine without any special processing. A local variable *rp* is used here to prevent *rawecho*'s own call to the output routine from changing the value of *tp->tty_reprint*.

When a backspace is found by *in_process*, the next function, *back_over* (line 14721), is called. It manipulates the input queue to remove the previous head of the queue if backing up is possible—if the queue is empty or if the last character is a line break, then backing up is not possible. Here the *tp->tty_reprint* flag mentioned in the discussions of *echo* and *rawecho* is tested. If it is *TRUE*, then *reprint* is called (line 14732) to put a clean copy of the output line on the screen. Then the *len* field of the last character displayed (the *cccc* field of Fig. 3-40) is consulted to find out how many characters have to be deleted on the display, and for each character a sequence of backspace-space-backspace characters is sent through *rawecho* to remove the unwanted character from the screen and have it replaced by a space.

Reprint is the next function. In addition to being called by *back_over*, it may be invoked by the user pressing the *REPRINT* key (CTRL-R). The loop on lines 14764 to 14769 searches backward through the input queue for the last line break. If it is found in the last position filled, there is nothing to do and *reprint* returns. Otherwise, it echos the CTRL-R, which appears on the display as the two character sequence "^R", and then moves to the next line and redisplays the queue from the last line break to the end.

Now we have arrived at *out_process* (line 14789). Like *in_process*, it is called by device-specific output routines, but it is simpler. It is called by the RS-232 and pseudo terminal device-specific output routines, but not by the console routine. *Out_process* works upon a circular buffer of bytes but does not remove them from the buffer. The only change it makes to the array is to insert a *CR* character ahead of an *NL* character in the buffer if the *OPOST* (enable output processing) and *ONLCR* (map NL to CR-NL) bits in *tp->tty_termios.oflag* are both set. Both bits are set by default in MINIX 3. Its job is to keep the *tp->tty_position* variable in the device's *tty* structure up to date. Tabs and backspaces complicate life.

The next routine is *dev_ioctl* (line 14874). It supports *do_ioctl* in carrying out the *tcdrain* function and the *tcsetattr* function when it is called with either the *TCSADRAIN* or *TCSAFLUSH* options. In these cases, *do_ioctl* cannot complete the action immediately if output is incomplete, so information about the request is stored in the parts of the *tty* structure reserved for delayed ioctl operations. Whenever *handle_events* runs, it first checks the *tp−>tty_ioreq* field after calling the device-specific output routine and calls *dev_ioctl* if an operation is pending. *Dev_ioctl* tests *tp−>tty_outleft* to see if output is complete, and if so, carries out the same actions that *do_ioctl* would have carried out immediately if there had been no delay. To service *tcdrain*, the only action is to reset the *tp−>tty_ioreq* field and send the reply message to the FS, telling it to wake up the process that made the original call. The *TCSAFLUSH* variant of *tcsetattr* calls *tty_icancel* to cancel input. For both variants of *tcsetattr*, the *termios* structure whose address was passed in the original call to ioctl is copied to the device's *tp−>tty_termios* structure. *Setattr* is then called, followed, as with *tcdrain*, by sending a reply message to wake up the blocked original caller.

Setattr (line 14899) is the next procedure. As we have seen, it is called by *do_ioctl* or *dev_ioctl* to change the attributes of a terminal device, and by *do_close* to reset the attributes back to the default settings. *Setattr* is always called after copying a new *termios* structure into a device's *tty* structure, because merely copying the parameters is not enough. If the device being controlled is now in noncanonical mode, the first action is to mark all characters currently in the input queue with the *IN_EOT* bit, as would have been done when these characters were originally entered in the queue if noncanonical mode had been in effect then. It is easier just to go ahead and do this (lines 14913 to 14919) than to test whether the characters already have the bit set. There is no way to know which attributes have just been changed and which still retain their old values.

The next action is to check the *MIN* and *TIME* values. In canonical mode *tp−>tty_min* is always 1; that is set on line 14926. In noncanonical mode the combination of the two values allows for four different modes of operation, as we saw in Fig. 3-31. On lines 14931 to 14933 *tp−>tty_min* is first set up with the value passed in *tp−>tty_termios.cc[VMIN]*, which is then modified if it is zero and *tp−>tty_termios.cc[VTIME]* is not zero.

Finally, *setattr* makes sure output is not stopped if XON/XOFF control is disabled, sends a *SIGHUP* signal if the output speed is set to zero, and makes an indirect call to the device-specific routine pointed to by *tp−>tty_ioctl* to do what can only be done at the device level.

The next function, *tty_reply* (line 14952) has been mentioned many times in the preceding discussion. Its action is entirely straightforward, constructing a message and sending it. If for some reason the reply fails, a panic ensues. The following functions are equally simple. *Sigchar* (line 14973) asks MM to send a signal. If the *NOFLSH* flag is not set, queued input is removed—the count of characters or lines received is zeroed and the pointers to the tail and head of the queue are equated. This is the default action. When a *SIGHUP* signal is to be caught, *NOFLSH* can be set, to allow input and output to resume after catching the signal. *Tty_icancel* (line 15000) unconditionally discards pending input in the way described for *sigchar*, and in addition calls the device-specific function pointed to by *tp−>tty_icancel*, to cancel input that may exist in the device itself or be buffered in the low-level code.

Tty_init (line 15013) is called when *tty_task* first starts. It loops through all possible terminals and sets up defaults. Initially, a pointer to *tty_devnop*, a dummy function that does nothing, is set into the *tp−>tty_icancel*, *tp−>tty_ocancel*, *tp−>tty_ioctl*, and *tp−>tty_close* variables. *Tty_init* then calls a device-specific initialization functions for the appropriate category of terminal (console, serial line, or pseudo terminal). These set up the real pointers to indirectly called device-specific functions. Recall that if there are no devices at all configured in a particular device category, a macro that returns immediately is created, so no part of the code for a nonconfigured device need be compiled. The call to *scr_init* initializes the console driver and also calls the initialization routine for the keyboard.

The next three functions support timers. A watchdog timer is initialized with a pointer to a function to run when the timer expires. *Tty_timed_out* is that function for most timers set by the terminal task. It sets the events flag to force processing of input and output. *Expire_timers* handles the terminal driver's timer queue. Recall that this is the function called from the main loop of *tty_task* when a *SYN_ALARM* message is received. A library routine, *tmrs_exptimers*, is used to traverse the linked list of timers, expiring and calling the watchdog functions of any that have timed out. On returning from the library function, if the queue is still active a sys_setalarm kernel call is made to ask for another *SYN_ALARM*. Finally, *settimer* (line 15089), sets timers for determining when to return from a read call in noncanonical mode. It is called with parameters of *tty_ptr*, a pointer to a *tty* structure, and *enable*, an integer which represents *TRUE* or *FALSE*. Library functions *tmrs_settimer* and *tmrs_clrtimer* are used to enable or disable a timer as determined by the *enable* argument. When a timer is enabled, the watchdog function is always *tty_timed_out*, described previously.

A description of *tty_devnop* (line 15125) is necessarily longer than its executable code, since it has none. It is a "no-operation" function to be indirectly addressed where a device does not require a service. We have seen *tty_devnop* used in *tty_init* as the default value entered into various function pointers before calling the initialization routine for a device.

The final item in *tty.c* needs some explanation. Select is a system call used when multiple I/O devices may require service at unpredictable times by a single process. A classic example is a communications program which needs to pay attention to a local keyboard and a remote system, perhaps connected by a modem. The select call allows opening several device files and monitoring all of them to see when they can be read from or written to without blocking. Without select it is necessary to use two processes to handle two-way communication, one acting as a master and handling communication in one direction, the other a slave handling communication in the other direction. Select is an example of a feature that is very nice to have, but which substantially complicates the system. One of the design goals of MINIX 3 is to be simple enough to be understood with reasonable effort in a reasonable time, and we have to set some limits. For that reason we will not discuss *do_select* (line 15135) and the support routines *select_try* (line 14313) and *select_retry* (line 14348) here.

3.8.5 Implementation of the Keyboard Driver

Now we turn to the device-dependent code that supports the MINIX 3 console, which consists of an IBM PC keyboard and a memory-mapped display. The physical devices that support these are entirely separate: on a standard desktop system the display uses an adapter card (of which there are at least a half-dozen basic types) plugged into the backplane, while the keyboard is supported by circuitry built into the parentboard which interfaces with an 8-bit single-chip computer inside the keyboard unit. The two subdevices require entirely separate software support, which is found in the files *keyboard.c* and *console.c*.

The operating system sees the keyboard and console as parts of the same device, */dev/console*. If there is enough memory available on the display adapter, **virtual console** support may be compiled, and in addition to */dev/console* there may be additional logical devices, */dev/ttyc1*, */dev/ttyc2*, and so on. Output from only one goes to the display at any given time, and there is only one keyboard to use for input to whichever console is active. Logically the keyboard is subservient to the console, but this is manifested in only two relatively minor ways. First, *tty_table* contains a *tty* structure for the console, and where separate fields are provided for input and output, for instance, the *tty_devread* and *tty_devwrite* fields, pointers to functions in *keyboard.c* and *console.c* are filled in at startup time. However, there is only one *tty_priv* field, and this points to the console's data structures only. Second, before entering its main loop, *tty_task* calls each logical device once to initialize it. The routine called for */dev/console* is in *console.c*, and the initialization code for the keyboard is called from there. The implied hierarchy could just as well have been reversed, however. We have always looked at input before output in dealing with I/O devices and we will continue that pattern, discussing *keyboard.c* in this section and leaving the discussion of *console.c* for the following section.

Keyboard.c begins, like most source files we have seen, with several #include statements. One of these is unusual, however. The file *keymaps/us-std.src* (included on line 15218) is not an ordinary header; it is a C source file that results in compilation of the default keymap within *keyboard.o* as an initialized array. The keymap source file is not included in Appendix B because of its size, but some representative entries are illustrated in Fig. 3-37. Following the #include statements are macros to define various constants. The first group are used in low-level interaction with the keyboard controller. Many of these are I/O port addresses or bit combinations that have meaning in these interactions. The next group includes symbolic names for special keys. On line 15249 the size of the circular keyboard input buffer is symbolically defined as *KB_IN_BYTES*, with a value of 32, and the buffer itself and variables to manage it are defined next. Since there is only one of these buffers care must be taken to make sure all of its contents are processed before virtual consoles are changed.

The next group of variables are used to hold various states that must be remembered to properly interpret a key press. They are used in different ways. For instance, the value of the *caps_down* flag (line 15266) is toggled between *TRUE* and *FALSE* each time the Caps Lock key is pressed. The *shift* flag (line 15264) is set to *TRUE* when either Shift key is pressed and to *FALSE* when both Shift keys are released. The *esc* variable is set when a scan code escape is received. It is always reset upon receipt of the following character.

Map_key0 (line 15297) is defined as a macro. It returns the ASCII code that corresponds to a scan code, ignoring modifiers. This is equivalent to the first column (unshifted) in the keymap array. Its big brother is *map_key* (line 15303), which performs the complete mapping of a scan code to an ASCII code, including accounting for (multiple) modifier keys that are depressed at the same time as ordinary keys.

The keyboard interrupt service routine is *kbd_interrupt* (line 15335), called whenever a key is pressed or released. It calls *scode* to get the scan code from the keyboard controller chip. The most significant bit of the scan code is set when a key release causes the interrupt, such codes could be ignored unless they were one of the modifier keys. However, in the interest of doing as little as possible in order to service an interrupt as quickly as possible, all raw scan codes are placed in the circular buffer and the *tp->tty_events* flag for the current console is raised (line 15350). For purposes of this discussion we will assume, as we did earlier, that no select calls have been made, and that *kbd_interrupt* returns immediately after this. Figure 3-41 shows scan codes in the buffer for a short line of input that contains two upper case characters, each preceded by the scan code for depression of a shift key and followed by the code for the release of the shift key. Initially codes for both key presses and releases are stored.

When a *HARD_INT* from the keyboard is received by *tty_task*, the complete main loop is not executed. A continue statement at line 13795 causes a new iteration of the main loop to begin immediately, at line 13764. (This is slightly simplified, we left some conditional code in the listing to show that if the serial line driver is enabled its user-space interrupt handler could also be called.) When execution transfers to the top of the loop the *tp->tty_events* flag for the console device is now found to be set, and *kb_read* (line 15360), the device-specific routine, is called using the pointer in the *tp->tty_devread* field of the console's *tty* structure.

42	35	163	170	18	146	38	166	38	166	24	152	57	185
L+	h+	h-	L-	e+	e-	l+	l-	l+	l-	o+	o-	SP+	SP-

54	17	145	182	24	152	19	147	38	166	32	160	28	156
R+	w+	w-	R-	o+	o-	r+	r-	l+	l-	d+	d-	CR+	CR-

Figure 3-41. Scan codes in the input buffer, with corresponding key actions below, for a line of text entered at the keyboard. L and R represent the left and right Shift keys. + and - indicate a key press and a key release. The code for a release is 128 more than the code for a press of the same key.

Kb_read takes scan codes from the keyboard's circular buffer and places ASCII codes in its local buffer, which is large enough to hold the escape sequences that must be generated in response to some scan codes from the numeric keypad. Then it calls *in_process* in the hardware-independent code to put the characters into the input queue. On line 15379 *icount* is decremented. The call to *make_break* returns the ASCII code as an integer. Special keys, such as keypad and function keys, have values greater than 0xFF at this point. Codes in the range from *HOME* to *INSRT* (0x101 to 0x10C, defined in file *include/minix/keymap.h*) result from pressing the numeric keypad, and are converted into 3-character escape sequences shown in Fig. 3-42 using the *numpad_map* array.

The sequences are then passed to *in_process* (lines 15392 to 15397). Higher codes are not passed on to *in_process*. Instead, a check is made for the codes for ALT-LEFT-ARROW, ALT-RIGHT-ARROW, and ALT-F1 through ALT-F12, and if one of these is found, *select_console* is called to switch virtual consoles. CTRL-F1 through CTRL-F12 are similarly given special handling. CTRL-F1 shows the mappings of function keys (more on this later). CTRL-F3 toggles between hardware scrolling and software scrolling of the console screen. CTRL-F7, CTRL-F8, and CTRL-F9 generate signals with the same effects as CTRL-\, CTRL-C, and CTRL-U, respectively, except these cannot be changed by the stty command.

Make_break (line 15431) converts scan codes into ASCII and then updates the variables that keep track of the state of modifier keys. First, however, it checks for the magic CTRL-ALT-DEL combination that PC users all know as the way to force a reboot under MS-DOS. Note the comment that it would be better to do this at a lower level. However, the simplicity of MINIX 3 interrupt handling in kernel space makes detecting CTRL-ALT-DEL impossible there, when an interrupt notification is sent the scan code has not yet been read.

An orderly shutdown is desirable, so rather than try to start the PC BIOS routines, a sys_kill kernel call is made to initiate sending a *SIGKILL* signal TO *init*, the parent process of all other processes (line 15448). *Init* is expected to catch

Key	Scan code	"ASCII"	Escape sequence
Home	71	0x101	ESC [H
Up Arrow	72	0x103	ESC [A
Pg Up	73	0x107	ESC [V
–	74	0x10A	ESC [S
Left Arrow	75	0x105	ESC [D
5	76	0x109	ESC [G
Right Arrow	77	0x106	ESC [C
+	78	0x10B	ESC [T
End	79	0x102	ESC [Y
Down Arrow	80	0x104	ESC [B
Pg Dn	81	0x108	ESC [U
Ins	82	0x10C	ESC [@

Figure 3-42. Escape codes generated by the numeric keypad. When scan codes for ordinary keys are translated into ASCII codes the special keys are assigned "pseudo ASCII" codes with values greater than 0xFF.

this signal and interpret it as a command to begin an orderly process of shutting down, prior to causing a return to the boot monitor, from which a full restart of the system or a reboot of MINIX 3 can be commanded.

Of course, it is not realistic to expect this to work every time. Most users understand the dangers of an abrupt shutdown and do not press CTRL-ALT-DEL until something is really going wrong and normal control of the system has become impossible. At this point it is likely that the system may be so disrupted that signaling another process may be impossible. This is why there is a *static* variable *CAD_count* in *make_break*. Most system crashes leave the interrupt system still functioning, so keyboard input can still be received and the terminal driver will remain active. Here MINIX 3 takes advantage of the expected behavior of computer users, who are likely to bang on the keys repeatedly when something does not seem to work correctly (possibly evidence our ancestors really were apes). If the attempt to kill *init* fails and the user presses CTRL-ALT-DEL twice more, a sys_abort kernel call is made, causing a return to the monitor without going through the call to *init*.

The main part of *make_break* is not hard to follow. The variable *make* records whether the scan code was generated by a key press or a key release, and then the call to *map_key* returns the ASCII code to *ch*. Next is a switch on *ch* (lines 15460 to 15499). Let us consider two cases, an ordinary key and a special key. For an ordinary key, none of the cases match, and in the default case (line 15498), the key code is returned if *make* is true. If somehow an ordinary key code is accepted at key release, a value of −1 is substituted here, and this is ignored by the caller, *kb_read*. A special key, for example *CTRL*, is identified at the appropriate place in the switch, in this case on line 15461. The corresponding variable, in this case *ctrl*, records the state of *make*, and −1 is substituted for the character code to be returned (and ignored). The handling of the *ALT*, *CALOCK*, *NLOCK*, and *SLOCK* keys is more complicated, but for all of these special keys the effect is similar: a variable records either the current state (for keys that are only effective while pressed) or toggles the previous state (for the lock keys).

There is one more case to consider, that of the *EXTKEY* code and the *esc* variable. This is not to be confused with the ESC key on the keyboard, which returns the ASCII code 0x1B. There is no way to generate the *EXTKEY* code alone by pressing any key or combination of keys; it is the PC keyboard's **extended key prefix**, the first byte of a 2-byte scan code that signifies that a key that was not part of the original PC's complement of keys but that has the same scan code, has been pressed. In many cases software treats the two keys identically. For instance, this is almost always the case for the normal "/" key and the gray "/" key on the numeric keyboard. In other cases, one would like to distinguish between such keys. For instance, many keyboard layouts for languages other than English treat the left and right ALT keys differently, to support keys that must generate three different character codes. Both ALT keys generate the same scan code (56), but the *EXTKEY* code precedes this when the right-hand ALT is pressed. When the *EXTKEY* code is returned, the *esc* flag is set. In this case, *make_break* returns from within the switch, thus bypassing the last step before a normal return, which sets *esc* to zero in every other case (line 15458). This has the effect of making the *esc* effective only for the very next code received. If you are familiar with the intricacies of the PC keyboard as it is ordinarily used, this will be both familiar and yet a little strange, because the PC BIOS does not allow one to read the scan code for an ALT key and returns a different value for the extended code than does MINIX 3.

Set_leds (line 15508) turns on and off the lights that indicate whether the Num Lock, Caps Lock, or Scroll Lock keys on a PC keyboard have been pressed. A control byte, *LED_CODE*, is written to an output port to instruct the keyboard that the next byte written to that port is for control of the lights, and the status of the three lights is encoded in 3 bits of that next byte. These operations are, of course, carried out by kernel calls which ask the system task write to the outport ports. The next two functions support this operation. *Kb_wait* (line 15530) is called to determine that the keyboard is ready to receive a command sequence, and *kb_ack* (line 15552) is called to verify that the command has been acknowledged. Both of these commands use busy waiting, continually reading until a desired code is seen. This is not a recommended technique for handling most I/O operations, but turning lights on and off on the keyboard is not going to be done very often and doing it inefficiently does not waste much time. Note also that both *kb_wait* and *kb_ack* could fail, and one can determine from the return code if this happens. Timeouts are handled by limiting the number of retries by means of a counter in the loop. But setting the light on the keyboard is not important enough to merit checking the value returned by either call, and *set_leds* just proceeds blindly.

Since the keyboard is part of the console, its initialization routine, *kb_init* (line 15572), is called from *scr_init* in *console.c*, not directly from *tty_init* in *tty.c*. If virtual consoles are enabled, (i.e., *NR_CONS* in *include/minix/config.h* is greater than 1), *kb_init* is called once for each logical console. The next function, *kb_init_once* (line 15583), is called just once, as its name implies. It sets the lights on the keyboard, and scans the keyboard to be sure no leftover keystroke is read. Then it initializes two arrays, *fkey_obs* and *sfkey_obs* which are used to bind function keys to the processes that must respond to them. When all is ready, it makes two kernel calls, sys_irqsetpolicy and sys_irqenable to set up the IRQ for the keyboard and configure it to automatically reenable, so a notification message will be sent to *tty_task* whenever a key is pressed or released.

Although we will soon have more opportunities to discuss how function keys work, this is a good place to describe the *fkey_obs* and *sfkey_obs* arrays. Each has twelve elements, since modern PC keyboards have twelve F-keys. The first array is for unmodified F-keys, the second is used when a shifted F-key is detected. They are composed of elements of type *obs_t*, which is a structure that can hold a process number and an integer. This structure and these arrays are declared in *keyboard.c* on lines 15279 to 15281. Initialization stores a special value, symbolically represented as *NONE*, in the *proc_nr* component of the structure to indicate it is not in use. *NONE* is a value outside the range of valid process numbers. Note that the process number is not a *pid*, it identifies a slot in the process table. This terminology may be confusing. But to send a notification a process number rather than a *pid* is used, because process numbers are used to index the *priv* table which determines whether a process is allowed to receive notifications. The integer *events* is also initially set to zero. It will be used to count events.

The next three functions are all rather simple. *Kbd_loadmap* (line 15610) is almost trivial. It is called by *do_ioctl* in *tty.c* to do the copying of a keymap from user space to overwrite the default keymap. The default is compiled by the inclusion of a keymap source file at the start of *keyboard.c*.

From its first release, MINIX has always provided for dumps of various kinds of system information or other special actions in response to pressing the function keys F1, F2, etc., on the system console. This is not a service generally provided in other operating systems, but MINIX was always intended to be a teaching tool. Users are encouraged to tinker with it, which means users may need extra help for debugging. In many cases the output produced by pressing one of the F-keys will be available even when the system has crashed. Figure 3-43 summarizes these keys and their effects.

These keys fall into two categories. As noted earlier, the CTRL-F1 through CTRL-F12 key combinations are detected by *kb_read*. These trigger events that

Key	Purpose
F1	Kernel process table
F2	Process memory maps
F3	Boot image
F4	Process privileges
F5	Boot monitor parameters
F6	IRQ hooks and policies
F7	Kernel messages
F10	Kernel parameters
F11	Timing details (if enabled)
F12	Scheduling queues
SF1	Process manager process table
SF2	Signals
SF3	File system process table
SF4	Device/driver mapping
SF5	Print key mappings
SF9	Ethernet statistics (RTL8139 only)
CF1	Show key mappings
CF3	Toggle software/hardware console scrolling
CF7	Send SIGQUIT, same effect as CTRL-\
CF8	Send SIGINT, same effect as CTRL-C
CF9	Send SIGKILL, same effect as CTRL-U

Figure 3-43. The function keys detected by *func_key()*.

can be handled by the terminal driver. These events are not necessarily display dumps. In fact, currently only CTRL-F1 provides an information display; it lists function key bindings. CTRL-F3 toggles hardware and software scrolling of the console screen, and the others cause signals.

Function keys pressed by themselves or together with the shift key are used to trigger events that cannot be handled by the terminal driver. They may result in notification messages to a server or driver. Because servers and drivers can be loaded, enabled, and disabled after MINIX 3 is already running, static binding of these keys at compilation time is not satisfactory. To enable run-time changes *tty_task* accepts messages of type *FKEY_CONTROL*. *Do_fkey_ctl* (line 15624) services such requests. Request types are *FKEY_MAP*, *FKEY_UNMAP*, or *FKEY_EVENTS*. The first two register or unregister a process with a key specified in a bitmap in the message, and the third message type returns a bitmap of keys belonging to the caller which have been pressed and resets the *events* field for these keys. A server process, the **information server**, (or **IS**) initializes the settings for processes in the boot image and also mediates generating responses. But individual drivers can also register to respond to a function key. Ethernet drivers typically do this, as a dump that shows packet statistics can be helpful in solving network problems.

Func_key (line 15715) is called from *kb_read* to see if a special key meant for local processing has been pressed. This is done for every scan code received, prior to any other processing. If it is not a function key at most three comparisons are made before control is returned to *kb_read*. If a function key is registered a notification message is sent to the appropriate process. If the process is one that has registered only one key the notification by itself is adequate for the process to know what to do. If a process is the information server or another that has registered several keys, a dialogue is required—the process must send an *FKEY_EVENTS* request to the terminal driver, to be processed by *do_fkey_ctl* which will inform the caller which keys have been active. The caller can then dispatch to the routine for each key that has been pressed.

Scan_keyboard (line 15800) works at the hardware interface level, by reading and writing bytes from I/O ports. The keyboard controller is informed that a character has been read by the sequence on lines 15809 and 15810, which reads a byte, writes it again with the most significant bit set to 1, and then rewrites it with the same bit rest to 0. This prevents the same data from being read on a subsequent read. There is no status checking in reading the keyboard, but there should be no problems in any case, since *scan_keyboard* is only called in response to an interrupt.

The last function in *keyboard.c* is *do_panic_dumps* (line 15819). If invoked as a result of a system panic, it provides an opportunity for the user to use the function keys to display debugging information. The loop on lines 15830 to 15854 is another example of busy waiting. The keyboard is read repeatedly until an ESC is typed. Certainly no one can claim that a more efficient technique is needed after a crash, while awaiting a command to reboot. Within the loop, the rarely-used nonblocking receive operation, nb_receive, is used to permit alternately accepting messages, if available, and testing the keyboard for input, which can be expected to be one of the options suggested in the message

    Hit ESC to reboot, DEL to shutdown, F-keys for debug dumps

printed on entering this function. In the next section we will see the code that implements *do_newkmess* and *do_diagnostics*.

3.8.6 Implementation of the Display Driver

The IBM PC display may be configured as several virtual terminals, if sufficient memory is available. We will examine the console's device-dependent code in this section. We will also look at the debug dump routines that use low-level services of the keyboard and display. These provide support for limited interaction with the user at the console, even when other parts of the MINIX 3 system are not functioning and can provide useful information even following a near-total system crash.

Hardware-specific support for console output to the PC memory-mapped screen is in *console.c*. The *console* structure is defined on lines 15981 to 15998. In a sense this structure is an extension of the *tty* structure defined in *tty.c*. At initialization the *tp−>tty_priv* field of a console's *tty* structure is assigned a pointer to its own *console* structure. The first item in the *console* structure is a pointer back to the corresponding *tty* structure. The components of a *console* structure are what one would expect for a video display: variables to record the row and column of the cursor location, the memory addresses of the start and limit of memory used for the display, the memory address pointed to by the controller chip's base pointer, and the current address of the cursor. Other variables are used for managing escape sequences. Since characters are initially received as 8-bit bytes and must be combined with attribute bytes and transferred as 16-bit words to video memory, a block to be transferred is built up in *c_ramqueue*, an array big enough to hold an entire 80-column row of 16-bit character-attribute pairs. Each virtual console needs one *console* structure, and the storage is allocated in the array *cons_table* (line 16001). As we have done with the *tty* and other structures, we will usually refer to the elements of a *console* structure using a pointer, for example, *cons−>c_tty*.

The function whose address is stored in each console's *tp−>tty_devwrite* entry is *cons_write* (line 16036). It is called from only one place, *handle_events* in *tty.c*. Most of the other functions in *console.c* exist to support this function. When it is called for the first time after a client process makes a write call, the data to be output are in the client's buffer, which can be found using the *tp−>tty_outproc* and *tp−>out_vir* fields in the *tty* structure. The *tp−>tty_outleft* field tells how many characters are to be transferred, and the *tp−>tty_outcum* field is initially zero, indicating none have yet been transferred. This is the usual situation upon entry to *cons_write*, because normally, once called, it transfers all the data requested in the original call. However, if the user wants to slow the process in order to review the data on the screen, he may enter a *STOP* (CTRL-S) character at the keyboard, resulting in raising of the *tp−>tty_inhibited* flag. *Cons_write* returns immediately when this flag is raised, even though the write has not been completed. In such a case *handle_events* will continue to call *cons_write*, and when *tp−>tty_inhibited* is finally reset, by the user entering a *START* (CTRL-Q) character, *cons_write* continues with the interrupted transfer.

Cons_write's first argument is a pointer to the particular console's *tty* structure, so the first thing that must be done is to initialize *cons*, the pointer to this console's *console* structure (line 16049). Then, because *handle_events* calls *cons_write* whenever it runs, the first action is a test to see if there really is work to be done. A quick return is made if not (line 16056). Following this the main loop on lines 16061 to 16089 is entered. This loop is similar in structure to the main loop of *in_transfer* in *tty.c*. A local buffer that can hold 64 characters is filled by using the *sys_vircopy* kernel call to get the data from the client's buffer. Following this, the pointer to the source and the counts are updated, and then each character in the local buffer is transferred to the *cons−>c_ramqueue* array, along with an attribute byte, for later transfer to the screen by *flush*.

The transfer of characters from *cons−>c_ramqueue* can be done in more than one way, as we saw in Fig. 3-35. *Out_char* can be called to do this for each character, but it is predictable that none of the special services of *out_char* will be needed if the character is a visible character, an escape sequence is not in progress, the screen width has not been exceeded, and *cons−>c_ramqueue* is not full. If the full service of *out_char* is not needed, the character is placed directly into *cons−>c_ramqueue*, along with the attribute byte (which is retrieved from *cons−>c_attr*), and *cons−>c_rwords* (which is the index into the queue), *cons−>c_column* (which keeps track of the column on the screen), and *tbuf*, the pointer into the buffer, are all incremented. This direct placement of characters into *cons−>c_ramqueue* corresponds to the dashed line on the left side of Fig. 3-35. If needed, *out_char* is called (line 16082). It does all of the bookkeeping, and additionally calls *flush*, which does the final transfer to screen memory, when necessary.

The transfer from the user buffer to the local buffer to the queue is repeated as long as *tp−>tty_outleft* indicates there are still characters to be transferred and the flag *tp−>tty_inhibited* has not been raised. When the transfer stops, whether because the write operation is complete or because *tp−>tty_inhibited* has been raised, *flush* is called again to transfer the last characters in the queue to screen memory. If the operation is complete (tested by seeing if *tp−>tty_outleft* is zero), a reply message is sent by calling *tty_reply* lines 16096 and 16097).

In addition to calls to *cons_write* from *handle_events*, characters to be displayed are also sent to the console by *echo* and *rawecho* in the hardware-independent part of the terminal driver. If the console is the current output device, calls via the *tp−>tty_echo* pointer are directed to the next function, *cons_echo* (line 16105). *Cons_echo* does all of its work by calling *out_char* and then *flush*. Input from the keyboard arrives character by character and the person doing the typing wants to see the echo with no perceptible delay, so putting characters into the output queue would be unsatisfactory.

Out_char (line 16119). does a test to see if an escape sequence is in progress, calling *parse_escape* and then returning immediately if so (lines 16124 to 16126). Otherwise, a switch is entered to check for special cases: null, backspace, the bell character, and so on. The handling of most of these is easy to follow. The linefeed and the tab are the most complicated, since they involve complicated changes to the position of the cursor on the screen and may require scrolling as well. The last test is for the *ESC* code. If it is found, the *cons−>c_esc_state* flag is set (line 16181), and future calls to *out_char* are diverted to *parse_escape* until the sequence is complete. At the end, the default is taken for printable characters. If the screen width has been exceeded, the screen may need to be scrolled, and *flush* is called. Before a character is placed in the output queue a test is made to see that the queue is not full, and *flush* is called if it is. Putting a character into the queue requires the same bookkeeping we saw earlier in *cons_write*.

The next function is *scroll_screen* (line 16205). *Scroll_screen* handles both scrolling up, the normal situation that must be dealt with whenever the bottom line on the screen is full, and scrolling down, which occurs when cursor positioning commands attempt to move the cursor beyond the top line of the screen. For each direction of scroll there are three possible methods. These are required to support different kinds of video cards.

We will look at the scrolling up case. To begin, *chars* is assigned the size of the screen minus one line. Softscrolling is accomplished by a single call to *vid_vid_copy* to move *chars* characters lower in memory, the size of the move being the number of characters in a line. *Vid_vid_copy* can wrap, that is, if asked to move a block of memory that overflows the upper end of the block assigned to the video display, it fetches the overflow portion from the low end of the memory block and moves it to an address higher than the part that is moved lower, treating the entire block as a circular array. The simplicity of the call hides a fairly slow operation, even though *vid_vid_copy* is an assembly language routine (defined in *drivers/tty/vidcopy.s*, not listed in Appendix B). This call requires the CPU to move 3840 bytes, which is a large job even in assembly language.

The softscroll method is never the default; the operator is supposed to select it only if hardware scrolling does not work or is not desired for some reason. One reason might be a desire to use the *screendump* command, either to save the screen memory in a file or to view the main console display when working from a remote terminal. When hardware scrolling is in effect, *screendump* is likely to give unexpected results, because the start of the screen memory is likely not to coincide with the start of the visible display.

On line 16226 the *wrap* variable is tested as the first part of a compound test. *Wrap* is true for older displays that can support hardware scrolling, and if the test fails, simple hardware scrolling occurs on line 16230, where the origin pointer used by the video controller chip, *cons->c_org*, is updated to point to the first character to be displayed at the upper-left corner of the display. If *wrap* is *FALSE*, the compound test continues with a test of whether the block to be moved up in the scroll operation overflows the bounds of the memory block designated for this console. If this is so, *vid_vid_copy* is called again to make a wrapped move of the block to the start of the console's allocated memory, and the origin pointer is updated. If there is no overlap, control passes to the simple hardware scrolling method always used by older video controllers. This consists of adjusting *cons->c_org* and then putting the new origin in the correct register of the controller chip. The call to do this is executed later, as is a call to blank the bottom line on the screen to achieve the "scrolling" effect.

The code for scrolling down is very similar to that for scrolling up. Finally, *mem_vid_copy* is called to blank out the line at the bottom (or top) addressed by *new_line*. Then *set_6845* is called to write the new origin from *cons->c_org* into the appropriate registers, and *flush* makes sure all changes become visible on the screen.

We have mentioned *flush* (line 16259) several times. It transfers the characters in the queue to the video memory using *mem_vid_copy*, updates some variables, and then makes sure the row and column numbers are reasonable, adjusting them if, for instance, an escape sequence has tried to move the cursor to a negative column position. Finally, a calculation of where the cursor ought to be is made and is compared with *cons->c_cur*. If they do not agree, and if the video memory that is currently being handled belongs to the current virtual console, a call to *set_6845* is made to set the correct value in the controller's cursor register.

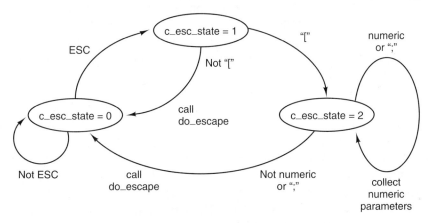

Figure 3-44. Finite state machine for processing escape sequences.

Figure 3-44 shows how escape sequence handling can be represented as a finite state machine. This is implemented by *parse_escape* (line 16293) which is called at the start of *out_char* if *cons->c_esc_state* is nonzero. An ESC itself is detected by *out_char* and makes *cons->c_esc_state* equal to 1. When the next character is received, *parse_escape* prepares for further processing by putting a "\0" in *cons->c_esc_intro*, a pointer to the start of the array of parameters, *cons->c_esc_parmv*[0] into *cons->c_esc_parmp*, and zeroes into the parameter array itself. Then the first character directly following the ESC is examined—valid values are either "[" or "M". In the first case the "[" is copied to *cons->c_esc_intro* and the state is advanced to 2. In the second case, *do_escape* is called to carry out the action, and the escape state is reset to zero. If the first character after the ESC is not one of the valid ones, it is ignored and succeeding characters are once again displayed normally.

When an ESC [sequence has been seen, the next character entered is processed by the escape state 2 code. There are three possibilities at this point. If the character is a numeric character, its value is extracted and added to 10 times the existing value in the position currently pointed to by *cons->c_esc_parmp*, initially *cons->c_esc_parmv*[0] (which was initialized to zero). The escape state does not change. This makes it possible to enter a series of decimal digits and accumulate a large numeric parameter, although the maximum value currently recognized by MINIX 3 is 80, used by the sequence that moves the cursor to an arbitrary position (lines 16335 to 16337). If the character is a semicolon there is another parameter, so the pointer to the parameter string is advanced, allowing succeeding numeric values to be accumulated in the second parameter (lines 16339 to 16341). If *MAX_ESC_PARMS* were to be changed to allocate a larger array for the parameters, this code would not have to be altered to accumulate additional numeric values after entry of additional parameters. Finally, if the character is neither a numeric digit nor a semicolon, *do_escape* is called.

Do_escape (line 16352) is one of the longer functions in the MINIX 3 system source code, even though MINIX 3's complement of recognized escape sequences is relatively modest. For all its length, however, the code should be easy to follow. After an initial call to *flush* to make sure the video display is fully updated, there is a simple if choice, depending upon whether the character immediately following the ESC character was a special control sequence introducer or not. If not, there is only one valid action, moving the cursor up one line if the sequence was ESC M. Note that the test for the "M" is done within a switch with a default action, as a validity check and in anticipation of addition of other sequences that do not use the ESC [format. The action is typical of many escape sequences: the *cons->c_row* variable is inspected to determine if scrolling is required. If the cursor is already on row 0, a *SCROLL_DOWN* call is made to *scroll_screen*; otherwise the cursor is moved up one line. The latter is accomplished just by decrementing *cons->c_row* and then calling *flush*. If a control sequence introducer is found, the code following the else on line 16377 is taken. A test is made for "[", the only control sequence introducer currently recognized by MINIX 3. If the sequence is valid, the first parameter found in the escape sequence, or zero if no numeric parameter was entered, is assigned to *value* (line 16380). If the sequence is invalid, nothing happens except that the large switch that ensues (lines 16381 to 16586) is skipped and the escape state is reset to zero before returning from *do_escape*. In the more interesting case that the sequence is valid, the switch is entered. We will not discuss all the cases; we will just note several that are representative of the types of actions governed by escape sequences.

The first five sequences are generated, with no numeric arguments, by the four "arrow" keys and the Home key on the IBM PC keyboard. The first two, ESC [A and ESC [B, are similar to ESC M, except they can accept a numeric parameter and move up and down by more than one line, and they do not scroll the screen if the parameter specifies a move that exceeds the bounds of the screen. In such cases, *flush* catches requests to move out of bounds and limits the move to the last row or the first row, as appropriate. The next two sequences, ESC [C and

ESC [D, which move the cursor right and left, are similarly limited by *flush*. When generated by the "arrow" keys there is no numeric argument, and thus the default movement of one line or column occurs.

ESC [H can take two numeric parameters, for instance, ESC [20;60H. The parameters specify an absolute position rather than one relative to the current position and are converted from 1-based numbers to 0-based numbers for proper interpretation. The Home key generates the default (no parameters) sequence which moves the cursor to position (1, 1).

ESC [*s*J and ESC [*s*K clear a part of either the entire screen or the current line, depending upon the parameter that is entered. In each case a count of characters is calculated. For instance, for ESC [1J, *count* gets the number of characters from the start of the screen to the cursor position, and the count and a position parameter, *dst*, which may be the start of the screen, *cons->c_org*, or the current cursor position, *cons->c_cur*, are used as parameters to a call to *mem_vid_copy*. This procedure is called with a parameter that causes it to fill the specified region with the current background color.

The next four sequences insert and delete lines and spaces at the cursor position, and their actions do not require detailed explanation. The last case, ESC [*n*m (note the *n* represents a numeric parameter, but the "m" is a literal character) has its effect upon *cons->c_attr*, the attribute byte that is interleaved between the character codes when they are written to video memory.

The next function, *set_6845* (line 16594), is used whenever it is necessary to update the video controller chip. The 6845 has internal 16-bit registers that are programmed 8 bits at a time, and writing a single register requires four I/O port write operations. These are carried out by setting up an array (vector) of (port, value) pairs and invoking a sys_voutb kernel call to get the system task to do the I/O. Some of the registers of the 6845 video controller chip are shown in Fig. 3-45

Registers	Function
10 – 11	Cursor size
12 – 13	Start address for drawing screen
14 – 15	Cursor position

Figure 3-45. Some of the 6845's registers.

The next function is *get_6845* (line 16613), which returns the values of readable video controller registers. It also uses kernel calls to accomplish its job. It does not appear to be called from anywhere in the current MINIX 3 code, but it may be useful for future enhancements such as adding graphics support.

The *beep* function (line 16629) is called when a CTRL-G character must be output. It takes advantage of the built-in support provided by the PC for making sounds by sending a square wave to the speaker. The sound is initiated by more of the kind of magic manipulation of I/O ports that only assembly language programmers can love. The more interesting part of the code is using the ability to set an alarm to turn off the beep. As a process with system privileges (i.e., a slot in the *priv* table), the terminal driver is allowed to set a timer using the library function *tmrs_settimers*. On line 16655 this is done, with the next function, *stop_beep*, specified as the function to run when the timer expires. This timer is put into the terminal task's own timer queue. The sys_setalarm kernel call that follows asks the system task to set a timer in the kernel. When that expires, a SYN_ALARM message is detected by the main loop of the terminal driver, *tty_task*, which calls *expire_timers* to deal with all timers belonging to the terminal driver, one of which is the one set by beep.

The next routine, *stop_beep* (line 16666), is the one whose address is put into the *tmr_func* field of the timer initiated by *beep*. It stops the beep after the designated time has elapsed and also resets the *beeping* flag. This prevents superfluous calls to the beep routine from having any effect.

Scr_init (line 16679) is called by *tty_init NR_CONS* times. Each time its argument is a pointer to a *tty* structure, one element of the *tty_table*. On lines 16693 and 16694 *line*, to be used as the index into the *cons_table* array, is calculated, tested for validity, and, if valid, used to initialize *cons*, the pointer to the current console table entry. At this point the *cons−>c_tty* field can be initialized with the pointer to the main *tty* structure for the device, and, in turn, *tp−>tty_priv* can be pointed to this device's *console_t* structure. Next, *kb_init* is called to initialize the keyboard, and then the pointers to device specific routines are set up, *tp−>tty_devwrite* pointing to *cons_write*, *tp−>tty_echo* pointing to *cons_echo*, and *tp−>tty_ioctl* pointing to *cons_ioctl*. The I/O address of the base register of the CRT controller is fetched from the BIOS, the address and size of the video memory are determined on lines 16708 to 16731, and the *wrap* flag (used to determine how to scroll) is set according to the class of video controller in use. On line 16735 the segment descriptor for the video memory is initialized in the global descriptor table by the system task.

Next comes the initialization of virtual consoles. Each time *scr_init* is called, the argument is a different value of *tp*, and thus a different *line* and *cons* are used on lines 16750 to 16753 to provide each virtual console with its own share of the available video memory. Each screen is then blanked, ready to start, and finally console 0 is selected to be the first active one.

Several routines display output on behalf of the terminal driver itself, the kernel, or another system component. The first one, *kputc* (line 16775) just calls *putk*, a routine to output text a byte at a time, to be described below. This routine is here because the library routine that provides the *printf* function used within system components is written to be linked to a character printing routine with this name, but other functions in the terminal driver expect one named *putk*.

Do_new_kmess (line 16784) is used to print messages from the kernel. Actually, "messages" is not the best word to use here; we do not mean messages as used for interprocess communication. This function is for displaying text on the console to report information, warnings, or errors to the user.

The kernel needs a special mechanism to display information. It needs to be robust, too, so it can be used during startup, before all components of MINIX 3 are running, or during a panic, another time when major parts of the system may be unavailable. The kernel writes text into a circular character buffer, part of a structure that also contains pointers to the next byte to write and the size of the yet-to-be processed text. The kernel sends a *SYS_SIG* message to the terminal driver when there is new text, and *do_new_kmess* is called when the main loop in *tty_task* is running. When things are not going so smoothly, (i.e., when the system crashes) the *SYS_SIG* will be detected by the loop that includes a nonblocking read operation in *do_panic_dumps*, which we saw in *keyboard.c*, and *do_new_kmess* will be called from there. In either case, the kernel call sys_getkmessages retrieves a copy of the kernel structure, and the bytes are displayed, one by one, by passing them to *putk*, followed by a final call to *putk* with a null byte to force it to flush the output. A local static variable is used to keep track of the position in the buffer between messages.

Do_diagnostics (line 16823) has a function similar to that of *do_new_kmess*, but *do_diagnostics* is used to display messages from system processes, rather than the kernel. A *DIAGNOSTICS* message can be received either by the *tty_task* main loop or the loop in *do_panic_dumps*, and in either case a call is made to *do_diagnostics*. The message contains a pointer to a buffer in the calling process and a count of the size of the message. No local buffer is used; instead repeated sys_vircopy kernel calls are made to get the text one byte at a time. This protects the terminal driver; if something goes wrong and a process starts generates an excessive amount of output there is no buffer to overrun. The characters are output one by one by calling *putk*, followed by a null byte.

Putk (line 16850) can print characters on behalf of any code linked into the terminal driver, and is used by the functions just described to output text on behalf of the kernel or other system components. It just calls *out_char* for each non-null byte received, and then calls *flush* for the null byte at the end of the string.

The remaining routines in *console.c* are short and simple and we will review them quickly. *Toggle_scroll* (line 16869) does what its name says, it toggles the flag that determines whether hardware or software scrolling is used. It also displays a message at the current cursor position to identify the selected mode. *Cons_stop* (line 16881) reinitializes the console to the state that the boot monitor expects, prior to a shutdown or reboot. *Cons_org0* (line 16893) is used only when a change of scrolling mode is forced by the F3 key, or when preparing to shut down. *Select_console* (line 16917) selects a virtual console. It is called with the new index and calls *set_6845* twice to get the video controller to display the proper part of the video memory.

The next two routines are highly hardware-specific. *Con_loadfont* (line 16931) loads a font into a graphics adapter, in support of the ioctl *TIOCSFON* operation. It calls *ga_program* (line 16971) to do a series of magical writes to an I/O port that cause the video adapter's font memory, which is normally not addressable by the CPU, to be visible. Then *phys_copy* is called to copy the font data to this area of memory, and another magic sequence is invoked to return the graphics adapter to its normal mode of operation.

The last function is *cons_ioctl* (line 16987). It performs only one function, setting the screen size, and is called only by *scr_init*, which uses values obtained from the BIOS. If there were a need for a real ioctl call to change the sizeMINIX 3screen code to provide the new dimensions would have to be written.

3.9 SUMMARY

Input/output is an important topic that is often neglected. A substantial fraction of any operating system is concerned with I/O. But I/O device drivers are often responsible for operating system problems. Drivers are often written by programmers working for device manufacturers. Conventional operating system designs usually require allowing drivers to have access to critical resources, such as interrupts, I/O ports, and memory belonging to other processes. The design of MINIX 3 isolates drivers as independent processes with limited privileges, so a bug in a driver cannot crash the entire system.

We started out by looking at I/O hardware, and the relation of I/O devices to I/O controllers, which are what the software has to deal with. Then we moved on to the four levels of I/O software: the interrupt routines, the device drivers, the device-independent I/O software, and the I/O libraries and spoolers that run in user space.

Then we examined the problem of deadlock and how it can be tackled. Deadlock occurs when a group of processes each have been granted exclusive access to some resources, and each one wants yet another resource that belongs to another process in the group. All of them are blocked and none will ever run again. Deadlock can be prevented by structuring the system so it can never occur, for example, by allowing a process to hold only one resource at any instant. It can also be avoided by examining each resource request to see if it leads to a situation in which deadlock is possible (an unsafe state) and denying or delaying those that lead to trouble.

Device drivers in MINIX 3 are implemented as independent processes running in user space. We have looked at the RAM disk driver, hard disk driver, and terminal driver. Each of these drivers has a main loop that gets requests and processes them, eventually sending back replies to report on what happened. Source code for the main loops and common functions of the RAM disk, hard disk, and floppy disk drivers is provided in a common driver library, but each driver is compiled and linked with its own copy of the library routines. Each device driver runs in its own address space. Several different terminals, using the system console, the serial lines, and network connections, are all supported by a single terminal driver process.

Device drivers have varying relationships to the interrupt system. Devices which can complete their work rapidly, such as the RAM disk and the memory-mapped display, do not use interrupts at all. The hard disk driver does most of its work in the driver code itself, and the interrupt handlers just return status information. Interrupts are always expected, and a receive can be done to wait for one. A keyboard interrupt can happen at any time. Messages generated by all interrupts for the terminal driver are received and processed in the main loop of the driver. When a keyboard interrupt occurs the first stage of processing the input is done as quickly as possible in order to be ready for subsequent interrupts.

MINIX 3 drivers have limited privileges, and cannot handle interrupts or access I/O ports on their own. Interrupts are handled by the system task, which sends a message to notify a driver when an interrupt occurs. Access to I/O ports is similarly mediated by the system task. Drivers cannot read or write I/O ports directly.

PROBLEMS

1. A 1x DVD reader can deliver data at a rate of 1.32 MB/sec. What is the highest speed DVD drive that could be connected over a USB 2.0 connection without losing data?

2. Many disks contain an ECC at the end of each sector. If the ECC is wrong, what actions might be taken and by which piece of hardware or software?

3. What is memory-mapped I/O? Why is it sometimes used?

4. Explain what DMA is and why it is used.

5. Although DMA does not use the CPU, the maximum transfer rate is still limited. Consider reading a block from the disk. Name three factors that might ultimately limit the rate of transfer.

6. CD-quality music requires sampling the sound signal 44,100 times per second. Suppose that a timer generates an interrupt at this rate and that each interrupt takes 1 microsec to handle on a 1-GHz CPU. What is the slowest clock rate that could be used and not lose any data? Assume that the number of instructions to be processed for an interrupt is constant, so halving the clock speed doubles the interrupt handling time.

7. An alternative to interrupts is polling. Are there any circumstances you can think of in which polling is a better choice?

8. Disk controllers have internal buffers and they are getting larger with each new model. Why?

9. Each device driver has two different interfaces with the operating system. One interface is a set of function calls that the operating system makes on the driver. The other is a set of calls that the driver makes on the operating system. Name one likely call in each interface.

10. Why do operating system designers attempt to provide device-independent I/O wherever it is possible?

11. In which of the four I/O software layers is each of the following done?

    (a) Computing the track, sector, and head for a disk read.
    (b) Maintaining a cache of recently used blocks.
    (c) Writing commands to the device registers.
    (d) Checking to see if the user is permitted to use the device.
    (e) Converting binary integers to ASCII for printing.

12. Why are output files for the printer normally spooled on disk before being printed?

13. Give an example of a deadlock that could occur in the physical world.

14. Consider Fig. 3-10. Suppose that in step (o) C requested S instead of requesting R. Would this lead to deadlock? Suppose that it requested both S and R?

15. Take a careful look at Fig. 3-13(b). If D asks for one more unit, does this lead to a safe state or an unsafe one? What if the request came from C instead of D?

16. All the trajectories in Fig. 3-14 are horizontal or vertical. Can you envision any circumstances in which diagonal trajectories were also possible?

17. Suppose that process A in Fig. 3-15 requests the last tape drive. Does this action lead to a deadlock?

18. A computer has six tape drives, with n processes competing for them. Each process may need two drives. For which values of n is the system deadlock free?

19. Can a system be in a state that is neither deadlocked nor safe? If so, give an example. If not, prove that all states are either deadlocked or safe.

20. A distributed system using mailboxes has two IPC primitives, SEND and RECEIVE. The latter primitive specifies a process to receive from, and blocks if no message from that process is available, even though messages may be waiting from other processes. There are no shared resources, but processes need to communicate frequently about other matters. Is deadlock possible? Discuss.

21. In an electronic funds transfer system, there are hundreds of identical processes that work as follows. Each process reads an input line specifying an amount of money, the account to be credited, and the account to be debited. Then it locks both accounts and transfers the money, releasing the locks when done. With many processes running in parallel, there is a very real danger that having locked account x it will be unable to lock y because y has been locked by a process now waiting for x. Devise a scheme that avoids deadlocks. Do not release an account record until you have completed the transactions. (In other words, solutions that lock one account and then release it immediately if the other is locked are not allowed.)

22. The banker's algorithm is being run in a system with m resource classes and n processes. In the limit of large m and n, the number of operations that must be performed to check a state for safety is proportional to $m^a n^b$. What are the values of a and b?

23. Consider the banker's algorithm of Fig. 3-15. Assume that processes A and D change their requests to an additional (1, 2, 1, 0) and (1, 2, 1, 0) respectively. Can these requests be met and the system still remain in a safe state?

24. Cinderella and the Prince are getting divorced. To divide their property, they have agreed on the following algorithm. Every morning, each one may send a letter to the other's lawyer requesting one item of property. Since it takes a day for letters to be delivered, they have agreed that if both discover that they have requested the same item on the same day, the next day they will send a letter canceling the request. Among their property is their dog, Woofer, Woofer's doghouse, their canary, Tweeter, and Tweeter's cage. The animals love their houses, so it has been agreed that any division of property separating an animal from its house is invalid, requiring the whole division to start over from scratch. Both Cinderella and the Prince desperately want Woofer. So they can go on (separate) vacations, each spouse has programmed a personal computer to handle the negotiation. When they come back from vacation, the computers are still negotiating. Why? Is deadlock possible? Is starvation (waiting forever) possible? Discuss.

25. Consider a disk with 1000 512-byte sectors/track, eight tracks per cylinder, and 10,000 cylinders with a rotation time of 10 msec. The track-to-track seek time is 1 msec. What is the maximum sustainable burst rate? How long can such a burst last?

26. A local area network is used as follows. The user issues a system call to write data packets to the network. The operating system then copies the data to a kernel buffer. Then it copies the data to the network controller board. When all the bytes are safely inside the controller, they are sent over the network at a rate of 10 megabits/sec. The receiving network controller stores each bit a microsecond after it is sent. When the last bit arrives, the destination CPU is interrupted, and the kernel copies the newly arrived packet to a kernel buffer to inspect it. Once it has figured out which user the packet is for, the kernel copies the data to the user space. If we assume that each interrupt and its associated processing takes 1 msec, that packets are 1024 bytes (ignore the headers), and that copying a byte takes 1 microsec, what is the maximum rate at which one process can pump data to another? Assume that the sender is blocked until the work is finished at the receiving side and an acknowledgement comes back. For simplicity, assume the time to get the acknowledgement back is so small it can be ignored.

27. The message format of Fig. 3-17 is used for sending request messages to drivers for block devices. Could any fields be omitted for character devices? Which ones?

28. Disk requests come in to the driver for cylinders 10, 22, 20, 2, 40, 6, and 38, in that order. A seek takes 6 msec per cylinder moved. How much seek time is needed for

(a) First-come, first served.
(b) Closest cylinder next.
(c) Elevator algorithm (initially moving upward).

In all cases, the arm is initially at cylinder 20.

29. A personal computer salesman visiting a university in South-West Amsterdam remarked during his sales pitch that his company had devoted substantial effort to making their version of UNIX very fast. As an example, he noted that their disk driver used the elevator algorithm and also queued multiple requests within a cylinder in sector order. A student, Harry Hacker, was impressed and bought one. He took it home and wrote a program to randomly read 10,000 blocks spread across the disk. To his amazement, the performance that he measured was identical to what would be expected from first-come, first-served. Was the salesman lying?

30. A UNIX process has two parts—the user part and the kernel part. Is the kernel part like a subroutine or a coroutine?

31. The clock interrupt handler on a certain computer requires 2 msec (including process switching overhead) per clock tick. The clock runs at 60 Hz. What fraction of the CPU is devoted to the clock?

32. Two examples of watchdog timers were given in the text: timing the startup of the floppy disk motor and allowing for carriage return on hardcopy terminals. Give a third example.

33. Why are RS232 terminals interrupt driven, but memory-mapped terminals not interrupt driven?

34. Consider how a terminal works. The driver outputs one character and then blocks. When the character has been printed, an interrupt occurs and a message is sent to the blocked driver, which outputs the next character and then blocks again. If the time to pass a message, output a character, and block is 4 msec, does this method work well on 110-baud lines? How about 4800-baud lines?

35. A bitmap terminal contains 1200 by 800 pixels. To scroll a window, the CPU (or controller) must move all the lines of text upward by copying their bits from one part of the video RAM to another. If a particular window is 66 lines high by 80 characters wide (5280 characters, total), and a character's box is 8 pixels wide by 12 pixels high, how long does it take to scroll the whole window at a copying rate of 500 nsec per byte? If all lines are 80 characters long, what is the equivalent baud rate of the terminal? Putting a character on the screen takes 50 microsec. Now compute the baud rate for the same terminal in color, with 4 bits/pixel. (Putting a character on the screen now takes 200 microsec.)

36. Why do operating systems provide escape characters, such as CTRL-V in MINIX?

37. After receiving a CTRL-C (SIGINT) character, the MINIX driver discards all output currently queued for that terminal. Why?

38. Many RS232 terminals have escape sequences for deleting the current line and moving all the lines below it up one line. How do you think this feature is implemented inside the terminal?

39. On the original IBM PC's color display, writing to the video RAM at any time other than during the CRT beam's vertical retrace caused ugly spots to appear all over the screen. A screen image is 25 by 80 characters, each of which fits in a box 8 pixels by 8 pixels. Each row of 640 pixels is drawn on a single horizontal scan of the beam, which takes 63.6 microsec, including the horizontal retrace. The screen is redrawn 60

times a second, each of which requires a vertical retrace period to get the beam back to the top. What fraction of the time is the video RAM available for writing in?

40. Write a graphics driver for the IBM color display, or some other suitable bitmap display. The driver should accept commands to set and clear individual pixels, move rectangles around the screen, and any other features you think are interesting. User programs interface to the driver by opening */dev/graphics* and writing commands to it.

41. Modify the MINIX floppy disk driver to do track-at-a-time caching.

42. Implement a floppy disk driver that works as a character, rather than a block device, to bypass the file system's block cache. In this way, users can read large chunks of data from the disk, which are DMA'ed directly to user space, greatly improving performance. This driver would primarily be of interest to programs that need to read the raw bits on the disk, without regard to the file system. File system checkers fall into this category.

43. Implement the UNIX PROFIL system call, which is missing from MINIX.

44. Modify the terminal driver so that in addition to a having a special key to erase the previous character, there is a key to erase the previous word.

45. A new hard disk device with removable media has been added to a MINIX 3 system. This device must spin up to speed every time the media are changed, and the spin up time is quite long. It is anticipated media changes will be made frequently while the system is running. Suddenly the *waitfor* routine in *at_wini.c* is unsatisfactory. Design a new *waitfor* routine in which, if the bit pattern being awaited is not found after 1 second of busy waiting, a phase will be entered in which the disk driver will sleep for 1 second, test the port, and go back to sleep for another second until either the sought-for pattern is found or the preset *TIMEOUT* period expires.

4

MEMORY MANAGEMENT

Memory is an important resource that must be carefully managed. While the average home computer nowadays has two thousand times as much memory as the IBM 7094 (the largest computer in the world in the early 1960s), programs and the data they are expected to handle have also grown tremendously. To paraphrase Parkinson's law, "Programs and their data expand to fill the memory available to hold them." In this chapter we will study how operating systems manage memory.

Ideally, what every programmer would like is an infinitely large, infinitely fast memory that is also nonvolatile, that is, does not lose its contents when the electric power fails. While we are at it, why not also ask for it to be inexpensive, too? Unfortunately technology cannot turn such dreams into memories. Consequently, most computers have a **memory hierarchy**, with a small amount of very fast, expensive, volatile cache memory, hundreds of megabytes of medium-speed, medium-price, volatile main memory (RAM), and tens or hundreds of gigabytes of slow, cheap, nonvolatile disk storage. It is the job of the operating system to coordinate how these memories are used.

The part of the operating system that manages the memory hierarchy is usually called the **memory manager**. Its job is to keep track of which parts of memory are in use and which parts are not in use, to allocate memory to processes when they need it and deallocate it when they are done, and to manage swapping between main memory and disk when main memory is too small to hold all the processes. In most systems (but not MINIX 3), it is in the kernel.

In this chapter we will investigate a number of different memory management schemes, ranging from very simple to highly sophisticated. We will start at the beginning and look first at the simplest possible memory management system and then gradually progress to more and more elaborate ones.

As we pointed out in Chap. 1, history tends to repeat itself in the computer world: minicomputer software was initially like mainframe software and personal computer software was initially like minicomputer software. The cycle is now repeating itself with palmtops, PDAs, and embedded systems. In these systems, simple memory management schemes are still in use. For this reason, they are still worth studying.

4.1 BASIC MEMORY MANAGEMENT

Memory management systems can be divided into two basic classes: those that move processes back and forth between main memory and disk during execution (swapping and paging), and those that do not. The latter are simpler, so we will study them first. Later in the chapter we will examine swapping and paging. Throughout this chapter the reader should keep in mind that swapping and paging are largely artifacts caused by the lack of sufficient main memory to hold all programs and data at once. If main memory ever gets so large that there is truly enough of it, the arguments in favor of one kind of memory management scheme or another may become obsolete.

On the other hand, as mentioned above, software seems to grow as fast as memory, so efficient memory management may always be needed. In the 1980s, there were many universities that ran a timesharing system with dozens of (more-or-less satisfied) users on a 4 MB VAX. Now Microsoft recommends having at least 128 MB for a single-user Windows XP system. The trend toward multimedia puts even more demands on memory, so good memory management is probably going to be needed for the next decade at least.

4.1.1 Monoprogramming without Swapping or Paging

The simplest possible memory management scheme is to run just one program at a time, sharing the memory between that program and the operating system. Three variations on this theme are shown in Fig. 4-1. The operating system may be at the bottom of memory in RAM (Random Access Memory), as shown in Fig. 4-1(a), or it may be in ROM (Read-Only Memory) at the top of memory, as shown in Fig. 4-1(b), or the device drivers may be at the top of memory in a ROM and the rest of the system in RAM down below, as shown in Fig. 4-1(c). The first model was formerly used on mainframes and minicomputers but is rarely used any more. The second model is used on some palmtop computers and embedded systems. The third model was used by early personal computers (e.g., running MS-DOS), where the portion of the system in the ROM is called the **BIOS** (Basic Input Output System).

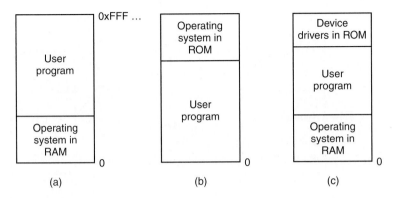

Figure 4-1. Three simple ways of organizing memory with an operating system and one user process. Other possibilities also exist.

When the system is organized in this way, only one process at a time can be running. As soon as the user types a command, the operating system copies the requested program from disk to memory and executes it. When the process finishes, the operating system displays a prompt character and waits for a new command. When it receives the command, it loads a new program into memory, overwriting the first one.

4.1.2 Multiprogramming with Fixed Partitions

Except on very simple embedded systems, monoprogramming is hardly used any more. Most modern systems allow multiple processes to run at the same time. Having multiple processes running at once means that when one process is blocked waiting for I/O to finish, another one can use the CPU. Thus multiprogramming increases the CPU utilization. Network servers always have the ability to run multiple processes (for different clients) at the same time, but most client (i.e., desktop) machines also have this ability nowadays.

The easiest way to achieve multiprogramming is simply to divide memory up into n (possibly unequal) partitions. This partitioning can, for example, be done manually when the system is started up.

When a job arrives, it can be put into the input queue for the smallest partition large enough to hold it. Since the partitions are fixed in this scheme, any space in a partition not used by a job is wasted while that job runs. In Fig. 4-2(a) we see how this system of fixed partitions and separate input queues looks.

The disadvantage of sorting the incoming jobs into separate queues becomes apparent when the queue for a large partition is empty but the queue for a small

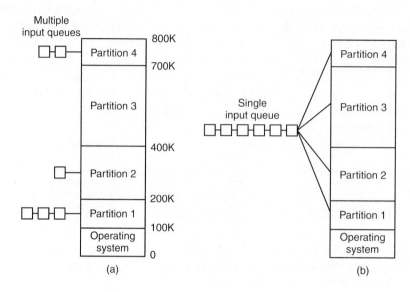

Figure 4-2. (a) Fixed memory partitions with separate input queues for each partition. (b) Fixed memory partitions with a single input queue.

partition is full, as is the case for partitions 1 and 3 in Fig. 4-2(a). Here small jobs have to wait to get into memory, even though plenty of memory is free. An alternative organization is to maintain a single queue as in Fig. 4-2(b). Whenever a partition becomes free, the job closest to the front of the queue that fits in it could be loaded into the empty partition and run. Since it is undesirable to waste a large partition on a small job, a different strategy is to search the whole input queue whenever a partition becomes free and pick the largest job that fits. Note that the latter algorithm discriminates against small jobs as being unworthy of having a whole partition, whereas usually it is desirable to give the smallest jobs (often interactive jobs) the best service, not the worst.

One way out is to have at least one small partition around. Such a partition will allow small jobs to run without having to allocate a large partition for them.

Another approach is to have a rule stating that a job that is eligible to run may not be skipped over more than k times. Each time it is skipped over, it gets one point. When it has acquired k points, it may not be skipped again.

This system, with fixed partitions set up by the operator in the morning and not changed thereafter, was used by OS/360 on large IBM mainframes for many years. It was called **MFT** (Multiprogramming with a Fixed number of Tasks or OS/MFT). it is simple to understand and equally simple to implement: incoming jobs are queued until a suitable partition is available, at which time the job is loaded into that partition and run until it terminates. However, nowadays, few, if any, operating systems, support this model, even on mainframe batch systems.

4.1.3 Relocation and Protection

Multiprogramming introduces two essential problems that must be solved—relocation and protection. Look at Fig. 4-2. From the figure it is clear that different jobs will be run at different addresses. When a program is linked (i.e., the main program, user-written procedures, and library procedures are combined into a single address space), the linker must know at what address the program will begin in memory.

For example, suppose that the first instruction is a call to a procedure at absolute address 100 within the binary file produced by the linker. If this program is loaded in partition 1 (at address 100K), that instruction will jump to absolute address 100, which is inside the operating system. What is needed is a call to 100K + 100. If the program is loaded into partition 2, it must be carried out as a call to 200K + 100, and so on. This problem is known as the **relocation** problem.

One possible solution is to actually modify the instructions as the program is loaded into memory. Programs loaded into partition 1 have 100K added to each address, programs loaded into partition 2 have 200K added to addresses, and so forth. To perform relocation during loading like this, the linker must include in the binary program a list or bitmap telling which program words are addresses to be relocated and which are opcodes, constants, or other items that must not be relocated. OS/MFT worked this way.

Relocation during loading does not solve the protection problem. A malicious program can always construct a new instruction and jump to it. Because programs in this system use absolute memory addresses rather than addresses relative to a register, there is no way to stop a program from building an instruction that reads or writes any word in memory. In multiuser systems, it is highly undesirable to let processes read and write memory belonging to other users.

The solution that IBM chose for protecting the 360 was to divide memory into blocks of 2-KB bytes and assign a 4-bit protection code to each block. The PSW (Program Status Word) contained a 4-bit key. The 360 hardware trapped any attempt by a running process to access memory whose protection code differed from the PSW key. Since only the operating system could change the protection codes and key, user processes were prevented from interfering with one another and with the operating system itself.

An alternative solution to both the relocation and protection problems is to equip the machine with two special hardware registers, called the **base** and **limit** registers. When a process is scheduled, the base register is loaded with the address of the start of its partition, and the limit register is loaded with the length of the partition. Every memory address generated automatically has the base register contents added to it before being sent to memory. Thus if the base register contains the value 100K, a CALL 100 instruction is effectively turned into a CALL 100K + 100 instruction, without the instruction itself being modified. Addresses are also checked against the limit register to make sure that they do not attempt to address memory outside the current partition. The hardware protects the base and limit registers to prevent user programs from modifying them.

A disadvantage of this scheme is the need to perform an addition and a comparison on every memory reference. Comparisons can be done fast, but additions are slow due to carry propagation time unless special addition circuits are used.

The CDC 6600—the world's first supercomputer—used this scheme. The Intel 8088 CPU used for the original IBM PC used a slightly weaker version of this scheme—base registers, but no limit registers. Few computers use it now.

4.2 SWAPPING

With a batch system, organizing memory into fixed partitions is simple and effective. Each job is loaded into a partition when it gets to the head of the queue. It stays in memory until it has finished. As long as enough jobs can be kept in memory to keep the CPU busy all the time, there is no reason to use anything more complicated.

With timesharing systems or graphics-oriented personal computers, the situation is different. Sometimes there is not enough main memory to hold all the currently active processes, so excess processes must be kept on disk and brought in to run dynamically.

Two general approaches to memory management can be used, depending (in part) on the available hardware. The simplest strategy, called **swapping**, consists of bringing in each process in its entirety, running it for a while, then putting it back on the disk. The other strategy, called **virtual memory**, allows programs to run even when they are only partially in main memory. Below we will study swapping; in Sec. 4.3 we will examine virtual memory.

The operation of a swapping system is illustrated in Fig. 4-3. Initially, only process A is in memory. Then processes B and C are created or swapped in from disk. In Fig. 4-3(d) A is swapped out to disk. Then D comes in and B goes out. Finally A comes in again. Since A is now at a different location, addresses contained in it must be relocated, either by software when it is swapped in or (more likely) by hardware during program execution.

The main difference between the fixed partitions of Fig. 4-2 and the variable partitions of Fig. 4-3 is that the number, location, and size of the partitions vary dynamically in the latter as processes come and go, whereas they are fixed in the former. The flexibility of not being tied to a fixed number of partitions that may be too large or too small improves memory utilization, but it also complicates allocating and deallocating memory, as well as keeping track of it.

When swapping creates multiple holes in memory, it is possible to combine them all into one big one by moving all the processes downward as far as possible. This technique is known as **memory compaction**. It is usually not done because it requires a lot of CPU time. For example, on a 1-GB machine that can

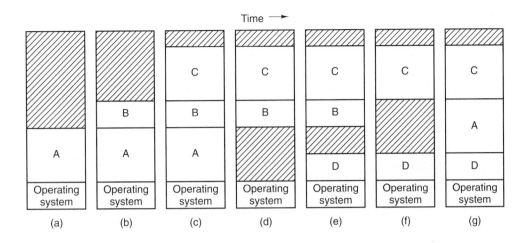

Figure 4-3. Memory allocation changes as processes come into memory and leave it. The shaded regions are unused memory.

copy at a rate of 2 GB/sec (0.5 nsec/byte) it takes about 0.5 sec to compact all of memory. That may not seem like much time, but it would be noticeably disruptive to a user watching a video stream.

A point that is worth making concerns how much memory should be allocated for a process when it is created or swapped in. If processes are created with a fixed size that never changes, then the allocation is simple: the operating system allocates exactly what is needed, no more and no less.

If, however, processes' data segments can grow, for example, by dynamically allocating memory from a heap, as in many programming languages, a problem occurs whenever a process tries to grow. If a hole is adjacent to the process, it can be allocated and the process can be allowed to grow into the hole. On the other hand, if the process is adjacent to another process, the growing process will either have to be moved to a hole in memory large enough for it, or one or more processes will have to be swapped out to create a large enough hole. If a process cannot grow in memory and the swap area on the disk is full, the process will have to wait or be killed.

If it is expected that most processes will grow as they run, it is probably a good idea to allocate a little extra memory whenever a process is swapped in or moved, to reduce the overhead associated with moving or swapping processes that no longer fit in their allocated memory. However, when swapping processes to disk, only the memory actually in use should be swapped; it is wasteful to swap the extra memory as well. In Fig. 4-4(a) we see a memory configuration in which space for growth has been allocated to two processes.

If processes can have two growing segments, for example, the data segment being used as a heap for variables that are dynamically allocated and released and

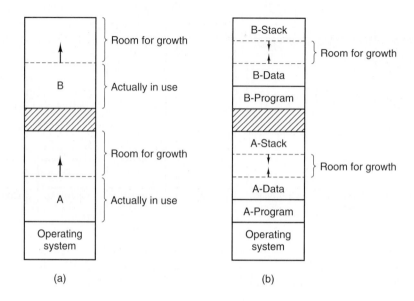

Figure 4-4. (a) Allocating space for a growing data segment. (b) Allocating space for a growing stack and a growing data segment.

a stack segment for the normal local variables and return addresses, an alternative arrangement suggests itself, namely that of Fig. 4-4(b). In this figure we see that each process illustrated has a stack at the top of its allocated memory that is growing downward, and a data segment just beyond the program text that is growing upward. The memory between them can be used for either segment. If it runs out, either the process will have to be moved to a hole with sufficient space, swapped out of memory until a large enough hole can be created, or killed.

4.2.1 Memory Management with Bitmaps

When memory is assigned dynamically, the operating system must manage it. In general terms, there are two ways to keep track of memory usage: bitmaps and free lists. In this section and the next one we will look at these two methods in turn.

With a bitmap, memory is divided up into allocation units, perhaps as small as a few words and perhaps as large as several kilobytes. Corresponding to each allocation unit is a bit in the bitmap, which is 0 if the unit is free and 1 if it is occupied (or vice versa). Figure 4-5 shows part of memory and the corresponding bitmap.

The size of the allocation unit is an important design issue. The smaller the allocation unit, the larger the bitmap. However, even with an allocation unit as small as 4 bytes, 32 bits of memory will require only 1 bit of the map. A memory

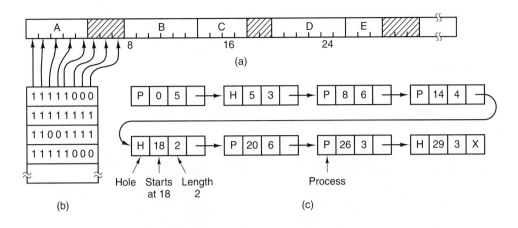

Figure 4-5. (a) A part of memory with five processes and three holes. The tick marks show the memory allocation units. The shaded regions (0 in the bitmap) are free. (b) The corresponding bitmap. (c) The same information as a list.

of $32n$ bits will use n map bits, so the bitmap will take up only 1/33 of memory. If the allocation unit is chosen large, the bitmap will be smaller, but appreciable memory may be wasted in the last unit of the process if the process size is not an exact multiple of the allocation unit.

A bitmap provides a simple way to keep track of memory words in a fixed amount of memory because the size of the bitmap depends only on the size of memory and the size of the allocation unit. The main problem with it is that when it has been decided to bring a k unit process into memory, the memory manager must search the bitmap to find a run of k consecutive 0 bits in the map. Searching a bitmap for a run of a given length is a slow operation (because the run may straddle word boundaries in the map); this is an argument against bitmaps.

4.2.2 Memory Management with Linked Lists

Another way of keeping track of memory is to maintain a linked list of allocated and free memory segments, where a segment is either a process or a hole between two processes. The memory of Fig. 4-5(a) is represented in Fig. 4-5(c) as a linked list of segments. Each entry in the list specifies a hole (H) or process (P), the address at which it starts, the length, and a pointer to the next entry.

In this example, the segment list is kept sorted by address. Sorting this way has the advantage that when a process terminates or is swapped out, updating the list is straightforward. A terminating process normally has two neighbors (except when it is at the very top or very bottom of memory). These may be either processes or holes, leading to the four combinations shown in Fig. 4-6. In Fig. 4-6(a) updating the list requires replacing a P by an H. In Fig. 4-6(b) and also in Fig. 4-

6(c), two entries are coalesced into one, and the list becomes one entry shorter. In Fig. 4-6(d), three entries are merged and two items are removed from the list. Since the process table slot for the terminating process will normally point to the list entry for the process itself, it may be more convenient to have the list as a double-linked list, rather than the single-linked list of Fig. 4-5(c). This structure makes it easier to find the previous entry and to see if a merge is possible.

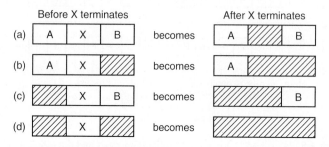

Figure 4-6. Four neighbor combinations for the terminating process, *X*.

When the processes and holes are kept on a list sorted by address, several algorithms can be used to allocate memory for a newly created process (or an existing process being swapped in from disk). We assume that the memory manager knows how much memory to allocate. The simplest algorithm is **first fit**. The process manager scans along the list of segments until it finds a hole that is big enough. The hole is then broken up into two pieces, one for the process and one for the unused memory, except in the statistically unlikely case of an exact fit. First fit is a fast algorithm because it searches as little as possible.

A minor variation of first fit is **next fit**. It works the same way as first fit, except that it keeps track of where it is whenever it finds a suitable hole. The next time it is called to find a hole, it starts searching the list from the place where it left off last time, instead of always at the beginning, as first fit does. Simulations by Bays (1977) show that next fit gives slightly worse performance than first fit.

Another well-known algorithm is **best fit**. Best fit searches the entire list and takes the smallest hole that is adequate. Rather than breaking up a big hole that might be needed later, best fit tries to find a hole that is close to the actual size needed.

As an example of first fit and best fit, consider Fig. 4-5 again. If a block of size 2 is needed, first fit will allocate the hole at 5, but best fit will allocate the hole at 18.

Best fit is slower than first fit because it must search the entire list every time it is called. Somewhat surprisingly, it also results in more wasted memory than first fit or next fit because it tends to fill up memory with tiny, useless holes. First fit generates larger holes on the average.

To get around the problem of breaking up nearly exact matches into a process and a tiny hole, one could think about **worst fit**, that is, always take the largest available hole, so that the hole broken off will be big enough to be useful. Simulation has shown that worst fit is not a very good idea either.

All four algorithms can be speeded up by maintaining separate lists for processes and holes. In this way, all of them devote their full energy to inspecting holes, not processes. The inevitable price that is paid for this speedup on allocation is the additional complexity and slowdown when deallocating memory, since a freed segment has to be removed from the process list and inserted into the hole list.

If distinct lists are maintained for processes and holes, the hole list may be kept sorted on size, to make best fit faster. When best fit searches a list of holes from smallest to largest, as soon as it finds a hole that fits, it knows that the hole is the smallest one that will do the job, hence the best fit. No further searching is needed, as it is with the single list scheme. With a hole list sorted by size, first fit and best fit are equally fast, and next fit is pointless.

When the holes are kept on separate lists from the processes, a small optimization is possible. Instead of having a separate set of data structures for maintaining the hole list, as is done in Fig. 4-5(c), the holes themselves can be used. The first word of each hole could be the hole size, and the second word a pointer to the following entry. The nodes of the list of Fig. 4-5(c), which require three words and one bit (P/H), are no longer needed.

Yet another allocation algorithm is **quick fit**, which maintains separate lists for some of the more common sizes requested. For example, it might have a table with n entries, in which the first entry is a pointer to the head of a list of 4-KB holes, the second entry is a pointer to a list of 8-KB holes, the third entry a pointer to 12-KB holes, and so on. Holes of say, 21 KB, could either be put on the 20-KB list or on a special list of odd-sized holes. With quick fit, finding a hole of the required size is extremely fast, but it has the same disadvantage as all schemes that sort by hole size, namely, when a process terminates or is swapped out, finding its neighbors to see if a merge is possible is expensive. If merging is not done, memory will quickly fragment into a large number of small holes into which no processes fit.

4.3 VIRTUAL MEMORY

Many years ago people were first confronted with programs that were too big to fit in the available memory. The solution usually adopted was to split the program into pieces, called **overlays**. Overlay 0 would start running first. When it was done, it would call another overlay. Some overlay systems were highly complex, allowing multiple overlays in memory at once. The overlays were kept on the disk and swapped in and out of memory by the operating system, dynamically, as needed.

Although the actual work of swapping overlays in and out was done by the system, the decision of how to split the program into pieces had to be done by the programmer. Splitting up large programs into small, modular pieces was time consuming and boring. It did not take long before someone thought of a way to turn the whole job over to the computer.

The method that was devised has come to be known as **virtual memory** (Fotheringham, 1961). The basic idea behind virtual memory is that the combined size of the program, data, and stack may exceed the amount of physical memory available for it. The operating system keeps those parts of the program currently in use in main memory, and the rest on the disk. For example, a 512-MB program can run on a 256-MB machine by carefully choosing which 256 MB to keep in memory at each instant, with pieces of the program being swapped between disk and memory as needed.

Virtual memory can also work in a multiprogramming system, with bits and pieces of many programs in memory at once. While a program is waiting for part of itself to be brought in, it is waiting for I/O and cannot run, so the CPU can be given to another process, the same way as in any other multiprogramming system.

4.3.1 Paging

Most virtual memory systems use a technique called **paging**, which we will now describe. On any computer, there exists a set of memory addresses that programs can produce. When a program uses an instruction like

    MOV REG,1000

it does this to copy the contents of memory address 1000 to REG (or vice versa, depending on the computer). Addresses can be generated using indexing, base registers, segment registers, and other ways.

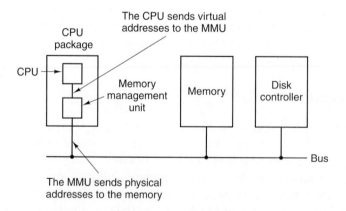

Figure 4-7. The position and function of the MMU. Here the MMU is shown as being a part of the CPU chip because it commonly is nowadays. However, logically it could be a separate chip and was in years gone by.

These program-generated addresses are called **virtual addresses** and form the **virtual address space**. On computers without virtual memory, the virtual address is put directly onto the memory bus and causes the physical memory word with the same address to be read or written. When virtual memory is used, the virtual addresses do not go directly to the memory bus. Instead, they go to an **MMU** (**Memory Management Unit**) that maps the virtual addresses onto the physical memory addresses as illustrated in Fig. 4-7.

A very simple example of how this mapping works is shown in Fig. 4-8. In this example, we have a computer that can generate 16-bit addresses, from 0 up to 64K. These are the virtual addresses. This computer, however, has only 32 KB of physical memory, so although 64-KB programs can be written, they cannot be loaded into memory in their entirety and run. A complete copy of a program's memory image, up to 64 KB, must be present on the disk, however, so that pieces can be brought in as needed.

The virtual address space is divided up into units called **pages**. The corresponding units in the physical memory are called **page frames**. The pages and page frames are always the same size. In this example they are 4 KB, but page sizes from 512 bytes to 1 MB have been used in real systems. With 64 KB of virtual address space and 32 KB of physical memory, we get 16 virtual pages and 8 page frames. Transfers between RAM and disk are always in units of a page.

When the program tries to access address 0, for example, using the instruction

        MOV REG,0

virtual address 0 is sent to the MMU. The MMU sees that this virtual address falls in page 0 (0 to 4095), which according to its mapping is page frame 2 (8192 to 12287). It thus transforms the address to 8192 and outputs address 8192 onto the bus. The memory knows nothing at all about the MMU and just sees a request for reading or writing address 8192, which it honors. Thus, the MMU has effectively mapped all virtual addresses between 0 and 4095 onto physical addresses 8192 to 12287.

Similarly, an instruction

        MOV REG,8192

is effectively transformed into

        MOV REG,24576

because virtual address 8192 is in virtual page 2 and this page is mapped onto physical page frame 6 (physical addresses 24576 to 28671). As a third example, virtual address 20500 is 20 bytes from the start of virtual page 5 (virtual addresses 20480 to 24575) and maps onto physical address 12288 + 20 = 12308.

By itself, this ability to map the 16 virtual pages onto any of the eight page frames by setting the MMU's map appropriately does not solve the problem that

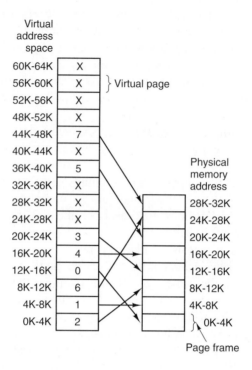

Figure 4-8. The relation between virtual addresses and physical memory addresses is given by the page table.

the virtual address space is larger than the physical memory. Since we have only eight physical page frames, only eight of the virtual pages in Fig. 4-8 are mapped onto physical memory. The others, shown as crosses in the figure, are not mapped. In the actual hardware, a **present/absent bit** keeps track of which pages are physically present in memory.

What happens if the program tries to use an unmapped page, for example, by using the instruction

    MOV REG,32780

which is byte 12 within virtual page 8 (starting at 32768)? The MMU notices that the page is unmapped (indicated by a cross in the figure) and causes the CPU to trap to the operating system. This trap is called a **page fault**. The operating system picks a little-used page frame and writes its contents back to the disk. It then fetches the page just referenced into the page frame just freed, changes the map, and restarts the trapped instruction.

For example, if the operating system decided to evict page frame 1, it would load virtual page 8 at physical address 4K and make two changes to the MMU map. First, it would mark virtual page 1's entry as unmapped, to trap any future accesses to virtual addresses between 4K and 8K. Then it would replace the cross in virtual page 8's entry with a 1, so that when the trapped instruction is re-executed, it will map virtual address 32780 onto physical address 4108.

Now let us look inside the MMU to see how it works and why we have chosen to use a page size that is a power of 2. In Fig. 4-9 we see an example of a virtual address, 8196 (0010000000000100 in binary), being mapped using the MMU map of Fig. 4-8. The incoming 16-bit virtual address is split into a 4-bit page number and a 12-bit offset. With 4 bits for the page number, we can have 16 pages, and with 12 bits for the offset, we can address all 4096 bytes within a page.

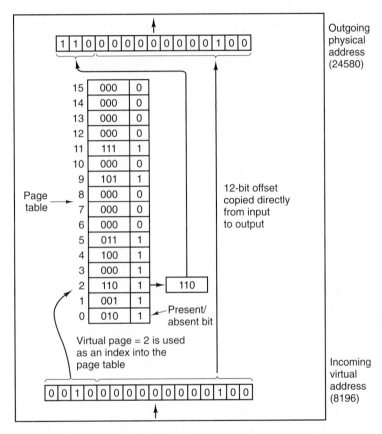

Figure 4-9. The internal operation of the MMU with 16 4-KB pages.

The page number is used as an index into the **page table**, yielding the number of the page frame corresponding to that virtual page. If the *present/absent* bit is 0, a trap to the operating system is caused. If the bit is 1, the page frame number found in the page table is copied to the high-order 3 bits of the output register, along with the 12-bit offset, which is copied unmodified from the incoming virtual address. Together they form a 15-bit physical address. The output register is then put onto the memory bus as the physical memory address.

4.3.2 Page Tables

In the simplest case, the mapping of virtual addresses onto physical addresses is as we have just described it. The virtual address is split into a virtual page number (high-order bits) and an offset (low-order bits). For example, with a 16-bit address and a 4-KB page size, the upper 4 bits could specify one of the 16 virtual pages and the lower 12 bits would then specify the byte offset (0 to 4095) within the selected page. However a split with 3 or 5 or some other number of bits for the page is also possible. Different splits imply different page sizes.

The virtual page number is used as an index into the page table to find the entry for that virtual page. From the page table entry, the page frame number (if any) is found. The page frame number is attached to the high-order end of the offset, replacing the virtual page number, to form a physical address that can be sent to the memory.

The purpose of the page table is to map virtual pages onto page frames. Mathematically speaking, the page table is a function, with the virtual page number as argument and the physical frame number as result. Using the result of this function, the virtual page field in a virtual address can be replaced by a page frame field, thus forming a physical memory address.

Despite this simple description, two major issues must be faced:

1. The page table can be extremely large.

2. The mapping must be fast.

The first point follows from the fact that modern computers use virtual addresses of at least 32 bits. With, say, a 4-KB page size, a 32-bit address space has 1 million pages, and a 64-bit address space has more than you want to contemplate. With 1 million pages in the virtual address space, the page table must have 1 million entries. And remember that each process needs its own page table (because it has its own virtual address space).

The second point is a consequence of the fact that the virtual-to-physical mapping must be done on every memory reference. A typical instruction has an instruction word, and often a memory operand as well. Consequently, it is necessary to make one, two, or sometimes more page table references per instruction. If an instruction takes, say, 1 nsec, the page table lookup must be done in under 250 psec to avoid becoming a major bottleneck.

The need for large, fast page mapping is a significant constraint on the way computers are built. Although the problem is most serious with top-of-the-line machines that must be very fast, it is also an issue at the low end as well, where cost and the price/performance ratio are critical In this section and the following ones, we will look at page table design in detail and show a number of hardware solutions that have been used in actual computers.

The simplest design (at least conceptually) is to have a single page table consisting of an array of fast hardware registers, with one entry for each virtual page, indexed by virtual page number, as shown in Fig. 4-9. When a process is started up, the operating system loads the registers with the process' page table, taken from a copy kept in main memory. During process execution, no more memory references are needed for the page table. The advantages of this method are that it is straightforward and requires no memory references during mapping. A disadvantage is that it is potentially expensive (if the page table is large). Also, having to load the full page table at every context switch hurts performance.

At the other extreme, the page table can be entirely in main memory. All the hardware needs then is a single register that points to the start of the page table. This design allows the memory map to be changed at a context switch by reloading one register. Of course, it has the disadvantage of requiring one or more memory references to read page table entries during the execution of each instruction. For this reason, this approach is rarely used in its most pure form, but below we will study some variations that have much better performance.

Multilevel Page Tables

To get around the problem of having to store huge page tables in memory all the time, many computers use a multilevel page table. A simple example is shown in Fig. 4-10. In Fig. 4-10(a) we have a 32-bit virtual address that is partitioned into a 10-bit *PT1* field, a 10-bit *PT2* field, and a 12-bit *Offset* field. Since offsets are 12 bits, pages are 4 KB, and there are a total of 2^{20} of them.

The secret to the multilevel page table method is to avoid keeping all the page tables in memory all the time. In particular, those that are not needed should not be kept around. Suppose, for example, that a process needs 12 megabytes, the bottom 4 megabytes of memory for program text, the next 4 megabytes for data, and the top 4 megabytes for the stack. In between the top of the data and the bottom of the stack is a gigantic hole that is not used.

In Fig. 4-10(b) we see how the two-level page table works in this example. On the left we have the top-level page table, with 1024 entries, corresponding to the 10-bit *PT1* field. When a virtual address is presented to the MMU, it first extracts the *PT1* field and uses this value as an index into the top-level page table. Each of these 1024 entries represents 4M because the entire 4-gigabyte (i.e., 32-bit) virtual address space has been chopped into chunks of 1024 bytes.

The entry located by indexing into the top-level page table yields the address or the page frame number of a second-level page table. Entry 0 of the top-level page table points to the page table for the program text, entry 1 points to the page table for the data, and entry 1023 points to the page table for the stack. The other (shaded) entries are not used. The *PT2* field is now used as an index into the selected second-level page table to find the page frame number for the page itself.

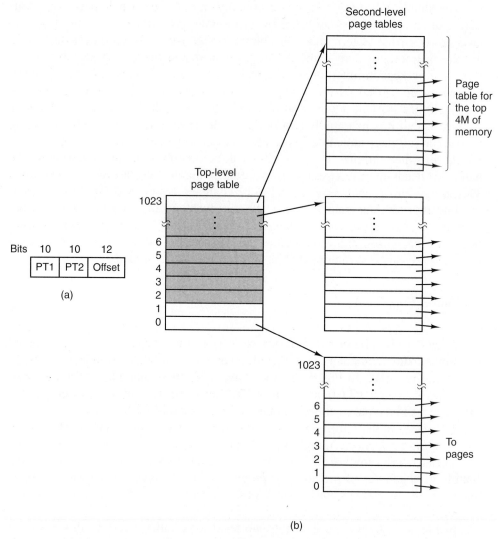

Figure 4-10. (a) A 32-bit address with two page table fields. (b) Two-level page tables.

As an example, consider the 32-bit virtual address 0x00403004 (4,206,596 decimal), which is 12,292 bytes into the data. This virtual address corresponds to $PT1 = 1$, $PT2 = 2$, and $Offset = 4$. The MMU first uses $PT1$ to index into the top-level page table and obtain entry 1, which corresponds to addresses 4M to 8M. It then uses $PT2$ to index into the second-level page table just found and extract entry 3, which corresponds to addresses 12,288 to 16,383 within its 4M chunk (i.e., absolute addresses 4,206,592 to 4,210,687). This entry contains the page frame number of the page containing virtual address 0x00403004. If that page is not in memory, the *present/absent* bit in the page table entry will be zero, causing a page fault. If the page is in memory, the page frame number taken from the second-level page table is combined with the offset (4) to construct a physical address. This address is put on the bus and sent to memory.

The interesting thing to note about Fig. 4-10 is that although the address space contains over a million pages, only four page tables are actually needed: the top-level table, the second-level tables for 0 to 4M, 4M to 8M, and the top 4M. The *present/absent* bits in 1021 entries of the top-level page table are set to 0, forcing a page fault if they are ever accessed. Should this occur, the operating system will notice that the process is trying to reference memory that it is not supposed to and will take appropriate action, such as sending it a signal or killing it. In this example we have chosen round numbers for the various sizes and have picked *PT1* equal to *PT2* but in actual practice other values are also possible, of course.

The two-level page table system of Fig. 4-10 can be expanded to three, four, or more levels. Additional levels give more flexibility, but it is doubtful that the additional complexity is worth it beyond two levels.

Structure of a Page Table Entry

Let us now turn from the structure of the page tables in the large, to the details of a single page table entry. The exact layout of an entry is highly machine dependent, but the kind of information present is roughly the same from machine to machine. In Fig. 4-11 we give a sample page table entry. The size varies from computer to computer, but 32 bits is a common size. The most important field is the *page frame number*. After all, the goal of the page mapping is to locate this value. Next to it we have the *present/absent* bit. If this bit is 1, the entry is valid and can be used. If it is 0, the virtual page to which the entry belongs is not currently in memory. Accessing a page table entry with this bit set to 0 causes a page fault.

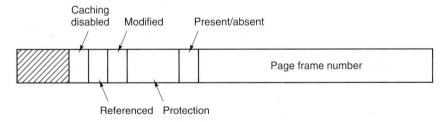

Figure 4-11. A typical page table entry.

The *protection* bits tell what kinds of access are permitted. In the simplest form, this field contains 1 bit, with 0 for read/write and 1 for read only. A more sophisticated arrangement is having 3 independent bits, one bit each for individually enabling reading, writing, and executing the page.

The *modified* and *referenced* bits keep track of page usage. When a page is written to, the hardware automatically sets the *modified* bit. This bit is used when the operating system decides to reclaim a page frame. If the page in it has been modified (i.e., is "dirty"), it must be written back to the disk. If it has not been modified (i.e., is "clean"), it can just be abandoned, since the disk copy is still valid. The bit is sometimes called the **dirty bit**, since it reflects the page's state.

The *referenced* bit is set whenever a page is referenced, either for reading or writing. Its value is to help the operating system choose a page to evict when a page fault occurs. Pages that are not being used are better candidates than pages that are, and this bit plays an important role in several of the page replacement algorithms that we will study later in this chapter.

Finally, the last bit allows caching to be disabled for the page. This feature is important for pages that map onto device registers rather than memory. If the operating system is sitting in a tight loop waiting for some I/O device to respond to a command it was just given, it is essential that the hardware keep fetching the word from the device, and not use an old cached copy. With this bit, caching can be turned off. Machines that have a separate I/O space and do not use memory mapped I/O do not need this bit.

Note that the disk address used to hold the page when it is not in memory is not part of the page table. The reason is simple. The page table holds only that information the hardware needs to translate a virtual address to a physical address. Information the operating system needs to handle page faults is kept in software tables inside the operating system. The hardware does not need it.

4.3.3 TLBs—Translation Lookaside Buffers

In most paging schemes, the page tables are kept in memory, due to their large size. Potentially, this design has an enormous impact on performance. Consider, for example, an instruction that copies one register to another. In the absence of paging, this instruction makes only one memory reference, to fetch the instruction. With paging, additional memory references will be needed to access the page table. Since execution speed is generally limited by the rate the CPU can get instructions and data out of the memory, having to make two page table references per memory reference reduces performance by 2/3. Under these conditions, no one would use it.

Computer designers have known about this problem for years and have come up with a solution. Their solution is based on the observation that most programs tend to make a large number of references to a small number of pages, and not the other way around. Thus only a small fraction of the page table entries are heavily read; the rest are barely used at all. This is an example of **locality of reference**, a concept we will come back to in a later section.

The solution that has been devised is to equip computers with a small hardware device for rapidly mapping virtual addresses to physical addresses without going through the page table. The device, called a **TLB** (**Translation Lookaside Buffer**) or sometimes an **associative memory**, is illustrated in Fig. 4-12. It is usually inside the MMU and consists of a small number of entries, eight in this example, but rarely more than 64. Each entry contains information about one page, including the virtual page number, a bit that is set when the page is modified, the protection code (read/write/execute permissions), and the physical page frame in which the page is located. These fields have a one-to-one correspondence with the fields in the page table. Another bit indicates whether the entry is valid (i.e., in use) or not.

Valid	Virtual page	Modified	Protection	Page frame
1	140	1	RW	31
1	20	0	R X	38
1	130	1	RW	29
1	129	1	RW	62
1	19	0	R X	50
1	21	0	R X	45
1	860	1	RW	14
1	861	1	RW	75

Figure 4-12. A TLB to speed up paging.

An example that might generate the TLB of Fig. 4-12 is a process in a loop that spans virtual pages 19, 20, and 21, so these TLB entries have protection codes for reading and executing. The main data currently being used (say, an array being processed) are on pages 129 and 130. Page 140 contains the indices used in the array calculations. Finally, the stack is on pages 860 and 861.

Let us now see how the TLB functions. When a virtual address is presented to the MMU for translation, the hardware first checks to see if its virtual page number is present in the TLB by comparing it to all the entries simultaneously (i.e., in parallel). If a valid match is found and the access does not violate the protection bits, the page frame is taken directly from the TLB, without going to the page table. If the virtual page number is present in the TLB but the instruction is trying to write on a read-only page, a protection fault is generated, the same way as it would be from the page table itself.

The interesting case is what happens when the virtual page number is not in the TLB. The MMU detects the miss and does an ordinary page table lookup. It then evicts one of the entries from the TLB and replaces it with the page table entry just looked up. Thus if that page is used again soon, the second time around it will result in a hit rather than a miss. When an entry is purged from the TLB, the modified bit is copied back into the page table entry in memory. The other values are already there. When the TLB is loaded from the page table, all the fields are taken from memory.

Software TLB Management

Up until now, we have assumed that every machine with paged virtual memory has page tables recognized by the hardware, plus a TLB. In this design, TLB management and handling TLB faults are done entirely by the MMU hardware. Traps to the operating system occur only when a page is not in memory.

In the past, this assumption was true. However, many modern RISC machines, including the SPARC, MIPS, HP PA, and PowerPC, do nearly all of this page management in software. On these machines, the TLB entries are explicitly loaded by the operating system. When a TLB miss occurs, instead of the MMU just going to the page tables to find and fetch the needed page reference, it just generates a TLB fault and tosses the problem into the lap of the operating system. The system must find the page, remove an entry from the TLB, enter the new one, and restart the instruction that faulted. And, of course, all of this must be done in a handful of instructions because TLB misses occur much more frequently than page faults.

Surprisingly enough, if the TLB is reasonably large (say, 64 entries) to reduce the miss rate, software management of the TLB turns out to be acceptably efficient. The main gain here is a much simpler MMU, which frees up a considerable amount of area on the CPU chip for caches and other features that can improve performance. Software TLB management is discussed by Uhlig et al. (1994).

Various strategies have been developed to improve performance on machines that do TLB management in software. One approach attacks both reducing TLB misses and reducing the cost of a TLB miss when it does occur (Bala et al., 1994). To reduce TLB misses, sometimes the operating system can use its intuition to figure out which pages are likely to be used next and to preload entries for them in the TLB. For example, when a client process sends a message to a server process on the same machine, it is very likely that the server will have to run soon. Knowing this, while processing the trap to do the send, the system can also check to see where the server's code, data, and stack pages are and map them in before they can cause TLB faults.

The normal way to process a TLB miss, whether in hardware or in software, is to go to the page table and perform the indexing operations to locate the page referenced. The problem with doing this search in software is that the pages holding the page table may not be in the TLB, which will cause additional TLB faults during the processing. These faults can be reduced by maintaining a large (e.g., 4-KB or larger) software cache of TLB entries in a fixed location whose page is always kept in the TLB. By first checking the software cache, the operating system can substantially reduce the number of TLB misses.

4.3.4 Inverted Page Tables

Traditional page tables of the type described so far require one entry per virtual page, since they are indexed by virtual page number. If the address space consists of 2^{32} bytes, with 4096 bytes per page, then over 1 million page table entries are needed. As a bare minimum, the page table will have to be at least 4 megabytes. On large systems, this size is probably doable.

However, as 64-bit computers become more common, the situation changes drastically. If the address space is now 2^{64} bytes, with 4-KB pages, we need a page table with 2^{52} entries. If each entry is 8 bytes, the table is over 30 million gigabytes. Tying up 30 million gigabytes just for the page table is not doable, not now and not for years to come, if ever. Consequently, a different solution is needed for 64-bit paged virtual address spaces.

One such solution is the **inverted page table**. In this design, there is one entry per page frame in real memory, rather than one entry per page of virtual address space. For example, with 64-bit virtual addresses, a 4-KB page, and 256 MB of RAM, an inverted page table only requires 65,536 entries. The entry keeps track of which (process, virtual page) is located in the page frame.

Although inverted page tables save vast amounts of space, at least when the virtual address space is much larger than the physical memory, they have a serious downside: virtual-to-physical translation becomes much harder. When process n references virtual page p, the hardware can no longer find the physical page by using p as an index into the page table. Instead, it must search the entire inverted page table for an entry (n, p). Furthermore, this search must be done on every memory reference, not just on page faults. Searching a 64K table on every memory reference is definitely not a good way to make your machine blindingly fast.

The way out of this dilemma is to use the TLB. If the TLB can hold all of the heavily used pages, translation can happen just as fast as with regular page tables. On a TLB miss, however, the inverted page table has to be searched in software. One feasible way to accomplish this search is to have a hash table hashed on the virtual address. All the virtual pages currently in memory that have the same hash value are chained together, as shown in Fig. 4-13. If the hash table has as many slots as the machine has physical pages, the average chain will be only one entry long, greatly speeding up the mapping. Once the page frame number has been found, the new (virtual, physical) pair is entered into the TLB and the faulting instruction restarted.

Inverted page tables are currently used on IBM, Sun, and Hewlett-Packard workstations and will become more common as 64-bit machines become widespread. Inverted page tables are essential on this machines. Other approaches to handling large virtual memories can be found in Huck and Hays (1993), Talluri and Hill (1994), and Talluri et al. (1995). Some hardware issues in implementation of virtual memory are discussed by Jacob and Mudge (1998).

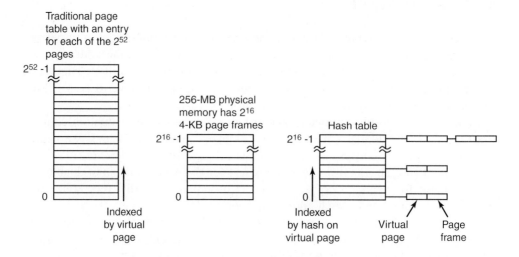

Figure 4-13. Comparison of a traditional page table with an inverted page table.

4.4 PAGE REPLACEMENT ALGORITHMS

When a page fault occurs, the operating system has to choose a page to re-move from memory to make room for the page that has to be brought in. If the page to be removed has been modified while in memory, it must be rewritten to the disk to bring the disk copy up to date. If, however, the page has not been changed (e.g., it contains program text), the disk copy is already up to date, so no rewrite is needed. The page to be read in just overwrites the page being evicted.

While it would be possible to pick a random page to evict at each page fault, system performance is much better if a page that is not heavily used is chosen. If a heavily used page is removed, it will probably have to be brought back in quickly, resulting in extra overhead. Much work has been done on the subject of page replacement algorithms, both theoretical and experimental. Below we will describe some of the most important algorithms.

It is worth noting that the problem of "page replacement" occurs in other areas of computer design as well. For example, most computers have one or more memory caches consisting of recently used 32-byte or 64-byte memory blocks. When the cache is full, some block has to be chosen for removal. This problem is precisely the same as page replacement except on a shorter time scale (it has to be done in a few nanoseconds, not milliseconds as with page replacement). The rea-son for the shorter time scale is that cache block misses are satisfied from main memory, which has no seek time and no rotational latency.

A second example is in a web browser. The browser keeps copies of previ-ously accessed web pages in its cache on the disk. Usually, the maximum cache size is fixed in advance, so the cache is likely to be full if the browser is used a lot. Whenever a web page is referenced, a check is made to see if a copy is in the cache and if so, if the page on the web is newer. If the cached copy is up to date, it is used; otherwise, a fresh copy is fetched from the Web. If the page is not in the cache at all or a newer version is available, it is downloaded. If it is a newer copy of a cached page it replaces the one in the cache. When the cache is full a decision has to be made to evict some other page in the case of a new page or a page that is larger than an older version. The considerations are similar to pages of virtual memory, except for the fact that the Web pages are never modified in the cache and thus are never written back to the web server. In a virtual memory system, pages in main memory may be either clean or dirty.

4.4.1 The Optimal Page Replacement Algorithm

The best possible page replacement algorithm is easy to describe but impossible to implement. It goes like this. At the moment that a page fault occurs, some set of pages is in memory. One of these pages will be referenced on the very next instruction (the page containing that instruction). Other pages may not be referenced until 10, 100, or perhaps 1000 instructions later. Each page can be labeled with the number of instructions that will be executed before that page is first referenced.

The optimal page algorithm simply says that the page with the highest label should be removed. If one page will not be used for 8 million instructions and another page will not be used for 6 million instructions, removing the former pushes the page fault that will fetch it back as far into the future as possible. Computers, like people, try to put off unpleasant events for as long as they can.

The only problem with this algorithm is that it is unrealizable. At the time of the page fault, the operating system has no way of knowing when each of the pages will be referenced next. (We saw a similar situation earlier with the shortest-job-first scheduling algorithm—how can the system tell which job is shortest?) Still, by running a program on a simulator and keeping track of all page references, it is possible to implement optimal page replacement on the *second* run by using the page reference information collected during the *first* run.

In this way it is possible to compare the performance of realizable algorithms with the best possible one. If an operating system achieves a performance of, say, only 1 percent worse than the optimal algorithm, effort spent in looking for a better algorithm will yield at most a 1 percent improvement.

To avoid any possible confusion, it should be made clear that this log of page references refers only to the one program just measured and then with only one specific input. The page replacement algorithm derived from it is thus specific to that one program and input data. Although this method is useful for evaluating page replacement algorithms, it is of no use in practical systems. Below we will study algorithms that *are* useful on real systems.

4.4.2 The Not Recently Used Page Replacement Algorithm

In order to allow the operating system to collect useful statistics about which pages are being used and which ones are not, most computers with virtual memory have two status bits associated with each page. R is set whenever the page is referenced (read or written). M is set when the page is written to (i.e., modified). The bits are contained in each page table entry, as shown in Fig. 4-11. It is important to realize that these bits must be updated on every memory reference, so it is essential that they be set by the hardware. Once a bit has been set to 1, it stays 1 until the operating system resets it to 0 in software.

If the hardware does not have these bits, they can be simulated as follows. When a process is started up, all of its page table entries are marked as not in memory. As soon as any page is referenced, a page fault will occur. The operating system then sets the R bit (in its internal tables), changes the page table entry to point to the correct page, with mode READ ONLY, and restarts the instruction. If the page is subsequently written on, another page fault will occur, allowing the operating system to set the M bit as well and change the page's mode to READ/WRITE.

The R and M bits can be used to build a simple paging algorithm as follows. When a process is started up, both page bits for all its pages are set to 0 by the operating system. Periodically (e.g., on each clock interrupt), the R bit is cleared, to distinguish pages that have not been referenced recently from those that have been.

When a page fault occurs, the operating system inspects all the pages and divides them into four categories based on the current values of their R and M bits:

    Class 0: not referenced, not modified.
    Class 1: not referenced, modified.
    Class 2: referenced, not modified.
    Class 3: referenced, modified.

Although class 1 pages seem, at first glance, impossible, they occur when a class 3 page has its R bit cleared by a clock interrupt. Clock interrupts do not clear the M bit because this information is needed to know whether the page has to be rewritten to disk or not. Clearing R but not M leads to a class 1 page.

The **NRU** (**Not Recently Used**) algorithm removes a page at random from the lowest numbered nonempty class. Implicit in this algorithm is that it is better to remove a modified page that has not been referenced in at least one clock tick (typically 20 msec) than a clean page that is in heavy use. The main attraction of NRU is that it is easy to understand, moderately efficient to implement, and gives a performance that, while certainly not optimal, may be adequate.

4.4.3 The First-In, First-Out (FIFO) Page Replacement Algorithm

Another low-overhead paging algorithm is the **FIFO (First-In, First-Out)** algorithm. To illustrate how this works, consider a supermarket that has enough shelves to display exactly k different products. One day, some company introduces a new convenience food—instant, freeze-dried, organic yogurt that can be reconstituted in a microwave oven. It is an immediate success, so our finite supermarket has to get rid of one old product in order to stock it.

One possibility is to find the product that the supermarket has been stocking the longest (i.e., something it began selling 120 years ago) and get rid of it on the grounds that no one is interested any more. In effect, the supermarket maintains a linked list of all the products it currently sells in the order they were introduced. The new one goes on the back of the list; the one at the front of the list is dropped.

As a page replacement algorithm, the same idea is applicable. The operating system maintains a list of all pages currently in memory, with the page at the head of the list the oldest one and the page at the tail the most recent arrival. On a page fault, the page at the head is removed and the new page added to the tail of the list. When applied to stores, FIFO might remove mustache wax, but it might also remove flour, salt, or butter. When applied to computers the same problem arises. For this reason, FIFO in its pure form is rarely used.

4.4.4 The Second Chance Page Replacement Algorithm

A simple modification to FIFO that avoids the problem of throwing out a heavily used page is to inspect the R bit of the oldest page. If it is 0, the page is both old and unused, so it is replaced immediately. If the R bit is 1, the bit is cleared, the page is put onto the end of the list of pages, and its load time is updated as though it had just arrived in memory. Then the search continues.

The operation of this algorithm, called **second chance**, is shown in Fig. 4-14. In Fig. 4-14(a) we see pages A through H kept on a linked list and sorted by the time they arrived in memory.

Suppose that a page fault occurs at time 20. The oldest page is A, which arrived at time 0, when the process started. If A has the R bit cleared, it is evicted from memory, either by being written to the disk (if it is dirty), or just abandoned (if it is clean). On the other hand, if the R bit is set, A is put onto the end of the list and its "load time" is reset to the current time (20). The R bit is also cleared. The search for a suitable page continues with B.

What second chance is doing is looking for an old page that has not been referenced in the previous clock interval. If all the pages have been referenced, second chance degenerates into pure FIFO. Specifically, imagine that all the pages in Fig. 4-14(a) have their R bits set. One by one, the operating system moves the pages to the end of the list, clearing the R bit each time it appends a page to the end of the list. Eventually, it comes back to page A, which now has its R bit cleared. At this point A is evicted. Thus the algorithm always terminates.

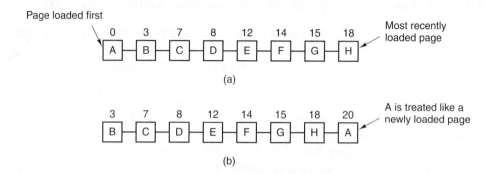

Figure 4-14. Operation of second chance. (a) Pages sorted in FIFO order. (b) Page list if a page fault occurs at time 20 and *A* has its *R* bit set. The numbers above the pages are their loading times.

4.4.5 The Clock Page Replacement Algorithm

Although second chance is a reasonable algorithm, it is unnecessarily inefficient because it is constantly moving pages around on its list. A better approach
is to keep all the page frames on a circular list in the form of a clock, as shown in
Fig. 4-15. A hand points to the oldest page.

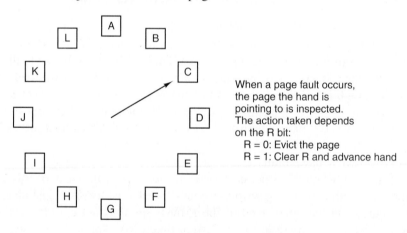

Figure 4-15. The clock page replacement algorithm.

When a page fault occurs, the page being pointed to by the hand is inspected.
If its *R* bit is 0, the page is evicted, the new page is inserted into the clock in its
place, and the hand is advanced one position. If *R* is 1, it is cleared and the hand
is advanced to the next page. This process is repeated until a page is found with
R = 0. Not surprisingly, this algorithm is called **clock**. It differs from second
chance only in the implementation, not in the page selected.

4.4.6 The Least Recently Used (LRU) Page Replacement Algorithm

A good approximation to the optimal algorithm is based on the observation that pages that have been heavily used in the last few instructions will probably be heavily used again in the next few. Conversely, pages that have not been used for ages will probably remain unused for a long time. This idea suggests a realizable algorithm: when a page fault occurs, throw out the page that has been unused for the longest time. This strategy is called **LRU (Least Recently Used)** paging.

Although LRU is theoretically realizable, it is not cheap. To fully implement LRU, it is necessary to maintain a linked list of all pages in memory, with the most recently used page at the front and the least recently used page at the rear. The difficulty is that the list must be updated on every memory reference. Finding a page in the list, deleting it, and then moving it to the front is a very time-consuming operation, even in hardware (assuming that such hardware could be built).

However, there are other ways to implement LRU with special hardware. Let us consider the simplest way first. This method requires equipping the hardware with a 64-bit counter, C, that is automatically incremented after each instruction. Furthermore, each page table entry must also have a field large enough to contain the counter. After each memory reference, the current value of C is stored in the page table entry for the page just referenced. When a page fault occurs, the operating system examines all the counters in the page table to find the lowest one. That page is the least recently used.

Now let us look at a second hardware LRU algorithm. For a machine with n page frames, the LRU hardware can maintain a matrix of $n \times n$ bits, initially all zero. Whenever page frame k is referenced, the hardware first sets all the bits of row k to 1, then sets all the bits of column k to 0. At any instant, the row whose binary value is lowest is the least recently used, the row whose value is next lowest is next least recently used, and so forth. The workings of this algorithm are given in Fig. 4-16 for four page frames and page references in the order

0 1 2 3 2 1 0 3 2 3

After page 0 is referenced, we have the situation of Fig. 4-16(a). After page 1 is referenced, we have the situation of Fig. 4-16(b), and so forth.

4.4.7 Simulating LRU in Software

Although both of the previous LRU algorithms are realizable in principle, few, if any, machines have this hardware, so they are of little use to the operating system designer who is making a system for a machine that does not have this hardware. Instead, a solution that can be implemented in software is needed. One possible software solution is called the **NFU (Not Frequently Used)** algorithm.

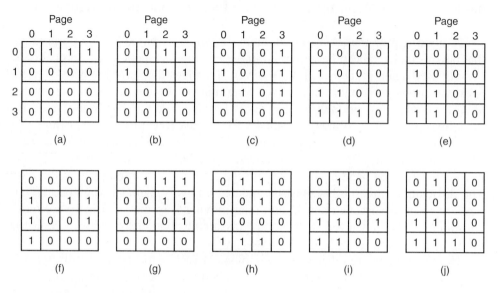

Figure 4-16. LRU using a matrix when pages are referenced in the order 0, 1, 2, 3, 2, 1, 0, 3, 2, 3.

It requires a software counter associated with each page, initially zero. At each clock interrupt, the operating system scans all the pages in memory. For each page, the R bit, which is 0 or 1, is added to the counter. In effect, the counters are an attempt to keep track of how often each page has been referenced. When a page fault occurs, the page with the lowest counter is chosen for replacement.

The main problem with NFU is that it never forgets anything. For example, in a multipass compiler, pages that were heavily used during pass 1 may still have a high count well into later passes. In fact, if pass 1 happens to have the longest execution time of all the passes, the pages containing the code for subsequent passes may always have lower counts than the pass 1 pages. Thus the operating system will remove useful pages instead of pages no longer in use.

Fortunately, a small modification to NFU makes it able to simulate LRU quite well. The modification has two parts. First, the counters are each shifted right 1 bit before the R bit is added in. Second, the R bit is added to the leftmost, rather than the rightmost bit.

Figure 4-17 illustrates how the modified algorithm, known as **aging**, works. Suppose that after the first clock tick the R bits for pages 0 to 5 have the values 1, 0, 1, 0, 1, and 1, respectively (page 0 is 1, page 1 is 0, page 2 is 1, etc.). In other words, between tick 0 and tick 1, pages 0, 2, 4, and 5 were referenced, setting their R bits to 1, while the other ones remain 0. After the six corresponding counters have been shifted and the R bit inserted at the left, they have the values shown in Fig. 4-17(a). The four remaining columns show the values of the six counters after the next four clock ticks, respectively.

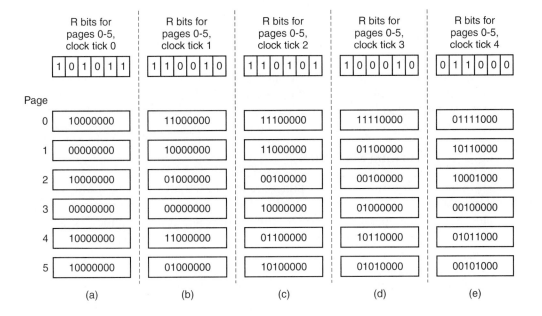

Figure 4-17. The aging algorithm simulates LRU in software. Shown are six pages for five clock ticks. The five clock ticks are represented by (a) to (e).

When a page fault occurs, the page whose counter is the lowest is removed. It is clear that a page that has not been referenced for, say, four clock ticks will have four leading zeros in its counter and thus will have a lower value than a counter that has not been referenced for three clock ticks.

This algorithm differs from LRU in two ways. Consider pages 3 and 5 in Fig. 4-17(e). Neither has been referenced for two clock ticks; both were referenced in the tick prior to that. According to LRU, if a page must be replaced, we should choose one of these two. The trouble is, we do not know which of these two was referenced last in the interval between tick 1 and tick 2. By recording only one bit per time interval, we have lost the ability to distinguish references early in the clock interval from those occurring later. All we can do is remove page 3, because page 5 was also referenced two ticks earlier and page 3 was not referenced then.

The second difference between LRU and aging is that in aging the counters have a finite number of bits, 8 bits in this example. Suppose that two pages each have a counter value of 0. All we can do is pick one of them at random. In reality, it may well be that one of the pages was last referenced 9 ticks ago and the other was last referenced 1000 ticks ago. We have no way of seeing that. In practice, however, 8 bits is generally enough if a clock tick is around 20 msec. If a page has not been referenced in 160 msec, it probably is not that important.

4.5 DESIGN ISSUES FOR PAGING SYSTEMS

In the previous sections we have explained how paging works and have given a few of the basic page replacement algorithms and shown how to model them. But knowing the bare mechanics is not enough. To design a system, you have to know a lot more to make it work well. It is like the difference between knowing how to move the rook, knight, and other pieces in chess, and being a good player. In the following sections, we will look at other issues that operating system designers must consider in order to get good performance from a paging system.

4.5.1 The Working Set Model

In the purest form of paging, processes are started up with none of their pages in memory. As soon as the CPU tries to fetch the first instruction, it gets a page fault, causing the operating system to bring in the page containing the first instruction. Other page faults for global variables and the stack usually follow quickly. After a while, the process has most of the pages it needs and settles down to run with relatively few page faults. This strategy is called **demand paging** because pages are loaded only on demand, not in advance.

Of course, it is easy enough to write a test program that systematically reads all the pages in a large address space, causing so many page faults that there is not enough memory to hold them all. Fortunately, most processes do not work this way. They exhibit a **locality of reference**, meaning that during any phase of execution, the process references only a relatively small fraction of its pages. Each pass of a multipass compiler, for example, references only a fraction of the pages, and a different fraction at that. The concept of locality of reference is widely applicable in computer science, for a history see Denning (2005).

The set of pages that a process is currently using is called its **working set** (Denning, 1968a; Denning, 1980). If the entire working set is in memory, the process will run without causing many faults until it moves into another execution phase (e.g., the next pass of the compiler). If the available memory is too small to hold the entire working set, the process will cause numerous page faults and run slowly since executing an instruction takes a few nanoseconds and reading in a page from the disk typically takes 10 milliseconds. At a rate of one or two instructions per 10 milliseconds, it will take ages to finish. A program causing page faults every few instructions is said to be **thrashing** (Denning, 1968b).

In a multiprogramming system, processes are frequently moved to disk (i.e., all their pages are removed from memory) to let other processes have a turn at the CPU. The question arises of what to do when a process is brought back in again. Technically, nothing need be done. The process will just cause page faults until its working set has been loaded. The problem is that having 20, 100, or even 1000 page faults every time a process is loaded is slow, and it also wastes considerable CPU time, since it takes the operating system a few milliseconds of CPU time to process a page fault, not to mention a fair amount of disk I/O.

Therefore, many paging systems try to keep track of each process' working set and make sure that it is in memory before letting the process run. This approach is called the **working set model** (Denning, 1970). It is designed to greatly reduce the page fault rate. Loading the pages *before* letting processes run is also called **prepaging.** Note that the working set changes over time.

It has long been known that most programs do not reference their address space uniformly Instead the references tend to cluster on a small number of pages. A memory reference may fetch an instruction, it may fetch data, or it may store data. At any instant of time, t, there exists a set consisting of all the pages used by the k most recent memory references. This set, $w(k, t)$, is the working set. Because a larger value of k means looking further into the past, the number of pages counted as part of the working set cannot decrease as k is made larger. So $w(k, t)$ is a monotonically nondecreasing function of k. The limit of $w(k, t)$ as k becomes large is finite because a program cannot reference more pages than its address space contains, and few programs will use every single page. Figure 4-18 depicts the size of the working set as a function of k.

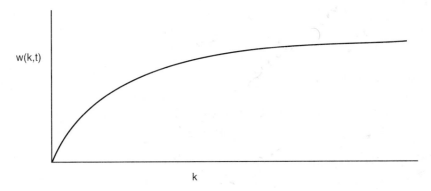

Figure 4-18. The working set is the set of pages used by the k most recent memory references. The function $w(k, t)$ is the size of the working set at time t.

The fact that most programs randomly access a small number of pages, but that this set changes slowly in time explains the initial rapid rise of the curve and then the slow rise for large k. For example, a program that is executing a loop occupying two pages using data on four pages, may reference all six pages every 1000 instructions, but the most recent reference to some other page may be a million instructions earlier, during the initialization phase. Due to this asymptotic behavior, the contents of the working set is not sensitive to the value of k chosen. To put it differently, there exists a wide range of k values for which the working set is unchanged. Because the working set varies slowly with time, it is possible to make a reasonable guess as to which pages will be needed when the program is restarted on the basis of its working set when it was last stopped. Prepaging consists of loading these pages before the process is allowed to run again.

To implement the working set model, it is necessary for the operating system to keep track of which pages are in the working set. One way to monitor this information is to use the aging algorithm discussed above. Any page containing a 1 bit among the high order n bits of the counter is considered to be a member of the working set. If a page has not been referenced in n consecutive clock ticks, it is dropped from the working set. The parameter n has to be determined experimentally for each system, but the system performance is usually not especially sensitive to the exact value.

Information about the working set can be used to improve the performance of the clock algorithm. Normally, when the hand points to a page whose R bit is 0, the page is evicted. The improvement is to check to see if that page is part of the working set of the current process. If it is, the page is spared. This algorithm is called **wsclock**.

4.5.2 Local versus Global Allocation Policies

In the preceding sections we have discussed several algorithms for choosing a page to replace when a fault occurs. A major issue associated with this choice (which we have carefully swept under the rug until now) is how memory should be allocated among the competing runnable processes.

Take a look at Fig. 4-19(a). In this figure, three processes, A, B, and C, make up the set of runnable processes. Suppose A gets a page fault. Should the page replacement algorithm try to find the least recently used page considering only the six pages currently allocated to A, or should it consider all the pages in memory? If it looks only at A's pages, the page with the lowest age value is $A5$, so we get the situation of Fig. 4-19(b).

On the other hand, if the page with the lowest age value is removed without regard to whose page it is, page $B3$ will be chosen and we will get the situation of Fig. 4-19(c). The algorithm of Fig. 4-19(b) is said to be a **local** page replacement algorithm, whereas that of Fig. 4-19(c) is said to be a **global** algorithm. Local algorithms effectively correspond to allocating every process a fixed fraction of the memory. Global algorithms dynamically allocate page frames among the runnable processes. Thus the number of page frames assigned to each process varies in time.

In general, global algorithms work better, especially when the working set size can vary over the lifetime of a process. If a local algorithm is used and the working set grows, thrashing will result, even if there are plenty of free page frames. If the working set shrinks, local algorithms waste memory. If a global algorithm is used, the system must continually decide how many page frames to assign to each process. One way is to monitor the working set size as indicated by the aging bits, but this approach does not necessarily prevent thrashing. The working set may change size in microseconds, whereas the aging bits are a crude measure spread over a number of clock ticks.

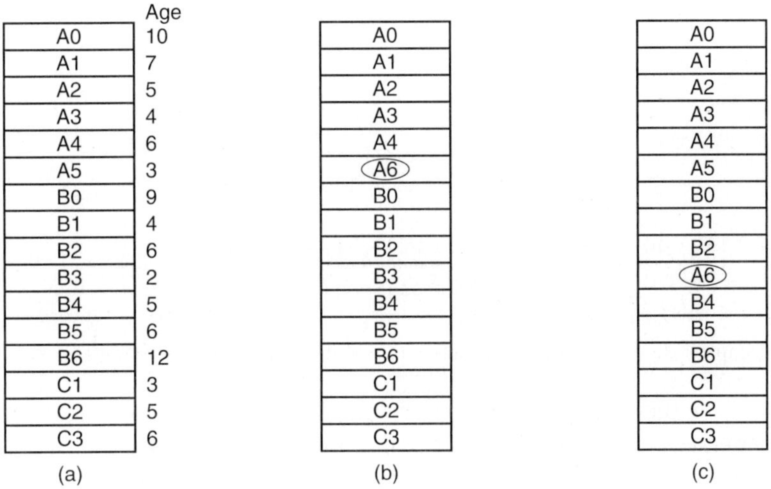

	Age
A0	10
A1	7
A2	5
A3	4
A4	6
A5	3
B0	9
B1	4
B2	6
B3	2
B4	5
B5	6
B6	12
C1	3
C2	5
C3	6

(a)

A0
A1
A2
A3
A4
(A6)
B0
B1
B2
B3
B4
B5
B6
C1
C2
C3

(b)

A0
A1
A2
A3
A4
A5
B0
B1
B2
(A6)
B4
B5
B6
C1
C2
C3

(c)

Figure 4-19. Local versus global page replacement. (a) Original configuration. (b) Local page replacement. (c) Global page replacement.

Another approach is to have an algorithm for allocating page frames to processes. One way is to periodically determine the number of running processes and allocate each process an equal share. Thus with 12,416 available (i.e., nonoperating system) page frames and 10 processes, each process gets 1241 frames. The remaining 6 go into a pool to be used when page faults occur.

Although this method seems fair, it makes little sense to give equal shares of the memory to a 10-KB process and a 300-KB process. Instead, pages can be allocated in proportion to each process' total size, with a 300-KB process getting 30 times the allotment of a 10-KB process. It is probably wise to give each process some minimum number, so it can run, no matter how small it is. On some machines, for example, a single two-operand instruction may need as many as six pages because the instruction itself, the source operand, and the destination operand may all straddle page boundaries. With an allocation of only five pages, programs containing such instructions cannot execute at all.

If a global algorithm is used, it may be possible to start each process up with some number of pages proportional to the process' size, but the allocation has to be updated dynamically as the processes run. One way to manage the allocation is to use the **PFF** (**Page Fault Frequency**) algorithm. It tells when to increase or decrease a process' page allocation but says nothing about which page to replace on a fault. It just controls the size of the allocation set.

For a large class of page replacement algorithms, including LRU, it is known that the fault rate decreases as more pages are assigned, as we discussed above. This is the assumption behind PFF. This property is illustrated in Fig. 4-20.

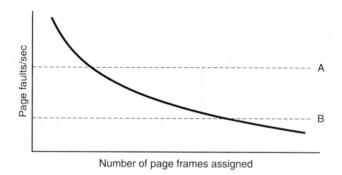

Figure 4-20. Page fault rate as a function of the number of page frames assigned.

Measuring the page fault rate is straightforward: just count the number of faults per second, possibly taking a running mean over past seconds as well. One easy way to do this is to add the present second's value to the current running mean and divide by two. The dashed line marked *A* corresponds to a page fault rate that is unacceptably high, so the faulting process is given more page frames to reduce the fault rate. The dashed line marked *B* corresponds to a page fault rate so low that it can be concluded that the process has too much memory. In this case, page frames may be taken away from it. Thus, PFF tries to keep the paging rate for each process within acceptable bounds.

If it discovers that there are so many processes in memory that it is not possible to keep all of them below *A*, then some process is removed from memory, and its page frames are divided up among the remaining processes or put into a pool of available pages that can be used on subsequent page faults. The decision to remove a process from memory is a form of **load control**. It shows that even with paging, swapping is still needed, only now swapping is used to reduce potential demand for memory, rather than to reclaim blocks of it for immediate use. Swapping processes out to relieve the load on memory is reminiscent of two-level scheduling, in which some processes are put on disk and a short-term scheduler is used to schedule the remaining processes. Clearly, the two ideas can be combined, with just enough processes swapped out to make the page-fault rate acceptable.

4.5.3 Page Size

The page size is often a parameter that can be chosen by the operating system. Even if the hardware has been designed with, for example, 512-byte pages, the operating system can easily regard pages 0 and 1, 2 and 3, 4 and 5, and so on, as 1-KB pages by always allocating two consecutive 512-byte page frames for them.

Determining the best page size requires balancing several competing factors. As a result, there is no overall optimum. To start with, there are two factors that argue for a small page size. A randomly chosen text, data, or stack segment will not fill an integral number of pages. On the average, half of the final page will be empty. The extra space in that page is wasted. This wastage is called **internal fragmentation**. With n segments in memory and a page size of p bytes, $np/2$ bytes will be wasted on internal fragmentation. This argues for a small page size.

Another argument for a small page size becomes apparent if we think about a program consisting of eight sequential phases of 4 KB each. With a 32-KB page size, the program must be allocated 32 KB all the time. With a 16-KB page size, it needs only 16 KB. With a page size of 4 KB or smaller, it requires only 4 KB at any instant. In general, a large page size will cause more unused program to be in memory than a small page size.

On the other hand, small pages mean that programs will need many pages, hence a large page table. A 32-KB program needs only four 8-KB pages, but 64 512-byte pages. Transfers to and from the disk are generally a page at a time, with most of the time being for the seek and rotational delay, so that transferring a small page takes almost as much time as transferring a large page. It might take 64×10 msec to load 64 512-byte pages, but only 4×10.1 msec to load four 8-KB pages.

On some machines, the page table must be loaded into hardware registers every time the CPU switches from one process to another. On these machines having a small page size means that the time required to load the page registers gets longer as the page size gets smaller. Furthermore, the space occupied by the page table increases as the page size decreases.

This last point can be analyzed mathematically. Let the average process size be s bytes and the page size be p bytes. Furthermore, assume that each page entry requires e bytes. The approximate number of pages needed per process is then s/p, occupying se/p bytes of page table space. The wasted memory in the last page of the process due to internal fragmentation is $p/2$. Thus, the total overhead due to the page table and the internal fragmentation loss is given by the sum of these two terms:

$$\text{overhead} = se/p + p/2$$

The first term (page table size) is large when the page size is small. The second term (internal fragmentation) is large when the page size is large. The optimum must lie somewhere in between. By taking the first derivative with respect to p and equating it to zero, we get the equation

$$-se/p^2 + 1/2 = 0$$

From this equation we can derive a formula that gives the optimum page size (considering only memory wasted in fragmentation and page table size). The result is:

$$p = \sqrt{2se}$$

For s = 1MB and e = 8 bytes per page table entry, the optimum page size is 4 KB. Commercially available computers have used page sizes ranging from 512 bytes to 1 MB. A typical value used to 1 KB, but nowadays 4 KB or 8 KB are more common. As memories get larger, the page size tends to get larger as well (but not linearly). Quadrupling the RAM size rarely even doubles the page size.

4.5.4 Virtual Memory Interface

Up until now, our whole discussion has assumed that virtual memory is transparent to processes and programmers. That is, all they see is a large virtual address space on a computer with a small(er) physical memory. With many systems, that is true, but in some advanced systems, programmers have some control over the memory map and can use it in nontraditional ways to enhance program behavior. In this section, we will briefly look at a few of these.

One reason for giving programmers control over their memory map is to allow two or more processes to share the same memory. If programmers can name regions of their memory, it may be possible for one process to give another process the name of a memory region so that process can also map it in. With two (or more) processes sharing the same pages, high bandwidth sharing becomes possible: one process writes into the shared memory and another one reads from it.

Sharing of pages can also be used to implement a high-performance message-passing system. Normally, when messages are passed, the data are copied from one address space to another, at considerable cost. If processes can control their page map, a message can be passed by having the sending process unmap the page(s) containing the message, and the receiving process mapping them in. Here only the page names have to be copied, instead of all the data.

Yet another advanced memory management technique is **distributed shared memory** (Feeley et al., 1995; Li and Hudak, 1989; and Zekauskas et al., 1994). The idea here is to allow multiple processes over a network to share a set of pages, possibly, but not necessarily, as a single shared linear address space. When a process references a page that is not currently mapped in, it gets a page fault. The page fault handler, which may be in the kernel or in user space, then locates the machine holding the page and sends it a message asking it to unmap the page and send it over the network. When the page arrives, it is mapped in and the faulting instruction is restarted.

4.6 SEGMENTATION

The virtual memory discussed so far is one-dimensional because the virtual addresses go from 0 to some maximum address, one address after another. For many problems, having two or more separate virtual address spaces may be much better than having only one. For example, a compiler has many tables that are built up as compilation proceeds, possibly including

1. The source text being saved for the printed listing (on batch systems).

2. The symbol table, containing the names and attributes of variables.

3. The table containing all the integer and floating-point constants used.

4. The parse tree, containing the syntactic analysis of the program.

5. The stack used for procedure calls within the compiler.

Each of the first four tables grows continuously as compilation proceeds. The last one grows and shrinks in unpredictable ways during compilation. In a one-dimensional memory, these five tables would have to be allocated contiguous chunks of virtual address space, as in Fig. 4-21.

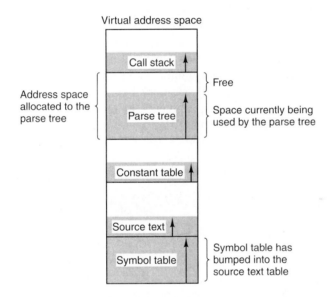

Figure 4-21. In a one-dimensional address space with growing tables, one table may bump into another.

Consider what happens if a program has an exceptionally large number of variables but a normal amount of everything else. The chunk of address space allocated for the symbol table may fill up, but there may be lots of room in the other tables. The compiler could, of course, simply issue a message saying that the compilation cannot continue due to too many variables, but doing so does not seem very sporting when unused space is left in the other tables.

Another possibility is to play Robin Hood, taking space from the tables with an excess of room and giving it to the tables with little room. This shuffling can be done, but it is analogous to managing one's own overlays—a nuisance at best and a great deal of tedious, unrewarding work at worst.

What is really needed is a way of freeing the programmer from having to manage the expanding and contracting tables, in the same way that virtual memory eliminates the worry of organizing the program into overlays.

A straightforward and extremely general solution is to provide the machine with many completely independent address spaces, called **segments**. Each segment consists of a linear sequence of addresses, from 0 to some maximum. The length of each segment may be anything from 0 to the maximum allowed. Different segments may, and usually do, have different lengths. Moreover, segment lengths may change during execution. The length of a stack segment may be increased whenever something is pushed onto the stack and decreased whenever something is popped off the stack.

Because each segment constitutes a separate address space, different segments can grow or shrink independently, without affecting each other. If a stack in a certain segment needs more address space to grow, it can have it, because there is nothing else in its address space to bump into. Of course, a segment can fill up but segments are usually very large, so this occurrence is rare. To specify an address in this segmented or two-dimensional memory, the program must supply a two-part address, a segment number, and an address within the segment. Figure 4-22 illustrates a segmented memory being used for the compiler tables discussed earlier. Five independent segments are shown here.

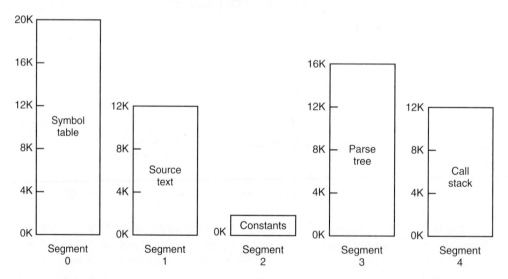

Figure 4-22. A segmented memory allows each table to grow or shrink independently of the other tables.

We emphasize that in its purest form, a segment is a logical entity, which the programmer is aware of and uses as a logical entity. A segment might contain one or more procedures, or an array, or a stack, or a collection of scalar variables, but usually it does not contain a mixture of different types.

A segmented memory has other advantages besides simplifying the handling of data structures that are growing or shrinking. If each procedure occupies a separate segment, with address 0 as its starting address, the linking up of procedures compiled separately is greatly simplified. After all the procedures that constitute a program have been compiled and linked up, a procedure call to the procedure in segment n will use the two-part address (n, 0) to address word 0 (the entry point).

If the procedure in segment n is subsequently modified and recompiled, no other procedures need be changed (because no starting addresses have been modified), even if the new version is larger than the old one. With a one-dimensional memory, the procedures are packed tightly next to each other, with no address space between them. Consequently, changing one procedure's size can affect the starting address of other, unrelated procedures. This, in turn, requires modifying all procedures that call any of the moved procedures, in order to incorporate their new starting addresses. If a program contains hundreds of procedures, this process can be costly.

Segmentation also facilitates sharing procedures or data between several processes. A common example is the **shared library**. Modern workstations that run advanced window systems often have extremely large graphical libraries compiled into nearly every program. In a segmented system, the graphical library can be put in a segment and shared by multiple processes, eliminating the need for having it in every process' address space. While it is also possible to have shared libraries in pure paging systems, it is much more complicated. In effect, these systems do it by simulating segmentation.

Because each segment forms a logical entity of which the programmer is aware, such as a procedure, or an array, or a stack, different segments can have different kinds of protection. A procedure segment can be specified as execute only, prohibiting attempts to read from it or store into it. A floating-point array can be specified as read/write but not execute, and attempts to jump to it will be caught. Such protection is helpful in catching programming errors.

You should try to understand why protection makes sense in a segmented memory but not in a one-dimensional paged memory. In a segmented memory the user is aware of what is in each segment. Normally, a segment would not contain a procedure and a stack, for example, but one or the other. Since each segment contains only one type of object, the segment can have the protection appropriate for that particular type. Paging and segmentation are compared in Fig. 4-23.

The contents of a page are, in a certain sense, accidental. The programmer is unaware of the fact that paging is even occurring. Although putting a few bits in each entry of the page table to specify the access allowed would be possible, to utilize this feature the programmer would have to keep track of where in his address space all the page boundaries were. However, that is precisely the sort of complex administration that paging was invented to eliminate. Because the user

Consideration	Paging	Segmentation
Need the programmer be aware that this technique is being used?	No	Yes
How many linear address spaces are there?	1	Many
Can the total address space exceed the size of physical memory?	Yes	Yes
Can procedures and data be distinguished and separately protected?	No	Yes
Can tables whose size fluctuates be accommodated easily?	No	Yes
Is sharing of procedures between users facilitated?	No	Yes
Why was this technique invented?	To get a large linear address space without having to buy more physical memory	To allow programs and data to be broken up into logically independent address spaces and to aid sharing and protection

Figure 4-23. Comparison of paging and segmentation.

of a segmented memory has the illusion that all segments are in main memory all the time—that is, he can address them as though they were—he can protect each segment separately, without having to be concerned with the administration of overlaying them.

4.6.1 Implementation of Pure Segmentation

The implementation of segmentation differs from paging in an essential way: pages are fixed size and segments are not. Figure 4-24(a) shows an example of physical memory initially containing five segments. Now consider what happens if segment 1 is evicted and segment 7, which is smaller, is put in its place. We arrive at the memory configuration of Fig. 4-24(b). Between segment 7 and segment 2 is an unused area—that is, a hole. Then segment 4 is replaced by segment 5, as in Fig. 4-24(c), and segment 3 is replaced by segment 6, as in Fig. 4-24(d). After the system has been running for a while, memory will be divided up into a number of chunks, some containing segments and some containing holes. This phenomenon, called **checkerboarding** or **external fragmentation**, wastes memory in the holes. It can be dealt with by compaction, as shown in Fig. 4-24(e).

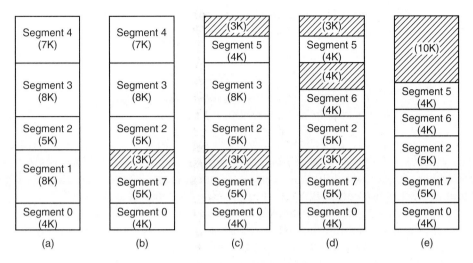

Figure 4-24. (a)-(d) Development of checkerboarding. (e) Removal of the checkerboarding by compaction.

4.6.2 Segmentation with Paging: The Intel Pentium

The Pentium supports up to 16K segments, each with up to 2^{32} bytes of virtual address space. The Pentium can be set up (by the operating system) to use only segmentation, only paging, or both. Most operating systems, including Windows XP and all flavors of UNIX, use the pure paging model, in which each process has a single segment of 2^{32} bytes. Since the Pentium is capable of providing processes with a much larger address space, and one operating system (OS/2) did actually use the full power of the addressing, we will describe how Pentium virtual memory works in its full generality.

The heart of the Pentium virtual memory consists of two tables, the **LDT** (**Local Descriptor Table**) and the **GDT** (**Global Descriptor Table**). Each program has its own LDT, but there is a single GDT, shared by all the programs on the computer. The LDT describes segments local to each program, including its code, data, stack, and so on, whereas the GDT describes system segments, including the operating system itself.

To access a segment, a Pentium program first loads a selector for that segment into one of the machine's six segment registers. During execution, the CS register holds the selector for the code segment and the DS register holds the selector for the data segment. The other segment registers are less important. Each selector is a 16-bit number, as shown in Fig. 4-25.

One of the selector bits tells whether the segment is local or global (i.e., whether it is in the LDT or GDT). Thirteen other bits specify the LDT or GDT entry number; thus tables are each restricted to holding 8K segment descriptors.

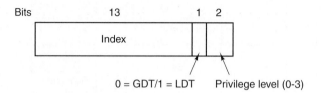

Figure 4-25. A Pentium selector.

The other 2 bits relate to protection, and will be described later. Descriptor 0 is forbidden. It may be safely loaded into a segment register to indicate that the segment register is not currently available. It causes a trap if used.

At the time a selector is loaded into a segment register, the corresponding descriptor is fetched from the LDT or GDT and stored in microprogram registers, so it can be accessed quickly. A descriptor consists of 8 bytes, including the segment's base address, size, and other information, as depicted in Fig. 4-26.

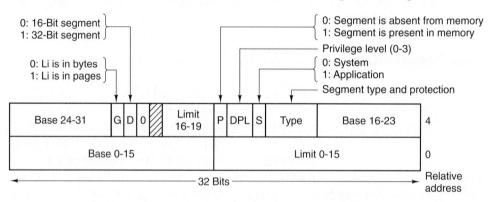

Figure 4-26. Pentium code segment descriptor. Data segments differ slightly.

The format of the selector has been cleverly chosen to make locating the descriptor easy. First either the LDT or GDT is selected, based on selector bit 2. Then the selector is copied to an internal scratch register, and the 3 low-order bits set to 0. Finally, the address of either the LDT or GDT table is added to it, to give a direct pointer to the descriptor. For example, selector 72 refers to entry 9 in the GDT, which is located at address GDT + 72.

Let us trace the steps by which a (selector, offset) pair is converted to a physical address. As soon as the microprogram knows which segment register is being used, it can find the complete descriptor corresponding to that selector in its internal registers. If the segment does not exist (selector 0), or is currently paged out, a trap occurs.

It then checks to see if the offset is beyond the end of the segment, in which case a trap also occurs. Logically, there should simply be a 32-bit field in the descriptor giving the size of the segment, but there are only 20 bits available, so a different scheme is used. If the *gbit* (Granularity) field is 0, the *limit* field is the exact segment size, up to 1 MB. If it is 1, the *limit* field gives the segment size in pages instead of bytes. The Pentium page size is fixed at 4 KB, so 20 bits are enough for segments up to 2^{32} bytes.

Assuming that the segment is in memory and the offset is in range, the Pentium then adds the 32-bit *base* field in the descriptor to the offset to form what is called a **linear address**, as shown in Fig. 4-27. The *base* field is broken up into three pieces and spread all over the descriptor for compatibility with the 286, in which the *base* is only 24 bits. In effect, the *base* field allows each segment to start at an arbitrary place within the 32-bit linear address space.

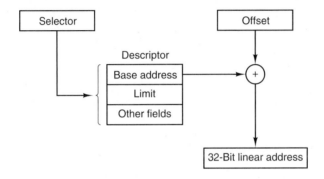

Figure 4-27. Conversion of a (selector, offset) pair to a linear address.

If paging is disabled (by a bit in a global control register), the linear address is interpreted as the physical address and sent to the memory for the read or write. Thus with paging disabled, we have a pure segmentation scheme, with each segment's base address given in its descriptor. Segments are permitted to overlap, incidentally, probably because it would be too much trouble and take too much time to verify that they were all disjoint.

On the other hand, if paging is enabled, the linear address is interpreted as a virtual address and mapped onto the physical address using page tables, pretty much as in our earlier examples. The only real complication is that with a 32-bit virtual address and a 4-KB page, a segment might contain 1 million pages, so a two-level mapping is used to reduce the page table size for small segments.

Each running program has a **page directory** consisting of 1024 32-bit entries. It is located at an address pointed to by a global register. Each entry in this directory points to a page table also containing 1024 32-bit entries. The page table entries point to page frames. The scheme is shown in Fig. 4-28.

In Fig. 4-28(a) we see a linear address divided into three fields, *dir*, *page*, and *offset*. The *dir* field is used to index into the page directory to locate a pointer to the proper page table. Then the *page* field is used as an index into the page table

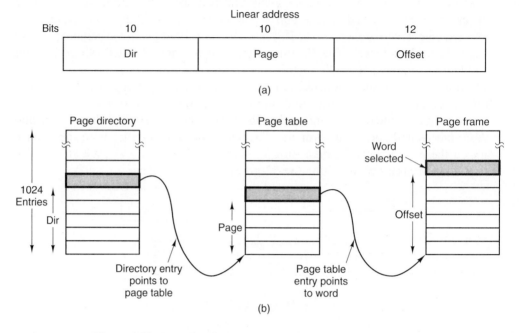

Figure 4-28. Mapping of a linear address onto a physical address.

to find the physical address of the page frame. Finally, *offset* is added to the address of the page frame to get the physical address of the byte or word needed.

The page table entries are 32 bits each, 20 of which contain a page frame number. The remaining bits contain access and dirty bits, set by the hardware for the benefit of the operating system, protection bits, and other utility bits.

Each page table has entries for 1024 4-KB page frames, so a single page table handles 4 megabytes of memory. A segment shorter than 4-MB will have a page directory with a single entry, a pointer to its one and only page table. In this way, the overhead for short segments is only two pages, instead of the million pages that would be needed in a one-level page table.

To avoid making repeated references to memory, the Pentium has a small TLB that directly maps the most recently used *dir–page* combinations onto the physical address of the page frame. Only when the current combination is not present in the TLB is the mechanism of Fig. 4-28 actually carried out and the TLB updated. As long as TLB misses are rare, performance is good.

A little thought will reveal the fact that when paging is used, there is really no point in having the *base* field in the descriptor be nonzero. All that *base* does is cause a small offset to use an entry in the middle of the page directory, instead of at the beginning. The real reason for including *base* at all is to allow pure (non-paged) segmentation, and for compatibility with the 286, which always has paging disabled (i.e., the 286 has only pure segmentation, but not paging).

It is also worth noting that if some application does not need segmentation but is content with a single, paged, 32-bit address space, that model is possible. All the segment registers can be set up with the same selector, whose descriptor has *base* = 0 and *limit* set to the maximum. The instruction offset will then be the linear address, with only a single address space used—in effect, normal paging. In fact, all current operating systems for the Pentium work this way. OS/2 was the only one that used the full power of the Intel MMU architecture.

All in all, one has to give credit to the Pentium designers. Given the conflicting goals of implementing pure paging, pure segmentation, and paged segments, while at the same time being compatible with the 286, and doing all of this efficiently, the resulting design is surprisingly simple and clean.

Although we have covered the complete architecture of the Pentium virtual memory, albeit briefly, it is worth saying a few words about protection, since this subject is intimately related to the virtual memory. The Pentium supports four protection levels with level 0 being the most privileged and level 3 the least. These are shown in Fig. 4-29. At each instant, a running program is at a certain level, indicated by a 2-bit field in its PSW. Each segment in the system also has a level.

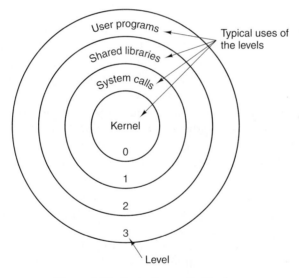

Figure 4-29. Protection on the Pentium.

As long as a program restricts itself to using segments at its own level, everything works fine. Attempts to access data at a higher level are permitted. Attempts to access data at a lower level are illegal and cause traps. Attempts to call procedures at a different level (higher or lower) are allowed, but in a carefully controlled way. To make an interlevel call, the CALL instruction must contain a selector instead of an address. This selector designates a descriptor called a **call gate**, which gives the address of the procedure to be called. Thus it is not possible to jump into the middle of an arbitrary code segment at a different level. Only official entry points may be used.

A typical use for this mechanism is suggested in Fig. 4-29. At level 0, we find the kernel of the operating system, which handles I/O, memory management, and other critical matters. At level 1, the system call handler is present. User programs may call procedures here to have system calls carried out, but only a specific and protected list of procedures may be called. Level 2 contains library procedures, possibly shared among many running programs. User programs may call these procedures and read their data, but they may not modify them. Finally, user programs run at level 3, which has the least protection.

Traps and interrupts use a mechanism similar to the call gates. They, too, reference descriptors, rather than absolute addresses, and these descriptors point to specific procedures to be executed. The *type* field in Fig. 4-26 distinguishes between code segments, data segments, and the various kinds of gates.

4.7 OVERVIEW OF THE MINIX 3 PROCESS MANAGER

Memory management in MINIX 3 is simple: paging is not used at all. MINIX 3 memory management as we will discuss it here does not include swapping either. Swapping code is available in the complete source and could be activated to make MINIX 3 work on a system with limited physical memory. In practice, memories are so large now that swapping is rarely needed.

In this chapter we will study a user-space server designated the **process manager**, or **PM** for short. The process manager handles system calls relating to process management. Of these some are intimately involved with memory management. The fork, exec, and brk calls are in this category. Process management also includes processing system calls related to signals, setting and examining process properties such as user and group ownership, and reporting CPU usage times. The MINIX 3 process manager also handles setting and querying the real time clock.

Sometimes when we are referring to that part of the process manager that handles memory management, we will refer to it as the "memory manager." It is possible that in a future release, process management and memory management will be completely separated, but in MINIX 3 the two functions are merged into one process.

The PM maintains a list of holes sorted in numerical memory address order. When memory is needed, either due to a fork or an exec system call, the hole list is searched using first fit for a hole that is big enough. Without swapping, a process that has been placed in memory remains in exactly the same place during its entire execution. It is never moved to another place in memory, nor does its allocated memory area ever grow or shrink.

This strategy for managing memory is somewhat unusual and deserves some explanation. It was originally derived from three factors:

1. The desire to keep the system easy to understand.

2. The architecture of the original IBM PC CPU (an Intel 8088),

3. The goal of making MINIX 3 easy to port to other hardware,

First, as a teaching system, avoiding complexity was highly desirable; a source code listing of nearly 250 pages was deemed long enough. Second, the system was designed for the original IBM PC, which did not even have an MMU, so including paging was impossible to start with. Third, since other computers of its era also lacked MMUs, this memory management strategy made porting to the Macintosh, Atari, Amiga, and other machines easier.

Of course, one can rightly ask if such a strategy still makes sense. The first point is still valid, although the system has definitely grown over the years. However, several new factors also play a role now. Modern PCs have more than 1000 times as much memory available as the original IBM PC. While programs are bigger, most systems have so much memory that swapping and paging are hardly needed. Finally, MINIX 3 is targeted to some extent at low-end systems such as embedded systems. Nowadays, digital cameras, DVD players, stereos, cell phones, and other products have operating systems, but certainly do not support swapping or paging. MINIX 3 is quite a reasonable choice in this world, so swapping and paging are not a high priority. Nevertheless, some work is in progress to see what can be done in the area of virtual memory in the simplest possible way. The Web site should be consulted to follow current developments.

It is also worth pointing out another way in which implementation of memory management in MINIX 3 differs from that of many other operating systems. The PM is not part of the kernel. Instead, it is a process that runs in user space and communicates with the kernel by the standard message mechanism. The position of the PM is shown in Fig. 2-29.

Moving the PM out of the kernel is an example of the separation of **policy** and **mechanism**. The decisions about which process will be placed where in memory (policy) are made by the PM. The actual setting of memory maps for processes (mechanism) is done by the system task within the kernel. This split makes it relatively easy to change the memory management policy (algorithms, etc.) without having to modify the lowest layers of the operating system.

Most of the PM code is devoted to handling the MINIX 3 system calls that involve creating processes, primarily fork and exec, rather than just manipulating lists of processes and holes. In the next section we will look at the memory layout, and in subsequent sections we will take a bird's-eye view of how the process management system calls are handled by the PM.

4.7.1 Memory Layout

MINIX 3 programs may be compiled to use **combined I and D space**, in which all parts of the process (text, data, and stack) share a block of memory which is allocated and released as one block. This was the default for the original version of MINIX. In MINIX 3, however, the default is to compile programs to use **separate I and D space**. For clarity, allocation of memory for the simpler combined model will be discussed first. Processes using separate I and D space can use memory more efficiently, but taking advantage of this feature complicates things. We will discuss the complications after the simple case has been outlined.

In normal MINIX 3 operation memory is allocated on two occasions. First, when a process forks, the amount of memory needed by the child is allocated. Second, when a process changes its memory image via the exec system call, the space occupied by the old image is returned to the free list as a hole, and memory is allocated for the new image. The new image may be in a part of memory different from the released memory. Its location will depend upon where an adequate hole is found. Memory is also released whenever a process terminates, either by exiting or by being killed by a signal. There is a third case: a system process can request memory for its own use; for instance, the memory driver can request memory for the RAM disk. This can only happen during system initialization.

Figure 4-30 shows memory allocation during a fork and an exec. In Fig. 4-30(a) we see two processes, A and B, in memory. If A forks, we get the situation of Fig. 4-30(b). The child is an exact copy of A. If the child now execs the file C, the memory looks like Fig. 4-30(c). The child's image is replaced by C.

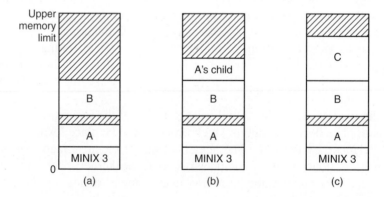

Figure 4-30. Memory allocation. (a) Originally. (b) After a fork. (c) After the child does an exec. The shaded regions are unused memory. The process is a common I&D one.

Note that the old memory for the child is released before the new memory for C is allocated, so that C can use the child's memory. In this way, a series of fork and exec pairs (such as the shell setting up a pipeline) can result in all the processes being adjacent, with no holes between them, assuming a large block of unallocated memory exists. Holes would remain if the new memory had been allocated before the old memory had been released.

Doing it this way is not trivial. Consider the possible error condition that there is not enough memory to perform an exec. A test for sufficient memory to complete the operation should be performed before the child's memory is released, so the child can respond to the error somehow. This means the child's memory must be considered as if it were a hole while it is still in use.

When memory is allocated, either by the fork or exec system calls, a certain amount of it is taken for the new process. In the former case, the amount taken is identical to what the parent process has. In the latter case, the PM takes the amount specified in the header of the file executed. Once this allocation has been made, under no conditions is the process ever allocated any more total memory.

What has been said so far applies to programs that have been compiled with combined I and D space. Programs with separate I and D space take advantage of an enhanced mode of memory management called **shared text**. When such a process does a fork, only the amount of memory needed for a copy of the new process' data and stack is allocated. Both the parent and the child share the executable code already in use by the parent. When such a process does an exec, the process table is searched to see if another process is already using the executable code needed. If one is found, new memory is allocated only for the data and stack, and the text already in memory is shared. Shared text complicates termination of a process. When a process terminates it always releases the memory occupied by its data and stack. But it only releases the memory occupied by its text segment after a search of the process table reveals that no other current process is sharing that memory. Thus a process may be allocated more memory when it starts than it releases when it terminates, if it loaded its own text when it started but that text is being shared by one or more other processes when the first process terminates.

Figure 4-31 shows how a program is stored as a disk file and how this is transferred to the internal memory layout of a MINIX 3 process. The header on the disk file contains information about the sizes of the different parts of the image, as well as the total size. In the header of a program with common I and D space, a field specifies the total size of the text and data parts; these parts are copied directly to the memory image. The data part in the image is enlarged by the amount specified in the *bss* field in the header. This area is cleared to contain all zeroes and is used for uninitialized static data. The total amount of memory to be allocated is specified by the *total* field in the header. If, for example, a program has 4 KB of text, 2 KB of data plus bss, and 1 KB of stack, and the header says to allocate 40 KB total, the gap of unused memory between the data segment and the stack segment will be 33 KB. A program file on the disk may also contain a symbol table. This is for use in debugging and is not copied into memory.

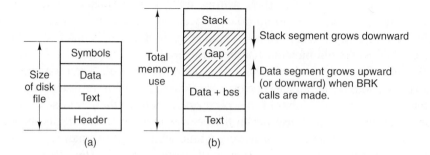

Figure 4-31. (a) A program as stored in a disk file. (b) Internal memory layout for a single process. In both parts of the figure the lowest disk or memory address is at the bottom and the highest address is at the top.

If the programmer knows that the total memory needed for the combined growth of the data and stack segments for the file *a.out* is at most 10 KB, he can give the command

    chmem =10240 a.out

which changes the header field so that upon **exec** the PM allocates a space 10240 bytes more than the sum of the initial text and data segments. For the above example, a total of 16 KB will be allocated on all subsequent **execs** of the file. Of this amount, the topmost 1 KB will be used for the stack, and 9 KB will be in the gap, where it can be used by growth of the stack, the data area, or both, as actually needed.

For a program using separate I and D space (indicated by a bit in the header that is set by the linker), the total field in the header applies to the combined data and stack space only. A program with 4 KB of text, 2 KB of data, 1 KB of stack, and a total size of 64 KB will be allocated 68 KB (4 KB instruction space, 64 KB stack and data space), leaving 61 KB for the data segment and stack to consume during execution. The boundary of the data segment can be moved only by the brk system call. All brk does is check to see if the new data segment bumps into the current stack pointer, and if not, notes the change in some internal tables. This is entirely internal to the memory originally allocated to the process; no additional memory is allocated by the operating system. If the new data segment bumps into the stack, the call fails.

This is a good place to mention a possible semantic difficulty. When we use the word "segment," we refer to an area of memory defined by the operating system. Intel processors have a set of internal **segment registers** and **segment descriptor tables** which provide hardware support for "segments." The Intel hardware designers' concept of a segment is similar to, but not always the same as, the segments used and defined by MINIX 3. All references to segments in this text should be interpreted as references to memory areas delineated by MINIX 3 data structures. We will refer explicitly to "segment registers" or "segment descriptors" when talking about the hardware.

This warning can be generalized. Hardware designers often try to provide support for the operating systems that they expect to be used on their machines, and the terminology used to describe registers and other aspects of a processor's architecture usually reflects an idea of how the features will be used. Such features are often useful to the implementer of an operating system, but they may not be used in the same way the hardware designer foresaw. This can lead to misunderstandings when the same word has different meanings when used to describe an aspect of an operating system or of the underlying hardware.

4.7.2 Message Handling

Like all the other components of MINIX 3, the process manager is message driven. After the system has been initialized, PM enters its main loop, which consists of waiting for a message, carrying out the request contained in the message, and sending a reply.

Two message categories may be received by the process manager. For high priority communication between the kernel and system servers such as PM, a **system notification message** is used. These are special cases to be discussed in the implementation section of this chapter. The majority of messages received by the process manager result from system calls originated by user processes. For this category, Figure 4-32 gives the list of legal message types, input parameters, and values sent back in the reply message.

Fork, exit, wait, waitpid, brk, and exec are clearly closely related to memory allocation and deallocation. The calls kill, alarm, and pause are all related to signals, as are sigaction, sigsuspend, sigpending, sigmask, and sigreturn. These also can affect what is in memory, because when a signal kills a process the memory used by that process is deallocated. The seven get/set calls have nothing to do with memory management at all, but they certainly relate to process management. Other calls could go either in the file system or the PM, since every system call is handled by one or the other. They were put here simply because the file system was large enough already. The time, stime, and times calls were put here for this reason, as was ptrace, which is used in debugging.

Reboot has effects throughout the operating system, but its first job is to send signals to terminate all processes in a controlled way, so the PM is a good place for it. The same is true of svrctl, whose most important use is to enable or disable swapping in the PM.

You may have noticed that the last two calls mentioned here, reboot and svrctl, were not listed in Fig. 1-9. This also true of the remaining calls in Fig. 4-32, getsysinfo, getprocnr, memalloc, memfree, and getsetpriority. None of these are intended for use by ordinary user processes, and they are not parts of the POSIX standard. They are provided because they are needed in a system like

MINIX 3. In a system with a monolithic kernel the operations provided by these calls could be provided by calls to functions compiled into the kernel. But in MINIX 3 components that are normally considered part of the operating system run in user space, and additional system calls are needed. Some of these do little more than implement an interface to a kernel call, a term we use for calls that request kernel services via the system task.

As mentioned in Chap. 1, although there is a library routine *sbrk*, there is no system call sbrk. The library routine computes the amount of memory needed by adding the increment or decrement specified as parameter to the current size and makes a brk call to set the size. Similarly, there are no separate system calls for *geteuid* and *getegid*. The calls getuid and getgid return both the effective and real identifiers. In like manner, getpid returns the PID of both the calling process and its parent.

A key data structure used for message processing is the *call_vec* table declared in *table.c*. It contains pointers to the procedures that handle the various message types. When a message comes in to the PM, the main loop extracts the message type and puts it in the global variable *call_nr*. This value is then used to index into *call_vec* to find the pointer to the procedure that handles the newly arrived message. That procedure is then called to execute the system call. The value that it returns is sent back to the caller in the reply message to report on the success or failure of the call. The mechanism is similar to the table of pointers to system call handlers used in step 7 of Fig. 1-16, only in user space rather than in the kernel.

4.7.3 Process Manager Data Structures and Algorithms

Two key data structures are used by the process manager: the process table and the hole table. We will now look at each of these in turn.

In Fig. 2-4 we saw that some process table fields are needed by the kernel, others by the process manager, and yet others by the file system. In MINIX 3, each of these three pieces of the operating system has its own process table, containing just those fields that it needs. With a few exceptions, entries correspond exactly, to keep things simple. Thus, slot *k* of the PM's table refers to the same process as slot *k* of the file system's table. When a process is created or destroyed, all three parts update their tables to reflect the new situation, in order to keep them synchronized.

The exceptions are processes that are not known outside of the kernel, either because they are compiled into the kernel, like the *CLOCK* and *SYSTEM* tasks, or because they are place holders like *IDLE*, and *KERNEL*. In the kernel process table their slots are designated by negative numbers. These slots do not exist in the process manager or file system process tables. Thus, strictly speaking, what was said above about slot *k* in the tables is true for *k* equal to or greater than zero.

Message type	Input parameters	Reply value
fork	(none)	Child's PID, (to child: 0)
exit	Exit status	(No reply if successful)
wait	(none)	Status
waitpid	Process identifier and flags	Status
brk	New size	New size
exec	Pointer to initial stack	(No reply if successful)
kill	Process identifier and signal	Status
alarm	Number of seconds to wait	Residual time
pause	(none)	(No reply if successful)
sigaction	Signal number, action, old action	Status
sigsuspend	Signal mask	(No reply if successful)
sigpending	(none)	Status
sigprocmask	How, set, old set	Status
sigreturn	Context	Status
getuid	(none)	Uid, effective uid
getgid	(none)	Gid, effective gid
getpid	(none)	PID, parent PID
setuid	New uid	Status
setgid	New gid	Status
setsid	New sid	Process group
getpgrp	New gid	Process group
time	Pointer to place where current time goes	Status
stime	Pointer to current time	Status
times	Pointer to buffer for process and child times	Uptime since boot
ptrace	Request, PID, address, data	Status
reboot	How (halt, reboot, or panic)	(No reply if successful)
svrctl	Request, data (depends upon function)	Status
getsysinfo	Request, data (depends upon function)	Status
getprocnr	(none)	Proc number
memalloc	Size, pointer to address	Status
memfree	Size, address	Status
getpriority	Pid, type, value	Priority (nice value)
setpriority	Pid, type, value	Priority (nice value)
gettimeofday	(none)	Time, uptime

Figure 4-32. The message types, input parameters, and reply values used for communicating with the PM.

Processes in Memory

The PM's process table is called *mproc* and its definition is given in *src/servers/pm/mproc.h*. It contains all the fields related to a process' memory allocation, as well as some additional items. The most important field is the array *mp_seg*, which has three entries, for the text, data, and stack segments, respectively. Each entry is a structure containing the virtual address, physical address, and length of the segment, all measured in **clicks** rather than in bytes. The size of a click is implementation dependent. In early MINIX versions it was 256 bytes. For MINIX 3 it is 1024 bytes. All segments must start on a click boundary and occupy an integral number of clicks.

The method used for recording memory allocation is shown in Fig. 4-33. In this figure we have a process with 3 KB of text, 4 KB of data, a gap of 1 KB, and then a 2-KB stack, for a total memory allocation of 10 KB. In Fig. 4-33(b) we see what the virtual, physical, and length fields for each of the three segments are, assuming that the process does not have separate I and D space. In this model, the text segment is always empty, and the data segment contains both text and data. When a process references virtual address 0, either to jump to it or to read it (i.e., as instruction space or as data space), physical address 0x32000 (in decimal, 200K) will be used. This address is at click 0xc8.

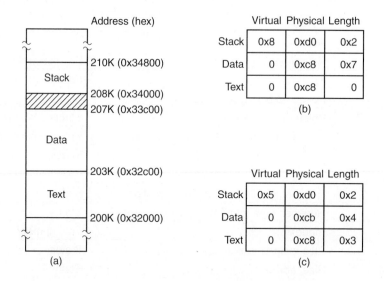

Figure 4-33. (a) A process in memory. (b) Its memory representation for combined I and D space. (c) Its memory representation for separate I and D space.

Note that the virtual address at which the stack begins depends initially on the total amount of memory allocated to the process. If the *chmem* command were used to modify the file header to provide a larger dynamic allocation area (bigger gap between data and stack segments), the next time the file was executed, the stack would start at a higher virtual address. If the stack grows longer by one click, the stack entry *should* change from the triple (0x8, 0xd0, 0x2) to the triple (0x7, 0xcf, 0x3). Note that, in this example, growth of the stack by one click would reduce the gap to nothing if there were no increase of the total memory allocation.

The 8088 hardware does not have a stack limit trap, and MINIX defined the stack in a way that will not trigger the trap on 32-bit processors until the stack has already overwritten the data segment. Thus, this change will not be made until the next brk system call, at which point the operating system explicitly reads SP and recomputes the segment entries. On a machine with a stack trap, the stack segment's entry could be updated as soon as the stack outgrew its segment. This is not done by MINIX 3 on 32-bit Intel processors, for reasons we will now discuss.

We mentioned previously that the efforts of hardware designers may not always produce exactly what the software designer needs. Even in protected mode on a Pentium, MINIX 3 does not trap when the stack outgrows its segment. Although in protected mode the Intel hardware detects attempted access to memory outside a segment (as defined by a segment descriptor such as the one in Fig. 4-26), in MINIX 3 the data segment descriptor and the stack segment descriptor are always identical. The MINIX 3 data and stack segments each use part of this space, and thus either or both can expand into the gap between them. However, only MINIX 3 can manage this. The CPU has no way to detect errors involving the gap, since as far as the hardware is concerned the gap is a valid part of both the data area and the stack area. Of course, the hardware can detect a very large error, such as an attempt to access memory outside the combined data-gap-stack area. This will protect one process from the mistakes of another process but is not enough to protect a process from itself.

A design decision was made here. We recognize an argument can be made for abandoning the shared hardware-defined segment that allows MINIX 3 to dynamically reallocate the gap area. The alternative, using the hardware to define nonoverlapping stack and data segments, would offer somewhat more security from certain errors but would make MINIX 3 more memory-hungry. The source code is available to anybody who wants to evaluate the other approach.

Fig. 4-33(c) shows the segment entries for the memory layout of Fig. 4-33(a) for separate I and D space. Here both the text and data segments are nonzero in length. The *mp_seg* array shown in Fig. 4-33(b) or (c) is primarily used to map virtual addresses onto physical memory addresses. Given a virtual address and the space to which it belongs, it is a simple matter to see whether the virtual address is legal or not (i.e., falls inside a segment), and if legal, what the corresponding physical address is. The kernel procedure *umap_local* performs this mapping for the I/O tasks and for copying to and from user space, for example.

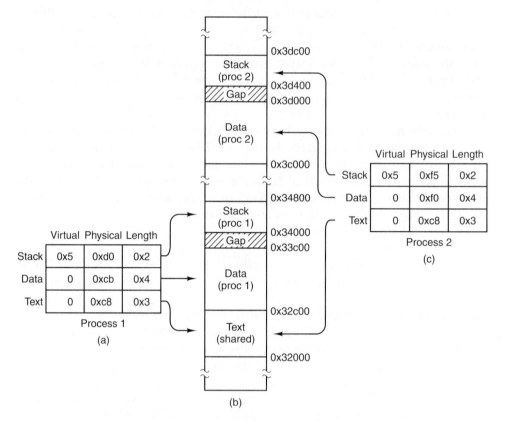

Figure 4-34. (a) The memory map of a separate I and D space process, as in the previous figure. (b) The layout in memory after a second process starts, executing the same program image with shared text. (c) The memory map of the second process.

Shared Text

The contents of the data and stack areas belonging to a process may change as the process executes, but the text does not change. It is common for several processes to be executing copies of the same program, for instance several users may be executing the same shell. Memory efficiency is improved by using **shared text**. When exec is about to load a process, it opens the file holding the disk image of the program to be loaded and reads the file header. If the process uses separate I and D space, a search of the *mp_dev*, *mp_ino*, and *mp_ctime* fields in each slot of *mproc* is made. These hold the device and i-node numbers and changed-status times of the images being executed by other processes. If a process in memory is found to be executing the same program that is about to be loaded, there is no need to allocate memory for another copy of the text. Instead the $mp\_seg[T]$ portion of the new process' memory map is initialized to point to the same place where the text segment is already loaded, and only the data and stack portions are set up in a new memory allocation. This is shown in Fig. 4-34. If the program uses combined I and D space or no match is found, memory is allocated as shown in Fig. 4-33 and the text and data for the new process are copied in from the disk.

In addition to the segment information, *mproc* also holds additional information about the process. This includes the process ID (PID) of the process itself and of its parent, the UIDs and GIDs (both real and effective), information about signals, and the exit status, if the process has already terminated but its parent has not yet done a wait for it. Also in *mproc* there are fields for a timer for sigalarm and for accumulated user and system time use by child processes. The kernel was responsible for these items in earlier versions of MINIX, but responsibility for them has been shifted to the process manager in MINIX 3.

The Hole List

The other major process manager data structure is the **hole table**, *hole*, defined in *src/servers/pm/alloc.c*, which lists every hole in memory in order of increasing memory address. The gaps between the data and stack segments are not considered holes; they have already been allocated to processes. Consequently, they are not contained in the free hole list. Each hole list entry has three fields: the base address of the hole, in clicks; the length of the hole, in clicks; and a pointer to the next entry on the list. The list is singly linked, so it is easy to find the next hole starting from any given hole, but to find the previous hole, you have to search the entire list from the beginning until you come to the given hole. Because of space limitations *alloc.c* is not included in the printed listing although it is on the CD-ROM. But the code defining the hole list is simple, and is shown in Fig. 4-35.

```
PRIVATE struct hole {
        struct hole *h_next;        /* pointer to next entry on the list */
        phys_clicks h_base;         /* where does the hole begin? */
        phys_clicks h_len;          /* how big is the hole? */
} hole[NR_HOLES];
```

Figure 4-35. The hole list is an array of struct hole.

The reason for recording everything about segments and holes in clicks rather than bytes is simple: it is much more efficient. In 16-bit mode, 16-bit integers are used for recording memory addresses, so with 1024-byte clicks, up to 64 MB of memory can be supported. In 32-bit mode, address fields can refer to up to as many as $2^{32} \times 2^{10} = 2^{42}$ bytes, which is 4 terabytes (4096 gigabytes).

The principal operations on the hole list are allocating a piece of memory of a given size and returning an existing allocation. To allocate memory, the hole list is searched, starting at the hole with the lowest address, until a hole that is large enough is found (first fit). The segment is then allocated by reducing the hole by the amount needed for the segment, or in the rare case of an exact fit, removing the hole from the list. This scheme is fast and simple but suffers from both a small amount of internal fragmentation (up to 1023 bytes may be wasted in the final click, since an integral number of clicks is always taken) and external fragmentation.

When a process terminates and is cleaned up, its data and stack memory are returned to the free list. If it uses combined I and D, this releases all its memory, since such programs never have a separate allocation of memory for text. If the program uses separate I and D and a search of the process table reveals no other process is sharing the text, the text allocation will also be returned. Since with shared text the text and data regions are not necessarily contiguous, two regions of memory may be returned. For each region returned, if either or both of the region's neighbors are holes, they are merged, so adjacent holes never occur. In this way, the number, location, and sizes of the holes vary continuously during system operation. Whenever all user processes have terminated, all of available memory is once again ready for allocation. This is not necessarily a single hole, however, since physical memory may be interrupted by regions unusable by the operating system, as in IBM compatible systems where read-only memory (ROM) and memory reserved for I/O transfers separate usable memory below address 640K from memory above 1 MB.

4.7.4 The FORK, EXIT, and WAIT System Calls

When processes are created or destroyed, memory must be allocated or deallocated. Also, the process table must be updated, including the parts held by the kernel and FS. The PM coordinates all this activity. Process creation is done by fork, and carried out in the series of steps shown in Fig. 4-36.

It is difficult and inconvenient to stop a fork call part way through, so the PM maintains a count at all times of the number of processes currently in existence in order to see easily if a process table slot is available. If the table is not full, an attempt is made to allocate memory for the child. If the program is one with separate I and D space, only enough memory for new data and stack allocations is requested. If this step also succeeds, the fork is guaranteed to work. The newly allocated memory is then filled in, a process slot is located and filled in, a PID is chosen, and the other parts of the system are informed that a new process has been created.

A process fully terminates when two events have both happened: (1) the process itself has exited (or has been killed by a signal), and (2) its parent has executed a wait system call to find out what happened. A process that has exited or

1. Check to see if process table is full.
2. Try to allocate memory for the child's data and stack.
3. Copy the parent's data and stack to the child's memory.
4. Find a free process slot and copy parent's slot to it.
5. Enter child's memory map in process table.
6. Choose a PID for the child.
7. Tell kernel and file system about child.
8. Report child's memory map to kernel.
9. Send reply messages to parent and child.

Figure 4-36. The steps required to carry out the fork system call.

has been killed, but whose parent has not (yet) done a wait for it, enters a kind of suspended animation, sometimes known as **zombie state**. It is prevented from being scheduled and has its alarm timer turned off (if it was on), but it is not removed from the process table. Its memory is freed. Zombie state is temporary and rarely lasts long. When the parent finally does the wait, the process table slot is freed, and the file system and kernel are informed.

A problem arises if the parent of an exiting process is itself already dead. If no special action were taken, the exiting process would remain a zombie forever. Instead, the tables are changed to make it a child of the *init* process. When the system comes up, *init* reads the */etc/ttytab* file to get a list of all terminals, and then forks off a login process to handle each one. It then blocks, waiting for processes to terminate. In this way, orphan zombies are cleaned up quickly.

4.7.5 The EXEC System Call

When a command is typed at the terminal, the shell forks off a new process, which then executes the command requested. It would have been possible to have a single system call to do both fork and exec at once, but they were provided as two distinct calls for a very good reason: to make it easy to implement I/O redirection. When the shell forks, if standard input is redirected, the child closes standard input and then opens the new standard input before executing the command. In this way the newly started process inherits the redirected standard input. Standard output is handled the same way.

Exec is the most complex system call in MINIX 3. It must replace the current memory image with a new one, including setting up a new stack. The new image must be a binary executable file, of course. An executable file may also be a script that must be interpreted by another program, such as the shell or *perl*. In that case the file whose image must be placed in memory is the binary of the interpreter, with the name of the script as an argument. In this section we discuss the simple case of an exec call that refers to a binary executable. Later, when we discuss implementation of exec, the additional processing required to execute a script will be described.

Exec carries out its job in a series of steps, as shown in Fig. 4-37.

1. Check permissions—is the file executable?
2. Read the header to get the segment and total sizes.
3. Fetch the arguments and environment from the caller.
4. Allocate new memory and release unneeded old memory.
5. Copy stack to new memory image.
6. Copy data (and possibly text) segment to new memory image.
7. Check for and handle setuid, setgid bits.
8. Fix up process table entry.
9. Tell kernel that process is now runnable.

Figure 4-37. The steps required to carry out the exec system call.

Each step consists, in turn, of yet smaller steps, some of which can fail. For example, there might be insufficient memory available. The order in which the tests are made has been carefully chosen to make sure the old memory image is not released until it is certain that the exec will succeed, to avoid the embarrassing situation of not being able to set up a new memory image, but not having the old one to go back to, either. Normally exec does not return, but if it fails, the calling process must get control again, with an error indication.

A few steps in Fig. 4-37 deserve some more comment. First is the question of whether or not there is enough room. After determining how much memory is needed, which requires determining if the text memory of another process can be shared, the hole list is searched to check whether there is sufficient physical memory *before* freeing the old memory. If the old memory were freed first and there were insufficient memory, it would be hard to get the old image back again and we would be up a tree.

However, this test is overly strict. It sometimes rejects exec calls that, in fact, could succeed. Suppose, for example, the process doing the exec call occupies 20 KB and its text is not shared by any other process. Further suppose that there is a 30-KB hole available and that the new image requires 50 KB. By testing before releasing, we will discover that only 30 KB is available and reject the call. If we had released first, we might have succeeded, depending on whether or not the new 20-KB hole were adjacent to, and thus now merged with, the 30 KB hole. A more sophisticated implementation could handle this situation a little better.

Another possible improvement would be to search for two holes, one for the text segment and one for the data segment, if the process to be execed uses separate I and D space. The segments do not need to be contiguous.

A more subtle issue is whether the executable file fits in the *virtual* address space. The problem is that memory is allocated not in bytes, but in 1024-byte clicks. Each click must belong to a single segment, and may not be, for example, half data, half stack, because the entire memory administration is in clicks.

To see how this restriction can give trouble, note that the address space on 16-bit Intel processors (8086 and 80286) is limited to 64 KB, which with a click size of 1024 allows 64 clicks. Suppose that a separate I and D space program has 40,000 bytes of text, 32,770 bytes of data, and 32,760 bytes of stack. The data segment occupies 33 clicks, although only 2 bytes of the last click is used; still, the whole click must be alloted for the data segment. The stack segment is 32 clicks. Together they exceed 64 clicks, and thus cannot co-exist, even though the number of *bytes* needed fits in the virtual address space (barely). In theory this problem exists on all machines whose click size is larger than 1 byte, but in practice it rarely occurs on Pentium-class processors, since they permit large (4-GB) segments. Unfortunately, the code has to check for this case. A system that does not check for rare, but possible, conditions is likely to crash in an unexpected way if one of them ever occurs.

Another important issue is how the initial stack is set up. The library call normally used to invoke exec with arguments and an environment is

    execve(name, argv, envp);

where *name* is a pointer to the name of the file to be executed, *argv* is a pointer to an array of pointers, each one pointing to an argument, and *envp* is a pointer to an array of pointers, each one pointing to an environment string.

It would be easy enough to implement exec by just putting the three pointers in the message to the PM and letting it fetch the file name and two arrays by itself. Then it would have to fetch each argument and each string one at a time. Doing it this way requires at least one message to the system task per argument or string and probably more, since the PM has no way of knowing in advance the size of each one.

To avoid the overhead of multiple messages to read all these pieces, a completely different strategy has been chosen. The *execve* library procedure builds the entire initial stack inside itself and passes its base address and size to the PM. Building the new stack within the user space is highly efficient, because references to the arguments and strings are just local memory references, not references to a different address space.

To make this mechanism clearer, consider an example. When a user types

    ls –l f.c g.c

to the shell, the shell interprets it and then makes the call

    execve("/bin/ls", argv, envp);

to the library procedure. The contents of the two pointer arrays are shown in Fig. 4-38(a). The procedure *execve*, within the shell's address space, now builds

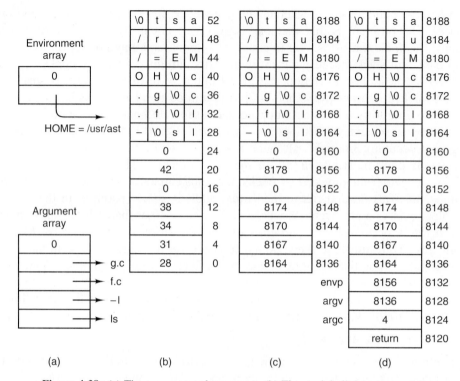

(a)

Environment array

0

HOME = /usr/ast

Argument array

0
→ g.c
→ f.c
→ −l
→ ls

(b)

\0	t	s	a	52
/	r	s	u	48
/	=	E	M	44
O	H	\0	c	40
.	g	\0	c	36
.	f	\0	l	32
−	\0	s	l	28
0				24
42				20
0				16
38				12
34				8
31				4
28				0

(c)

\0	t	s	a	8188
/	r	s	u	8184
/	=	E	M	8180
O	H	\0	c	8176
.	g	\0	c	8172
.	f	\0	l	8168
−	\0	s	l	8164
0				8160
8178				8156
0				8152
8174				8148
8170				8144
8167				8140
8164				8136

(d)

\0	t	s	a	8188
/	r	s	u	8184
/	=	E	M	8180
O	H	\0	c	8176
.	g	\0	c	8172
.	f	\0	l	8168
−	\0	s	l	8164
0				8160
8178				8156
0				8152
8174				8148
8170				8144
8167				8140
8164				8136
envp				8132
argv				8128
argc			4	8124
return				8120

Figure 4-38. (a) The arrays passed to *execve*. (b) The stack built by *execve*. (c) The stack after relocation by the PM. (d) The stack as it appears to *main* at the start of execution.

the initial stack, as shown in Fig. 4-38(b). This stack is eventually copied intact to the PM during the processing of the exec call.

When the stack is finally copied to the user process, it will not be put at virtual address 0. Instead, it will be put at the end of the memory allocation, as determined by the total memory size field in the executable file's header. As an example, let us arbitrarily assume that the total size is 8192 bytes, so the last byte available to the program is at address 8191. It is up to the PM to relocate the pointers within the stack so that when deposited into the new address, the stack looks like Fig. 4-38(c).

When the exec call completes and the program starts running, the stack will indeed look exactly like Fig. 4-38(c), with the stack pointer having the value 8136. However, another problem is yet to be dealt with. The main program of the executed file is probably declared something like this:

```
main(argc, argv, envp);
```

As far as the C compiler is concerned, *main* is just another function. It does not know that *main* is special, so it compiles code to access the three parameters on the assumption that they will be passed on the stack according to the standard C calling convention, last parameter first. With one integer and two pointers, the three parameters are expected to occupy the three words just before the return address. Of course, the stack of Fig. 4-38(c) does not look like that at all.

The solution is that programs do not begin with *main*. Instead, a small, assembly language routine called the **C run-time, start-off** procedure, or **crtso**, is always linked in at text address 0 so it gets control first. Its job is to push three more words onto the stack and then to call *main* using the standard call instruction. This results in the stack of Fig. 4-38(d) at the time that *main* starts executing. Thus, *main* is tricked into thinking it was called in the usual way (actually, it is not really a trick; it *is* called that way).

If the programmer neglects to call *exit* at the end of *main*, control will pass back to the C run-time, start-off routine when main is finished. Again, the compiler just sees *main* as an ordinary procedure and generates the usual code to return from it after the last statement. Thus *main* returns to its caller, the C run-time, start-off routine which then calls *exit* itself. Most of the code of 32-bit *crtso* is shown in Fig. 4-39. The comments should make its operation clear. Left out are initialization of the environment if not defined by the programmer, code to load the registers that are pushed and a few lines that set a flag that indicates if a floating point coprocessor is present or not. The complete source is in the file *src/lib/i386/rts/crtso.s*.

```
push   ecx           ! push environ
push   edx           ! push argv
push   eax           ! push argc
call   _main         ! main(argc, argv, envp)
push   eax           ! push exit status
call   _exit
hlt                  ! force a trap if exit fails
```

Figure 4-39. The key part of *crtso*, the C run-time, start-off routine.

4.7.6 The BRK System Call

The library procedures *brk* and *sbrk* are used to adjust the upper bound of the data segment. The former takes an absolute size (in bytes) and calls brk. The latter takes a positive or negative increment to the current size, computes the new data segment size, and then calls brk. Actually, there is no sbrk system call.

An interesting question is: "How does *sbrk* keep track of the current size, so it can compute the new size?" The answer is that a variable, *brksize*, always holds the current size so *sbrk* can find it. This variable is initialized to a compiler generated symbol giving the initial size of text plus data (combined I and D) or just data (separate I and D). The name, and, in fact, very existence of such a symbol is compiler dependent, and thus it will not be found defined in any header file in the source file directories. It is defined in the library, in the file *brksize.s*. Exactly where it will be found depends on the system, but it will be in the same directory as *crtso.s*.

Carrying out brk is easy for the process manager. All that must be done is to check to see that everything still fits in the address space, adjust the tables, and tell the kernel.

4.7.7 Signal Handling

In Chap. 1, **signals** were described as a mechanism to convey information to a process that is not necessarily waiting for input. A defined set of signals exists, and each signal has a default action—either kill the process to which it is directed, or ignore the signal. Signal processing would be easy to understand and to implement if these were the only alternatives. However, processes can use system calls to alter these responses. A process can request that any signal (except for the special sigkill signal) be ignored. Furthermore, a user process can prepare to **catch** a signal by requesting that a **signal handler** procedure internal to the process be activated instead of the default action for any signal (except, again, for sigkill). Thus to the programmer it appears that there are two distinct times when the operating system deals with signals: a preparation phase when a process may modify its response to a future signal, and a response phase when a signal is generated and acted upon. The action can be execution of a custom-written signal handler. A third phase also occurs, as shown in Fig. 4-40. When a user-written handler terminates, a special system call cleans up and restores normal operation of the signaled process. The programmer does not need to know about this third phase. He writes a signal handler just like any other function. The operating system takes care of the details of invoking and terminating the handler and managing the stack.

| Preparation: program code prepares for possible signal. |
| Response: signal is received and action is taken. |
| Cleanup: restore normal operation of the process. |

Figure 4-40. Three phases of dealing with signals.

In the preparation phase there are several system calls that a process can execute at any time to change its response to a signal. The most general of these is sigaction, which can specify that the process ignore some signal, catch some signal (replacing the default action with execution of user-defined signal-handling code within the process), or restore the default response to some signal. Another system call, sigprocmask, can block a signal, causing it to be queued and to be acted upon only when and if the process unblocks that particular signal at a later time. These calls may be made at any time, even from within a signal catching function. In MINIX 3 the preparation phase of signal processing is handled entirely by the PM, since the necessary data structures are all in the PM's part of the process table. For each process there are several *sigset_t* variables. These are bitmaps, in which each possible signal is represented by a bit. One such variable defines a set of signals to be ignored, another defines a set to be caught, and so on. For each process there is also an array of *sigaction* structures, one for each signal. The structure is defined in Fig. 4-41. Each element of the *sigaction* structure contains a variable to hold the address of a custom handler for that signal and an additional *sigset_t* variable to map signals to be blocked while that handler is executing. The field used for the address of the handler can instead hold special values signifying that the signal is to be ignored or is to be handled in the default way defined for that signal.

```
struct sigaction {
    __sighandler_t sa_handler;    /* SIG_DFL, SIG_IGN, SIG_MESS;
                                     or pointer to function */
    sigset_t sa_mask;             /* signals to be blocked during handler */
    int sa_flags;                 /* special flags */
}
```

Figure 4-41. The sigaction structure.

This is a good place to mention that a system process, such as the process manager itself, cannot catch signals. System processes use a a new handler type *SIG_MESS* that tells PM to forward a signal by means of a *SYS_SIG* notification message. No cleanup is needed for *SIG_MESS*-type signals.

When a signal is generated, multiple parts of the MINIX 3 system may become involved. The response begins in the PM, which figures out which processes should get the signal using the data structures just mentioned. If the signal is to be caught, it must be delivered to the target process. This requires saving information about the state of the process, so normal execution can be resumed. The information is stored on the stack of the signaled process, and a check must be made to determine that there is sufficient stack space. The PM does this checking, since this is within its realm, and then calls the system task in the kernel to put the information on the stack. The system task also manipulates the program counter of the process, so the process can execute the handler code. When the handler terminates, a sigreturn system call is made. Through this call, both the PM and the kernel participate in restoring the signal context and registers of the signaled process so it can resume normal execution. If the signal is not caught, the default action is taken, which may involve calling the file system to produce a **core dump** (writing the memory image of the process to a file that may be examined with a debugger), as well as killing the process, which involves all of the PM, file system, and kernel. The PM may direct one or more repetitions of these actions, since a single signal may need to be delivered to a group of processes.

The signals known to MINIX 3 are defined in *include/signal.h*, a file required by the POSIX standard. They are listed in Fig. 4-42. All of the mandatory POSIX signals are defined in MINIX 3, but not all the optional ones are. For instance, POSIX requires several signals related to job control, the ability to put a running program into the background and bring it back. MINIX 3 does not support job control, but programs that might generate these signals can be ported to MINIX 3. These signals will be ignored if generated. Job control has not been implemented because it was intended to provide a way to start a program running, then detach from it to allow the user to do something else. With MINIX 3, after starting a program, a user can just hit ALT+F2 to switch to a new virtual terminal to do something else while the program runs. Virtual terminals are a kind of poor man's windowing system, but eliminate the need for job control and its signals, at least if you are working on the local console. MINIX 3 also defines some non-POSIX signals for internal use and some synonyms for POSIX names for compatibility with older source code.

In a traditional UNIX system, signals can be generated in two ways: by the kill system call, and by the kernel. Some user-space processes in MINIX 3 do things that would be done by the kernel in a traditional system. Fig. 4-42 shows all signals known to MINIX 3 and their origins. Sigint, sigquit, and sigkill can be initiated by pressing special key combinations on the keyboard. Sigalrm is managed by the process manager. Sigpipe is generated by the file system. The *kill* program can be used to cause any signal to be sent to any process. Some kernel signals depend upon hardware support. For instance, the 8086 and 8088 processors do not support detection of illegal instruction operation codes, but this capability is available on the 286 and above, which trap on an attempt to execute an illegal opcode. This service is provided by the hardware. The implementer of the operating system must provide code to generate a signal in response to the trap. We saw in Chap. 2 that *kernel/exception.c* contains code to do just this for a number of different conditions. Thus a sigill signal will be generated in response to an illegal instruction when MINIX 3 runs on a 286 or higher processor; on the original 8088 it was never seen.

Just because the hardware can trap on a certain condition does not mean the capability can be used fully by the operating system implementer. For instance, several kinds of violations of memory integrity result in exceptions on all Intel processors beginning with the 286. Code in *kernel/exception.c* translates these exceptions into sigsegv signals. Separate exceptions are generated for violations of the limits of the hardware-defined stack segment and for other segments, since these might need to be treated differently. However, because of the way MINIX 3 uses memory, the hardware cannot detect all the errors that might occur. The hardware defines a base and a limit for each segment. The stack and data segments are combined in a single harware segment. The hardware-defined data segment base is the same as the MINIX 3 data segment base, but the hardware-defined data segment limit is higher than the limit that MINIX 3 enforces in software. In

Signal	Description	Generated by
SIGHUP	Hangup	KILL system call
SIGINT	Interrupt	TTY
SIGQUIT	Quit	TTY
SIGILL	Illegal instruction	Kernel (*)
SIGTRAP	Trace trap	Kernel (M)
SIGABRT	Abnormal termination	TTY
SIGFPE	Floating point exception	Kernel (*)
SIGKILL	Kill (cannot be caught or ignored)	KILL system call
SIGUSR1	User-defined signal # 1	Not supported
SIGSEGV	Segmentation violation	Kernel (*)
SIGUSR2	User defined signal # 2	Not supported
SIGPIPE	Write on a pipe with no one to read it	FS
SIGALRM	Alarm clock, timeout	PM
SIGTERM	Software termination signal from kill	KILL system call
SIGCHLD	Child process terminated or stopped	PM
SIGCONT	Continue if stopped	Not supported
SIGSTOP	Stop signal	Not supported
SIGTSTP	Interactive stop signal	Not supported
SIGTTIN	Background process wants to read	Not supported
SIGTTOU	Background process wants to write	Not supported
SIGKMESS	Kernel message	Kernel
SIGKSIG	Kernel signal pending	Kernel
SIGKSTOP	Kernel shutting down	Kernel

Figure 4-42. Signals defined by POSIX and MINIX 3. Signals indicated by (*) depend upon hardware support. Signals marked (M) are not defined by POSIX, but are defined by MINIX 3 for compatibility with older programs. Kernel signals are MINIX 3 specific signals generated by the kernel, and used to inform system processes about system events. Several obsolete names and synonyms are not listed here.

other words, the hardware defines the data segment as the maximum amount of memory that MINIX 3 could possibly use for data, if somehow the stack could shrink to nothing. Similarly, the hardware defines the stack as the maximum amount of memory the MINIX 3 stack could use if the data area could shrink to nothing. Although certain violations can be detected by the hardware, the hardware cannot detect the most probable stack violation, growth of the stack into the data area, since as far as the hardware registers and descriptor tables are concerned the data area and the stack area overlap.

Conceivably some code could be added to the kernel that would check the register contents of a process after each time the process gets a chance to run and generate a sigsegv signal upon detection of a violation of the integrity of the MINIX 3-defined data or stack areas. Whether this would be worthwhile is unclear; hardware traps can catch a violation immediately. A software check might not get a chance to do its work until many thousands of additional instructions had been executed, and at that point there might be very little a signal handler could do to try to recover.

Whatever their origin, the PM processes all signals the same way. For each process to be signaled, a variety of checks are made to see if the signal is feasible. One process can signal another if the signaler is the superuser or if the real or effective UID of the signaler is equal to either the real or effective UID of the signaled process. But there are several conditions that can prevent a signal being sent. Zombies cannot be signaled, for example. A process cannot be signaled if it has explicitly called sigaction to ignore the signal or sigprocmask to block it. Blocking a signal is distinct from ignoring it; receipt of a blocked signal is remembered, and it is delivered when and if the signaled process removes the block. Finally, if its stack space is not adequate the signaled process is killed.

If all the conditions are met, the signal can be sent. If the process has not arranged for the signal to be caught, no information needs to be passed to the process. In this case the PM executes the default action for the signal, which is usually to kill the process, possibly also producing a core dump. For a few signals the default action is to ignore the signal. The signals marked "Not supported" in Fig. 4-42 are required to be defined by POSIX but are ignored by MINIX 3, as permitted by the standard.

Catching a signal means executing custom signal-handling code, the address of which is stored in a *sigaction* structure in the process table. In Chap. 2 we saw how the stackframe within its process table entry receives the information needed to restart a process when it is interrupted. By modifying the stackframe of a process to be signaled, it can be arranged that when the process next is allowed to execute the signal handler will run. By modifying the stack of the process in user space, it can be arranged that when the signal handler terminates the sigreturn system call will be made. This system call is never invoked by user-written code. It is executed after the kernel puts its address on the stack in such a way that its address becomes the return address popped from the stack when a signal handler terminates. Sigreturn restores the original stackframe of the signaled process, so it can resume execution at the point where it was interrupted by the signal.

Although the final stage of sending a signal is done by the system task, this is a good place to summarize how it is done, since the data used are passed to the kernel from the PM. Catching a signal requires something much like the context switch that occurs when one process is taken out of execution and another process is put into execution, since when the handler terminates the process ought to be able to continue as if nothing had happened. However, there is only room in the process table to store one copy of the contents of all the CPU registers that are needed to restore the process to its original state. The solution to this problem is shown in Fig. 4-43. Part (a) of the figure is a simplified view of the stack of a process and part of its process table entry just after it has been taken out of execution following an interrupt. At the time of suspension the contents of all of the CPU registers are copied into the stackframe structure in the process table entry for the suspended process in the kernel part of the process table. This will be the situation at the moment a signal is generated. A signal is generated by a process or task different from the intended recipient, so the recipient cannot be running at that time.

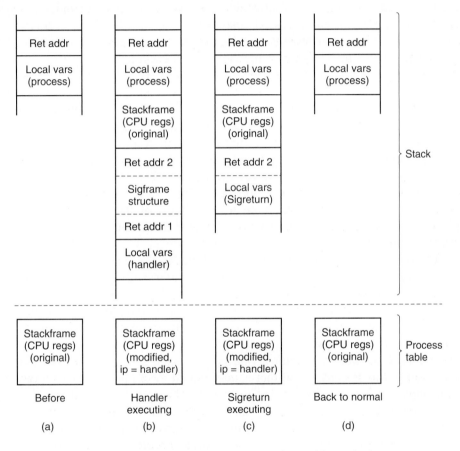

Figure 4-43. The stack of a process (above) and its stackframe in the process table (below) corresponding to phases in handling a signal. (a) State as process is taken out of execution. (b) State as handler begins execution. (c) State while sigreturn is executing. (d) State after sigreturn completes execution.

In preparation for handling the signal, the stackframe from the process table is copied onto the stack of the receiving process as a *sigcontext* structure, thus preserving it. Then a *sigframe* structure is placed on the stack. This structure contains information to be used by sigreturn after the handler finishes. It also contains the address of the library procedure that invokes sigreturn itself, *ret addr1*, and another return address, *ret addr2*, which is the address where execution of the interrupted program will resume. As will be seen, however, the latter address is not used during normal execution.

Although the handler is written as an ordinary procedure by the programmer, it is not called by a call instruction. The instruction pointer (program counter) field in the stackframe in the process table is altered to cause the signal handler to begin executing when *restart* puts the signaled process back into execution. Figure 4-43(b) shows the situation after this preparation has been completed and as the signal handler executes. Recall that the signal handler is an ordinary procedure, so when it terminates, *ret addr1* is popped and sigreturn executes.

Part (c) shows the situation while sigreturn is executing. The rest of the sigframe structure is now sigreturn's local variables. Part of sigreturn's action is to adjust its own stack pointer so that if it were to terminate like an ordinary function, it would use *ret addr2* as its return address. However, sigreturn does not actually terminate this way. It terminates like other system calls, allowing the scheduler in the kernel to decide which process to restart. Eventually, the signaled process will be rescheduled and will restart at this address, because the address is also in the process' original stackframe. The reason this address is on the stack is that a user might want to trace a program using a debugger, and this fools the debugger into a reasonable interpretation of the stack while a signal handler is being traced. In each phase the stack looks like that of an ordinary process, with local variables on top of a return address.

The real work of sigreturn is to restore things to the state they were in before the signal was received, and to clean up. Most importantly, the stackframe in the process table is restored to its original state, using the copy that was saved on the signaled process' stack. When sigreturn terminates, the situation will be as in Fig. 4-43(d), which shows the process waiting to be put back into execution in the same state it was in when interrupted.

For most signals the default action is to kill the signaled process. The PM takes care of this for any signal that is not ignored by default, and which the recipient process has not been enabled to handle, block, or ignore. If the parent is waiting for it, the killed process is cleaned up and removed from the process table. If the parent is not waiting, it becomes a zombie. For certain signals (e.g., SIGQUIT), the PM also writes a core dump of the process to the current directory.

It can easily happen that a signal is sent to a process that is currently blocked waiting for a read on a terminal for which no input is available. If the process has not specified that the signal is to be caught, it is just killed in the usual way. If, however, the signal is caught, the issue arises of what to do after the signal interrupt has been processed. Should the process go back to waiting, or should it continue with the next statement? Decisions, decisions.

What MINIX 3 does is this: the system call is terminated in such a way as to return the error code *EINTR*, so the process can see that the call was broken off by a signal. Determining that a signaled process was blocked on a system call is not entirely trivial. The PM must ask the file system to check for it.

This behavior is suggested, but not required, by POSIX, which also allows a read to return the number of bytes read so far at the time of receipt of the signal. Returning *EINTR* makes it possible to set an alarm and to catch sigalrm. This is an easy way to implement a timeout, for instance to terminate *login* and hang up a modem line if a user does not respond within a certain period.

User-Space Timers

Generating an alarm to wake up a process after a preset period of time is one of the most common uses of signals. In a conventional operating system, alarms would be managed entirely by the kernel, or a clock driver running in kernel space. In MINIX 3 responsibility for alarms to user processes is delegated to the process manager. The idea is to lighten the kernel's load, and simplify the code that runs in kernel space. If it is true that some number *b* of bugs are inevitable per some number *l* of lines of code, it is reasonable to expect that a smaller kernel will mean fewer bugs in the kernel. Even if the total number of bugs remains the same, their effects should be less serious if they occur in user-space operating system components rather than in the kernel itself.

Can we handle alarms without depending upon kernel-space code at all? In MINIX 3, at least, the answer is no, of course not. Alarms are managed in the first place by the kernel-space clock task, which maintains a linked list, or queue, of timers, as schematized in Fig. 2-49. On every interrupt from the clock chip the expiration time of the timer at the head of the queue is compared to the current time, and if it has expired the clock task main loop is activated. The clock task then causes a notification to be sent to the process that requested the alarm.

The innovation in MINIX 3 is that timers in kernel space are maintained only for system processes. The process manager maintains another queue of timers on behalf of user processes that have requested alarms. The process manager requests an alarm from the clock only for the timer at the head of its queue. If a new request is not added to the head of the queue no request to the clock is necessary at the time it is added. (Actually, of course, an alarm request is made through the system task, since the clock task does not communicate directly with any other process.) When expiration of an alarm is detected after a clock interrupt a notification comes to the process manager. The PM then does all the work of checking its own timer queue, signaling user processes, and possibly requesting another alarm if there is still an active alarm request at the head of its list.

So far this does not sound as if it saves much effort at the kernel level, but there are several other considerations. First there is the possibility that more than one timer may be found to have expired on a particular clock tick. It may seem improbable that two processes would request alarms at the same time. However, although the clock checks for timer expirations on every interrupt from the clock chip, interrupts are sometimes disabled, as we have seen. A call to the PC BIOS can cause enough interrupts to be missed that special provision is made to catch up. This means the time maintained by the clock task can jump by multiple ticks, making it possible that multiple timeouts may need to be handled at once. If these are handled by the process manager the kernel-space code does not have to traverse its own linked list, cleaning it up and generating multiple notifications.

Second, alarms can be cancelled. A user process may terminate before a timer set on its behalf expires. Or a timer may have been set as a backup to prevent a process from waiting forever for an event that might never occur. When the event does occur the alarm can be cancelled. Clearly, it eases the load on the kernel-space code if cancellation of timers is done on a queue maintained by the process manager, and not in the kernel. The kernel-space queue only needs attention when the timer at its head expires or when the process manager makes a change to the head of its queue.

The implementation of timers will be easier to understand if we take a quick tour of the functions used in handling an alarm now. Many functions in the process manager and in the kernel are involved, and it is hard to see the whole picture when looking at details, one function at a time.

When the PM sets an alarm on behalf of a user process a timer is initialized by *set_alarm*. The timer structure has fields for the expiration time, the process on behalf of which the alarm is set, and a pointer to a function to execute. For alarms that function is always *cause_sigalarm*. Then the system task is asked to set a kernel-space alarm. When this timer expires the watchdog process in the kernel, *cause_alarm*, is executed and sends a notification to the process manager. Several functions and macros are involved in this, but eventually this notification is received by the PM's *get_work* function, and detected as a message of type *SYN_ALARM* in the PM's main loop, which calls the PM's *pm_expire_timers* function. Now several more functions in the process manager's space are used. A library function, *tmrs_exptimers* causes the watchdog *cause_sigalrm* to be executed, which calls *checksig*, which calls *sig_proc*. Next, *sig_proc* decides whether to kill the process or send it the *SIGALRM*. Finally, sending the signal requires asking the system task in kernel space for help, of course, since data in the process table and in the stack space of the signaled process are manipulated, as was described in Fig. 4-43.

4.7.8 Other System Calls

The PM also handles a few more simple system calls. Time and stime deal with the real time clock. The times call gets process accounting times. They are handled here largely because the PM is a convenient place to put them. (We will discuss another time-related call, utime, when we come to file systems in Chap. 5, since it stores file modification times in i-nodes.)

The library functions *getuid* and *geteuid* both invoke the getuid system call, which returns both values in its return message. Similarly, the getgid system call also returns real and effective values for use by the *getgid* and *getegid* functions. getpid works the same way to return both the process ID and the ID of the parent process, and setuid and setgid can each set both real and effective values in one call. Two additional system calls exist in this group, getpgrp and setsid. The former returns the process group ID, and the latter sets it to the current PID value. These seven calls are the simplest MINIX 3 system calls.

The ptrace and reboot system calls are also handled by the PM. The former supports debugging of programs. The latter affects many aspects of the system. It is appropriate to place it in the PM because its first action is to send signals to kill all processes except init. After that, it calls upon the file system and the system task to complete its work.

4.8 IMPLEMENTATION OF THE MINIX 3 PROCESS MANAGER

Armed with a general overview of how the PM works, let us now turn to the code itself. The PM is written entirely in C, is straightforward, and contains a substantial amount of commentary in the code itself, so our treatment of most parts need not be long or involved. We will first look briefly at the header files, then the main program, and finally the files for the various system call groups discussed previously.

4.8.1 The Header Files and Data Structures

Several header files in the PM source directory have the same names as files in the kernel directory; these names will be seen again in the file system. These files have similar functions in their own contexts. The parallel structure is designed to make it easier to understand the organization of the whole MINIX 3 system. The PM also has a number of headers with unique names. As in other parts of the system, storage for global variables is reserved when the PM's version of *table.c* is compiled. In this section we will look at all of the header files, as well as *table.c*.

As with the other major parts of MINIX 3, the PM has a master header file, *pm.h* (line 17000). It is included in every compilation, and it in turn includes all the system-wide header files from */usr/include* and its subdirectories that are needed by every object module. Most of the files that are included in *kernel/kernel.h* are also included here. The PM also needs some definitions in *include/fcntl.h* and *include/unistd.h*. The PM's own versions of *const.h*, *type.h*, *proto.h*, and *glo.h* also are included. We saw a similar structure with the kernel.

Const.h (line 17100) defines some constants used by the PM.

Type.h is currently unused and exists in skeletal form just so the PM files will have the same organization as the other parts of MINIX 3. *Proto.h* (line 17300) collects in one place function prototypes needed throughout the PM. Dummy definitions of some functions needed when swapping is compiled into MINIX 3 are found on lines 17313 and 17314. Putting these macros here simplifies compiling a version without swapping; otherwise many other source files would have to be modified to remove calls to these functions.

The PM's global variables are declared in *glo.h* (line 17500). The same trick used in the kernel with *EXTERN* is used here, namely, *EXTERN* is normally a macro that expands to *extern*, except in the file *table.c*. There it becomes the null string so storage can be reserved for the variables declared as *EXTERN*.

The first of these variables, *mp*, is a pointer to an *mproc* structure, the PM part of the process table for the process whose system call is being processed. The second variable, *procs_in_use*, keeps track of how many process slots are currently in use, making it easy to see if a fork call is feasible.

The message buffer *m_in* is for the request messages. *Who* is the index of the current process; it is related to *mp* by

```
mp = &mproc[who];
```

When a message comes in, the system call number is extracted from it and put in *call_nr*.

MINIX 3 writes an image of a process to a core file when a process terminates abnormally. *Core_name* defines the name this file will have, *core_sset* is a bitmap which defines which signals should produce core dumps, and *ign_sset* is a bitmap telling which signals should be ignored. Note that *core_name* is defined *extern*, not *EXTERN*. The array *call_vec* is also declared as *extern*. The reason for making both of these declarations this way will be explained when we discuss *table.c*.

The PM's part of the process table is in the next file, *mproc.h* (line 17600). Most of the fields are adequately described by their comments. Several fields deal with signal handling. *Mp_ignore*, *mp_catch*, *mp_sig2mess*, *mp_sigmask*, *mp_sigmask2*, and *mp_sigpending* are bitmaps, in which each bit represents one of the signals that can be sent to a process. The type *sigset_t* is a 32-bit integer, so MINIX 3 could support up to 32 signals. Currently 22 signals are defined, although some are not supported, as permitted by the POSIX standard. Signal 1 is the least significant (rightmost) bit. In any case, POSIX requires standard functions to add or delete members of the signal sets represented by these bitmaps, so all necessary manipulations can be done without the programmer being aware of these details. The array *mp_sigact* is important for handling signals. An element is provided for each signal type, and each element is a *sigaction* structure (defined in the file *include/signal.h*). Each *sigaction* structure consists of three fields:

1. The *sa_handler* field defines whether the signal is to be handled in the default way, ignored, or handled by a special handler.

2. The *sa_mask* field is a *sigset_t* that defines which signals are to be blocked when the signal is being handled by a custom handler.

3. The *sa_flags* field is a set of flags that apply to the signal.

This array makes possible a great deal of flexibility in handling signals.

The *mp_flags* field is used to hold a miscellaneous collection of bits, as indicated at the end of the file. This field is an unsigned integer, 16 bits on low-end CPUs or 32 bits on a 386 and up.

The next field in the process table is *mp_procargs*. When a new process is started, a stack like the one shown in Fig. 4-38 is built, and a pointer to the start of the new process' *argv* array is stored here. This is used by the *ps* command. For instance, for the example of Fig. 4-38, the value 8164 would be stored here, making it possible for *ps* to display the command line,

ls –l f.c g.c

if executed while the *ls* command is active.

The *mp_swapq* field is not used in MINIX 3 as described here. It is used when swapping is enabled, and points to a queue of processes waiting to be swapped. The *mp_reply* field is where a reply message is built. In earlier versions of MINIX, one such field was provided, defined in *glo.h* and thus compiled when *table.c* was compiled. In MINIX 3, a space for building a reply message is provided for every process. Providing a place for a reply in each process table slot allows the PM to go on to handle another incoming message if a reply cannot be sent immediately upon completion of building the reply. The PM cannot handle two requests at once, but it can postpone replies if necessary, and catch up by trying to send all pending replies each time it completes a request.

The last two items in the process table might be regarded as frills. *Mp_nice* provides a place for each process to be assigned a nice value, so users can lower the priority of their processes, for example, to allow one running process to defer to another, more important, one. However, MINIX 3 uses this field internally to provide system processes (servers and drivers) with different priorities, depending upon their needs. The *mp_name* field is convenient for debugging, to help the programmer identify a process table slot in a memory dump. A system call is available to search the process table for a process name and return a process ID.

Finally, note that the process manager's part of the process table is declared as an array of size *NR_PROCS* (line 17655). Recall that the kernel's part of the process table was declared as an array of size *NR_TASKS + NR_PROCS* in *kernel/proc.h* (line 5593). As mentioned previously, processes compiled into the kernel are not known to user space components of the operating system such as the process manager. They are not really first-class processes.

The next file is *param.h* (line 17700), which contains macros for many of the system call parameters contained in the request message. It also contains twelve macros for fields in the reply message, and three macros used only in messages to the file system. For example, if the statement

    k = m_in.pid;

appears in any file in which *param.h* is included, the C preprocessor converts it to

    k = m_in.m1_i1;

before feeding it to the compiler proper (line 17707).

Before we continue with the executable code, let us look at *table.c* (line 17800). Compilation of this file reserves storage for the various *EXTERN* variables and structures we have seen in *glo.h* and *mproc.h*. The statement

    #define _TABLE

causes *EXTERN* to become the null string. This is the same mechanism that we saw in the kernel code. As we mentioned earlier, *core_name* was declared as *extern*, not *EXTERN* in *glo.h*. Now we can see why. Here *core_name* is declared with an initialization string. Initialization is not possible within an *extern* definition.

The other major feature of *table.c* is the array *call_vec* (line 17815). It is also an initialized array, and thus could not be declared as *EXTERN* in *glo.h*. When a request message arrives, the system call number is extracted from it and used as an index into *call_vec* to locate the procedure that carries out that system call. System call numbers that are not valid calls all invoke *no_sys*, which just returns an error code. Note that although the *_PROTOTYPE* macro is used in defining *call_vec*, this is not a declaration of a prototype; it is the definition of an initialized array. However, it is an array of functions, and use of *_PROTOTYPE* is the easiest way to do this that is compatible with both classic (Kernighan & Ritchie) C and Standard C.

A final note on header files: because MINIX 3 is still being actively developed, there are still some rough edges. One of these is that some source files in *pm/* include header files from the kernel directory. It may be hard to find some important definitions if you are not aware of this. Arguably definitions used by more than one major component of MINIX 3 should be consolidated into header files in the *include/* directory.

4.8.2 The Main Program

The PM is compiled and linked independently from the kernel and the file system. Consequently, it has its own main program, which is started up after the kernel has finished initializing itself. The entry point is at line 18041 in *main.c*. After doing its own initialization by calling *pm_init*, the PM enters its loop on line 18051. In this loop, it calls *get_work* to wait for an incoming request message. Then it calls one of its *do_XXX* procedures via the *call_vec* table to carry out the request. Finally, it sends a reply, if needed. This construction should be familiar by now: it is the same one used by the I/O tasks.

The preceding description is slightly simplified. As mentioned in Chap. 2, **notification messages** can be sent to any process. These are identified by special values in the *call_nr* field. In lines 18055 to 18062 a test is made for the two types of notification messages the PM can receive, and special action is taken in these cases. Also, a test is made for a valid *call_nr* on line 18064 before an attempt is made to carry out a request (on line 18067). Although an invalid request is unlikely, the test is cheap and the consequences of an invalid request would be serious.

Another point worth noting is the call to *swap_in* at line 18073. As we mentioned in the context of *proto.h*, in MINIX 3 as configured for description in this text this is a dummy call. But if the system is compiled with the full set of source code with swapping enabled, this is where a test is made to see if a process could be swapped in.

Finally, although the comment on line 18070 indicates this is where a reply is sent back, that is also a simplification. The call to *setreply* constructs a reply in the space we mentioned earlier, in the process table entry for the current process. Then in lines 18078 to 18091 of the loop, all entries in the process table are checked and all pending replies that can be sent are sent, skipping over any that cannot be sent at this time.

The procedures *get_work* (line 18099) and *setreply* (line 18116) handle the actual receiving and sending, respectively. The former does a little trick to make it look like a message from the kernel was actually from the PM itself, since the kernel does not have a process table slot of its own. The latter function does not really send the reply, it sets it up to be sent later, as mentioned above.

Initialization of the Process Manager

The longest procedure in *main.c* is *pm_init*, which initializes the PM. It is not used after the system has started running. Even though drivers and servers are compiled separately and run as separate processes, some of them are loaded as part of the **boot image** by the boot monitor. It is hard to see how any operating system could be started without a PM and a file system, so these components probably will always need to be loaded into memory by the boot monitor. Some device drivers are also loaded as part of the image. Although it is a goal to make as many MINIX 3 drivers as possible independently loadable, it is hard to see, for instance, how to avoid loading some disk driver early in the game.

Most of the work of *pm_init* is to initialize the PM's tables so all of the preloaded processes can run. As noted earlier the PM maintains two important data structures, the **hole table** (or **free memory table**) and a part of the process

table. We will consider the hole table first. Initialization of memory is complicated. It will be easier to understand the description that follows if we first show
how memory is organized when the PM is activated. MINIX 3 provides all the
information we need for this.

Before the MINIX 3 boot image itself is loaded into memory, the boot monitor
determines the layout of available memory. From the boot menu, you can press
the ESC key to see the boot parameters. One line in the display shows blocks of
unused memory, and looks like this:

memory = 800:923e0,100000:3df0000

(After MINIX 3 starts you can also see this information using the *sysenv* command
or the F5 key. The exact numbers you see may be different, of course.)

This shows two blocks of free memory. In addition, there are two blocks of
used memory. Memory below 0x800 is used for BIOS data and by the master
boot record and the bootblock. It really does not matter how it is used, it is not
available by the time the boot monitor starts up. The free memory beginning at
0x800 is the "base memory" of IBM-compatible computers. In this example,
starting at address 0x800 (2048) there are 0x923e0 (599008) bytes available.
Above this is the 640 KB to 1 MB "upper memory area" which is off limits to
ordinary programs—it is reserved for ROM and dedicated RAM on I/O adapters.
Finally, at address 0x100000 (1 MB) there are 0x3df0000 bytes free. This range
is commonly referred to as "extended memory." This example indicates the computer has a total of 64 MB of RAM installed.

If you have been keeping track of these numbers you will have noticed that
the amount of free base memory is less than the 638 KB you might have expected.
The MINIX 3 boot monitor loads itself as high as possible in this range, and in this
case requires about 52 KB. In this example about 584 KB is really free. This is a
good place to note that memory use could be more complicated than is in this example. For instance, one method of running MINIX, not yet ported to MINIX 3 at
the time this is being written, uses an MS-DOS file to simulate a MINIX disk. The
technique requires loading some components of MS-DOS before starting the
MINIX 3 boot monitor. If these are not loaded adjacent to memory regions
already in use more than two regions of free memory will be reported by the boot
monitor.

When the boot monitor loads the boot image into memory information about
the image components is displayed on the console screen. Fig. 4-44 shows part of
such a display. In this example (typical but possibly not identical to what you will
see as this was from a pre-release version of MINIX 3), the boot monitor loaded
the kernel into the free memory at address 0x800. The PM, file system, reincarnation server, and other components not shown in the figure are installed in the
block of free memory that starts at 1 MB. This was an arbitrary design choice;
enough memory remains below the 588 KB limit for some of these components.
However, when MINIX 3 is compiled with a large block cache, as is true in this

example, the file system cannot fit into the space just above the kernel. It was easier, but by no means essential, just to load everything in the higher region of memory. Nothing is lost by this, the memory manager can make use of the hole in memory below 588 KB once the system is running and user processes are started.

cs	ds	text	data	bss	stack	
0000800	0005800	19552	3140	30076	0	kernel
0100000	0104c00	19456	2356	48612	1024	pm
0111800	011c400	43216	5912	6224364	2048	fs
070e000	070f400	4352	616	4696	131072	rs

Figure 4-44. Boot monitor display of memory usage of the first few boot image components.

Initialization of the PM starts by looping through the process table to disable the timer for each slot so no spurious alarms can occur. Then global variables that define the default sets of signals that will be ignored or that will cause core dumps are initialized. Next the information we have seen about memory use is processed. On line 18182 the system task retrieves the boot monitor's *memory* string that we saw above. In our example there are two base:size pairs showing blocks of free memory. The call to *get_mem_chunks* (line 18184) converts the data in the ASCII string into binary, and enters the base and size values into the array *mem_chunks* (line 18192) the elements of which are defined as

    struct memory {phys_clicks base; phys_clicks size;};

Mem_chunks is not the hole list yet, it is just a small array in which this information is collected prior to initializing the hole list.

After querying the kernel and converting information about kernel memory use into units of clicks, *patch_mem_chunks* is called to subtract the kernel usage from *mem_chunks* array. Now memory that was in use before MINIX 3 started is accounted for, as is memory used by the kernel. *Mem_chunks* is not complete, but memory used by normal processes in the boot image will be accounted for within the loop on lines 18201 to 18239 which initializes process table entries.

Information about attributes of all processes that are part of the boot image are in the *image* table that was declared in *kernel/table.c* (lines 6095 to 6109). Before entering the main loop the sys_getimage kernel call on line 18197 provides the process manager with a copy of the *image* table. (Strictly speaking, this is not exactly a kernel call; it is one of more than a dozen macros defined in *include/minix/syslib.h* that provide easily-used interfaces to the sys_getinfo kernel call.) Kernel processes are not known in user space and the PM (and FS) parts of the process table do not need initialization for kernel processes. In fact, space is not reserved for kernel process slots. These each have a negative process number (process table index), and they are ignored by the test on line 18202. Also, it is not necessary to call *patch_mem_chunks* for kernel processes; the allowance made for the kernel's memory use also takes care of the tasks that are compiled into the kernel.

System processes and user processes need to be added to the process table, although they get slightly different treatments (lines 18210 to 18219). The only user process loaded in the boot image is *init*, thus a test is made for *INIT_PROC_NR* (line 18210). All of the other processes in the boot image are system processes. System processes are special—they cannot be swapped, they each have a dedicated slot in the *priv* table in the kernel, and they have special privileges as indicated by their flags. For each process, the proper defaults are set for signal processing (with some differences between the defaults for system processes and *init*). Then the memory map of each process is obtained from the kernel, using *get_mem_map*, which ultimately invokes the sys_getinfo kernel call, and *patch_mem_chunks* is called to adjust the *mem_chunks* array (lines 18225 to 18230) accordingly.

Finally, a message is sent to the file system so an entry for each process can be initialized in the FS part of the process table (lines 18233 to 18236). The message contains only the process number and the PID; this is sufficient to initialize the FS process table slot, as all the processes in the system boot image belong to the superuser and can be given the same default values. Each message is dispatched with a send operation, so no reply is expected. After sending the message the name of the process is displayed on the console (line 18237):

> Building process table: pm fs rs tty memory log driver init

In this display driver is a stand-in for the default disk driver; multiple disk drivers may be compiled into the boot image, with one selected as the default by a *label=* assignment in the boot parameters.

The PM's own process table entry is a special case. After the main loop is complete the PM makes some changes to its own entry and then sends a final message to the file system with a symbolic value of *NONE* as the process number. This message is sent with a sendrec call, and the process manager blocks expecting a response. While the PM has been looping through the initialization code the file system has been executing a *receive* loop (on lines 24189 to 24202, if you want to peek at code to be described in the next chapter). Receiving the message with process number *NONE* tells the FS that all system processes have been initialized, so it can exit its loop and send a synchronization message to unblock the PM.

Now the FS is free to continue its own initialization, and here in the PM initialization is also almost complete. On line 18253, *mem_init* is called. This function takes the information that has been collected in the *mem_chunks* array and initializes the linked list of free memory regions and related variables that will be used for memory management once the system is running. Normal memory management begins after printing a message on the console listing total memory, memory in use by MINIX 3, and available memory:

Physical memory: total 63996 KB, system 12834 KB, free 51162 KB.

The next function is *get_nice_value* (line 18263). It is called to determine the "nice level" of each process in the boot image. The *image* table provides a *queue* value for each boot image process which defines on which priority queue the process will be scheduled. These range from 0 for high priority processes like *CLOCK* to 15 for *IDLE*. But the traditional meaning of "nice level" in UNIX systems is a value that can be either positive or negative. Thus *get_nice_value* scales the kernel priority values on a scale centered on zero for user processes. This is done using constants defined as macros in *include/sys/resource.h* (not listed), *PRIO_MIN* and *PRIO_MAX*, with values of -20 and +20. These are scaled between *MIN_USER_Q* and *MAX_USER_Q*, defined in *kernel/proc.h*, so if a decision is made to provide fewer or more scheduling queues the *nice* command will still work. *Init*, the root process in the user process tree, is scheduled in priority queue 7 and receives a "nice" value of 0, which is inherited by a child after a fork.

The last two functions contained in *main.c* have already been mentioned in passing. *Get_mem_chunks* (line 18280) is called only once. It takes the memory information returned by the boot monitor as an ASCII string of hexadecimal base:size pairs, converts the information into units of clicks, and stores the information in the *mem_chunks* array. *Patch_mem_chunks* (line 18333) continues building the free memory list, and is called several times, once for the kernel itself and once for *init* and each of the system processes initialized during the main loop of *pm_init*. It corrects the raw boot monitor information. Its job is easier because it gets its data in click units. For each process, *pm_init* is passed the base and size of the text and data allocations for that process. For each process, the base of the last element in the array of free blocks is increased by the sum of the lengths of the text and data segments. Then the size of that block is decreased by the same amount to mark the memory for that process as in use.

4.8.3 Implementation of FORK, EXIT, and WAIT

The fork, exit, and wait system calls are implemented by the procedures *do_fork*, *do_pm_exit*, and *do_waitpid* in the file *forkexit.c*. The procedure *do_fork* (line 18430) follows the steps shown in Fig. 4-36. Notice that the second call to *procs_in_use* (line 18445) reserves the last few process table slots for the superuser. In computing how much memory the child needs, the gap between the data and stack segments is included, but the text segment is not. Either the parent's text is shared, or, if the process has common I and D space, its text segment is of zero length. After doing the computation, a call is made to *alloc_mem* to get the memory. If this is successful, the base addresses of child and parent are converted from clicks into absolute bytes, and sys_copy is called to send a message to the system task to get the copying done.

Now a slot is found in the process table. The test involving *procs_in_use* earlier guarantees that one will exist. After the slot has been found, it is filled in, first by copying the parent's slot there, and then updating the fields *mp_parent*, *mp_flags*, *mp_child_utime*, *mp_child_stime*, *mp_seg*, *mp_exitstatus*, and *mp_sigstatus*. Some of these fields need special handling. Only certain bits in the *mp_flags* field are inherited. The *mp_seg* field is an array containing elements for the text, data, and stack segments, and the text portion is left pointing to the parent's text segment if the flags indicate this is a separate I and D program that can share text.

The next step is assigning a PID to the child. The call to *get_free_pid* does what its name indicates. This is not as simple as one might think, and we will describe the function further on.

Sys_fork and *tell_fs* inform the kernel and file system, respectively, that a new process has been created, so they can update their process tables. (All the procedures beginning with *sys_* are library routines that send a message to the system task in the kernel to request one of the services of Fig. 2-45.) Process creation and destruction are always initiated by the PM and then propagated to the kernel and file system when completed.

The reply message to the child is sent explicitly at the end of *do_fork*. The reply to the parent, containing the child's PID, is sent by the loop in *main*, as the normal reply to a request.

The next system call handled by the PM is exit. The procedure *do_pm_exit* (line 18509) accepts the call, but most of the work is done by the call to *pm_exit*, a few lines further down. The reason for this division of labor is that *pm_exit* is also called to take care of processes terminated by a signal. The work is the same, but the parameters are different, so it is convenient to split things up this way.

The first thing *pm_exit* does is to stop the timer, if the process has one running. Then the time used by the child is added to the parent's account. Next, the kernel and file system are notified that the process is no longer runnable (lines 18550 and 18551). The sys_exit kernel call sends a message to the system task telling it to clear the slot used by this process in the kernel's process table. Next the memory is released. A call to *find_share* determines whether the text segment is being shared by another process, and if not the text segment is released by a call to *free_mem*. This is followed by another call to the same procedure to release the data and stack. It is not worth the trouble to decide whether all the memory could be released in one call to *free_mem*. If the parent is waiting, *cleanup* is called to release the process table slot. If the parent is not waiting, the process becomes a zombie, indicated by the *ZOMBIE* bit in the *mp_flags* word, and the parent is sent a *SIGCHILD* signal.

Whether the process is completely eliminated or made into a zombie, the final action of *pm_exit* is to loop through the process table and look for children of the process it has just terminated (lines 18582 to 18589). If any are found, they are disinherited and become children of *init*. If *init* is waiting and a child is hanging, *cleanup* is then called for that child. This deals with situations such as the one shown in Fig. 4-45(a). In this figure we see that process 12 is about to exit, and that its parent, 7, is waiting for it. *Cleanup* will be called to get rid of 12, so 52 and 53 are turned into children of *init*, as shown in Fig. 4-45(b). Now we have the situation that 53, which has already exited, is the child of a process doing a wait. Consequently, it can also be cleaned up.

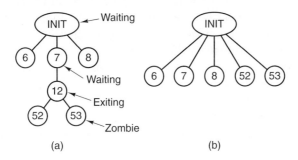

(a)   (b)

Figure 4-45. (a) The situation as process 12 is about to exit. (b) The situation after it has exited.

When the parent process does a wait or a waitpid, control comes to procedure *do_waitpid* on line 18598. The parameters supplied by the two calls are different, and the actions expected are also different, but the setup done in lines 18613 to 18615 prepares internal variables so *do_waitpid* can perform the actions of either call. The loop on lines 18623 to 18642 scans the entire process table to see if the process has any children at all, and if so, checks to see if any are zombies that can now be cleaned up. If a zombie is found (line 18630), it is cleaned up and *do_waitpid* returns the *SUSPEND* return code. If a traced child is found, the reply message being constructed is modified to indicate the process is stopped, and *do_waitpid* returns.

If the process doing the wait has no children, it simply receives an error return (line 18653). If it has children, but none are zombies or are being traced, a test is made to see if *do_waitpid* was called with a bit set indicating the parent did not want to wait. If not (the usual case), then a bit is set on line 18648 to indicate that it is waiting, and the parent is suspended until a child terminates.

When a process has exited and its parent is waiting for it, in whichever order these events occur, the procedure *cleanup* (line 18660) is called to perform the last rites. Not much remains to be done by this point. The parent is awakened from its wait or waitpid call and is given the PID of the terminated child, as well as its exit and signal status. The file system has already released the child's memory, and the kernel has already suspended scheduling and freed up the child's slot in the process table. At this point, the child process is gone forever.

4.8.4 Implementation of EXEC

The code for **exec** follows the outline of Fig. 4-40. It is contained in the procedure *do_exec* (line 18747) in *exec.c*. After making a few validity checks, the PM fetches the name of the file to be executed from user space (lines 18773 to 18776). Recall that the library procedures which implement **exec** build a stack within the old core image, as we saw in Fig. 4-38. This stack is fetched into the PM's memory space next (line 18782).

The next few steps are written as a loop (lines 18789 to 18801). However, for ordinary binary executables only one pass through the loop takes place. We will first describe this case. On line 18791 a message to the file system switches to the user's directory so the path to the file will be interpreted relative to the user's, rather than to PM's, working directory. Then *allowed* is called—if execution is allowed it opens the file. If the test fails a negative number is returned instead of a valid file descriptor, and *do_exit* terminates indicating failure. If the file is present and executable, the PM calls *read_header* and gets the segment sizes. For an ordinary binary the return code from *read_header* will cause an exit from the loop at line 18800.

Now we will look at what happens if the executable is a script. MINIX 3, like most UNIX-like operating systems, supports executable scripts. *Read_header* tests the first two bytes of the file for the magic **shebang** (#!) sequence and returns a special code if this is found, indicating a script. The first line of a script marked this way specifies the interpreter for the script, and possibly also specifies flags and options for the interpreter. For instance, a script can be written with a first line like

```
#! /bin/sh
```

to show it is to be interpreted by the Bourne shell, or

```
#! /usr/local/bin/perl −wT
```

to be interpreted with Perl with flags set to warn of possible problems. This complicates the job of **exec**, however. When a script is to be run, the file that *do_exec* must load into memory is not the script itself. Instead the binary for the interpreter must be loaded. When a script is identified *patch_stack* is called on line 18801 at the bottom of the loop.

What *patch_stack* does can be illustrated by an example. Suppose that a Perl script is called with a few arguments on the command line, like this:

```
perl_prog.pl file1 file2
```

If the perl script was written with a shebang line similar to the one we saw above *patch_stack* creates a stack to execute the perl binary as if the command line were:

```
/usr/local/bin/perl -wT perl_prog.pl file1 file2
```

If it is successful in this, the first part of this line, that is, the path to the binary executable of the interpreter, is returned. Then the body of the loop is executed once more, this time reading the file header and getting the segment sizes of the file to be executed. It is not permitted for the first line of a script to point to another script as its interpreter. That is why the variable *r* is used. It can only be incremented once, allowing only one chance to call *patch_stack*. If on the second time through the loop the code indicating a script is encountered, the test on line 18800 will break the loop. The code for a script, represented symbolically as *ESCRIPT*, is a negative number (defined on line 18741). In this case the test on line 18803 will cause *do_exit* to return with an error code telling whether the problem is a file that canot be executed or a command line that is too long.

Some work remains to be done to complete the exec operation. *Find_share* checks to see if the new process can share text with a process that is already running (line 18809), and *new_mem* allocates memory for the new image and releases the old memory. Both the image in memory and the process table need to be made ready before the exec-ed program can run. On lines 18819 to 18821 the executable file's i-node, filesystem, and modification time are saved in the process table. Then the stack is fixed up as in Fig. 4-38(c) and copied to the new image in memory. Next the text (if not already sharing text) and data segments are copied from the disk to the memory image by calling *rw_seg* (lines 18834 to 18841). If the *setuid* or *setgid* bits are set the file system needs to be notified to put the effective id information into the FS part of process table entry (lines 18845 to 18852). In the PM's part of the file table a pointer to the arguments to the new program is saved so the *ps* command will be able to show the command line, signal bitmasks are initialized, the FS is notified to close any file descriptors that should be closed after an exec, and the name of the command is saved for display by *ps* or during debugging (lines 18856 to 18877). Usually, the last step is to tell the kernel, but if tracing is enabled a signal must be sent (lines 18878 to 18881).

In describing the work of *do_exec* we mentioned a number of supporting functions provided in *exec.c*. *Read_header* (line 18889) not only reads the header and returns the segment sizes, it also verifies that the file is a valid MINIX 3 executable for the same CPU type as the operating system is compiled for. The constant value *A_I80386* on line 18944 is determined by a *#ifdef ... #endif* sequence at compile time. Binary executable programs for 32-bit MINIX 3 on Intel platforms must have this constant in their headers to be acceptable. If MINIX 3 were to be compiled to run in 16-bit mode the value here would be *A_I8086*. If you are curious, you can see values defined for other CPUs in *include/a.out.h*.

Procedure *new_mem* (line 18980) checks to see if sufficient memory is available for the new memory image. It searches for a hole big enough for just the data and stack if the text is being shared; otherwise it searches for a single hole big enough for the combined text, data, and stack. A possible improvement here would be to search for two separate holes. In earlier versions of MINIX it was required that the text and data/stack segments be contiguous, but this is not necessary in MINIX 3. If sufficient memory is found, the old memory is released and the new memory is acquired. If insufficient memory is available, the exec call fails. After the new memory is allocated, *new_mem* updates the memory map (in *mp_seg*) and reports it to the kernel with the sys_newmap kernel call.

The final job of *new_mem* is to zero the bss segment, gap, and stack segment. (The bss segment is that part of the data segment that contains all the uninitialized global variables.) The work is done by the system task, called by sys_memset at line 19064. Many compilers generate explicit code to zero the bss segment, but doing it here allows MINIX 3 to work even with compilers that do not. The gap between data and stack segments is also zeroed, so that when the data segment is extended by brk, the newly acquired memory will contain zeroes. This is not only a convenience for the programmer, who can count on new variables having an initial value of zero, it is also a security feature on a multiuser operating system, where a process previously using this memory may have been using data that should not be seen by other processes.

The next procedure, *patch_ptr* (line 19074), relocates pointers like those of Fig. 4-38(b) to the form of Fig. 4-38(c). The work is simple: examine the stack to find all the pointers and add the base address to each one.

The next two functions work together. We described their purpose earlier. When a script is exec-ed the binary for the interpreter of the script is the executable that must be run. *Insert_arg* (line 19106) inserts strings into the PM copy of the stack. This is directed by *patch_stack* (line 19162), which finds all of the strings on the shebang line of the script, and calls *insert_arg*. The pointers have to be corrected, too, of course. *Insert_arg*'s job is straightforward, but there are a number of things that can go wrong and must be tested. This is a good place to mention that checking for problems when dealing with scripts is particularly important. Scripts, after all, can be written by users, and all computer professionals recognize that users are often the major cause of problems. But, seriously, a major difference between a script and a compiled binary is that you can generally trust the compiler to have refused to produce output for a wide range of errors in the source code. A script is not validated this way.

Fig. 4-46 shows how this would work for a call to a shell script, *s.sh*, which operates on a file *f1*. The command line looks like this:

    s.sh f1

and the shebang line of the script indicates it is to be interpreted by the Bourne shell:

    #! /bin/sh

In part (a) of the figure is the stack copied from the caller's space. Part (b) shows how this is transformed by *patch_stack* and *insert_arg*. Both of these diagrams correspond to Fig.4-38(b).

The next function defined in *exec.c* is *rw_seg* (line 19208). Is called once or twice per exec, possibly to load the text segment and always to load the data

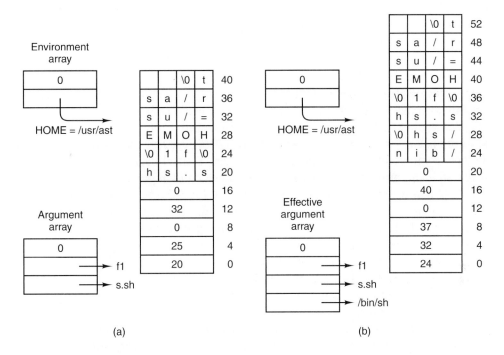

Figure 4-46. a. Arrays passed to *execve* and the stack created when a script is executed. b. After processing by *patch_stack*, the arrays and the stack look like this. The script name is passed to the program which interprets the script.

segment. Rather than just reading the file block by block and then copying the blocks to the user, a trick is used to allow the file system to load the entire segment directly to the user space. In effect, the call is decoded by the file system in a slightly special way so that it appears to be a read of the entire segment by the user process itself. Only a few lines at the beginning of the file system's read routine know that some monkey business is going on here. Loading is appreciably speeded up by this maneuver.

The final procedure in *exec.c* is *find_share* (line 19256). It searches for a process that can share text by comparing the i-node, device, and modification times of the file to be executed with those of existing processes. This is just a straightforward search of the appropriate fields in *mproc*. Of course, it must ignore the process on behalf of which the search is being made.

4.8.5 Implementation of BRK

As we have just seen, the basic memory model used by MINIX 3 is quite simple: each process is given a single contiguous allocation for its data and stack when it is created. It is never moved around in memory, it never grows, and it never shrinks. All that can happen is that the data segment can eat away at the gap from the low end, and the stack can eat away at it from the high end. Under these circumstances, the implementation of the brk call in *break.c* is especially easy. It consists of verifying that the new sizes are feasible and then updating the tables to reflect them.

The top-level procedure is *do_brk* (line 19328), but most of the work is done in *adjust* (line 19361). The latter checks to see if the stack and data segments have collided. If they have, the brk call cannot be carried out, but the process is not killed immediately. A safety factor, *SAFETY_BYTES*, is added to the top of the data segment before making the test, so (hopefully) the decision that the stack has grown too far can be made while there is still enough room on the stack for the process to continue for a short while. It gets control back (with an error message), so it can print appropriate messages and shut down gracefully.

Note that *SAFETY_BYTES* and *SAFETY_CLICKS* are defined using #define statements in the middle of the procedure (line 19393). This use is rather unusual; normally such definitions appear at the beginning of files, or in separate header files. The associated comment reveals that the programmer found deciding upon the size of the safety factor to be difficult. No doubt this definition was done in this way to attract attention and, perhaps, to stimulate additional experimentation.

The base of the data segment is constant, so if *adjust* has to adjust the data segment, all it does is update the length field. The stack grows downward from a fixed end point, so if *adjust* also notices that the stack pointer, which is given to it as a parameter, has grown beyond the stack segment (to a lower address), both the origin and length are updated.

4.8.6 Implementation of Signal Handling

Eight POSIX system calls are related to signals. These calls are summarized in Fig. 4-47. These system calls, as well as the signals themselves, are processed in the file *signal.c*.

System call	Purpose
sigaction	Modify response to future signal
sigprocmask	Change set of blocked signals
kill	Send signal to another process
alarm	Send ALRM signal to self after delay
pause	Suspend self until future signal
sigsuspend	Change set of blocked signals, then PAUSE
sigpending	Examine set of pending (blocked) signals
sigreturn	Clean up after signal handler

Figure 4-47. System calls relating to signals.

The sigaction system call supports the *sigaction* and *signal* functions, which allow a process to alter how it will respond to signals. *Sigaction* is required by

POSIX and is the preferred call for most purposes, but the *signal* library function is required by Standard C, and programs that must be portable to non-POSIX systems should be written using it. The code for *do_sigaction* (line 19544) begins with checks for a valid signal number and verification that the call is not an attempt to change the response to a sigkill signal (lines 19550 and 19551). (It is not permitted to ignore, catch, or block sigkill. Sigkill is the ultimate means by which a user can control his processes and a system manager can control his users.) *Sigaction* is called with pointers to a *sigaction* structure, *sig_osa*, which receives the old signal attributes that were in effect before the call, and another such structure, *sig_nsa*, containing a new set of attributes.

The first step is to call the system task to copy the current attributes into the structure pointed to by *sig_osa*. *Sigaction* can be called with a *NULL* pointer in *sig_nsa* to examine the old signal attributes without changing them. In this case *do_sigaction* returns immediately (line 19560). If *sig_nsa* is not *NULL*, the structure defining the new signal action is copied to the PM's space.

The code in lines 19567 to 19585 modifies the *mp_catch*, *mp_ignore*, and *mp_sigpending* bitmaps according to whether the new action is to be to ignore the signal, to use the default handler, or to catch the signal. The *sa_handler* field of the *sigaction* structure is used to pass a pointer to the procedure to the function to be executed if a signal is to be caught, or one of the special codes *SIG_IGN* or *SIG_DFL*, whose meanings should be clear if you understand the POSIX standards for signal handling discussed earlier. A special MINIX 3-specific code, *SIG_MESS* is also possible; this will be explained below.

The library functions *sigaddset* and *sigdelset* are used, to modify the signal bitmaps, although the actions are straightforward bit manipulation operations that could have been implemented with simple macros. However, these functions are required by the POSIX standard in order to make programs that use them easily portable, even to systems in which the number of signals exceeds the number of bits available in an integer. Using the library functions helps to make MINIX 3 itself easily portable to different architectures.

We mentioned a special case above. The *SIG_MESS* code detected on line 19576 is available only for privileged (system) processes. Such processes are normally blocked, waiting for request messages. Thus the ordinary method of receiving a signal, in which the PM asks the kernel to put a signal frame on the recipients stack, will be delayed until a message wakes up the recipient. A *SIG_MESS* code tells the PM to deliver a notification message, which has higher priority than normal messages. A notification message contains the set of pending signals as an argument, allowing multiple signals to be passed in one message.

Finally, the other signal-related fields in the PM's part of the process table are filled in. For each potential signal there is a bitmap, the *sa_mask*, which defines which signals are to be blocked while a handler for that signal is executing. For each signal there is also a pointer, *sa_handler*. It can contain a pointer to the handler function, or special values to indicate the signal is to be ignored, handled in the default way, or used to generate a message. The address of the library routine that invokes sigreturn when the handler terminates is stored in *mp_sigreturn*. This address is one of the fields in the message received by the PM.

POSIX allows a process to manipulate its own signal handling, even while within a signal handler. This can be used to change signal response to subsequent signals while a signal is being processed, and then to restore the normal set of responses. The next group of system calls support these signal-manipulation features. Sigpending is handled by *do_sigpending* (line 19597), which returns the *mp_sigpending* bitmap, so a process can determine if it has pending signals. Sigprocmask, handled by *do_sigprocmask*, returns the set of signals that are currently blocked, and can also be used to change the state of a single signal in the set, or to replace the entire set with a new one. The moment that a signal is unblocked is an appropriate time to check for pending signals, and this is done by calls to *check_pending* on line 19635 and line 19641. *Do_sigsuspend* (line 19657) carries out the sigsuspend system call. This call suspends a process until a signal is received. Like the other functions we have discussed here, it manipulates bitmaps. It also sets the sigsuspended bit in *mp_flags*, which is all it takes to prevent execution of the process. Again, this is a good time to make a call to *check_pending*. Finally, *do_sigreturn* handles sigreturn, which is used to return from a custom handler. It restores the signal context that existed when the handler was entered, and it also calls *check_pending* on line 19682.

When a user process, such as the *kill* command, invokes the kill system call, the PM's *do_kill* function (line 19689) is invoked. A single call to kill may require delivery of signals to a group of several processes, and *do_kill* just calls *check_sig*, which checks the entire process table for eligible recipients.

Some signals, such as sigint, originate in the kernel itself. *Ksig_pending* (line 19699) is activated when a message from the kernel about pending signals is sent to the PM. There may be more than one process with pending signals, so the loop on lines 19714 to 19722 repeatedly asks the system task for a pending signal, passes it on to *handle_sig*, and then tells the system task it is done, until there are no more processes with signals pending. The messages come with a bitmap, allowing the kernel to generate multiple signals with one message. The next function, *handle_sig*, processes the bitmap one bit at a time on lines 19750 to 19763. Some kernel signals need special attention: the process ID is changed in some cases to cause the signal to be delivered to a group of processes (lines 19753 to 19757). Otherwise, each set bit results in a call to *check_sig*, just as in *do_kill*.

Alarms and Timers

The alarm system call is handled by *do_alarm* (line 19769). It calls the next function, *set_alarm*, which is a separate function because it is also used to turn off a timer when a process exits with a timer still on. This is done by calling *set_alarm* with an alarm time of zero. *Set_alarm* does its work with timers maintained within the process manager. It first determines if a timer is already set on behalf of the requesting process, and if so, whether it has expired, so the system call can return the time in seconds remaining on a previous alarm, or zero if no timer was set. A comment within the code explains some problems with dealing with long times. Some rather ugly code on line 19918 multiplies the argument to the call, a time in seconds, by the constant *HZ*, the number of clock ticks per second, to get a time in tick units. Three casts are needed to make the result the correct *clock_t* data type. Then on the next line the calculation is reversed with *ticks* cast from *clock_t* to *unsigned long*. The result is compared with a cast of the original alarm time argument cast to *unsigned long*. If they are not equal it means the requested time resulted in a number that was out of range of one of the data types used, and a value which means "never" is substituted. Finally, either *pm_set_timer* or *pm_cancel_timer* is called to add or remove a timer from the process manager's timer queue. The key argument to the former call is *cause_sigalarm*, the watchdog function to be executed when the timer expires.

Any interaction with the timer maintained in kernel space is hidden in the calls to the *pm_XXX_timer* routines. Every request for an alarm that eventually culminates in an alarm will normally result in a request to set a timer in kernel space. The only exception would be if more than one request for a timeout at the exact same time were to occur. However, processes may cancel their alarms or terminate before their alarms expire. A kernel call to request setting a timer in kernel space only needs to be made when there is a change to the timer at the head of the process manager's timer queue.

Upon expiration of a timer in the kernel-space timer queue that was set on behalf of the PM, the system task announces the fact by sending the PM a notification message, detected as type *SYN_ALARM* by the main loop of the PM. This results in a call to *pm_expire_timers*, which ultimately results in execution of the next function, *cause_sigalrm*.

Cause_sigalarm (line 19935) is the watchdog, mentioned above. It gets the process number of the process to be signaled, checks some flags, resets the *ALARM_ON* flag, and calls *check_sig* to send the *SIGALRM* signal.

The default action of the *SIGALRM* signal is to kill the process if it is not caught. If the *SIGALRM* is to be caught, a handler must be installed by sigaction. Fig. 4-48 shows the complete sequence of events for a *SIGALRM* signal with a custom handler. The figure shows that three sequences of messages occur. First, in message (1) the user does an alarm call via a message to the PM. At this point the process manager sets up a timer in the queue of timers it maintains for user processes, and acknowledges with message (2). Nothing more may happen for a while. When the timer for this request reaches the head of the PM's timer queue, because timers ahead of it have expired or have been cancelled, message (3) is sent to the system task to have it set up a new kernel-space timer for the process manager, and is acknowledged by message (4). Again, some time will pass before anything more happens. But after this timer reaches the head of the kernel-

space timer queue the clock interrupt handler will find it has expired. The
remaining messages in the sequence will follow quickly. The clock interupt
handler sends a *HARD_INT* message (5) to the clock task, which causes it to run
and update its timers. The timer watchdog function, *cause_alarm*, initiates message (6), a notification to the PM. The PM now updates its timers, and after
determining from its part of the process table that a handler is installed for
SIGALRM in the target process, sends message (7) to the system task to have it do
the stack manipulations needed to send the signal to the user process. This is
acknowledged by message (8). The user process will be scheduled and will execute the handler, and then will make a sigreturn call (9) to the process manager.
The process manager then sends message (10) to the system task to complete the
cleanup, and this is acknowledged by message (11). Not shown in this diagram is
another pair of messages from the PM to the system task to get the uptime, made
before message (3).

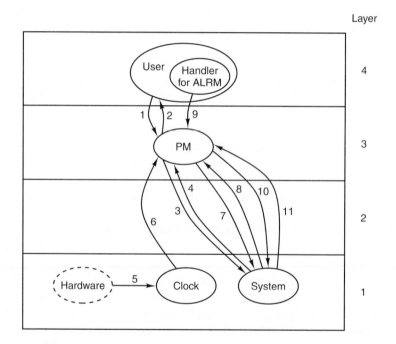

Figure 4-48. Messages for an alarm. The most important are: (1) User does
alarm. (3) PM asks system task to set timer. (6) Clock tells PM time has expired. (7) PM requests signal to user. (9) Handler terminates with call to sigreturn. See text for details.

The next function, *do_pause*, takes care of the pause system call (line
19853). It isn't really related to alarms and timers, although it can be used in a
program to suspend execution until an alarm (or some other signal) is received.

All that is necessary is to set a bit and return the *SUSPEND* code, which causes the main loop of the PM to refrain from replying, thus keeping the caller blocked. The kernel need not even be informed, since it knows that the caller is blocked.

Support Functions for Signals

Several support functions in *signal.c* have been mentioned in passing. We will now look at them in more detail. By far the most important is *sig_proc* (line 19864), which actually sends a signal. First a number of tests are made. Attempts to send to dead or zombie processes are serious problems that cause a system panic (lines 19889 to 19893). A process that is currently being traced is stopped when signaled (lines 19894 to 19899). If the signal is to be ignored, *sig_proc*'s work is complete on line 19902. This is the default action for some signals, for instance, those signals that are required to be there by POSIX but do not have to (and are not) supported by MINIX 3. If the signal is blocked, the only action that needs to be taken is to set a bit in that process' *mp_sigpending* bitmap. The key test (line 19910) is to distinguish processes that have been enabled to catch signals from those that have not. With the exception of signals that are converted into messages to be sent to system services all other special considerations have been eliminated by this point and a process that cannot catch the signal must be terminated.

First we will look at the processing of signals that are eligible to be caught (lines 19911 to 19950). A message is constructed to be sent to the kernel, some parts of which are copies of information in the PM's part of the process table. If the process to be signaled was previously suspended by sigsuspend, the signal mask that was saved at the time of suspension is included in the message; otherwise the current signal mask is included (line 19914). Other items included in the message are several addresses in the space of the signaled process space: the signal handler, the address of the *sigreturn* library routine to be called on completion of the handler, and the current stack pointer.

Next, space is allocated on the process' stack. Figure 4-49 shows the structure that is put on the stack. The *sigcontext* portion is put on the stack to preserve it for later restoration, since the corresponding structure in the process table itself is altered in preparation for execution of the signal handler. The *sigframe* part provides a return address for the signal handler and data needed by sigreturn to complete restoration of the process' state when the handler is done. The return address and frame pointer are not actually used by any part of MINIX 3. They are there to fool a debugger if anyone should ever try to trace execution of a signal handler.

The structure to be put on the signaled process' stack is fairly large. The code in lines 19923 and 19924 reserves space for it, following which a call to *adjust* tests to see whether there is enough room on the process' stack. If there is not

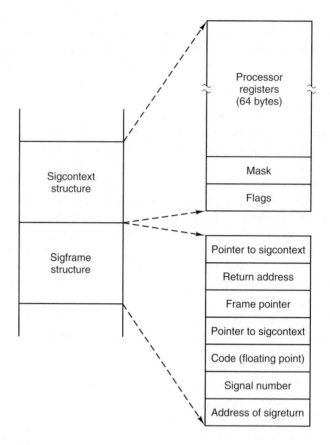

Figure 4-49. The sigcontext and sigframe structures pushed on the stack to prepare for a signal handler. The processor registers are a copy of the stack-frame used during a context switch.

enough stack space, the process is killed by jumping to the label *doterminate* using the seldom-used C goto (lines 19926 and 19927).

The call to *adjust* has a potential problem. Recall from our discussion of the implementation of brk that *adjust* returns an error if the stack is within *SAFETY_BYTES* of running into the data segment. The extra margin of error is provided because the validity of the stack can only be checked occasionally by software. This margin of error is probably excessive in the present instance, since it is known exactly how much space is needed on the stack for the signal, and additional space is needed only for the signal handler, presumably a relatively simple function. It is possible that some processes may be terminated unnecessarily because the call to *adjust* fails. This is certainly better than having programs fail mysteriously at other times, but finer tuning of these tests may be possible at some time in the future.

If there is enough room on the stack for the struct, two more flags are checked. The *SA_NODEFER* flag indicates if the signaled process is to block further signals of the same type while handling a signal. The *SA_RESETHAND* flag tells if the signal handler is to be reset upon receiving this signal. (This provides faithful emulation of the old *signal* call. Although this "feature" is often considered a fault in the old call, support of old features requires supporting their faults as well.) The kernel is then notified, using the sys_sigsend kernel call (line 19940) to put the sigframe on the stack. Finally, the bit indicating that a signal is pending is cleared, and *unpause* is called to terminate any system call on which the process may be hanging. When the signaled process next executes, the signal handler will run. If for some reason all of the tests above failed, the PM panics (line 19949).

The exception mentioned above—signals converted into messages for system services—is tested for on line 19951, and carried out by the sys_kill kernel call that follows. This causes the system task to send a notification message to the signaled process. Recall that, unlike most other notifications, a notification from the system task carries a payload in addition to the basic information about its origin and a timestamp. It also transmits a bitmap of signals, so the signaled system process learns of all pending signals. If the sys_kill call fails, the PM panics. If it succeeds *sig_proc* returns (line 19954). If the test on line 19951 failed, execution falls through to the *doterminate* label.

Now let us look at the termination code marked by the label *doterminate* (line 19957). The label and a goto are the easiest way to handle the possible failure of the call to *adjust*. Here signals are processed that for one reason or another cannot or should not be caught. It is possible that the signal was one to be ignored, in which case *sig_proc* just returns. Otherwise the process must be terminated. The only question is whether a core dump is also needed. Finally, the process is terminated as if it had exited, through a call to *pm_exit* (line 19967).

Check_sig (line 19973) is where the PM checks to see if a signal can be sent. The call

```
kill(0, sig);
```

causes the indicated signal to be sent to all the processes in the caller's group (i.e., all the processes started from the same terminal). Signals originating in the kernel and the reboot system call also may affect multiple processes. For this reason, *check_sig* loops on lines 19996 to 20026 to scan through the process table to find all the processes to which a signal should be sent. The loop contains a large number of tests. Only if all of them are passed is the signal sent, by calling *sig_proc* on line 20023.

Check_pending (line 20036) is another important function called several times in the code we have just reviewed. It loops through all the bits in the *mp_sigpending* bitmap for the process referred to by *do_sigmask*, *do_sigreturn*, or *do_sigsuspend*, to see if any blocked signal has become unblocked. It calls *sig_proc* to send the first unblocked pending signal it finds. Since all signal handlers eventually cause execution of *do_sigreturn*, this code suffices eventually to deliver all pending unmasked signals.

The procedure *unpause* (line 20065) has to do with signals that are sent to processes suspended on pause, wait, read, write, or sigsuspend calls. Pause, wait, and sigsuspend can be checked by consulting the PM's part of the process table, but if none of these are found, the file system must be asked to use its own *do_unpause* function to check for a possible hangup on read or write. In every case the action is the same: an error reply is sent to the waiting call and the flag bit that corresponds to the cause of the wait is reset so the process may resume execution and process the signal.

The final procedure in this file is *dump_core* (line 20093), which writes core dumps to the disk. A core dump consists of a header with information about the size of the segments occupied by a process, a copy of all the process' state information, obtained by copying the kernel process table information for the process, and the memory image of each of the segments. A debugger can interpret this information to help the programmer determine what went wrong during execution of the process.

The code to write the file is straightforward. The potential problem mentioned in the previous section again raises its head, but in a somewhat different form. To be sure the stack segment to be recorded in the core dump is up to date, *adjust* is called on line 20120. This call may fail because of the safety margin built into it. The success of the call is not checked by *dump_core*, so the core dump will be written in any case, but within the file the information about the stack may be incorrect.

Support Functions for Timers

The MINIX 3 process manager handles requests for alarms from user processes, which are not allowed to contact the kernel or the system task directly themselves. All details of scheduling an alarm at the clock task are hidden behind this interface. Only system processes are allowed to set an alarm timer at the kernel. Support for this is provided in the file *timers.c* (line 20200).

The process manager maintains a list of requests for alarms, and asks the system task to notify it when it is time for an alarm. When an alarm comes from the kernel the process manager passes it on to the process that should receive it.

Three functions are provided here to support timers. *Pm_set_timer* sets a timer and adds it to the PM's list of timers, *pm_expire_timer* checks for expired timers and *pm_cancel_timer* removes a timer from the PM's list. All three of these take advantage of functions in the timers library, declared in *include/-timers.h*. The function *Pm_set_timer* calls *tmrs_settimer*, *pm_expire_timer* calls *tmrs_exptimers*, and *pm_cancel_timer* calls *tmrs_clrtimers*. These all manage the business of traversing a linked list and inserting or removing an item, as required. Only when an item is inserted at or removed from the head of the queue does it become necessary to involve the system task in order to adjust the kernel-space timer queue. In such cases each of the *pm_XXX_timer* functions uses a sys_setalarm kernel call to request help at the kernel level.

4.8.7 Implementation of Other System Calls

The process manager handles three system calls that involve time in *time.c*: time, stime, and times. They are summarized in Fig. 4-50.

Call	Function
time	Get current real time and uptime in seconds
stime	Set the real time clock
times	Get the process accounting times

Figure 4-50. Three system calls involving time.

The real time is maintained by the clock task within the kernel, but the clock task itself does not exchange messages with any process except the system task. As a consequence, the only way to get or set the real time is to send a message to the system task. This is, in fact, what *do_time* (line 20320) and *do_stime* (line 20341) both do. The real time is measured in seconds since Jan 1, 1970.

Accounting information is also maintained by the kernel for each process. At each clock tick it charges one tick to some process. The kernel doesn't know about parent-child relationships, so it falls to the process manager to accumulate time information for the children of a process. When a child exits, its times are accumulated in the parent's slot in the PM's part of the process table. *Do_times* (line 20366) retrieves the time usage of a parent process from the system task with a sys_times kernel call, then fills in a reply message with user and system time charged to children.

The file *getset.c* contains one procedure, *do_getset* (line 20415), which carries out seven POSIX-required PM system calls. They are shown in Fig. 4-51. They are all so simple that they are not worth an entire procedure each. The getuid and getgid calls both return the real and effective UID or GID.

Setting the uid or gid is slightly more complex than just reading it. A check has to be made to see if the caller is authorized to set the uid or gid. If the caller passes the test, the file system must be informed of the new uid or gid, since file protection depends on it. The setsid call creates a new session, and a process which is already a process group leader is not allowed to do this. The test on line 20463 checks this. The file system completes the job of making a process into a session leader with no controlling terminal.

In contrast to the system calls considered so far in this chapter, the calls in *misc.c* are not required by POSIX. These calls are necessary because the user-

System Call	Description
getuid	Return real and effective UID
getgid	Return real and effective GID
getpid	Return PIDs of process and its parent
setuid	Set caller's real and effective UID
setgid	Set caller's real and effective GID
setsid	Create new session, return PID
getpgrp	Return ID of process group

Figure 4-51. The system calls supported in *servers/pm/getset.c*.

space device drivers and servers of MINIX 3 need support for communication with the kernel that is not necessary in monolithic operating systems. Fig. 4-52 shows these calls and their purposes.

System Call	Description
do_allocmem	Allocate a chunk of memory
do_freemem	Deallocate a chunk of memory
do_getsysinfo	Get info about PM from kernel
do_getprocnr	Get index to proc table from PID or name
do_reboot	Kill all processes, tell FS and kernel
do_getsetpriority	Get or set system priority
do_svrctrl	Make a process into a server

Figure 4-52. Special-purpose MINIX 3 system calls in *servers/pm/misc.c*.

The first two are handled entirely by the PM. *do_allocmem* reads the request from a received message, converts it into click units, and calls *alloc_mem*. This is used, for example, by the memory driver to allocate memory for the RAM disk. *Do_freemem* is similar, but calls *free_mem*.

The next calls usually need help from other parts of the system. They may be thought of as interfaces to the system task. *Do_getsysinfo* (line 20554) can do several things, depending on the request in the message received. It can call the system task to get information about the kernel contained in the *kinfo* structure (defined in the file *include/minix/type.h*). It can also be used to provide the address of the PM's own part of the process table or a copy of the entire process table to another process upon request. The final action is carried out by a call to *sys_datacopy* (line 20582). *Do_getprocnr* can find an index into the process table in its own section if given PID, and calls the system task for help if all it has to work with is the name of the target process.

The next two calls, although not required by POSIX, will probably be found in some form in most UNIX-like systems. *Do_reboot* sends a *KILL* signal to all processes, and tells the file system to get ready for a reboot. Only after the file system has been synched is the kernel notified with a *sys_abort* call (line 20667). A reboot may be the result of a panic, or a request from the superuser to halt or restart, and the kernel needs to know which case applies. *Do_getsetpriority*, supports the famous UNIX *nice* utility, which allows a user to reduce the priority of a process in order to be a good neighbor to other processes (possibly his own). More importantly, this call is used by the MINIX 3 system to provide fine-grained control of relative priorities of system components. A network or disk device that must handle a rapid stream of data can be given priority over one that receives data more slowly, such as a keyboard. Also, a high-priority process that is stuck in a loop and preventing other processes from running may have its priority lowered temporarily. Changing priority is done by scheduling the process on a lower (or higher) priority queue, as described in the discussion of implementation of scheduling in Chap. 2. When this is initiated by the scheduler in the kernel there is no need to involve the PM, of course, but an ordinary process must use a system call. At the level of the PM it is just a matter of reading the current value returned in a message or generating a message with a new value. A kernel call, *sys_nice* sends the new value to the system task.

The last function in *misc.c* is *do_svrctl*. It is currently used to enable and disable swapping. Other functions once served by this call are expected to be implemented in the reincarnation server.

The last system call we will consider in this chapter is ptrace, handled by *trace.c*. This file is not listed in Appendix B, but may be found on the CD-ROM and the MINIX 3 Web site. Ptrace is used by debugging programs. The parameter to this call can be one of eleven commands. These are shown in Fig. 4-53. In the PM *do_trace* processes four of them: *T_OK*, *T_RESUME*, I T_EXIT , *T_STEP*. Requests to enable and exit tracing are completed here. All other commands are passed on to the system task, which has access to the kernel's part of the process table. This is done by calling the *sys_trace* library function. Two support functions for tracing are provided. *Find_proc* searches the process table for the process to be traced, and *stop_proc* stops a traced process when it is signaled.

4.8.8 Memory Management Utilities

We will end this chapter by describing briefly two more files which provide support functions for the process manager. These are *alloc.c* and *utility.c*. Because internal details of these files are not discussed here, they are not printed in Appendix B (to keep this already fat book from becoming even fatter). However, they are available on the CD-ROM and the MINIX 3 Web site.

Alloc.c is where the system keeps track of which parts of memory are in use and which are free. It has three entry points:

Command	Description
T_STOP	Stop the process
T_OK	Enable tracing by parent for this process
T_GETINS	Return value from text (instruction) space
T_GETDATA	Return value from data space
T_GETUSER	Return value from user process table
T_SETINS	Set value in instruction space
T_SETDATA	Set value in data space
T_SETUSER	Set value in user process table
T_RESUME	Resume execution
T_EXIT	Exit
T_STEP	Set trace bit

Figure 4-53. Debugging commands supported by *servers/pm/trace.c*.

1. *alloc_mem* – request a block of memory of a given size.

2. *free_mem* – return memory that is no longer needed.

3. *mem_init* – initialize the free list when the PM starts running.

As we have said before, *alloc_mem* uses first fit on a list of holes sorted by memory address. If it finds a piece that is too big, it takes what it needs and leaves the rest on the free list, but reduced in size by the amount taken. If an entire hole is needed, *del_slot* is called to remove the entry from the free list.

Free_mem's job is to check if a newly released piece of memory can be merged with holes on either side. If it can, *merge* is called to join the holes and update the lists.

Mem_init builds the initial free list, consisting of all available memory.

The last file to be described is *utility.c*, which holds a few miscellaneous procedures used in various places in the PM. As with *alloc.c*, *utility.c* is not listed in Appendix B.

Get_free_pid finds a free PID for a child process. It avoids a problem that conceivably could occur. The maximum PID value is 30,000. It ought to be the maximum value that can be in *PID_t*, but this value was chosen to avoid problems with some older programs that use a smaller type. After assigning, say, PID 20 to a very long-lived process, 30,000 more processes might be created and destroyed, and simply incrementing a variable each time a new PID is needed and wrapping around to zero when the limit is reached could bring us back to 20 again. Assigning a PID that was still in use would be a disaster (suppose someone later tried to signal process 20). A variable holding the last PID assigned is incremented and if it exceeds a fixed maximum value, a fresh start is made with PID 2 (because *init* always has PID 1). Then the whole process table is searched to make sure that the PID to be assigned is not already in use. If it is in use the procedure is repeated until a free PID is found.

The procedure *allowed* checks to see if a given access is allowed to a file. For example, *do_exec* needs to know if a file is executable.

The procedure *no_sys* should never be called. It is provided just in case a user ever calls the PM with an invalid system call number.

Panic is called only when the PM has detected an error from which it cannot recover. It reports the error to the system task, which then brings MINIX 3 to a screeching halt. It is not called lightly.

The next function in *utility.c* is *tell_fs*, which constructs a message and sends it to the file system when the latter needs to be informed of events handled by the PM.

Find_param is used to parse the monitor parameters. Its current use is to extract information about memory use before MINIX 3 is loaded into memory, but it could be used to find other information if there were a need.

The next two functions in this file provide interfaces to the library function *sys_getproc*, which calls the system task to get information from the kernel's part of the process table. *Sys_getproc*, in turn, is actually a macro defined in *include/minix/syslib.h* which passes parameters to the sys_getinfo kernel call. *Get_mem_map* gets the memory map of a process. *Get_stack_ptr* gets the stack pointer. Both of these need a process number, that is, an index into the process table, which is not the same as a PID. The last function in *utility.c* is *proc_from_pid* which provides this support—it is called with a PID and returns an index to the process table.

4.9 SUMMARY

In this chapter we have examined memory management, both in general and in MINIX 3. We saw that the simplest systems do not swap or page at all. Once a program is loaded into memory, it remains there until it finishes. Embedded systems usually work like this, possibly with the code even in ROM. Some operating systems allow only one process at a time in memory, while others support multiprogramming.

The next step up is swapping. When swapping is used, the system can handle more processes than it has room for in memory. Processes for which there is no room are swapped out to the disk. Free space in memory and on disk can be kept track of with a bitmap or a hole list.

More advanced computers often have some form of virtual memory. In the simplest form, each process' address space is divided up into uniformly sized blocks called pages, which can be placed into any available page frame in memory. Many page replacement algorithms have been proposed. Two of the better known ones are second chance and aging. To make paging systems work well, choosing an algorithm is not enough; attention to issues such as determining the working set, memory allocation policy, and page size are required.

Segmentation helps in handling data structures that change size during execution and simplifies linking and sharing. It also facilitates providing different protection for different segments. Sometimes segmentation and paging are combined to provide a two-dimensional virtual memory. The Intel Pentium supports segmentation and paging.

Memory management in MINIX 3 is simple. Memory is allocated when a process executes a fork or exec system call. The memory so allocated is never increased or decreased as long as the process lives. On Intel processors there are two memory models used by MINIX 3. Small programs can have instructions and data in the same memory segment. Larger programs use separate instruction and data space (separate I and D). Processes with separate I and D space can share the text portion of their memory, so only data and stack memory must be allocated during a fork. This may also be true during an exec if another process already is using the text needed by the new program.

Most of the work of the PM is concerned not with keeping track of free memory, which it does using a hole list and the first fit algorithm, but rather with carrying out the system calls relating to process management. A number of system calls support POSIX-style signals, and since the default action of most signals is to terminate the signaled process, it is appropriate to handle them in the PM, which initiates termination of all processes. Several system calls not directly related to memory are also handled by the PM, mainly because it is smaller than the file system, and thus it was most convenient to put them here.

PROBLEMS

1. A computer system has enough room to hold four programs in its main memory. These programs are each idle half the time waiting for I/O. What fraction of the CPU time is wasted?

2. Consider a swapping system in which memory consists of the following hole sizes in memory order: 10 KB, 4 KB, 20 KB, 18 KB, 7 KB, 9 KB, 12 KB, and 15 KB. Which hole is taken for successive segment requests of

   (a) 12 KB
   (b) 10 KB
   (c) 9 KB

   for first fit? Now repeat the question for best fit, worst fit, and next fit.

3. A computer has 1 GB of RAM allocated in units of 64 KB. How many KB are needed if a bitmap is used to keep track of free memory?

4. Now revisit the previous question using a hole list. How much memory is needed for the list in the best case and in the worst case? Assume the operating system occupies the bottom 512 KB of memory.

5. What is the difference between a physical address and a virtual address?

6. Using the page mapping of Fig. 4-8, give the physical address corresponding to each of the following virtual addresses:

   (a) 20
   (b) 4100
   (c) 8300

7. In Fig. 4-9, the page field of the virtual address is 4 bits and the page field of the physical address is 3 bits. In general, is it permitted for the number of page bits of the virtual address to be smaller, equal to, or larger than the number of page bits of the physical address? Discuss your answer.

8. The Intel 8086 processor does not support virtual memory. Nevertheless, some companies previously sold systems that contained an unmodified 8086 CPU and do paging. Make an educated guess as to how they did it. (*Hint*: think about the logical location of the MMU.)

9. If an instruction takes 1 nsec and a page fault takes an additional n nsec, give a formula for the effective instruction time if page faults occur every k instructions.

10. A machine has a 32-bit address space and an 8 KB page. The page table is entirely in hardware, with one 32-bit word per entry. When a process starts, the page table is copied to the hardware from memory, at one word every 100 nsec. If each process runs for 100 msec (including the time to load the page table), what fraction of the CPU time is devoted to loading the page tables?

11. A computer with a 32-bit address uses a two-level page table. Virtual addresses are split into a 9-bit top-level page table field, an 11-bit second-level page table field, and an offset. How large are the pages and how many are there in the address space?

12. Below is the listing of a short assembly language program for a computer with 512-byte pages. The program is located at address 1020, and its stack pointer is at 8192 (the stack grows toward 0). Give the page reference string generated by this program. Each instruction occupies 4 bytes (1 word), and both instruction and data references count in the reference string.

   Load word 6144 into register 0
   Push register 0 onto the stack
   Call a procedure at 5120, stacking the return address
   Subtract the immediate constant 16 from the stack pointer
   Compare the actual parameter to the immediate constant 4
   Jump if equal to 5152

13. Suppose that a 32-bit virtual address is broken up into four fields, a, b, c, and d. The first three are used for a three-level page table system. The fourth field, d, is the

offset. Does the number of pages depend on the sizes of all four fields? If not, which ones matter and which ones do not?

14. A computer whose processes have 1024 pages in their address spaces keeps its page tables in memory. The overhead required for reading a word from the page table is 500 nsec. To reduce this overhead, the computer has a TLB, which holds 32 (virtual page, physical page frame) pairs, and can do a look up in 100 nsec. What hit rate is needed to reduce the mean overhead to 200 nsec?

15. The TLB on the VAX did not contain an R bit. Was this omission just an artifact of its era (1980s) or is there some other reason for its absence?

16. A machine has 48-bit virtual addresses and 32-bit physical addresses. Pages are 8 KB. How many entries are needed for the page table?

17. A RISC CPU with 64-bit virtual addresses and 8 GB of RAM uses an inverted page table with 8-KB pages. What is the minimum size of the TLB?

18. A computer has four page frames. The time of loading, time of last access, and the R and M bits for each page are as shown below (the times are in clock ticks):

Page	Loaded	Last ref.	R	M
0	126	279	0	0
1	230	260	1	0
2	120	272	1	1
3	160	280	1	1

(a) Which page will NRU replace?
(b) Which page will FIFO replace?
(c) Which page will LRU replace?
(d) Which page will second chance replace?

19. If FIFO page replacement is used with four page frames and eight pages, how many page faults will occur with the reference string 0172327103 if the four frames are initially empty? Now repeat this problem for LRU.

20. A small computer has 8 page frames, each containing a page. The page frames contain virtual pages A, C, G, H, B, L, N, D, and F in that order. Their respective load times were 18, 23, 5, 7, 32, 19, 3, and 8. Their reference bits are 1, 0, 1, 1, 0, 1, 1, and 0 and their modified bits are 1, 1, 1, 0, 0, 0, 1, and 1, respectively. What is the order that second chance considers pages and which one is selected?

21. Are there *any* circumstances in which clock and second chance choose different pages to replace? If so, what are they?

22. Suppose that a computer uses the PFF page replacement algorithm but there is sufficient memory to hold all the processes without page faults. What happens?

23. A small computer has four page frames. At the first clock tick, the R bits are 0111 (page 0 is 0, the rest are 1). At subsequent clock ticks, the values are 1011, 1010, 1101, 0010, 1010, 1100, and 0001. If the aging algorithm is used with an 8-bit counter, give the values of the four counters after the last tick.

24. How long does it take to load a 64-KB program from a disk whose average seek time is 10 msec, whose rotation time is 8 msec, and whose tracks hold 1 MB

    (a) for a 2-KB page size?
    (b) for a 4-KB page size?
    (c) for a 64-KB page size

The pages are spread randomly around the disk.

25. Given the results of the previous problem, why are pages so small? Name two disadvantages of 64-KB pages with respect to 4-KB pages.

26. One of the first timesharing machines, the PDP-1, had a memory of 4-KB 18-bit words. It held one process at a time in memory. When the scheduler decided to run another process, the process in memory was written to a paging drum, with 4K 18-bit words around the circumference of the drum. The drum could start writing (or reading) at any word, rather than only at word 0. Why do you suppose this drum was chosen?

27. An embedded computer provides each process with 65,536 bytes of address space divided into pages of 4096 bytes. A particular program has a text size of 32,768 bytes, a data size of 16,386 bytes, and a stack size of 15,870 bytes. Will this program fit in the address space? If the page size were 512 bytes, would it fit? Remember that a page may not contain parts of two different segments.

28. It has been observed that the number of instructions executed between page faults is directly proportional to the number of page frames allocated to a program. If the available memory is doubled, the mean interval between page faults is also doubled. Suppose that a normal instruction takes 1 microsec, but if a page fault occurs, it takes 2001 microsec (i.e., 2 msec) to handle the fault. If a program takes 60 sec to run, during which time it gets 15,000 page faults, how long would it take to run if twice as much memory were available?

29. A group of operating system designers for the Frugal Computer Company are thinking about ways of reducing the amount of backing store needed in their new operating system. The head guru has just suggested not bothering to save the program text in the swap area at all, but just page it in directly from the binary file whenever it is needed. Are there any problems with this approach?

30. Explain the difference between internal fragmentation and external fragmentation. Which one occurs in paging systems? Which one occurs in systems using pure segmentation?

31. When segmentation and paging are both being used, as in the Pentium, first the segment descriptor must be looked up, then the page descriptor. Does the TLB also work this way, with two levels of lookup?

32. Why does the MINIX 3 memory management scheme make it necessary to have a program like *chmem*?

33. Figure 4-44 shows the initial memory usage of the first four components of a MINIX 3 system. What will be the cs value for the next component loaded after rs?

34. IBM-compatible computers have ROM and I/O device memory not available for program use in the range from 640 KB to 1 MB, and after the MINIX 3 boot monitor relocates itself below the 640-KB limit the memory available for program use is further reduced. In Fig. 4-44, how much memory is available for loading a program in the region between the kernel and the unavailable region if the boot monitor has 52256 bytes allocated to it?

35. In the previous problem does it matter whether the boot monitor takes exactly as much memory as it needs or if it is rounded up to units of clicks?

36. In Sec. 4.7.5, it was pointed out that on an **exec** call, by testing for an adequate hole before releasing the current process' memory, a suboptimal implementation is achieved. Reprogram this algorithm to do better.

37. In Sec. 4.8.4, it was pointed out that it would be better to search for holes for the text and data segments separately. Implement this improvement.

38. Redesign *adjust* to avoid the problem of signaled processes being killed unnecessarily because of a too-strict test for stack space.

39. To tell the current memory allocation of a MINIX 3 process you can use the command

    chmem +0 a.out

but this has the annoying side effect of rewriting the file, and thus changing its date and time information. Modify *chmem* to make a new command *showmem*, which simply displays the current memory allocation of its argument.

5

FILE SYSTEMS

All computer applications need to store and retrieve information. While a process is running, it can store a limited amount of information within its own address space. However, the storage capacity is restricted to the size of the virtual address space. For some applications this size is adequate, but for others, such as airline reservations, banking, or corporate record keeping, it is far too small.

A second problem with keeping information within a process' address space is that when the process terminates, the information is lost. For many applications, (e.g., for databases), the information must be retained for weeks, months, or even forever. Having it vanish when the process using it terminates is unacceptable. Furthermore, it must not go away when a computer crash kills the process.

A third problem is that it is frequently necessary for multiple processes to access (parts of) the information at the same time. If we have an online telephone directory stored inside the address space of a single process, only that process can access it. The way to solve this problem is to make the information itself independent of any one process.

Thus we have three essential requirements for long-term information storage:

1. It must be possible to store a very large amount of information.

2. The information must survive the termination of the process using it.

3. Multiple processes must be able to access the information concurrently.

The usual solution to all these problems is to store information on disks and other external media in units called **files**. Processes can then read them and write new ones if need be. Information stored in files must be **persistent**, that is, not be affected by process creation and termination. A file should only disappear when its owner explicitly removes it.

Files are managed by the operating system. How they are structured, named, accessed, used, protected, and implemented are major topics in operating system design. As a whole, that part of the operating system dealing with files is known as the **file system** and is the subject of this chapter.

From the users' standpoint, the most important aspect of a file system is how it appears to them, that is, what constitutes a file, how files are named and protected, what operations are allowed on files, and so on. The details of whether linked lists or bitmaps are used to keep track of free storage and how many sectors there are in a logical block are of less interest, although they are of great importance to the designers of the file system. For this reason, we have structured the chapter as several sections. The first two are concerned with the user interface to files and directories, respectively. Then comes a discussion of alternative ways a file system can be implemented. Following a discussion of security and protection mechanisms, we conclude with a description of the MINIX 3 file system.

5.1 FILES

In the following pages we will look at files from the user's point of view, that is, how they are used and what properties they have.

5.1.1 File Naming

Files are an abstraction mechanism. They provide a way to store information on the disk and read it back later. This must be done in such a way as to shield the user from the details of how and where the information is stored, and how the disks actually work.

Probably the most important characteristic of any abstraction mechanism is the way the objects being managed are named, so we will start our examination of file systems with the subject of file naming. When a process creates a file, it gives the file a name. When the process terminates, the file continues to exist and can be accessed by other processes using its name.

The exact rules for file naming vary somewhat from system to system, but all current operating systems allow strings of one to eight letters as legal file names. Thus *andrea*, *bruce*, and *cathy* are possible file names. Frequently digits and special characters are also permitted, so names like *2*, *urgent!*, and *Fig.2-14* are often valid as well. Many file systems support names as long as 255 characters.

Some file systems distinguish between upper- and lower-case letters, whereas others do not. UNIX (including all its variants) falls in the first category; MS-DOS falls in the second. Thus a UNIX system can have all of the following as three distinct files: *maria*, *Maria*, and *MARIA*. In MS-DOS, all these names refer to the same file.

Windows falls in between these extremes. The Windows 95 and Windows 98 file systems are both based upon the MS-DOS file system, and thus inherit many of its properties, such as how file names are constructed. With each new version improvements were added but the features we will discuss are mostly common to MS-DOS and "classic" Windows versions. In addition, Windows NT, Windows 2000, and Windows XP support the MS-DOS file system. However, the latter systems also have a native file system (**NTFS**) that has different properties (such as file names in Unicode). This file system also has seen changes in successive versions. In this chapter, we will refer to the older systems as the Windows 98 file system. If a feature does not apply to the MS-DOS or Windows 95 versions we will say so. Likewise, we will refer to the newer system as either NTFS or the Windows XP file system, and we will point it out if an aspect under discussion does not also apply to the file systems of Windows NT or Windows 2000. When we say just Windows, we mean all Windows file systems since Windows 95.

Many operating systems support two-part file names, with the two parts separated by a period, as in *prog.c*. The part following the period is called the **file extension** and usually indicates something about the file, in this example that it is a C programming language source file. In MS-DOS, for example, file names are 1 to 8 characters, plus an optional extension of 1 to 3 characters. In UNIX, the size of the extension, if any, is up to the user, and a file may even have two or more extensions, as in *prog.c.bz2*, where *.bz2* is commonly used to indicate that the file (*prog.c*) has been compressed using the bzip2 compression algorithm. Some of the more common file extensions and their meanings are shown in Fig. 5-1.

In some systems (e.g., UNIX), file extensions are just conventions and are not enforced by the operating system. A file named *file.txt* might be some kind of text file, but that name is more to remind the owner than to convey any actual information to the computer. On the other hand, a C compiler may actually insist that files it is to compile end in *.c*, and it may refuse to compile them if they do not.

Conventions like this are especially useful when the same program can handle several different kinds of files. The C compiler, for example, can be given a list of files to compile and link together, some of them C files (e.g., *foo.c*), some of them assembly language files (e.g., *bar.s*), and some of them object files (e.g., *other.o*). The extension then becomes essential for the compiler to tell which are C files, which are assembly files, and which are object files.

In contrast, Windows is very much aware of the extensions and assigns meaning to them. Users (or processes) can register extensions with the operating system and specify which program "owns" which one. When a user double clicks on a file name, the program assigned to its file extension is launched and given

Extension	Meaning
file.bak	Backup file
file.c	C source program
file.gif	Graphical Interchange Format image
file.html	World Wide Web HyperText Markup Language document
file.iso	ISO image of a CD-ROM (for burning to CD)
file.jpg	Still picture encoded with the JPEG standard
file.mp3	Music encoded in MPEG layer 3 audio format
file.mpg	Movie encoded with the MPEG standard
file.o	Object file (compiler output, not yet linked)
file.pdf	Portable Document Format file
file.ps	PostScript file
file.tex	Input for the TEX formatting program
file.txt	General text file
file.zip	Compressed archive

Figure 5-1. Some typical file extensions.

the name of the file as parameter. For example, double clicking on *file.doc* starts Microsoft *Word* with *file.doc* as the initial file to edit.

Some might think it odd that Microsoft chose to make common extensions invisible by default since they are so important. Fortunately most of the "wrong by default" settings of Windows can be changed by a sophisticated user who knows where to look.

5.1.2 File Structure

Files can be structured in any one of several ways. Three common possibilities are depicted in Fig. 5-2. The file in Fig. 5-2(a) is just an unstructured sequence of bytes. In effect, the operating system does not know or care what is in the file. All it sees are bytes. Any meaning must be imposed by user-level programs. Both UNIX and Windows 98 use this approach.

Having the operating system regard files as nothing more than byte sequences provides the maximum flexibility. User programs can put anything they want in their files and name them any way that is convenient. The operating system does not help, but it also does not get in the way. For users who want to do unusual things, the latter can be very important.

The first step up in structure is shown in Fig. 5-2(b). In this model, a file is a sequence of fixed-length records, each with some internal structure. Central to the idea of a file being a sequence of records is the idea that the read operation returns one record and the write operation overwrites or appends one record. As a

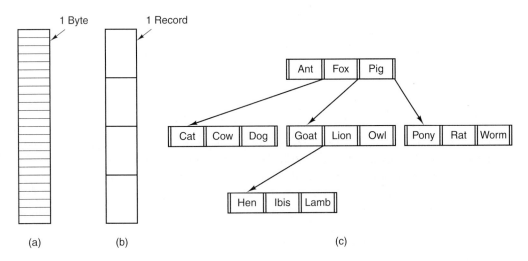

Figure 5-2. Three kinds of files. (a) Byte sequence. (b) Record sequence. (c) Tree.

historical note, when the 80-column punched card was king many (mainframe) operating systems based their file systems on files consisting of 80-character records, in effect, card images. These systems also supported files of 132-character records, which were intended for the line printer (which in those days were big chain printers having 132 columns). Programs read input in units of 80 characters and wrote it in units of 132 characters, although the final 52 could be spaces, of course. No current general-purpose system works this way.

The third kind of file structure is shown in Fig. 5-2(c). In this organization, a file consists of a tree of records, not necessarily all the same length, each containing a **key** field in a fixed position in the record. The tree is sorted on the key field, to allow rapid searching for a particular key.

The basic operation here is not to get the "next" record, although that is also possible, but to get the record with a specific key. For the zoo file of Fig. 5-2(c), one could ask the system to get the record whose key is *pony*, for example, without worrying about its exact position in the file. Furthermore, new records can be added to the file, with the operating system, and not the user, deciding where to place them. This type of file is clearly quite different from the unstructured byte streams used in UNIX and Windows 98 but is widely used on the large mainframe computers still used in some commercial data processing.

5.1.3 File Types

Many operating systems support several types of files. UNIX and Windows, for example, have regular files and directories. UNIX also has character and block special files. Windows XP also uses **metadata** files, which we will mention later.

Regular files are the ones that contain user information. All the files of Fig. 5-2 are regular files. **Directories** are system files for maintaining the structure of the file system. We will study directories below. **Character special files** are related to input/output and used to model serial I/O devices such as terminals, printers, and networks. **Block special files** are used to model disks. In this chapter we will be primarily interested in regular files.

Regular files are generally either ASCII files or binary files. ASCII files consist of lines of text. In some systems each line is terminated by a carriage return character. In others, the line feed character is used. Some systems (e.g., Windows) use both. Lines need not all be of the same length.

The great advantage of ASCII files is that they can be displayed and printed as is, and they can be edited with any text editor. Furthermore, if large numbers of programs use ASCII files for input and output, it is easy to connect the output of one program to the input of another, as in shell pipelines. (The interprocess plumbing is not any easier, but interpreting the information certainly is if a standard convention, such as ASCII, is used for expressing it.)

Other files are binary files, which just means that they are not ASCII files. Listing them on the printer gives an incomprehensible listing full of what is apparently random junk. Usually, they have some internal structure known to programs that use them.

For example, in Fig. 5-3(a) we see a simple executable binary file taken from an early version of UNIX. Although technically the file is just a sequence of bytes, the operating system will only execute a file if it has the proper format. It has five sections: header, text, data, relocation bits, and symbol table. The header starts with a so-called **magic number**, identifying the file as an executable file (to prevent the accidental execution of a file not in this format). Then come the sizes of the various pieces of the file, the address at which execution starts, and some flag bits. Following the header are the text and data of the program itself. These are loaded into memory and relocated using the relocation bits. The symbol table is used for debugging.

Our second example of a binary file is an archive, also from UNIX. It consists of a collection of library procedures (modules) compiled but not linked. Each one is prefaced by a header telling its name, creation date, owner, protection code, and size. Just as with the executable file, the module headers are full of binary numbers. Copying them to the printer would produce complete gibberish.

Every operating system must recognize at least one file type: its own executable file, but some operating systems recognize more. The old TOPS-20 system (for the DECsystem 20) went so far as to examine the creation time of any file to be executed. Then it located the source file and saw if the source had been modified since the binary was made. If it had been, it automatically recompiled the source. In UNIX terms, the *make* program had been built into the shell. The file extensions were mandatory so the operating system could tell which binary program was derived from which source.

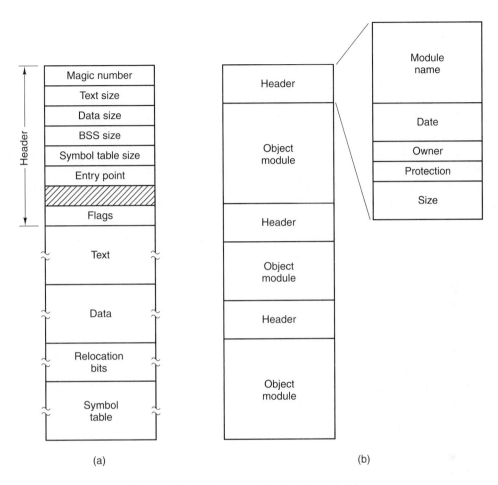

Figure 5-3. (a) An executable file. (b) An archive.

Having strongly typed files like this causes problems whenever the user does anything that the system designers did not expect. Consider, as an example, a system in which program output files have extension *.dat* (data files). If a user writes a program formatter that reads a *.c* file (C program), transforms it (e.g., by converting it to a standard indentation layout), and then writes the transformed file as output, the output file will be of type *.dat*. If the user tries to offer this to the C compiler to compile it, the system will refuse because it has the wrong extension. Attempts to copy *file.dat* to *file.c* will be rejected by the system as invalid (to protect the user against mistakes).

While this kind of "user friendliness" may help novices, it drives experienced users up the wall since they have to devote considerable effort to circumventing the operating system's idea of what is reasonable and what is not.

5.1.4 File Access

Early operating systems provided only a single kind of file access: **sequential access**. In these systems, a process could read all the bytes or records in a file in order, starting at the beginning, but could not skip around and read them out of order. Sequential files could be rewound, however, so they could be read as often as needed. Sequential files were convenient when the storage medium was magnetic tape, rather than disk.

When disks came into use for storing files, it became possible to read the bytes or records of a file out of order, or to access records by key, rather than by position. Files whose bytes or records can be read in any order are called **random access files**. They are required by many applications.

Random access files are essential for many applications, for example, database systems. If an airline customer calls up and wants to reserve a seat on a particular flight, the reservation program must be able to access the record for that flight without having to read the records for thousands of other flights first.

Two methods are used for specifying where to start reading. In the first one, every read operation gives the position in the file to start reading at. In the second one, a special operation, seek, is provided to set the current position. After a seek, the file can be read sequentially from the now-current position.

In some older mainframe operating systems, files are classified as being either sequential or random access at the time they are created. This allows the system to use different storage techniques for the two classes. Modern operating systems do not make this distinction. All their files are automatically random access.

5.1.5 File Attributes

Every file has a name and its data. In addition, all operating systems associate other information with each file, for example, the date and time the file was created and the file's size. We will call these extra items the file's **attributes** although some people called them **metadata**. The list of attributes varies considerably from system to system. The table of Fig. 5-4 shows some of the possibilities, but others also exist. No existing system has all of these, but each is present in some system.

The first four attributes relate to the file's protection and tell who may access it and who may not. All kinds of schemes are possible, some of which we will study later. In some systems the user must present a password to access a file, in which case the password must be one of the attributes.

The flags are bits or short fields that control or enable some specific property. Hidden files, for example, do not appear in listings of the files. The archive flag is a bit that keeps track of whether the file has been backed up. The backup program clears it, and the operating system sets it whenever a file is changed. In this

Attribute	Meaning
Protection	Who can access the file and in what way
Password	Password needed to access the file
Creator	ID of the person who created the file
Owner	Current owner
Read-only flag	0 for read/write; 1 for read only
Hidden flag	0 for normal; 1 for do not display in listings
System flag	0 for normal files; 1 for system file
Archive flag	0 for has been backed up; 1 for needs to be backed up
ASCII/binary flag	0 for ASCII file; 1 for binary file
Random access flag	0 for sequential access only; 1 for random access
Temporary flag	0 for normal; 1 for delete file on process exit
Lock flags	0 for unlocked; nonzero for locked
Record length	Number of bytes in a record
Key position	Offset of the key within each record
Key length	Number of bytes in the key field
Creation time	Date and time the file was created
Time of last access	Date and time the file was last accessed
Time of last change	Date and time the file has last changed
Current size	Number of bytes in the file
Maximum size	Number of bytes the file may grow to

Figure 5-4. Some possible file attributes.

way, the backup program can tell which files need backing up. The temporary flag allows a file to be marked for automatic deletion when the process that created it terminates.

The record length, key position, and key length fields are only present in files whose records can be looked up using a key. They provide the information required to find the keys.

The various times keep track of when the file was created, most recently accessed and most recently modified. These are useful for a variety of purposes. For example, a source file that has been modified after the creation of the corresponding object file needs to be recompiled. These fields provide the necessary information.

The current size tells how big the file is at present. Some old mainframe operating systems require the maximum size to be specified when the file is created, in order to let the operating system reserve the maximum amount of storage in advance. Modern operating systems are clever enough to do without this feature.

5.1.6 File Operations

Files exist to store information and allow it to be retrieved later. Different systems provide different operations to allow storage and retrieval. Below is a discussion of the most common system calls relating to files.

1. Create. The file is created with no data. The purpose of the call is to announce that the file is coming and to set some of the attributes.

2. Delete. When the file is no longer needed, it has to be deleted to free up disk space. A system call for this purpose is always provided.

3. Open. Before using a file, a process must open it. The purpose of the open call is to allow the system to fetch the attributes and list of disk addresses into main memory for rapid access on later calls.

4. Close. When all the accesses are finished, the attributes and disk addresses are no longer needed, so the file should be closed to free up some internal table space. Many systems encourage this by imposing a maximum number of open files on processes. A disk is written in blocks, and closing a file forces writing of the file's last block, even though that block may not be entirely full yet.

5. Read. Data are read from file. Usually, the bytes come from the current position. The caller must specify how much data are needed and must also provide a buffer to put them in.

6. Write. Data are written to the file, again, usually at the current position. If the current position is the end of the file, the file's size increases. If the current position is in the middle of the file, existing data are overwritten and lost forever.

7. Append. This call is a restricted form of write. It can only add data to the end of the file. Systems that provide a minimal set of system calls do not generally have append, but many systems provide multiple ways of doing the same thing, and these systems sometimes have append.

8. Seek. For random access files, a method is needed to specify from where to take the data. One common approach is a system call, seek, that repositions the file pointer to a specific place in the file. After this call has completed, data can be read from, or written to, that position.

9. Get attributes. Processes often need to read file attributes to do their work. For example, the UNIX *make* program is commonly used to manage software development projects consisting of many source files. When *make* is called, it examines the modification times of all

the source and object files and arranges for the minimum number of compilations required to bring everything up to date. To do its job, it must look at the attributes, namely, the modification times.

10. Set attributes. Some of the attributes are user settable and can be changed after the file has been created. This system call makes that possible. The protection mode information is an obvious example. Most of the flags also fall in this category.

11. Rename. It frequently happens that a user needs to change the name of an existing file. This system call makes that possible. It is not always strictly necessary, because the file can usually be copied to a new file with the new name, and the old file then deleted.

12. Lock. Locking a file or a part of a file prevents multiple simultaneous access by different process. For an airline reservation system, for instance, locking the database while making a reservation prevents reservation of a seat for two different travelers.

5.2 DIRECTORIES

To keep track of files, file systems normally have **directories** or **folders**, which, in many systems, are themselves files. In this section we will discuss directories, their organization, their properties, and the operations that can be performed on them.

5.2.1 Simple Directories

A directory typically contains a number of entries, one per file. One possibility is shown in Fig. 5-5(a), in which each entry contains the file name, the file attributes, and the disk addresses where the data are stored. Another possibility is shown in Fig. 5-5(b). Here a directory entry holds the file name and a pointer to another data structure where the attributes and disk addresses are found. Both of these systems are commonly used.

When a file is opened, the operating system searches its directory until it finds the name of the file to be opened. It then extracts the attributes and disk addresses, either directly from the directory entry or from the data structure pointed to, and puts them in a table in main memory. All subsequent references to the file use the information in main memory.

The number of directories varies from system to system. The simplest form of directory system is a single directory containing all files for all users, as illustrated in Fig. 5-6(a). On early personal computers, this single-directory system was common, in part because there was only one user.

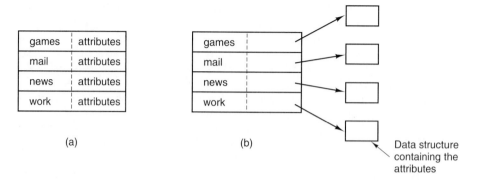

Figure 5-5. (a) Attributes in the directory entry. (b) Attributes elsewhere.

The problem with having only one directory in a system with multiple users is that different users may accidentally use the same names for their files. For example, if user *A* creates a file called *mailbox*, and then later user *B* also creates a file called *mailbox*, *B*'s file will overwrite *A*'s file. Consequently, this scheme is not used on multiuser systems any more, but could be used on a small embedded system, for example, a handheld personal digital assistant or a cellular telephone.

To avoid conflicts caused by different users choosing the same file name for their own files, the next step up is giving each user a private directory. In that way, names chosen by one user do not interfere with names chosen by a different user and there is no problem caused by the same name occurring in two or more directories. This design leads to the system of Fig. 5-6(b). This design could be used, for example, on a multiuser computer or on a simple network of personal computers that shared a common file server over a local area network.

Implicit in this design is that when a user tries to open a file, the operating system knows which user it is in order to know which directory to search. As a consequence, some kind of login procedure is needed, in which the user specifies a login name or identification, something not required with a single-level directory system.

When this system is implemented in its most basic form, users can only access files in their own directories.

5.2.2 Hierarchical Directory Systems

The two-level hierarchy eliminates file name conflicts between users. But another problem is that users with many files may want to group them in smaller subgroups, for instance a professor might want to separate handouts for a class from drafts of chapters of a new textbook. What is needed is a general hierarchy (i.e., a tree of directories). With this approach, each user can have as many directories as are needed so that files can be grouped together in natural ways. This approach is shown in Fig. 5-6(c). Here, the directories *A*, *B*, and *C* contained in

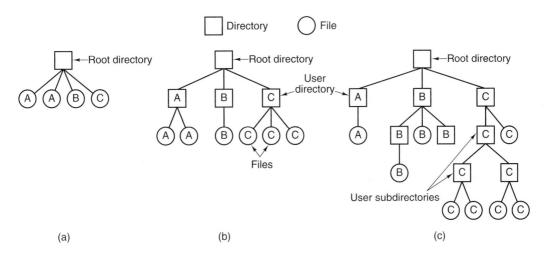

Figure 5-6. Three file system designs. (a) Single directory shared by all users. (b) One directory per user. (c) Arbitrary tree per user. The letters indicate the directory or file's owner.

the root directory each belong to a different user, two of whom have created subdirectories for projects they are working on.

The ability to create an arbitrary number of subdirectories provides a powerful structuring tool for users to organize their work. For this reason nearly all modern PC and server file systems are organized this way.

However, as we have pointed out before, history often repeats itself with new technologies. Digital cameras have to record their images somewhere, usually on a flash memory card. The very first digital cameras had a single directory and named the files *DSC0001.JPG, DSC0002.JPG*, etc. However, it did not take very long for camera manufacturers to build file systems with multiple directories, as in Fig. 5-6(b). What difference does it make that none of the camera owners understand how to use multiple directories, and probably could not conceive of any use for this feature even if they did understand it? It is only (embedded) software, after all, and thus costs the camera manufacturer next to nothing to provide. Can digital cameras with full-blown hierarchical file systems, multiple login names, and 255-character file names be far behind?

5.2.3 Path Names

When the file system is organized as a directory tree, some way is needed for specifying file names. Two different methods are commonly used. In the first method, each file is given an **absolute path name** consisting of the path from the root directory to the file. As an example, the path */usr/ast/mailbox* means that the root directory contains a subdirectory *usr/*, which in turn contains a subdirectory *ast/*, which contains the file *mailbox*. Absolute path names always start at the root directory and are unique. In UNIX the components of the path are separated by /. In Windows the separator is \. Thus the same path name would be written as follows in these two systems:

```
Windows        \usr\ast\mailbox
UNIX           /usr/ast/mailbox
```

No matter which character is used, if the first character of the path name is the separator, then the path is absolute.

The other kind of name is the **relative path name**. This is used in conjunction with the concept of the **working directory** (also called the **current directory**). A user can designate one directory as the current working directory, in which case all path names not beginning at the root directory are taken relative to the working directory. For example, if the current working directory is */usr/ast*, then the file whose absolute path is */usr/ast/mailbox* can be referenced simply as *mailbox*. In other words, the UNIX command

```
cp /usr/ast/mailbox /usr/ast/mailbox.bak
```

and the command

```
cp mailbox mailbox.bak
```

do exactly the same thing if the working directory is */usr/ast/*. The relative form is often more convenient, but it does the same thing as the absolute form.

Some programs need to access a specific file without regard to what the working directory is. In that case, they should always use absolute path names. For example, a spelling checker might need to read */usr/lib/dictionary* to do its work. It should use the full, absolute path name in this case because it does not know what the working directory will be when it is called. The absolute path name will always work, no matter what the working directory is.

Of course, if the spelling checker needs a large number of files from */usr/lib/*, an alternative approach is for it to issue a system call to change its working directory to */usr/lib/*, and then use just *dictionary* as the first parameter to open. By explicitly changing the working directory, it knows for sure where it is in the directory tree, so it can then use relative paths.

Each process has its own working directory, so when a process changes its working directory and later exits, no other processes are affected and no traces of the change are left behind in the file system. In this way it is always perfectly safe for a process to change its working directory whenever that is convenient. On the other hand, if a *library procedure* changes the working directory and does not change back to where it was when it is finished, the rest of the program may not work since its assumption about where it is may now suddenly be invalid. For this reason, library procedures rarely change the working directory, and when they must, they always change it back again before returning.

Most operating systems that support a hierarchical directory system have two special entries in every directory, "." and "..", generally pronounced "dot" and "dotdot." Dot refers to the current directory; dotdot refers to its parent. To see how these are used, consider the UNIX file tree of Fig. 5-7. A certain process has */usr/ast/* as its working directory. It can use .. to go up the tree. For example, it can copy the file */usr/lib/dictionary* to its own directory using the command

cp ../lib/dictionary .

The first path instructs the system to go upward (to the *usr* directory), then to go down to the directory *lib/* to find the file *dictionary*.

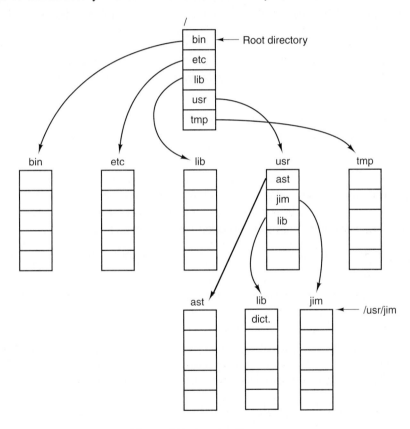

Figure 5-7. A UNIX directory tree.

The second argument (dot) names the current directory. When the *cp* command gets a directory name (including dot) as its last argument, it copies all the files there. Of course, a more normal way to do the copy would be to type

cp /usr/lib/dictionary .

Here the use of dot saves the user the trouble of typing *dictionary* a second time.

Nevertheless, typing

cp /usr/lib/dictionary dictionary

also works fine, as does

cp /usr/lib/dictionary /usr/ast/dictionary

All of these do exactly the same thing.

5.2.4 Directory Operations

The system calls for managing directories exhibit more variation from system to system than system calls for files. To give an impression of what they are and how they work, we will give a sample (taken from UNIX).

1. Create. A directory is created. It is empty except for dot and dotdot, which are put there automatically by the system (or in a few cases, by the *mkdir* program).

2. Delete. A directory is deleted. Only an empty directory can be deleted. A directory containing only dot and dotdot is considered empty as these cannot usually be deleted.

3. Opendir. Directories can be read. For example, to list all the files in a directory, a listing program opens the directory to read out the names of all the files it contains. Before a directory can be read, it must be opened, analogous to opening and reading a file.

4. Closedir. When a directory has been read, it should be closed to free up internal table space.

5. Readdir. This call returns the next entry in an open directory. Formerly, it was possible to read directories using the usual read system call, but that approach has the disadvantage of forcing the programmer to know and deal with the internal structure of directories. In contrast, readdir always returns one entry in a standard format, no matter which of the possible directory structures is being used.

6. Rename. In many respects, directories are just like files and can be renamed the same way files can be.

7. Link. Linking is a technique that allows a file to appear in more than one directory. This system call specifies an existing file and a path name, and creates a link from the existing file to the name specified by the path. In this way, the same file may appear in multiple directories. A link of this kind, which increments the counter in the file's i-node (to keep track of the number of directory entries containing the file), is sometimes called a **hard link**.

8. Unlink. A directory entry is removed. If the file being unlinked is only present in one directory (the normal case), it is removed from the file system. If it is present in multiple directories, only the path name specified is removed. The others remain. In UNIX, the system call for deleting files (discussed earlier) is, in fact, unlink.

The above list gives the most important calls, but there are a few others as well, for example, for managing the protection information associated with a directory.

5.3 FILE SYSTEM IMPLEMENTATION

Now it is time to turn from the user's view of the file system to the implementer's view. Users are concerned with how files are named, what operations are allowed on them, what the directory tree looks like, and similar interface issues. Implementers are interested in how files and directories are stored, how disk space is managed, and how to make everything work efficiently and reliably. In the following sections we will examine a number of these areas to see what the issues and trade-offs are.

5.3.1 File System Layout

File systems usually are stored on disks. We looked at basic disk layout in Chap. 2, in the section on bootstrapping MINIX 3. To review this material briefly, most disks can be divided up into partitions, with independent file systems on each partition. Sector 0 of the disk is called the **MBR** (**Master Boot Record**) and is used to boot the computer. The end of the MBR contains the partition table. This table gives the starting and ending addresses of each partition. One of the partitions in the table may be marked as active. When the computer is booted, the BIOS reads in and executes the code in the MBR. The first thing the MBR program does is locate the active partition, read in its first block, called the **boot block**, and execute it. The program in the boot block loads the operating system contained in that partition. For uniformity, every partition starts with a boot block, even if it does not contain a bootable operating system. Besides, it might contain one in the some time in the future, so reserving a boot block is a good idea anyway.

The above description must be true, regardless of the operating system in use, for any hardware platform on which the BIOS is to be able to start more than one operating system. The terminology may differ with different operating systems. For instance the master boot record may sometimes be called the **IPL** (**Initial Program Loader**), **Volume Boot Code**, or simply **masterboot**. Some operating systems do not require a partition to be marked active to be booted, and provide a menu for the user to choose a partition to boot, perhaps with a timeout after which a default choice is automatically taken. Once the BIOS has loaded an MBR or boot sector the actions may vary. For instance, more than one block of a partition may be used to contain the program that loads the operating system. The BIOS can be counted on only to load the first block, but that block may then load additional blocks if the implementer of the operating system writes the boot block that way. An implementer can also supply a custom MBR, but it must work with a standard partition table if multiple operating systems are to be supported.

On PC-compatible systems there can be no more than four **primary partitions** because there is only room for a four-element array of partition descriptors between the master boot record and the end of the first 512-byte sector. Some operating systems allow one entry in the partition table to be an **extended partition** which points to a linked list of **logical partitions**. This makes it possible to have any number of additional partitions. The BIOS cannot start an operating system from a logical partition, so initial startup from a primary partition is required to load code that can manage logical partitions.

An alternative to extended partitions is used by MINIX 3, which allows a partition to contain a **subpartition table**. An advantage of this is that the same code that manages a primary partition table can manage a subpartition table, which has the same structure. Potential uses for subpartitions are to have different ones for the root device, swapping, the system binaries, and the users' files. In this way, problems in one subpartition cannot propagate to another one, and a new version of the operating system can be easily installed by replacing the contents of some of the subpartitions but not all.

Not all disks are partitioned. Floppy disks usually start with a boot block in the first sector. The BIOS reads the first sector of a disk and looks for a magic number which identifies it as valid executable code, to prevent an attempt to execute the first sector of an unformatted or corrupted disk. A master boot record and a boot block use the same magic number, so the executable code may be either one. Also, what we say here is not limited to electromechanical disk devices. A device such as a camera or personal digital assistant that uses nonvolatile (e.g., flash) memory typically has part of the memory organized to simulate a disk.

Other than starting with a boot block, the layout of a disk partition varies considerably from file system to file system. A UNIX-like file system will contain some of the items shown in Fig. 5-8. The first one is the **superblock**. It contains all the key parameters about the file system and is read into memory when the computer is booted or the file system is first touched.

Next might come information about free blocks in the file system. This might be followed by the i-nodes, an array of data structures, one per file, telling all about the file and where its blocks are located. After that might come the root directory, which contains the top of the file system tree. Finally, the remainder of the disk typically contains all the other directories and files.

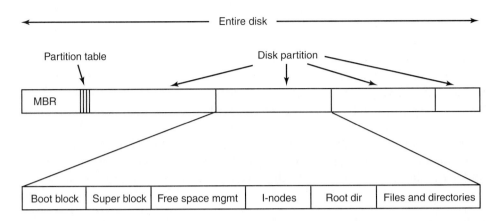

Figure 5-8. A possible file system layout.

5.3.2 Implementing Files

Probably the most important issue in implementing file storage is keeping track of which disk blocks go with which file. Various methods are used in different operating systems. In this section, we will examine a few of them.

Contiguous Allocation

The simplest allocation scheme is to store each file as a contiguous run of disk blocks. Thus on a disk with 1-KB blocks, a 50-KB file would be allocated 50 consecutive blocks. Contiguous disk space allocation has two significant advantages. First, it is simple to implement because keeping track of where a file's blocks are is reduced to remembering two numbers: the disk address of the first block and the number of blocks in the file. Given the number of the first block, the number of any other block can be found by a simple addition.

Second, the read performance is excellent because the entire file can be read from the disk in a single operation. Only one seek is needed (to the first block). After that, no more seeks or rotational delays are needed so data come in at the full bandwidth of the disk. Thus contiguous allocation is simple to implement and has high performance.

Unfortunately, contiguous allocation also has a major drawback: in time, the disk becomes fragmented, consisting of files and holes. Initially, this fragmentation is not a problem since each new file can be written at the end of disk, following the previous one. However, eventually the disk will fill up and it will become necessary to either compact the disk, which is prohibitively expensive, or to reuse the free space in the holes. Reusing the space requires maintaining a list of holes, which is doable. However, when a new file is to be created, it is necessary to know its final size in order to choose a hole of the correct size to place it in.

As we mentioned in Chap. 1, history may repeat itself in computer science as new generations of technology occur. Contiguous allocation was actually used on magnetic disk file systems years ago due to its simplicity and high performance (user friendliness did not count for much then). Then the idea was dropped due to the nuisance of having to specify final file size at file creation time. But with the advent of CD-ROMs, DVDs, and other write-once optical media, suddenly contiguous files are a good idea again. For such media, contiguous allocation is feasible and, in fact, widely used. Here all the file sizes are known in advance and will never change during subsequent use of the CD-ROM file system. It is thus important to study old systems and ideas that were conceptually clean and simple because they may be applicable to future systems in surprising ways.

Linked List Allocation

The second method for storing files is to keep each one as a linked list of disk blocks, as shown in Fig. 5-9. The first word of each block is used as a pointer to the next one. The rest of the block is for data.

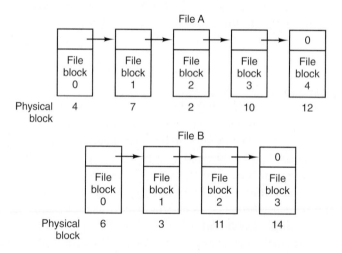

Figure 5-9. Storing a file as a linked list of disk blocks.

Unlike contiguous allocation, every disk block can be used in this method. No space is lost to disk fragmentation (except for internal fragmentation in the last block of each file). Also, it is sufficient for the directory entry to merely store the disk address of the first block. The rest can be found starting there.

On the other hand, although reading a file sequentially is straightforward, random access is extremely slow. To get to block n, the operating system has to start at the beginning and read the $n - 1$ blocks prior to it, one at a time. Clearly, doing so many reads will be painfully slow.

Also, the amount of data storage in a block is no longer a power of two be-cause the pointer takes up a few bytes. While not fatal, having a peculiar size is less efficient because many programs read and write in blocks whose size is a power of two. With the first few bytes of each block occupied to a pointer to the next block, reads of the full block size require acquiring and concatenating infor-mation from two disk blocks, which generates extra overhead due to the copying.

Linked List Allocation Using a Table in Memory

Both disadvantages of the linked list allocation can be eliminated by taking the pointer word from each disk block and putting it in a table in memory. Figure 5-10 shows what the table looks like for the example of Fig. 5-9. In both figures, we have two files. File *A* uses disk blocks 4, 7, 2, 10, and 12, in that order, and file *B* uses disk blocks 6, 3, 11, and 14, in that order. Using the table of Fig. 5-10, we can start with block 4 and follow the chain all the way to the end. The same can be done starting with block 6. Both chains are terminated with a special marker (e.g., −1) that is not a valid block number. Such a table in main memory is called a **FAT** (**File Allocation Table**).

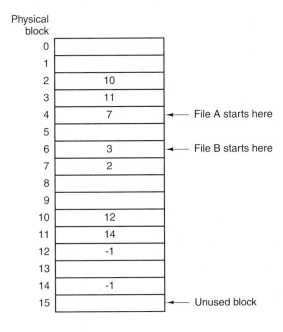

Figure 5-10. Linked list allocation using a file allocation table in main memory.

Using this organization, the entire block is available for data. Furthermore, random access is much easier. Although the chain must still be followed to find a given offset within the file, the chain is entirely in memory, so it can be followed without making any disk references. Like the previous method, it is sufficient for the directory entry to keep a single integer (the starting block number) and still be able to locate all the blocks, no matter how large the file is.

The primary disadvantage of this method is that the entire table must be in memory all the time. With a 20-GB disk and a 1-KB block size, the table needs 20 million entries, one for each of the 20 million disk blocks. Each entry has to be a minimum of 3 bytes. For speed in lookup, they should be 4 bytes. Thus the table will take up 60 MB or 80 MB of main memory all the time, depending on whether the system is optimized for space or time. Conceivably the table could be put in pageable memory, but it would still occupy a great deal of virtual memory and disk space as well as generating paging traffic. MS-DOS and Windows 98 use only FAT file systems and later versions of Windows also support it.

I-Nodes

Our last method for keeping track of which blocks belong to which file is to associate with each file a data structure called an **i-node** (**index-node**), which lists the attributes and disk addresses of the file's blocks. A simple example is depicted in Fig. 5-11. Given the i-node, it is then possible to find all the blocks of the file. The big advantage of this scheme over linked files using an in-memory table is that the i-node need only be in memory when the corresponding file is open. If each i-node occupies n bytes and a maximum of k files may be open at once, the total memory occupied by the array holding the i-nodes for the open files is only kn bytes. Only this much space need be reserved in advance.

This array is usually far smaller than the space occupied by the file table described in the previous section. The reason is simple. The table for holding the linked list of all disk blocks is proportional in size to the disk itself. If the disk has n blocks, the table needs n entries. As disks grow larger, this table grows linearly with them. In contrast, the i-node scheme requires an array in memory whose size is proportional to the maximum number of files that may be open at once. It does not matter if the disk is 1 GB or 10 GB or 100 GB.

One problem with i-nodes is that if each one has room for a fixed number of disk addresses, what happens when a file grows beyond this limit? One solution is to reserve the last disk address not for a data block, but instead for the address of an **indirect block** containing more disk block addresses. This idea can be extended to use **double indirect blocks** and **triple indirect blocks**, as shown in Fig. 5-11.

5.3.3 Implementing Directories

Before a file can be read, it must be opened. When a file is opened, the operating system uses the path name supplied by the user to locate the directory entry. Finding a directory entry means, of course, that the root directory must be

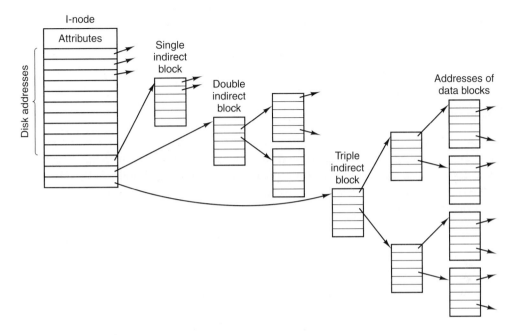

Figure 5-11. An i-node with three levels of indirect blocks.

located first. The root directory may be in a fixed location relative to the start of a partition. Alternatively, its position may be determined from other information, for instance, in a classic UNIX file system the superblock contains information about the size of the file system data structures that precede the data area. From the superblock the location of the i-nodes can be found. The first i-node will point to the root directory, which is created when a UNIX file system is made. In Windows XP, information in the boot sector (which is really much bigger than one sector) locates the **MFT** (**Master File Table**), which is used to locate other parts of the file system.

Once the root directory is located a search through the directory tree finds the desired directory entry. The directory entry provides the information needed to find the disk blocks. Depending on the system, this information may be the disk address of the entire file (contiguous allocation), the number of the first block (both linked list schemes), or the number of the i-node. In all cases, the main function of the directory system is to map the ASCII name of the file onto the information needed to locate the data.

A closely related issue is where the attributes should be stored. Every file system maintains file attributes, such as each file's owner and creation time, and they must be stored somewhere. One obvious possibility is to store them directly in the directory entry. In its simplest form, a directory consists of a list of fixed-size entries, one per file, containing a (fixed-length) file name, a structure of the file attributes, and one or more disk addresses (up to some maximum) telling where the disk blocks are, as we saw in Fig. 5-5(a).

For systems that use i-nodes, another possibility for storing the attributes is in the i-nodes, rather than in the directory entries, as in Fig. 5-5(b). In this case, the directory entry can be shorter: just a file name and an i-node number.

Shared Files

In Chap. 1 we briefly mentioned **links** between files, which make it easy for several users working together on a project to share files. Figure 5-12 shows the file system of Fig. 5-6(c) again, only with one of *C*'s files now present in one of *B*'s directories as well.

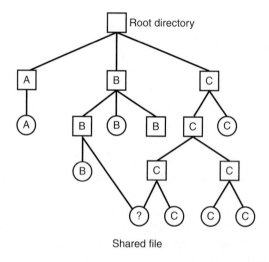

Figure 5-12. File system containing a shared file.

In UNIX the use of i-nodes for storing file attributes makes sharing easy; any number of directory entries can point to a single i-node. The i-node contains a field which is incremented when a new link is added, and which is decremented when a link is deleted. Only when the link count reaches zero are the actual data and the i-node itself deleted.

This kind of link is sometimes called a **hard link**. Sharing files using hard links is not always possible. A major limitation is that directories and i-nodes are data structures of a single file system (partition), so a directory in one file system cannot point to an i-node on another file system. Also, a file can have only one owner and one set of permissions. If the owner of a shared file deletes his own directory entry for that file, another user could be stuck with a file in his directory that he cannot delete if the permissions do not allow it.

An alternative way to share files is to create a new kind of file whose data is the path to another file. This kind of link will work across mounted file systems. In fact, if a means is provided for path names to include network addresses, such a link can refer to a file on a different computer. This second kind of link is called a **symbolic link** in UNIX-like systems, a **shortcut** in Windows, and an **alias** in Apple's Mac OS. Symbolic links can be used on systems where attributes are stored within directory entries. A little thought should convince you that multiple directory entries containing file attributes would be difficult to synchronize. Any change to a file would have to affect every directory entry for that file. But the extra directory entries for symbolic links do not contain the attributes of the file to which they point. A disadvantage of symbolic links is that when a file is deleted, or even just renamed, a link becomes an orphan.

Directories in Windows 98

The file system of the original release of Windows 95 was identical to the MS-DOS file system, but a second release added support for longer file names and bigger files. We will refer to this as the Windows 98 file system, even though it is found on some Windows 95 systems. Two types of directory entry exist in Windows 98. We will call the first one, shown in Fig. 5-13, a base entry.

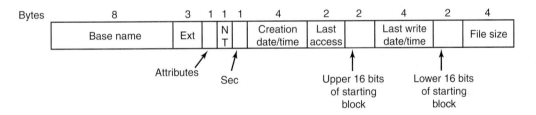

Figure 5-13. A Windows 98 base directory entry.

The base directory entry has all the information that was in the directory entries of older Windows versions, and more. The 10 bytes starting with the *NT* field are additions to the older Windows 95 structure, which fortunately (or more likely deliberately, with later improvement in mind) were not previously used. The most important upgrade is the field that increases the number of bits available for pointing to the starting block from 16 to 32. This increases the maximum potential size of the file system from 2^{16} blocks to 2^{32} blocks.

This structure provides only for the old-style 8 + 3 character filenames inherited from MS-DOS (and CP/M). How about long file names? The answer to the problem of providing long file names while retaining compatibility with the older systems was to use additional directory entries. Fig. 5-14 shows an alternative form of directory entry that can contain up to 13 characters of a long file name. For files with long names a shortened form of the name is generated automatically

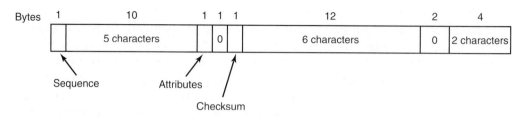

Figure 5-14. An entry for (part of) a long file name in Windows 98.

and placed in the *Base name* and *Ext* fields of an Fig. 5-13-style base directory entry. As many entries like that of Fig. 5-14 as are needed to contain the long file name are placed before the base entry, in reverse order. The *Attributes* field of each long name entry contains the value 0x0F, which is an impossible value for older (MS-DOS and Windows 95) files systems, so these entries will be ignored if the directory is read by an older system (on a floppy disk, for instance). A bit in the *Sequence* field tells the system which is the last entry.

If this seems rather complex, well, it is. Providing backward compatibility so an earlier simpler system can continue to function while providing additional features for a newer system is likely to be messy. A purist might decide not to go to so much trouble. However, a purist would probably not become rich selling new versions of operating systems.

Directories in UNIX

The traditional UNIX directory structure is extremely simple, as shown in Fig. 5-15. Each entry contains just a file name and its i-node number. All the information about the type, size, times, ownership, and disk blocks is contained in the i-node. Some UNIX systems have a different layout, but in all cases, a directory entry ultimately contains only an ASCII string and an i-node number.

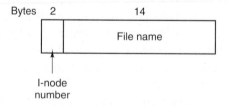

Figure 5-15. A Version 7 UNIX directory entry.

When a file is opened, the file system must take the file name supplied and locate its disk blocks. Let us consider how the path name */usr/ast/mbox* is looked up. We will use UNIX as an example, but the algorithm is basically the same for all hierarchical directory systems. First the system locates the root directory. The i-nodes form a simple array which is located using information in the superblock. The first entry in this array is the i-node of the root directory.

The file system looks up the first component of the path, *usr*, in the root direc-tory to find the i-node number of the file */usr/*. Locating an i-node from its number is straightforward, since each one has a fixed location relative to the first one. From this i-node, the system locates the directory for */usr/* and looks up the next component, *ast*, in it. When it has found the entry for *ast*, it has the i-node for the directory */usr/ast/*. From this i-node it can find the directory itself and look up *mbox*. The i-node for this file is then read into memory and kept there until the file is closed. The lookup process is illustrated in Fig. 5-16.

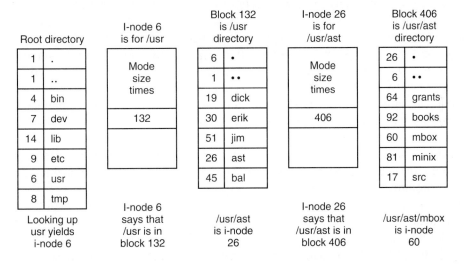

Figure 5-16. The steps in looking up */usr/ast/mbox*.

Relative path names are looked up the same way as absolute ones, only start-ing from the working directory instead of starting from the root directory. Every directory has entries for . and .. which are put there when the directory is created. The entry . has the i-node number for the current directory, and the entry for .. has the i-node number for the parent directory. Thus, a procedure looking up *../dick/prog.c* simply looks up .. in the working directory, finds the i-node number for the parent directory, and searches that directory for *dick*. No special mechan-ism is needed to handle these names. As far as the directory system is concerned, they are just ordinary ASCII strings, just the same as any other names.

Directories in NTFS

Microsoft's **NTFS (New Technology File System)** is the default file system. We do not have space for a detailed description of NTFS, but will just briefly look at some of the problems NTFS deals with and the solutions used.

One problem is long file and path names. NTFS allows long file names (up to 255 characters) and path names (up to 32,767 characters). But since older versions of Windows cannot read NTFS file systems, a complicated backward-compatible directory structure is not needed, and filename fields are variable length. Provision is made to have a second 8 + 3 character name so an older system can access NTFS files over a network.

NTFS provides for multiple character sets by using Unicode for filenames. Unicode uses 16 bits for each character, enough to represent multiple languages with very large symbol sets (e.g., Japanese). But using multiple languages raises problems in addition to representation of different character sets. Even among Latin-derived languages there are subtleties. For instance, in Spanish some combinations of two characters count as single characters when sorting. Words beginning with "ch" or "ll" should appear in sorted lists after words that begin with "cz" or "lz", respectively. The problem of case mapping is more complex. If the default is to make filenames case sensitive, there may still be a need to do case-insensitive searches. For Latin-based languages it is obvious how to do that, at least to native users of these languages. In general, if only one language is in use, users will probably know the rules. However, Unicode allows a mixture of languages: Greek, Russian, and Japanese filenames could all appear in a single directory at an international organization. The NTFS solution is an attribute for each file that defines the case conventions for the language of the filename.

More attributes is the NTFS solution to many problems. In UNIX, a file is a sequence of bytes. In NTFS a file is a collection of attributes, and each attribute is a stream of bytes. The basic NTFS data structure is the **MFT** (**Master File Table**) that provides for 16 attributes, each of which can have a length of up to 1 KB within the MFT. If that is not enough, an attribute within the MFT can be a header that points to an additional file with an extension of the attribute values. This is known as a **nonresident attribute**. The MFT itself is a file, and it has an entry for every file and directory in the file system. Since it can grow very large, when an NTFS file system is created about 12.5% of the space on the partition is reserved for growth of the MFT. Thus it can grow without becoming fragmented, at least until the initial reserved space is used, after which another large chunk of space will be reserved. So if the MFT becomes fragmented it will consists of a small number of very large fragments.

What about data in NTFS? Data is just another attribute. In fact an NTFS file may have more than one data stream. This feature was originally provided to allow Windows servers to serve files to Apple MacIntosh clients. In the original MacIntosh operating system (through Mac OS 9) all files had two data streams, called the resource fork and the data fork. Multiple data streams have other uses, for instance a large graphic image may have a smaller thumbnail image associated with it. A stream can contain up to 2^{64} bytes. At the other extreme, NTFS can handle small files by putting a few hundred bytes in the attribute header. This is called an **immediate file** (Mullender and Tanenbaum, 1984).

We have only touched upon a few ways that NTFS deals with issues not addressed by older and simpler file systems. NTFS also provides features such as a sophisticated protection system, encryption, and data compression. Describing all these features and their implementation would require much more space than we can spare here. For a more throrough look at NTFS see Tanenbaum (2001) or look on the World Wide Web for more information.

5.3.4 Disk Space Management

Files are normally stored on disk, so management of disk space is a major concern to file system designers. Two general strategies are possible for storing an *n* byte file: *n* consecutive bytes of disk space are allocated, or the file is split up into a number of (not necessarily) contiguous blocks. The same trade-off is present in memory management systems between pure segmentation and paging.

As we have seen, storing a file as a contiguous sequence of bytes has the obvious problem that if a file grows, it will probably have to be moved on the disk. The same problem holds for segments in memory, except that moving a segment in memory is a relatively fast operation compared to moving a file from one disk position to another. For this reason, nearly all file systems chop files up into fixed-size blocks that need not be adjacent.

Block Size

Once it has been decided to store files in fixed-size blocks, the question arises of how big the blocks should be. Given the way disks are organized, the sector, the track and the cylinder are obvious candidates for the unit of allocation (although these are all device dependent, which is a minus). In a paging system, the page size is also a major contender. However, having a large allocation unit, such as a cylinder, means that every file, even a 1-byte file, ties up an entire cylinder.

On the other hand, using a small allocation unit means that each file will consist of many blocks. Reading each block normally requires a seek and a rotational delay, so reading a file consisting of many small blocks will be slow.

As an example, consider a disk with 131,072 bytes/track, a rotation time of 8.33 msec, and an average seek time of 10 msec. The time in milliseconds to read a block of *k* bytes is then the sum of the seek, rotational delay, and transfer times:

$$10 + 4.165 + (k/131072) \times 8.33$$

The solid curve of Fig. 5-17 shows the data rate for such a disk as a function of block size.

To compute the space efficiency, we need to make an assumption about the mean file size. An early study showed that the mean file size in UNIX environments is about 1 KB (Mullender and Tanenbaum, 1984). A measurement made in

2005 at the department of one of the authors (AST), which has 1000 users and over 1 million UNIX disk files, gives a median size of 2475 bytes, meaning that half the files are smaller than 2475 bytes and half are larger. As an aside, the median is a better metric than the mean because a very small number of files can influence the mean enormously, but not the median. A few 100-MB hardware manuals or a promotional videos or to can greatly skew the mean but have little effect on the median.

In an experiment to see if Windows NT file usage was appreciably different from UNIX file usage, Vogels (1999) made measurements on files at Cornell University. He observed that NT file usage is more complicated than on UNIX. He wrote:

> *When we type a few characters in the* notepad *text editor, saving this to a file will trigger 26 system calls, including 3 failed open attempts, 1 file overwrite and 4 additional open and close sequences.*

Nevertheless, he observed a median size (weighted by usage) of files just read at 1 KB, files just written as 2.3 KB and files read and written as 4.2 KB. Given the fact that Cornell has considerable large-scale scientific computing and the difference in measurement technique (static versus dynamic), the results are reasonably consistent with a median file size of around 2 KB.

For simplicity, let us assume all files are 2 KB, which leads to the dashed curve in Fig. 5-17 for the disk space efficiency.

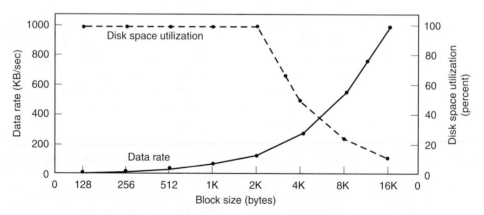

Figure 5-17. The solid curve (left-hand scale) gives the data rate of a disk. The dashed curve (right-hand scale) gives the disk space efficiency. All files are 2 KB.

The two curves can be understood as follows. The access time for a block is completely dominated by the seek time and rotational delay, so given that it is going to cost 14 msec to access a block, the more data that are fetched, the better. Hence the data rate goes up with block size (until the transfers take so long that the transfer time begins to dominate). With small blocks that are powers of two and 2-KB files, no space is wasted in a block. However, with 2-KB files and 4 KB or larger blocks, some disk space is wasted. In reality, few files are a multiple of the disk block size, so some space is always wasted in the last block of a file.

What the curves show, however, is that performance and space utilization are inherently in conflict. Small blocks are bad for performance but good for disk space utilization. A compromise size is needed. For this data, 4 KB might be a good choice, but some operating systems made their choices a long time ago, when the disk parameters and file sizes were different. For UNIX, 1 KB is commonly used. For MS-DOS the block size can be any power of two from 512 bytes to 32 KB, but is determined by the disk size and for reasons unrelated to these arguments (the maximum number of blocks on a disk partition is 2^{16}, which forces large blocks on large disks).

Keeping Track of Free Blocks

Once a block size has been chosen, the next issue is how to keep track of free blocks. Two methods are widely used, as shown in Fig. 5-18. The first one consists of using a linked list of disk blocks, with each block holding as many free disk block numbers as will fit. With a 1-KB block and a 32-bit disk block number, each block on the free list holds the numbers of 255 free blocks. (One slot is needed for the pointer to the next block). A 256-GB disk needs a free list of maximum 1,052,689 blocks to hold all 2^{28} disk block numbers. Often free blocks are used to hold the free list.

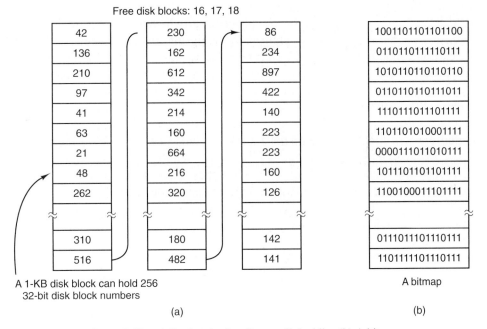

Free disk blocks: 16, 17, 18

A 1-KB disk block can hold 256 32-bit disk block numbers

A bitmap

(a)   (b)

Figure 5-18. (a) Storing the free list on a linked list. (b) A bitmap.

The other free space management technique is the bitmap. A disk with n blocks requires a bitmap with n bits. Free blocks are represented by 1s in the map, allocated blocks by 0s (or vice versa). A 256-GB disk has 2^{28} 1-KB blocks and thus requires 2^{28} bits for the map, which requires 32,768 blocks. It is not surprising that the bitmap requires less space, since it uses 1 bit per block, versus 32 bits in the linked list model. Only if the disk is nearly full (i.e., has few free blocks) will the linked list scheme require fewer blocks than the bitmap. On the other hand, if there are many blocks free, some of them can be borrowed to hold the free list without any loss of disk capacity.

When the free list method is used, only one block of pointers need be kept in main memory. When a file is created, the needed blocks are taken from the block of pointers. When it runs out, a new block of pointers is read in from the disk. Similarly, when a file is deleted, its blocks are freed and added to the block of pointers in main memory. When this block fills up, it is written to disk.

5.3.5 File System Reliability

Destruction of a file system is often a far greater disaster than destruction of a computer. If a computer is destroyed by fire, lightning surges, or a cup of coffee poured onto the keyboard, it is annoying and will cost money, but generally a replacement can be purchased with a minimum of fuss. Inexpensive personal computers can even be replaced within an hour by just going to the dealer (except at universities, where issuing a purchase order takes three committees, five signatures, and 90 days).

If a computer's file system is irrevocably lost, whether due to hardware, software, or rats gnawing on the backup tapes, restoring all the information will be difficult and time consuming at best, and in many cases will be impossible. For the people whose programs, documents, customer files, tax records, databases, marketing plans, or other data are gone forever, the consequences can be catastrophic. While the file system cannot offer any protection against physical destruction of the equipment and media, it can help protect the information. In this section we will look at some of the issues involved in safeguarding the file system.

Floppy disks are generally perfect when they leave the factory, but they can develop bad blocks during use. It is arguable that this is more likely now than it was in the days when floppy disks were more widely used. Networks and large capacity removable devices such as writeable CDs have led to floppy disks being used infrequently. Cooling fans draw air and airborne dust in through floppy disk drives, and a drive that has not been used for a long time may be so dirty that it ruins the next disk that is inserted. A floppy drive that is used frequently is less likely to damage a disk.

Hard disks frequently have bad blocks right from the start: it is just too expensive to manufacture them completely free of all defects. As we saw in Chap. 3, bad blocks on hard disks are generally handled by the controller by replacing bad sectors with spares provided for that purpose. On these disks, tracks are at least one sector bigger than needed, so that at least one bad spot can be skipped by leaving it in a gap between two consecutive sectors. A few spare sectors are provided on each cylinder so the controller can do automatic sector remapping if it notices that a sector needs more than a certain number of retries to be read or written. Thus the user is usually unaware of bad blocks or their management. Nevertheless, when a modern IDE or SCSI disk fails, it will usually fail horribly, because it has run out of spare sectors. SCSI disks provide a "recovered error" when they remap a block. If the driver notes this and displays a message on the monitor the user will know it is time to buy a new disk when these messages begin to appear frequently.

A simple software solution to the bad block problem exists, suitable for use on older disks. This approach requires the user or file system to carefully construct a file containing all the bad blocks. This technique removes them from the free list, so they will never occur in data files. As long as the bad block file is never read or written, no problems will arise. Care has to be taken during disk backups to avoid reading this file and trying to back it up.

Backups

Most people do not think making backups of their files is worth the time and effort—until one fine day their disk abruptly dies, at which time most of them undergo a deathbed conversion. Companies, however, (usually) well understand the value of their data and generally do a backup at least once a day, usually to tape. Modern tapes hold tens or sometimes even hundreds of gigabytes and cost pennies per gigabyte. Nevertheless, making backups is not quite as trivial as it sounds, so we will examine some of the related issues below.

Backups to tape are generally made to handle one of two potential problems:

1. Recover from disaster.
2. Recover from stupidity.

The first one covers getting the computer running again after a disk crash, fire, flood, or other natural catastrophe. In practice, these things do not happen very often, which is why many people do not bother with backups. These people also tend not to have fire insurance on their houses for the same reason.

The second reason is that users often accidentally remove files that they later need again. This problem occurs so often that when a file is "removed" in Windows, it is not deleted at all, but just moved to a special directory, the **recycle bin**, so it can be fished out and restored easily later. Backups take this principle further and allow files that were removed days, even weeks ago, to be restored from old backup tapes.

Making a backup takes a long time and occupies a large amount of space, so doing it efficiently and conveniently is important. These considerations raise the following issues. First, should the entire file system be backed up or only part of it? At many installations, the executable (binary) programs are kept in a limited part of the file system tree. It is not necessary to back up these files if they can all be reinstalled from the manufacturers' CD-ROMs. Also, most systems have a directory for temporary files. There is usually no reason to back it up either. In UNIX, all the special files (I/O devices) are kept in a directory */dev/*. Not only is backing up this directory not necessary, it is downright dangerous because the backup program would hang forever if it tried to read each of these to completion. In short, it is usually desirable to back up only specific directories and everything in them rather than the entire file system.

Second, it is wasteful to back up files that have not changed since the last backup, which leads to the idea of **incremental dumps**. The simplest form of incremental dumping is to make a complete dump (backup) periodically, say weekly or monthly, and to make a daily dump of only those files that have been modified since the last full dump. Even better is to dump only those files that have changed since they were last dumped. While this scheme minimizes dumping time, it makes recovery more complicated because first the most recent full dump has to be restored, followed by all the incremental dumps in reverse order, oldest one first. To ease recovery, more sophisticated incremental dumping schemes are often used.

Third, since immense amounts of data are typically dumped, it may be desirable to compress the data before writing them to tape. However, with many compression algorithms, a single bad spot on the backup tape can foil the decompression algorithm and make an entire file or even an entire tape unreadable. Thus the decision to compress the backup stream must be carefully considered.

Fourth, it is difficult to perform a backup on an active file system. If files and directories are being added, deleted, and modified during the dumping process, the resulting dump may be inconsistent. However, since making a dump may take hours, it may be necessary to take the system offline for much of the night to make the backup, something that is not always acceptable. For this reason, algorithms have been devised for making rapid snapshots of the file system state by copying critical data structures, and then requiring future changes to files and directories to copy the blocks instead of updating them in place (Hutchinson et al., 1999). In this way, the file system is effectively frozen at the moment of the snapshot, so it can be backed up at leisure afterward.

Fifth and last, making backups introduces many nontechnical problems into an organization. The best online security system in the world may be useless if the system administrator keeps all the backup tapes in his office and leaves it open and unguarded whenever he walks down the hall to get output from the printer. All a spy has to do is pop in for a second, put one tiny tape in his pocket, and saunter off jauntily. Goodbye security. Also, making a daily backup has little use if the fire that burns down the computers also burns up all the backup tapes. For this reason, backup tapes should be kept off-site, but that introduces more security risks. For a thorough discussion of these and other practical administration issues, see Nemeth et al. (2001). Below we will discuss only the technical issues involved in making file system backups.

Two strategies can be used for dumping a disk to tape: a physical dump or a logical dump. A **physical dump** starts at block 0 of the disk, writes all the disk blocks onto the output tape in order, and stops when it has copied the last one. Such a program is so simple that it can probably be made 100% bug free, something that can probably not be said about any other useful program.

Nevertheless, it is worth making several comments about physical dumping. For one thing, there is no value in backing up unused disk blocks. If the dumping program can get access to the free block data structure, it can avoid dumping unused blocks. However, skipping unused blocks requires writing the number of each block in front of the block (or the equivalent), since it is no longer true that block k on the tape was block k on the disk.

A second concern is dumping bad blocks. If all bad blocks are remapped by the disk controller and hidden from the operating system as we described in Sec. 5.4.4, physical dumping works fine. On the other hand, if they are visible to the operating system and maintained in one or more "bad block files" or bitmaps, it is absolutely essential that the physical dumping program get access to this information and avoid dumping them to prevent endless disk read errors during the dumping process.

The main advantages of physical dumping are simplicity and great speed (basically, it can run at the speed of the disk). The main disadvantages are the inability to skip selected directories, make incremental dumps, and restore individual files upon request. For these reasons, most installations make logical dumps.

A **logical dump** starts at one or more specified directories and recursively dumps all files and directories found there that have changed since some given base date (e.g., the last backup for an incremental dump or system installation for a full dump). Thus in a logical dump, the dump tape gets a series of carefully identified directories and files, which makes it easy to restore a specific file or directory upon request.

In order to be able to properly restore even a single file correctly, all information needed to recreate the path to that file must be saved to the backup medium. Thus the first step in doing a logical dump is doing an analysis of the directory tree. Obviously, we need to save any file or directory that has been modified. But for proper restoration, all directories, even unmodified ones, that lie on the path to a modified file or directory must be saved. This means saving not just the data (file names and pointers to i-nodes), all the attributes of the directories must be saved, so they can be restored with the original permissions. The directories and their attributes are written to the tape first, and then modified files (with their attributes) are saved. This makes it possible to restore the dumped files and directories to a fresh file system on a different computer. In this way, the dump and restore programs can be used to transport entire file systems between computers.

A second reason for dumping unmodified directories above modified files is to make it possible to incrementally restore a single file (possibly to handle recovery from accidental deletion). Suppose that a full file system dump is done Sunday evening and an incremental dump is done on Monday evening. On Tuesday the directory */usr/jhs/proj/nr3/* is removed, along with all the directories and files under it. On Wednesday morning bright and early, a user wants to restore the file */usr/jhs/proj/nr3/plans/summary* However, is not possible to just restore the file *summary* because there is no place to put it. The directories *nr3/* and *plans/* must be restored first. To get their owners, modes, times, etc., correct, these directories must be present on the dump tape even though they themselves were not modified since the previous full dump.

Restoring a file system from the dump tapes is straightforward. To start with, an empty file system is created on the disk. Then the most recent full dump is restored. Since the directories appear first on the tape, they are all restored first, giving a skeleton of the file system. Then the files themselves are restored. This process is then repeated with the first incremental dump made after the full dump, then the next one, and so on.

Although logical dumping is straightforward, there are a few tricky issues. For one, since the free block list is not a file, it is not dumped and hence it must be reconstructed from scratch after all the dumps have been restored. Doing so is always possible since the set of free blocks is just the complement of the set of blocks contained in all the files combined.

Another issue is links. If a file is linked to two or more directories, it is important that the file is restored only one time and that all the directories that are supposed to point to it do so.

Still another issue is the fact that UNIX files may contain holes. It is legal to open a file, write a few bytes, then seek to a distant file offset and write a few more bytes. The blocks in between are not part of the file and should not be dumped and not be restored. Core dump files often have a large hole between the data segment and the stack. If not handled properly, each restored core file will fill this area with zeros and thus be the same size as the virtual address space (e.g., 2^{32} bytes, or worse yet, 2^{64} bytes).

Finally, special files, named pipes, and the like should never be dumped, no matter in which directory they may occur (they need not be confined to */dev/*). For more information about file system backups, see Chervenak et al. (1998) and Zwicky (1991).

File System Consistency

Another area where reliability is an issue is file system consistency. Many file systems read blocks, modify them, and write them out later. If the system crashes before all the modified blocks have been written out, the file system can be left in an inconsistent state. This problem is especially critical if some of the blocks that have not been written out are i-node blocks, directory blocks, or blocks containing the free list.

To deal with the problem of inconsistent file systems, most computers have a utility program that checks file system consistency. For example, UNIX has *fsck* and Windows has *chkdsk* (or *scandisk* in earlier versions). This utility can be run whenever the system is booted, especially after a crash. The description below tells how *fsck* works. *Chkdsk* is somewhat different because it works on a different file system, but the general principle of using the file system's inherent redundancy to repair it is still valid. All file system checkers verify each file system (disk partition) independently of the other ones.

Two kinds of consistency checks can be made: blocks and files. To check for block consistency, the program builds two tables, each one containing a counter for each block, initially set to 0. The counters in the first table keep track of how many times each block is present in a file; the counters in the second table record how often each block is present in the free list (or the bitmap of free blocks).

The program then reads all the i-nodes. Starting from an i-node, it is possible to build a list of all the block numbers used in the corresponding file. As each block number is read, its counter in the first table is incremented. The program then examines the free list or bitmap, to find all the blocks that are not in use. Each occurrence of a block in the free list results in its counter in the second table being incremented.

If the file system is consistent, each block will have a 1 either in the first table or in the second table, as illustrated in Fig. 5-19(a). However, as a result of a crash, the tables might look like Fig. 5-19(b), in which block 2 does not occur in either table. It will be reported as being a **missing block**. While missing blocks do no real harm, they do waste space and thus reduce the capacity of the disk. The solution to missing blocks is straightforward: the file system checker just adds them to the free list.

Another situation that might occur is that of Fig. 5-19(c). Here we see a block, number 4, that occurs twice in the free list. (Duplicates can occur only if the free list is really a list; with a bitmap it is impossible.) The solution here is also simple: rebuild the free list.

The worst thing that can happen is that the same data block is present in two or more files, as shown in Fig. 5-19(d) with block 5. If either of these files is removed, block 5 will be put on the free list, leading to a situation in which the same block is both in use and free at the same time. If both files are removed, the block will be put onto the free list twice.

The appropriate action for the file system checker to take is to allocate a free block, copy the contents of block 5 into it, and insert the copy into one of the files. In this way, the information content of the files is unchanged (although almost assuredly one is garbled), but the file system structure is at least made consistent. The error should be reported, to allow the user to inspect the damage.

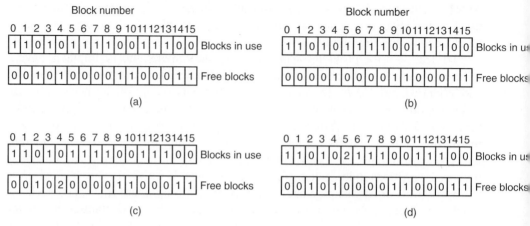

Figure 5-19. File system states. (a) Consistent. (b) Missing block. (c) Duplicate block in free list. (d) Duplicate data block.

In addition to checking to see that each block is properly accounted for, the file system checker also checks the directory system. It, too, uses a table of counters, but these are per file, rather than per block. It starts at the root directory and recursively descends the tree, inspecting each directory in the file system. For every file in every directory, it increments a counter for that file's usage count. Remember that due to hard links, a file may appear in two or more directories. Symbolic links do not count and do not cause the counter for the target file to be incremented.

When it is all done, it has a list, indexed by i-node number, telling how many directories contain each file. It then compares these numbers with the link counts stored in the i-nodes themselves. These counts start at 1 when a file is created and are incremented each time a (hard) link is made to the file. In a consistent file system, both counts will agree. However, two kinds of errors can occur: the link count in the i-node can be too high or it can be too low.

If the link count is higher than the number of directory entries, then even if all the files are removed from the directories, the count will still be nonzero and the i-node will not be removed. This error is not serious, but it wastes space on the disk with files that are not in any directory. It should be fixed by setting the link count in the i-node to the correct value.

The other error is potentially catastrophic. If two directory entries are linked to a file, but the i-node says that there is only one, when either directory entry is removed, the i-node count will go to zero. When an i-node count goes to zero, the file system marks it as unused and releases all of its blocks. This action will result in one of the directories now pointing to an unused i-node, whose blocks may soon be assigned to other files. Again, the solution is just to force the link count in the i-node to the actual number of directory entries.

These two operations, checking blocks and checking directories, are often integrated for efficiency reasons (i.e., only one pass over the i-nodes is required). Other checks are also possible. For example, directories have a definite format, with i-node numbers and ASCII names. If an i-node number is larger than the number of i-nodes on the disk, the directory has been damaged.

Furthermore, each i-node has a mode, some of which are legal but strange, such as 0007, which allows the owner and his group no access at all, but allows outsiders to read, write, and execute the file. It might be useful to at least report files that give outsiders more rights than the owner. Directories with more than, say, 1000 entries are also suspicious. Files located in user directories, but which are owned by the superuser and have the SETUID bit on, are potential security problems because such files acquire the powers of the superuser when executed by any user. With a little effort, one can put together a fairly long list of technically legal but still peculiar situations that might be worth reporting.

The previous paragraphs have discussed the problem of protecting the user against crashes. Some file systems also worry about protecting the user against himself. If the user intends to type

        rm *.o

to remove all the files ending with .o (compiler generated object files), but accidentally types

        rm * .o

(note the space after the asterisk), rm will remove all the files in the current directory and then complain that it cannot find .o. In some systems, when a file is removed, all that happens is that a bit is set in the directory or i-node marking the file as removed. No disk blocks are returned to the free list until they are actually needed. Thus, if the user discovers the error immediately, it is possible to run a special utility program that "unremoves" (i.e., restores) the removed files. In Windows, files that are removed are placed in the recycle bin, from which they can later be retrieved if need be. Of course, no storage is reclaimed until they are actually deleted from this directory.

Mechanisms like this are insecure. A secure system would actually overwrite the data blocks with zeros or random bits when a disk is deleted, so another user could not retrieve it. Many users are unaware how long data can live. Confidential or sensitive data can often be recovered from disks that have been discarded (Garfinkel and Shelat, 2003).

5.3.6 File System Performance

Access to disk is much slower than access to memory. Reading a memory word might take 10 nsec. Reading from a hard disk might proceed at 10 MB/sec, which is forty times slower per 32-bit word, and to this must be added 5–10 msec to seek to the track and then wait for the desired sector to arrive under the read head. If only a single word is needed, the memory access is on the order of a million times as fast as disk access. As a result of this difference in access time, many file systems have been designed with various optimizations to improve performance. In this section we will cover three of them.

Caching

The most common technique used to reduce disk accesses is the **block cache** or **buffer cache**. (Cache is pronounced "cash" and is derived from the French *cacher*, meaning to hide.) In this context, a cache is a collection of blocks that logically belong on the disk but are being kept in memory for performance reasons.

Various algorithms can be used to manage the cache, but a common one is to check all read requests to see if the needed block is in the cache. If it is, the read request can be satisfied without a disk access. If the block is not in the cache, it is first read into the cache, and then copied to wherever it is needed. Subsequent requests for the same block can be satisfied from the cache.

Operation of the cache is illustrated in Fig. 5-20. Since there are many (often thousands of) blocks in the cache, some way is needed to determine quickly if a given block is present. The usual way is to hash the device and disk address and look up the result in a hash table. All the blocks with the same hash value are chained together on a linked list so the collision chain can be followed.

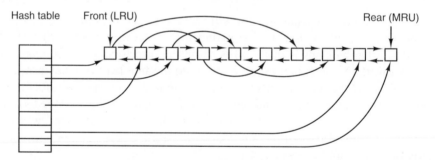

Figure 5-20. The buffer cache data structures.

When a block has to be loaded into a full cache, some block has to be removed (and rewritten to the disk if it has been modified since being brought in). This situation is very much like paging, and all the usual page replacement algorithms described in Chap. 4, such as FIFO, second chance, and LRU, are applicable. One pleasant difference between paging and caching is that cache references are relatively infrequent, so that it is feasible to keep all the blocks in exact LRU order with linked lists.

In Fig. 5-20, we see that in addition to the collision chains starting at the hash table, there is also a bidirectional list running through all the blocks in the order of usage, with the least recently used block on the front of this list and the most recently used block at the end of this list. When a block is referenced, it can be removed from its position on the bidirectional list and put at the end. In this way, exact LRU order can be maintained.

Unfortunately, there is a catch. Now that we have a situation in which exact LRU is possible, it turns out that LRU is undesirable. The problem has to do with the crashes and file system consistency discussed in the previous section. If a critical block, such as an i-node block, is read into the cache and modified, but not rewritten to the disk, a crash will leave the file system in an inconsistent state. If the i-node block is put at the end of the LRU chain, it may be quite a while before it reaches the front and is rewritten to the disk.

Furthermore, some blocks, such as i-node blocks, are rarely referenced twice within a short interval. These considerations lead to a modified LRU scheme, taking two factors into account:

1. Is the block likely to be needed again soon?

2. Is the block essential to the consistency of the file system?

For both questions, blocks can be divided into categories such as i-node blocks, indirect blocks, directory blocks, full data blocks, and partially full data blocks. Blocks that will probably not be needed again soon go on the front, rather than the rear of the LRU list, so their buffers will be reused quickly. Blocks that might be needed again soon, such as a partly full block that is being written, go on the end of the list, so they will stay around for a long time.

The second question is independent of the first one. If the block is essential to the file system consistency (basically, everything except data blocks), and it has been modified, it should be written to disk immediately, regardless of which end of the LRU list it is put on. By writing critical blocks quickly, we greatly reduce the probability that a crash will wreck the file system. While a user may be unhappy if one of his files is ruined in a crash, he is likely to be far more unhappy if the whole file system is lost.

Even with this measure to keep the file system integrity intact, it is undesirable to keep data blocks in the cache too long before writing them out. Consider the plight of someone who is using a personal computer to write a book. Even if our writer periodically tells the editor to write the file being edited to the disk, there is a good chance that everything will still be in the cache and nothing on the disk. If the system crashes, the file system structure will not be corrupted, but a whole day's work will be lost.

This situation need not happen very often before we have a fairly unhappy user. Systems take two approaches to dealing with it. The UNIX way is to have a system call, sync, which forces all the modified blocks out onto the disk immediately. When the system is started up, a program, usually called *update*, is started up in the background to sit in an endless loop issuing sync calls, sleeping for 30 sec between calls. As a result, no more than 30 seconds of work is lost due to a system crash, a comforting thought for many people.

The Windows way is to write every modified block to disk as soon as it has been written. Caches in which all modified blocks are written back to the disk immediately are called **write-through caches**. They require more disk I/O than nonwrite-through caches. The difference between these two approaches can be seen when a program writes a 1-KB block full, one character at a time. UNIX will collect all the characters in the cache and write the block out once every 30 seconds, or whenever the block is removed from the cache. Windows will make a disk access for every character written. Of course, most programs do internal buffering, so they normally write not a character, but a line or a larger unit on each write system call.

A consequence of this difference in caching strategy is that just removing a (floppy) disk from a UNIX system without doing a sync will almost always result in lost data, and frequently in a corrupted file system as well. With Windows, no problem arises. These differing strategies were chosen because UNIX was developed in an environment in which all disks were hard disks and not removable, whereas Windows started out in the floppy disk world. As hard disks became the norm, the UNIX approach, with its better efficiency, became the norm, and is also used now on Windows for hard disks.

Block Read Ahead

A second technique for improving perceived file system performance is to try to get blocks into the cache before they are needed to increase the hit rate. In particular, many files are read sequentially. When the file system is asked to produce block k in a file, it does that, but when it is finished, it makes a sneaky check in the cache to see if block $k + 1$ is already there. If it is not, it schedules a read for block $k + 1$ in the hope that when it is needed, it will have already arrived in the cache. At the very least, it will be on the way.

Of course, this read ahead strategy only works for files that are being read sequentially. If a file is being randomly accessed, read ahead does not help. In fact, it hurts by tying up disk bandwidth reading in useless blocks and removing potentially useful blocks from the cache (and possibly tying up more disk bandwidth writing them back to disk if they are dirty). To see whether read ahead is worth doing, the file system can keep track of the access patterns to each open file. For example, a bit associated with each file can keep track of whether the file is in "sequential access mode" or "random access mode." Initially, the file is given the benefit of the doubt and put in sequential access mode. However, whenever a seek is done, the bit is cleared. If sequential reads start happening again, the bit is set once again. In this way, the file system can make a reasonable guess about whether it should read ahead or not. If it gets it wrong once it a while, it is not a disaster, just a little bit of wasted disk bandwidth.

Reducing Disk Arm Motion

Caching and read ahead are not the only ways to increase file system performance. Another important technique is to reduce the amount of disk arm motion by putting blocks that are likely to be accessed in sequence close to each other, preferably in the same cylinder. When an output file is written, the file system has to allocate the blocks one at a time, as they are needed. If the free blocks are recorded in a bitmap, and the whole bitmap is in main memory, it is easy enough to choose a free block as close as possible to the previous block. With a free list, part of which is on disk, it is much harder to allocate blocks close together.

However, even with a free list, some block clustering can be done. The trick is to keep track of disk storage not in blocks, but in groups of consecutive blocks. If sectors consist of 512 bytes, the system could use 1-KB blocks (2 sectors) but allocate disk storage in units of 2 blocks (4 sectors). This is not the same as having a 2-KB disk blocks, since the cache would still use 1-KB blocks and disk transfers would still be 1 KB but reading a file sequentially on an otherwise idle system would reduce the number of seeks by a factor of two, considerably improving performance. A variation on the same theme is to take account of rotational positioning. When allocating blocks, the system attempts to place consecutive blocks in a file in the same cylinder.

Another performance bottleneck in systems that use i-nodes or anything equivalent to i-nodes is that reading even a short file requires two disk accesses: one for the i-node and one for the block. The usual i-node placement is shown in Fig. 5-21(a). Here all the i-nodes are near the beginning of the disk, so the average distance between an i-node and its blocks will be about half the number of cylinders, requiring long seeks.

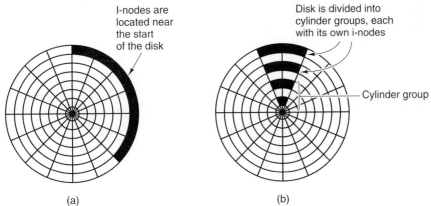

Figure 5-21. (a) I-nodes placed at the start of the disk. (b) Disk divided into cylinder groups, each with its own blocks and i-nodes.

One easy performance improvement is to put the i-nodes in the middle of the disk, rather than at the start, thus reducing the average seek between the i-node and the first block by a factor of two. Another idea, shown in Fig. 5-21(b), is to divide the disk into cylinder groups, each with its own i-nodes, blocks, and free list (McKusick et al., 1984). When creating a new file, any i-node can be chosen, but an attempt is made to find a block in the same cylinder group as the i-node. If none is available, then a block in a nearby cylinder group is used.

5.3.7 Log-Structured File Systems

Changes in technology are putting pressure on current file systems. In particular, CPUs keep getting faster, disks are becoming much bigger and cheaper (but not much faster), and memories are growing exponentially in size. The one parameter that is not improving by leaps and bounds is disk seek time. The combination of these factors means that a performance bottleneck is arising in many file systems. Research done at Berkeley attempted to alleviate this problem by designing a completely new kind of file system, LFS (the **Log-structured File System**). In this section we will briefly describe how LFS works. For a more complete treatment, see Rosenblum and Ousterhout (1991).

The idea that drove the LFS design is that as CPUs get faster and RAM memories get larger, disk caches are also increasing rapidly. Consequently, it is now possible to satisfy a very substantial fraction of all read requests directly from the file system cache, with no disk access needed. It follows from this observation, that in the future, most disk accesses will be writes, so the read-ahead mechanism used in some file systems to fetch blocks before they are needed no longer gains much performance.

To make matters worse, in most file systems, writes are done in very small chunks. Small writes are highly inefficient, since a 50-μsec disk write is often preceded by a 10-msec seek and a 4-msec rotational delay. With these parameters, disk efficiency drops to a fraction of 1 percent.

To see where all the small writes come from, consider creating a new file on a UNIX system. To write this file, the i-node for the directory, the directory block, the i-node for the file, and the file itself must all be written. While these writes can be delayed, doing so exposes the file system to serious consistency problems if a crash occurs before the writes are done. For this reason, the i-node writes are generally done immediately.

From this reasoning, the LFS designers decided to re-implement the UNIX file system in such a way as to achieve the full bandwidth of the disk, even in the face of a workload consisting in large part of small random writes. The basic idea is to structure the entire disk as a log. Periodically, and also when there is a special need for it, all the pending writes being buffered in memory are collected into a single segment and written to the disk as a single contiguous segment at the end of the log. A single segment may thus contain i-nodes, directory blocks, data blocks, and other kinds of blocks all mixed together. At the start of each segment is a segment summary, telling what can be found in the segment. If the average segment can be made to be about 1 MB, almost the full bandwidth of the disk can be utilized.

In this design, i-nodes still exist and have the same structure as in UNIX, but they are now scattered all over the log, instead of being at a fixed position on the disk. Nevertheless, when an i-node is located, locating the blocks is done in the usual way. Of course, finding an i-node is now much harder, since its address cannot simply be calculated from its i-node number, as in UNIX. To make it possible to find i-nodes, an i-node map, indexed by i-node number, is maintained. Entry *i* in this map points to i-node *i* on the disk. The map is kept on disk, but it is also cached, so the most heavily used parts will be in memory most of the time in order to improve performance.

To summarize what we have said so far, all writes are initially buffered in memory, and periodically all the buffered writes are written to the disk in a single segment, at the end of the log. Opening a file now consists of using the map to locate the i-node for the file. Once the i-node has been located, the addresses of the blocks can be found from it. All of the blocks will themselves be in segments, somewhere in the log.

If disks were infinitely large, the above description would be the entire story. However, real disks are finite, so eventually the log will occupy the entire disk, at which time no new segments can be written to the log. Fortunately, many existing segments may have blocks that are no longer needed, for example, if a file is overwritten, its i-node will now point to the new blocks, but the old ones will still be occupying space in previously written segments.

To deal with this problem, LFS has a **cleaner** thread that spends its time scanning the log circularly to compact it. It starts out by reading the summary of the first segment in the log to see which i-nodes and files are there. It then checks the current i-node map to see if the i-nodes are still current and file blocks are still in use. If not, that information is discarded. The i-nodes and blocks that are still in use go into memory to be written out in the next segment. The original segment is then marked as free, so the log can use it for new data. In this manner, the cleaner moves along the log, removing old segments from the back and putting any live data into memory for rewriting in the next segment. Consequently, the disk is a big circular buffer, with the writer thread adding new segments to the front and the cleaner thread removing old ones from the back.

The bookkeeping here is nontrivial, since when a file block is written back to a new segment, the i-node of the file (somewhere in the log) must be located, updated, and put into memory to be written out in the next segment. The i-node map must then be updated to point to the new copy. Nevertheless, it is possible to do the administration, and the performance results show that all this complexity is worthwhile. Measurements given in the papers cited above show that LFS outperforms UNIX by an order of magnitude on small writes, while having a performance that is as good as or better than UNIX for reads and large writes.

5.4 SECURITY

File systems generally contain information that is highly valuable to their users. Protecting this information against unauthorized usage is therefore a major concern of all file systems. In the following sections we will look at a variety of issues concerned with security and protection. These issues apply equally well to timesharing systems as to networks of personal computers connected to shared servers via local area networks.

5.4.1 The Security Environment

People frequently use the terms "security" and "protection" interchangeably. Nevertheless, it is frequently useful to make a distinction between the general problems involved in making sure that files are not read or modified by unauthorized persons, which include technical, administrative, legal, and political issues on the one hand, and the specific operating system mechanisms used to provide security, on the other. To avoid confusion, we will use the term **security** to refer to the overall problem, and the term **protection mechanisms** to refer to the specific operating system mechanisms used to safeguard information in the computer. The boundary between them is not well defined, however. First we will look at security to see what the nature of the problem is. Later on in the chapter we will look at the protection mechanisms and models available to help achieve security.

Security has many facets. Three of the more important ones are the nature of the threats, the nature of intruders, and accidental data loss. We will now look at these in turn.

Threats

From a security perspective, computer systems have three general goals, with corresponding threats to them, as listed in Fig. 5-22. The first one, **data confidentiality**, is concerned with having secret data remain secret. More specifically, if the owner of some data has decided that these data are only to be made available to certain people and no others, the system should guarantee that release of the data to unauthorized people does not occur. As a bare minimum, the owner should be able to specify who can see what, and the system should enforce these specifications.

The second goal, **data integrity**, means that unauthorized users should not be able to modify any data without the owner's permission. Data modification in this context includes not only changing the data, but also removing data and adding false data as well. If a system cannot guarantee that data deposited in it remain unchanged until the owner decides to change them, it is not worth much as an information system. Integrity is usually more important than confidentiality.

Goal	Threat
Data confidentiality	Exposure of data
Data integrity	Tampering with data
System availability	Denial of service

Figure 5-22. Security goals and threats.

The third goal, **system availability**, means that nobody can disturb the system to make it unusable. Such **denial of service** attacks are increasingly common. For example, if a computer is an Internet server, sending a flood of requests to it may cripple it by eating up all of its CPU time just examining and discarding incoming requests. If it takes, say, 100 µsec to process an incoming request to read a Web page, then anyone who manages to send 10,000 requests/sec can wipe it out. Reasonable models and technology for dealing with attacks on confidentiality and integrity are available; foiling denial-of-services attacks is much harder.

Another aspect of the security problem is **privacy**: protecting individuals from misuse of information about them. This quickly gets into many legal and moral issues. Should the government compile dossiers on everyone in order to catch X-cheaters, where X is "welfare" or "tax," depending on your politics? Should the police be able to look up anything on anyone in order to stop organized crime? Do employers and insurance companies have rights? What happens when these rights conflict with individual rights? All of these issues are extremely important but are beyond the scope of this book.

Intruders

Most people are pretty nice and obey the law, so why worry about security? Because there are unfortunately a few people around who are not so nice and want to cause trouble (possibly for their own commercial gain). In the security literature, people who are nosing around places where they have no business being are called **intruders** or sometimes **adversaries**. Intruders act in two different ways. Passive intruders just want to read files they are not authorized to read. Active intruders are more malicious; they want to make unauthorized changes. When designing a system to be secure against intruders, it is important to keep in mind the kind of intruder one is trying to protect against. Some common categories are

1. Casual prying by nontechnical users. Many people have personal computers on their desks that are connected to a shared file server, and human nature being what it is, some of them will read other people's electronic mail and other files if no barriers are placed in the way. Most UNIX systems, for example, have the default that all newly created files are publicly readable.

2. Snooping by insiders. Students, system programmers, operators, and other technical personnel often consider it to be a personal challenge to break the security of the local computer system. They often are highly skilled and are willing to devote a substantial amount of time to the effort.

3. Determined attempts to make money. Some bank programmers have attempted to steal from the bank they were working for. Schemes have varied from changing the software to truncate rather than round interest, keeping the fraction of a cent for themselves, to siphoning off accounts not used in years, to blackmail ("Pay me or I will destroy all the bank's records.").

4. Commercial or military espionage. Espionage refers to a serious and well-funded attempt by a competitor or a foreign country to steal programs, trade secrets, patentable ideas, technology, circuit designs, business plans, and so forth. Often this attempt will involve wiretapping or even erecting antennas directed at the computer to pick up its electromagnetic radiation.

It should be clear that trying to keep a hostile foreign government from stealing military secrets is quite a different matter from trying to keep students from inserting a funny message-of-the-day into the system. The amount of effort needed for security and protection clearly depends on who the enemy is thought to be.

Malicious Programs

Another category of security pest is malicious programs, sometimes called **malware**. In a sense, a writer of malware is also an intruder, often with high technical skills. The difference between a conventional intruder and malware is that the former refers to a person who is personally trying to break into a system to cause damage whereas the latter is a program written by such a person and then released into the world. Some malware seems to have been written just to cause damage, but some is targeted more specifically. It is becoming a huge problem and a great deal has been written about it (Aycock and Barker, 2005; Cerf, 2005; Ledin, 2005; McHugh and Deek, 2005; Treese, 2004; and Weiss, 2005)

The most well known kind of malware is the **virus**. Basically a virus is a piece of code that can reproduce itself by attaching a copy of itself to another program, analogous to how biological viruses reproduce. The virus can do other things in addition to reproducing itself. For example, it can type a message, display an image on the screen, play music, or something else harmless. Unfortunately, it can also modify, destroy, or steal files (by e-mailing them somewhere).

Another thing a virus can do is to render the computer unusable as long as the virus is running. This is called a **DOS (Denial Of Service)** attack. The usual approach is to consume resources wildly, such as the CPU, or filling up the disk with junk. Viruses (and the other forms of malware to be described) can also be used to cause a **DDOS (Distributed Denial Of Service)** attack. In this case the virus does not do anything immediately upon infecting a computer. At a predetermined date and time thousands of copies of the virus on computers all over the world start requesting web pages or other network services from their target, for instance the Web site of a political party or a corporation. This can overload the targeted server and the networks that service it.

Malware is frequently created for profit. Much (if not most) unwanted junk e-mail ("spam") is relayed to its final destinations by networks of computers that have been infected by viruses or other forms of malware. A computer infected by such a rogue program becomes a slave, and reports its status to its master, somewhere on the Internet. The master then sends spam to be relayed to all the e-mail addresses that can be gleaned from e-mail address books and other files on the slave. Another kind of malware for profit scheme installs a **key logger** on an infected computer. A key logger records everything typed at the keyboard. It is not too difficult to filter this data and extract information such as username—password combinations or credit card numbers and expiration dates. This information is then sent back to a master where it can be used or sold for criminal use.

Related to the virus is the **worm**. Whereas a virus is spread by attaching itself to another program, and is executed when its host program is executed, a worm is a free-standing program. Worms spread by using networks to transmit copies of themselves to other computers. Windows systems always have a *Startup* directory for each user; any program in that folder will be executed when the user logs in. So all the worm has to do is arrange to put itself (or a shortcut to itself) in the *Startup* directory on a remote system. Other ways exist, some much more difficult to detect, to cause a remote computer to execute a program file that has been copied to its file system. The effects of a worm can be the same as those of a virus. Indeed, the distinction between a virus and a worm is not always clear; some malware uses both methods to spread.

Another category of malware is the **Trojan horse**. This is a program that apparently performs a valid function—perhaps it is a game or a supposedly "improved" version of a useful utility. But when the Trojan horse is executed some other function is performed, perhaps launching a worm or virus or performing one of the nasty things that malware does. The effects of a Trojan horse are likely to be subtle and stealthy. Unlike worms and viruses, Trojan horses are voluntarily downloaded by users, and as soon as they are recognized for what they are and the word gets out, a Trojan horse will be deleted from reputable download sites.

Another kind of malware is the **logic bomb**. This device is a piece of code written by one of a company's (currently employed) programmers and secretly inserted into the production operating system. As long as the programmer feeds it its daily password, it does nothing. However, if the programmer is suddenly fired and physically removed from the premises without warning, the next day the logic bomb does not get its password, so it goes off.

Going off might involve clearing the disk, erasing files at random, carefully making hard-to-detect changes to key programs, or encrypting essential files. In the latter case, the company has a tough choice about whether to call the police (which may or may not result in a conviction many months later) or to give in to this blackmail and to rehire the ex-programmer as a "consultant" for an astronomical sum to fix the problem (and hope that he does not plant new logic bombs while doing so).

Yet another form of malware is **spyware**. This is usually obtained by visiting a Web site. In its simplest form spyware may be nothing more than a **cookie**. Cookies are small files exchanged between web browsers and web servers. They have a legitimate purpose. A cookie contains some information that will allow the Web site to identify you. It is like the ticket you get when you leave a bicycle to be repaired. When you return to the shop, your half of the ticket gets matched with your bicycle (and its repair bill). Web connections are not persistent, so, for example, if you indicate an interest in buying this book when visiting an online bookstore, the bookstore asks your browser to accept a cookie. When you have finished browsing and perhaps have selected other books to buy, you click on the page where your order is finalized. At that point the web server asks your browser to return the cookies it has stored from the current session, It can use the information in these to generate the list of items you have said you want to buy.

Normally, cookies used for a purpose like this expire quickly. They are quite useful, and e-commerce depends upon them. But some Web sites use cookies for purposes that are not so benign. For instance, advertisements on Web sites are often furnished by companies other than the information provider. Advertisers pay Web site owners for this privilege. If a cookie is placed when you visit a page with information about, say, bicycle equipment, and you then go to another Web site that sells clothing, the same advertising company may provide ads on this page, and may collect cookies you obtained elsewhere. Thus you may suddenly find yourself viewing ads for special gloves or jackets especially made for cyclists. Advertisers can collect a lot of information about your interests this way; you may not want to share so much information about yourself.

What is worse, there are various ways a Web site may be able to download executable program code to your computer. Most browsers accept **plug-ins** to add additional function, such as displaying new kinds of files. Users often accept offers for new plugins without knowing much about what the plugin does. Or a user may willingly accept an offer to be provided with a new cursor for the desktop that looks like a dancing kitten. And a bug in a web browser may allow a remote site to install an unwanted program, perhaps after luring the user to a page that has been carefully constructed to take advantage of the vulnerability. Any time a program is accepted from another source, voluntarily or not, there is a risk it could contain code that does you harm.

Accidental Data Loss

In addition to threats caused by malicious intruders, valuable data can be lost by accident. Some of the common causes of accidental data loss are

1. Acts of God: fires, floods, earthquakes, wars, riots, or rats gnawing tapes or floppy disks.

2. Hardware or software errors: CPU malfunctions, unreadable disks or tapes, telecommunication errors, program bugs.

3. Human errors: incorrect data entry, wrong tape or disk mounted, wrong program run, lost disk or tape, or some other mistake.

Most of these can be dealt with by maintaining adequate backups, preferably far away from the original data. While protecting data against accidental loss may seem mundane compared to protecting against clever intruders, in practice, probably more damage is caused by the former than the latter.

5.4.2 Generic Security Attacks

Finding security flaws is not easy. The usual way to test a system's security is to hire a group of experts, known as **tiger teams** or **penetration teams**, to see if they can break in. Hebbard et al. (1980) tried the same thing with graduate students. In the course of the years, these penetration teams have discovered a number of areas in which systems are likely to be weak. Below we have listed some of the more common attacks that are often successful. When designing a system, be sure it can withstand attacks like these.

1. Request memory pages, disk space, or tapes and just read them. Many systems do not erase them before allocating them, and they may be full of interesting information written by the previous owner.

2. Try illegal system calls, or legal system calls with illegal parameters, or even legal system calls with legal but unreasonable parameters. Many systems can easily be confused.

3. Start logging in and then hit DEL, RUBOUT or BREAK halfway through the login sequence. In some systems, the password checking program will be killed and the login considered successful.

4. Try modifying complex operating system structures kept in user space (if any). In some systems (especially on mainframes), to open a file, the program builds a large data structure containing the file name and many other parameters and passes it to the system. As the file is read and written, the system sometimes updates the structure itself. Changing these fields can wreak havoc with the security.

5. Spoof the user by writing a program that types "login:" on the screen and go away. Many users will walk up to the terminal and willingly tell it their login name and password, which the program carefully records for its evil master.

6. Look for manuals that say "Do not do *X*." Try as many variations of *X* as possible.

7. Convince a system programmer to change the system to skip certain vital security checks for any user with your login name. This attack is known as a **trapdoor**.

8. All else failing, the penetrator might find the computer center director's secretary and offer a large bribe. The secretary probably has easy access to all kinds of wonderful information, and is usually poorly paid. Do not underestimate problems caused by personnel.

These and other attacks are discussed by Linde (1975). Many other sources of information on security and testing security can be found, especially on the Web. A recent Windows-oriented work is Johansson and Riley (2005).

5.4.3 Design Principles for Security

Saltzer and Schroeder (1975) have identified several general principles that can be used as a guide to designing secure systems. A brief summary of their ideas (based on experience with MULTICS) is given below.

First, the system design should be public. Assuming that the intruder will not know how the system works serves only to delude the designers.

Second, the default should be no access. Errors in which legitimate access is refused will be reported much faster than errors in which unauthorized access is allowed.

Third, check for current authority. The system should not check for permission, determine that access is permitted, and then squirrel away this information for subsequent use. Many systems check for permission when a file is opened, and not afterward. This means that a user who opens a file, and keeps it open for weeks, will continue to have access, even if the owner has long since changed the file protection.

Fourth, give each process the least privilege possible. If an editor has only the authority to access the file to be edited (specified when the editor is invoked), editors with Trojan horses will not be able to do much damage. This principle implies a fine-grained protection scheme. We will discuss such schemes later in this chapter.

Fifth, the protection mechanism should be simple, uniform, and built into the lowest layers of the system. Trying to retrofit security to an existing insecure system is nearly impossible. Security, like correctness, is not an add-on feature.

Sixth, the scheme chosen must be psychologically acceptable. If users feel that protecting their files is too much work, they just will not do it. Nevertheless, they will complain loudly if something goes wrong. Replies of the form "It is your own fault" will generally not be well received.

5.4.4 User Authentication

Many protection schemes are based on the assumption that the system knows the identity of each user. The problem of identifying users when they log in is called **user authentication**. Most authentication methods are based on identifying something the user knows, something the user has, or something the user is.

Passwords

The most widely used form of authentication is to require the user to type a password. Password protection is easy to understand and easy to implement. In UNIX it works like this: The login program asks the user to type his name and password. The password is immediately encrypted. The login program then reads the password file, which is a series of ASCII lines, one per user, until it finds the line containing the user's login name. If the (encrypted) password contained in this line matches the encrypted password just computed, the login is permitted, otherwise it is refused.

Password authentication is easy to defeat. One frequently reads about groups of high school, or even junior high school students who, with the aid of their trusty home computers, have broken into some top secret system owned by a large corporation or government agency. Virtually all the time the break-in consists of guessing a user name and password combination.

Although more recent studies have been made (e.g., Klein, 1990) the classic work on password security remains the one done by Morris and Thompson (1979) on UNIX systems. They compiled a list of likely passwords: first and last names, street names, city names, words from a moderate-sized dictionary (also words spelled backward), license plate numbers, and short strings of random characters.

They then encrypted each of these using the known password encryption algorithm and checked to see if any of the encrypted passwords matched entries in their list. Over 86 percent of all passwords turned up in their list.

If all passwords consisted of 7 characters chosen at random from the 95 printable ASCII characters, the search space becomes 95^7, which is about 7×10^{13}. At 1000 encryptions per second, it would take 2000 years to build the list to check the password file against. Furthermore, the list would fill 20 million magnetic tapes. Even requiring passwords to contain at least one lowercase character, one uppercase character, and one special character, and be at least seven characters long would be a major improvement over unrestricted user-chosen passwords.

Even if it is considered politically impossible to require users to pick reasonable passwords, Morris and Thompson have described a technique that renders their own attack (encrypting a large number of passwords in advance) almost useless. Their idea is to associate an n-bit random number with each password. The random number is changed whenever the password is changed. The random number is stored in the password file in unencrypted form, so that everyone can read it. Instead of just storing the encrypted password in the password file, the password and the random number are first concatenated and then encrypted together. This encrypted result is stored in the password file.

Now consider the implications for an intruder who wants to build up a list of likely passwords, encrypt them, and save the results in a sorted file, f, so that any encrypted password can be looked up easily. If an intruder suspects that *Marilyn* might be a password, it is no longer sufficient just to encrypt *Marilyn* and put the result in f. He has to encrypt 2^n strings, such as *Marilyn0000, Marilyn0001, Marilyn0002*, and so forth and enter all of them in f. This technique increases the size of f by 2^n. UNIX uses this method with $n = 12$. It is known as **salting** the password file. Some versions of UNIX make the password file itself unreadable but provide a program to look up entries upon request, adding just enough delay to greatly slow down any attacker.

Although this method offers protection against intruders who try to precompute a large list of encrypted passwords, it does little to protect a user *David* whose password is also *David*. One way to encourage people to pick better passwords is to have the computer offer advice. Some computers have a program that generates random easy-to-pronounce nonsense words, such as *fotally*, *garbungy*, or *bipitty* that can be used as passwords (preferably with some upper case and special characters thrown in).

Other computers require users to change their passwords regularly, to limit the damage done if a password leaks out. The most extreme form of this approach is the **one-time password**. When one-time passwords are used, the user gets a book containing a list of passwords. Each login uses the next password in the list. If an intruder ever discovers a password, it will not do him any good, since next time a different password must be used. It is suggested that the user try to avoid losing the password book.

It goes almost without saying that while a password is being typed in, the computer should not display the typed characters, to keep them from prying eyes near the terminal. What is less obvious is that passwords should never be stored in the computer in unencrypted form. Furthermore, not even the computer center management should have unencrypted copies. Keeping unencrypted passwords anywhere is looking for trouble.

A variation on the password idea is to have each new user provide a long list of questions and answers that are then stored in the computer in encrypted form. The questions should be chosen so that the user does not need to write them down. In other words, they should be things no one forgets. Typical questions are:

1. Who is Marjolein's sister?

2. On what street was your elementary school?

3. What did Mrs. Woroboff teach?

At login, the computer asks one of them at random and checks the answer.

Another variation is **challenge-response**. When this is used, the user picks an algorithm when signing up as a user, for example x^2. When the user logs in, the computer types an argument, say 7, in which case the user types 49. The algorithm can be different in the morning and afternoon, on different days of the week, from different terminals, and so on.

Physical Identification

A completely different approach to authorization is to check to see if the user has some item, normally a plastic card with a magnetic stripe on it. The card is inserted into the terminal, which then checks to see whose card it is. This method can be combined with a password, so a user can only log in if he (1) has the card and (2) knows the password. Automated cash-dispensing machines usually work this way.

Yet another approach is to measure physical characteristics that are hard to forge. For example, a fingerprint or a voiceprint reader in the terminal could verify the user's identity. (It makes the search go faster if the user tells the computer who he is, rather than making the computer compare the given fingerprint to the entire data base.) Direct visual recognition is not yet feasible but may be one day.

Another technique is signature analysis. The user signs his name with a special pen connected to the terminal, and the computer compares it to a known specimen stored on line. Even better is not to compare the signature, but compare the pen motions made while writing it. A good forger may be able to copy the signature, but will not have a clue as to the exact order in which the strokes were made.

Finger length analysis is surprisingly practical. When this is used, each terminal has a device like the one of Fig. 5-23. The user inserts his hand into it, and the length of each of his fingers is measured and checked against the data base.

We could go on and on with more examples, but two more will help make an important point. Cats and other animals mark off their territory by urinating around its perimeter. Apparently cats can identify each other this way. Suppose that someone comes up with a tiny device capable of doing an instant urinalysis, thereby providing a foolproof identification. Each terminal could be equipped with one of these devices, along with a discreet sign reading: "For login, please deposit sample here." This might be an absolutely unbreakable system, but it would probably have a fairly serious user acceptance problem.

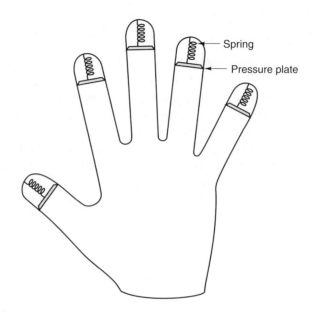

Figure 5-23. A device for measuring finger length.

The same could be said of a system consisting of a thumbtack and a small spectrograph. The user would be requested to jab his thumb against the thumbtack, thus extracting a drop of blood for spectrographic analysis. The point is that any authentication scheme must be psychologically acceptable to the user community. Finger-length measurements probably will not cause any problem, but even something as nonintrusive as storing fingerprints on line may be unacceptable to many people.

Countermeasures

Computer installations that are really serious about security—and few are until the day after an intruder has broken in and done major damage—often take steps to make unauthorized entry much harder. For example, each user could be allowed to log in only from a specific terminal, and only during certain days of the week and hours of the day.

Dial-up telephone lines could be made to work as follows. Anyone can dial up and log in, but after a successful login, the system immediately breaks the connection and calls the user back at an agreed upon number. This measure means than an intruder cannot just try breaking in from any phone line; only the user's (home) phone will do. In any event, with or without call back, the system should take at least 10 seconds to check any password typed in on a dial-up line, and should increase this time after several consecutive unsuccessful login attempts, in order to reduce the rate at which intruders can try. After three failed login attempts, the line should be disconnected for 10 minutes and security personnel notified.

All logins should be recorded. When a user logs in, the system should report the time and terminal of the previous login, so he can detect possible break ins.

The next step up is laying baited traps to catch intruders. A simple scheme is to have one special login name with an easy password (e.g., login name: guest, password: guest). Whenever anyone logs in using this name, the system security specialists are immediately notified. Other traps can be easy-to-find bugs in the operating system and similar things, designed for the purpose of catching intruders in the act. Stoll (1989) has written an entertaining account of the traps he set to track down a spy who broke into a university computer in search of military secrets.

5.5 PROTECTION MECHANISMS

In the previous sections we have looked at many potential problems, some of them technical, some of them not. In the following sections we will concentrate on some of the detailed technical ways that are used in operating systems to protect files and other things. All of these techniques make a clear distinction between policy (whose data are to be protected from whom) and mechanism (how the system enforces the policy). The separation of policy and mechanism is discussed by Sandhu (1993). Our emphasis will be on mechanisms, not policies.

In some systems, protection is enforced by a program called a **reference monitor**. Every time an access to a potentially protected resource is attempted, the system first asks the reference monitor to check its legality. The reference monitor then looks at its policy tables and makes a decision. Below we will describe the environment in which a reference monitor operates.

5.5.1 Protection Domains

A computer system contains many "objects" that need to be protected. These objects can be hardware (e.g., CPUs, memory segments, disk drives, or printers), or they can be software (e.g., processes, files, databases, or semaphores).

Each object has a unique name by which it is referenced, and a finite set of operations that processes are allowed to carry out on it. The read and write operations are appropriate to a file; up and down make sense on a semaphore.

It is obvious that a way is needed to prohibit processes from accessing objects that they are not authorized to access. Furthermore, this mechanism must also make it possible to restrict processes to a subset of the legal operations when that is needed. For example, process A may be entitled to read, but not write, file F.

In order to discuss different protection mechanisms, it is useful to introduce the concept of a domain. A **domain** is a set of (object, rights) pairs. Each pair specifies an object and some subset of the operations that can be performed on it. A **right** in this context means permission to perform one of the operations. Often a domain corresponds to a single user, telling what the user can do and not do, but a domain can also be more general than just one user.

Figure 5-24 shows three domains, showing the objects in each domain and the rights [Read, Write, eXecute] available on each object. Note that *Printer1* is in two domains at the same time. Although not shown in this example, it is possible for the same object to be in multiple domains, with *different* rights in each one.

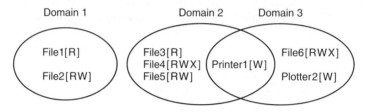

Figure 5-24. Three protection domains.

At every instant of time, each process runs in some protection domain. In other words, there is some collection of objects it can access, and for each object it has some set of rights. Processes can also switch from domain to domain during execution. The rules for domain switching are highly system dependent.

To make the idea of a protection domain more concrete, let us look at UNIX. In UNIX, the domain of a process is defined by its UID and GID. Given any (UID, GID) combination, it is possible to make a complete list of all objects (files, including I/O devices represented by special files, etc.) that can be accessed, and whether they can be accessed for reading, writing, or executing. Two processes with the same (UID, GID) combination will have access to exactly the same set of objects. Processes with different (UID, GID) values will have access to a different set of files, although there may be considerable overlap in most cases.

Furthermore, each process in UNIX has two halves: the user part and the kernel part. When the process does a system call, it switches from the user part to the kernel part. The kernel part has access to a different set of objects from the user part. For example, the kernel can access all the pages in physical memory, the entire disk, and all the other protected resources. Thus, a system call causes a domain switch.

When a process does an **exec** on a file with the SETUID or SETGID bit on, it acquires a new effective UID or GID. With a different (UID, GID) combination, it has a different set of files and operations available. Running a program with SETUID or SETGID is also a domain switch, since the rights available change.

An important question is how the system keeps track of which object belongs to which domain. Conceptually, at least, one can envision a large matrix, with the rows being domains and the columns being objects. Each box lists the rights, if any, that the domain contains for the object. The matrix for Fig. 5-24 is shown in Fig. 5-25. Given this matrix and the current domain number, the system can tell if an access to a given object in a particular way from a specified domain is allowed.

	File1	File2	File3	File4	File5	File6	Printer1	Plotter2
Domain 1	Read	Read Write						
2			Read	Read Write Execute	Read Write		Write	
3						Read Write Execute	Write	Write

Figure 5-25. A protection matrix.

Domain switching itself can be easily included in the matrix model by realizing that a domain is itself an object, with the operation enter. Figure 5-26 shows the matrix of Fig. 5-25 again, only now with the three domains as objects themselves. Processes in domain 1 can switch to domain 2, but once there, they cannot go back. This situation models executing a SETUID program in UNIX. No other domain switches are permitted in this example.

	File1	File2	File3	File4	File5	File6	Printer1	Plotter2	Domain1	Domain2	Domain3
Domain 1	Read	Read Write								Enter	
2			Read	Read Write Execute	Read Write		Write				
3						Read Write Execute	Write	Write			

Figure 5-26. A protection matrix with domains as objects.

5.5.2 Access Control Lists

In practice, actually storing the matrix of Fig. 5-26 is rarely done because it is large and sparse. Most domains have no access at all to most objects, so storing a very large, mostly empty, matrix is a waste of disk space. Two methods that are practical, however, are storing the matrix by rows or by columns, and then storing only the nonempty elements. The two approaches are surprisingly different. In this section we will look at storing it by column; in the next one we will study storing it by row.

The first technique consists of associating with each object an (ordered) list containing all the domains that may access the object, and how. This list is called the **Access Control List** or **ACL** and is illustrated in Fig. 5-27. Here we see three processes, each belonging to a different domain. A, B, and C, and three files *F1*, *F2*, and *F3*. For simplicity, we will assume that each domain corresponds to exactly one user, in this case, users A, B, and C. Often in the security literature, the users are called **subjects** or **principals**, to contrast them with the things owned, the **objects**, such as files.

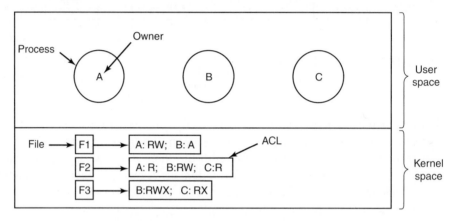

Figure 5-27. Use of access control lists to manage file access.

Each file has an ACL associated with it. File *F1* has two entries in its ACL (separated by a semicolon). The first entry says that any process owned by user *A* may read and write the file. The second entry says that any process owned by user *B* may read the file. All other accesses by these users and all accesses by other users are forbidden. Note that the rights are granted by user, not by process. As far as the protection system goes, any process owned by user *A* can read and write file *F1*. It does not matter if there is one such process or 100 of them. It is the owner, not the process ID, that matters.

File *F2* has three entries in its ACL: *A*, *B*, and *C* can all read the file, and in addition *B* can also write it. No other accesses are allowed. File *F3* is apparently an executable program, since *B* and *C* can both read and execute it. *B* can also write it.

This example illustrates the most basic form of protection with ACLs. More sophisticated systems are often used in practice. To start with, we have only shown three rights so far: read, write, and execute. There may be additional rights as well. Some of these may be generic, that is, apply to all objects, and some may be object specific. Examples of generic rights are destroy object and copy object.

These could hold for any object, no matter what type it is. Object-specific rights might include append message for a mailbox object and sort alphabetically for a directory object.

So far, our ACL entries have been for individual users. Many systems support the concept of a **group** of users. Groups have names and can be included in ACLs. Two variations on the semantics of groups are possible. In some systems, each process has a user ID (UID) and group ID (GID). In such systems, an ACL entry contains entries of the form

UID1, GID1: rights1; UID2, GID2: rights2; ...

Under these conditions, when a request is made to access an object, a check is made using the caller's UID and GID. If they are present in the ACL, the rights listed are available. If the (UID, GID) combination is not in the list, the access is not permitted.

Using groups this way effectively introduces the concept of a **role**. Consider an installation in which Tana is system administrator, and thus in the group *sysadm*. However, suppose that the company also has some clubs for employees and Tana is a member of the pigeon fanciers club. Club members belong to the group *pigfan* and have access to the company's computers for managing their pigeon database. A portion of the ACL might be as shown in Fig. 5-28.

File	Access control list
Password	tana, sysadm: RW
Pigeon_data	bill, pigfan: RW; tana, pigfan: RW; ...

Figure 5-28. Two access control lists.

If Tana tries to access one of these files, the result depends on which group she is currently logged in as. When she logs in, the system may ask her to choose which of her groups she is currently using, or there might even be different login names and/or passwords to keep them separate. The point of this scheme is to prevent Tana from accessing the password file when she currently has her pigeon fancier's hat on. She can only do that when logged in as the system administrator.

In some cases, a user may have access to certain files independent of which group she is currently logged in as. That case can be handled by introducing **wildcards**, which mean everyone. For example, the entry

tana, *: RW

for the password file would give Tana access no matter which group she was currently in as.

Yet another possibility is that if a user belongs to any of the groups that have certain access rights, the access is permitted. In this case, a user belonging to multiple groups does not have to specify which group to use at login time. All of them count all of the time. A disadvantage of this approach is that it provides less encapsulation: Tana can edit the password file during a pigeon club meeting.

The use of groups and wildcards introduces the possibility of selectively blocking a specific user from accessing a file. For example, the entry

virgil, *: (none); *, *: RW

gives the entire world except for Virgil read and write access to the file. This works because the entries are scanned in order, and the first one that applies is taken; subsequent entries are not even examined. A match is found for Virgil on the first entry and the access rights, in this case, (none) are found and applied. The search is terminated at that point. The fact that the rest of the world has access is never even seen.

The other way of dealing with groups is not to have ACL entries consist of (UID, GID) pairs, but to have each entry be a UID or a GID. For example, an entry for the file *pigeon_data* could be

debbie: RW; phil: RW; pigfan: RW

meaning that Debbie and Phil, and all members of the *pigfan* group have read and write access to the file.

It sometimes occurs that a user or a group has certain permissions with respect to a file that the file owner later wishes to revoke. With access control lists, it is relatively straightforward to revoke a previously granted access. All that has to be done is edit the ACL to make the change. However, if the ACL is checked only when a file is opened, most likely the change will only take effect on future calls to open. Any file that is already open will continue to have the rights it had when it was opened, even if the user is no longer authorized to access the file at all.

5.5.3 Capabilities

The other way of slicing up the matrix of Fig. 5-26 is by rows. When this method is used, associated with each process is a list of objects that may be accessed, along with an indication of which operations are permitted on each, in other words, its domain. This list is called a **capability list** or **C-list** and the individual items on it are called **capabilities** (Dennis and Van Horn, 1966; Fabry, 1974). A set of three processes and their capability lists is shown in Fig. 5-29.

Each capability grants the owner certain rights on a certain object. In Fig. 5-29, the process owned by user *A* can read files *F1* and *F2*, for example. Usually, a capability consists of a file (or more generally, an object) identifier and a bitmap for the various rights. In a UNIX-like system, the file identifier would probably be the i-node number. Capability lists are themselves objects and may be pointed to from other capability lists, thus facilitating sharing of subdomains.

It is fairly obvious that capability lists must be protected from user tampering. Three methods of protecting them are known. The first way requires a **tagged**

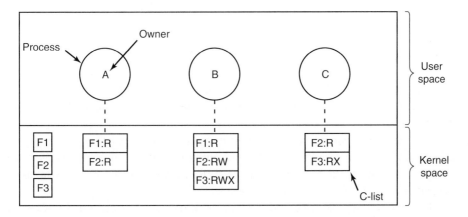

Figure 5-29. When capabilities are used, each process has a capability list.

architecture, a hardware design in which each memory word has an extra (or tag) bit that tells whether the word contains a capability or not. The tag bit is not used by arithmetic, comparison, or similar ordinary instructions, and it can be modified only by programs running in kernel mode (i.e., the operating system). Tagged-architecture machines have been built and can be made to work well (Feustal, 1972). The IBM AS/400 is a popular example.

The second way is to keep the C-list inside the operating system. Capabilities are then referred to by their position in the capability list. A process might say: "Read 1 KB from the file pointed to by capability 2." This form of addressing is similar to using file descriptors in UNIX. Hydra worked this way (Wulf et al., 1974).

The third way is to keep the C-list in user space, but manage the capabilities cryptographically so that users cannot tamper with them. This approach is particularly suited to distributed systems and works as follows. When a client process sends a message to a remote server, for example, a file server, to create an object for it, the server creates the object and generates a long random number, the check field, to go with it. A slot in the server's file table is reserved for the object and the check field is stored there along with the addresses of the disk blocks, etc. In UNIX terms, the check field is stored on the server in the i-node. It is not sent back to the user and never put on the network. The server then generates and returns a capability to the user of the form shown in Fig. 5-30.

Figure 5-30. A cryptographically-protected capability.

The capability returned to the user contains the server's identifier, the object number (the index into the server's tables, essentially, the i-node number), and the rights, stored as a bitmap. For a newly created object, all the rights bits are turned on. The last field consists of the concatenation of the object, rights, and check field run through a cryptographically-secure one-way function, f, of the kind we discussed earlier.

When the user wishes to access the object, it sends the capability to the server as part of the request. The server then extracts the object number to index into its tables to find the object. It then computes $f(Object, Rights, Check)$ taking the first two parameters from the capability itself and the third one from its own tables. If the result agrees with the fourth field in the capability, the request is honored; otherwise, it is rejected. If a user tries to access someone else's object, he will not be able to fabricate the fourth field correctly since he does not know the check field, and the request will be rejected.

A user can ask the server to produce and return a weaker capability, for example, for read-only access. First the server verifies that the capability is valid. If so, if computes $f(Object, New\_rights, Check)$ and generates a new capability putting this value in the fourth field. Note that the original $Check$ value is used because other outstanding capabilities depend on it.

This new capability is sent back to the requesting process. The user can now give this to a friend by just sending it in a message. If the friend turns on rights bits that should be off, the server will detect this when the capability is used since the f value will not correspond to the false rights field. Since the friend does not know the true check field, he cannot fabricate a capability that corresponds to the false rights bits. This scheme was developed for the Amoeba system and used extensively there (Tanenbaum et al., 1990).

In addition to the specific object-dependent rights, such as read and execute, capabilities (both kernel and cryptographically-protected) usually have **generic rights** which are applicable to all objects. Examples of generic rights are

1. Copy capability: create a new capability for the same object.

2. Copy object: create a duplicate object with a new capability.

3. Remove capability: delete an entry from the C-list; object unaffected.

4. Destroy object: permanently remove an object and a capability.

A last remark worth making about capability systems is that revoking access to an object is quite difficult in the kernel-managed version. It is hard for the system to find all the outstanding capabilities for any object to take them back, since they may be stored in C-lists all over the disk. One approach is to have each capability point to an indirect object, rather than to the object itself. By having the indirect object point to the real object, the system can always break that connection, thus invalidating the capabilities. (When a capability to the indirect object is later presented to the system, the user will discover that the indirect object is now pointing to a null object.)

In the Amoeba scheme, revocation is easy. All that needs to be done is change the check field stored with the object. In one blow, all existing capabilities are invalidated. However, neither scheme allows selective revocation, that is, taking back, say, John's permission, but nobody else's. This defect is generally recognized to be a problem with all capability systems.

Another general problem is making sure the owner of a valid capability does not give a copy to 1000 of his best friends. Having the kernel manage capabilities, as in Hydra, solves this problem, but this solution does not work well in a distributed system such as Amoeba.

On the other hand, capabilities solve the problem of sandboxing mobile code very elegantly. When a foreign program is started, it is given a capability list containing only those capabilities that the machine owner wants to give it, such as the ability to write on the screen and the ability to read and write files in one scratch directory just created for it. If the mobile code is put into its own process with only these limited capabilities, it will not be able to access any other system resources and thus be effectively confined to a sandbox without the need to modify its code or run it interpretively. Running code with as few access rights as possible is known as the **principle of least privilege** and is a powerful guideline for producing secure systems.

Briefly summarized, ACLs and capabilities have somewhat complementary properties. Capabilities are very efficient because if a process says "Open the file pointed to by capability 3," no checking is needed. With ACLs, a (potentially long) search of the ACL may be needed. If groups are not supported, then granting everyone read access to a file requires enumerating all users in the ACL. Capabilities also allow a process to be encapsulated easily, whereas ACLs do not. On the other hand, ACLs allow selective revocation of rights, which capabilities do not. Finally, if an object is removed and the capabilities are not or the capabilities are removed and an object is not, problems arise. ACLs do not suffer from this problem.

5.5.4 Covert Channels

Even with access control lists and capabilities, security leaks can still occur. In this section we discuss how information can still leak out even when it has been rigorously proven that such leakage is mathematically impossible. These ideas are due to Lampson (1973).

Lampson's model was originally formulated in terms of a single timesharing system, but the same ideas can be adapted to LANs and other multiuser environments. In the purest form, it involves three processes on some protected machine. The first process is the client, which wants some work performed by the second one, the server. The client and the server do not entirely trust each other. For example, the server's job is to help clients with filling out their tax forms. The clients are worried that the server will secretly record their financial data, for example, maintaining a secret list of who earns how much, and then selling the list. The server is worried that the clients will try to steal the valuable tax program.

The third process is the collaborator, which is conspiring with the server to indeed steal the client's confidential data. The collaborator and server are typically owned by the same person. These three processes are shown in Fig. 5-31. The object of this exercise is to design a system in which it is impossible for the server process to leak to the collaborator process the information that it has legitimately received from the client process. Lampson called this the **confinement problem**.

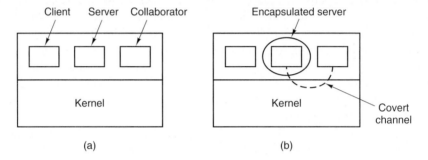

Figure 5-31. (a) The client, server, and collaborator processes. (b) The encapsulated server can still leak to the collaborator via covert channels.

From the system designer's point of view, the goal is to encapsulate or confine the server in such a way that it cannot pass information to the collaborator. Using a protection matrix scheme we can easily guarantee that the server cannot communicate with the collaborator by writing a file to which the collaborator has read access. We can probably also ensure that the server cannot communicate with the collaborator using the system's normal interprocess communication mechanism.

Unfortunately, more subtle communication channels may be available. For example, the server can try to communicate a binary bit stream as follows: To send a 1 bit, it computes as hard as it can for a fixed interval of time. To send a 0 bit, it goes to sleep for the same length of time.

The collaborator can try to detect the bit stream by carefully monitoring its response time. In general, it will get better response when the server is sending a 0 than when the server is sending a 1. This communication channel is known as a **covert channel**, and is illustrated in Fig. 5-31(b).

Of course, the covert channel is a noisy channel, containing a lot of extraneous information, but information can be reliably sent over a noisy channel by using an error-correcting code (e.g., a Hamming code, or even something more sophisticated). The use of an error-correcting code reduces the already low bandwidth of the covert channel even more, but it still may be enough to leak substantial information. It is fairly obvious that no protection model based on a matrix of objects and domains is going to prevent this kind of leakage.

Modulating the CPU usage is not the only covert channel. The paging rate can also be modulated (many page faults for a 1, no page faults for a 0). In fact, almost any way of degrading system performance in a clocked way is a candidate. If the system provides a way of locking files, then the server can lock some file to indicate a 1, and unlock it to indicate a 0. On some systems, it may be possible for a process to detect the status of a lock even on a file that it cannot access. This covert channel is illustrated in Fig. 5-32, with the file locked or unlocked for some fixed time interval known to both the server and collaborator. In this example, the secret bit stream 11010100 is being transmitted.

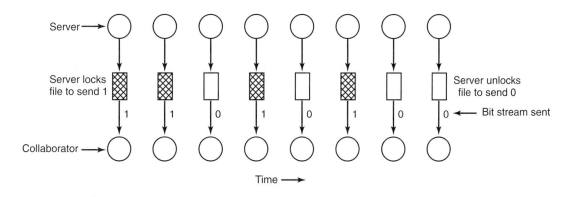

Figure 5-32. A covert channel using file locking.

Locking and unlocking a prearranged file, S is not an especially noisy channel, but it does require fairly accurate timing unless the bit rate is very low. The reliability and performance can be increased even more using an acknowledgement protocol. This protocol uses two more files, $F1$ and $F2$, locked by the server and collaborator, respectively to keep the two processes synchronized. After the server locks or unlocks S, it flips the lock status of $F1$ to indicate that a bit has been sent. As soon as the collaborator has read out the bit, it flips $F2$'s lock status to tell the server it is ready for another bit and waits until $F1$ is flipped again to indicate that another bit is present in S. Since timing is no longer involved, this protocol is fully reliable, even in a busy system and can proceed as fast as the two processes can get scheduled. To get higher bandwidth, why not use two files per bit time, or make it a byte-wide channel with eight signaling files, $S0$ through $S7$.

Acquiring and releasing dedicated resources (tape drives, plotters, etc.) can also be used for signaling. The server acquires the resource to send a 1 and releases it to send a 0. In UNIX, the server could create a file to indicate a 1 and remove it to indicate a 0; the collaborator could use the access system call to see if the file exists. This call works even though the collaborator has no permission to use the file. Unfortunately, many other covert channels exist.

Lampson also mentioned a way of leaking information to the (human) owner of the server process. Presumably the server process will be entitled to tell its owner how much work it did on behalf of the client, so the client can be billed. If the actual computing bill is, say, $100 and the client's income is $53,000 dollars, the server could report the bill as $100.53 to its owner.

Just finding all the covert channels, let alone blocking them, is extremely difficult. In practice, there is little that can be done. Introducing a process that causes page faults at random, or otherwise spends its time degrading system performance in order to reduce the bandwidth of the covert channels is not an attractive proposition.

5.6 OVERVIEW OF THE MINIX 3 FILE SYSTEM

Like any file system, the MINIX 3 file system must deal with all the issues we have just studied. It must allocate and deallocate space for files, keep track of disk blocks and free space, provide some way to protect files against unauthorized usage, and so on. In the remainder of this chapter we will look closely at MINIX 3 to see how it accomplishes these goals.

In the first part of this chapter, we have repeatedly referred to UNIX rather than to MINIX 3 for the sake of generality, although the external interfaces of the two is virtually identical. Now we will concentrate on the internal design of MINIX 3. For information about the UNIX internals, see Thompson (1978), Bach (1987), Lions (1996), and Vahalia (1996).

The MINIX 3 file system is just a big C program that runs in user space (see Fig. 2-29). To read and write files, user processes send messages to the file system telling what they want done. The file system does the work and then sends back a reply. The file system is, in fact, a network file server that happens to be running on the same machine as the caller.

This design has some important implications. For one thing, the file system can be modified, experimented with, and tested almost completely independently of the rest of MINIX 3. For another, it is very easy to move the file system to any computer that has a C compiler, compile it there, and use it as a free-standing UNIX-like remote file server. The only changes that need to be made are in the area of how messages are sent and received, which differs from system to system.

In the following sections, we will present an overview of many of the key areas of the file system design. Specifically, we will look at messages, the file system layout, the bitmaps, i-nodes, the block cache, directories and paths, file descriptors, file locking, and special files (plus pipes). After studying these topics, we will show a simple example of how the pieces fit together by tracing what happens when a user process executes the read system call.

Messages from users	Input parameters	Reply value
access	File name, access mode	Status
chdir	Name of new working directory	Status
chmod	File name, new mode	Status
chown	File name, new owner, group	Status
chroot	Name of new root directory	Status
close	File descriptor of file to close	Status
creat	Name of file to be created, mode	File descriptor
dup	File descriptor (for dup2, two fds)	New file descriptor
fcntl	File descriptor, function code, arg	Depends on function
fstat	Name of file, buffer	Status
ioctl	File descriptor, function code, arg	Status
link	Name of file to link to, name of link	Status
lseek	File descriptor, offset, whence	New position
mkdir	File name, mode	Status
mknod	Name of dir or special, mode, address	Status
mount	Special file, where to mount, ro flag	Status
open	Name of file to open, r/w flag	File descriptor
pipe	Pointer to 2 file descriptors (modified)	Status
read	File descriptor, buffer, how many bytes	# Bytes read
rename	File name, file name	Status
rmdir	File name	Status
stat	File name, status buffer	Status
stime	Pointer to current time	Status
sync	(None)	Always OK
time	Pointer to place where current time goes	Status
times	Pointer to buffer for process and child times	Status
umask	Complement of mode mask	Always OK
umount	Name of special file to unmount	Status
unlink	Name of file to unlink	Status
utime	File name, file times	Always OK
write	File descriptor, buffer, how many bytes	# Bytes written
Messages from PM	**Input parameters**	**Reply value**
exec	Pid	Status
exit	Pid	Status
fork	Parent pid, child pid	Status
setgid	Pid, real and effective gid	Status
setsid	Pid	Status
setuid	Pid, real and effective uid	Status
Other messages	**Input parameters**	**Reply value**
revive	Process to revive	(No reply)
unpause	Process to check	(See text)

Figure 5-33. File system messages. File name parameters are always pointers to the name. The code status as reply value means *OK* or *ERROR*.

5.6.1 Messages

The file system accepts 39 types of messages requesting work. All but two are for MINIX 3 system calls. The two exceptions are messages generated by other parts of MINIX 3. Of the system calls, 31 are accepted from user processes. Six system call messages are for system calls which are handled first by the process manager, which then calls the file system to do a part of the work. Two other messages are also handled by the file system. The messages are shown in Fig. 5-33.

The structure of the file system is basically the same as that of the process manager and all the I/O device drivers. It has a main loop that waits for a message to arrive. When a message arrives, its type is extracted and used as an index into a table containing pointers to the procedures within the file system that handle all the types. Then the appropriate procedure is called, it does its work and returns a status value. The file system then sends a reply back to the caller and goes back to the top of the loop to wait for the next message.

5.6.2 File System Layout

A MINIX 3 file system is a logical, self-contained entity with i-nodes, directories, and data blocks. It can be stored on any block device, such as a floppy disk or a hard disk partition. In all cases, the layout of the file system has the same structure. Figure 5-34 shows this layout for a floppy disk or a small hard disk partition with 64 i-nodes and a 1-KB block size. In this simple example, the zone bitmap is just one 1-KB block, so it can keep track of no more than 8192 1-KB zones (blocks), thus limiting the file system to 8 MB. Even for a floppy disk, only 64 i-nodes puts a severe limit on the number of files, so rather than the four blocks reserved for i-nodes in the figure, more would probably be used. Reserving eight blocks for i-nodes would be more practical but our diagram would not look as nice. For a modern hard disk, both the i-node and zone bitmaps will be much larger than 1 block, of course. The relative size of the various components in Fig. 5-34 may vary from file system to file system, depending on their sizes, how many files are allowed maximum, and so on. But all the components are always present and in the same order.

Each file system begins with a **boot block**. This contains executable code. The size of a boot block is always 1024 bytes (two disk sectors), even though MINIX 3 may (and by default does) use a larger block size elsewhere. When the computer is turned on, the hardware reads the boot block from the boot device into memory, jumps to it, and begins executing its code. The boot block code begins the process of loading the operating system itself. Once the system has been booted, the boot block is not used any more. Not every disk drive can be used as a boot device, but to keep the structure uniform, every block device has a block reserved for boot block code. At worst this strategy wastes one block. To prevent the hardware from trying to boot an unbootable device, a **magic number**

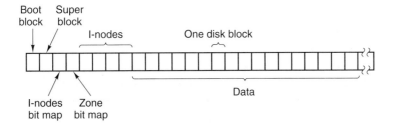

Figure 5-34. Disk layout for a floppy disk or small hard disk partition, with 64 i-nodes and a 1-KB block size (i.e., two consecutive 512-byte sectors are treated as a single block).

is placed at a known location in the boot block when and only when the executable code is written to the device. When booting from a device, the hardware (actually, the BIOS code) will refuse to attempt to load from a device lacking the magic number. Doing this prevents inadvertently using garbage as a boot program.

The **superblock** contains information describing the layout of the file system. Like the boot block, the superblock is always 1024 bytes, regardless of the block size used for the rest of the file system. It is illustrated in Fig. 5-35.

The main function of the superblock is to tell the file system how big the various pieces of the file system are. Given the block size and the number of i-nodes, it is easy to calculate the size of the i-node bitmap and the number of blocks of i-nodes. For example, for a 1-KB block, each block of the bitmap has 1024 bytes (8192 bits), and thus can keep track of the status of up to 8192 i-nodes. (Actually the first block can handle only up to 8191 i-nodes, since there is no 0th i-node, but it is given a bit in the bitmap, anyway). For 10,000 i-nodes, two bitmap blocks are needed. Since i-nodes each occupy 64 bytes, a 1-KB block holds up to 16 i-nodes. With 64 i-nodes, four disk blocks are needed to contain them all.

We will explain the difference between zones and blocks in detail later, but for the time being it is sufficient to say that disk storage can be allocated in units (zones) of 1, 2, 4, 8, or in general 2^n blocks. The zone bitmap keeps track of free storage in zones, not blocks. For all standard disks used by MINIX 3 the zone and block sizes are the same (4 KB by default), so to a first approximation a zone is the same as a block on these devices. Until we come to the details of storage allocation later in the chapter, it is adequate to think "block" whenever you see "zone."

Note that the number of blocks per zone is not stored in the superblock, as it is never needed. All that is needed is the base 2 logarithm of the zone to block ratio, which is used as the shift count to convert zones to blocks and vice versa. For example, with 8 blocks per zone, $\log_2 8 = 3$, so to find the zone containing block 128 we shift 128 right 3 bits to get zone 16.

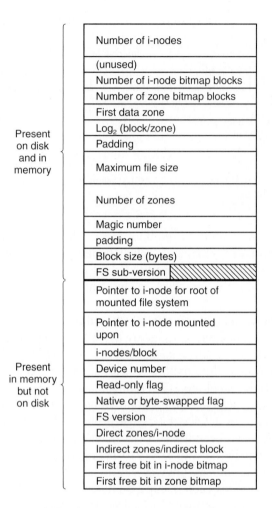

Present on disk and in memory

- Number of i-nodes
- (unused)
- Number of i-node bitmap blocks
- Number of zone bitmap blocks
- First data zone
- Log_2 (block/zone)
- Padding
- Maximum file size
- Number of zones
- Magic number
- padding
- Block size (bytes)
- FS sub-version

Present in memory but not on disk

- Pointer to i-node for root of mounted file system
- Pointer to i-node mounted upon
- i-nodes/block
- Device number
- Read-only flag
- Native or byte-swapped flag
- FS version
- Direct zones/i-node
- Indirect zones/indirect block
- First free bit in i-node bitmap
- First free bit in zone bitmap

Figure 5-35. The MINIX 3 superblock.

The zone bitmap includes only the data zones (i.e., the blocks used for the bitmaps and i-nodes are not in the map), with the first data zone designated zone 1 in the bitmap. As with the i-node bitmap, bit 0 in the map is unused, so the first block in the zone bitmap can map 8191 zones and subsequent blocks can map 8192 zones each. If you examine the bitmaps on a newly formatted disk, you will find that both the i-node and zone bitmaps have 2 bits set to 1. One is for the nonexistent 0th i-node or zone; the other is for the i-node and zone used by the root directory on the device, which is placed there when the file system is created.

The information in the superblock is redundant because sometimes it is needed in one form and sometimes in another. With 1 KB devoted to the superblock, it makes sense to compute this information in all the forms it is needed, rather than having to recompute it frequently during execution. The zone number of the first data zone on the disk, for example, can be calculated from the block size, zone size, number of i-nodes, and number of zones, but it is faster just to keep it in the superblock. The rest of the superblock is wasted anyhow, so using up another word of it costs nothing.

When MINIX 3 is booted, the superblock for the root device is read into a table in memory. Similarly, as other file systems are mounted, their superblocks are also brought into memory. The superblock table holds a number of fields not present on the disk. These include flags that allow a device to be specified as read-only or as following a byte-order convention opposite to the standard, and fields to speed access by indicating points in the bitmaps below which all bits are marked used. In addition, there is a field describing the device from which the superblock came.

Before a disk can be used as a MINIX 3 file system, it must be given the structure of Fig. 5-34. The utility program *mkfs* has been provided to build file systems. This program can be called either by a command like

    mkfs /dev/fd1 1440

to build an empty 1440 block file system on the floppy disk in drive 1, or it can be given a prototype file listing directories and files to include in the new file system. This command also puts a magic number in the superblock to identify the file system as a valid MINIX file system. The MINIX file system has evolved, and some aspects of the file system (for instance, the size of i-nodes) were different previously. The magic number identifies the version of *mkfs* that created the file system, so differences can be accommodated. Attempts to mount a file system not in MINIX 3 format, such as an MS-DOS diskette, will be rejected by the mount system call, which checks the superblock for a valid magic number and other things.

5.6.3 Bitmaps

MINIX 3 keeps tracks of which i-nodes and zones are free by using two bitmaps. When a file is removed, it is then a simple matter to calculate which block of the bitmap contains the bit for the i-node being freed and to find it using the normal cache mechanism. Once the block is found, the bit corresponding to the freed i-node is set to 0. Zones are released from the zone bitmap in the same way.

Logically, when a file is to be created, the file system must search through the bit-map blocks one at a time for the first free i-node. This i-node is then allocated for the new file. In fact, the in-memory copy of the superblock has a field which points to the first free i-node, so no search is necessary until after a node is used, when the pointer must be updated to point to the new next free i-node, which will often turn out to be the next one, or a close one. Similarly, when an i-node is freed, a check is made to see if the free i-node comes before the currently-pointed-to one, and the pointer is updated if necessary. If every i-node slot on the disk is full, the search routine returns a 0, which is why i-node 0 is not used (i.e., so it can be used to indicate the search failed). (When *mkfs* creates a new file system, it zeroes i-node 0 and sets the lowest bit in the bitmap to 1, so the file system will never attempt to allocate it.) Everything that has been said here about the i-node bitmaps also applies to the zone bitmap; logically it is searched for the first free zone when space is needed, but a pointer to the first free zone is maintained to eliminate most of the need for sequential searches through the bitmap.

With this background, we can now explain the difference between zones and blocks. The idea behind zones is to help ensure that disk blocks that belong to the same file are located on the same cylinder, to improve performance when the file is read sequentially. The approach chosen is to make it possible to allocate several blocks at a time. If, for example, the block size is 1 KB and the zone size is 4 KB, the zone bitmap keeps track of zones, not blocks. A 20-MB disk has 5K zones of 4 KB, hence 5K bits in its zone map.

Most of the file system works with blocks. Disk transfers are always a block at a time, and the buffer cache also works with individual blocks. Only a few parts of the system that keep track of physical disk addresses (e.g., the zone bitmap and the i-nodes) know about zones.

Some design decisions had to be made in developing the MINIX 3 file system. In 1985, when MINIX was conceived, disk capacities were small, and it was expected that many users would have only floppy disks. A decision was made to restrict disk addresses to 16 bits in the V1 file system, primarily to be able to store many of them in the indirect blocks. With a 16-bit zone number and a 1-KB zone, only 64-KB zones can be addressed, limiting disks to 64 MB. This was an enormous amount of storage in those days, and it was thought that as disks got larger, it would be easy to switch to 2-KB or 4-KB zones, without changing the block size. The 16-bit zone numbers also made it easy to keep the i-node size to 32 bytes.

As MINIX developed, and larger disks became much more common, it was obvious that changes were desirable. Many files are smaller than 1 KB, so increasing the block size would mean wasting disk bandwidth, reading and writing mostly empty blocks and wasting precious main memory storing them in the buffer cache. The zone size could have been increased, but a larger zone size means more wasted disk space, and it was still desirable to retain efficient operation on small disks. Another reasonable alternative would have been to have different zone sizes on large and small devices.

In the end it was decided to increase the size of disk pointers to 32 bits. This made it possible for the MINIX V2 file system to deal with device sizes up to 4 terabytes with 1-KB blocks and zones and 16 TB with 4-KB blocks and zones (the default value now). However, other factors restrict this size (e.g., with 32-bit pointers, raw devices are limited to 4 GB). Increasing the size of disk pointers required an increase in the size of i-nodes. This is not necessarily a bad thing—it means the MINIX V2 (and now, V3) i-node is compatible with standard UNIX i-nodes, with room for three time values, more indirect and double indirect zones, and room for later expansion with triple indirect zones.

Zones also introduce an unexpected problem, best illustrated by a simple example, again with 4-KB zones and 1-KB blocks. Suppose that a file is of length 1-KB, meaning that one zone has been allocated for it. The three blocks between offsets 1024 and 4095 contain garbage (residue from the previous owner), but no structural harm is done to the file system because the file size is clearly marked in the i-node as 1 KB In fact, the blocks containing garbage will not be read into the block cache, since reads are done by blocks, not by zones. Reads beyond the end of a file always return a count of 0 and no data.

Now someone seeks to 32,768 and writes 1 byte. The file size is now set to 32,769. Subsequent seeks to byte 1024 followed by attempts to read the data will now be able to read the previous contents of the block, a major security breach.

The solution is to check for this situation when a write is done beyond the end of a file, and explicitly zero all the not-yet-allocated blocks in the zone that was previously the last one. Although this situation rarely occurs, the code has to deal with it, making the system slightly more complex.

5.6.4 I-Nodes

The layout of the MINIX 3 i-node is given in Fig. 5-36. It is almost the same as a standard UNIX i-node. The disk zone pointers are 32-bit pointers, and there are only 9 pointers, 7 direct and 2 indirect. The MINIX 3 i-nodes occupy 64 bytes, the same as standard UNIX i-nodes, and there is space available for a 10th (triple indirect) pointer, although its use is not supported by the standard version of the FS. The MINIX 3 i-node access, modification time and i-node change times are standard, as in UNIX. The last of these is updated for almost every file operation except a read of the file.

When a file is opened, its i-node is located and brought into the *inode* table in memory, where it remains until the file is closed. The *inode* table has a few additional fields not present on the disk, such as the i-node's device and number, so the file system knows where to rewrite the i-node if it is modified while in memory. It also has a counter per i-node. If the same file is opened more than once, only one copy of the i-node is kept in memory, but the counter is incremented each time the file is opened and decremented each time the file is closed. Only when the counter finally reaches zero is the i-node removed from the table. If it has been modified since being loaded into memory, it is also rewritten to the disk.

The main function of a file's i-node is to tell where the data blocks are. The first seven zone numbers are given right in the i-node itself. For the standard distribution, with zones and blocks both 1 KB, files up to 7 KB do not need indirect blocks. Beyond 7 KB, indirect zones are needed, using the scheme of Fig. 5-10,

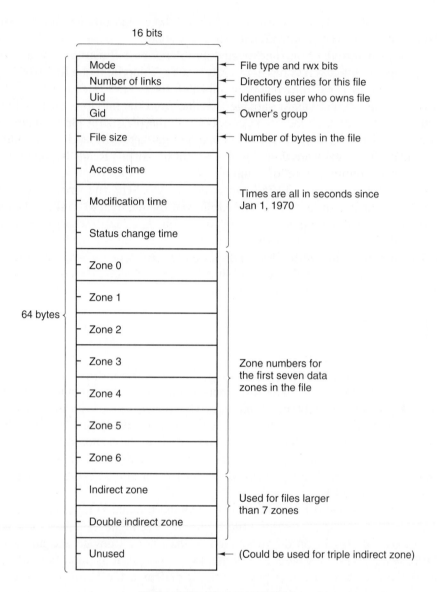

Figure 5-36. The MINIX i-node.

except that only the single and double indirect blocks are used. With 1-KB blocks and zones and 32-bit zone numbers, a single indirect block holds 256 entries, representing a quarter megabyte of storage. The double indirect block points to 256 single indirect blocks, giving access to up to 64 megabytes. With 4-KB blocks, the double indirect block leads to 1024×1024 blocks, which is over a million 4-KB blocks, making the maximum file zie over 4 GB. In practice the use of 32-bit numbers as file offsets limits the maximum file size to $2^{32} - 1$ bytes. As a consequence of these numbers, when 4-KB disk blocks are used MINIX 3 has no need for triple indirect blocks; the maximum file size is limited by the pointer size, not the ability to keep track of enough blocks.

The i-node also holds the mode information, which tells what kind of a file it is (regular, directory, block special, character special, or pipe), and gives the protection and SETUID and SETGID bits. The *link* field in the i-node records how many directory entries point to the i-node, so the file system knows when to release the file's storage. This field should not be confused with the counter (present only in the *inode* table in memory, not on the disk) that tells how many times the file is currently open, typically by different processes.

As a final note on i-nodes, we mention that the structure of Fig. 5-36 may be modified for special purposes. An example used in MINIX 3 is the i-nodes for block and character device special files. These do not need zone pointers, because they don't have to reference data areas on the disk. The major and minor device numbers are stored in the *Zone-0* space in Fig. 5-36. Another way an i-node could be used, although not implemented in MINIX 3, is as an immediate file with a small amount of data stored in the i-node itself.

5.6.5 The Block Cache

MINIX 3 uses a block cache to improve file system performance. The cache is implemented as a fixed array of buffers, each consisting of a header containing pointers, counters, and flags, and a body with room for one disk block. All the buffers that are not in use are chained together in a double-linked list, from most recently used (MRU) to least recently used (LRU) as illustrated in Fig. 5-37.

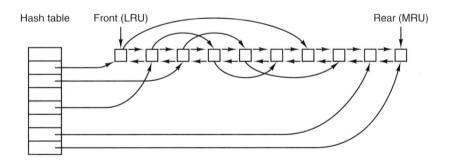

Figure 5-37. The linked lists used by the block cache.

In addition, to be able to quickly determine if a given block is in the cache or not, a hash table is used. All the buffers containing a block that has hash code k are linked together on a single-linked list pointed to by entry k in the hash table. The hash function just extracts the low-order n bits from the block number, so blocks from different devices appear on the same hash chain. Every buffer is on one of these chains. When the file system is initialized after MINIX 3 is booted, all buffers are unused, of course, and all are in a single chain pointed to by the 0th hash table entry. At that time all the other hash table entries contain a null pointer, but once the system starts, buffers will be removed from the 0th chain and other chains will be built.

When the file system needs to acquire a block, it calls a procedure, *get_block*, which computes the hash code for that block and searches the appropriate list. *Get_block* is called with a device number as well as a block number, and the search compares both numbers with the corresponding fields in the buffer chain. If a buffer containing the block is found, a counter in the buffer header is incremented to show that the block is in use, and a pointer to it is returned. If a block is not found on the hash list, the first buffer on the LRU list can be used; it is guaranteed not to be still in use, and the block it contains may be evicted to free up the buffer.

Once a block has been chosen for eviction from the block cache, another flag in its header is checked to see if the block has been modified since being read in. If so, it is rewritten to the disk. At this point the block needed is read in by sending a message to the disk driver. The file system is suspended until the block arrives, at which time it continues and a pointer to the block is returned to the caller.

When the procedure that requested the block has completed its job, it calls another procedure, *put_block*, to free the block. Normally, a block will be used immediately and then released, but since it is possible that additional requests for a block will be made before it has been released, *put_block* decrements the use counter and puts the buffer back onto the LRU list only when the use counter has gone back to zero. While the counter is nonzero, the block remains in limbo.

One of the parameters to *put_block* tells what class of block (e.g., i-nodes, directory, data) is being freed. Depending on the class, two key decisions are made:

1. Whether to put the block on the front or rear of the LRU list.

2. Whether to write the block (if modified) to disk immediately or not.

Almost all blocks go on the rear of the list in true LRU fashion. The exception is blocks from the RAM disk; since they are already in memory there is little advantage to keeping them in the block cache.

A modified block is not rewritten until either one of two events occurs:

1. It reaches the front of the LRU chain and is evicted.

2. A sync system call is executed.

Sync does not traverse the LRU chain but instead indexes through the array of buffers in the cache. Even if a buffer has not been released yet, if it has been modified, sync will find it and ensure that the copy on disk is updated.

Policies like this invite tinkering. In an older version of MINIX a superblock was modified when a file system was mounted, and was always rewritten immediately to reduce the chance of corrupting the file system in the event of a crash. Superblocks are modified only if the size of a RAM disk must be adjusted at startup time because the RAM disk was created bigger than the RAM image device. However, the superblock is not read or written as a normal block, because it is always 1024 bytes in size, like the boot block, regardless of the block size used for blocks handled by the cache. Another abandoned experiment is that in older versions of MINIX there was a *ROBUST* macro definable in the system configuration file, *include/minix/config.h*, which, if defined, caused the file system to mark i-node, directory, indirect, and bit-map blocks to be written immediately upon release. This was intended to make the file system more robust; the price paid was slower operation. It turned out this was not effective. A power failure occurring when all blocks have not been yet been written is going to cause a headache whether it is an i-node or a data block that is lost.

Note that the header flag indicating that a block has been modified is set by the procedure within the file system that requested and used the block. The procedures *get_block* and *put_block* are concerned just with manipulating the linked lists. They have no idea which file system procedure wants which block or why.

5.6.6 Directories and Paths

Another important subsystem within the file system manages directories and path names. Many system calls, such as open, have a file name as a parameter. What is really needed is the i-node for that file, so it is up to the file system to look up the file in the directory tree and locate its i-node.

A MINIX directory is a file that in previous versions contained 16-byte entries, 2 bytes for an i-node number and 14 bytes for the file name. This design limited disk partitions to 64-KB files and file names to 14 characters, the same as V7 UNIX. As disks have grown file names have also grown. In MINIX 3 the V3 file system provides 64 bytes directory entries, with 4 bytes for the i-node number and 60 bytes for the file name. Having up to 4 billion files per disk partition is effectively infinite and any programmer choosing a file name longer than 60 characters should be sent back to programming school.

Note that *paths* such as

/usr/ast/course_material_for_this_year/operating_systems/examination-1.ps

are not limited to 60 characters—just the individual component names. The use of fixed-length directory entries, in this case, 64 bytes, is an example of a trade-off involving simplicity, speed, and storage. Other operating systems typically organize directories as a heap, with a fixed header for each file pointing to a name on the heap at the end of the directory. The MINIX 3 scheme is very simple and required practically no code changes from V2. It is also very fast for both looking up names and storing new ones, since no heap management is ever required. The price paid is wasted disk storage, because most files are much shorter than 60 characters.

It is our firm belief that optimizing to save disk storage (and some RAM storage since directories are occasionally in memory) is the wrong choice. Code simplicity and correctness should come first and speed should come second. With modern disks usually exceeding 100 GB, saving a small amount of disk space at the price of more complicated and slower code is generally not a good idea. Unfortunately, many programmers grew up in an era of tiny disks and even tinier RAMs, and were trained from day 1 to resolve all trade-offs between code complexity, speed, and space in favor of minimizing space requirements. This implicit assumption really has to be reexamined in light of current realities.

Now let us see how the path /usr/ast/mbox/ is looked up. The system first looks up *usr* in the root directory, then it looks up *ast* in /usr/, and finally it looks up *mbox* in /usr/ast/. The actual lookup proceeds one path component at a time, as illustrated in Fig. 5-16.

The only complication is what happens when a mounted file system is encountered. The usual configuration for MINIX 3 and many other UNIX-like systems is to have a small root file system containing the files needed to start the system and to do basic system maintenance, and to have the majority of the files, including users' directories, on a separate device mounted on /usr. This is a good time to look at how mounting is done. When the user types the command

mount /dev/c0d1p2 /usr

on the terminal, the file system contained on hard disk 1, partition 2 is mounted on top of /usr/ in the root file system. The file systems before and after mounting are shown in Fig. 5-38.

The key to the whole mount business is a flag set in the memory copy of the i-node of /usr after a successful mount. This flag indicates that the i-node is mounted on. The mount call also loads the superblock for the newly mounted file system into the *super_block* table and sets two pointers in it. Furthermore, it puts the root i-node of the mounted file system in the *inode* table.

In Fig. 5-35 we see that superblocks in memory contain two fields related to mounted file systems. The first of these, the *i-node-for-root-of-mounted-file-system*, is set to point to the root i-node of the newly mounted file system. The second, the *i-node-mounted-upon*, is set to point to the i-node mounted on, in this case the i-node for /usr. These two pointers serve to connect the mounted file system to the root and represent the "glue" that holds the mounted file system to the root [shown as the dots in Fig. 5-38(c)]. This glue is what makes mounted file systems work.

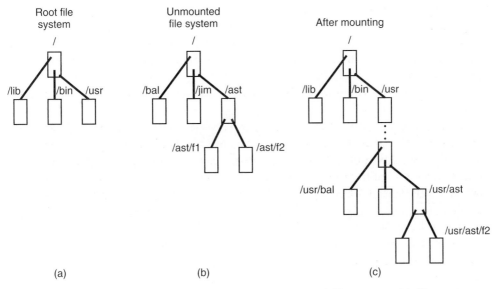

Figure 5-38. (a) Root file system. (b) An unmounted file system. (c) The result of mounting the file system of (b) on */usr/*.

When a path such as */usr/ast/f2* is being looked up, the file system will see a flag in the i-node for */usr/* and realize that it must continue searching at the root i-node of the file system mounted on */usr/*. The question is: "How does it find this root i-node?"

The answer is straightforward. The system searches all the superblocks in memory until it finds the one whose *i-node mounted on* field points to */usr/*. This must be the superblock for the file system mounted on */usr/*. Once it has the superblock, it is easy to follow the other pointer to find the root i-node for the mounted file system. Now the file system can continue searching. In this example, it looks for *ast* in the root directory of hard disk partition 2.

5.6.7 File Descriptors

Once a file has been opened, a file descriptor is returned to the user process for use in subsequent read and write calls. In this section we will look at how file descriptors are managed within the file system.

Like the kernel and the process manager, the file system maintains part of the process table within its address space. Three of its fields are of particular interest. The first two are pointers to the i-nodes for the root directory and the working directory. Path searches, such as that of Fig. 5-16, always begin at one or the other, depending on whether the path is absolute or relative. These pointers are changed by the chroot and chdir system calls to point to the new root or new working directory, respectively.

The third interesting field in the process table is an array indexed by file descripttor number. It is used to locate the proper file when a file descriptor is presented. At first glance, it might seem sufficient to have the k-th entry in this array just point to the i-node for the file belonging to file descriptor k. After all, the i-node is fetched into memory when the file is opened and kept there until it is closed, so it is sure to be available.

Unfortunately, this simple plan fails because files can be shared in subtle ways in MINIX 3 (as well as in UNIX). The trouble arises because associated with each file is a 32-bit number that indicates the next byte to be read or written. It is this number, called the **file position**, that is changed by the lseek system call. The problem can be stated easily: "Where should the file pointer be stored?"

The first possibility is to put it in the i-node. Unfortunately, if two or more processes have the same file open at the same time, they must all have their own file pointers, since it would hardly do to have an lseek by one process affect the next read of a different process. Conclusion: the file position cannot go in the i-node.

What about putting it in the process table? Why not have a second array, paralleling the file descriptor array, giving the current position of each file? This idea does not work either, but the reasoning is more subtle. Basically, the trouble comes from the semantics of the fork system call. When a process forks, both the parent and the child are required to share a single pointer giving the current position of each open file.

To better understand the problem, consider the case of a shell script whose output has been redirected to a file. When the shell forks off the first program, its file position for standard output is 0. This position is then inherited by the child, which writes, say, 1 KB of output. When the child terminates, the shared file position must now be 1024.

Now the shell reads some more of the shell script and forks off another child. It is essential that the second child inherit a file position of 1024 from the shell, so it will begin writing at the place where the first program left off. If the shell did not share the file position with its children, the second program would overwrite the output from the first one, instead of appending to it.

As a result, it is not possible to put the file position in the process table. It really must be shared. The solution used in UNIX and MINIX 3 is to introduce a new, shared table, *filp*, which contains all the file positions. Its use is illustrated in Fig. 5-39. By having the file position truly shared, the semantics of fork can be implemented correctly, and shell scripts work properly.

Although the only thing that the *filp* table really must contain is the shared file position, it is convenient to put the i-node pointer there, too. In this way, all that the file descriptor array in the process table contains is a pointer to a *filp* entry. The *filp* entry also contains the file mode (permission bits), some flags indicating

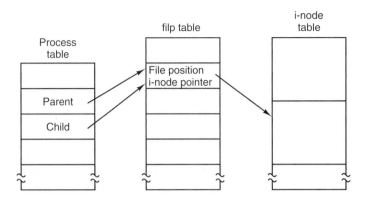

Figure 5-39. How file positions are shared between a parent and a child.

whether the file was opened in a special mode, and a count of the number of proc-esses using it, so the file system can tell when the last process using the entry has terminated, in order to reclaim the slot.

5.6.8 File Locking

Yet another aspect of file system management requires a special table. This is file locking. MINIX 3 supports the POSIX interprocess communication mechanism of **advisory file locking**. This permits any part, or multiple parts, of a file to be marked as locked. The operating system does not enforce locking, but processes are expected to be well behaved and to look for locks on a file before doing any-thing that would conflict with another process.

The reasons for providing a separate table for locks are similar to the justifica-tions for the *filp* table discussed in the previous section. A single process can have more than one lock active, and different parts of a file may be locked by more than one process (although, of course, the locks cannot overlap), so neither the process table nor the *filp* table is a good place to record locks. Since a file may have more than one lock placed upon it, the i-node is not a good place either.

MINIX 3 uses another table, the *file_lock* table, to record all locks. Each slot in this table has space for a lock type, indicating if the file is locked for reading or writing, the process ID holding the lock, a pointer to the i-node of the locked file, and the offsets of the first and last bytes of the locked region.

5.6.9 Pipes and Special Files

Pipes and special files differ from ordinary files in an important way. When a process tries to read or write a block of data from a disk file, it is almost certain that the operation will complete within a few hundred milliseconds at most. In the worst case, two or three disk accesses might be needed, not more. When reading from a pipe, the situation is different: if the pipe is empty, the reader will have to wait until some other process puts data in the pipe, which might take hours. Similarly, when reading from a terminal, a process will have to wait until somebody types something.

As a consequence, the file system's normal rule of handling a request until it is finished does not work. It is necessary to suspend these requests and restart them later. When a process tries to read or write from a pipe, the file system can check the state of the pipe immediately to see if the operation can be completed. If it can be, it is, but if it cannot be, the file system records the parameters of the system call in the process table, so it can restart the process when the time comes.

Note that the file system need not take any action to have the caller suspended. All it has to do is refrain from sending a reply, leaving the caller blocked waiting for the reply. Thus, after suspending a process, the file system goes back to its main loop to wait for the next system call. As soon as another process modifies the pipe's state so that the suspended process can complete, the file system sets a flag so that next time through the main loop it extracts the suspended process' parameters from the process table and executes the call.

The situation with terminals and other character special files is slightly different. The i-node for each special file contains two numbers, the major device and the minor device. The major device number indicates the device class (e.g., RAM disk, floppy disk, hard disk, terminal). It is used as an index into a file system table that maps it onto the number of the corresponding I/O device driver. In effect, the major device determines which I/O driver to call. The minor device number is passed to the driver as a parameter. It specifies which device is to be used, for example, terminal 2 or drive 1.

In some cases, most notably terminal devices, the minor device number encodes some information about a category of devices handled by a driver. For instance, the primary MINIX 3 console, */dev/console*, is device 4, 0 (major, minor). Virtual consoles are handled by the same part of the driver software. These are devices */dev/ttyc1* (4,1), */dev/ttyc2* (4,2), and so on. Serial line terminals need different low-level software, and these devices, */dev/tty00*, and */dev/tty01* are assigned device numbers 4, 16 and 4, 17. Similarly, network terminals use pseudo-terminal drivers, and these also need different low-level software. In MINIX 3 these devices, *ttyp0*, *ttyp1*, etc., are assigned device numbers such as 4, 128 and 4, 129. These pseudo devices each have an associated device, *ptyp0*, *ptyp1*, etc. The major, minor device number pairs for these are 4,192 and 4,193, etc. These numbers are chosen to make it easy for the device driver to call the low-level functions required for each group of devices. It is not expected that anyone is going to equip a MINIX 3 system with 192 or more terminals.

When a process reads from a special file, the file system extracts the major and minor device numbers from the file's i-node, and uses the major device number as an index into a file system table to map it onto the process number of the corresponding device driver. Once it has identified the driver, the file system sends it a message, including as parameters the minor device, the operation to be performed, the caller's process number and buffer address, and the number of bytes to be transferred. The format is the same as in Fig. 3-15, except that *POSITION* is not used.

If the driver is able to carry out the work immediately (e.g., a line of input has already been typed on the terminal), it copies the data from its own internal buffers to the user and sends the file system a reply message saying that the work is done. The file system then sends a reply message to the user, and the call is finished. Note that the driver does not copy the data to the file system. Data from block devices go through the block cache, but data from character special files do not.

On the other hand, if the driver is not able to carry out the work, it records the message parameters in its internal tables, and immediately sends a reply to the file system saying that the call could not be completed. At this point, the file system is in the same situation as having discovered that someone is trying to read from an empty pipe. It records the fact that the process is suspended and waits for the next message.

When the driver has acquired enough data to complete the call, it transfers them to the buffer of the still-blocked user and then sends the file system a message reporting what it has done. All the file system has to do is send a reply message to the user to unblock it and report the number of bytes transferred.

5.6.10 An Example: The READ System Call

As we shall see shortly, most of the code of the file system is devoted to carrying out system calls. Therefore, it is appropriate that we conclude this overview with a brief sketch of how the most important call, read, works.

When a user program executes the statement

```
n = read(fd, buffer, nbytes);
```

to read an ordinary file, the library procedure *read* is called with three parameters. It builds a message containing these parameters, along with the code for read as the message type, sends the message to the file system, and blocks waiting for the reply. When the message arrives, the file system uses the message type as an index into its tables to call the procedure that handles reading.

This procedure extracts the file descriptor from the message and uses it to locate the *filp* entry and then the i-node for the file to be read (see Fig. 5-39). The request is then broken up into pieces such that each piece fits within a block. For example, if the current file position is 600 and 1024 bytes have been requested, the request is split into two parts, for 600 to 1023, and for 1024 to 1623 (assuming 1-KB blocks).

For each of these pieces in turn, a check is made to see if the relevant block is in the cache. If the block is not present, the file system picks the least recently used buffer not currently in use and claims it, sending a message to the disk device driver to rewrite it if it is dirty. Then the disk driver is asked to fetch the block to be read.

Once the block is in the cache, the file system sends a message to the system task asking it to copy the data to the appropriate place in the user's buffer (i.e., bytes 600 to 1023 to the start of the buffer, and bytes 1024 to 1623 to offset 424 within the buffer). After the copy has been done, the file system sends a reply message to the user specifying how many bytes have been copied.

When the reply comes back to the user, the library function *read* extracts the reply code and returns it as the function value to the caller.

One extra step is not really part of the read call itself. After the file system completes a read and sends a reply, it initiates reading additional blocks, provided that the read is from a block device and certain other conditions are met. Since sequential file reads are common, it is reasonable to expect that the next blocks in a file will be requested in the next read request, and this makes it likely that the desired block will already be in the cache when it is needed. The number of blocks requested depends upon the size of the block cache; as many as 32 additional blocks may be requested. The device driver does not necessarily return this many blocks, and if at least one block is returned a request is considered successful.

5.7 IMPLEMENTATION OF THE MINIX 3 FILE SYSTEM

The MINIX 3 file system is relatively large (more than 100 pages of C) but quite straightforward. Requests to carry out system calls come in, are carried out, and replies are sent. In the following sections we will go through it a file at a time, pointing out the highlights. The code itself contains many comments to aid the reader.

In looking at the code for other parts of MINIX 3 we have generally looked at the main loop of a process first and then looked at the routines that handle the different message types. We will organize our approach to the file system differently. First we will go through the major subsystems (cache management, i-node management, etc.). Then we will look at the main loop and the system calls that operate upon files. Next we will look at systems call that operate upon directories, and then, we will discuss the remaining system calls that fall into neither category. Finally we will see how device special files are handled.

5.7.1 Header Files and Global Data Structures

Like the kernel and process manager, various data structures and tables used in the file system are defined in header files. Some of these data structures are placed in system-wide header files in *include/* and its subdirectories. For instance, *include/sys/stat.h* defines the format by which system calls can provide i-node information to other programs and the structure of a directory entry is defined in *include/sys/dir.h*. Both of these files are required by POSIX. The file system is affected by a number of definitions contained in the global configuration file *include/minix/config.h*, such as *NR_BUFS* and *NR_BUF_HASH*, which control the size of the block cache.

File System Headers

The file system's own header files are in the file system source directory *src/fs/*. Many file names will be familiar from studying other parts of the MINIX 3 system. The FS master header file, *fs.h* (line 20900), is quite analogous to *src/kernel/kernel.h* and *src/pm/pm.h*. It includes other header files needed by all the C source files in the file system. As in the other parts of MINIX 3, the file system master header includes the file system's own *const.h*, *type.h*, *proto.h*, and *glo.h*. We will look at these next.

Const.h (line 21000) defines some constants, such as table sizes and flags, that are used throughout the file system. MINIX 3 already has a history. Earlier versions of MINIX had different file systems. Although MINIX 3 does not support the old *V1* and *V2* file systems, some definitions have been retained, both for reference and in expectation that someone will add support for these later. Support for older versions is useful not only for accessing files on older MINIX file systems, it may also be useful for exchanging files.

Other operating systems may use older MINIX file systems—for instance, Linux originally used and still supports MINIX file systems. (It is perhaps somewhat ironic that Linux still supports the original MINIX file system but MINIX 3 does not.) Some utilities are available for MS-DOS and Windows to access older MINIX directories and files. The superblock of a file system contains a **magic number** to allow the operating system to identify the file system's type; the constants *SUPER_MAGIC*, *SUPER_V2*, and *SUPER_V3* define these numbers for the three versions of the MINIX file system. There are also *_REV*-suffixed versions of these for V1 and V2, in which the bytes of the magic number are reversed. These were used with ports of older MINIX versions to systems with a different byte order (little-endian rather than big-endian) so a removable disk written on a machine with a different byte order could be identified as such. As of the release of MINIX 3.1.0 defining a *SUPER_V3_REV* magic number has not been necessary, but it is likely this definition will be added in the future.

Type.h (line 21100) defines both the old V1 and new V2 i-node structures as they are laid out on the disk. The i-node is one structure that did not change in MINIX 3, so the V2 i-node is used with the V-3 file system. The V2 i-node is twice as big as the old one, which was designed for compactness on systems with no hard drive and 360-KB diskettes. The new version provides space for the three time fields which UNIX systems provide. In the V1 i-node there was only one time field, but a stat or fstat would "fake it" and return a *stat* structure containing all three fields. There is a minor difficulty in providing support for the two file system versions. This is flagged by the comment on line 21116. Older MINIX 3 software expected the *gid_t* type to be an 8-bit quantity, so *d2_gid* must be declared as type *u16_t*.

Proto.h (line 21200) provides function prototypes in forms acceptable to either old K&R or newer ANSI Standard C compilers. It is a long file, but not of great interest. However, there is one point to note: because there are so many different system calls handled by the file system, and because of the way the file system is organized, the various *do_XXX* functions are scattered through a number of files. *Proto.h* is organized by file and is a handy way to find the file to consult when you want to see the code that handles a particular system call.

Finally, *glo.h* (line 21400) defines global variables. The message buffers for the incoming and reply messages are also here. The now-familiar trick with the *EXTERN* macro is used, so these variables can be accessed by all parts of the file system. As in the other parts of MINIX 3, the storage space will be reserved when *table.c* is compiled.

The file system's part of the process table is contained in *fproc.h* (line 21500). The *fproc* array is declared with the *EXTERN* macro. It holds the mode mask, pointers to the i-nodes for the current root directory and working directory, the file descriptor array, uid, gid, and terminal number for each process. The process id and the process group id are also found here. The process id is duplicated in the part of the process table located in the process manager.

Several fields are used to store the parameters of those system calls that may be suspended part way through, such as reads from an empty pipe. The fields *fp_suspended* and *fp_revived* actually require only single bits, but nearly all compilers generate better code for characters than bit fields. There is also a field for the *FD_CLOEXEC* bits called for by the POSIX standard. These are used to indicate that a file should be closed when an **exec** call is made.

Now we come to files that define other tables maintained by the file system. The first, *buf.h* (line 21600), defines the block cache. The structures here are all declared with *EXTERN*. The array *buf* holds all the buffers, each of which contains a data part, *b*, and a header full of pointers, flags, and counters. The data part is declared as a union of five types (lines 21618 to 21632) because sometimes it is convenient to refer to the block as a character array, sometimes as a directory, etc.

The truly proper way to refer to the data part of buffer 3 as a character array is *buf*[3].*b.b_ _data* because *buf*[3].*b* refers to the union as a whole, from which the *b_ _data* field is selected. Although this syntax is correct, it is cumbersome, so on line 21649 we define a macro *b_data*, which allows us to write *buf*[3].*b_data* instead. Note that *b_ _data* (the field of the union) contains two underscores, whereas *b_data* (the macro) contains just one, to distinguish them. Macros for other ways of accessing the block are defined on lines 21650 to 21655.

The buffer hash table, *buf_hash*, is defined on line 21657. Each entry points to a list of buffers. Originally all the lists are empty. Macros at the end of *buf.h* define different block types. The *WRITE_IMMED* bit signals that a block must be rewritten to the disk immediately if it is changed, and the *ONE_SHOT* bit is used to indicate a block is unlikely to be needed soon. Neither of these is used currently but they remain available for anyone who has a bright idea about improving performance or reliability by modifying the way blocks in the cache are queued.

Finally, in the last line *HASH_MASK* is defined, based upon the value of *NR_BUF_HASH* configured in *include/minix/config.h*. *HASH_MASK* is ANDed with a block number to determine which entry in *buf_hash* to use as the starting point in a search for a block buffer.

File.h (line 21700) contains the intermediate table *filp* (declared as *EXTERN*), used to hold the current file position and i-node pointer (see Fig. 5-39). It also tells whether the file was opened for reading, writing, or both, and how many file descriptors are currently pointing to the entry.

The file locking table, *file_lock* (declared as *EXTERN*), is in *lock.h* (line 21800). The size of the array is determined by *NR_LOCKS*, which is defined as 8 in *const.h*. This number should be increased if it is desired to implement a multi-user data base on a MINIX 3 system.

In *inode.h* (line 21900) the i-node table *inode* is declared (using *EXTERN*). It holds i-nodes that are currently in use. As we said earlier, when a file is opened its i-node is read into memory and kept there until the file is closed. The *inode* structure definition provides for information that is kept in memory, but is not written to the disk i-node. Notice that there is only one version, and nothing is version-specific here. When the i-node is read in from the disk, differences between V1 and V2/V3 file systems are handled. The rest of the file system does not need to know about the file system format on the disk, at least until the time comes to write back modified information.

Most of the fields should be self-explanatory at this point. However, *i_seek* deserves some comment. It was mentioned earlier that, as an optimization, when the file system notices that a file is being read sequentially, it tries to read blocks into the cache even before they are asked for. For randomly accessed files there is no read ahead. When an lseek call is made, the field *i_seek* is set to inhibit read ahead.

The file *param.h* (line 22000) is analogous to the file of the same name in the process manager. It defines names for message fields containing parameters, so the code can refer to, for example, *m_in.buffer*, instead of *m_in.m1_p1*, which selects one of the fields of the message buffer *m_in*.

In *super.h* (line 22100), we have the declaration of the superblock table. When the system is booted, the superblock for the root device is loaded here. As file systems are mounted, their superblocks go here as well. As with other tables, *super_block* is declared as *EXTERN*.

File System Storage Allocation

The last file we will discuss in this section is not a header. However, just as we did when discussing the process manager, it seems appropriate to discuss *table.c* immediately after reviewing the header files, since they are all included when *table.c* (line 22200) is compiled. Most of the data structures we have mentioned—the block cache, the *filp* table, and so on—are defined with the *EXTERN* macro, as are also the file system's global variables and the file system's part of the process table. In the same way we have seen in other parts of the MINIX 3 system, the storage is actually reserved when *table.c* is compiled. This file also contains one major initialized array. *Call_vector* contains the pointer array used in the main loop for determining which procedure handles which system call number. We saw a similar table inside the process manager.

5.7.2 Table Management

Associated with each of the main tables—blocks, i-nodes, superblocks, and so forth—is a file that contains procedures that manage the table. These procedures are heavily used by the rest of the file system and form the principal interface between tables and the file system. For this reason, it is appropriate to begin our study of the file system code with them.

Block Management

The block cache is managed by the procedures in the file *cache.c*. This file contains the nine procedures listed in Fig. 5-40. The first one, *get_block* (line 22426), is the standard way the file system gets data blocks. When a file system procedure needs to read a user data block, a directory block, a superblock, or any other kind of block, it calls *get_block*, specifying the device and block number.

When *get_block* is called, it first examines the block cache to see if the requested block is there. If so, it returns a pointer to it. Otherwise, it has to read the block in. The blocks in the cache are linked together on *NR_BUF_HASH* linked lists. *NR_BUF_HASH* is a tunable parameter, along with *NR_BUFS*, the size of the block cache. Both of these are set in *include/minix/config.h*. At the end of this section we will say a few words about optimizing the size of the block cache and the hash table. The *HASH_MASK* is *NR_BUF_HASH* − 1. With 256 hash lists, the mask is 255, so all the blocks on each list have block numbers that end with the same string of 8 bits, that is 00000000, 00000001, ..., or 11111111.

The first step is usually to search a hash chain for a block, although there is a special case, when a hole in a sparse file is being read, where this search is skipped. This is the reason for the test on line 22454. Otherwise, the next two

Procedure	Function
get_block	Fetch a block for reading or writing
put_block	Return a block previously requested with get_block
alloc_zone	Allocate a new zone (to make a file longer)
free_zone	Release a zone (when a file is removed)
rw_block	Transfer a block between disk and cache
invalidate	Purge all the cache blocks for some device
flushall	Flush all dirty blocks for one device
rw_scattered	Read or write scattered data from or to a device
rm_lru	Remove a block from its LRU chain

Figure 5-40. Procedures used for block management.

lines set *bp* to point to the start of the list on which the requested block would be, if it were in the cache, applying *HASH_MASK* to the block number. The loop on the next line searches this list to see if the block can be found. If it is found and is not in use, it is removed from the LRU list. If it is already in use, it is not on the LRU list anyway. The pointer to the found block is returned to the caller on line 22463.

If the block is not on the hash list, it is not in the cache, so the least recently used block from the LRU list is taken. The buffer chosen is removed from its hash chain, since it is about to acquire a new block number and hence belongs on a different hash chain. If it is dirty, it is rewritten to the disk on line 22495. Doing this with a call to *flushall* rewrites any other dirty blocks for the same device. This call is is the way most blocks get written. Blocks that are currently in use are never chosen for eviction, since they are not on the LRU chain. Blocks will hardly ever be found to be in use, however; normally a block is released by *put_block* immediately upon being used.

As soon as the buffer is available, all of the fields, including *b_dev*, are updated with the new parameters (lines 22499 to 22504), and the block may be read in from the disk. However, there are two occasions when it may not be necessary to read the block from the disk. *Get_block* is called with a parameter *only_search*. This may indicate that this is a prefetch. During a prefetch an available buffer is found, writing the old contents to the disk if necessary, and a new block number is assigned to the buffer, but the *b_dev* field is set to *NO_DEV* to signal there are as yet no valid data in this block. We will see how this is used when we discuss the *rw_scattered* function. *Only_search* can also be used to signal that the file system needs a block just to rewrite all of it. In this case it is wasteful to first read the old version in. In either of these cases the parameters are updated, but the actual disk read is omitted (lines 22507 to 22513). When the new block has been read in, *get_block* returns to its caller with a pointer to it.

Suppose that the file system needs a directory block temporarily, to look up a file name. It calls *get_block* to acquire the directory block. When it has looked up its file name, it calls *put_block* (line 22520) to return the block to the cache, thus making the buffer available in case it is needed later for a different block.

Put_block takes care of putting the newly returned block on the LRU list, and in some cases, rewriting it to the disk. At line 22544 a decision is made to put it on the front or rear of the LRU list. Blocks on a RAM disk are always put on the front of the queue. The block cache does not really do very much for a RAM disk, since its data are already in memory and accessible without actual I/O. The *ONE_SHOT* flag is tested to see if the block has been marked as one not likely to be needed again soon, and such blocks are put on the front, where they will be reused quickly. However, this is used rarely, if at all. Almost all blocks except those from the RAM disk are put on the rear, in case they are needed again soon.

After the block has been repositioned on the LRU list, another check is made to see if the block should be rewritten to disk immediately. Like the previous test, the test for *WRITE_IMMED* is a vestige of an abandoned experiment; currently no blocks are marked for immediate writing.

As a file grows, from time to time a new zone must be allocated to hold the new data. The procedure *alloc_zone* (line 22580) takes care of allocating new zones. It does this by finding a free zone in the zone bitmap. There is no need to search through the bitmap if this is to be the first zone in a file; the *s_zsearch* field in the superblock, which always points to the first available zone on the device, is consulted. Otherwise an attempt is made to find a zone close to the last existing zone of the current file, in order to keep the zones of a file together. This is done by starting the search of the bitmap at this last zone (line 22603). The mapping between the bit number in the bitmap and the zone number is handled on line 22615, with bit 1 corresponding to the first data zone.

When a file is removed, its zones must be returned to the bitmap. *Free_zone* (line 22621) is responsible for returning these zones. All it does is call *free_bit*, passing the zone map and the bit number as parameters. *Free_bit* is also used to return free i-nodes, but then with the i-node map as the first parameter, of course.

Managing the cache requires reading and writing blocks. To provide a simple disk interface, the procedure *rw_block* (line 22641) has been provided. It reads or writes one block. Analogously, *rw_inode* exists to read and write i-nodes.

The next procedure in the file is *invalidate* (line 22680). It is called when a disk is unmounted, for example, to remove from the cache all the blocks belonging to the file system just unmounted. If this were not done, then when the device were reused (with a different floppy disk), the file system might find the old blocks instead of the new ones.

We mentioned earlier that *flushall* (line 22694), called from *get_block* whenever a dirty block is removed from the LRU list, is the function responsible for writing most data. It is also called by the sync system call to flush to disk all dirty buffers belonging to a specific device. Sync is activated periodically by the update daemon, and calls *flushall* once for each mounted device. *Flushall* treats the buffer cache as a linear array, so all dirty buffers are found, even ones that are currently in use and are not in the LRU list. All buffers in the cache are scanned, and those that belong to the device to be flushed and that need to be written are added to an array of pointers, *dirty*. This array is declared as *static* to keep it off the stack. It is then passed to *rw_scattered*.

In MINIX 3 scheduling of disk writing has been removed from the disk device drivers and made the sole responsibility of *rw_scattered* (line 22711). This function receives a device identifier, a pointer to an array of pointers to buffers, the size of the array, and a flag indicating whether to read or write. The first thing it does is sort the array it receives on the block numbers, so the actual read or write operation will be performed in an efficient order. It then constructs vectors of contiguous blocks to send to the the device driver with a call to *dev_io*. The driver does not have to do any additional scheduling. It is likely with a modern disk that the drive electronics will further optimize the order of requests, but this is not visible to MINIX 3. *Rw_scattered* is called with the *WRITING* flag only from the *flushall* function described above. In this case the origin of these block numbers is easy to understand. They are buffers which contain data from blocks previously read but now modified. The only call to *rw_scattered* for a read operation is from *rahead* in *read.c*. At this point, we just need to know that before calling *rw_scattered*, *get_block* has been called repeatedly in prefetch mode, thus reserving a group of buffers. These buffers contain block numbers, but no valid device parameter. This is not a problem, since *rw_scattered* is called with a device parameter as one of its arguments.

There is an important difference in the way a device driver may respond to a read (as opposed to a write) request, from *rw_scattered*. A request to write a number of blocks *must* be honored completely, but a request to read a number of blocks may be handled differently by different drivers, depending upon what is most efficient for the particular driver. *Rahead* often calls *rw_scattered* with a request for a list of blocks that may not actually be needed, so the best response is to get as many blocks as can be gotten easily, but not to go wildly seeking all over a device that may have a substantial seek time. For instance, the floppy driver may stop at a track boundary, and many other drivers will read only consecutive blocks. When the read is complete, *rw_scattered* marks the blocks read by filling in the device number field in their block buffers.

The last function in Fig. 5-40 is *rm_lru* (line 22809). This function is used to remove a block from the LRU list. It is used only by *get_block* in this file, so it is declared *PRIVATE* instead of *PUBLIC* to hide it from procedures outside the file.

Before we leave the block cache, let us say a few words about fine-tuning it. *NR_BUF_HASH* must be a power of 2. If it is larger than *NR_BUFS*, the average length of a hash chain will be less than one. If there is enough memory for a large number of buffers, there is space for a large number of hash chains, so the usual choice is to make *NR_BUF_HASH* the next power of 2 greater than

NR_BUFS. The listing in the text shows settings of 128 blocks and 128 hash lists. The optimal size depends upon how the system is used, since that determines how much must be buffered. The full source code used to compile the standard MINIX 3 binaries that are installed from the CD-ROM that accommpanies this text has settings of 1280 buffers and 2048 hash chains. Empirically it was found that increasing the number of buffers beyond this did not improve performance when recompiling the MINIX 3 system, so apparently this is large enough to hold the binaries for all compiler passes. For some other kind of work a smaller size might be adequate or a larger size might improve performance.

The buffers for the standard MINIX 3 system on the CD-ROM occupy more than 5 MB of RAM. An additional binary, designated *image_small* is provided that was compiled with just 128 buffers in the block cache, and the buffers for this system need only a little more than 0.5 MB. This one can be installed on a system with only 8 MB of RAM. The standard version requires 16 MB of RAM. With some tweaking, it could no doubt be shoehorned into a memory of 4 MB or smaller.

I-Node Management

The block cache is not the only file system table that needs support procedures. The i-node table does, too. Many of the procedures are similar in function to the block management procedures. They are listed in Fig. 5-41.

Procedure	Function
get_inode	Fetch an i-node into memory
put_inode	Return an i-node that is no longer needed
alloc_inode	Allocate a new i-node (for a new file)
wipe_inode	Clear some fields in an i-node
free_inode	Release an i-node (when a file is removed)
update_times	Update time fields in an i-node
rw_inode	Transfer an i-node between memory and disk
old_icopy	Convert i-node contents to write to V1 disk i-node
new_icopy	Convert data read from V1 file system disk i-node
dup_inode	Indicate that someone else is using an i-node

Figure 5-41. Procedures used for i-node management.

The procedure *get_inode* (line 22933) is analogous to *get_block*. When any part of the file system needs an i-node, it calls *get_inode* to acquire it. *Get_inode* first searches the *inode* table to see if the i-node is already present. If so, it increments the usage counter and returns a pointer to it. This search is contained on lines 22945 to 22955. If the i-node is not present in memory, the i-node is loaded by calling *rw_inode*.

When the procedure that needed the i-node is finished with it, the i-node is returned by calling the procedure *put_inode* (line 22976), which decrements the usage count *i_count*. If the count is then zero, the file is no longer in use, and the i-node can be removed from the table. If it is dirty, it is rewritten to disk.

If the *i_link* field is zero, no directory entry is pointing to the file, so all its zones can be freed. Note that the usage count going to zero and the number of links going to zero are different events, with different causes and different consequences. If the i-node is for a pipe, all the zones must be released, even though the number of links may not be zero. This happens when a process reading from a pipe releases the pipe. There is no sense in having a pipe for one process.

When a new file is created, an i-node must be allocated by *alloc_inode* (line 23003). MINIX 3 allows mounting of devices in read-only mode, so the superblock is checked to make sure the device is writable. Unlike zones, where an attempt is made to keep the zones of a file close together, any i-node will do. In order to save the time of searching the i-node bitmap, advantage is taken of the field in the superblock where the first unused i-node is recorded.

After the i-node has been acquired, *get_inode* is called to fetch the i-node into the table in memory. Then its fields are initialized, partly in-line (lines 23038 to 23044) and partly using the procedure *wipe_inode* (line 23060). This particular division of labor has been chosen because *wipe_inode* is also needed elsewhere in the file system to clear certain i-node fields (but not all of them).

When a file is removed, its i-node is freed by calling *free_inode* (line 23079). All that happens here is that the corresponding bit in the i-node bitmap is set to 0 and the superblock's record of the first unused i-node is updated.

The next function, *update_times* (line 23099), is called to get the time from the system clock and change the time fields that require updating. *Update_times* is also called by the stat and fstat system calls, so it is declared *PUBLIC*.

The procedure *rw_inode* (line 23125) is analogous to *rw_block*. Its job is to fetch an i-node from the disk. It does its work by carrying out the following steps:

1. Calculate which block contains the required i-node.

2. Read in the block by calling *get_block*.

3. Extract the i-node and copy it to the *inode* table.

4. Return the block by calling *put_block*.

Rw_inode is a bit more complex than the basic outline given above, so some additional functions are needed. First, because getting the current time requires a kernel call, any need for a change to the time fields in the i-node is only marked by setting bits in the i-node's *i_update* field while the i-node is in memory. If this field is nonzero when an i-node must be written, *update_times* is called.

Second, the history of MINIX adds a complication: in the old *V1* file system the i-nodes on the disk have a different structure from *V2*. Two functions, *old_icopy* (line 23168) and *new_icopy* (line 23214) are provided to take care of the conversions. The first converts between i-node information in memory and the format used by the *V1* filesystem. The second does the same conversion for *V2* and *V3* filesystem disks. Both of these functions are called only from within this file, so they are declared *PRIVATE*. Each function handles conversions in both directions (disk to memory or memory to disk).

Older versions of MINIX were ported to systems which used a different byte order from Intel processors and MINIX 3 is also likely to be ported to such architectures in the future. Every implementation uses the native byte order on its disk; the *sp->native* field in the superblock identifies which order is used. Both *old_icopy* and *new_icopy* call functions *conv2* and *conv4* to swap byte orders, if necessary. Of course, much of what we have just described is not used by MINIX 3, since it does not support the V1 filesystem to the extent that V1 disks can be used. And as of this writing nobody has ported MINIX 3 to a platform that uses a different byte order. But these bits and pieces remain in place for the day when someone decides to make MINIX 3 more versatile.

The procedure *dup_inode* (line 23257) just increments the usage count of the i-node. It is called when an open file is opened again. On the second open, the i-node need not be fetched from disk again.

Superblock Management

The file *super.c* contains procedures that manage the superblock and the bitmaps. Six procedures are defined in this file, listed in Fig. 5-42.

Procedure	Function
alloc_bit	Allocate a bit from the zone or i-node map
free_bit	Free a bit in the zone or i-node map
get_super	Search the superblock table for a device
get_block_size	Find block size to use
mounted	Report whether given i-node is on a mounted (or root) file system
read_super	Read a superblock

Figure 5-42. Procedures used to manage the superblock and bitmaps.

When an i-node or zone is needed, *alloc_inode* or *alloc_zone* is called, as we have seen above. Both of these call *alloc_bit* (line 23324) to actually search the relevant bitmap. The search involves three nested loops, as follows:

1. The outer one loops on all the blocks of a bitmap.

2. The middle one loops on all the words of a block.

3. The inner one loops on all the bits of a word.

The middle loop works by seeing if the current word is equal to the one's complement of zero, that is, a complete word full of 1s. If so, it has no free i-nodes or zones, so the next word is tried. When a word with a different value is found, it must have at least one 0 bit in it, so the inner loop is entered to find the free (i.e., 0) bit. If all the blocks have been tried without success, there are no free i-nodes or zones, so the code *NO_BIT* (0) is returned. Searches like this can consume a lot of processor time, but the use of the superblock fields that point to the first unused i-node and zone, passed to *alloc_bit* in *origin*, helps to keep these searches short.

Freeing a bit is simpler than allocating one, because no search is required. *Free_bit* (line 23400) calculates which bitmap block contains the bit to free and sets the proper bit to 0 by calling *get_block*, zeroing the bit in memory and then calling *put_block*.

The next procedure, *get_super* (line 23445), is used to search the superblock table for a specific device. For example, when a file system is to be mounted, it is necessary to check that it is not already mounted. This check can be performed by asking *get_super* to find the file system's device. If it does not find the device, then the file system is not mounted.

In MINIX 3 the file system server is capable of handling file systems with different block sizes, although within a given disk partition only a single block size can be used. The *get_block_size* function (line 23467) is meant to determine the block size of a file system. It searches the superblock table for the given device and returns the block size of the device if it is mounted. Otherwise the minimum block size, *MIN_BLOCK_SIZE* is returned.

The next function, *mounted* (line 23489), is called only when a block device is closed. Normally, all cached data for a device are discarded when it is closed. But, if the device happens to be mounted, this is not desirable. *Mounted* is called with a pointer to the i-node for a device. It just returns *TRUE* if the device is the root device, or if it is a mounted device.

Finally, we have *read_super* (line 23509). This is partially analogous to *rw_block* and *rw_inode*, but it is called only to read. The superblock is not read into the block cache at all, a request is made directly to the device for 1024 bytes starting at an offset of the same amount from the beginning of the device. Writing a superblock is not necessary in the normal operation of the system. *Read_super* checks the version of the file system from which it has just read and performs conversions, if necessary, so the copy of the superblock in memory will have the standard structure even when read from a disk with a different superblock structure or byte order.

Even though it is not currently used in MINIX 3, the method of determining whether a disk was written on a system with a different byte order is clever and worth noting. The magic number of a superblock is written with the native byte order of the system upon which the file system was created, and when a super-block is read a test for reversed-byte-order superblocks is made.

File Descriptor Management

MINIX 3 contains special procedures to manage file descriptors and the *filp* table (see Fig. 5-39). They are contained in the file *filedes.c*. When a file is created or opened, a free file descriptor and a free *filp* slot are needed. The pro-cedure *get_fd* (line 23716) is used to find them. They are not marked as in use, however, because many checks must first be made before it is known for sure that the creat or open will succeed.

Get_filp (line 23761) is used to see if a file descriptor is in range, and if so, returns its *filp* pointer.

The last procedure in this file is *find_filp* (line 23774). It is needed to find out when a process is writing on a broken pipe (i.e., a pipe not open for reading by any other process). It locates potential readers by a brute force search of the *filp* table. If it cannot find one, the pipe is broken and the write fails.

File Locking

The POSIX record locking functions are shown in Fig. 5-43. A part of a file can be locked for reading and writing, or for writing only, by an fcntl call specify-ing a *F_SETLK* or *F_SETLKW* request. Whether a lock exists over a part of a file can be determined using the *F_GETLK* request.

Operation	Meaning
F_SETLK	Lock region for both reading and writing
F_SETLKW	Lock region for writing
F_GETLK	Report if region is locked

Figure 5-43. The POSIX advisory record locking operations. These operations are requested by using an FCNTL system call.

The file *lock.c* contains only two functions. *Lock_op* (line 23820) is called by the fcntl system call with a code for one of the operations shown in Fig. 5-43. It does some error checking to be sure the region specified is valid. When a lock is being set, it must not conflict with an existing lock, and when a lock is being cleared, an existing lock must not be split in two. When any lock is cleared, the other function in this file, *lock_revive* (line 23964), is called. It wakes up all the processes that are blocked waiting for locks.

This strategy is a compromise; it would take extra code to figure out exactly which processes were waiting for a particular lock to be released. Those processes that are still waiting for a locked file will block again when they start. This strategy is based on an assumption that locking will be used infrequently. If a major multiuser data base were to be built upon a MINIX 3 system, it might be desirable to reimplement this.

Lock_revive is also called when a locked file is closed, as might happen, for instance, if a process is killed before it finishes using a locked file.

5.7.3 The Main Program

The main loop of the file system is contained in file *main.c*, (line 24040). After a call to *fs_init* for initialization, the main loop is entered. Structurally, this is very similar to the main loop of the process manager and the I/O device drivers. The call to *get_work* waits for the next request message to arrive (unless a process previously suspended on a pipe or terminal can now be handled). It also sets a global variable, *who*, to the caller's process table slot number and another global variable, *call_nr*, to the number of the system call to be carried out.

Once back in the main loop the variable *fp* is pointed to the caller's process table slot, and the *super_user* flag tells whether the caller is the superuser or not. Notification messages are high priority, and a *SYS_SIG* message is checked for first, to see if the system is shutting down. The second highest priority is a *SYN_ALARM*, which means that a timer set by the file system has expired. A *NOTIFY_MESSAGE* means a device driver is ready for attention, and is dispatched to *dev_status*. Then comes the main attraction—the call to the procedure that carries out the system call. The procedure to call is selected by using *call_nr* as an index into the array of procedure pointers, *call_vecs*.

When control comes back to the main loop, if *dont_reply* has been set, the reply is inhibited (e.g., a process has blocked trying to read from an empty pipe). Otherwise a reply is sent by calling *reply* (line 24087). The final statement in the main loop has been designed to detect that a file is being read sequentially and to load the next block into the cache before it is actually requested, to improve performance.

Two other functions in this file are intimately involved with the file system's main loop. *Get_work* (line 24099) checks to see if any previously blocked procedures have now been revived. If so, these have priority over new messages. When there is no internal work to do the file system calls the kernel to get a message, on line 24124. Skipping ahead a few lines, we find *reply* (line 24159) which is called after a system call has been completed, successfully or otherwise. It sends a reply back to the caller. The process may have been killed by a signal, so the status code returned by the kernel is ignored. In this case there is nothing to be done anyway.

Initialization of the File System

The functions that remain to be discussed in *main.c* are used at system startup. The major player is *fs_init*, which is called by the file system before it enters its main loop during startup of the entire system. In the context of discussing process scheduling in Chapter 2 we showed in Fig. 2-43 the initial queueing of processes as the MINIX 3 system starts up. The file system is scheduled on a queue with lower priority than the process manager, so we can be sure that at startup time the process manager will get a chance to run before the file system. In Chapter 4 we examined the initialization of the process manager. As the PM builds its part of the process table, adding entries for itself and all other processes in the boot image, it sends a message to the file system for each one so the FS can initialize the corresponding entry in the FS part of the file system. Now we can see the other half of this interaction.

When the file system starts it immediately enters a loop of its own in *fs_init*, on lines 24189 to 24202. The first statement in the loop is a call to receive, to get a message sent at line 18235 in the PM's *pm_init* initialization function. Each message contains a process number and a PID. The first is used as an index into the file system's process table and the second is saved in the *fp_pid* field of each selected slot. Following this the real and effective uid and gid for the superuser and a ~0 (all bits set) umask is set up for each selected slot. When a message with the symbolic value *NONE* in the process number field is received the loop terminates and a message is sent back to the process manager to tell it all is OK.

Next, the file system's own initialization is completed. First important constants are tested for valid values. Then several other functions are invoked to initialize the block cache and the device table, to load the RAM disk if necessary, and to load the root device superblock. At this point the root device can be accessed, and another loop is made through the FS part of the process table, so each process loaded from the boot image will recognize the root directory and use the root directory as its working directory (lines 24228 to 24235).

The first function called by *fs_init* after it finshes its interaction with the process manager is *buf_pool*, which begins on line 24132. It builds the linked lists used by the block cache. Figure 5-37 shows the normal state of the block cache, in which all blocks are linked on both the LRU chain and a hash chain. It may be helpful to see how the situation of Fig. 5-37 comes about. Immediately after the cache is initialized by *buf_pool*, all the buffers will be on the LRU chain, and all will be linked into the 0th hash chain, as in Fig. 5-44(a). When a buffer is requested, and while it is in use, we have the situation of Fig. 5-44(b), in which we see that a block has been removed from the LRU chain and is now on a different hash chain.

Normally, blocks are released and returned to the LRU chain immediately. Figure 5-44(c) shows the situation after the block has been returned to the LRU chain. Although it is no longer in use, it can be accessed again to provide the same data, if need be, and so it is retained on the hash chain. After the system has been in operation for awhile, almost all of the blocks can be expected to have been used and to be distributed among the different hash chains at random. Then the LRU chain will look like Fig. 5-37.

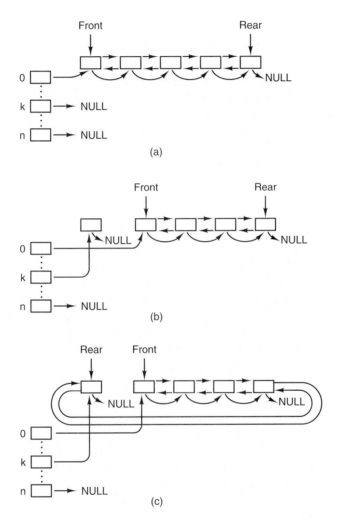

Figure 5-44. Block cache initialization. (a) Before any buffers have been used. (b) After one block has been requested. (c) After the block has been released.

The next thing called after *buf_pool* is *build_dmap*, which we will describe later, along with other functions dealing with device files. After that, *load_ram* is called, which uses the next function we will examine, *igetenv* (line 2641). This function retrieves a numeric device identifier from the kernel, using the name of a boot parameter as a key. If you have used the *sysenv* command to to look at the boot parameters on a working MINIX 3 system, you have seen that *sysenv* reports devices numerically, displaying strings like

    rootdev=912

The file system uses numbers like this to identify devices. The number is simply 256 x *major* + *minor*, where *major* and *minor* are the major and minor device numbers. In this example, the major, minor pair is 3, 144, which corresponds to */dev/c0d1p0s0*, a typical place to install MINIX 3 on a system with two disk drives.

Load_ram (line 24260) allocates space for a RAM disk, and loads the root file system on it, if required by the boot parameters. It uses *igetenv* to get the *rootdev*, *ramimagedev*, and *ramsize* parameters set in the boot environment (lines 24278 to 24280). If the boot parameters specify

    rootdev = ram

the root file system is copied from the device named by *ramimagedev* to the RAM disk block by block, starting with the boot block, with no interpretation of the various file system data structures. If the *ramsize* boot parameter is smaller than the size of *ramimagedev*, the RAM disk is made large enough to hold it. If *ramsize* specifies a size larger than the boot device file system the requested size is allocated and the RAM disk file system is adjusted to use the full size specified (lines 24404 to 24420). This is the only time that the file system ever writes a superblock, but, just as with reading a superblock, the block cache is not used and the data is written directly to the device using *dev_io*.

Two items merit note at this point. The first is the code on lines 24291 to 24307 which deals with the case of booting from a CD-ROM. The *cdprobe* function, not discussed in this text, is used. Interested readers are referred to the code in *fs/cdprobe.c*, which can be found on the CD-ROM or the Web site. Second, regardless of the disk block size used by MINIX 3 for ordinary disk access, the boot block is always a 1 KB block and the superblock is loaded from the second 1 KB of the disk device. Anything else would be complicated, since the block size cannot be known until the superblock has been loaded.

Load_ram allocates space for an empty RAM disk if a nonzero *ramsize* is specified without a request to use the RAM disk as the root file system. In this case, since no file system structures are copied, the RAM device cannot be used as a file system until it has been initialized by the *mkfs* command. Alternatively, such a RAM disk can be used for a secondary cache if support for this is compiled into the file system.

The last function in *main.c* is *load_super* (line 24426). It initializes the superblock table and reads in the superblock of the root device.

5.7.4 Operations on Individual Files

In this section we will look at the system calls that operate on individual files one at a time (as opposed to, say, operations on directories). We will start with how files are created, opened, and closed. After that we will examine in some detail the mechanism by which files are read and written. Then that we will look at pipes and how operations on them differ from those on files.

Creating, Opening, and Closing Files

The file *open.c* contains the code for six system calls: creat, open, mknod, mkdir, close, and lseek. We will examine creat and open together, and then look at each of the others.

In older versions of UNIX, the creat and open calls had distinct purposes. Trying to open a file that did not exist was an error, and a new file had to be created with creat, which could also be used to truncate an existing file to zero length. The need for two distinct calls is no longer present in a POSIX system, however. Under POSIX, the open call now allows creating a new file or truncating an old file, so the creat call now represents a subset of the possible uses of the open call and is really only necessary for compatibility with older programs. The procedures that handle creat and open are *do_creat* (line 24537) and *do_open* (line 24550). (As in the process manager, the convention is used in the file system that system call **XXX** is performed by procedure *do_XXX*.) Opening or creating a file involves three steps:

1. Finding the i-node (allocating and initializing if the file is new).

2. Finding or creating the directory entry.

3. Setting up and returning a file descriptor for the file.

Both the creat and the open calls do two things: they fetch the name of a file and then they call *common_open* which takes care of tasks common to both calls.

Common_open (line 24573) starts by making sure that free file descriptor and *filp* table slots are available. If the calling function specified creation of a new file (by calling with the *O_CREAT* bit set), *new_node* is called on line 24594. *New_node* returns a pointer to an existing i-node if the directory entry already exists; otherwise it will create both a new directory entry and i-node. If the i-node cannot be created, *new_node* sets the global variable *err_code*. An error code does not always mean an error. If *new_node* finds an existing file, the error code returned will indicate that the file exists, but in this case that error is acceptable (line 24597). If the *O_CREAT* bit is not set, a search is made for the i-node using an alternative method, the *eat_path* function in *path.c*, which we will discuss further on. At this point, the important thing to understand is that if an i-node is not found or successfully created, *common_open* will terminate with an error before line 24606 is reached. Otherwise, execution continues here with assignment of a file descriptor and claiming of a slot in the *filp* table, Following this, if a new file has just been created, lines 24612 to 24680 are skipped.

If the file is not new, then the file system must test to see what kind of a file it is, what its mode is, and so on, to determine whether it can be opened. The call to *forbidden* on line 24614 first makes a general check of the *rwx* bits. If the file is a regular file and *common_open* was called with the *O_TRUNC* bit set, it is truncated to length zero and *forbidden* is called again (line 24620), this time to be sure the file may be written. If the permissions allow, *wipe_inode* and *rw_inode* are called to re-initialize the i-node and write it to the disk. Other file types (directories, special files, and named pipes) are subjected to appropriate tests. In the case of a device, a call is made on line 24640 (using the *dmap* structure) to the appropriate routine to open the device. In the case of a named pipe, a call is made to *pipe_open* (line 24646), and various tests relevant to pipes are made.

The code of *common_open*, as well as many other file system procedures, contains a large amount of code that checks for various errors and illegal combinations. While not glamorous, this code is essential to having an error-free, robust file system. If something is wrong, the file descriptor and *filp* slot previously allocated are deallocated and the i-node is released (lines 24683 to 24689). In this case the value returned by *common_open* will be a negative number, indicating an error. If there are no problems the file descriptor, a positive value, is returned.

This is a good place to discuss in more detail the operation of *new_node* (line 24697), which does the allocation of the i-node and the entering of the path name into the file system for creat and open calls. It is also used for the mknod and mkdir calls, yet to be discussed. The statement on line 24711 parses the path name (i.e., looks it up component by component) as far as the final directory; the call to *advance* three lines later tries to see if the final component can be opened.

For example, on the call

    fd = creat("/usr/ast/foobar", 0755);

last_dir tries to load the i-node for */usr/ast/* into the tables and return a pointer to it. If the file does not exist, we will need this i-node shortly in order to add *foobar* to the directory. All the other system calls that add or delete files also use *last_dir* to first open the final directory in the path.

If *new_node* discovers that the file does not exist, it calls *alloc_inode* on line 24717 to allocate and load a new i-node, returning a pointer to it. If no free i-nodes are left, *new_node* fails and returns *NIL_INODE*.

If an i-node can be allocated, the operation continues at line 24727, filling in some of the fields, writing it back to the disk, and entering the file name in the final directory (on line 24732). Again we see that the file system must constantly check for errors, and upon encountering one, carefully release all the resources, such as i-nodes and blocks that it is holding. If we were prepared to just let

MINIX 3 panic when we ran out of, say, i-nodes, rather than undoing all the effects of the current call and returning an error code to the caller, the file system would be appreciably simpler.

As mentioned above, pipes require special treatment. If there is not at least one reader/writer pair for a pipe, *pipe_open* (line 24758) suspends the caller. Otherwise, it calls *release*, which looks through the process table for processes that are blocked on the pipe. If it is successful, the processes are revived.

The mknod call is handled by *do_mknod* (line 24785). This procedure is similar to *do_creat*, except that it just creates the i-node and makes a directory entry for it. In fact, most of the work is done by the call to *new_node* on line 24797. If the i-node already exists, an error code will be returned. This is the same error code that was an acceptable result from *new_node* when it was called by *common_open*; in this case, however, the error code is passed back to the caller, which presumably will act accordingly. The case-by-case analysis we saw in *common_open* is not needed here.

The mkdir call is handled by the function *do_mkdir* (line 24805). As with the other system calls we have discussed here, *new_node* plays an important part. Directories, unlike files, always have links and are never completely empty because every directory must contain two entries from the time of its creation: the "." and ".." entries that refer to the directory itself and to its parent directory. The number of links a file may have is limited, it is *LINK_MAX* (defined in *include/limits.h* as *SHRT_MAX,* 32767 for MINIX 3 on a standard 32-bit Intel system). Since the reference to a parent directory in a child is a link to the parent, the first thing *do_mkdir* does is to see if it is possible to make another link in the parent directory (lines 24819 and 24820). Once this test has been passed, *new_node* is called. If *new_node* succeeds, then the directory entries for "." and ".." are made (lines 24841 and 24842). All of this is straightforward, but there could be failures (for instance, if the disk is full), so to avoid making a mess of things provision is made for undoing the initial stages of the process if it can not be completed.

Closing a file is easier than opening one. The work is done by *do_close* (line 24865). Pipes and special files need some attention, but for regular files, almost all that needs to be done is to decrement the *filp* counter and check to see if it is zero, in which case the i-node is returned with *put_inode*. The final step is to remove any locks and to revive any process that may have been suspended waiting for a lock on the file to be released.

Note that returning an i-node means that its counter in the *inode* table is decremented, so it can be removed from the table eventually. This operation has nothing to do with freeing the i-node (i.e., setting a bit in the bitmap saying that it is available). The i-node is only freed when the file has been removed from all directories.

The final procedure in *open.c* is *do_lseek* (line 24939). When a seek is done, this procedure is called to set the file position to a new value. On line 24968 reading ahead is inhibited; an explicit attempt to seek to a position in a file is incompatible with sequential access.

Reading a File

Once a file has been opened, it can be read or written. Many functions are used during both reading and writing. These are found in the file *read.c*. We will discuss these first and then proceed to the following file, *write.c*, to look at code specifically used for writing. Reading and writing differ in a number of ways, but they have enough similarities that all that is required of *do_read* (line 25030) is to call the common procedure *read_write* with a flag set to *READING*. We will see in the next section that *do_write* is equally simple.

Read_write begins on line 25038. Some special code on lines 25063 to 25066 is used by the process manager to have the file system load entire segments in user space for it. Normal calls are processed starting on line 25068. Some validity checks follow (e.g., reading from a file opened only for writing) and some variables are initialized. Reads from character special files do not go through the block cache, so they are filtered out on line 25122.

The tests on lines 25132 to 25145 apply only to writes and have to do with files that may get bigger than the device can hold, or writes that will create a hole in the file by writing *beyond* the end-of-file. As we discussed in the MINIX 3 overview, the presence of multiple blocks per zone causes problems that must be dealt with explicitly. Pipes are also special and are checked for.

The heart of the read mechanism, at least for ordinary files, is the loop starting on line 25157. This loop breaks the request up into chunks, each of which fits in a single disk block. A chunk begins at the current position and extends until one of the following conditions is met:

1. All the bytes have been read.

2. A block boundary is encountered.

3. The end-of-file is hit.

These rules mean that a chunk never requires two disk blocks to satisfy it. Figure 5-45 shows three examples of how the chunk size is determined, for chunk sizes of 6, 2, and 1 bytes, respectively. The actual calculation is done on lines 25159 to 25169.

The actual reading of the chunk is done by *rw_chunk*. When control returns, various counters and pointers are incremented, and the next iteration begins. When the loop terminates, the file position and other variables may be updated (e.g., pipe pointers).

Finally, if read ahead is called for, the i-node to read from and the position to read from are stored in global variables, so that after the reply message is sent to the user, the file system can start getting the next block. In many cases the file

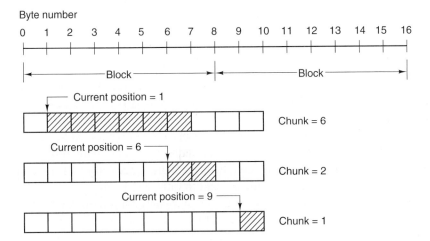

Figure 5-45. Three examples of how the first chunk size is determined for a 10-byte file. The block size is 8 bytes, and the number of bytes requested is 6. The chunk is shown shaded.

system will block, waiting for the next disk block, during which time the user process will be able to work on the data it just received. This arrangement overlaps processing and I/O and can improve performance substantially.

The procedure *rw_chunk* (line 25251) is concerned with taking an i-node and a file position, converting them into a physical disk block number, and requesting the transfer of that block (or a portion of it) to the user space. The mapping of the relative file position to the physical disk address is done by *read_map*, which understands about i-nodes and indirect blocks. For an ordinary file, the variables *b* and *dev* on line 25280 and line 25281 contain the physical block number and device number, respectively. The call to *get_block* on line 25303 is where the cache handler is asked to find the block, reading it in if need be. Calling *rahead* on line 25295 then ensures that the block is read into the cache.

Once we have a pointer to the block, the *sys_vircopy* kernel call on line 25317 takes care of transferring the required portion of it to the user space. The block is then released by *put_block*, so that it can be evicted from the cache later. (After being acquired by *get_block*, it will not be in the LRU queue and it will not be returned there while the counter in the block's header shows that it is in use, so it will be exempt from eviction; *put_block* decrements the counter and returns the block to the LRU queue when the counter reaches zero.) The code on line 25327 indicates whether a write operation filled the block. However, the value passed to *put_block* in *n* does not affect how the block is placed on the queue; all blocks are now placed on the rear of the LRU chain.

Read_map (line 25337) converts a logical file position to the physical block number by inspecting the i-node. For blocks close enough to the beginning of the file that they fall within one of the first seven zones (the ones right in the i-node), a simple calculation is sufficient to determine which zone is needed, and then which block. For blocks further into the file, one or more indirect blocks may have to be read.

Rd_indir (line 25400) is called to read an indirect block. The comments for this function are a bit out of date; code to support the 68000 processor has been removed and the support for the MINIX V1 file system is not used and could also be dropped. However, it is worth noting that if someone wanted to add support for other file system versions or other platforms where data might have a different format on the disk, problems of different data types and byte orders could be relegated to this file. If messy conversions were necessary, doing them here would let the rest of the file system see data in only one form.

Read_ahead (line 25432) converts the logical position to a physical block number, calls *get_block* to make sure the block is in the cache (or bring it in), and then returns the block immediately. It cannot do anything with the block, after all. It just wants to improve the chance that the block is around if it is needed soon,

Note that *read_ahead* is called only from the main loop in *main*. It is not called as part of the processing of the read system call. It is important to realize that the call to *read_ahead* is performed *after* the reply is sent, so that the user will be able to continue running even if the file system has to wait for a disk block while reading ahead.

Read_ahead by itself is designed to ask for just one more block. It calls the last function in *read.c*, *rahead*, to actually get the job done. *Rahead* (line 25451) works according to the theory that if a little more is good, a lot more is better. Since disks and other storage devices often take a relatively long time to locate the first block requested but then can relatively quickly read in a number of adjacent blocks, it may be possible to get many more blocks read with little additional effort. A prefetch request is made to *get_block*, which prepares the block cache to receive a number of blocks at once. Then *rw_scattered* is called with a list of blocks. We have previously discussed this; recall that when the device drivers are actually called by *rw_scattered*, each one is free to answer only as much of the request as it can efficiently handle. This all sounds fairly complicated, but the complications make possible a significant speedup of applications which read large amounts of data from the disk.

Figure 5-46 shows the relations between some of the major procedures involved in reading a file–in particular, who calls whom.

Writing a File

The code for writing to files is in *write.c*. Writing a file is similar to reading one, and *do_write* (line 25625) just calls *read_write* with the *WRITING* flag. A major difference between reading and writing is that writing requires allocating new disk blocks. *Write_map* (line 25635) is analogous to *read_map*, only instead

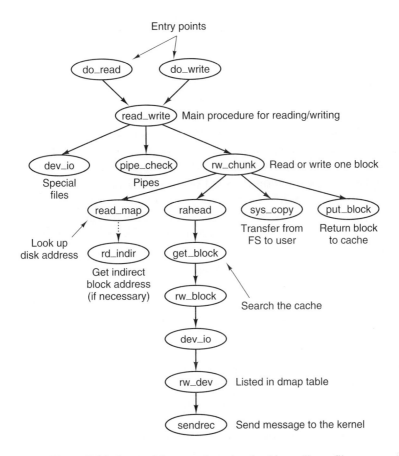

Figure 5-46. Some of the procedures involved in reading a file.

of looking up physical block numbers in the i-node and its indirect blocks, it enters new ones there (to be precise, it enters zone numbers, not block numbers).

The code of *write_map* is long and detailed because it must deal with several cases. If the zone to be inserted is close to the beginning of the file, it is just inserted into the i-node on (line 25658).

The worst case is when a file exceeds the size that can be handled by a single-indirect block, so a double-indirect block is now required. Next, a single-indirect block must be allocated and its address put into the double-indirect block. As with reading, a separate procedure, *wr_indir*, is called. If the double-indirect block is acquired correctly, but the disk is full so the single-indirect block cannot be allocated, then the double one must be returned to avoid corrupting the bitmap.

Again, if we could just toss in the sponge and panic at this point, the code would be much simpler. However, from the user's point of view it is much nicer that running out of disk space just returns an error from write, rather than crashing the computer with a corrupted file system.

Wr_indir (line 25726) calls the conversion routines, *conv4* to do any necessary data conversion and puts a new zone number into an indirect block. (Again, there is leftover code here to handle the old V1 filesystem, but only the V2 code is currently used.) Keep in mind that the name of this function, like the names of many other functions that involve reading and writing, is not literally true. The actual writing to the disk is handled by the functions that maintain the block cache.

The next procedure in *write.c* is *clear_zone* (line 25747), which takes care of the problem of erasing blocks that are suddenly in the middle of a file. This happens when a seek is done beyond the end of a file, followed by a write of some data. Fortunately, this situation does not occur very often.

New_block (line 25787) is called by *rw_chunk* whenever a new block is needed. Figure 5-47 shows six successive stages of the growth of a sequential file. The block size is 1-KB and the zone size is 2-KB in this example.

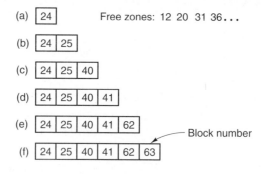

Figure 5-47. (a) – (f) The successive allocation of 1-KB blocks with a 2-KB zone.

The first time *new_block* is called, it allocates zone 12 (blocks 24 and 25). The next time it uses block 25, which has already been allocated but is not yet in use. On the third call, zone 20 (blocks 40 and 41) is allocated, and so on. *Zero_block* (line 25839) clears a block, erasing its previous contents. This description is considerably longer than the actual code.

Pipes

Pipes are similar to ordinary files in many respects. In this section we will focus on the differences. The code we will discuss is all in *pipe.c*.

First of all, pipes are created differently, by the pipe call, rather than the creat call. The pipe call is handled by *do_pipe* (line 25933). All *do_pipe* really does is allocate an i-node for the pipe and return two file descriptors for it. Pipes are owned by the system, not by the user, and are located on the designated pipe device (configured in *include/minix/config.h*), which could very well be a RAM disk, since pipe data do not have to be preserved permanently.

Reading and writing a pipe is slightly different from reading and writing a file, because a pipe has a finite capacity. An attempt to write to a pipe that is already full will cause the writer to be suspended. Similarly, reading from an empty pipe will suspend the reader. In effect, a pipe has two pointers, the current position (used by readers) and the size (used by writers), to determine where data come from or go to.

The various checks to see if an operation on a pipe is possible are carried out by *pipe_check* (line 25986). In addition to the above tests, which may lead to the caller being suspended, *pipe_check* calls *release* to see if a process previously suspended due to no data or too much data can now be revived. These revivals are done on line 26017 and line 26052, for sleeping writers and readers, respectively. Writing on a broken pipe (no readers) is also detected here.

The act of suspending a process is done by *suspend* (line 26073). All it does is save the parameters of the call in the process table and set the flag *dont_reply* to *TRUE*, to inhibit the file system's reply message.

The procedure *release* (line 26099) is called to check if a process that was suspended on a pipe can now be allowed to continue. If it finds one, it calls *revive* to set a flag so that the main loop will notice it later. This function is not a system call, but is listed in Fig. 5-33(c) because it uses the message-passing mechanism.

The last procedure in *pipe.c* is *do_unpause* (line 26189). When the process manager is trying to signal a process, it must find out if that process is hanging on a pipe or special file (in which case it must be awakened with an *EINTR* error). Since the process manager knows nothing about pipes or special files, it sends a message to the file system to ask. That message is processed by *do_unpause*, which revives the process, if it is blocked. Like *revive*, *do_unpause* has some similarity to a system call, although it is not one.

The last two functions in *pipe.c*, *select_request_pipe* (line 26247) and *select_match_pipe* (line 26278), support the select call, which is not discussed here.

5.7.5 Directories and Paths

We have now finished looking at how files are read and written. Our next task is to see how path names and directories are handled.

Converting a Path to an I-Node

Many system calls (e.g., open, unlink, and mount) have path names (i.e., file names) as a parameter. Most of these calls must fetch the i-node for the named file before they can start working on the call itself. How a path name is converted to an i-node is a subject we will now look at in detail. We already saw the general outline in Fig. 5-16.

The parsing of path names is done in the file *path.c*. The first procedure, *eat_path* (line 26327), accepts a pointer to a path name, parses it, arranges for its i-node to be loaded into memory, and returns a pointer to the i-node. It does its work by calling *last_dir* to get the i-node to the final directory and then calling *advance* to get the final component of the path. If the search fails, for example, because one of the directories along the path does not exist, or exists but is protected against being searched, *NIL_INODE* is returned instead of a pointer to the i-node.

Path names may be absolute or relative and may have arbitrarily many components, separated by slashes. These issues are dealt with by *last_dir*, which begins by examining the first character of the path name to see if it is an absolute path or a relative one (line 26371). For absolute paths, *rip* is set to point to the root i-node; for relative ones, it is set to point to the i-node for the current working directory.

At this point, *last_dir* has the path name and a pointer to the i-node of the directory to look up the first component in. It enters a loop on line 26382 now, parsing the path name, component by component. When it gets to the end, it returns a pointer to the final directory.

Get_name (line 26413) is a utility procedure that extracts components from strings. More interesting is *advance* (line 26454), which takes as parameters a directory pointer and a string, and looks up the string in the directory. If it finds the string, *advance* returns a pointer to its i-node. The details of transferring across mounted file systems are handled here.

Although *advance* controls the string lookup, the actual comparison of the string against the directory entries is done in *search_dir* (line 26535), which is the only place in the file system where directory files are actually examined. It contains two nested loops, one to loop over the blocks in a directory, and one to loop over the entries in a block. *Search_dir* is also used to enter and delete names from directories. Figure 5-48 shows the relationships between some of the major procedures used in looking up path names.

Mounting File Systems

Two system calls that affect the file system as a whole are mount and umount. They allow independent file systems on different minor devices to be "glued" together to form a single, seamless naming tree. Mounting, as we saw in Fig. 5-38, is effectively achieved by reading in the root i-node and superblock of the file system to be mounted and setting two pointers in its superblock. One of them points to the i-node mounted on, and the other points to the root i-node of the mounted file system. These pointers hook the file systems together.

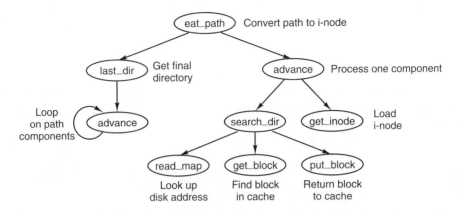

Figure 5-48. Some of the procedures used in looking up path names.

The setting of these pointers is done in the file *mount.c* by *do_mount* on lines 26819 and 26820. The two pages of code that precede setting the pointers are almost entirely concerned with checking for all the errors that can occur while mounting a file system, among them:

1. The special file given is not a block device.

2. The special file is a block device but is already mounted.

3. The file system to be mounted has a rotten magic number.

4. The file system to be mounted is invalid (e.g., no i-nodes).

5. The file to be mounted on does not exist or is a special file.

6. There is no room for the mounted file system's bitmaps.

7. There is no room for the mounted file system's superblock.

8. There is no room for the mounted file system's root i-node.

Perhaps it seems inappropriate to keep harping on this point, but the reality of any practical operating system is that a substantial fraction of the code is devoted to doing minor chores that are not intellectually very exciting but are crucial to making a system usable. If a user attempts to mount the wrong floppy disk by accident, say, once a month, and this leads to a crash and a corrupted file system, the user will perceive the system as being unreliable and blame the designer, not himself.

The famous inventor Thomas Edison once made a remark that is relevant here. He said that "genius" is 1 percent inspiration and 99 percent perspiration. The difference between a good system and a mediocre one is not the brilliance of the former's scheduling algorithm, but its attention to getting all the details right.

Unmounting a file system is easier than mounting one—there are fewer things that can go wrong. *Do_umount* (line 26828) is called to start the job, which is divided into two parts. *Do_umount* itself checks that the call was made by the superuser, converts the name into a device number, and then calls *unmount* (line 26846), which completes the operation. The only real issue is making sure that no process has any open files or working directories on the file system to be removed. This check is straightforward: just scan the whole i-node table to see if any i-nodes in memory belong to the file system to be removed (other than the root i-node). If so, the umount call fails.

The last procedure in *mount.c* is *name_to_dev* (line 26893), which takes a special file pathname, gets its i-node, and extracts its major and minor device numbers. These are stored in the i-node itself, in the place where the first zone would normally go. This slot is available because special files do not have zones.

Linking and Unlinking Files

The next file to consider is *link.c*, which deals with linking and unlinking files. The procedure *do_link* (line 27034) is very much like *do_mount* in that nearly all of the code is concerned with error checking. Some of the possible errors that can occur in the call

    link(file_name, link_name);

are listed below:

1. *File_name* does not exist or cannot be accessed.

2. *File_name* already has the maximum number of links.

3. *File_name* is a directory (only superuser can link to it).

4. *Link_name* already exists.

5. *File_name* and *link_name* are on different devices.

If no errors are present, a new directory entry is made with the string *link_name* and the i-node number of *file_name*. In the code, *name1* corresponds to *file_name* and *name2* corresponds to *link_name*. The actual entry is made by *search_dir*, called from *do_link* on line 27086.

Files and directories are removed by unlinking them. The work of both the unlink and rmdir system calls is done by *do_unlink* (line 27104). Again, a variety of checks must be made; testing that a file exists and that a directory is not a mount point are done by the common code in *do_unlink*, and then either *remove_dir* or *unlink_file* is called, depending upon the system call being supported. We will discuss these shortly.

The other system call supported in *link.c* is rename. UNIX users are familiar with the *mv* shell command which ultimately uses this call; its name reflects another aspect of the call. Not only can it change the name of a file within a directory, it can also effectively move the file from one directory to another, and it can do this atomically, which prevents certain race conditions. The work is done by *do_rename* (line 27162). Many conditions must be tested before this command can be completed. Among these are:

1. The original file must exist (line 27177).

2. The old pathname must not be a directory above the new pathname in the directory tree (lines 27195 to 27212).

3. Neither . nor .. is acceptable as an old or new name (lines 27217 and 27218).

4. Both parent directories must be on the same device (line 27221).

5. Both parent directories must be writable, searchable, and on a writable device (lines 27224 and 27225).

6. Neither the old nor the new name may be a directory with a file system mounted upon it.

Some other conditions must be checked if the new name already exists. Most importantly it must be possible to remove an existing file with the new name.

In the code for *do_rename* there are a few examples of design decisions that were taken to minimize the possibility of certain problems. Renaming a file to a name that already exists could fail on a full disk, even though in the end no additional space is used, if the old file were not removed first, and this is what is done at lines 27260 to 27266. The same logic is used at line 27280, removing the old file name before creating a new name in the same directory, to avoid the possibility that the directory might need to acquire an additional block. However, if the new file and the old file are to be in different directories, that concern is not relevant, and at line 27285 a new file name is created (in a different directory) before the old one is removed, because from a system integrity standpoint a crash that left two filenames pointing to an i-node would be much less serious than a crash that left an i-node not pointed to by any directory entry. The probability of running out of space during a rename operation is low, and that of a system crash even lower, but in these cases it costs nothing more to be prepared for the worst case.

The remaining functions in *link.c* support the ones that we have already discussed. In addition, the first of them, *truncate* (line 27316), is called from several other places in the file system. It steps through an i-node one zone at a time, freeing all the zones it finds, as well as the indirect blocks. *Remove_dir* (line 27375) carries out a number of additional tests to be sure the directory can be removed, and then it in turn calls *unlink_file* (line 27415). If no errors are found, the directory entry is cleared and the link count in the i-node is reduced by one.

5.7.6 Other System Calls

The last group of system calls is a mixed bag of things involving status, directories, protection, time, and other services.

Changing Directories and File Status

The file *stadir.c* contains the code for six system calls: chdir, fchdir, chroot, stat, fstat, and fstatfs. In studying *last_dir* we saw how path searches start out by looking at the first character of the path, to see if it is a slash or not. Depending on the result, a pointer is then set to the working directory or the root directory.

Changing from one working directory (or root directory) to another is just a matter of changing these two pointers within the caller's process table. These changes are made by *do_chdir* (line 27542) and *do_chroot* (line 27580). Both of them do the necessary checking and then call *change* (line 27594), which does some more tests, then calls *change_into* (line 27611) to open the new directory and replace the old one.

Do_fchdir (line 27529) supports fchdir, which is an alternate way of effecting the same operation as chdir, with the calling argument a file descriptor rather than a path. It tests for a valid descriptor, and if the descriptor is valid it calls *change_into* to do the job.

In *do_chdir* the code on lines 27552 to 27570 is not executed on chdir calls made by user processes. It is specifically for calls made by the process manager, to change to a user's directory for the purpose of handling exec calls. When a user tries to execute a file, say, *a.out* in his working directory, it is easier for the process manager to change to that directory than to try to figure out where it is.

The two system calls stat and fstat are basically the same, except for how the file is specified. The former gives a path name, whereas the latter provides the file descriptor of an open file, similar to what we saw for chdir and fchdir. The top-level procedures, *do_stat* (line 27638) and *do_fstat* (line 27658), both call *stat_inode* to do the work. Before calling *stat_inode*, *do_stat* opens the file to get its i-node. In this way, both *do_stat* and *do_fstat* pass an i-node pointer to *stat_inode*.

All *stat_inode* (line 27673) does is to extract information from the i-node and copy it into a buffer. The buffer must be explicitly copied to user space by a sys_datacopy kernel call on lines 27713 and 27714 because it is too large to fit in a message.

Finally, we come to *do_fstatfs* (line 27721). Fstatfs is not a POSIX call, although POSIX defines a similar fstatvfs call which returns a much bigger data structure. The MINIX 3 fstatfs returns only one piece of information, the block size of a file system. The prototype for the call is

_PROTOTYPE(int fstatfs, (int fd, struct statfs *st)   );

The *statfs* structure it uses is simple, and can be displayed on a single line:

    struct statfs { off_t f_bsize;   /* file system block size */ };

These definitions are in *include/sys/statfs.h*, which is not listed in Appendix B.

Protection

The MINIX 3 protection mechanism uses the *rwx* bits. Three sets of bits are present for each file: for the owner, for his group, and for others. The bits are set by the chmod system call, which is carried out by *do_chmod*, in file *protect.c* (line 27824). After making a series of validity checks, the mode is changed on line 27850.

The chown system call is similar to chmod in that both of them change an internal i-node field in some file. The implementation is also similar although *do_chown* (line 27862) can be used to change the owner only by the superuser. Ordinary users can use this call to change the group of their own files.

The umask system call allows the user to set a mask (stored in the process table), which then masks out bits in subsequent creat system calls. The complete implementation would be only one statement, line 27907, except that the call must return the old mask value as its result. This additional burden triples the number of lines of code required (lines 27906 to 27908).

The access system call makes it possible for a process to find out if it can access a file in a specified way (e.g., for reading). It is implemented by *do_access* (line 27914), which fetches the file's i-node and calls the internal procedure, *forbidden* (line 27938), to see if the access is forbidden. *Forbidden* checks the uid and gid, as well as the information in the i-node. Depending on what it finds, it selects one of the three *rwx* groups and checks to see if the access is permitted or forbidden.

Read_only (line 27999) is a little internal procedure that tells whether the file system on which its i-node parameter is located is mounted read only or read-write. It is needed to prevent writes on file systems mounted read only.

5.7.7 The I/O Device Interface

As we have mentioned more than once, a design goal was to make MINIX 3 a more robust operating system by having all device drivers run as user-space processes without direct access to kernel data structures or kernel code. The primary advantage of this approach is that a faulty device driver will not cause the entire system to crash, but there are some other implications of this approach. One is that device drivers not needed immediately upon startup can be started at any time after startup is complete. This also implies that a device driver can be stopped, restarted, or replaced by a different driver for the same device at any time while the system is running. This flexibility is subject, of course to some restrictions—you cannot start multiple drivers for the same device. However, if the hard disk driver crashes, it can be restarted from a copy on the RAM disk.

MINIX 3 device drivers are accessed from the file system. In response to user requests for I/O the file system sends messages to the user-space device drivers. The *dmap* table has an entry for every possible major device type. It provides the mapping between the major device number and the corresponding device driver. The next two files we will consider deal with the *dmap* table. The table itself is declared in *dmap.c*. This file also supports initialization of the table and a new system call, devctl, which is intended to support starting, stopping, and restarting of device drivers. After that we will look at *device.c* which supports normal run-time operations on devices, such as open, close, read, write, and ioctl.

When a device is opened, closed, read, or written, *dmap* provides the name of the procedure to call to handle the operation. All of these procedures are located in the file system's address space. Many of these procedures do nothing, but some call a device driver to request actual I/O. The process number corresponding to each major device is also provided by the table.

Whenever a new major device is added to MINIX 3, a line must be added to this table telling what action, if any, is to be taken when the device is opened, closed, read, or written. As a simple example, if a tape drive is added to MINIX 3, when its special file is opened, the procedure in the table could check to see if the tape drive is already in use.

Dmap.c begins with a macro definition, *DT* (lines 28115 to 28117), which is used to initialize the *dmap* table. This macro makes it easier to add a new device driver when reconfiguring MINIX 3. Elements of the *dmap* table are defined in *include/minix/dmap.h*; each element consists of a pointer to a function to be called on an open or close, another pointer to a function to be called on a read or write, a process number (index into process table, not a PID), and a set of flags. The actual table is an array of such elements, declared on line 28132. This table is globally available within the file server. The size of the table is *NR_DEVICES*, which is 32 in the version of MINIX 3 described here, and almost twice as big as needed for the number of devices currently supported. Fortunately, the C language behavior of setting all uninitialized variables to zero will ensure that no spurious information appears in unused slots.

Following the declaration of *dmap* is a *PRIVATE* declaration of *init_dmap*. It is defined by an array of *DT* macros, one for each possible major device. Each of these macros expands to initialize an entry in the global array at compile time. A look at a few of the macros will help with understanding how they are used. *Init_dmap[1]* defines the entry for the memory driver, which is major device 1. The macro looks like this:

```
DT(1, gen_opcl, gen_io, MEM_PROC_NR, 0)
```

The memory driver is always present and is loaded with the system boot image. The "1" as first parameter means that this driver must be present. In this case, a pointer to *gen_opcl* will be entered as the function to call to open or close, and a pointer to *gen_io* will be entered to specify the function to call for reading or writing, *MEM_PROC_NR* tells which slot in the process table the memory driver uses, and "0" means no flags are set. Now look at the next entry, *init_dmap[2]*. This is the entry for the floppy disk driver, and it looks like this:

```
DT(0, no_dev, 0,  0,  DMAP_MUTABLE)
```

The first "0" indicates this entry is for a driver not required to be in the boot image. The default for the first pointer field specifies a call to *no_dev* on an attempt to open the device. This function returns an *ENODEV* "no such device" error to the caller. The next two zeros are also defaults: since the device cannot be opened there is no need to specify a function to call to do I/O, and a zero in the process table slot is interpreted as no process specified. The meaning of the flag *DMAP_MUTABLE* is that changes to this entry are permitted. (Note that the absence of this flag for the memory driver entry means its entry cannot be changed after initialization.) MINIX 3 can be configured with or without a floppy disk driver in the boot image. If the floppy disk driver is in the boot image and it is specified by a *label=FLOPPY* boot parameter to be the default disk device, this entry will be changed when the file system starts. If the floppy driver is not in the boot image, or if it is in the image but is not specified to be the default disk device, this field will not be changed when FS starts. However, it is still possible for the floppy driver to be activated later. Typically this is done by the */etc/rc* script run when *init* is run.

Do_devctl (line 28157) is the first function executed to service a devctl call. The current version is very simple, it recognizes two requests, *DEV_MAP* and *DEV_UNMAP*, and the latter returns a *ENOSYS* error, which means "function not implemented." Obviously, this is a stopgap. In the case of *DEV_MAP* the next function, *map_driver* is called.

It might be helpful to describe how the devctl call is used, and plans for its use in the future. A server process, the **reincarnation server** (**RS**) is used in MINIX 3 to support starting user-space servers and drivers after the operating system is up and running. The interface to the reincarnation server is the *service* utility, and examples of its use can be seen in */etc/rc*. An example is

```
service up /sbin/floppy –dev /dev/fd0
```

This action results in the reincarnation server making a devctl call to start the binary */sbin/floppy* as the device driver for the device special file */dev/fd0*. To do this, RS execs the specified binary, but sets a flag that inhibits it from running until it has been transformed into a system process. Once the process is in memory and its slot number in the process table is known, the major device number for the specified device is determined. This information is then included in a message to the file server that requested the devctl *DEV_MAP* operation. This is the most important part of the reincarnation server's job from the point of view of initializing the I/O interface. For the sake of completeness we will also mention that to complete initialization of the device driver, RS also makes a sys_privctl call to have the system task initialize the driver process's *priv* table entry and allow it to execute. Recall from Chapter 2 that a dedicated *priv* table slot is what makes an otherwise ordinary user-space process into a system process.

The reincarnation server is new, and in the release of MINIX 3 described here it is still rudimentary. Plans for future releases of MINIX 3 include a more powerful reincarnation server that will be able to stop and restart drivers in addition to starting them. It will also be able to monitor drivers and restart them automatically if problems develop. Check the Web site (*www.minix3.org*) and the newsgroup (*comp.os.minix*) for the current status.

Continuing with *dmap.c*, the function *map_driver* begins on line 28178. Its operation is straightforward. If the *DMAP_MUTABLE* flag is set for the entry in the *dmap* table, appropriate values are written into each entry. Three different variants of the function for handling opening and closing of the device are available; one is selected by a *style* parameter passed in the message from RS to the file system (lines 28204 to 28206). Notice that *dmap_flags* is not altered. If the entry was marked *DMAP_MUTABLE* originally it retains this status after the devctl call .

The third function in *dmap.c* is *build_map*. This is called by *fs_init* when the file system is first started, before it enters its main loop. The first thing done is to loop over all of the entries in the local *init_dmap* table and copy the expanded macros to the global *dmap* table for each entry that does not have *no_dev* specified as the *dmap_opcl* member. This correctly initializes these entries. Otherwise the default values for an uninitialized driver are set in place in *dmap*. The rest of *build_map* is more interesting. A boot image can be built with multiple disk device drivers. By default *at_wini*, *bios_wini*, and *floppy* drivers are added to the boot image by the *Makefile* in the *src/tools/*. A label is added to each of these, and a *label=* item in the boot parameters determines which one will actually be loaded in the image and activated as the default disk driver. The *env_get_param* calls on line 28248 and line 28250 use library routines that ultimately use the sys_getinfo kernel call to get the *label* and *controller* boot parameter strings. Finally, *build_map* is called on line 28267 to modify the entry in *dmap* that corresponds to the boot device. The key thing here is setting the process number to *DRVR_PROC_NR*, which happens to be slot 6 in the process table. This slot is magic; the driver in this slot is the default driver.

Now we come to the file *device.c*, which contains the procedures needed for device I/O at run time.

The first one is *dev_open* (line 28334). It is called by other parts of the file system, most often from *common_open* in *main.c* when a open operation is determined to be accessing a device special file, but also from *load_ram* and *do_mount*. Its operation is typical of several procedures we will see here. It determines the major device number, verifies that it is valid, and then uses it to set a pointer to an entry in the *dmap* table, and then makes a call to the function pointed to in that entry, at line 28349:

```
r = (*dp->dmap_opcl)(DEV_OPEN, dev, proc, flags)
```

In the case of a disk drive, the function called will be *gen_opcl*, in the case of a terminal device it will be *tty_opcl*. If a *SUSPEND* return code is received there is a serious problem; an open call should not fail this way.

The next call, *dev_close* (line 28357) is simpler. It is not expected that a call will be made to an invalid device, and no harm is done if a close operation fails, so the code is shorter than this text describing it, just one line that will end up calling the same *_opcl* procedure as *dev_open* called when the device was opened.

When the file system receives a notification message from a device driver *dev_status* (line 28366) is called. A notification means an event has occurred, and this function is responsible for finding out what kind of event and initiating appropriate action. The origin of the notification is specified as a process number, so the first step is to search through the *dmap* table to find an entry that corresponds to the notifying process (lines 18371 to 18373). It is possible the notification could have been bogus, so it is not an error if no corresponding entry is found and *dev_status* returns without finding a match. If a match is found, the loop on lines 28378 to 28398 is entered. On each iteration a message is sent to the driver process requesting its status. Three possible reply types are expected. A *DEV_REVIVE* message may be received if the process that originally requested I/O was previously suspended. In this case *revive* (in *pipe.c*, line 26146) is called. A *DEV_IO_READY* message may be received if a select call has been made on the device. Finally, a *DEV_NO_STATUS* message may be received, and is, in fact expected, but possibly not until one or both of the first two message types are received. For this reason, the *get_more* variable is used to cause the loop to repeat until the *DEV_NO_STATUS* message is received.

When actual device I/O is needed, *dev_io* (line 28406) is called from *read_write* (line 25124) to handle character special files, and from *rw_block* (line 22661) to handle block special files. It builds a standard message (see Fig. 3-17) and sends it to the specified device driver by calling either *gen_io* or *ctty_io* as specified in the *dp->dmap_driver* field of the *dmap*table. While *dev_io* is waiting for a reply from the driver, the file system waits. It has no internal multiprogramming. Usually, these waits are quite short though (e.g., 50 msec). But it is possible no data will be available—this is especially likely if the data was requested from a terminal device. In that case the reply message may indicate *SUSPEND*, to temporarily suspend the calling application but let the file system continue.

The procedure *gen_opcl* (line 28455) is called for disk devices, whether floppy disks, hard disks, or memory-based devices. A message is constructed, and, as with reading and writing, the *dmap* table is used to determine whether *gen_io* or *ctty_io* will be used to send the message to the driver process for the device. *Gen_opcl* is also used to close the same devices.

To open a terminal device *tty_opcl* (line 28482) is called. It calls *gen_opcl* after possibly modifying the flags, and if the call made the tty the controlling tty for the active process this is recorded in the process table *fp_tty* entry for that process.

The device */dev/tty* is a fiction which does not correspond to any particular device. This is a magic designation that an interactive user can use to refer to his own terminal, no matter which physical terminal is actually in use. To open or close */dev/tty*, a call is made to *ctty_opcl* (line 28518). It determines whether the *fp_tty* process table entry for the current process has indeed been modified by a previous *ctty_opcl* call to indicate a controlling tty.

The setsid system call requires some work by the file system, and this is performed by *do_setsid* (line 28534). It modifies the process table entry for the current process to record that the process is a session leader and has no controlling process.

One system call, ioctl, is handled primarily in *device.c*. This call has been put here because it is closely tied to the device driver interface. When an ioctl is done, *do_ioctl* (line 28554) is called to build a message and send it to the proper device driver.

To control terminal devices one of the functions declared in *include/termios.h* should be used in programs written to be POSIX compliant. The C library will translate such functions into ioctl calls. For devices other than terminals ioctl is used for many operations, many of which were described in Chap. 3.

The next function, *gen_io* (line 28575), is the real workhorse of this file. Whether the operation on a device is an open or a close, a read or a write, or an ioctl this function is called to complete the work. Since */dev/tty* is not a physical device, when a message that refers to it must be sent, the next function, *ctty_io* (line 28652), finds the correct major and minor device and substitutes them into the message before passing the message on. The call is made using the *dmap* entry for the physical device that is actually in use. As MINIX 3 is currently configured a call to *gen_io* will result.

The function *no_dev* (line 28677), is called from slots in the table for which a device does not exist, for example when a network device is referenced on a machine with no network support. It returns an *ENODEV* status. It prevents crashes when nonexistent devices are accessed.

The last function in *device.c* is *clone_opcl* (line 28691). Some devices need special processing upon open. Such a device is "cloned," that is, on a successful open it is replaced by a new device with a new unique minor device number. In MINIX 3 as described here this capability is not used. However, it is used when networking is enabled. A device that needs this will, of course, have an entry in the *dmap* table that specifies *clone_opcl* in the *dmap_opcl* field. This is accomplished by a call from the reincarnation server that specifies *STYLE_CLONE*.

When *clone_opcl* opens a device the operation starts in exactly the same way as *gen_opcl*, but on the return a new minor device number may be returned in the *REP_STATUS* field of the reply message. If so, a temporary file is created if it is possible to allocate a new i-node. A visible directory entry is not created. That is not necessary, since the file is already open.

Time

Associated with each file are three 32-bit numbers relating to time. Two of these record the times when the file was last accessed and last modified. The third records when the status of the i-node itself was last changed. This time will change for almost every access to a file except a read or exec. These times are kept in the i-node. With the utime system call, the access and modification times can be set by the owner of the file or the superuser. The procedure *do_utime* (line 28818) in file *time.c* performs the system call by fetching the i-node and storing the time in it. At line 28848 the flags that indicate a time update is required are reset, so the system will not make an expensive and redundant call to *clock_time*.

As we saw in the previous chapter, the real time is determined by adding the time since the system was started (maintained by the clock task) to the real time when startup occurred. The stime system call returns the real time. Most of its work is done by the process manager, but the file system also maintains a record of the startup time in a global variable, *boottime*. The process manager sends a message to the file system whenever a stime call is made. The file system's *do_stime* (line 28859) updates *boottime* from this message.

5.7.8 Additional System Call Support

There are a number of files that are not listed in Appendix B, but which are required to compile a working system. In this section we will review some files that support additional system calls. In the next section we will mention files and functions that provide more general support for the file system.

The file *misc.c* contains procedures for a few system and kernel calls that do not fit in anywhere else.

Do_getsysinfo is an interface to the sys_datacopy kernel call. It is meant to support the information server (IS) for debugging purposes. It allows IS to request a copy of file system data structures so it can display them to the user.

The dup system call duplicates a file descriptor. In other words, it creates a new file descriptor that points to the same file as its argument. The call has a variant dup2. Both versions of the call are handled by *do_dup* This function is included in MINIX 3 to support old binary programs. Both of these calls are obsolete. The current version of the MINIX 3 C library will invoke the fcntl system call when either of these are encountered in a C source file.

Operation	Meaning
F_DUPFD	Duplicate a file descriptor
F_GETFD	Get the close-on-exec flag
F_SETFD	Set the close-on-exec flag
F_GETFL	Get file status flags
F_SETFL	Set file status flags
F_GETLK	Get lock status of a file
F_SETLK	Set read/write lock on a file
F_SETLKW	Set write lock on a file

Figure 5-49. The POSIX request parameters for the FCNTL system call.

Fcntl, handled by *do_fcntl* is the preferred way to request operations on an open file. Services are requested using POSIX-defined flags described in Fig. 5-49. The call is invoked with a file descriptor, a request code, and additional arguments as necessary for the particular request. For instance, the equivalent of the old call

    dup2(fd, fd2);

would be

    fcntl(fd, F_DUPFD, fd2);

Several of these requests set or read a flag; the code consists of just a few lines. For instance, the *F_SETFD* request sets a bit that forces closing of a file when its owner process does an exec. The *F_GETFD* request is used to determine whether a file must be closed when an exec call is made. The *F_SETFL* and *F_GETFL* requests permit setting flags to indicate a particular file is available in nonblocking mode or for append operations.

Do_fcntl handles file locking, also. A call with the *F_GETLK*, *F_SETLK*, or *F_SETLKW* command specified is translated into a call to *lock_op*, discussed in an earlier section.

The next system call is sync, which copies all blocks and i-nodes that have been modified since being loaded back to the disk. The call is processed by *do_sync*. It simply searches through all the tables looking for dirty entries. The i-nodes must be processed first, since *rw_inode* leaves its results in the block cache. After all dirty i-nodes are written to the block cache, then all dirty blocks are written to the disk.

The system calls fork, exec, exit, and set are really process manager calls, but the results have to be posted here as well. When a process forks, it is essential that the kernel, process manager, and file system all know about it. These "system calls" do not come from user processes, but from the process manager.

Do_fork, *do_exit*, and *do_set* record the relevant information in the file system's part of the process table. *Do_exec* searches for and closes (using *do_close*) any files marked to be closed-on-exec.

The last function in *misc.c* is not really a system call but is handled like one. *Do_revive* is called when a device driver that was previously unable to complete work that the file system had requested, such as providing input data for a user process, has now completed the work. The file system then revives the process and sends it the reply message.

One system call merits a header file as well as a C source file to support it. *Select.h* and *select.c* provide support for the select system call. Select is used when a single process has to do deal with multiple I/O streams, as, for instance, a communications or network program. Describing it in detail is beyond the scope of this book.

5.7.9 File System Utilities

The file system contains a few general purpose utility procedures that are used in various places. They are collected together in the file *utility.c*.

Clock_time sends messages to the system task to find out what the current real time is.

Fetch_name is needed because many system calls have a file name as parameter. If the file name is short, it is included in the message from the user to the file system. If it is long, a pointer to the name in user space is put in the message. *Fetch_name* checks for both cases, and either way, gets the name.

Two functions here handle general classes of errors. *No_sys* is the error handler that is called when the file system receives a system call that is not one of its calls. *Panic* prints a message and tells the kernel to throw in the towel when something catastrophic happens. Similar functions can be found in *pm/utility.c* in the process manager's source directory.

The last two functions, *conv2* and *conv4*, exist to help MINIX 3 deal with the problem of differences in byte order between different CPU families. These routines are called when reading from or writing to a disk data structure, such as an i-node or bitmap. The byte order in the system that created the disk is recorded in the superblock. If it is different from the order used by the local processor the order will be swapped. The rest of the file system does not need to know anything about the byte order on the disk.

Finally, there are two other files that provide specialized utility services to the file manager. The file system can ask the system task to set an alarm for it, but if it needs more than one timer it can maintain its own linked list of timers, similar to what we saw for the process manager in the previous chapter. The file *timers.c* provides this support for the file system. Finally, MINIX 3 implements a unique way of using a CD-ROM that hides a simulated MINIX 3 disk with several partitions on a CD-ROM, and allows booting a live MINIX 3 system from the CD-

ROM. The MINIX 3 files are not visible to operating systems that support only standard CD-ROM file formats. The file *cdprobe.c* is used at boot time to locate a CD-ROM device and the files on it needed to start MINIX 3.

5.7.10 Other MINIX 3 Components

The process manager discussed in the previous chapter and the file system discussed in this chapter are user-space servers which provide support that would be integrated into a monolithic kernel in an operating system of conventional design. These are not the only server processes in a MINIX 3 system, however. There are other user-space processes that have system privileges and should be considered part of the operating system. We do not have enough space in this book to discuss their internals, but we should at least mention them here.

One we have already mentioned in this chapter. This is the reincarnation server, RS, which can start an ordinary process and turn it into a system process. It is used in the current version of MINIX 3 to launch device drivers that are not part of the system boot image. In future releases it will also be able to stop and restart drivers, and, indeed, to monitor drivers and stop and restart them automatically if they seem to be malfunctioning. The source code for the reincarnation server is in the *src/servers/rs/* directory.

Another server that has been mentioned in passing is the information server, IS. It is used to generate the debugging dumps that can be triggered by pressing the function keys on a PC-style keyboard. The source code for the information server is in the *src/servers/is/* directory.

The information server and the reincarnation servers are relatively small programs. There is a third, optional, server, the network server, or INET. It is quite large. The INET program image on disk is comparable in size to the MINIX 3 boot image. It is started by the reincarnation server in much the same way that device drivers are started. The inet source code is in the *src/servers/inet/* directory.

Finally, we will mention one other system component which is considered a device driver, not a server. This is the log driver. With so many different components of the operating system running as independent processes, it is desirable to provide a standardized way of handling diagnostic, warning, and error messages. The MINIX 3 solution is to have a device driver for a pseudo-device known as */dev/klog* which can receive messages and handle writing them to a file. The source code for the log driver is in the *src/drivers/log/* directory.

5.8 SUMMARY

When seen from the outside, a file system is a collection of files and directories, plus operations on them. Files can be read and written, directories can be created and destroyed, and files can be moved from directory to directory. Most modern file systems support a hierarchical directory system, in which directories may have subdirectories ad infinitum.

When seen from the inside, a file system looks quite different. The file system designers have to be concerned with how storage is allocated, and how the system keeps track of which block goes with which file. We have also seen how different systems have different directory structures. File system reliability and performance are also important issues.

Security and protection are of vital concern to both the system users and system designers. We discussed some security flaws in older systems, and generic problems that many systems have. We also looked at authentication, with and without passwords, access control lists, and capabilities, as well as a matrix model for thinking about protection.

Finally, we studied the MINIX 3 file system in detail. It is large but not very complicated. It accepts requests for work from user processes, indexes into a table of procedure pointers, and calls that procedure to carry out the requested system call. Due to its modular structure and position outside the kernel, it can be removed from MINIX 3 and used as a free-standing network file server with only minor modifications.

Internally, MINIX 3 buffers data in a block cache and attempts to read ahead when making sequential access to file. If the cache is made large enough, most program text will be found to be already in memory during operations that repeatedly access a particular set of programs, such as a compilation.

PROBLEMS

1. NTFS uses Unicode for naming files. Unicode supports 16-bit characters. Give an advantage of Unicode file naming over ASCII file naming.

2. Some files begin with a magic number. Of what use is this?

3. Fig. 5-4 lists some file attributes. Not listed in this table is parity. Would that be a useful file attribute? If so, how might it be used?

4. Give 5 different path names for the file */etc/passwd*. (*Hint:* think about the directory entries "." and "..".)

5. Systems that support sequential files always have an operation to rewind files. Do systems that support random access files need this too?

6. Some operating systems provide a system call rename to give a file a new name. Is there any difference at all between using this call to rename a file, and just copying the file to a new file with the new name, followed by deleting the old one?

7. Consider the directory tree of Fig. 5-7. If */usr/jim/* is the working directory, what is the absolute path name for the file whose relative path name is *../ast/x*?

8. Consider the following proposal. Instead of having a single root for the file system, give each user a personal root. Does that make the system more flexible? Why or why not?

9. The UNIX file system has a call chroot that changes the root to a given directory. Does this have any security implications? If so, what are they?

10. The UNIX system has a call to read a directory entry. Since directories are just files, why is it necessary to have a special call? Can users not just read the raw directories themselves?

11. A standard PC can hold only four operating systems at once. Is there any way to increase this limit? What consequences would your proposal have?

12. Contiguous allocation of files leads to disk fragmentation, as mentioned in the text. Is this internal fragmentation or external fragmentation? Make an analogy with something discussed in the previous chapter.

13. Figure 5-10 shows the structure of the original FAT file system used on MS-DOS. Originally this file system had only 4096 blocks, so a table with 4096 (12-bit) entries was enough. If that scheme were to be directly extended to file systems with 2^{32} blocks, how much space would the FAT occupy?

14. An operating system only supports a single directory but allows that directory to have arbitrarily many files with arbitrarily long file names. Can something approximating a hierarchical file system be simulated? How?

15. Free disk space can be kept track of using a free list or a bitmap. Disk addresses require D bits. For a disk with B blocks, F of which are free, state the condition under which the free list uses less space than the bitmap. For D having the value 16 bits, express your answer as a percentage of the disk space that must be free.

16. It has been suggested that the first part of each UNIX file be kept in the same disk block as its i-node. What good would this do?

17. The performance of a file system depends upon the cache hit rate (fraction of blocks found in the cache). If it takes 1 msec to satisfy a request from the cache, but 40 msec to satisfy a request if a disk read is needed, give a formula for the mean time required to satisfy a request if the hit rate is h. Plot this function for values of h from 0 to 1.0.

18. What is the difference between a hard link and a symbolic link? Give an advantage of each one.

19. Name three pitfalls to watch out for when backing up a file system.

20. A disk has 4000 cylinders, each with 8 tracks of 512 blocks. A seek takes 1 msec per cylinder moved. If no attempt is made to put the blocks of a file close to each other, two blocks that are logically consecutive (i.e., follow one another in the file) will require an average seek, which takes 5 msec. If, however, the operating system makes an attempt to cluster related blocks, the mean interblock distance can be reduced to 2 cylinders and the seek time reduced to 100 microsec. How long does it take to read a 100 block file in both cases, if the rotational latency is 10 msec and the transfer time is 20 microsec per block?

21. Would compacting disk storage periodically be of any conceivable value? Explain.

22. What is the difference between a virus and a worm? How do they each reproduce?

23. After getting your degree, you apply for a job as director of a large university computer center that has just put its ancient operating system out to pasture and switched over to UNIX. You get the job. Fifteen minutes after starting work, your assistant bursts into your office screaming: "Some students discovered the algorithm we use for encrypting passwords and posted it on the Internet." What should you do?

24. Two computer science students, Carolyn and Elinor, are having a discussion about i-nodes. Carolyn maintains that memories have gotten so large and so cheap that when a file is opened, it is simpler and faster just to fetch a new copy of the i-node into the i-node table, rather than search the entire table to see if it is already there. Elinor disagrees. Who is right?

25. The Morris-Thompson protection scheme with the *n*-bit random numbers was designed to make it difficult for an intruder to discover a large number of passwords by encrypting common strings in advance. Does the scheme also offer protection against a student user who is trying to guess the superuser password on his machine?

26. A computer science department has a large collection of UNIX machines on its local network. Users on any machine can issue a command of the form

　　machine4 who

and have it executed on *machine4*, without having the user log in on the remote machine. This feature is implemented by having the user's kernel send the command and his uid to the remote machine. Is this scheme secure if the kernels are all trustworthy (e.g., large timeshared minicomputers with protection hardware)? What if some of the machines are students' personal computers, with no protection hardware?

27. When a file is removed, its blocks are generally put back on the free list, but they are not erased. Do you think it would be a good idea to have the operating system erase each block before releasing it? Consider both security and performance factors in your answer, and explain the effect of each.

28. Three different protection mechanisms that we have discussed are capabilities, access control lists, and the UNIX *rwx* bits. For each of the following protection problems, tell which of these mechanisms can be used.

(a) Ken wants his files readable by everyone except his office mate.
(b) Mitch and Steve want to share some secret files.
(c) Linda wants some of her files to be public.

For UNIX, assume that groups are categories such as faculty, students, secretaries, etc.

29. Can the Trojan horse attack work in a system protected by capabilities?

30. The size of the *filp* table is currently defined as a constant, *NR_FILPS*, in *fs/const.h*. In order to accommodate more users on a networked system you want to increase *NR_PROCS* in *include/minix/config.h*. How should *NR_FILPS* be defined as a function of *NR_PROCS*?

31. Suppose that a technological breakthrough occurs, and that nonvolatile RAM, which retains its contents reliably following a power failure, becomes available with no price or performance disadvantage over conventional RAM. What aspects of file system design would be affected by this development?

32. Symbolic links are files that point to other files or directories indirectly. Unlike ordinary links such as those currently implemented in MINIX 3, a symbolic link has its own i-node, which points to a data block. The data block contains the path to the file being linked to, and the i-node makes it possible for the link to have different ownership and permissions from the file linked to. A symbolic link and the file or directory to which it points can be located on different devices. Symbolic links are not part of MINIX 3. Implement symbolic links for MINIX 3.

33. Although the current limit to a MINIX 3 file size is determined by the 32-file pointer, in the future, with 64-bit file pointers, files larger than $2^{32} - 1$ bytes may be allowed, in which case triple indirect blocks may be needed. Modify FS to add triple indirect blocks.

34. Show if setting the (now-unused) ROBUST flag might make the file system more or less robust in the face of a crash. Whether this is the case in the current version of MINIX 3 has not been researched, so it may be either way. Take a good look at what happens when a modified block is evicted from the cache. Take into account that a modified data block may be accompanied by a modified i-node and bitmap.

35. Design a mechanism to add support for a "foreign" file system, so that one could, for instance, mount an MS-DOS file system on a directory in the MINIX 3 file system.

36. Write a pair of programs, in C or as shell scripts, to send and receive a message by a covert channel on a MINIX 3 system. *Hint*: A permission bit can be seen even when a file is otherwise inaccessible, and the *sleep* command or system call is guaranteed to delay for a fixed time, set by its argument. Measure the data rate on an idle system. Then create an artificially heavy load by starting up numerous different background processes and measure the data rate again.

37. Implement immediate files in MINIX 3, that is small files actually stored in the i-node itself, thus saving a disk access to retrieve them.

6

READING LIST AND BIBLIOGRAPHY

In the previous five chapters we have touched upon a variety of topics. This chapter is intended as an aid to readers interested in pursuing their study of operating systems further. Section 6.1 is a list of suggested readings. Section 6.2 is an alphabetical bibliography of all books and articles cited in this book.

In addition to the references given below, the *Proceedings of the n-th ACM Symposium on Operating Systems Principles* (ACM) held every other year and the *Proceedings of the n-th International Conference on Distributed Computing Systems* (IEEE) held every year are good places to look for recent papers on operating systems. So is the USENIX *Symposium on Operating Systems Design and Implementation*. Furthermore, *ACM Transactions on Computer Systems* and *Operating Systems Review* are two journals that often have relevant articles.

6.1 SUGGESTIONS FOR FURTHER READING

Below is a list of suggested readings keyed by chapter.

6.1.1 Introduction and General Works

Bovet and Cesati, *Understanding the Linux Kernel,* 3rd Ed.
For anyone wishing to understand how the Linux kernel works internally, this book is probably your best bet.

Brinch Hansen, *Classic Operating Systems*

Operating system have been around long enough now that some of them can be considered classic: systems that changed how the world looked at computers. This book is a collection of 24 papers about seminal operating systems, categorized as open shop, batch, multiprogramming, timesharing, personal computer, and distributed operating systems. Anyone interested in the history of operating systems should read this book.

Brooks, *The Mythical Man-Month: Essays on Software Engineering*

A witty, amusing, and informative book on how *not* to write an operating system by someone who learned the hard way. Full of good advice.

Corbató, "On Building Systems That Will Fail"

In his Turing Award lecture, the father of timesharing addresses many of the same concerns that Brooks does in the *Mythical Man-Month*. His conclusion is that all complex systems will ultimately fail, and that to have any chance for success at all, it is absolutely essential to avoid complexity and strive for simplicity and elegance in design.

Deitel et al, *Operating Systems,* 3rd Ed.

A general textbook on operating systems. In addition to the standard material, it contains detailed case studies of Linux and Windows XP.

Dijkstra, "My Recollections of Operating System Design"

Reminiscences by one of the pioneers of operating system design, starting back in the days when the term "operating system" was not yet known.

IEEE, *Information Technology—Portable Operating System Interface (POSIX), Part 1: System Application Program Interface (API) [C Language]*

This is the standard. Some parts are actually quite readable, especially Annex B, "Rationale and Notes," which sheds light on why things are done as they are. One advantage of referring to the standard document is that, by definition, there are no errors. If a typographical error in a macro name makes it through the editing process it is no longer an error, it is official.

Lampson, "Hints for Computer System Design"

Butler Lampson, one of the world's leading designers of innovative operating systems, has collected many hints, suggestions, and guidelines from his years of experience and put them together in this entertaining and informative article. Like Brooks' book, this is required reading for every aspiring operating system designer.

Lewine, *POSIX Programmer's Guide*

This book describes the POSIX standard in a much more readable way than the standards document itself, and includes discussions on how to convert older programs to POSIX and how to develop new programs for the POSIX environment. There are numerous examples of code, including several complete programs. All POSIX-required library functions and header files are described.

McKusick and Neville-Neil, *The Design and Implementation of the FreeBSD Operating System*

For a thorough explanation of how a modern version of UNIX, in this case FreeBSD, works inside, this is the place to look. It covers processes, I/O, memory management, networking, and just about everything else.

Milojicic, "Operating Systems: Now and in the Future,"

Suppose you were to ask six of the world's leading experts in operating systems a series of questions about the field and where it was going. Would you get the same answers? *Hint*: No. Find out what they said here.

Ray and Ray, *Visual Quickstart Guide: UNIX,* 2nd Ed.

It will help you understand examples in this book if you are comfortable as a UNIX user. This is just one of a number of available beginners' guides to working with the UNIX operating system. Although implemented differently, MINIX looks like UNIX to a user, and this or a similar book will also be helpful in your work with MINIX.

Russinovich and Solomon, *Microsoft Windows Internals,* 4th Ed.

Ever wondered how Windows works inside? Wonder no more. This book tells you everything you conceivably wanted to know about processes, memory management, I/O, networking, security, and a great deal more.

Silberschatz et al, *Operating System Concepts,* 7th Ed.

Another textbook on operating systems. It covers processes, storage management, files, and distributed systems. Two case studies are given: Linux and Windows XP.

Stallings, *Operating Systems,* 5th Ed.

Still another textbook on operating systems. It covers all the usual topics, and also includes a small amount of material on distributed systems, plus an appendix on queueing theory.

Stevens and Rago, *Advanced Programming in the UNIX Environment,* 2nd Ed.

This book tells how to write C programs that use the UNIX system call interface and the standard C library. Examples have been tested on FreeBSD 5.2.1,

Linux 2.4.22 kernel; Solaris 9; and Darwin 7.4.0, and the FreeBSD/Mach base of Mac OS X 10.3. The relationship of these implementations to POSIX is described in detail.

6.1.2 Processes

Andrews and Schneider, "Concepts and Notations for Concurrent Programming"
A tutorial and survey of processes and interprocess communication, including busy waiting, semaphores, monitors, message passing, and other techniques. The article also shows how these concepts are embedded in various programming languages.

Ben-Ari, *Principles of Concurrent and Distributed Programming*
This book consists of three parts; the first has chapters on mutual exclusion, semaphores, monitors, and the dining philosophers problem, among others. The second part discusses distributed programming and languages useful for distributed programming. The third part is on principles of implementation of concurrency.

Bic and Shaw, *Operating System Principles*
This operating systems textbook has four chapters on processes, including not only the usual principles, but also quite a bit of material on implementation.

Milo et al., "Process Migration"
As clusters of PCs gradually replace supercomputers, the issue of moving processes from one machine to another (e.g., for load balancing) is becoming more relevant. In this survey, the authors discuss how process migration works, along with its benefits and pitfalls.

Silberschatz et al, *Operating System Concepts,* 7th Ed.
Chapters 3 through 7 cover processes and interprocess communication, including scheduling, critical sections, semaphores, monitors, and classical interprocess communication problems.

6.1.3 Input/Output

Chen et al., "RAID: High Performance Reliable Secondary Storage"
The use of multiple disk drives in parallel for fast I/O is a trend in high end systems. The authors discuss this idea and examine different organizations in terms of performance, cost, and reliability.

Coffman et al., "System Deadlocks"
A short introduction to deadlocks, what causes them, and how they can be prevented or detected.

Corbet et al., *Linux Device Drivers,* 3rd Ed.

If you really really really want to know how I/O works, try writing a device driver. This book tells you how to do it for Linux.

Geist and Daniel, "A Continuum of Disk Scheduling Algorithms"

A generalized disk arm scheduling algorithm is presented. Extensive simulation and experimental results are given.

Holt, "Some Deadlock Properties of Computer Systems"

A discussion of deadlocks. Holt introduces a directed graph model that can be used to analyze some deadlock situations.

IEEE *Computer* Magazine, March 1994

This issue of *Computer* contains eight articles on advanced I/O, and covers simulation, high performance storage, caching, I/O for parallel computers, and multimedia.

Levine, "Defining Deadlocks"

In this short article, Levine raises interesting questions about conventional definitions and examples of deadlock.

Swift et al., "Recovering Device Drivers"

Device drivers have an error rate an order of magnitude higher than other operating system code. Is there anything that can be done to improve reliability then? This paper describes how shadow drivers can be used to achieve this goal.

Tsegaye and Foss, "A Comparison of the Linux and Windows Device Driver Architecture"

Linux and Windows have quite different architectures for their device drivers. This papers discusses both of them and shows how they are similar and how they are different.

Wilkes et al., "The HP AutoRAID Hierarchical Storage System"

An important new development in high-performance disk systems is RAID (Redundant Array of Inexpensive Disks), in which an array of small disks work together to produce a high-bandwidth system. In this paper, the authors describe in some detail the system they built at HP Labs.

6.1.4 Memory Management

Bic and Shaw, *Operating System Principles*

Three chapters of this book are devoted to memory management, physical memory, virtual memory, and shared memory.

Denning, "Virtual Memory"

A classic paper on many aspects of virtual memory. Denning was one of the pioneers in this field, and was the inventor of the working set concept.

Denning, "Working Sets Past and Present"

A good overview of numerous memory management and paging algorithms. A comprehensive bibliography is included.

Denning, "The Locality Principle"

A recent look back at the history of the locality principle and a discussion of its applicability to a number of problems beyond memory paging issues.

Halpern, "VIM: Taming Software with Hardware"

In this provocative article, Halpern argues that a tremendous amount of money is being spent to produce, debug, and maintain software that deals with memory optimization, not only in operating systems, but also in compilers and other software. He argues that seen macro-economically, it would be better to spend this money just buying more memory and having simple straightforward, more reliable software.

Knuth, *The Art of Computer Programming,* Vol. 1

First fit, best fit, and other memory management algorithms are discussed and compared in this book.

Silberschatz et al, *Operating System Concepts,* 7th Ed.

Chapters 8 and 9 deal with memory management, including swapping, paging, and segmentation. A variety of paging algorithms are mentioned.

6.1.5 File Systems

Denning, "The United States vs. Craig Neidorf"

When a young hacker discovered and published information about how the telephone system works, he was indicted for computer fraud. This article describes the case, which involved many fundamental issues, including freedom of speech. The article is followed by some dissenting views and a rebuttal by Denning.

Ghemawat et al., "The Google File System"

Suppose you decided you wanted to store the entire Internet at home so you could find things really quickly. How would you go about it? Step 1 would be to buy, say, 200,000 PCs. Ordinary garden-variety PCs will do. Nothing fancy needed. Step 2 would be to read this paper to find out how Google does it.

Hafner and Markoff, *Cyberpunk: Outlaws and Hackers on the Computer Frontier*
Three compelling tales of young hackers breaking into computers around the world are told here by the New York Times computer reporter who broke the Internet worm story and his coauthor.

Harbron, *File Systems: Structures and Algorithms*
A book on file system design, applications, and performance. Both structure and algorithms are covered.

Harris et al., *Gray Hat Hacking: The Ethical Hacker's Handbook*
This book discusses legal and ethical aspects of testing computer systems for vulnerabilities, as well as providing technical information about how they are created and how they can be detected.

McKusick et al., "A Fast File System for UNIX"
The UNIX file system was completely reimplemented for 4.2 BSD. This paper describes the design of the new file system, and discusses its performance.

Satyanarayanan, "The Evolution of Coda"
As mobile computing becomes more common, the need to integrate and synchronize mobile and fixed file systems becomes more urgent. Coda was a pioneer in this area. Its evolution and operation is described in this paper.

Silberschatz et al *Operating System Concepts,* 7th Ed.
Chapters 10 and 11 are about file systems. They cover file operations, access methods, consistency semantics, directories, and protection, and implementation, among other topics.

Stallings, *Operating Systems,* 5th Ed.
Chapter 16 contains a fair amount of material about the security environment especially about hackers, viruses and other threats.

Uppuluri et al., "Preventing Race Condition Attacks on File Systems"
Situations exist in which a process assumes that two operations will be performed atomically, with no intervening operations. If another process manages to sneak in and perform an operation between them, security may be breached. This paper discusses the problem and proposes a solution.

Yang et al., "Using Model Checking to Find Serious File System Errors"
File system errors can lead to lost data, so getting them debugged is very important. This paper describes a formal technique that helps detect file system errors before they can do any damage. The results of using the model checker on actual file system code is presented.

6.2 ALPHABETICAL BIBLIOGRAPHY

ANDERSON, T.E., BERSHAD, B.N., LAZOWSKA, E.D., and LEVY, H.M.: "Scheduler Activations: Effective Kernel Support for the User-Level Management of Parallelism," *ACM Trans. on Computer Systems*, vol. 10, pp. 53-79, Feb. 1992.

ANDREWS, G.R., and SCHNEIDER, F.B.: "Concepts and Notations for Concurrent Programming," *Computing Surveys*, vol. 15, pp. 3-43, March 1983.

AYCOCK, J., and BARKER, K.: "Viruses 101," *Proc. Tech. Symp. on Comp. Sci. Education*, ACM, pp. 152-156, 2005.

BACH, M.J.: *The Design of the UNIX Operating System*, Upper Saddle River, NJ: Prentice Hall, 1987.

BALA, K., KAASHOEK, M.F., and WEIHL, W.: "Software Prefetching and Caching for Translation Lookaside Buffers," *Proc. First Symp. on Oper. Syst. Design and Implementation*, USENIX, pp. 243-254, 1994.

BASILI, V.R., and PERRICONE, B.T.: "Software errors and Complexity: An Empirical Investigation," *Commun. of the ACM*, vol. 27, pp. 43-52, Jan. 1984.

BAYS, C.: "A Comparison of Next-Fit, First-Fit, and Best-Fit," *Commun. of the ACM*, vol. 20, pp. 191-192, March 1977.

BEN-ARI, M: *Principles of Concurrent and Distributed Programming*, Upper Saddle River, NJ: Prentice Hall, 1990.

BIC, L.F., and SHAW, A.C.: *Operating System Principles*, Upper Saddle River, NJ: Prentice Hall, 2003.

BOEHM, H.-J.: "Threads Cannot be Implemented as a Library," *Proc. 2004 ACM SIGPLAN Conf. on Prog. Lang. Design and Impl.*, ACM, pp. 261-268, 2005.

BOVET, D.P., and CESATI, M.: *Understanding the Linux Kernel,* 2nd Ed., Sebastopol, CA, O'Reilly, 2002.

BRINCH HANSEN, P.: *Operating System Principles* Upper Saddle River, NJ: Prentice Hall, 1973.

BRINCH HANSEN, P.: *Classic Operating Systems*, New York: Springer-Verlag, 2001.

BROOKS, F. P., Jr.: *The Mythical Man-Month: Essays on Software Engineering*, Anniversary Ed., Boston: Addison-Wesley, 1995.

CERF, V.G.: "Spam, Spim, and Spit," *Commun. of the ACM*, vol. 48, pp. 39-43, April 2005.

CHEN, H, WAGNER, D., and DEAN, D.: "Setuid Demystified," *Proc. 11th USENIX Security Symposium*, pp. 171-190, 2002.

CHEN, P.M., LEE, E.K., GIBSON, G.A., KATZ, R.H., and PATTERSON, D.A.: "RAID: High Performance Reliable Secondary Storage," *Computing Surveys*, vol. 26, pp. 145-185, June 1994.

CHERITON, D.R.: "An Experiment Using Registers for Fast Message-Based Interprocess Communication," *Operating Systems Review*, vol. 18, pp. 12-20, Oct. 1984.

CHERVENAK, A., VELLANSKI, V., and KURMAS, Z.: "Protecting File Systems: A Survey of Backup Techniques," *Proc. 15th Symp. on Mass Storage Systems*, IEEE, 1998

CHOU, A., YANG, J.-F., CHELF, B., and HALLEM, S.: "An Empirical Study of Operating System Errors," *Proc. 18th Symp. on Oper. Syst. Prin.*, ACM, pp. 73-88, 2001.

COFFMAN, E.G., ELPHICK, M.J., and SHOSHANI, A.: "System Deadlocks," *Computing Surveys*, vol. 3, pp. 67-78, June 1971.

CORBATO´, F.J.: "On Building Systems That Will Fail," *Commun. of the ACM*, vol. 34, pp. 72-81, Sept. 1991.

CORBATO´, F.J., MERWIN-DAGGETT, M., and DALEY, R.C: "An Experimental Time-Sharing System," *Proc. AFIPS Fall Joint Computer Conf.*, AFIPS, pp. 335-344, 1962.

CORBATO´, F.J., SALTZER, J.H., and CLINGEN, C.T.: "MULTICS—The First Seven Years," *Proc. AFIPS Spring Joint Computer Conf.*, AFIPS, pp. 571-583, 1972.

CORBATO´, F.J., and VYSSOTSKY, V.A.: "Introduction and Overview of the MULTICS System," *Proc. AFIPS Fall Joint Computer Conf.*, AFIPS, pp. 185-196, 1965.

CORBET, J., RUBINI, A., and KROAH-HARTMAN, G.: *Linux Device Drivers,* 3rd Ed. Sebastopol, CA: O'Reilly, 2005.

COURTOIS, P.J., HEYMANS, F., and PARNAS, D.L.: "Concurrent Control with Readers and Writers," *Commun. of the ACM*, vol. 10, pp. 667-668, Oct. 1971.

DALEY, R.C., and DENNIS, J.B.: "Virtual Memory, Processes, and Sharing in MULTICS," *Commun. of the ACM*, vol. 11, pp. 306-312, May 1968.

DEITEL, H.M., DEITEL, P. J., and CHOFFNES, D. R. : *Operating Systems,* 3rd Ed., Upper Saddle River, NJ: Prentice-Hall, 2004.

DENNING, D.: "The United states vs. Craig Neidorf," *Commun. of the ACM*, vol. 34, pp. 22-43, March 1991.

DENNING, P.J.: "The Working Set Model for Program Behavior," *Commun. of the ACM*, vol. 11, pp. 323-333, 1968a.

DENNING, P.J.: "Thrashing: Its Causes and Prevention," *Proc. AFIPS National Computer Conf.*, AFIPS, pp. 915-922, 1968b.

DENNING, P.J.: "Virtual Memory," *Computing Surveys*, vol. 2, pp. 153-189, Sept. 1970.

DENNING, P.J.: "Working Sets Past and Present," *IEEE Trans. on Software Engineering*, vol. SE-6, pp. 64-84, Jan. 1980.

DENNING, P.J.: "The Locality Principle," *Commun. of the ACM*, vol. 48, pp. 19-24, July 2005.

DENNIS, J.B., and VAN HORN, E.C.: "Programming Semantics for Multiprogrammed Computations," *Commun. of the ACM*, vol. 9, pp. 143-155, March 1966.

DIBONA, C., OCKMAN, S., and STONE, M. eds.: *Open Sources: Voices from the Open Source Revolution*, Sebastopol, CA: O'Reilly, 1999.

DIJKSTRA, E.W.: "Co-operating Sequential Processes," in *Programming Languages*, Genuys, F. (Ed.), London: Academic Press, 1965.

DIJKSTRA, E.W.: "The Structure of THE Multiprogramming System," *Commun. of the ACM*, vol. 11, pp. 341-346, May 1968.

DIJKSTRA, E.W.: "My Recollections of Operating System Design," *Operating Systems Review*, vol. 39, pp. 4-40, April 2005.

DODGE, C., IRVINE, C., and NGUYEN, T.: "A Study of Initialization in Linux and OpenBSD," *Operating Systems Review*, vol. 39, pp. 79-93 April 2005.

ENGLER, D., CHEN, D.Y., and CHOU, A.: "Bugs as Inconsistent Behavior: A General Approach to Inferring Errors in Systems Code," *Proc. 18th Symp. on Oper. Syst. Prin.*, ACM, pp. 57-72, 2001.

ENGLER, D.R., KAASHOEK, M.F., and O'TOOLE, J. Jr.: "Exokernel: An Operating System Architecture for Application-Level Resource Management," *Proc. 15th Symp. on Oper. Syst. Prin.*, ACM, pp. 251-266, 1995.

FABRY, R.S.: "Capability-Based Addressing," *Commun. of the ACM*, vol. 17, pp. 403-412, July 1974.

FEELEY, M.J., MORGAN, W.E., PIGHIN, F.H., KARLIN, A.R., LEVY, H.M., and THEKKATH, C.A.: "Implementing Global Memory Management in a Workstation CLuster," *Proc. 15th Symp. on Oper. Syst. Prin.*, ACM, pp. 201-212, 1995.

FEUSTAL, E.A.: "The Rice Research Computer—A Tagged Architecture," *Proc. AFIPS Conf.* 1972.

FOTHERINGHAM, J.: "Dynamic Storage Allocation in the Atlas Including an Automatic Use of a Backing Store," *Commun. of the ACM*, vol. 4, pp. 435-436, Oct. 1961.

GARFINKEL, S.L., and SHELAT, A.: "Remembrance of Data Passed: A Study of Disk Sanitization Practices," *IEEE Security & Privacy*, vol. 1, pp. 17-27, Jan.-Feb. 2003.

GEIST, R., and DANIEL, S.: "A Continuum of Disk Scheduling Algorithms," *ACM Trans. on Computer Systems*, vol. 5, pp. 77-92, Feb. 1987.

GHEMAWAT, S., GOBIOFF, H., and LEUNG., S.-T.: "The Google File System," *Proc. 19th Symp. on Oper. Syst. Prin.*, ACM, pp. 29-43, 2003.

GRAHAM, R.: "Use of High-Level Languages for System Programming," Project MAC Report TM-13, M.I.T., Sept. 1970.

HAFNER, K., and MARKOFF, J.: *Cyberpunk: Outlaws and Hackers on the Computer Frontier*, New York: Simon and Schuster, 1991.

HALPERN, M.: "VIM: Taming Software with Hardware," *IEEE Computer*, vol. 36, pp. 21-25, Oct. 2003.

HARBRON, T.R.: *File Systems: Structures and Algorithms*, Upper Saddle River, NJ: Prentice Hall, 1988.

HARRIS, S., HARPER, A., EAGLE, C., NESS, J., and LESTER, M.: *Gray Hat Hacking: The Ethical Hacker's Handbook*, New York: McGraw-Hill Osborne Media, 2004.

HAUSER, C., JACOBI, C., THEIMER, M., WELCH, B., and WEISER, M.: "Using Threads in Interactive Systems: A Case Study," *Proc. 14th Symp. on Oper. Syst. Prin.*, ACM, pp. 94-105, 1993.

HEBBARD, B. et al.: "A Penetration Analysis of the Michigan Terminal System," *Operating Systems Review*, vol. 14, pp. 7-20, Jan. 1980.

HERBORTH, C.: *UNIX Advanced: Visual Quickpro Guide*, Berkeley, CA: Peachpit Press, 2005

HERDER, J.N.: "Towards a True Microkernel Operating System," M.S. Thesis, Vrije Universiteit, Amsterdam, Feb. 2005.

HOARE, C.A.R.: "Monitors, An Operating System Structuring Concept," *Commun. of the ACM*, vol. 17, pp. 549-557, Oct. 1974; Erratum in *Commun. of the ACM*, vol. 18, p. 95, Feb. 1975.

HOLT, R.C: "Some Deadlock Properties of Computer Systems," *Computing Surveys*, vol. 4, pp. 179-196, Sept. 1972.

HUCK, J., and HAYS, J.: "Architectural Support for Translation Table Management in Large Address Space Machines," *Proc. 20th Annual Int'l Symp. on Computer Arch.*, ACM, pp. 39-50, 1993.

HUTCHINSON, N.C., MANLEY, S., FEDERWISCH, M., HARRIS, G., HITZ, D, KLEIMAN, S, and O'MALLEY, S.: "Logical vs. Physical File System Backup," *Proc. Third USENIX Symp. on Oper. Syst. Design and Implementation*, USENIX, pp. 239-249, 1999.

IEEE: *Information technology—Portable Operating System Interface (POSIX), Part 1: System Application Program Interface (API) [C Language]*, New York: IEEE, 1990.

JACOB, B., and MUDGE, T.: "Virtual Memory: Issues of Implementation," *IEEE Computer*, vol. 31, pp. 33-43, June 1998.

JOHANSSON, J., and RILEY, S: *Protect Your Windows Network: From Perimeter to Data*, Boston: Addison-Wesley, 2005.

KERNIGHAN, B.W., and RITCHIE, D.M.: *The C Programming Language*, 2nd Ed., Upper Saddle River, NJ: Prentice Hall, 1988.

KLEIN, D.V.: "Foiling the Cracker: A Survey of, and Improvements to, Password Security," *Proc. UNIX Security Workshop II*, USENIX, Aug. 1990.

KLEINROCK, L.: *Queueing Systems, Vol. 1*, New York: John Wiley, 1975.

KNUTH, D.E.: *The Art of Computer Programming, Volume 1: Fundamental Algorithms*, 3rd Ed., Boston: Addison-Wesley, 1997.

LAMPSON, B.W.: "A Scheduling Philosophy for Multiprogramming Systems," *Commun. of the ACM*, vol. 11, pp. 347-360, May 1968.

LAMPSON, B.W.: "A Note on the Confinement Problem," *Commun. of the ACM*, vol. 10, pp. 613-615, Oct. 1973.

LAMPSON, B.W.: "Hints for Computer System Design," *IEEE Software*, vol. 1, pp. 11-28, Jan. 1984.

LEDIN, G., Jr.: "Not Teaching Viruses and Worms is Harmful," *Commun. of the ACM*, vol. 48, p. 144, Jan. 2005.

LESCHKE, T.: "Achieving Speed and Flexibility by Separating Management from Protection: Embracing the Exokernel Operating System," *Operating Systems Review*, vol. 38, pp. 5-19, Oct. 2004.

LEVINE, G.N.: "Defining Deadlocks," *Operating Systems Review* vol. 37, pp. 54-64, Jan. 2003a.

LEVINE, G.N.: "Defining Deadlock with Fungible Resources," *Operating Systems Review*, vol. 37, pp. 5-11, July 2003b.

LEVINE, G.N.: "The Classification of Deadlock Prevention and Avoidance is Erroneous," *Operating Systems Review*, vol. 39, 47-50, April 2005.

LEWINE, D.: *POSIX Programmer's Guide*, Sebastopol, CA: O'Reilly & Associates, 1991.

LI, K., and HUDAK, P.: "Memory Coherence in Shared Virtual Memory Systems," *ACM Trans. on Computer Systems*, vol. 7, pp. 321-359, Nov. 1989.

LINDE, R.R.: "Operating System Penetration," *Proc. AFIPS National Computer Conf.*, AFIPS, pp. 361-368, 1975.

LIONS, J.: *Lions' Commentary on Unix 6th Edition, with Source Code*, San Jose, CA: Peer-to-Peer Communications, 1996.

MARSH, B.D., SCOTT, M.L., LEBLANC, T.J., and MARKATOS, E.P.: "First-Class User-Level Threads," *Proc. 13th Symp. on Oper. Syst. Prin.*, ACM, pp. 110-121, 1991.

McHUGH, J.A.M., and DEEK, F.P.: "An Incentive System for Reducing Malware Attacks," *Commun. of the ACM*, vol. 48, pp. 94-99, June 2005.

McKUSICK, M.K., JOY, W.N., LEFFLER, S.J., and FABRY, R.S.: "A Fast File System for UNIX," *ACM Trans. on Computer Systems*, vol. 2, pp. 181-197, Aug. 1984.

McKUSICK, M.K., and NEVILLE-NEIL, G.V.: *The Design and Implementation of the FreeBSD Operating System*, Addison-Wesley: Boston, 2005.

MILO, D., DOUGLIS, F., PAINDAVEINE, Y, WHEELER, R., and ZHOU, S.: "Process Migration," *ACM Computing Surveys*, vol. 32, pp. 241-299, July-Sept. 2000.

MILOJICIC, D.: "Operating Systems: Now and in the Future," *IEEE Concurrency*, vol. 7, pp. 12-21, Jan.-March 1999.

MOODY, G.: *Rebel Code* Cambridge, MA: Perseus, 2001.

MORRIS, R., and THOMPSON, K.: "Password Security: A Case History," *Commun. of the ACM*, vol. 22, pp. 594-597, Nov. 1979.

MULLENDER, S.J., and TANENBAUM, A.S.: "Immediate Files," *Software—Practice and Experience*, vol. 14, pp. 365-368, April 1984.

NAUGHTON, J.: *A Brief History of the Future*, Woodstock, NY: Overlook Books, 2000.

NEMETH, E., SNYDER, G., SEEBASS, S., and HEIN, T. R.: *UNIX System Administration*, 3rd Ed., Upper Saddle River, NJ, Prentice Hall, 2000.

ORGANICK, E.I.: *The Multics System*, Cambridge, MA: M.I.T. Press, 1972.

OSTRAND, T.J., WEYUKER, E.J., and BELL, R.M.: "Where the Bugs Are," *Proc. 2004 ACM Symp. on Softw. Testing and Analysis*, ACM, 86-96, 2004.

PETERSON, G.L.: "Myths about the Mutual Exclusion Problem," *Information Processing Letters*, vol. 12, pp. 115-116, June 1981.

PRECHELT, L.: "An Empirical Comparison of Seven Programming Languages," *IEEE Computer*, vol. 33, pp. 23-29, Oct. 2000.

RAY, D.S., and RAY, E.J.: *Visual Quickstart Guide: UNIX,* 2nd Ed., Berkeley, CA: Peachpit Press, 2003.

ROSENBLUM, M., and OUSTERHOUT, J.K.: "The Design and Implementation of a Log-Structured File System," *Proc. 13th Symp. on Oper. Syst. Prin.*, ACM, pp. 1-15, 1991.

RUSSINOVICH, M.E., and SOLOMON, D.A.: *Microsoft Windows Internals*, 4th Ed., Redmond, WA: Microsoft Press, 2005.

SALTZER, J.H.: "Protection and Control of Information Sharing in MULTICS," *Commun. of the ACM*, vol. 17, pp. 388-402, July 1974.

SALTZER, J.H., and SCHROEDER, M.D.: "The Protection of Information in Computer Systems," *Proc. IEEE*, vol. 63, pp. 1278-1308, Sept. 1975.

SALUS, P.H.: *A Quarter Century of UNIX*, Boston: Addison-Wesley, 1994.

SANDHU, R.S.: "Lattice-Based Access Control Models," *Computer*, vol. 26, pp. 9-19, Nov. 1993.

SATYANARAYANAN, M.: "The Evolution of Coda," *ACM Trans. on Computer Systems*, vol. 20, pp. 85-124, May 2002.

SEAWRIGHT, L.H., and MACKINNON, R.A.: "VM/370—A Study of Multiplicity and Usefulness," *IBM Systems Journal*, vol. 18, pp. 4-17, 1979.

SILBERSCHATZ, A., GALVIN, P.B., and GAGNE, G.: *Operating System Concepts,* 7th Ed., New York: John Wiley, 2004.

STALLINGS, W.: *Operating Systems,* 5th Ed., Upper Saddle River, NJ: Prentice Hall, 2005.

STEVENS, W.R., and RAGO, S. A.: *Advanced Programming in the UNIX Environment,* 2nd Ed., Boston: Addison-Wesley, 2005.

STOLL, C.: *The Cuckoo's Egg: Tracking a Spy through the Maze of Computer Espionage,* New York: Doubleday, 1989.

SWIFT, M.M., ANNAMALAI, M., BERSHAD, B.N., and LEVY, H.M.: "Recovering Device Drivers," *Proc. Sixth Symp. on Oper. Syst. Design and Implementation,* USENIX, pp. 1-16, 2004.

TAI, K.C., and CARVER, R.H.: "VP: A New Operation for Semaphores," *Operating Systems Review,* vol. 30, pp. 5-11, July 1996.

TALLURI, M., and HILL, M.D.: "Surpassing the TLB Performance of Superpages with Less Operating System Support," *Proc. Sixth Int'l Conf. on Architectural Support for Progr. Lang. and Operating Systems,* ACM, pp. 171-182, 1994.

TALLURI, M., HILL, M.D., and KHALIDI, Y.A.: "A New Page Table for 64-bit Address Spaces," *Proc. 15th Symp. on Oper. Syst. Prin.,* ACM, pp. 184-200, 1995.

TANENBAUM, A.S.: *Modern Operating Systems,* 2nd Ed., Upper Saddle River: NJ, Prentice Hall, 2001

TANENBAUM, A.S., VAN RENESSE, R., STAVEREN, H. VAN, SHARP, G.J., MULLENDER, S.J., JANSEN, J., and ROSSUM, G. VAN: "Experiences with the Amoeba Distributed Operating System," *Commun. of the ACM,* vol. 33, pp. 46-63, Dec. 1990.

TANENBAUM, A.S., and VAN STEEN, M.R.: *Distributed Systems: Principles and Paradigms,* Upper Saddle River, NJ, Prentice Hall, 2002.

TEORY, T.J.: "Properties of Disk Scheduling Policies in Multiprogrammed Computer Systems," *Proc. AFIPS Fall Joint Computer Conf.,* AFIPS, pp. 1-11, 1972.

THOMPSON, K.: "UNIX Implementation," *Bell System Technical Journal,* vol. 57, pp. 1931-1946, July-Aug. 1978.

TREESE, W.: "The State of Security on the Internet," *NetWorker,* vol. 8, pp. 13-15, Sept. 2004.

TSEGAYE, M., and FOSS, R.: "A Comparison of the Linux and Windows Device Driver Architectures," *Operating Systems Review,* vol. 38, pp. 8-33, April 2004.

UHLIG, R., NAGLE, D., STANLEY, T, MUDGE, T., SECREST, S., and BROWN, R: "Design Tradeoffs for Software-Managed TLBs," *ACM Trans. on Computer Systems,* vol. 12, pp. 175-205, Aug. 1994.

UPPULURI, P., JOSHI, U., and RAY, A.: "Preventing Race Condition Attacks on File Systems," *Proc. 2005 ACM Symp. on Applied Computing*, ACM, pp. 346-353, 2005.

VAHALIA, U.: *UNIX Internals—The New Frontiers,* 2nd Ed., Upper Saddle River, NJ: Prentice Hall, 1996.

VOGELS, W.: "File System Usage in Windows NT 4.0," *Proc. ACM Symp. on Operating System Principles*, ACM, pp. 93-109, 1999.

WALDSPURGER, C.A., and WEIHL, W.E.: "Lottery Scheduling: Flexible Proportional-Share Resource Management," *Proc. First Symp. on Oper. Syst. Design and Implementation*, USENIX, pp. 1-11, 1994.

WEISS, A.: "Spyware Be Gone," *NetWorker*, vol. 9, pp. 18-25, March 2005.

WILKES, J., GOLDING, R., STAELIN, C, abd SULLIVAN, T.: "The HP AutoRAID Hierarchical Storage System," *ACM Trans. on Computer Systems*, vol. 14, pp. 108-136, Feb. 1996.

WULF, W.A., COHEN, E.S., CORWIN, W.M., JONES, A.K., LEVIN, R., PIERSON, C., and POLLACK, F.J.: "HYDRA: The Kernel of a Multiprocessor Operating System," *Commun. of the ACM*, vol. 17, pp. 337-345, June 1974.

YANG, J., TWOHEY, P., ENGLER, D. and MUSUVATHI, M.: "Using Model Checking to Find Serious File System Errors," *Proc. Sixth Symp. on Oper. Syst. Design and Implementation*, USENIX, 2004.

ZEKAUSKAS, M.J., SAWDON, W.A., and BERSHAD, B.N.: "Software Write Detection for a Distributed Shared Memory," *Proc. First Symp. on Oper. Syst. Design and Implementation*, USENIX, pp. 87-100, 1994.

ZWICKY, E.D.: "Torture-Testing Backup and Archive Programs: Things You Ought to Know but Probably Would Rather Not," *Prof. Fifth Conf. on Large Installation Systems Admin.*, USENIX, pp. 181-190, 1991.

APPENDIX A

INSTALLING MINIX

A

INSTALLING MINIX 3

This appendix explains how to install MINIX 3. A complete MINIX 3 installation requires a Pentium (or compatible) with at least 16-MB of RAM, 1 GB of free disk space, an IDE CD-ROM and an IDE hard disk. A minimal installation (without the commands sources) requires 8 MB RAM and 50 MB of disk space. Serial ATA, USB, and SCSI disks are not supported at present. For USB CD-ROMS, see the Website: *www.minix3.org*.

A.1 PREPARATION

If you already have the CD-ROM (e.g., from the book), you can skip steps 1 and 2, but it is wise to check *www.minix3.org* to see if a newer version is available. If you want to run MINIX 3 on a simulator instead of native, see Part V first. If you do not have an IDE CD-ROM, either get the special USB CD-ROM boot image or use a simulator.

1. **Download the MINIX 3 CD-ROM image**
Download the MINIX 3 CD-ROM image from the MINIX 3 Website at *www.minix3.org*.

2. **Create a bootable MINIX 3 CD-ROM**
Decompress the downloaded file. You will get a CD-ROM image file with extension *.iso* and this manual. The *.iso* file is a bit-for-bit CD-ROM image. Burn it to a CD-ROM to make a bootable CD-ROM.

If you are using *Easy CD Creator 5*, select "Record CD from CD image" from the File menu and change the file type from *.cif* to *.iso* in the dialog box that appears. Select the image file and click "Open." Then click "Start Recording."

If you are using *Nero Express 5*, choose "Disc Image or Saved Project" and change the type to "Image Files," select the image file and click "Open." Select your CD recorder and click on "Next."

If you are running Windows XP and do not have a CD-ROM burning program, take a look at *alexfeinman.brinkster.net/isorecorder.htm* for a free one and use it to create a CD image.

3. Determine which Ethernet Chip you have

MINIX 3 supports several Ethernet chips for networking over LAN, ADSL, and cable. These include Intel Pro/100, RealTek 8029 and 8139, AMD LANCE, and several 3Com chips. During setup you will be asked which Ethernet chip you have, if any. Determine that now by looking at your documentation. Alternatively, if you are using Windows, go to the device manager as follows:

Windows 2000: Start > Settings > Control Panel > System > Hardware > Device Manager
Windows XP: Start > Control Panel > System > Hardware > Device Manager

System requires double clicking; the rest are single. Expand the + next to "Network adapters" to see what you have. Write it down. If you do not have a supported chip, you can still run MINIX 3, but without Ethernet.

4. Partition your hard disk

You can boot the computer from your CD-ROM if you like and MINIX 3 will start, but to do anything useful, you have to create a partition for it on your hard disk. But before partitioning, be sure to **back up your data to an external medium like CD-ROM or DVD** as a safety precaution, just in case something goes wrong. Your files are valuable; protect them.

Unless you are sure you are an expert on disk partitioning with much experience, it is strongly suggested that you read the online tutorial on disk partitioning at *www.minix3.org/doc/partitions.html*. If you already know how to manage partitions, create a contiguous chunk of free disk space of at least 50 MB, or, if you want all the commands sources, 1 GB. If you do not know how to manage partitions but have a partitioning program like *Partition Magic*, use it to create a region of free disk space. Also make sure there is at least one primary partition (i.e., Master Boot Record slot) free. The MINIX 3 setup script will guide you through creating a MINIX partition in the free space, which can be on either the first or second IDE disk.

If you are running Windows 95, 98, ME, or 2000 *and* your disk consists of a single FAT partition, you can use the *presz134.exe* program on the CD-ROM (also available at *zeleps.com*) to reduce its size to leave room for MINIX. In all other cases, please read the online tutorial cited above.

If your disk is larger than 128 GB, the MINIX 3 partition must fall entirely in the first 128 GB (due to the way disk blocks are addressed).

WARNING: If you make a mistake during disk partitioning, you can lose all the data on the disk, so be sure to back it up to CD-ROM or DVD before starting. Disk partitioning requires great care, so proceed with caution.

A.2 BOOTING

By now you should have allocated some free space on your disk. If you have not done so yet, please do it now unless there is an existing partition you are willing to convert to MINIX 3.

1. **Boot from the CD-ROM**

Insert the CD-ROM into your CD-ROM drive and boot the computer from it. If you have 16 MB of RAM or more, choose "Regular;" if you have only 8 MB choose "small." If the computer boots from the hard disk instead of the CD-ROM, boot again and enter the BIOS setup program to change the order of boot devices, putting the CD-ROM before the hard disk.

2. **Login as root**

When the *login* prompt appears, login as *root.* After a successful login as root, you will see the shell prompt (#). At this point you are running fully-operational MINIX 3. If you type:

```
ls /usr/bin | more
```

you can see what software is available. Hit space to scroll the list. To see what program *foo* does, type:

```
man foo
```

The manual pages are also available at *www.minix3.org/manpages.*

3. **Start the setup script**

To start the installation of MINIX 3 on the hard disk, type

```
setup
```

After this and all other commands, be sure to type ENTER (RETURN). When the installation script ends a screen with a colon, hit ENTER to continue. If the screen suddenly goes blank, press CTRL-F3 to select software scrolling (should only be needed on very old computers). Note that CTRL-key means depress the CTRL key and while holding it down, press "key."

A.3 INSTALLING TO THE HARD DISK

These steps correspond to the steps on the screen.

1. Select keyboard type

When you are asked to select your national keyboard, do so. This and other steps have a default choice, in square brackets. If you agree with it, just hit ENTER. In most steps, the default is generally a good choice for beginners. The us-swap keyboard interchanges the CAPS LOCK and CTRL keys, as is conventional on UNIX systems.

2. Select your Ethernet chip

You will now be asked which of the available Ethernet drivers you want installed (or none). Please choose one of the options.

3. Basic minimal or full distribution?

If you are tight on disk space, select M for a minimal installation which includes all the binaries but only the system sources installed. The minimal option does not install the sources of the commands. 50 MB is enough for a bare-bones system. If you have 1 GB or more, choose F for a full installation.

4. Create or select a partition for MINIX 3

You will first be asked if you are an expert in MINIX 3 disk partitioning. If so, you will be placed in the *part* program to give you full power to edit the Master Boot Record (and enough rope to hang yourself). If you are not an expert, press ENTER for the default action, which is an automated step-by-step guide to formatting a disk partition for MINIX 3.

Substep 4.1: Select a disk to install MINIX 3

An IDE controller may have up to four disks. The *setup* script will now look for each one. Just ignore any error messages. When the drives are listed, select one. and confirm your choice. If you have two hard disks and you decide to install MINIX 3 to the second one and have trouble booting from it, please see *www.minix3.org/doc/using2disks.html* for the solution.

Substep 4.2: Select a disk region

Now choose a region to install MINIX 3 into. You have three choices:

(1) Select a free region
(2) Select a partition to overwrite
(3) Delete a partition to free up space and merge with adjacent free space

For choices (1) and (2), type the region number. For (3) type

    delete

then give the region number when asked. This region will be overwritten and its previous contents lost forever.

Substep 4.3: Confirm your choices

You have now reached the point of no return. You will be asked if you want to continue. **If you do, the data in the selected region will be lost forever.** If you are sure, type:

    yes

and then ENTER. To exit the setup script without changing the partition table, hit CTRL-C.

5. Reinstall choice

If you chose an existing MINIX 3 partition, in this step you will be offered a choice between a Full install, which erases everything in the partition, and a Reinstall, which does not affect your existing */home* partition. This design means that you can put your personal files on */home* and reinstall a newer version of MINIX 3 when it is available without losing your personal files.

6. Select the size of /home

The selected partition will be divided into three subpartitions: root, */usr*, and */home*. The latter is for your own personal files. Specify how much of the partition should be set aside for your files. You will be asked to confirm your choice.

7. Select a block size

Disk block sizes of 1-KB, 2-KB, 4-KB, and 8-KB are supported, but to use a size larger than 4-KB you have to change a constant and recompile the system. If your memory is 16 MB or more, use the default (4 KB); otherwise, use 1 KB.

8. Wait for bad block detection

The setup script will now scan each partition for bad disk blocks. This will take several minutes, possibly 10 minutes or more on a large partition. Please be patient. If you are absolutely certain there are no bad blocks, you can kill each scan by hitting CTRL-C.

9. Wait for files to be copied

When the scan finishes, files will be automatically copied from the CD-ROM to the hard disk. Every file will be announced as it is copied. When the copying is complete, MINIX 3 is installed. Shut the system down by typing

    shutdown

Always stop MINIX 3 this way to avoid data loss as MINIX 3 keeps some files on the RAM disk and only copies them back to the hard disk at shutdown time.

A.4 TESTING

This section tells you how to test your installation, rebuild the system after modifying it, and boot it later. To start, boot your new MINIX 3 system. For example, if you used controller 0, disk 0, partition 3, type

```
boot c0d0p3
```

and log in as root. Under very rare conditions the drive number seen by the BIOS (and used by the boot monitor) may not agree with the one used by MINIX 3. Try the one announced by the setup script first. This is a good time to create a root password. See *man passwd* for help.

1. **Compile the test suite**
   To test MINIX 3, at the command prompt (#) type

```
cd /usr/src/test
make
```

and wait until it completes all 40 compilations. Log out by typing CTRL-D,

2. **Run the test suite**
   To test the system, log in as bin (required) and type

```
cd /usr/src/test
./run
```

to run the test programs. They should all run correctly but they can take 20 min on a fast machine and over an hour on a slow one. *Note*: It is necessary to compile the test suite when running as root but execute it as bin in order to see if the setuid bit works correctly.

3. **Rebuild the entire operating system**
   If all the tests work correctly, you can now rebuild the system. Doing so is not necessary since it comes prebuilt, but if you plan to modify the system, you will need to know how to rebuild it. Besides, rebuilding the system is a good test to see if it works. Type:

```
cd /usr/src/tools
make
```

to see the various options available. Now make a new bootable image by typing

```
su
make clean
time make image
```

You just rebuilt the operating system, including all the kernel and user-mode parts. That did not take very long, did it? If you have a legacy floppy disk drive, you can make a bootable floppy for use later by inserting a formatted floppy and typing

    make fdboot

When you are asked to complete the path, type:

    fd0

This approach does not currently work with USB floppies since there is no MINIX 3 USB floppy disk driver yet. To update the boot image currently installed on the hard disk, type

    make hdboot

4. Shut down and reboot the new system

To boot the new system, first shut down by typing:

    shutdown

This command saves certain files and returns you to the MINIX 3 boot monitor. To get a summary of what the boot monitor can do, while in it, type:

    help

For more details, see *www.minix3.org/manpages/man8/boot.8.html.* You can now remove any CD-ROM or floppy disk and turn off the computer.

5. Booting Tomorrow

If you have a legacy floppy disk drive, the simplest way to boot MINIX 3 is by inserting your new boot floppy and turning on the power. It takes only a few seconds. Alternatively, boot from the MINIX 3 CD-ROM, login as bin and type:

    shutdown

to get back to the MINIX 3 boot monitor. Now type:

    boot c0d0p0

to boot from the operating system image file on controller 0, driver 0, partition 0. Of course, if you put MINIX 3 on drive 0 partition 1, use:

    boot c0d0p1

and so on.

A third possibility for booting is to make the MINIX 3 partition the active one, and use the MINIX 3 boot monitor to start MINIX 3 or any other operating system. For details see *www.minix3.org/manpages/man8/boot.8.html.*

Finally, a fourth option is for you to install a multiboot loader such as LILO or GRUB (*www.gnu.org/software/grub*). Then you can boot any of your operating systems easily. Discussion of multiboot loaders is beyond the scope of this guide, but there is some information on the subject at *www.minix3.org/doc*.

A.5 USING A SIMULATOR

A completely different approach to running MINIX 3 is to run it on top of another operating system instead of native on the bare metal. Various virtual machines, simulators, and emulators are available for this purpose. Some of the most popular ones are:

- VMware (www.vmware.com)
- Bochs (www.bochs.org)
- QEMU (www.qemu.org)

See the documentation for each of them. Running a program on a simulator is similar to running it on the actual machine, so you should go back to Part I and acquire the latest CD-ROM and continue from there.

APPENDIX B

THE MINIX SOURCE CODE

```
++++++++++++++++++++++++++++++++++++++++++++++++++++++++++++++++++++++++++
                              include/ansi.h
++++++++++++++++++++++++++++++++++++++++++++++++++++++++++++++++++++++++++
00000   /* The <ansi.h> header attempts to decide whether the compiler has enough
00001    * conformance to Standard C for Minix to take advantage of.  If so, the
00002    * symbol _ANSI is defined (as 31459).  Otherwise _ANSI is not defined
00003    * here, but it may be defined by applications that want to bend the rules.
00004    * The magic number in the definition is to inhibit unnecessary bending
00005    * of the rules.  (For consistency with the new '#ifdef _ANSI" tests in
00006    * the headers, _ANSI should really be defined as nothing, but that would
00007    * break many library routines that use "#if _ANSI".)
00008    *
00009    * If _ANSI ends up being defined, a macro
00010    *
00011    *        _PROTOTYPE(function, params)
00012    *
00013    * is defined.  This macro expands in different ways, generating either
00014    * ANSI Standard C prototypes or old-style K&R (Kernighan & Ritchie)
00015    * prototypes, as needed.  Finally, some programs use _CONST, _VOIDSTAR etc
00016    * in such a way that they are portable over both ANSI and K&R compilers.
00017    * The appropriate macros are defined here.
00018    */
00019
00020   #ifndef _ANSI_H
00021   #define _ANSI_H
00022
00023   #if __STDC__ == 1
00024   #define _ANSI           31459   /* compiler claims full ANSI conformance */
00025   #endif
00026
00027   #ifdef __GNUC__
00028   #define _ANSI           31459   /* gcc conforms enough even in non-ANSI mode */
00029   #endif
00030
00031   #ifdef _ANSI
00032
00033   /* Keep everything for ANSI prototypes. */
00034   #define _PROTOTYPE(function, params)     function params
00035   #define _ARGS(params)                    params
00036
00037   #define _VOIDSTAR       void *
00038   #define _VOID           void
00039   #define _CONST          const
00040   #define _VOLATILE       volatile
00041   #define _SIZET          size_t
00042
00043   #else
00044
00045   /* Throw away the parameters for K&R prototypes. */
00046   #define _PROTOTYPE(function, params)     function()
00047   #define _ARGS(params)                    ()
00048
00049   #define _VOIDSTAR       void *
00050   #define _VOID           void
00051   #define _CONST
00052   #define _VOLATILE
00053   #define _SIZET          int
00054
```

```
00055  #endif /* _ANSI */
00056
00057  /* This should be defined as restrict when a C99 compiler is used. */
00058  #define _RESTRICT
00059
00060  /* Setting any of _MINIX, _POSIX_C_SOURCE or _POSIX2_SOURCE implies
00061   * _POSIX_SOURCE.  (Seems wrong to put this here in ANSI space.)
00062   */
00063  #if defined(_MINIX) || _POSIX_C_SOURCE > 0 || defined(_POSIX2_SOURCE)
00064  #undef _POSIX_SOURCE
00065  #define _POSIX_SOURCE    1
00066  #endif
00067
00068  #endif /* ANSI_H */
```

```
+++++++++++++++++++++++++++++++++++++++++++++++++++++++++++++++++++++++++++++
                              include/limits.h
+++++++++++++++++++++++++++++++++++++++++++++++++++++++++++++++++++++++++++++
```

```
00100  /* The <limits.h> header defines some basic sizes, both of the language types
00101   * (e.g., the number of bits in an integer), and of the operating system (e.g.
00102   * the number of characters in a file name.
00103   */
00104
00105  #ifndef _LIMITS_H
00106  #define _LIMITS_H
00107
00108  /* Definitions about chars (8 bits in MINIX, and signed). */
00109  #define CHAR_BIT         8      /* # bits in a char */
00110  #define CHAR_MIN      -128      /* minimum value of a char */
00111  #define CHAR_MAX       127      /* maximum value of a char */
00112  #define SCHAR_MIN     -128      /* minimum value of a signed char */
00113  #define SCHAR_MAX      127      /* maximum value of a signed char */
00114  #define UCHAR_MAX      255      /* maximum value of an unsigned char */
00115  #define MB_LEN_MAX       1      /* maximum length of a multibyte char */
00116
00117  /* Definitions about shorts (16 bits in MINIX). */
00118  #define SHRT_MIN   (-32767-1)   /* minimum value of a short */
00119  #define SHRT_MAX       32767    /* maximum value of a short */
00120  #define USHRT_MAX      0xFFFF   /* maximum value of unsigned short */
00121
00122  /* _EM_WSIZE is a compiler-generated symbol giving the word size in bytes. */
00123  #define INT_MIN (-2147483647-1) /* minimum value of a 32-bit int */
00124  #define INT_MAX   2147483647    /* maximum value of a 32-bit int */
00125  #define UINT_MAX  0xFFFFFFFF    /* maximum value of an unsigned 32-bit int */
00126
00127  /*Definitions about longs (32 bits in MINIX). */
00128  #define LONG_MIN (-2147483647L-1)/* minimum value of a long */
00129  #define LONG_MAX  2147483647L   /* maximum value of a long */
00130  #define ULONG_MAX 0xFFFFFFFFL   /* maximum value of an unsigned long */
00131
00132  #include <sys/dir.h>
00133
00134  /* Minimum sizes required by the POSIX P1003.1 standard (Table 2-3). */
00135  #ifdef _POSIX_SOURCE            /* these are only visible for POSIX */
00136  #define _POSIX_ARG_MAX    4096  /* exec() may have 4K worth of args */
00137  #define _POSIX_CHILD_MAX     6  /* a process may have 6 children */
00138  #define _POSIX_LINK_MAX      8  /* a file may have 8 links */
00139  #define _POSIX_MAX_CANON   255  /* size of the canonical input queue */
```

```
00140   #define _POSIX_MAX_INPUT    255   /* you can type 255 chars ahead */
00141   #define _POSIX_NAME_MAX DIRSIZ    /* a file name may have 14 chars */
00142   #define _POSIX_NGROUPS_MAX    0   /* supplementary group IDs are optional */
00143   #define _POSIX_OPEN_MAX      16   /* a process may have 16 files open */
00144   #define _POSIX_PATH_MAX     255   /* a pathname may contain 255 chars */
00145   #define _POSIX_PIPE_BUF     512   /* pipes writes of 512 bytes must be atomic */
00146   #define _POSIX_STREAM_MAX     8   /* at least 8 FILEs can be open at once */
00147   #define _POSIX_TZNAME_MAX     3   /* time zone names can be at least 3 chars */
00148   #define _POSIX_SSIZE_MAX 32767    /* read() must support 32767 byte reads */
00149
00150   /* Values actually implemented by MINIX (Tables 2-4, 2-5, 2-6, and 2-7). */
00151   /* Some of these old names had better be defined when not POSIX. */
00152   #define _NO_LIMIT           100   /* arbitrary number; limit not enforced */
00153
00154   #define NGROUPS_MAX           0   /* supplemental group IDs not available */
00155   #define ARG_MAX           16384   /* # bytes of args + environ for exec() */
00156   #define CHILD_MAX     _NO_LIMIT   /* MINIX does not limit children */
00157   #define OPEN_MAX             20   /* # open files a process may have */
00158   #define LINK_MAX       SHRT_MAX   /* # links a file may have */
00159   #define MAX_CANON           255   /* size of the canonical input queue */
00160   #define MAX_INPUT           255   /* size of the type-ahead buffer */
00161   #define NAME_MAX         DIRSIZ   /* # chars in a file name */
00162   #define PATH_MAX            255   /* # chars in a path name */
00163   #define PIPE_BUF           7168   /* # bytes in atomic write to a pipe */
00164   #define STREAM_MAX           20   /* must be the same as FOPEN_MAX in stdio.h */
00165   #define TZNAME_MAX            3   /* maximum bytes in a time zone name is 3 */
00166   #define SSIZE_MAX         32767   /* max defined byte count for read() */
00167
00168   #endif /* _POSIX_SOURCE */
00169
00170   #endif /* _LIMITS_H */
```

```
+++++++++++++++++++++++++++++++++++++++++++++++++++++++++++++++++++++++++++++
                             include/errno.h
+++++++++++++++++++++++++++++++++++++++++++++++++++++++++++++++++++++++++++++

00200   /* The <errno.h> header defines the numbers of the various errors that can
00201    * occur during program execution.  They are visible to user programs and
00202    * should be small positive integers.  However, they are also used within
00203    * MINIX, where they must be negative.  For example, the READ system call is
00204    * executed internally by calling do_read().  This function returns either a
00205    * (negative) error number or a (positive) number of bytes actually read.
00206    *
00207    * To solve the problem of having the error numbers be negative inside the
00208    * the system and positive outside, the following mechanism is used.  All the
00209    * definitions are are the form:
00210    *
00211    *        #define EPERM           (_SIGN 1)
00212    *
00213    * If the macro _SYSTEM is defined, then  _SIGN is set to "-", otherwise it is
00214    * set to "".  Thus when compiling the operating system, the  macro _SYSTEM
00215    * will be defined, setting EPERM to (- 1), whereas when when this
00216    * file is included in an ordinary user program, EPERM has the value ( 1).
00217    */
00218
00219   #ifndef _ERRNO_H                    /* check if <errno.h> is already included */
```

```
00220  #define _ERRNO_H                      /* it is not included; note that fact */
00221
00222  /* Now define _SIGN as "" or "-" depending on _SYSTEM. */
00223  #ifdef _SYSTEM
00224  #   define _SIGN          -
00225  #   define OK             0
00226  #else
00227  #   define _SIGN
00228  #endif
00229
00230  extern int errno;                      /* place where the error numbers go */
00231
00232  /* Here are the numerical values of the error numbers. */
00233  #define _NERROR               70  /* number of errors */
00234
00235  #define EGENERIC     (_SIGN 99)  /* generic error */
00236  #define EPERM        (_SIGN 1)   /* operation not permitted */
00237  #define ENOENT       (_SIGN 2)   /* no such file or directory */
00238  #define ESRCH        (_SIGN 3)   /* no such process */
00239  #define EINTR        (_SIGN 4)   /* interrupted function call */
00240  #define EIO          (_SIGN 5)   /* input/output error */
00241  #define ENXIO        (_SIGN 6)   /* no such device or address */
00242  #define E2BIG        (_SIGN 7)   /* arg list too long */
00243  #define ENOEXEC      (_SIGN 8)   /* exec format error */
00244  #define EBADF        (_SIGN 9)   /* bad file descriptor */
00245  #define ECHILD       (_SIGN 10)  /* no child process */
00246  #define EAGAIN       (_SIGN 11)  /* resource temporarily unavailable */
00247  #define ENOMEM       (_SIGN 12)  /* not enough space */
00248  #define EACCES       (_SIGN 13)  /* permission denied */
00249  #define EFAULT       (_SIGN 14)  /* bad address */
00250  #define ENOTBLK      (_SIGN 15)  /* Extension: not a block special file */
00251  #define EBUSY        (_SIGN 16)  /* resource busy */
00252  #define EEXIST       (_SIGN 17)  /* file exists */
00253  #define EXDEV        (_SIGN 18)  /* improper link */
00254  #define ENODEV       (_SIGN 19)  /* no such device */
00255  #define ENOTDIR      (_SIGN 20)  /* not a directory */
00256  #define EISDIR       (_SIGN 21)  /* is a directory */
00257  #define EINVAL       (_SIGN 22)  /* invalid argument */
00258  #define ENFILE       (_SIGN 23)  /* too many open files in system */
00259  #define EMFILE       (_SIGN 24)  /* too many open files */
00260  #define ENOTTY       (_SIGN 25)  /* inappropriate I/O control operation */
00261  #define ETXTBSY      (_SIGN 26)  /* no longer used */
00262  #define EFBIG        (_SIGN 27)  /* file too large */
00263  #define ENOSPC       (_SIGN 28)  /* no space left on device */
00264  #define ESPIPE       (_SIGN 29)  /* invalid seek */
00265  #define EROFS        (_SIGN 30)  /* read-only file system */
00266  #define EMLINK       (_SIGN 31)  /* too many links */
00267  #define EPIPE        (_SIGN 32)  /* broken pipe */
00268  #define EDOM         (_SIGN 33)  /* domain error     (from ANSI C std) */
00269  #define ERANGE       (_SIGN 34)  /* result too large  (from ANSI C std) */
00270  #define EDEADLK      (_SIGN 35)  /* resource deadlock avoided */
00271  #define ENAMETOOLONG (_SIGN 36)  /* file name too long */
00272  #define ENOLCK       (_SIGN 37)  /* no locks available */
00273  #define ENOSYS       (_SIGN 38)  /* function not implemented */
00274  #define ENOTEMPTY    (_SIGN 39)  /* directory not empty */
00275
00276  /* The following errors relate to networking. */
00277  #define EPACKSIZE    (_SIGN 50)  /* invalid packet size for some protocol */
00278  #define EOUTOFBUFS   (_SIGN 51)  /* not enough buffers left */
00279  #define EBADIOCTL    (_SIGN 52)  /* illegal ioctl for device */
```

```
00280   #define EBADMODE        (_SIGN 53)  /* badmode in ioctl */
00281   #define EWOULDBLOCK     (_SIGN 54)
00282   #define EBADDEST        (_SIGN 55)  /* not a valid destination address */
00283   #define EDSTNOTRCH      (_SIGN 56)  /* destination not reachable */
00284   #define EISCONN         (_SIGN 57)  /* all ready connected */
00285   #define EADDRINUSE      (_SIGN 58)  /* address in use */
00286   #define ECONNREFUSED    (_SIGN 59)  /* connection refused */
00287   #define ECONNRESET      (_SIGN 60)  /* connection reset */
00288   #define ETIMEDOUT       (_SIGN 61)  /* connection timed out */
00289   #define EURG            (_SIGN 62)  /* urgent data present */
00290   #define ENOURG          (_SIGN 63)  /* no urgent data present */
00291   #define ENOTCONN        (_SIGN 64)  /* no connection (yet or anymore) */
00292   #define ESHUTDOWN       (_SIGN 65)  /* a write call to a shutdown connection */
00293   #define ENOCONN         (_SIGN 66)  /* no such connection */
00294   #define EAFNOSUPPORT    (_SIGN 67)  /* address family not supported */
00295   #define EPROTONOSUPPORT (_SIGN 68) /* protocol not supported by AF */
00296   #define EPROTOTYPE      (_SIGN 69)  /* Protocol wrong type for socket */
00297   #define EINPROGRESS     (_SIGN 70)  /* Operation now in progress */
00298   #define EADDRNOTAVAIL   (_SIGN 71)  /* Can't assign requested address */
00299   #define EALREADY        (_SIGN 72)  /* Connection already in progress */
00300   #define EMSGSIZE        (_SIGN 73)  /* Message too long */
00301
00302   /* The following are not POSIX errors, but they can still happen.
00303    * All of these are generated by the kernel and relate to message passing.
00304    */
00305   #define ELOCKED         (_SIGN 101) /* can't send message due to deadlock */
00306   #define EBADCALL        (_SIGN 102) /* illegal system call number */
00307   #define EBADSRCDST      (_SIGN 103) /* bad source or destination process */
00308   #define ECALLDENIED     (_SIGN 104) /* no permission for system call */
00309   #define EDEADDST        (_SIGN 105) /* send destination is not alive */
00310   #define ENOTREADY       (_SIGN 106) /* source or destination is not ready */
00311   #define EBADREQUEST     (_SIGN 107) /* destination cannot handle request */
00312   #define EDONTREPLY      (_SIGN 201) /* pseudo-code: don't send a reply */
00313
00314   #endif /* _ERRNO_H */
```

```
+++++++++++++++++++++++++++++++++++++++++++++++++++++++++++++++++++++++++++++
                              include/unistd.h
+++++++++++++++++++++++++++++++++++++++++++++++++++++++++++++++++++++++++++++

00400   /* The <unistd.h> header contains a few miscellaneous manifest constants. */
00401
00402   #ifndef _UNISTD_H
00403   #define _UNISTD_H
00404
00405   #ifndef _TYPES_H
00406   #include <sys/types.h>
00407   #endif
00408
00409   /* Values used by access().  POSIX Table 2-8. */
00410   #define F_OK             0   /* test if file exists */
00411   #define X_OK             1   /* test if file is executable */
00412   #define W_OK             2   /* test if file is writable */
00413   #define R_OK             4   /* test if file is readable */
00414
00415   /* Values used for whence in lseek(fd, offset, whence).  POSIX Table 2-9. */
00416   #define SEEK_SET         0   /* offset is absolute  */
00417   #define SEEK_CUR         1   /* offset is relative to current position */
00418   #define SEEK_END         2   /* offset is relative to end of file */
00419
```

```
00420  /* This value is required by POSIX Table 2-10. */
00421  #define _POSIX_VERSION 199009L  /* which standard is being conformed to */
00422
00423  /* These three definitions are required by POSIX Sec. 8.2.1.2. */
00424  #define STDIN_FILENO     0     /* file descriptor for stdin */
00425  #define STDOUT_FILENO    1     /* file descriptor for stdout */
00426  #define STDERR_FILENO    2     /* file descriptor for stderr */
00427
00428  #ifdef _MINIX
00429  /* How to exit the system or stop a server process. */
00430  #define RBT_HALT         0
00431  #define RBT_REBOOT       1
00432  #define RBT_PANIC        2     /* a server panics */
00433  #define RBT_MONITOR      3     /* let the monitor do this */
00434  #define RBT_RESET        4     /* hard reset the system */
00435  #endif
00436
00437  /* What system info to retrieve with sysgetinfo(). */
00438  #define SI_KINFO         0     /* get kernel info via PM */
00439  #define SI_PROC_ADDR     1     /* address of process table */
00440  #define SI_PROC_TAB      2     /* copy of entire process table */
00441  #define SI_DMAP_TAB      3     /* get device <-> driver mappings */
00442
00443  /* NULL must be defined in <unistd.h> according to POSIX Sec. 2.7.1. */
00444  #define NULL     ((void *)0)
00445
00446  /* The following relate to configurable system variables. POSIX Table 4-2. */
00447  #define _SC_ARG_MAX        1
00448  #define _SC_CHILD_MAX      2
00449  #define _SC_CLOCKS_PER_SEC 3
00450  #define _SC_CLK_TCK        3
00451  #define _SC_NGROUPS_MAX    4
00452  #define _SC_OPEN_MAX       5
00453  #define _SC_JOB_CONTROL    6
00454  #define _SC_SAVED_IDS      7
00455  #define _SC_VERSION        8
00456  #define _SC_STREAM_MAX     9
00457  #define _SC_TZNAME_MAX     10
00458
00459  /* The following relate to configurable pathname variables. POSIX Table 5-2. */
00460  #define _PC_LINK_MAX       1   /* link count */
00461  #define _PC_MAX_CANON      2   /* size of the canonical input queue */
00462  #define _PC_MAX_INPUT      3   /* type-ahead buffer size */
00463  #define _PC_NAME_MAX       4   /* file name size */
00464  #define _PC_PATH_MAX       5   /* pathname size */
00465  #define _PC_PIPE_BUF       6   /* pipe size */
00466  #define _PC_NO_TRUNC       7   /* treatment of long name components */
00467  #define _PC_VDISABLE       8   /* tty disable */
00468  #define _PC_CHOWN_RESTRICTED 9 /* chown restricted or not */
00469
00470  /* POSIX defines several options that may be implemented or not, at the
00471   * implementer's whim.  This implementer has made the following choices:
00472   *
00473   * _POSIX_JOB_CONTROL       not defined:        no job control
00474   * _POSIX_SAVED_IDS         not defined:        no saved uid/gid
00475   * _POSIX_NO_TRUNC          defined as -1:      long path names are truncated
00476   * _POSIX_CHOWN_RESTRICTED  defined:            you can't give away files
00477   * _POSIX_VDISABLE          defined:            tty functions can be disabled
00478   */
00479  #define _POSIX_NO_TRUNC          (-1)
```

```
00480    #define _POSIX_CHOWN_RESTRICTED  1
00481
00482    /* Function Prototypes. */
00483    _PROTOTYPE( void _exit, (int _status)                                    );
00484    _PROTOTYPE( int access, (const char *_path, int _amode)                  );
00485    _PROTOTYPE( unsigned int alarm, (unsigned int _seconds)                  );
00486    _PROTOTYPE( int chdir, (const char *_path)                               );
00487    _PROTOTYPE( int fchdir, (int fd)                                         );
00488    _PROTOTYPE( int chown, (const char *_path, _mnx_Uid_t _owner, _mnx_Gid_t _group)     );
00489    _PROTOTYPE( int close, (int _fd)                                         );
00490    _PROTOTYPE( char *ctermid, (char *_s)                                    );
00491    _PROTOTYPE( char *cuserid, (char *_s)                                    );
00492    _PROTOTYPE( int dup, (int _fd)                                           );
00493    _PROTOTYPE( int dup2, (int _fd, int _fd2)                                );
00494    _PROTOTYPE( int execl, (const char *_path, const char *_arg, ...)        );
00495    _PROTOTYPE( int execle, (const char *_path, const char *_arg, ...)       );
00496    _PROTOTYPE( int execlp, (const char *_file, const char *_arg, ...)       );
00497    _PROTOTYPE( int execv, (const char *_path, char *const _argv[])          );
00498    _PROTOTYPE( int execve, (const char *_path, char *const _argv[],
00499                                                 char *const _envp[])        );
00500    _PROTOTYPE( int execvp, (const char *_file, char *const _argv[])         );
00501    _PROTOTYPE( pid_t fork, (void)                                           );
00502    _PROTOTYPE( long fpathconf, (int _fd, int _name)                         );
00503    _PROTOTYPE( char *getcwd, (char *_buf, size_t _size)                     );
00504    _PROTOTYPE( gid_t getegid, (void)                                        );
00505    _PROTOTYPE( uid_t geteuid, (void)                                        );
00506    _PROTOTYPE( gid_t getgid, (void)                                         );
00507    _PROTOTYPE( int getgroups, (int _gidsetsize, gid_t _grouplist[])         );
00508    _PROTOTYPE( char *getlogin, (void)                                       );
00509    _PROTOTYPE( pid_t getpgrp, (void)                                        );
00510    _PROTOTYPE( pid_t getpid, (void)                                         );
00511    _PROTOTYPE( pid_t getppid, (void)                                        );
00512    _PROTOTYPE( uid_t getuid, (void)                                         );
00513    _PROTOTYPE( int isatty, (int _fd)                                        );
00514    _PROTOTYPE( int link, (const char *_existing, const char *_new)          );
00515    _PROTOTYPE( off_t lseek, (int _fd, off_t _offset, int _whence)           );
00516    _PROTOTYPE( long pathconf, (const char *_path, int _name)                );
00517    _PROTOTYPE( int pause, (void)                                            );
00518    _PROTOTYPE( int pipe, (int _fildes[2])                                   );
00519    _PROTOTYPE( ssize_t read, (int _fd, void *_buf, size_t _n)               );
00520    _PROTOTYPE( int rmdir, (const char *_path)                               );
00521    _PROTOTYPE( int setgid, (_mnx_Gid_t _gid)                                );
00522    _PROTOTYPE( int setpgid, (pid_t _pid, pid_t _pgid)                       );
00523    _PROTOTYPE( pid_t setsid, (void)                                         );
00524    _PROTOTYPE( int setuid, (_mnx_Uid_t _uid)                                );
00525    _PROTOTYPE( unsigned int sleep, (unsigned int _seconds)                  );
00526    _PROTOTYPE( long sysconf, (int _name)                                    );
00527    _PROTOTYPE( pid_t tcgetpgrp, (int _fd)                                   );
00528    _PROTOTYPE( int tcsetpgrp, (int _fd, pid_t _pgrp_id)                     );
00529    _PROTOTYPE( char *ttyname, (int _fd)                                     );
00530    _PROTOTYPE( int unlink, (const char *_path)                              );
00531    _PROTOTYPE( ssize_t write, (int _fd, const void *_buf, size_t _n)        );
00532
00533    /* Open Group Base Specifications Issue 6 (not complete) */
00534    _PROTOTYPE( int symlink, (const char *path1, const char *path2)          );
00535    _PROTOTYPE( int getopt, (int _argc, char **_argv, char *_opts)           );
00536    extern char *optarg;
00537    extern int optind, opterr, optopt;
00538    _PROTOTYPE( int usleep, (useconds_t _useconds)                           );
00539
```

```
00540  #ifdef _MINIX
00541  #ifndef _TYPE_H
00542  #include <minix/type.h>
00543  #endif
00544  _PROTOTYPE( int brk, (char *_addr)                                      );
00545  _PROTOTYPE( int chroot, (const char *_name)                             );
00546  _PROTOTYPE( int mknod, (const char *_name, _mnx_Mode_t _mode, Dev_t _addr)   );
00547  _PROTOTYPE( int mknod4, (const char *_name, _mnx_Mode_t _mode, Dev_t _addr,
00548             long _size)                                                  );
00549  _PROTOTYPE( char *mktemp, (char *_template)                             );
00550  _PROTOTYPE( int mount, (char *_spec, char *_name, int _flag)            );
00551  _PROTOTYPE( long ptrace, (int _req, pid_t _pid, long _addr, long _data) );
00552  _PROTOTYPE( char *sbrk, (int _incr)                                     );
00553  _PROTOTYPE( int sync, (void)                                            );
00554  _PROTOTYPE( int fsync, (int fd)                                         );
00555  _PROTOTYPE( int umount, (const char *_name)                             );
00556  _PROTOTYPE( int reboot, (int _how, ...)                                 );
00557  _PROTOTYPE( int gethostname, (char *_hostname, size_t _len)             );
00558  _PROTOTYPE( int getdomainname, (char *_domain, size_t _len)             );
00559  _PROTOTYPE( int ttyslot, (void)                                         );
00560  _PROTOTYPE( int fttyslot, (int _fd)                                     );
00561  _PROTOTYPE( char *crypt, (const char *_key, const char *_salt)          );
00562  _PROTOTYPE( int getsysinfo, (int who, int what, void *where)            );
00563  _PROTOTYPE( int getprocnr, (void)                                       );
00564  _PROTOTYPE( int findproc, (char *proc_name, int *proc_nr)               );
00565  _PROTOTYPE( int allocmem, (phys_bytes size, phys_bytes *base)           );
00566  _PROTOTYPE( int freemem, (phys_bytes size, phys_bytes base)             );
00567  #define DEV_MAP 1
00568  #define DEV_UNMAP 2
00569  #define mapdriver(driver, device, style) devctl(DEV_MAP, driver, device, style)
00570  #define unmapdriver(device) devctl(DEV_UNMAP, 0, device, 0)
00571  _PROTOTYPE( int devctl, (int ctl_req, int driver, int device, int style));
00572
00573  /* For compatibility with other Unix systems */
00574  _PROTOTYPE( int getpagesize, (void)                                     );
00575  _PROTOTYPE( int setgroups, (int ngroups, const gid_t *gidset)           );
00576
00577  #endif
00578
00579  _PROTOTYPE( int readlink, (const char *, char *, int));
00580  _PROTOTYPE( int getopt, (int, char **, char *));
00581  extern int optind, opterr, optopt;
00582
00583  #endif /* _UNISTD_H */
```

```
++++++++++++++++++++++++++++++++++++++++++++++++++++++++++++++++++++++++++++
                          include/string.h
++++++++++++++++++++++++++++++++++++++++++++++++++++++++++++++++++++++++++++
```

```
00600  /* The <string.h> header contains prototypes for the string handling
00601   * functions.
00602   */
00603
00604  #ifndef _STRING_H
00605  #define _STRING_H
00606
00607  #define NULL     ((void *)0)
00608
00609  #ifndef _SIZE_T
```

```
00610   #define _SIZE_T
00611   typedef unsigned int size_t;     /* type returned by sizeof */
00612   #endif /*_SIZE_T */
00613
00614   /* Function Prototypes. */
00615   #ifndef _ANSI_H
00616   #include <ansi.h>
00617   #endif
00618
00619   _PROTOTYPE( void *memchr, (const void *_s, int _c, size_t _n)          );
00620   _PROTOTYPE( int memcmp, (const void *_s1, const void *_s2, size_t _n)  );
00621   _PROTOTYPE( void *memcpy, (void *_s1, const void *_s2, size_t _n)      );
00622   _PROTOTYPE( void *memmove, (void *_s1, const void *_s2, size_t _n)     );
00623   _PROTOTYPE( void *memset, (void *_s, int _c, size_t _n)                );
00624   _PROTOTYPE( char *strcat, (char *_s1, const char *_s2)                 );
00625   _PROTOTYPE( char *strchr, (const char *_s, int _c)                     );
00626   _PROTOTYPE( int strncmp, (const char *_s1, const char *_s2, size_t _n) );
00627   _PROTOTYPE( int strcmp, (const char *_s1, const char *_s2)             );
00628   _PROTOTYPE( int strcoll, (const char *_s1, const char *_s2)            );
00629   _PROTOTYPE( char *strcpy, (char *_s1, const char *_s2)                 );
00630   _PROTOTYPE( size_t strcspn, (const char *_s1, const char *_s2)         );
00631   _PROTOTYPE( char *strerror, (int _errnum)                             );
00632   _PROTOTYPE( size_t strlen, (const char *_s)                            );
00633   _PROTOTYPE( char *strncat, (char *_s1, const char *_s2, size_t _n)     );
00634   _PROTOTYPE( char *strncpy, (char *_s1, const char *_s2, size_t _n)     );
00635   _PROTOTYPE( char *strpbrk, (const char *_s1, const char *_s2)          );
00636   _PROTOTYPE( char *strrchr, (const char *_s, int _c)                    );
00637   _PROTOTYPE( size_t strspn, (const char *_s1, const char *_s2)          );
00638   _PROTOTYPE( char *strstr, (const char *_s1, const char *_s2)           );
00639   _PROTOTYPE( char *strtok, (char *_s1, const char *_s2)                 );
00640   _PROTOTYPE( size_t strxfrm, (char *_s1, const char *_s2, size_t _n)    );
00641
00642   #ifdef _POSIX_SOURCE
00643   /* Open Group Base Specifications Issue 6 (not complete) */
00644    char *strdup(const char *_s1);
00645   #endif
00646
00647   #ifdef _MINIX
00648   /* For backward compatibility. */
00649   _PROTOTYPE( char *index, (const char *_s, int _charwanted)             );
00650   _PROTOTYPE( char *rindex, (const char *_s, int _charwanted)            );
00651   _PROTOTYPE( void bcopy, (const void *_src, void *_dst, size_t _length) );
00652   _PROTOTYPE( int bcmp, (const void *_s1, const void *_s2, size_t _length));
00653   _PROTOTYPE( void bzero, (void *_dst, size_t _length)                   );
00654   _PROTOTYPE( void *memccpy, (char *_dst, const char *_src, int _ucharstop,
00655                                             size_t _size)        );
00656
00657   /* Misc. extra functions */
00658   _PROTOTYPE( int strcasecmp, (const char *_s1, const char *_s2)         );
00659   _PROTOTYPE( int strncasecmp, (const char *_s1, const char *_s2,
00660                                             size_t _len)        );
00661   _PROTOTYPE( size_t strnlen, (const char *_s, size_t _n)                );
00662   #endif
00663
00664   #endif /* _STRING_H */
```

```
++++++++++++++++++++++++++++++++++++++++++++++++++++++++++++++++++++++++++++++
                              include/signal.h
++++++++++++++++++++++++++++++++++++++++++++++++++++++++++++++++++++++++++++++
00700   /* The <signal.h> header defines all the ANSI and POSIX signals.
00701    * MINIX supports all the signals required by POSIX. They are defined below.
00702    * Some additional signals are also supported.
00703    */
00704
00705   #ifndef _SIGNAL_H
00706   #define _SIGNAL_H
00707
00708   #ifndef _ANSI_H
00709   #include <ansi.h>
00710   #endif
00711   #ifdef _POSIX_SOURCE
00712   #ifndef _TYPES_H
00713   #include <sys/types.h>
00714   #endif
00715   #endif
00716
00717   /* Here are types that are closely associated with signal handling. */
00718   typedef int sig_atomic_t;
00719
00720   #ifdef _POSIX_SOURCE
00721   #ifndef _SIGSET_T
00722   #define _SIGSET_T
00723   typedef unsigned long sigset_t;
00724   #endif
00725   #endif
00726
00727   #define _NSIG              20      /* number of signals used */
00728
00729   #define SIGHUP              1      /* hangup */
00730   #define SIGINT              2      /* interrupt (DEL) */
00731   #define SIGQUIT             3      /* quit (ASCII FS) */
00732   #define SIGILL              4      /* illegal instruction */
00733   #define SIGTRAP             5      /* trace trap (not reset when caught) */
00734   #define SIGABRT             6      /* IOT instruction */
00735   #define SIGIOT              6      /* SIGABRT for people who speak PDP-11 */
00736   #define SIGUNUSED           7      /* spare code */
00737   #define SIGFPE              8      /* floating point exception */
00738   #define SIGKILL             9      /* kill (cannot be caught or ignored) */
00739   #define SIGUSR1            10      /* user defined signal # 1 */
00740   #define SIGSEGV            11      /* segmentation violation */
00741   #define SIGUSR2            12      /* user defined signal # 2 */
00742   #define SIGPIPE            13      /* write on a pipe with no one to read it */
00743   #define SIGALRM            14      /* alarm clock */
00744   #define SIGTERM            15      /* software termination signal from kill */
00745   #define SIGCHLD            17      /* child process terminated or stopped */
00746
00747   #define SIGEMT              7      /* obsolete */
00748   #define SIGBUS             10      /* obsolete */
00749
00750   /* MINIX specific signals. These signals are not used by user proceses,
00751    * but meant to inform system processes, like the PM, about system events.
00752    */
00753   #define SIGKMESS           18      /* new kernel message */
00754   #define SIGKSIG            19      /* kernel signal pending */
```

```
00755    #define SIGKSTOP           20     /* kernel shutting down */
00756
00757    /* POSIX requires the following signals to be defined, even if they are
00758     * not supported.  Here are the definitions, but they are not supported.
00759     */
00760    #define SIGCONT            18     /* continue if stopped */
00761    #define SIGSTOP            19     /* stop signal */
00762    #define SIGTSTP            20     /* interactive stop signal */
00763    #define SIGTTIN            21     /* background process wants to read */
00764    #define SIGTTOU            22     /* background process wants to write */
00765
00766    /* The sighandler_t type is not allowed unless _POSIX_SOURCE is defined. */
00767    typedef void _PROTOTYPE( (*__sighandler_t), (int) );
00768
00769    /* Macros used as function pointers. */
00770    #define SIG_ERR     ((__sighandler_t) -1)       /* error return */
00771    #define SIG_DFL     ((__sighandler_t)  0)       /* default signal handling */
00772    #define SIG_IGN     ((__sighandler_t)  1)       /* ignore signal */
00773    #define SIG_HOLD    ((__sighandler_t)  2)       /* block signal */
00774    #define SIG_CATCH   ((__sighandler_t)  3)       /* catch signal */
00775    #define SIG_MESS    ((__sighandler_t)  4)       /* pass as message (MINIX) */
00776
00777    #ifdef _POSIX_SOURCE
00778    struct sigaction {
00779      __sighandler_t sa_handler;    /* SIG_DFL, SIG_IGN, or pointer to function */
00780      sigset_t sa_mask;             /* signals to be blocked during handler */
00781      int sa_flags;                 /* special flags */
00782    };
00783
00784    /* Fields for sa_flags. */
00785    #define SA_ONSTACK   0x0001     /* deliver signal on alternate stack */
00786    #define SA_RESETHAND 0x0002     /* reset signal handler when signal caught */
00787    #define SA_NODEFER   0x0004     /* don't block signal while catching it */
00788    #define SA_RESTART   0x0008     /* automatic system call restart */
00789    #define SA_SIGINFO   0x0010     /* extended signal handling */
00790    #define SA_NOCLDWAIT 0x0020     /* don't create zombies */
00791    #define SA_NOCLDSTOP 0x0040     /* don't receive SIGCHLD when child stops */
00792
00793    /* POSIX requires these values for use with sigprocmask(2). */
00794    #define SIG_BLOCK          0    /* for blocking signals */
00795    #define SIG_UNBLOCK        1    /* for unblocking signals */
00796    #define SIG_SETMASK        2    /* for setting the signal mask */
00797    #define SIG_INQUIRE        4    /* for internal use only */
00798    #endif /* _POSIX_SOURCE */
00799
00800    /* POSIX and ANSI function prototypes. */
00801    _PROTOTYPE( int raise, (int _sig)                                      );
00802    _PROTOTYPE( __sighandler_t signal, (int _sig, __sighandler_t _func)    );
00803
00804    #ifdef _POSIX_SOURCE
00805    _PROTOTYPE( int kill, (pid_t _pid, int _sig)                           );
00806    _PROTOTYPE( int sigaction,
00807        (int _sig, const struct sigaction *_act, struct sigaction *_oact)  );
00808    _PROTOTYPE( int sigaddset, (sigset_t *_set, int _sig)                  );
00809    _PROTOTYPE( int sigdelset, (sigset_t *_set, int _sig)                  );
00810    _PROTOTYPE( int sigemptyset, (sigset_t *_set)                          );
00811    _PROTOTYPE( int sigfillset, (sigset_t *_set)                           );
00812    _PROTOTYPE( int sigismember, (const sigset_t *_set, int _sig)          );
00813    _PROTOTYPE( int sigpending, (sigset_t *_set)                           );
00814    _PROTOTYPE( int sigprocmask,
```

```
00815                (int _how, const sigset_t *_set, sigset_t *_oset)          );
00816  _PROTOTYPE( int sigsuspend, (const sigset_t *_sigmask)                   );
00817  #endif
00818
00819  #endif /* _SIGNAL_H */


+++++++++++++++++++++++++++++++++++++++++++++++++++++++++++++++++++++++++++++++
                               include/fcntl.h
+++++++++++++++++++++++++++++++++++++++++++++++++++++++++++++++++++++++++++++++

00900  /* The <fcntl.h> header is needed by the open() and fcntl() system calls,
00901   * which  have a variety of parameters and flags.  They are described here.
00902   * The formats of the calls to each of these are:
00903   *
00904   *        open(path, oflag [,mode])        open a file
00905   *        fcntl(fd, cmd [,arg])            get or set file attributes
00906   *
00907   */
00908
00909  #ifndef _FCNTL_H
00910  #define _FCNTL_H
00911
00912  #ifndef _TYPES_H
00913  #include <sys/types.h>
00914  #endif
00915
00916  /* These values are used for cmd in fcntl().  POSIX Table 6-1. */
00917  #define F_DUPFD            0    /* duplicate file descriptor */
00918  #define F_GETFD            1    /* get file descriptor flags */
00919  #define F_SETFD            2    /* set file descriptor flags */
00920  #define F_GETFL            3    /* get file status flags */
00921  #define F_SETFL            4    /* set file status flags */
00922  #define F_GETLK            5    /* get record locking information */
00923  #define F_SETLK            6    /* set record locking information */
00924  #define F_SETLKW           7    /* set record locking info; wait if blocked */
00925
00926  /* File descriptor flags used for fcntl().  POSIX Table 6-2. */
00927  #define FD_CLOEXEC         1    /* close on exec flag for third arg of fcntl */
00928
00929  /* L_type values for record locking with fcntl().  POSIX Table 6-3. */
00930  #define F_RDLCK            1    /* shared or read lock */
00931  #define F_WRLCK            2    /* exclusive or write lock */
00932  #define F_UNLCK            3    /* unlock */
00933
00934  /* Oflag values for open().  POSIX Table 6-4. */
00935  #define O_CREAT        00100    /* creat file if it doesn't exist */
00936  #define O_EXCL         00200    /* exclusive use flag */
00937  #define O_NOCTTY       00400    /* do not assign a controlling terminal */
00938  #define O_TRUNC        01000    /* truncate flag */
00939
00940  /* File status flags for open() and fcntl().  POSIX Table 6-5. */
00941  #define O_APPEND       02000    /* set append mode */
00942  #define O_NONBLOCK     04000    /* no delay */
00943
00944  /* File access modes for open() and fcntl().  POSIX Table 6-6. */
00945  #define O_RDONLY           0    /* open(name, O_RDONLY) opens read only */
00946  #define O_WRONLY           1    /* open(name, O_WRONLY) opens write only */
00947  #define O_RDWR             2    /* open(name, O_RDWR) opens read/write */
00948
00949  /* Mask for use with file access modes.  POSIX Table 6-7. */
```

```
00950  #define O_ACCMODE          03     /* mask for file access modes */
00951
00952  /* Struct used for locking.  POSIX Table 6-8. */
00953  struct flock {
00954    short l_type;                  /* type: F_RDLCK, F_WRLCK, or F_UNLCK */
00955    short l_whence;                /* flag for starting offset */
00956    off_t l_start;                 /* relative offset in bytes */
00957    off_t l_len;                   /* size; if 0, then until EOF */
00958    pid_t l_pid;                   /* process id of the locks' owner */
00959  };
00960
00961  /* Function Prototypes. */
00962  _PROTOTYPE( int creat, (const char *_path, _mnx_Mode_t _mode)          );
00963  _PROTOTYPE( int fcntl, (int _filedes, int _cmd, ...)                   );
00964  _PROTOTYPE( int open,  (const char *_path, int _oflag, ...)            );
00965
00966  #endif /* _FCNTL_H */
```

```
++++++++++++++++++++++++++++++++++++++++++++++++++++++++++++++++++++++++++++
                          include/termios.h
++++++++++++++++++++++++++++++++++++++++++++++++++++++++++++++++++++++++++++

01000  /* The <termios.h> header is used for controlling tty modes. */
01001
01002  #ifndef _TERMIOS_H
01003  #define _TERMIOS_H
01004
01005  typedef unsigned short tcflag_t;
01006  typedef unsigned char cc_t;
01007  typedef unsigned int speed_t;
01008
01009  #define NCCS              20     /* size of cc_c array, some extra space
01010                                  * for extensions. */
01011
01012  /* Primary terminal control structure. POSIX Table 7-1. */
01013  struct termios {
01014    tcflag_t c_iflag;              /* input modes */
01015    tcflag_t c_oflag;              /* output modes */
01016    tcflag_t c_cflag;              /* control modes */
01017    tcflag_t c_lflag;              /* local modes */
01018    speed_t  c_ispeed;             /* input speed */
01019    speed_t  c_ospeed;             /* output speed */
01020    cc_t c_cc[NCCS];               /* control characters */
01021  };
01022
01023  /* Values for termios c_iflag bit map.  POSIX Table 7-2. */
01024  #define BRKINT            0x0001 /* signal interrupt on break */
01025  #define ICRNL             0x0002 /* map CR to NL on input */
01026  #define IGNBRK            0x0004 /* ignore break */
01027  #define IGNCR             0x0008 /* ignore CR */
01028  #define IGNPAR            0x0010 /* ignore characters with parity errors */
01029  #define INLCR             0x0020 /* map NL to CR on input */
01030  #define INPCK             0x0040 /* enable input parity check */
01031  #define ISTRIP            0x0080 /* mask off 8th bit */
01032  #define IXOFF             0x0100 /* enable start/stop input control */
01033  #define IXON              0x0200 /* enable start/stop output control */
01034  #define PARMRK            0x0400 /* mark parity errors in the input queue */
```

```
01035
01036  /* Values for termios c_oflag bit map.  POSIX Sec. 7.1.2.3. */
01037  #define OPOST             0x0001  /* perform output processing */
01038
01039  /* Values for termios c_cflag bit map.  POSIX Table 7-3. */
01040  #define CLOCAL            0x0001  /* ignore modem status lines */
01041  #define CREAD             0x0002  /* enable receiver */
01042  #define CSIZE             0x000C  /* number of bits per character */
01043  #define        CS5        0x0000  /* if CSIZE is CS5, characters are 5 bits */
01044  #define        CS6        0x0004  /* if CSIZE is CS6, characters are 6 bits */
01045  #define        CS7        0x0008  /* if CSIZE is CS7, characters are 7 bits */
01046  #define        CS8        0x000C  /* if CSIZE is CS8, characters are 8 bits */
01047  #define CSTOPB            0x0010  /* send 2 stop bits if set, else 1 */
01048  #define HUPCL             0x0020  /* hang up on last close */
01049  #define PARENB            0x0040  /* enable parity on output */
01050  #define PARODD            0x0080  /* use odd parity if set, else even */
01051
01052  /* Values for termios c_lflag bit map.  POSIX Table 7-4. */
01053  #define ECHO              0x0001  /* enable echoing of input characters */
01054  #define ECHOE             0x0002  /* echo ERASE as backspace */
01055  #define ECHOK             0x0004  /* echo KILL */
01056  #define ECHONL            0x0008  /* echo NL */
01057  #define ICANON            0x0010  /* canonical input (erase and kill enabled) */
01058  #define IEXTEN            0x0020  /* enable extended functions */
01059  #define ISIG              0x0040  /* enable signals */
01060  #define NOFLSH            0x0080  /* disable flush after interrupt or quit */
01061  #define TOSTOP            0x0100  /* send SIGTTOU (job control, not implemented*/
01062
01063  /* Indices into c_cc array.  Default values in parentheses. POSIX Table 7-5. */
01064  #define VEOF                  0  /* cc_c[VEOF] = EOF char (^D) */
01065  #define VEOL                  1  /* cc_c[VEOL] = EOL char (undef) */
01066  #define VERASE                2  /* cc_c[VERASE] = ERASE char (^H) */
01067  #define VINTR                 3  /* cc_c[VINTR] = INTR char (DEL) */
01068  #define VKILL                 4  /* cc_c[VKILL] = KILL char (^U) */
01069  #define VMIN                  5  /* cc_c[VMIN] = MIN value for timer */
01070  #define VQUIT                 6  /* cc_c[VQUIT] = QUIT char (^\) */
01071  #define VTIME                 7  /* cc_c[VTIME] = TIME value for timer */
01072  #define VSUSP                 8  /* cc_c[VSUSP] = SUSP (^Z, ignored) */
01073  #define VSTART                9  /* cc_c[VSTART] = START char (^S) */
01074  #define VSTOP                10  /* cc_c[VSTOP] = STOP char (^Q) */
01075
01076  #define _POSIX_VDISABLE   (cc_t)0xFF   /* You can't even generate this
01077                                         * character with 'normal' keyboards.
01078                                         * But some language specific keyboards
01079                                         * can generate 0xFF. It seems that all
01080                                         * 256 are used, so cc_t should be a
01081                                         * short...
01082                                         */
01083
01084  /* Values for the baud rate settings.  POSIX Table 7-6. */
01085  #define B0                0x0000  /* hang up the line */
01086  #define B50               0x1000  /* 50 baud */
01087  #define B75               0x2000  /* 75 baud */
01088  #define B110              0x3000  /* 110 baud */
01089  #define B134              0x4000  /* 134.5 baud */
01090  #define B150              0x5000  /* 150 baud */
01091  #define B200              0x6000  /* 200 baud */
01092  #define B300              0x7000  /* 300 baud */
01093  #define B600              0x8000  /* 600 baud */
01094  #define B1200             0x9000  /* 1200 baud */
```

```
01095   #define B1800             0xA000  /* 1800 baud */
01096   #define B2400             0xB000  /* 2400 baud */
01097   #define B4800             0xC000  /* 4800 baud */
01098   #define B9600             0xD000  /* 9600 baud */
01099   #define B19200            0xE000  /* 19200 baud */
01100   #define B38400            0xF000  /* 38400 baud */
01101
01102   /* Optional actions for tcsetattr().  POSIX Sec. 7.2.1.2. */
01103   #define TCSANOW           1   /* changes take effect immediately */
01104   #define TCSADRAIN         2   /* changes take effect after output is done */
01105   #define TCSAFLUSH         3   /* wait for output to finish and flush input */
01106
01107   /* Queue_selector values for tcflush().  POSIX Sec. 7.2.2.2. */
01108   #define TCIFLUSH          1   /* flush accumulated input data */
01109   #define TCOFLUSH          2   /* flush accumulated output data */
01110   #define TCIOFLUSH         3   /* flush accumulated input and output data */
01111
01112   /* Action values for tcflow().  POSIX Sec. 7.2.2.2. */
01113   #define TCOOFF            1   /* suspend output */
01114   #define TCOON             2   /* restart suspended output */
01115   #define TCIOFF            3   /* transmit a STOP character on the line */
01116   #define TCION             4   /* transmit a START character on the line */
01117
01118   /* Function Prototypes. */
01119   #ifndef _ANSI_H
01120   #include <ansi.h>
01121   #endif
01122
01123   _PROTOTYPE( int tcsendbreak, (int _fildes, int _duration)                );
01124   _PROTOTYPE( int tcdrain, (int _filedes)                                  );
01125   _PROTOTYPE( int tcflush, (int _filedes, int _queue_selector)             );
01126   _PROTOTYPE( int tcflow, (int _filedes, int _action)                      );
01127   _PROTOTYPE( speed_t cfgetispeed, (const struct termios *_termios_p)      );
01128   _PROTOTYPE( speed_t cfgetospeed, (const struct termios *_termios_p)      );
01129   _PROTOTYPE( int cfsetispeed, (struct termios *_termios_p, speed_t _speed) );
01130   _PROTOTYPE( int cfsetospeed, (struct termios *_termios_p, speed_t _speed) );
01131   _PROTOTYPE( int tcgetattr, (int _filedes, struct termios *_termios_p)    );
01132   _PROTOTYPE( int tcsetattr, \
01133           (int _filedes, int _opt_actions, const struct termios *_termios_p)   );
01134
01135   #define cfgetispeed(termios_p)          ((termios_p)->c_ispeed)
01136   #define cfgetospeed(termios_p)          ((termios_p)->c_ospeed)
01137   #define cfsetispeed(termios_p, speed)   ((termios_p)->c_ispeed = (speed), 0)
01138   #define cfsetospeed(termios_p, speed)   ((termios_p)->c_ospeed = (speed), 0)
01139
01140   #ifdef _MINIX
01141   /* Here are the local extensions to the POSIX standard for Minix. Posix
01142    * conforming programs are not able to access these, and therefore they are
01143    * only defined when a Minix program is compiled.
01144    */
01145
01146   /* Extensions to the termios c_iflag bit map.  */
01147   #define IXANY             0x0800  /* allow any key to continue ouptut */
01148
01149   /* Extensions to the termios c_oflag bit map. They are only active iff
01150    * OPOST is enabled. */
01151   #define ONLCR             0x0002  /* Map NL to CR-NL on output */
01152   #define XTABS             0x0004  /* Expand tabs to spaces */
01153   #define ONOEOT            0x0008  /* discard EOT's (^D) on output) */
01154
```

```
01155   /* Extensions to the termios c_lflag bit map.  */
01156   #define LFLUSHO         0x0200  /* Flush output. */
01157
01158   /* Extensions to the c_cc array. */
01159   #define VREPRINT        11      /* cc_c[VREPRINT] (^R) */
01160   #define VLNEXT          12      /* cc_c[VLNEXT] (^V) */
01161   #define VDISCARD        13      /* cc_c[VDISCARD] (^O) */
01162
01163   /* Extensions to baud rate settings. */
01164   #define B57600          0x0100  /* 57600 baud */
01165   #define B115200         0x0200  /* 115200 baud */
01166
01167   /* These are the default settings used by the kernel and by 'stty sane' */
01168
01169   #define TCTRL_DEF       (CREAD | CS8 | HUPCL)
01170   #define TINPUT_DEF      (BRKINT | ICRNL | IXON | IXANY)
01171   #define TOUTPUT_DEF     (OPOST | ONLCR)
01172   #define TLOCAL_DEF      (ISIG | IEXTEN | ICANON | ECHO | ECHOE)
01173   #define TSPEED_DEF      B9600
01174
01175   #define TEOF_DEF        '\4'    /* ^D */
01176   #define TEOL_DEF        _POSIX_VDISABLE
01177   #define TERASE_DEF      '\10'   /* ^H */
01178   #define TINTR_DEF       '\3'    /* ^C */
01179   #define TKILL_DEF       '\25'   /* ^U */
01180   #define TMIN_DEF        1
01181   #define TQUIT_DEF       '\34'   /* ^\ */
01182   #define TSTART_DEF      '\21'   /* ^Q */
01183   #define TSTOP_DEF       '\23'   /* ^S */
01184   #define TSUSP_DEF       '\32'   /* ^Z */
01185   #define TTIME_DEF       0
01186   #define TREPRINT_DEF    '\22'   /* ^R */
01187   #define TLNEXT_DEF      '\26'   /* ^V */
01188   #define TDISCARD_DEF    '\17'   /* ^O */
01189
01190   /* Window size. This information is stored in the TTY driver but not used.
01191    * This can be used for screen based applications in a window environment.
01192    * The ioctls TIOCGWINSZ and TIOCSWINSZ can be used to get and set this
01193    * information.
01194    */
01195
01196   struct winsize
01197   {
01198           unsigned short  ws_row;         /* rows, in characters */
01199           unsigned short  ws_col;         /* columns, in characters */
01200           unsigned short  ws_xpixel;      /* horizontal size, pixels */
01201           unsigned short  ws_ypixel;      /* vertical size, pixels */
01202   };
01203   #endif /* _MINIX */
01204
01205   #endif /* _TERMIOS_H */
```

```
++++++++++++++++++++++++++++++++++++++++++++++++++++++++++++++++++++++++++++
                             include/timers.h
++++++++++++++++++++++++++++++++++++++++++++++++++++++++++++++++++++++++++++
01300  /* This library provides generic watchdog timer management functionality.
01301   * The functions operate on a timer queue provided by the caller. Note that
01302   * the timers must use absolute time to allow sorting. The library provides:
01303   *
01304   *    tmrs_settimer:     (re)set a new watchdog timer in the timers queue
01305   *    tmrs_clrtimer:     remove a timer from both the timers queue
01306   *    tmrs_exptimers:    check for expired timers and run watchdog functions
01307   *
01308   * Author:
01309   *    Jorrit N. Herder <jnherder@cs.vu.nl>
01310   *    Adapted from tmr_settimer and tmr_clrtimer in src/kernel/clock.c.
01311   *    Last modified: September 30, 2004.
01312   */
01313
01314  #ifndef _TIMERS_H
01315  #define _TIMERS_H
01316
01317  #include <limits.h>
01318  #include <sys/types.h>
01319
01320  struct timer;
01321  typedef void (*tmr_func_t)(struct timer *tp);
01322  typedef union { int ta_int; long ta_long; void *ta_ptr; } tmr_arg_t;
01323
01324  /* A timer_t variable must be declare for each distinct timer to be used.
01325   * The timers watchdog function and expiration time are automatically set
01326   * by the library function tmrs_settimer, but its argument is not.
01327   */
01328  typedef struct timer
01329  {
01330    struct timer   *tmr_next;      /* next in a timer chain */
01331    clock_t        tmr_exp_time;   /* expiration time */
01332    tmr_func_t     tmr_func;       /* function to call when expired */
01333    tmr_arg_t      tmr_arg;        /* random argument */
01334  } timer_t;
01335
01336  /* Used when the timer is not active. */
01337  #define TMR_NEVER    ((clock_t) -1 < 0) ? ((clock_t) LONG_MAX) : ((clock_t) -1)
01338  #undef TMR_NEVER
01339  #define TMR_NEVER         ((clock_t) LONG_MAX)
01340
01341  /* These definitions can be used to set or get data from a timer variable. */
01342  #define tmr_arg(tp) (&(tp)->tmr_arg)
01343  #define tmr_exp_time(tp) (&(tp)->tmr_exp_time)
01344
01345  /* Timers should be initialized once before they are being used. Be careful
01346   * not to reinitialize a timer that is in a list of timers, or the chain
01347   * will be broken.
01348   */
01349  #define tmr_inittimer(tp) (void)((tp)->tmr_exp_time = TMR_NEVER, \
01350          (tp)->tmr_next = NULL)
01351
01352  /* The following generic timer management functions are available. They
01353   * can be used to operate on the lists of timers. Adding a timer to a list
01354   * automatically takes care of removing it.
```

```
01355    */
01356    _PROTOTYPE( clock_t tmrs_clrtimer, (timer_t **tmrs, timer_t *tp, clock_t *new_head)
01357    _PROTOTYPE( void tmrs_exptimers, (timer_t **tmrs, clock_t now, clock_t *new_head)
01358    _PROTOTYPE( clock_t tmrs_settimer, (timer_t **tmrs, timer_t *tp,
01359             clock_t exp_time, tmr_func_t watchdog, clock_t *new_head)
01360
01361    #endif /* _TIMERS_H */
01362
```

```
++++++++++++++++++++++++++++++++++++++++++++++++++++++++++++++++++++++++++++++
                            include/sys/types.h
++++++++++++++++++++++++++++++++++++++++++++++++++++++++++++++++++++++++++++++
```

```
01400    /* The <sys/types.h> header contains important data type definitions.
01401     * It is considered good programming practice to use these definitions,
01402     * instead of the underlying base type.  By convention, all type names end
01403     * with _t.
01404     */
01405
01406    #ifndef _TYPES_H
01407    #define _TYPES_H
01408
01409    #ifndef _ANSI_H
01410    #include <ansi.h>
01411    #endif
01412
01413    /* The type size_t holds all results of the sizeof operator.  At first glance,
01414     * it seems obvious that it should be an unsigned int, but this is not always
01415     * the case. For example, MINIX-ST (68000) has 32-bit pointers and 16-bit
01416     * integers. When one asks for the size of a 70K struct or array, the result
01417     * requires 17 bits to express, so size_t must be a long type.  The type
01418     * ssize_t is the signed version of size_t.
01419     */
01420    #ifndef _SIZE_T
01421    #define _SIZE_T
01422    typedef unsigned int size_t;
01423    #endif
01424
01425    #ifndef _SSIZE_T
01426    #define _SSIZE_T
01427    typedef int ssize_t;
01428    #endif
01429
01430    #ifndef _TIME_T
01431    #define _TIME_T
01432    typedef long time_t;                  /* time in sec since 1 Jan 1970 0000 GMT */
01433    #endif
01434
01435    #ifndef _CLOCK_T
01436    #define _CLOCK_T
01437    typedef long clock_t;                 /* unit for system accounting */
01438    #endif
01439
01440    #ifndef _SIGSET_T
01441    #define _SIGSET_T
01442    typedef unsigned long sigset_t;
01443    #endif
01444
```

```
01445   /* Open Group Base Specifications Issue 6 (not complete) */
01446   typedef long usecond_t;          /* Time in microseconds */
01447
01448   /* Types used in disk, inode, etc. data structures. */
01449   typedef short          dev_t;      /* holds (major|minor) device pair */
01450   typedef char           gid_t;      /* group id */
01451   typedef unsigned long  ino_t;      /* i-node number (V3 filesystem) */
01452   typedef unsigned short mode_t;     /* file type and permissions bits */
01453   typedef short          nlink_t;    /* number of links to a file */
01454   typedef unsigned long  off_t;      /* offset within a file */
01455   typedef int            pid_t;      /* process id (must be signed) */
01456   typedef short          uid_t;      /* user id */
01457   typedef unsigned long  zone_t;     /* zone number */
01458   typedef unsigned long  block_t;    /* block number */
01459   typedef unsigned long  bit_t;      /* bit number in a bit map */
01460   typedef unsigned short zone1_t;    /* zone number for V1 file systems */
01461   typedef unsigned short bitchunk_t; /* collection of bits in a bitmap */
01462
01463   typedef unsigned char  u8_t;       /* 8 bit type */
01464   typedef unsigned short u16_t;      /* 16 bit type */
01465   typedef unsigned long  u32_t;      /* 32 bit type */
01466
01467   typedef char           i8_t;       /* 8 bit signed type */
01468   typedef short          i16_t;      /* 16 bit signed type */
01469   typedef long           i32_t;      /* 32 bit signed type */
01470
01471   typedef struct { u32_t _[2]; } u64_t;
01472
01473   /* The following types are needed because MINIX uses K&R style function
01474    * definitions (for maximum portability). When a short, such as dev_t, is
01475    * passed to a function with a K&R definition, the compiler automatically
01476    * promotes it to an int. The prototype must contain an int as the parameter,
01477    * not a short, because an int is what an old-style function definition
01478    * expects. Thus using dev_t in a prototype would be incorrect. It would be
01479    * sufficient to just use int instead of dev_t in the prototypes, but Dev_t
01480    * is clearer.
01481    */
01482   typedef int            Dev_t;
01483   typedef int            _mnx_Gid_t;
01484   typedef int            Nlink_t;
01485   typedef int            _mnx_Uid_t;
01486   typedef int            U8_t;
01487   typedef unsigned long  U32_t;
01488   typedef int            I8_t;
01489   typedef int            I16_t;
01490   typedef long           I32_t;
01491
01492   /* ANSI C makes writing down the promotion of unsigned types very messy. When
01493    * sizeof(short) == sizeof(int), there is no promotion, so the type stays
01494    * unsigned. When the compiler is not ANSI, there is usually no loss of
01495    * unsignedness, and there are usually no prototypes so the promoted type
01496    * doesn't matter. The use of types like Ino_t is an attempt to use ints
01497    * (which are not promoted) while providing information to the reader.
01498    */
01499
01500   typedef unsigned long  Ino_t;
01501
01502   #if _EM_WSIZE == 2
01503   /*typedef unsigned int      Ino_t; Ino_t is now 32 bits */
01504   typedef unsigned int   Zone1_t;
```

```
01505    typedef unsigned int Bitchunk_t;
01506    typedef unsigned int       U16_t;
01507    typedef unsigned int   _mnx_Mode_t;
01508
01509    #else /* _EM_WSIZE == 4, or _EM_WSIZE undefined */
01510    /*typedef int            Ino_t; Ino_t is now 32 bits */
01511    typedef int            Zone1_t;
01512    typedef int            Bitchunk_t;
01513    typedef int               U16_t;
01514    typedef int           _mnx_Mode_t;
01515
01516    #endif /* _EM_WSIZE == 2, etc */
01517
01518    /* Signal handler type, e.g. SIG_IGN */
01519    typedef void _PROTOTYPE( (*sighandler_t), (int) );
01520
01521    /* Compatibility with other systems */
01522    typedef unsigned char    u_char;
01523    typedef unsigned short   u_short;
01524    typedef unsigned int     u_int;
01525    typedef unsigned long    u_long;
01526    typedef char             *caddr_t;
01527
01528    #endif /* _TYPES_H */
```

```
++++++++++++++++++++++++++++++++++++++++++++++++++++++++++++++++++++++++++++++
                        include/sys/sigcontext.h
++++++++++++++++++++++++++++++++++++++++++++++++++++++++++++++++++++++++++++++
```

```
01600    #ifndef _SIGCONTEXT_H
01601    #define _SIGCONTEXT_H
01602
01603    /* The sigcontext structure is used by the sigreturn(2) system call.
01604     * sigreturn() is seldom called by user programs, but it is used internally
01605     * by the signal catching mechanism.
01606     */
01607
01608    #ifndef _ANSI_H
01609    #include <ansi.h>
01610    #endif
01611
01612    #ifndef _MINIX_SYS_CONFIG_H
01613    #include <minix/sys_config.h>
01614    #endif
01615
01616    #if !defined(_MINIX_CHIP)
01617    #include "error, configuration is not known"
01618    #endif
01619
01620    /* The following structure should match the stackframe_s structure used
01621     * by the kernel's context switching code.  Floating point registers should
01622     * be added in a different struct.
01623     */
01624    struct sigregs {
01625      short sr_gs;
01626      short sr_fs;
01627      short sr_es;
01628      short sr_ds;
01629      int sr_di;
```

```
01630      int sr_si;
01631      int sr_bp;
01632      int sr_st;                      /* stack top -- used in kernel */
01633      int sr_bx;
01634      int sr_dx;
01635      int sr_cx;
01636      int sr_retreg;
01637      int sr_retadr;                  /* return address to caller of save -- used
01638                                       * in kernel */
01639      int sr_pc;
01640      int sr_cs;
01641      int sr_psw;
01642      int sr_sp;
01643      int sr_ss;
01644    };
01645
01646    struct sigframe {               /* stack frame created for signalled process */
01647      _PROTOTYPE( void (*sf_retadr), (void) );
01648      int sf_signo;
01649      int sf_code;
01650      struct sigcontext *sf_scp;
01651      int sf_fp;
01652      _PROTOTYPE( void (*sf_retadr2), (void) );
01653      struct sigcontext *sf_scpcopy;
01654    };
01655
01656    struct sigcontext {
01657      int sc_flags;                   /* sigstack state to restore */
01658      long sc_mask;                   /* signal mask to restore */
01659      struct sigregs sc_regs;         /* register set to restore */
01660    };
01661
01662    #define sc_gs sc_regs.sr_gs
01663    #define sc_fs sc_regs.sr_fs
01664    #define sc_es sc_regs.sr_es
01665    #define sc_ds sc_regs.sr_ds
01666    #define sc_di sc_regs.sr_di
01667    #define sc_si sc_regs.sr_si
01668    #define sc_fp sc_regs.sr_bp
01669    #define sc_st sc_regs.sr_st                 /* stack top -- used in kernel */
01670    #define sc_bx sc_regs.sr_bx
01671    #define sc_dx sc_regs.sr_dx
01672    #define sc_cx sc_regs.sr_cx
01673    #define sc_retreg sc_regs.sr_retreg
01674    #define sc_retadr sc_regs.sr_retadr         /* return address to caller of
01675                                                save -- used in kernel */
01676    #define sc_pc sc_regs.sr_pc
01677    #define sc_cs sc_regs.sr_cs
01678    #define sc_psw sc_regs.sr_psw
01679    #define sc_sp sc_regs.sr_sp
01680    #define sc_ss sc_regs.sr_ss
01681
01682    /* Values for sc_flags.  Must agree with <minix/jmp_buf.h>. */
01683    #define SC_SIGCONTEXT   2           /* nonzero when signal context is included */
01684    #define SC_NOREGLOCALS  4           /* nonzero when registers are not to be
01685                                                saved and restored */
01686
01687    _PROTOTYPE( int sigreturn, (struct sigcontext *_scp)                 );
01688
01689    #endif /* _SIGCONTEXT_H */
```

```
++++++++++++++++++++++++++++++++++++++++++++++++++++++++++++++++++++++++++++++
                            include/sys/stat.h
++++++++++++++++++++++++++++++++++++++++++++++++++++++++++++++++++++++++++++++
01700  /* The <sys/stat.h> header defines a struct that is used in the stat() and
01701   * fstat functions.  The information in this struct comes from the i-node of
01702   * some file.  These calls are the only approved way to inspect i-nodes.
01703   */
01704
01705  #ifndef _STAT_H
01706  #define _STAT_H
01707
01708  #ifndef _TYPES_H
01709  #include <sys/types.h>
01710  #endif
01711
01712  struct stat {
01713    dev_t st_dev;                   /* major/minor device number */
01714    ino_t st_ino;                   /* i-node number */
01715    mode_t st_mode;                 /* file mode, protection bits, etc. */
01716    short int st_nlink;             /* # links; TEMPORARY HACK: should be nlink_t*/
01717    uid_t st_uid;                   /* uid of the file's owner */
01718    short int st_gid;               /* gid; TEMPORARY HACK: should be gid_t */
01719    dev_t st_rdev;
01720    off_t st_size;                  /* file size */
01721    time_t st_atime;                /* time of last access */
01722    time_t st_mtime;                /* time of last data modification */
01723    time_t st_ctime;                /* time of last file status change */
01724  };
01725
01726  /* Traditional mask definitions for st_mode. */
01727  /* The ugly casts on only some of the definitions are to avoid suprising sign
01728   * extensions such as S_IFREG != (mode_t) S_IFREG when ints are 32 bits.
01729   */
01730  #define S_IFMT   ((mode_t) 0170000)      /* type of file */
01731  #define S_IFLNK  ((mode_t) 0120000)      /* symbolic link, not implemented */
01732  #define S_IFREG  ((mode_t) 0100000)      /* regular */
01733  #define S_IFBLK  0060000                 /* block special */
01734  #define S_IFDIR  0040000                 /* directory */
01735  #define S_IFCHR  0020000                 /* character special */
01736  #define S_IFIFO  0010000                 /* this is a FIFO */
01737  #define S_ISUID  0004000                 /* set user id on execution */
01738  #define S_ISGID  0002000                 /* set group id on execution */
01739                                           /* next is reserved for future use */
01740  #define S_ISVTX    01000                 /* save swapped text even after use */
01741
01742  /* POSIX masks for st_mode. */
01743  #define S_IRWXU    00700         /* owner:  rwx------ */
01744  #define S_IRUSR    00400         /* owner:  r-------- */
01745  #define S_IWUSR    00200         /* owner:  -w------- */
01746  #define S_IXUSR    00100         /* owner:  --x------ */
01747
01748  #define S_IRWXG    00070         /* group:  ---rwx--- */
01749  #define S_IRGRP    00040         /* group:  ---r----- */
01750  #define S_IWGRP    00020         /* group:  ----w---- */
01751  #define S_IXGRP    00010         /* group:  -----x--- */
01752
01753  #define S_IRWXO    00007         /* others: ------rwx */
01754  #define S_IROTH    00004         /* others: ------r-- */
```

```
01755   #define S_IWOTH    00002        /* others: -------w- */
01756   #define S_IXOTH    00001        /* others: --------x */
01757
01758   /* The following macros test st_mode (from POSIX Sec. 5.6.1.1). */
01759   #define S_ISREG(m)     (((m) & S_IFMT) == S_IFREG)    /* is a reg file */
01760   #define S_ISDIR(m)     (((m) & S_IFMT) == S_IFDIR)    /* is a directory */
01761   #define S_ISCHR(m)     (((m) & S_IFMT) == S_IFCHR)    /* is a char spec */
01762   #define S_ISBLK(m)     (((m) & S_IFMT) == S_IFBLK)    /* is a block spec */
01763   #define S_ISFIFO(m)    (((m) & S_IFMT) == S_IFIFO)    /* is a pipe/FIFO */
01764   #define S_ISLNK(m)     (((m) & S_IFMT) == S_IFLNK)    /* is a sym link */
01765
01766   /* Function Prototypes. */
01767   _PROTOTYPE( int chmod, (const char *_path, _mnx_Mode_t _mode)       );
01768   _PROTOTYPE( int fstat, (int _fildes, struct stat *_buf)             );
01769   _PROTOTYPE( int mkdir, (const char *_path, _mnx_Mode_t _mode)       );
01770   _PROTOTYPE( int mkfifo, (const char *_path, _mnx_Mode_t _mode)      );
01771   _PROTOTYPE( int stat, (const char *_path, struct stat *_buf)        );
01772   _PROTOTYPE( mode_t umask, (_mnx_Mode_t _cmask)                      );
01773
01774   /* Open Group Base Specifications Issue 6 (not complete) */
01775   _PROTOTYPE( int lstat, (const char *_path, struct stat *_buf)       );
01776
01777   #endif /* _STAT_H */
```

```
++++++++++++++++++++++++++++++++++++++++++++++++++++++++++++++++++++++++++++++
                            include/sys/dir.h
++++++++++++++++++++++++++++++++++++++++++++++++++++++++++++++++++++++++++++++

01800   /* The <dir.h> header gives the layout of a directory. */
01801
01802   #ifndef _DIR_H
01803   #define _DIR_H
01804
01805   #include <sys/types.h>
01806
01807   #define DIRBLKSIZ      512      /* size of directory block */
01808
01809   #ifndef DIRSIZ
01810   #define DIRSIZ   60
01811   #endif
01812
01813   struct direct {
01814     ino_t d_ino;
01815     char d_name[DIRSIZ];
01816   };
01817
01818   #endif /* _DIR_H */
```

```
++++++++++++++++++++++++++++++++++++++++++++++++++++++++++++++++++++++++++++++
                            include/sys/wait.h
++++++++++++++++++++++++++++++++++++++++++++++++++++++++++++++++++++++++++++++

01900   /* The <sys/wait.h> header contains macros related to wait(). The value
01901    * returned by wait() and waitpid() depends on whether the process
01902    * terminated by an exit() call, was killed by a signal, or was stopped
01903    * due to job control, as follows:
01904    *
```

```
01905    *                              High byte   Low byte
01906    *                           +--------------------+
01907    *        exit(status)       |  status  |    0    |
01908    *                           +--------------------+
01909    *    killed by signal       |    0     | signal  |
01910    *                           +--------------------+
01911    *    stopped (job control)  |  signal  |  0177   |
01912    *                           +--------------------+
01913    */
01914
01915    #ifndef _WAIT_H
01916    #define _WAIT_H
01917
01918    #ifndef _TYPES_H
01919    #include <sys/types.h>
01920    #endif
01921
01922    #define _LOW(v)         ( (v) & 0377)
01923    #define _HIGH(v)        ( ((v) >> 8) & 0377)
01924
01925    #define WNOHANG         1       /* do not wait for child to exit */
01926    #define WUNTRACED       2       /* for job control; not implemented */
01927
01928    #define WIFEXITED(s)    (_LOW(s) == 0)                   /* normal exit */
01929    #define WEXITSTATUS(s)  (_HIGH(s))                       /* exit status */
01930    #define WTERMSIG(s)     (_LOW(s) & 0177)                 /* sig value */
01931    #define WIFSIGNALED(s)  (((unsigned int)(s)-1 & 0xFFFF) < 0xFF) /* signaled */
01932    #define WIFSTOPPED(s)   (_LOW(s) == 0177)                /* stopped */
01933    #define WSTOPSIG(s)     (_HIGH(s) & 0377)                /* stop signal */
01934
01935    /* Function Prototypes. */
01936    _PROTOTYPE( pid_t wait, (int *_stat_loc)                        );
01937    _PROTOTYPE( pid_t waitpid, (pid_t _pid, int *_stat_loc, int _options)   );
01938
01939    #endif /* _WAIT_H */


+++++++++++++++++++++++++++++++++++++++++++++++++++++++++++++++++++++++++++++++++
                          include/sys/ioctl.h
+++++++++++++++++++++++++++++++++++++++++++++++++++++++++++++++++++++++++++++++++

02000    /*      sys/ioctl.h - All ioctl() command codes.      Author: Kees J. Bot
02001     *                                                    23 Nov 2002
02002     *
02003     * This header file includes all other ioctl command code headers.
02004     */
02005
02006    #ifndef _S_IOCTL_H
02007    #define _S_IOCTL_H
02008
02009    /* A driver that uses ioctls claims a character for its series of commands.
02010     * For instance:  #define TCGETS  _IOR('T', 8, struct termios)
02011     * This is a terminal ioctl that uses the character 'T'.  The character(s)
02012     * used in each header file are shown in the comment following.
02013     */
02014
02015    #include <sys/ioc_tty.h>        /* 'T' 't' 'k'          */
02016    #include <sys/ioc_disk.h>       /* 'd'                  */
02017    #include <sys/ioc_memory.h>     /* 'm'                  */
02018    #include <sys/ioc_cmos.h>       /* 'c'                  */
02019
```

```
02020   #endif /* _S_IOCTL_H */
```

```
++++++++++++++++++++++++++++++++++++++++++++++++++++++++++++++++++++++++++++++
                            include/sys/ioc_disk.h
++++++++++++++++++++++++++++++++++++++++++++++++++++++++++++++++++++++++++++++
02100   /*      sys/ioc_disk.h - Disk ioctl() command codes.    Author: Kees J. Bot
02101    *                                                               23 Nov 2002
02102    *
02103    */
02104
02105   #ifndef _S_I_DISK_H
02106   #define _S_I_DISK_H
02107
02108   #include <minix/ioctl.h>
02109
02110   #define DIOCSETP        _IOW('d', 3, struct partition)
02111   #define DIOCGETP        _IOR('d', 4, struct partition)
02112   #define DIOCEJECT       _IO ('d', 5)
02113   #define DIOCTIMEOUT     _IOW('d', 6, int)
02114   #define DIOCOPENCT      _IOR('d', 7, int)
02115
02116   #endif /* _S_I_DISK_H */
```

```
++++++++++++++++++++++++++++++++++++++++++++++++++++++++++++++++++++++++++++++
                            include/minix/ioctl.h
++++++++++++++++++++++++++++++++++++++++++++++++++++++++++++++++++++++++++++++
02200   /*      minix/ioctl.h - Ioctl helper definitions.    Author: Kees J. Bot
02201    *                                                            23 Nov 2002
02202    *
02203    * This file is included by every header file that defines ioctl codes.
02204    */
02205
02206   #ifndef _M_IOCTL_H
02207   #define _M_IOCTL_H
02208
02209   #ifndef _TYPES_H
02210   #include <sys/types.h>
02211   #endif
02212
02213   #if _EM_WSIZE >= 4
02214   /* Ioctls have the command encoded in the low-order word, and the size
02215    * of the parameter in the high-order word. The 3 high bits of the high-
02216    * order word are used to encode the in/out/void status of the parameter.
02217    */
02218   #define _IOCPARM_MASK   0x1FFF
02219   #define _IOC_VOID       0x20000000
02220   #define _IOCTYPE_MASK   0xFFFF
02221   #define _IOC_IN         0x40000000
02222   #define _IOC_OUT        0x80000000
02223   #define _IOC_INOUT      (_IOC_IN | _IOC_OUT)
02224
```

```
02225   #define _IO(x,y)          ((x << 8) | y | _IOC_VOID)
02226   #define _IOR(x,y,t)       ((x << 8) | y | ((sizeof(t) & _IOCPARM_MASK) << 16) |\
02227                             _IOC_OUT)
02228   #define _IOW(x,y,t)       ((x << 8) | y | ((sizeof(t) & _IOCPARM_MASK) << 16) |\
02229                             _IOC_IN)
02230   #define _IORW(x,y,t)      ((x << 8) | y | ((sizeof(t) & _IOCPARM_MASK) << 16) |\
02231                             _IOC_INOUT)
02232   #else
02233   /* No fancy encoding on a 16-bit machine. */
02234
02235   #define _IO(x,y)          ((x << 8) | y)
02236   #define _IOR(x,y,t)       _IO(x,y)
02237   #define _IOW(x,y,t)       _IO(x,y)
02238   #define _IORW(x,y,t)      _IO(x,y)
02239   #endif
02240
02241   int ioctl(int _fd, int _request, void *_data);
02242
02243   #endif /* _M_IOCTL_H */
```

```
++++++++++++++++++++++++++++++++++++++++++++++++++++++++++++++++++++++++++++
                              include/minix/config.h
++++++++++++++++++++++++++++++++++++++++++++++++++++++++++++++++++++++++++++
```

```
02300   #ifndef _CONFIG_H
02301   #define _CONFIG_H
02302
02303   /* Minix release and version numbers. */
02304   #define OS_RELEASE "3"
02305   #define OS_VERSION "1.0"
02306
02307   /* This file sets configuration parameters for the MINIX kernel, FS, and PM.
02308    * It is divided up into two main sections.  The first section contains
02309    * user-settable parameters.  In the second section, various internal system
02310    * parameters are set based on the user-settable parameters.
02311    *
02312    * Parts of config.h have been moved to sys_config.h, which can be included
02313    * by other include files that wish to get at the configuration data, but
02314    * don't want to pollute the users namespace. Some editable values have
02315    * gone there.
02316    *
02317    * This is a modified version of config.h for compiling a small Minix system
02318    * with only the options described in the text, Operating Systems Design and
02319    * Implementation, 3rd edition. See the version of config.h in the full
02320    * source code directory for information on alternatives omitted here.
02321    */
02322
02323   /* The MACHINE (called _MINIX_MACHINE) setting can be done
02324    * in <minix/machine.h>.
02325    */
02326   #include <minix/sys_config.h>
02327
02328   #define MACHINE        _MINIX_MACHINE
02329
02330   #define IBM_PC         _MACHINE_IBM_PC
02331   #define SUN_4          _MACHINE_SUN_4
02332   #define SUN_4_60       _MACHINE_SUN_4_60
02333   #define ATARI          _MACHINE_ATARI
02334   #define MACINTOSH      _MACHINE_MACINTOSH
```

```
02335
02336  /* Number of slots in the process table for non-kernel processes. The number
02337   * of system processes defines how many processes with special privileges
02338   * there can be. User processes share the same properties and count for one.
02339   *
02340   * These can be changed in sys_config.h.
02341   */
02342  #define NR_PROCS              _NR_PROCS
02343  #define NR_SYS_PROCS          _NR_SYS_PROCS
02344
02345  #define NR_BUFS 128
02346  #define NR_BUF_HASH 128
02347
02348  /* Number of controller tasks (/dev/cN device classes). */
02349  #define NR_CTRLRS             2
02350
02351  /* Enable or disable the second level file system cache on the RAM disk. */
02352  #define ENABLE_CACHE2         0
02353
02354  /* Enable or disable swapping processes to disk. */
02355  #define ENABLE_SWAP           0
02356
02357  /* Include or exclude an image of /dev/boot in the boot image.
02358   * Please update the makefile in /usr/src/tools/ as well.
02359   */
02360  #define ENABLE_BOOTDEV        0      /* load image of /dev/boot at boot time */
02361
02362  /* DMA_SECTORS may be increased to speed up DMA based drivers. */
02363  #define DMA_SECTORS           1      /* DMA buffer size (must be >= 1) */
02364
02365  /* Include or exclude backwards compatibility code. */
02366  #define ENABLE_BINCOMPAT   0      /* for binaries using obsolete calls */
02367  #define ENABLE_SRCCOMPAT   0      /* for sources using obsolete calls */
02368
02369  /* Which process should receive diagnostics from the kernel and system?
02370   * Directly sending it to TTY only displays the output. Sending it to the
02371   * log driver will cause the diagnostics to be buffered and displayed.
02372   */
02373  #define OUTPUT_PROC_NR   LOG_PROC_NR      /* TTY_PROC_NR or LOG_PROC_NR */
02374
02375  /* NR_CONS, NR_RS_LINES, and NR_PTYS determine the number of terminals the
02376   * system can handle.
02377   */
02378  #define NR_CONS            4      /* # system consoles (1 to 8) */
02379  #define NR_RS_LINES        0      /* # rs232 terminals (0 to 4) */
02380  #define NR_PTYS            0      /* # pseudo terminals (0 to 64) */
02381
02382  /*===========================================================================*
02383   *        There are no user-settable parameters after this line              *
02384   *===========================================================================*/
02385  /* Set the CHIP type based on the machine selected. The symbol CHIP is actually
02386   * indicative of more than just the CPU.  For example, machines for which
02387   * CHIP == INTEL are expected to have 8259A interrrupt controllers and the
02388   * other properties of IBM PC/XT/AT/386 types machines in general. */
02389  #define INTEL             _CHIP_INTEL   /* CHIP type for PC, XT, AT, 386 and clones */
02390  #define M68000            _CHIP_M68000  /* CHIP type for Atari, Amiga, Macintosh    */
02391  #define SPARC             _CHIP_SPARC   /* CHIP type for SUN-4 (e.g. SPARCstation)  */
02392
02393  /* Set the FP_FORMAT type based on the machine selected, either hw or sw    */
02394  #define FP_NONE  _FP_NONE          /* no floating point support             */
```

```
02395   #define FP_IEEE   _FP_IEEE          /* conform IEEE floating point standard      */
02396
02397   /* _MINIX_CHIP is defined in sys_config.h. */
02398   #define CHIP     _MINIX_CHIP
02399
02400   /* _MINIX_FP_FORMAT is defined in sys_config.h. */
02401   #define FP_FORMAT        _MINIX_FP_FORMAT
02402
02403   /* _ASKDEV and _FASTLOAD are defined in sys_config.h. */
02404   #define ASKDEV _ASKDEV
02405   #define FASTLOAD _FASTLOAD
02406
02407   #endif /* _CONFIG_H */




++++++++++++++++++++++++++++++++++++++++++++++++++++++++++++++++++++++++++++++++++
                            include/minix/sys_config.h
++++++++++++++++++++++++++++++++++++++++++++++++++++++++++++++++++++++++++++++++++
02500   #ifndef _MINIX_SYS_CONFIG_H
02501   #define _MINIX_SYS_CONFIG_H 1
02502
02503   /* This is a modified sys_config.h for compiling a small Minix system
02504    * with only the options described in the text, Operating Systems Design and
02505    * Implementation, 3rd edition. See the sys_config.h in the full
02506    * source code directory for information on alternatives omitted here.
02507    */
02508
02509   /*=============================================================================*
02510    *                This section contains user-settable parameters              *
02511    *=============================================================================*/
02512   #define _MINIX_MACHINE        _MACHINE_IBM_PC
02513
02514   #define _MACHINE_IBM_PC                1   /* any  8088 or 80x86-based system */
02515
02516   /* Word size in bytes (a constant equal to sizeof(int)). */
02517   #if __ACK__ || __GNUC__
02518   #define _WORD_SIZE        _EM_WSIZE
02519   #define _PTR_SIZE         _EM_WSIZE
02520   #endif
02521
02522   #define _NR_PROCS        64
02523   #define _NR_SYS_PROCS    32
02524
02525   /* Set the CHIP type based on the machine selected. The symbol CHIP is actually
02526    * indicative of more than just the CPU.  For example, machines for which
02527    * CHIP == INTEL are expected to have 8259A interrrupt controllers and the
02528    * other properties of IBM PC/XT/AT/386 types machines in general. */
02529   #define _CHIP_INTEL      1         /* CHIP type for PC, XT, AT, 386 and clones */
02530
02531   /* Set the FP_FORMAT type based on the machine selected, either hw or sw      */
02532   #define _FP_NONE         0         /* no floating point support               */
02533   #define _FP_IEEE         1         /* conform IEEE floating point standard    */
02534
02535   #define _MINIX_CHIP            _CHIP_INTEL
02536
02537   #define _MINIX_FP_FORMAT    _FP_NONE
02538
02539   #ifndef _MINIX_MACHINE
```

```
02540    error "In <minix/sys_config.h> please define _MINIX_MACHINE"
02541    #endif
02542
02543    #ifndef _MINIX_CHIP
02544    error "In <minix/sys_config.h> please define _MINIX_MACHINE to have a legal value"
02545    #endif
02546
02547    #if (_MINIX_MACHINE == 0)
02548    error "_MINIX_MACHINE has incorrect value (0)"
02549    #endif
02550
02551    #endif /* _MINIX_SYS_CONFIG_H */
02552
02553
```

```
++++++++++++++++++++++++++++++++++++++++++++++++++++++++++++++++++++++++++++
                             include/minix/const.h
++++++++++++++++++++++++++++++++++++++++++++++++++++++++++++++++++++++++++++
```

```
02600    /* Copyright (C) 2001 by Prentice-Hall, Inc.  See the copyright notice in
02601     * the file /usr/src/LICENSE.
02602     */
02603
02604    #ifndef CHIP
02605    #error CHIP is not defined
02606    #endif
02607
02608    #define EXTERN         extern     /* used in *.h files */
02609    #define PRIVATE        static     /* PRIVATE x limits the scope of x */
02610    #define PUBLIC                    /* PUBLIC is the opposite of PRIVATE */
02611    #define FORWARD        static     /* some compilers require this to be 'static'*/
02612
02613    #define TRUE               1      /* used for turning integers into Booleans */
02614    #define FALSE              0      /* used for turning integers into Booleans */
02615
02616    #define HZ                60      /* clock freq (software settable on IBM-PC) */
02617
02618    #define SUPER_USER (uid_t) 0      /* uid_t of superuser */
02619
02620    /* Devices. */
02621    #define MAJOR              8      /* major device = (dev>>MAJOR) & 0377 */
02622    #define MINOR              0      /* minor device = (dev>>MINOR) & 0377 */
02623
02624    #define NULL       ((void *)0)    /* null pointer */
02625    #define CPVEC_NR          16      /* max # of entries in a SYS_VCOPY request */
02626    #define CPVVEC_NR         64      /* max # of entries in a SYS_VCOPY request */
02627    #define NR_IOREQS      MIN(NR_BUFS, 64)
02628                                     /* maximum number of entries in an iorequest */
02629
02630    /* Message passing constants. */
02631    #define MESS_SIZE (sizeof(message))       /* might need usizeof from FS here */
02632    #define NIL_MESS ((message *) 0)          /* null pointer */
02633
02634    /* Memory related constants. */
02635    #define SEGMENT_TYPE  0xFF00     /* bit mask to get segment type */
02636    #define SEGMENT_INDEX 0x00FF     /* bit mask to get segment index */
02637
02638    #define LOCAL_SEG     0x0000     /* flags indicating local memory segment */
02639    #define NR_LOCAL_SEGS      3     /* # local segments per process (fixed) */
```

```
02640  #define T                    0    /* proc[i].mem_map[T] is for text */
02641  #define D                    1    /* proc[i].mem_map[D] is for data */
02642  #define S                    2    /* proc[i].mem_map[S] is for stack */
02643
02644  #define REMOTE_SEG      0x0100    /* flags indicating remote memory segment */
02645  #define NR_REMOTE_SEGS       3    /* # remote memory regions (variable) */
02646
02647  #define BIOS_SEG        0x0200    /* flags indicating BIOS memory segment */
02648  #define NR_BIOS_SEGS         3    /* # BIOS memory regions (variable) */
02649
02650  #define PHYS_SEG        0x0400    /* flag indicating entire physical memory */
02651
02652  /* Labels used to disable code sections for different reasons. */
02653  #define DEAD_CODE            0    /* unused code in normal configuration */
02654  #define FUTURE_CODE          0    /* new code to be activated + tested later */
02655  #define TEMP_CODE            1    /* active code to be removed later */
02656
02657  /* Process name length in the PM process table, including '\0'. */
02658  #define PROC_NAME_LEN       16
02659
02660  /* Miscellaneous */
02661  #define BYTE              0377    /* mask for 8 bits */
02662  #define READING              0    /* copy data to user */
02663  #define WRITING              1    /* copy data from user */
02664  #define NO_NUM          0x8000    /* used as numerical argument to panic() */
02665  #define NIL_PTR     (char *) 0    /* generally useful expression */
02666  #define HAVE_SCATTERED_IO    1    /* scattered I/O is now standard */
02667
02668  /* Macros. */
02669  #define MAX(a, b)    ((a) > (b) ? (a) : (b))
02670  #define MIN(a, b)    ((a) < (b) ? (a) : (b))
02671
02672  /* Memory is allocated in clicks. */
02673  #if (CHIP == INTEL)
02674  #define CLICK_SIZE        1024    /* unit in which memory is allocated */
02675  #define CLICK_SHIFT         10    /* log2 of CLICK_SIZE */
02676  #endif
02677
02678  #if (CHIP == SPARC) || (CHIP == M68000)
02679  #define CLICK_SIZE        4096    /* unit in which memory is allocated */
02680  #define CLICK_SHIFT         12    /* log2 of CLICK_SIZE */
02681  #endif
02682
02683  /* Click to byte conversions (and vice versa). */
02684  #define HCLICK_SHIFT         4    /* log2 of HCLICK_SIZE */
02685  #define HCLICK_SIZE         16    /* hardware segment conversion magic */
02686  #if CLICK_SIZE >= HCLICK_SIZE
02687  #define click_to_hclick(n) ((n) << (CLICK_SHIFT - HCLICK_SHIFT))
02688  #else
02689  #define click_to_hclick(n) ((n) >> (HCLICK_SHIFT - CLICK_SHIFT))
02690  #endif
02691  #define hclick_to_physb(n) ((phys_bytes) (n) << HCLICK_SHIFT)
02692  #define physb_to_hclick(n) ((n) >> HCLICK_SHIFT)
02693
02694  #define ABS               -999    /* this process means absolute memory */
02695
02696  /* Flag bits for i_mode in the inode. */
02697  #define I_TYPE          0170000 /* this field gives inode type */
02698  #define I_REGULAR       0100000 /* regular file, not dir or special */
02699  #define I_BLOCK_SPECIAL 0060000 /* block special file */
```

```
02700  #define I_DIRECTORY     0040000 /* file is a directory */
02701  #define I_CHAR_SPECIAL  0020000 /* character special file */
02702  #define I_NAMED_PIPE    0010000 /* named pipe (FIFO) */
02703  #define I_SET_UID_BIT   0004000 /* set effective uid_t on exec */
02704  #define I_SET_GID_BIT   0002000 /* set effective gid_t on exec */
02705  #define ALL_MODES       0006777 /* all bits for user, group and others */
02706  #define RWX_MODES       0000777 /* mode bits for RWX only */
02707  #define R_BIT           0000004 /* Rwx protection bit */
02708  #define W_BIT           0000002 /* rWx protection bit */
02709  #define X_BIT           0000001 /* rwX protection bit */
02710  #define I_NOT_ALLOC     0000000 /* this inode is free */
02711
02712  /* Flag used only in flags argument of dev_open. */
02713  #define RO_BIT          0200000 /* Open device readonly; fail if writable. */
02714
02715  /* Some limits. */
02716  #define MAX_BLOCK_NR  ((block_t) 077777777)    /* largest block number */
02717  #define HIGHEST_ZONE   ((zone_t) 077777777)    /* largest zone number */
02718  #define MAX_INODE_NR ((ino_t) 037777777777)    /* largest inode number */
02719  #define MAX_FILE_POS ((off_t) 037777777777)    /* largest legal file offset */
02720
02721  #define NO_BLOCK              ((block_t) 0)    /* absence of a block number */
02722  #define NO_ENTRY                ((ino_t) 0)    /* absence of a dir entry */
02723  #define NO_ZONE                ((zone_t) 0)    /* absence of a zone number */
02724  #define NO_DEV                  ((dev_t) 0)    /* absence of a device numb */
```

++
                          include/minix/type.h
++

```
02800  #ifndef _TYPE_H
02801  #define _TYPE_H
02802
02803  #ifndef _MINIX_SYS_CONFIG_H
02804  #include <minix/sys_config.h>
02805  #endif
02806
02807  #ifndef _TYPES_H
02808  #include <sys/types.h>
02809  #endif
02810
02811  /* Type definitions. */
02812  typedef unsigned int vir_clicks;        /*  virtual addr/length in clicks */
02813  typedef unsigned long phys_bytes;       /* physical addr/length in bytes */
02814  typedef unsigned int phys_clicks;       /* physical addr/length in clicks */
02815
02816  #if (_MINIX_CHIP == _CHIP_INTEL)
02817  typedef unsigned int vir_bytes; /* virtual addresses and lengths in bytes */
02818  #endif
02819
02820  #if (_MINIX_CHIP == _CHIP_M68000)
02821  typedef unsigned long vir_bytes;/* virtual addresses and lengths in bytes */
02822  #endif
02823
02824  #if (_MINIX_CHIP == _CHIP_SPARC)
02825  typedef unsigned long vir_bytes;/* virtual addresses and lengths in bytes */
02826  #endif
02827
02828  /* Memory map for local text, stack, data segments. */
02829  struct mem_map {
```

```
02830    vir_clicks mem_vir;           /* virtual address */
02831    phys_clicks mem_phys;         /* physical address */
02832    vir_clicks mem_len;           /* length */
02833  };
02834
02835  /* Memory map for remote memory areas, e.g., for the RAM disk. */
02836  struct far_mem {
02837    int in_use;                   /* entry in use, unless zero */
02838    phys_clicks mem_phys;         /* physical address */
02839    vir_clicks mem_len;           /* length */
02840  };
02841
02842  /* Structure for virtual copying by means of a vector with requests. */
02843  struct vir_addr {
02844    int proc_nr;
02845    int segment;
02846    vir_bytes offset;
02847  };
02848
02849  #define phys_cp_req vir_cp_req
02850  struct vir_cp_req {
02851    struct vir_addr src;
02852    struct vir_addr dst;
02853    phys_bytes count;
02854  };
02855
02856  typedef struct {
02857    vir_bytes iov_addr;           /* address of an I/O buffer */
02858    vir_bytes iov_size;           /* sizeof an I/O buffer */
02859  } iovec_t;
02860
02861  /* PM passes the address of a structure of this type to KERNEL when
02862   * sys_sendsig() is invoked as part of the signal catching mechanism.
02863   * The structure contain all the information that KERNEL needs to build
02864   * the signal stack.
02865   */
02866  struct sigmsg {
02867    int sm_signo;                 /* signal number being caught */
02868    unsigned long sm_mask;        /* mask to restore when handler returns */
02869    vir_bytes sm_sighandler;      /* address of handler */
02870    vir_bytes sm_sigreturn;       /* address of _sigreturn in C library */
02871    vir_bytes sm_stkptr;          /* user stack pointer */
02872  };
02873
02874  /* This is used to obtain system information through SYS_GETINFO. */
02875  struct kinfo {
02876    phys_bytes code_base;         /* base of kernel code */
02877    phys_bytes code_size;
02878    phys_bytes data_base;         /* base of kernel data */
02879    phys_bytes data_size;
02880    vir_bytes proc_addr;          /* virtual address of process table */
02881    phys_bytes kmem_base;         /* kernel memory layout (/dev/kmem) */
02882    phys_bytes kmem_size;
02883    phys_bytes bootdev_base;      /* boot device from boot image (/dev/boot) */
02884    phys_bytes bootdev_size;
02885    phys_bytes bootdev_mem;
02886    phys_bytes params_base;       /* parameters passed by boot monitor */
02887    phys_bytes params_size;
02888    int nr_procs;                 /* number of user processes */
02889    int nr_tasks;                 /* number of kernel tasks */
```

```
02890    char release[6];              /* kernel release number */
02891    char version[6];              /* kernel version number */
02892    int relocking;                /* relocking check (for debugging) */
02893  };
02894
02895  struct machine {
02896    int pc_at;
02897    int ps_mca;
02898    int processor;
02899    int protected;
02900    int vdu_ega;
02901    int vdu_vga;
02902  };
02903
02904  #endif /* _TYPE_H */
```

```
+++++++++++++++++++++++++++++++++++++++++++++++++++++++++++++++++++++++++++
                         include/minix/ipc.h
+++++++++++++++++++++++++++++++++++++++++++++++++++++++++++++++++++++++++++
```

```
03000  #ifndef _IPC_H
03001  #define _IPC_H
03002
03003  /*========================================================================*
03004   * Types relating to messages.                                            *
03005   *========================================================================*/
03006
03007  #define M1              1
03008  #define M3              3
03009  #define M4              4
03010  #define M3_STRING       14
03011
03012  typedef struct {int m1i1, m1i2, m1i3; char *m1p1, *m1p2, *m1p3;} mess_1;
03013  typedef struct {int m2i1, m2i2, m2i3; long m2l1, m2l2; char *m2p1;} mess_2;
03014  typedef struct {int m3i1, m3i2; char *m3p1; char m3ca1[M3_STRING];} mess_3;
03015  typedef struct {long m4l1, m4l2, m4l3, m4l4, m4l5;} mess_4;
03016  typedef struct {short m5c1, m5c2; int m5i1, m5i2; long m5l1, m5l2, m5l3;}mess_5;
03017  typedef struct {int m7i1, m7i2, m7i3, m7i4; char *m7p1, *m7p2;} mess_7;
03018  typedef struct {int m8i1, m8i2; char *m8p1, *m8p2, *m8p3, *m8p4;} mess_8;
03019
03020  typedef struct {
03021    int m_source;                 /* who sent the message */
03022    int m_type;                   /* what kind of message is it */
03023    union {
03024          mess_1 m_m1;
03025          mess_2 m_m2;
03026          mess_3 m_m3;
03027          mess_4 m_m4;
03028          mess_5 m_m5;
03029          mess_7 m_m7;
03030          mess_8 m_m8;
03031    } m_u;
03032  } message;
03033
03034  /* The following defines provide names for useful members. */
03035  #define m1_i1   m_u.m_m1.m1i1
03036  #define m1_i2   m_u.m_m1.m1i2
03037  #define m1_i3   m_u.m_m1.m1i3
03038  #define m1_p1   m_u.m_m1.m1p1
03039  #define m1_p2   m_u.m_m1.m1p2
```

```
03040   #define m1_p3   m_u.m_m1.m1p3
03041
03042   #define m2_i1   m_u.m_m2.m2i1
03043   #define m2_i2   m_u.m_m2.m2i2
03044   #define m2_i3   m_u.m_m2.m2i3
03045   #define m2_l1   m_u.m_m2.m2l1
03046   #define m2_l2   m_u.m_m2.m2l2
03047   #define m2_p1   m_u.m_m2.m2p1
03048
03049   #define m3_i1   m_u.m_m3.m3i1
03050   #define m3_i2   m_u.m_m3.m3i2
03051   #define m3_p1   m_u.m_m3.m3p1
03052   #define m3_ca1  m_u.m_m3.m3ca1
03053
03054   #define m4_l1   m_u.m_m4.m4l1
03055   #define m4_l2   m_u.m_m4.m4l2
03056   #define m4_l3   m_u.m_m4.m4l3
03057   #define m4_l4   m_u.m_m4.m4l4
03058   #define m4_l5   m_u.m_m4.m4l5
03059
03060   #define m5_c1   m_u.m_m5.m5c1
03061   #define m5_c2   m_u.m_m5.m5c2
03062   #define m5_i1   m_u.m_m5.m5i1
03063   #define m5_i2   m_u.m_m5.m5i2
03064   #define m5_l1   m_u.m_m5.m5l1
03065   #define m5_l2   m_u.m_m5.m5l2
03066   #define m5_l3   m_u.m_m5.m5l3
03067
03068   #define m7_i1   m_u.m_m7.m7i1
03069   #define m7_i2   m_u.m_m7.m7i2
03070   #define m7_i3   m_u.m_m7.m7i3
03071   #define m7_i4   m_u.m_m7.m7i4
03072   #define m7_p1   m_u.m_m7.m7p1
03073   #define m7_p2   m_u.m_m7.m7p2
03074
03075   #define m8_i1   m_u.m_m8.m8i1
03076   #define m8_i2   m_u.m_m8.m8i2
03077   #define m8_p1   m_u.m_m8.m8p1
03078   #define m8_p2   m_u.m_m8.m8p2
03079   #define m8_p3   m_u.m_m8.m8p3
03080   #define m8_p4   m_u.m_m8.m8p4
03081
03082   /*========================================================================*
03083    * Minix run-time system (IPC).                                          *
03084    *========================================================================*/
03085
03086   /* Hide names to avoid name space pollution. */
03087   #define echo            _echo
03088   #define notify          _notify
03089   #define sendrec         _sendrec
03090   #define receive         _receive
03091   #define send            _send
03092   #define nb_receive      _nb_receive
03093   #define nb_send         _nb_send
03094
03095   _PROTOTYPE( int echo, (message *m_ptr)                            );
03096   _PROTOTYPE( int notify, (int dest)                               );
03097   _PROTOTYPE( int sendrec, (int src_dest, message *m_ptr)          );
03098   _PROTOTYPE( int receive, (int src, message *m_ptr)               );
03099   _PROTOTYPE( int send, (int dest, message *m_ptr)                 );
```

```
03100    _PROTOTYPE( int nb_receive, (int src, message *m_ptr)              );
03101    _PROTOTYPE( int nb_send, (int dest, message *m_ptr)               );
03102
03103    #endif /* _IPC_H */


++++++++++++++++++++++++++++++++++++++++++++++++++++++++++++++++++++++++++++
                         include/minix/syslib.h
++++++++++++++++++++++++++++++++++++++++++++++++++++++++++++++++++++++++++++

03200    /* Prototypes for system library functions. */
03201
03202    #ifndef _SYSLIB_H
03203    #define _SYSLIB_H
03204
03205    #ifndef _TYPES_H
03206    #include <sys/types.h>
03207    #endif
03208
03209    #ifndef _IPC_H
03210    #include <minix/ipc.h>
03211    #endif
03212
03213    #ifndef _DEVIO_H
03214    #include <minix/devio.h>
03215    #endif
03216
03217    /* Forward declaration */
03218    struct reg86u;
03219
03220    #define SYSTASK SYSTEM
03221
03222    /*===========================================================================*
03223     * Minix system library.                                                     *
03224     *===========================================================================*/
03225    _PROTOTYPE( int _taskcall, (int who, int syscallnr, message *msgptr));
03226
03227    _PROTOTYPE( int sys_abort, (int how, ...));
03228    _PROTOTYPE( int sys_exec, (int proc, char *ptr,
03229                                      char *aout, vir_bytes initpc));
03230    _PROTOTYPE( int sys_fork, (int parent, int child));
03231    _PROTOTYPE( int sys_newmap, (int proc, struct mem_map *ptr));
03232    _PROTOTYPE( int sys_exit, (int proc));
03233    _PROTOTYPE( int sys_trace, (int req, int proc, long addr, long *data_p));
03234
03235    _PROTOTYPE( int sys_svrctl, (int proc, int req, int priv,vir_bytes argp));
03236    _PROTOTYPE( int sys_nice, (int proc, int priority));
03237
03238    _PROTOTYPE( int sys_int86, (struct reg86u *reg86p));
03239
03240    /* Shorthands for sys_sdevio() system call. */
03241    #define sys_insb(port, proc_nr, buffer, count) \
03242            sys_sdevio(DIO_INPUT, port, DIO_BYTE, proc_nr, buffer, count)
03243    #define sys_insw(port, proc_nr, buffer, count) \
03244            sys_sdevio(DIO_INPUT, port, DIO_WORD, proc_nr, buffer, count)
03245    #define sys_outsb(port, proc_nr, buffer, count) \
03246            sys_sdevio(DIO_OUTPUT, port, DIO_BYTE, proc_nr, buffer, count)
03247    #define sys_outsw(port, proc_nr, buffer, count) \
03248            sys_sdevio(DIO_OUTPUT, port, DIO_WORD, proc_nr, buffer, count)
03249    _PROTOTYPE( int sys_sdevio, (int req, long port, int type, int proc_nr,
```

```
03250                 void *buffer, int count));
03251
03252  /* Clock functionality: get system times or (un)schedule an alarm call. */
03253  _PROTOTYPE( int sys_times, (int proc_nr, clock_t *ptr));
03254  _PROTOTYPE(int sys_setalarm, (clock_t exp_time, int abs_time));
03255
03256  /* Shorthands for sys_irqctl() system call. */
03257  #define sys_irqdisable(hook_id) \
03258      sys_irqctl(IRQ_DISABLE, 0, 0, hook_id)
03259  #define sys_irqenable(hook_id) \
03260      sys_irqctl(IRQ_ENABLE, 0, 0, hook_id)
03261  #define sys_irqsetpolicy(irq_vec, policy, hook_id) \
03262      sys_irqctl(IRQ_SETPOLICY, irq_vec, policy, hook_id)
03263  #define sys_irqrmpolicy(irq_vec, hook_id) \
03264      sys_irqctl(IRQ_RMPOLICY, irq_vec, 0, hook_id)
03265  _PROTOTYPE ( int sys_irqctl, (int request, int irq_vec, int policy,
03266      int *irq_hook_id) );
03267
03268  /* Shorthands for sys_vircopy() and sys_physcopy() system calls. */
03269  #define sys_biosin(bios_vir, dst_vir, bytes) \
03270          sys_vircopy(SELF, BIOS_SEG, bios_vir, SELF, D, dst_vir, bytes)
03271  #define sys_biosout(src_vir, bios_vir, bytes) \
03272          sys_vircopy(SELF, D, src_vir, SELF, BIOS_SEG, bios_vir, bytes)
03273  #define sys_datacopy(src_proc, src_vir, dst_proc, dst_vir, bytes) \
03274          sys_vircopy(src_proc, D, src_vir, dst_proc, D, dst_vir, bytes)
03275  #define sys_textcopy(src_proc, src_vir, dst_proc, dst_vir, bytes) \
03276          sys_vircopy(src_proc, T, src_vir, dst_proc, T, dst_vir, bytes)
03277  #define sys_stackcopy(src_proc, src_vir, dst_proc, dst_vir, bytes) \
03278          sys_vircopy(src_proc, S, src_vir, dst_proc, S, dst_vir, bytes)
03279  _PROTOTYPE(int sys_vircopy, (int src_proc, int src_seg, vir_bytes src_vir,
03280          int dst_proc, int dst_seg, vir_bytes dst_vir, phys_bytes bytes));
03281
03282  #define sys_abscopy(src_phys, dst_phys, bytes) \
03283          sys_physcopy(NONE, PHYS_SEG, src_phys, NONE, PHYS_SEG, dst_phys, bytes)
03284  _PROTOTYPE(int sys_physcopy, (int src_proc, int src_seg, vir_bytes src_vir,
03285          int dst_proc, int dst_seg, vir_bytes dst_vir, phys_bytes bytes));
03286  _PROTOTYPE(int sys_memset, (unsigned long pattern,
03287                  phys_bytes base, phys_bytes bytes));
03288
03289  /* Vectored virtual / physical copy calls. */
03290  #if DEAD_CODE            /* library part not yet implemented */
03291  _PROTOTYPE(int sys_virvcopy, (phys_cp_req *vec_ptr,int vec_size,int *nr_ok));
03292  _PROTOTYPE(int sys_physvcopy, (phys_cp_req *vec_ptr,int vec_size,int *nr_ok));
03293  #endif
03294
03295  _PROTOTYPE(int sys_umap, (int proc_nr, int seg, vir_bytes vir_addr,
03296          vir_bytes bytes, phys_bytes *phys_addr));
03297  _PROTOTYPE(int sys_segctl, (int *index, u16_t *seg, vir_bytes *off,
03298          phys_bytes phys, vir_bytes size));
03299
03300  /* Shorthands for sys_getinfo() system call. */
03301  #define sys_getkmessages(dst)    sys_getinfo(GET_KMESSAGES, dst, 0,0,0)
03302  #define sys_getkinfo(dst)        sys_getinfo(GET_KINFO, dst, 0,0,0)
03303  #define sys_getmachine(dst)      sys_getinfo(GET_MACHINE, dst, 0,0,0)
03304  #define sys_getproctab(dst)      sys_getinfo(GET_PROCTAB, dst, 0,0,0)
03305  #define sys_getprivtab(dst)      sys_getinfo(GET_PRIVTAB, dst, 0,0,0)
03306  #define sys_getproc(dst,nr)      sys_getinfo(GET_PROC, dst, 0,0, nr)
03307  #define sys_getrandomness(dst)   sys_getinfo(GET_RANDOMNESS, dst, 0,0,0)
03308  #define sys_getimage(dst)        sys_getinfo(GET_IMAGE, dst, 0,0,0)
03309  #define sys_getirqhooks(dst)     sys_getinfo(GET_IRQHOOKS, dst, 0,0,0)
```

```
03310  #define sys_getmonparams(v,vl)  sys_getinfo(GET_MONPARAMS, v,vl, 0,0)
03311  #define sys_getschedinfo(v1,v2) sys_getinfo(GET_SCHEDINFO, v1,0, v2,0)
03312  #define sys_getlocktimings(dst) sys_getinfo(GET_LOCKTIMING, dst, 0,0,0)
03313  #define sys_getbiosbuffer(virp, sizep) sys_getinfo(GET_BIOSBUFFER, virp, \
03314          sizeof(*virp), sizep, sizeof(*sizep))
03315  _PROTOTYPE(int sys_getinfo, (int request, void *val_ptr, int val_len,
03316                              void *val_ptr2, int val_len2)            );
03317
03318  /* Signal control. */
03319  _PROTOTYPE(int sys_kill, (int proc, int sig) );
03320  _PROTOTYPE(int sys_sigsend, (int proc_nr, struct sigmsg *sig_ctxt) );
03321  _PROTOTYPE(int sys_sigreturn, (int proc_nr, struct sigmsg *sig_ctxt) );
03322  _PROTOTYPE(int sys_getksig, (int *k_proc_nr, sigset_t *k_sig_map) );
03323  _PROTOTYPE(int sys_endksig, (int proc_nr) );
03324
03325  /* NOTE: two different approaches were used to distinguish the device I/O
03326   * types 'byte', 'word', 'long': the latter uses #define and results in a
03327   * smaller implementation, but looses the static type checking.
03328   */
03329  _PROTOTYPE(int sys_voutb, (pvb_pair_t *pvb_pairs, int nr_ports)      );
03330  _PROTOTYPE(int sys_voutw, (pvw_pair_t *pvw_pairs, int nr_ports)      );
03331  _PROTOTYPE(int sys_voutl, (pvl_pair_t *pvl_pairs, int nr_ports)      );
03332  _PROTOTYPE(int sys_vinb, (pvb_pair_t *pvb_pairs, int nr_ports)       );
03333  _PROTOTYPE(int sys_vinw, (pvw_pair_t *pvw_pairs, int nr_ports)       );
03334  _PROTOTYPE(int sys_vinl, (pvl_pair_t *pvl_pairs, int nr_ports)       );
03335
03336  /* Shorthands for sys_out() system call. */
03337  #define sys_outb(p,v)   sys_out((p), (unsigned long) (v), DIO_BYTE)
03338  #define sys_outw(p,v)   sys_out((p), (unsigned long) (v), DIO_WORD)
03339  #define sys_outl(p,v)   sys_out((p), (unsigned long) (v), DIO_LONG)
03340  _PROTOTYPE(int sys_out, (int port, unsigned long value, int type)    );
03341
03342  /* Shorthands for sys_in() system call. */
03343  #define sys_inb(p,v)    sys_in((p), (unsigned long*) (v), DIO_BYTE)
03344  #define sys_inw(p,v)    sys_in((p), (unsigned long*) (v), DIO_WORD)
03345  #define sys_inl(p,v)    sys_in((p), (unsigned long*) (v), DIO_LONG)
03346  _PROTOTYPE(int sys_in, (int port, unsigned long *value, int type)    );
03347
03348  #endif /* _SYSLIB_H */
03349
```

```
++++++++++++++++++++++++++++++++++++++++++++++++++++++++++++++++++++++++++++
                          include/minix/sysutil.h
++++++++++++++++++++++++++++++++++++++++++++++++++++++++++++++++++++++++++++
```

```
03400  #ifndef _EXTRALIB_H
03401  #define _EXTRALIB_H
03402
03403  /* Extra system library definitions to support device drivers and servers.
03404   *
03405   * Created:
03406   *     Mar 15, 2004 by Jorrit N. Herder
03407   *
03408   * Changes:
03409   *     May 31, 2005: added printf, kputc (relocated from syslib)
03410   *     May 31, 2005: added getuptime
03411   *     Mar 18, 2005: added tickdelay
03412   *     Oct 01, 2004: added env_parse, env_prefix, env_panic
03413   *     Jul 13, 2004: added fkey_ctl
03414   *     Apr 28, 2004: added report, panic
```

```
03415    *        Mar 31, 2004: setup like other libraries, such as syslib
03416    */
03417
03418   /*===========================================================================*
03419    * Miscellaneous helper functions.
03420    *===========================================================================*/
03421
03422   /* Environment parsing return values. */
03423   #define EP_BUF_SIZE    128        /* local buffer for env value */
03424   #define EP_UNSET        0         /* variable not set */
03425   #define EP_OFF          1         /* var = off */
03426   #define EP_ON           2         /* var = on (or field left blank) */
03427   #define EP_SET          3         /* var = 1:2:3 (nonblank field) */
03428   #define EP_EGETKENV     4         /* sys_getkenv() failed ... */
03429
03430   _PROTOTYPE( void env_setargs, (int argc, char *argv[])                 );
03431   _PROTOTYPE( int env_get_param, (char *key, char *value, int max_size) );
03432   _PROTOTYPE( int env_prefix, (char *env, char *prefix)                 );
03433   _PROTOTYPE( void env_panic, (char *key)                               );
03434   _PROTOTYPE( int env_parse, (char *env, char *fmt, int field, long *param,
03435                               long min, long max)                       );
03436
03437   #define fkey_map(fkeys, sfkeys) fkey_ctl(FKEY_MAP, (fkeys), (sfkeys))
03438   #define fkey_unmap(fkeys, sfkeys) fkey_ctl(FKEY_UNMAP, (fkeys), (sfkeys))
03439   #define fkey_events(fkeys, sfkeys) fkey_ctl(FKEY_EVENTS, (fkeys), (sfkeys))
03440   _PROTOTYPE( int fkey_ctl, (int req, int *fkeys, int *sfkeys)          );
03441
03442   _PROTOTYPE( int printf, (const char *fmt, ...));
03443   _PROTOTYPE( void kputc, (int c));
03444   _PROTOTYPE( void report, (char *who, char *mess, int num));
03445   _PROTOTYPE( void panic, (char *who, char *mess, int num));
03446   _PROTOTYPE( int getuptime, (clock_t *ticks));
03447   _PROTOTYPE( int tickdelay, (clock_t ticks));
03448
03449   #endif /* _EXTRALIB_H */
03450
```

```
++++++++++++++++++++++++++++++++++++++++++++++++++++++++++++++++++++++++++++++
                            include/minix/callnr.h
++++++++++++++++++++++++++++++++++++++++++++++++++++++++++++++++++++++++++++++
```

```
03500   #define NCALLS          91      /* number of system calls allowed */
03501
03502   #define EXIT            1
03503   #define FORK            2
03504   #define READ            3
03505   #define WRITE           4
03506   #define OPEN            5
03507   #define CLOSE           6
03508   #define WAIT            7
03509   #define CREAT           8
03510   #define LINK            9
03511   #define UNLINK          10
03512   #define WAITPID         11
03513   #define CHDIR           12
03514   #define TIME            13
```

```
03515   #define MKNOD            14
03516   #define CHMOD            15
03517   #define CHOWN            16
03518   #define BRK              17
03519   #define STAT             18
03520   #define LSEEK            19
03521   #define GETPID           20
03522   #define MOUNT            21
03523   #define UMOUNT           22
03524   #define SETUID           23
03525   #define GETUID           24
03526   #define STIME            25
03527   #define PTRACE           26
03528   #define ALARM            27
03529   #define FSTAT            28
03530   #define PAUSE            29
03531   #define UTIME            30
03532   #define ACCESS           33
03533   #define SYNC             36
03534   #define KILL             37
03535   #define RENAME           38
03536   #define MKDIR            39
03537   #define RMDIR            40
03538   #define DUP              41
03539   #define PIPE             42
03540   #define TIMES            43
03541   #define SETGID           46
03542   #define GETGID           47
03543   #define SIGNAL           48
03544   #define IOCTL            54
03545   #define FCNTL            55
03546   #define EXEC             59
03547   #define UMASK            60
03548   #define CHROOT           61
03549   #define SETSID           62
03550   #define GETPGRP          63
03551
03552   /* The following are not system calls, but are processed like them. */
03553   #define UNPAUSE          65      /* to MM or FS: check for EINTR */
03554   #define REVIVE           67      /* to FS: revive a sleeping process */
03555   #define TASK_REPLY       68      /* to FS: reply code from tty task */
03556
03557   /* Posix signal handling. */
03558   #define SIGACTION        71
03559   #define SIGSUSPEND       72
03560   #define SIGPENDING       73
03561   #define SIGPROCMASK      74
03562   #define SIGRETURN        75
03563
03564   #define REBOOT           76      /* to PM */
03565
03566   /* MINIX specific calls, e.g., to support system services. */
03567   #define SVRCTL           77
03568                                    /* unused */
03569   #define GETSYSINFO       79      /* to PM or FS */
03570   #define GETPROCNR        80      /* to PM */
03571   #define DEVCTL           81      /* to FS */
03572   #define FSTATFS          82      /* to FS */
03573   #define ALLOCMEM         83      /* to PM */
03574   #define FREEMEM          84      /* to PM */
```

```
03575   #define SELECT            85      /* to FS */
03576   #define FCHDIR            86      /* to FS */
03577   #define FSYNC             87      /* to FS */
03578   #define GETPRIORITY       88      /* to PM */
03579   #define SETPRIORITY       89      /* to PM */
03580   #define GETTIMEOFDAY      90      /* to PM */
```

```
++++++++++++++++++++++++++++++++++++++++++++++++++++++++++++++++++++++++++++++
                              include/minix/com.h
++++++++++++++++++++++++++++++++++++++++++++++++++++++++++++++++++++++++++++++
03600   #ifndef _MINIX_COM_H
03601   #define _MINIX_COM_H
03602
03603   /*===========================================================================*
03604    *                      Magic process numbers                              *
03605    *===========================================================================*/
03606
03607   #define ANY             0x7ace  /* used to indicate 'any process' */
03608   #define NONE            0x6ace  /* used to indicate 'no process at all' */
03609   #define SELF            0x8ace  /* used to indicate 'own process' */
03610
03611   /*===========================================================================*
03612    *          Process numbers of processes in the system image               *
03613    *===========================================================================*/
03614
03615   /* The values of several task numbers depend on whether they or other tasks
03616    * are enabled. They are defined as (PREVIOUS_TASK - ENABLE_TASK) in general.
03617    * ENABLE_TASK is either 0 or 1, so a task either gets a new number, or gets
03618    * the same number as the previous task and is further unused. Note that the
03619    * order should correspond to the order in the task table defined in table.c.
03620    */
03621
03622   /* Kernel tasks. These all run in the same address space. */
03623   #define IDLE             -4      /* runs when no one else can run */
03624   #define CLOCK            -3      /* alarms and other clock functions */
03625   #define SYSTEM           -2      /* request system functionality */
03626   #define KERNEL           -1      /* pseudo-process for IPC and scheduling */
03627   #define HARDWARE      KERNEL      /* for hardware interrupt handlers */
03628
03629   /* Number of tasks. Note that NR_PROCS is defined in <minix/config.h>. */
03630   #define NR_TASKS          4
03631
03632   /* User-space processes, that is, device drivers, servers, and INIT. */
03633   #define PM_PROC_NR        0      /* process manager */
03634   #define FS_PROC_NR        1      /* file system */
03635   #define RS_PROC_NR        2      /* reincarnation server */
03636   #define MEM_PROC_NR       3      /* memory driver (RAM disk, null, etc.) */
03637   #define LOG_PROC_NR       4      /* log device driver */
03638   #define TTY_PROC_NR       5      /* terminal (TTY) driver */
03639   #define DRVR_PROC_NR      6      /* device driver for boot medium */
03640   #define INIT_PROC_NR      7      /* init -- goes multiuser */
03641
03642   /* Number of processes contained in the system image. */
03643   #define NR_BOOT_PROCS   (NR_TASKS + INIT_PROC_NR + 1)
03644
```

```
03645   /*===========================================================================*
03646    *                      Kernel notification types                            *
03647    *===========================================================================*/
03648
03649   /* Kernel notification types. In principle, these can be sent to any process,
03650    * so make sure that these types do not interfere with other message types.
03651    * Notifications are prioritized because of the way they are unhold() and
03652    * blocking notifications are delivered. The lowest numbers go first. The
03653    * offset are used for the per-process notification bit maps.
03654    */
03655   #define NOTIFY_MESSAGE            0x1000
03656   #define NOTIFY_FROM(p_nr)        (NOTIFY_MESSAGE | ((p_nr) + NR_TASKS))
03657   #   define SYN_ALARM     NOTIFY_FROM(CLOCK)      /* synchronous alarm */
03658   #   define SYS_SIG       NOTIFY_FROM(SYSTEM)     /* system signal */
03659   #   define HARD_INT      NOTIFY_FROM(HARDWARE)   /* hardware interrupt */
03660   #   define NEW_KSIG      NOTIFY_FROM(HARDWARE)   /* new kernel signal */
03661   #   define FKEY_PRESSED  NOTIFY_FROM(TTY_PROC_NR)/* function key press */
03662
03663   /* Shorthands for message parameters passed with notifications. */
03664   #define NOTIFY_SOURCE            m_source
03665   #define NOTIFY_TYPE              m_type
03666   #define NOTIFY_ARG               m2_l1
03667   #define NOTIFY_TIMESTAMP         m2_l2
03668   #define NOTIFY_FLAGS             m2_i1
03669
03670   /*===========================================================================*
03671    *             Messages for BLOCK and CHARACTER device drivers               *
03672    *===========================================================================*/
03673
03674   /* Message types for device drivers. */
03675   #define DEV_RQ_BASE    0x400     /* base for device request types */
03676   #define DEV_RS_BASE    0x500     /* base for device response types */
03677
03678   #define CANCEL          (DEV_RQ_BASE +  0) /* general req to force a task to cancel */
03679   #define DEV_READ        (DEV_RQ_BASE +  3) /* read from minor device */
03680   #define DEV_WRITE       (DEV_RQ_BASE +  4) /* write to minor device */
03681   #define DEV_IOCTL       (DEV_RQ_BASE +  5) /* I/O control code */
03682   #define DEV_OPEN        (DEV_RQ_BASE +  6) /* open a minor device */
03683   #define DEV_CLOSE       (DEV_RQ_BASE +  7) /* close a minor device */
03684   #define DEV_SCATTER     (DEV_RQ_BASE +  8) /* write from a vector */
03685   #define DEV_GATHER      (DEV_RQ_BASE +  9) /* read into a vector */
03686   #define TTY_SETPGRP     (DEV_RQ_BASE + 10) /* set process group */
03687   #define TTY_EXIT        (DEV_RQ_BASE + 11) /* process group leader exited */
03688   #define DEV_SELECT      (DEV_RQ_BASE + 12) /* request select() attention */
03689   #define DEV_STATUS      (DEV_RQ_BASE + 13) /* request driver status */
03690
03691   #define DEV_REPLY       (DEV_RS_BASE + 0) /* general task reply */
03692   #define DEV_CLONED      (DEV_RS_BASE + 1) /* return cloned minor */
03693   #define DEV_REVIVE      (DEV_RS_BASE + 2) /* driver revives process */
03694   #define DEV_IO_READY    (DEV_RS_BASE + 3) /* selected device ready */
03695   #define DEV_NO_STATUS   (DEV_RS_BASE + 4) /* empty status reply */
03696
03697   /* Field names for messages to block and character device drivers. */
03698   #define DEVICE          m2_i1    /* major-minor device */
03699   #define PROC_NR         m2_i2    /* which (proc) wants I/O? */
03700   #define COUNT           m2_i3    /* how many bytes to transfer */
03701   #define REQUEST         m2_i3    /* ioctl request code */
03702   #define POSITION        m2_l1    /* file offset */
03703   #define ADDRESS         m2_p1    /* core buffer address */
03704
```

```
03705   /* Field names for DEV_SELECT messages to device drivers. */
03706   #define DEV_MINOR       m2_i1   /* minor device */
03707   #define DEV_SEL_OPS     m2_i2   /* which select operations are requested */
03708   #define DEV_SEL_WATCH   m2_i3   /* request notify if no operations are ready */
03709
03710   /* Field names used in reply messages from tasks. */
03711   #define REP_PROC_NR     m2_i1   /* # of proc on whose behalf I/O was done */
03712   #define REP_STATUS      m2_i2   /* bytes transferred or error number */
03713   #  define SUSPEND       -998    /* status to suspend caller, reply later */
03714
03715   /* Field names for messages to TTY driver. */
03716   #define TTY_LINE        DEVICE  /* message parameter: terminal line */
03717   #define TTY_REQUEST     COUNT   /* message parameter: ioctl request code */
03718   #define TTY_SPEK        POSITION/* message parameter: ioctl speed, erasing */
03719   #define TTY_FLAGS       m2_l2   /* message parameter: ioctl tty mode */
03720   #define TTY_PGRP        m2_i3   /* message parameter: process group */
03721
03722   /* Field names for the QIC 02 status reply from tape driver */
03723   #define TAPE_STAT0      m2_l1
03724   #define TAPE_STAT1      m2_l2
03725
03726   /*===========================================================================*
03727    *                      Messages for networking layer                        *
03728    *===========================================================================*/
03729
03730   /* Message types for network layer requests. This layer acts like a driver. */
03731   #define NW_OPEN         DEV_OPEN
03732   #define NW_CLOSE        DEV_CLOSE
03733   #define NW_READ         DEV_READ
03734   #define NW_WRITE        DEV_WRITE
03735   #define NW_IOCTL        DEV_IOCTL
03736   #define NW_CANCEL       CANCEL
03737
03738   /* Base type for data link layer requests and responses. */
03739   #define DL_RQ_BASE      0x800
03740   #define DL_RS_BASE      0x900
03741
03742   /* Message types for data link layer requests. */
03743   #define DL_WRITE        (DL_RQ_BASE + 3)
03744   #define DL_WRITEV       (DL_RQ_BASE + 4)
03745   #define DL_READ         (DL_RQ_BASE + 5)
03746   #define DL_READV        (DL_RQ_BASE + 6)
03747   #define DL_INIT         (DL_RQ_BASE + 7)
03748   #define DL_STOP         (DL_RQ_BASE + 8)
03749   #define DL_GETSTAT      (DL_RQ_BASE + 9)
03750
03751   /* Message type for data link layer replies. */
03752   #define DL_INIT_REPLY   (DL_RS_BASE + 20)
03753   #define DL_TASK_REPLY   (DL_RS_BASE + 21)
03754
03755   /* Field names for data link layer messages. */
03756   #define DL_PORT         m2_i1
03757   #define DL_PROC         m2_i2
03758   #define DL_COUNT        m2_i3
03759   #define DL_MODE         m2_l1
03760   #define DL_CLCK         m2_l2
03761   #define DL_ADDR         m2_p1
03762   #define DL_STAT         m2_l1
03763
03764   /* Bits in 'DL_STAT' field of DL replies. */
```

```
03765   #  define DL_PACK_SEND         0x01
03766   #  define DL_PACK_RECV         0x02
03767   #  define DL_READ_IP           0x04
03768
03769   /* Bits in 'DL_MODE' field of DL requests. */
03770   #  define DL_NOMODE            0x0
03771   #  define DL_PROMISC_REQ       0x2
03772   #  define DL_MULTI_REQ         0x4
03773   #  define DL_BROAD_REQ         0x8
03774
03775   /*===========================================================================*
03776    *                 SYSTASK request types and field names                     *
03777    *===========================================================================*/
03778
03779   /* System library calls are dispatched via a call vector, so be careful when
03780    * modifying the system call numbers. The numbers here determine which call
03781    * is made from the call vector.
03782    */
03783   #define KERNEL_CALL      0x600    /* base for kernel calls to SYSTEM */
03784
03785   #  define SYS_FORK       (KERNEL_CALL + 0)       /* sys_fork() */
03786   #  define SYS_EXEC       (KERNEL_CALL + 1)       /* sys_exec() */
03787   #  define SYS_EXIT       (KERNEL_CALL + 2)       /* sys_exit() */
03788   #  define SYS_NICE       (KERNEL_CALL + 3)       /* sys_nice() */
03789   #  define SYS_PRIVCTL    (KERNEL_CALL + 4)       /* sys_privctl() */
03790   #  define SYS_TRACE      (KERNEL_CALL + 5)       /* sys_trace() */
03791   #  define SYS_KILL       (KERNEL_CALL + 6)       /* sys_kill() */
03792
03793   #  define SYS_GETKSIG    (KERNEL_CALL + 7)       /* sys_getsig() */
03794   #  define SYS_ENDKSIG    (KERNEL_CALL + 8)       /* sys_endsig() */
03795   #  define SYS_SIGSEND    (KERNEL_CALL + 9)       /* sys_sigsend() */
03796   #  define SYS_SIGRETURN  (KERNEL_CALL + 10)      /* sys_sigreturn() */
03797
03798   #  define SYS_NEWMAP     (KERNEL_CALL + 11)      /* sys_newmap() */
03799   #  define SYS_SEGCTL     (KERNEL_CALL + 12)      /* sys_segctl() */
03800   #  define SYS_MEMSET     (KERNEL_CALL + 13)      /* sys_memset() */
03801
03802   #  define SYS_UMAP       (KERNEL_CALL + 14)      /* sys_umap() */
03803   #  define SYS_VIRCOPY    (KERNEL_CALL + 15)      /* sys_vircopy() */
03804   #  define SYS_PHYSCOPY   (KERNEL_CALL + 16)      /* sys_physcopy() */
03805   #  define SYS_VIRVCOPY   (KERNEL_CALL + 17)      /* sys_virvcopy() */
03806   #  define SYS_PHYSVCOPY  (KERNEL_CALL + 18)      /* sys_physvcopy() */
03807
03808   #  define SYS_IRQCTL     (KERNEL_CALL + 19)      /* sys_irqctl() */
03809   #  define SYS_INT86      (KERNEL_CALL + 20)      /* sys_int86() */
03810   #  define SYS_DEVIO      (KERNEL_CALL + 21)      /* sys_devio() */
03811   #  define SYS_SDEVIO     (KERNEL_CALL + 22)      /* sys_sdevio() */
03812   #  define SYS_VDEVIO     (KERNEL_CALL + 23)      /* sys_vdevio() */
03813
03814   #  define SYS_SETALARM   (KERNEL_CALL + 24)      /* sys_setalarm() */
03815   #  define SYS_TIMES      (KERNEL_CALL + 25)      /* sys_times() */
03816   #  define SYS_GETINFO    (KERNEL_CALL + 26)      /* sys_getinfo() */
03817   #  define SYS_ABORT      (KERNEL_CALL + 27)      /* sys_abort() */
03818
03819   #define NR_SYS_CALLS    28       /* number of system calls */
03820
03821   /* Field names for SYS_MEMSET, SYS_SEGCTL. */
03822   #define MEM_PTR         m2_p1    /* base */
03823   #define MEM_COUNT       m2_l1    /* count */
03824   #define MEM_PATTERN     m2_l2    /* pattern to write */
```

```
03825 #define MEM_CHUNK_BASE   m4_l1   /* physical base address */
03826 #define MEM_CHUNK_SIZE   m4_l2   /* size of mem chunk */
03827 #define MEM_TOT_SIZE     m4_l3   /* total memory size */
03828 #define MEM_CHUNK_TAG    m4_l4   /* tag to identify chunk of mem */
03829
03830 /* Field names for SYS_DEVIO, SYS_VDEVIO, SYS_SDEVIO. */
03831 #define DIO_REQUEST      m2_i3   /* device in or output */
03832 #    define DIO_INPUT       0    /* input */
03833 #    define DIO_OUTPUT      1    /* output */
03834 #define DIO_TYPE         m2_i1   /* flag indicating byte, word, or long */
03835 #    define DIO_BYTE      'b'    /* byte type values */
03836 #    define DIO_WORD      'w'    /* word type values */
03837 #    define DIO_LONG      'l'    /* long type values */
03838 #define DIO_PORT         m2_l1   /* single port address */
03839 #define DIO_VALUE        m2_l2   /* single I/O value */
03840 #define DIO_VEC_ADDR     m2_p1   /* address of buffer or (p,v)-pairs */
03841 #define DIO_VEC_SIZE     m2_l2   /* number of elements in vector */
03842 #define DIO_VEC_PROC     m2_i2   /* number of process where vector is */
03843
03844 /* Field names for SYS_SIGNARLM, SYS_FLAGARLM, SYS_SYNCALRM. */
03845 #define ALRM_EXP_TIME    m2_l1   /* expire time for the alarm call */
03846 #define ALRM_ABS_TIME    m2_i2   /* set to 1 to use absolute alarm time */
03847 #define ALRM_TIME_LEFT   m2_l1   /* how many ticks were remaining */
03848 #define ALRM_PROC_NR     m2_i1   /* which process wants the alarm? */
03849 #define ALRM_FLAG_PTR    m2_p1   /* virtual address of timeout flag */
03850
03851 /* Field names for SYS_IRQCTL. */
03852 #define IRQ_REQUEST      m5_c1   /* what to do? */
03853 #    define IRQ_SETPOLICY   1    /* manage a slot of the IRQ table */
03854 #    define IRQ_RMPOLICY    2    /* remove a slot of the IRQ table */
03855 #    define IRQ_ENABLE      3    /* enable interrupts */
03856 #    define IRQ_DISABLE     4    /* disable interrupts */
03857 #define IRQ_VECTOR       m5_c2   /* irq vector */
03858 #define IRQ_POLICY       m5_i1   /* options for IRQCTL request */
03859 #    define IRQ_REENABLE  0x001  /* reenable IRQ line after interrupt */
03860 #    define IRQ_BYTE      0x100  /* byte values */
03861 #    define IRQ_WORD      0x200  /* word values */
03862 #    define IRQ_LONG      0x400  /* long values */
03863 #define IRQ_PROC_NR      m5_i2   /* process number, SELF, NONE */
03864 #define IRQ_HOOK_ID      m5_l3   /* id of irq hook at kernel */
03865
03866 /* Field names for SYS_SEGCTL. */
03867 #define SEG_SELECT       m4_l1   /* segment selector returned */
03868 #define SEG_OFFSET       m4_l2   /* offset in segment returned */
03869 #define SEG_PHYS         m4_l3   /* physical address of segment */
03870 #define SEG_SIZE         m4_l4   /* segment size */
03871 #define SEG_INDEX        m4_l5   /* segment index in remote map */
03872
03873 /* Field names for SYS_VIDCOPY. */
03874 #define VID_REQUEST      m4_l1   /* what to do? */
03875 #    define VID_VID_COPY    1    /* request vid_vid_copy() */
03876 #    define MEM_VID_COPY    2    /* request mem_vid_copy() */
03877 #define VID_SRC_ADDR     m4_l2   /* virtual address in memory */
03878 #define VID_SRC_OFFSET   m4_l3   /* offset in video memory */
03879 #define VID_DST_OFFSET   m4_l4   /* offset in video memory */
03880 #define VID_CP_COUNT     m4_l5   /* number of words to be copied */
03881
03882 /* Field names for SYS_ABORT. */
03883 #define ABRT_HOW         m1_i1   /* RBT_REBOOT, RBT_HALT, etc. */
03884 #define ABRT_MON_PROC    m1_i2   /* process where monitor params are */
```

```
03885   #define ABRT_MON_LEN    m1_i3    /* length of monitor params */
03886   #define ABRT_MON_ADDR   m1_p1    /* virtual address of monitor params */
03887
03888   /* Field names for _UMAP, _VIRCOPY, _PHYSCOPY. */
03889   #define CP_SRC_SPACE    m5_c1    /* T or D space (stack is also D) */
03890   #define CP_SRC_PROC_NR  m5_i1    /* process to copy from */
03891   #define CP_SRC_ADDR     m5_l1    /* address where data come from */
03892   #define CP_DST_SPACE    m5_c2    /* T or D space (stack is also D) */
03893   #define CP_DST_PROC_NR  m5_i2    /* process to copy to */
03894   #define CP_DST_ADDR     m5_l2    /* address where data go to */
03895   #define CP_NR_BYTES     m5_l3    /* number of bytes to copy */
03896
03897   /* Field names for SYS_VCOPY and SYS_VVIRCOPY. */
03898   #define VCP_NR_OK       m1_i2    /* number of successfull copies */
03899   #define VCP_VEC_SIZE    m1_i3    /* size of copy vector */
03900   #define VCP_VEC_ADDR    m1_p1    /* pointer to copy vector */
03901
03902   /* Field names for SYS_GETINFO. */
03903   #define I_REQUEST       m7_i3    /* what info to get */
03904   #    define GET_KINFO        0    /* get kernel information structure */
03905   #    define GET_IMAGE        1    /* get system image table */
03906   #    define GET_PROCTAB      2    /* get kernel process table */
03907   #    define GET_RANDOMNESS   3    /* get randomness buffer */
03908   #    define GET_MONPARAMS    4    /* get monitor parameters */
03909   #    define GET_KENV         5    /* get kernel environment string */
03910   #    define GET_IRQHOOKS     6    /* get the IRQ table */
03911   #    define GET_KMESSAGES    7    /* get kernel messages */
03912   #    define GET_PRIVTAB      8    /* get kernel privileges table */
03913   #    define GET_KADDRESSES   9    /* get various kernel addresses */
03914   #    define GET_SCHEDINFO   10    /* get scheduling queues */
03915   #    define GET_PROC        11    /* get process slot if given process */
03916   #    define GET_MACHINE     12    /* get machine information */
03917   #    define GET_LOCKTIMING  13    /* get lock()/unlock() latency timing */
03918   #    define GET_BIOSBUFFER  14    /* get a buffer for BIOS calls */
03919   #define I_PROC_NR       m7_i4    /* calling process */
03920   #define I_VAL_PTR       m7_p1    /* virtual address at caller */
03921   #define I_VAL_LEN       m7_i1    /* max length of value */
03922   #define I_VAL_PTR2      m7_p2    /* second virtual address */
03923   #define I_VAL_LEN2      m7_i2    /* second length, or proc nr */
03924
03925   /* Field names for SYS_TIMES. */
03926   #define T_PROC_NR       m4_l1    /* process to request time info for */
03927   #define T_USER_TIME     m4_l1    /* user time consumed by process */
03928   #define T_SYSTEM_TIME   m4_l2    /* system time consumed by process */
03929   #define T_CHILD_UTIME   m4_l3    /* user time consumed by process' children */
03930   #define T_CHILD_STIME   m4_l4    /* sys time consumed by process' children */
03931   #define T_BOOT_TICKS    m4_l5    /* number of clock ticks since boot time */
03932
03933   /* Field names for SYS_TRACE, SYS_SVRCTL. */
03934   #define CTL_PROC_NR     m2_i1    /* process number of the caller */
03935   #define CTL_REQUEST     m2_i2    /* server control request */
03936   #define CTL_MM_PRIV     m2_i3    /* privilege as seen by PM */
03937   #define CTL_ARG_PTR     m2_p1    /* pointer to argument */
03938   #define CTL_ADDRESS     m2_l1    /* address at traced process' space */
03939   #define CTL_DATA        m2_l2    /* data field for tracing */
03940
03941   /* Field names for SYS_KILL, SYS_SIGCTL */
03942   #define SIG_REQUEST     m2_l2    /* PM signal control request */
03943   #define S_GETSIG            0    /* get pending kernel signal */
03944   #define S_ENDSIG            1    /* finish a kernel signal */
```

```
03945 #define S_SENDSIG          2       /* POSIX style signal handling */
03946 #define S_SIGRETURN        3       /* return from POSIX handling */
03947 #define S_KILL             4       /* servers kills process with signal */
03948 #define SIG_PROC      m2_i1        /* process number for inform */
03949 #define SIG_NUMBER    m2_i2        /* signal number to send */
03950 #define SIG_FLAGS     m2_i3        /* signal flags field */
03951 #define SIG_MAP       m2_l1        /* used by kernel to pass signal bit map */
03952 #define SIG_CTXT_PTR  m2_p1        /* pointer to info to restore signal context */
03953
03954 /* Field names for SYS_FORK, _EXEC, _EXIT, _NEWMAP. */
03955 #define PR_PROC_NR    m1_i1        /* indicates a (child) process */
03956 #define PR_PRIORITY   m1_i2        /* process priority */
03957 #define PR_PPROC_NR   m1_i2        /* indicates a (parent) process */
03958 #define PR_PID        m1_i3        /* process id at process manager */
03959 #define PR_STACK_PTR  m1_p1        /* used for stack ptr in sys_exec, sys_getsp */
03960 #define PR_TRACING    m1_i3        /* flag to indicate tracing is on/ off */
03961 #define PR_NAME_PTR   m1_p2        /* tells where program name is for dmp */
03962 #define PR_IP_PTR     m1_p3        /* initial value for ip after exec */
03963 #define PR_MEM_PTR    m1_p1        /* tells where memory map is for sys_newmap */
03964
03965 /* Field names for SYS_INT86 */
03966 #define INT86_REG86   m1_p1      /* pointer to registers */
03967
03968 /* Field names for SELECT (FS). */
03969 #define SEL_NFDS      m8_i1
03970 #define SEL_READFDS   m8_p1
03971 #define SEL_WRITEFDS  m8_p2
03972 #define SEL_ERRORFDS  m8_p3
03973 #define SEL_TIMEOUT   m8_p4
03974
03975 /*===========================================================================*
03976  *              Messages for system management server                       *
03977  *===========================================================================*/
03978
03979 #define SRV_RQ_BASE           0x700
03980
03981 #define SRV_UP         (SRV_RQ_BASE + 0)     /* start system service */
03982 #define SRV_DOWN       (SRV_RQ_BASE + 1)     /* stop system service */
03983 #define SRV_STATUS     (SRV_RQ_BASE + 2)     /* get service status */
03984
03985 #  define SRV_PATH_ADDR       m1_p1          /* path of binary */
03986 #  define SRV_PATH_LEN        m1_i1          /* length of binary */
03987 #  define SRV_ARGS_ADDR       m1_p2          /* arguments to be passed */
03988 #  define SRV_ARGS_LEN        m1_i2          /* length of arguments */
03989 #  define SRV_DEV_MAJOR       m1_i3          /* major device number */
03990 #  define SRV_PRIV_ADDR       m1_p3          /* privileges string */
03991 #  define SRV_PRIV_LEN        m1_i3          /* length of privileges */
03992
03993 /*===========================================================================*
03994  *              Miscellaneous messages used by TTY                          *
03995  *===========================================================================*/
03996
03997 /* Miscellaneous request types and field names, e.g. used by IS server. */
03998 #define PANIC_DUMPS           97      /* debug dumps at the TTY on RBT_PANIC */
03999 #define FKEY_CONTROL          98      /* control a function key at the TTY */
04000 #  define FKEY_REQUEST      m2_i1     /* request to perform at TTY */
04001 #  define   FKEY_MAP        10        /* observe function key */
04002 #  define   FKEY_UNMAP      11        /* stop observing function key */
04003 #  define   FKEY_EVENTS     12        /* request open key presses */
04004 #  define FKEY_FKEYS        m2_l1     /* F1-F12 keys pressed */
```

```
04005   #  define FKEY_SFKEYS        m2_l2      /* Shift-F1-F12 keys pressed */
04006   #define DIAGNOSTICS       100      /* output a string without FS in between */
04007   #  define DIAG_PRINT_BUF     m1_p1
04008   #  define DIAG_BUF_COUNT     m1_i1
04009   #  define DIAG_PROC_NR       m1_i2
04010
04011   #endif /* _MINIX_COM_H */
```

```
++++++++++++++++++++++++++++++++++++++++++++++++++++++++++++++++++++++++++++
                          include/minix/devio.h
++++++++++++++++++++++++++++++++++++++++++++++++++++++++++++++++++++++++++++
```

```
04100   /* This file provides basic types and some constants for the
04101    * SYS_DEVIO and SYS_VDEVIO system calls, which allow user-level
04102    * processes to perform device I/O.
04103    *
04104    * Created:
04105    *      Apr 08, 2004 by Jorrit N. Herder
04106    */
04107
04108   #ifndef _DEVIO_H
04109   #define _DEVIO_H
04110
04111   #include <minix/sys_config.h>      /* needed to include <minix/type.h> */
04112   #include <sys/types.h>            /* u8_t, u16_t, u32_t needed */
04113
04114   typedef u16_t port_t;
04115   typedef U16_t Port_t;
04116
04117   /* We have different granularities of port I/O: 8, 16, 32 bits.
04118    * Also see <ibm/portio.h>, which has functions for bytes, words,
04119    * and longs. Hence, we need different (port,value)-pair types.
04120    */
04121   typedef struct { u16_t port;  u8_t value; } pvb_pair_t;
04122   typedef struct { u16_t port; u16_t value; } pvw_pair_t;
04123   typedef struct { u16_t port; u32_t value; } pvl_pair_t;
04124
04125   /* Macro shorthand to set (port,value)-pair. */
04126   #define pv_set(pv, p, v) ((pv).port = (p), (pv).value = (v))
04127   #define pv_ptr_set(pv_ptr, p, v) ((pv_ptr)->port = (p), (pv_ptr)->value = (v))
04128
04129   #endif  /* _DEVIO_H */
```

```
++++++++++++++++++++++++++++++++++++++++++++++++++++++++++++++++++++++++++++
                          include/minix/dmap.h
++++++++++++++++++++++++++++++++++++++++++++++++++++++++++++++++++++++++++++
```

```
04200   #ifndef _DMAP_H
04201   #define _DMAP_H
04202
04203   #include <minix/sys_config.h>
04204   #include <minix/ipc.h>
04205
```

```
04206  /*===========================================================================*
04207   *                          Device <-> Driver Table                          *
04208   *===========================================================================*/
04209
04210  /* Device table.  This table is indexed by major device number.  It provides
04211   * the link between major device numbers and the routines that process them.
04212   * The table can be update dynamically. The field 'dmap_flags' describe an
04213   * entry's current status and determines what control options are possible.
04214   */
04215  #define DMAP_MUTABLE            0x01   /* mapping can be overtaken */
04216  #define DMAP_BUSY               0x02   /* driver busy with request */
04217
04218  enum dev_style { STYLE_DEV, STYLE_NDEV, STYLE_TTY, STYLE_CLONE };
04219
04220  extern struct dmap {
04221    int _PROTOTYPE ((*dmap_opcl), (int, Dev_t, int, int) );
04222    void _PROTOTYPE ((*dmap_io), (int, message *) );
04223    int dmap_driver;
04224    int dmap_flags;
04225  } dmap[];
04226
04227  /*===========================================================================*
04228   *                      Major and minor device numbers                       *
04229   *===========================================================================*/
04230
04231  /* Total number of different devices. */
04232  #define NR_DEVICES              32                      /* number of (major) devices */
04233
04234  /* Major and minor device numbers for MEMORY driver. */
04235  #define MEMORY_MAJOR            1     /* major device for memory devices */
04236  #  define RAM_DEV              0     /* minor device for /dev/ram */
04237  #  define MEM_DEV              1     /* minor device for /dev/mem */
04238  #  define KMEM_DEV             2     /* minor device for /dev/kmem */
04239  #  define NULL_DEV             3     /* minor device for /dev/null */
04240  #  define BOOT_DEV             4     /* minor device for /dev/boot */
04241  #  define ZERO_DEV             5     /* minor device for /dev/zero */
04242
04243  #define CTRLR(n) ((n)==0 ? 3 : (8 + 2*((n)-1))) /* magic formula */
04244
04245  /* Full device numbers that are special to the boot monitor and FS. */
04246  #  define DEV_RAM             0x0100   /* device number of /dev/ram */
04247  #  define DEV_BOOT            0x0104   /* device number of /dev/boot */
04248
04249  #define FLOPPY_MAJOR            2     /* major device for floppy disks */
04250  #define TTY_MAJOR               4     /* major device for ttys */
04251  #define CTTY_MAJOR              5     /* major device for /dev/tty */
04252
04253  #define INET_MAJOR              7     /* major device for inet */
04254
04255  #define LOG_MAJOR               15    /* major device for log driver */
04256  #  define IS_KLOG_DEV          0     /* minor device for /dev/klog */
04257
04258  #endif /* _DMAP_H */
```

```
++++++++++++++++++++++++++++++++++++++++++++++++++++++++++++++++++++++++++++++
                            include/ibm/portio.h
++++++++++++++++++++++++++++++++++++++++++++++++++++++++++++++++++++++++++++++

04300   /*
04301   ibm/portio.h
04302
04303   Created:        Jan 15, 1992 by Philip Homburg
04304   */
04305
04306   #ifndef _PORTIO_H_
04307   #define _PORTIO_H_
04308
04309   #ifndef _TYPES_H
04310   #include <sys/types.h>
04311   #endif
04312
04313   unsigned inb(U16_t _port);
04314   unsigned inw(U16_t _port);
04315   unsigned inl(U32_t _port);
04316   void outb(U16_t _port, U8_t _value);
04317   void outw(U16_t _port, U16_t _value);
04318   void outl(U16_t _port, U32_t _value);
04319   void insb(U16_t _port, void *_buf, size_t _count);
04320   void insw(U16_t _port, void *_buf, size_t _count);
04321   void insl(U16_t _port, void *_buf, size_t _count);
04322   void outsb(U16_t _port, void *_buf, size_t _count);
04323   void outsw(U16_t _port, void *_buf, size_t _count);
04324   void outsl(U16_t _port, void *_buf, size_t _count);
04325   void intr_disable(void);
04326   void intr_enable(void);
04327
04328   #endif /* _PORTIO_H_ */


++++++++++++++++++++++++++++++++++++++++++++++++++++++++++++++++++++++++++++++
                            include/ibm/interrupt.h
++++++++++++++++++++++++++++++++++++++++++++++++++++++++++++++++++++++++++++++

04400   /* Interrupt numbers and hardware vectors. */
04401
04402   #ifndef _INTERRUPT_H
04403   #define _INTERRUPT_H
04404
04405   #if (CHIP == INTEL)
04406
04407   /* 8259A interrupt controller ports. */
04408   #define INT_CTL          0x20    /* I/O port for interrupt controller */
04409   #define INT_CTLMASK      0x21    /* setting bits in this port disables ints */
04410   #define INT2_CTL         0xA0    /* I/O port for second interrupt controller */
04411   #define INT2_CTLMASK     0xA1    /* setting bits in this port disables ints */
04412
04413   /* Magic numbers for interrupt controller. */
04414   #define END_OF_INT       0x20    /* code used to re-enable after an interrupt */
04415
04416   /* Interrupt vectors defined/reserved by processor. */
04417   #define DIVIDE_VECTOR     0      /* divide error */
04418   #define DEBUG_VECTOR      1      /* single step (trace) */
04419   #define NMI_VECTOR        2      /* non-maskable interrupt */
```

```
04420   #define BREAKPOINT_VECTOR   3     /* software breakpoint */
04421   #define OVERFLOW_VECTOR     4     /* from INTO */
04422
04423   /* Fixed system call vector. */
04424   #define SYS_VECTOR          32    /* system calls are made with int SYSVEC */
04425   #define SYS386_VECTOR       33    /* except 386 system calls use this */
04426   #define LEVEL0_VECTOR       34    /* for execution of a function at level 0 */
04427
04428   /* Suitable irq bases for hardware interrupts.  Reprogram the 8259(s) from
04429    * the PC BIOS defaults since the BIOS doesn't respect all the processor's
04430    * reserved vectors (0 to 31).
04431    */
04432   #define BIOS_IRQ0_VEC       0x08  /* base of IRQ0-7 vectors used by BIOS */
04433   #define BIOS_IRQ8_VEC       0x70  /* base of IRQ8-15 vectors used by BIOS */
04434   #define IRQ0_VECTOR         0x50  /* nice vectors to relocate IRQ0-7 to */
04435   #define IRQ8_VECTOR         0x70  /* no need to move IRQ8-15 */
04436
04437   /* Hardware interrupt numbers. */
04438   #define NR_IRQ_VECTORS      16
04439   #define CLOCK_IRQ           0
04440   #define KEYBOARD_IRQ        1
04441   #define CASCADE_IRQ         2     /* cascade enable for 2nd AT controller */
04442   #define ETHER_IRQ           3     /* default ethernet interrupt vector */
04443   #define SECONDARY_IRQ       3     /* RS232 interrupt vector for port 2 */
04444   #define RS232_IRQ           4     /* RS232 interrupt vector for port 1 */
04445   #define XT_WINI_IRQ         5     /* xt winchester */
04446   #define FLOPPY_IRQ          6     /* floppy disk */
04447   #define PRINTER_IRQ         7
04448   #define AT_WINI_0_IRQ       14    /* at winchester controller 0 */
04449   #define AT_WINI_1_IRQ       15    /* at winchester controller 1 */
04450
04451   /* Interrupt number to hardware vector. */
04452   #define BIOS_VECTOR(irq)          \
04453           (((irq) < 8 ? BIOS_IRQ0_VEC : BIOS_IRQ8_VEC) + ((irq) & 0x07))
04454   #define VECTOR(irq)       \
04455           (((irq) < 8 ? IRQ0_VECTOR : IRQ8_VECTOR) + ((irq) & 0x07))
04456
04457   #endif /* (CHIP == INTEL) */
04458
04459   #endif /* _INTERRUPT_H */
```

```
++++++++++++++++++++++++++++++++++++++++++++++++++++++++++++++++++++++++++++++++
                            include/ibm/ports.h
++++++++++++++++++++++++++++++++++++++++++++++++++++++++++++++++++++++++++++++++
```

```
04500   /* Addresses and magic numbers for miscellaneous ports. */
04501
04502   #ifndef _PORTS_H
04503   #define _PORTS_H
04504
04505   #if (CHIP == INTEL)
04506
04507   /* Miscellaneous ports. */
04508   #define PCR                 0x65  /* Planar Control Register */
04509   #define PORT_B              0x61  /* I/O port for 8255 port B (kbd, beeper...) */
04510   #define TIMER0              0x40  /* I/O port for timer channel 0 */
04511   #define TIMER2              0x42  /* I/O port for timer channel 2 */
04512   #define TIMER_MODE          0x43  /* I/O port for timer mode control */
04513
04514   #endif /* (CHIP == INTEL) */
```

```
04515
04516   #endif /* _PORTS_H */
```

```
++++++++++++++++++++++++++++++++++++++++++++++++++++++++++++++++++++++++++++++
                                kernel/kernel.h
++++++++++++++++++++++++++++++++++++++++++++++++++++++++++++++++++++++++++++++

04600   #ifndef KERNEL_H
04601   #define KERNEL_H
04602
04603   /* This is the master header for the kernel.  It includes some other files
04604    * and defines the principal constants.
04605    */
04606   #define _POSIX_SOURCE    1    /* tell headers to include POSIX stuff */
04607   #define _MINIX           1    /* tell headers to include MINIX stuff */
04608   #define _SYSTEM          1    /* tell headers that this is the kernel */
04609
04610   /* The following are so basic, all the *.c files get them automatically. */
04611   #include <minix/config.h>      /* global configuration, MUST be first */
04612   #include <ansi.h>             /* C style: ANSI or K&R, MUST be second */
04613   #include <sys/types.h>        /* general system types */
04614   #include <minix/const.h>      /* MINIX specific constants */
04615   #include <minix/type.h>       /* MINIX specific types, e.g. message */
04616   #include <minix/ipc.h>        /* MINIX run-time system */
04617   #include <timers.h>           /* watchdog timer management */
04618   #include <errno.h>            /* return codes and error numbers */
04619   #include <ibm/portio.h>       /* device I/O and toggle interrupts */
04620
04621   /* Important kernel header files. */
04622   #include "config.h"           /* configuration, MUST be first */
04623   #include "const.h"            /* constants, MUST be second */
04624   #include "type.h"             /* type definitions, MUST be third */
04625   #include "proto.h"            /* function prototypes */
04626   #include "glo.h"              /* global variables */
04627   #include "ipc.h"              /* IPC constants */
04628   /* #include "debug.h" */       /* debugging, MUST be last kernel header */
04629
04630   #endif /* KERNEL_H */
04631
```

```
++++++++++++++++++++++++++++++++++++++++++++++++++++++++++++++++++++++++++++++
                                kernel/config.h
++++++++++++++++++++++++++++++++++++++++++++++++++++++++++++++++++++++++++++++

04700   #ifndef CONFIG_H
04701   #define CONFIG_H
04702
04703   /* This file defines the kernel configuration. It allows to set sizes of some
04704    * kernel buffers and to enable or disable debugging code, timing features,
04705    * and individual kernel calls.
04706    *
04707    * Changes:
04708    *    Jul 11, 2005      Created.  (Jorrit N. Herder)
04709    */
```

```
04710
04711  /* In embedded and sensor applications, not all the kernel calls may be
04712   * needed. In this section you can specify which kernel calls are needed
04713   * and which are not. The code for unneeded kernel calls is not included in
04714   * the system binary, making it smaller. If you are not sure, it is best
04715   * to keep all kernel calls enabled.
04716   */
04717  #define USE_FORK            1      /* fork a new process */
04718  #define USE_NEWMAP          1      /* set a new memory map */
04719  #define USE_EXEC            1      /* update process after execute */
04720  #define USE_EXIT            1      /* clean up after process exit */
04721  #define USE_TRACE           1      /* process information and tracing */
04722  #define USE_GETKSIG         1      /* retrieve pending kernel signals */
04723  #define USE_ENDKSIG         1      /* finish pending kernel signals */
04724  #define USE_KILL            1      /* send a signal to a process */
04725  #define USE_SIGSEND         1      /* send POSIX-style signal */
04726  #define USE_SIGRETURN       1      /* sys_sigreturn(proc_nr, ctxt_ptr, flags) */
04727  #define USE_ABORT           1      /* shut down MINIX */
04728  #define USE_GETINFO         1      /* retrieve a copy of kernel data */
04729  #define USE_TIMES           1      /* get process and system time info */
04730  #define USE_SETALARM        1      /* schedule a synchronous alarm */
04731  #define USE_DEVIO           1      /* read or write a single I/O port */
04732  #define USE_VDEVIO          1      /* process vector with I/O requests */
04733  #define USE_SDEVIO          1      /* perform I/O request on a buffer */
04734  #define USE_IRQCTL          1      /* set an interrupt policy */
04735  #define USE_SEGCTL          1      /* set up a remote segment */
04736  #define USE_PRIVCTL         1      /* system privileges control */
04737  #define USE_NICE            1      /* change scheduling priority */
04738  #define USE_UMAP            1      /* map virtual to physical address */
04739  #define USE_VIRCOPY         1      /* copy using virtual addressing */
04740  #define USE_VIRVCOPY        1      /* vector with virtual copy requests */
04741  #define USE_PHYSCOPY        1      /* copy using physical addressing */
04742  #define USE_PHYSVCOPY       1      /* vector with physical copy requests */
04743  #define USE_MEMSET          1      /* write char to a given memory area */
04744
04745  /* Length of program names stored in the process table. This is only used
04746   * for the debugging dumps that can be generated with the IS server. The PM
04747   * server keeps its own copy of the program name.
04748   */
04749  #define P_NAME_LEN          8
04750
04751  /* Kernel diagnostics are written to a circular buffer. After each message,
04752   * a system server is notified and a copy of the buffer can be retrieved to
04753   * display the message. The buffers size can safely be reduced.
04754   */
04755  #define KMESS_BUF_SIZE    256
04756
04757  /* Buffer to gather randomness. This is used to generate a random stream by
04758   * the MEMORY driver when reading from /dev/random.
04759   */
04760  #define RANDOM_ELEMENTS    32
04761
04762  /* This section contains defines for valuable system resources that are used
04763   * by device drivers. The number of elements of the vectors is determined by
04764   * the maximum needed by any given driver. The number of interrupt hooks may
04765   * be incremented on systems with many device drivers.
04766   */
04767  #define NR_IRQ_HOOKS       16              /* number of interrupt hooks */
04768  #define VDEVIO_BUF_SIZE    64              /* max elements per VDEVIO request */
04769  #define VCOPY_VEC_SIZE     16              /* max elements per VCOPY request */
```

```
04770
04771   /* How many bytes for the kernel stack. Space allocated in mpx.s. */
04772   #define K_STACK_BYTES   1024
04773
04774   /* This section allows to enable kernel debugging and timing functionality.
04775    * For normal operation all options should be disabled.
04776    */
04777   #define DEBUG_SCHED_CHECK  0     /* sanity check of scheduling queues */
04778   #define DEBUG_LOCK_CHECK   0     /* kernel lock() sanity check */
04779   #define DEBUG_TIME_LOCKS   0     /* measure time spent in locks */
04780
04781   #endif /* CONFIG_H */
04782
```

```
++++++++++++++++++++++++++++++++++++++++++++++++++++++++++++++++++++++++++++++
                              kernel/const.h
++++++++++++++++++++++++++++++++++++++++++++++++++++++++++++++++++++++++++++++
```

```
04800   /* General macros and constants used by the kernel. */
04801   #ifndef CONST_H
04802   #define CONST_H
04803
04804   #include <ibm/interrupt.h>       /* interrupt numbers and hardware vectors */
04805   #include <ibm/ports.h>           /* port addresses and magic numbers */
04806   #include <ibm/bios.h>            /* BIOS addresses, sizes and magic numbers */
04807   #include <ibm/cpu.h>             /* BIOS addresses, sizes and magic numbers */
04808   #include <minix/config.h>
04809   #include "config.h"
04810
04811   /* To translate an address in kernel space to a physical address.  This is
04812    * the same as umap_local(proc_ptr, D, vir, sizeof(*vir)), but less costly.
04813    */
04814   #define vir2phys(vir)    (kinfo.data_base + (vir_bytes) (vir))
04815
04816   /* Map a process number to a privilege structure id. */
04817   #define s_nr_to_id(n)    (NR_TASKS + (n) + 1)
04818
04819   /* Translate a pointer to a field in a structure to a pointer to the structure
04820    * itself. So it translates '&struct_ptr->field' back to 'struct_ptr'.
04821    */
04822   #define structof(type, field, ptr) \
04823           ((type *) (((char *) (ptr)) - offsetof(type, field)))
04824
04825   /* Constants used in virtual_copy(). Values must be 0 and 1, respectively. */
04826   #define _SRC_   0
04827   #define _DST_   1
04828
04829   /* Number of random sources */
04830   #define RANDOM_SOURCES  16
04831
04832   /* Constants and macros for bit map manipulation. */
04833   #define BITCHUNK_BITS    (sizeof(bitchunk_t) * CHAR_BIT)
04834   #define BITMAP_CHUNKS(nr_bits) (((nr_bits)+BITCHUNK_BITS-1)/BITCHUNK_BITS)
04835   #define MAP_CHUNK(map,bit) (map)[((bit)/BITCHUNK_BITS)]
04836   #define CHUNK_OFFSET(bit) ((bit)%BITCHUNK_BITS)
04837   #define GET_BIT(map,bit) ( MAP_CHUNK(map,bit) & (1 << CHUNK_OFFSET(bit) )
04838   #define SET_BIT(map,bit) ( MAP_CHUNK(map,bit) |= (1 << CHUNK_OFFSET(bit) )
04839   #define UNSET_BIT(map,bit) ( MAP_CHUNK(map,bit) &= ~(1 << CHUNK_OFFSET(bit) )
```

```
04840
04841   #define get_sys_bit(map,bit) \
04842           ( MAP_CHUNK(map.chunk,bit) & (1 << CHUNK_OFFSET(bit) )
04843   #define set_sys_bit(map,bit) \
04844           ( MAP_CHUNK(map.chunk,bit) |= (1 << CHUNK_OFFSET(bit) )
04845   #define unset_sys_bit(map,bit) \
04846           ( MAP_CHUNK(map.chunk,bit) &= ~(1 << CHUNK_OFFSET(bit) )
04847   #define NR_SYS_CHUNKS    BITMAP_CHUNKS(NR_SYS_PROCS)
04848
04849   /* Program stack words and masks. */
04850   #define INIT_PSW        0x0200     /* initial psw */
04851   #define INIT_TASK_PSW 0x1200      /* initial psw for tasks (with IOPL 1) */
04852   #define TRACEBIT        0x0100     /* OR this with psw in proc[] for tracing */
04853   #define SETPSW(rp, new)            /* permits only certain bits to be set */ \
04854           ((rp)->p_reg.psw = (rp)->p_reg.psw & ~0xCD5 | (new) & 0xCD5)
04855   #define IF_MASK 0x00000200
04856   #define IOPL_MASK 0x003000
04857
04858   /* Disable/ enable hardware interrupts. The parameters of lock() and unlock()
04859    * are used when debugging is enabled. See debug.h for more information.
04860    */
04861   #define lock(c, v)      intr_disable();
04862   #define unlock(c)       intr_enable();
04863
04864   /* Sizes of memory tables. The boot monitor distinguishes three memory areas,
04865    * namely low mem below 1M, 1M-16M, and mem after 16M. More chunks are needed
04866    * for DOS MINIX.
04867    */
04868   #define NR_MEMS              8
04869
04870   #endif /* CONST_H */
04871
04872
04873
04874
04875
```

```
++++++++++++++++++++++++++++++++++++++++++++++++++++++++++++++++++++++++++++++++
                              kernel/type.h
++++++++++++++++++++++++++++++++++++++++++++++++++++++++++++++++++++++++++++++++
```

```
04900   #ifndef TYPE_H
04901   #define TYPE_H
04902
04903   typedef _PROTOTYPE( void task_t, (void) );
04904
04905   /* Process table and system property related types. */
04906   typedef int proc_nr_t;                    /* process table entry number */
04907   typedef short sys_id_t;                   /* system process index */
04908   typedef struct {                          /* bitmap for system indexes */
04909     bitchunk_t chunk[BITMAP_CHUNKS(NR_SYS_PROCS)];
04910   } sys_map_t;
04911
04912   struct boot_image {
04913     proc_nr_t proc_nr;                      /* process number to use */
04914     task_t *initial_pc;                     /* start function for tasks */
```

```
04915      int flags;                          /* process flags */
04916      unsigned char quantum;              /* quantum (tick count) */
04917      int priority;                       /* scheduling priority */
04918      int stksize;                        /* stack size for tasks */
04919      short trap_mask;                    /* allowed system call traps */
04920      bitchunk_t ipc_to;                  /* send mask protection */
04921      long call_mask;                     /* system call protection */
04922      char proc_name[P_NAME_LEN];         /* name in process table */
04923  };
04924
04925  struct memory {
04926      phys_clicks base;                   /* start address of chunk */
04927      phys_clicks size;                   /* size of memory chunk */
04928  };
04929
04930  /* The kernel outputs diagnostic messages in a circular buffer. */
04931  struct kmessages {
04932      int km_next;                        /* next index to write */
04933      int km_size;                        /* current size in buffer */
04934      char km_buf[KMESS_BUF_SIZE];        /* buffer for messages */
04935  };
04936
04937  struct randomness {
04938      struct {
04939          int r_next;                              /* next index to write */
04940          int r_size;                              /* number of random elements */
04941          unsigned short r_buf[RANDOM_ELEMENTS]; /* buffer for random info */
04942      } bin[RANDOM_SOURCES];
04943  };
04944
04945  #if (CHIP == INTEL)
04946  typedef unsigned reg_t;            /* machine register */
04947
04948  /* The stack frame layout is determined by the software, but for efficiency
04949   * it is laid out so the assembly code to use it is as simple as possible.
04950   * 80286 protected mode and all real modes use the same frame, built with
04951   * 16-bit registers.  Real mode lacks an automatic stack switch, so little
04952   * is lost by using the 286 frame for it.  The 386 frame differs only in
04953   * having 32-bit registers and more segment registers.  The same names are
04954   * used for the larger registers to avoid differences in the code.
04955   */
04956  struct stackframe_s {           /* proc_ptr points here */
04957  #if _WORD_SIZE == 4
04958      u16_t gs;                   /* last item pushed by save */
04959      u16_t fs;                   /*  ^ */
04960  #endif
04961      u16_t es;                   /*  | */
04962      u16_t ds;                   /*  | */
04963      reg_t di;                   /* di through cx are not accessed in C */
04964      reg_t si;                   /* order is to match pusha/popa */
04965      reg_t fp;                   /* bp */
04966      reg_t st;                   /* hole for another copy of sp */
04967      reg_t bx;                   /*  | */
04968      reg_t dx;                   /*  | */
04969      reg_t cx;                   /*  | */
04970      reg_t retreg;               /* ax and above are all pushed by save */
04971      reg_t retadr;               /* return address for assembly code save() */
04972      reg_t pc;                   /*  ^  last item pushed by interrupt */
04973      reg_t cs;                   /*  | */
04974      reg_t psw;                  /*  | */
```

```
04975       reg_t sp;                       /*  | */
04976       reg_t ss;                       /* these are pushed by CPU during interrupt */
04977   };
04978
04979   struct segdesc_s {                  /* segment descriptor for protected mode */
04980       u16_t limit_low;
04981       u16_t base_low;
04982       u8_t base_middle;
04983       u8_t access;                    /* |P|DL|1|X|E|R|A| */
04984       u8_t granularity;               /* |G|X|O|A|LIMT| */
04985       u8_t base_high;
04986   };
04987
04988   typedef unsigned long irq_policy_t;
04989   typedef unsigned long irq_id_t;
04990
04991   typedef struct irq_hook {
04992       struct irq_hook *next;                   /* next hook in chain */
04993       int (*handler)(struct irq_hook *);       /* interrupt handler */
04994       int irq;                                 /* IRQ vector number */
04995       int id;                                  /* id of this hook */
04996       int proc_nr;                             /* NONE if not in use */
04997       irq_id_t notify_id;                      /* id to return on interrupt */
04998       irq_policy_t policy;                     /* bit mask for policy */
04999   } irq_hook_t;
05000
05001   typedef int (*irq_handler_t)(struct irq_hook *);
05002
05003   #endif /* (CHIP == INTEL) */
05004
05005   #if (CHIP == M68000)
05006   /* M68000 specific types go here. */
05007   #endif /* (CHIP == M68000) */
05008
05009   #endif /* TYPE_H */
```

```
++++++++++++++++++++++++++++++++++++++++++++++++++++++++++++++++++++++++++++++++
                                kernel/proto.h
++++++++++++++++++++++++++++++++++++++++++++++++++++++++++++++++++++++++++++++++
```

```
05100   /* Function prototypes. */
05101
05102   #ifndef PROTO_H
05103   #define PROTO_H
05104
05105   /* Struct declarations. */
05106   struct proc;
05107   struct timer;
05108
05109   /* clock.c */
05110   _PROTOTYPE( void clock_task, (void)                                      );
05111   _PROTOTYPE( void clock_stop, (void)                                      );
05112   _PROTOTYPE( clock_t get_uptime, (void)                                   );
05113   _PROTOTYPE( unsigned long read_clock, (void)                             );
05114   _PROTOTYPE( void set_timer, (struct timer *tp, clock_t t, tmr_func_t f)  );
05115   _PROTOTYPE( void reset_timer, (struct timer *tp)                         );
05116
05117   /* main.c */
05118   _PROTOTYPE( void main, (void)                                            );
05119   _PROTOTYPE( void prepare_shutdown, (int how)                             );
```

```
05120
05121   /* utility.c */
05122   _PROTOTYPE( void kprintf, (const char *fmt, ...)                  );
05123   _PROTOTYPE( void panic, (_CONST char *s, int n)                  );
05124
05125   /* proc.c */
05126   _PROTOTYPE( int sys_call, (int function, int src_dest, message *m_ptr)  );
05127   _PROTOTYPE( int lock_notify, (int src, int dst)                  );
05128   _PROTOTYPE( int lock_send, (int dst, message *m_ptr)             );
05129   _PROTOTYPE( void lock_enqueue, (struct proc *rp)                 );
05130   _PROTOTYPE( void lock_dequeue, (struct proc *rp)                 );
05131
05132   /* start.c */
05133   _PROTOTYPE( void cstart, (U16_t cs, U16_t ds, U16_t mds,
05134                               U16_t parmoff, U16_t parmsize)         );
05135
05136   /* system.c */
05137   _PROTOTYPE( int get_priv, (register struct proc *rc, int proc_type)  );
05138   _PROTOTYPE( void send_sig, (int proc_nr, int sig_nr)             );
05139   _PROTOTYPE( void cause_sig, (int proc_nr, int sig_nr)            );
05140   _PROTOTYPE( void sys_task, (void)                               );
05141   _PROTOTYPE( void get_randomness, (int source)                    );
05142   _PROTOTYPE( int virtual_copy, (struct vir_addr *src, struct vir_addr *dst,
05143                               vir_bytes bytes)                      );
05144   #define numap_local(proc_nr, vir_addr, bytes) \
05145           umap_local(proc_addr(proc_nr), D, (vir_addr), (bytes))
05146   _PROTOTYPE( phys_bytes umap_local, (struct proc *rp, int seg,
05147                   vir_bytes vir_addr, vir_bytes bytes)              );
05148   _PROTOTYPE( phys_bytes umap_remote, (struct proc *rp, int seg,
05149                   vir_bytes vir_addr, vir_bytes bytes)              );
05150   _PROTOTYPE( phys_bytes umap_bios, (struct proc *rp, vir_bytes vir_addr,
05151                   vir_bytes bytes)                                  );
05152
05153   /* exception.c */
05154   _PROTOTYPE( void exception, (unsigned vec_nr)                    );
05155
05156   /* i8259.c */
05157   _PROTOTYPE( void intr_init, (int mine)                          );
05158   _PROTOTYPE( void intr_handle, (irq_hook_t *hook)                 );
05159   _PROTOTYPE( void put_irq_handler, (irq_hook_t *hook, int irq,
05160                               irq_handler_t handler)  );
05161   _PROTOTYPE( void rm_irq_handler, (irq_hook_t *hook)              );
05162
05163   /* klib*.s */
05164   _PROTOTYPE( void int86, (void)                                  );
05165   _PROTOTYPE( void cp_mess, (int src,phys_clicks src_clicks,vir_bytes src_offset,
05166                   phys_clicks dst_clicks, vir_bytes dst_offset)    );
05167   _PROTOTYPE( void enable_irq, (irq_hook_t *hook)                  );
05168   _PROTOTYPE( int disable_irq, (irq_hook_t *hook)                  );
05169   _PROTOTYPE( u16_t mem_rdw, (U16_t segm, vir_bytes offset)         );
05170   _PROTOTYPE( void phys_copy, (phys_bytes source, phys_bytes dest,
05171                   phys_bytes count)                                );
05172   _PROTOTYPE( void phys_memset, (phys_bytes source, unsigned long pattern,
05173                   phys_bytes count)                                );
05174   _PROTOTYPE( void phys_insb, (U16_t port, phys_bytes buf, size_t count)  );
05175   _PROTOTYPE( void phys_insw, (U16_t port, phys_bytes buf, size_t count)  );
05176   _PROTOTYPE( void phys_outsb, (U16_t port, phys_bytes buf, size_t count) );
05177   _PROTOTYPE( void phys_outsw, (U16_t port, phys_bytes buf, size_t count) );
05178   _PROTOTYPE( void reset, (void)                                  );
05179   _PROTOTYPE( void level0, (void (*func)(void))                    );
```

```
05180   _PROTOTYPE( void monitor, (void)                              );
05181   _PROTOTYPE( void read_tsc, (unsigned long *high, unsigned long *low)   );
05182   _PROTOTYPE( unsigned long read_cpu_flags, (void)              );
05183
05184   /* mpx*.s */
05185   _PROTOTYPE( void idle_task, (void)                            );
05186   _PROTOTYPE( void restart, (void)                              );
05187
05188   /* The following are never called from C (pure asm procs). */
05189
05190   /* Exception handlers (real or protected mode), in numerical order. */
05191   void _PROTOTYPE( int00, (void) ), _PROTOTYPE( divide_error, (void) );
05192   void _PROTOTYPE( int01, (void) ), _PROTOTYPE( single_step_exception, (void) );
05193   void _PROTOTYPE( int02, (void) ), _PROTOTYPE( nmi, (void) );
05194   void _PROTOTYPE( int03, (void) ), _PROTOTYPE( breakpoint_exception, (void) );
05195   void _PROTOTYPE( int04, (void) ), _PROTOTYPE( overflow, (void) );
05196   void _PROTOTYPE( int05, (void) ), _PROTOTYPE( bounds_check, (void) );
05197   void _PROTOTYPE( int06, (void) ), _PROTOTYPE( inval_opcode, (void) );
05198   void _PROTOTYPE( int07, (void) ), _PROTOTYPE( copr_not_available, (void) );
05199   void                             _PROTOTYPE( double_fault, (void) );
05200   void                             _PROTOTYPE( copr_seg_overrun, (void) );
05201   void                             _PROTOTYPE( inval_tss, (void) );
05202   void                             _PROTOTYPE( segment_not_present, (void) );
05203   void                             _PROTOTYPE( stack_exception, (void) );
05204   void                             _PROTOTYPE( general_protection, (void) );
05205   void                             _PROTOTYPE( page_fault, (void) );
05206   void                             _PROTOTYPE( copr_error, (void) );
05207
05208   /* Hardware interrupt handlers. */
05209   _PROTOTYPE( void hwint00, (void) );
05210   _PROTOTYPE( void hwint01, (void) );
05211   _PROTOTYPE( void hwint02, (void) );
05212   _PROTOTYPE( void hwint03, (void) );
05213   _PROTOTYPE( void hwint04, (void) );
05214   _PROTOTYPE( void hwint05, (void) );
05215   _PROTOTYPE( void hwint06, (void) );
05216   _PROTOTYPE( void hwint07, (void) );
05217   _PROTOTYPE( void hwint08, (void) );
05218   _PROTOTYPE( void hwint09, (void) );
05219   _PROTOTYPE( void hwint10, (void) );
05220   _PROTOTYPE( void hwint11, (void) );
05221   _PROTOTYPE( void hwint12, (void) );
05222   _PROTOTYPE( void hwint13, (void) );
05223   _PROTOTYPE( void hwint14, (void) );
05224   _PROTOTYPE( void hwint15, (void) );
05225
05226   /* Software interrupt handlers, in numerical order. */
05227   _PROTOTYPE( void trp, (void) );
05228   _PROTOTYPE( void s_call, (void) ), _PROTOTYPE( p_s_call, (void) );
05229   _PROTOTYPE( void level0_call, (void) );
05230
05231   /* protect.c */
05232   _PROTOTYPE( void prot_init, (void)                            );
05233   _PROTOTYPE( void init_codeseg, (struct segdesc_s *segdp, phys_bytes base,
05234                   vir_bytes size, int privilege)               );
05235   _PROTOTYPE( void init_dataseg, (struct segdesc_s *segdp, phys_bytes base,
05236                   vir_bytes size, int privilege)               );
05237   _PROTOTYPE( phys_bytes seg2phys, (U16_t seg)                  );
05238   _PROTOTYPE( void phys2seg, (u16_t *seg, vir_bytes *off, phys_bytes phys));
05239   _PROTOTYPE( void enable_iop, (struct proc *pp)                );
```

```
05240    _PROTOTYPE( void alloc_segments, (struct proc *rp)                        );
05241
05242    #endif /* PROTO_H */
05243
05244
```

```
+++++++++++++++++++++++++++++++++++++++++++++++++++++++++++++++++++++++++++
                              kernel/glo.h
+++++++++++++++++++++++++++++++++++++++++++++++++++++++++++++++++++++++++++
05300    #ifndef GLO_H
05301    #define GLO_H
05302
05303    /* Global variables used in the kernel. This file contains the declarations;
05304     * storage space for the variables is allocated in table.c, because EXTERN is
05305     * defined as extern unless the _TABLE definition is seen. We rely on the
05306     * compiler's default initialization (0) for several global variables.
05307     */
05308    #ifdef _TABLE
05309    #undef EXTERN
05310    #define EXTERN
05311    #endif
05312
05313    #include <minix/config.h>
05314    #include "config.h"
05315
05316    /* Variables relating to shutting down MINIX. */
05317    EXTERN char kernel_exception;             /* TRUE after system exceptions */
05318    EXTERN char shutdown_started;             /* TRUE after shutdowns / reboots */
05319
05320    /* Kernel information structures. This groups vital kernel information. */
05321    EXTERN phys_bytes aout;                   /* address of a.out headers */
05322    EXTERN struct kinfo kinfo;                /* kernel information for users */
05323    EXTERN struct machine machine;            /* machine information for users */
05324    EXTERN struct kmessages kmess;            /* diagnostic messages in kernel */
05325    EXTERN struct randomness krandom;         /* gather kernel random information */
05326
05327    /* Process scheduling information and the kernel reentry count. */
05328    EXTERN struct proc *prev_ptr;    /* previously running process */
05329    EXTERN struct proc *proc_ptr;    /* pointer to currently running process */
05330    EXTERN struct proc *next_ptr;    /* next process to run after restart() */
05331    EXTERN struct proc *bill_ptr;    /* process to bill for clock ticks */
05332    EXTERN char k_reenter;           /* kernel reentry count (entry count less 1) */
05333    EXTERN unsigned lost_ticks;      /* clock ticks counted outside clock task */
05334
05335    /* Interrupt related variables. */
05336    EXTERN irq_hook_t irq_hooks[NR_IRQ_HOOKS];      /* hooks for general use */
05337    EXTERN irq_hook_t *irq_handlers[NR_IRQ_VECTORS];/* list of IRQ handlers */
05338    EXTERN int irq_actids[NR_IRQ_VECTORS];          /* IRQ ID bits active */
05339    EXTERN int irq_use;                             /* map of all in-use irq's */
05340
05341    /* Miscellaneous. */
05342    EXTERN reg_t mon_ss, mon_sp;              /* boot monitor stack */
05343    EXTERN int mon_return;                    /* true if we can return to monitor */
05344
05345    /* Variables that are initialized elsewhere are just extern here. */
05346    extern struct boot_image image[];         /* system image processes */
05347    extern char *t_stack[];                   /* task stack space */
05348    extern struct segdesc_s gdt[];            /* global descriptor table */
05349
```

```
05350   EXTERN _PROTOTYPE( void (*level0_func), (void) );
05351
05352   #endif /* GLO_H */
05353
05354
05355
05356
05357
```

```
++++++++++++++++++++++++++++++++++++++++++++++++++++++++++++++++++++++++++++
                              kernel/ipc.h
++++++++++++++++++++++++++++++++++++++++++++++++++++++++++++++++++++++++++++
```

```
05400   #ifndef IPC_H
05401   #define IPC_H
05402
05403   /* This header file defines constants for MINIX inter-process communication.
05404    * These definitions are used in the file proc.c.
05405    */
05406   #include <minix/com.h>
05407
05408   /* Masks and flags for system calls. */
05409   #define SYSCALL_FUNC     0x0F    /* mask for system call function */
05410   #define SYSCALL_FLAGS    0xF0    /* mask for system call flags */
05411   #define NON_BLOCKING     0x10    /* prevent blocking, return error */
05412
05413   /* System call numbers that are passed when trapping to the kernel. The
05414    * numbers are carefully defined so that it can easily be seen (based on
05415    * the bits that are on) which checks should be done in sys_call().
05416    */
05417   #define SEND              1      /* 0 0 0 1 : blocking send */
05418   #define RECEIVE           2      /* 0 0 1 0 : blocking receive */
05419   #define SENDREC           3      /* 0 0 1 1 : SEND + RECEIVE */
05420   #define NOTIFY            4      /* 0 1 0 0 : nonblocking notify */
05421   #define ECHO              8      /* 1 0 0 0 : echo a message */
05422
05423   /* The following bit masks determine what checks that should be done. */
05424   #define CHECK_PTR        0x0B    /* 1 0 1 1 : validate message buffer */
05425   #define CHECK_DST        0x05    /* 0 1 0 1 : validate message destination */
05426   #define CHECK_SRC        0x02    /* 0 0 1 0 : validate message source */
05427
05428   #endif /* IPC_H */
```

```
++++++++++++++++++++++++++++++++++++++++++++++++++++++++++++++++++++++++++++
                              kernel/proc.h
++++++++++++++++++++++++++++++++++++++++++++++++++++++++++++++++++++++++++++
```

```
05500   #ifndef PROC_H
05501   #define PROC_H
05502
05503   /* Here is the declaration of the process table.  It contains all process
05504    * data, including registers, flags, scheduling priority, memory map,
05505    * accounting, message passing (IPC) information, and so on.
05506    *
05507    * Many assembly code routines reference fields in it.  The offsets to these
05508    * fields are defined in the assembler include file sconst.h.  When changing
05509    * struct proc, be sure to change sconst.h to match.
```

```
05510    */
05511    #include <minix/com.h>
05512    #include "protect.h"
05513    #include "const.h"
05514    #include "priv.h"
05515
05516    struct proc {
05517      struct stackframe_s p_reg;      /* process' registers saved in stack frame */
05518      reg_t p_ldt_sel;               /* selector in gdt with ldt base and limit */
05519      struct segdesc_s p_ldt[2+NR_REMOTE_SEGS]; /* CS, DS and remote segments */
05520
05521      proc_nr_t p_nr;                /* number of this process (for fast access) */
05522      struct priv *p_priv;           /* system privileges structure */
05523      char p_rts_flags;              /* SENDING, RECEIVING, etc. */
05524
05525      char p_priority;               /* current scheduling priority */
05526      char p_max_priority;           /* maximum scheduling priority */
05527      char p_ticks_left;             /* number of scheduling ticks left */
05528      char p_quantum_size;           /* quantum size in ticks */
05529
05530      struct mem_map p_memmap[NR_LOCAL_SEGS];   /* memory map (T, D, S) */
05531
05532      clock_t p_user_time;           /* user time in ticks */
05533      clock_t p_sys_time;            /* sys time in ticks */
05534
05535      struct proc *p_nextready;      /* pointer to next ready process */
05536      struct proc *p_caller_q;       /* head of list of procs wishing to send */
05537      struct proc *p_q_link;         /* link to next proc wishing to send */
05538      message *p_messbuf;            /* pointer to passed message buffer */
05539      proc_nr_t p_getfrom;           /* from whom does process want to receive? */
05540      proc_nr_t p_sendto;            /* to whom does process want to send? */
05541
05542      sigset_t p_pending;            /* bit map for pending kernel signals */
05543
05544      char p_name[P_NAME_LEN];       /* name of the process, including \0 */
05545    };
05546
05547    /* Bits for the runtime flags. A process is runnable iff p_rts_flags == 0. */
05548    #define SLOT_FREE        0x01    /* process slot is free */
05549    #define NO_MAP           0x02    /* keeps unmapped forked child from running */
05550    #define SENDING          0x04    /* process blocked trying to SEND */
05551    #define RECEIVING        0x08    /* process blocked trying to RECEIVE */
05552    #define SIGNALED         0x10    /* set when new kernel signal arrives */
05553    #define SIG_PENDING      0x20    /* unready while signal being processed */
05554    #define P_STOP           0x40    /* set when process is being traced */
05555    #define NO_PRIV          0x80    /* keep forked system process from running */
05556
05557    /* Scheduling priorities for p_priority. Values must start at zero (highest
05558     * priority) and increment.  Priorities of the processes in the boot image
05559     * can be set in table.c. IDLE must have a queue for itself, to prevent low
05560     * priority user processes to run round-robin with IDLE.
05561     */
05562    #define NR_SCHED_QUEUES   16     /* MUST equal minimum priority + 1 */
05563    #define TASK_Q             0     /* highest, used for kernel tasks */
05564    #define MAX_USER_Q         0     /* highest priority for user processes */
05565    #define USER_Q             7     /* default (should correspond to nice 0) */
05566    #define MIN_USER_Q        14     /* minimum priority for user processes */
05567    #define IDLE_Q            15     /* lowest, only IDLE process goes here */
05568
05569    /* Magic process table addresses. */
```

```
05570   #define BEG_PROC_ADDR (&proc[0])
05571   #define BEG_USER_ADDR (&proc[NR_TASKS])
05572   #define END_PROC_ADDR (&proc[NR_TASKS + NR_PROCS])
05573
05574   #define NIL_PROC              ((struct proc *) 0)
05575   #define NIL_SYS_PROC          ((struct proc *) 1)
05576   #define cproc_addr(n)         (&(proc + NR_TASKS)[(n)])
05577   #define proc_addr(n)          (pproc_addr + NR_TASKS)[(n)]
05578   #define proc_nr(p)            ((p)->p_nr)
05579
05580   #define isokprocn(n)          ((unsigned) ((n) + NR_TASKS) < NR_PROCS + NR_TASKS)
05581   #define isemptyn(n)           isemptyp(proc_addr(n))
05582   #define isemptyp(p)           ((p)->p_rts_flags == SLOT_FREE)
05583   #define iskernelp(p)          iskerneln((p)->p_nr)
05584   #define iskerneln(n)          ((n) < 0)
05585   #define isuserp(p)            isusern((p)->p_nr)
05586   #define isusern(n)            ((n) >= 0)
05587
05588   /* The process table and pointers to process table slots. The pointers allow
05589    * faster access because now a process entry can be found by indexing the
05590    * pproc_addr array, while accessing an element i requires a multiplication
05591    * with sizeof(struct proc) to determine the address.
05592    */
05593   EXTERN struct proc proc[NR_TASKS + NR_PROCS];   /* process table */
05594   EXTERN struct proc *pproc_addr[NR_TASKS + NR_PROCS];
05595   EXTERN struct proc *rdy_head[NR_SCHED_QUEUES]; /* ptrs to ready list headers */
05596   EXTERN struct proc *rdy_tail[NR_SCHED_QUEUES]; /* ptrs to ready list tails */
05597
05598   #endif /* PROC_H */
```

```
++++++++++++++++++++++++++++++++++++++++++++++++++++++++++++++++++++++++++++++
                            kernel/sconst.h
++++++++++++++++++++++++++++++++++++++++++++++++++++++++++++++++++++++++++++++
```

```
05600   ! Miscellaneous constants used in assembler code.
05601   W              =        _WORD_SIZE      ! Machine word size.
05602
05603   ! Offsets in struct proc. They MUST match proc.h.
05604   P_STACKBASE    =        0
05605   GSREG          =        P_STACKBASE
05606   FSREG          =        GSREG + 2       ! 386 introduces FS and GS segments
05607   ESREG          =        FSREG + 2
05608   DSREG          =        ESREG + 2
05609   DIREG          =        DSREG + 2
05610   SIREG          =        DIREG + W
05611   BPREG          =        SIREG + W
05612   STREG          =        BPREG + W       ! hole for another SP
05613   BXREG          =        STREG + W
05614   DXREG          =        BXREG + W
05615   CXREG          =        DXREG + W
05616   AXREG          =        CXREG + W
05617   RETADR         =        AXREG + W       ! return address for save() call
05618   PCREG          =        RETADR + W
05619   CSREG          =        PCREG + W
05620   PSWREG         =        CSREG + W
05621   SPREG          =        PSWREG + W
05622   SSREG          =        SPREG + W
05623   P_STACKTOP     =        SSREG + W
05624   P_LDT_SEL      =        P_STACKTOP
```

```
05625   P_LDT           =       P_LDT_SEL + W
05626
05627   Msize           =       9                       ! size of a message in 32-bit words
```

```
++++++++++++++++++++++++++++++++++++++++++++++++++++++++++++++++++++++++++
                            kernel/priv.h
++++++++++++++++++++++++++++++++++++++++++++++++++++++++++++++++++++++++++
05700   #ifndef PRIV_H
05701   #define PRIV_H
05702
05703   /* Declaration of the system privileges structure. It defines flags, system
05704    * call masks, an synchronous alarm timer, I/O privileges, pending hardware
05705    * interrupts and notifications, and so on.
05706    * System processes each get their own structure with properties, whereas all
05707    * user processes share one structure. This setup provides a clear separation
05708    * between common and privileged process fields and is very space efficient.
05709    *
05710    * Changes:
05711    *    Jul 01, 2005      Created.  (Jorrit N. Herder)
05712    */
05713   #include <minix/com.h>
05714   #include "protect.h"
05715   #include "const.h"
05716   #include "type.h"
05717
05718   struct priv {
05719     proc_nr_t s_proc_nr;          /* number of associated process */
05720     sys_id_t s_id;                /* index of this system structure */
05721     short s_flags;                /* PREEMTIBLE, BILLABLE, etc. */
05722
05723     short s_trap_mask;            /* allowed system call traps */
05724     sys_map_t s_ipc_from;        /* allowed callers to receive from */
05725     sys_map_t s_ipc_to;          /* allowed destination processes */
05726     long s_call_mask;            /* allowed kernel calls */
05727
05728     sys_map_t s_notify_pending;   /* bit map with pending notifications */
05729     irq_id_t s_int_pending;       /* pending hardware interrupts */
05730     sigset_t s_sig_pending;       /* pending signals */
05731
05732     timer_t s_alarm_timer;        /* synchronous alarm timer */
05733     struct far_mem s_farmem[NR_REMOTE_SEGS];  /* remote memory map */
05734     reg_t *s_stack_guard;         /* stack guard word for kernel tasks */
05735   };
05736
05737   /* Guard word for task stacks. */
05738   #define STACK_GUARD     ((reg_t) (sizeof(reg_t) == 2 ? 0xBEEF : 0xDEADBEEF))
05739
05740   /* Bits for the system property flags. */
05741   #define PREEMPTIBLE     0x01    /* kernel tasks are not preemptible */
05742   #define BILLABLE        0x04    /* some processes are not billable */
05743   #define SYS_PROC        0x10    /* system processes are privileged */
05744   #define SENDREC_BUSY    0x20    /* sendrec() in progress */
05745
05746   /* Magic system structure table addresses. */
05747   #define BEG_PRIV_ADDR (&priv[0])
05748   #define END_PRIV_ADDR (&priv[NR_SYS_PROCS])
05749
```

```
05750  #define priv_addr(i)       (ppriv_addr)[(i)]
05751  #define priv_id(rp)        ((rp)->p_priv->s_id)
05752  #define priv(rp)           ((rp)->p_priv)
05753
05754  #define id_to_nr(id)     priv_addr(id)->s_proc_nr
05755  #define nr_to_id(nr)     priv(proc_addr(nr))->s_id
05756
05757  /* The system structures table and pointers to individual table slots. The
05758   * pointers allow faster access because now a process entry can be found by
05759   * indexing the psys_addr array, while accessing an element i requires a
05760   * multiplication with sizeof(struct sys) to determine the address.
05761   */
05762  EXTERN struct priv priv[NR_SYS_PROCS];          /* system properties table */
05763  EXTERN struct priv *ppriv_addr[NR_SYS_PROCS];   /* direct slot pointers */
05764
05765  /* Unprivileged user processes all share the same privilege structure.
05766   * This id must be fixed because it is used to check send mask entries.
05767   */
05768  #define USER_PRIV_ID     0
05769
05770  /* Make sure the system can boot. The following sanity check verifies that
05771   * the system privileges table is large enough for the number of processes
05772   * in the boot image.
05773   */
05774  #if (NR_BOOT_PROCS > NR_SYS_PROCS)
05775  #error NR_SYS_PROCS must be larger than NR_BOOT_PROCS
05776  #endif
05777
05778  #endif /* PRIV_H */
```

```
++++++++++++++++++++++++++++++++++++++++++++++++++++++++++++++++++++++++++++
                              kernel/protect.h
++++++++++++++++++++++++++++++++++++++++++++++++++++++++++++++++++++++++++++
```

```
05800  /* Constants for protected mode. */
05801
05802  /* Table sizes. */
05803  #define GDT_SIZE (FIRST_LDT_INDEX + NR_TASKS + NR_PROCS)
05804                                        /* spec. and LDT's */
05805  #define IDT_SIZE (IRQ8_VECTOR + 8)      /* only up to the highest vector */
05806  #define LDT_SIZE (2 + NR_REMOTE_SEGS)   /* CS, DS and remote segments */
05807
05808  /* Fixed global descriptors.  1 to 7 are prescribed by the BIOS. */
05809  #define GDT_INDEX          1  /* GDT descriptor */
05810  #define IDT_INDEX          2  /* IDT descriptor */
05811  #define DS_INDEX           3  /* kernel DS */
05812  #define ES_INDEX           4  /* kernel ES (386: flag 4 Gb at startup) */
05813  #define SS_INDEX           5  /* kernel SS (386: monitor SS at startup) */
05814  #define CS_INDEX           6  /* kernel CS */
05815  #define MON_CS_INDEX       7  /* temp for BIOS (386: monitor CS at startup) */
05816  #define TSS_INDEX          8  /* kernel TSS */
05817  #define DS_286_INDEX       9  /* scratch 16-bit source segment */
05818  #define ES_286_INDEX      10  /* scratch 16-bit destination segment */
05819  #define A_INDEX           11  /* 64K memory segment at A0000 */
05820  #define B_INDEX           12  /* 64K memory segment at B0000 */
05821  #define C_INDEX           13  /* 64K memory segment at C0000 */
05822  #define D_INDEX           14  /* 64K memory segment at D0000 */
05823  #define FIRST_LDT_INDEX   15  /* rest of descriptors are LDT's */
05824
```

```
05825   #define GDT_SELECTOR        0x08  /* (GDT_INDEX * DESC_SIZE) bad for asld */
05826   #define IDT_SELECTOR        0x10  /* (IDT_INDEX * DESC_SIZE) */
05827   #define DS_SELECTOR         0x18  /* (DS_INDEX * DESC_SIZE) */
05828   #define ES_SELECTOR         0x20  /* (ES_INDEX * DESC_SIZE) */
05829   #define FLAT_DS_SELECTOR    0x21  /* less privileged ES */
05830   #define SS_SELECTOR         0x28  /* (SS_INDEX * DESC_SIZE) */
05831   #define CS_SELECTOR         0x30  /* (CS_INDEX * DESC_SIZE) */
05832   #define MON_CS_SELECTOR     0x38  /* (MON_CS_INDEX * DESC_SIZE) */
05833   #define TSS_SELECTOR        0x40  /* (TSS_INDEX * DESC_SIZE) */
05834   #define DS_286_SELECTOR     0x49  /* (DS_286_INDEX*DESC_SIZE+TASK_PRIVILEGE) */
05835   #define ES_286_SELECTOR     0x51  /* (ES_286_INDEX*DESC_SIZE+TASK_PRIVILEGE) */
05836
05837   /* Fixed local descriptors. */
05838   #define CS_LDT_INDEX        0  /* process CS */
05839   #define DS_LDT_INDEX        1  /* process DS=ES=FS=GS=SS */
05840   #define EXTRA_LDT_INDEX     2  /* first of the extra LDT entries */
05841
05842   /* Privileges. */
05843   #define INTR_PRIVILEGE      0  /* kernel and interrupt handlers */
05844   #define TASK_PRIVILEGE      1  /* kernel tasks */
05845   #define USER_PRIVILEGE      3  /* servers and user processes */
05846
05847   /* 286 hardware constants. */
05848
05849   /* Exception vector numbers. */
05850   #define BOUNDS_VECTOR        5  /* bounds check failed */
05851   #define INVAL_OP_VECTOR      6  /* invalid opcode */
05852   #define COPROC_NOT_VECTOR    7  /* coprocessor not available */
05853   #define DOUBLE_FAULT_VECTOR  8
05854   #define COPROC_SEG_VECTOR    9  /* coprocessor segment overrun */
05855   #define INVAL_TSS_VECTOR    10  /* invalid TSS */
05856   #define SEG_NOT_VECTOR      11  /* segment not present */
05857   #define STACK_FAULT_VECTOR  12  /* stack exception */
05858   #define PROTECTION_VECTOR   13  /* general protection */
05859
05860   /* Selector bits. */
05861   #define TI                 0x04  /* table indicator */
05862   #define RPL                0x03  /* requester privilege level */
05863
05864   /* Descriptor structure offsets. */
05865   #define DESC_BASE           2  /* to base_low */
05866   #define DESC_BASE_MIDDLE    4  /* to base_middle */
05867   #define DESC_ACCESS         5  /* to access byte */
05868   #define DESC_SIZE           8  /* sizeof (struct segdesc_s) */
05869
05870   /* Base and limit sizes and shifts. */
05871   #define BASE_MIDDLE_SHIFT   16  /* shift for base --> base_middle */
05872
05873   /* Access-byte and type-byte bits. */
05874   #define PRESENT            0x80  /* set for descriptor present */
05875   #define DPL                0x60  /* descriptor privilege level mask */
05876   #define DPL_SHIFT           5
05877   #define SEGMENT            0x10  /* set for segment-type descriptors */
05878
05879   /* Access-byte bits. */
05880   #define EXECUTABLE         0x08  /* set for executable segment */
05881   #define CONFORMING         0x04  /* set for conforming segment if executable */
05882   #define EXPAND_DOWN        0x04  /* set for expand-down segment if !executable*/
05883   #define READABLE           0x02  /* set for readable segment if executable */
05884   #define WRITEABLE          0x02  /* set for writeable segment if !executable */
```

```
05885  #define TSS_BUSY          0x02  /* set if TSS descriptor is busy */
05886  #define ACCESSED          0x01  /* set if segment accessed */
05887
05888  /* Special descriptor types. */
05889  #define AVL_286_TSS          1  /* available 286 TSS */
05890  #define LDT                  2  /* local descriptor table */
05891  #define BUSY_286_TSS         3  /* set transparently to the software */
05892  #define CALL_286_GATE        4  /* not used */
05893  #define TASK_GATE            5  /* only used by debugger */
05894  #define INT_286_GATE         6  /* interrupt gate, used for all vectors */
05895  #define TRAP_286_GATE        7  /* not used */
05896
05897  /* Extra 386 hardware constants. */
05898
05899  /* Exception vector numbers. */
05900  #define PAGE_FAULT_VECTOR   14
05901  #define COPROC_ERR_VECTOR   16  /* coprocessor error */
05902
05903  /* Descriptor structure offsets. */
05904  #define DESC_GRANULARITY     6  /* to granularity byte */
05905  #define DESC_BASE_HIGH       7  /* to base_high */
05906
05907  /* Base and limit sizes and shifts. */
05908  #define BASE_HIGH_SHIFT     24  /* shift for base --> base_high */
05909  #define BYTE_GRAN_MAX   0xFFFFFL  /* maximum size for byte granular segment */
05910  #define GRANULARITY_SHIFT   16  /* shift for limit --> granularity */
05911  #define OFFSET_HIGH_SHIFT   16  /* shift for (gate) offset --> offset_high */
05912  #define PAGE_GRAN_SHIFT     12  /* extra shift for page granular limits */
05913
05914  /* Type-byte bits. */
05915  #define DESC_386_BIT 0x08  /* 386 types are obtained by ORing with this */
05916                            /* LDT's and TASK_GATE's don't need it */
05917
05918  /* Granularity byte. */
05919  #define GRANULAR          0x80  /* set for 4K granularilty */
05920  #define DEFAULT           0x40  /* set for 32-bit defaults (executable seg) */
05921  #define BIG               0x40  /* set for "BIG" (expand-down seg) */
05922  #define AVL               0x10  /* 0 for available */
05923  #define LIMIT_HIGH        0x0F  /* mask for high bits of limit */
```

```
++++++++++++++++++++++++++++++++++++++++++++++++++++++++++++++++++++++++++++++
                              kernel/table.c
++++++++++++++++++++++++++++++++++++++++++++++++++++++++++++++++++++++++++++++
```

```
06000  /* The object file of "table.c" contains most kernel data. Variables that
06001   * are declared in the *.h files appear with EXTERN in front of them, as in
06002   *
06003   *     EXTERN int x;
06004   *
06005   * Normally EXTERN is defined as extern, so when they are included in another
06006   * file, no storage is allocated.  If EXTERN were not present, but just say,
06007   *
06008   *     int x;
06009   *
06010   * then including this file in several source files would cause 'x' to be
06011   * declared several times.  While some linkers accept this, others do not,
06012   * so they are declared extern when included normally.  However, it must be
06013   * declared for real somewhere.  That is done here, by redefining EXTERN as
06014   * the null string, so that inclusion of all *.h files in table.c actually
```

```
06015     * generates storage for them.
06016     *
06017     * Various variables could not be declared EXTERN, but are declared PUBLIC
06018     * or PRIVATE. The reason for this is that extern variables cannot have a
06019     * default initialization. If such variables are shared, they must also be
06020     * declared in one of the *.h files without the initialization.  Examples
06021     * include 'boot_image' (this file) and 'idt' and 'gdt' (protect.c).
06022     *
06023     * Changes:
06024     *    Aug 02, 2005   set privileges and minimal boot image (Jorrit N. Herder)
06025     *    Oct 17, 2004   updated above and tasktab comments  (Jorrit N. Herder)
06026     *    May 01, 2004   changed struct for system image  (Jorrit N. Herder)
06027     */
06028    #define _TABLE
06029
06030    #include "kernel.h"
06031    #include "proc.h"
06032    #include "ipc.h"
06033    #include <minix/com.h>
06034    #include <ibm/int86.h>
06035
06036    /* Define stack sizes for the kernel tasks included in the system image. */
06037    #define NO_STACK        0
06038    #define SMALL_STACK     (128 * sizeof(char *))
06039    #define IDL_S   SMALL_STACK     /* 3 intr, 3 temps, 4 db for Intel */
06040    #define HRD_S   NO_STACK        /* dummy task, uses kernel stack */
06041    #define TSK_S   SMALL_STACK     /* system and clock task */
06042
06043    /* Stack space for all the task stacks.  Declared as (char *) to align it. */
06044    #define TOT_STACK_SPACE (IDL_S + HRD_S + (2 * TSK_S))
06045    PUBLIC char *t_stack[TOT_STACK_SPACE / sizeof(char *)];
06046
06047    /* Define flags for the various process types. */
06048    #define IDL_F   (SYS_PROC | PREEMPTIBLE | BILLABLE)     /* idle task */
06049    #define TSK_F   (SYS_PROC)                              /* kernel tasks */
06050    #define SRV_F   (SYS_PROC | PREEMPTIBLE)                /* system services */
06051    #define USR_F   (BILLABLE | PREEMPTIBLE)                /* user processes */
06052
06053    /* Define system call traps for the various process types. These call masks
06054     * determine what system call traps a process is allowed to make.
06055     */
06056    #define TSK_T   (1 << RECEIVE)                   /* clock and system */
06057    #define SRV_T   (~0)                             /* system services */
06058    #define USR_T   ((1 << SENDREC) | (1 << ECHO))   /* user processes */
06059
06060    /* Send masks determine to whom processes can send messages or notifications.
06061     * The values here are used for the processes in the boot image. We rely on
06062     * the initialization code in main() to match the s_nr_to_id() mapping for the
06063     * processes in the boot image, so that the send mask that is defined here
06064     * can be directly copied onto map[0] of the actual send mask. Privilege
06065     * structure 0 is shared by user processes.
06066     */
06067    #define s(n)            (1 << s_nr_to_id(n))
06068    #define SRV_M (~0)
06069    #define SYS_M (~0)
06070    #define USR_M (s(PM_PROC_NR) | s(FS_PROC_NR) | s(RS_PROC_NR))
06071    #define DRV_M (USR_M | s(SYSTEM) | s(CLOCK) | s(LOG_PROC_NR) | s(TTY_PROC_NR))
06072
06073    /* Define kernel calls that processes are allowed to make. This is not looking
06074     * very nice, but we need to define the access rights on a per call basis.
```

```
06075     * Note that the reincarnation server has all bits on, because it should
06076     * be allowed to distribute rights to services that it starts.
06077     */
06078   #define c(n)      (1 << ((n)-KERNEL_CALL))
06079   #define RS_C      ~0
06080   #define PM_C      ~(c(SYS_DEVIO) | c(SYS_SDEVIO) | c(SYS_VDEVIO) \
06081       | c(SYS_IRQCTL) | c(SYS_INT86))
06082   #define FS_C      (c(SYS_KILL) | c(SYS_VIRCOPY) | c(SYS_VIRVCOPY) | c(SYS_UMAP) \
06083       | c(SYS_GETINFO) | c(SYS_EXIT) | c(SYS_TIMES) | c(SYS_SETALARM))
06084   #define DRV_C   (FS_C | c(SYS_SEGCTL) | c(SYS_IRQCTL) | c(SYS_INT86) \
06085       | c(SYS_DEVIO) | c(SYS_VDEVIO) | c(SYS_SDEVIO))
06086   #define MEM_C   (DRV_C | c(SYS_PHYSCOPY) | c(SYS_PHYSVCOPY))
06087
06088   /* The system image table lists all programs that are part of the boot image.
06089    * The order of the entries here MUST agree with the order of the programs
06090    * in the boot image and all kernel tasks must come first.
06091    * Each entry provides the process number, flags, quantum size (qs), scheduling
06092    * queue, allowed traps, ipc mask, and a name for the process table. The
06093    * initial program counter and stack size is also provided for kernel tasks.
06094    */
06095   PUBLIC struct boot_image image[] = {
06096   /* process nr,   pc, flags, qs,  queue, stack, traps, ipcto, call,  name */
06097   { IDLE,  idle_task, IDL_F,  8, IDLE_Q, IDL_S,    0,     0,    0, "IDLE"  },
06098   { CLOCK,clock_task, TSK_F, 64, TASK_Q, TSK_S, TSK_T,    0,    0, "CLOCK" },
06099   { SYSTEM, sys_task, TSK_F, 64, TASK_Q, TSK_S, TSK_T,    0,    0, "SYSTEM"},
06100   { HARDWARE,       0, TSK_F, 64, TASK_Q, HRD_S,    0,     0,    0, "KERNEL"},
06101   { PM_PROC_NR,     0, SRV_F, 32,      3, 0,    SRV_T, SRV_M,  PM_C, "pm"   },
06102   { FS_PROC_NR,     0, SRV_F, 32,      4, 0,    SRV_T, SRV_M,  FS_C, "fs"   },
06103   { RS_PROC_NR,     0, SRV_F,  4,      3, 0,    SRV_T, SYS_M,  RS_C, "rs"   },
06104   { TTY_PROC_NR,    0, SRV_F,  4,      1, 0,    SRV_T, SYS_M, DRV_C, "tty"  },
06105   { MEM_PROC_NR,    0, SRV_F,  4,      2, 0,    SRV_T, DRV_M, MEM_C, "memory"},
06106   { LOG_PROC_NR,    0, SRV_F,  4,      2, 0,    SRV_T, SYS_M, DRV_C, "log"  },
06107   { DRVR_PROC_NR,   0, SRV_F,  4,      2, 0,    SRV_T, SYS_M, DRV_C, "driver"},
06108   { INIT_PROC_NR,   0, USR_F,  8, USER_Q, 0,    USR_T, USR_M,    0, "init" },
06109   };
06110
06111   /* Verify the size of the system image table at compile time. Also verify that
06112    * the first chunk of the ipc mask has enough bits to accommodate the processes
06113    * in the image.
06114    * If a problem is detected, the size of the 'dummy' array will be negative,
06115    * causing a compile time error. Note that no space is actually allocated
06116    * because 'dummy' is declared extern.
06117    */
06118   extern int dummy[(NR_BOOT_PROCS==sizeof(image)/
06119          sizeof(struct boot_image))?1:-1];
06120   extern int dummy[(BITCHUNK_BITS > NR_BOOT_PROCS - 1) ? 1 : -1];
06121
```

```
++++++++++++++++++++++++++++++++++++++++++++++++++++++++++++++++++++++++++++++
                              kernel/mpx.s
++++++++++++++++++++++++++++++++++++++++++++++++++++++++++++++++++++++++++++++
```

```
06200   #
06201   ! Chooses between the 8086 and 386 versions of the Minix startup code.
06202
06203   #include <minix/config.h>
06204   #if _WORD_SIZE == 2
```

```
06205    #include "mpx88.s"
06206    #else
06207    #include "mpx386.s"
06208    #endif
```

```
++++++++++++++++++++++++++++++++++++++++++++++++++++++++++++++++++++++++++++
                            kernel/mpx386.s
++++++++++++++++++++++++++++++++++++++++++++++++++++++++++++++++++++++++++++
```

```
06300    #
06301    ! This file, mpx386.s, is included by mpx.s when Minix is compiled for
06302    ! 32-bit Intel CPUs. The alternative mpx88.s is compiled for 16-bit CPUs.
06303
06304    ! This file is part of the lowest layer of the MINIX kernel.  (The other part
06305    ! is "proc.c".)  The lowest layer does process switching and message handling.
06306    ! Furthermore it contains the assembler startup code for Minix and the 32-bit
06307    ! interrupt handlers.  It cooperates with the code in "start.c" to set up a
06308    ! good environment for main().
06309
06310    ! Every transition to the kernel goes through this file.  Transitions to the
06311    ! kernel may be nested.  The initial entry may be with a system call (i.e.,
06312    ! send or receive a message), an exception or a hardware interrupt;  kernel
06313    ! reentries may only be made by hardware interrupts.  The count of reentries
06314    ! is kept in "k_reenter". It is important for deciding whether to switch to
06315    ! the kernel stack and for protecting the message passing code in "proc.c".
06316
06317    ! For the message passing trap, most of the machine state is saved in the
06318    ! proc table.  (Some of the registers need not be saved.)  Then the stack is
06319    ! switched to "k_stack", and interrupts are reenabled.  Finally, the system
06320    ! call handler (in C) is called.  When it returns, interrupts are disabled
06321    ! again and the code falls into the restart routine, to finish off held-up
06322    ! interrupts and run the process or task whose pointer is in "proc_ptr".
06323
06324    ! Hardware interrupt handlers do the same, except  (1) The entire state must
06325    ! be saved.  (2) There are too many handlers to do this inline, so the save
06326    ! routine is called.  A few cycles are saved by pushing the address of the
06327    ! appropiate restart routine for a return later.  (3) A stack switch is
06328    ! avoided when the stack is already switched.  (4) The (master) 8259 interrupt
06329    ! controller is reenabled centrally in save().  (5) Each interrupt handler
06330    ! masks its interrupt line using the 8259 before enabling (other unmasked)
06331    ! interrupts, and unmasks it after servicing the interrupt.  This limits the
06332    ! nest level to the number of lines and protects the handler from itself.
06333
06334    ! For communication with the boot monitor at startup time some constant
06335    ! data are compiled into the beginning of the text segment. This facilitates
06336    ! reading the data at the start of the boot process, since only the first
06337    ! sector of the file needs to be read.
06338
06339    ! Some data storage is also allocated at the end of this file. This data
06340    ! will be at the start of the data segment of the kernel and will be read
06341    ! and modified by the boot monitor before the kernel starts.
06342
06343    ! sections
06344
06345    .sect .text
06346    begtext:
06347    .sect .rom
06348    begrom:
06349    .sect .data
```

```
06350   begdata:
06351   .sect .bss
06352   begbss:
06353
06354   #include <minix/config.h>
06355   #include <minix/const.h>
06356   #include <minix/com.h>
06357   #include <ibm/interrupt.h>
06358   #include "const.h"
06359   #include "protect.h"
06360   #include "sconst.h"
06361
06362   /* Selected 386 tss offsets. */
06363   #define TSS3_S_SP0      4
06364
06365   ! Exported functions
06366   ! Note: in assembly language the .define statement applied to a function name
06367   ! is loosely equivalent to a prototype in C code -- it makes it possible to
06368   ! link to an entity declared in the assembly code but does not create
06369   ! the entity.
06370
06371   .define _restart
06372   .define save
06373
06374   .define _divide_error
06375   .define _single_step_exception
06376   .define _nmi
06377   .define _breakpoint_exception
06378   .define _overflow
06379   .define _bounds_check
06380   .define _inval_opcode
06381   .define _copr_not_available
06382   .define _double_fault
06383   .define _copr_seg_overrun
06384   .define _inval_tss
06385   .define _segment_not_present
06386   .define _stack_exception
06387   .define _general_protection
06388   .define _page_fault
06389   .define _copr_error
06390
06391   .define _hwint00          ! handlers for hardware interrupts
06392   .define _hwint01
06393   .define _hwint02
06394   .define _hwint03
06395   .define _hwint04
06396   .define _hwint05
06397   .define _hwint06
06398   .define _hwint07
06399   .define _hwint08
06400   .define _hwint09
06401   .define _hwint10
06402   .define _hwint11
06403   .define _hwint12
06404   .define _hwint13
06405   .define _hwint14
06406   .define _hwint15
06407
06408   .define _s_call
06409   .define _p_s_call
```

```
06410          .define  _level0_call
06411
06412  ! Exported variables.
06413          .define  begbss
06414          .define  begdata
06415
06416          .sect .text
06417  !*===================================================================*
06418  !*                              MINIX                                 *
06419  !*===================================================================*
06420  MINIX:                          ! this is the entry point for the MINIX kernel
06421          jmp     over_flags      ! skip over the next few bytes
06422          .data2  CLICK_SHIFT     ! for the monitor: memory granularity
06423  flags:
06424          .data2  0x01FD          ! boot monitor flags:
06425                                  !       call in 386 mode, make bss, make stack,
06426                                  !       load high, don't patch, will return,
06427                                  !       uses generic INT, memory vector,
06428                                  !       new boot code return
06429          nop                     ! extra byte to sync up disassembler
06430  over_flags:
06431
06432  ! Set up a C stack frame on the monitor stack.  (The monitor sets cs and ds
06433  ! right.  The ss descriptor still references the monitor data segment.)
06434          movzx   esp, sp         ! monitor stack is a 16 bit stack
06435          push    ebp
06436          mov     ebp, esp
06437          push    esi
06438          push    edi
06439          cmp     4(ebp), 0       ! monitor return vector is
06440          jz      noret           ! nonzero if return possible
06441          inc     (_mon_return)
06442  noret:  mov     (_mon_sp), esp  ! save stack pointer for later return
06443
06444  ! Copy the monitor global descriptor table to the address space of kernel and
06445  ! switch over to it.  Prot_init() can then update it with immediate effect.
06446
06447          sgdt    (_gdt+GDT_SELECTOR)              ! get the monitor gdtr
06448          mov     esi, (_gdt+GDT_SELECTOR+2)       ! absolute address of GDT
06449          mov     ebx, _gdt                       ! address of kernel GDT
06450          mov     ecx, 8*8                        ! copying eight descriptors
06451  copygdt:
06452   eseg   movb    al, (esi)
06453          movb    (ebx), al
06454          inc     esi
06455          inc     ebx
06456          loop    copygdt
06457          mov     eax, (_gdt+DS_SELECTOR+2)        ! base of kernel data
06458          and     eax, 0x00FFFFFF                 ! only 24 bits
06459          add     eax, _gdt                       ! eax = vir2phys(gdt)
06460          mov     (_gdt+GDT_SELECTOR+2), eax       ! set base of GDT
06461          lgdt    (_gdt+GDT_SELECTOR)              ! switch over to kernel GDT
06462
06463  ! Locate boot parameters, set up kernel segment registers and stack.
06464          mov     ebx, 8(ebp)     ! boot parameters offset
06465          mov     edx, 12(ebp)    ! boot parameters length
06466          mov     eax, 16(ebp)    ! address of a.out headers
06467          mov     (_aout), eax
06468          mov     ax, ds          ! kernel data
06469          mov     es, ax
```

```
06470          mov     fs, ax
06471          mov     gs, ax
06472          mov     ss, ax
06473          mov     esp, k_stktop   ! set sp to point to the top of kernel stack
06474
06475  ! Call C startup code to set up a proper environment to run main().
06476          push    edx
06477          push    ebx
06478          push    SS_SELECTOR
06479          push    DS_SELECTOR
06480          push    CS_SELECTOR
06481          call    _cstart          ! cstart(cs, ds, mds, parmoff, parmlen)
06482          add     esp, 5*4
06483
06484  ! Reload gdtr, idtr and the segment registers to global descriptor table set
06485  ! up by prot_init().
06486
06487          lgdt    (_gdt+GDT_SELECTOR)
06488          lidt    (_gdt+IDT_SELECTOR)
06489
06490          jmpf    CS_SELECTOR:csinit
06491  csinit:
06492      o16 mov     ax, DS_SELECTOR
06493          mov     ds, ax
06494          mov     es, ax
06495          mov     fs, ax
06496          mov     gs, ax
06497          mov     ss, ax
06498      o16 mov     ax, TSS_SELECTOR        ! no other TSS is used
06499          ltr     ax
06500          push    0                       ! set flags to known good state
06501          popf                            ! esp, clear nested task and int enable
06502
06503          jmp     _main                   ! main()
06504
06505
06506  !*===========================================================================*
06507  !*                             interrupt handlers                            *
06508  !*                   interrupt handlers for 386 32-bit protected mode        *
06509  !*===========================================================================*
06510
06511  !*===========================================================================*
06512  !*                                hwint00 - 07                               *
06513  !*===========================================================================*
06514  ! Note this is a macro, it just looks like a subroutine.
06515  #define hwint_master(irq)           \
06516          call    save                    /* save interrupted process state */;\
06517          push    (_irq_handlers+4*irq)   /* irq_handlers[irq]              */;\
06518          call    _intr_handle            /* intr_handle(irq_handlers[irq]) */;\
06519          pop     ecx                                                       ;\
06520          cmp     (_irq_actids+4*irq), 0  /* interrupt still active?        */;\
06521          jz      0f                                                        ;\
06522          inb     INT_CTLMASK             /* get current mask */            ;\
06523          orb     al, [1<<irq]            /* mask irq */                    ;\
06524          outb    INT_CTLMASK             /* disable the irq                */;\
06525  0:      movb    al, END_OF_INT                                            ;\
06526          outb    INT_CTL                 /* reenable master 8259           */;\
06527          ret                             /* restart (another) process      */
06528
06529  ! Each of these entry points is an expansion of the hwint_master macro
```

```
06530             .align  16
06531    _hwint00:                     ! Interrupt routine for irq 0 (the clock).
06532             hwint_master(0)
06533
06534             .align  16
06535    _hwint01:                     ! Interrupt routine for irq 1 (keyboard)
06536             hwint_master(1)
06537
06538             .align  16
06539    _hwint02:                     ! Interrupt routine for irq 2 (cascade!)
06540             hwint_master(2)
06541
06542             .align  16
06543    _hwint03:                     ! Interrupt routine for irq 3 (second serial)
06544             hwint_master(3)
06545
06546             .align  16
06547    _hwint04:                     ! Interrupt routine for irq 4 (first serial)
06548             hwint_master(4)
06549
06550             .align  16
06551    _hwint05:                     ! Interrupt routine for irq 5 (XT winchester)
06552             hwint_master(5)
06553
06554             .align  16
06555    _hwint06:                     ! Interrupt routine for irq 6 (floppy)
06556             hwint_master(6)
06557
06558             .align  16
06559    _hwint07:                     ! Interrupt routine for irq 7 (printer)
06560             hwint_master(7)
06561
06562    !*===========================================================================*
06563    !*                              hwint08 - 15                                 *
06564    !*===========================================================================*
06565    ! Note this is a macro, it just looks like a subroutine.
06566    #define hwint_slave(irq)         \
06567             call     save                        /* save interrupted process state */;\
06568             push     (_irq_handlers+4*irq)       /* irq_handlers[irq]              */;\
06569             call     _intr_handle                /* intr_handle(irq_handlers[irq]) */;\
06570             pop      ecx                                                            ;\
06571             cmp      (_irq_actids+4*irq), 0 /* interrupt still active?       */;\
06572             jz       0f                                                            ;\
06573             inb      INT2_CTLMASK                                                  ;\
06574             orb      al, [1<<[irq-8]]                                              ;\
06575             outb     INT2_CTLMASK                /* disable the irq              */;\
06576    0:       movb     al, END_OF_INT                                                ;\
06577             outb     INT_CTL                     /* reenable master 8259         */;\
06578             outb     INT2_CTL                    /* reenable slave 8259          */;\
06579             ret                                  /* restart (another) process    */
06580
06581    ! Each of these entry points is an expansion of the hwint_slave macro
06582             .align  16
06583    _hwint08:                     ! Interrupt routine for irq 8 (realtime clock)
06584             hwint_slave(8)
06585
06586             .align  16
06587    _hwint09:                     ! Interrupt routine for irq 9 (irq 2 redirected)
06588             hwint_slave(9)
06589
```

```
06590                  .align   16
06591   _hwint10:                      ! Interrupt routine for irq 10
06592                  hwint_slave(10)
06593
06594                  .align   16
06595   _hwint11:                      ! Interrupt routine for irq 11
06596                  hwint_slave(11)
06597
06598                  .align   16
06599   _hwint12:                      ! Interrupt routine for irq 12
06600                  hwint_slave(12)
06601
06602                  .align   16
06603   _hwint13:                      ! Interrupt routine for irq 13 (FPU exception)
06604                  hwint_slave(13)
06605
06606                  .align   16
06607   _hwint14:                      ! Interrupt routine for irq 14 (AT winchester)
06608                  hwint_slave(14)
06609
06610                  .align   16
06611   _hwint15:                      ! Interrupt routine for irq 15
06612                  hwint_slave(15)
06613
06614   !*===========================================================================*
06615   !*                              save                                         *
06616   !*===========================================================================*
06617   ! Save for protected mode.
06618   ! This is much simpler than for 8086 mode, because the stack already points
06619   ! into the process table, or has already been switched to the kernel stack.
06620
06621                  .align   16
06622   save:
06623                  cld                         ! set direction flag to a known value
06624                  pushad                      ! save "general" registers
06625        o16 push  ds                          ! save ds
06626        o16 push  es                          ! save es
06627        o16 push  fs                          ! save fs
06628        o16 push  gs                          ! save gs
06629                  mov     dx, ss              ! ss is kernel data segment
06630                  mov     ds, dx              ! load rest of kernel segments
06631                  mov     es, dx              ! kernel does not use fs, gs
06632                  mov     eax, esp            ! prepare to return
06633                  incb    (_k_reenter)        ! from -1 if not reentering
06634                  jnz     set_restart1        ! stack is already kernel stack
06635                  mov     esp, k_stktop
06636                  push    _restart            ! build return address for int handler
06637                  xor     ebp, ebp            ! for stacktrace
06638                  jmp     RETADR-P_STACKBASE(eax)
06639
06640                  .align   4
06641   set_restart1:
06642                  push    restart1
06643                  jmp     RETADR-P_STACKBASE(eax)
06644
06645   !*===========================================================================*
06646   !*                              _s_call                                      *
06647   !*===========================================================================*
06648                  .align   16
06649   _s_call:
```

```
06650   _p_s_call:
06651           cld                          ! set direction flag to a known value
06652           sub     esp, 6*4             ! skip RETADR, eax, ecx, edx, ebx, est
06653           push    ebp                  ! stack already points into proc table
06654           push    esi
06655           push    edi
06656   o16 push    ds
06657   o16 push    es
06658   o16 push    fs
06659   o16 push    gs
06660           mov     dx, ss
06661           mov     ds, dx
06662           mov     es, dx
06663           incb    (_k_reenter)
06664           mov     esi, esp             ! assumes P_STACKBASE == 0
06665           mov     esp, k_stktop
06666           xor     ebp, ebp             ! for stacktrace
06667                                        ! end of inline save
06668                                        ! now set up parameters for sys_call()
06669           push    ebx                  ! pointer to user message
06670           push    eax                  ! src/dest
06671           push    ecx                  ! SEND/RECEIVE/BOTH
06672           call    _sys_call            ! sys_call(function, src_dest, m_ptr)
06673                                        ! caller is now explicitly in proc_ptr
06674           mov     AXREG(esi), eax ! sys_call MUST PRESERVE si
06675
06676   ! Fall into code to restart proc/task running.
06677
06678   !*===========================================================================*
06679   !*                              restart                                      *
06680   !*===========================================================================*
06681   _restart:
06682
06683   ! Restart the current process or the next process if it is set.
06684
06685           cmp     (_next_ptr), 0       ! see if another process is scheduled
06686           jz      0f
06687           mov     eax, (_next_ptr)
06688           mov     (_proc_ptr), eax     ! schedule new process
06689           mov     (_next_ptr), 0
06690   0:      mov     esp, (_proc_ptr)     ! will assume P_STACKBASE == 0
06691           lldt    P_LDT_SEL(esp)       ! enable process' segment descriptors
06692           lea     eax, P_STACKTOP(esp) ! arrange for next interrupt
06693           mov     (_tss+TSS3_S_SP0), eax ! to save state in process table
06694   restart1:
06695           decb    (_k_reenter)
06696   o16 pop     gs
06697   o16 pop     fs
06698   o16 pop     es
06699   o16 pop     ds
06700           popad
06701           add     esp, 4               ! skip return adr
06702           iretd                        ! continue process
06703
06704   !*===========================================================================*
06705   !*                         exception handlers                                *
06706   !*===========================================================================*
06707   _divide_error:
06708           push    DIVIDE_VECTOR
06709           jmp     exception
```

```
06710
06711   _single_step_exception:
06712           push    DEBUG_VECTOR
06713           jmp     exception
06714
06715   _nmi:
06716           push    NMI_VECTOR
06717           jmp     exception
06718
06719   _breakpoint_exception:
06720           push    BREAKPOINT_VECTOR
06721           jmp     exception
06722
06723   _overflow:
06724           push    OVERFLOW_VECTOR
06725           jmp     exception
06726
06727   _bounds_check:
06728           push    BOUNDS_VECTOR
06729           jmp     exception
06730
06731   _inval_opcode:
06732           push    INVAL_OP_VECTOR
06733           jmp     exception
06734
06735   _copr_not_available:
06736           push    COPROC_NOT_VECTOR
06737           jmp     exception
06738
06739   _double_fault:
06740           push    DOUBLE_FAULT_VECTOR
06741           jmp     errexception
06742
06743   _copr_seg_overrun:
06744           push    COPROC_SEG_VECTOR
06745           jmp     exception
06746
06747   _inval_tss:
06748           push    INVAL_TSS_VECTOR
06749           jmp     errexception
06750
06751   _segment_not_present:
06752           push    SEG_NOT_VECTOR
06753           jmp     errexception
06754
06755   _stack_exception:
06756           push    STACK_FAULT_VECTOR
06757           jmp     errexception
06758
06759   _general_protection:
06760           push    PROTECTION_VECTOR
06761           jmp     errexception
06762
06763   _page_fault:
06764           push    PAGE_FAULT_VECTOR
06765           jmp     errexception
06766
06767   _copr_error:
06768           push    COPROC_ERR_VECTOR
06769           jmp     exception
```

```
06770
06771  !*===========================================================================*
06772  !*                              exception                                    *
06773  !*===========================================================================*
06774  ! This is called for all exceptions which do not push an error code.
06775
06776          .align  16
06777  exception:
06778   sseg   mov     (trap_errno), 0             ! clear trap_errno
06779   sseg   pop     (ex_number)
06780          jmp     exception1
06781
06782  !*===========================================================================*
06783  !*                              errexception                                 *
06784  !*===========================================================================*
06785  ! This is called for all exceptions which push an error code.
06786
06787          .align  16
06788  errexception:
06789   sseg   pop     (ex_number)
06790   sseg   pop     (trap_errno)
06791  exception1:                                 ! Common for all exceptions.
06792          push    eax                         ! eax is scratch register
06793          mov     eax, 0+4(esp)               ! old eip
06794   sseg   mov     (old_eip), eax
06795          movzx   eax, 4+4(esp)               ! old cs
06796   sseg   mov     (old_cs), eax
06797          mov     eax, 8+4(esp)               ! old eflags
06798   sseg   mov     (old_eflags), eax
06799          pop     eax
06800          call    save
06801          push    (old_eflags)
06802          push    (old_cs)
06803          push    (old_eip)
06804          push    (trap_errno)
06805          push    (ex_number)
06806          call    _exception                  ! (ex_number, trap_errno, old_eip,
06807                                              !       old_cs, old_eflags)
06808          add     esp, 5*4
06809          ret
06810
06811  !*===========================================================================*
06812  !*                              level0_call                                  *
06813  !*===========================================================================*
06814  _level0_call:
06815          call    save
06816          jmp     (_level0_func)
06817
06818  !*===========================================================================*
06819  !*                              data                                         *
06820  !*===========================================================================*
06821
06822  .sect .rom      ! Before the string table please
06823          .data2  0x526F              ! this must be the first data entry (magic #)
06824
06825  .sect .bss
06826  k_stack:
06827          .space  K_STACK_BYTES       ! kernel stack
06828  k_stktop:                           ! top of kernel stack
06829          .comm   ex_number, 4
```

```
06830            .comm    trap_errno, 4
06831            .comm    old_eip, 4
06832            .comm    old_cs, 4
06833            .comm    old_eflags, 4


++++++++++++++++++++++++++++++++++++++++++++++++++++++++++++++++++++++++++++++
                               kernel/start.c
++++++++++++++++++++++++++++++++++++++++++++++++++++++++++++++++++++++++++++++
06900  /* This file contains the C startup code for Minix on Intel processors.
06901   * It cooperates with mpx.s to set up a good environment for main().
06902   *
06903   * This code runs in real mode for a 16 bit kernel and may have to switch
06904   * to protected mode for a 286.
06905   * For a 32 bit kernel this already runs in protected mode, but the selectors
06906   * are still those given by the BIOS with interrupts disabled, so the
06907   * descriptors need to be reloaded and interrupt descriptors made.
06908   */
06909
06910  #include "kernel.h"
06911  #include "protect.h"
06912  #include "proc.h"
06913  #include <stdlib.h>
06914  #include <string.h>
06915
06916  FORWARD _PROTOTYPE( char *get_value, (_CONST char *params, _CONST char *key));
06917  /*===========================================================================*
06918   *                                cstart                                     *
06919   *===========================================================================*/
06920  PUBLIC void cstart(cs, ds, mds, parmoff, parmsize)
06921  U16_t cs, ds;                     /* kernel code and data segment */
06922  U16_t mds;                        /* monitor data segment */
06923  U16_t parmoff, parmsize;          /* boot parameters offset and length */
06924  {
06925  /* Perform system initializations prior to calling main(). Most settings are
06926   * determined with help of the environment strings passed by MINIX' loader.
06927   */
06928    char params[128*sizeof(char *)];              /* boot monitor parameters */
06929    register char *value;                         /* value in key=value pair */
06930    extern int etext, end;
06931
06932    /* Decide if mode is protected; 386 or higher implies protected mode.
06933     * This must be done first, because it is needed for, e.g., seg2phys().
06934     * For 286 machines we cannot decide on protected mode, yet. This is
06935     * done below.
06936     */
06937  #if _WORD_SIZE != 2
06938    machine.protected = 1;
06939  #endif
06940
06941    /* Record where the kernel and the monitor are. */
06942    kinfo.code_base = seg2phys(cs);
06943    kinfo.code_size = (phys_bytes) &etext;         /* size of code segment */
06944    kinfo.data_base = seg2phys(ds);
06945    kinfo.data_size = (phys_bytes) &end;           /* size of data segment */
06946
06947    /* Initialize protected mode descriptors. */
06948    prot_init();
06949
```

```
06950        /* Copy the boot parameters to the local buffer. */
06951        kinfo.params_base = seg2phys(mds) + parmoff;
06952        kinfo.params_size = MIN(parmsize,sizeof(params)-2);
06953        phys_copy(kinfo.params_base, vir2phys(params), kinfo.params_size);
06954
06955        /* Record miscellaneous information for user-space servers. */
06956        kinfo.nr_procs = NR_PROCS;
06957        kinfo.nr_tasks = NR_TASKS;
06958        strncpy(kinfo.release, OS_RELEASE, sizeof(kinfo.release));
06959        kinfo.release[sizeof(kinfo.release)-1] = '\0';
06960        strncpy(kinfo.version, OS_VERSION, sizeof(kinfo.version));
06961        kinfo.version[sizeof(kinfo.version)-1] = '\0';
06962        kinfo.proc_addr = (vir_bytes) proc;
06963        kinfo.kmem_base = vir2phys(0);
06964        kinfo.kmem_size = (phys_bytes) &end;
06965
06966      · /* Processor?  86, 186, 286, 386, ...
06967        * Decide if mode is protected for older machines.
06968        */
06969        machine.processor=atoi(get_value(params, "processor"));
06970    #if _WORD_SIZE == 2
06971        machine.protected = machine.processor >= 286;
06972    #endif
06973        if (! machine.protected) mon_return = 0;
06974
06975        /* XT, AT or MCA bus? */
06976        value = get_value(params, "bus");
06977        if (value == NIL_PTR || strcmp(value, "at") == 0) {
06978            machine.pc_at = TRUE;                      /* PC-AT compatible hardware */
06979        } else if (strcmp(value, "mca") == 0) {
06980            machine.pc_at = machine.ps_mca = TRUE;     /* PS/2 with micro channel */
06981        }
06982
06983        /* Type of VDU: */
06984        value = get_value(params, "video");           /* EGA or VGA video unit */
06985        if (strcmp(value, "ega") == 0) machine.vdu_ega = TRUE;
06986        if (strcmp(value, "vga") == 0) machine.vdu_vga = machine.vdu_ega = TRUE;
06987
06988        /* Return to assembler code to switch to protected mode (if 286),
06989        * reload selectors and call main().
06990        */
06991    }

06993    /*===========================================================================*
06994     *                              get_value                                     *
06995     *===========================================================================*/
06996
06997    PRIVATE char *get_value(params, name)
06998    _CONST char *params;                              /* boot monitor parameters */
06999    _CONST char *name;                                /* key to look up */
07000    {
07001    /* Get environment value - kernel version of getenv to avoid setting up the
07002     * usual environment array.
07003     */
07004      register _CONST char *namep;
07005      register char *envp;
07006
07007      for (envp = (char *) params; *envp != 0;) {
07008          for (namep = name; *namep != 0 && *namep == *envp; namep++, envp++)
07009              ;
```

```
07010            if (*namep == '\0' && *envp == '=') return(envp + 1);
07011            while (*envp++ != 0)
07012                    ;
07013    }
07014    return(NIL_PTR);
07015  }




++++++++++++++++++++++++++++++++++++++++++++++++++++++++++++++++++++++++++++
                                kernel/main.c
++++++++++++++++++++++++++++++++++++++++++++++++++++++++++++++++++++++++++++

07100  /* This file contains the main program of MINIX as well as its shutdown code.
07101   * The routine main() initializes the system and starts the ball rolling by
07102   * setting up the process table, interrupt vectors, and scheduling each task
07103   * to run to initialize itself.
07104   * The routine shutdown() does the opposite and brings down MINIX.
07105   *
07106   * The entries into this file are:
07107   *   main:             MINIX main program
07108   *   prepare_shutdown: prepare to take MINIX down
07109   *
07110   * Changes:
07111   *   Nov 24, 2004   simplified main() with system image  (Jorrit N. Herder)
07112   *   Aug 20, 2004   new prepare_shutdown() and shutdown()  (Jorrit N. Herder)
07113   */
07114  #include "kernel.h"
07115  #include <signal.h>
07116  #include <string.h>
07117  #include <unistd.h>
07118  #include <a.out.h>
07119  #include <minix/callnr.h>
07120  #include <minix/com.h>
07121  #include "proc.h"
07122
07123  /* Prototype declarations for PRIVATE functions. */
07124  FORWARD _PROTOTYPE( void announce, (void));
07125  FORWARD _PROTOTYPE( void shutdown, (timer_t *tp));
07126
07127  /*===========================================================================*
07128   *                                  main                                     *
07129   *===========================================================================*/
07130  PUBLIC void main()
07131  {
07132  /* Start the ball rolling. */
07133    struct boot_image *ip;        /* boot image pointer */
07134    register struct proc *rp;      /* process pointer */
07135    register struct priv *sp;      /* privilege structure pointer */
07136    register int i, s;
07137    int hdrindex;                  /* index to array of a.out headers */
07138    phys_clicks text_base;
07139    vir_clicks text_clicks, data_clicks;
07140    reg_t ktsb;                    /* kernel task stack base */
07141    struct exec e_hdr;             /* for a copy of an a.out header */
07142
07143    /* Initialize the interrupt controller. */
07144    intr_init(1);
```

```
07145
07146     /* Clear the process table. Anounce each slot as empty and set up mappings
07147      * for proc_addr() and proc_nr() macros. Do the same for the table with
07148      * privilege structures for the system processes.
07149      */
07150     for (rp = BEG_PROC_ADDR, i = -NR_TASKS; rp < END_PROC_ADDR; ++rp, ++i) {
07151         rp->p_rts_flags = SLOT_FREE;          /* initialize free slot */
07152         rp->p_nr = i;                         /* proc number from ptr */
07153         (pproc_addr + NR_TASKS)[i] = rp;      /* proc ptr from number */
07154     }
07155     for (sp = BEG_PRIV_ADDR, i = 0; sp < END_PRIV_ADDR; ++sp, ++i) {
07156         sp->s_proc_nr = NONE;                 /* initialize as free */
07157         sp->s_id = i;                         /* priv structure index */
07158         ppriv_addr[i] = sp;                   /* priv ptr from number */
07159     }
07160
07161     /* Set up proc table entries for tasks and servers.  The stacks of the
07162      * kernel tasks are initialized to an array in data space.  The stacks
07163      * of the servers have been added to the data segment by the monitor, so
07164      * the stack pointer is set to the end of the data segment.  All the
07165      * processes are in low memory on the 8086.  On the 386 only the kernel
07166      * is in low memory, the rest is loaded in extended memory.
07167      */
07168
07169     /* Task stacks. */
07170     ktsb = (reg_t) t_stack;
07171
07172     for (i=0; i < NR_BOOT_PROCS; ++i) {
07173         ip = &image[i];                        /* process' attributes */
07174         rp = proc_addr(ip->proc_nr);           /* get process pointer */
07175         rp->p_max_priority = ip->priority;     /* max scheduling priority */
07176         rp->p_priority = ip->priority;         /* current priority */
07177         rp->p_quantum_size = ip->quantum;      /* quantum size in ticks */
07178         rp->p_ticks_left = ip->quantum;        /* current credit */
07179         strncpy(rp->p_name, ip->proc_name, P_NAME_LEN); /* set process name */
07180         (void) get_priv(rp, (ip->flags & SYS_PROC));   /* assign structure */
07181         priv(rp)->s_flags = ip->flags;         /* process flags */
07182         priv(rp)->s_trap_mask = ip->trap_mask; /* allowed traps */
07183         priv(rp)->s_call_mask = ip->call_mask; /* kernel call mask */
07184         priv(rp)->s_ipc_to.chunk[0] = ip->ipc_to;  /* restrict targets */
07185         if (iskerneln(proc_nr(rp))) {          /* part of the kernel? */
07186             if (ip->stksize > 0) {             /* HARDWARE stack size is 0 */
07187                 rp->p_priv->s_stack_guard = (reg_t *) ktsb;
07188                 *rp->p_priv->s_stack_guard = STACK_GUARD;
07189             }
07190             ktsb += ip->stksize;        /* point to high end of stack */
07191             rp->p_reg.sp = ktsb;        /* this task's initial stack ptr */
07192             text_base = kinfo.code_base >> CLICK_SHIFT;
07193                                         /* processes that are in the kernel */
07194             hdrindex = 0;               /* all use the first a.out header */
07195         } else {
07196             hdrindex = 1 + i-NR_TASKS;      /* servers, drivers, INIT */
07197         }
07198
07199         /* The bootstrap loader created an array of the a.out headers at
07200          * absolute address 'aout'. Get one element to e_hdr.
07201          */
07202         phys_copy(aout + hdrindex * A_MINHDR, vir2phys(&e_hdr),
07203                                         (phys_bytes) A_MINHDR);
07204         /* Convert addresses to clicks and build process memory map */
```

```
07205                text_base = e_hdr.a_syms >> CLICK_SHIFT;
07206                text_clicks = (e_hdr.a_text + CLICK_SIZE-1) >> CLICK_SHIFT;
07207                if (!(e_hdr.a_flags & A_SEP)) text_clicks = 0;      /* common I&D */
07208                data_clicks = (e_hdr.a_total + CLICK_SIZE-1) >> CLICK_SHIFT;
07209                rp->p_memmap[T].mem_phys = text_base;
07210                rp->p_memmap[T].mem_len  = text_clicks;
07211                rp->p_memmap[D].mem_phys = text_base + text_clicks;
07212                rp->p_memmap[D].mem_len  = data_clicks;
07213                rp->p_memmap[S].mem_phys = text_base + text_clicks + data_clicks;
07214                rp->p_memmap[S].mem_vir  = data_clicks; /* empty - stack is in data */
07215
07216                /* Set initial register values.  The processor status word for tasks
07217                 * is different from that of other processes because tasks can
07218                 * access I/O; this is not allowed to less-privileged processes
07219                 */
07220                rp->p_reg.pc = (reg_t) ip->initial_pc;
07221                rp->p_reg.psw = (iskernelp(rp)) ? INIT_TASK_PSW : INIT_PSW;
07222
07223                /* Initialize the server stack pointer. Take it down one word
07224                 * to give crtso.s something to use as "argc".
07225                 */
07226                if (isusern(proc_nr(rp))) {                 /* user-space process? */
07227                        rp->p_reg.sp = (rp->p_memmap[S].mem_vir +
07228                                        rp->p_memmap[S].mem_len) << CLICK_SHIFT;
07229                        rp->p_reg.sp -= sizeof(reg_t);
07230                }
07231
07232                /* Set ready. The HARDWARE task is never ready. */
07233                if (rp->p_nr != HARDWARE) {
07234                        rp->p_rts_flags = 0;                /* runnable if no flags */
07235                        lock_enqueue(rp);                   /* add to scheduling queues */
07236                } else {
07237                        rp->p_rts_flags = NO_MAP;           /* prevent from running */
07238                }
07239
07240                /* Code and data segments must be allocated in protected mode. */
07241                alloc_segments(rp);
07242        }
07243
07244        /* We're definitely not shutting down. */
07245        shutdown_started = 0;
07246
07247        /* MINIX is now ready. All boot image processes are on the ready queue.
07248         * Return to the assembly code to start running the current process.
07249         */
07250        bill_ptr = proc_addr(IDLE);             /* it has to point somewhere */
07251        announce();                             /* print MINIX startup banner */
07252        restart();
07253 }
07254
07255 /*===========================================================================*
07256  *                              announce                                     *
07257  *===========================================================================*/
07258 PRIVATE void announce(void)
07259 {
07260   /* Display the MINIX startup banner. */
07261   kprintf("MINIX %s.%s."
07262        "Copyright 2006, Vrije Universiteit, Amsterdam, The Netherlands\n",
07263        OS_RELEASE, OS_VERSION);
07264
```

```
07265      /* Real mode, or 16/32-bit protected mode? */
07266      kprintf("Executing in %s mode.\n\n",
07267          machine.protected ? "32-bit protected" : "real");
07268  }

07270  /*===========================================================================*
07271   *                          prepare_shutdown                                 *
07272   *===========================================================================*/
07273  PUBLIC void prepare_shutdown(how)
07274  int how;
07275  {
07276  /* This function prepares to shutdown MINIX. */
07277      static timer_t shutdown_timer;
07278      register struct proc *rp;
07279      message m;
07280
07281      /* Show debugging dumps on panics. Make sure that the TTY task is still
07282       * available to handle them. This is done with help of a non-blocking send.
07283       * We rely on TTY to call sys_abort() when it is done with the dumps.
07284       */
07285      if (how == RBT_PANIC) {
07286          m.m_type = PANIC_DUMPS;
07287          if (nb_send(TTY_PROC_NR,&m)==OK)    /* don't block if TTY isn't ready */
07288              return;                         /* await sys_abort() from TTY */
07289      }
07290
07291      /* Send a signal to all system processes that are still alive to inform
07292       * them that the MINIX kernel is shutting down. A proper shutdown sequence
07293       * should be implemented by a user-space server. This mechanism is useful
07294       * as a backup in case of system panics, so that system processes can still
07295       * run their shutdown code, e.g, to synchronize the FS or to let the TTY
07296       * switch to the first console.
07297       */
07298      kprintf("Sending SIGKSTOP to system processes ...\n");
07299      for (rp=BEG_PROC_ADDR; rp<END_PROC_ADDR; rp++) {
07300          if (!isemptyp(rp) && (priv(rp)->s_flags & SYS_PROC) && !iskernelp(rp))
07301              send_sig(proc_nr(rp), SIGKSTOP);
07302      }
07303
07304      /* We're shutting down. Diagnostics may behave differently now. */
07305      shutdown_started = 1;
07306
07307      /* Notify system processes of the upcoming shutdown and allow them to be
07308       * scheduled by setting a watchog timer that calls shutdown(). The timer
07309       * argument passes the shutdown status.
07310       */
07311      kprintf("MINIX will now be shut down ...\n");
07312      tmr_arg(&shutdown_timer)->ta_int = how;
07313
07314      /* Continue after 1 second, to give processes a chance to get
07315       * scheduled to do shutdown work.
07316       */
07317      set_timer(&shutdown_timer, get_uptime() + HZ, shutdown);
07318  }

07320  /*===========================================================================*
07321   *                              shutdown                                     *
07322   *===========================================================================*/
07323  PRIVATE void shutdown(tp)
07324  timer_t *tp;
```

```
07325   {
07326   /* This function is called from prepare_shutdown or stop_sequence to bring
07327    * down MINIX. How to shutdown is in the argument: RBT_HALT (return to the
07328    * monitor), RBT_MONITOR (execute given code), RBT_RESET (hard reset).
07329    */
07330     int how = tmr_arg(tp)->ta_int;
07331     u16_t magic;
07332
07333     /* Now mask all interrupts, including the clock, and stop the clock. */
07334     outb(INT_CTLMASK, ~0);
07335     clock_stop();
07336
07337     if (mon_return && how != RBT_RESET) {
07338         /* Reinitialize the interrupt controllers to the BIOS defaults. */
07339         intr_init(0);
07340         outb(INT_CTLMASK, 0);
07341         outb(INT2_CTLMASK, 0);
07342
07343         /* Return to the boot monitor. Set the program if not already done. */
07344         if (how != RBT_MONITOR) phys_copy(vir2phys(""), kinfo.params_base, 1);
07345         level0(monitor);
07346     }
07347
07348     /* Reset the system by jumping to the reset address (real mode), or by
07349      * forcing a processor shutdown (protected mode). First stop the BIOS
07350      * memory test by setting a soft reset flag.
07351      */
07352     magic = STOP_MEM_CHECK;
07353     phys_copy(vir2phys(&magic), SOFT_RESET_FLAG_ADDR, SOFT_RESET_FLAG_SIZE);
07354     level0(reset);
07355   }
```

```
++++++++++++++++++++++++++++++++++++++++++++++++++++++++++++++++++++++++++++++
                              kernel/proc.c
++++++++++++++++++++++++++++++++++++++++++++++++++++++++++++++++++++++++++++++
```

```
07400   /* This file contains essentially all of the process and message handling.
07401    * Together with "mpx.s" it forms the lowest layer of the MINIX kernel.
07402    * There is one entry point from the outside:
07403    *
07404    *   sys_call:        a system call, i.e., the kernel is trapped with an INT
07405    *
07406    * As well as several entry points used from the interrupt and task level:
07407    *
07408    *   lock_notify:     notify a process of a system event
07409    *   lock_send:       send a message to a process
07410    *   lock_enqueue:    put a process on one of the scheduling queues
07411    *   lock_dequeue:    remove a process from the scheduling queues
07412    *
07413    * Changes:
07414    *   Aug 19, 2005     rewrote scheduling code  (Jorrit N. Herder)
07415    *   Jul 25, 2005     rewrote system call handling  (Jorrit N. Herder)
07416    *   May 26, 2005     rewrote message passing functions  (Jorrit N. Herder)
07417    *   May 24, 2005     new notification system call  (Jorrit N. Herder)
07418    *   Oct 28, 2004     nonblocking send and receive calls  (Jorrit N. Herder)
07419    *
```

```
07420        * The code here is critical to make everything work and is important for the
07421        * overall performance of the system. A large fraction of the code deals with
07422        * list manipulation. To make this both easy to understand and fast to execute
07423        * pointer pointers are used throughout the code. Pointer pointers prevent
07424        * exceptions for the head or tail of a linked list.
07425        *
07426        *   node_t *queue, *new_node;    // assume these as global variables
07427        *   node_t **xpp = &queue;       // get pointer pointer to head of queue
07428        *   while (*xpp != NULL)         // find last pointer of the linked list
07429        *       xpp = &(*xpp)->next;     // get pointer to next pointer
07430        *   *xpp = new_node;             // now replace the end (the NULL pointer)
07431        *   new_node->next = NULL;       // and mark the new end of the list
07432        *
07433        * For example, when adding a new node to the end of the list, one normally
07434        * makes an exception for an empty list and looks up the end of the list for
07435        * nonempty lists. As shown above, this is not required with pointer pointers.
07436        */
07437
07438       #include <minix/com.h>
07439       #include <minix/callnr.h>
07440       #include "kernel.h"
07441       #include "proc.h"
07442
07443       /* Scheduling and message passing functions. The functions are available to
07444        * other parts of the kernel through lock_...(). The lock temporarily disables
07445        * interrupts to prevent race conditions.
07446        */
07447       FORWARD _PROTOTYPE( int mini_send, (struct proc *caller_ptr, int dst,
07448                       message *m_ptr, unsigned flags) );
07449       FORWARD _PROTOTYPE( int mini_receive, (struct proc *caller_ptr, int src,
07450                       message *m_ptr, unsigned flags) );
07451       FORWARD _PROTOTYPE( int mini_notify, (struct proc *caller_ptr, int dst) );
07452
07453       FORWARD _PROTOTYPE( void enqueue, (struct proc *rp) );
07454       FORWARD _PROTOTYPE( void dequeue, (struct proc *rp) );
07455       FORWARD _PROTOTYPE( void sched, (struct proc *rp, int *queue, int *front) );
07456       FORWARD _PROTOTYPE( void pick_proc, (void) );
07457
07458       #define BuildMess(m_ptr, src, dst_ptr) \
07459               (m_ptr)->m_source = (src);                                      \
07460               (m_ptr)->m_type = NOTIFY_FROM(src);                             \
07461               (m_ptr)->NOTIFY_TIMESTAMP = get_uptime();                       \
07462               switch (src) {                                                  \
07463               case HARDWARE:                                                  \
07464                       (m_ptr)->NOTIFY_ARG = priv(dst_ptr)->s_int_pending;     \
07465                       priv(dst_ptr)->s_int_pending = 0;                       \
07466                       break;                                                  \
07467               case SYSTEM:                                                    \
07468                       (m_ptr)->NOTIFY_ARG = priv(dst_ptr)->s_sig_pending;     \
07469                       priv(dst_ptr)->s_sig_pending = 0;                       \
07470                       break;                                                  \
07471               }
07472
07473       #define CopyMess(s,sp,sm,dp,dm) \
07474               cp_mess(s, (sp)->p_memmap[D].mem_phys,  \
07475                       (vir_bytes)sm, (dp)->p_memmap[D].mem_phys, (vir_bytes)dm)
07476
```

```
07477  /*===========================================================================*
07478   *                              sys_call                                     *
07479   *===========================================================================*/
07480  PUBLIC int sys_call(call_nr, src_dst, m_ptr)
07481  int call_nr;                       /* system call number and flags */
07482  int src_dst;                       /* src to receive from or dst to send to */
07483  message *m_ptr;                    /* pointer to message in the caller's space */
07484  {
07485  /* System calls are done by trapping to the kernel with an INT instruction.
07486   * The trap is caught and sys_call() is called to send or receive a message
07487   * (or both). The caller is always given by 'proc_ptr'.
07488   */
07489    register struct proc *caller_ptr = proc_ptr;  /* get pointer to caller */
07490    int function = call_nr & SYSCALL_FUNC;        /* get system call function */
07491    unsigned flags = call_nr & SYSCALL_FLAGS;     /* get flags */
07492    int mask_entry;                               /* bit to check in send mask */
07493    int result;                                   /* the system call's result */
07494    vir_clicks vlo, vhi;            /* virtual clicks containing message to send */
07495
07496    /* Check if the process has privileges for the requested call. Calls to the
07497     * kernel may only be SENDREC, because tasks always reply and may not block
07498     * if the caller doesn't do receive().
07499     */
07500    if (! (priv(caller_ptr)->s_trap_mask & (1 << function)) ||
07501            (iskerneln(src_dst) && function != SENDREC
07502             && function != RECEIVE)) {
07503        kprintf("sys_call: trap %d not allowed, caller %d, src_dst %d\n",
07504            function, proc_nr(caller_ptr), src_dst);
07505        return(ECALLDENIED);                    /* trap denied by mask or kernel */
07506    }
07507
07508    /* Require a valid source and/ or destination process, unless echoing. */
07509    if (! (isokprocn(src_dst) || src_dst == ANY || function == ECHO)) {
07510        kprintf("sys_call: invalid src_dst, src_dst %d, caller %d\n",
07511            src_dst, proc_nr(caller_ptr));
07512        return(EBADSRCDST);                     /* invalid process number */
07513    }
07514
07515    /* If the call involves a message buffer, i.e., for SEND, RECEIVE, SENDREC,
07516     * or ECHO, check the message pointer. This check allows a message to be
07517     * anywhere in data or stack or gap. It will have to be made more elaborate
07518     * for machines which don't have the gap mapped.
07519     */
07520    if (function & CHECK_PTR) {
07521        vlo = (vir_bytes) m_ptr >> CLICK_SHIFT;
07522        vhi = ((vir_bytes) m_ptr + MESS_SIZE - 1) >> CLICK_SHIFT;
07523        if (vlo < caller_ptr->p_memmap[D].mem_vir || vlo > vhi ||
07524                vhi >= caller_ptr->p_memmap[S].mem_vir +
07525                caller_ptr->p_memmap[S].mem_len) {
07526            kprintf("sys_call: invalid message pointer, trap %d, caller %d\n",
07527                function, proc_nr(caller_ptr));
07528            return(EFAULT);                     /* invalid message pointer */
07529        }
07530    }
07531
07532    /* If the call is to send to a process, i.e., for SEND, SENDREC or NOTIFY,
07533     * verify that the caller is allowed to send to the given destination and
07534     * that the destination is still alive.
07535     */
07536    if (function & CHECK_DST) {
```

```
07537            if (! get_sys_bit(priv(caller_ptr)->s_ipc_to, nr_to_id(src_dst))) {
07538                kprintf("sys_call: ipc mask denied %d sending to %d\n",
07539                    proc_nr(caller_ptr), src_dst);
07540                return(ECALLDENIED);              /* call denied by ipc mask */
07541            }
07542
07543            if (isemptyn(src_dst) && !shutdown_started) {
07544                kprintf("sys_call: dead dest; %d, %d, %d\n",
07545                    function, proc_nr(caller_ptr), src_dst);
07546                return(EDEADDST);                /* cannot send to the dead */
07547            }
07548        }
07549
07550        /* Now check if the call is known and try to perform the request. The only
07551         * system calls that exist in MINIX are sending and receiving messages.
07552         *   - SENDREC: combines SEND and RECEIVE in a single system call
07553         *   - SEND:    sender blocks until its message has been delivered
07554         *   - RECEIVE: receiver blocks until an acceptable message has arrived
07555         *   - NOTIFY:  nonblocking call; deliver notification or mark pending
07556         *   - ECHO:    nonblocking call; directly echo back the message
07557         */
07558        switch(function) {
07559        case SENDREC:
07560            /* A flag is set so that notifications cannot interrupt SENDREC. */
07561            priv(caller_ptr)->s_flags |= SENDREC_BUSY;
07562            /* fall through */
07563        case SEND:
07564            result = mini_send(caller_ptr, src_dst, m_ptr, flags);
07565            if (function == SEND || result != OK) {
07566                break;                                  /* done, or SEND failed */
07567            }                                           /* fall through for SENDREC */
07568        case RECEIVE:
07569            if (function == RECEIVE)
07570                priv(caller_ptr)->s_flags &= ~SENDREC_BUSY;
07571            result = mini_receive(caller_ptr, src_dst, m_ptr, flags);
07572            break;
07573        case NOTIFY:
07574            result = mini_notify(caller_ptr, src_dst);
07575            break;
07576        case ECHO:
07577            CopyMess(caller_ptr->p_nr, caller_ptr, m_ptr, caller_ptr, m_ptr);
07578            result = OK;
07579            break;
07580        default:
07581            result = EBADCALL;                       /* illegal system call */
07582        }
07583
07584        /* Now, return the result of the system call to the caller. */
07585        return(result);
07586    }
07587
07588    /*===========================================================================*
07589     *                                mini_send                                   *
07590     *===========================================================================*/
07591    PRIVATE int mini_send(caller_ptr, dst, m_ptr, flags)
07592    register struct proc *caller_ptr;    /* who is trying to send a message? */
07593    int dst;                             /* to whom is message being sent? */
07594    message *m_ptr;                       /* pointer to message buffer */
07595    unsigned flags;                      /* system call flags */
07596    {
```

```
07597   /* Send a message from 'caller_ptr' to 'dst'. If 'dst' is blocked waiting
07598    * for this message, copy the message to it and unblock 'dst'. If 'dst' is
07599    * not waiting at all, or is waiting for another source, queue 'caller_ptr'.
07600    */
07601     register struct proc *dst_ptr = proc_addr(dst);
07602     register struct proc **xpp;
07603     register struct proc *xp;
07604
07605     /* Check for deadlock by 'caller_ptr' and 'dst' sending to each other. */
07606     xp = dst_ptr;
07607     while (xp->p_rts_flags & SENDING) {            /* check while sending */
07608             xp = proc_addr(xp->p_sendto);         /* get xp's destination */
07609             if (xp == caller_ptr) return(ELOCKED); /* deadlock if cyclic */
07610     }
07611
07612     /* Check if 'dst' is blocked waiting for this message. The destination's
07613      * SENDING flag may be set when its SENDREC call blocked while sending.
07614      */
07615     if ( (dst_ptr->p_rts_flags & (RECEIVING | SENDING)) == RECEIVING &&
07616         (dst_ptr->p_getfrom == ANY || dst_ptr->p_getfrom == caller_ptr->p_nr)) {
07617             /* Destination is indeed waiting for this message. */
07618             CopyMess(caller_ptr->p_nr, caller_ptr, m_ptr, dst_ptr,
07619                     dst_ptr->p_messbuf);
07620             if ((dst_ptr->p_rts_flags &= ~RECEIVING) == 0) enqueue(dst_ptr);
07621     } else if ( ! (flags & NON_BLOCKING)) {
07622             /* Destination is not waiting.  Block and dequeue caller. */
07623             caller_ptr->p_messbuf = m_ptr;
07624             if (caller_ptr->p_rts_flags == 0) dequeue(caller_ptr);
07625             caller_ptr->p_rts_flags |= SENDING;
07626             caller_ptr->p_sendto = dst;
07627
07628             /* Process is now blocked.  Put in on the destination's queue. */
07629             xpp = &dst_ptr->p_caller_q;               /* find end of list */
07630             while (*xpp != NIL_PROC) xpp = &(*xpp)->p_q_link;
07631             *xpp = caller_ptr;                        /* add caller to end */
07632             caller_ptr->p_q_link = NIL_PROC;          /* mark new end of list */
07633     } else {
07634             return(ENOTREADY);
07635     }
07636     return(OK);
07637   }

07639   /*===========================================================================*
07640    *                              mini_receive                                 *
07641    *===========================================================================*/
07642   PRIVATE int mini_receive(caller_ptr, src, m_ptr, flags)
07643   register struct proc *caller_ptr;        /* process trying to get message */
07644   int src;                                 /* which message source is wanted */
07645   message *m_ptr;                           /* pointer to message buffer */
07646   unsigned flags;                          /* system call flags */
07647   {
07648   /* A process or task wants to get a message.  If a message is already queued,
07649    * acquire it and deblock the sender.  If no message from the desired source
07650    * is available block the caller, unless the flags don't allow blocking.
07651    */
07652     register struct proc **xpp;
07653     register struct notification **ntf_q_pp;
07654     message m;
07655     int bit_nr;
07656     sys_map_t *map;
```

```
07657          bitchunk_t *chunk;
07658          int i, src_id, src_proc_nr;
07659
07660          /* Check to see if a message from desired source is already available.
07661           * The caller's SENDING flag may be set if SENDREC couldn't send. If it is
07662           * set, the process should be blocked.
07663           */
07664          if (!(caller_ptr->p_rts_flags & SENDING)) {
07665
07666              /* Check if there are pending notifications, except for SENDREC. */
07667              if (! (priv(caller_ptr)->s_flags & SENDREC_BUSY)) {
07668
07669                  map = &priv(caller_ptr)->s_notify_pending;
07670                  for (chunk=&map->chunk[0]; chunk<&map->chunk[NR_SYS_CHUNKS]; chunk++) {
07671
07672                      /* Find a pending notification from the requested source. */
07673                      if (! *chunk) continue;                       /* no bits in chunk */
07674                      for (i=0; ! (*chunk & (1<<i)); ++i) {}        /* look up the bit */
07675                      src_id = (chunk - &map->chunk[0]) * BITCHUNK_BITS + i;
07676                      if (src_id >= NR_SYS_PROCS) break;            /* out of range */
07677                      src_proc_nr = id_to_nr(src_id);               /* get source proc */
07678                      if (src!=ANY && src!=src_proc_nr) continue; /* source not ok */
07679                      *chunk &= ~(1 << i);                          /* no longer pending */
07680
07681                      /* Found a suitable source, deliver the notification message. */
07682                      BuildMess(&m, src_proc_nr, caller_ptr);       /* assemble message */
07683                      CopyMess(src_proc_nr, proc_addr(HARDWARE), &m, caller_ptr, m_ptr);
07684                      return(OK);                                   /* report success */
07685                  }
07686              }
07687
07688              /* Check caller queue. Use pointer pointers to keep code simple. */
07689              xpp = &caller_ptr->p_caller_q;
07690              while (*xpp != NIL_PROC) {
07691                  if (src == ANY || src == proc_nr(*xpp)) {
07692                      /* Found acceptable message. Copy it and update status. */
07693                      CopyMess((*xpp)->p_nr, *xpp, (*xpp)->p_messbuf, caller_ptr, m_ptr);
07694                      if (((*xpp)->p_rts_flags &= ~SENDING) == 0) enqueue(*xpp);
07695                      *xpp = (*xpp)->p_q_link;                      /* remove from queue */
07696                      return(OK);                                   /* report success */
07697                  }
07698                  xpp = &(*xpp)->p_q_link;                          /* proceed to next */
07699              }
07700          }
07701
07702          /* No suitable message is available or the caller couldn't send in SENDREC.
07703           * Block the process trying to receive, unless the flags tell otherwise.
07704           */
07705          if ( ! (flags & NON_BLOCKING)) {
07706              caller_ptr->p_getfrom = src;
07707              caller_ptr->p_messbuf = m_ptr;
07708              if (caller_ptr->p_rts_flags == 0) dequeue(caller_ptr);
07709              caller_ptr->p_rts_flags |= RECEIVING;
07710              return(OK);
07711          } else {
07712              return(ENOTREADY);
07713          }
07714      }
```

```
07716  /*===========================================================================*
07717   *                              mini_notify                                  *
07718   *===========================================================================*/
07719  PRIVATE int mini_notify(caller_ptr, dst)
07720  register struct proc *caller_ptr;       /* sender of the notification */
07721  int dst;                                 /* which process to notify */
07722  {
07723    register struct proc *dst_ptr = proc_addr(dst);
07724    int src_id;                            /* source id for late delivery */
07725    message m;                             /* the notification message */
07726
07727    /* Check to see if target is blocked waiting for this message. A process
07728     * can be both sending and receiving during a SENDREC system call.
07729     */
07730    if ((dst_ptr->p_rts_flags & (RECEIVING|SENDING)) == RECEIVING &&
07731        ! (priv(dst_ptr)->s_flags & SENDREC_BUSY) &&
07732        (dst_ptr->p_getfrom == ANY || dst_ptr->p_getfrom == caller_ptr->p_nr)) {
07733
07734        /* Destination is indeed waiting for a message. Assemble a notification
07735         * message and deliver it. Copy from pseudo-source HARDWARE, since the
07736         * message is in the kernel's address space.
07737         */
07738        BuildMess(&m, proc_nr(caller_ptr), dst_ptr);
07739        CopyMess(proc_nr(caller_ptr), proc_addr(HARDWARE), &m,
07740            dst_ptr, dst_ptr->p_messbuf);
07741        dst_ptr->p_rts_flags &= ~RECEIVING;       /* deblock destination */
07742        if (dst_ptr->p_rts_flags == 0) enqueue(dst_ptr);
07743        return(OK);
07744    }
07745
07746    /* Destination is not ready to receive the notification. Add it to the
07747     * bit map with pending notifications. Note the indirectness: the system id
07748     * instead of the process number is used in the pending bit map.
07749     */
07750    src_id = priv(caller_ptr)->s_id;
07751    set_sys_bit(priv(dst_ptr)->s_notify_pending, src_id);
07752    return(OK);
07753  }

07755  /*===========================================================================*
07756   *                              lock_notify                                  *
07757   *===========================================================================*/
07758  PUBLIC int lock_notify(src, dst)
07759  int src;                                 /* sender of the notification */
07760  int dst;                                 /* who is to be notified */
07761  {
07762  /* Safe gateway to mini_notify() for tasks and interrupt handlers. The sender
07763   * is explicitly given to prevent confusion where the call comes from. MINIX
07764   * kernel is not reentrant, which means to interrupts are disabled after
07765   * the first kernel entry (hardware interrupt, trap, or exception). Locking
07766   * is done by temporarily disabling interrupts.
07767   */
07768    int result;
07769
07770    /* Exception or interrupt occurred, thus already locked. */
07771    if (k_reenter >= 0) {
07772        result = mini_notify(proc_addr(src), dst);
07773    }
07774
07775    /* Call from task level, locking is required. */
```

```
07776        else {
07777            lock(0, "notify");
07778            result = mini_notify(proc_addr(src), dst);
07779            unlock(0);
07780        }
07781        return(result);
07782    }

07784    /*===========================================================================*
07785     *                                enqueue                                     *
07786     *===========================================================================*/
07787    PRIVATE void enqueue(rp)
07788    register struct proc *rp;        /* this process is now runnable */
07789    {
07790    /* Add 'rp' to one of the queues of runnable processes.  This function is
07791     * responsible for inserting a process into one of the scheduling queues.
07792     * The mechanism is implemented here.   The actual scheduling policy is
07793     * defined in sched() and pick_proc().
07794     */
07795      int q;                                 /* scheduling queue to use */
07796      int front;                             /* add to front or back */
07797
07798      /* Determine where to insert to process. */
07799      sched(rp, &q, &front);
07800
07801      /* Now add the process to the queue. */
07802      if (rdy_head[q] == NIL_PROC) {         /* add to empty queue */
07803          rdy_head[q] = rdy_tail[q] = rp;    /* create a new queue */
07804          rp->p_nextready = NIL_PROC;        /* mark new end */
07805      }
07806      else if (front) {                      /* add to head of queue */
07807          rp->p_nextready = rdy_head[q];     /* chain head of queue */
07808          rdy_head[q] = rp;                  /* set new queue head */
07809      }
07810      else {                                 /* add to tail of queue */
07811          rdy_tail[q]->p_nextready = rp;     /* chain tail of queue */
07812          rdy_tail[q] = rp;                  /* set new queue tail */
07813          rp->p_nextready = NIL_PROC;        /* mark new end */
07814      }
07815
07816      /* Now select the next process to run. */
07817      pick_proc();
07818    }

07820    /*===========================================================================*
07821     *                                dequeue                                     *
07822     *===========================================================================*/
07823    PRIVATE void dequeue(rp)
07824    register struct proc *rp;        /* this process is no longer runnable */
07825    {
07826    /* A process must be removed from the scheduling queues, for example, because
07827     * it has blocked.  If the currently active process is removed, a new process
07828     * is picked to run by calling pick_proc().
07829     */
07830      register int q = rp->p_priority;        /* queue to use */
07831      register struct proc **xpp;             /* iterate over queue */
07832      register struct proc *prev_xp;
07833
07834      /* Side-effect for kernel: check if the task's stack still is ok? */
07835      if (iskernelp(rp)) {
```

```
07836             if (*priv(rp)->s_stack_guard != STACK_GUARD)
07837                     panic("stack overrun by task", proc_nr(rp));
07838     }
07839
07840     /* Now make sure that the process is not in its ready queue. Remove the
07841      * process if it is found. A process can be made unready even if it is not
07842      * running by being sent a signal that kills it.
07843      */
07844     prev_xp = NIL_PROC;
07845     for (xpp = &rdy_head[q]; *xpp != NIL_PROC; xpp = &(*xpp)->p_nextready) {
07846
07847         if (*xpp == rp) {                          /* found process to remove */
07848             *xpp = (*xpp)->p_nextready;            /* replace with next chain */
07849             if (rp == rdy_tail[q])                 /* queue tail removed */
07850                 rdy_tail[q] = prev_xp;             /* set new tail */
07851             if (rp == proc_ptr || rp == next_ptr) /* active process removed */
07852                 pick_proc();                       /* pick new process to run */
07853             break;
07854         }
07855         prev_xp = *xpp;                            /* save previous in chain */
07856     }
07857 }


07859 /*===========================================================================*
07860  *                              sched                                         *
07861  *===========================================================================*/
07862 PRIVATE void sched(rp, queue, front)
07863 register struct proc *rp;                      /* process to be scheduled */
07864 int *queue;                                    /* return: queue to use */
07865 int *front;                                    /* return: front or back */
07866 {
07867 /* This function determines the scheduling policy.  It is called whenever a
07868  * process must be added to one of the scheduling queues to decide where to
07869  * insert it.  As a side-effect the process' priority may be updated.
07870  */
07871   static struct proc *prev_ptr = NIL_PROC;     /* previous without time */
07872   int time_left = (rp->p_ticks_left > 0);      /* quantum fully consumed */
07873   int penalty = 0;                             /* change in priority */
07874
07875   /* Check whether the process has time left. Otherwise give a new quantum
07876    * and possibly raise the priority.  Processes using multiple quantums
07877    * in a row get a lower priority to catch infinite loops in high priority
07878    * processes (system servers and drivers).
07879    */
07880   if ( ! time_left) {                           /* quantum consumed ? */
07881       rp->p_ticks_left = rp->p_quantum_size;   /* give new quantum */
07882       if (prev_ptr == rp) penalty ++;          /* catch infinite loops */
07883       else penalty --;                         /* give slow way back */
07884       prev_ptr = rp;                           /* store ptr for next */
07885   }
07886
07887   /* Determine the new priority of this process. The bounds are determined
07888    * by IDLE's queue and the maximum priority of this process. Kernel tasks
07889    * and the idle process are never changed in priority.
07890    */
07891   if (penalty != 0 && ! iskernelp(rp)) {
07892       rp->p_priority += penalty;               /* update with penalty */
07893       if (rp->p_priority < rp->p_max_priority) /* check upper bound */
07894           rp->p_priority=rp->p_max_priority;
07895       else if (rp->p_priority > IDLE_Q-1)      /* check lower bound */
```

```
07896                rp->p_priority = IDLE_Q-1;
07897      }
07898
07899      /* If there is time left, the process is added to the front of its queue,
07900       * so that it can immediately run. The queue to use simply is always the
07901       * process' current priority.
07902       */
07903      *queue = rp->p_priority;
07904      *front = time_left;
07905  }

07907  /*===========================================================================*
07908   *                              pick_proc                                     *
07909   *===========================================================================*/
07910  PRIVATE void pick_proc()
07911  {
07912  /* Decide who to run now.  A new process is selected by setting 'next_ptr'.
07913   * When a billable process is selected, record it in 'bill_ptr', so that the
07914   * clock task can tell who to bill for system time.
07915   */
07916    register struct proc *rp;                      /* process to run */
07917    int q;                                          /* iterate over queues */
07918
07919    /* Check each of the scheduling queues for ready processes. The number of
07920     * queues is defined in proc.h, and priorities are set in the image table.
07921     * The lowest queue contains IDLE, which is always ready.
07922     */
07923    for (q=0; q < NR_SCHED_QUEUES; q++) {
07924        if ( (rp = rdy_head[q]) != NIL_PROC) {
07925            next_ptr = rp;                          /* run process 'rp' next */
07926            if (priv(rp)->s_flags & BILLABLE)
07927                bill_ptr = rp;                      /* bill for system time */
07928            return;
07929        }
07930    }
07931  }

07933  /*===========================================================================*
07934   *                              lock_send                                     *
07935   *===========================================================================*/
07936  PUBLIC int lock_send(dst, m_ptr)
07937  int dst;                        /* to whom is message being sent? */
07938  message *m_ptr;                 /* pointer to message buffer */
07939  {
07940  /* Safe gateway to mini_send() for tasks. */
07941    int result;
07942    lock(2, "send");
07943    result = mini_send(proc_ptr, dst, m_ptr, NON_BLOCKING);
07944    unlock(2);
07945    return(result);
07946  }

07948  /*===========================================================================*
07949   *                              lock_enqueue                                  *
07950   *===========================================================================*/
07951  PUBLIC void lock_enqueue(rp)
07952  struct proc *rp;                /* this process is now runnable */
07953  {
07954  /* Safe gateway to enqueue() for tasks. */
07955    lock(3, "enqueue");
```

```
07956      enqueue(rp);
07957      unlock(3);
07958    }

07960    /*===========================================================================*
07961     *                              lock_dequeue                                 *
07962     *===========================================================================*/
07963    PUBLIC void lock_dequeue(rp)
07964    struct proc *rp;                    /* this process is no longer runnable */
07965    {
07966    /* Safe gateway to dequeue() for tasks. */
07967      lock(4, "dequeue");
07968      dequeue(rp);
07969      unlock(4);
07970    }
```

```
++++++++++++++++++++++++++++++++++++++++++++++++++++++++++++++++++++++++++++
                            kernel/exception.c
++++++++++++++++++++++++++++++++++++++++++++++++++++++++++++++++++++++++++++

08000    /* This file contains a simple exception handler.  Exceptions in user
08001     * processes are converted to signals. Exceptions in a kernel task cause
08002     * a panic.
08003     */
08004
08005    #include "kernel.h"
08006    #include <signal.h>
08007    #include "proc.h"
08008
08009    /*===========================================================================*
08010     *                              exception                                    *
08011     *===========================================================================*/
08012    PUBLIC void exception(vec_nr)
08013    unsigned vec_nr;
08014    {
08015    /* An exception or unexpected interrupt has occurred. */
08016
08017      struct ex_s {
08018          char *msg;
08019          int signum;
08020          int minprocessor;
08021      };
08022      static struct ex_s ex_data[] = {
08023          { "Divide error", SIGFPE, 86 },
08024          { "Debug exception", SIGTRAP, 86 },
08025          { "Nonmaskable interrupt", SIGBUS, 86 },
08026          { "Breakpoint", SIGEMT, 86 },
08027          { "Overflow", SIGFPE, 86 },
08028          { "Bounds check", SIGFPE, 186 },
08029          { "Invalid opcode", SIGILL, 186 },
08030          { "Coprocessor not available", SIGFPE, 186 },
08031          { "Double fault", SIGBUS, 286 },
08032          { "Copressor segment overrun", SIGSEGV, 286 },
08033          { "Invalid TSS", SIGSEGV, 286 },
08034          { "Segment not present", SIGSEGV, 286 },
```

```
08035              { "Stack exception", SIGSEGV, 286 },     /* STACK_FAULT already used */
08036              { "General protection", SIGSEGV, 286 },
08037              { "Page fault", SIGSEGV, 386 },          /* not close */
08038              { NIL_PTR, SIGILL, 0 },                  /* probably software trap */
08039              { "Coprocessor error", SIGFPE, 386 },
08040      };
08041      register struct ex_s *ep;
08042      struct proc *saved_proc;
08043
08044      /* Save proc_ptr, because it may be changed by debug statements. */
08045      saved_proc = proc_ptr;
08046
08047      ep = &ex_data[vec_nr];
08048
08049      if (vec_nr == 2) {              /* spurious NMI on some machines */
08050          kprintf("got spurious NMI\n");
08051          return;
08052      }
08053
08054      /* If an exception occurs while running a process, the k_reenter variable
08055       * will be zero. Exceptions in interrupt handlers or system traps will make
08056       * k_reenter larger than zero.
08057       */
08058      if (k_reenter == 0 && ! iskernelp(saved_proc)) {
08059          cause_sig(proc_nr(saved_proc), ep->signum);
08060          return;
08061      }
08062
08063      /* Exception in system code. This is not supposed to happen. */
08064      if (ep->msg == NIL_PTR || machine.processor < ep->minprocessor)
08065          kprintf("\nIntel-reserved exception %d\n", vec_nr);
08066      else
08067          kprintf("\n%s\n", ep->msg);
08068      kprintf("k_reenter = %d ", k_reenter);
08069      kprintf("process %d (%s), ", proc_nr(saved_proc), saved_proc->p_name);
08070      kprintf("pc = %u:0x%x", (unsigned) saved_proc->p_reg.cs,
08071      (unsigned) saved_proc->p_reg.pc);
08072
08073      panic("exception in a kernel task", NO_NUM);
08074  }
```

```
+++++++++++++++++++++++++++++++++++++++++++++++++++++++++++++++++++++++++++++
                              kernel/i8259.c
+++++++++++++++++++++++++++++++++++++++++++++++++++++++++++++++++++++++++++++
08100  /* This file contains routines for initializing the 8259 interrupt controller:
08101   *      put_irq_handler: register an interrupt handler
08102   *      rm_irq_handler: deregister an interrupt handler
08103   *      intr_handle:    handle a hardware interrupt
08104   *      intr_init:      initialize the interrupt controller(s)
08105   */
08106
08107  #include "kernel.h"
08108  #include "proc.h"
08109  #include <minix/com.h>
```

```
08110
08111  #define ICW1_AT          0x11      /* edge triggered, cascade, need ICW4 */
08112  #define ICW1_PC          0x13      /* edge triggered, no cascade, need ICW4 */
08113  #define ICW1_PS          0x19      /* level triggered, cascade, need ICW4 */
08114  #define ICW4_AT_SLAVE    0x01      /* not SFNM, not buffered, normal EOI, 8086 */
08115  #define ICW4_AT_MASTER   0x05      /* not SFNM, not buffered, normal EOI, 8086 */
08116  #define ICW4_PC_SLAVE    0x09      /* not SFNM, buffered, normal EOI, 8086 */
08117  #define ICW4_PC_MASTER   0x0D      /* not SFNM, buffered, normal EOI, 8086 */
08118
08119  #define set_vec(nr, addr)        ((void)0)
08120
08121  /*===========================================================================*
08122   *                              intr_init                                    *
08123   *===========================================================================*/
08124  PUBLIC void intr_init(mine)
08125  int mine;
08126  {
08127  /* Initialize the 8259s, finishing with all interrupts disabled.  This is
08128   * only done in protected mode, in real mode we don't touch the 8259s, but
08129   * use the BIOS locations instead.  The flag "mine" is set if the 8259s are
08130   * to be programmed for MINIX, or to be reset to what the BIOS expects.
08131   */
08132    int i;
08133
08134    intr_disable();
08135
08136      /* The AT and newer PS/2 have two interrupt controllers, one master,
08137       * one slaved at IRQ 2.  (We don't have to deal with the PC that
08138       * has just one controller, because it must run in real mode.)
08139       */
08140      outb(INT_CTL, machine.ps_mca ? ICW1_PS : ICW1_AT);
08141      outb(INT_CTLMASK, mine ? IRQ0_VECTOR : BIOS_IRQ0_VEC);
08142                                                    /* ICW2 for master */
08143      outb(INT_CTLMASK, (1 << CASCADE_IRQ));        /* ICW3 tells slaves */
08144      outb(INT_CTLMASK, ICW4_AT_MASTER);
08145      outb(INT_CTLMASK, ~(1 << CASCADE_IRQ));       /* IRQ 0-7 mask */
08146      outb(INT2_CTL, machine.ps_mca ? ICW1_PS : ICW1_AT);
08147      outb(INT2_CTLMASK, mine ? IRQ8_VECTOR : BIOS_IRQ8_VEC);
08148                                                    /* ICW2 for slave */
08149      outb(INT2_CTLMASK, CASCADE_IRQ);          /* ICW3 is slave nr */
08150      outb(INT2_CTLMASK, ICW4_AT_SLAVE);
08151      outb(INT2_CTLMASK, ~0);                       /* IRQ 8-15 mask */
08152
08153      /* Copy the BIOS vectors from the BIOS to the Minix location, so we
08154       * can still make BIOS calls without reprogramming the i8259s.
08155       */
08156      phys_copy(BIOS_VECTOR(0) * 4L, VECTOR(0) * 4L, 8 * 4L);
08157  }

08159  /*===========================================================================*
08160   *                            put_irq_handler                                *
08161   *===========================================================================*/
08162  PUBLIC void put_irq_handler(hook, irq, handler)
08163  irq_hook_t *hook;
08164  int irq;
08165  irq_handler_t handler;
08166  {
08167  /* Register an interrupt handler. */
08168    int id;
08169    irq_hook_t **line;
```

```
08170
08171      if (irq < 0 || irq >= NR_IRQ_VECTORS)
08172          panic("invalid call to put_irq_handler", irq);
08173
08174      line = &irq_handlers[irq];
08175      id = 1;
08176      while (*line != NULL) {
08177          if (hook == *line) return;         /* extra initialization */
08178          line = &(*line)->next;
08179          id <<= 1;
08180      }
08181      if (id == 0) panic("Too many handlers for irq", irq);
08182
08183      hook->next = NULL;
08184      hook->handler = handler;
08185      hook->irq = irq;
08186      hook->id = id;
08187      *line = hook;
08188
08189      irq_use |= 1 << irq;
08190  }

08192  /*===========================================================================*
08193   *                              rm_irq_handler                               *
08194   *===========================================================================*/
08195  PUBLIC void rm_irq_handler(hook)
08196  irq_hook_t *hook;
08197  {
08198  /* Unregister an interrupt handler. */
08199      int irq = hook->irq;
08200      int id = hook->id;
08201      irq_hook_t **line;
08202
08203      if (irq < 0 || irq >= NR_IRQ_VECTORS)
08204          panic("invalid call to rm_irq_handler", irq);
08205
08206      line = &irq_handlers[irq];
08207      while (*line != NULL) {
08208          if ((*line)->id == id) {
08209              (*line) = (*line)->next;
08210              if (! irq_handlers[irq]) irq_use &= ~(1 << irq);
08211              return;
08212          }
08213          line = &(*line)->next;
08214      }
08215      /* When the handler is not found, normally return here. */
08216  }

08218  /*===========================================================================*
08219   *                              intr_handle                                  *
08220   *===========================================================================*/
08221  PUBLIC void intr_handle(hook)
08222  irq_hook_t *hook;
08223  {
08224  /* Call the interrupt handlers for an interrupt with the given hook list.
08225   * The assembly part of the handler has already masked the IRQ, reenabled the
08226   * controller(s) and enabled interrupts.
08227   */
08228
08229      /* Call list of handlers for an IRQ. */
```

```
08230        while (hook != NULL) {
08231            /* For each handler in the list, mark it active by setting its ID bit,
08232             * call the function, and unmark it if the function returns true.
08233             */
08234            irq_actids[hook->irq] |= hook->id;
08235            if ((*hook->handler)(hook)) irq_actids[hook->irq] &= ~hook->id;
08236            hook = hook->next;
08237        }
08238
08239        /* The assembly code will now disable interrupts, unmask the IRQ if and only
08240         * if all active ID bits are cleared, and restart a process.
08241         */
08242    }
```

```
++++++++++++++++++++++++++++++++++++++++++++++++++++++++++++++++++++++++++++++
                              kernel/protect.c
++++++++++++++++++++++++++++++++++++++++++++++++++++++++++++++++++++++++++++++
```

```
08300    /* This file contains code for initialization of protected mode, to initialize
08301     * code and data segment descriptors, and to initialize global descriptors
08302     * for local descriptors in the process table.
08303     */
08304
08305    #include "kernel.h"
08306    #include "proc.h"
08307    #include "protect.h"
08308
08309    #define INT_GATE_TYPE    (INT_286_GATE | DESC_386_BIT)
08310    #define TSS_TYPE         (AVL_286_TSS  | DESC_386_BIT)
08311
08312    struct desctableptr_s {
08313      char limit[sizeof(u16_t)];
08314      char base[sizeof(u32_t)];                /* really u24_t + pad for 286 */
08315    };
08316
08317    struct gatedesc_s {
08318      u16_t offset_low;
08319      u16_t selector;
08320      u8_t pad;                          /* |000|XXXXX| ig & trpg, |XXXXXXXX| task g */
08321      u8_t p_dpl_type;                   /* |P|DL|0|TYPE| */
08322      u16_t offset_high;
08323    };
08324
08325    struct tss_s {
08326      reg_t backlink;
08327      reg_t sp0;                         /* stack pointer to use during interrupt */
08328      reg_t ss0;                         /* "   segment "  "       "        " */
08329      reg_t sp1;
08330      reg_t ss1;
08331      reg_t sp2;
08332      reg_t ss2;
08333      reg_t cr3;
08334      reg_t ip;
08335      reg_t flags;
08336      reg_t ax;
08337      reg_t cx;
08338      reg_t dx;
08339      reg_t bx;
```

```
08340        reg_t sp;
08341        reg_t bp;
08342        reg_t si;
08343        reg_t di;
08344        reg_t es;
08345        reg_t cs;
08346        reg_t ss;
08347        reg_t ds;
08348        reg_t fs;
08349        reg_t gs;
08350        reg_t ldt;
08351        u16_t trap;
08352        u16_t iobase;
08353   /* u8_t iomap[0]; */
08354   };
08355
08356   PUBLIC struct segdesc_s gdt[GDT_SIZE];          /* used in klib.s and mpx.s */
08357   PRIVATE struct gatedesc_s idt[IDT_SIZE];        /* zero-init so none present */
08358   PUBLIC struct tss_s tss;                        /* zero init */
08359
08360   FORWARD _PROTOTYPE( void int_gate, (unsigned vec_nr, vir_bytes offset,
08361                   unsigned dpl_type) );
08362   FORWARD _PROTOTYPE( void sdesc, (struct segdesc_s *segdp, phys_bytes base,
08363                   vir_bytes size) );
08364
08365   /*===========================================================================*
08366    *                              prot_init                                     *
08367    *===========================================================================*/
08368   PUBLIC void prot_init()
08369   {
08370   /* Set up tables for protected mode.
08371    * All GDT slots are allocated at compile time.
08372    */
08373     struct gate_table_s *gtp;
08374     struct desctableptr_s *dtp;
08375     unsigned ldt_index;
08376     register struct proc *rp;
08377
08378     static struct gate_table_s {
08379           _PROTOTYPE( void (*gate), (void) );
08380           unsigned char vec_nr;
08381           unsigned char privilege;
08382     }
08383     gate_table[] = {
08384           { divide_error, DIVIDE_VECTOR, INTR_PRIVILEGE },
08385           { single_step_exception, DEBUG_VECTOR, INTR_PRIVILEGE },
08386           { nmi, NMI_VECTOR, INTR_PRIVILEGE },
08387           { breakpoint_exception, BREAKPOINT_VECTOR, USER_PRIVILEGE },
08388           { overflow, OVERFLOW_VECTOR, USER_PRIVILEGE },
08389           { bounds_check, BOUNDS_VECTOR, INTR_PRIVILEGE },
08390           { inval_opcode, INVAL_OP_VECTOR, INTR_PRIVILEGE },
08391           { copr_not_available, COPROC_NOT_VECTOR, INTR_PRIVILEGE },
08392           { double_fault, DOUBLE_FAULT_VECTOR, INTR_PRIVILEGE },
08393           { copr_seg_overrun, COPROC_SEG_VECTOR, INTR_PRIVILEGE },
08394           { inval_tss, INVAL_TSS_VECTOR, INTR_PRIVILEGE },
08395           { segment_not_present, SEG_NOT_VECTOR, INTR_PRIVILEGE },
08396           { stack_exception, STACK_FAULT_VECTOR, INTR_PRIVILEGE },
08397           { general_protection, PROTECTION_VECTOR, INTR_PRIVILEGE },
08398           { page_fault, PAGE_FAULT_VECTOR, INTR_PRIVILEGE },
08399           { copr_error, COPROC_ERR_VECTOR, INTR_PRIVILEGE },
```

```
08400              { hwint00, VECTOR( 0), INTR_PRIVILEGE },
08401              { hwint01, VECTOR( 1), INTR_PRIVILEGE },
08402              { hwint02, VECTOR( 2), INTR_PRIVILEGE },
08403              { hwint03, VECTOR( 3), INTR_PRIVILEGE },
08404              { hwint04, VECTOR( 4), INTR_PRIVILEGE },
08405              { hwint05, VECTOR( 5), INTR_PRIVILEGE },
08406              { hwint06, VECTOR( 6), INTR_PRIVILEGE },
08407              { hwint07, VECTOR( 7), INTR_PRIVILEGE },
08408              { hwint08, VECTOR( 8), INTR_PRIVILEGE },
08409              { hwint09, VECTOR( 9), INTR_PRIVILEGE },
08410              { hwint10, VECTOR(10), INTR_PRIVILEGE },
08411              { hwint11, VECTOR(11), INTR_PRIVILEGE },
08412              { hwint12, VECTOR(12), INTR_PRIVILEGE },
08413              { hwint13, VECTOR(13), INTR_PRIVILEGE },
08414              { hwint14, VECTOR(14), INTR_PRIVILEGE },
08415              { hwint15, VECTOR(15), INTR_PRIVILEGE },
08416              { s_call, SYS386_VECTOR, USER_PRIVILEGE },        /* 386 system call */
08417              { level0_call, LEVEL0_VECTOR, TASK_PRIVILEGE },
08418          };
08419
08420          /* Build gdt and idt pointers in GDT where the BIOS expects them. */
08421          dtp= (struct desctableptr_s *) &gdt[GDT_INDEX];
08422          * (u16_t *) dtp->limit = (sizeof gdt) - 1;
08423          * (u32_t *) dtp->base = vir2phys(gdt);
08424
08425          dtp= (struct desctableptr_s *) &gdt[IDT_INDEX];
08426          * (u16_t *) dtp->limit = (sizeof idt) - 1;
08427          * (u32_t *) dtp->base = vir2phys(idt);
08428
08429          /* Build segment descriptors for tasks and interrupt handlers. */
08430          init_codeseg(&gdt[CS_INDEX],
08431                  kinfo.code_base, kinfo.code_size, INTR_PRIVILEGE);
08432          init_dataseg(&gdt[DS_INDEX],
08433                  kinfo.data_base, kinfo.data_size, INTR_PRIVILEGE);
08434          init_dataseg(&gdt[ES_INDEX], 0L, 0, TASK_PRIVILEGE);
08435
08436          /* Build scratch descriptors for functions in klib88. */
08437          init_dataseg(&gdt[DS_286_INDEX], 0L, 0, TASK_PRIVILEGE);
08438          init_dataseg(&gdt[ES_286_INDEX], 0L, 0, TASK_PRIVILEGE);
08439
08440          /* Build local descriptors in GDT for LDT's in process table.
08441           * The LDT's are allocated at compile time in the process table, and
08442           * initialized whenever a process' map is initialized or changed.
08443           */
08444          for (rp = BEG_PROC_ADDR, ldt_index = FIRST_LDT_INDEX;
08445               rp < END_PROC_ADDR; ++rp, ldt_index++) {
08446              init_dataseg(&gdt[ldt_index], vir2phys(rp->p_ldt),
08447                                      sizeof(rp->p_ldt), INTR_PRIVILEGE);
08448              gdt[ldt_index].access = PRESENT | LDT;
08449              rp->p_ldt_sel = ldt_index * DESC_SIZE;
08450          }
08451
08452          /* Build main TSS.
08453           * This is used only to record the stack pointer to be used after an
08454           * interrupt.
08455           * The pointer is set up so that an interrupt automatically saves the
08456           * current process's registers ip:cs:f:sp:ss in the correct slots in the
08457           * process table.
08458           */
08459          tss.ss0 = DS_SELECTOR;
```

```
08460    init_dataseg(&gdt[TSS_INDEX], vir2phys(&tss), sizeof(tss), INTR_PRIVILEGE);
08461    gdt[TSS_INDEX].access = PRESENT | (INTR_PRIVILEGE << DPL_SHIFT) | TSS_TYPE;
08462
08463    /* Build descriptors for interrupt gates in IDT. */
08464    for (gtp = &gate_table[0];
08465        gtp < &gate_table[sizeof gate_table / sizeof gate_table[0]]; ++gtp) {
08466        int_gate(gtp->vec_nr, (vir_bytes) gtp->gate,
08467                PRESENT | INT_GATE_TYPE | (gtp->privilege << DPL_SHIFT));
08468    }
08469
08470    /* Complete building of main TSS. */
08471    tss.iobase = sizeof tss;        /* empty i/o permissions map */
08472  }

08474  /*===========================================================================*
08475   *                              init_codeseg                                 *
08476   *===========================================================================*/
08477  PUBLIC void init_codeseg(segdp, base, size, privilege)
08478  register struct segdesc_s *segdp;
08479  phys_bytes base;
08480  vir_bytes size;
08481  int privilege;
08482  {
08483  /* Build descriptor for a code segment. */
08484    sdesc(segdp, base, size);
08485    segdp->access = (privilege << DPL_SHIFT)
08486                | (PRESENT | SEGMENT | EXECUTABLE | READABLE);
08487                /* CONFORMING = 0, ACCESSED = 0 */
08488  }

08490  /*===========================================================================*
08491   *                              init_dataseg                                 *
08492   *===========================================================================*/
08493  PUBLIC void init_dataseg(segdp, base, size, privilege)
08494  register struct segdesc_s *segdp;
08495  phys_bytes base;
08496  vir_bytes size;
08497  int privilege;
08498  {
08499  /* Build descriptor for a data segment. */
08500    sdesc(segdp, base, size);
08501    segdp->access = (privilege << DPL_SHIFT) | (PRESENT | SEGMENT | WRITEABLE);
08502                /* EXECUTABLE = 0, EXPAND_DOWN = 0, ACCESSED = 0 */
08503  }

08505  /*===========================================================================*
08506   *                                 sdesc                                     *
08507   *===========================================================================*/
08508  PRIVATE void sdesc(segdp, base, size)
08509  register struct segdesc_s *segdp;
08510  phys_bytes base;
08511  vir_bytes size;
08512  {
08513  /* Fill in the size fields (base, limit and granularity) of a descriptor. */
08514    segdp->base_low = base;
08515    segdp->base_middle = base >> BASE_MIDDLE_SHIFT;
08516    segdp->base_high = base >> BASE_HIGH_SHIFT;
08517
08518    --size;                            /* convert to a limit, 0 size means 4G */
08519    if (size > BYTE_GRAN_MAX) {
```

```
08520                    segdp->limit_low = size >> PAGE_GRAN_SHIFT;
08521                    segdp->granularity = GRANULAR | (size >>
08522                                            (PAGE_GRAN_SHIFT + GRANULARITY_SHIFT));
08523          } else {
08524                    segdp->limit_low = size;
08525                    segdp->granularity = size >> GRANULARITY_SHIFT;
08526          }
08527          segdp->granularity |= DEFAULT;         /* means BIG for data seg */
08528    }

08530    /*===========================================================================*
08531     *                              seg2phys                                     *
08532     *===========================================================================*/
08533    PUBLIC phys_bytes seg2phys(seg)
08534    U16_t seg;
08535    {
08536    /* Return the base address of a segment, with seg being either a 8086 segment
08537     * register, or a 286/386 segment selector.
08538     */
08539      phys_bytes base;
08540      struct segdesc_s *segdp;
08541
08542      if (! machine.protected) {
08543            base = hclick_to_physb(seg);
08544      } else {
08545            segdp = &gdt[seg >> 3];
08546            base =    ((u32_t) segdp->base_low << 0)
08547                    | ((u32_t) segdp->base_middle << 16)
08548                    | ((u32_t) segdp->base_high << 24);
08549      }
08550      return base;
08551    }

08553    /*===========================================================================*
08554     *                              phys2seg                                     *
08555     *===========================================================================*/
08556    PUBLIC void phys2seg(seg, off, phys)
08557    u16_t *seg;
08558    vir_bytes *off;
08559    phys_bytes phys;
08560    {
08561    /* Return a segment selector and offset that can be used to reach a physical
08562     * address, for use by a driver doing memory I/O in the A0000 - DFFFF range.
08563     */
08564      *seg = FLAT_DS_SELECTOR;
08565      *off = phys;
08566    }

08568    /*===========================================================================*
08569     *                              int_gate                                     *
08570     *===========================================================================*/
08571    PRIVATE void int_gate(vec_nr, offset, dpl_type)
08572    unsigned vec_nr;
08573    vir_bytes offset;
08574    unsigned dpl_type;
08575    {
08576    /* Build descriptor for an interrupt gate. */
08577      register struct gatedesc_s *idp;
08578
08579      idp = &idt[vec_nr];
```

```
08580      idp->offset_low = offset;
08581      idp->selector = CS_SELECTOR;
08582      idp->p_dpl_type = dpl_type;
08583      idp->offset_high = offset >> OFFSET_HIGH_SHIFT;
08584    }

08586    /*===========================================================================*
08587     *                              enable_iop                                    *
08588     *===========================================================================*/
08589    PUBLIC void enable_iop(pp)
08590    struct proc *pp;
08591    {
08592    /* Allow a user process to use I/O instructions.  Change the I/O Permission
08593     * Level bits in the psw. These specify least-privileged Current Permission
08594     * Level allowed to execute I/O instructions. Users and servers have CPL 3.
08595     * You can't have less privilege than that. Kernel has CPL 0, tasks CPL 1.
08596     */
08597      pp->p_reg.psw |= 0x3000;
08598    }

08600    /*===========================================================================*
08601     *                              alloc_segments                                *
08602     *===========================================================================*/
08603    PUBLIC void alloc_segments(rp)
08604    register struct proc *rp;
08605    {
08606    /* This is called at system initialization from main() and by do_newmap().
08607     * The code has a separate function because of all hardware-dependencies.
08608     * Note that IDLE is part of the kernel and gets TASK_PRIVILEGE here.
08609     */
08610      phys_bytes code_bytes;
08611      phys_bytes data_bytes;
08612      int privilege;
08613
08614      if (machine.protected) {
08615          data_bytes = (phys_bytes) (rp->p_memmap[S].mem_vir +
08616              rp->p_memmap[S].mem_len) << CLICK_SHIFT;
08617          if (rp->p_memmap[T].mem_len == 0)
08618              code_bytes = data_bytes;        /* common I&D, poor protect */
08619          else
08620              code_bytes = (phys_bytes) rp->p_memmap[T].mem_len << CLICK_SHIFT;
08621          privilege = (iskernelp(rp)) ? TASK_PRIVILEGE : USER_PRIVILEGE;
08622          init_codeseg(&rp->p_ldt[CS_LDT_INDEX],
08623              (phys_bytes) rp->p_memmap[T].mem_phys << CLICK_SHIFT,
08624              code_bytes, privilege);
08625          init_dataseg(&rp->p_ldt[DS_LDT_INDEX],
08626              (phys_bytes) rp->p_memmap[D].mem_phys << CLICK_SHIFT,
08627              data_bytes, privilege);
08628          rp->p_reg.cs = (CS_LDT_INDEX * DESC_SIZE) | TI | privilege;
08629          rp->p_reg.gs =
08630          rp->p_reg.fs =
08631          rp->p_reg.ss =
08632          rp->p_reg.es =
08633          rp->p_reg.ds = (DS_LDT_INDEX*DESC_SIZE) | TI | privilege;
08634      } else {
08635          rp->p_reg.cs = click_to_hclick(rp->p_memmap[T].mem_phys);
08636          rp->p_reg.ss =
08637          rp->p_reg.es =
08638          rp->p_reg.ds = click_to_hclick(rp->p_memmap[D].mem_phys);
08639      }
```

```
08640    }




++++++++++++++++++++++++++++++++++++++++++++++++++++++++++++++++++++++++++++++
                                kernel/klib.s
++++++++++++++++++++++++++++++++++++++++++++++++++++++++++++++++++++++++++++++

08700    #
08701    ! Chooses between the 8086 and 386 versions of the low level kernel code.
08702
08703    #include <minix/config.h>
08704    #if _WORD_SIZE == 2
08705    #include "klib88.s"
08706    #else
08707    #include "klib386.s"
08708    #endif




++++++++++++++++++++++++++++++++++++++++++++++++++++++++++++++++++++++++++++++
                              kernel/klib386.s
++++++++++++++++++++++++++++++++++++++++++++++++++++++++++++++++++++++++++++++

08800    #
08801    ! sections
08802
08803    .sect .text; .sect .rom; .sect .data; .sect .bss
08804
08805    #include <minix/config.h>
08806    #include <minix/const.h>
08807    #include "const.h"
08808    #include "sconst.h"
08809    #include "protect.h"
08810
08811    ! This file contains a number of assembly code utility routines needed by the
08812    ! kernel.  They are:
08813
08814    .define _monitor          ! exit Minix and return to the monitor
08815    .define _int86            ! let the monitor make an 8086 interrupt call
08816    .define _cp_mess          ! copies messages from source to destination
08817    .define _exit             ! dummy for library routines
08818    .define __exit            ! dummy for library routines
08819    .define ___exit           ! dummy for library routines
08820    .define ___main           ! dummy for GCC
08821    .define _phys_insw        ! transfer data from (disk controller) port to memory
08822    .define _phys_insb        ! likewise byte by byte
08823    .define _phys_outsw       ! transfer data from memory to (disk controller) port
08824    .define _phys_outsb       ! likewise byte by byte
08825    .define _enable_irq       ! enable an irq at the 8259 controller
08826    .define _disable_irq      ! disable an irq
08827    .define _phys_copy        ! copy data from anywhere to anywhere in memory
08828    .define _phys_memset      ! write pattern anywhere in memory
08829    .define _mem_rdw          ! copy one word from [segment:offset]
08830    .define _reset            ! reset the system
08831    .define _idle_task        ! task executed when there is no work
08832    .define _level0           ! call a function at level 0
08833    .define _read_tsc         ! read the cycle counter (Pentium and up)
08834    .define _read_cpu_flags   ! read the cpu flags
```

```
08835
08836   ! The routines only guarantee to preserve the registers the C compiler
08837   ! expects to be preserved (ebx, esi, edi, ebp, esp, segment registers, and
08838   ! direction bit in the flags).
08839
08840   .sect .text
08841   !*===========================================================================*
08842   !*                              monitor                                      *
08843   !*===========================================================================*
08844   ! PUBLIC void monitor();
08845   ! Return to the monitor.
08846
08847   _monitor:
08848           mov     esp, (_mon_sp)          ! restore monitor stack pointer
08849       o16 mov     dx, SS_SELECTOR         ! monitor data segment
08850           mov     ds, dx
08851           mov     es, dx
08852           mov     fs, dx
08853           mov     gs, dx
08854           mov     ss, dx
08855           pop     edi
08856           pop     esi
08857           pop     ebp
08858       o16 retf                            ! return to the monitor
08859
08860
08861   !*===========================================================================*
08862   !*                              int86                                        *
08863   !*===========================================================================*
08864   ! PUBLIC void int86();
08865   _int86:
08866           cmpb    (_mon_return), 0        ! is the monitor there?
08867           jnz     0f
08868           movb    ah, 0x01                ! an int 13 error seems appropriate
08869           movb    (_reg86+ 0), ah         ! reg86.w.f = 1 (set carry flag)
08870           movb    (_reg86+13), ah         ! reg86.b.ah = 0x01 = "invalid command"
08871           ret
08872   0:      push    ebp                     ! save C registers
08873           push    esi
08874           push    edi
08875           push    ebx
08876           pushf                           ! save flags
08877           cli                             ! no interruptions
08878
08879           inb     INT2_CTLMASK
08880           movb    ah, al
08881           inb     INT_CTLMASK
08882           push    eax                     ! save interrupt masks
08883           mov     eax, (_irq_use)         ! map of in-use IRQ's
08884           and     eax, ~[1<<CLOCK_IRQ]    ! keep the clock ticking
08885           outb    INT_CTLMASK             ! enable all unused IRQ's and vv.
08886           movb    al, ah
08887           outb    INT2_CTLMASK
08888
08889           mov     eax, SS_SELECTOR        ! monitor data segment
08890           mov     ss, ax
08891           xchg    esp, (_mon_sp)          ! switch stacks
08892           push    (_reg86+36)             ! parameters used in INT call
08893           push    (_reg86+32)
08894           push    (_reg86+28)
```

```
08895              push      (_reg86+24)
08896              push      (_reg86+20)
08897              push      (_reg86+16)
08898              push      (_reg86+12)
08899              push      (_reg86+ 8)
08900              push      (_reg86+ 4)
08901              push      (_reg86+ 0)
08902              mov       ds, ax                  ! remaining data selectors
08903              mov       es, ax
08904              mov       fs, ax
08905              mov       gs, ax
08906              push      cs
08907              push      return                  ! kernel return address and selector
08908        o16 jmpf       20+2*4+10*4+2*4(esp)    ! make the call
08909   return:
08910              pop       (_reg86+ 0)
08911              pop       (_reg86+ 4)
08912              pop       (_reg86+ 8)
08913              pop       (_reg86+12)
08914              pop       (_reg86+16)
08915              pop       (_reg86+20)
08916              pop       (_reg86+24)
08917              pop       (_reg86+28)
08918              pop       (_reg86+32)
08919              pop       (_reg86+36)
08920              lgdt      (_gdt+GDT_SELECTOR)      ! reload global descriptor table
08921              jmpf      CS_SELECTOR:csinit       ! restore everything
08922   csinit: mov        eax, DS_SELECTOR
08923              mov       ds, ax
08924              mov       es, ax
08925              mov       fs, ax
08926              mov       gs, ax
08927              mov       ss, ax
08928              xchg      esp, (_mon_sp)          ! unswitch stacks
08929              lidt      (_gdt+IDT_SELECTOR)      ! reload interrupt descriptor table
08930              andb      (_gdt+TSS_SELECTOR+DESC_ACCESS), ~0x02  ! clear TSS busy bit
08931              mov       eax, TSS_SELECTOR
08932              ltr       ax                      ! set TSS register
08933
08934              pop       eax
08935              outb      INT_CTLMASK             ! restore interrupt masks
08936              movb      al, ah
08937              outb      INT2_CTLMASK
08938
08939              add       (_lost_ticks), ecx      ! record lost clock ticks
08940
08941              popf                              ! restore flags
08942              pop       ebx                     ! restore C registers
08943              pop       edi
08944              pop       esi
08945              pop       ebp
08946              ret
08947
08948
08949   !*===========================================================================*
08950   !*                              cp_mess                                      *
08951   !*===========================================================================*
08952   ! PUBLIC void cp_mess(int src, phys_clicks src_clicks, vir_bytes src_offset,
08953   !                      phys_clicks dst_clicks, vir_bytes dst_offset);
08954   ! This routine makes a fast copy of a message from anywhere in the address
```

```
08955    ! space to anywhere else.  It also copies the source address provided as a
08956    ! parameter to the call into the first word of the destination message.
08957    !
08958    ! Note that the message size, "Msize" is in DWORDS (not bytes) and must be set
08959    ! correctly.  Changing the definition of message in the type file and not
08960    ! changing it here will lead to total disaster.
08961
08962    CM_ARGS =        4 + 4 + 4 + 4 + 4        ! 4 + 4 + 4 + 4 + 4
08963    !                es  ds edi esi eip        proc scl sof dcl dof
08964    !
08965            .align  16
08966    _cp_mess:
08967            cld
08968            push    esi
08969            push    edi
08970            push    ds
08971            push    es
08972
08973            mov     eax, FLAT_DS_SELECTOR
08974            mov     ds, ax
08975            mov     es, ax
08976
08977            mov     esi, CM_ARGS+4(esp)              ! src clicks
08978            shl     esi, CLICK_SHIFT
08979            add     esi, CM_ARGS+4+4(esp)            ! src offset
08980            mov     edi, CM_ARGS+4+4+4(esp)          ! dst clicks
08981            shl     edi, CLICK_SHIFT
08982            add     edi, CM_ARGS+4+4+4+4(esp)        ! dst offset
08983
08984            mov     eax, CM_ARGS(esp)        ! process number of sender
08985            stos                             ! copy number of sender to dest message
08986            add     esi, 4                   ! do not copy first word
08987            mov     ecx, Msize - 1           ! remember, first word does not count
08988            rep
08989            movs                             ! copy the message
08990
08991            pop     es
08992            pop     ds
08993            pop     edi
08994            pop     esi
08995            ret                              ! that is all folks!
08996
08997
08998    !*========================================================================*
08999    !*                              exit                                      *
09000    !*========================================================================*
09001    ! PUBLIC void exit();
09002    ! Some library routines use exit, so provide a dummy version.
09003    ! Actual calls to exit cannot occur in the kernel.
09004    ! GNU CC likes to call ___main from main() for nonobvious reasons.
09005
09006    _exit:
09007    __exit:
09008    ___exit:
09009            sti
09010            jmp     ___exit
09011
09012    ___main:
09013            ret
09014
```

```
09015
09016   !*===========================================================================*
09017   !*                              phys_insw                                    *
09018   !*===========================================================================*
09019   ! PUBLIC void phys_insw(Port_t port, phys_bytes buf, size_t count);
09020   ! Input an array from an I/O port.  Absolute address version of insw().
09021
09022   _phys_insw:
09023           push    ebp
09024           mov     ebp, esp
09025           cld
09026           push    edi
09027           push    es
09028           mov     ecx, FLAT_DS_SELECTOR
09029           mov     es, cx
09030           mov     edx, 8(ebp)             ! port to read from
09031           mov     edi, 12(ebp)            ! destination addr
09032           mov     ecx, 16(ebp)            ! byte count
09033           shr     ecx, 1                  ! word count
09034   rep o16 ins                             ! input many words
09035           pop     es
09036           pop     edi
09037           pop     ebp
09038           ret
09039
09040
09041   !*===========================================================================*
09042   !*                              phys_insb                                    *
09043   !*===========================================================================*
09044   ! PUBLIC void phys_insb(Port_t port, phys_bytes buf, size_t count);
09045   ! Input an array from an I/O port.  Absolute address version of insb().
09046
09047   _phys_insb:
09048           push    ebp
09049           mov     ebp, esp
09050           cld
09051           push    edi
09052           push    es
09053           mov     ecx, FLAT_DS_SELECTOR
09054           mov     es, cx
09055           mov     edx, 8(ebp)             ! port to read from
09056           mov     edi, 12(ebp)            ! destination addr
09057           mov     ecx, 16(ebp)            ! byte count
09058   !       shr     ecx, 1                  ! word count
09059      rep  insb                            ! input many bytes
09060           pop     es
09061           pop     edi
09062           pop     ebp
09063           ret
09064
09065
09066   !*===========================================================================*
09067   !*                              phys_outsw                                   *
09068   !*===========================================================================*
09069   ! PUBLIC void phys_outsw(Port_t port, phys_bytes buf, size_t count);
09070   ! Output an array to an I/O port.  Absolute address version of outsw().
09071
09072           .align  16
09073   _phys_outsw:
09074           push    ebp
```

```
09075              mov       ebp, esp
09076              cld
09077              push      esi
09078              push      ds
09079              mov       ecx, FLAT_DS_SELECTOR
09080              mov       ds, cx
09081              mov       edx, 8(ebp)           ! port to write to
09082              mov       esi, 12(ebp)          ! source addr
09083              mov       ecx, 16(ebp)          ! byte count
09084              shr       ecx, 1                ! word count
09085   rep o16 outs                              ! output many words
09086              pop       ds
09087              pop       esi
09088              pop       ebp
09089              ret
09090
09091
09092   !*===========================================================================*
09093   !*                            phys_outsb                                     *
09094   !*===========================================================================*
09095   ! PUBLIC void phys_outsb(Port_t port, phys_bytes buf, size_t count);
09096   ! Output an array to an I/O port.  Absolute address version of outsb().
09097
09098              .align    16
09099   _phys_outsb:
09100              push      ebp
09101              mov       ebp, esp
09102              cld
09103              push      esi
09104              push      ds
09105              mov       ecx, FLAT_DS_SELECTOR
09106              mov       ds, cx
09107              mov       edx, 8(ebp)           ! port to write to
09108              mov       esi, 12(ebp)          ! source addr
09109              mov       ecx, 16(ebp)          ! byte count
09110      rep   outsb                            ! output many bytes
09111              pop       ds
09112              pop       esi
09113              pop       ebp
09114              ret
09115
09116
09117   !*===========================================================================*
09118   !*                            enable_irq                                     *
09119   !*===========================================================================*/
09120   ! PUBLIC void enable_irq(irq_hook_t *hook)
09121   ! Enable an interrupt request line by clearing an 8259 bit.
09122   ! Equivalent C code for hook->irq < 8:
09123   !    if ((irq_actids[hook->irq] &= ~hook->id) == 0)
09124   !        outb(INT_CTLMASK, inb(INT_CTLMASK) & ~(1 << irq));
09125
09126              .align    16
09127   _enable_irq:
09128              push      ebp
09129              mov       ebp, esp
09130              pushf
09131              cli
09132              mov       eax, 8(ebp)           ! hook
09133              mov       ecx, 8(eax)           ! irq
09134              mov       eax, 12(eax)          ! id bit
```

```
09135              not     eax
09136              and     _irq_actids(ecx*4), eax ! clear this id bit
09137              jnz     en_done                 ! still masked by other handlers?
09138              movb    ah, ~1
09139              rolb    ah, cl                  ! ah = ~(1 << (irq % 8))
09140              mov     edx, INT_CTLMASK        ! enable irq < 8 at the master 8259
09141              cmpb    cl, 8
09142              jb      0f
09143              mov     edx, INT2_CTLMASK       ! enable irq >= 8 at the slave 8259
09144      0:      inb     dx
09145              andb    al, ah
09146              outb    dx                      ! clear bit at the 8259
09147      en_done:popf
09148              leave
09149              ret
09150
09151
09152      !*===========================================================================*
09153      !*                              disable_irq                                  *
09154      !*===========================================================================*/
09155      ! PUBLIC int disable_irq(irq_hook_t *hook)
09156      ! Disable an interrupt request line by setting an 8259 bit.
09157      ! Equivalent C code for irq < 8:
09158      !    irq_actids[hook->irq] |= hook->id;
09159      !    outb(INT_CTLMASK, inb(INT_CTLMASK) | (1 << irq));
09160      ! Returns true iff the interrupt was not already disabled.
09161
09162              .align  16
09163      _disable_irq:
09164              push    ebp
09165              mov     ebp, esp
09166              pushf
09167              cli
09168              mov     eax, 8(ebp)             ! hook
09169              mov     ecx, 8(eax)             ! irq
09170              mov     eax, 12(eax)            ! id bit
09171              or      _irq_actids(ecx*4), eax ! set this id bit
09172              movb    ah, 1
09173              rolb    ah, cl                  ! ah = (1 << (irq % 8))
09174              mov     edx, INT_CTLMASK        ! disable irq < 8 at the master 8259
09175              cmpb    cl, 8
09176              jb      0f
09177              mov     edx, INT2_CTLMASK       ! disable irq >= 8 at the slave 8259
09178      0:      inb     dx
09179              testb   al, ah
09180              jnz     dis_already             ! already disabled?
09181              orb     al, ah
09182              outb    dx                      ! set bit at the 8259
09183              mov     eax, 1                  ! disabled by this function
09184              popf
09185              leave
09186              ret
09187      dis_already:
09188              xor     eax, eax                ! already disabled
09189              popf
09190              leave
09191              ret
09192
09193
```

```
09194    !*===========================================================================*
09195    !*                                  phys_copy                                *
09196    !*===========================================================================*
09197    ! PUBLIC void phys_copy(phys_bytes source, phys_bytes destination,
09198    !                        phys_bytes bytecount);
09199    ! Copy a block of physical memory.
09200
09201    PC_ARGS =         4 + 4 + 4 + 4    ! 4 + 4 + 4
09202    !                 es edi esi eip   src dst len
09203
09204            .align  16
09205    _phys_copy:
09206            cld
09207            push    esi
09208            push    edi
09209            push    es
09210
09211            mov     eax, FLAT_DS_SELECTOR
09212            mov     es, ax
09213
09214            mov     esi, PC_ARGS(esp)
09215            mov     edi, PC_ARGS+4(esp)
09216            mov     eax, PC_ARGS+4+4(esp)
09217
09218            cmp     eax, 10                  ! avoid align overhead for small counts
09219            jb      pc_small
09220            mov     ecx, esi                 ! align source, hope target is too
09221            neg     ecx
09222            and     ecx, 3                   ! count for alignment
09223            sub     eax, ecx
09224            rep
09225      eseg movsb
09226            mov     ecx, eax
09227            shr     ecx, 2                   ! count of dwords
09228            rep
09229      eseg movs
09230            and     eax, 3
09231    pc_small:
09232            xchg    ecx, eax                 ! remainder
09233            rep
09234      eseg movsb
09235
09236            pop     es
09237            pop     edi
09238            pop     esi
09239            ret
09240
09241    !*===========================================================================*
09242    !*                                phys_memset                                *
09243    !*===========================================================================*
09244    ! PUBLIC void phys_memset(phys_bytes source, unsigned long pattern,
09245    !        phys_bytes bytecount);
09246    ! Fill a block of physical memory with pattern.
09247
09248            .align  16
09249    _phys_memset:
09250            push    ebp
09251            mov     ebp, esp
09252            push    esi
09253            push    ebx
```

```
09254          push      ds
09255          mov       esi, 8(ebp)
09256          mov       eax, 16(ebp)
09257          mov       ebx, FLAT_DS_SELECTOR
09258          mov       ds, bx
09259          mov       ebx, 12(ebp)
09260          shr       eax, 2
09261   fill_start:
09262          mov       (esi), ebx
09263          add       esi, 4
09264          dec       eax
09265          jnz       fill_start
09266          ! Any remaining bytes?
09267          mov       eax, 16(ebp)
09268          and       eax, 3
09269   remain_fill:
09270          cmp       eax, 0
09271          jz        fill_done
09272          movb      bl, 12(ebp)
09273          movb      (esi), bl
09274          add       esi, 1
09275          inc       ebp
09276          dec       eax
09277          jmp       remain_fill
09278   fill_done:
09279          pop       ds
09280          pop       ebx
09281          pop       esi
09282          pop       ebp
09283          ret
09284
09285   !*========================================================================*
09286   !*                              mem_rdw                                   *
09287   !*========================================================================*
09288   ! PUBLIC u16_t mem_rdw(U16_t segment, u16_t *offset);
09289   ! Load and return word at far pointer segment:offset.
09290
09291          .align    16
09292   _mem_rdw:
09293          mov       cx, ds
09294          mov       ds, 4(esp)              ! segment
09295          mov       eax, 4+4(esp)           ! offset
09296          movzx     eax, (eax)              ! word to return
09297          mov       ds, cx
09298          ret
09299
09300
09301   !*========================================================================*
09302   !*                              reset                                     *
09303   !*========================================================================*
09304   ! PUBLIC void reset();
09305   ! Reset the system by loading IDT with offset 0 and interrupting.
09306
09307   _reset:
09308          lidt      (idt_zero)
09309          int       3                       ! anything goes, the 386 will not like it
09310   .sect .data
09311   idt_zero:      .data4  0, 0
09312   .sect .text
09313
```

```
09314
09315    !*===========================================================================*
09316    !*                              idle_task                                    *
09317    !*===========================================================================*
09318    _idle_task:
09319    ! This task is called when the system has nothing else to do.  The HLT
09320    ! instruction puts the processor in a state where it draws minimum power.
09321            push    halt
09322            call    _level0         ! level0(halt)
09323            pop     eax
09324            jmp     _idle_task
09325    halt:
09326            sti
09327            hlt
09328            cli
09329            ret
09330
09331    !*===========================================================================*
09332    !*                              level0                                       *
09333    !*===========================================================================*
09334    ! PUBLIC void level0(void (*func)(void))
09335    ! Call a function at permission level 0.  This allows kernel tasks to do
09336    ! things that are only possible at the most privileged CPU level.
09337    !
09338    _level0:
09339            mov     eax, 4(esp)
09340            mov     (_level0_func), eax
09341            int     LEVEL0_VECTOR
09342            ret
09343
09344
09345    !*===========================================================================*
09346    !*                              read_tsc                                     *
09347    !*===========================================================================*
09348    ! PUBLIC void read_tsc(unsigned long *high, unsigned long *low);
09349    ! Read the cycle counter of the CPU. Pentium and up.
09350    .align 16
09351    _read_tsc:
09352    .data1 0x0f              ! this is the RDTSC instruction
09353    .data1 0x31              ! it places the TSC in EDX:EAX
09354            push ebp
09355            mov ebp, 8(esp)
09356            mov (ebp), edx
09357            mov ebp, 12(esp)
09358            mov (ebp), eax
09359            pop ebp
09360            ret
09361
09362    !*===========================================================================*
09363    !*                              read_flags                                   *
09364    !*===========================================================================*
09365    ! PUBLIC unsigned long read_cpu_flags(void);
09366    ! Read CPU status flags from C.
09367    .align 16
09368    _read_cpu_flags:
09369            pushf
09370            mov eax, (esp)
09371            popf
09372            ret
09373
```

```
++++++++++++++++++++++++++++++++++++++++++++++++++++++++++++++++++++++++++
                          kernel/utility.c
++++++++++++++++++++++++++++++++++++++++++++++++++++++++++++++++++++++++++
09400  /* This file contains a collection of miscellaneous procedures:
09401   *   panic:          abort MINIX due to a fatal error
09402   *   kprintf:        diagnostic output for the kernel
09403   *
09404   * Changes:
09405   *   Dec 10, 2004   kernel printing to circular buffer  (Jorrit N. Herder)
09406   *
09407   * This file contains the routines that take care of kernel messages, i.e.,
09408   * diagnostic output within the kernel. Kernel messages are not directly
09409   * displayed on the console, because this must be done by the output driver.
09410   * Instead, the kernel accumulates characters in a buffer and notifies the
09411   * output driver when a new message is ready.
09412   */
09413
09414  #include <minix/com.h>
09415  #include "kernel.h"
09416  #include <stdarg.h>
09417  #include <unistd.h>
09418  #include <stddef.h>
09419  #include <stdlib.h>
09420  #include <signal.h>
09421  #include "proc.h"
09422
09423  #define END_OF_KMESS    -1
09424  FORWARD _PROTOTYPE(void kputc, (int c));
09425
09426  /*===========================================================================*
09427   *                              panic                                        *
09428   *===========================================================================*/
09429  PUBLIC void panic(mess,nr)
09430  _CONST char *mess;
09431  int nr;
09432  {
09433  /* The system has run aground of a fatal kernel error. Terminate execution. */
09434    static int panicking = 0;
09435    if (panicking ++) return;              /* prevent recursive panics */
09436
09437    if (mess != NULL) {
09438        kprintf("\nKernel panic: %s", mess);
09439        if (nr != NO_NUM) kprintf(" %d", nr);
09440        kprintf("\n",NO_NUM);
09441    }
09442
09443    /* Abort MINIX. */
09444    prepare_shutdown(RBT_PANIC);
09445  }
09446
09447  /*===========================================================================*
09448   *                              kprintf                                      *
09449   *===========================================================================*/
09450  PUBLIC void kprintf(const char *fmt, ...)      /* format to be printed */
09451  {
09452    int c;                                       /* next character in fmt */
09453    int d;
09454    unsigned long u;                             /* hold number argument */
```

```
09455    int base;                                       /* base of number arg */
09456    int negative = 0;                               /* print minus sign */
09457    static char x2c[] = "0123456789ABCDEF";          /* nr conversion table */
09458    char ascii[8 * sizeof(long) / 3 + 2];           /* string for ascii number */
09459    char *s = NULL;                                  /* string to be printed */
09460    va_list argp;                                    /* optional arguments */
09461
09462    va_start(argp, fmt);                            /* init variable arguments */
09463
09464    while((c=*fmt++) != 0) {
09465
09466        if (c == '%') {                             /* expect format '%key' */
09467            switch(c = *fmt++) {                    /* determine what to do */
09468
09469            /* Known keys are %d, %u, %x, %s, and %%. This is easily extended
09470             * with number types like %b and %o by providing a different base.
09471             * Number type keys don't set a string to 's', but use the general
09472             * conversion after the switch statement.
09473             */
09474            case 'd':                               /* output decimal */
09475                d = va_arg(argp, signed int);
09476                if (d < 0) { negative = 1; u = -d; }  else { u = d; }
09477                base = 10;
09478                break;
09479            case 'u':                               /* output unsigned long */
09480                u = va_arg(argp, unsigned long);
09481                base = 10;
09482                break;
09483            case 'x':                               /* output hexadecimal */
09484                u = va_arg(argp, unsigned long);
09485                base = 0x10;
09486                break;
09487            case 's':                               /* output string */
09488                s = va_arg(argp, char *);
09489                if (s == NULL) s = "(null)";
09490                break;
09491            case '%':                               /* output percent */
09492                s = "%";
09493                break;
09494
09495            /* Unrecognized key. */
09496            default:                                /* echo back %key */
09497                s = "%?";
09498                s[1] = c;                           /* set unknown key */
09499            }
09500
09501            /* Assume a number if no string is set. Convert to ascii. */
09502            if (s == NULL) {
09503                s = ascii + sizeof(ascii)-1;
09504                *s = 0;
09505                do { *--s = x2c[(u % base)]; }        /* work backwards */
09506                while ((u /= base) > 0);
09507            }
09508
09509            /* This is where the actual output for format "%key" is done. */
09510            if (negative) kputc('-');                /* print sign if negative */
09511            while(*s != 0) { kputc(*s++); }          /* print string/ number */
09512            s = NULL;                                /* reset for next round */
09513        }
09514        else {
```

```
09515              kputc(c);                              /* print and continue */
09516          }
09517      }
09518      kputc(END_OF_KMESS);                           /* terminate output */
09519      va_end(argp);                                  /* end variable arguments */
09520  }

09522  /*===========================================================================*
09523   *                              kputc                                        *
09524   *===========================================================================*/
09525  PRIVATE void kputc(c)
09526  int c;                                    /* character to append */
09527  {
09528  /* Accumulate a single character for a kernel message. Send a notification
09529   * to the output driver if an END_OF_KMESS is encountered.
09530   */
09531      if (c != END_OF_KMESS) {
09532          kmess.km_buf[kmess.km_next] = c;   /* put normal char in buffer */
09533          if (kmess.km_size < KMESS_BUF_SIZE)
09534              kmess.km_size += 1;
09535          kmess.km_next = (kmess.km_next + 1) % KMESS_BUF_SIZE;
09536      } else {
09537          send_sig(OUTPUT_PROC_NR, SIGKMESS);
09538      }
09539  }
```

```
++++++++++++++++++++++++++++++++++++++++++++++++++++++++++++++++++++++++++++++
                              kernel/system.h
++++++++++++++++++++++++++++++++++++++++++++++++++++++++++++++++++++++++++++++
```

```
09600  /* Function prototypes for the system library.
09601   * The implementation is contained in src/kernel/system/.
09602   *
09603   * The system library allows access to system services by doing a kernel call.
09604   * Kernel calls are transformed into request messages to the SYS task that is
09605   * responsible for handling the call. By convention, sys_call() is transformed
09606   * into a message with type SYS_CALL that is handled in a function do_call().
09607   */
09608
09609  #ifndef SYSTEM_H
09610  #define SYSTEM_H
09611
09612  /* Common includes for the system library. */
09613  #include "kernel.h"
09614  #include "proto.h"
09615  #include "proc.h"
09616
09617  /* Default handler for unused kernel calls. */
09618  _PROTOTYPE( int do_unused, (message *m_ptr) );
09619  _PROTOTYPE( int do_exec, (message *m_ptr) );
09620  _PROTOTYPE( int do_fork, (message *m_ptr) );
09621  _PROTOTYPE( int do_newmap, (message *m_ptr) );
09622  _PROTOTYPE( int do_exit, (message *m_ptr) );
09623  _PROTOTYPE( int do_trace, (message *m_ptr) );
09624  _PROTOTYPE( int do_nice, (message *m_ptr) );
```

```
09625    _PROTOTYPE( int do_copy, (message *m_ptr) );
09626    #define do_vircopy        do_copy
09627    #define do_physcopy       do_copy
09628    _PROTOTYPE( int do_vcopy, (message *m_ptr) );
09629    #define do_virvcopy       do_vcopy
09630    #define do_physvcopy      do_vcopy
09631    _PROTOTYPE( int do_umap, (message *m_ptr) );
09632    _PROTOTYPE( int do_memset, (message *m_ptr) );
09633    _PROTOTYPE( int do_abort, (message *m_ptr) );
09634    _PROTOTYPE( int do_getinfo, (message *m_ptr) );
09635    _PROTOTYPE( int do_privctl, (message *m_ptr) );
09636    _PROTOTYPE( int do_segctl, (message *m_ptr) );
09637    _PROTOTYPE( int do_irqctl, (message *m_ptr) );
09638    _PROTOTYPE( int do_devio, (message *m_ptr) );
09639    _PROTOTYPE( int do_vdevio, (message *m_ptr) );
09640    _PROTOTYPE( int do_int86, (message *m_ptr) );
09641    _PROTOTYPE( int do_sdevio, (message *m_ptr) );
09642    _PROTOTYPE( int do_kill, (message *m_ptr) );
09643    _PROTOTYPE( int do_getksig, (message *m_ptr) );
09644    _PROTOTYPE( int do_endksig, (message *m_ptr) );
09645    _PROTOTYPE( int do_sigsend, (message *m_ptr) );
09646    _PROTOTYPE( int do_sigreturn, (message *m_ptr) );
09647    _PROTOTYPE( int do_times, (message *m_ptr) );
09648    _PROTOTYPE( int do_setalarm, (message *m_ptr) );
09649
09650    #endif   /* SYSTEM_H */
09651
09652
09653



++++++++++++++++++++++++++++++++++++++++++++++++++++++++++++++++++++++++++++
                            kernel/system.c
++++++++++++++++++++++++++++++++++++++++++++++++++++++++++++++++++++++++++++

09700    /* This task provides an interface between the kernel and user-space system
09701     * processes. System services can be accessed by doing a kernel call. Kernel
09702     * calls are  transformed into request messages, which are handled by this
09703     * task. By convention, a sys_call() is transformed in a SYS_CALL request
09704     * message that is handled in a function named do_call().
09705     *
09706     * A private call vector is used to map all kernel calls to the functions that
09707     * handle them. The actual handler functions are contained in separate files
09708     * to keep this file clean. The call vector is used in the system task's main
09709     * loop to handle all incoming requests.
09710     *
09711     * In addition to the main sys_task() entry point, which starts the main loop,
09712     * there are several other minor entry points:
09713     *    get_priv:        assign privilege structure to user or system process
09714     *    send_sig:        send a signal directly to a system process
09715     *    cause_sig:       take action to cause a signal to occur via PM
09716     *    umap_local:      map virtual address in LOCAL_SEG to physical
09717     *    umap_remote:     map virtual address in REMOTE_SEG to physical
09718     *    umap_bios:       map virtual address in BIOS_SEG to physical
09719     *    virtual_copy:    copy bytes from one virtual address to another
09720     *    get_randomness:  accumulate randomness in a buffer
09721     *
09722     * Changes:
09723     *    Aug 04, 2005   check if kernel call is allowed  (Jorrit N. Herder)
09724     *    Jul 20, 2005   send signal to services with message  (Jorrit N. Herder)
```

```
09725   *    Jan 15, 2005   new, generalized virtual copy function  (Jorrit N. Herder)
09726   *    Oct 10, 2004   dispatch system calls from call vector  (Jorrit N. Herder)
09727   *    Sep 30, 2004   source code documentation updated  (Jorrit N. Herder)
09728   */
09729
09730   #include "kernel.h"
09731   #include "system.h"
09732   #include <stdlib.h>
09733   #include <signal.h>
09734   #include <unistd.h>
09735   #include <sys/sigcontext.h>
09736   #include <ibm/memory.h>
09737   #include "protect.h"
09738
09739   /* Declaration of the call vector that defines the mapping of kernel calls
09740    * to handler functions. The vector is initialized in sys_init() with map(),
09741    * which makes sure the kernel call numbers are ok. No space is allocated,
09742    * because the dummy is declared extern. If an illegal call is given, the
09743    * array size will be negative and this won't compile.
09744    */
09745   PUBLIC int (*call_vec[NR_SYS_CALLS])(message *m_ptr);
09746
09747   #define map(call_nr, handler) \
09748       {extern int dummy[NR_SYS_CALLS>(unsigned)(call_nr-KERNEL_CALL) ? 1:-1];} \
09749       call_vec[(call_nr-KERNEL_CALL)] = (handler)
09750
09751   FORWARD _PROTOTYPE( void initialize, (void));
09752
09753   /*===========================================================================*
09754    *                              sys_task                                     *
09755    *===========================================================================*/
09756   PUBLIC void sys_task()
09757   {
09758   /* Main entry point of sys_task.  Get the message and dispatch on type. */
09759     static message m;
09760     register int result;
09761     register struct proc *caller_ptr;
09762     unsigned int call_nr;
09763     int s;
09764
09765     /* Initialize the system task. */
09766     initialize();
09767
09768     while (TRUE) {
09769         /* Get work. Block and wait until a request message arrives. */
09770         receive(ANY, &m);
09771         call_nr = (unsigned) m.m_type - KERNEL_CALL;
09772         caller_ptr = proc_addr(m.m_source);
09773
09774         /* See if the caller made a valid request and try to handle it. */
09775         if (! (priv(caller_ptr)->s_call_mask & (1<<call_nr))) {
09776             kprintf("SYSTEM: request %d from %d denied.\n", call_nr,m.m_source);
09777             result = ECALLDENIED;                    /* illegal message type */
09778         } else if (call_nr >= NR_SYS_CALLS) {                /* check call number */
09779             kprintf("SYSTEM: illegal request %d from %d.\n", call_nr,m.m_source);
09780             result = EBADREQUEST;                    /* illegal message type */
09781         }
09782         else {
09783             result = (*call_vec[call_nr])(&m);   /* handle the kernel call */
09784         }
```

```
09785
09786              /* Send a reply, unless inhibited by a handler function. Use the kernel
09787               * function lock_send() to prevent a system call trap. The destination
09788               * is known to be blocked waiting for a message.
09789               */
09790              if (result != EDONTREPLY) {
09791                  m.m_type = result;                      /* report status of call */
09792                  if (OK != (s=lock_send(m.m_source, &m))) {
09793                      kprintf("SYSTEM, reply to %d failed: %d\n", m.m_source, s);
09794                  }
09795              }
09796          }
09797  }


09799  /*===========================================================================*
09800   *                              initialize                                   *
09801   *===========================================================================*/
09802  PRIVATE void initialize(void)
09803  {
09804      register struct priv *sp;
09805      int i;
09806
09807      /* Initialize IRQ handler hooks. Mark all hooks available. */
09808      for (i=0; i<NR_IRQ_HOOKS; i++) {
09809          irq_hooks[i].proc_nr = NONE;
09810      }
09811
09812      /* Initialize all alarm timers for all processes. */
09813      for (sp=BEG_PRIV_ADDR; sp < END_PRIV_ADDR; sp++) {
09814          tmr_inittimer(&(sp->s_alarm_timer));
09815      }
09816
09817      /* Initialize the call vector to a safe default handler. Some kernel calls
09818       * may be disabled or nonexistant. Then explicitly map known calls to their
09819       * handler functions. This is done with a macro that gives a compile error
09820       * if an illegal call number is used. The ordering is not important here.
09821       */
09822      for (i=0; i<NR_SYS_CALLS; i++) {
09823          call_vec[i] = do_unused;
09824      }
09825
09826      /* Process management. */
09827      map(SYS_FORK, do_fork);                  /* a process forked a new process */
09828      map(SYS_EXEC, do_exec);                  /* update process after execute */
09829      map(SYS_EXIT, do_exit);                  /* clean up after process exit */
09830      map(SYS_NICE, do_nice);                  /* set scheduling priority */
09831      map(SYS_PRIVCTL, do_privctl);            /* system privileges control */
09832      map(SYS_TRACE, do_trace);                /* request a trace operation */
09833
09834      /* Signal handling. */
09835      map(SYS_KILL, do_kill);                  /* cause a process to be signaled */
09836      map(SYS_GETKSIG, do_getksig);            /* PM checks for pending signals */
09837      map(SYS_ENDKSIG, do_endksig);            /* PM finished processing signal */
09838      map(SYS_SIGSEND, do_sigsend);            /* start POSIX-style signal */
09839      map(SYS_SIGRETURN, do_sigreturn);        /* return from POSIX-style signal */
09840
09841      /* Device I/O. */
09842      map(SYS_IRQCTL, do_irqctl);              /* interrupt control operations */
09843      map(SYS_DEVIO, do_devio);                /* inb, inw, inl, outb, outw, outl */
09844      map(SYS_SDEVIO, do_sdevio);              /* phys_insb, _insw, _outsb, _outsw */
```

```
09845       map(SYS_VDEVIO, do_vdevio);          /* vector with devio requests */
09846       map(SYS_INT86, do_int86);            /* real-mode BIOS calls */
09847
09848       /* Memory management. */
09849       map(SYS_NEWMAP, do_newmap);          /* set up a process memory map */
09850       map(SYS_SEGCTL, do_segctl);          /* add segment and get selector */
09851       map(SYS_MEMSET, do_memset);          /* write char to memory area */
09852
09853       /* Copying. */
09854       map(SYS_UMAP, do_umap);              /* map virtual to physical address */
09855       map(SYS_VIRCOPY, do_vircopy);        /* use pure virtual addressing */
09856       map(SYS_PHYSCOPY, do_physcopy);      /* use physical addressing */
09857       map(SYS_VIRVCOPY, do_virvcopy);      /* vector with copy requests */
09858       map(SYS_PHYSVCOPY, do_physvcopy);    /* vector with copy requests */
09859
09860       /* Clock functionality. */
09861       map(SYS_TIMES, do_times);            /* get uptime and process times */
09862       map(SYS_SETALARM, do_setalarm);      /* schedule a synchronous alarm */
09863
09864       /* System control. */
09865       map(SYS_ABORT, do_abort);            /* abort MINIX */
09866       map(SYS_GETINFO, do_getinfo);        /* request system information */
09867   }

09869   /*===========================================================================*
09870    *                              get_priv                                     *
09871    *===========================================================================*/
09872   PUBLIC int get_priv(rc, proc_type)
09873   register struct proc *rc;                    /* new (child) process pointer */
09874   int proc_type;                               /* system or user process flag */
09875   {
09876   /* Get a privilege structure. All user processes share the same privilege
09877    * structure. System processes get their own privilege structure.
09878    */
09879     register struct priv *sp;                    /* privilege structure */
09880
09881     if (proc_type == SYS_PROC) {                 /* find a new slot */
09882         for (sp = BEG_PRIV_ADDR; sp < END_PRIV_ADDR; ++sp)
09883             if (sp->s_proc_nr == NONE && sp->s_id != USER_PRIV_ID) break;
09884         if (sp->s_proc_nr != NONE) return(ENOSPC);
09885         rc->p_priv = sp;                         /* assign new slot */
09886         rc->p_priv->s_proc_nr = proc_nr(rc);     /* set association */
09887         rc->p_priv->s_flags = SYS_PROC;          /* mark as privileged */
09888     } else {
09889         rc->p_priv = &priv[USER_PRIV_ID];        /* use shared slot */
09890         rc->p_priv->s_proc_nr = INIT_PROC_NR;    /* set association */
09891         rc->p_priv->s_flags = 0;                 /* no initial flags */
09892     }
09893     return(OK);
09894   }

09896   /*===========================================================================*
09897    *                              get_randomness                               *
09898    *===========================================================================*/
09899   PUBLIC void get_randomness(source)
09900   int source;
09901   {
09902   /* On machines with the RDTSC (cycle counter read instruction - pentium
09903    * and up), use that for high-resolution raw entropy gathering. Otherwise,
09904    * use the realtime clock (tick resolution).
```

```
09905      *
09906      * Unfortunately this test is run-time - we don't want to bother with
09907      * compiling different kernels for different machines.
09908      *
09909      * On machines without RDTSC, we use read_clock().
09910      */
09911       int r_next;
09912       unsigned long tsc_high, tsc_low;
09913
09914       source %= RANDOM_SOURCES;
09915       r_next= krandom.bin[source].r_next;
09916       if (machine.processor > 486) {
09917           read_tsc(&tsc_high, &tsc_low);
09918           krandom.bin[source].r_buf[r_next] = tsc_low;
09919       } else {
09920           krandom.bin[source].r_buf[r_next] = read_clock();
09921       }
09922       if (krandom.bin[source].r_size < RANDOM_ELEMENTS) {
09923           krandom.bin[source].r_size ++;
09924       }
09925       krandom.bin[source].r_next = (r_next + 1 ) % RANDOM_ELEMENTS;
09926    }

09928    /*===========================================================================*
09929     *                             send_sig                                      *
09930     *===========================================================================*/
09931    PUBLIC void send_sig(proc_nr, sig_nr)
09932    int proc_nr;                    /* system process to be signalled */
09933    int sig_nr;                     /* signal to be sent, 1 to _NSIG */
09934    {
09935    /* Notify a system process about a signal. This is straightforward. Simply
09936     * set the signal that is to be delivered in the pending signals map and
09937     * send a notification with source SYSTEM.
09938     */
09939       register struct proc *rp;
09940
09941       rp = proc_addr(proc_nr);
09942       sigaddset(&priv(rp)->s_sig_pending, sig_nr);
09943       lock_notify(SYSTEM, proc_nr);
09944    }

09946    /*===========================================================================*
09947     *                             cause_sig                                     *
09948     *===========================================================================*/
09949    PUBLIC void cause_sig(proc_nr, sig_nr)
09950    int proc_nr;                    /* process to be signalled */
09951    int sig_nr;                     /* signal to be sent, 1 to _NSIG */
09952    {
09953    /* A system process wants to send a signal to a process.  Examples are:
09954     *  - HARDWARE wanting to cause a SIGSEGV after a CPU exception
09955     *  - TTY wanting to cause SIGINT upon getting a DEL
09956     *  - FS wanting to cause SIGPIPE for a broken pipe
09957     * Signals are handled by sending a message to PM.  This function handles the
09958     * signals and makes sure the PM gets them by sending a notification. The
09959     * process being signaled is blocked while PM has not finished all signals
09960     * for it.
09961     * Race conditions between calls to this function and the system calls that
09962     * process pending kernel signals cannot exist. Signal related functions are
09963     * only called when a user process causes a CPU exception and from the kernel
09964     * process level, which runs to completion.
```

```
09965    */
09966      register struct proc *rp;
09967
09968      /* Check if the signal is already pending. Process it otherwise. */
09969      rp = proc_addr(proc_nr);
09970      if (! sigismember(&rp->p_pending, sig_nr)) {
09971          sigaddset(&rp->p_pending, sig_nr);
09972          if (! (rp->p_rts_flags & SIGNALED)) {            /* other pending */
09973              if (rp->p_rts_flags == 0) lock_dequeue(rp);  /* make not ready */
09974              rp->p_rts_flags |= SIGNALED | SIG_PENDING;   /* update flags */
09975              send_sig(PM_PROC_NR, SIGKSIG);
09976          }
09977      }
09978  }

09980  /*===========================================================================*
09981   *                              umap_local                                   *
09982   *===========================================================================*/
09983  PUBLIC phys_bytes umap_local(rp, seg, vir_addr, bytes)
09984  register struct proc *rp;      /* pointer to proc table entry for process */
09985  int seg;                       /* T, D, or S segment */
09986  vir_bytes vir_addr;            /* virtual address in bytes within the seg */
09987  vir_bytes bytes;               /* # of bytes to be copied */
09988  {
09989  /* Calculate the physical memory address for a given virtual address. */
09990    vir_clicks vc;               /* the virtual address in clicks */
09991    phys_bytes pa;               /* intermediate variables as phys_bytes */
09992    phys_bytes seg_base;
09993
09994    /* If 'seg' is D it could really be S and vice versa.  T really means T.
09995     * If the virtual address falls in the gap,  it causes a problem. On the
09996     * 8088 it is probably a legal stack reference, since "stackfaults" are
09997     * not detected by the hardware.  On 8088s, the gap is called S and
09998     * accepted, but on other machines it is called D and rejected.
09999     * The Atari ST behaves like the 8088 in this respect.
10000     */
10001
10002    if (bytes <= 0) return( (phys_bytes) 0);
10003    if (vir_addr + bytes <= vir_addr) return 0;   /* overflow */
10004    vc = (vir_addr + bytes - 1) >> CLICK_SHIFT;   /* last click of data */
10005
10006    if (seg != T)
10007        seg = (vc < rp->p_memmap[D].mem_vir + rp->p_memmap[D].mem_len ? D : S);
10008
10009    if ((vir_addr>>CLICK_SHIFT) >= rp->p_memmap[seg].mem_vir +
10010        rp->p_memmap[seg].mem_len) return( (phys_bytes) 0 );
10011
10012    if (vc >= rp->p_memmap[seg].mem_vir +
10013        rp->p_memmap[seg].mem_len) return( (phys_bytes) 0 );
10014
10015    seg_base = (phys_bytes) rp->p_memmap[seg].mem_phys;
10016    seg_base = seg_base << CLICK_SHIFT;   /* segment origin in bytes */
10017    pa = (phys_bytes) vir_addr;
10018    pa -= rp->p_memmap[seg].mem_vir << CLICK_SHIFT;
10019    return(seg_base + pa);
10020  }
```

```
10022  /*===========================================================================*
10023   *                              umap_remote                                  *
10024   *===========================================================================*/
10025  PUBLIC phys_bytes umap_remote(rp, seg, vir_addr, bytes)
10026  register struct proc *rp;        /* pointer to proc table entry for process */
10027  int seg;                         /* index of remote segment */
10028  vir_bytes vir_addr;              /* virtual address in bytes within the seg */
10029  vir_bytes bytes;                 /* # of bytes to be copied */
10030  {
10031  /* Calculate the physical memory address for a given virtual address. */
10032    struct far_mem *fm;
10033
10034    if (bytes <= 0) return( (phys_bytes) 0);
10035    if (seg < 0 || seg >= NR_REMOTE_SEGS) return( (phys_bytes) 0);
10036
10037    fm = &rp->p_priv->s_farmem[seg];
10038    if (! fm->in_use) return( (phys_bytes) 0);
10039    if (vir_addr + bytes > fm->mem_len) return( (phys_bytes) 0);
10040
10041    return(fm->mem_phys + (phys_bytes) vir_addr);
10042  }

10044  /*===========================================================================*
10045   *                              umap_bios                                    *
10046   *===========================================================================*/
10047  PUBLIC phys_bytes umap_bios(rp, vir_addr, bytes)
10048  register struct proc *rp;        /* pointer to proc table entry for process */
10049  vir_bytes vir_addr;              /* virtual address in BIOS segment */
10050  vir_bytes bytes;                 /* # of bytes to be copied */
10051  {
10052  /* Calculate the physical memory address at the BIOS. Note: currently, BIOS
10053   * address zero (the first BIOS interrupt vector) is not considered as an
10054   * error here, but since the physical address will be zero as well, the
10055   * calling function will think an error occurred. This is not a problem,
10056   * since no one uses the first BIOS interrupt vector.
10057   */
10058
10059    /* Check all acceptable ranges. */
10060    if (vir_addr >= BIOS_MEM_BEGIN && vir_addr + bytes <= BIOS_MEM_END)
10061        return (phys_bytes) vir_addr;
10062    else if (vir_addr >= BASE_MEM_TOP && vir_addr + bytes <= UPPER_MEM_END)
10063        return (phys_bytes) vir_addr;
10064    kprintf("Warning, error in umap_bios, virtual address 0x%x\n", vir_addr);
10065    return 0;
10066  }

10068  /*===========================================================================*
10069   *                              virtual_copy                                 *
10070   *===========================================================================*/
10071  PUBLIC int virtual_copy(src_addr, dst_addr, bytes)
10072  struct vir_addr *src_addr;       /* source virtual address */
10073  struct vir_addr *dst_addr;       /* destination virtual address */
10074  vir_bytes bytes;                 /* # of bytes to copy  */
10075  {
10076  /* Copy bytes from virtual address src_addr to virtual address dst_addr.
10077   * Virtual addresses can be in ABS, LOCAL_SEG, REMOTE_SEG, or BIOS_SEG.
10078   */
10079    struct vir_addr *vir_addr[2]; /* virtual source and destination address */
10080    phys_bytes phys_addr[2];      /* absolute source and destination */
10081    int seg_index;
```

```
10082    int i;
10083
10084    /* Check copy count. */
10085    if (bytes <= 0) return(EDOM);
10086
10087    /* Do some more checks and map virtual addresses to physical addresses. */
10088    vir_addr[_SRC_] = src_addr;
10089    vir_addr[_DST_] = dst_addr;
10090    for (i=_SRC_; i<=_DST_; i++) {
10091
10092        /* Get physical address. */
10093        switch((vir_addr[i]->segment & SEGMENT_TYPE)) {
10094        case LOCAL_SEG:
10095            seg_index = vir_addr[i]->segment & SEGMENT_INDEX;
10096            phys_addr[i] = umap_local( proc_addr(vir_addr[i]->proc_nr),
10097                seg_index, vir_addr[i]->offset, bytes );
10098            break;
10099        case REMOTE_SEG:
10100            seg_index = vir_addr[i]->segment & SEGMENT_INDEX;
10101            phys_addr[i] = umap_remote( proc_addr(vir_addr[i]->proc_nr),
10102                seg_index, vir_addr[i]->offset, bytes );
10103            break;
10104        case BIOS_SEG:
10105            phys_addr[i] = umap_bios( proc_addr(vir_addr[i]->proc_nr),
10106                vir_addr[i]->offset, bytes );
10107            break;
10108        case PHYS_SEG:
10109            phys_addr[i] = vir_addr[i]->offset;
10110            break;
10111        default:
10112            return(EINVAL);
10113        }
10114
10115        /* Check if mapping succeeded. */
10116        if (phys_addr[i] <= 0 && vir_addr[i]->segment != PHYS_SEG)
10117            return(EFAULT);
10118    }
10119
10120    /* Now copy bytes between physical addresseses. */
10121    phys_copy(phys_addr[_SRC_], phys_addr[_DST_], (phys_bytes) bytes);
10122    return(OK);
10123 }
```

```
++++++++++++++++++++++++++++++++++++++++++++++++++++++++++++++++++++++++++++
                        kernel/system/do_setalarm.c
++++++++++++++++++++++++++++++++++++++++++++++++++++++++++++++++++++++++++++

10200    /* The kernel call implemented in this file:
10201     *   m_type:    SYS_SETALARM
10202     *
10203     * The parameters for this kernel call are:
10204     *    m2_l1:    ALRM_EXP_TIME       (alarm's expiration time)
10205     *    m2_i2:    ALRM_ABS_TIME       (expiration time is absolute?)
10206     *    m2_l1:    ALRM_TIME_LEFT      (return seconds left of previous)
10207     */
10208
10209 #include "../system.h"
```

```
10210
10211   #if USE_SETALARM
10212
10213   FORWARD _PROTOTYPE( void cause_alarm, (timer_t *tp) );
10214
10215   /*===========================================================================*
10216    *                              do_setalarm                                  *
10217    *===========================================================================*/
10218   PUBLIC int do_setalarm(m_ptr)
10219   message *m_ptr;                        /* pointer to request message */
10220   {
10221   /* A process requests a synchronous alarm, or wants to cancel its alarm. */
10222     register struct proc *rp;      /* pointer to requesting process */
10223     int proc_nr;                   /* which process wants the alarm */
10224     long exp_time;                 /* expiration time for this alarm */
10225     int use_abs_time;              /* use absolute or relative time */
10226     timer_t *tp;                   /* the process' timer structure */
10227     clock_t uptime;                /* placeholder for current uptime */
10228
10229     /* Extract shared parameters from the request message. */
10230     exp_time = m_ptr->ALRM_EXP_TIME;       /* alarm's expiration time */
10231     use_abs_time = m_ptr->ALRM_ABS_TIME;   /* flag for absolute time */
10232     proc_nr = m_ptr->m_source;             /* process to interrupt later */
10233     rp = proc_addr(proc_nr);
10234     if (! (priv(rp)->s_flags & SYS_PROC)) return(EPERM);
10235
10236     /* Get the timer structure and set the parameters for this alarm. */
10237     tp = &(priv(rp)->s_alarm_timer);
10238     tmr_arg(tp)->ta_int = proc_nr;
10239     tp->tmr_func = cause_alarm;
10240
10241     /* Return the ticks left on the previous alarm. */
10242     uptime = get_uptime();
10243     if ((tp->tmr_exp_time != TMR_NEVER) && (uptime < tp->tmr_exp_time) ) {
10244         m_ptr->ALRM_TIME_LEFT = (tp->tmr_exp_time - uptime);
10245     } else {
10246         m_ptr->ALRM_TIME_LEFT = 0;
10247     }
10248
10249     /* Finally, (re)set the timer depending on the expiration time. */
10250     if (exp_time == 0) {
10251         reset_timer(tp);
10252     } else {
10253         tp->tmr_exp_time = (use_abs_time) ? exp_time : exp_time + get_uptime();
10254         set_timer(tp, tp->tmr_exp_time, tp->tmr_func);
10255     }
10256     return(OK);
10257   }
10258
10259   /*===========================================================================*
10260    *                              cause_alarm                                  *
10261    *===========================================================================*/
10262   PRIVATE void cause_alarm(tp)
10263   timer_t *tp;
10264   {
10265   /* Routine called if a timer goes off and the process requested a synchronous
10266    * alarm. The process number is stored in timer argument 'ta_int'. Notify that
10267    * process with a notification message from CLOCK.
10268    */
10269     int proc_nr = tmr_arg(tp)->ta_int;            /* get process number */
```

```
10270       lock_notify(CLOCK, proc_nr);                    /* notify process */
10271   }

10273   #endif /* USE_SETALARM */


++++++++++++++++++++++++++++++++++++++++++++++++++++++++++++++++++++++++++++++++
                              kernel/system/do_exec.c
++++++++++++++++++++++++++++++++++++++++++++++++++++++++++++++++++++++++++++++++
10300   /* The kernel call implemented in this file:
10301    *    m_type:     SYS_EXEC
10302    *
10303    * The parameters for this kernel call are:
10304    *     m1_i1:      PR_PROC_NR                  (process that did exec call)
10305    *     m1_p1:      PR_STACK_PTR                (new stack pointer)
10306    *     m1_p2:      PR_NAME_PTR                 (pointer to program name)
10307    *     m1_p3:      PR_IP_PTR                   (new instruction pointer)
10308    */
10309   #include "../system.h"
10310   #include <string.h>
10311   #include <signal.h>
10312
10313   #if USE_EXEC
10314
10315   /*===========================================================================*
10316    *                              do_exec                                       *
10317    *===========================================================================*/
10318   PUBLIC int do_exec(m_ptr)
10319   register message *m_ptr;           /* pointer to request message */
10320   {
10321   /* Handle sys_exec().  A process has done a successful EXEC. Patch it up. */
10322     register struct proc *rp;
10323     reg_t sp;                        /* new sp */
10324     phys_bytes phys_name;
10325     char *np;
10326
10327     rp = proc_addr(m_ptr->PR_PROC_NR);
10328     sp = (reg_t) m_ptr->PR_STACK_PTR;
10329     rp->p_reg.sp = sp;               /* set the stack pointer */
10330     phys_memset(vir2phys(&rp->p_ldt[EXTRA_LDT_INDEX]), 0,
10331         (LDT_SIZE - EXTRA_LDT_INDEX) * sizeof(rp->p_ldt[0]));
10332     rp->p_reg.pc = (reg_t) m_ptr->PR_IP_PTR;    /* set pc */
10333     rp->p_rts_flags &= ~RECEIVING;   /* PM does not reply to EXEC call */
10334     if (rp->p_rts_flags == 0) lock_enqueue(rp);
10335
10336     /* Save command name for debugging, ps(1) output, etc. */
10337     phys_name = numap_local(m_ptr->m_source, (vir_bytes) m_ptr->PR_NAME_PTR,
10338                             (vir_bytes) P_NAME_LEN - 1);
10339     if (phys_name != 0) {
10340         phys_copy(phys_name, vir2phys(rp->p_name), (phys_bytes) P_NAME_LEN - 1);
10341         for (np = rp->p_name; (*np & BYTE) >= ' '; np++) {}
10342         *np = 0;                                   /* mark end */
10343     } else {
10344         strncpy(rp->p_name, "<unset>", P_NAME_LEN);
10345     }
10346     return(OK);
10347   }
10348   #endif /* USE_EXEC */
```

```
++++++++++++++++++++++++++++++++++++++++++++++++++++++++++++++++++++++++++
                          kernel/clock.c
++++++++++++++++++++++++++++++++++++++++++++++++++++++++++++++++++++++++++
10400   /* This file contains the clock task, which handles time related functions.
10401    * Important events that are handled by the CLOCK include setting and
10402    * monitoring alarm timers and deciding when to (re)schedule processes.
10403    * The CLOCK offers a direct interface to kernel processes. System services
10404    * can access its services through system calls, such as sys_setalarm(). The
10405    * CLOCK task thus is hidden from the outside world.
10406    *
10407    * Changes:
10408    *   Oct 08, 2005   reordering and comment editing (A. S. Woodhull)
10409    *   Mar 18, 2004   clock interface moved to SYSTEM task (Jorrit N. Herder)
10410    *   Sep 30, 2004   source code documentation updated  (Jorrit N. Herder)
10411    *   Sep 24, 2004   redesigned alarm timers  (Jorrit N. Herder)
10412    *
10413    * The function do_clocktick() is triggered by the clock's interrupt
10414    * handler when a watchdog timer has expired or a process must be scheduled.
10415    *
10416    * In addition to the main clock_task() entry point, which starts the main
10417    * loop, there are several other minor entry points:
10418    *   clock_stop:       called just before MINIX shutdown
10419    *   get_uptime:       get realtime since boot in clock ticks
10420    *   set_timer:        set a watchdog timer (+)
10421    *   reset_timer:      reset a watchdog timer (+)
10422    *   read_clock:       read the counter of channel 0 of the 8253A timer
10423    *
10424    * (+) The CLOCK task keeps tracks of watchdog timers for the entire kernel.
10425    * The watchdog functions of expired timers are executed in do_clocktick().
10426    * It is crucial that watchdog functions not block, or the CLOCK task may
10427    * be blocked. Do not send() a message when the receiver is not expecting it.
10428    * Instead, notify(), which always returns, should be used.
10429    */
10430
10431   #include "kernel.h"
10432   #include "proc.h"
10433   #include <signal.h>
10434   #include <minix/com.h>
10435
10436   /* Function prototype for PRIVATE functions. */
10437   FORWARD _PROTOTYPE( void init_clock, (void) );
10438   FORWARD _PROTOTYPE( int clock_handler, (irq_hook_t *hook) );
10439   FORWARD _PROTOTYPE( int do_clocktick, (message *m_ptr) );
10440
10441   /* Clock parameters. */
10442   #define COUNTER_FREQ (2*TIMER_FREQ) /* counter frequency using square wave */
10443   #define LATCH_COUNT     0x00    /* cc00xxxx, c = channel, x = any */
10444   #define SQUARE_WAVE     0x36    /* ccaammmb, a = access, m = mode, b = BCD */
10445                                  /*    11x11, 11 = LSB then MSB, x11 = sq wave */
10446   #define TIMER_COUNT ((unsigned) (TIMER_FREQ/HZ)) /* initial value for counter*/
10447   #define TIMER_FREQ  1193182L    /* clock frequency for timer in PC and AT */
10448
10449   #define CLOCK_ACK_BIT   0x80    /* PS/2 clock interrupt acknowledge bit */
10450
10451   /* The CLOCK's timers queue. The functions in <timers.h> operate on this.
10452    * Each system process possesses a single synchronous alarm timer. If other
10453    * kernel parts want to use additional timers, they must declare their own
10454    * persistent (static) timer structure, which can be passed to the clock
```

```
10455      * via (re)set_timer().
10456      * When a timer expires its watchdog function is run by the CLOCK task.
10457      */
10458     PRIVATE timer_t *clock_timers;          /* queue of CLOCK timers */
10459     PRIVATE clock_t next_timeout;           /* realtime that next timer expires */
10460
10461     /* The time is incremented by the interrupt handler on each clock tick. */
10462     PRIVATE clock_t realtime;               /* real time clock */
10463     PRIVATE irq_hook_t clock_hook;          /* interrupt handler hook */
10464
10465     /*========================================================================*
10466      *                              clock_task                               *
10467      *========================================================================*/
10468     PUBLIC void clock_task()
10469     {
10470     /* Main program of clock task. If the call is not HARD_INT it is an error.
10471      */
10472       message m;                        /* message buffer for both input and output */
10473       int result;                       /* result returned by the handler */
10474
10475       init_clock();                     /* initialize clock task */
10476
10477       /* Main loop of the clock task.  Get work, process it. Never reply. */
10478       while (TRUE) {
10479
10480           /* Go get a message. */
10481           receive(ANY, &m);
10482
10483           /* Handle the request. Only clock ticks are expected. */
10484           switch (m.m_type) {
10485           case HARD_INT:
10486               result = do_clocktick(&m);     /* handle clock tick */
10487               break;
10488           default:                          /* illegal request type */
10489               kprintf("CLOCK: illegal request %d from %d.\n", m.m_type,m.m_source);
10490           }
10491       }
10492     }
10494     /*========================================================================*
10495      *                              do_clocktick                             *
10496      *========================================================================*/
10497     PRIVATE int do_clocktick(m_ptr)
10498     message *m_ptr;                         /* pointer to request message */
10499     {
10500     /* Despite its name, this routine is not called on every clock tick. It
10501      * is called on those clock ticks when a lot of work needs to be done.
10502      */
10503
10504       /* A process used up a full quantum. The interrupt handler stored this
10505        * process in 'prev_ptr'.  First make sure that the process is not on the
10506        * scheduling queues.  Then announce the process ready again. Since it has
10507        * no more time left, it gets a new quantum and is inserted at the right
10508        * place in the queues.  As a side-effect a new process will be scheduled.
10509        */
10510       if (prev_ptr->p_ticks_left <= 0 && priv(prev_ptr)->s_flags & PREEMPTIBLE) {
10511           lock_dequeue(prev_ptr);                /* take it off the queues */
10512           lock_enqueue(prev_ptr);                /* and reinsert it again */
10513       }
10514
```

```
10515        /* Check if a clock timer expired and run its watchdog function. */
10516        if (next_timeout <= realtime) {
10517                tmrs_exptimers(&clock_timers, realtime, NULL);
10518                next_timeout = clock_timers == NULL ?
10519                        TMR_NEVER : clock_timers->tmr_exp_time;
10520        }
10521
10522        /* Inhibit sending a reply. */
10523        return(EDONTREPLY);
10524  }
10525
10526  /*===========================================================================*
10527   *                              init_clock                                   *
10528   *===========================================================================*/
10529  PRIVATE void init_clock()
10530  {
10531        /* Initialize the CLOCK's interrupt hook. */
10532        clock_hook.proc_nr = CLOCK;
10533
10534        /* Initialize channel 0 of the 8253A timer to, e.g., 60 Hz. */
10535        outb(TIMER_MODE, SQUARE_WAVE);          /* set timer to run continuously */
10536        outb(TIMER0, TIMER_COUNT);              /* load timer low byte */
10537        outb(TIMER0, TIMER_COUNT >> 8);         /* load timer high byte */
10538        put_irq_handler(&clock_hook, CLOCK_IRQ, clock_handler);/* register handler */
10539        enable_irq(&clock_hook);                /* ready for clock interrupts */
10540  }
10541
10542  /*===========================================================================*
10543   *                              clock_stop                                   *
10544   *===========================================================================*/
10545  PUBLIC void clock_stop()
10546  {
10547  /* Reset the clock to the BIOS rate. (For rebooting) */
10548        outb(TIMER_MODE, 0x36);
10549        outb(TIMER0, 0);
10550        outb(TIMER0, 0);
10551  }
10552
10553  /*===========================================================================*
10554   *                              clock_handler                                *
10555   *===========================================================================*/
10556  PRIVATE int clock_handler(hook)
10557  irq_hook_t *hook;
10558  {
10559  /* This executes on each clock tick (i.e., every time the timer chip generates
10560   * an interrupt). It does a little bit of work so the clock task does not have
10561   * to be called on every tick.  The clock task is called when:
10562   *
10563   *      (1) the scheduling quantum of the running process has expired, or
10564   *      (2) a timer has expired and the watchdog function should be run.
10565   *
10566   * Many global global and static variables are accessed here.  The safety of
10567   * this must be justified. All scheduling and message passing code acquires a
10568   * lock by temporarily disabling interrupts, so no conflicts with calls from
10569   * the task level can occur. Furthermore, interrupts are not reentrant, the
10570   * interrupt handler cannot be bothered by other interrupts.
10571   *
10572   * Variables that are updated in the clock's interrupt handler:
10573   *      lost_ticks:
10574   *              Clock ticks counted outside the clock task. This for example
```

```
10575   *                    is used when the boot monitor processes a real mode interrupt.
10576   *      realtime:
10577   *                    The current uptime is incremented with all outstanding ticks.
10578   *      proc_ptr, bill_ptr:
10579   *                    These are used for accounting.  It does not matter if proc.c
10580   *                    is changing them, provided they are always valid pointers,
10581   *                    since at worst the previous process would be billed.
10582   */
10583   register unsigned ticks;
10584
10585   /* Acknowledge the PS/2 clock interrupt. */
10586   if (machine.ps_mca) outb(PORT_B, inb(PORT_B) | CLOCK_ACK_BIT);
10587
10588   /* Get number of ticks and update realtime. */
10589   ticks = lost_ticks + 1;
10590   lost_ticks = 0;
10591   realtime += ticks;
10592
10593   /* Update user and system accounting times. Charge the current process for
10594    * user time. If the current process is not billable, that is, if a non-user
10595    * process is running, charge the billable process for system time as well.
10596    * Thus the unbillable process' user time is the billable user's system time.
10597    */
10598   proc_ptr->p_user_time += ticks;
10599   if (priv(proc_ptr)->s_flags & PREEMPTIBLE) {
10600       proc_ptr->p_ticks_left -= ticks;
10601   }
10602   if (! (priv(proc_ptr)->s_flags & BILLABLE)) {
10603       bill_ptr->p_sys_time += ticks;
10604       bill_ptr->p_ticks_left -= ticks;
10605   }
10606
10607   /* Check if do_clocktick() must be called. Done for alarms and scheduling.
10608    * Some processes, such as the kernel tasks, cannot be preempted.
10609    */
10610   if ((next_timeout <= realtime) || (proc_ptr->p_ticks_left <= 0)) {
10611       prev_ptr = proc_ptr;                      /* store running process */
10612       lock_notify(HARDWARE, CLOCK);             /* send notification */
10613   }
10614   return(1);                                    /* reenable interrupts */
10615 }

10617 /*===========================================================================*
10618  *                              get_uptime                                    *
10619  *===========================================================================*/
10620 PUBLIC clock_t get_uptime()
10621 {
10622 /* Get and return the current clock uptime in ticks. */
10623   return(realtime);
10624 }

10626 /*===========================================================================*
10627  *                              set_timer                                     *
10628  *===========================================================================*/
10629 PUBLIC void set_timer(tp, exp_time, watchdog)
10630 struct timer *tp;              /* pointer to timer structure */
10631 clock_t exp_time;             /* expiration realtime */
10632 tmr_func_t watchdog;          /* watchdog to be called */
10633 {
10634 /* Insert the new timer in the active timers list. Always update the
```

```
10635        * next timeout time by setting it to the front of the active list.
10636        */
10637        tmrs_settimer(&clock_timers, tp, exp_time, watchdog, NULL);
10638        next_timeout = clock_timers->tmr_exp_time;
10639    }

10641    /*===========================================================================*
10642     *                              reset_timer                                  *
10643     *===========================================================================*/
10644    PUBLIC void reset_timer(tp)
10645    struct timer *tp;                       /* pointer to timer structure */
10646    {
10647    /* The timer pointed to by 'tp' is no longer needed. Remove it from both the
10648     * active and expired lists. Always update the next timeout time by setting
10649     * it to the front of the active list.
10650     */
10651        tmrs_clrtimer(&clock_timers, tp, NULL);
10652        next_timeout = (clock_timers == NULL) ?
10653            TMR_NEVER : clock_timers->tmr_exp_time;
10654    }

10656    /*===========================================================================*
10657     *                              read_clock                                   *
10658     *===========================================================================*/
10659    PUBLIC unsigned long read_clock()
10660    {
10661    /* Read the counter of channel 0 of the 8253A timer.  This counter counts
10662     * down at a rate of TIMER_FREQ and restarts at TIMER_COUNT-1 when it
10663     * reaches zero. A hardware interrupt (clock tick) occurs when the counter
10664     * gets to zero and restarts its cycle.
10665     */
10666        unsigned count;

10668        outb(TIMER_MODE, LATCH_COUNT);
10669        count = inb(TIMER0);
10670        count |= (inb(TIMER0) << 8);

10672        return count;
10673    }


++++++++++++++++++++++++++++++++++++++++++++++++++++++++++++++++++++++++++++
                              drivers/drivers.h
++++++++++++++++++++++++++++++++++++++++++++++++++++++++++++++++++++++++++++

10700    /* This is the master header for all device drivers. It includes some other
10701     * files and defines the principal constants.
10702     */
10703    #define _POSIX_SOURCE      1    /* tell headers to include POSIX stuff */
10704    #define _MINIX             1    /* tell headers to include MINIX stuff */
10705    #define _SYSTEM            1    /* get negative error number in <errno.h> */

10707    /* The following are so basic, all the *.c files get them automatically. */
10708    #include <minix/config.h>       /* MUST be first */
10709    #include <ansi.h>               /* MUST be second */
10710    #include <minix/type.h>
10711    #include <minix/com.h>
10712    #include <minix/dmap.h>
10713    #include <minix/callnr.h>
10714    #include <sys/types.h>
```

```
10715   #include <minix/const.h>
10716   #include <minix/devio.h>
10717   #include <minix/syslib.h>
10718   #include <minix/sysutil.h>
10719   #include <minix/bitmap.h>
10720
10721   #include <ibm/interrupt.h>      /* IRQ vectors and miscellaneous ports */
10722   #include <ibm/bios.h>           /* BIOS index numbers */
10723   #include <ibm/ports.h>          /* Well-known ports */
10724
10725   #include <string.h>
10726   #include <signal.h>
10727   #include <stdlib.h>
10728   #include <limits.h>
10729   #include <stddef.h>
10730   #include <errno.h>
10731   #include <unistd.h>
10732
```

```
+++++++++++++++++++++++++++++++++++++++++++++++++++++++++++++++++++++++++++++++
                          drivers/libdriver/driver.h
+++++++++++++++++++++++++++++++++++++++++++++++++++++++++++++++++++++++++++++++
```

```
10800   /* Types and constants shared between the generic and device dependent
10801    * device driver code.
10802    */
10803
10804   #define _POSIX_SOURCE      1     /* tell headers to include POSIX stuff */
10805   #define _MINIX             1     /* tell headers to include MINIX stuff */
10806   #define _SYSTEM            1     /* get negative error number in <errno.h> */
10807
10808   /* The following are so basic, all the *.c files get them automatically. */
10809   #include <minix/config.h>        /* MUST be first */
10810   #include <ansi.h>                /* MUST be second */
10811   #include <minix/type.h>
10812   #include <minix/ipc.h>
10813   #include <minix/com.h>
10814   #include <minix/callnr.h>
10815   #include <sys/types.h>
10816   #include <minix/const.h>
10817   #include <minix/syslib.h>
10818   #include <minix/sysutil.h>
10819
10820   #include <string.h>
10821   #include <limits.h>
10822   #include <stddef.h>
10823   #include <errno.h>
10824
10825   #include <minix/partition.h>
10826   #include <minix/u64.h>
10827
10828   /* Info about and entry points into the device dependent code. */
10829   struct driver {
10830     _PROTOTYPE( char *(*dr_name), (void) );
10831     _PROTOTYPE( int (*dr_open), (struct driver *dp, message *m_ptr) );
10832     _PROTOTYPE( int (*dr_close), (struct driver *dp, message *m_ptr) );
10833     _PROTOTYPE( int (*dr_ioctl), (struct driver *dp, message *m_ptr) );
10834     _PROTOTYPE( struct device *(*dr_prepare), (int device) );
```

```
10835        _PROTOTYPE( int (*dr_transfer), (int proc_nr, int opcode, off_t position,
10836                                           iovec_t *iov, unsigned nr_req) );
10837        _PROTOTYPE( void (*dr_cleanup), (void) );
10838        _PROTOTYPE( void (*dr_geometry), (struct partition *entry) );
10839        _PROTOTYPE( void (*dr_signal), (struct driver *dp, message *m_ptr) );
10840        _PROTOTYPE( void (*dr_alarm), (struct driver *dp, message *m_ptr) );
10841        _PROTOTYPE( int (*dr_cancel), (struct driver *dp, message *m_ptr) );
10842        _PROTOTYPE( int (*dr_select), (struct driver *dp, message *m_ptr) );
10843        _PROTOTYPE( int (*dr_other), (struct driver *dp, message *m_ptr) );
10844        _PROTOTYPE( int (*dr_hw_int), (struct driver *dp, message *m_ptr) );
10845 };
10846
10847 #if (CHIP == INTEL)
10848
10849 /* Number of bytes you can DMA before hitting a 64K boundary: */
10850 #define dma_bytes_left(phys)     \
10851    ((unsigned) (sizeof(int) == 2 ? 0 : 0x10000) - (unsigned) ((phys) & 0xFFFF))
10852
10853 #endif /* CHIP == INTEL */
10854
10855 /* Base and size of a partition in bytes. */
10856 struct device {
10857   u64_t dv_base;
10858   u64_t dv_size;
10859 };
10860
10861 #define NIL_DEV          ((struct device *) 0)
10862
10863 /* Functions defined by driver.c: */
10864 _PROTOTYPE( void driver_task, (struct driver *dr) );
10865 _PROTOTYPE( char *no_name, (void) );
10866 _PROTOTYPE( int do_nop, (struct driver *dp, message *m_ptr) );
10867 _PROTOTYPE( struct device *nop_prepare, (int device) );
10868 _PROTOTYPE( void nop_cleanup, (void) );
10869 _PROTOTYPE( void nop_task, (void) );
10870 _PROTOTYPE( void nop_signal, (struct driver *dp, message *m_ptr) );
10871 _PROTOTYPE( void nop_alarm, (struct driver *dp, message *m_ptr) );
10872 _PROTOTYPE( int nop_cancel, (struct driver *dp, message *m_ptr) );
10873 _PROTOTYPE( int nop_select, (struct driver *dp, message *m_ptr) );
10874 _PROTOTYPE( int do_diocntl, (struct driver *dp, message *m_ptr) );
10875
10876 /* Parameters for the disk drive. */
10877 #define SECTOR_SIZE      512     /* physical sector size in bytes */
10878 #define SECTOR_SHIFT       9     /* for division */
10879 #define SECTOR_MASK      511     /* and remainder */
10880
10881 /* Size of the DMA buffer buffer in bytes. */
10882 #define USE_EXTRA_DMA_BUF  0     /* usually not needed */
10883 #define DMA_BUF_SIZE     (DMA_SECTORS * SECTOR_SIZE)
10884
10885 #if (CHIP == INTEL)
10886 extern u8_t *tmp_buf;                    /* the DMA buffer */
10887 #else
10888 extern u8_t tmp_buf[];                   /* the DMA buffer */
10889 #endif
10890 extern phys_bytes tmp_phys;              /* phys address of DMA buffer */
```

```
++++++++++++++++++++++++++++++++++++++++++++++++++++++++++++++++++++++++++++
                           drivers/libdriver/drvlib.h
++++++++++++++++++++++++++++++++++++++++++++++++++++++++++++++++++++++++++++

10900   /* IBM device driver definitions                  Author: Kees J. Bot
10901    *                                                        7 Dec 1995
10902    */
10903
10904   #include <ibm/partition.h>
10905
10906   _PROTOTYPE( void partition, (struct driver *dr, int device, int style, int atapi) );
10907
10908   /* BIOS parameter table layout. */
10909   #define bp_cylinders(t)          (* (u16_t *) (&(t)[0]))
10910   #define bp_heads(t)              (* (u8_t *)  (&(t)[2]))
10911   #define bp_reduced_wr(t)         (* (u16_t *) (&(t)[3]))
10912   #define bp_precomp(t)            (* (u16_t *) (&(t)[5]))
10913   #define bp_max_ecc(t)            (* (u8_t *)  (&(t)[7]))
10914   #define bp_ctlbyte(t)            (* (u8_t *)  (&(t)[8]))
10915   #define bp_landingzone(t)        (* (u16_t *) (&(t)[12]))
10916   #define bp_sectors(t)            (* (u8_t *)  (&(t)[14]))
10917
10918   /* Miscellaneous. */
10919   #define DEV_PER_DRIVE   (1 + NR_PARTITIONS)
10920   #define MINOR_t0        64
10921   #define MINOR_r0        120
10922   #define MINOR_d0p0s0    128
10923   #define MINOR_fd0p0     (28<<2)
10924   #define P_FLOPPY        0
10925   #define P_PRIMARY       1
10926   #define P_SUB           2




++++++++++++++++++++++++++++++++++++++++++++++++++++++++++++++++++++++++++++
                           drivers/libdriver/driver.c
++++++++++++++++++++++++++++++++++++++++++++++++++++++++++++++++++++++++++++

11000   /* This file contains device independent device driver interface.
11001    *
11002    * Changes:
11003    *    Jul 25, 2005   added SYS_SIG type for signals  (Jorrit N. Herder)
11004    *    Sep 15, 2004   added SYN_ALARM type for timeouts  (Jorrit N. Herder)
11005    *    Jul 23, 2004   removed kernel dependencies  (Jorrit N. Herder)
11006    *    Apr 02, 1992   constructed from AT wini and floppy driver  (Kees J. Bot)
11007    *
11008    *
11009    * The drivers support the following operations (using message format m2):
11010    *
11011    *    m_type      DEVICE    PROC_NR    COUNT    POSITION  ADRRESS
11012    * ----------------------------------------------------------------
11013    * | DEV_OPEN  | device | proc nr |         |         |         |
11014    * |-----------+--------+---------+---------+---------+---------|
11015    * | DEV_CLOSE | device | proc nr |         |         |         |
11016    * |-----------+--------+---------+---------+---------+---------|
11017    * | DEV_READ  | device | proc nr |  bytes  | offset  | buf ptr |
11018    * |-----------+--------+---------+---------+---------+---------|
11019    * | DEV_WRITE | device | proc nr |  bytes  | offset  | buf ptr |
```

```
11020    *  |------------+---------+---------+---------+---------+---------|
11021    *  | DEV_GATHER | device  | proc nr | iov len |  offset | iov ptr |
11022    *  |------------+---------+---------+---------+---------+---------|
11023    *  | DEV_SCATTER| device  | proc nr | iov len |  offset | iov ptr |
11024    *  |------------+---------+---------+---------+---------+---------|
11025    *  |  DEV_IOCTL | device  | proc nr |func code|         | buf ptr |
11026    *  |------------+---------+---------+---------+---------+---------|
11027    *  |  CANCEL    | device  | proc nr | r/w     |         |         |
11028    *  |------------+---------+---------+---------+---------+---------|
11029    *  |  HARD_STOP |         |         |         |         |         |
11030    *  -------------------------------------------------------------
11031    *
11032    * The file contains one entry point:
11033    *
11034    *    driver_task:      called by the device dependent task entry
11035    */
11036
11037   #include "../drivers.h"
11038   #include <sys/ioc_disk.h>
11039   #include "driver.h"
11040
11041   #define BUF_EXTRA        0
11042
11043   /* Claim space for variables. */
11044   PRIVATE u8_t buffer[(unsigned) 2 * DMA_BUF_SIZE + BUF_EXTRA];
11045   u8_t *tmp_buf;                    /* the DMA buffer eventually */
11046   phys_bytes tmp_phys;             /* phys address of DMA buffer */
11047
11048   FORWARD _PROTOTYPE( void init_buffer, (void) );
11049   FORWARD _PROTOTYPE( int do_rdwt, (struct driver *dr, message *mp) );
11050   FORWARD _PROTOTYPE( int do_vrdwt, (struct driver *dr, message *mp) );
11051
11052   int device_caller;
11053
11054   /*===========================================================================*
11055    *                              driver_task                                  *
11056    *===========================================================================*/
11057   PUBLIC void driver_task(dp)
11058   struct driver *dp;       /* Device dependent entry points. */
11059   {
11060   /* Main program of any device driver task. */
11061
11062     int r, proc_nr;
11063     message mess;
11064
11065     /* Get a DMA buffer. */
11066     init_buffer();
11067
11068     /* Here is the main loop of the disk task.  It waits for a message, carries
11069      * it out, and sends a reply.
11070      */
11071     while (TRUE) {
11072
11073         /* Wait for a request to read or write a disk block. */
11074         if(receive(ANY, &mess) != OK) continue;
11075
11076         device_caller = mess.m_source;
11077         proc_nr = mess.PROC_NR;
11078
11079         /* Now carry out the work. */
```

```
11080          switch(mess.m_type) {
11081          case DEV_OPEN:          r = (*dp->dr_open)(dp, &mess);  break;
11082          case DEV_CLOSE:         r = (*dp->dr_close)(dp, &mess); break;
11083          case DEV_IOCTL:         r = (*dp->dr_ioctl)(dp, &mess); break;
11084          case CANCEL:            r = (*dp->dr_cancel)(dp, &mess);break;
11085          case DEV_SELECT:        r = (*dp->dr_select)(dp, &mess);break;
11086
11087          case DEV_READ:
11088          case DEV_WRITE:   r = do_rdwt(dp, &mess);        break;
11089          case DEV_GATHER:
11090          case DEV_SCATTER: r = do_vrdwt(dp, &mess);       break;
11091
11092          case HARD_INT:          /* leftover interrupt or expired timer. */
11093                                  if(dp->dr_hw_int) {
11094                                          (*dp->dr_hw_int)(dp, &mess);
11095                                  }
11096                                  continue;
11097          case SYS_SIG:           (*dp->dr_signal)(dp, &mess);
11098                                  continue;       /* don't reply */
11099          case SYN_ALARM:         (*dp->dr_alarm)(dp, &mess);
11100                                  continue;       /* don't reply */
11101          default:
11102                  if(dp->dr_other)
11103                          r = (*dp->dr_other)(dp, &mess);
11104                  else
11105                          r = EINVAL;
11106                  break;
11107          }
11108
11109          /* Clean up leftover state. */
11110          (*dp->dr_cleanup)();
11111
11112          /* Finally, prepare and send the reply message. */
11113          if (r != EDONTREPLY) {
11114                  mess.m_type = TASK_REPLY;
11115                  mess.REP_PROC_NR = proc_nr;
11116                  /* Status is # of bytes transferred or error code. */
11117                  mess.REP_STATUS = r;
11118                  send(device_caller, &mess);
11119          }
11120    }
11121  }

11123  /*===========================================================================*
11124   *                              init_buffer                                  *
11125   *===========================================================================*/
11126  PRIVATE void init_buffer()
11127  {
11128  /* Select a buffer that can safely be used for DMA transfers.  It may also
11129   * be used to read partition tables and such.  Its absolute address is
11130   * 'tmp_phys', the normal address is 'tmp_buf'.
11131   */
11132
11133    unsigned left;
11134
11135    tmp_buf = buffer;
11136    sys_umap(SELF, D, (vir_bytes)buffer, (phys_bytes)sizeof(buffer), &tmp_phys);
11137
11138    if ((left = dma_bytes_left(tmp_phys)) < DMA_BUF_SIZE) {
11139          /* First half of buffer crosses a 64K boundary, can't DMA into that */
```

```
11140              tmp_buf += left;
11141              tmp_phys += left;
11142      }
11143  }

11145  /*===========================================================================*
11146   *                              do_rdwt                                      *
11147   *===========================================================================*/
11148  PRIVATE int do_rdwt(dp, mp)
11149  struct driver *dp;              /* device dependent entry points */
11150  message *mp;                    /* pointer to read or write message */
11151  {
11152  /* Carry out a single read or write request. */
11153    iovec_t iovec1;
11154    int r, opcode;
11155    phys_bytes phys_addr;
11156
11157    /* Disk address?  Address and length of the user buffer? */
11158    if (mp->COUNT < 0) return(EINVAL);
11159
11160    /* Check the user buffer. */
11161    sys_umap(mp->PROC_NR, D, (vir_bytes) mp->ADDRESS, mp->COUNT, &phys_addr);
11162    if (phys_addr == 0) return(EFAULT);
11163
11164    /* Prepare for I/O. */
11165    if ((*dp->dr_prepare)(mp->DEVICE) == NIL_DEV) return(ENXIO);
11166
11167    /* Create a one element scatter/gather vector for the buffer. */
11168    opcode = mp->m_type == DEV_READ ? DEV_GATHER : DEV_SCATTER;
11169    iovec1.iov_addr = (vir_bytes) mp->ADDRESS;
11170    iovec1.iov_size = mp->COUNT;
11171
11172    /* Transfer bytes from/to the device. */
11173    r = (*dp->dr_transfer)(mp->PROC_NR, opcode, mp->POSITION, &iovec1, 1);
11174
11175    /* Return the number of bytes transferred or an error code. */
11176    return(r == OK ? (mp->COUNT - iovec1.iov_size) : r);
11177  }

11179  /*===========================================================================*
11180   *                              do_vrdwt                                     *
11181   *===========================================================================*/
11182  PRIVATE int do_vrdwt(dp, mp)
11183  struct driver *dp;         /* device dependent entry points */
11184  message *mp;               /* pointer to read or write message */
11185  {
11186  /* Carry out an device read or write to/from a vector of user addresses.
11187   * The "user addresses" are assumed to be safe, i.e. FS transferring to/from
11188   * its own buffers, so they are not checked.
11189   */
11190    static iovec_t iovec[NR_IOREQS];
11191    iovec_t *iov;
11192    phys_bytes iovec_size;
11193    unsigned nr_req;
11194    int r;
11195
11196    nr_req = mp->COUNT;    /* Length of I/O vector */
11197
11198    if (mp->m_source < 0) {
11199      /* Called by a task, no need to copy vector. */
```

```
11200          iov = (iovec_t *) mp->ADDRESS;
11201        } else {
11202          /* Copy the vector from the caller to kernel space. */
11203          if (nr_req > NR_IOREQS) nr_req = NR_IOREQS;
11204          iovec_size = (phys_bytes) (nr_req * sizeof(iovec[0]));
11205
11206          if (OK != sys_datacopy(mp->m_source, (vir_bytes) mp->ADDRESS,
11207                      SELF, (vir_bytes) iovec, iovec_size))
11208              panic((*dp->dr_name)(),"bad I/O vector by", mp->m_source);
11209          iov = iovec;
11210        }
11211
11212        /* Prepare for I/O. */
11213        if ((*dp->dr_prepare)(mp->DEVICE) == NIL_DEV) return(ENXIO);
11214
11215        /* Transfer bytes from/to the device. */
11216        r = (*dp->dr_transfer)(mp->PROC_NR, mp->m_type, mp->POSITION, iov, nr_req);
11217
11218        /* Copy the I/O vector back to the caller. */
11219        if (mp->m_source >= 0) {
11220          sys_datacopy(SELF, (vir_bytes) iovec,
11221              mp->m_source, (vir_bytes) mp->ADDRESS, iovec_size);
11222        }
11223        return(r);
11224      }

11226      /*===========================================================================*
11227       *                              no_name                                      *
11228       *===========================================================================*/
11229      PUBLIC char *no_name()
11230      {
11231      /* Use this default name if there is no specific name for the device. This was
11232       * originally done by fetching the name from the task table for this process:
11233       * "return(tasktab[proc_number(proc_ptr) + NR_TASKS].name);", but currently a
11234       * real "noname" is returned. Perhaps, some system information service can be
11235       * queried for a name at a later time.
11236       */
11237        static char name[] = "noname";
11238        return name;
11239      }

11241      /*===========================================================================*
11242       *                              do_nop                                       *
11243       *===========================================================================*/
11244      PUBLIC int do_nop(dp, mp)
11245      struct driver *dp;
11246      message *mp;
11247      {
11248      /* Nothing there, or nothing to do. */
11249
11250        switch (mp->m_type) {
11251        case DEV_OPEN:       return(ENODEV);
11252        case DEV_CLOSE:      return(OK);
11253        case DEV_IOCTL:      return(ENOTTY);
11254        default:             return(EIO);
11255        }
11256      }
```

```
11258  /*===========================================================*
11259   *                        nop_signal                         *
11260   *===========================================================*/
11261  PUBLIC void nop_signal(dp, mp)
11262  struct driver *dp;
11263  message *mp;
11264  {
11265  /* Default action for signal is to ignore. */
11266  }

11268  /*===========================================================*
11269   *                        nop_alarm                          *
11270   *===========================================================*/
11271  PUBLIC void nop_alarm(dp, mp)
11272  struct driver *dp;
11273  message *mp;
11274  {
11275  /* Ignore the leftover alarm. */
11276  }

11278  /*===========================================================*
11279   *                        nop_prepare                        *
11280   *===========================================================*/
11281  PUBLIC struct device *nop_prepare(device)
11282  {
11283  /* Nothing to prepare for. */
11284    return(NIL_DEV);
11285  }

11287  /*===========================================================*
11288   *                        nop_cleanup                        *
11289   *===========================================================*/
11290  PUBLIC void nop_cleanup()
11291  {
11292  /* Nothing to clean up. */
11293  }

11295  /*===========================================================*
11296   *                        nop_cancel                         *
11297   *===========================================================*/
11298  PUBLIC int nop_cancel(struct driver *dr, message *m)
11299  {
11300  /* Nothing to do for cancel. */
11301    return(OK);
11302  }

11304  /*===========================================================*
11305   *                        nop_select                         *
11306   *===========================================================*/
11307  PUBLIC int nop_select(struct driver *dr, message *m)
11308  {
11309  /* Nothing to do for select. */
11310    return(OK);
11311  }

11313  /*===========================================================*
11314   *                        do_diocntl                         *
11315   *===========================================================*/
11316  PUBLIC int do_diocntl(dp, mp)
11317  struct driver *dp;
```

```
11318  message *mp;                        /* pointer to ioctl request */
11319  {
11320  /* Carry out a partition setting/getting request. */
11321    struct device *dv;
11322    struct partition entry;
11323    int s;
11324
11325    if (mp->REQUEST != DIOCSETP && mp->REQUEST != DIOCGETP) {
11326          if(dp->dr_other) {
11327                  return dp->dr_other(dp, mp);
11328          } else return(ENOTTY);
11329    }
11330
11331    /* Decode the message parameters. */
11332    if ((dv = (*dp->dr_prepare)(mp->DEVICE)) == NIL_DEV) return(ENXIO);
11333
11334    if (mp->REQUEST == DIOCSETP) {
11335          /* Copy just this one partition table entry. */
11336          if (OK != (s=sys_datacopy(mp->PROC_NR, (vir_bytes) mp->ADDRESS,
11337                  SELF, (vir_bytes) &entry, sizeof(entry))))
11338              return s;
11339          dv->dv_base = entry.base;
11340          dv->dv_size = entry.size;
11341    } else {
11342          /* Return a partition table entry and the geometry of the drive. */
11343          entry.base = dv->dv_base;
11344          entry.size = dv->dv_size;
11345          (*dp->dr_geometry)(&entry);
11346          if (OK != (s=sys_datacopy(SELF, (vir_bytes) &entry,
11347                  mp->PROC_NR, (vir_bytes) mp->ADDRESS, sizeof(entry))))
11348              return s;
11349    }
11350    return(OK);
11351  }
```

```
++++++++++++++++++++++++++++++++++++++++++++++++++++++++++++++++++++++++++++
                          drivers/libdriver/drvlib.c
++++++++++++++++++++++++++++++++++++++++++++++++++++++++++++++++++++++++++++
11400  /* IBM device driver utility functions.        Author: Kees J. Bot
11401   *                                                    7 Dec 1995
11402   * Entry point:
11403   *   partition: partition a disk to the partition table(s) on it.
11404   */
11405
11406  #include "driver.h"
11407  #include "drvlib.h"
11408  #include <unistd.h>
11409
11410  /* Extended partition? */
11411  #define ext_part(s)     ((s) == 0x05 || (s) == 0x0F)
11412
11413  FORWARD _PROTOTYPE( void extpartition, (struct driver *dp, int extdev,
11414                                          unsigned long extbase) );
11415  FORWARD _PROTOTYPE( int get_part_table, (struct driver *dp, int device,
11416                          unsigned long offset, struct part_entry *table));
11417  FORWARD _PROTOTYPE( void sort, (struct part_entry *table) );
11418
11419  #ifndef CD_SECTOR_SIZE
```

```
11420    #define CD_SECTOR_SIZE 2048
11421    #endif
11422
11423    /*===========================================================================*
11424     *                              partition                                     *
11425     *===========================================================================*/
11426    PUBLIC void partition(dp, device, style, atapi)
11427    struct driver *dp;          /* device dependent entry points */
11428    int device;                 /* device to partition */
11429    int style;                  /* partitioning style: floppy, primary, sub. */
11430    int atapi;                  /* atapi device */
11431    {
11432    /* This routine is called on first open to initialize the partition tables
11433     * of a device.  It makes sure that each partition falls safely within the
11434     * device's limits.  Depending on the partition style we are either making
11435     * floppy partitions, primary partitions or subpartitions.  Only primary
11436     * partitions are sorted, because they are shared with other operating
11437     * systems that expect this.
11438     */
11439      struct part_entry table[NR_PARTITIONS], *pe;
11440      int disk, par;
11441      struct device *dv;
11442      unsigned long base, limit, part_limit;
11443
11444      /* Get the geometry of the device to partition */
11445      if ((dv = (*dp->dr_prepare)(device)) == NIL_DEV
11446                              || cmp64u(dv->dv_size, 0) == 0) return;
11447      base = div64u(dv->dv_base, SECTOR_SIZE);
11448      limit = base + div64u(dv->dv_size, SECTOR_SIZE);
11449
11450      /* Read the partition table for the device. */
11451      if(!get_part_table(dp, device, 0L, table)) {
11452            return;
11453      }
11454
11455      /* Compute the device number of the first partition. */
11456      switch (style) {
11457      case P_FLOPPY:
11458            device += MINOR_fd0p0;
11459            break;
11460      case P_PRIMARY:
11461            sort(table);            /* sort a primary partition table */
11462            device += 1;
11463            break;
11464      case P_SUB:
11465            disk = device / DEV_PER_DRIVE;
11466            par = device % DEV_PER_DRIVE - 1;
11467            device = MINOR_d0p0s0 + (disk * NR_PARTITIONS + par) * NR_PARTITIONS;
11468      }
11469
11470      /* Find an array of devices. */
11471      if ((dv = (*dp->dr_prepare)(device)) == NIL_DEV) return;
11472
11473      /* Set the geometry of the partitions from the partition table. */
11474      for (par = 0; par < NR_PARTITIONS; par++, dv++) {
11475            /* Shrink the partition to fit within the device. */
11476            pe = &table[par];
11477            part_limit = pe->lowsec + pe->size;
11478            if (part_limit < pe->lowsec) part_limit = limit;
11479            if (part_limit > limit) part_limit = limit;
```

```
11480          if (pe->lowsec < base) pe->lowsec = base;
11481          if (part_limit < pe->lowsec) part_limit = pe->lowsec;
11482
11483          dv->dv_base = mul64u(pe->lowsec, SECTOR_SIZE);
11484          dv->dv_size = mul64u(part_limit - pe->lowsec, SECTOR_SIZE);
11485
11486          if (style == P_PRIMARY) {
11487                  /* Each Minix primary partition can be subpartitioned. */
11488                  if (pe->sysind == MINIX_PART)
11489                          partition(dp, device + par, P_SUB, atapi);
11490
11491                  /* An extended partition has logical partitions. */
11492                  if (ext_part(pe->sysind))
11493                          extpartition(dp, device + par, pe->lowsec);
11494          }
11495   }
11496 }

11498 /*===========================================================================*
11499  *                              extpartition                                 *
11500  *===========================================================================*/
11501 PRIVATE void extpartition(dp, extdev, extbase)
11502 struct driver *dp;       /* device dependent entry points */
11503 int extdev;              /* extended partition to scan */
11504 unsigned long extbase;   /* sector offset of the base extended partition */
11505 {
11506 /* Extended partitions cannot be ignored alas, because people like to move
11507  * files to and from DOS partitions.  Avoid reading this code, it's no fun.
11508  */
11509   struct part_entry table[NR_PARTITIONS], *pe;
11510   int subdev, disk, par;
11511   struct device *dv;
11512   unsigned long offset, nextoffset;
11513
11514   disk = extdev / DEV_PER_DRIVE;
11515   par = extdev % DEV_PER_DRIVE - 1;
11516   subdev = MINOR_d0p0s0 + (disk * NR_PARTITIONS + par) * NR_PARTITIONS;
11517
11518   offset = 0;
11519   do {
11520          if (!get_part_table(dp, extdev, offset, table)) return;
11521          sort(table);
11522
11523          /* The table should contain one logical partition and optionally
11524           * another extended partition.  (It's a linked list.)
11525           */
11526          nextoffset = 0;
11527          for (par = 0; par < NR_PARTITIONS; par++) {
11528                  pe = &table[par];
11529                  if (ext_part(pe->sysind)) {
11530                          nextoffset = pe->lowsec;
11531                  } else
11532                  if (pe->sysind != NO_PART) {
11533                          if ((dv = (*dp->dr_prepare)(subdev)) == NIL_DEV) return;
11534
11535                          dv->dv_base = mul64u(extbase + offset + pe->lowsec,
11536                                                              SECTOR_SIZE);
11537                          dv->dv_size = mul64u(pe->size, SECTOR_SIZE);
11538
11539                          /* Out of devices? */
```

```
11540                               if (++subdev % NR_PARTITIONS == 0) return;
11541                      }
11542              }
11543      } while ((offset = nextoffset) != 0);
11544  }

11546  /*===========================================================================*
11547   *                              get_part_table                               *
11548   *===========================================================================*/
11549  PRIVATE int get_part_table(dp, device, offset, table)
11550  struct driver *dp;
11551  int device;
11552  unsigned long offset;          /* sector offset to the table */
11553  struct part_entry *table;      /* four entries */
11554  {
11555  /* Read the partition table for the device, return true iff there were no
11556   * errors.
11557   */
11558    iovec_t iovec1;
11559    off_t position;
11560    static unsigned char partbuf[CD_SECTOR_SIZE];
11561
11562    position = offset << SECTOR_SHIFT;
11563    iovec1.iov_addr = (vir_bytes) partbuf;
11564    iovec1.iov_size = CD_SECTOR_SIZE;
11565    if ((*dp->dr_prepare)(device) != NIL_DEV) {
11566          (void) (*dp->dr_transfer)(SELF, DEV_GATHER, position, &iovec1, 1);
11567    }
11568    if (iovec1.iov_size != 0) {
11569          return 0;
11570    }
11571    if (partbuf[510] != 0x55 || partbuf[511] != 0xAA) {
11572          /* Invalid partition table. */
11573          return 0;
11574    }
11575    memcpy(table, (partbuf + PART_TABLE_OFF), NR_PARTITIONS * sizeof(table[0]));
11576    return 1;
11577  }

11579  /*===========================================================================*
11580   *                              sort                                          *
11581   *===========================================================================*/
11582  PRIVATE void sort(table)
11583  struct part_entry *table;
11584  {
11585  /* Sort a partition table. */
11586    struct part_entry *pe, tmp;
11587    int n = NR_PARTITIONS;
11588
11589    do {
11590          for (pe = table; pe < table + NR_PARTITIONS-1; pe++) {
11591                  if (pe[0].sysind == NO_PART
11592                      || (pe[0].lowsec > pe[1].lowsec
11593                                      && pe[1].sysind != NO_PART)) {
11594                      tmp = pe[0]; pe[0] = pe[1]; pe[1] = tmp;
11595                  }
11596          }
11597    } while (--n > 0);
11598  }
```

```
++++++++++++++++++++++++++++++++++++++++++++++++++++++++++++++++++++++++++
                         drivers/memory/memory.c
++++++++++++++++++++++++++++++++++++++++++++++++++++++++++++++++++++++++++
11600   /* This file contains the device dependent part of the drivers for the
11601    * following special files:
11602    *      /dev/ram        - RAM disk
11603    *      /dev/mem        - absolute memory
11604    *      /dev/kmem       - kernel virtual memory
11605    *      /dev/null       - null device (data sink)
11606    *      /dev/boot       - boot device loaded from boot image
11607    *      /dev/zero       - null byte stream generator
11608    *
11609    *  Changes:
11610    *      Apr 29, 2005    added null byte generator  (Jorrit N. Herder)
11611    *      Apr 09, 2005    added support for boot device  (Jorrit N. Herder)
11612    *      Jul 26, 2004    moved RAM driver to user-space  (Jorrit N. Herder)
11613    *      Apr 20, 1992    device dependent/independent split  (Kees J. Bot)
11614    */
11615
11616   #include "../drivers.h"
11617   #include "../libdriver/driver.h"
11618   #include <sys/ioc_memory.h>
11619   #include "../../kernel/const.h"
11620   #include "../../kernel/config.h"
11621   #include "../../kernel/type.h"
11622
11623   #include "assert.h"
11624
11625   #define NR_DEVS            6              /* number of minor devices */
11626
11627   PRIVATE struct device m_geom[NR_DEVS];  /* base and size of each device */
11628   PRIVATE int m_seg[NR_DEVS];             /* segment index of each device */
11629   PRIVATE int m_device;                   /* current device */
11630   PRIVATE struct kinfo kinfo;             /* kernel information */
11631   PRIVATE struct machine machine;         /* machine information */
11632
11633   extern int errno;                       /* error number for PM calls */
11634
11635   FORWARD _PROTOTYPE( char *m_name, (void)                          );
11636   FORWARD _PROTOTYPE( struct device *m_prepare, (int device)       );
11637   FORWARD _PROTOTYPE( int m_transfer, (int proc_nr, int opcode, off_t position,
11638                                       iovec_t *iov, unsigned nr_req)  );
11639   FORWARD _PROTOTYPE( int m_do_open, (struct driver *dp, message *m_ptr)  );
11640   FORWARD _PROTOTYPE( void m_init, (void) );
11641   FORWARD _PROTOTYPE( int m_ioctl, (struct driver *dp, message *m_ptr)    );
11642   FORWARD _PROTOTYPE( void m_geometry, (struct partition *entry)          );
11643
11644   /* Entry points to this driver. */
11645   PRIVATE struct driver m_dtab = {
11646     m_name,         /* current device's name */
11647     m_do_open,      /* open or mount */
11648     do_nop,         /* nothing on a close */
11649     m_ioctl,        /* specify ram disk geometry */
11650     m_prepare,      /* prepare for I/O on a given minor device */
11651     m_transfer,     /* do the I/O */
11652     nop_cleanup,    /* no need to clean up */
11653     m_geometry,     /* memory device "geometry" */
11654     nop_signal,     /* system signals */
```

```
11655      nop_alarm,
11656      nop_cancel,
11657      nop_select,
11658      NULL,
11659      NULL
11660  };
11661
11662  /* Buffer for the /dev/zero null byte feed. */
11663  #define ZERO_BUF_SIZE                    1024
11664  PRIVATE char dev_zero[ZERO_BUF_SIZE];
11665
11666  #define click_to_round_k(n) \
11667          ((unsigned) ((((unsigned long) (n) << CLICK_SHIFT) + 512) / 1024))
11668
11669  /*===========================================================================*
11670   *                              main                                         *
11671   *===========================================================================*/
11672  PUBLIC int main(void)
11673  {
11674  /* Main program. Initialize the memory driver and start the main loop. */
11675    m_init();
11676    driver_task(&m_dtab);
11677    return(OK);
11678  }
11679
11680  /*===========================================================================*
11681   *                              m_name                                       *
11682   *===========================================================================*/
11683  PRIVATE char *m_name()
11684  {
11685  /* Return a name for the current device. */
11686    static char name[] = "memory";
11687    return name;
11688  }
11689
11690  /*===========================================================================*
11691   *                              m_prepare                                    *
11692   *===========================================================================*/
11693  PRIVATE struct device *m_prepare(device)
11694  int device;
11695  {
11696  /* Prepare for I/O on a device: check if the minor device number is ok. */
11697    if (device < 0 || device >= NR_DEVS) return(NIL_DEV);
11698    m_device = device;
11699
11700    return(&m_geom[device]);
11701  }
11702
11703  /*===========================================================================*
11704   *                              m_transfer                                   *
11705   *===========================================================================*/
11706  PRIVATE int m_transfer(proc_nr, opcode, position, iov, nr_req)
11707  int proc_nr;                    /* process doing the request */
11708  int opcode;                     /* DEV_GATHER or DEV_SCATTER */
11709  off_t position;                 /* offset on device to read or write */
11710  iovec_t *iov;                   /* pointer to read or write request vector */
11711  unsigned nr_req;                /* length of request vector */
11712  {
11713  /* Read or write one the driver's minor devices. */
11714    phys_bytes mem_phys;
```

```
11715     int seg;
11716     unsigned count, left, chunk;
11717     vir_bytes user_vir;
11718     struct device *dv;
11719     unsigned long dv_size;
11720     int s;
11721
11722     /* Get minor device number and check for /dev/null. */
11723     dv = &m_geom[m_device];
11724     dv_size = cv64ul(dv->dv_size);
11725
11726     while (nr_req > 0) {
11727
11728             /* How much to transfer and where to / from. */
11729             count = iov->iov_size;
11730             user_vir = iov->iov_addr;
11731
11732             switch (m_device) {
11733
11734             /* No copying; ignore request. */
11735             case NULL_DEV:
11736                 if (opcode == DEV_GATHER) return(OK);        /* always at EOF */
11737                 break;
11738
11739             /* Virtual copying. For RAM disk, kernel memory and boot device. */
11740             case RAM_DEV:
11741             case KMEM_DEV:
11742             case BOOT_DEV:
11743                 if (position >= dv_size) return(OK);        /* check for EOF */
11744                 if (position + count > dv_size) count = dv_size - position;
11745                 seg = m_seg[m_device];
11746
11747                 if (opcode == DEV_GATHER) {                 /* copy actual data */
11748                     sys_vircopy(SELF,seg,position, proc_nr,D,user_vir, count);
11749                 } else {
11750                     sys_vircopy(proc_nr,D,user_vir, SELF,seg,position, count);
11751                 }
11752                 break;
11753
11754             /* Physical copying. Only used to access entire memory. */
11755             case MEM_DEV:
11756                 if (position >= dv_size) return(OK);        /* check for EOF */
11757                 if (position + count > dv_size) count = dv_size - position;
11758                 mem_phys = cv64ul(dv->dv_base) + position;
11759
11760                 if (opcode == DEV_GATHER) {                 /* copy data */
11761                     sys_physcopy(NONE, PHYS_SEG, mem_phys,
11762                             proc_nr, D, user_vir, count);
11763                 } else {
11764                     sys_physcopy(proc_nr, D, user_vir,
11765                             NONE, PHYS_SEG, mem_phys, count);
11766                 }
11767                 break;
11768
11769             /* Null byte stream generator. */
11770             case ZERO_DEV:
11771                 if (opcode == DEV_GATHER) {
11772                     left = count;
11773                     while (left > 0) {
11774                         chunk = (left > ZERO_BUF_SIZE) ? ZERO_BUF_SIZE : left;
```

```
11775                             if (OK != (s=sys_vircopy(SELF, D, (vir_bytes) dev_zero,
11776                                 proc_nr, D, user_vir, chunk)))
11777                             report("MEM","sys_vircopy failed", s);
11778                         left -= chunk;
11779                         user_vir += chunk;
11780                     }
11781                 }
11782             break;
11783
11784         /* Unknown (illegal) minor device. */
11785         default:
11786             return(EINVAL);
11787         }
11788
11789         /* Book the number of bytes transferred. */
11790         position += count;
11791         iov->iov_addr += count;
11792         if ((iov->iov_size -= count) == 0) { iov++; nr_req--; }
11793
11794     }
11795     return(OK);
11796 }

11798 /*===========================================================================*
11799  *                              m_do_open                                    *
11800  *===========================================================================*/
11801 PRIVATE int m_do_open(dp, m_ptr)
11802 struct driver *dp;
11803 message *m_ptr;
11804 {
11805 /* Check device number on open.  (This used to give I/O privileges to a
11806  * process opening /dev/mem or /dev/kmem. This may be needed in case of
11807  * memory mapped I/O. With system calls to do I/O this is no longer needed.)
11808  */
11809     if (m_prepare(m_ptr->DEVICE) == NIL_DEV) return(ENXIO);
11810
11811     return(OK);
11812 }

11814 /*===========================================================================*
11815  *                              m_init                                       *
11816  *===========================================================================*/
11817 PRIVATE void m_init()
11818 {
11819     /* Initialize this task. All minor devices are initialized one by one. */
11820     int i, s;
11821
11822     if (OK != (s=sys_getkinfo(&kinfo))) {
11823         panic("MEM","Couldn't get kernel information.",s);
11824     }
11825
11826     /* Install remote segment for /dev/kmem memory. */
11827     m_geom[KMEM_DEV].dv_base = cvul64(kinfo.kmem_base);
11828     m_geom[KMEM_DEV].dv_size = cvul64(kinfo.kmem_size);
11829     if (OK != (s=sys_segctl(&m_seg[KMEM_DEV], (u16_t *) &s, (vir_bytes *) &s,
11830                 kinfo.kmem_base, kinfo.kmem_size))) {
11831         panic("MEM","Couldn't install remote segment.",s);
11832     }
11833
11834     /* Install remote segment for /dev/boot memory, if enabled. */
```

```
11835      m_geom[BOOT_DEV].dv_base = cvul64(kinfo.bootdev_base);
11836      m_geom[BOOT_DEV].dv_size = cvul64(kinfo.bootdev_size);
11837      if (kinfo.bootdev_base > 0) {
11838          if (OK != (s=sys_segctl(&m_seg[BOOT_DEV], (u16_t *) &s, (vir_bytes *) &s,
11839                  kinfo.bootdev_base, kinfo.bootdev_size))) {
11840              panic("MEM","Couldn't install remote segment.",s);
11841          }
11842      }
11843
11844      /* Initialize /dev/zero. Simply write zeros into the buffer. */
11845      for (i=0; i<ZERO_BUF_SIZE; i++) {
11846          dev_zero[i] = '\0';
11847      }
11848
11849      /* Set up memory ranges for /dev/mem. */
11850      if (OK != (s=sys_getmachine(&machine))) {
11851          panic("MEM","Couldn't get machine information.",s);
11852      }
11853      if (! machine.protected) {
11854          m_geom[MEM_DEV].dv_size =   cvul64(0x100000); /* 1M for 8086 systems */
11855      } else {
11856          m_geom[MEM_DEV].dv_size = cvul64(0xFFFFFFFF); /* 4G-1 for 386 systems */
11857      }
11858  }

11860  /*===========================================================================*
11861   *                              m_ioctl                                      *
11862   *===========================================================================*/
11863  PRIVATE int m_ioctl(dp, m_ptr)
11864  struct driver *dp;                          /* pointer to driver structure */
11865  message *m_ptr;                             /* pointer to control message */
11866  {
11867  /* I/O controls for the memory driver. Currently there is one I/O control:
11868   * - MIOCRAMSIZE: to set the size of the RAM disk.
11869   */
11870    struct device *dv;
11871    if ((dv = m_prepare(m_ptr->DEVICE)) == NIL_DEV) return(ENXIO);
11872
11873    switch (m_ptr->REQUEST) {
11874      case MIOCRAMSIZE: {
11875          /* FS wants to create a new RAM disk with the given size. */
11876          phys_bytes ramdev_size;
11877          phys_bytes ramdev_base;
11878          int s;
11879
11880          if (m_ptr->PROC_NR != FS_PROC_NR) {
11881              report("MEM", "warning, MIOCRAMSIZE called by", m_ptr->PROC_NR);
11882              return(EPERM);
11883          }
11884
11885          /* Try to allocate a piece of memory for the RAM disk. */
11886          ramdev_size = m_ptr->POSITION;
11887          if (allocmem(ramdev_size, &ramdev_base) < 0) {
11888              report("MEM", "warning, allocmem failed", errno);
11889              return(ENOMEM);
11890          }
11891          dv->dv_base = cvul64(ramdev_base);
11892          dv->dv_size = cvul64(ramdev_size);
11893
11894          if (OK != (s=sys_segctl(&m_seg[RAM_DEV], (u16_t *) &s, (vir_bytes *) &s,
```

```
11895                      ramdev_base, ramdev_size))) {
11896                  panic("MEM","Couldn't install remote segment.",s);
11897          }
11898          break;
11899      }
11900
11901    default:
11902        return(do_diocntl(&m_dtab, m_ptr));
11903    }
11904    return(OK);
11905  }
11906
11907  /*===========================================================================*
11908   *                              m_geometry                                   *
11909   *===========================================================================*/
11910  PRIVATE void m_geometry(entry)
11911  struct partition *entry;
11912  {
11913    /* Memory devices don't have a geometry, but the outside world insists. */
11914    entry->cylinders = div64u(m_geom[m_device].dv_size, SECTOR_SIZE) / (64 * 32);
11915    entry->heads = 64;
11916    entry->sectors = 32;
11917  }
```

```
++++++++++++++++++++++++++++++++++++++++++++++++++++++++++++++++++++++++++++
                         drivers/at_wini/at_wini.h
++++++++++++++++++++++++++++++++++++++++++++++++++++++++++++++++++++++++++++

12000  #include "../drivers.h"
12001  #include "../libdriver/driver.h"
12002  #include "../libdriver/drvlib.h"
12003
12004  _PROTOTYPE(int main, (void));
12005
12006  #define VERBOSE          0    /* display identify messages during boot */
12007  #define ENABLE_ATAPI     0    /* add ATAPI cd-rom support to driver */
```

```
++++++++++++++++++++++++++++++++++++++++++++++++++++++++++++++++++++++++++++
                         drivers/at_wini/at_wini.c
++++++++++++++++++++++++++++++++++++++++++++++++++++++++++++++++++++++++++++

12100  /* This file contains the device dependent part of a driver for the IBM-AT
12101   * winchester controller.  Written by Adri Koppes.
12102   *
12103   * The file contains one entry point:
12104   *
12105   *   at_winchester_task:        main entry when system is brought up
12106   *
12107   * Changes:
12108   *    Aug 19, 2005    ata pci support, supports SATA  (Ben Gras)
12109   *    Nov 18, 2004    moved AT disk driver to user-space  (Jorrit N. Herder)
12110   *    Aug 20, 2004    watchdogs replaced by sync alarms  (Jorrit N. Herder)
12111   *    Mar 23, 2000    added ATAPI CDROM support  (Michael Temari)
12112   *    May 14, 2000    d-d/i rewrite  (Kees J. Bot)
12113   *    Apr 13, 1992    device dependent/independent split  (Kees J. Bot)
12114   */
```

```
12115
12116   #include "at_wini.h"
12117   #include "../libpci/pci.h"
12118
12119   #include <minix/sysutil.h>
12120   #include <minix/keymap.h>
12121   #include <sys/ioc_disk.h>
12122
12123   #define ATAPI_DEBUG          0    /* To debug ATAPI code. */
12124
12125   /* I/O Ports used by winchester disk controllers. */
12126
12127   /* Read and write registers */
12128   #define REG_CMD_BASE0    0x1F0    /* command base register of controller 0 */
12129   #define REG_CMD_BASE1    0x170    /* command base register of controller 1 */
12130   #define REG_CTL_BASE0    0x3F6    /* control base register of controller 0 */
12131   #define REG_CTL_BASE1    0x376    /* control base register of controller 1 */
12132
12133   #define REG_DATA             0    /* data register (offset from the base reg.) */
12134   #define REG_PRECOMP          1    /* start of write precompensation */
12135   #define REG_COUNT            2    /* sectors to transfer */
12136   #define REG_SECTOR           3    /* sector number */
12137   #define REG_CYL_LO           4    /* low byte of cylinder number */
12138   #define REG_CYL_HI           5    /* high byte of cylinder number */
12139   #define REG_LDH              6    /* lba, drive and head */
12140   #define    LDH_DEFAULT     0xA0    /* ECC enable, 512 bytes per sector */
12141   #define    LDH_LBA         0x40    /* Use LBA addressing */
12142   #define    ldh_init(drive)    (LDH_DEFAULT | ((drive) << 4))
12143
12144   /* Read only registers */
12145   #define REG_STATUS           7    /* status */
12146   #define    STATUS_BSY      0x80    /* controller busy */
12147   #define    STATUS_RDY      0x40    /* drive ready */
12148   #define    STATUS_WF       0x20    /* write fault */
12149   #define    STATUS_SC       0x10    /* seek complete (obsolete) */
12150   #define    STATUS_DRQ      0x08    /* data transfer request */
12151   #define    STATUS_CRD      0x04    /* corrected data */
12152   #define    STATUS_IDX      0x02    /* index pulse */
12153   #define    STATUS_ERR      0x01    /* error */
12154   #define    STATUS_ADMBSY  0x100    /* administratively busy (software) */
12155   #define REG_ERROR            1    /* error code */
12156   #define    ERROR_BB        0x80    /* bad block */
12157   #define    ERROR_ECC       0x40    /* bad ecc bytes */
12158   #define    ERROR_ID        0x10    /* id not found */
12159   #define    ERROR_AC        0x04    /* aborted command */
12160   #define    ERROR_TK        0x02    /* track zero error */
12161   #define    ERROR_DM        0x01    /* no data address mark */
12162
12163   /* Write only registers */
12164   #define REG_COMMAND          7    /* command */
12165   #define    CMD_IDLE        0x00    /* for w_command: drive idle */
12166   #define    CMD_RECALIBRATE 0x10    /* recalibrate drive */
12167   #define    CMD_READ        0x20    /* read data */
12168   #define    CMD_READ_EXT    0x24    /* read data (LBA48 addressed) */
12169   #define    CMD_WRITE       0x30    /* write data */
12170   #define    CMD_WRITE_EXT   0x34    /* write data (LBA48 addressed) */
12171   #define    CMD_READVERIFY  0x40    /* read verify */
12172   #define    CMD_FORMAT      0x50    /* format track */
12173   #define    CMD_SEEK        0x70    /* seek cylinder */
12174   #define    CMD_DIAG        0x90    /* execute device diagnostics */
```

```
12175  #define   CMD_SPECIFY          0x91     /* specify parameters */
12176  #define   ATA_IDENTIFY         0xEC     /* identify drive */
12177  /* #define REG_CTL              0x206   */ /* control register */
12178  #define REG_CTL           0        /* control register */
12179  #define   CTL_NORETRY          0x80     /* disable access retry */
12180  #define   CTL_NOECC            0x40     /* disable ecc retry */
12181  #define   CTL_EIGHTHEADS       0x08     /* more than eight heads */
12182  #define   CTL_RESET            0x04     /* reset controller */
12183  #define   CTL_INTDISABLE       0x02     /* disable interrupts */
12184
12185  #define REG_STATUS          7     /* status */
12186  #define   STATUS_BSY           0x80     /* controller busy */
12187  #define   STATUS_DRDY          0x40     /* drive ready */
12188  #define   STATUS_DMADF         0x20     /* dma ready/drive fault */
12189  #define   STATUS_SRVCDSC       0x10     /* service or dsc */
12190  #define   STATUS_DRQ           0x08     /* data transfer request */
12191  #define   STATUS_CORR          0x04     /* correctable error occurred */
12192  #define   STATUS_CHECK         0x01     /* check error */
12193
12194  /* Interrupt request lines. */
12195  #define NO_IRQ             0     /* no IRQ set yet */
12196
12197  #define ATAPI_PACKETSIZE       12
12198  #define SENSE_PACKETSIZE       18
12199
12200  /* Common command block */
12201  struct command {
12202    u8_t  precomp;          /* REG_PRECOMP, etc. */
12203    u8_t  count;
12204    u8_t  sector;
12205    u8_t  cyl_lo;
12206    u8_t  cyl_hi;
12207    u8_t  ldh;
12208    u8_t  command;
12209  };
12210
12211  /* Error codes */
12212  #define ERR               (-1)    /* general error */
12213  #define ERR_BAD_SECTOR    (-2)    /* block marked bad detected */
12214
12215  /* Some controllers don't interrupt, the clock will wake us up. */
12216  #define WAKEUP            (32*HZ) /* drive may be out for 31 seconds max */
12217
12218  /* Miscellaneous. */
12219  #define MAX_DRIVES         8
12220  #define COMPAT_DRIVES      4
12221  #define MAX_SECS           256    /* controller can transfer this many sectors */
12222  #define MAX_ERRORS         4      /* how often to try rd/wt before quitting */
12223  #define NR_MINORS         (MAX_DRIVES * DEV_PER_DRIVE)
12224  #define SUB_PER_DRIVE     (NR_PARTITIONS * NR_PARTITIONS)
12225  #define NR_SUBDEVS        (MAX_DRIVES * SUB_PER_DRIVE)
12226  #define DELAY_USECS        1000   /* controller timeout in microseconds */
12227  #define DELAY_TICKS        1      /* controller timeout in ticks */
12228  #define DEF_TIMEOUT_TICKS      300      /* controller timeout in ticks */
12229  #define RECOVERY_USECS 500000    /* controller recovery time in microseconds */
12230  #define RECOVERY_TICKS     30     /* controller recovery time in ticks */
12231  #define INITIALIZED        0x01   /* drive is initialized */
12232  #define DEAF               0x02   /* controller must be reset */
12233  #define SMART              0x04   /* drive supports ATA commands */
12234  #define ATAPI              0      /* don't bother with ATAPI; optimise out */
```

```
12235   #define IDENTIFIED      0x10    /* w_identify done successfully */
12236   #define IGNORING        0x20    /* w_identify failed once */
12237
12238   /* Timeouts and max retries. */
12239   int timeout_ticks = DEF_TIMEOUT_TICKS, max_errors = MAX_ERRORS;
12240   int wakeup_ticks = WAKEUP;
12241   long w_standard_timeouts = 0, w_pci_debug = 0, w_instance = 0,
12242    w_lba48 = 0, atapi_debug = 0;
12243
12244   int w_testing = 0, w_silent = 0;
12245
12246   int w_next_drive = 0;
12247
12248   /* Variables. */
12249
12250   /* wini is indexed by controller first, then drive (0-3).
12251    * controller 0 is always the 'compatability' ide controller, at
12252    * the fixed locations, whether present or not.
12253    */
12254   PRIVATE struct wini {            /* main drive struct, one entry per drive */
12255     unsigned state;               /* drive state: deaf, initialized, dead */
12256     unsigned w_status;            /* device status register */
12257     unsigned base_cmd;            /* command base register */
12258     unsigned base_ctl;            /* control base register */
12259     unsigned irq;                 /* interrupt request line */
12260     unsigned irq_mask;            /* 1 << irq */
12261     unsigned irq_need_ack;        /* irq needs to be acknowledged */
12262     int irq_hook_id;              /* id of irq hook at the kernel */
12263     int lba48;                    /* supports lba48 */
12264     unsigned lcylinders;          /* logical number of cylinders (BIOS) */
12265     unsigned lheads;              /* logical number of heads */
12266     unsigned lsectors;            /* logical number of sectors per track */
12267     unsigned pcylinders;          /* physical number of cylinders (translated) */
12268     unsigned pheads;              /* physical number of heads */
12269     unsigned psectors;            /* physical number of sectors per track */
12270     unsigned ldhpref;             /* top four bytes of the LDH (head) register */
12271     unsigned precomp;             /* write precompensation cylinder / 4 */
12272     unsigned max_count;           /* max request for this drive */
12273     unsigned open_ct;             /* in-use count */
12274     struct device part[DEV_PER_DRIVE];      /* disks and partitions */
12275     struct device subpart[SUB_PER_DRIVE]; /* subpartitions */
12276   } wini[MAX_DRIVES], *w_wn;
12277
12278   PRIVATE int w_device = -1;
12279   PRIVATE int w_controller = -1;
12280   PRIVATE int w_major = -1;
12281   PRIVATE char w_id_string[40];
12282
12283   PRIVATE int win_tasknr;                      /* my task number */
12284   PRIVATE int w_command;                       /* current command in execution */
12285   PRIVATE u8_t w_byteval;                       /* used for SYS_IRQCTL */
12286   PRIVATE int w_drive;                          /* selected drive */
12287   PRIVATE int w_controller;                     /* selected controller */
12288   PRIVATE struct device *w_dv;                  /* device's base and size */
12289
12290   FORWARD _PROTOTYPE( void init_params, (void)                        );
12291   FORWARD _PROTOTYPE( void init_drive, (struct wini *, int, int, int, int, int, int));
12292   FORWARD _PROTOTYPE( void init_params_pci, (int)                     );
12293   FORWARD _PROTOTYPE( int w_do_open, (struct driver *dp, message *m_ptr) );
12294   FORWARD _PROTOTYPE( struct device *w_prepare, (int dev)             );
```

```
12295   FORWARD _PROTOTYPE( int w_identify, (void)                        );
12296   FORWARD _PROTOTYPE( char *w_name, (void)                         );
12297   FORWARD _PROTOTYPE( int w_specify, (void)                        );
12298   FORWARD _PROTOTYPE( int w_io_test, (void)                        );
12299   FORWARD _PROTOTYPE( int w_transfer, (int proc_nr, int opcode, off_t position,
12300                                        iovec_t *iov, unsigned nr_req) );
12301   FORWARD _PROTOTYPE( int com_out, (struct command *cmd)           );
12302   FORWARD _PROTOTYPE( void w_need_reset, (void)                    );
12303   FORWARD _PROTOTYPE( void ack_irqs, (unsigned int)                );
12304   FORWARD _PROTOTYPE( int w_do_close, (struct driver *dp, message *m_ptr) );
12305   FORWARD _PROTOTYPE( int w_other, (struct driver *dp, message *m_ptr)  );
12306   FORWARD _PROTOTYPE( int w_hw_int, (struct driver *dp, message *m_ptr) );
12307   FORWARD _PROTOTYPE( int com_simple, (struct command *cmd)        );
12308   FORWARD _PROTOTYPE( void w_timeout, (void)                       );
12309   FORWARD _PROTOTYPE( int w_reset, (void)                          );
12310   FORWARD _PROTOTYPE( void w_intr_wait, (void)                     );
12311   FORWARD _PROTOTYPE( int at_intr_wait, (void)                     );
12312   FORWARD _PROTOTYPE( int w_waitfor, (int mask, int value)         );
12313   FORWARD _PROTOTYPE( void w_geometry, (struct partition *entry)   );
12314
12315   /* Entry points to this driver. */
12316   PRIVATE struct driver w_dtab = {
12317     w_name,                 /* current device's name */
12318     w_do_open,              /* open or mount request, initialize device */
12319     w_do_close,             /* release device */
12320     do_diocntl,             /* get or set a partition's geometry */
12321     w_prepare,              /* prepare for I/O on a given minor device */
12322     w_transfer,             /* do the I/O */
12323     nop_cleanup,            /* nothing to clean up */
12324     w_geometry,             /* tell the geometry of the disk */
12325     nop_signal,             /* no cleanup needed on shutdown */
12326     nop_alarm,              /* ignore leftover alarms */
12327     nop_cancel,             /* ignore CANCELs */
12328     nop_select,             /* ignore selects */
12329     w_other,                /* catch-all for unrecognized commands and ioctls */
12330     w_hw_int                /* leftover hardware interrupts */
12331   };
12332
12333   /*===========================================================================*
12334    *                          at_winchester_task                               *
12335    *===========================================================================*/
12336   PUBLIC int main()
12337   {
12338   /* Set special disk parameters then call the generic main loop. */
12339     init_params();
12340     driver_task(&w_dtab);
12341     return(OK);
12342   }
12343
12344   /*===========================================================================*
12345    *                              init_params                                   *
12346    *===========================================================================*/
12347   PRIVATE void init_params()
12348   {
12349   /* This routine is called at startup to initialize the drive parameters. */
12350
12351     u16_t parv[2];
12352     unsigned int vector, size;
12353     int drive, nr_drives;
12354     struct wini *wn;
```

```
12355    u8_t params[16];
12356    int s;
12357
12358    /* Boot variables. */
12359    env_parse("ata_std_timeout", "d", 0, &w_standard_timeouts, 0, 1);
12360    env_parse("ata_pci_debug", "d", 0, &w_pci_debug, 0, 1);
12361    env_parse("ata_instance", "d", 0, &w_instance, 0, 8);
12362    env_parse("ata_lba48", "d", 0, &w_lba48, 0, 1);
12363    env_parse("atapi_debug", "d", 0, &atapi_debug, 0, 1);
12364
12365    if (w_instance == 0) {
12366            /* Get the number of drives from the BIOS data area */
12367            if ((s=sys_vircopy(SELF, BIOS_SEG, NR_HD_DRIVES_ADDR,
12368                            SELF, D, (vir_bytes) params, NR_HD_DRIVES_SIZE)) != OK)
12369                    panic(w_name(), "Couldn't read BIOS", s);
12370            if ((nr_drives = params[0]) > 2) nr_drives = 2;
12371
12372            for (drive = 0, wn = wini; drive < COMPAT_DRIVES; drive++, wn++) {
12373                    if (drive < nr_drives) {
12374                            /* Copy the BIOS parameter vector */
12375                            vector = (drive == 0) ? BIOS_HD0_PARAMS_ADDR:BIOS_HD1_PARAMS_ADDR;
12376                            size = (drive == 0) ? BIOS_HD0_PARAMS_SIZE:BIOS_HD1_PARAMS_SIZE;
12377                            if ((s=sys_vircopy(SELF, BIOS_SEG, vector,
12378                                            SELF, D, (vir_bytes) parv, size)) != OK)
12379                                    panic(w_name(), "Couldn't read BIOS", s);
12380
12381                            /* Calculate the address of the parameters and copy them */
12382                            if ((s=sys_vircopy(
12383                                    SELF, BIOS_SEG, hclick_to_physb(parv[1]) + parv[0],
12384                                    SELF, D, (phys_bytes) params, 16L))!=OK)
12385                                    panic(w_name(),"Couldn't copy parameters", s);
12386
12387                            /* Copy the parameters to the structures of the drive */
12388                            wn->lcylinders = bp_cylinders(params);
12389                            wn->lheads = bp_heads(params);
12390                            wn->lsectors = bp_sectors(params);
12391                            wn->precomp = bp_precomp(params) >> 2;
12392                    }
12393
12394                    /* Fill in non-BIOS parameters. */
12395                    init_drive(wn,
12396                            drive < 2 ? REG_CMD_BASE0 : REG_CMD_BASE1,
12397                            drive < 2 ? REG_CTL_BASE0 : REG_CTL_BASE1,
12398                            NO_IRQ, 0, 0, drive);
12399                    w_next_drive++;
12400            }
12401    }
12402
12403    /* Look for controllers on the pci bus. Skip none the first instance,
12404     * skip one and then 2 for every instance, for every next instance.
12405     */
12406    if (w_instance == 0)
12407            init_params_pci(0);
12408    else
12409            init_params_pci(w_instance*2-1);
12410
12411 }

12413 #define ATA_IF_NOTCOMPAT1 (1L << 0)
12414 #define ATA_IF_NOTCOMPAT2 (1L << 2)
```

```
12415
12416   /*===========================================================================*
12417    *                              init_drive                                   *
12418    *===========================================================================*/
12419   PRIVATE void init_drive(struct wini *w int base_cmd int base_ctl int irq int ack ...
12420   {
12421           w->state = 0;
12422           w->w_status = 0;
12423           w->base_cmd = base_cmd;
12424           w->base_ctl = base_ctl;
12425           w->irq = irq;
12426           w->irq_mask = 1 << irq;
12427           w->irq_need_ack = ack;
12428           w->irq_hook_id = hook;
12429           w->ldhpref = ldh_init(drive);
12430           w->max_count = MAX_SECS << SECTOR_SHIFT;
12431           w->lba48 = 0;
12432   }


12434   /*===========================================================================*
12435    *                            init_params_pci                                *
12436    *===========================================================================*/
12437   PRIVATE void init_params_pci(int skip)
12438   {
12439     int r, devind, drive;
12440     u16_t vid, did;
12441     pci_init();
12442     for(drive = w_next_drive; drive < MAX_DRIVES; drive++)
12443             wini[drive].state = IGNORING;
12444     for(r = pci_first_dev(&devind, &vid, &did);
12445             r!=0&&w_next_drive<MAX_DRIVES; r=pci_next_dev(&devind,&vid, &did)) {
12446             int interface, irq, irq_hook;
12447             /* Base class must be 01h (mass storage), subclass must
12448              * be 01h (ATA).
12449              */
12450             if (pci_attr_r8(devind, PCI_BCR) != 0x01 ||
12451               pci_attr_r8(devind, PCI_SCR) != 0x01) {
12452               continue;
12453             }
12454             /* Found a controller.
12455              * Programming interface register tells us more.
12456              */
12457             interface = pci_attr_r8(devind, PCI_PIFR);
12458             irq = pci_attr_r8(devind, PCI_ILR);
12459
12460             /* Any non-compat drives? */
12461             if (interface & (ATA_IF_NOTCOMPAT1 | ATA_IF_NOTCOMPAT2)) {
12462                     int s;
12463                     irq_hook = irq;
12464                     if (skip > 0) {
12465                      if(w_pci_debug)printf("atapci skipping contr. (remain %d)\n",skip);
12466                             skip--;
12467                             continue;
12468                     }
12469                     if ((s=sys_irqsetpolicy(irq, 0, &irq_hook)) != OK) {
12470                             printf("atapci: couldn't set IRQ policy %d\n", irq);
12471                             continue;
12472                     }
12473                     if ((s=sys_irqenable(&irq_hook)) != OK) {
12474                             printf("atapci: couldn't enable IRQ line %d\n", irq);
```

```
12475                                    continue;
12476                              }
12477                  } else {
12478                          /* If not.. this is not the ata-pci controller we're
12479                           * looking for.
12480                           */
12481                          if (w_pci_debug) printf("atapci skipping compatability controller\n");
12482                          continue;
12483                  }
12484
12485                  /* Primary channel not in compatability mode? */
12486                  if (interface & ATA_IF_NOTCOMPAT1) {
12487                          u32_t base_cmd, base_ctl;
12488                          base_cmd = pci_attr_r32(devind, PCI_BAR) & 0xfffffffe0;
12489                          base_ctl = pci_attr_r32(devind, PCI_BAR_2) & 0xfffffffe0;
12490                          if (base_cmd != REG_CMD_BASE0 && base_cmd != REG_CMD_BASE1) {
12491                                  init_drive(&wini[w_next_drive],
12492                                          base_cmd, base_ctl, irq, 1, irq_hook, 0);
12493                                  init_drive(&wini[w_next_drive+1],
12494                                          base_cmd, base_ctl, irq, 1, irq_hook, 1);
12495                                  if (w_pci_debug)
12496                          printf("atapci %d: 0x%x 0x%x irq %d\n",devind,base_cmd,base_ctl,irq)
12497                          } else printf("atapci: ignored drives on pri, base: %x\n",base_cmd);
12498                  }
12499
12500                  /* Secondary channel not in compatability mode? */
12501                  if (interface & ATA_IF_NOTCOMPAT2) {
12502                          u32_t base_cmd, base_ctl;
12503                          base_cmd = pci_attr_r32(devind, PCI_BAR_3) & 0xfffffffe0;
12504                          base_ctl = pci_attr_r32(devind, PCI_BAR_4) & 0xfffffffe0;
12505                          if (base_cmd != REG_CMD_BASE0 && base_cmd != REG_CMD_BASE1) {
12506                                  init_drive(&wini[w_next_drive+2],
12507                                          base_cmd, base_ctl, irq, 1, irq_hook, 2);
12508                                  init_drive(&wini[w_next_drive+3],
12509                                          base_cmd, base_ctl, irq, 1, irq_hook, 3);
12510                                  if (w_pci_debug)
12511                          printf("atapci %d: 0x%x 0x%x irq %d\n",devind,base_cmd,base_ctl,irq);
12512                          } else printf("atapci: ignored drives on secondary %x\n", base_cmd);
12513                  }
12514          w_next_drive += 4;
12515      }
12516  }

12518  /*===========================================================================*
12519   *                              w_do_open                                    *
12520   *===========================================================================*/
12521  PRIVATE int w_do_open(dp, m_ptr)
12522  struct driver *dp;
12523  message *m_ptr;
12524  {
12525  /* Device open: Initialize the controller and read the partition table. */
12526
12527      struct wini *wn;
12528
12529      if (w_prepare(m_ptr->DEVICE) == NIL_DEV) return(ENXIO);
12530
12531      wn = w_wn;
12532
12533      /* If we've probed it before and it failed, don't probe it again. */
12534      if (wn->state & IGNORING) return ENXIO;
```

```
12535
12536        /* If we haven't identified it yet, or it's gone deaf,
12537         * (re-)identify it.
12538         */
12539        if (!(wn->state & IDENTIFIED) || (wn->state & DEAF)) {
12540                /* Try to identify the device. */
12541                if (w_identify() != OK) {
12542                        if (wn->state & DEAF) w_reset();
12543                        wn->state = IGNORING;
12544                        return(ENXIO);
12545                }
12546                  /* Do a test transaction unless it's a CD drive (then
12547                   * we can believe the controller, and a test may fail
12548                   * due to no CD being in the drive). If it fails, ignore
12549                   * the device forever.
12550                   */
12551                if (!(wn->state & ATAPI) && w_io_test() != OK) {
12552                        wn->state |= IGNORING;
12553                        return(ENXIO);
12554                }
12555        }
12556
12557        /* If it's not an ATAPI device, then don't open with RO_BIT. */
12558        if (!(wn->state & ATAPI) && (m_ptr->COUNT & RO_BIT)) return EACCES;
12559
12560        /* Partition the drive if it's being opened for the first time,
12561         * or being opened after being closed.
12562         */
12563        if (wn->open_ct == 0) {
12564
12565                /* Partition the disk. */
12566                memset(wn->part, sizeof(wn->part), 0);
12567                memset(wn->subpart, sizeof(wn->subpart), 0);
12568                partition(&w_dtab, w_drive * DEV_PER_DRIVE, P_PRIMARY, wn->state & ATAPI);
12569        }
12570        wn->open_ct++;
12571        return(OK);
12572 }


12574 /*===========================================================================*
12575  *                            w_prepare                                      *
12576  *===========================================================================*/
12577 PRIVATE struct device *w_prepare(int device)
12578 {
12579 /* Prepare for I/O on a device. */
12580 struct wini *prev_wn;
12581 prev_wn = w_wn;
12582   w_device = device;
12583
12584   if (device < NR_MINORS) {                         /* d0, d0p[0-3], d1, ... */
12585        w_drive = device / DEV_PER_DRIVE;            /* save drive number */
12586        w_wn = &wini[w_drive];
12587        w_dv = &w_wn->part[device % DEV_PER_DRIVE];
12588   } else
12589   if ((unsigned) (device -= MINOR_d0p0s0) < NR_SUBDEVS) {/*d[0-7]p[0-3]s[0-3]*/
12590        w_drive = device / SUB_PER_DRIVE;
12591        w_wn = &wini[w_drive];
12592        w_dv = &w_wn->subpart[device % SUB_PER_DRIVE];
12593   } else {
12594        w_device = -1;
```

```
12595                return(NIL_DEV);
12596        }
12597        return(w_dv);
12598  }

12600  /*===========================================================================*
12601   *                             w_identify                                    *
12602   *===========================================================================*/
12603  PRIVATE int w_identify()
12604  {
12605  /* Find out if a device exists, if it is an old AT disk, or a newer ATA
12606   * drive, a removable media device, etc.
12607   */
12608
12609    struct wini *wn = w_wn;
12610    struct command cmd;
12611    int i, s;
12612    unsigned long size;
12613  #define id_byte(n)      (&tmp_buf[2 * (n)])
12614  #define id_word(n)      (((u16_t) id_byte(n)[0] <<  0) \
12615                          |((u16_t) id_byte(n)[1] <<  8))
12616  #define id_longword(n)  (((u32_t) id_byte(n)[0] <<  0) \
12617                          |((u32_t) id_byte(n)[1] <<  8) \
12618                          |((u32_t) id_byte(n)[2] << 16) \
12619                          |((u32_t) id_byte(n)[3] << 24))
12620
12621    /* Try to identify the device. */
12622    cmd.ldh     = wn->ldhpref;
12623    cmd.command = ATA_IDENTIFY;
12624    if (com_simple(&cmd) == OK) {
12625            /* This is an ATA device. */
12626            wn->state |= SMART;
12627
12628            /* Device information. */
12629            if ((s=sys_insw(wn->base_cmd + REG_DATA, SELF, tmp_buf, SECTOR_SIZE)) != OK)
12630                    panic(w_name(),"Call to sys_insw() failed", s);
12631
12632            /* Why are the strings byte swapped??? */
12633            for (i = 0; i < 40; i++) w_id_string[i] = id_byte(27)[i^1];
12634
12635            /* Preferred CHS translation mode. */
12636            wn->pcylinders = id_word(1);
12637            wn->pheads = id_word(3);
12638            wn->psectors = id_word(6);
12639            size = (u32_t) wn->pcylinders * wn->pheads * wn->psectors;
12640
12641            if ((id_byte(49)[1] & 0x02) && size > 512L*1024*2) {
12642                    /* Drive is LBA capable and is big enough to trust it to
12643                     * not make a mess of it.
12644                     */
12645                    wn->ldhpref |= LDH_LBA;
12646                    size = id_longword(60);
12647
12648                    if (w_lba48 && ((id_word(83)) & (1L << 10))) {
12649                            /* Drive is LBA48 capable (and LBA48 is turned on). */
12650                            if (id_word(102) || id_word(103)) {
12651                                    /* If no. of sectors doesn't fit in 32 bits,
12652                                     * trunacte to this. So it's LBA32 for now.
12653                                     * This can still address devices up to 2TB
12654                                     * though.
```

```
12655                                          */
12656                                  size = ULONG_MAX;
12657                          } else {
12658                                  /* Actual number of sectors fits in 32 bits. */
12659                                  size = id_longword(100);
12660                          }
12661
12662                          wn->lba48 = 1;
12663                  }
12664          }
12665
12666          if (wn->lcylinders == 0) {
12667                  /* No BIOS parameters?  Then make some up. */
12668                  wn->lcylinders = wn->pcylinders;
12669                  wn->lheads = wn->pheads;
12670                  wn->lsectors = wn->psectors;
12671                  while (wn->lcylinders > 1024) {
12672                          wn->lheads *= 2;
12673                          wn->lcylinders /= 2;
12674                  }
12675          }
12676  } else {
12677          /* Not an ATA device; no translations, no special features.  Don't
12678           * touch it unless the BIOS knows about it.
12679           */
12680          if (wn->lcylinders == 0) { return(ERR); }        /* no BIOS parameters */
12681          wn->pcylinders = wn->lcylinders;
12682          wn->pheads = wn->lheads;
12683          wn->psectors = wn->lsectors;
12684          size = (u32_t) wn->pcylinders * wn->pheads * wn->psectors;
12685  }
12686
12687  /* Size of the whole drive */
12688  wn->part[0].dv_size = mul64u(size, SECTOR_SIZE);
12689
12690  /* Reset/calibrate (where necessary) */
12691  if (w_specify() != OK && w_specify() != OK) {
12692          return(ERR);
12693  }
12694
12695  if (wn->irq == NO_IRQ) {
12696          /* Everything looks OK; register IRQ so we can stop polling. */
12697          wn->irq = w_drive < 2 ? AT_WINI_0_IRQ : AT_WINI_1_IRQ;
12698          wn->irq_hook_id = wn->irq;      /* id to be returned if interrupt occurs */
12699          if ((s=sys_irqsetpolicy(wn->irq, IRQ_REENABLE, &wn->irq_hook_id)) != OK)
12700                  panic(w_name(), "couldn't set IRQ policy", s);
12701          if ((s=sys_irqenable(&wn->irq_hook_id)) != OK)
12702                  panic(w_name(), "couldn't enable IRQ line", s);
12703  }
12704  wn->state |= IDENTIFIED;
12705  return(OK);
12706  }

12708  /*===========================================================================*
12709   *                              w_name                                       *
12710   *===========================================================================*/
12711  PRIVATE char *w_name()
12712  {
12713  /* Return a name for the current device. */
12714    static char name[] = "AT-D0";
```

```
12715
12716      name[4] = '0' + w_drive;
12717      return name;
12718  }

12720  /*===========================================================================*
12721   *                              w_io_test                                    *
12722   *===========================================================================*/
12723  PRIVATE int w_io_test(void)
12724  {
12725          int r, save_dev;
12726          int save_timeout, save_errors, save_wakeup;
12727          iovec_t iov;
12728          static char buf[SECTOR_SIZE];
12729          iov.iov_addr = (vir_bytes) buf;
12730          iov.iov_size = sizeof(buf);
12731          save_dev = w_device;
12732
12733          /* Reduce timeout values for this test transaction. */
12734          save_timeout = timeout_ticks;
12735          save_errors = max_errors;
12736          save_wakeup = wakeup_ticks;
12737
12738          if (!w_standard_timeouts) {
12739                  timeout_ticks = HZ * 4;
12740                  wakeup_ticks = HZ * 6;
12741                  max_errors = 3;
12742          }
12743
12744          w_testing = 1;
12745
12746          /* Try I/O on the actual drive (not any (sub)partition). */
12747          if (w_prepare(w_drive * DEV_PER_DRIVE) == NIL_DEV)
12748                  panic(w_name(), "Couldn't switch devices", NO_NUM);
12749
12750          r = w_transfer(SELF, DEV_GATHER, 0, &iov, 1);
12751
12752          /* Switch back. */
12753          if (w_prepare(save_dev) == NIL_DEV)
12754                  panic(w_name(), "Couldn't switch back devices", NO_NUM);
12755
12756          /* Restore parameters. */
12757          timeout_ticks = save_timeout;
12758          max_errors = save_errors;
12759          wakeup_ticks = save_wakeup;
12760          w_testing = 0;
12761
12762          /* Test if everything worked. */
12763          if (r != OK || iov.iov_size != 0) {
12764                  return ERR;
12765          }
12766
12767          /* Everything worked. */
12768
12769          return OK;
12770  }
```

```
12772  /*===========================================================================*
12773   *                            w_specify                                     *
12774   *===========================================================================*/
12775  PRIVATE int w_specify()
12776  {
12777  /* Routine to initialize the drive after boot or when a reset is needed. */
12778
12779    struct wini *wn = w_wn;
12780    struct command cmd;
12781
12782    if ((wn->state & DEAF) && w_reset() != OK) {
12783          return(ERR);
12784    }
12785
12786    if (!(wn->state & ATAPI)) {
12787          /* Specify parameters: precompensation, number of heads and sectors. */
12788          cmd.precomp = wn->precomp;
12789          cmd.count   = wn->psectors;
12790          cmd.ldh     = w_wn->ldhpref | (wn->pheads - 1);
12791          cmd.command = CMD_SPECIFY;              /* Specify some parameters */
12792
12793          /* Output command block and see if controller accepts the parameters. */
12794          if (com_simple(&cmd) != OK) return(ERR);
12795
12796          if (!(wn->state & SMART)) {
12797                /* Calibrate an old disk. */
12798                cmd.sector  = 0;
12799                cmd.cyl_lo  = 0;
12800                cmd.cyl_hi  = 0;
12801                cmd.ldh     = w_wn->ldhpref;
12802                cmd.command = CMD_RECALIBRATE;
12803
12804                if (com_simple(&cmd) != OK) return(ERR);
12805          }
12806    }
12807    wn->state |= INITIALIZED;
12808    return(OK);
12809  }

12811  /*===========================================================================*
12812   *                            do_transfer                                   *
12813   *===========================================================================*/
12814  PRIVATE int do_transfer(struct wini *wn, unsigned int precomp, unsigned int count,
12815          unsigned int sector, unsigned int opcode)
12816  {
12817          struct command cmd;
12818          unsigned secspcyl = wn->pheads * wn->psectors;
12819
12820          cmd.precomp = precomp;
12821          cmd.count   = count;
12822          cmd.command = opcode == DEV_SCATTER ? CMD_WRITE : CMD_READ;
12823          /*
12824          if (w_lba48 && wn->lba48) {
12825          } else */
12826          if (wn->ldhpref & LDH_LBA) {
12827                cmd.sector  = (sector >>  0) & 0xFF;
12828                cmd.cyl_lo  = (sector >>  8) & 0xFF;
12829                cmd.cyl_hi  = (sector >> 16) & 0xFF;
12830                cmd.ldh     = wn->ldhpref | ((sector >> 24) & 0xF);
12831          } else {
```

```
12832                     int cylinder, head, sec;
12833                     cylinder = sector / secspcyl;
12834                     head = (sector % secspcyl) / wn->psectors;
12835                     sec = sector % wn->psectors;
12836                     cmd.sector  = sec + 1;
12837                     cmd.cyl_lo  = cylinder & BYTE;
12838                     cmd.cyl_hi  = (cylinder >> 8) & BYTE;
12839                     cmd.ldh     = wn->ldhpref | head;
12840             }
12841
12842         return com_out(&cmd);
12843 }
12844
12845 /*===========================================================================*
12846  *                              w_transfer                                   *
12847  *===========================================================================*/
12848 PRIVATE int w_transfer(proc_nr, opcode, position, iov, nr_req)
12849 int proc_nr;                        /* process doing the request */
12850 int opcode;                         /* DEV_GATHER or DEV_SCATTER */
12851 off_t position;                     /* offset on device to read or write */
12852 iovec_t *iov;                       /* pointer to read or write request vector */
12853 unsigned nr_req;                    /* length of request vector */
12854 {
12855   struct wini *wn = w_wn;
12856   iovec_t *iop, *iov_end = iov + nr_req;
12857   int r, s, errors;
12858   unsigned long block;
12859   unsigned long dv_size = cv64ul(w_dv->dv_size);
12860   unsigned cylinder, head, sector, nbytes;
12861
12862   /* Check disk address. */
12863   if ((position & SECTOR_MASK) != 0) return(EINVAL);
12864
12865   errors = 0;
12866
12867   while (nr_req > 0) {
12868         /* How many bytes to transfer? */
12869         nbytes = 0;
12870         for (iop = iov; iop < iov_end; iop++) nbytes += iop->iov_size;
12871         if ((nbytes & SECTOR_MASK) != 0) return(EINVAL);
12872
12873         /* Which block on disk and how close to EOF? */
12874         if (position >= dv_size) return(OK);            /* At EOF */
12875         if (position + nbytes > dv_size) nbytes = dv_size - position;
12876         block = div64u(add64ul(w_dv->dv_base, position), SECTOR_SIZE);
12877
12878         if (nbytes >= wn->max_count) {
12879                 /* The drive can't do more then max_count at once. */
12880                 nbytes = wn->max_count;
12881         }
12882
12883         /* First check to see if a reinitialization is needed. */
12884         if (!(wn->state & INITIALIZED) && w_specify() != OK) return(EIO);
12885
12886         /* Tell the controller to transfer nbytes bytes. */
12887         r = do_transfer(wn, wn->precomp, ((nbytes >> SECTOR_SHIFT) & BYTE),
12888                 block, opcode);
12889
12890         while (r == OK && nbytes > 0) {
12891                 /* For each sector, wait for an interrupt and fetch the data
```

```
12892                             * (read), or supply data to the controller and wait for an
12893                             * interrupt (write).
12894                             */
12895
12896                    if (opcode == DEV_GATHER) {
12897                            /* First an interrupt, then data. */
12898                            if ((r = at_intr_wait()) != OK) {
12899                                    /* An error, send data to the bit bucket. */
12900                                    if (w_wn->w_status & STATUS_DRQ) {
12901             if ((s=sys_insw(wn->base_cmd + REG_DATA, SELF, tmp_buf, SECTOR_SIZE)) != OK)
12902                    panic(w_name(),"Call to sys_insw() failed", s);
12903                                    }
12904                                    break;
12905                            }
12906                    }
12907
12908                    /* Wait for data transfer requested. */
12909                    if (!w_waitfor(STATUS_DRQ, STATUS_DRQ)) { r = ERR; break; }
12910
12911                    /* Copy bytes to or from the device's buffer. */
12912                    if (opcode == DEV_GATHER) { if((s=sys_insw(wn->base_cmd+REG_DATA,
12913                                    proc_nr,(void*)iov->iov_addr,SECTOR_SIZE))!=OK)
12914                    panic(w_name(),"Call to sys_insw() failed", s);
12915                    } else { if((s=sys_outsw(wn->base_cmd+REG_DATA,proc_nr,
12916                                    (void *) iov->iov_addr,SECTOR_SIZE))!=OK)
12917                    panic(w_name(),"Call to sys_insw() failed", s);
12918
12919                            /* Data sent, wait for an interrupt. */
12920                            if ((r = at_intr_wait()) != OK) break;
12921                    }
12922
12923                    /* Book the bytes successfully transferred. */
12924                    nbytes -= SECTOR_SIZE;
12925                    position += SECTOR_SIZE;
12926                    iov->iov_addr += SECTOR_SIZE;
12927                    if ((iov->iov_size -= SECTOR_SIZE) == 0) { iov++; nr_req--; }
12928            }
12929
12930            /* Any errors? */
12931            if (r != OK) {
12932                    /* Don't retry if sector marked bad or too many errors. */
12933                    if (r == ERR_BAD_SECTOR || ++errors == max_errors) {
12934                            w_command = CMD_IDLE;
12935                            return(EIO);
12936                    }
12937            }
12938    }
12939
12940  w_command = CMD_IDLE;
12941  return(OK);
12942 }
12943
12944 /*===========================================================================*
12945  *                            com_out                                        *
12946  *===========================================================================*/
12947 PRIVATE int com_out(cmd)
12948 struct command *cmd;              /* Command block */
12949 {
12950 /* Output the command block to the winchester controller and return status */
12951
```

```
12952      struct wini *wn = w_wn;
12953      unsigned base_cmd = wn->base_cmd;
12954      unsigned base_ctl = wn->base_ctl;
12955      pvb_pair_t outbyte[7];                    /* vector for sys_voutb() */
12956      int s;                                    /* status for sys_(v)outb() */
12957
12958      if (w_wn->state & IGNORING) return ERR;
12959
12960      if (!w_waitfor(STATUS_BSY, 0)) {
12961            printf("%s: controller not ready\n", w_name());
12962            return(ERR);
12963      }
12964
12965      /* Select drive. */
12966      if ((s=sys_outb(base_cmd + REG_LDH, cmd->ldh)) != OK)
12967            panic(w_name(),"Couldn't write register to select drive",s);
12968
12969      if (!w_waitfor(STATUS_BSY, 0)) {
12970            printf("%s: com_out: drive not ready\n", w_name());
12971            return(ERR);
12972      }
12973
12974      /* Schedule a wakeup call, some controllers are flaky. This is done with
12975       * a synchronous alarm. If a timeout occurs a SYN_ALARM message is sent
12976       * from HARDWARE, so that w_intr_wait() can call w_timeout() in case the
12977       * controller was not able to execute the command. Leftover timeouts are
12978       * simply ignored by the main loop.
12979       */
12980      sys_setalarm(wakeup_ticks, 0);
12981
12982      wn->w_status = STATUS_ADMBSY;
12983      w_command = cmd->command;
12984      pv_set(outbyte[0], base_ctl + REG_CTL, wn->pheads >= 8 ? CTL_EIGHTHEADS : 0);
12985      pv_set(outbyte[1], base_cmd + REG_PRECOMP, cmd->precomp);
12986      pv_set(outbyte[2], base_cmd + REG_COUNT, cmd->count);
12987      pv_set(outbyte[3], base_cmd + REG_SECTOR, cmd->sector);
12988      pv_set(outbyte[4], base_cmd + REG_CYL_LO, cmd->cyl_lo);
12989      pv_set(outbyte[5], base_cmd + REG_CYL_HI, cmd->cyl_hi);
12990      pv_set(outbyte[6], base_cmd + REG_COMMAND, cmd->command);
12991      if ((s=sys_voutb(outbyte,7)) != OK)
12992            panic(w_name(),"Couldn't write registers with sys_voutb()",s);
12993      return(OK);
12994  }


12996  /*===========================================================================*
12997   *                            w_need_reset                                   *
12998   *===========================================================================*/
12999  PRIVATE void w_need_reset()
13000  {
13001  /* The controller needs to be reset. */
13002    struct wini *wn;
13003    int dr = 0;
13004
13005    for (wn = wini; wn < &wini[MAX_DRIVES]; wn++, dr++) {
13006          if (wn->base_cmd == w_wn->base_cmd) {
13007                wn->state |= DEAF;
13008                wn->state &= ~INITIALIZED;
13009          }
13010    }
13011  }
```

```
13013  /*===========================================================================*
13014   *                              w_do_close                                   *
13015   *===========================================================================*/
13016  PRIVATE int w_do_close(dp, m_ptr)
13017  struct driver *dp;
13018  message *m_ptr;
13019  {
13020  /* Device close: Release a device. */
13021    if (w_prepare(m_ptr->DEVICE) == NIL_DEV)
13022          return(ENXIO);
13023    w_wn->open_ct--;
13024    return(OK);
13025  }

13027  /*===========================================================================*
13028   *                              com_simple                                   *
13029   *===========================================================================*/
13030  PRIVATE int com_simple(cmd)
13031  struct command *cmd;              /* Command block */
13032  {
13033  /* A simple controller command, only one interrupt and no data-out phase. */
13034    int r;
13035
13036    if (w_wn->state & IGNORING) return ERR;
13037
13038    if ((r = com_out(cmd)) == OK) r = at_intr_wait();
13039    w_command = CMD_IDLE;
13040    return(r);
13041  }

13043  /*===========================================================================*
13044   *                              w_timeout                                     *
13045   *===========================================================================*/
13046  PRIVATE void w_timeout(void)
13047  {
13048    struct wini *wn = w_wn;
13049
13050    switch (w_command) {
13051    case CMD_IDLE:
13052          break;               /* fine */
13053    case CMD_READ:
13054    case CMD_WRITE:
13055          /* Impossible, but not on PC's:  The controller does not respond. */
13056
13057          /* Limiting multisector I/O seems to help. */
13058          if (wn->max_count > 8 * SECTOR_SIZE) {
13059                wn->max_count = 8 * SECTOR_SIZE;
13060          } else {
13061                wn->max_count = SECTOR_SIZE;
13062          }
13063          /*FALL THROUGH*/
13064    default:
13065          /* Some other command. */
13066          if (w_testing)  wn->state |= IGNORING;  /* Kick out this drive. */
13067          else if (!w_silent) printf("%s: timeout on command %02x\n", w_name(), w_command);
13068          w_need_reset();
13069          wn->w_status = 0;
13070    }
13071  }
```

```
13073   /*===========================================================================*
13074    *                              w_reset                                      *
13075    *===========================================================================*/
13076   PRIVATE int w_reset()
13077   {
13078   /* Issue a reset to the controller.  This is done after any catastrophe,
13079    * like the controller refusing to respond.
13080    */
13081     int s;
13082     struct wini *wn = w_wn;
13083
13084     /* Don't bother if this drive is forgotten. */
13085     if (w_wn->state & IGNORING) return ERR;
13086
13087     /* Wait for any internal drive recovery. */
13088     tickdelay(RECOVERY_TICKS);
13089
13090     /* Strobe reset bit */
13091     if ((s=sys_outb(wn->base_ctl + REG_CTL, CTL_RESET)) != OK)
13092         panic(w_name(),"Couldn't strobe reset bit",s);
13093     tickdelay(DELAY_TICKS);
13094     if ((s=sys_outb(wn->base_ctl + REG_CTL, 0)) != OK)
13095         panic(w_name(),"Couldn't strobe reset bit",s);
13096     tickdelay(DELAY_TICKS);
13097
13098     /* Wait for controller ready */
13099     if (!w_waitfor(STATUS_BSY, 0)) {
13100         printf("%s: reset failed, drive busy\n", w_name());
13101         return(ERR);
13102     }
13103
13104     /* The error register should be checked now, but some drives mess it up. */
13105
13106     for (wn = wini; wn < &wini[MAX_DRIVES]; wn++) {
13107         if (wn->base_cmd == w_wn->base_cmd) {
13108             wn->state &= ~DEAF;
13109             if (w_wn->irq_need_ack) {
13110                 /* Make sure irq is actually enabled.. */
13111                 sys_irqenable(&w_wn->irq_hook_id);
13112             }
13113         }
13114     }
13115
13116
13117     return(OK);
13118   }

13120   /*===========================================================================*
13121    *                              w_intr_wait                                  *
13122    *===========================================================================*/
13123   PRIVATE void w_intr_wait()
13124   {
13125   /* Wait for a task completion interrupt. */
13126
13127     message m;
13128
13129     if (w_wn->irq != NO_IRQ) {
13130         /* Wait for an interrupt that sets w_status to "not busy". */
13131         while (w_wn->w_status & (STATUS_ADMBSY|STATUS_BSY)) {
```

```
13132                    receive(ANY, &m);                   /* expect HARD_INT message */
13133                    if (m.m_type == SYN_ALARM) {    /* but check for timeout */
13134                        w_timeout();                /* a.o. set w_status */
13135                    } else if (m.m_type == HARD_INT) {
13136                        sys_inb(w_wn->base_cmd + REG_STATUS, &w_wn->w_status);
13137                        ack_irqs(m.NOTIFY_ARG);
13138                    } else {
13139                        printf("AT_WINI got unexpected message %d from %d\n",
13140                            m.m_type, m.m_source);
13141                    }
13142                }
13143        } else {
13144            /* Interrupt not yet allocated; use polling. */
13145            (void) w_waitfor(STATUS_BSY, 0);
13146        }
13147  }

13149  /*===========================================================================*
13150   *                              at_intr_wait                                 *
13151   *===========================================================================*/
13152  PRIVATE int at_intr_wait()
13153  {
13154  /* Wait for an interrupt, study the status bits and return error/success. */
13155    int r;
13156    int s,inbval;              /* read value with sys_inb */
13157
13158    w_intr_wait();
13159    if ((w_wn->w_status & (STATUS_BSY | STATUS_WF | STATUS_ERR)) == 0) {
13160        r = OK;
13161    } else {
13162        if ((s=sys_inb(w_wn->base_cmd + REG_ERROR, &inbval)) != OK)
13163            panic(w_name(),"Couldn't read register",s);
13164        if ((w_wn->w_status & STATUS_ERR) && (inbval & ERROR_BB)) {
13165            r = ERR_BAD_SECTOR;      /* sector marked bad, retries won't help */
13166        } else {
13167            r = ERR;                 /* any other error */
13168        }
13169    }
13170    w_wn->w_status |= STATUS_ADMBSY;    /* assume still busy with I/O */
13171    return(r);
13172  }

13174  /*===========================================================================*
13175   *                              w_waitfor                                    *
13176   *===========================================================================*/
13177  PRIVATE int w_waitfor(mask, value)
13178  int mask;                          /* status mask */
13179  int value;                         /* required status */
13180  {
13181  /* Wait until controller is in the required state.  Return zero on timeout.
13182   * An alarm that set a timeout flag is used. TIMEOUT is in micros, we need
13183   * ticks. Disabling the alarm is not needed, because a static flag is used
13184   * and a leftover timeout cannot do any harm.
13185   */
13186    clock_t t0, t1;
13187    int s;
13188    getuptime(&t0);
13189    do {
13190        if ((s=sys_inb(w_wn->base_cmd + REG_STATUS, &w_wn->w_status)) != OK)
13191            panic(w_name(),"Couldn't read register",s);
```

```
13192                 if ((w_wn->w_status & mask) == value) {
13193                         return 1;
13194                 }
13195         } while ((s=getuptime(&t1)) == OK && (t1-t0) < timeout_ticks );
13196         if (OK != s) printf("AT_WINI: warning, get_uptime failed: %d\n",s);
13197
13198         w_need_reset();                         /* controller gone deaf */
13199         return(0);
13200 }

13202 /*===========================================================================*
13203  *                              w_geometry                                   *
13204  *===========================================================================*/
13205 PRIVATE void w_geometry(entry)
13206 struct partition *entry;
13207 {
13208         struct wini *wn = w_wn;
13209
13210         if (wn->state & ATAPI) {                 /* Make up some numbers. */
13211                 entry->cylinders = div64u(wn->part[0].dv_size, SECTOR_SIZE) / (64*32);
13212                 entry->heads = 64;
13213                 entry->sectors = 32;
13214         } else {                                 /* Return logical geometry. */
13215                 entry->cylinders = wn->lcylinders;
13216                 entry->heads = wn->lheads;
13217                 entry->sectors = wn->lsectors;
13218         }
13219 }

13221 /*===========================================================================*
13222  *                              w_other                                      *
13223  *===========================================================================*/
13224 PRIVATE int w_other(dr, m)
13225 struct driver *dr;
13226 message *m;
13227 {
13228         int r, timeout, prev;
13229
13230         if (m->m_type != DEV_IOCTL ) {
13231                 return EINVAL;
13232         }
13233
13234         if (m->REQUEST == DIOCTIMEOUT) {
13235                 if ((r=sys_datacopy(m->PROC_NR, (vir_bytes)m->ADDRESS,
13236                         SELF, (vir_bytes)&timeout, sizeof(timeout))) != OK)
13237                         return r;
13238
13239                 if (timeout == 0) {
13240                         /* Restore defaults. */
13241                         timeout_ticks = DEF_TIMEOUT_TICKS;
13242                         max_errors = MAX_ERRORS;
13243                         wakeup_ticks = WAKEUP;
13244                         w_silent = 0;
13245                 } else if (timeout < 0) {
13246                         return EINVAL;
13247                 } else  {
13248                         prev = wakeup_ticks;
13249
13250                         if (!w_standard_timeouts) {
13251                                 /* Set (lower) timeout, lower error
```

```
13252                                         * tolerance and set silent mode.
13253                                         */
13254                                        wakeup_ticks = timeout;
13255                                        max_errors = 3;
13256                                        w_silent = 1;
13257
13258                                        if (timeout_ticks > timeout)
13259                                                timeout_ticks = timeout;
13260                                }
13261
13262                                if ((r=sys_datacopy(SELF, (vir_bytes)&prev,
13263                                  m->PROC_NR,(vir_bytes)m->ADDRESS,sizeof(prev)))!=OK)
13264                                        return r;
13265                        }
13266
13267                        return OK;
13268                } else  if (m->REQUEST == DIOCOPENCT) {
13269                        int count;
13270                        if (w_prepare(m->DEVICE) == NIL_DEV) return ENXIO;
13271                        count = w_wn->open_ct;
13272                        if ((r=sys_datacopy(SELF, (vir_bytes)&count,
13273                                m->PROC_NR, (vir_bytes)m->ADDRESS, sizeof(count))) != OK)
13274                                return r;
13275                        return OK;
13276                }
13277        return EINVAL;
13278 }

13280 /*===========================================================================*
13281  *                              w_hw_int                                     *
13282  *===========================================================================*/
13283 PRIVATE int w_hw_int(dr, m)
13284 struct driver *dr;
13285 message *m;
13286 {
13287   /* Leftover interrupt(s) received; ack it/them. */
13288   ack_irqs(m->NOTIFY_ARG);
13289
13290   return OK;
13291 }


13294 /*===========================================================================*
13295  *                              ack_irqs                                     *
13296  *===========================================================================*/
13297 PRIVATE void ack_irqs(unsigned int irqs)
13298 {
13299   unsigned int drive;
13300   for (drive = 0; drive < MAX_DRIVES && irqs; drive++) {
13301        if (!(wini[drive].state & IGNORING) && wini[drive].irq_need_ack &&
13302        (wini[drive].irq_mask & irqs)) {
13303        if (sys_inb((wini[drive].base_cmd+REG_STATUS),&wini[drive].w_status)!=OK)
13304                printf("couldn't ack irq on drive %d\n", drive);
13305        if (sys_irqenable(&wini[drive].irq_hook_id) != OK)
13306                printf("couldn't re-enable drive %d\n", drive);
13307        irqs &= ~wini[drive].irq_mask;
13308        }
13309    }
13310 }
```

```
13313  #define STSTR(a) if (status & STATUS_ ## a) { strcat(str, #a); strcat(str, " "); }
13314  #define ERRSTR(a) if (e & ERROR_ ## a) { strcat(str, #a); strcat(str, " "); }
13315  char *strstatus(int status)
13316  {
13317          static char str[200];
13318          str[0] = '\0';
13319
13320          STSTR(BSY);
13321          STSTR(DRDY);
13322          STSTR(DMADF);
13323          STSTR(SRVCDSC);
13324          STSTR(DRQ);
13325          STSTR(CORR);
13326          STSTR(CHECK);
13327          return str;
13328  }

13330  char *strerr(int e)
13331  {
13332          static char str[200];
13333          str[0] = '\0';
13334
13335          ERRSTR(BB);
13336          ERRSTR(ECC);
13337          ERRSTR(ID);
13338          ERRSTR(AC);
13339          ERRSTR(TK);
13340          ERRSTR(DM);
13341
13342          return str;
13343  }
```

```
++++++++++++++++++++++++++++++++++++++++++++++++++++++++++++++++++++++++++++++++
                             drivers/tty/tty.h
++++++++++++++++++++++++++++++++++++++++++++++++++++++++++++++++++++++++++++++++
```

```
13400  /*      tty.h - Terminals      */
13401
13402  #include <timers.h>
13403
13404  /* First minor numbers for the various classes of TTY devices. */
13405  #define CONS_MINOR        0
13406  #define LOG_MINOR         15
13407  #define RS232_MINOR       16
13408  #define TTYPX_MINOR       128
13409  #define PTYPX_MINOR       192
13410
13411  #define LINEWRAP          1      /* console.c - wrap lines at column 80 */
13412
13413  #define TTY_IN_BYTES      256    /* tty input queue size */
13414  #define TAB_SIZE          8      /* distance between tab stops */
13415  #define TAB_MASK          7      /* mask to compute a tab stop position */
13416
13417  #define ESC               '\33'  /* escape */
13418
13419  #define O_NOCTTY          00400  /* from <fcntl.h>, or cc will choke */
```

```
13420    #define O_NONBLOCK       04000
13421
13422    struct tty;
13423    typedef _PROTOTYPE( int (*devfun_t), (struct tty *tp, int try_only) );
13424    typedef _PROTOTYPE( void (*devfunarg_t), (struct tty *tp, int c) );
13425
13426    typedef struct tty {
13427      int tty_events;                  /* set when TTY should inspect this line */
13428      int tty_index;                   /* index into TTY table */
13429      int tty_minor;                   /* device minor number */
13430
13431      /* Input queue.  Typed characters are stored here until read by a program. */
13432      u16_t *tty_inhead;               /* pointer to place where next char goes */
13433      u16_t *tty_intail;               /* pointer to next char to be given to prog */
13434      int tty_incount;                 /* # chars in the input queue */
13435      int tty_eotct;                   /* number of "line breaks" in input queue */
13436      devfun_t tty_devread;            /* routine to read from low level buffers */
13437      devfun_t tty_icancel;            /* cancel any device input */
13438      int tty_min;                     /* minimum requested #chars in input queue */
13439      timer_t tty_tmr;                 /* the timer for this tty */
13440
13441      /* Output section. */
13442      devfun_t tty_devwrite;           /* routine to start actual device output */
13443      devfunarg_t tty_echo;            /* routine to echo characters input */
13444      devfun_t tty_ocancel;            /* cancel any ongoing device output */
13445      devfun_t tty_break;              /* let the device send a break */
13446
13447      /* Terminal parameters and status. */
13448      int tty_position;                /* current position on the screen for echoing */
13449      char tty_reprint;                /* 1 when echoed input messed up, else 0 */
13450      char tty_escaped;                /* 1 when LNEXT (^V) just seen, else 0 */
13451      char tty_inhibited;              /* 1 when STOP (^S) just seen (stops output) */
13452      char tty_pgrp;                   /* slot number of controlling process */
13453      char tty_openct;                 /* count of number of opens of this tty */
13454
13455      /* Information about incomplete I/O requests is stored here. */
13456      char tty_inrepcode;              /* reply code, TASK_REPLY or REVIVE */
13457      char tty_inrevived;              /* set to 1 if revive callback is pending */
13458      char tty_incaller;               /* process that made the call (usually FS) */
13459      char tty_inproc;                 /* process that wants to read from tty */
13460      vir_bytes tty_in_vir;            /* virtual address where data is to go */
13461      int tty_inleft;                  /* how many chars are still needed */
13462      int tty_incum;                   /* # chars input so far */
13463      char tty_outrepcode;             /* reply code, TASK_REPLY or REVIVE */
13464      char tty_outrevived;             /* set to 1 if revive callback is pending */
13465      char tty_outcaller;              /* process that made the call (usually FS) */
13466      char tty_outproc;                /* process that wants to write to tty */
13467      vir_bytes tty_out_vir;           /* virtual address where data comes from */
13468      int tty_outleft;                 /* # chars yet to be output */
13469      int tty_outcum;                  /* # chars output so far */
13470      char tty_iocaller;               /* process that made the call (usually FS) */
13471      char tty_ioproc;                 /* process that wants to do an ioctl */
13472      int tty_ioreq;                   /* ioctl request code */
13473      vir_bytes tty_iovir;             /* virtual address of ioctl buffer */
13474
13475      /* select() data */
13476      int tty_select_ops;              /* which operations are interesting */
13477      int tty_select_proc;             /* which process wants notification */
13478
13479      /* Miscellaneous. */
```

```
13480        devfun_t tty_ioctl;              /* set line speed, etc. at the device level */
13481        devfun_t tty_close;              /* tell the device that the tty is closed */
13482        void *tty_priv;                  /* pointer to per device private data */
13483        struct termios tty_termios;      /* terminal attributes */
13484        struct winsize tty_winsize;      /* window size (#lines and #columns) */
13485
13486        u16_t tty_inbuf[TTY_IN_BYTES];/* tty input buffer */
13487
13488 } tty_t;
13489
13490 /* Memory allocated in tty.c, so extern here. */
13491 extern tty_t tty_table[NR_CONS+NR_RS_LINES+NR_PTYS];
13492 extern int ccurrent;                     /* currently visible console */
13493 extern int irq_hook_id;                  /* hook id for keyboard irq */
13494
13495 extern unsigned long kbd_irq_set;
13496 extern unsigned long rs_irq_set;
13497
13498 /* Values for the fields. */
13499 #define NOT_ESCAPED       0       /* previous character is not LNEXT (^V) */
13500 #define ESCAPED           1       /* previous character was LNEXT (^V) */
13501 #define RUNNING           0       /* no STOP (^S) has been typed to stop output */
13502 #define STOPPED           1       /* STOP (^S) has been typed to stop output */
13503
13504 /* Fields and flags on characters in the input queue. */
13505 #define IN_CHAR      0x00FF       /* low 8 bits are the character itself */
13506 #define IN_LEN       0x0F00       /* length of char if it has been echoed */
13507 #define IN_LSHIFT         8       /* length = (c & IN_LEN) >> IN_LSHIFT */
13508 #define IN_EOT       0x1000       /* char is a line break (^D, LF) */
13509 #define IN_EOF       0x2000       /* char is EOF (^D), do not return to user */
13510 #define IN_ESC       0x4000       /* escaped by LNEXT (^V), no interpretation */
13511
13512 /* Times and timeouts. */
13513 #define force_timeout() ((void) (0))
13514
13515 /* Memory allocated in tty.c, so extern here. */
13516 extern timer_t *tty_timers;              /* queue of TTY timers */
13517 extern clock_t tty_next_timeout;         /* next TTY timeout */
13518
13519 /* Number of elements and limit of a buffer. */
13520 #define buflen(buf)      (sizeof(buf) / sizeof((buf)[0]))
13521 #define bufend(buf)      ((buf) + buflen(buf))
13522
13523 /* Memory allocated in tty.c, so extern here. */
13524 extern struct machine machine;  /* machine information (a.o.: pc_at, ega) */
13525
13526 /* Function prototypes for TTY driver. */
13527 /* tty.c */
13528 _PROTOTYPE( void handle_events, (struct tty *tp)                       );
13529 _PROTOTYPE( void sigchar, (struct tty *tp, int sig)                   );
13530 _PROTOTYPE( void tty_task, (void)                                     );
13531 _PROTOTYPE( int in_process, (struct tty *tp, char *buf, int count)    );
13532 _PROTOTYPE( void out_process, (struct tty *tp, char *bstart, char *bpos,
13533                               char *bend, int *icount, int *ocount)   );
13534 _PROTOTYPE( void tty_wakeup, (clock_t now)                            );
13535 _PROTOTYPE( void tty_reply, (int code, int replyee, int proc_nr,
13536                                              int status)              );
13537 _PROTOTYPE( int tty_devnop, (struct tty *tp, int try)                 );
13538 _PROTOTYPE( int select_try, (struct tty *tp, int ops)                 );
13539 _PROTOTYPE( int select_retry, (struct tty *tp)                        );
```

```
13540
13541    /* console.c */
13542    _PROTOTYPE( void kputc, (int c)                                   );
13543    _PROTOTYPE( void cons_stop, (void)                                );
13544    _PROTOTYPE( void do_new_kmess, (message *m)                       );
13545    _PROTOTYPE( void do_diagnostics, (message *m)                     );
13546    _PROTOTYPE( void scr_init, (struct tty *tp)                       );
13547    _PROTOTYPE( void toggle_scroll, (void)                            );
13548    _PROTOTYPE( int con_loadfont, (message *m)                        );
13549    _PROTOTYPE( void select_console, (int cons_line)                  );
13550
13551    /* keyboard.c */
13552    _PROTOTYPE( void kb_init, (struct tty *tp)                        );
13553    _PROTOTYPE( void kb_init_once, (void)                             );
13554    _PROTOTYPE( int kbd_loadmap, (message *m)                         );
13555    _PROTOTYPE( void do_panic_dumps, (message *m)                     );
13556    _PROTOTYPE( void do_fkey_ctl, (message *m)                        );
13557    _PROTOTYPE( void kbd_interrupt, (message *m)                      );
13558
13559    /* vidcopy.s */
13560    _PROTOTYPE( void vid_vid_copy, (unsigned src, unsigned dst, unsigned count));
13561    _PROTOTYPE( void mem_vid_copy, (u16_t *src, unsigned dst, unsigned count));
```

```
++++++++++++++++++++++++++++++++++++++++++++++++++++++++++++++++++++++++++++
                               drivers/tty/tty.c
++++++++++++++++++++++++++++++++++++++++++++++++++++++++++++++++++++++++++++
```

```
13600    /* This file contains the terminal driver, both for the IBM console and regular
13601     * ASCII terminals.  It handles only the device-independent part of a TTY, the
13602     * device dependent parts are in console.c, rs232.c, etc.  This file contains
13603     * two main entry points, tty_task() and tty_wakeup(), and several minor entry
13604     * points for use by the device-dependent code.
13605     *
13606     * The device-independent part accepts "keyboard" input from the device-
13607     * dependent part, performs input processing (special key interpretation),
13608     * and sends the input to a process reading from the TTY.  Output to a TTY
13609     * is sent to the device-dependent code for output processing and "screen"
13610     * display.  Input processing is done by the device by calling 'in_process'
13611     * on the input characters, output processing may be done by the device itself
13612     * or by calling 'out_process'.  The TTY takes care of input queuing, the
13613     * device does the output queuing.  If a device receives an external signal,
13614     * like an interrupt, then it causes tty_wakeup() to be run by the CLOCK task
13615     * to, you guessed it, wake up the TTY to check if input or output can
13616     * continue.
13617     *
13618     * The valid messages and their parameters are:
13619     *
13620     *    HARD_INT:       output has been completed or input has arrived
13621     *    SYS_SIG:        e.g., MINIX wants to shutdown; run code to cleanly stop
13622     *    DEV_READ:       a process wants to read from a terminal
13623     *    DEV_WRITE:      a process wants to write on a terminal
13624     *    DEV_IOCTL:      a process wants to change a terminal's parameters
13625     *    DEV_OPEN:       a tty line has been opened
13626     *    DEV_CLOSE:      a tty line has been closed
13627     *    DEV_SELECT:     start select notification request
13628     *    DEV_STATUS:     FS wants to know status for SELECT or REVIVE
13629     *    CANCEL:         terminate a previous incomplete system call immediately
```

```
13630   *
13631   *      m_type     TTY_LINE   PROC_NR    COUNT   TTY_SPEK  TTY_FLAGS  ADDRESS
13632   * -------------------------------------------------------------------------
13633   * | HARD_INT   |          |          |         |          |          |         |
13634   * |-----------+----------+----------+--------+---------+---------+---------|
13635   * | SYS_SIG    | sig set  |          |         |          |          |         |
13636   * |-----------+----------+----------+--------+---------+---------+---------|
13637   * | DEV_READ   |minor dev| proc nr  | count  |         O_NONBLOCK| buf ptr |
13638   * |-----------+----------+----------+--------+---------+---------+---------|
13639   * | DEV_WRITE  |minor dev| proc nr  | count  |         |         | buf ptr |
13640   * |-----------+----------+----------+--------+---------+---------+---------|
13641   * | DEV_IOCTL  |minor dev| proc nr  |func code|erase etc|  flags  |         |
13642   * |-----------+----------+----------+--------+---------+---------+---------|
13643   * | DEV_OPEN   |minor dev| proc nr  | O_NOCTTY|         |          |         |
13644   * |-----------+----------+----------+--------+---------+---------+---------|
13645   * | DEV_CLOSE  |minor dev| proc nr  |         |          |          |         |
13646   * |-----------+----------+----------+--------+---------+---------+---------|
13647   * | DEV_STATUS |          |          |         |          |          |         |
13648   * |-----------+----------+----------+--------+---------+---------+---------|
13649   * | CANCEL     |minor dev| proc nr  |         |          |          |         |
13650   * -------------------------------------------------------------------------
13651   *
13652   * Changes:
13653   *    Jan 20, 2004    moved TTY driver to user-space   (Jorrit N. Herder)
13654   *    Sep 20, 2004    local timer management/ sync alarms  (Jorrit N. Herder)
13655   *    Jul 13, 2004    support for function key observers  (Jorrit N. Herder)
13656   */
13657
13658   #include "../drivers.h"
13659   #include "../drivers.h"
13660   #include <termios.h>
13661   #include <sys/ioc_tty.h>
13662   #include <signal.h>
13663   #include <minix/callnr.h>
13664   #include <minix/keymap.h>
13665   #include "tty.h"
13666
13667   #include <sys/time.h>
13668   #include <sys/select.h>
13669
13670   extern int irq_hook_id;
13671
13672   unsigned long kbd_irq_set = 0;
13673   unsigned long rs_irq_set = 0;
13674
13675   /* Address of a tty structure. */
13676   #define tty_addr(line)   (&tty_table[line])
13677
13678   /* Macros for magic tty types. */
13679   #define isconsole(tp)    ((tp) < tty_addr(NR_CONS))
13680   #define ispty(tp)        ((tp) >= tty_addr(NR_CONS+NR_RS_LINES))
13681
13682   /* Macros for magic tty structure pointers. */
13683   #define FIRST_TTY        tty_addr(0)
13684   #define END_TTY          tty_addr(sizeof(tty_table) / sizeof(tty_table[0]))
13685
13686   /* A device exists if at least its 'devread' function is defined. */
13687   #define tty_active(tp)   ((tp)->tty_devread != NULL)
13688
13689   /* RS232 lines or pseudo terminals can be completely configured out. */
```

```
13690    #if NR_RS_LINES == 0
13691    #define rs_init(tp)       ((void) 0)
13692    #endif
13693    #if NR_PTYS == 0
13694    #define pty_init(tp)      ((void) 0)
13695    #define do_pty(tp, mp)    ((void) 0)
13696    #endif
13697
13698    FORWARD _PROTOTYPE( void tty_timed_out, (timer_t *tp)          );
13699    FORWARD _PROTOTYPE( void expire_timers, (void)                );
13700    FORWARD _PROTOTYPE( void settimer, (tty_t *tty_ptr, int enable) );
13701    FORWARD _PROTOTYPE( void do_cancel, (tty_t *tp, message *m_ptr) );
13702    FORWARD _PROTOTYPE( void do_ioctl, (tty_t *tp, message *m_ptr) );
13703    FORWARD _PROTOTYPE( void do_open, (tty_t *tp, message *m_ptr)  );
13704    FORWARD _PROTOTYPE( void do_close, (tty_t *tp, message *m_ptr) );
13705    FORWARD _PROTOTYPE( void do_read, (tty_t *tp, message *m_ptr)  );
13706    FORWARD _PROTOTYPE( void do_write, (tty_t *tp, message *m_ptr) );
13707    FORWARD _PROTOTYPE( void do_select, (tty_t *tp, message *m_ptr) );
13708    FORWARD _PROTOTYPE( void do_status, (message *m_ptr)          );
13709    FORWARD _PROTOTYPE( void in_transfer, (tty_t *tp)             );
13710    FORWARD _PROTOTYPE( int tty_echo, (tty_t *tp, int ch)         );
13711    FORWARD _PROTOTYPE( void rawecho, (tty_t *tp, int ch)         );
13712    FORWARD _PROTOTYPE( int back_over, (tty_t *tp)                );
13713    FORWARD _PROTOTYPE( void reprint, (tty_t *tp)                 );
13714    FORWARD _PROTOTYPE( void dev_ioctl, (tty_t *tp)               );
13715    FORWARD _PROTOTYPE( void setattr, (tty_t *tp)                 );
13716    FORWARD _PROTOTYPE( void tty_icancel, (tty_t *tp)             );
13717    FORWARD _PROTOTYPE( void tty_init, (void)                     );
13718
13719    /* Default attributes. */
13720    PRIVATE struct termios termios_defaults = {
13721      TINPUT_DEF, TOUTPUT_DEF, TCTRL_DEF, TLOCAL_DEF, TSPEED_DEF, TSPEED_DEF,
13722      {
13723            TEOF_DEF, TEOL_DEF, TERASE_DEF, TINTR_DEF, TKILL_DEF, TMIN_DEF,
13724            TQUIT_DEF, TTIME_DEF, TSUSP_DEF, TSTART_DEF, TSTOP_DEF,
13725            TREPRINT_DEF, TLNEXT_DEF, TDISCARD_DEF,
13726      },
13727    };
13728    PRIVATE struct winsize winsize_defaults;        /* = all zeroes */
13729
13730    /* Global variables for the TTY task (declared extern in tty.h). */
13731    PUBLIC tty_t tty_table[NR_CONS+NR_RS_LINES+NR_PTYS];
13732    PUBLIC int ccurrent;                        /* currently active console */
13733    PUBLIC timer_t *tty_timers;                 /* queue of TTY timers */
13734    PUBLIC clock_t tty_next_timeout;            /* time that the next alarm is due */
13735    PUBLIC struct machine machine;              /* kernel environment variables */
13736
13737    /*===========================================================================*
13738     *                              tty_task                                      *
13739     *===========================================================================*/
13740    PUBLIC void main(void)
13741    {
13742    /* Main routine of the terminal task. */
13743
13744      message tty_mess;                 /* buffer for all incoming messages */
13745      unsigned line;
13746      int s;
13747      char *types[] = {"task","driver","server", "user"};
13748      register struct proc *rp;
13749      register tty_t *tp;
```

```
13750
13751    /* Initialize the TTY driver. */
13752    tty_init();
13753
13754    /* Get kernel environment (protected_mode, pc_at and ega are needed). */
13755    if (OK != (s=sys_getmachine(&machine))) {
13756      panic("TTY","Couldn't obtain kernel environment.", s);
13757    }
13758
13759    /* Final one-time keyboard initialization. */
13760    kb_init_once();
13761
13762    printf("\n");
13763
13764    while (TRUE) {
13765
13766        /* Check for and handle any events on any of the ttys. */
13767        for (tp = FIRST_TTY; tp < END_TTY; tp++) {
13768            if (tp->tty_events) handle_events(tp);
13769        }
13770
13771        /* Get a request message. */
13772        receive(ANY, &tty_mess);
13773
13774        /* First handle all kernel notification types that the TTY supports.
13775         *  - An alarm went off, expire all timers and handle the events.
13776         *  - A hardware interrupt also is an invitation to check for events.
13777         *  - A new kernel message is available for printing.
13778         *  - Reset the console on system shutdown.
13779         * Then see if this message is different from a normal device driver
13780         * request and should be handled separately. These extra functions
13781         * do not operate on a device, in constrast to the driver requests.
13782         */
13783        switch (tty_mess.m_type) {
13784        case SYN_ALARM:                /* fall through */
13785            expire_timers();           /* run watchdogs of expired timers */
13786            continue;                  /* contine to check for events */
13787        case HARD_INT: {               /* hardware interrupt notification */
13788            if (tty_mess.NOTIFY_ARG & kbd_irq_set)
13789                kbd_interrupt(&tty_mess);/* fetch chars from keyboard */
13790 #if NR_RS_LINES > 0
13791            if (tty_mess.NOTIFY_ARG & rs_irq_set)
13792                rs_interrupt(&tty_mess);/* serial I/O */
13793 #endif
13794            expire_timers();           /* run watchdogs of expired timers */
13795            continue;                  /* contine to check for events */
13796        }
13797        case SYS_SIG: {                /* system signal */
13798            sigset_t sigset = (sigset_t) tty_mess.NOTIFY_ARG;
13799
13800            if (sigismember(&sigset, SIGKSTOP)) {
13801                cons_stop();           /* switch to primary console */
13802                if (irq_hook_id != -1) {
13803                    sys_irqdisable(&irq_hook_id);
13804                    sys_irqrmpolicy(KEYBOARD_IRQ, &irq_hook_id);
13805                }
13806            }
13807            if (sigismember(&sigset, SIGTERM)) cons_stop();
13808            if (sigismember(&sigset, SIGKMESS)) do_new_kmess(&tty_mess);
13809            continue;
```

```
13810                }
13811                case PANIC_DUMPS:                /* allow panic dumps */
13812                        cons_stop();             /* switch to primary console */
13813                        do_panic_dumps(&tty_mess);
13814                        continue;
13815                case DIAGNOSTICS:                /* a server wants to print some */
13816                        do_diagnostics(&tty_mess);
13817                        continue;
13818                case FKEY_CONTROL:               /* (un)register a fkey observer */
13819                        do_fkey_ctl(&tty_mess);
13820                        continue;
13821                default:                         /* should be a driver request */
13822                        ;                        /* do nothing; end switch */
13823                }
13824
13825                /* Only device requests should get to this point. All requests,
13826                 * except DEV_STATUS, have a minor device number. Check this
13827                 * exception and get the minor device number otherwise.
13828                 */
13829                if (tty_mess.m_type == DEV_STATUS) {
13830                        do_status(&tty_mess);
13831                        continue;
13832                }
13833                line = tty_mess.TTY_LINE;
13834                if ((line - CONS_MINOR) < NR_CONS) {
13835                        tp = tty_addr(line - CONS_MINOR);
13836                } else if (line == LOG_MINOR) {
13837                        tp = tty_addr(0);
13838                } else if ((line - RS232_MINOR) < NR_RS_LINES) {
13839                        tp = tty_addr(line - RS232_MINOR + NR_CONS);
13840                } else if ((line - TTYPX_MINOR) < NR_PTYS) {
13841                        tp = tty_addr(line - TTYPX_MINOR + NR_CONS + NR_RS_LINES);
13842                } else if ((line - PTYPX_MINOR) < NR_PTYS) {
13843                        tp = tty_addr(line - PTYPX_MINOR + NR_CONS + NR_RS_LINES);
13844                        if (tty_mess.m_type != DEV_IOCTL) {
13845                                do_pty(tp, &tty_mess);
13846                                continue;
13847                        }
13848                } else {
13849                        tp = NULL;
13850                }
13851
13852                /* If the device doesn't exist or is not configured return ENXIO. */
13853                if (tp == NULL || ! tty_active(tp)) {
13854                        printf("Warning, TTY got illegal request %d from %d\n",
13855                                tty_mess.m_type, tty_mess.m_source);
13856                        tty_reply(TASK_REPLY, tty_mess.m_source,
13857                                                        tty_mess.PROC_NR, ENXIO);
13858                        continue;
13859                }
13860
13861                /* Execute the requested device driver function. */
13862                switch (tty_mess.m_type) {
13863                    case DEV_READ:      do_read(tp, &tty_mess);      break;
13864                    case DEV_WRITE:     do_write(tp, &tty_mess);     break;
13865                    case DEV_IOCTL:     do_ioctl(tp, &tty_mess);     break;
13866                    case DEV_OPEN:      do_open(tp, &tty_mess);      break;
13867                    case DEV_CLOSE:     do_close(tp, &tty_mess);     break;
13868                    case DEV_SELECT:    do_select(tp, &tty_mess);    break;
13869                    case CANCEL:        do_cancel(tp, &tty_mess);    break;
```

```
13870                    default:
13871                        printf("Warning, TTY got unexpected request %d from %d\n",
13872                            tty_mess.m_type, tty_mess.m_source);
13873                    tty_reply(TASK_REPLY, tty_mess.m_source,
13874                                            tty_mess.PROC_NR, EINVAL);
13875            }
13876    }
13877 }

13879 /*===========================================================================*
13880  *                              do_status                                    *
13881  *===========================================================================*/
13882 PRIVATE void do_status(m_ptr)
13883 message *m_ptr;
13884 {
13885   register struct tty *tp;
13886   int event_found;
13887   int status;
13888   int ops;
13889
13890   /* Check for select or revive events on any of the ttys. If we found an,
13891    * event return a single status message for it. The FS will make another
13892    * call to see if there is more.
13893    */
13894   event_found = 0;
13895   for (tp = FIRST_TTY; tp < END_TTY; tp++) {
13896        if ((ops = select_try(tp, tp->tty_select_ops)) &&
13897                        tp->tty_select_proc == m_ptr->m_source) {
13898
13899                /* I/O for a selected minor device is ready. */
13900                m_ptr->m_type = DEV_IO_READY;
13901                m_ptr->DEV_MINOR = tp->tty_index;
13902                m_ptr->DEV_SEL_OPS = ops;
13903
13904                tp->tty_select_ops &= ~ops;     /* unmark select event */
13905                event_found = 1;
13906                break;
13907        }
13908        else if (tp->tty_inrevived && tp->tty_incaller == m_ptr->m_source) {
13909
13910                /* Suspended request finished. Send a REVIVE. */
13911                m_ptr->m_type = DEV_REVIVE;
13912                m_ptr->REP_PROC_NR = tp->tty_inproc;
13913                m_ptr->REP_STATUS = tp->tty_incum;
13914
13915                tp->tty_inleft = tp->tty_incum = 0;
13916                tp->tty_inrevived = 0;          /* unmark revive event */
13917                event_found = 1;
13918                break;
13919        }
13920        else if (tp->tty_outrevived && tp->tty_outcaller == m_ptr->m_source) {
13921
13922                /* Suspended request finished. Send a REVIVE. */
13923                m_ptr->m_type = DEV_REVIVE;
13924                m_ptr->REP_PROC_NR = tp->tty_outproc;
13925                m_ptr->REP_STATUS = tp->tty_outcum;
13926
13927                tp->tty_outcum = 0;
13928                tp->tty_outrevived = 0;         /* unmark revive event */
13929                event_found = 1;
```

```
13930                          break;
13931              }
13932      }
13933
13934  #if NR_PTYS > 0
13935      if (!event_found)
13936              event_found = pty_status(m_ptr);
13937  #endif
13938
13939      if (! event_found) {
13940              /* No events of interest were found. Return an empty message. */
13941              m_ptr->m_type = DEV_NO_STATUS;
13942      }
13943
13944      /* Almost done. Send back the reply message to the caller. */
13945      if ((status = send(m_ptr->m_source, m_ptr)) != OK) {
13946              panic("TTY","send in do_status failed, status\n", status);
13947      }
13948  }

13950  /*===========================================================================*
13951   *                              do_read                                      *
13952   *===========================================================================*/
13953  PRIVATE void do_read(tp, m_ptr)
13954  register tty_t *tp;             /* pointer to tty struct */
13955  register message *m_ptr;        /* pointer to message sent to the task */
13956  {
13957  /* A process wants to read from a terminal. */
13958    int r, status;
13959    phys_bytes phys_addr;
13960
13961    /* Check if there is already a process hanging in a read, check if the
13962     * parameters are correct, do I/O.
13963     */
13964    if (tp->tty_inleft > 0) {
13965            r = EIO;
13966    } else
13967    if (m_ptr->COUNT <= 0) {
13968            r = EINVAL;
13969    } else
13970    if (sys_umap(m_ptr->PROC_NR, D, (vir_bytes) m_ptr->ADDRESS, m_ptr->COUNT,
13971                    &phys_addr) != OK) {
13972            r = EFAULT;
13973    } else {
13974            /* Copy information from the message to the tty struct. */
13975            tp->tty_inrepcode = TASK_REPLY;
13976            tp->tty_incaller = m_ptr->m_source;
13977            tp->tty_inproc = m_ptr->PROC_NR;
13978            tp->tty_in_vir = (vir_bytes) m_ptr->ADDRESS;
13979            tp->tty_inleft = m_ptr->COUNT;
13980
13981            if (!(tp->tty_termios.c_lflag & ICANON)
13982                                    && tp->tty_termios.c_cc[VTIME] > 0) {
13983                    if (tp->tty_termios.c_cc[VMIN] == 0) {
13984                            /* MIN & TIME specify a read timer that finishes the
13985                             * read in TIME/10 seconds if no bytes are available.
13986                             */
13987                            settimer(tp, TRUE);
13988                            tp->tty_min = 1;
13989                    } else {
```

```
13990                                   /* MIN & TIME specify an inter-byte timer that may
13991                                    * have to be cancelled if there are no bytes yet.
13992                                    */
13993                                   if (tp->tty_eotct == 0) {
13994                                           settimer(tp, FALSE);
13995                                           tp->tty_min = tp->tty_termios.c_cc[VMIN];
13996                                   }
13997                           }
13998                   }
13999
14000           /* Anything waiting in the input buffer? Clear it out... */
14001           in_transfer(tp);
14002           /* ...then go back for more. */
14003           handle_events(tp);
14004           if (tp->tty_inleft == 0)  {
14005                   if (tp->tty_select_ops)
14006                           select_retry(tp);
14007                   return;                  /* already done */
14008           }
14009
14010           /* There were no bytes in the input queue available, so either suspend
14011            * the caller or break off the read if nonblocking.
14012            */
14013           if (m_ptr->TTY_FLAGS & O_NONBLOCK) {
14014                   r = EAGAIN;                              /* cancel the read */
14015                   tp->tty_inleft = tp->tty_incum = 0;
14016           } else {
14017                   r = SUSPEND;                             /* suspend the caller */
14018                   tp->tty_inrepcode = REVIVE;
14019           }
14020   }
14021   tty_reply(TASK_REPLY, m_ptr->m_source, m_ptr->PROC_NR, r);
14022   if (tp->tty_select_ops)
14023           select_retry(tp);
14024 }

14026 /*===========================================================================*
14027  *                              do_write                                     *
14028  *===========================================================================*/
14029 PRIVATE void do_write(tp, m_ptr)
14030 register tty_t *tp;
14031 register message *m_ptr;         /* pointer to message sent to the task */
14032 {
14033 /* A process wants to write on a terminal. */
14034   int r;
14035   phys_bytes phys_addr;
14036
14037   /* Check if there is already a process hanging in a write, check if the
14038    * parameters are correct, do I/O.
14039    */
14040   if (tp->tty_outleft > 0) {
14041           r = EIO;
14042   } else
14043   if (m_ptr->COUNT <= 0) {
14044           r = EINVAL;
14045   } else
14046   if (sys_umap(m_ptr->PROC_NR, D, (vir_bytes) m_ptr->ADDRESS, m_ptr->COUNT,
14047                   &phys_addr) != OK) {
14048           r = EFAULT;
14049   } else {
```

```
14050              /* Copy message parameters to the tty structure. */
14051              tp->tty_outrepcode = TASK_REPLY;
14052              tp->tty_outcaller = m_ptr->m_source;
14053              tp->tty_outproc = m_ptr->PROC_NR;
14054              tp->tty_out_vir = (vir_bytes) m_ptr->ADDRESS;
14055              tp->tty_outleft = m_ptr->COUNT;
14056
14057              /* Try to write. */
14058              handle_events(tp);
14059              if (tp->tty_outleft == 0)
14060                      return; /* already done */
14061
14062              /* None or not all the bytes could be written, so either suspend the
14063               * caller or break off the write if nonblocking.
14064               */
14065              if (m_ptr->TTY_FLAGS & O_NONBLOCK) {          /* cancel the write */
14066                      r = tp->tty_outcum > 0 ? tp->tty_outcum : EAGAIN;
14067                      tp->tty_outleft = tp->tty_outcum = 0;
14068              } else {
14069                      r = SUSPEND;                           /* suspend the caller */
14070                      tp->tty_outrepcode = REVIVE;
14071              }
14072      }
14073      tty_reply(TASK_REPLY, m_ptr->m_source, m_ptr->PROC_NR, r);
14074 }

14076 /*===========================================================================*
14077  *                              do_ioctl                                     *
14078  *===========================================================================*/
14079 PRIVATE void do_ioctl(tp, m_ptr)
14080 register tty_t *tp;
14081 message *m_ptr;                  /* pointer to message sent to task */
14082 {
14083 /* Perform an IOCTL on this terminal. Posix termios calls are handled
14084  * by the IOCTL system call
14085  */
14086
14087   int r;
14088   union {
14089         int i;
14090   } param;
14091   size_t size;
14092
14093   /* Size of the ioctl parameter. */
14094   switch (m_ptr->TTY_REQUEST) {
14095     case TCGETS:        /* Posix tcgetattr function */
14096     case TCSETS:        /* Posix tcsetattr function, TCSANOW option */
14097     case TCSETSW:       /* Posix tcsetattr function, TCSADRAIN option */
14098     case TCSETSF:       /* Posix tcsetattr function, TCSAFLUSH option */
14099         size = sizeof(struct termios);
14100         break;
14101
14102     case TCSBRK:        /* Posix tcsendbreak function */
14103     case TCFLOW:        /* Posix tcflow function */
14104     case TCFLSH:        /* Posix tcflush function */
14105     case TIOCGPGRP:     /* Posix tcgetpgrp function */
14106     case TIOCSPGRP:     /* Posix tcsetpgrp function */
14107         size = sizeof(int);
14108         break;
14109
```

```
14110        case TIOCGWINSZ:     /* get window size (not Posix) */
14111        case TIOCSWINSZ:     /* set window size (not Posix) */
14112            size = sizeof(struct winsize);
14113            break;
14114
14115        case KIOCSMAP:       /* load keymap (Minix extension) */
14116            size = sizeof(keymap_t);
14117            break;
14118
14119        case TIOCSFON:       /* load font (Minix extension) */
14120            size = sizeof(u8_t [8192]);
14121            break;
14122
14123        case TCDRAIN:        /* Posix tcdrain function -- no parameter */
14124        default:             size = 0;
14125  }
14126
14127  r = OK;
14128  switch (m_ptr->TTY_REQUEST) {
14129    case TCGETS:
14130        /* Get the termios attributes. */
14131        r = sys_vircopy(SELF, D, (vir_bytes) &tp->tty_termios,
14132                m_ptr->PROC_NR, D, (vir_bytes) m_ptr->ADDRESS,
14133                (vir_bytes) size);
14134        break;
14135
14136    case TCSETSW:
14137    case TCSETSF:
14138    case TCDRAIN:
14139        if (tp->tty_outleft > 0) {
14140                /* Wait for all ongoing output processing to finish. */
14141                tp->tty_iocaller = m_ptr->m_source;
14142                tp->tty_ioproc = m_ptr->PROC_NR;
14143                tp->tty_ioreq = m_ptr->REQUEST;
14144                tp->tty_iovir = (vir_bytes) m_ptr->ADDRESS;
14145                r = SUSPEND;
14146                break;
14147        }
14148        if (m_ptr->TTY_REQUEST == TCDRAIN) break;
14149        if (m_ptr->TTY_REQUEST == TCSETSF) tty_icancel(tp);
14150        /*FALL THROUGH*/
14151    case TCSETS:
14152        /* Set the termios attributes. */
14153        r = sys_vircopy( m_ptr->PROC_NR, D, (vir_bytes) m_ptr->ADDRESS,
14154                SELF, D, (vir_bytes) &tp->tty_termios, (vir_bytes) size);
14155        if (r != OK) break;
14156        setattr(tp);
14157        break;
14158
14159    case TCFLSH:
14160        r = sys_vircopy( m_ptr->PROC_NR, D, (vir_bytes) m_ptr->ADDRESS,
14161                SELF, D, (vir_bytes) &param.i, (vir_bytes) size);
14162        if (r != OK) break;
14163        switch (param.i) {
14164            case TCIFLUSH:      tty_icancel(tp);                          break;
14165            case TCOFLUSH:      (*tp->tty_ocancel)(tp, 0);               break;
14166            case TCIOFLUSH:     tty_icancel(tp); (*tp->tty_ocancel)(tp, 0); break;
14167            default:            r = EINVAL;
14168        }
14169        break;
```

```
14170
14171         case TCFLOW:
14172             r = sys_vircopy( m_ptr->PROC_NR, D, (vir_bytes) m_ptr->ADDRESS,
14173                     SELF, D, (vir_bytes) &param.i, (vir_bytes) size);
14174             if (r != OK) break;
14175             switch (param.i) {
14176                 case TCOOFF:
14177                 case TCOON:
14178                     tp->tty_inhibited = (param.i == TCOOFF);
14179                     tp->tty_events = 1;
14180                     break;
14181                 case TCIOFF:
14182                     (*tp->tty_echo)(tp, tp->tty_termios.c_cc[VSTOP]);
14183                     break;
14184                 case TCION:
14185                     (*tp->tty_echo)(tp, tp->tty_termios.c_cc[VSTART]);
14186                     break;
14187                 default:
14188                     r = EINVAL;
14189             }
14190             break;
14191
14192         case TCSBRK:
14193             if (tp->tty_break != NULL) (*tp->tty_break)(tp,0);
14194             break;
14195
14196         case TIOCGWINSZ:
14197             r = sys_vircopy(SELF, D, (vir_bytes) &tp->tty_winsize,
14198                     m_ptr->PROC_NR, D, (vir_bytes) m_ptr->ADDRESS,
14199                     (vir_bytes) size);
14200             break;
14201
14202         case TIOCSWINSZ:
14203             r = sys_vircopy( m_ptr->PROC_NR, D, (vir_bytes) m_ptr->ADDRESS,
14204                     SELF, D, (vir_bytes) &tp->tty_winsize, (vir_bytes) size);
14205             /* SIGWINCH... */
14206             break;
14207
14208         case KIOCSMAP:
14209             /* Load a new keymap (only /dev/console). */
14210             if (isconsole(tp)) r = kbd_loadmap(m_ptr);
14211             break;
14212
14213         case TIOCSFON:
14214             /* Load a font into an EGA or VGA card (hs@hck.hr) */
14215             if (isconsole(tp)) r = con_loadfont(m_ptr);
14216             break;
14217
14218 /* These Posix functions are allowed to fail if _POSIX_JOB_CONTROL is
14219  * not defined.
14220  */
14221         case TIOCGPGRP:
14222         case TIOCSPGRP:
14223         default:
14224             r = ENOTTY;
14225     }
14226
14227     /* Send the reply. */
14228     tty_reply(TASK_REPLY, m_ptr->m_source, m_ptr->PROC_NR, r);
14229 }
```

```
14231  /*===========================================================================*
14232   *                              do_open                                       *
14233   *===========================================================================*/
14234  PRIVATE void do_open(tp, m_ptr)
14235  register tty_t *tp;
14236  message *m_ptr;                 /* pointer to message sent to task */
14237  {
14238  /* A tty line has been opened.  Make it the callers controlling tty if
14239   * O_NOCTTY is *not* set and it is not the log device.  1 is returned if
14240   * the tty is made the controlling tty, otherwise OK or an error code.
14241   */
14242    int r = OK;
14243
14244    if (m_ptr->TTY_LINE == LOG_MINOR) {
14245          /* The log device is a write-only diagnostics device. */
14246          if (m_ptr->COUNT & R_BIT) r = EACCES;
14247    } else {
14248          if (!(m_ptr->COUNT & O_NOCTTY)) {
14249                  tp->tty_pgrp = m_ptr->PROC_NR;
14250                  r = 1;
14251          }
14252          tp->tty_openct++;
14253    }
14254    tty_reply(TASK_REPLY, m_ptr->m_source, m_ptr->PROC_NR, r);
14255  }

14257  /*===========================================================================*
14258   *                              do_close                                      *
14259   *===========================================================================*/
14260  PRIVATE void do_close(tp, m_ptr)
14261  register tty_t *tp;
14262  message *m_ptr;                 /* pointer to message sent to task */
14263  {
14264  /* A tty line has been closed.  Clean up the line if it is the last close. */
14265
14266    if (m_ptr->TTY_LINE != LOG_MINOR && --tp->tty_openct == 0) {
14267          tp->tty_pgrp = 0;
14268          tty_icancel(tp);
14269          (*tp->tty_ocancel)(tp, 0);
14270          (*tp->tty_close)(tp, 0);
14271          tp->tty_termios = termios_defaults;
14272          tp->tty_winsize = winsize_defaults;
14273          setattr(tp);
14274    }
14275    tty_reply(TASK_REPLY, m_ptr->m_source, m_ptr->PROC_NR, OK);
14276  }

14278  /*===========================================================================*
14279   *                              do_cancel                                     *
14280   *===========================================================================*/
14281  PRIVATE void do_cancel(tp, m_ptr)
14282  register tty_t *tp;
14283  message *m_ptr;                 /* pointer to message sent to task */
14284  {
14285  /* A signal has been sent to a process that is hanging trying to read or write.
14286   * The pending read or write must be finished off immediately.
14287   */
14288
14289    int proc_nr;
```

```
14290      int mode;
14291
14292      /* Check the parameters carefully, to avoid cancelling twice. */
14293      proc_nr = m_ptr->PROC_NR;
14294      mode = m_ptr->COUNT;
14295      if ((mode & R_BIT) && tp->tty_inleft != 0 && proc_nr == tp->tty_inproc) {
14296              /* Process was reading when killed.  Clean up input. */
14297              tty_icancel(tp);
14298              tp->tty_inleft = tp->tty_incum = 0;
14299      }
14300      if ((mode & W_BIT) && tp->tty_outleft != 0 && proc_nr == tp->tty_outproc) {
14301              /* Process was writing when killed.  Clean up output. */
14302              (*tp->tty_ocancel)(tp, 0);
14303              tp->tty_outleft = tp->tty_outcum = 0;
14304      }
14305      if (tp->tty_ioreq != 0 && proc_nr == tp->tty_ioproc) {
14306              /* Process was waiting for output to drain. */
14307              tp->tty_ioreq = 0;
14308      }
14309      tp->tty_events = 1;
14310      tty_reply(TASK_REPLY, m_ptr->m_source, proc_nr, EINTR);
14311  }
14312
14313  PUBLIC int select_try(struct tty *tp, int ops)
14314  {
14315          int ready_ops = 0;
14316
14317          /* Special case. If line is hung up, no operations will block.
14318           * (and it can be seen as an exceptional condition.)
14319           */
14320          if (tp->tty_termios.c_ospeed == B0) {
14321                  ready_ops |= ops;
14322          }
14323
14324          if (ops & SEL_RD) {
14325                  /* will i/o not block on read? */
14326                  if (tp->tty_inleft > 0) {
14327                          ready_ops |= SEL_RD;     /* EIO - no blocking */
14328                  } else if (tp->tty_incount > 0) {
14329                          /* Is a regular read possible? tty_incount
14330                           * says there is data. But a read will only succeed
14331                           * in canonical mode if a newline has been seen.
14332                           */
14333                          if (!(tp->tty_termios.c_lflag & ICANON) ||
14334                                  tp->tty_eotct > 0) {
14335                                  ready_ops |= SEL_RD;
14336                          }
14337                  }
14338          }
14339
14340          if (ops & SEL_WR)  {
14341                  if (tp->tty_outleft > 0)  ready_ops |= SEL_WR;
14342                  else if ((*tp->tty_devwrite)(tp, 1)) ready_ops |= SEL_WR;
14343          }
14344
14345          return ready_ops;
14346  }
14347
14348  PUBLIC int select_retry(struct tty *tp)
14349  {
```

```
14350              if (select_try(tp, tp->tty_select_ops))
14351                      notify(tp->tty_select_proc);
14352              return OK;
14353  }

14355  /*===========================================================================*
14356   *                              handle_events                                *
14357   *===========================================================================*/
14358  PUBLIC void handle_events(tp)
14359  tty_t *tp;                              /* TTY to check for events. */
14360  {
14361  /* Handle any events pending on a TTY.  These events are usually device
14362   * interrupts.
14363   *
14364   * Two kinds of events are prominent:
14365   *      - a character has been received from the console or an RS232 line.
14366   *      - an RS232 line has completed a write request (on behalf of a user).
14367   * The interrupt handler may delay the interrupt message at its discretion
14368   * to avoid swamping the TTY task.  Messages may be overwritten when the
14369   * lines are fast or when there are races between different lines, input
14370   * and output, because MINIX only provides single buffering for interrupt
14371   * messages (in proc.c).  This is handled by explicitly checking each line
14372   * for fresh input and completed output on each interrupt.
14373   */
14374    char *buf;
14375    unsigned count;
14376    int status;

14378    do {
14379          tp->tty_events = 0;

14381          /* Read input and perform input processing. */
14382          (*tp->tty_devread)(tp, 0);

14384          /* Perform output processing and write output. */
14385          (*tp->tty_devwrite)(tp, 0);

14387          /* Ioctl waiting for some event? */
14388          if (tp->tty_ioreq != 0) dev_ioctl(tp);
14389    } while (tp->tty_events);

14391    /* Transfer characters from the input queue to a waiting process. */
14392    in_transfer(tp);

14394    /* Reply if enough bytes are available. */
14395    if (tp->tty_incum >= tp->tty_min && tp->tty_inleft > 0) {
14396          if (tp->tty_inrepcode == REVIVE) {
14397                  notify(tp->tty_incaller);
14398                  tp->tty_inrevived = 1;
14399          } else {
14400                  tty_reply(tp->tty_inrepcode, tp->tty_incaller,
14401                          tp->tty_inproc, tp->tty_incum);
14402                  tp->tty_inleft = tp->tty_incum = 0;
14403          }
14404    }
14405    if (tp->tty_select_ops)
14406          select_retry(tp);
14407  #if NR_PTYS > 0
14408    if (ispty(tp))
14409          select_retry_pty(tp);
```

```
14410   #endif
14411   }

14413   /*===========================================================================*
14414    *                              in_transfer                                  *
14415    *===========================================================================*/
14416   PRIVATE void in_transfer(tp)
14417   register tty_t *tp;              /* pointer to terminal to read from */
14418   {
14419   /* Transfer bytes from the input queue to a process reading from a terminal. */

14421     int ch;
14422     int count;
14423     char buf[64], *bp;

14425     /* Force read to succeed if the line is hung up, looks like EOF to reader. */
14426     if (tp->tty_termios.c_ospeed == B0) tp->tty_min = 0;

14428     /* Anything to do? */
14429     if (tp->tty_inleft == 0 || tp->tty_eotct < tp->tty_min) return;

14431     bp = buf;
14432     while (tp->tty_inleft > 0 && tp->tty_eotct > 0) {
14433             ch = *tp->tty_intail;

14435             if (!(ch & IN_EOF)) {
14436                     /* One character to be delivered to the user. */
14437                     *bp = ch & IN_CHAR;
14438                     tp->tty_inleft--;
14439                     if (++bp == bufend(buf)) {
14440                             /* Temp buffer full, copy to user space. */
14441                             sys_vircopy(SELF, D, (vir_bytes) buf,
14442                                     tp->tty_inproc, D, tp->tty_in_vir,
14443                                     (vir_bytes) buflen(buf));
14444                             tp->tty_in_vir += buflen(buf);
14445                             tp->tty_incum += buflen(buf);
14446                             bp = buf;
14447                     }
14448             }

14450             /* Remove the character from the input queue. */
14451             if (++tp->tty_intail == bufend(tp->tty_inbuf))
14452                     tp->tty_intail = tp->tty_inbuf;
14453             tp->tty_incount--;
14454             if (ch & IN_EOT) {
14455                     tp->tty_eotct--;
14456                     /* Don't read past a line break in canonical mode. */
14457                     if (tp->tty_termios.c_lflag & ICANON) tp->tty_inleft = 0;
14458             }
14459     }

14461     if (bp > buf) {
14462             /* Leftover characters in the buffer. */
14463             count = bp - buf;
14464             sys_vircopy(SELF, D, (vir_bytes) buf,
14465                     tp->tty_inproc, D, tp->tty_in_vir, (vir_bytes) count);
14466             tp->tty_in_vir += count;
14467             tp->tty_incum += count;
14468     }
14469
```

```
14470          /* Usually reply to the reader, possibly even if incum == 0 (EOF). */
14471          if (tp->tty_inleft == 0) {
14472                  if (tp->tty_inrepcode == REVIVE) {
14473                          notify(tp->tty_incaller);
14474                          tp->tty_inrevived = 1;
14475                  } else {
14476                          tty_reply(tp->tty_inrepcode, tp->tty_incaller,
14477                                  tp->tty_inproc, tp->tty_incum);
14478                          tp->tty_inleft = tp->tty_incum = 0;
14479                  }
14480          }
14481  }

14483  /*===========================================================================*
14484   *                              in_process                                   *
14485   *===========================================================================*/
14486  PUBLIC int in_process(tp, buf, count)
14487  register tty_t *tp;                     /* terminal on which character has arrived */
14488  char *buf;                              /* buffer with input characters */
14489  int count;                              /* number of input characters */
14490  {
14491  /* Characters have just been typed in.  Process, save, and echo them.  Return
14492   * the number of characters processed.
14493   */
14494
14495    int ch, sig, ct;
14496    int timeset = FALSE;
14497    static unsigned char csize_mask[] = { 0x1F, 0x3F, 0x7F, 0xFF };
14498
14499    for (ct = 0; ct < count; ct++) {
14500          /* Take one character. */
14501          ch = *buf++ & BYTE;
14502
14503          /* Strip to seven bits? */
14504          if (tp->tty_termios.c_iflag & ISTRIP) ch &= 0x7F;
14505
14506          /* Input extensions? */
14507          if (tp->tty_termios.c_lflag & IEXTEN) {
14508
14509                  /* Previous character was a character escape? */
14510                  if (tp->tty_escaped) {
14511                          tp->tty_escaped = NOT_ESCAPED;
14512                          ch |= IN_ESC;    /* protect character */
14513                  }
14514
14515                  /* LNEXT (^V) to escape the next character? */
14516                  if (ch == tp->tty_termios.c_cc[VLNEXT]) {
14517                          tp->tty_escaped = ESCAPED;
14518                          rawecho(tp, '^');
14519                          rawecho(tp, '\b');
14520                          continue;        /* do not store the escape */
14521                  }
14522
14523                  /* REPRINT (^R) to reprint echoed characters? */
14524                  if (ch == tp->tty_termios.c_cc[VREPRINT]) {
14525                          reprint(tp);
14526                          continue;
14527                  }
14528          }
14529
```

```
14530                  /* _POSIX_VDISABLE is a normal character value, so better escape it. */
14531                  if (ch == _POSIX_VDISABLE) ch |= IN_ESC;
14532
14533                  /* Map CR to LF, ignore CR, or map LF to CR. */
14534                  if (ch == '\r') {
14535                          if (tp->tty_termios.c_iflag & IGNCR) continue;
14536                          if (tp->tty_termios.c_iflag & ICRNL) ch = '\n';
14537                  } else
14538                  if (ch == '\n') {
14539                          if (tp->tty_termios.c_iflag & INLCR) ch = '\r';
14540                  }
14541
14542                  /* Canonical mode? */
14543                  if (tp->tty_termios.c_lflag & ICANON) {
14544
14545                          /* Erase processing (rub out of last character). */
14546                          if (ch == tp->tty_termios.c_cc[VERASE]) {
14547                                  (void) back_over(tp);
14548                                  if (!(tp->tty_termios.c_lflag & ECHOE)) {
14549                                          (void) tty_echo(tp, ch);
14550                                  }
14551                                  continue;
14552                          }
14553
14554                          /* Kill processing (remove current line). */
14555                          if (ch == tp->tty_termios.c_cc[VKILL]) {
14556                                  while (back_over(tp)) {}
14557                                  if (!(tp->tty_termios.c_lflag & ECHOE)) {
14558                                          (void) tty_echo(tp, ch);
14559                                          if (tp->tty_termios.c_lflag & ECHOK)
14560                                                  rawecho(tp, '\n');
14561                                  }
14562                                  continue;
14563                          }
14564
14565                          /* EOF (^D) means end-of-file, an invisible "line break". */
14566                          if (ch == tp->tty_termios.c_cc[VEOF]) ch |= IN_EOT | IN_EOF;
14567
14568                          /* The line may be returned to the user after an LF. */
14569                          if (ch == '\n') ch |= IN_EOT;
14570
14571                          /* Same thing with EOL, whatever it may be. */
14572                          if (ch == tp->tty_termios.c_cc[VEOL]) ch |= IN_EOT;
14573                  }
14574
14575                  /* Start/stop input control? */
14576                  if (tp->tty_termios.c_iflag & IXON) {
14577
14578                          /* Output stops on STOP (^S). */
14579                          if (ch == tp->tty_termios.c_cc[VSTOP]) {
14580                                  tp->tty_inhibited = STOPPED;
14581                                  tp->tty_events = 1;
14582                                  continue;
14583                          }
14584
14585                          /* Output restarts on START (^Q) or any character if IXANY. */
14586                          if (tp->tty_inhibited) {
14587                                  if (ch == tp->tty_termios.c_cc[VSTART]
14588                                                  || (tp->tty_termios.c_iflag & IXANY)) {
14589                                          tp->tty_inhibited = RUNNING;
```

```
14590                                       tp->tty_events = 1;
14591                                       if (ch == tp->tty_termios.c_cc[VSTART])
14592                                               continue;
14593                               }
14594                       }
14595               }
14596
14597               if (tp->tty_termios.c_lflag & ISIG) {
14598                       /* Check for INTR (^?) and QUIT (^\) characters. */
14599                       if (ch == tp->tty_termios.c_cc[VINTR]
14600                                               || ch == tp->tty_termios.c_cc[VQUIT]) {
14601                               sig = SIGINT;
14602                               if (ch == tp->tty_termios.c_cc[VQUIT]) sig = SIGQUIT;
14603                               sigchar(tp, sig);
14604                               (void) tty_echo(tp, ch);
14605                               continue;
14606                       }
14607               }
14608
14609               /* Is there space in the input buffer? */
14610               if (tp->tty_incount == buflen(tp->tty_inbuf)) {
14611                       /* No space; discard in canonical mode, keep in raw mode. */
14612                       if (tp->tty_termios.c_lflag & ICANON) continue;
14613                       break;
14614               }
14615
14616               if (!(tp->tty_termios.c_lflag & ICANON)) {
14617                       /* In raw mode all characters are "line breaks". */
14618                       ch |= IN_EOT;
14619
14620                       /* Start an inter-byte timer? */
14621                       if (!timeset && tp->tty_termios.c_cc[VMIN] > 0
14622                                       && tp->tty_termios.c_cc[VTIME] > 0) {
14623                               settimer(tp, TRUE);
14624                               timeset = TRUE;
14625                       }
14626               }
14627
14628               /* Perform the intricate function of echoing. */
14629               if (tp->tty_termios.c_lflag & (ECHO|ECHONL)) ch = tty_echo(tp, ch);
14630
14631               /* Save the character in the input queue. */
14632               *tp->tty_inhead++ = ch;
14633               if (tp->tty_inhead == bufend(tp->tty_inbuf))
14634                       tp->tty_inhead = tp->tty_inbuf;
14635               tp->tty_incount++;
14636               if (ch & IN_EOT) tp->tty_eotct++;
14637
14638               /* Try to finish input if the queue threatens to overflow. */
14639               if (tp->tty_incount == buflen(tp->tty_inbuf)) in_transfer(tp);
14640       }
14641   return ct;
14642 }
14643
14644 /*===========================================================================*
14645  *                              echo                                         *
14646  *===========================================================================*/
14647 PRIVATE int tty_echo(tp, ch)
14648 register tty_t *tp;              /* terminal on which to echo */
14649 register int ch;                /* pointer to character to echo */
```

```
14650   {
14651   /* Echo the character if echoing is on.  Some control characters are echoed
14652    * with their normal effect, other control characters are echoed as "^X",
14653    * normal characters are echoed normally.  EOF (^D) is echoed, but immediately
14654    * backspaced over.  Return the character with the echoed length added to its
14655    * attributes.
14656    */
14657     int len, rp;
14658
14659     ch &= ~IN_LEN;
14660     if (!(tp->tty_termios.c_lflag & ECHO)) {
14661           if (ch == ('\n' | IN_EOT) && (tp->tty_termios.c_lflag
14662                                      & (ICANON|ECHONL)) == (ICANON|ECHONL))
14663                   (*tp->tty_echo)(tp, '\n');
14664           return(ch);
14665     }
14666
14667     /* "Reprint" tells if the echo output has been messed up by other output. */
14668     rp = tp->tty_incount == 0 ? FALSE : tp->tty_reprint;
14669
14670     if ((ch & IN_CHAR) < ' ') {
14671           switch (ch & (IN_ESC|IN_EOF|IN_EOT|IN_CHAR)) {
14672               case '\t':
14673                   len = 0;
14674                   do {
14675                           (*tp->tty_echo)(tp, ' ');
14676                           len++;
14677                   } while (len < TAB_SIZE && (tp->tty_position & TAB_MASK) != 0);
14678                   break;
14679               case '\r' | IN_EOT:
14680               case '\n' | IN_EOT:
14681                   (*tp->tty_echo)(tp, ch & IN_CHAR);
14682                   len = 0;
14683                   break;
14684               default:
14685                   (*tp->tty_echo)(tp, '^');
14686                   (*tp->tty_echo)(tp, '@' + (ch & IN_CHAR));
14687                   len = 2;
14688           }
14689     } else
14690     if ((ch & IN_CHAR) == '\177') {
14691           /* A DEL prints as "^?". */
14692           (*tp->tty_echo)(tp, '^');
14693           (*tp->tty_echo)(tp, '?');
14694           len = 2;
14695     } else {
14696           (*tp->tty_echo)(tp, ch & IN_CHAR);
14697           len = 1;
14698     }
14699     if (ch & IN_EOF) while (len > 0) { (*tp->tty_echo)(tp, '\b'); len--; }
14700
14701     tp->tty_reprint = rp;
14702     return(ch | (len << IN_LSHIFT));
14703   }

14705   /*===========================================================================*
14706    *                              rawecho                                       *
14707    *===========================================================================*/
14708   PRIVATE void rawecho(tp, ch)
14709   register tty_t *tp;
```

```
14710    int ch;
14711    {
14712    /* Echo without interpretation if ECHO is set. */
14713      int rp = tp->tty_reprint;
14714      if (tp->tty_termios.c_lflag & ECHO) (*tp->tty_echo)(tp, ch);
14715      tp->tty_reprint = rp;
14716    }

14718    /*===========================================================================*
14719     *                              back_over                                     *
14720     *===========================================================================*/
14721    PRIVATE int back_over(tp)
14722    register tty_t *tp;
14723    {
14724    /* Backspace to previous character on screen and erase it. */
14725      u16_t *head;
14726      int len;
14727
14728      if (tp->tty_incount == 0) return(0);    /* queue empty */
14729      head = tp->tty_inhead;
14730      if (head == tp->tty_inbuf) head = bufend(tp->tty_inbuf);
14731      if (*--head & IN_EOT) return(0);                /* can't erase "line breaks" */
14732      if (tp->tty_reprint) reprint(tp);               /* reprint if messed up */
14733      tp->tty_inhead = head;
14734      tp->tty_incount--;
14735      if (tp->tty_termios.c_lflag & ECHOE) {
14736              len = (*head & IN_LEN) >> IN_LSHIFT;
14737              while (len > 0) {
14738                      rawecho(tp, '\b');
14739                      rawecho(tp, ' ');
14740                      rawecho(tp, '\b');
14741                      len--;
14742              }
14743      }
14744      return(1);                              /* one character erased */
14745    }

14747    /*===========================================================================*
14748     *                              reprint                                       *
14749     *===========================================================================*/
14750    PRIVATE void reprint(tp)
14751    register tty_t *tp;              /* pointer to tty struct */
14752    {
14753    /* Restore what has been echoed to screen before if the user input has been
14754     * messed up by output, or if REPRINT (^R) is typed.
14755     */
14756      int count;
14757      u16_t *head;
14758
14759      tp->tty_reprint = FALSE;
14760
14761      /* Find the last line break in the input. */
14762      head = tp->tty_inhead;
14763      count = tp->tty_incount;
14764      while (count > 0) {
14765              if (head == tp->tty_inbuf) head = bufend(tp->tty_inbuf);
14766              if (head[-1] & IN_EOT) break;
14767              head--;
14768              count--;
14769      }
```

```
14770        if (count == tp->tty_incount) return;          /* no reason to reprint */
14771
14772        /* Show REPRINT (^R) and move to a new line. */
14773        (void) tty_echo(tp, tp->tty_termios.c_cc[VREPRINT] | IN_ESC);
14774        rawecho(tp, '\r');
14775        rawecho(tp, '\n');
14776
14777        /* Reprint from the last break onwards. */
14778        do {
14779                if (head == bufend(tp->tty_inbuf)) head = tp->tty_inbuf;
14780                *head = tty_echo(tp, *head);
14781                head++;
14782                count++;
14783        } while (count < tp->tty_incount);
14784    }

14786    /*===========================================================================*
14787     *                              out_process                                  *
14788     *===========================================================================*/
14789    PUBLIC void out_process(tp, bstart, bpos, bend, icount, ocount)
14790    tty_t *tp;
14791    char *bstart, *bpos, *bend;    /* start/pos/end of circular buffer */
14792    int *icount;                   /* # input chars / input chars used */
14793    int *ocount;                   /* max output chars / output chars used */
14794    {
14795    /* Perform output processing on a circular buffer.  *icount is the number of
14796     * bytes to process, and the number of bytes actually processed on return.
14797     * *ocount is the space available on input and the space used on output.
14798     * (Naturally *icount < *ocount.)  The column position is updated modulo
14799     * the TAB size, because we really only need it for tabs.
14800     */
14801
14802      int tablen;
14803      int ict = *icount;
14804      int oct = *ocount;
14805      int pos = tp->tty_position;
14806
14807      while (ict > 0) {
14808            switch (*bpos) {
14809            case '\7':
14810                    break;
14811            case '\b':
14812                    pos--;
14813                    break;
14814            case '\r':
14815                    pos = 0;
14816                    break;
14817            case '\n':
14818                    if ((tp->tty_termios.c_oflag & (OPOST|ONLCR))
14819                                                 == (OPOST|ONLCR)) {
14820                            /* Map LF to CR+LF if there is space.  Note that the
14821                             * next character in the buffer is overwritten, so
14822                             * we stop at this point.
14823                             */
14824                            if (oct >= 2) {
14825                                    *bpos = '\r';
14826                                    if (++bpos == bend) bpos = bstart;
14827                                    *bpos = '\n';
14828                                    pos = 0;
14829                                    ict--;
```

```
14830                                oct -= 2;
14831                        }
14832                        goto out_done;  /* no space or buffer got changed */
14833                    }
14834                break;
14835          case '\t':
14836                /* Best guess for the tab length. */
14837                tablen = TAB_SIZE - (pos & TAB_MASK);
14838
14839                if ((tp->tty_termios.c_oflag & (OPOST|XTABS))
14840                                            == (OPOST|XTABS)) {
14841                    /* Tabs must be expanded. */
14842                    if (oct >= tablen) {
14843                        pos += tablen;
14844                        ict--;
14845                        oct -= tablen;
14846                        do {
14847                                *bpos = ' ';
14848                                if (++bpos == bend) bpos = bstart;
14849                        } while (--tablen != 0);
14850                    }
14851                    goto out_done;
14852                }
14853                /* Tabs are output directly. */
14854                pos += tablen;
14855                break;
14856          default:
14857                /* Assume any other character prints as one character. */
14858                pos++;
14859          }
14860          if (++bpos == bend) bpos = bstart;
14861          ict--;
14862          oct--;
14863    }
14864  out_done:
14865    tp->tty_position = pos & TAB_MASK;
14866
14867    *icount -= ict;      /* [io]ct are the number of chars not used */
14868    *ocount -= oct;      /* *[io]count are the number of chars that are used */
14869  }

14871  /*===========================================================================*
14872   *                              dev_ioctl                                     *
14873   *===========================================================================*/
14874  PRIVATE void dev_ioctl(tp)
14875  tty_t *tp;
14876  {
14877  /* The ioctl's TCSETSW, TCSETSF and TCDRAIN wait for output to finish to make
14878   * sure that an attribute change doesn't affect the processing of current
14879   * output.  Once output finishes the ioctl is executed as in do_ioctl().
14880   */
14881    int result;
14882
14883    if (tp->tty_outleft > 0) return;              /* output not finished */
14884
14885    if (tp->tty_ioreq != TCDRAIN) {
14886          if (tp->tty_ioreq == TCSETSF) tty_icancel(tp);
14887          result = sys_vircopy(tp->tty_ioproc, D, tp->tty_iovir,
14888                        SELF, D, (vir_bytes) &tp->tty_termios,
14889                        (vir_bytes) sizeof(tp->tty_termios));
```

```
14890              setattr(tp);
14891      }
14892      tp->tty_ioreq = 0;
14893      tty_reply(REVIVE, tp->tty_iocaller, tp->tty_ioproc, result);
14894  }

14896  /*===========================================================================*
14897   *                              setattr                                      *
14898   *===========================================================================*/
14899  PRIVATE void setattr(tp)
14900  tty_t *tp;
14901  {
14902  /* Apply the new line attributes (raw/canonical, line speed, etc.) */
14903    u16_t *inp;
14904    int count;
14905
14906    if (!(tp->tty_termios.c_lflag & ICANON)) {
14907              /* Raw mode; put a "line break" on all characters in the input queue.
14908               * It is undefined what happens to the input queue when ICANON is
14909               * switched off, a process should use TCSAFLUSH to flush the queue.
14910               * Keeping the queue to preserve typeahead is the Right Thing, however
14911               * when a process does use TCSANOW to switch to raw mode.
14912               */
14913              count = tp->tty_eotct = tp->tty_incount;
14914              inp = tp->tty_intail;
14915              while (count > 0) {
14916                      *inp |= IN_EOT;
14917                      if (++inp == bufend(tp->tty_inbuf)) inp = tp->tty_inbuf;
14918                      --count;
14919              }
14920      }
14921
14922    /* Inspect MIN and TIME. */
14923    settimer(tp, FALSE);
14924    if (tp->tty_termios.c_lflag & ICANON) {
14925              /* No MIN & TIME in canonical mode. */
14926              tp->tty_min = 1;
14927      } else {
14928              /* In raw mode MIN is the number of chars wanted, and TIME how long
14929               * to wait for them.  With interesting exceptions if either is zero.
14930               */
14931              tp->tty_min = tp->tty_termios.c_cc[VMIN];
14932              if (tp->tty_min == 0 && tp->tty_termios.c_cc[VTIME] > 0)
14933                      tp->tty_min = 1;
14934      }
14935
14936    if (!(tp->tty_termios.c_iflag & IXON)) {
14937              /* No start/stop output control, so don't leave output inhibited. */
14938              tp->tty_inhibited = RUNNING;
14939              tp->tty_events = 1;
14940      }
14941
14942    /* Setting the output speed to zero hangs up the phone. */
14943    if (tp->tty_termios.c_ospeed == B0) sigchar(tp, SIGHUP);
14944
14945    /* Set new line speed, character size, etc at the device level. */
14946    (*tp->tty_ioctl)(tp, 0);
14947  }
```

```
14949  /*===========================================================================*
14950   *                              tty_reply                                    *
14951   *===========================================================================*/
14952  PUBLIC void tty_reply(code, replyee, proc_nr, status)
14953  int code;                           /* TASK_REPLY or REVIVE */
14954  int replyee;                        /* destination address for the reply */
14955  int proc_nr;                        /* to whom should the reply go? */
14956  int status;                         /* reply code */
14957  {
14958  /* Send a reply to a process that wanted to read or write data. */
14959    message tty_mess;
14960
14961    tty_mess.m_type = code;
14962    tty_mess.REP_PROC_NR = proc_nr;
14963    tty_mess.REP_STATUS = status;
14964
14965    if ((status = send(replyee, &tty_mess)) != OK) {
14966        panic("TTY","tty_reply failed, status\n", status);
14967    }
14968  }


14970  /*===========================================================================*
14971   *                              sigchar                                      *
14972   *===========================================================================*/
14973  PUBLIC void sigchar(tp, sig)
14974  register tty_t *tp;
14975  int sig;                            /* SIGINT, SIGQUIT, SIGKILL or SIGHUP */
14976  {
14977  /* Process a SIGINT, SIGQUIT or SIGKILL char from the keyboard or SIGHUP from
14978   * a tty close, "stty 0", or a real RS-232 hangup.  MM will send the signal to
14979   * the process group (INT, QUIT), all processes (KILL), or the session leader
14980   * (HUP).
14981   */
14982    int status;
14983
14984    if (tp->tty_pgrp != 0)
14985        if (OK != (status = sys_kill(tp->tty_pgrp, sig)))
14986            panic("TTY","Error, call to sys_kill failed", status);
14987
14988    if (!(tp->tty_termios.c_lflag & NOFLSH)) {
14989        tp->tty_incount = tp->tty_eotct = 0;      /* kill earlier input */
14990        tp->tty_intail = tp->tty_inhead;
14991        (*tp->tty_ocancel)(tp, 0);                        /* kill all output */
14992        tp->tty_inhibited = RUNNING;
14993        tp->tty_events = 1;
14994    }
14995  }


14997  /*===========================================================================*
14998   *                              tty_icancel                                  *
14999   *===========================================================================*/
15000  PRIVATE void tty_icancel(tp)
15001  register tty_t *tp;
15002  {
15003  /* Discard all pending input, tty buffer or device. */
15004
15005    tp->tty_incount = tp->tty_eotct = 0;
15006    tp->tty_intail = tp->tty_inhead;
15007    (*tp->tty_icancel)(tp, 0);
15008  }
```

```
15010  /*===========================================================================*
15011   *                              tty_init                                     *
15012   *===========================================================================*/
15013  PRIVATE void tty_init()
15014  {
15015  /* Initialize tty structure and call device initialization routines. */
15016
15017    register tty_t *tp;
15018    int s;
15019    struct sigaction sigact;
15020
15021    /* Initialize the terminal lines. */
15022    for (tp = FIRST_TTY,s=0; tp < END_TTY; tp++,s++) {
15023
15024          tp->tty_index = s;
15025
15026          tmr_inittimer(&tp->tty_tmr);
15027
15028          tp->tty_intail = tp->tty_inhead = tp->tty_inbuf;
15029          tp->tty_min = 1;
15030          tp->tty_termios = termios_defaults;
15031          tp->tty_icancel = tp->tty_ocancel = tp->tty_ioctl = tp->tty_close =
15032                                                            tty_devnop;
15033          if (tp < tty_addr(NR_CONS)) {
15034                  scr_init(tp);
15035                  tp->tty_minor = CONS_MINOR + s;
15036          } else
15037          if (tp < tty_addr(NR_CONS+NR_RS_LINES)) {
15038                  rs_init(tp);
15039                  tp->tty_minor = RS232_MINOR + s-NR_CONS;
15040          } else {
15041                  pty_init(tp);
15042                  tp->tty_minor = s - (NR_CONS+NR_RS_LINES) + TTYPX_MINOR;
15043          }
15044    }
15045  }


15047  /*===========================================================================*
15048   *                              tty_timed_out                                *
15049   *===========================================================================*/
15050  PRIVATE void tty_timed_out(timer_t *tp)
15051  {
15052  /* This timer has expired. Set the events flag, to force processing. */
15053    tty_t *tty_ptr;
15054    tty_ptr = &tty_table[tmr_arg(tp)->ta_int];
15055    tty_ptr->tty_min = 0;                      /* force read to succeed */
15056    tty_ptr->tty_events = 1;
15057  }


15059  /*===========================================================================*
15060   *                              expire_timers                                *
15061   *===========================================================================*/
15062  PRIVATE void expire_timers(void)
15063  {
15064  /* A synchronous alarm message was received. Check if there are any expired
15065   * timers. Possibly set the event flag and reschedule another alarm.
15066   */
15067    clock_t now;                               /* current time */
15068    int s;
```

```
15069
15070     /* Get the current time to compare the timers against. */
15071     if ((s=getuptime(&now)) != OK)
15072         panic("TTY","Couldn't get uptime from clock.", s);
15073
15074     /* Scan the queue of timers for expired timers. This dispatch the watchdog
15075      * functions of expired timers. Possibly a new alarm call must be scheduled.
15076      */
15077     tmrs_exptimers(&tty_timers, now, NULL);
15078     if (tty_timers == NULL) tty_next_timeout = TMR_NEVER;
15079     else {                                          /* set new sync alarm */
15080         tty_next_timeout = tty_timers->tmr_exp_time;
15081         if ((s=sys_setalarm(tty_next_timeout, 1)) != OK)
15082             panic("TTY","Couldn't set synchronous alarm.", s);
15083     }
15084 }

15086 /*===========================================================================*
15087  *                              settimer                                     *
15088  *===========================================================================*/
15089 PRIVATE void settimer(tty_ptr, enable)
15090 tty_t *tty_ptr;                    /* line to set or unset a timer on */
15091 int enable;                        /* set timer if true, otherwise unset */
15092 {
15093   clock_t now;                              /* current time */
15094   clock_t exp_time;
15095   int s;
15096
15097     /* Get the current time to calculate the timeout time. */
15098     if ((s=getuptime(&now)) != OK)
15099         panic("TTY","Couldn't get uptime from clock.", s);
15100     if (enable) {
15101         exp_time = now + tty_ptr->tty_termios.c_cc[VTIME] * (HZ/10);
15102         /* Set a new timer for enabling the TTY events flags. */
15103         tmrs_settimer(&tty_timers, &tty_ptr->tty_tmr,
15104                 exp_time, tty_timed_out, NULL);
15105     } else {
15106         /* Remove the timer from the active and expired lists. */
15107         tmrs_clrtimer(&tty_timers, &tty_ptr->tty_tmr, NULL);
15108     }
15109
15110     /* Now check if a new alarm must be scheduled. This happens when the front
15111      * of the timers queue was disabled or reinserted at another position, or
15112      * when a new timer was added to the front.
15113      */
15114     if (tty_timers == NULL) tty_next_timeout = TMR_NEVER;
15115     else if (tty_timers->tmr_exp_time != tty_next_timeout) {
15116         tty_next_timeout = tty_timers->tmr_exp_time;
15117         if ((s=sys_setalarm(tty_next_timeout, 1)) != OK)
15118             panic("TTY","Couldn't set synchronous alarm.", s);
15119     }
15120 }

15122 /*===========================================================================*
15123  *                              tty_devnop                                   *
15124  *===========================================================================*/
15125 PUBLIC int tty_devnop(tp, try)
15126 tty_t *tp;
15127 int try;
15128 {
```

```
15129        /* Some functions need not be implemented at the device level. */
15130    }

15132    /*========================================================================*
15133     *                           do_select                                   *
15134     *========================================================================*/
15135    PRIVATE void do_select(tp, m_ptr)
15136    register tty_t *tp;              /* pointer to tty struct */
15137    register message *m_ptr;         /* pointer to message sent to the task */
15138    {
15139            int ops, ready_ops = 0, watch;
15140
15141            ops = m_ptr->PROC_NR & (SEL_RD|SEL_WR|SEL_ERR);
15142            watch = (m_ptr->PROC_NR & SEL_NOTIFY) ? 1 : 0;
15143
15144            ready_ops = select_try(tp, ops);
15145
15146            if (!ready_ops && ops && watch) {
15147                    tp->tty_select_ops |= ops;
15148                    tp->tty_select_proc = m_ptr->m_source;
15149            }
15150
15151            tty_reply(TASK_REPLY, m_ptr->m_source, m_ptr->PROC_NR, ready_ops);
15152
15153            return;
15154    }
```

```
++++++++++++++++++++++++++++++++++++++++++++++++++++++++++++++++++++++++++++++
                            drivers/tty/keyboard.c
++++++++++++++++++++++++++++++++++++++++++++++++++++++++++++++++++++++++++++++

15200    /* Keyboard driver for PC's and AT's.
15201     *
15202     * Changes:
15203     *      Jul 13, 2004    processes can observe function keys  (Jorrit N. Herder)
15204     *      Jun 15, 2004    removed wreboot(), except panic dumps (Jorrit N. Herder)
15205     *      Feb 04, 1994    loadable keymaps  (Marcus Hampel)
15206     */

15208    #include "../drivers.h"
15209    #include <sys/time.h>
15210    #include <sys/select.h>
15211    #include <termios.h>
15212    #include <signal.h>
15213    #include <unistd.h>
15214    #include <minix/callnr.h>
15215    #include <minix/com.h>
15216    #include <minix/keymap.h>
15217    #include "tty.h"
15218    #include "keymaps/us-std.src"
15219    #include "../../kernel/const.h"
15220    #include "../../kernel/config.h"
15221    #include "../../kernel/type.h"
15222    #include "../../kernel/proc.h"
15223
15224    int irq_hook_id = -1;
```

```
15225
15226  /* Standard and AT keyboard.  (PS/2 MCA implies AT throughout.) */
15227  #define KEYBD              0x60    /* I/O port for keyboard data */
15228
15229  /* AT keyboard. */
15230  #define KB_COMMAND         0x64    /* I/O port for commands on AT */
15231  #define KB_STATUS          0x64    /* I/O port for status on AT */
15232  #define KB_ACK             0xFA    /* keyboard ack response */
15233  #define KB_OUT_FULL        0x01    /* status bit set when keypress char pending */
15234  #define KB_IN_FULL         0x02    /* status bit set when not ready to receive */
15235  #define LED_CODE           0xED    /* command to keyboard to set LEDs */
15236  #define MAX_KB_ACK_RETRIES 0x1000      /* max #times to wait for kb ack */
15237  #define MAX_KB_BUSY_RETRIES 0x1000     /* max #times to loop while kb busy */
15238  #define KBIT               0x80    /* bit used to ack characters to keyboard */
15239
15240  /* Miscellaneous. */
15241  #define ESC_SCAN           0x01    /* reboot key when panicking */
15242  #define SLASH_SCAN         0x35    /* to recognize numeric slash */
15243  #define RSHIFT_SCAN        0x36    /* to distinguish left and right shift */
15244  #define HOME_SCAN          0x47    /* first key on the numeric keypad */
15245  #define INS_SCAN           0x52    /* INS for use in CTRL-ALT-INS reboot */
15246  #define DEL_SCAN           0x53    /* DEL for use in CTRL-ALT-DEL reboot */
15247
15248  #define CONSOLE              0     /* line number for console */
15249  #define KB_IN_BYTES         32     /* size of keyboard input buffer */
15250  PRIVATE char ibuf[KB_IN_BYTES]; /* input buffer */
15251  PRIVATE char *ihead = ibuf;      /* next free spot in input buffer */
15252  PRIVATE char *itail = ibuf;      /* scan code to return to TTY */
15253  PRIVATE int icount;              /* # codes in buffer */
15254
15255  PRIVATE int esc;                 /* escape scan code detected? */
15256  PRIVATE int alt_l;               /* left alt key state */
15257  PRIVATE int alt_r;               /* right alt key state */
15258  PRIVATE int alt;                 /* either alt key */
15259  PRIVATE int ctrl_l;              /* left control key state */
15260  PRIVATE int ctrl_r;              /* right control key state */
15261  PRIVATE int ctrl;                /* either control key */
15262  PRIVATE int shift_l;             /* left shift key state */
15263  PRIVATE int shift_r;             /* right shift key state */
15264  PRIVATE int shift;               /* either shift key */
15265  PRIVATE int num_down;            /* num lock key depressed */
15266  PRIVATE int caps_down;           /* caps lock key depressed */
15267  PRIVATE int scroll_down;         /* scroll lock key depressed */
15268  PRIVATE int locks[NR_CONS];      /* per console lock keys state */
15269
15270  /* Lock key active bits.  Chosen to be equal to the keyboard LED bits. */
15271  #define SCROLL_LOCK        0x01
15272  #define NUM_LOCK           0x02
15273  #define CAPS_LOCK          0x04
15274
15275  PRIVATE char numpad_map[] =
15276              {'H', 'Y', 'A', 'B', 'D', 'C', 'V', 'U', 'G', 'S', 'T', '@'};
15277
15278  /* Variables and definition for observed function keys. */
15279  typedef struct observer { int proc_nr; int events; } obs_t;
15280  PRIVATE obs_t  fkey_obs[12];     /* observers for F1-F12 */
15281  PRIVATE obs_t sfkey_obs[12];     /* observers for SHIFT F1-F12 */
15282
15283  FORWARD _PROTOTYPE( int kb_ack, (void)                           );
15284  FORWARD _PROTOTYPE( int kb_wait, (void)                          );
```

```
15285   FORWARD _PROTOTYPE( int func_key, (int scode)                         );
15286   FORWARD _PROTOTYPE( int scan_keyboard, (void)                         );
15287   FORWARD _PROTOTYPE( unsigned make_break, (int scode)                  );
15288   FORWARD _PROTOTYPE( void set_leds, (void)                             );
15289   FORWARD _PROTOTYPE( void show_key_mappings, (void)                    );
15290   FORWARD _PROTOTYPE( int kb_read, (struct tty *tp, int try)            );
15291   FORWARD _PROTOTYPE( unsigned map_key, (int scode)                     );
15292
15293   /*===========================================================================*
15294    *                              map_key0                                     *
15295    *===========================================================================*/
15296   /* Map a scan code to an ASCII code ignoring modifiers. */
15297   #define map_key0(scode)   \
15298           ((unsigned) keymap[(scode) * MAP_COLS])
15299
15300   /*===========================================================================*
15301    *                              map_key                                      *
15302    *===========================================================================*/
15303   PRIVATE unsigned map_key(scode)
15304   int scode;
15305   {
15306   /* Map a scan code to an ASCII code. */
15307
15308     int caps, column, lk;
15309     u16_t *keyrow;
15310
15311     if (scode == SLASH_SCAN && esc) return '/';    /* don't map numeric slash */
15312
15313     keyrow = &keymap[scode * MAP_COLS];
15314
15315     caps = shift;
15316     lk = locks[ccurrent];
15317     if ((lk & NUM_LOCK) && HOME_SCAN <= scode && scode <= DEL_SCAN) caps = !caps;
15318     if ((lk & CAPS_LOCK) && (keyrow[0] & HASCAPS)) caps = !caps;
15319
15320     if (alt) {
15321           column = 2;
15322           if (ctrl || alt_r) column = 3;   /* Ctrl + Alt == AltGr */
15323           if (caps) column = 4;
15324     } else {
15325           column = 0;
15326           if (caps) column = 1;
15327           if (ctrl) column = 5;
15328     }
15329     return keyrow[column] & ~HASCAPS;
15330   }
15331
15332   /*===========================================================================*
15333    *                              kbd_interrupt                                *
15334    *===========================================================================*/
15335   PUBLIC void kbd_interrupt(m_ptr)
15336   message *m_ptr;
15337   {
15338   /* A keyboard interrupt has occurred.  Process it. */
15339     int scode;
15340     static timer_t timer;             /* timer must be static! */
15341
15342     /* Fetch the character from the keyboard hardware and acknowledge it. */
15343     scode = scan_keyboard();
15344
```

```
15345        /* Store the scancode in memory so the task can get at it later. */
15346        if (icount < KB_IN_BYTES) {
15347                *ihead++ = scode;
15348                if (ihead == ibuf + KB_IN_BYTES) ihead = ibuf;
15349                icount++;
15350                tty_table[ccurrent].tty_events = 1;
15351                if (tty_table[ccurrent].tty_select_ops & SEL_RD) {
15352                        select_retry(&tty_table[ccurrent]);
15353                }
15354        }
15355  }


15357  /*===========================================================================*
15358   *                              kb_read                                      *
15359   *===========================================================================*/
15360  PRIVATE int kb_read(tp, try)
15361  tty_t *tp;
15362  int try;
15363  {
15364  /* Process characters from the circular keyboard buffer. */
15365        char buf[3];
15366        int scode;
15367        unsigned ch;
15368
15369        tp = &tty_table[ccurrent];              /* always use the current console */
15370
15371        if (try) {
15372                if (icount > 0) return 1;
15373                return 0;
15374        }
15375
15376        while (icount > 0) {
15377                scode = *itail++;                       /* take one key scan code */
15378                if (itail == ibuf + KB_IN_BYTES) itail = ibuf;
15379                icount--;
15380
15381                /* Function keys are being used for debug dumps. */
15382                if (func_key(scode)) continue;
15383
15384                /* Perform make/break processing. */
15385                ch = make_break(scode);
15386
15387                if (ch <= 0xFF) {
15388                        /* A normal character. */
15389                        buf[0] = ch;
15390                        (void) in_process(tp, buf, 1);
15391                } else
15392                if (HOME <= ch && ch <= INSRT) {
15393                        /* An ASCII escape sequence generated by the numeric pad. */
15394                        buf[0] = ESC;
15395                        buf[1] = '[';
15396                        buf[2] = numpad_map[ch - HOME];
15397                        (void) in_process(tp, buf, 3);
15398                } else
15399                if (ch == ALEFT) {
15400                        /* Choose lower numbered console as current console. */
15401                        select_console(ccurrent - 1);
15402                        set_leds();
15403                } else
15404                if (ch == ARIGHT) {
```

```
15405                        /* Choose higher numbered console as current console. */
15406                        select_console(ccurrent + 1);
15407                        set_leds();
15408              } else
15409              if (AF1 <= ch && ch <= AF12) {
15410                        /* Alt-F1 is console, Alt-F2 is ttyc1, etc. */
15411                        select_console(ch - AF1);
15412                        set_leds();
15413              } else
15414              if (CF1 <= ch && ch <= CF12) {
15415                   switch(ch) {
15416                        case CF1: show_key_mappings(); break;
15417                        case CF3: toggle_scroll(); break; /* hardware <-> software */
15418                        case CF7: sigchar(&tty_table[CONSOLE], SIGQUIT); break;
15419                        case CF8: sigchar(&tty_table[CONSOLE], SIGINT); break;
15420                        case CF9: sigchar(&tty_table[CONSOLE], SIGKILL); break;
15421                   }
15422              }
15423       }
15424
15425       return 1;
15426  }
15427
15428  /*===========================================================================*
15429   *                              make_break                                   *
15430   *===========================================================================*/
15431  PRIVATE unsigned make_break(scode)
15432  int scode;                     /* scan code of key just struck or released */
15433  {
15434  /* This routine can handle keyboards that interrupt only on key depression,
15435   * as well as keyboards that interrupt on key depression and key release.
15436   * For efficiency, the interrupt routine filters out most key releases.
15437   */
15438    int ch, make, escape;
15439    static int CAD_count = 0;
15440
15441    /* Check for CTRL-ALT-DEL, and if found, halt the computer. This would
15442     * be better done in keyboard() in case TTY is hung, except control and
15443     * alt are set in the high level code.
15444     */
15445    if (ctrl && alt && (scode == DEL_SCAN || scode == INS_SCAN))
15446    {
15447          if (++CAD_count == 3) sys_abort(RBT_HALT);
15448          sys_kill(INIT_PROC_NR, SIGABRT);
15449          return -1;
15450    }
15451
15452    /* High-order bit set on key release. */
15453    make = (scode & KEY_RELEASE) == 0;                 /* true if pressed */
15454
15455    ch = map_key(scode &= ASCII_MASK);                 /* map to ASCII */
15456
15457    escape = esc;         /* Key is escaped? (true if added since the XT) */
15458    esc = 0;
15459
15460    switch (ch) {
15461         case CTRL:                      /* Left or right control key */
15462                  *(escape ? &ctrl_r : &ctrl_l) = make;
15463                  ctrl = ctrl_l | ctrl_r;
15464                  break;
```

```
15465          case SHIFT:              /* Left or right shift key */
15466                  *(scode == RSHIFT_SCAN ? &shift_r : &shift_l) = make;
15467                  shift = shift_l | shift_r;
15468                  break;
15469          case ALT:                /* Left or right alt key */
15470                  *(escape ? &alt_r : &alt_l) = make;
15471                  alt = alt_l | alt_r;
15472                  break;
15473          case CALOCK:             /* Caps lock - toggle on 0 -> 1 transition */
15474                  if (caps_down < make) {
15475                          locks[ccurrent] ^= CAPS_LOCK;
15476                          set_leds();
15477                  }
15478                  caps_down = make;
15479                  break;
15480          case NLOCK:              /* Num lock */
15481                  if (num_down < make) {
15482                          locks[ccurrent] ^= NUM_LOCK;
15483                          set_leds();
15484                  }
15485                  num_down = make;
15486                  break;
15487          case SLOCK:              /* Scroll lock */
15488                  if (scroll_down < make) {
15489                          locks[ccurrent] ^= SCROLL_LOCK;
15490                          set_leds();
15491                  }
15492                  scroll_down = make;
15493                  break;
15494          case EXTKEY:             /* Escape keycode */
15495                  esc = 1;                 /* Next key is escaped */
15496                  return(-1);
15497          default:                 /* A normal key */
15498                  if (make) return(ch);
15499      }
15500
15501   /* Key release, or a shift type key. */
15502   return(-1);
15503 }
15504
15505 /*===========================================================================*
15506  *                              set_leds                                      *
15507  *===========================================================================*/
15508 PRIVATE void set_leds()
15509 {
15510 /* Set the LEDs on the caps, num, and scroll lock keys */
15511   int s;
15512   if (! machine.pc_at) return;   /* PC/XT doesn't have LEDs */
15513
15514   kb_wait();                      /* wait for buffer empty  */
15515   if ((s=sys_outb(KEYBD, LED_CODE)) != OK)
15516       printf("Warning, sys_outb couldn't prepare for LED values: %d\n", s);
15517                                  /* prepare keyboard to accept LED values */
15518   kb_ack();                       /* wait for ack response  */
15519
15520   kb_wait();                      /* wait for buffer empty  */
15521   if ((s=sys_outb(KEYBD, locks[ccurrent])) != OK)
15522       printf("Warning, sys_outb couldn't give LED values: %d\n", s);
15523                                  /* give keyboard LED values */
15524   kb_ack();                       /* wait for ack response  */
```

```
15525    }

15527    /*===========================================================================*
15528     *                              kb_wait                                       *
15529     *===========================================================================*/
15530    PRIVATE int kb_wait()
15531    {
15532    /* Wait until the controller is ready; return zero if this times out. */
15533
15534      int retries, status, temp;
15535      int s;
15536
15537      retries = MAX_KB_BUSY_RETRIES + 1;     /* wait until not busy */
15538      do {
15539          s = sys_inb(KB_STATUS, &status);
15540          if (status & KB_OUT_FULL) {
15541              s = sys_inb(KEYBD, &temp);     /* discard value */
15542          }
15543          if (! (status & (KB_IN_FULL|KB_OUT_FULL)) )
15544              break;                          /* wait until ready */
15545      } while (--retries != 0);               /* continue unless timeout */
15546      return(retries);                 /* zero on timeout, positive if ready */
15547    }

15549    /*===========================================================================*
15550     *                              kb_ack                                        *
15551     *===========================================================================*/
15552    PRIVATE int kb_ack()
15553    {
15554    /* Wait until kbd acknowledges last command; return zero if this times out. */
15555
15556      int retries, s;
15557      u8_t u8val;
15558
15559      retries = MAX_KB_ACK_RETRIES + 1;
15560      do {
15561          s = sys_inb(KEYBD, &u8val);
15562          if (u8val == KB_ACK)
15563              break;                  /* wait for ack */
15564      } while(--retries != 0);        /* continue unless timeout */
15565
15566      return(retries);                /* nonzero if ack received */
15567    }

15569    /*===========================================================================*
15570     *                              kb_init                                       *
15571     *===========================================================================*/
15572    PUBLIC void kb_init(tp)
15573    tty_t *tp;
15574    {
15575    /* Initialize the keyboard driver. */
15576
15577      tp->tty_devread = kb_read;     /* input function */
15578    }

15580    /*===========================================================================*
15581     *                              kb_init_once                                  *
15582     *===========================================================================*/
15583    PUBLIC void kb_init_once(void)
15584    {
```

```
15585        int i;
15586
15587        set_leds();                      /* turn off numlock led */
15588        scan_keyboard();                 /* discard leftover keystroke */
15589
15590            /* Clear the function key observers array. Also see func_key(). */
15591            for (i=0; i<12; i++) {
15592                fkey_obs[i].proc_nr = NONE;     /* F1-F12 observers */
15593                fkey_obs[i].events = 0;         /* F1-F12 observers */
15594                sfkey_obs[i].proc_nr = NONE;    /* Shift F1-F12 observers */
15595                sfkey_obs[i].events = 0;        /* Shift F1-F12 observers */
15596            }
15597
15598            /* Set interrupt handler and enable keyboard IRQ. */
15599            irq_hook_id = KEYBOARD_IRQ;          /* id to be returned on interrupt */
15600            if ((i=sys_irqsetpolicy(KEYBOARD_IRQ, IRQ_REENABLE, &irq_hook_id)) != OK)
15601                panic("TTY",  "Couldn't set keyboard IRQ policy", i);
15602            if ((i=sys_irqenable(&irq_hook_id)) != OK)
15603                panic("TTY", "Couldn't enable keyboard IRQs", i);
15604            kbd_irq_set |= (1 << KEYBOARD_IRQ);
15605        }

15607    /*===========================================================================*
15608     *                              kbd_loadmap                                   *
15609     *===========================================================================*/
15610    PUBLIC int kbd_loadmap(m)
15611    message *m;
15612    {
15613    /* Load a new keymap. */
15614      int result;
15615      result = sys_vircopy(m->PROC_NR, D, (vir_bytes) m->ADDRESS,
15616            SELF, D, (vir_bytes) keymap,
15617            (vir_bytes) sizeof(keymap));
15618      return(result);
15619    }

15621    /*===========================================================================*
15622     *                              do_fkey_ctl                                   *
15623     *===========================================================================*/
15624    PUBLIC void do_fkey_ctl(m_ptr)
15625    message *m_ptr;                          /* pointer to the request message */
15626    {
15627    /* This procedure allows processes to register a function key to receive
15628     * notifications if it is pressed. At most one binding per key can exist.
15629     */
15630      int i;
15631      int result;
15632
15633      switch (m_ptr->FKEY_REQUEST) {          /* see what we must do */
15634      case FKEY_MAP:                          /* request for new mapping */
15635          result = OK;                        /* assume everything will be ok*/
15636          for (i=0; i < 12; i++) {            /* check F1-F12 keys */
15637              if (bit_isset(m_ptr->FKEY_FKEYS, i+1) ) {
15638                  if (fkey_obs[i].proc_nr == NONE) {
15639                      fkey_obs[i].proc_nr = m_ptr->m_source;
15640                      fkey_obs[i].events = 0;
15641                      bit_unset(m_ptr->FKEY_FKEYS, i+1);
15642                  } else {
15643                      printf("WARNING, fkey_map failed F%d\n", i+1);
15644                      result = EBUSY;          /* report failure, but try rest */
```

```
15645                    }
15646                }
15647            }
15648            for (i=0; i < 12; i++) {            /* check Shift+F1-F12 keys */
15649                if (bit_isset(m_ptr->FKEY_SFKEYS, i+1) ) {
15650                    if (sfkey_obs[i].proc_nr == NONE) {
15651                        sfkey_obs[i].proc_nr = m_ptr->m_source;
15652                        sfkey_obs[i].events = 0;
15653                        bit_unset(m_ptr->FKEY_SFKEYS, i+1);
15654                    } else {
15655                        printf("WARNING, fkey_map failed Shift F%d\n", i+1);
15656                        result = EBUSY;          /* report failure but try rest */
15657                    }
15658                }
15659            }
15660            break;
15661        case FKEY_UNMAP:
15662            result = OK;                         /* assume everything will be ok*/
15663            for (i=0; i < 12; i++) {            /* check F1-F12 keys */
15664                if (bit_isset(m_ptr->FKEY_FKEYS, i+1) ) {
15665                    if (fkey_obs[i].proc_nr == m_ptr->m_source) {
15666                        fkey_obs[i].proc_nr = NONE;
15667                        fkey_obs[i].events = 0;
15668                        bit_unset(m_ptr->FKEY_FKEYS, i+1);
15669                    } else {
15670                        result = EPERM;          /* report failure, but try rest */
15671                    }
15672                }
15673            }
15674            for (i=0; i < 12; i++) {            /* check Shift+F1-F12 keys */
15675                if (bit_isset(m_ptr->FKEY_SFKEYS, i+1) ) {
15676                    if (sfkey_obs[i].proc_nr == m_ptr->m_source) {
15677                        sfkey_obs[i].proc_nr = NONE;
15678                        sfkey_obs[i].events = 0;
15679                        bit_unset(m_ptr->FKEY_SFKEYS, i+1);
15680                    } else {
15681                        result = EPERM;          /* report failure, but try rest */
15682                    }
15683                }
15684            }
15685            break;
15686        case FKEY_EVENTS:
15687            m_ptr->FKEY_FKEYS = m_ptr->FKEY_SFKEYS = 0;
15688            for (i=0; i < 12; i++) {            /* check (Shift+) F1-F12 keys */
15689                if (fkey_obs[i].proc_nr == m_ptr->m_source) {
15690                    if (fkey_obs[i].events) {
15691                        bit_set(m_ptr->FKEY_FKEYS, i+1);
15692                        fkey_obs[i].events = 0;
15693                    }
15694                }
15695                if (sfkey_obs[i].proc_nr == m_ptr->m_source) {
15696                    if (sfkey_obs[i].events) {
15697                        bit_set(m_ptr->FKEY_SFKEYS, i+1);
15698                        sfkey_obs[i].events = 0;
15699                    }
15700                }
15701            }
15702            break;
15703        default:
15704            result = EINVAL;                     /* key cannot be observed */
```

```
15705    }
15706
15707    /* Almost done, return result to caller. */
15708    m_ptr->m_type = result;
15709    send(m_ptr->m_source, m_ptr);
15710  }

15712  /*===========================================================================*
15713   *                              func_key                                     *
15714   *===========================================================================*/
15715  PRIVATE int func_key(scode)
15716  int scode;                         /* scan code for a function key */
15717  {
15718  /* This procedure traps function keys for debugging purposes. Observers of
15719   * function keys are kept in a global array. If a subject (a key) is pressed
15720   * the observer is notified of the event. Initialization of the arrays is done
15721   * in kb_init, where NONE is set to indicate there is no interest in the key.
15722   * Returns FALSE on a key release or if the key is not observable.
15723   */
15724    message m;
15725    int key;
15726    int proc_nr;
15727    int i,s;
15728
15729    /* Ignore key releases. If this is a key press, get full key code. */
15730    if (scode & KEY_RELEASE) return(FALSE);       /* key release */
15731    key = map_key(scode);                         /* include modifiers */
15732
15733    /* Key pressed, now see if there is an observer for the pressed key.
15734     *              F1-F12      observers are in fkey_obs array.
15735     *      SHIFT   F1-F12      observers are in sfkey_req array.
15736     *      CTRL    F1-F12      reserved (see kb_read)
15737     *      ALT     F1-F12      reserved (see kb_read)
15738     * Other combinations are not in use. Note that Alt+Shift+F1-F12 is yet
15739     * defined in <minix/keymap.h>, and thus is easy for future extensions.
15740     */
15741    if (F1 <= key && key <= F12) {                /* F1-F12 */
15742        proc_nr = fkey_obs[key - F1].proc_nr;
15743        fkey_obs[key - F1].events ++ ;
15744    } else if (SF1 <= key && key <= SF12) {       /* Shift F2-F12 */
15745        proc_nr = sfkey_obs[key - SF1].proc_nr;
15746        sfkey_obs[key - SF1].events ++;
15747    }
15748    else {
15749        return(FALSE);                            /* not observable */
15750    }
15751
15752    /* See if an observer is registered and send it a message. */
15753    if (proc_nr != NONE) {
15754        m.NOTIFY_TYPE = FKEY_PRESSED;
15755        notify(proc_nr);
15756    }
15757    return(TRUE);
15758  }

15760  /*===========================================================================*
15761   *                          show_key_mappings                                *
15762   *===========================================================================*/
15763  PRIVATE void show_key_mappings()
15764  {
```

```
15765        int i,s;
15766        struct proc proc;
15767
15768        printf("\n");
15769        printf("System information.   Known function key mappings to request debug dumps:\n");
15770        printf("------------------------------------------------------------------------\n");
15771        for (i=0; i<12; i++) {
15772
15773          printf(" %sF%d: ", i+1<10? " ":"", i+1);
15774          if (fkey_obs[i].proc_nr != NONE) {
15775              if ((s=sys_getproc(&proc, fkey_obs[i].proc_nr))!=OK)
15776                  printf("sys_getproc: %d\n", s);
15777              printf("%-14.14s", proc.p_name);
15778          } else {
15779              printf("%-14.14s", "<none>");
15780          }
15781
15782          printf("   %sShift-F%d: ", i+1<10? " ":"", i+1);
15783          if (sfkey_obs[i].proc_nr != NONE) {
15784              if ((s=sys_getproc(&proc, sfkey_obs[i].proc_nr))!=OK)
15785                  printf("sys_getproc: %d\n", s);
15786              printf("%-14.14s", proc.p_name);
15787          } else {
15788              printf("%-14.14s", "<none>");
15789          }
15790          printf("\n");
15791        }
15792        printf("\n");
15793        printf("Press one of the registered function keys to trigger a debug dump.\n");
15794        printf("\n");
15795   }

15797   /*===========================================================================*
15798    *                              scan_keyboard                                *
15799    *===========================================================================*/
15800   PRIVATE int scan_keyboard()
15801   {
15802   /* Fetch the character from the keyboard hardware and acknowledge it. */
15803     pvb_pair_t byte_in[2], byte_out[2];
15804
15805     byte_in[0].port = KEYBD;        /* get the scan code for the key struck */
15806     byte_in[1].port = PORT_B;       /* strobe the keyboard to ack the char */
15807     sys_vinb(byte_in, 2);           /* request actual input */
15808
15809     pv_set(byte_out[0], PORT_B, byte_in[1].value | KBIT); /* strobe bit high */
15810     pv_set(byte_out[1], PORT_B, byte_in[1].value);        /* then strobe low */
15811     sys_voutb(byte_out, 2);         /* request actual output */
15812
15813     return(byte_in[0].value);                 /* return scan code */
15814   }

15816   /*===========================================================================*
15817    *                              do_panic_dumps                               *
15818    *===========================================================================*/
15819   PUBLIC void do_panic_dumps(m)
15820   message *m;                      /* request message to TTY */
15821   {
15822   /* Wait for keystrokes for printing debugging info and reboot. */
15823     int quiet, code;
15824
```

```
15825   /* A panic! Allow debug dumps until user wants to shutdown. */
15826   printf("\nHit ESC to reboot, DEL to shutdown, F-keys for debug dumps\n");
15827
15828   (void) scan_keyboard();         /* ack any old input */
15829   quiet = scan_keyboard();/* quiescent value (0 on PC, last code on AT)*/
15830   for (;;) {
15831         tickdelay(10);
15832         /* See if there are pending request for output, but don't block.
15833          * Diagnostics can span multiple printf()s, so do it in a loop.
15834          */
15835         while (nb_receive(ANY, m) == OK) {
15836                 switch(m->m_type) {
15837                 case FKEY_CONTROL: do_fkey_ctl(m);      break;
15838                 case SYS_SIG:      do_new_kmess(m);     break;
15839                 case DIAGNOSTICS:  do_diagnostics(m);   break;
15840                 default:        ;       /* do nothing */
15841                 }
15842                 tickdelay(1);           /* allow more */
15843         }
15844         code = scan_keyboard();
15845         if (code != quiet) {
15846                 /* A key has been pressed. */
15847                 switch (code) {                 /* possibly abort MINIX */
15848                 case ESC_SCAN: sys_abort(RBT_REBOOT); return;
15849                 case DEL_SCAN: sys_abort(RBT_HALT);   return;
15850                 }
15851                 (void) func_key(code);          /* check for function key */
15852                 quiet = scan_keyboard();
15853         }
15854   }
15855   }
```

```
++++++++++++++++++++++++++++++++++++++++++++++++++++++++++++++++++++++++++++++++
                             drivers/tty/console.c
++++++++++++++++++++++++++++++++++++++++++++++++++++++++++++++++++++++++++++++++
```

```
15900   /* Code and data for the IBM console driver.
15901    *
15902    * The 6845 video controller used by the IBM PC shares its video memory with
15903    * the CPU somewhere in the 0xB0000 memory bank.  To the 6845 this memory
15904    * consists of 16-bit words.  Each word has a character code in the low byte
15905    * and a so-called attribute byte in the high byte.  The CPU directly modifies
15906    * video memory to display characters, and sets two registers on the 6845 that
15907    * specify the video origin and the cursor position.  The video origin is the
15908    * place in video memory where the first character (upper left corner) can
15909    * be found.  Moving the origin is a fast way to scroll the screen.  Some
15910    * video adapters wrap around the top of video memory, so the origin can
15911    * move without bounds.  For other adapters screen memory must sometimes be
15912    * moved to reset the origin.  All computations on video memory use character
15913    * (word) addresses for simplicity and assume there is no wrapping.  The
15914    * assembly support functions translate the word addresses to byte addresses
15915    * and the scrolling function worries about wrapping.
15916    */
15917
15918   #include "../drivers.h"
15919   #include <termios.h>
```

```
15920   #include <minix/callnr.h>
15921   #include <minix/com.h>
15922   #include "tty.h"
15923
15924   #include "../../kernel/const.h"
15925   #include "../../kernel/config.h"
15926   #include "../../kernel/type.h"
15927
15928   /* Definitions used by the console driver. */
15929   #define MONO_BASE    0xB0000L    /* base of mono video memory */
15930   #define COLOR_BASE   0xB8000L    /* base of color video memory */
15931   #define MONO_SIZE    0x1000      /* 4K mono video memory */
15932   #define COLOR_SIZE   0x4000      /* 16K color video memory */
15933   #define EGA_SIZE     0x8000      /* EGA & VGA have at least 32K */
15934   #define BLANK_COLOR  0x0700      /* determines cursor color on blank screen */
15935   #define SCROLL_UP    0          /* scroll forward */
15936   #define SCROLL_DOWN  1          /* scroll backward */
15937   #define BLANK_MEM ((u16_t *) 0) /* tells mem_vid_copy() to blank the screen */
15938   #define CONS_RAM_WORDS   80      /* video ram buffer size */
15939   #define MAX_ESC_PARMS    4       /* number of escape sequence params allowed */
15940
15941   /* Constants relating to the controller chips. */
15942   #define M_6845       0x3B4       /* port for 6845 mono */
15943   #define C_6845       0x3D4       /* port for 6845 color */
15944   #define INDEX        0           /* 6845's index register */
15945   #define DATA         1           /* 6845's data register */
15946   #define STATUS       6           /* 6845's status register */
15947   #define VID_ORG      12          /* 6845's origin register */
15948   #define CURSOR       14          /* 6845's cursor register */
15949
15950   /* Beeper. */
15951   #define BEEP_FREQ    0x0533      /* value to put into timer to set beep freq */
15952   #define B_TIME       3           /* length of CTRL-G beep is ticks */
15953
15954   /* definitions used for font management */
15955   #define GA_SEQUENCER_INDEX   0x3C4
15956   #define GA_SEQUENCER_DATA    0x3C5
15957   #define GA_GRAPHICS_INDEX    0x3CE
15958   #define GA_GRAPHICS_DATA     0x3CF
15959   #define GA_VIDEO_ADDRESS     0xA0000L
15960   #define GA_FONT_SIZE         8192
15961
15962   /* Global variables used by the console driver and assembly support. */
15963   PUBLIC int vid_index;           /* index of video segment in remote mem map */
15964   PUBLIC u16_t vid_seg;
15965   PUBLIC vir_bytes vid_off;       /* video ram is found at vid_seg:vid_off */
15966   PUBLIC unsigned vid_size;       /* 0x2000 for color or 0x0800 for mono */
15967   PUBLIC unsigned vid_mask;       /* 0x1FFF for color or 0x07FF for mono */
15968   PUBLIC unsigned blank_color = BLANK_COLOR; /* display code for blank */
15969
15970   /* Private variables used by the console driver. */
15971   PRIVATE int vid_port;           /* I/O port for accessing 6845 */
15972   PRIVATE int wrap;               /* hardware can wrap? */
15973   PRIVATE int softscroll;         /* 1 = software scrolling, 0 = hardware */
15974   PRIVATE int beeping;            /* speaker is beeping? */
15975   PRIVATE unsigned font_lines;    /* font lines per character */
15976   PRIVATE unsigned scr_width;     /* # characters on a line */
15977   PRIVATE unsigned scr_lines;     /* # lines on the screen */
15978   PRIVATE unsigned scr_size;      /* # characters on the screen */
15979
```

```
15980  /* Per console data. */
15981  typedef struct console {
15982    tty_t *c_tty;                    /* associated TTY struct */
15983    int c_column;                    /* current column number (0-origin) */
15984    int c_row;                       /* current row (0 at top of screen) */
15985    int c_rwords;                    /* number of WORDS (not bytes) in outqueue */
15986    unsigned c_start;                /* start of video memory of this console */
15987    unsigned c_limit;                /* limit of this console's video memory */
15988    unsigned c_org;                  /* location in RAM where 6845 base points */
15989    unsigned c_cur;                  /* current position of cursor in video RAM */
15990    unsigned c_attr;                 /* character attribute */
15991    unsigned c_blank;                /* blank attribute */
15992    char c_reverse;                  /* reverse video */
15993    char c_esc_state;                /* 0=normal, 1=ESC, 2=ESC[ */
15994    char c_esc_intro;                /* Distinguishing character following ESC */
15995    int *c_esc_parmp;                /* pointer to current escape parameter */
15996    int c_esc_parmv[MAX_ESC_PARMS];      /* list of escape parameters */
15997    u16_t c_ramqueue[CONS_RAM_WORDS];    /* buffer for video RAM */
15998  } console_t;
15999
16000  PRIVATE int nr_cons= 1;          /* actual number of consoles */
16001  PRIVATE console_t cons_table[NR_CONS];
16002  PRIVATE console_t *curcons;      /* currently visible */
16003
16004  /* Color if using a color controller. */
16005  #define color   (vid_port == C_6845)
16006
16007  /* Map from ANSI colors to the attributes used by the PC */
16008  PRIVATE int ansi_colors[8] = {0, 4, 2, 6, 1, 5, 3, 7};
16009
16010  /* Structure used for font management */
16011  struct sequence {
16012          unsigned short index;
16013          unsigned char port;
16014          unsigned char value;
16015  };
16016
16017  FORWARD _PROTOTYPE( int cons_write, (struct tty *tp, int try)        );
16018  FORWARD _PROTOTYPE( void cons_echo, (tty_t *tp, int c)              );
16019  FORWARD _PROTOTYPE( void out_char, (console_t *cons, int c)         );
16020  FORWARD _PROTOTYPE( void putk, (int c)                             );
16021  FORWARD _PROTOTYPE( void beep, (void)                             );
16022  FORWARD _PROTOTYPE( void do_escape, (console_t *cons, int c)        );
16023  FORWARD _PROTOTYPE( void flush, (console_t *cons)                  );
16024  FORWARD _PROTOTYPE( void parse_escape, (console_t *cons, int c)     );
16025  FORWARD _PROTOTYPE( void scroll_screen, (console_t *cons, int dir)  );
16026  FORWARD _PROTOTYPE( void set_6845, (int reg, unsigned val)          );
16027  FORWARD _PROTOTYPE( void get_6845, (int reg, unsigned *val)         );
16028  FORWARD _PROTOTYPE( void stop_beep, (timer_t *tmrp)                 );
16029  FORWARD _PROTOTYPE( void cons_org0, (void)                         );
16030  FORWARD _PROTOTYPE( int ga_program, (struct sequence *seq)          );
16031  FORWARD _PROTOTYPE( int cons_ioctl, (tty_t *tp, int)               );
16032
16033  /*===========================================================================*
16034   *                              cons_write                                   *
16035   *===========================================================================*/
16036  PRIVATE int cons_write(tp, try)
16037  register struct tty *tp;        /* tells which terminal is to be used */
16038  int try;
16039  {
```

```
16040    /* Copy as much data as possible to the output queue, then start I/O.  On
16041     * memory-mapped terminals, such as the IBM console, the I/O will also be
16042     * finished, and the counts updated.  Keep repeating until all I/O done.
16043     */
16044
16045    int count;
16046    int result;
16047    register char *tbuf;
16048    char buf[64];
16049    console_t *cons = tp->tty_priv;
16050
16051    if (try) return 1;      /* we can always write to console */
16052
16053    /* Check quickly for nothing to do, so this can be called often without
16054     * unmodular tests elsewhere.
16055     */
16056    if ((count = tp->tty_outleft) == 0 || tp->tty_inhibited) return;
16057
16058    /* Copy the user bytes to buf[] for decent addressing. Loop over the
16059     * copies, since the user buffer may be much larger than buf[].
16060     */
16061    do {
16062            if (count > sizeof(buf)) count = sizeof(buf);
16063            if ((result = sys_vircopy(tp->tty_outproc, D, tp->tty_out_vir,
16064                            SELF, D, (vir_bytes) buf, (vir_bytes) count)) != OK)
16065                    break;
16066            tbuf = buf;
16067
16068            /* Update terminal data structure. */
16069            tp->tty_out_vir += count;
16070            tp->tty_outcum += count;
16071            tp->tty_outleft -= count;
16072
16073            /* Output each byte of the copy to the screen.  Avoid calling
16074             * out_char() for the "easy" characters, put them into the buffer
16075             * directly.
16076             */
16077            do {
16078                    if ((unsigned) *tbuf < ' ' || cons->c_esc_state > 0
16079                            || cons->c_column >= scr_width
16080                            || cons->c_rwords >= buflen(cons->c_ramqueue))
16081                    {
16082                            out_char(cons, *tbuf++);
16083                    } else {
16084                            cons->c_ramqueue[cons->c_rwords++] =
16085                                            cons->c_attr | (*tbuf++ & BYTE);
16086                            cons->c_column++;
16087                    }
16088            } while (--count != 0);
16089    } while ((count = tp->tty_outleft) != 0 && !tp->tty_inhibited);
16090
16091    flush(cons);                            /* transfer anything buffered to the screen */
16092
16093    /* Reply to the writer if all output is finished or if an error occured. */
16094    if (tp->tty_outleft == 0 || result != OK) {
16095            /* REVIVE is not possible. I/O on memory mapped consoles finishes. */
16096            tty_reply(tp->tty_outrepcode, tp->tty_outcaller, tp->tty_outproc,
16097                                            tp->tty_outcum);
16098            tp->tty_outcum = 0;
16099    }
```

```
16100  }

16102  /*===========================================================================*
16103   *                              cons_echo                                    *
16104   *===========================================================================*/
16105  PRIVATE void cons_echo(tp, c)
16106  register tty_t *tp;              /* pointer to tty struct */
16107  int c;                          /* character to be echoed */
16108  {
16109  /* Echo keyboard input (print & flush). */
16110    console_t *cons = tp->tty_priv;
16111
16112    out_char(cons, c);
16113    flush(cons);
16114  }

16116  /*===========================================================================*
16117   *                              out_char                                     *
16118   *===========================================================================*/
16119  PRIVATE void out_char(cons, c)
16120  register console_t *cons;        /* pointer to console struct */
16121  int c;                          /* character to be output */
16122  {
16123  /* Output a character on the console.  Check for escape sequences first. */
16124    if (cons->c_esc_state > 0) {
16125          parse_escape(cons, c);
16126          return;
16127    }
16128
16129    switch(c) {
16130        case 000:               /* null is typically used for padding */
16131                return;         /* better not do anything */
16132
16133        case 007:               /* ring the bell */
16134                flush(cons);    /* print any chars queued for output */
16135                beep();
16136                return;
16137
16138        case '\b':              /* backspace */
16139                if (--cons->c_column < 0) {
16140                        if (--cons->c_row >= 0) cons->c_column += scr_width;
16141                }
16142                flush(cons);
16143                return;
16144
16145        case '\n':              /* line feed */
16146                if ((cons->c_tty->tty_termios.c_oflag & (OPOST|ONLCR))
16147                                        == (OPOST|ONLCR)) {
16148                        cons->c_column = 0;
16149                }
16150                /*FALL THROUGH*/
16151        case 013:               /* CTRL-K */
16152        case 014:               /* CTRL-L */
16153                if (cons->c_row == scr_lines-1) {
16154                        scroll_screen(cons, SCROLL_UP);
16155                } else {
16156                        cons->c_row++;
16157                }
16158                flush(cons);
16159                return;
```

```
16160
16161            case '\r':                   /* carriage return */
16162                    cons->c_column = 0;
16163                    flush(cons);
16164                    return;
16165
16166            case '\t':                   /* tab */
16167                    cons->c_column = (cons->c_column + TAB_SIZE) & ~TAB_MASK;
16168                    if (cons->c_column > scr_width) {
16169                            cons->c_column -= scr_width;
16170                            if (cons->c_row == scr_lines-1) {
16171                                    scroll_screen(cons, SCROLL_UP);
16172                            } else {
16173                                    cons->c_row++;
16174                            }
16175                    }
16176                    flush(cons);
16177                    return;
16178
16179            case 033:                    /* ESC - start of an escape sequence */
16180                    flush(cons);     /* print any chars queued for output */
16181                    cons->c_esc_state = 1;  /* mark ESC as seen */
16182                    return;
16183
16184            default:                     /* printable chars are stored in ramqueue */
16185                    if (cons->c_column >= scr_width) {
16186                            if (!LINEWRAP) return;
16187                            if (cons->c_row == scr_lines-1) {
16188                                    scroll_screen(cons, SCROLL_UP);
16189                            } else {
16190                                    cons->c_row++;
16191                            }
16192                            cons->c_column = 0;
16193                            flush(cons);
16194                    }
16195                    if (cons->c_rwords == buflen(cons->c_ramqueue)) flush(cons);
16196                    cons->c_ramqueue[cons->c_rwords++] = cons->c_attr | (c & BYTE);
16197                    cons->c_column++;                       /* next column */
16198                    return;
16199      }
16200  }

16202  /*===========================================================================*
16203   *                              scroll_screen                                *
16204   *===========================================================================*/
16205  PRIVATE void scroll_screen(cons, dir)
16206  register console_t *cons;       /* pointer to console struct */
16207  int dir;                        /* SCROLL_UP or SCROLL_DOWN */
16208  {
16209    unsigned new_line, new_org, chars;
16210
16211    flush(cons);
16212    chars = scr_size - scr_width;            /* one screen minus one line */
16213
16214    /* Scrolling the screen is a real nuisance due to the various incompatible
16215     * video cards.  This driver supports software scrolling (Hercules?),
16216     * hardware scrolling (mono and CGA cards) and hardware scrolling without
16217     * wrapping (EGA cards).  In the latter case we must make sure that
16218     *            c_start <= c_org && c_org + scr_size <= c_limit
16219     * holds, because EGA doesn't wrap around the end of video memory.
```

```
16220        */
16221        if (dir == SCROLL_UP) {
16222                /* Scroll one line up in 3 ways: soft, avoid wrap, use origin. */
16223                if (softscroll) {
16224                        vid_vid_copy(cons->c_start + scr_width, cons->c_start, chars);
16225                } else
16226                if (!wrap && cons->c_org + scr_size + scr_width >= cons->c_limit) {
16227                        vid_vid_copy(cons->c_org + scr_width, cons->c_start, chars);
16228                        cons->c_org = cons->c_start;
16229                } else {
16230                        cons->c_org = (cons->c_org + scr_width) & vid_mask;
16231                }
16232                new_line = (cons->c_org + chars) & vid_mask;
16233        } else {
16234                /* Scroll one line down in 3 ways: soft, avoid wrap, use origin. */
16235                if (softscroll) {
16236                        vid_vid_copy(cons->c_start, cons->c_start + scr_width, chars);
16237                } else
16238                if (!wrap && cons->c_org < cons->c_start + scr_width) {
16239                        new_org = cons->c_limit - scr_size;
16240                        vid_vid_copy(cons->c_org, new_org + scr_width, chars);
16241                        cons->c_org = new_org;
16242                } else {
16243                        cons->c_org = (cons->c_org - scr_width) & vid_mask;
16244                }
16245                new_line = cons->c_org;
16246        }
16247        /* Blank the new line at top or bottom. */
16248        blank_color = cons->c_blank;
16249        mem_vid_copy(BLANK_MEM, new_line, scr_width);
16250
16251        /* Set the new video origin. */
16252        if (cons == curcons) set_6845(VID_ORG, cons->c_org);
16253        flush(cons);
16254    }


16256    /*===========================================================================*
16257     *                              flush                                         *
16258     *===========================================================================*/
16259    PRIVATE void flush(cons)
16260    register console_t *cons;         /* pointer to console struct */
16261    {
16262    /* Send characters buffered in 'ramqueue' to screen memory, check the new
16263     * cursor position, compute the new hardware cursor position and set it.
16264     */
16265      unsigned cur;
16266      tty_t *tp = cons->c_tty;
16267
16268      /* Have the characters in 'ramqueue' transferred to the screen. */
16269      if (cons->c_rwords > 0) {
16270          mem_vid_copy(cons->c_ramqueue, cons->c_cur, cons->c_rwords);
16271          cons->c_rwords = 0;
16272
16273          /* TTY likes to know the current column and if echoing messed up. */
16274          tp->tty_position = cons->c_column;
16275          tp->tty_reprint = TRUE;
16276      }
16277
16278      /* Check and update the cursor position. */
16279      if (cons->c_column < 0) cons->c_column = 0;
```

```
16280        if (cons->c_column > scr_width) cons->c_column = scr_width;
16281        if (cons->c_row < 0) cons->c_row = 0;
16282        if (cons->c_row >= scr_lines) cons->c_row = scr_lines - 1;
16283        cur = cons->c_org + cons->c_row * scr_width + cons->c_column;
16284        if (cur != cons->c_cur) {
16285                if (cons == curcons) set_6845(CURSOR, cur);
16286                cons->c_cur = cur;
16287        }
16288  }


16290  /*===========================================================================*
16291   *                              parse_escape                                 *
16292   *===========================================================================*/
16293  PRIVATE void parse_escape(cons, c)
16294  register console_t *cons;          /* pointer to console struct */
16295  char c;                            /* next character in escape sequence */
16296  {
16297  /* The following ANSI escape sequences are currently supported.
16298   * If n and/or m are omitted, they default to 1.
16299   *     ESC [nA moves up n lines
16300   *     ESC [nB moves down n lines
16301   *     ESC [nC moves right n spaces
16302   *     ESC [nD moves left n spaces
16303   *     ESC [m;nH" moves cursor to (m,n)
16304   *     ESC [J clears screen from cursor
16305   *     ESC [K clears line from cursor
16306   *     ESC [nL inserts n lines ar cursor
16307   *     ESC [nM deletes n lines at cursor
16308   *     ESC [nP deletes n chars at cursor
16309   *     ESC [n@ inserts n chars at cursor
16310   *     ESC [nm enables rendition n (0=normal, 4=bold, 5=blinking, 7=reverse)
16311   *     ESC M scrolls the screen backwards if the cursor is on the top line
16312   */

16314    switch (cons->c_esc_state) {
16315      case 1:                        /* ESC seen */
16316          cons->c_esc_intro = '\0';
16317          cons->c_esc_parmp = bufend(cons->c_esc_parmv);
16318          do {
16319                  *--cons->c_esc_parmp = 0;
16320          } while (cons->c_esc_parmp > cons->c_esc_parmv);
16321          switch (c) {
16322              case '[':   /* Control Sequence Introducer */
16323                  cons->c_esc_intro = c;
16324                  cons->c_esc_state = 2;
16325                  break;
16326              case 'M':   /* Reverse Index */
16327                  do_escape(cons, c);
16328                  break;
16329              default:
16330                  cons->c_esc_state = 0;
16331          }
16332          break;

16334      case 2:                              /* ESC [ seen */
16335          if (c >= '0' && c <= '9') {
16336                  if (cons->c_esc_parmp < bufend(cons->c_esc_parmv))
16337                          *cons->c_esc_parmp = *cons->c_esc_parmp * 10 + (c-'0');
16338          } else
16339          if (c == ';') {
```

```
16340                    if (cons->c_esc_parmp < bufend(cons->c_esc_parmv))
16341                            cons->c_esc_parmp++;
16342            } else {
16343                    do_escape(cons, c);
16344            }
16345            break;
16346      }
16347  }

16349  /*===========================================================================*
16350   *                              do_escape                                    *
16351   *===========================================================================*/
16352  PRIVATE void do_escape(cons, c)
16353  register console_t *cons;            /* pointer to console struct */
16354  char c;                              /* next character in escape sequence */
16355  {
16356    int value, n;
16357    unsigned src, dst, count;
16358    int *parmp;
16359
16360    /* Some of these things hack on screen RAM, so it had better be up to date */
16361    flush(cons);
16362
16363    if (cons->c_esc_intro == '\0') {
16364            /* Handle a sequence beginning with just ESC */
16365            switch (c) {
16366                case 'M':           /* Reverse Index */
16367                    if (cons->c_row == 0) {
16368                            scroll_screen(cons, SCROLL_DOWN);
16369                    } else {
16370                            cons->c_row--;
16371                    }
16372                    flush(cons);
16373                    break;
16374
16375                default: break;
16376            }
16377    } else
16378    if (cons->c_esc_intro == '[') {
16379            /* Handle a sequence beginning with ESC [ and parameters */
16380            value = cons->c_esc_parmv[0];
16381            switch (c) {
16382                case 'A':               /* ESC [nA moves up n lines */
16383                    n = (value == 0 ? 1 : value);
16384                    cons->c_row -= n;
16385                    flush(cons);
16386                    break;
16387
16388                case 'B':               /* ESC [nB moves down n lines */
16389                    n = (value == 0 ? 1 : value);
16390                    cons->c_row += n;
16391                    flush(cons);
16392                    break;
16393
16394                case 'C':               /* ESC [nC moves right n spaces */
16395                    n = (value == 0 ? 1 : value);
16396                    cons->c_column += n;
16397                    flush(cons);
16398                    break;
16399
```

```
16400                    case 'D':              /* ESC [nD moves left n spaces */
16401                        n = (value == 0 ? 1 : value);
16402                        cons->c_column -= n;
16403                        flush(cons);
16404                        break;
16405
16406                    case 'H':              /* ESC [m;nH" moves cursor to (m,n) */
16407                        cons->c_row = cons->c_esc_parmv[0] - 1;
16408                        cons->c_column = cons->c_esc_parmv[1] - 1;
16409                        flush(cons);
16410                        break;
16411
16412                    case 'J':              /* ESC [sJ clears in display */
16413                        switch (value) {
16414                            case 0:    /* Clear from cursor to end of screen */
16415                                count = scr_size - (cons->c_cur - cons->c_org);
16416                                dst = cons->c_cur;
16417                                break;
16418                            case 1:    /* Clear from start of screen to cursor */
16419                                count = cons->c_cur - cons->c_org;
16420                                dst = cons->c_org;
16421                                break;
16422                            case 2:    /* Clear entire screen */
16423                                count = scr_size;
16424                                dst = cons->c_org;
16425                                break;
16426                            default:   /* Do nothing */
16427                                count = 0;
16428                                dst = cons->c_org;
16429                        }
16430                        blank_color = cons->c_blank;
16431                        mem_vid_copy(BLANK_MEM, dst, count);
16432                        break;
16433
16434                    case 'K':              /* ESC [sK clears line from cursor */
16435                        switch (value) {
16436                            case 0:    /* Clear from cursor to end of line */
16437                                count = scr_width - cons->c_column;
16438                                dst = cons->c_cur;
16439                                break;
16440                            case 1:    /* Clear from beginning of line to cursor */
16441                                count = cons->c_column;
16442                                dst = cons->c_cur - cons->c_column;
16443                                break;
16444                            case 2:    /* Clear entire line */
16445                                count = scr_width;
16446                                dst = cons->c_cur - cons->c_column;
16447                                break;
16448                            default:   /* Do nothing */
16449                                count = 0;
16450                                dst = cons->c_cur;
16451                        }
16452                        blank_color = cons->c_blank;
16453                        mem_vid_copy(BLANK_MEM, dst, count);
16454                        break;
16455
16456                    case 'L':              /* ESC [nL inserts n lines at cursor */
16457                        n = value;
16458                        if (n < 1) n = 1;
16459                        if (n > (scr_lines - cons->c_row))
```

```
16460                              n = scr_lines - cons->c_row;
16461
16462                      src = cons->c_org + cons->c_row * scr_width;
16463                      dst = src + n * scr_width;
16464                      count = (scr_lines - cons->c_row - n) * scr_width;
16465                      vid_vid_copy(src, dst, count);
16466                      blank_color = cons->c_blank;
16467                      mem_vid_copy(BLANK_MEM, src, n * scr_width);
16468                      break;
16469
16470              case 'M':            /* ESC [nM deletes n lines at cursor */
16471                      n = value;
16472                      if (n < 1) n = 1;
16473                      if (n > (scr_lines - cons->c_row))
16474                              n = scr_lines - cons->c_row;
16475
16476                      dst = cons->c_org + cons->c_row * scr_width;
16477                      src = dst + n * scr_width;
16478                      count = (scr_lines - cons->c_row - n) * scr_width;
16479                      vid_vid_copy(src, dst, count);
16480                      blank_color = cons->c_blank;
16481                      mem_vid_copy(BLANK_MEM, dst + count, n * scr_width);
16482                      break;
16483
16484              case '@':            /* ESC [n@ inserts n chars at cursor */
16485                      n = value;
16486                      if (n < 1) n = 1;
16487                      if (n > (scr_width - cons->c_column))
16488                              n = scr_width - cons->c_column;
16489
16490                      src = cons->c_cur;
16491                      dst = src + n;
16492                      count = scr_width - cons->c_column - n;
16493                      vid_vid_copy(src, dst, count);
16494                      blank_color = cons->c_blank;
16495                      mem_vid_copy(BLANK_MEM, src, n);
16496                      break;
16497
16498              case 'P':            /* ESC [nP deletes n chars at cursor */
16499                      n = value;
16500                      if (n < 1) n = 1;
16501                      if (n > (scr_width - cons->c_column))
16502                              n = scr_width - cons->c_column;
16503
16504                      dst = cons->c_cur;
16505                      src = dst + n;
16506                      count = scr_width - cons->c_column - n;
16507                      vid_vid_copy(src, dst, count);
16508                      blank_color = cons->c_blank;
16509                      mem_vid_copy(BLANK_MEM, dst + count, n);
16510                      break;
16511
16512              case 'm':            /* ESC [nm enables rendition n */
16513                      for (parmp = cons->c_esc_parmv; parmp <= cons->c_esc_parmp
16514                              && parmp < bufend(cons->c_esc_parmv); parmp++) {
16515                              if (cons->c_reverse) {
16516                                      /* Unswap fg and bg colors */
16517                                      cons->c_attr =  ((cons->c_attr & 0x7000) >> 4) |
16518                                                      ((cons->c_attr & 0x0700) << 4) |
16519                                                      ((cons->c_attr & 0x8800));
```

```
16520                           }
16521                           switch (n = *parmp) {
16522                               case 0:     /* NORMAL */
16523                                   cons->c_attr = cons->c_blank = BLANK_COLOR;
16524                                   cons->c_reverse = FALSE;
16525                                   break;
16526
16527                               case 1:     /* BOLD */
16528                                   /* Set intensity bit */
16529                                   cons->c_attr |= 0x0800;
16530                                   break;
16531
16532                               case 4:     /* UNDERLINE */
16533                                   if (color) {
16534                                           /* Change white to cyan, i.e. lose red
16535                                           */
16536                                           cons->c_attr = (cons->c_attr & 0xBBFF);
16537                                   } else {
16538                                           /* Set underline attribute */
16539                                           cons->c_attr = (cons->c_attr & 0x99FF);
16540                                   }
16541                                   break;
16542
16543                               case 5:     /* BLINKING */
16544                                   /* Set the blink bit */
16545                                   cons->c_attr |= 0x8000;
16546                                   break;
16547
16548                               case 7:     /* REVERSE */
16549                                   cons->c_reverse = TRUE;
16550                                   break;
16551
16552                               default:    /* COLOR */
16553                                   if (n == 39) n = 37;     /* set default color */
16554                                   if (n == 49) n = 40;
16555
16556                                   if (!color) {
16557                                           /* Don't mess up a monochrome screen */
16558                                   } else
16559                                   if (30 <= n && n <= 37) {
16560                                           /* Foreground color */
16561                                           cons->c_attr =
16562                                                   (cons->c_attr & 0xF8FF) |
16563                                                   (ansi_colors[(n - 30)] << 8);
16564                                           cons->c_blank =
16565                                                   (cons->c_blank & 0xF8FF) |
16566                                                   (ansi_colors[(n - 30)] << 8);
16567                                   } else
16568                                   if (40 <= n && n <= 47) {
16569                                           /* Background color */
16570                                           cons->c_attr =
16571                                                   (cons->c_attr & 0x8FFF) |
16572                                                   (ansi_colors[(n - 40)] << 12);
16573                                           cons->c_blank =
16574                                                   (cons->c_blank & 0x8FFF) |
16575                                                   (ansi_colors[(n - 40)] << 12);
16576                                   }
16577                           }
16578                           if (cons->c_reverse) {
16579                                   /* Swap fg and bg colors */
```

```
16580                                          cons->c_attr = ((cons->c_attr & 0x7000) >> 4) |
16581                                                          ((cons->c_attr & 0x0700) << 4) |
16582                                                          ((cons->c_attr & 0x8800));
16583                                  }
16584                          }
16585                  break;
16586              }
16587      }
16588      cons->c_esc_state = 0;
16589  }

16591  /*===========================================================================*
16592   *                              set_6845                                      *
16593   *===========================================================================*/
16594  PRIVATE void set_6845(reg, val)
16595  int reg;                        /* which register pair to set */
16596  unsigned val;                   /* 16-bit value to set it to */
16597  {
16598  /* Set a register pair inside the 6845.
16599   * Registers 12-13 tell the 6845 where in video ram to start
16600   * Registers 14-15 tell the 6845 where to put the cursor
16601   */
16602      pvb_pair_t char_out[4];
16603      pv_set(char_out[0], vid_port + INDEX, reg);      /* set index register */
16604      pv_set(char_out[1], vid_port + DATA, (val>>8) & BYTE);   /* high byte */
16605      pv_set(char_out[2], vid_port + INDEX, reg + 1);          /* again */
16606      pv_set(char_out[3], vid_port + DATA, val&BYTE);          /* low byte */
16607      sys_voutb(char_out, 4);                              /* do actual output */
16608  }

16610  /*===========================================================================*
16611   *                              get_6845                                      *
16612   *===========================================================================*/
16613  PRIVATE void get_6845(reg, val)
16614  int reg;                        /* which register pair to set */
16615  unsigned *val;                  /* 16-bit value to set it to */
16616  {
16617      char v1, v2;
16618  /* Get a register pair inside the 6845.  */
16619      sys_outb(vid_port + INDEX, reg);
16620      sys_inb(vid_port + DATA, &v1);
16621      sys_outb(vid_port + INDEX, reg+1);
16622      sys_inb(vid_port + DATA, &v2);
16623      *val = (v1 << 8) | v2;
16624  }

16626  /*===========================================================================*
16627   *                              beep                                          *
16628   *===========================================================================*/
16629  PRIVATE void beep()
16630  {
16631  /* Making a beeping sound on the speaker (output for CRTL-G).
16632   * This routine works by turning on the bits 0 and 1 in port B of the 8255
16633   * chip that drive the speaker.
16634   */
16635      static timer_t tmr_stop_beep;
16636      pvb_pair_t char_out[3];
16637      clock_t now;
16638      int port_b_val, s;
16639
```

```
16640          /* Fetch current time in advance to prevent beeping delay. */
16641          if ((s=getuptime(&now)) != OK)
16642                  panic("TTY","Console couldn't get clock's uptime.", s);
16643          if (!beeping) {
16644                  /* Set timer channel 2, square wave, with given frequency. */
16645                  pv_set(char_out[0], TIMER_MODE, 0xB6);
16646                  pv_set(char_out[1], TIMER2, (BEEP_FREQ >> 0) & BYTE);
16647                  pv_set(char_out[2], TIMER2, (BEEP_FREQ >> 8) & BYTE);
16648                  if (sys_voutb(char_out, 3)==OK) {
16649                          if (sys_inb(PORT_B, &port_b_val)==OK &&
16650                              sys_outb(PORT_B, (port_b_val|3))==OK)
16651                                  beeping = TRUE;
16652                  }
16653          }
16654          /* Add a timer to the timers list. Possibly reschedule the alarm. */
16655          tmrs_settimer(&tty_timers, &tmr_stop_beep, now+B_TIME, stop_beep, NULL);
16656          if (tty_timers->tmr_exp_time != tty_next_timeout) {
16657                  tty_next_timeout = tty_timers->tmr_exp_time;
16658                  if ((s=sys_setalarm(tty_next_timeout, 1)) != OK)
16659                          panic("TTY","Console couldn't set alarm.", s);
16660          }
16661  }

16663  /*===========================================================================*
16664   *                              stop_beep                                    *
16665   *===========================================================================*/
16666  PRIVATE void stop_beep(tmrp)
16667  timer_t *tmrp;
16668  {
16669  /* Turn off the beeper by turning off bits 0 and 1 in PORT_B. */
16670    int port_b_val;
16671    if (sys_inb(PORT_B, &port_b_val)==OK &&
16672        sys_outb(PORT_B, (port_b_val & ~3))==OK)
16673                  beeping = FALSE;
16674  }

16676  /*===========================================================================*
16677   *                              scr_init                                     *
16678   *===========================================================================*/
16679  PUBLIC void scr_init(tp)
16680  tty_t *tp;
16681  {
16682  /* Initialize the screen driver. */
16683    console_t *cons;
16684    phys_bytes vid_base;
16685    u16_t bios_columns, bios_crtbase, bios_fontlines;
16686    u8_t bios_rows;
16687    int line;
16688    int s;
16689    static int vdu_initialized = 0;
16690    unsigned page_size;

16692    /* Associate console and TTY. */
16693    line = tp - &tty_table[0];
16694    if (line >= nr_cons) return;
16695    cons = &cons_table[line];
16696    cons->c_tty = tp;
16697    tp->tty_priv = cons;

16699    /* Initialize the keyboard driver. */
```

```
16700     kb_init(tp);
16701
16702     /* Fill in TTY function hooks. */
16703     tp->tty_devwrite = cons_write;
16704     tp->tty_echo = cons_echo;
16705     tp->tty_ioctl = cons_ioctl;
16706
16707     /* Get the BIOS parameters that describe the VDU. */
16708     if (! vdu_initialized++) {
16709
16710             /* How about error checking? What to do on failure??? */
16711             s=sys_vircopy(SELF, BIOS_SEG, (vir_bytes) VDU_SCREEN_COLS_ADDR,
16712                     SELF, D, (vir_bytes) &bios_columns, VDU_SCREEN_COLS_SIZE);
16713             s=sys_vircopy(SELF, BIOS_SEG, (vir_bytes) VDU_CRT_BASE_ADDR,
16714                     SELF, D, (vir_bytes) &bios_crtbase, VDU_CRT_BASE_SIZE);
16715             s=sys_vircopy(SELF, BIOS_SEG, (vir_bytes) VDU_SCREEN_ROWS_ADDR,
16716                     SELF, D, (vir_bytes) &bios_rows, VDU_SCREEN_ROWS_SIZE);
16717             s=sys_vircopy(SELF, BIOS_SEG, (vir_bytes) VDU_FONTLINES_ADDR,
16718                     SELF, D, (vir_bytes) &bios_fontlines, VDU_FONTLINES_SIZE);
16719
16720             vid_port = bios_crtbase;
16721             scr_width = bios_columns;
16722             font_lines = bios_fontlines;
16723             scr_lines = machine.vdu_ega ? bios_rows+1 : 25;
16724
16725             if (color) {
16726                     vid_base = COLOR_BASE;
16727                     vid_size = COLOR_SIZE;
16728             } else {
16729                     vid_base = MONO_BASE;
16730                     vid_size = MONO_SIZE;
16731             }
16732             if (machine.vdu_ega) vid_size = EGA_SIZE;
16733             wrap = ! machine.vdu_ega;
16734
16735             s = sys_segctl(&vid_index, &vid_seg, &vid_off, vid_base, vid_size);
16736
16737             vid_size >>= 1;          /* word count */
16738             vid_mask = vid_size - 1;
16739
16740             /* Size of the screen (number of displayed characters.) */
16741             scr_size = scr_lines * scr_width;
16742
16743             /* There can be as many consoles as video memory allows. */
16744             nr_cons = vid_size / scr_size;
16745             if (nr_cons > NR_CONS) nr_cons = NR_CONS;
16746             if (nr_cons > 1) wrap = 0;
16747             page_size = vid_size / nr_cons;
16748     }
16749
16750     cons->c_start = line * page_size;
16751     cons->c_limit = cons->c_start + page_size;
16752     cons->c_cur = cons->c_org = cons->c_start;
16753     cons->c_attr = cons->c_blank = BLANK_COLOR;
16754
16755     if (line != 0) {
16756             /* Clear the non-console vtys. */
16757             blank_color = BLANK_COLOR;
16758             mem_vid_copy(BLANK_MEM, cons->c_start, scr_size);
16759     } else {
```

```
16760              int i, n;
16761              /* Set the cursor of the console vty at the bottom. c_cur
16762               * is updated automatically later.
16763               */
16764              scroll_screen(cons, SCROLL_UP);
16765              cons->c_row = scr_lines - 1;
16766              cons->c_column = 0;
16767          }
16768      select_console(0);
16769      cons_ioctl(tp, 0);
16770  }

16772  /*===========================================================================*
16773   *                              kputc                                        *
16774   *===========================================================================*/
16775  PUBLIC void kputc(c)
16776  int c;
16777  {
16778          putk(c);
16779  }

16781  /*===========================================================================*
16782   *                              do_new_kmess                                 *
16783   *===========================================================================*/
16784  PUBLIC void do_new_kmess(m)
16785  message *m;
16786  {
16787  /* Notification for a new kernel message. */
16788    struct kmessages kmess;                          /* kmessages structure */
16789    static int prev_next = 0;                        /* previous next seen */
16790    int size, next;
16791    int bytes;
16792    int r;
16793
16794    /* Try to get a fresh copy of the buffer with kernel messages. */
16795    sys_getkmessages(&kmess);
16796
16797    /* Print only the new part. Determine how many new bytes there are with
16798     * help of the current and previous 'next' index. Note that the kernel
16799     * buffer is circular. This works fine if less then KMESS_BUF_SIZE bytes
16800     * is new data; else we miss % KMESS_BUF_SIZE here.
16801     * Check for size being positive, the buffer might as well be emptied!
16802     */
16803    if (kmess.km_size > 0) {
16804        bytes = ((kmess.km_next + KMESS_BUF_SIZE) - prev_next) % KMESS_BUF_SIZE;
16805        r=prev_next;                                 /* start at previous old */
16806        while (bytes > 0) {
16807            putk( kmess.km_buf[(r%KMESS_BUF_SIZE)] );
16808            bytes --;
16809            r ++;
16810        }
16811        putk(0);                        /* terminate to flush output */
16812    }
16813
16814    /* Almost done, store 'next' so that we can determine what part of the
16815     * kernel messages buffer to print next time a notification arrives.
16816     */
16817    prev_next = kmess.km_next;
16818  }
```

```
16820   /*===========================================================================*
16821    *                              do_diagnostics                               *
16822    *===========================================================================*/
16823   PUBLIC void do_diagnostics(m_ptr)
16824   message *m_ptr;                         /* pointer to request message */
16825   {
16826   /* Print a string for a server. */
16827     char c;
16828     vir_bytes src;
16829     int count;
16830     int result = OK;
16831     int proc_nr = m_ptr->DIAG_PROC_NR;
16832     if (proc_nr == SELF) proc_nr = m_ptr->m_source;
16833
16834     src = (vir_bytes) m_ptr->DIAG_PRINT_BUF;
16835     for (count = m_ptr->DIAG_BUF_COUNT; count > 0; count--) {
16836           if (sys_vircopy(proc_nr, D, src++, SELF, D, (vir_bytes) &c, 1) != OK) {
16837                   result = EFAULT;
16838                   break;
16839           }
16840           putk(c);
16841     }
16842     putk(0);                             /* always terminate, even with EFAULT */
16843     m_ptr->m_type = result;
16844     send(m_ptr->m_source, m_ptr);
16845   }

16847   /*===========================================================================*
16848    *                                 putk                                      *
16849    *===========================================================================*/
16850   PRIVATE void putk(c)
16851   int c;                                 /* character to print */
16852   {
16853   /* This procedure is used by the version of printf() that is linked with
16854    * the TTY driver.  The one in the library sends a message to FS, which is
16855    * not what is needed for printing within the TTY. This version just queues
16856    * the character and starts the output.
16857    */
16858     if (c != 0) {
16859           if (c == '\n') putk('\r');
16860           out_char(&cons_table[0], (int) c);
16861     } else {
16862           flush(&cons_table[0]);
16863     }
16864   }

16866   /*===========================================================================*
16867    *                              toggle_scroll                                *
16868    *===========================================================================*/
16869   PUBLIC void toggle_scroll()
16870   {
16871   /* Toggle between hardware and software scroll. */
16872
16873     cons_org0();
16874     softscroll = !softscroll;
16875     printf("%sware scrolling enabled.\n", softscroll ? "Soft" : "Hard");
16876   }
```

```
16878  /*===========================================================================*
16879   *                          cons_stop                                        *
16880   *===========================================================================*/
16881  PUBLIC void cons_stop()
16882  {
16883  /* Prepare for halt or reboot. */
16884    cons_org0();
16885    softscroll = 1;
16886    select_console(0);
16887    cons_table[0].c_attr = cons_table[0].c_blank = BLANK_COLOR;
16888  }


16890  /*===========================================================================*
16891   *                          cons_org0                                        *
16892   *===========================================================================*/
16893  PRIVATE void cons_org0()
16894  {
16895  /* Scroll video memory back to put the origin at 0. */
16896    int cons_line;
16897    console_t *cons;
16898    unsigned n;
16899
16900    for (cons_line = 0; cons_line < nr_cons; cons_line++) {
16901          cons = &cons_table[cons_line];
16902          while (cons->c_org > cons->c_start) {
16903                  n = vid_size - scr_size;          /* amount of unused memory */
16904                  if (n > cons->c_org - cons->c_start)
16905                          n = cons->c_org - cons->c_start;
16906                  vid_vid_copy(cons->c_org, cons->c_org - n, scr_size);
16907                  cons->c_org -= n;
16908          }
16909          flush(cons);
16910    }
16911    select_console(ccurrent);
16912  }


16914  /*===========================================================================*
16915   *                          select_console                                   *
16916   *===========================================================================*/
16917  PUBLIC void select_console(int cons_line)
16918  {
16919  /* Set the current console to console number 'cons_line'. */
16920
16921    if (cons_line < 0 || cons_line >= nr_cons) return;
16922    ccurrent = cons_line;
16923    curcons = &cons_table[cons_line];
16924    set_6845(VID_ORG, curcons->c_org);
16925    set_6845(CURSOR, curcons->c_cur);
16926  }


16928  /*===========================================================================*
16929   *                          con_loadfont                                     *
16930   *===========================================================================*/
16931  PUBLIC int con_loadfont(m)
16932  message *m;
16933  {
16934  /* Load a font into the EGA or VGA adapter. */
16935    int result;
16936    static struct sequence seq1[7] = {
16937          { GA_SEQUENCER_INDEX, 0x00, 0x01 },
```

```
16938            { GA_SEQUENCER_INDEX, 0x02, 0x04 },
16939            { GA_SEQUENCER_INDEX, 0x04, 0x07 },
16940            { GA_SEQUENCER_INDEX, 0x00, 0x03 },
16941            { GA_GRAPHICS_INDEX, 0x04, 0x02 },
16942            { GA_GRAPHICS_INDEX, 0x05, 0x00 },
16943            { GA_GRAPHICS_INDEX, 0x06, 0x00 },
16944     };
16945     static struct sequence seq2[7] = {
16946            { GA_SEQUENCER_INDEX, 0x00, 0x01 },
16947            { GA_SEQUENCER_INDEX, 0x02, 0x03 },
16948            { GA_SEQUENCER_INDEX, 0x04, 0x03 },
16949            { GA_SEQUENCER_INDEX, 0x00, 0x03 },
16950            { GA_GRAPHICS_INDEX, 0x04, 0x00 },
16951            { GA_GRAPHICS_INDEX, 0x05, 0x10 },
16952            { GA_GRAPHICS_INDEX, 0x06,    0 },
16953     };
16954
16955     seq2[6].value= color ? 0x0E : 0x0A;
16956
16957     if (!machine.vdu_ega) return(ENOTTY);
16958     result = ga_program(seq1);     /* bring font memory into view */
16959
16960     result = sys_physcopy(m->PROC_NR, D, (vir_bytes) m->ADDRESS,
16961           NONE, PHYS_SEG, (phys_bytes) GA_VIDEO_ADDRESS, (phys_bytes)GA_FONT_SIZE);
16962
16963     result = ga_program(seq2);     /* restore */
16964
16965     return(result);
16966  }


16968  /*===========================================================================*
16969   *                               ga_program                                  *
16970   *===========================================================================*/
16971  PRIVATE int ga_program(seq)
16972  struct sequence *seq;
16973  {
16974    pvb_pair_t char_out[14];
16975    int i;
16976    for (i=0; i<7; i++) {
16977        pv_set(char_out[2*i], seq->index, seq->port);
16978        pv_set(char_out[2*i+1], seq->index+1, seq->value);
16979        seq++;
16980    }
16981    return sys_voutb(char_out, 14);
16982  }


16984  /*===========================================================================*
16985   *                               cons_ioctl                                  *
16986   *===========================================================================*/
16987  PRIVATE int cons_ioctl(tp, try)
16988  tty_t *tp;
16989  int try;
16990  {
16991  /* Set the screen dimensions. */
16992
16993     tp->tty_winsize.ws_row= scr_lines;
16994     tp->tty_winsize.ws_col= scr_width;
16995     tp->tty_winsize.ws_xpixel= scr_width * 8;
16996     tp->tty_winsize.ws_ypixel= scr_lines * font_lines;
16997  }
```

```
++++++++++++++++++++++++++++++++++++++++++++++++++++++++++++++++++++++++++++
                              servers/pm/pm.h
++++++++++++++++++++++++++++++++++++++++++++++++++++++++++++++++++++++++++++
17000    /* This is the master header for PM.  It includes some other files
17001     * and defines the principal constants.
17002     */
17003    #define _POSIX_SOURCE      1    /* tell headers to include POSIX stuff */
17004    #define _MINIX             1    /* tell headers to include MINIX stuff */
17005    #define _SYSTEM            1    /* tell headers that this is the kernel */
17006
17007    /* The following are so basic, all the *.c files get them automatically. */
17008    #include <minix/config.h>       /* MUST be first */
17009    #include <ansi.h>               /* MUST be second */
17010    #include <sys/types.h>
17011    #include <minix/const.h>
17012    #include <minix/type.h>
17013
17014    #include <fcntl.h>
17015    #include <unistd.h>
17016    #include <minix/syslib.h>
17017    #include <minix/sysutil.h>
17018
17019    #include <limits.h>
17020    #include <errno.h>
17021
17022    #include "const.h"
17023    #include "type.h"
17024    #include "proto.h"
17025    #include "glo.h"




++++++++++++++++++++++++++++++++++++++++++++++++++++++++++++++++++++++++++++
                              servers/pm/const.h
++++++++++++++++++++++++++++++++++++++++++++++++++++++++++++++++++++++++++++
17100    /* Constants used by the Process Manager. */
17101
17102    #define NO_MEM ((phys_clicks) 0)  /* returned by alloc_mem() with mem is up */
17103
17104    #define NR_PIDS        30000     /* process ids range from 0 to NR_PIDS-1.
17105                                      * (magic constant: some old applications use
17106                                      * a 'short' instead of pid_t.)
17107                                      */
17108
17109    #define PM_PID          0        /* PM's process id number */
17110    #define INIT_PID        1        /* INIT's process id number */
17111
```

```
++++++++++++++++++++++++++++++++++++++++++++++++++++++++++++++++++++++++++++++
                            servers/pm/type.h
++++++++++++++++++++++++++++++++++++++++++++++++++++++++++++++++++++++++++++++

17200   /* If there were any type definitions local to the Process Manager, they would
17201    * be here.  This file is included only for symmetry with the kernel and File
17202    * System, which do have some local type definitions.
17203    */
17204


++++++++++++++++++++++++++++++++++++++++++++++++++++++++++++++++++++++++++++++
                            servers/pm/proto.h
++++++++++++++++++++++++++++++++++++++++++++++++++++++++++++++++++++++++++++++

17300   /* Function prototypes. */
17301
17302   struct mproc;
17303   struct stat;
17304   struct mem_map;
17305   struct memory;
17306
17307   #include <timers.h>
17308
17309   /* alloc.c */
17310   _PROTOTYPE( phys_clicks alloc_mem, (phys_clicks clicks)              );
17311   _PROTOTYPE( void free_mem, (phys_clicks base, phys_clicks clicks)    );
17312   _PROTOTYPE( void mem_init, (struct memory *chunks, phys_clicks *free)  );
17313   #define swap_in()                        ((void)0)
17314   #define swap_inqueue(rmp)                ((void)0)
17315
17316   /* break.c */
17317   _PROTOTYPE( int adjust, (struct mproc *rmp,
17318                           vir_clicks data_clicks, vir_bytes sp)        );
17319   _PROTOTYPE( int do_brk, (void)                                       );
17320   _PROTOTYPE( int size_ok, (int file_type, vir_clicks tc, vir_clicks dc,
17321                           vir_clicks sc, vir_clicks dvir, vir_clicks s_vir) );
17322
17323   /* devio.c */
17324   _PROTOTYPE( int do_dev_io, (void) );
17325   _PROTOTYPE( int do_dev_io, (void) );
17326
17327   /* dmp.c */
17328   _PROTOTYPE( int do_fkey_pressed, (void)                                     );
17329
17330   /* exec.c */
17331   _PROTOTYPE( int do_exec, (void)                                      );
17332   _PROTOTYPE( void rw_seg, (int rw, int fd, int proc, int seg,
17333                                            phys_bytes seg_bytes)      );
17334   _PROTOTYPE( struct mproc *find_share, (struct mproc *mp_ign, Ino_t ino,
17335                           Dev_t dev, time_t ctime)                    );
17336
17337   /* forkexit.c */
17338   _PROTOTYPE( int do_fork, (void)                                      );
17339   _PROTOTYPE( int do_pm_exit, (void)                                   );
17340   _PROTOTYPE( int do_waitpid, (void)                                   );
17341   _PROTOTYPE( void pm_exit, (struct mproc *rmp, int exit_status)       );
17342
17343   /* getset.c */
17344   _PROTOTYPE( int do_getset, (void)                                    );
```

```
17345
17346  /* main.c */
17347  _PROTOTYPE( int main, (void)                                    );
17348
17349  /* misc.c */
17350  _PROTOTYPE( int do_reboot, (void)                              );
17351  _PROTOTYPE( int do_getsysinfo, (void)                          );
17352  _PROTOTYPE( int do_getprocnr, (void)                           );
17353  _PROTOTYPE( int do_svrctl, (void)                              );
17354  _PROTOTYPE( int do_allocmem, (void)                            );
17355  _PROTOTYPE( int do_freemem, (void)                             );
17356  _PROTOTYPE( int do_getsetpriority, (void)                              );
17357
17358  _PROTOTYPE( void setreply, (int proc_nr, int result)           );
17359
17360  /* signal.c */
17361  _PROTOTYPE( int do_alarm, (void)                               );
17362  _PROTOTYPE( int do_kill, (void)                                );
17363  _PROTOTYPE( int ksig_pending, (void)                           );
17364  _PROTOTYPE( int do_pause, (void)                               );
17365  _PROTOTYPE( int set_alarm, (int proc_nr, int sec)              );
17366  _PROTOTYPE( int check_sig, (pid_t proc_id, int signo)          );
17367  _PROTOTYPE( void sig_proc, (struct mproc *rmp, int sig_nr)     );
17368  _PROTOTYPE( int do_sigaction, (void)                           );
17369  _PROTOTYPE( int do_sigpending, (void)                          );
17370  _PROTOTYPE( int do_sigprocmask, (void)                         );
17371  _PROTOTYPE( int do_sigreturn, (void)                           );
17372  _PROTOTYPE( int do_sigsuspend, (void)                          );
17373  _PROTOTYPE( void check_pending, (struct mproc *rmp)            );
17374
17375  /* time.c */
17376  _PROTOTYPE( int do_stime, (void)                               );
17377  _PROTOTYPE( int do_time, (void)                                );
17378  _PROTOTYPE( int do_times, (void)                               );
17379  _PROTOTYPE( int do_gettimeofday, (void)                        );
17380
17381  /* timers.c */
17382  _PROTOTYPE( void pm_set_timer, (timer_t *tp, int delta,
17383          tmr_func_t watchdog, int arg));
17384  _PROTOTYPE( void pm_expire_timers, (clock_t now));
17385  _PROTOTYPE( void pm_cancel_timer, (timer_t *tp));
17386
17387  /* trace.c */
17388  _PROTOTYPE( int do_trace, (void)                               );
17389  _PROTOTYPE( void stop_proc, (struct mproc *rmp, int sig_nr)    );
17390
17391  /* utility.c */
17392  _PROTOTYPE( pid_t get_free_pid, (void)                         );
17393  _PROTOTYPE( int allowed, (char *name_buf, struct stat *s_buf, int mask) );
17394  _PROTOTYPE( int no_sys, (void)                                 );
17395  _PROTOTYPE( void panic, (char *who, char *mess, int num)       );
17396  _PROTOTYPE( void tell_fs, (int what, int p1, int p2, int p3)   );
17397  _PROTOTYPE( int get_stack_ptr, (int proc_nr, vir_bytes *sp)    );
17398  _PROTOTYPE( int get_mem_map, (int proc_nr, struct mem_map *mem_map)     );
17399  _PROTOTYPE( char *find_param, (const char *key));
17400  _PROTOTYPE( int proc_from_pid, (pid_t p));
```

```
+++++++++++++++++++++++++++++++++++++++++++++++++++++++++++++++++++++++++++++++++
                             servers/pm/glo.h
+++++++++++++++++++++++++++++++++++++++++++++++++++++++++++++++++++++++++++++++++
17500   /* EXTERN should be extern except in table.c */
17501   #ifdef _TABLE
17502   #undef EXTERN
17503   #define EXTERN
17504   #endif
17505
17506   /* Global variables. */
17507   EXTERN struct mproc *mp;        /* ptr to 'mproc' slot of current process */
17508   EXTERN int procs_in_use;       /* how many processes are marked as IN_USE */
17509   EXTERN char monitor_params[128*sizeof(char *)]; /* boot monitor parameters */
17510   EXTERN struct kinfo kinfo;                       /* kernel information */
17511
17512   /* The parameters of the call are kept here. */
17513   EXTERN message m_in;           /* the incoming message itself is kept here. */
17514   EXTERN int who;                /* caller's proc number */
17515   EXTERN int call_nr;            /* system call number */
17516
17517   extern _PROTOTYPE (int (*call_vec[]), (void) ); /* system call handlers */
17518   extern char core_name[];       /* file name where core images are produced */
17519   EXTERN sigset_t core_sset;     /* which signals cause core images */
17520   EXTERN sigset_t ign_sset;      /* which signals are by default ignored */
17521
```

```
+++++++++++++++++++++++++++++++++++++++++++++++++++++++++++++++++++++++++++++++++
                             servers/pm/mproc.h
+++++++++++++++++++++++++++++++++++++++++++++++++++++++++++++++++++++++++++++++++
17600   /* This table has one slot per process.  It contains all the process management
17601    * information for each process.  Among other things, it defines the text, data
17602    * and stack segments, uids and gids, and various flags.  The kernel and file
17603    * systems have tables that are also indexed by process, with the contents
17604    * of corresponding slots referring to the same process in all three.
17605    */
17606   #include <timers.h>
17607
17608   EXTERN struct mproc {
17609     struct mem_map mp_seg[NR_LOCAL_SEGS]; /* points to text, data, stack */
17610     char mp_exitstatus;          /* storage for status when process exits */
17611     char mp_sigstatus;           /* storage for signal # for killed procs */
17612     pid_t mp_pid;                /* process id */
17613     pid_t mp_procgrp;            /* pid of process group (used for signals) */
17614     pid_t mp_wpid;               /* pid this process is waiting for */
17615     int mp_parent;               /* index of parent process */
17616
17617     /* Child user and system times. Accounting done on child exit. */
17618     clock_t mp_child_utime;      /* cumulative user time of children */
17619     clock_t mp_child_stime;      /* cumulative sys time of children */
17620
17621     /* Real and effective uids and gids. */
17622     uid_t mp_realuid;            /* process' real uid */
17623     uid_t mp_effuid;             /* process' effective uid */
17624     gid_t mp_realgid;            /* process' real gid */
```

```
17625     gid_t mp_effgid;                /* process' effective gid */
17626
17627     /* File identification for sharing. */
17628     ino_t mp_ino;                   /* inode number of file */
17629     dev_t mp_dev;                   /* device number of file system */
17630     time_t mp_ctime;                /* inode changed time */
17631
17632     /* Signal handling information. */
17633     sigset_t mp_ignore;             /* 1 means ignore the signal, 0 means don't */
17634     sigset_t mp_catch;              /* 1 means catch the signal, 0 means don't */
17635     sigset_t mp_sig2mess;           /* 1 means transform into notify message */
17636     sigset_t mp_sigmask;            /* signals to be blocked */
17637     sigset_t mp_sigmask2;           /* saved copy of mp_sigmask */
17638     sigset_t mp_sigpending;         /* pending signals to be handled */
17639     struct sigaction mp_sigact[_NSIG + 1]; /* as in sigaction(2) */
17640     vir_bytes mp_sigreturn;         /* address of C library __sigreturn function */
17641     struct timer mp_timer;          /* watchdog timer for alarm(2) */
17642
17643     /* Backwards compatibility for signals. */
17644     sighandler_t mp_func;           /* all sigs vectored to a single user fcn */
17645
17646     unsigned mp_flags;              /* flag bits */
17647     vir_bytes mp_procargs;          /* ptr to proc's initial stack arguments */
17648     struct mproc *mp_swapq;         /* queue of procs waiting to be swapped in */
17649     message mp_reply;               /* reply message to be sent to one */
17650
17651     /* Scheduling priority. */
17652     signed int mp_nice;             /* nice is PRIO_MIN..PRIO_MAX, standard 0. */
17653
17654     char mp_name[PROC_NAME_LEN];    /* process name */
17655 } mproc[NR_PROCS];
17656
17657 /* Flag values */
17658 #define IN_USE          0x001   /* set when 'mproc' slot in use */
17659 #define WAITING         0x002   /* set by WAIT system call */
17660 #define ZOMBIE          0x004   /* set by EXIT, cleared by WAIT */
17661 #define PAUSED          0x008   /* set by PAUSE system call */
17662 #define ALARM_ON        0x010   /* set when SIGALRM timer started */
17663 #define SEPARATE        0x020   /* set if file is separate I & D space */
17664 #define TRACED          0x040   /* set if process is to be traced */
17665 #define STOPPED         0x080   /* set if process stopped for tracing */
17666 #define SIGSUSPENDED    0x100   /* set by SIGSUSPEND system call */
17667 #define REPLY           0x200   /* set if a reply message is pending */
17668 #define ONSWAP          0x400   /* set if data segment is swapped out */
17669 #define SWAPIN          0x800   /* set if on the "swap this in" queue */
17670 #define DONT_SWAP       0x1000  /* never swap out this process */
17671 #define PRIV_PROC       0x2000  /* system process, special privileges */
17672
17673 #define NIL_MPROC ((struct mproc *) 0)
17674
```

++
                          servers/pm/param.h
++

```
17700 /* The following names are synonyms for the variables in the input message. */
17701 #define addr            m1_p1
17702 #define exec_name       m1_p1
17703 #define exec_len        m1_i1
17704 #define func            m6_f1
```

```
17705   #define grp_id          m1_i1
17706   #define namelen         m1_i2
17707   #define pid             m1_i1
17708   #define procnr          m1_i1
17709   #define seconds         m1_i1
17710   #define sig             m6_i1
17711   #define stack_bytes     m1_i2
17712   #define stack_ptr       m1_p2
17713   #define status          m1_i1
17714   #define usr_id          m1_i1
17715   #define request         m2_i2
17716   #define taddr           m2_l1
17717   #define data            m2_l2
17718   #define sig_nr          m1_i2
17719   #define sig_nsa         m1_p1
17720   #define sig_osa         m1_p2
17721   #define sig_ret         m1_p3
17722   #define sig_set         m2_l1
17723   #define sig_how         m2_i1
17724   #define sig_flags       m2_i2
17725   #define sig_context     m2_p1
17726   #define info_what       m1_i1
17727   #define info_where      m1_p1
17728   #define reboot_flag     m1_i1
17729   #define reboot_code     m1_p1
17730   #define reboot_strlen   m1_i2
17731   #define svrctl_req      m2_i1
17732   #define svrctl_argp     m2_p1
17733   #define stime           m2_l1
17734   #define memsize         m4_l1
17735   #define membase         m4_l2
17736
17737   /* The following names are synonyms for the variables in a reply message. */
17738   #define reply_res       m_type
17739   #define reply_res2      m2_i1
17740   #define reply_ptr       m2_p1
17741   #define reply_mask      m2_l1
17742   #define reply_trace     m2_l2
17743   #define reply_time      m2_l1
17744   #define reply_utime     m2_l2
17745   #define reply_t1        m4_l1
17746   #define reply_t2        m4_l2
17747   #define reply_t3        m4_l3
17748   #define reply_t4        m4_l4
17749   #define reply_t5        m4_l5
17750
17751   /* The following names are used to inform the FS about certain events. */
17752   #define tell_fs_arg1    m1_i1
17753   #define tell_fs_arg2    m1_i2
17754   #define tell_fs_arg3    m1_i3
17755
```

```
++++++++++++++++++++++++++++++++++++++++++++++++++++++++++++++++++++++++++
                        servers/pm/table.c
++++++++++++++++++++++++++++++++++++++++++++++++++++++++++++++++++++++++++
17800   /* This file contains the table used to map system call numbers onto the
17801    * routines that perform them.
17802    */
17803
17804   #define _TABLE
17805
17806   #include "pm.h"
17807   #include <minix/callnr.h>
17808   #include <signal.h>
17809   #include "mproc.h"
17810   #include "param.h"
17811
17812   /* Miscellaneous */
17813   char core_name[] = "core";          /* file name where core images are produced */
17814
17815   _PROTOTYPE (int (*call_vec[NCALLS]), (void) ) = {
17816           no_sys,          /*  0 = unused  */
17817           do_pm_exit,      /*  1 = exit    */
17818           do_fork,         /*  2 = fork    */
17819           no_sys,          /*  3 = read    */
17820           no_sys,          /*  4 = write   */
17821           no_sys,          /*  5 = open    */
17822           no_sys,          /*  6 = close   */
17823           do_waitpid,      /*  7 = wait    */
17824           no_sys,          /*  8 = creat   */
17825           no_sys,          /*  9 = link    */
17826           no_sys,          /* 10 = unlink  */
17827           do_waitpid,      /* 11 = waitpid */
17828           no_sys,          /* 12 = chdir   */
17829           do_time,         /* 13 = time    */
17830           no_sys,          /* 14 = mknod   */
17831           no_sys,          /* 15 = chmod   */
17832           no_sys,          /* 16 = chown   */
17833           do_brk,          /* 17 = break   */
17834           no_sys,          /* 18 = stat    */
17835           no_sys,          /* 19 = lseek   */
17836           do_getset,       /* 20 = getpid  */
17837           no_sys,          /* 21 = mount   */
17838           no_sys,          /* 22 = umount  */
17839           do_getset,       /* 23 = setuid  */
17840           do_getset,       /* 24 = getuid  */
17841           do_stime,        /* 25 = stime   */
17842           do_trace,        /* 26 = ptrace  */
17843           do_alarm,        /* 27 = alarm   */
17844           no_sys,          /* 28 = fstat   */
17845           do_pause,        /* 29 = pause   */
17846           no_sys,          /* 30 = utime   */
17847           no_sys,          /* 31 = (stty)  */
17848           no_sys,          /* 32 = (gtty)  */
17849           no_sys,          /* 33 = access  */
17850           no_sys,          /* 34 = (nice)  */
17851           no_sys,          /* 35 = (ftime) */
17852           no_sys,          /* 36 = sync    */
17853           do_kill,         /* 37 = kill    */
17854           no_sys,          /* 38 = rename  */
```

```
17855          no_sys,          /* 39 = mkdir    */
17856          no_sys,          /* 40 = rmdir    */
17857          no_sys,          /* 41 = dup      */
17858          no_sys,          /* 42 = pipe     */
17859          do_times,        /* 43 = times    */
17860          no_sys,          /* 44 = (prof)   */
17861          no_sys,          /* 45 = unused   */
17862          do_getset,       /* 46 = setgid   */
17863          do_getset,       /* 47 = getgid   */
17864          no_sys,          /* 48 = (signal)*/
17865          no_sys,          /* 49 = unused   */
17866          no_sys,          /* 50 = unused   */
17867          no_sys,          /* 51 = (acct)   */
17868          no_sys,          /* 52 = (phys)   */
17869          no_sys,          /* 53 = (lock)   */
17870          no_sys,          /* 54 = ioctl    */
17871          no_sys,          /* 55 = fcntl    */
17872          no_sys,          /* 56 = (mpx)    */
17873          no_sys,          /* 57 = unused   */
17874          no_sys,          /* 58 = unused   */
17875          do_exec,         /* 59 = execve   */
17876          no_sys,          /* 60 = umask    */
17877          no_sys,          /* 61 = chroot   */
17878          do_getset,       /* 62 = setsid   */
17879          do_getset,       /* 63 = getpgrp */
17880
17881          no_sys,          /* 64 = unused */
17882          no_sys,          /* 65 = UNPAUSE */
17883          no_sys,          /* 66 = unused   */
17884          no_sys,          /* 67 = REVIVE   */
17885          no_sys,          /* 68 = TASK_REPLY   */
17886          no_sys,          /* 69 = unused   */
17887          no_sys,          /* 70 = unused   */
17888          do_sigaction,    /* 71 = sigaction    */
17889          do_sigsuspend,   /* 72 = sigsuspend   */
17890          do_sigpending,   /* 73 = sigpending   */
17891          do_sigprocmask,  /* 74 = sigprocmask */
17892          do_sigreturn,    /* 75 = sigreturn    */
17893          do_reboot,       /* 76 = reboot   */
17894          do_svrctl,       /* 77 = svrctl   */
17895
17896          no_sys,          /* 78 = unused */
17897          do_getsysinfo,   /* 79 = getsysinfo */
17898          do_getprocnr,    /* 80 = getprocnr */
17899          no_sys,          /* 81 = unused */
17900          no_sys,          /* 82 = fstatfs */
17901          do_allocmem,     /* 83 = memalloc */
17902          do_freemem,      /* 84 = memfree */
17903          no_sys,          /* 85 = select */
17904          no_sys,          /* 86 = fchdir */
17905          no_sys,          /* 87 = fsync */
17906          do_getsetpriority,       /* 88 = getpriority */
17907          do_getsetpriority,       /* 89 = setpriority */
17908          do_time,         /* 90 = gettimeofday */
17909  };
17910  /* This should not fail with "array size is negative": */
17911  extern int dummy[sizeof(call_vec) == NCALLS * sizeof(call_vec[0]) ? 1 : -1];
```

```
++++++++++++++++++++++++++++++++++++++++++++++++++++++++++++++++++++++++++++
                          servers/pm/main.c
++++++++++++++++++++++++++++++++++++++++++++++++++++++++++++++++++++++++++++
18000   /* This file contains the main program of the process manager and some related
18001    * procedures.  When MINIX starts up, the kernel runs for a little while,
18002    * initializing itself and its tasks, and then it runs PM and FS.  Both PM
18003    * and FS initialize themselves as far as they can. PM asks the kernel for
18004    * all free memory and starts serving requests.
18005    *
18006    * The entry points into this file are:
18007    *   main:       starts PM running
18008    *   setreply:   set the reply to be sent to process making an PM system call
18009    */
18010
18011   #include "pm.h"
18012   #include <minix/keymap.h>
18013   #include <minix/callnr.h>
18014   #include <minix/com.h>
18015   #include <signal.h>
18016   #include <stdlib.h>
18017   #include <fcntl.h>
18018   #include <sys/resource.h>
18019   #include <string.h>
18020   #include "mproc.h"
18021   #include "param.h"
18022
18023   #include "../../kernel/const.h"
18024   #include "../../kernel/config.h"
18025   #include "../../kernel/type.h"
18026   #include "../../kernel/proc.h"
18027
18028   FORWARD _PROTOTYPE( void get_work, (void)                        );
18029   FORWARD _PROTOTYPE( void pm_init, (void)                        );
18030   FORWARD _PROTOTYPE( int get_nice_value, (int queue)             );
18031   FORWARD _PROTOTYPE( void get_mem_chunks, (struct memory *mem_chunks)    );
18032   FORWARD _PROTOTYPE( void patch_mem_chunks, (struct memory *mem_chunks,
18033           struct mem_map *map_ptr)             );
18034
18035   #define click_to_round_k(n) \
18036           ((unsigned) ((((unsigned long) (n) << CLICK_SHIFT) + 512) / 1024))
18037
18038   /*===========================================================================*
18039    *                              main                                         *
18040    *===========================================================================*/
18041   PUBLIC int main()
18042   {
18043   /* Main routine of the process manager. */
18044     int result, s, proc_nr;
18045     struct mproc *rmp;
18046     sigset_t sigset;
18047
18048     pm_init();                       /* initialize process manager tables */
18049
18050     /* This is PM's main loop- get work and do it, forever and forever. */
18051     while (TRUE) {
18052           get_work();               /* wait for an PM system call */
18053
18054           /* Check for system notifications first. Special cases. */
```

```
18055               if (call_nr == SYN_ALARM) {
18056                       pm_expire_timers(m_in.NOTIFY_TIMESTAMP);
18057                       result = SUSPEND;              /* don't reply */
18058               } else if (call_nr == SYS_SIG) {       /* signals pending */
18059                       sigset = m_in.NOTIFY_ARG;
18060                       if (sigismember(&sigset, SIGKSIG))  (void) ksig_pending();
18061                       result = SUSPEND;              /* don't reply */
18062               }
18063               /* Else, if the system call number is valid, perform the call. */
18064               else if ((unsigned) call_nr >= NCALLS) {
18065                       result = ENOSYS;
18066               } else {
18067                       result = (*call_vec[call_nr])();
18068               }
18069
18070               /* Send the results back to the user to indicate completion. */
18071               if (result != SUSPEND) setreply(who, result);
18072
18073               swap_in();                /* maybe a process can be swapped in? */
18074
18075               /* Send out all pending reply messages, including the answer to
18076                * the call just made above.  The processes must not be swapped out.
18077                */
18078               for (proc_nr=0, rmp=mproc; proc_nr < NR_PROCS; proc_nr++, rmp++) {
18079                       /* In the meantime, the process may have been killed by a
18080                        * signal (e.g. if a lethal pending signal was unblocked)
18081                        * without the PM realizing it. If the slot is no longer in
18082                        * use or just a zombie, don't try to reply.
18083                        */
18084                       if ((rmp->mp_flags & (REPLY | ONSWAP | IN_USE | ZOMBIE)) ==
18085                          (REPLY | IN_USE)) {
18086                               if ((s=send(proc_nr, &rmp->mp_reply)) != OK) {
18087                                       panic(__FILE__,"PM can't reply to", proc_nr);
18088                               }
18089                               rmp->mp_flags &= ~REPLY;
18090                       }
18091               }
18092       }
18093   return(OK);
18094 }

18096 /*===========================================================================*
18097  *                              get_work                                     *
18098  *===========================================================================*/
18099 PRIVATE void get_work()
18100 {
18101 /* Wait for the next message and extract useful information from it. */
18102   if (receive(ANY, &m_in) != OK) panic(__FILE__,"PM receive error", NO_NUM);
18103   who = m_in.m_source;          /* who sent the message */
18104   call_nr = m_in.m_type;        /* system call number */
18105
18106   /* Process slot of caller. Misuse PM's own process slot if the kernel is
18107    * calling. This can happen in case of synchronous alarms (CLOCK) or or
18108    * event like pending kernel signals (SYSTEM).
18109    */
18110   mp = &mproc[who < 0 ? PM_PROC_NR : who];
18111 }
```

```
18113    /*===========================================================================*
18114     *                              setreply                                     *
18115     *===========================================================================*/
18116    PUBLIC void setreply(proc_nr, result)
18117    int proc_nr;                        /* process to reply to */
18118    int result;                         /* result of call (usually OK or error #) */
18119    {
18120    /* Fill in a reply message to be sent later to a user process.  System calls
18121     * may occasionally fill in other fields, this is only for the main return
18122     * value, and for setting the "must send reply" flag.
18123     */
18124      register struct mproc *rmp = &mproc[proc_nr];
18125
18126      rmp->mp_reply.reply_res = result;
18127      rmp->mp_flags |= REPLY;           /* reply pending */
18128
18129      if (rmp->mp_flags & ONSWAP)
18130            swap_inqueue(rmp);          /* must swap this process back in */
18131    }


18133    /*===========================================================================*
18134     *                              pm_init                                      *
18135     *===========================================================================*/
18136    PRIVATE void pm_init()
18137    {
18138    /* Initialize the process manager.
18139     * Memory use info is collected from the boot monitor, the kernel, and
18140     * all processes compiled into the system image. Initially this information
18141     * is put into an array mem_chunks. Elements of mem_chunks are struct memory,
18142     * and hold base, size pairs in units of clicks. This array is small, there
18143     * should be no more than 8 chunks. After the array of chunks has been built
18144     * the contents are used to initialize the hole list. Space for the hole list
18145     * is reserved as an array with twice as many elements as the maximum number
18146     * of processes allowed. It is managed as a linked list, and elements of the
18147     * array are struct hole, which, in addition to storage for a base and size in
18148     * click units also contain space for a link, a pointer to another element.
18149     */
18150      int s;
18151      static struct boot_image image[NR_BOOT_PROCS];
18152      register struct boot_image *ip;
18153      static char core_sigs[] = { SIGQUIT, SIGILL, SIGTRAP, SIGABRT,
18154                            SIGEMT, SIGFPE, SIGUSR1, SIGSEGV, SIGUSR2 };
18155      static char ign_sigs[] = { SIGCHLD };
18156      register struct mproc *rmp;
18157      register char *sig_ptr;
18158      phys_clicks total_clicks, minix_clicks, free_clicks;
18159      message mess;
18160      struct mem_map mem_map[NR_LOCAL_SEGS];
18161      struct memory mem_chunks[NR_MEMS];
18162
18163      /* Initialize process table, including timers. */
18164      for (rmp=&mproc[0]; rmp<&mproc[NR_PROCS]; rmp++) {
18165            tmr_inittimer(&rmp->mp_timer);
18166      }
18167
18168      /* Build the set of signals which cause core dumps, and the set of signals
18169       * that are by default ignored.
18170       */
18171      sigemptyset(&core_sset);
18172      for (sig_ptr = core_sigs; sig_ptr < core_sigs+sizeof(core_sigs); sig_ptr++)
```

```
18173            sigaddset(&core_sset, *sig_ptr);
18174    sigemptyset(&ign_sset);
18175    for (sig_ptr = ign_sigs; sig_ptr < ign_sigs+sizeof(ign_sigs); sig_ptr++)
18176            sigaddset(&ign_sset, *sig_ptr);
18177
18178    /* Obtain a copy of the boot monitor parameters and the kernel info struct.
18179     * Parse the list of free memory chunks. This list is what the boot monitor
18180     * reported, but it must be corrected for the kernel and system processes.
18181     */
18182    if ((s=sys_getmonparams(monitor_params, sizeof(monitor_params))) != OK)
18183        panic(__FILE__,"get monitor params failed",s);
18184    get_mem_chunks(mem_chunks);
18185    if ((s=sys_getkinfo(&kinfo)) != OK)
18186        panic(__FILE__,"get kernel info failed",s);
18187
18188    /* Get the memory map of the kernel to see how much memory it uses. */
18189    if ((s=get_mem_map(SYSTASK, mem_map)) != OK)
18190            panic(__FILE__,"couldn't get memory map of SYSTASK",s);
18191    minix_clicks = (mem_map[S].mem_phys+mem_map[S].mem_len)-mem_map[T].mem_phys;
18192    patch_mem_chunks(mem_chunks, mem_map);
18193
18194    /* Initialize PM's process table. Request a copy of the system image table
18195     * that is defined at the kernel level to see which slots to fill in.
18196     */
18197    if (OK != (s=sys_getimage(image)))
18198            panic(__FILE__,"couldn't get image table: %d\n", s);
18199    procs_in_use = 0;                        /* start populating table */
18200    printf("Building process table:");       /* show what's happening */
18201    for (ip = &image[0]; ip < &image[NR_BOOT_PROCS]; ip++) {
18202        if (ip->proc_nr >= 0) {              /* task have negative nrs */
18203            procs_in_use += 1;               /* found user process */
18204
18205            /* Set process details found in the image table. */
18206            rmp = &mproc[ip->proc_nr];
18207            strncpy(rmp->mp_name, ip->proc_name, PROC_NAME_LEN);
18208            rmp->mp_parent = RS_PROC_NR;
18209            rmp->mp_nice = get_nice_value(ip->priority);
18210            if (ip->proc_nr == INIT_PROC_NR) {     /* user process */
18211                rmp->mp_pid = INIT_PID;
18212                rmp->mp_flags |= IN_USE;
18213                sigemptyset(&rmp->mp_ignore);
18214            }
18215            else {                                 /* system process */
18216                rmp->mp_pid = get_free_pid();
18217                rmp->mp_flags |= IN_USE | DONT_SWAP | PRIV_PROC;
18218                sigfillset(&rmp->mp_ignore);
18219            }
18220            sigemptyset(&rmp->mp_sigmask);
18221            sigemptyset(&rmp->mp_catch);
18222            sigemptyset(&rmp->mp_sig2mess);
18223
18224            /* Get memory map for this process from the kernel. */
18225            if ((s=get_mem_map(ip->proc_nr, rmp->mp_seg)) != OK)
18226                    panic(__FILE__,"couldn't get process entry",s);
18227            if (rmp->mp_seg[T].mem_len != 0) rmp->mp_flags |= SEPARATE;
18228            minix_clicks += rmp->mp_seg[S].mem_phys +
18229                    rmp->mp_seg[S].mem_len - rmp->mp_seg[T].mem_phys;
18230            patch_mem_chunks(mem_chunks, rmp->mp_seg);
18231
18232            /* Tell FS about this system process. */
```

```
18233                        mess.PR_PROC_NR = ip->proc_nr;
18234                        mess.PR_PID = rmp->mp_pid;
18235                        if (OK != (s=send(FS_PROC_NR, &mess)))
18236                                panic(__FILE__,"can't sync up with FS", s);
18237                        printf(" %s", ip->proc_name);    /* display process name */
18238                }
18239        }
18240        printf(".\n");                                  /* last process done */
18241
18242        /* Override some details. PM is somewhat special. */
18243        mproc[PM_PROC_NR].mp_pid = PM_PID;              /* magically override pid */
18244        mproc[PM_PROC_NR].mp_parent = PM_PROC_NR;       /* PM doesn't have parent */
18245
18246        /* Tell FS that no more system processes follow and synchronize. */
18247        mess.PR_PROC_NR = NONE;
18248        if (sendrec(FS_PROC_NR, &mess) != OK || mess.m_type != OK)
18249                panic(__FILE__,"can't sync up with FS", NO_NUM);
18250
18251        /* Initialize tables to all physical memory and print memory information. */
18252        printf("Physical memory:");
18253        mem_init(mem_chunks, &free_clicks);
18254        total_clicks = minix_clicks + free_clicks;
18255        printf(" total %u KB,", click_to_round_k(total_clicks));
18256        printf(" system %u KB,", click_to_round_k(minix_clicks));
18257        printf(" free %u KB.\n", click_to_round_k(free_clicks));
18258   }

18260   /*===========================================================================*
18261    *                               get_nice_value                              *
18262    *===========================================================================*/
18263   PRIVATE int get_nice_value(queue)
18264   int queue;                                     /* store mem chunks here */
18265   {
18266   /* Processes in the boot image have a priority assigned. The PM doesn't know
18267    * about priorities, but uses 'nice' values instead. The priority is between
18268    * MIN_USER_Q and MAX_USER_Q. We have to scale between PRIO_MIN and PRIO_MAX.
18269    */
18270     int nice_val = (queue - USER_Q) * (PRIO_MAX-PRIO_MIN+1) /
18271         (MIN_USER_Q-MAX_USER_Q+1);
18272     if (nice_val > PRIO_MAX) nice_val = PRIO_MAX; /* shouldn't happen */
18273     if (nice_val < PRIO_MIN) nice_val = PRIO_MIN; /* shouldn't happen */
18274     return nice_val;
18275   }

18277   /*===========================================================================*
18278    *                               get_mem_chunks                              *
18279    *===========================================================================*/
18280   PRIVATE void get_mem_chunks(mem_chunks)
18281   struct memory *mem_chunks;                          /* store mem chunks here */
18282   {
18283   /* Initialize the free memory list from the 'memory' boot variable.  Translate
18284    * the byte offsets and sizes in this list to clicks, properly truncated. Also
18285    * make sure that we don't exceed the maximum address space of the 286 or the
18286    * 8086, i.e. when running in 16-bit protected mode or real mode.
18287    */
18288     long base, size, limit;
18289     char *s, *end;                              /* use to parse boot variable */
18290     int i, done = 0;
18291     struct memory *memp;
18292
```

```
18293          /* Initialize everything to zero. */
18294          for (i = 0; i < NR_MEMS; i++) {
18295                  memp = &mem_chunks[i];              /* next mem chunk is stored here */
18296                  memp->base = memp->size = 0;
18297          }
18298
18299          /* The available memory is determined by MINIX' boot loader as a list of
18300           * (base:size)-pairs in boothead.s. The 'memory' boot variable is set in
18301           * in boot.s.  The format is "b0:s0,b1:s1,b2:s2", where b0:s0 is low mem,
18302           * b1:s1 is mem between 1M and 16M, b2:s2 is mem above 16M. Pairs b1:s1
18303           * and b2:s2 are combined if the memory is adjacent.
18304           */
18305          s = find_param("memory");                   /* get memory boot variable */
18306          for (i = 0; i < NR_MEMS && !done; i++) {
18307                  memp = &mem_chunks[i];              /* next mem chunk is stored here */
18308                  base = size = 0;                    /* initialize next base:size pair */
18309                  if (*s != 0) {                      /* get fresh data, unless at end */
18310
18311                          /* Read fresh base and expect colon as next char. */
18312                          base = strtoul(s, &end, 0x10);            /* get number */
18313                          if (end != s && *end == ':') s = ++end;   /* skip ':' */
18314                          else *s=0;                      /* terminate, should not happen */
18315
18316                          /* Read fresh size and expect comma or assume end. */
18317                          size = strtoul(s, &end, 0x10);            /* get number */
18318                          if (end != s && *end == ',') s = ++end;   /* skip ',' */
18319                          else done = 1;
18320                  }
18321                  limit = base + size;
18322                  base = (base + CLICK_SIZE-1) & ~(long)(CLICK_SIZE-1);
18323                  limit &= ~(long)(CLICK_SIZE-1);
18324                  if (limit <= base) continue;
18325                  memp->base = base >> CLICK_SHIFT;
18326                  memp->size = (limit - base) >> CLICK_SHIFT;
18327          }
18328  }


18330  /*===========================================================================*
18331   *                              patch_mem_chunks                             *
18332   *===========================================================================*/
18333  PRIVATE void patch_mem_chunks(mem_chunks, map_ptr)
18334  struct memory *mem_chunks;                          /* store mem chunks here */
18335  struct mem_map *map_ptr;                            /* memory to remove */
18336  {
18337  /* Remove server memory from the free memory list. The boot monitor
18338   * promises to put processes at the start of memory chunks. The
18339   * tasks all use same base address, so only the first task changes
18340   * the memory lists. The servers and init have their own memory
18341   * spaces and their memory will be removed from the list.
18342   */
18343    struct memory *memp;
18344    for (memp = mem_chunks; memp < &mem_chunks[NR_MEMS]; memp++) {
18345          if (memp->base == map_ptr[T].mem_phys) {
18346                  memp->base += map_ptr[T].mem_len + map_ptr[D].mem_len;
18347                  memp->size -= map_ptr[T].mem_len + map_ptr[D].mem_len;
18348          }
18349    }
18350  }
```

```
++++++++++++++++++++++++++++++++++++++++++++++++++++++++++++++++++++++++++++
                          servers/pm/forkexit.c
++++++++++++++++++++++++++++++++++++++++++++++++++++++++++++++++++++++++++++
18400   /* This file deals with creating processes (via FORK) and deleting them (via
18401    * EXIT/WAIT).  When a process forks, a new slot in the 'mproc' table is
18402    * allocated for it, and a copy of the parent's core image is made for the
18403    * child.  Then the kernel and file system are informed.  A process is removed
18404    * from the 'mproc' table when two events have occurred: (1) it has exited or
18405    * been killed by a signal, and (2) the parent has done a WAIT.  If the process
18406    * exits first, it continues to occupy a slot until the parent does a WAIT.
18407    *
18408    * The entry points into this file are:
18409    *   do_fork:    perform the FORK system call
18410    *   do_pm_exit: perform the EXIT system call (by calling pm_exit())
18411    *   pm_exit:    actually do the exiting
18412    *   do_wait:    perform the WAITPID or WAIT system call
18413    */
18414
18415   #include "pm.h"
18416   #include <sys/wait.h>
18417   #include <minix/callnr.h>
18418   #include <minix/com.h>
18419   #include <signal.h>
18420   #include "mproc.h"
18421   #include "param.h"
18422
18423   #define LAST_FEW            2    /* last few slots reserved for superuser */
18424
18425   FORWARD _PROTOTYPE (void cleanup, (register struct mproc *child) );
18426
18427   /*===========================================================================*
18428    *                              do_fork                                       *
18429    *===========================================================================*/
18430   PUBLIC int do_fork()
18431   {
18432   /* The process pointed to by 'mp' has forked.  Create a child process. */
18433     register struct mproc *rmp;    /* pointer to parent */
18434     register struct mproc *rmc;    /* pointer to child */
18435     int child_nr, s;
18436     phys_clicks prog_clicks, child_base;
18437     phys_bytes prog_bytes, parent_abs, child_abs; /* Intel only */
18438     pid_t new_pid;
18439
18440     /* If tables might fill up during FORK, don't even start since recovery half
18441      * way through is such a nuisance.
18442      */
18443     rmp = mp;
18444     if ((procs_in_use == NR_PROCS) ||
18445                 (procs_in_use >= NR_PROCS-LAST_FEW && rmp->mp_effuid != 0))
18446     {
18447           printf("PM: warning, process table is full!\n");
18448           return(EAGAIN);
18449     }
18450
18451     /* Determine how much memory to allocate.  Only the data and stack need to
18452      * be copied, because the text segment is either shared or of zero length.
18453      */
18454     prog_clicks = (phys_clicks) rmp->mp_seg[S].mem_len;
```

```
18455        prog_clicks += (rmp->mp_seg[S].mem_vir - rmp->mp_seg[D].mem_vir);
18456        prog_bytes = (phys_bytes) prog_clicks << CLICK_SHIFT;
18457        if ( (child_base = alloc_mem(prog_clicks)) == NO_MEM) return(ENOMEM);
18458
18459        /* Create a copy of the parent's core image for the child. */
18460        child_abs = (phys_bytes) child_base << CLICK_SHIFT;
18461        parent_abs = (phys_bytes) rmp->mp_seg[D].mem_phys << CLICK_SHIFT;
18462        s = sys_abscopy(parent_abs, child_abs, prog_bytes);
18463        if (s < 0) panic(__FILE__,"do_fork can't copy", s);
18464
18465        /* Find a slot in 'mproc' for the child process.  A slot must exist. */
18466        for (rmc = &mproc[0]; rmc < &mproc[NR_PROCS]; rmc++)
18467                if ( (rmc->mp_flags & IN_USE) == 0) break;
18468
18469        /* Set up the child and its memory map; copy its 'mproc' slot from parent. */
18470        child_nr = (int)(rmc - mproc);          /* slot number of the child */
18471        procs_in_use++;
18472        *rmc = *rmp;                            /* copy parent's process slot to child's */
18473        rmc->mp_parent = who;                   /* record child's parent */
18474        /* inherit only these flags */
18475        rmc->mp_flags &= (IN_USE|SEPARATE|PRIV_PROC|DONT_SWAP);
18476        rmc->mp_child_utime = 0;                /* reset administration */
18477        rmc->mp_child_stime = 0;                /* reset administration */
18478
18479        /* A separate I&D child keeps the parents text segment.  The data and stack
18480         * segments must refer to the new copy.
18481         */
18482        if (!(rmc->mp_flags & SEPARATE)) rmc->mp_seg[T].mem_phys = child_base;
18483        rmc->mp_seg[D].mem_phys = child_base;
18484        rmc->mp_seg[S].mem_phys = rmc->mp_seg[D].mem_phys +
18485                             (rmp->mp_seg[S].mem_vir - rmp->mp_seg[D].mem_vir);
18486        rmc->mp_exitstatus = 0;
18487        rmc->mp_sigstatus = 0;
18488
18489        /* Find a free pid for the child and put it in the table. */
18490        new_pid = get_free_pid();
18491        rmc->mp_pid = new_pid;          /* assign pid to child */
18492
18493        /* Tell kernel and file system about the (now successful) FORK. */
18494        sys_fork(who, child_nr);
18495        tell_fs(FORK, who, child_nr, rmc->mp_pid);
18496
18497        /* Report child's memory map to kernel. */
18498        sys_newmap(child_nr, rmc->mp_seg);
18499
18500        /* Reply to child to wake it up. */
18501        setreply(child_nr, 0);                  /* only parent gets details */
18502        rmp->mp_reply.procnr = child_nr;        /* child's process number */
18503        return(new_pid);                        /* child's pid */
18504 }


18506 /*===========================================================================*
18507  *                              do_pm_exit                                   *
18508  *===========================================================================*/
18509 PUBLIC int do_pm_exit()
18510 {
18511 /* Perform the exit(status) system call. The real work is done by pm_exit(),
18512  * which is also called when a process is killed by a signal.
18513  */
18514    pm_exit(mp, m_in.status);
```

```
18515      return(SUSPEND);              /* can't communicate from beyond the grave */
18516    }

18518    /*===========================================================================*
18519     *                              pm_exit                                       *
18520     *===========================================================================*/
18521    PUBLIC void pm_exit(rmp, exit_status)
18522    register struct mproc *rmp;     /* pointer to the process to be terminated */
18523    int exit_status;               /* the process' exit status (for parent) */
18524    {
18525    /* A process is done.  Release most of the process' possessions.  If its
18526     * parent is waiting, release the rest, else keep the process slot and
18527     * become a zombie.
18528     */
18529      register int proc_nr;
18530      int parent_waiting, right_child;
18531      pid_t pidarg, procgrp;
18532      struct mproc *p_mp;
18533      clock_t t[5];

18535      proc_nr = (int) (rmp - mproc);         /* get process slot number */

18537      /* Remember a session leader's process group. */
18538      procgrp = (rmp->mp_pid == mp->mp_procgrp) ? mp->mp_procgrp : 0;

18540      /* If the exited process has a timer pending, kill it. */
18541      if (rmp->mp_flags & ALARM_ON) set_alarm(proc_nr, (unsigned) 0);

18543      /* Do accounting: fetch usage times and accumulate at parent. */
18544      sys_times(proc_nr, t);
18545      p_mp = &mproc[rmp->mp_parent];                      /* process' parent */
18546      p_mp->mp_child_utime += t[0] + rmp->mp_child_utime;   /* add user time */
18547      p_mp->mp_child_stime += t[1] + rmp->mp_child_stime;   /* add system time */

18549      /* Tell the kernel and FS that the process is no longer runnable. */
18550      tell_fs(EXIT, proc_nr, 0, 0);  /* file system can free the proc slot */
18551      sys_exit(proc_nr);

18553      /* Pending reply messages for the dead process cannot be delivered. */
18554      rmp->mp_flags &= ~REPLY;

18556      /* Release the memory occupied by the child. */
18557      if (find_share(rmp, rmp->mp_ino, rmp->mp_dev, rmp->mp_ctime) == NULL) {
18558          /* No other process shares the text segment, so free it. */
18559          free_mem(rmp->mp_seg[T].mem_phys, rmp->mp_seg[T].mem_len);
18560      }
18561      /* Free the data and stack segments. */
18562      free_mem(rmp->mp_seg[D].mem_phys,
18563          rmp->mp_seg[S].mem_vir
18564          + rmp->mp_seg[S].mem_len - rmp->mp_seg[D].mem_vir);

18566      /* The process slot can only be freed if the parent has done a WAIT. */
18567      rmp->mp_exitstatus = (char) exit_status;

18569      pidarg = p_mp->mp_wpid;                  /* who's being waited for? */
18570      parent_waiting = p_mp->mp_flags & WAITING;
18571      right_child =                            /* child meets one of the 3 tests? */
18572          (pidarg == -1 || pidarg == rmp->mp_pid || -pidarg == rmp->mp_procgrp);

18574      if (parent_waiting && right_child) {
```

```
18575              cleanup(rmp);                   /* tell parent and release child slot */
18576     } else {
18577              rmp->mp_flags = IN_USE|ZOMBIE;  /* parent not waiting, zombify child */
18578              sig_proc(p_mp, SIGCHLD);        /* send parent a "child died" signal */
18579     }
18580
18581     /* If the process has children, disinherit them.  INIT is the new parent. */
18582     for (rmp = &mproc[0]; rmp < &mproc[NR_PROCS]; rmp++) {
18583              if (rmp->mp_flags & IN_USE && rmp->mp_parent == proc_nr) {
18584                       /* 'rmp' now points to a child to be disinherited. */
18585                       rmp->mp_parent = INIT_PROC_NR;
18586                       parent_waiting = mproc[INIT_PROC_NR].mp_flags & WAITING;
18587                       if (parent_waiting && (rmp->mp_flags & ZOMBIE)) cleanup(rmp);
18588              }
18589     }
18590
18591     /* Send a hangup to the process' process group if it was a session leader. */
18592     if (procgrp != 0) check_sig(-procgrp, SIGHUP);
18593 }

18595 /*===========================================================================*
18596  *                                do_waitpid                                 *
18597  *===========================================================================*/
18598 PUBLIC int do_waitpid()
18599 {
18600 /* A process wants to wait for a child to terminate. If a child is already
18601  * waiting, go clean it up and let this WAIT call terminate.  Otherwise,
18602  * really wait.
18603  * A process calling WAIT never gets a reply in the usual way at the end
18604  * of the main loop (unless WNOHANG is set or no qualifying child exists).
18605  * If a child has already exited, the routine cleanup() sends the reply
18606  * to awaken the caller.
18607  * Both WAIT and WAITPID are handled by this code.
18608  */
18609   register struct mproc *rp;
18610   int pidarg, options, children;
18611
18612   /* Set internal variables, depending on whether this is WAIT or WAITPID. */
18613   pidarg  = (call_nr == WAIT ? -1 : m_in.pid);      /* 1st param of waitpid */
18614   options = (call_nr == WAIT ?  0 : m_in.sig_nr);   /* 3rd param of waitpid */
18615   if (pidarg == 0) pidarg = -mp->mp_procgrp;        /* pidarg < 0 ==> proc grp */
18616
18617   /* Is there a child waiting to be collected? At this point, pidarg != 0:
18618    *      pidarg  >  0 means pidarg is pid of a specific process to wait for
18619    *      pidarg == -1 means wait for any child
18620    *      pidarg  < -1 means wait for any child whose process group = -pidarg
18621    */
18622   children = 0;
18623   for (rp = &mproc[0]; rp < &mproc[NR_PROCS]; rp++) {
18624            if ( (rp->mp_flags & IN_USE) && rp->mp_parent == who) {
18625                     /* The value of pidarg determines which children qualify. */
18626                     if (pidarg  > 0 && pidarg != rp->mp_pid) continue;
18627                     if (pidarg < -1 && -pidarg != rp->mp_procgrp) continue;
18628
18629                     children++;                      /* this child is acceptable */
18630                     if (rp->mp_flags & ZOMBIE) {
18631                              /* This child meets the pid test and has exited. */
18632                              cleanup(rp);     /* this child has already exited */
18633                              return(SUSPEND);
18634                     }
```

```
18635                      if ((rp->mp_flags & STOPPED) && rp->mp_sigstatus) {
18636                              /* This child meets the pid test and is being traced.*/
18637                              mp->mp_reply.reply_res2 = 0177|(rp->mp_sigstatus << 8);
18638                              rp->mp_sigstatus = 0;
18639                              return(rp->mp_pid);
18640                      }
18641                  }
18642          }
18643
18644      /* No qualifying child has exited.  Wait for one, unless none exists. */
18645      if (children > 0) {
18646              /* At least 1 child meets the pid test exists, but has not exited. */
18647              if (options & WNOHANG) return(0);     /* parent does not want to wait */
18648              mp->mp_flags |= WAITING;              /* parent wants to wait */
18649              mp->mp_wpid = (pid_t) pidarg;         /* save pid for later */
18650              return(SUSPEND);                      /* do not reply, let it wait */
18651      } else {
18652              /* No child even meets the pid test.  Return error immediately. */
18653              return(ECHILD);                       /* no - parent has no children */
18654      }
18655  }

18657  /*===========================================================================*
18658   *                              cleanup                                       *
18659   *===========================================================================*/
18660  PRIVATE void cleanup(child)
18661  register struct mproc *child;    /* tells which process is exiting */
18662  {
18663  /* Finish off the exit of a process.  The process has exited or been killed
18664   * by a signal, and its parent is waiting.
18665   */
18666      struct mproc *parent = &mproc[child->mp_parent];
18667      int exitstatus;
18668
18669      /* Wake up the parent by sending the reply message. */
18670      exitstatus = (child->mp_exitstatus << 8) | (child->mp_sigstatus & 0377);
18671      parent->mp_reply.reply_res2 = exitstatus;
18672      setreply(child->mp_parent, child->mp_pid);
18673      parent->mp_flags &= ~WAITING;             /* parent no longer waiting */
18674
18675      /* Release the process table entry and reinitialize some field. */
18676      child->mp_pid = 0;
18677      child->mp_flags = 0;
18678      child->mp_child_utime = 0;
18679      child->mp_child_stime = 0;
18680      procs_in_use--;
18681  }
```

```
++++++++++++++++++++++++++++++++++++++++++++++++++++++++++++++++++++++++++++
                              servers/pm/exec.c
++++++++++++++++++++++++++++++++++++++++++++++++++++++++++++++++++++++++++++

18700  /* This file handles the EXEC system call.  It performs the work as follows:
18701   *      - see if the permissions allow the file to be executed
18702   *      - read the header and extract the sizes
18703   *      - fetch the initial args and environment from the user space
18704   *      - allocate the memory for the new process
```

```
18705   *    - copy the initial stack from PM to the process
18706   *    - read in the text and data segments and copy to the process
18707   *    - take care of setuid and setgid bits
18708   *    - fix up 'mproc' table
18709   *    - tell kernel about EXEC
18710   *    - save offset to initial argc (for ps)
18711   *
18712   * The entry points into this file are:
18713   *   do_exec:    perform the EXEC system call
18714   *   rw_seg:     read or write a segment from or to a file
18715   *   find_share: find a process whose text segment can be shared
18716   */
18717
18718   #include "pm.h"
18719   #include <sys/stat.h>
18720   #include <minix/callnr.h>
18721   #include <minix/com.h>
18722   #include <a.out.h>
18723   #include <signal.h>
18724   #include <string.h>
18725   #include "mproc.h"
18726   #include "param.h"
18727
18728   FORWARD _PROTOTYPE( int new_mem, (struct mproc *sh_mp, vir_bytes text_bytes,
18729                      vir_bytes data_bytes, vir_bytes bss_bytes,
18730                      vir_bytes stk_bytes, phys_bytes tot_bytes)        );
18731   FORWARD _PROTOTYPE( void patch_ptr, (char stack[ARG_MAX], vir_bytes base) );
18732   FORWARD _PROTOTYPE( int insert_arg, (char stack[ARG_MAX],
18733                      vir_bytes *stk_bytes, char *arg, int replace)     );
18734   FORWARD _PROTOTYPE( char *patch_stack, (int fd, char stack[ARG_MAX],
18735                      vir_bytes *stk_bytes, char *script)              );
18736   FORWARD _PROTOTYPE( int read_header, (int fd, int *ft, vir_bytes *text_bytes,
18737                      vir_bytes *data_bytes, vir_bytes *bss_bytes,
18738                      phys_bytes *tot_bytes, long *sym_bytes, vir_clicks sc,
18739                      vir_bytes *pc)                                   );
18740
18741   #define ESCRIPT (-2000) /* Returned by read_header for a #! script. */
18742   #define PTRSIZE sizeof(char *) /* Size of pointers in argv[] and envp[]. */
18743
18744   /*===========================================================================*
18745    *                              do_exec                                       *
18746    *===========================================================================*/
18747   PUBLIC int do_exec()
18748   {
18749   /* Perform the execve(name, argv, envp) call.  The user library builds a
18750    * complete stack image, including pointers, args, environ, etc.  The stack
18751    * is copied to a buffer inside PM, and then to the new core image.
18752    */
18753     register struct mproc *rmp;
18754     struct mproc *sh_mp;
18755     int m, r, fd, ft, sn;
18756     static char mbuf[ARG_MAX];     /* buffer for stack and zeroes */
18757     static char name_buf[PATH_MAX]; /* the name of the file to exec */
18758     char *new_sp, *name, *basename;
18759     vir_bytes src, dst, text_bytes, data_bytes, bss_bytes, stk_bytes, vsp;
18760     phys_bytes tot_bytes;           /* total space for program, including gap */
18761     long sym_bytes;
18762     vir_clicks sc;
18763     struct stat s_buf[2], *s_p;
18764     vir_bytes pc;
```

```
18765
18766        /* Do some validity checks. */
18767        rmp = mp;
18768        stk_bytes = (vir_bytes) m_in.stack_bytes;
18769        if (stk_bytes > ARG_MAX) return(ENOMEM);         /* stack too big */
18770        if (m_in.exec_len <= 0 || m_in.exec_len > PATH_MAX) return(EINVAL);
18771
18772        /* Get the exec file name and see if the file is executable. */
18773        src = (vir_bytes) m_in.exec_name;
18774        dst = (vir_bytes) name_buf;
18775        r = sys_datacopy(who, (vir_bytes) src,
18776                     PM_PROC_NR, (vir_bytes) dst, (phys_bytes) m_in.exec_len);
18777        if (r != OK) return(r);         /* file name not in user data segment */
18778
18779        /* Fetch the stack from the user before destroying the old core image. */
18780        src = (vir_bytes) m_in.stack_ptr;
18781        dst = (vir_bytes) mbuf;
18782        r = sys_datacopy(who, (vir_bytes) src,
18783                     PM_PROC_NR, (vir_bytes) dst, (phys_bytes)stk_bytes);
18784        /* can't fetch stack (e.g. bad virtual addr) */
18785        if (r != OK) return(EACCES);
18786
18787        r = 0;         /* r = 0 (first attempt), or 1 (interpreted script) */
18788        name = name_buf;     /* name of file to exec. */
18789        do {
18790              s_p = &s_buf[r];
18791              tell_fs(CHDIR, who, FALSE, 0);  /* switch to the user's FS environ */
18792              fd = allowed(name, s_p, X_BIT); /* is file executable? */
18793              if (fd < 0)  return(fd);                /* file was not executable */
18794
18795              /* Read the file header and extract the segment sizes. */
18796              sc = (stk_bytes + CLICK_SIZE - 1) >> CLICK_SHIFT;
18797
18798              m = read_header(fd, &ft, &text_bytes, &data_bytes, &bss_bytes,
18799                                        &tot_bytes, &sym_bytes, sc, &pc);
18800              if (m != ESCRIPT || ++r > 1) break;
18801        } while ((name = patch_stack(fd, mbuf, &stk_bytes, name_buf)) != NULL);
18802
18803        if (m < 0) {
18804              close(fd);                   /* something wrong with header */
18805              return(stk_bytes > ARG_MAX ? ENOMEM : ENOEXEC);
18806        }
18807
18808        /* Can the process' text be shared with that of one already running? */
18809        sh_mp = find_share(rmp, s_p->st_ino, s_p->st_dev, s_p->st_ctime);
18810
18811        /* Allocate new memory and release old memory.  Fix map and tell kernel. */
18812        r = new_mem(sh_mp, text_bytes, data_bytes, bss_bytes, stk_bytes, tot_bytes);
18813        if (r != OK) {
18814              close(fd);                   /* insufficient core or program too big */
18815              return(r);
18816        }
18817
18818        /* Save file identification to allow it to be shared. */
18819        rmp->mp_ino = s_p->st_ino;
18820        rmp->mp_dev = s_p->st_dev;
18821        rmp->mp_ctime = s_p->st_ctime;
18822
18823        /* Patch up stack and copy it from PM to new core image. */
18824        vsp = (vir_bytes) rmp->mp_seg[S].mem_vir << CLICK_SHIFT;
```

```
18825        vsp += (vir_bytes) rmp->mp_seg[S].mem_len << CLICK_SHIFT;
18826        vsp -= stk_bytes;
18827        patch_ptr(mbuf, vsp);
18828        src = (vir_bytes) mbuf;
18829        r = sys_datacopy(PM_PROC_NR, (vir_bytes) src,
18830                            who, (vir_bytes) vsp, (phys_bytes)stk_bytes);
18831        if (r != OK) panic(__FILE__,"do_exec stack copy err on", who);
18832
18833        /* Read in text and data segments. */
18834        if (sh_mp != NULL) {
18835                lseek(fd, (off_t) text_bytes, SEEK_CUR);   /* shared: skip text */
18836        } else {
18837                rw_seg(0, fd, who, T, text_bytes);
18838        }
18839        rw_seg(0, fd, who, D, data_bytes);
18840
18841        close(fd);                          /* don't need exec file any more */
18842
18843        /* Take care of setuid/setgid bits. */
18844        if ((rmp->mp_flags & TRACED) == 0) { /* suppress if tracing */
18845                if (s_buf[0].st_mode & I_SET_UID_BIT) {
18846                        rmp->mp_effuid = s_buf[0].st_uid;
18847                        tell_fs(SETUID,who, (int)rmp->mp_realuid, (int)rmp->mp_effuid);
18848                }
18849                if (s_buf[0].st_mode & I_SET_GID_BIT) {
18850                        rmp->mp_effgid = s_buf[0].st_gid;
18851                        tell_fs(SETGID,who, (int)rmp->mp_realgid, (int)rmp->mp_effgid);
18852                }
18853        }
18854
18855        /* Save offset to initial argc (for ps) */
18856        rmp->mp_procargs = vsp;
18857
18858        /* Fix 'mproc' fields, tell kernel that exec is done,  reset caught sigs. */
18859        for (sn = 1; sn <= _NSIG; sn++) {
18860                if (sigismember(&rmp->mp_catch, sn)) {
18861                        sigdelset(&rmp->mp_catch, sn);
18862                        rmp->mp_sigact[sn].sa_handler = SIG_DFL;
18863                        sigemptyset(&rmp->mp_sigact[sn].sa_mask);
18864                }
18865        }
18866
18867        rmp->mp_flags &= ~SEPARATE;    /* turn off SEPARATE bit */
18868        rmp->mp_flags |= ft;           /* turn it on for separate I & D files */
18869        new_sp = (char *) vsp;
18870
18871        tell_fs(EXEC, who, 0, 0);      /* allow FS to handle FD_CLOEXEC files */
18872
18873        /* System will save command line for debugging, ps(1) output, etc. */
18874        basename = strrchr(name, '/');
18875        if (basename == NULL) basename = name; else basename++;
18876        strncpy(rmp->mp_name, basename, PROC_NAME_LEN-1);
18877        rmp->mp_name[PROC_NAME_LEN] = '\0';
18878        sys_exec(who, new_sp, basename, pc);
18879
18880        /* Cause a signal if this process is traced. */
18881        if (rmp->mp_flags & TRACED) check_sig(rmp->mp_pid, SIGTRAP);
18882
18883        return(SUSPEND);                     /* no reply, new program just runs */
18884 }
```

```
18886   /*===========================================================================*
18887    *                          read_header                                      *
18888    *===========================================================================*/
18889   PRIVATE int read_header(fd, ft, text_bytes, data_bytes, bss_bytes,
18890                                           tot_bytes, sym_bytes, sc, pc)
18891   int fd;                         /* file descriptor for reading exec file */
18892   int *ft;                        /* place to return ft number */
18893   vir_bytes *text_bytes;          /* place to return text size */
18894   vir_bytes *data_bytes;          /* place to return initialized data size */
18895   vir_bytes *bss_bytes;           /* place to return bss size */
18896   phys_bytes *tot_bytes;          /* place to return total size */
18897   long *sym_bytes;                /* place to return symbol table size */
18898   vir_clicks sc;                  /* stack size in clicks */
18899   vir_bytes *pc;                  /* program entry point (initial PC) */
18900   {
18901   /* Read the header and extract the text, data, bss and total sizes from it. */
18902
18903     int m, ct;
18904     vir_clicks tc, dc, s_vir, dvir;
18905     phys_clicks totc;
18906     struct exec hdr;                /* a.out header is read in here */
18907
18908     /* Read the header and check the magic number.  The standard MINIX header
18909      * is defined in <a.out.h>.  It consists of 8 chars followed by 6 longs.
18910      * Then come 4 more longs that are not used here.
18911      *    Byte 0: magic number 0x01
18912      *    Byte 1: magic number 0x03
18913      *    Byte 2: normal = 0x10 (not checked, 0 is OK), separate I/D = 0x20
18914      *    Byte 3: CPU type, Intel 16 bit = 0x04, Intel 32 bit = 0x10,
18915      *            Motorola = 0x0B, Sun SPARC = 0x17
18916      *    Byte 4: Header length = 0x20
18917      *    Bytes 5-7 are not used.
18918      *
18919      *    Now come the 6 longs
18920      *    Bytes  8-11: size of text segments in bytes
18921      *    Bytes 12-15: size of initialized data segment in bytes
18922      *    Bytes 16-19: size of bss in bytes
18923      *    Bytes 20-23: program entry point
18924      *    Bytes 24-27: total memory allocated to program (text, data + stack)
18925      *    Bytes 28-31: size of symbol table in bytes
18926      * The longs are represented in a machine dependent order,
18927      * little-endian on the 8088, big-endian on the 68000.
18928      * The header is followed directly by the text and data segments, and the
18929      * symbol table (if any). The sizes are given in the header. Only the
18930      * text and data segments are copied into memory by exec. The header is
18931      * used here only. The symbol table is for the benefit of a debugger and
18932      * is ignored here.
18933      */
18934
18935     if ((m= read(fd, &hdr, A_MINHDR)) < 2) return(ENOEXEC);
18936
18937     /* Interpreted script? */
18938     if ((((char *) &hdr)[0] == '#' && ((char *) &hdr)[1] == '!') return(ESCRIPT);
18939
18940     if (m != A_MINHDR) return(ENOEXEC);
18941
18942     /* Check magic number, cpu type, and flags. */
18943     if (BADMAG(hdr)) return(ENOEXEC);
18944     if (hdr.a_cpu != A_I80386) return(ENOEXEC);
```

```
18945       if ((hdr.a_flags & ~(A_NSYM | A_EXEC | A_SEP)) != 0) return(ENOEXEC);
18946
18947       *ft = ( (hdr.a_flags & A_SEP) ? SEPARATE : 0);     /* separate I & D or not */
18948
18949       /* Get text and data sizes. */
18950       *text_bytes = (vir_bytes) hdr.a_text; /* text size in bytes */
18951       *data_bytes = (vir_bytes) hdr.a_data; /* data size in bytes */
18952       *bss_bytes  = (vir_bytes) hdr.a_bss;  /* bss size in bytes */
18953       *tot_bytes  = hdr.a_total;            /* total bytes to allocate for prog */
18954       *sym_bytes  = hdr.a_syms;             /* symbol table size in bytes */
18955       if (*tot_bytes == 0) return(ENOEXEC);
18956
18957       if (*ft != SEPARATE) {
18958           /* If I & D space is not separated, it is all considered data. Text=0*/
18959           *data_bytes += *text_bytes;
18960           *text_bytes = 0;
18961       }
18962       *pc = hdr.a_entry;    /* initial address to start execution */
18963
18964       /* Check to see if segment sizes are feasible. */
18965       tc = ((unsigned long) *text_bytes + CLICK_SIZE - 1) >> CLICK_SHIFT;
18966       dc = (*data_bytes + *bss_bytes + CLICK_SIZE - 1) >> CLICK_SHIFT;
18967       totc = (*tot_bytes + CLICK_SIZE - 1) >> CLICK_SHIFT;
18968       if (dc >= totc) return(ENOEXEC);        /* stack must be at least 1 click */
18969       dvir = (*ft == SEPARATE ? 0 : tc);
18970       s_vir = dvir + (totc - sc);
18971       m = (dvir + dc > s_vir) ? ENOMEM : OK;
18972       ct = hdr.a_hdrlen & BYTE;               /* header length */
18973       if (ct > A_MINHDR) lseek(fd, (off_t) ct, SEEK_SET); /* skip unused hdr */
18974       return(m);
18975 }

18977 /*===========================================================================*
18978  *                              new_mem                                       *
18979  *===========================================================================*/
18980 PRIVATE int new_mem(sh_mp, text_bytes, data_bytes,
18981           bss_bytes,stk_bytes,tot_bytes)
18982 struct mproc *sh_mp;               /* text can be shared with this process */
18983 vir_bytes text_bytes;             /* text segment size in bytes */
18984 vir_bytes data_bytes;             /* size of initialized data in bytes */
18985 vir_bytes bss_bytes;              /* size of bss in bytes */
18986 vir_bytes stk_bytes;              /* size of initial stack segment in bytes */
18987 phys_bytes tot_bytes;             /* total memory to allocate, including gap */
18988 {
18989 /* Allocate new memory and release the old memory.  Change the map and report
18990  * the new map to the kernel.  Zero the new core image's bss, gap and stack.
18991  */
18992
18993       register struct mproc *rmp = mp;
18994       vir_clicks text_clicks, data_clicks, gap_clicks, stack_clicks, tot_clicks;
18995       phys_clicks new_base;
18996       phys_bytes bytes, base, bss_offset;
18997       int s;
18998
18999       /* No need to allocate text if it can be shared. */
19000       if (sh_mp != NULL) text_bytes = 0;
19001
19002       /* Allow the old data to be swapped out to make room.  (Which is really a
19003        * waste of time, because we are going to throw it away anyway.)
19004        */
```

```
19005          rmp->mp_flags |= WAITING;
19006
19007          /* Acquire the new memory.  Each of the 4 parts: text, (data+bss), gap,
19008           * and stack occupies an integral number of clicks, starting at click
19009           * boundary.  The data and bss parts are run together with no space.
19010           */
19011          text_clicks = ((unsigned long) text_bytes + CLICK_SIZE - 1) >> CLICK_SHIFT;
19012          data_clicks = (data_bytes + bss_bytes + CLICK_SIZE - 1) >> CLICK_SHIFT;
19013          stack_clicks = (stk_bytes + CLICK_SIZE - 1) >> CLICK_SHIFT;
19014          tot_clicks = (tot_bytes + CLICK_SIZE - 1) >> CLICK_SHIFT;
19015          gap_clicks = tot_clicks - data_clicks - stack_clicks;
19016          if ( (int) gap_clicks < 0) return(ENOMEM);
19017
19018          /* Try to allocate memory for the new process. */
19019          new_base = alloc_mem(text_clicks + tot_clicks);
19020          if (new_base == NO_MEM) return(ENOMEM);
19021
19022          /* We've got memory for the new core image.  Release the old one. */
19023          rmp = mp;
19024
19025          if (find_share(rmp, rmp->mp_ino, rmp->mp_dev, rmp->mp_ctime) == NULL) {
19026                  /* No other process shares the text segment, so free it. */
19027                  free_mem(rmp->mp_seg[T].mem_phys, rmp->mp_seg[T].mem_len);
19028          }
19029          /* Free the data and stack segments. */
19030          free_mem(rmp->mp_seg[D].mem_phys,
19031           rmp->mp_seg[S].mem_vir + rmp->mp_seg[S].mem_len - rmp->mp_seg[D].mem_vir);
19032
19033          /* We have now passed the point of no return.  The old core image has been
19034           * forever lost, memory for a new core image has been allocated.  Set up
19035           * and report new map.
19036           */
19037          if (sh_mp != NULL) {
19038                  /* Share the text segment. */
19039                  rmp->mp_seg[T] = sh_mp->mp_seg[T];
19040          } else {
19041                  rmp->mp_seg[T].mem_phys = new_base;
19042                  rmp->mp_seg[T].mem_vir = 0;
19043                  rmp->mp_seg[T].mem_len = text_clicks;
19044          }
19045          rmp->mp_seg[D].mem_phys = new_base + text_clicks;
19046          rmp->mp_seg[D].mem_vir = 0;
19047          rmp->mp_seg[D].mem_len = data_clicks;
19048          rmp->mp_seg[S].mem_phys = rmp->mp_seg[D].mem_phys + data_clicks + gap_clicks;
19049          rmp->mp_seg[S].mem_vir = rmp->mp_seg[D].mem_vir + data_clicks + gap_clicks;
19050          rmp->mp_seg[S].mem_len = stack_clicks;
19051
19052          sys_newmap(who, rmp->mp_seg);    /* report new map to the kernel */
19053
19054          /* The old memory may have been swapped out, but the new memory is real. */
19055          rmp->mp_flags &= ~(WAITING|ONSWAP|SWAPIN);
19056
19057          /* Zero the bss, gap, and stack segment. */
19058          bytes = (phys_bytes)(data_clicks + gap_clicks + stack_clicks) << CLICK_SHIFT;
19059          base = (phys_bytes) rmp->mp_seg[D].mem_phys << CLICK_SHIFT;
19060          bss_offset = (data_bytes >> CLICK_SHIFT) << CLICK_SHIFT;
19061          base += bss_offset;
19062          bytes -= bss_offset;
19063
19064          if ((s=sys_memset(0, base, bytes)) != OK) {
```

```
19065                     panic(__FILE__,"new_mem can't zero", s);
19066        }
19067
19068     return(OK);
19069   }

19071   /*===========================================================================*
19072    *                               patch_ptr                                   *
19073    *===========================================================================*/
19074   PRIVATE void patch_ptr(stack, base)
19075   char stack[ARG_MAX];                  /* pointer to stack image within PM */
19076   vir_bytes base;                       /* virtual address of stack base inside user */
19077   {
19078   /* When doing an exec(name, argv, envp) call, the user builds up a stack
19079    * image with arg and env pointers relative to the start of the stack.  Now
19080    * these pointers must be relocated, since the stack is not positioned at
19081    * address 0 in the user's address space.
19082    */
19083
19084     char **ap, flag;
19085     vir_bytes v;
19086
19087     flag = 0;                           /* counts number of 0-pointers seen */
19088     ap = (char **) stack;               /* points initially to 'nargs' */
19089     ap++;                               /* now points to argv[0] */
19090     while (flag < 2) {
19091           if (ap >= (char **) &stack[ARG_MAX]) return;    /* too bad */
19092           if (*ap != NULL) {
19093                   v = (vir_bytes) *ap;    /* v is relative pointer */
19094                   v += base;              /* relocate it */
19095                   *ap = (char *) v;       /* put it back */
19096           } else {
19097                   flag++;
19098           }
19099           ap++;
19100     }
19101   }

19103   /*===========================================================================*
19104    *                               insert_arg                                  *
19105    *===========================================================================*/
19106   PRIVATE int insert_arg(stack, stk_bytes, arg, replace)
19107   char stack[ARG_MAX];                  /* pointer to stack image within PM */
19108   vir_bytes *stk_bytes;                 /* size of initial stack */
19109   char *arg;                            /* argument to prepend/replace as new argv[0] */
19110   int replace;
19111   {
19112   /* Patch the stack so that arg will become argv[0].  Be careful, the stack may
19113    * be filled with garbage, although it normally looks like this:
19114    *         nargs argv[0] ... argv[nargs-1] NULL envp[0] ... NULL
19115    * followed by the strings "pointed" to by the argv[i] and the envp[i].  The
19116    * pointers are really offsets from the start of stack.
19117    * Return true iff the operation succeeded.
19118    */
19119     int offset, a0, a1, old_bytes = *stk_bytes;
19120
19121     /* Prepending arg adds at least one string and a zero byte. */
19122     offset = strlen(arg) + 1;
19123
19124     a0 = (int) ((char **) stack)[1];      /* argv[0] */
```

```
19125        if (a0 < 4 * PTRSIZE || a0 >= old_bytes) return(FALSE);
19126
19127        a1 = a0;                        /* a1 will point to the strings to be moved */
19128        if (replace) {
19129                /* Move a1 to the end of argv[0][] (argv[1] if nargs > 1). */
19130                do {
19131                        if (a1 == old_bytes) return(FALSE);
19132                        --offset;
19133                } while (stack[a1++] != 0);
19134        } else {
19135                offset += PTRSIZE;      /* new argv[0] needs new pointer in argv[] */
19136                a0 += PTRSIZE;          /* location of new argv[0][]. */
19137        }
19138
19139        /* stack will grow by offset bytes (or shrink by -offset bytes) */
19140        if ((*stk_bytes += offset) > ARG_MAX) return(FALSE);
19141
19142        /* Reposition the strings by offset bytes */
19143        memmove(stack + a1 + offset, stack + a1, old_bytes - a1);
19144
19145        strcpy(stack + a0, arg);         /* Put arg in the new space. */
19146
19147        if (!replace) {
19148                /* Make space for a new argv[0]. */
19149                memmove(stack + 2 * PTRSIZE, stack + 1 * PTRSIZE, a0 - 2 * PTRSIZE);
19150
19151                ((char **) stack)[0]++; /* nargs++; */
19152        }
19153        /* Now patch up argv[] and envp[] by offset. */
19154        patch_ptr(stack, (vir_bytes) offset);
19155        ((char **) stack)[1] = (char *) a0;   /* set argv[0] correctly */
19156        return(TRUE);
19157 }
19158
19159 /*===========================================================================*
19160  *                              patch_stack                                  *
19161  *===========================================================================*/
19162 PRIVATE char *patch_stack(fd, stack, stk_bytes, script)
19163 int fd;                                 /* file descriptor to open script file */
19164 char stack[ARG_MAX];                    /* pointer to stack image within PM */
19165 vir_bytes *stk_bytes;                   /* size of initial stack */
19166 char *script;                           /* name of script to interpret */
19167 {
19168 /* Patch the argument vector to include the path name of the script to be
19169  * interpreted, and all strings on the #! line.  Returns the path name of
19170  * the interpreter.
19171  */
19172   char *sp, *interp = NULL;
19173   int n;
19174   enum { INSERT=FALSE, REPLACE=TRUE };
19175
19176   /* Make script[] the new argv[0]. */
19177   if (!insert_arg(stack, stk_bytes, script, REPLACE)) return(NULL);
19178
19179   if (lseek(fd, 2L, 0) == -1                   /* just behind the #! */
19180       || (n= read(fd, script, PATH_MAX)) < 0   /* read line one */
19181       || (sp= memchr(script, '\n', n)) == NULL /* must be a proper line */
19182           return(NULL);
19183
19184   /* Move sp backwards through script[], prepending each string to stack. */
```

```
19185    for (;;) {
19186        /* skip spaces behind argument. */
19187        while (sp > script && (*--sp == ' ' || *sp == '\t')) {}
19188        if (sp == script) break;
19189
19190        sp[1] = 0;
19191        /* Move to the start of the argument. */
19192        while (sp > script && sp[-1] != ' ' && sp[-1] != '\t') --sp;
19193
19194        interp = sp;
19195        if (!insert_arg(stack, stk_bytes, sp, INSERT)) return(NULL);
19196    }
19197
19198    /* Round *stk_bytes up to the size of a pointer for alignment contraints. */
19199    *stk_bytes= ((*stk_bytes + PTRSIZE - 1) / PTRSIZE) * PTRSIZE;
19200
19201    close(fd);
19202    return(interp);
19203  }
19204
19205  /*===========================================================================*
19206   *                              rw_seg                                       *
19207   *===========================================================================*/
19208  PUBLIC void rw_seg(rw, fd, proc, seg, seg_bytes0)
19209  int rw;                          /* 0 = read, 1 = write */
19210  int fd;                          /* file descriptor to read from / write to */
19211  int proc;                        /* process number */
19212  int seg;                         /* T, D, or S */
19213  phys_bytes seg_bytes0;           /* how much is to be transferred? */
19214  {
19215  /* Transfer text or data from/to a file and copy to/from a process segment.
19216   * This procedure is a little bit tricky.  The logical way to transfer a
19217   * segment would be block by block and copying each block to/from the user
19218   * space one at a time.  This is too slow, so we do something dirty here,
19219   * namely send the user space and virtual address to the file system in the
19220   * upper 10 bits of the file descriptor, and pass it the user virtual address
19221   * instead of a PM address.  The file system extracts these parameters when
19222   * gets a read or write call from the process manager, which is the only
19223   * process that is permitted to use this trick.  The file system then copies
19224   * the whole segment directly to/from user space, bypassing PM completely.
19225   *
19226   * The byte count on read is usually smaller than the segment count, because
19227   * a segment is padded out to a click multiple, and the data segment is only
19228   * partially initialized.
19229   */
19230
19231    int new_fd, bytes, r;
19232    char *ubuf_ptr;
19233    struct mem_map *sp = &mproc[proc].mp_seg[seg];
19234    phys_bytes seg_bytes = seg_bytes0;
19235
19236    new_fd = (proc << 7) | (seg << 5) | fd;
19237    ubuf_ptr = (char *) ((vir_bytes) sp->mem_vir << CLICK_SHIFT);
19238
19239    while (seg_bytes != 0) {
19240  #define PM_CHUNK_SIZE 8192
19241        bytes = MIN((INT_MAX / PM_CHUNK_SIZE) * PM_CHUNK_SIZE, seg_bytes);
19242        if (rw == 0) {
19243            r = read(new_fd, ubuf_ptr, bytes);
19244        } else {
```

```
19245                    r = write(new_fd, ubuf_ptr, bytes);
19246            }
19247            if (r != bytes) break;
19248            ubuf_ptr += bytes;
19249            seg_bytes -= bytes;
19250    }
19251 }

19253 /*===========================================================================*
19254  *                              find_share                                   *
19255  *===========================================================================*/
19256 PUBLIC struct mproc *find_share(mp_ign, ino, dev, ctime)
19257 struct mproc *mp_ign;            /* process that should not be looked at */
19258 ino_t ino;                       /* parameters that uniquely identify a file */
19259 dev_t dev;
19260 time_t ctime;
19261 {
19262 /* Look for a process that is the file <ino, dev, ctime> in execution.  Don't
19263  * accidentally "find" mp_ign, because it is the process on whose behalf this
19264  * call is made.
19265  */
19266   struct mproc *sh_mp;
19267   for (sh_mp = &mproc[0]; sh_mp < &mproc[NR_PROCS]; sh_mp++) {
19268
19269         if (!(sh_mp->mp_flags & SEPARATE)) continue;
19270         if (sh_mp == mp_ign) continue;
19271         if (sh_mp->mp_ino != ino) continue;
19272         if (sh_mp->mp_dev != dev) continue;
19273         if (sh_mp->mp_ctime != ctime) continue;
19274         return sh_mp;
19275   }
19276   return(NULL);
19277 }
```

```
++++++++++++++++++++++++++++++++++++++++++++++++++++++++++++++++++++++++++++++
                            servers/pm/break.c
++++++++++++++++++++++++++++++++++++++++++++++++++++++++++++++++++++++++++++++
```

```
19300 /* The MINIX model of memory allocation reserves a fixed amount of memory for
19301  * the combined text, data, and stack segments.  The amount used for a child
19302  * process created by FORK is the same as the parent had.  If the child does
19303  * an EXEC later, the new size is taken from the header of the file EXEC'ed.
19304  *
19305  * The layout in memory consists of the text segment, followed by the data
19306  * segment, followed by a gap (unused memory), followed by the stack segment.
19307  * The data segment grows upward and the stack grows downward, so each can
19308  * take memory from the gap.  If they meet, the process must be killed.  The
19309  * procedures in this file deal with the growth of the data and stack segments.
19310  *
19311  * The entry points into this file are:
19312  *   do_brk:    BRK/SBRK system calls to grow or shrink the data segment
19313  *   adjust:    see if a proposed segment adjustment is allowed
19314  *   size_ok:   see if the segment sizes are feasible
19315  */
19316
19317 #include "pm.h"
19318 #include <signal.h>
19319 #include "mproc.h"
```

```
19320  #include "param.h"
19321
19322  #define DATA_CHANGED       1      /* flag value when data segment size changed */
19323  #define STACK_CHANGED      2      /* flag value when stack size changed */
19324
19325  /*===========================================================================*
19326   *                              do_brk                                        *
19327   *===========================================================================*/
19328  PUBLIC int do_brk()
19329  {
19330  /* Perform the brk(addr) system call.
19331   *
19332   * The call is complicated by the fact that on some machines (e.g., 8088),
19333   * the stack pointer can grow beyond the base of the stack segment without
19334   * anybody noticing it.
19335   * The parameter, 'addr' is the new virtual address in D space.
19336   */
19337
19338    register struct mproc *rmp;
19339    int r;
19340    vir_bytes v, new_sp;
19341    vir_clicks new_clicks;
19342
19343    rmp = mp;
19344    v = (vir_bytes) m_in.addr;
19345    new_clicks = (vir_clicks) ( ((long) v + CLICK_SIZE - 1) >> CLICK_SHIFT);
19346    if (new_clicks < rmp->mp_seg[D].mem_vir) {
19347          rmp->mp_reply.reply_ptr = (char *) -1;
19348          return(ENOMEM);
19349    }
19350    new_clicks -= rmp->mp_seg[D].mem_vir;
19351    if ((r=get_stack_ptr(who, &new_sp)) != OK)     /* ask kernel for sp value */
19352          panic(__FILE__,"couldn't get stack pointer", r);
19353    r = adjust(rmp, new_clicks, new_sp);
19354    rmp->mp_reply.reply_ptr = (r == OK ? m_in.addr : (char *) -1);
19355    return(r);                              /* return new address or -1 */
19356  }

19358  /*===========================================================================*
19359   *                              adjust                                        *
19360   *===========================================================================*/
19361  PUBLIC int adjust(rmp, data_clicks, sp)
19362  register struct mproc *rmp;       /* whose memory is being adjusted? */
19363  vir_clicks data_clicks;          /* how big is data segment to become? */
19364  vir_bytes sp;                    /* new value of sp */
19365  {
19366  /* See if data and stack segments can coexist, adjusting them if need be.
19367   * Memory is never allocated or freed.  Instead it is added or removed from the
19368   * gap between data segment and stack segment.  If the gap size becomes
19369   * negative, the adjustment of data or stack fails and ENOMEM is returned.
19370   */
19371
19372    register struct mem_map *mem_sp, *mem_dp;
19373    vir_clicks sp_click, gap_base, lower, old_clicks;
19374    int changed, r, ft;
19375    long base_of_stack, delta;       /* longs avoid certain problems */
19376
19377    mem_dp = &rmp->mp_seg[D];         /* pointer to data segment map */
19378    mem_sp = &rmp->mp_seg[S];         /* pointer to stack segment map */
19379    changed = 0;                     /* set when either segment changed */
```

```
19380
19381        if (mem_sp->mem_len == 0) return(OK); /* don't bother init */
19382
19383        /* See if stack size has gone negative (i.e., sp too close to 0xFFFF...) */
19384        base_of_stack = (long) mem_sp->mem_vir + (long) mem_sp->mem_len;
19385        sp_click = sp >> CLICK_SHIFT; /* click containing sp */
19386        if (sp_click >= base_of_stack) return(ENOMEM);          /* sp too high */
19387
19388        /* Compute size of gap between stack and data segments. */
19389        delta = (long) mem_sp->mem_vir - (long) sp_click;
19390        lower = (delta > 0 ? sp_click : mem_sp->mem_vir);
19391
19392        /* Add a safety margin for future stack growth. Impossible to do right. */
19393 #define SAFETY_BYTES   (384 * sizeof(char *))
19394 #define SAFETY_CLICKS ((SAFETY_BYTES + CLICK_SIZE - 1) / CLICK_SIZE)
19395        gap_base = mem_dp->mem_vir + data_clicks + SAFETY_CLICKS;
19396        if (lower < gap_base) return(ENOMEM); /* data and stack collided */
19397
19398        /* Update data length (but not data orgin) on behalf of brk() system call. */
19399        old_clicks = mem_dp->mem_len;
19400        if (data_clicks != mem_dp->mem_len) {
19401              mem_dp->mem_len = data_clicks;
19402              changed |= DATA_CHANGED;
19403        }
19404
19405        /* Update stack length and origin due to change in stack pointer. */
19406        if (delta > 0) {
19407              mem_sp->mem_vir -= delta;
19408              mem_sp->mem_phys -= delta;
19409              mem_sp->mem_len += delta;
19410              changed |= STACK_CHANGED;
19411        }
19412
19413        /* Do the new data and stack segment sizes fit in the address space? */
19414        ft = (rmp->mp_flags & SEPARATE);
19415        r = (rmp->mp_seg[D].mem_vir + rmp->mp_seg[D].mem_len >
19416              rmp->mp_seg[S].mem_vir) ? ENOMEM : OK;
19417        if (r == OK) {
19418              if (changed) sys_newmap((int)(rmp - mproc), rmp->mp_seg);
19419              return(OK);
19420        }
19421
19422        /* New sizes don't fit or require too many page/segment registers. Restore.*/
19423        if (changed & DATA_CHANGED) mem_dp->mem_len = old_clicks;
19424        if (changed & STACK_CHANGED) {
19425              mem_sp->mem_vir += delta;
19426              mem_sp->mem_phys += delta;
19427              mem_sp->mem_len -= delta;
19428        }
19429     return(ENOMEM);
19430 }
```

```
++++++++++++++++++++++++++++++++++++++++++++++++++++++++++++++++++++++++++++
                            servers/pm/signal.c
++++++++++++++++++++++++++++++++++++++++++++++++++++++++++++++++++++++++++++
19500   /* This file handles signals, which are asynchronous events and are generally
19501    * a messy and unpleasant business.  Signals can be generated by the KILL
19502    * system call, or from the keyboard (SIGINT) or from the clock (SIGALRM).
19503    * In all cases control eventually passes to check_sig() to see which processes
19504    * can be signaled.  The actual signaling is done by sig_proc().
19505    *
19506    * The entry points into this file are:
19507    *   do_sigaction:   perform the SIGACTION system call
19508    *   do_sigpending:  perform the SIGPENDING system call
19509    *   do_sigprocmask: perform the SIGPROCMASK system call
19510    *   do_sigreturn:   perform the SIGRETURN system call
19511    *   do_sigsuspend:  perform the SIGSUSPEND system call
19512    *   do_kill:    perform the KILL system call
19513    *   do_alarm:   perform the ALARM system call by calling set_alarm()
19514    *   set_alarm: tell the clock task to start or stop a timer
19515    *   do_pause:  perform the PAUSE system call
19516    *   ksig_pending: the kernel notified about pending signals
19517    *   sig_proc:  interrupt or terminate a signaled process
19518    *   check_sig: check which processes to signal with sig_proc()
19519    *   check_pending:  check if a pending signal can now be delivered
19520    */
19521
19522   #include "pm.h"
19523   #include <sys/stat.h>
19524   #include <sys/ptrace.h>
19525   #include <minix/callnr.h>
19526   #include <minix/com.h>
19527   #include <signal.h>
19528   #include <sys/sigcontext.h>
19529   #include <string.h>
19530   #include "mproc.h"
19531   #include "param.h"
19532
19533   #define CORE_MODE       0777    /* mode to use on core image files */
19534   #define DUMPED          0200    /* bit set in status when core dumped */
19535
19536   FORWARD _PROTOTYPE( void dump_core, (struct mproc *rmp)              );
19537   FORWARD _PROTOTYPE( void unpause, (int pro)                         );
19538   FORWARD _PROTOTYPE( void handle_sig, (int proc_nr, sigset_t sig_map)   );
19539   FORWARD _PROTOTYPE( void cause_sigalrm, (struct timer *tp)          );
19540
19541   /*===========================================================================*
19542    *                            do_sigaction                                   *
19543    *===========================================================================*/
19544   PUBLIC int do_sigaction()
19545   {
19546     int r;
19547     struct sigaction svec;
19548     struct sigaction *svp;
19549
19550     if (m_in.sig_nr == SIGKILL) return(OK);
19551     if (m_in.sig_nr < 1 || m_in.sig_nr > _NSIG) return (EINVAL);
19552     svp = &mp->mp_sigact[m_in.sig_nr];
19553     if ((struct sigaction *) m_in.sig_osa != (struct sigaction *) NULL) {
19554         r = sys_datacopy(PM_PROC_NR,(vir_bytes) svp,
```

```
19555                         who, (vir_bytes) m_in.sig_osa, (phys_bytes) sizeof(svec));
19556                 if (r != OK) return(r);
19557         }
19558
19559         if ((struct sigaction *) m_in.sig_nsa == (struct sigaction *) NULL)
19560                 return(OK);
19561
19562         /* Read in the sigaction structure. */
19563         r = sys_datacopy(who, (vir_bytes) m_in.sig_nsa,
19564                         PM_PROC_NR, (vir_bytes) &svec, (phys_bytes) sizeof(svec));
19565         if (r != OK) return(r);
19566
19567         if (svec.sa_handler == SIG_IGN) {
19568                 sigaddset(&mp->mp_ignore, m_in.sig_nr);
19569                 sigdelset(&mp->mp_sigpending, m_in.sig_nr);
19570                 sigdelset(&mp->mp_catch, m_in.sig_nr);
19571                 sigdelset(&mp->mp_sig2mess, m_in.sig_nr);
19572         } else if (svec.sa_handler == SIG_DFL) {
19573                 sigdelset(&mp->mp_ignore, m_in.sig_nr);
19574                 sigdelset(&mp->mp_catch, m_in.sig_nr);
19575                 sigdelset(&mp->mp_sig2mess, m_in.sig_nr);
19576         } else if (svec.sa_handler == SIG_MESS) {
19577                 if (! (mp->mp_flags & PRIV_PROC)) return(EPERM);
19578                 sigdelset(&mp->mp_ignore, m_in.sig_nr);
19579                 sigaddset(&mp->mp_sig2mess, m_in.sig_nr);
19580                 sigdelset(&mp->mp_catch, m_in.sig_nr);
19581         } else {
19582                 sigdelset(&mp->mp_ignore, m_in.sig_nr);
19583                 sigaddset(&mp->mp_catch, m_in.sig_nr);
19584                 sigdelset(&mp->mp_sig2mess, m_in.sig_nr);
19585         }
19586         mp->mp_sigact[m_in.sig_nr].sa_handler = svec.sa_handler;
19587         sigdelset(&svec.sa_mask, SIGKILL);
19588         mp->mp_sigact[m_in.sig_nr].sa_mask = svec.sa_mask;
19589         mp->mp_sigact[m_in.sig_nr].sa_flags = svec.sa_flags;
19590         mp->mp_sigreturn = (vir_bytes) m_in.sig_ret;
19591         return(OK);
19592 }

19594 /*===========================================================================*
19595  *                              do_sigpending                                *
19596  *===========================================================================*/
19597 PUBLIC int do_sigpending()
19598 {
19599   mp->mp_reply.reply_mask = (long) mp->mp_sigpending;
19600   return OK;
19601 }

19603 /*===========================================================================*
19604  *                              do_sigprocmask                               *
19605  *===========================================================================*/
19606 PUBLIC int do_sigprocmask()
19607 {
19608 /* Note that the library interface passes the actual mask in sigmask_set,
19609  * not a pointer to the mask, in order to save a copy.  Similarly,
19610  * the old mask is placed in the return message which the library
19611  * interface copies (if requested) to the user specified address.
19612  *
19613  * The library interface must set SIG_INQUIRE if the 'act' argument
19614  * is NULL.
```

```
19615     */
19616
19617     int i;
19618
19619     mp->mp_reply.reply_mask = (long) mp->mp_sigmask;
19620
19621     switch (m_in.sig_how) {
19622         case SIG_BLOCK:
19623             sigdelset((sigset_t *)&m_in.sig_set, SIGKILL);
19624             for (i = 1; i <= _NSIG; i++) {
19625                     if (sigismember((sigset_t *)&m_in.sig_set, i))
19626                             sigaddset(&mp->mp_sigmask, i);
19627             }
19628             break;
19629
19630         case SIG_UNBLOCK:
19631             for (i = 1; i <= _NSIG; i++) {
19632                     if (sigismember((sigset_t *)&m_in.sig_set, i))
19633                             sigdelset(&mp->mp_sigmask, i);
19634             }
19635             check_pending(mp);
19636             break;
19637
19638         case SIG_SETMASK:
19639             sigdelset((sigset_t *) &m_in.sig_set, SIGKILL);
19640             mp->mp_sigmask = (sigset_t) m_in.sig_set;
19641             check_pending(mp);
19642             break;
19643
19644         case SIG_INQUIRE:
19645             break;
19646
19647         default:
19648             return(EINVAL);
19649             break;
19650     }
19651     return OK;
19652 }
19653
19654 /*===========================================================================*
19655  *                              do_sigsuspend                                *
19656  *===========================================================================*/
19657 PUBLIC int do_sigsuspend()
19658 {
19659   mp->mp_sigmask2 = mp->mp_sigmask;      /* save the old mask */
19660   mp->mp_sigmask = (sigset_t) m_in.sig_set;
19661   sigdelset(&mp->mp_sigmask, SIGKILL);
19662   mp->mp_flags |= SIGSUSPENDED;
19663   check_pending(mp);
19664   return(SUSPEND);
19665 }
19666
19667 /*===========================================================================*
19668  *                              do_sigreturn                                 *
19669  *===========================================================================*/
19670 PUBLIC int do_sigreturn()
19671 {
19672 /* A user signal handler is done.  Restore context and check for
19673  * pending unblocked signals.
19674  */
```

```
19675
19676    int r;
19677
19678    mp->mp_sigmask = (sigset_t) m_in.sig_set;
19679    sigdelset(&mp->mp_sigmask, SIGKILL);
19680
19681    r = sys_sigreturn(who, (struct sigmsg *) m_in.sig_context);
19682    check_pending(mp);
19683    return(r);
19684  }

19686  /*===========================================================================*
19687   *                              do_kill                                      *
19688   *===========================================================================*/
19689  PUBLIC int do_kill()
19690  {
19691  /* Perform the kill(pid, signo) system call. */
19692
19693    return check_sig(m_in.pid, m_in.sig_nr);
19694  }

19696  /*===========================================================================*
19697   *                              ksig_pending                                 *
19698   *===========================================================================*/
19699  PUBLIC int ksig_pending()
19700  {
19701  /* Certain signals, such as segmentation violations originate in the kernel.
19702   * When the kernel detects such signals, it notifies the PM to take further
19703   * action. The PM requests the kernel to send messages with the process
19704   * slot and bit map for all signaled processes. The File System, for example,
19705   * uses this mechanism to signal writing on broken pipes (SIGPIPE).
19706   *
19707   * The kernel has notified the PM about pending signals. Request pending
19708   * signals until all signals are handled. If there are no more signals,
19709   * NONE is returned in the process number field.
19710   */
19711    int proc_nr;
19712    sigset_t sig_map;
19713
19714    while (TRUE) {
19715      sys_getksig(&proc_nr, &sig_map);      /* get an arbitrary pending signal */
19716      if (NONE == proc_nr) {                /* stop if no more pending signals */
19717          break;
19718      } else {
19719          handle_sig(proc_nr, sig_map);     /* handle the received signal */
19720          sys_endksig(proc_nr);             /* tell kernel it's done */
19721      }
19722    }
19723    return(SUSPEND);                         /* prevents sending reply */
19724  }

19726  /*===========================================================================*
19727   *                              handle_sig                                   *
19728   *===========================================================================*/
19729  PRIVATE void handle_sig(proc_nr, sig_map)
19730  int proc_nr;
19731  sigset_t sig_map;
19732  {
19733    register struct mproc *rmp;
19734    int i;
```

```
19735    pid_t proc_id, id;
19736
19737    rmp = &mproc[proc_nr];
19738    if ((rmp->mp_flags & (IN_USE | ZOMBIE)) != IN_USE) return;
19739    proc_id = rmp->mp_pid;
19740    mp = &mproc[0];                          /* pretend signals are from PM */
19741    mp->mp_procgrp = rmp->mp_procgrp;        /* get process group right */
19742
19743    /* Check each bit in turn to see if a signal is to be sent.  Unlike
19744     * kill(), the kernel may collect several unrelated signals for a
19745     * process and pass them to PM in one blow.  Thus loop on the bit
19746     * map. For SIGINT and SIGQUIT, use proc_id 0 to indicate a broadcast
19747     * to the recipient's process group.  For SIGKILL, use proc_id -1 to
19748     * indicate a systemwide broadcast.
19749     */
19750    for (i = 1; i <= _NSIG; i++) {
19751            if (!sigismember(&sig_map, i)) continue;
19752            switch (i) {
19753                case SIGINT:
19754                case SIGQUIT:
19755                    id = 0; break;  /* broadcast to process group */
19756                case SIGKILL:
19757                    id = -1; break; /* broadcast to all except INIT */
19758                default:
19759                    id = proc_id;
19760                    break;
19761            }
19762            check_sig(id, i);
19763    }
19764 }

19766 /*===========================================================================*
19767  *                              do_alarm                                     *
19768  *===========================================================================*/
19769 PUBLIC int do_alarm()
19770 {
19771 /* Perform the alarm(seconds) system call. */
19772   return(set_alarm(who, m_in.seconds));
19773 }


19775 /*===========================================================================*
19776  *                              set_alarm                                    *
19777  *===========================================================================*/
19778 PUBLIC int set_alarm(proc_nr, sec)
19779 int proc_nr;                    /* process that wants the alarm */
19780 int sec;                        /* how many seconds delay before the signal */
19781 {
19782 /* This routine is used by do_alarm() to set the alarm timer.  It is also used
19783  * to turn the timer off when a process exits with the timer still on.
19784  */
19785   clock_t ticks;            /* number of ticks for alarm */
19786   clock_t exptime;          /* needed for remaining time on previous alarm */
19787   clock_t uptime;           /* current system time */
19788   int remaining;            /* previous time left in seconds */
19789   int s;
19790
19791   /* First determine remaining time of previous alarm, if set. */
19792   if (mproc[proc_nr].mp_flags & ALARM_ON) {
19793         if ( (s=getuptime(&uptime)) != OK)
19794                 panic(__FILE__,"set_alarm couldn't get uptime", s);
```

```
19795                 exptime = *tmr_exp_time(&mproc[proc_nr].mp_timer);
19796                 remaining = (int) ((exptime - uptime + (HZ-1))/HZ);
19797                 if (remaining < 0) remaining = 0;
19798         } else {
19799                 remaining = 0;
19800         }
19801
19802         /* Tell the clock task to provide a signal message when the time comes.
19803          *
19804          * Large delays cause a lot of problems.  First, the alarm system call
19805          * takes an unsigned seconds count and the library has cast it to an int.
19806          * That probably works, but on return the library will convert "negative"
19807          * unsigneds to errors.  Presumably no one checks for these errors, so
19808          * force this call through.  Second, If unsigned and long have the same
19809          * size, converting from seconds to ticks can easily overflow.  Finally,
19810          * the kernel has similar overflow bugs adding ticks.
19811          *
19812          * Fixing this requires a lot of ugly casts to fit the wrong interface
19813          * types and to avoid overflow traps.  ALRM_EXP_TIME has the right type
19814          * (clock_t) although it is declared as long.  How can variables like
19815          * this be declared properly without combinatorial explosion of message
19816          * types?
19817          */
19818         ticks = (clock_t) (HZ * (unsigned long) (unsigned) sec);
19819         if ( (unsigned long) ticks / HZ != (unsigned) sec)
19820                 ticks = LONG_MAX;        /* eternity (really TMR_NEVER) */
19821
19822         if (ticks != 0) {
19823                 pm_set_timer(&mproc[proc_nr].mp_timer, ticks, cause_sigalrm, proc_nr);
19824                 mproc[proc_nr].mp_flags |=  ALARM_ON;
19825         } else if (mproc[proc_nr].mp_flags & ALARM_ON) {
19826                 pm_cancel_timer(&mproc[proc_nr].mp_timer);
19827                 mproc[proc_nr].mp_flags &= ~ALARM_ON;
19828         }
19829         return(remaining);
19830 }

19832 /*===========================================================================*
19833  *                              cause_sigalrm                                *
19834  *===========================================================================*/
19835 PRIVATE void cause_sigalrm(tp)
19836 struct timer *tp;
19837 {
19838   int proc_nr;
19839   register struct mproc *rmp;
19840
19841   proc_nr = tmr_arg(tp)->ta_int;         /* get process from timer */
19842   rmp = &mproc[proc_nr];
19843
19844   if ((rmp->mp_flags & (IN_USE | ZOMBIE)) != IN_USE) return;
19845   if ((rmp->mp_flags & ALARM_ON) == 0) return;
19846   rmp->mp_flags &= ~ALARM_ON;
19847   check_sig(rmp->mp_pid, SIGALRM);
19848 }

19850 /*===========================================================================*
19851  *                              do_pause                                     *
19852  *===========================================================================*/
19853 PUBLIC int do_pause()
19854 {
```

```
19855   /* Perform the pause() system call. */
19856
19857     mp->mp_flags |= PAUSED;
19858     return(SUSPEND);
19859   }


19861   /*===========================================================================*
19862    *                              sig_proc                                      *
19863    *===========================================================================*/
19864   PUBLIC void sig_proc(rmp, signo)
19865   register struct mproc *rmp;      /* pointer to the process to be signaled */
19866   int signo;                      /* signal to send to process (1 to _NSIG) */
19867   {
19868   /* Send a signal to a process.  Check to see if the signal is to be caught,
19869    * ignored, tranformed into a message (for system processes) or blocked.
19870    *  - If the signal is to be transformed into a message, request the KERNEL to
19871    * send the target process a system notification with the pending signal as an
19872    * argument.
19873    *  - If the signal is to be caught, request the KERNEL to push a sigcontext
19874    * structure and a sigframe structure onto the catcher's stack.  Also, KERNEL
19875    * will reset the program counter and stack pointer, so that when the process
19876    * next runs, it will be executing the signal handler. When the signal handler
19877    * returns,  sigreturn(2) will be called.  Then KERNEL will restore the signal
19878    * context from the sigcontext structure.
19879    * If there is insufficient stack space, kill the process.
19880    */
19881
19882     vir_bytes new_sp;
19883     int s;
19884     int slot;
19885     int sigflags;
19886     struct sigmsg sm;
19887
19888     slot = (int) (rmp - mproc);
19889     if ((rmp->mp_flags & (IN_USE | ZOMBIE)) != IN_USE) {
19890           printf("PM: signal %d sent to %s process %d\n",
19891                 signo, (rmp->mp_flags & ZOMBIE) ? "zombie" : "dead", slot);
19892           panic(__FILE__,"", NO_NUM);
19893     }
19894     if ((rmp->mp_flags & TRACED) && signo != SIGKILL) {
19895           /* A traced process has special handling. */
19896           unpause(slot);
19897           stop_proc(rmp, signo);  /* a signal causes it to stop */
19898           return;
19899     }
19900     /* Some signals are ignored by default. */
19901     if (sigismember(&rmp->mp_ignore, signo)) {
19902           return;
19903     }
19904     if (sigismember(&rmp->mp_sigmask, signo)) {
19905           /* Signal should be blocked. */
19906           sigaddset(&rmp->mp_sigpending, signo);
19907           return;
19908     }
19909     sigflags = rmp->mp_sigact[signo].sa_flags;
19910     if (sigismember(&rmp->mp_catch, signo)) {
19911           if (rmp->mp_flags & SIGSUSPENDED)
19912                 sm.sm_mask = rmp->mp_sigmask2;
19913           else
19914                 sm.sm_mask = rmp->mp_sigmask;
```

```
19915                     sm.sm_signo = signo;
19916                     sm.sm_sighandler = (vir_bytes) rmp->mp_sigact[signo].sa_handler;
19917                     sm.sm_sigreturn = rmp->mp_sigreturn;
19918                     if ((s=get_stack_ptr(slot, &new_sp)) != OK)
19919                             panic(__FILE__,"couldn't get new stack pointer",s);
19920                     sm.sm_stkptr = new_sp;
19921
19922                     /* Make room for the sigcontext and sigframe struct. */
19923                     new_sp -= sizeof(struct sigcontext)
19924                                             + 3 * sizeof(char *) + 2 * sizeof(int);
19925
19926                     if (adjust(rmp, rmp->mp_seg[D].mem_len, new_sp) != OK)
19927                             goto doterminate;
19928
19929                     rmp->mp_sigmask |= rmp->mp_sigact[signo].sa_mask;
19930                     if (sigflags & SA_NODEFER)
19931                             sigdelset(&rmp->mp_sigmask, signo);
19932                     else
19933                             sigaddset(&rmp->mp_sigmask, signo);
19934
19935                     if (sigflags & SA_RESETHAND) {
19936                             sigdelset(&rmp->mp_catch, signo);
19937                             rmp->mp_sigact[signo].sa_handler = SIG_DFL;
19938                     }
19939
19940                     if (OK == (s=sys_sigsend(slot, &sm))) {
19941
19942                             sigdelset(&rmp->mp_sigpending, signo);
19943                             /* If process is hanging on PAUSE, WAIT, SIGSUSPEND, tty,
19944                              * pipe, etc., release it.
19945                              */
19946                             unpause(slot);
19947                             return;
19948                     }
19949             panic(__FILE__, "warning, sys_sigsend failed", s);
19950     }
19951   else if (sigismember(&rmp->mp_sig2mess, signo)) {
19952         if (OK != (s=sys_kill(slot,signo)))
19953                 panic(__FILE__, "warning, sys_kill failed", s);
19954         return;
19955   }
19956
19957 doterminate:
19958   /* Signal should not or cannot be caught.  Take default action. */
19959   if (sigismember(&ign_sset, signo)) return;
19960
19961   rmp->mp_sigstatus = (char) signo;
19962   if (sigismember(&core_sset, signo)) {
19963         /* Switch to the user's FS environment and dump core. */
19964         tell_fs(CHDIR, slot, FALSE, 0);
19965         dump_core(rmp);
19966   }
19967   pm_exit(rmp, 0);                      /* terminate process */
19968 }
19969
19970 /*===========================================================================*
19971  *                              check_sig                                     *
19972  *===========================================================================*/
19973 PUBLIC int check_sig(proc_id, signo)
19974 pid_t proc_id;                    /* pid of proc to sig, or 0 or -1, or -pgrp */
```

```
19975  int signo;                          /* signal to send to process (0 to _NSIG) */
19976  {
19977  /* Check to see if it is possible to send a signal.  The signal may have to be
19978   * sent to a group of processes.  This routine is invoked by the KILL system
19979   * call, and also when the kernel catches a DEL or other signal.
19980   */
19981
19982    register struct mproc *rmp;
19983    int count;                        /* count # of signals sent */
19984    int error_code;
19985
19986    if (signo < 0 || signo > _NSIG) return(EINVAL);
19987
19988    /* Return EINVAL for attempts to send SIGKILL to INIT alone. */
19989    if (proc_id == INIT_PID && signo == SIGKILL) return(EINVAL);
19990
19991    /* Search the proc table for processes to signal.  (See forkexit.c about
19992     * pid magic.)
19993     */
19994    count = 0;
19995    error_code = ESRCH;
19996    for (rmp = &mproc[0]; rmp < &mproc[NR_PROCS]; rmp++) {
19997          if (!(rmp->mp_flags & IN_USE)) continue;
19998          if ((rmp->mp_flags & ZOMBIE) && signo != 0) continue;
19999
20000          /* Check for selection. */
20001          if (proc_id > 0 && proc_id != rmp->mp_pid) continue;
20002          if (proc_id == 0 && mp->mp_procgrp != rmp->mp_procgrp) continue;
20003          if (proc_id == -1 && rmp->mp_pid <= INIT_PID) continue;
20004          if (proc_id < -1 && rmp->mp_procgrp != -proc_id) continue;
20005
20006          /* Check for permission. */
20007          if (mp->mp_effuid != SUPER_USER
20008              && mp->mp_realuid != rmp->mp_realuid
20009              && mp->mp_effuid != rmp->mp_realuid
20010              && mp->mp_realuid != rmp->mp_effuid
20011              && mp->mp_effuid != rmp->mp_effuid) {
20012                  error_code = EPERM;
20013                  continue;
20014          }
20015
20016          count++;
20017          if (signo == 0) continue;
20018
20019          /* 'sig_proc' will handle the disposition of the signal.  The
20020           * signal may be caught, blocked, ignored, or cause process
20021           * termination, possibly with core dump.
20022           */
20023          sig_proc(rmp, signo);
20024
20025          if (proc_id > 0) break; /* only one process being signaled */
20026    }
20027
20028    /* If the calling process has killed itself, don't reply. */
20029    if ((mp->mp_flags & (IN_USE | ZOMBIE)) != IN_USE) return(SUSPEND);
20030    return(count > 0 ? OK : error_code);
20031  }
```

```
20033  /*===========================================================================*
20034   *                               check_pending                               *
20035   *===========================================================================*/
20036  PUBLIC void check_pending(rmp)
20037  register struct mproc *rmp;
20038  {
20039    /* Check to see if any pending signals have been unblocked.  The
20040     * first such signal found is delivered.
20041     *
20042     * If multiple pending unmasked signals are found, they will be
20043     * delivered sequentially.
20044     *
20045     * There are several places in this file where the signal mask is
20046     * changed.  At each such place, check_pending() should be called to
20047     * check for newly unblocked signals.
20048     */
20049
20050    int i;
20051
20052    for (i = 1; i <= _NSIG; i++) {
20053          if (sigismember(&rmp->mp_sigpending, i) &&
20054                  !sigismember(&rmp->mp_sigmask, i)) {
20055                  sigdelset(&rmp->mp_sigpending, i);
20056                  sig_proc(rmp, i);
20057                  break;
20058          }
20059    }
20060  }

20062  /*===========================================================================*
20063   *                               unpause                                     *
20064   *===========================================================================*/
20065  PRIVATE void unpause(pro)
20066  int pro;                                /* which process number */
20067  {
20068  /* A signal is to be sent to a process.  If that process is hanging on a
20069   * system call, the system call must be terminated with EINTR.  Possible
20070   * calls are PAUSE, WAIT, READ and WRITE, the latter two for pipes and ttys.
20071   * First check if the process is hanging on an PM call.  If not, tell FS,
20072   * so it can check for READs and WRITEs from pipes, ttys and the like.
20073   */
20074
20075    register struct mproc *rmp;
20076
20077    rmp = &mproc[pro];
20078
20079    /* Check to see if process is hanging on a PAUSE, WAIT or SIGSUSPEND call. */
20080    if (rmp->mp_flags & (PAUSED | WAITING | SIGSUSPENDED)) {
20081          rmp->mp_flags &= ~(PAUSED | WAITING | SIGSUSPENDED);
20082          setreply(pro, EINTR);
20083          return;
20084    }
20085
20086    /* Process is not hanging on an PM call.  Ask FS to take a look. */
20087    tell_fs(UNPAUSE, pro, 0, 0);
20088  }
```

```
20090   /*===========================================================================*
20091    *                                dump_core                                  *
20092    *===========================================================================*/
20093   PRIVATE void dump_core(rmp)
20094   register struct mproc *rmp;        /* whose core is to be dumped */
20095   {
20096   /* Make a core dump on the file "core", if possible. */
20097
20098     int s, fd, seg, slot;
20099     vir_bytes current_sp;
20100     long trace_data, trace_off;
20101
20102     slot = (int) (rmp - mproc);
20103
20104     /* Can core file be written?  We are operating in the user's FS environment,
20105      * so no special permission checks are needed.
20106      */
20107     if (rmp->mp_realuid != rmp->mp_effuid) return;
20108     if ( (fd = open(core_name, O_WRONLY | O_CREAT | O_TRUNC | O_NONBLOCK,
20109                                        CORE_MODE)) < 0) return;
20110     rmp->mp_sigstatus |= DUMPED;
20111
20112     /* Make sure the stack segment is up to date.
20113      * We don't want adjust() to fail unless current_sp is preposterous,
20114      * but it might fail due to safety checking.  Also, we don't really want
20115      * the adjust() for sending a signal to fail due to safety checking.
20116      * Maybe make SAFETY_BYTES a parameter.
20117      */
20118     if ((s=get_stack_ptr(slot, &current_sp)) != OK)
20119         panic(__FILE__,"couldn't get new stack pointer",s);
20120     adjust(rmp, rmp->mp_seg[D].mem_len, current_sp);
20121
20122     /* Write the memory map of all segments to begin the core file. */
20123     if (write(fd, (char *) rmp->mp_seg, (unsigned) sizeof rmp->mp_seg)
20124         != (unsigned) sizeof rmp->mp_seg) {
20125         close(fd);
20126         return;
20127     }
20128
20129     /* Write out the whole kernel process table entry to get the regs. */
20130     trace_off = 0;
20131     while (sys_trace(T_GETUSER, slot, trace_off, &trace_data) == OK) {
20132         if (write(fd, (char *) &trace_data, (unsigned) sizeof (long))
20133             != (unsigned) sizeof (long)) {
20134                 close(fd);
20135                 return;
20136         }
20137         trace_off += sizeof (long);
20138     }
20139
20140     /* Loop through segments and write the segments themselves out. */
20141     for (seg = 0; seg < NR_LOCAL_SEGS; seg++) {
20142         rw_seg(1, fd, slot, seg,
20143                 (phys_bytes) rmp->mp_seg[seg].mem_len << CLICK_SHIFT);
20144     }
20145     close(fd);
20146   }
```

```
++++++++++++++++++++++++++++++++++++++++++++++++++++++++++++++++++++++++++
                            servers/pm/timers.c
++++++++++++++++++++++++++++++++++++++++++++++++++++++++++++++++++++++++++

20200    /* PM watchdog timer management. These functions in this file provide
20201     * a convenient interface to the timers library that manages a list of
20202     * watchdog timers. All details of scheduling an alarm at the CLOCK task
20203     * are hidden behind this interface.
20204     * Only system processes are allowed to set an alarm timer at the kernel.
20205     * Therefore, the PM maintains a local list of timers for user processes
20206     * that requested an alarm signal.
20207     *
20208     * The entry points into this file are:
20209     *    pm_set_timer:      reset and existing or set a new watchdog timer
20210     *    pm_expire_timers:  check for expired timers and run watchdog functions
20211     *    pm_cancel_timer:   remove a time from the list of timers
20212     *
20213     */

20215    #include "pm.h"

20217    #include <timers.h>
20218    #include <minix/syslib.h>
20219    #include <minix/com.h>

20221    PRIVATE timer_t *pm_timers = NULL;

20223    /*===========================================================================*
20224     *                              pm_set_timer                                 *
20225     *===========================================================================*/
20226    PUBLIC void pm_set_timer(timer_t *tp, int ticks, tmr_func_t watchdog, int arg)
20227    {
20228            int r;
20229            clock_t now, prev_time = 0, next_time;

20231            if ((r = getuptime(&now)) != OK)
20232                    panic(__FILE__, "PM couldn't get uptime", NO_NUM);

20234            /* Set timer argument and add timer to the list. */
20235            tmr_arg(tp)->ta_int = arg;
20236            prev_time = tmrs_settimer(&pm_timers,tp,now+ticks,watchdog,&next_time);

20238            /* Reschedule our synchronous alarm if necessary. */
20239            if (! prev_time || prev_time > next_time) {
20240                    if (sys_setalarm(next_time, 1) != OK)
20241                            panic(__FILE__, "PM set timer couldn't set alarm.", NO_NUM);
20242            }

20244            return;
20245    }

20247    /*===========================================================================*
20248     *                              pm_expire_timers                             *
20249     *===========================================================================*/
20250    PUBLIC void pm_expire_timers(clock_t now)
20251    {
20252            clock_t next_time;

20254            /* Check for expired timers and possibly reschedule an alarm. */
```

```
20255                  tmrs_exptimers(&pm_timers, now, &next_time);
20256                  if (next_time > 0) {
20257                          if (sys_setalarm(next_time, 1) != OK)
20258                                  panic(__FILE__, "PM expire timer couldn't set alarm.", NO_NUM);
20259                  }
20260      }

20262      /*===========================================================================*
20263       *                              pm_cancel_timer                              *
20264       *===========================================================================*/
20265      PUBLIC void pm_cancel_timer(timer_t *tp)
20266      {
20267              clock_t next_time, prev_time;
20268              prev_time = tmrs_clrtimer(&pm_timers, tp, &next_time);
20269
20270              /* If the earliest timer has been removed, we have to set the alarm to
20271           * the next timer, or cancel the alarm altogether if the last timer has
20272           * been cancelled (next_time will be 0 then).
20273              */
20274              if (prev_time < next_time || ! next_time) {
20275                      if (sys_setalarm(next_time, 1) != OK)
20276                              panic(__FILE__, "PM expire timer couldn't set alarm.", NO_NUM);
20277              }
20278      }


++++++++++++++++++++++++++++++++++++++++++++++++++++++++++++++++++++++++++++++++
                              servers/pm/time.c
++++++++++++++++++++++++++++++++++++++++++++++++++++++++++++++++++++++++++++++++

20300      /* This file takes care of those system calls that deal with time.
20301       *
20302       * The entry points into this file are
20303       *   do_time:          perform the TIME system call
20304       *   do_stime:         perform the STIME system call
20305       *   do_times:         perform the TIMES system call
20306       */
20307
20308      #include "pm.h"
20309      #include <minix/callnr.h>
20310      #include <minix/com.h>
20311      #include <signal.h>
20312      #include "mproc.h"
20313      #include "param.h"
20314
20315      PRIVATE time_t boottime;
20316
20317      /*===========================================================================*
20318       *                                 do_time                                   *
20319       *===========================================================================*/
20320      PUBLIC int do_time()
20321      {
20322      /* Perform the time(tp) system call. This returns the time in seconds since
20323       * 1.1.1970.  MINIX is an astrophysically naive system that assumes the earth
20324       * rotates at a constant rate and that such things as leap seconds do not
20325       * exist.
20326       */
20327        clock_t uptime;
20328        int s;
20329
```

```
20330      if ( (s=getuptime(&uptime)) != OK)
20331          panic(__FILE__,"do_time couldn't get uptime", s);
20332
20333      mp->mp_reply.reply_time = (time_t) (boottime + (uptime/HZ));
20334      mp->mp_reply.reply_utime = (uptime%HZ)*1000000/HZ;
20335      return(OK);
20336  }

20338  /*===========================================================================*
20339   *                              do_stime                                     *
20340   *===========================================================================*/
20341  PUBLIC int do_stime()
20342  {
20343  /* Perform the stime(tp) system call. Retrieve the system's uptime (ticks
20344   * since boot) and store the time in seconds at system boot in the global
20345   * variable 'boottime'.
20346   */
20347      clock_t uptime;
20348      int s;
20349
20350      if (mp->mp_effuid != SUPER_USER) {
20351          return(EPERM);
20352      }
20353      if ( (s=getuptime(&uptime)) != OK)
20354          panic(__FILE__,"do_stime couldn't get uptime", s);
20355      boottime = (long) m_in.stime - (uptime/HZ);
20356
20357      /* Also inform FS about the new system time. */
20358      tell_fs(STIME, boottime, 0, 0);
20359
20360      return(OK);
20361  }

20363  /*===========================================================================*
20364   *                              do_times                                     *
20365   *===========================================================================*/
20366  PUBLIC int do_times()
20367  {
20368  /* Perform the times(buffer) system call. */
20369      register struct mproc *rmp = mp;
20370      clock_t t[5];
20371      int s;
20372
20373      if (OK != (s=sys_times(who, t)))
20374          panic(__FILE__,"do_times couldn't get times", s);
20375      rmp->mp_reply.reply_t1 = t[0];                    /* user time */
20376      rmp->mp_reply.reply_t2 = t[1];                    /* system time */
20377      rmp->mp_reply.reply_t3 = rmp->mp_child_utime; /* child user time */
20378      rmp->mp_reply.reply_t4 = rmp->mp_child_stime; /* child system time */
20379      rmp->mp_reply.reply_t5 = t[4];                    /* uptime since boot */
20380
20381      return(OK);
20382  }
```

```
++++++++++++++++++++++++++++++++++++++++++++++++++++++++++++++++++++++++++++++
                               servers/pm/getset.c
++++++++++++++++++++++++++++++++++++++++++++++++++++++++++++++++++++++++++++++

20400   /* This file handles the 4 system calls that get and set uids and gids.
20401    * It also handles getpid(), setsid(), and getpgrp().  The code for each
20402    * one is so tiny that it hardly seemed worthwhile to make each a separate
20403    * function.
20404    */
20405
20406   #include "pm.h"
20407   #include <minix/callnr.h>
20408   #include <signal.h>
20409   #include "mproc.h"
20410   #include "param.h"
20411
20412   /*===========================================================================*
20413    *                              do_getset                                    *
20414    *===========================================================================*/
20415   PUBLIC int do_getset()
20416   {
20417   /* Handle GETUID, GETGID, GETPID, GETPGRP, SETUID, SETGID, SETSID.  The four
20418    * GETs and SETSID return their primary results in 'r'.  GETUID, GETGID, and
20419    * GETPID also return secondary results (the effective IDs, or the parent
20420    * process ID) in 'reply_res2', which is returned to the user.
20421    */
20422
20423     register struct mproc *rmp = mp;
20424     register int r;
20425
20426     switch(call_nr) {
20427         case GETUID:
20428                 r = rmp->mp_realuid;
20429                 rmp->mp_reply.reply_res2 = rmp->mp_effuid;
20430                 break;
20431
20432         case GETGID:
20433                 r = rmp->mp_realgid;
20434                 rmp->mp_reply.reply_res2 = rmp->mp_effgid;
20435                 break;
20436
20437         case GETPID:
20438                 r = mproc[who].mp_pid;
20439                 rmp->mp_reply.reply_res2 = mproc[rmp->mp_parent].mp_pid;
20440                 break;
20441
20442         case SETUID:
20443                 if (rmp->mp_realuid != (uid_t) m_in.usr_id &&
20444                                 rmp->mp_effuid != SUPER_USER)
20445                         return(EPERM);
20446                 rmp->mp_realuid = (uid_t) m_in.usr_id;
20447                 rmp->mp_effuid = (uid_t) m_in.usr_id;
20448                 tell_fs(SETUID, who, rmp->mp_realuid, rmp->mp_effuid);
20449                 r = OK;
20450                 break;
20451
20452         case SETGID:
20453                 if (rmp->mp_realgid != (gid_t) m_in.grp_id &&
20454                                 rmp->mp_effuid != SUPER_USER)
```

```
20455                          return(EPERM);
20456                  rmp->mp_realgid = (gid_t) m_in.grp_id;
20457                  rmp->mp_effgid = (gid_t) m_in.grp_id;
20458                  tell_fs(SETGID, who, rmp->mp_realgid, rmp->mp_effgid);
20459                  r = OK;
20460                  break;
20461
20462          case SETSID:
20463                  if (rmp->mp_procgrp == rmp->mp_pid) return(EPERM);
20464                  rmp->mp_procgrp = rmp->mp_pid;
20465                  tell_fs(SETSID, who, 0, 0);
20466                  /* fall through */
20467
20468          case GETPGRP:
20469                  r = rmp->mp_procgrp;
20470                  break;
20471
20472          default:
20473                  r = EINVAL;
20474                  break;
20475      }
20476      return(r);
20477  }
```

```
+++++++++++++++++++++++++++++++++++++++++++++++++++++++++++++++++++++++++++++++
                              servers/pm/misc.c
+++++++++++++++++++++++++++++++++++++++++++++++++++++++++++++++++++++++++++++++
```

```
20500  /* Miscellaneous system calls.                      Author: Kees J. Bot
20501   *                                                          31 Mar 2000
20502   * The entry points into this file are:
20503   *    do_reboot: kill all processes, then reboot system
20504   *    do_svrctl: process manager control
20505   *    do_getsysinfo: request copy of PM data structure  (Jorrit N. Herder)
20506   *    do_getprocnr: lookup process slot number  (Jorrit N. Herder)
20507   *    do_memalloc: allocate a chunk of memory  (Jorrit N. Herder)
20508   *    do_memfree: deallocate a chunk of memory  (Jorrit N. Herder)
20509   *    do_getsetpriority: get/set process priority
20510   */
20511
20512  #include "pm.h"
20513  #include <minix/callnr.h>
20514  #include <signal.h>
20515  #include <sys/svrctl.h>
20516  #include <sys/resource.h>
20517  #include <minix/com.h>
20518  #include <string.h>
20519  #include "mproc.h"
20520  #include "param.h"
20521
20522  /*===========================================================================*
20523   *                              do_allocmem                                   *
20524   *===========================================================================*/
20525  PUBLIC int do_allocmem()
20526  {
20527    vir_clicks mem_clicks;
20528    phys_clicks mem_base;
20529
```

```
20530      mem_clicks = (m_in.memsize + CLICK_SIZE -1 ) >> CLICK_SHIFT;
20531      mem_base = alloc_mem(mem_clicks);
20532      if (mem_base == NO_MEM) return(ENOMEM);
20533      mp->mp_reply.membase =  (phys_bytes) (mem_base << CLICK_SHIFT);
20534      return(OK);
20535  }

20537  /*===========================================================================*
20538   *                            do_freemem                                     *
20539   *===========================================================================*/
20540  PUBLIC int do_freemem()
20541  {
20542      vir_clicks mem_clicks;
20543      phys_clicks mem_base;
20544
20545      mem_clicks = (m_in.memsize + CLICK_SIZE -1 ) >> CLICK_SHIFT;
20546      mem_base = (m_in.membase + CLICK_SIZE -1 ) >> CLICK_SHIFT;
20547      free_mem(mem_base, mem_clicks);
20548      return(OK);
20549  }

20551  /*===========================================================================*
20552   *                            do_getsysinfo                                  *
20553   *===========================================================================*/
20554  PUBLIC int do_getsysinfo()
20555  {
20556      struct mproc *proc_addr;
20557      vir_bytes src_addr, dst_addr;
20558      struct kinfo kinfo;
20559      size_t len;
20560      int s;
20561
20562      switch(m_in.info_what) {
20563      case SI_KINFO:                       /* kernel info is obtained via PM */
20564            sys_getkinfo(&kinfo);
20565            src_addr = (vir_bytes) &kinfo;
20566            len = sizeof(struct kinfo);
20567            break;
20568      case SI_PROC_ADDR:                   /* get address of PM process table */
20569            proc_addr = &mproc[0];
20570            src_addr = (vir_bytes) &proc_addr;
20571            len = sizeof(struct mproc *);
20572            break;
20573      case SI_PROC_TAB:                    /* copy entire process table */
20574            src_addr = (vir_bytes) mproc;
20575            len = sizeof(struct mproc) * NR_PROCS;
20576            break;
20577      default:
20578            return(EINVAL);
20579      }
20580
20581      dst_addr = (vir_bytes) m_in.info_where;
20582      if (OK != (s=sys_datacopy(SELF, src_addr, who, dst_addr, len)))
20583            return(s);
20584      return(OK);
20585  }
```

```
20587   /*===========================================================================*
20588    *                              do_getprocnr                                 *
20589    *===========================================================================*/
20590   PUBLIC int do_getprocnr()
20591   {
20592     register struct mproc *rmp;
20593     static char search_key[PROC_NAME_LEN+1];
20594     int key_len;
20595     int s;
20596
20597     if (m_in.pid >= 0) {                              /* lookup process by pid */
20598           for (rmp = &mproc[0]; rmp < &mproc[NR_PROCS]; rmp++) {
20599                   if ((rmp->mp_flags & IN_USE) && (rmp->mp_pid==m_in.pid)) {
20600                           mp->mp_reply.procnr = (int) (rmp - mproc);
20601                           return(OK);
20602                   }
20603           }
20604           return(ESRCH);
20605     } else if (m_in.namelen > 0) {                   /* lookup process by name */
20606           key_len = MIN(m_in.namelen, PROC_NAME_LEN);
20607           if (OK != (s=sys_datacopy(who, (vir_bytes) m_in.addr,
20608                           SELF, (vir_bytes) search_key, key_len)))
20609                   return(s);
20610           search_key[key_len] = '\0';      /* terminate for safety */
20611           for (rmp = &mproc[0]; rmp < &mproc[NR_PROCS]; rmp++) {
20612                   if ((rmp->mp_flags & IN_USE) &&
20613                           strncmp(rmp->mp_name, search_key, key_len)==0) {
20614                           mp->mp_reply.procnr = (int) (rmp - mproc);
20615                           return(OK);
20616                   }
20617           }
20618           return(ESRCH);
20619     } else {                                      /* return own process number */
20620           mp->mp_reply.procnr = who;
20621     }
20622     return(OK);
20623   }


20625   /*===========================================================================*
20626    *                              do_reboot                                    *
20627    *===========================================================================*/
20628   #define REBOOT_CODE     "delay; boot"
20629   PUBLIC int do_reboot()
20630   {
20631     char monitor_code[32*sizeof(char *)];
20632     int code_len;
20633     int abort_flag;
20634
20635     if (mp->mp_effuid != SUPER_USER) return(EPERM);
20636
20637     switch (m_in.reboot_flag) {
20638     case RBT_HALT:
20639     case RBT_PANIC:
20640     case RBT_RESET:
20641           abort_flag = m_in.reboot_flag;
20642           break;
20643     case RBT_REBOOT:
20644           code_len = strlen(REBOOT_CODE) + 1;
20645           strncpy(monitor_code, REBOOT_CODE, code_len);
20646           abort_flag = RBT_MONITOR;
```

```
20647            break;
20648      case RBT_MONITOR:
20649            code_len = m_in.reboot_strlen + 1;
20650            if (code_len > sizeof(monitor_code)) return(EINVAL);
20651            if (sys_datacopy(who, (vir_bytes) m_in.reboot_code,
20652                    PM_PROC_NR, (vir_bytes) monitor_code,
20653                    (phys_bytes) (code_len)) != OK) return(EFAULT);
20654            if (monitor_code[code_len-1] != 0) return(EINVAL);
20655            abort_flag = RBT_MONITOR;
20656            break;
20657      default:
20658            return(EINVAL);
20659      }
20660
20661      check_sig(-1, SIGKILL);                   /* kill all processes except init */
20662      tell_fs(REBOOT,0,0,0);                    /* tell FS to prepare for shutdown */
20663
20664      /* Ask the kernel to abort. All system services, including the PM, will
20665       * get a HARD_STOP notification. Await the notification in the main loop.
20666       */
20667      sys_abort(abort_flag, PM_PROC_NR, monitor_code, code_len);
20668      return(SUSPEND);                          /* don't reply to killed process */
20669 }

20671 /*===========================================================================*
20672  *                            do_getsetpriority                              *
20673  *===========================================================================*/
20674 PUBLIC int do_getsetpriority()
20675 {
20676      int arg_which, arg_who, arg_pri;
20677      int rmp_nr;
20678      struct mproc *rmp;
20679
20680      arg_which = m_in.m1_i1;
20681      arg_who = m_in.m1_i2;
20682      arg_pri = m_in.m1_i3;     /* for SETPRIORITY */
20683
20684      /* Code common to GETPRIORITY and SETPRIORITY. */
20685
20686      /* Only support PRIO_PROCESS for now. */
20687      if (arg_which != PRIO_PROCESS)
20688              return(EINVAL);
20689
20690      if (arg_who == 0)
20691              rmp_nr = who;
20692      else
20693              if ((rmp_nr = proc_from_pid(arg_who)) < 0)
20694                      return(ESRCH);
20695
20696      rmp = &mproc[rmp_nr];
20697
20698      if (mp->mp_effuid != SUPER_USER &&
20699          mp->mp_effuid != rmp->mp_effuid && mp->mp_effuid != rmp->mp_realuid)
20700              return EPERM;
20701
20702      /* If GET, that's it. */
20703      if (call_nr == GETPRIORITY) {
20704              return(rmp->mp_nice - PRIO_MIN);
20705      }
20706
```

```
20707                    /* Only root is allowed to reduce the nice level. */
20708                    if (rmp->mp_nice > arg_pri && mp->mp_effuid != SUPER_USER)
20709                            return(EACCES);
20710
20711                    /* We're SET, and it's allowed. Do it and tell kernel. */
20712                    rmp->mp_nice = arg_pri;
20713                    return sys_nice(rmp_nr, arg_pri);
20714    }

20716    /*===========================================================================*
20717     *                                do_svrctl                                   *
20718     *===========================================================================*/
20719    PUBLIC int do_svrctl()
20720    {
20721      int s, req;
20722      vir_bytes ptr;
20723    #define MAX_LOCAL_PARAMS 2
20724      static struct {
20725              char name[30];
20726              char value[30];
20727      } local_param_overrides[MAX_LOCAL_PARAMS];
20728      static int local_params = 0;
20729
20730      req = m_in.svrctl_req;
20731      ptr = (vir_bytes) m_in.svrctl_argp;
20732
20733      /* Is the request indeed for the MM? */
20734      if (((req >> 8) & 0xFF) != 'M') return(EINVAL);
20735
20736      /* Control operations local to the PM. */
20737      switch(req) {
20738      case MMSETPARAM:
20739      case MMGETPARAM: {
20740          struct sysgetenv sysgetenv;
20741          char search_key[64];
20742          char *val_start;
20743          size_t val_len;
20744          size_t copy_len;
20745
20746          /* Copy sysgetenv structure to PM. */
20747          if (sys_datacopy(who, ptr, SELF, (vir_bytes) &sysgetenv,
20748                  sizeof(sysgetenv)) != OK) return(EFAULT);
20749
20750          /* Set a param override? */
20751          if (req == MMSETPARAM) {
20752            if (local_params >= MAX_LOCAL_PARAMS) return ENOSPC;
20753            if (sysgetenv.keylen <= 0
20754            || sysgetenv.keylen >=
20755                    sizeof(local_param_overrides[local_params].name)
20756            || sysgetenv.vallen <= 0
20757            || sysgetenv.vallen >=
20758                    sizeof(local_param_overrides[local_params].value))
20759                    return EINVAL;
20760
20761              if ((s = sys_datacopy(who, (vir_bytes) sysgetenv.key,
20762                SELF, (vir_bytes) local_param_overrides[local_params].name,
20763                  sysgetenv.keylen)) != OK)
20764                    return s;
20765              if ((s = sys_datacopy(who, (vir_bytes) sysgetenv.val,
20766                SELF, (vir_bytes) local_param_overrides[local_params].value,
```

```
20767                              sysgetenv.keylen)) != OK)
20768                          return s;
20769                      local_param_overrides[local_params].name[sysgetenv.keylen] = '\0';
20770                      local_param_overrides[local_params].value[sysgetenv.vallen] = '\0';
20771
20772                  local_params++;
20773
20774              return OK;
20775          }
20776
20777          if (sysgetenv.keylen == 0) {        /* copy all parameters */
20778              val_start = monitor_params;
20779              val_len = sizeof(monitor_params);
20780          }
20781          else {                              /* lookup value for key */
20782              int p;
20783              /* Try to get a copy of the requested key. */
20784              if (sysgetenv.keylen > sizeof(search_key)) return(EINVAL);
20785              if ((s = sys_datacopy(who, (vir_bytes) sysgetenv.key,
20786                      SELF, (vir_bytes) search_key, sysgetenv.keylen)) != OK)
20787                  return(s);
20788
20789              /* Make sure key is null-terminated and lookup value.
20790               * First check local overrides.
20791               */
20792              search_key[sysgetenv.keylen-1]= '\0';
20793              for(p = 0; p < local_params; p++) {
20794                      if (!strcmp(search_key, local_param_overrides[p].name)) {
20795                              val_start = local_param_overrides[p].value;
20796                              break;
20797                      }
20798              }
20799              if (p >= local_params && (val_start = find_param(search_key)) == NULL)
20800                      return(ESRCH);
20801              val_len = strlen(val_start) + 1;
20802          }
20803
20804          /* See if it fits in the client's buffer. */
20805          if (val_len > sysgetenv.vallen)
20806            return E2BIG;
20807
20808          /* Value found, make the actual copy (as far as possible). */
20809          copy_len = MIN(val_len, sysgetenv.vallen);
20810          if ((s=sys_datacopy(SELF, (vir_bytes) val_start,
20811              who, (vir_bytes) sysgetenv.val, copy_len)) != OK)
20812              return(s);
20813
20814          return OK;
20815      }
20816    default:
20817          return(EINVAL);
20818      }
20819  }
```

```
++++++++++++++++++++++++++++++++++++++++++++++++++++++++++++++++++++++++++++
                             servers/fs/fs.h
++++++++++++++++++++++++++++++++++++++++++++++++++++++++++++++++++++++++++++

20900   /* This is the master header for fs.  It includes some other files
20901    * and defines the principal constants.
20902    */
20903   #define _POSIX_SOURCE      1    /* tell headers to include POSIX stuff */
20904   #define _MINIX             1    /* tell headers to include MINIX stuff */
20905   #define _SYSTEM            1    /* tell headers that this is the kernel */
20906
20907   #define VERBOSE            0    /* show messages during initialization? */
20908
20909   /* The following are so basic, all the *.c files get them automatically. */
20910   #include <minix/config.h>       /* MUST be first */
20911   #include <ansi.h>               /* MUST be second */
20912   #include <sys/types.h>
20913   #include <minix/const.h>
20914   #include <minix/type.h>
20915   #include <minix/dmap.h>
20916
20917   #include <limits.h>
20918   #include <errno.h>
20919
20920   #include <minix/syslib.h>
20921   #include <minix/sysutil.h>
20922
20923   #include "const.h"
20924   #include "type.h"
20925   #include "proto.h"
20926   #include "glo.h"



++++++++++++++++++++++++++++++++++++++++++++++++++++++++++++++++++++++++++++
                             servers/fs/const.h
++++++++++++++++++++++++++++++++++++++++++++++++++++++++++++++++++++++++++++

21000   /* Tables sizes */
21001   #define V1_NR_DZONES       7    /* # direct zone numbers in a V1 inode */
21002   #define V1_NR_TZONES       9    /* total # zone numbers in a V1 inode */
21003   #define V2_NR_DZONES       7    /* # direct zone numbers in a V2 inode */
21004   #define V2_NR_TZONES      10    /* total # zone numbers in a V2 inode */
21005
21006   #define NR_FILPS         128    /* # slots in filp table */
21007   #define NR_INODES         64    /* # slots in "in core" inode table */
21008   #define NR_SUPERS          8    /* # slots in super block table */
21009   #define NR_LOCKS           8    /* # slots in the file locking table */
21010
21011   /* The type of sizeof may be (unsigned) long.  Use the following macro for
21012    * taking the sizes of small objects so that there are no surprises like
21013    * (small) long constants being passed to routines expecting an int.
21014    */
21015   #define usizeof(t) ((unsigned) sizeof(t))
21016
21017   /* File system types. */
21018   #define SUPER_MAGIC   0x137F     /* magic number contained in super-block */
21019   #define SUPER_REV     0x7F13     /* magic # when 68000 disk read on PC or vv */
```

```
21020  #define SUPER_V2       0x2468    /* magic # for V2 file systems */
21021  #define SUPER_V2_REV   0x6824    /* V2 magic written on PC, read on 68K or vv */
21022  #define SUPER_V3       0x4d5a    /* magic # for V3 file systems */
21023
21024  #define V1                   1   /* version number of V1 file systems */
21025  #define V2                   2   /* version number of V2 file systems */
21026  #define V3                   3   /* version number of V3 file systems */
21027
21028  /* Miscellaneous constants */
21029  #define SU_UID     ((uid_t) 0)    /* super_user's uid_t */
21030  #define SYS_UID    ((uid_t) 0)    /* uid_t for processes MM and INIT */
21031  #define SYS_GID    ((gid_t) 0)    /* gid_t for processes MM and INIT */
21032  #define NORMAL            0       /* forces get_block to do disk read */
21033  #define NO_READ           1       /* prevents get_block from doing disk read */
21034  #define PREFETCH          2       /* tells get_block not to read or mark dev */
21035
21036  #define XPIPE    (-NR_TASKS-1)    /* used in fp_task when susp'd on pipe */
21037  #define XLOCK    (-NR_TASKS-2)    /* used in fp_task when susp'd on lock */
21038  #define XPOPEN   (-NR_TASKS-3)    /* used in fp_task when susp'd on pipe open */
21039  #define XSELECT  (-NR_TASKS-4)    /* used in fp_task when susp'd on select */
21040
21041  #define NO_BIT     ((bit_t) 0)    /* returned by alloc_bit() to signal failure */
21042
21043  #define DUP_MASK          0100    /* mask to distinguish dup2 from dup */
21044
21045  #define LOOK_UP           0 /* tells search_dir to lookup string */
21046  #define ENTER             1 /* tells search_dir to make dir entry */
21047  #define DELETE            2 /* tells search_dir to delete entry */
21048  #define IS_EMPTY          3 /* tells search_dir to ret. OK or ENOTEMPTY */
21049
21050  #define CLEAN             0       /* disk and memory copies identical */
21051  #define DIRTY             1       /* disk and memory copies differ */
21052  #define ATIME           002       /* set if atime field needs updating */
21053  #define CTIME           004       /* set if ctime field needs updating */
21054  #define MTIME           010       /* set if mtime field needs updating */
21055
21056  #define BYTE_SWAP         0       /* tells conv2/conv4 to swap bytes */
21057
21058  #define END_OF_FILE    (-104)     /* eof detected */
21059
21060  #define ROOT_INODE        1               /* inode number for root directory */
21061  #define BOOT_BLOCK  ((block_t) 0)         /* block number of boot block */
21062  #define SUPER_BLOCK_BYTES (1024)          /* bytes offset */
21063  #define START_BLOCK    2                  /* first block of FS (not counting SB) */
21064
21065  #define DIR_ENTRY_SIZE       usizeof (struct direct)  /* # bytes/dir entry   */
21066  #define NR_DIR_ENTRIES(b)    ((b)/DIR_ENTRY_SIZE)  /* # dir entries/blk   */
21067  #define SUPER_SIZE     usizeof (struct super_block)  /* super_block size    */
21068  #define PIPE_SIZE(b)         (V1_NR_DZONES*(b))  /* pipe size in bytes   */
21069
21070  #define FS_BITMAP_CHUNKS(b) ((b)/usizeof (bitchunk_t))/* # map chunks/blk   */
21071  #define FS_BITCHUNK_BITS          (usizeof(bitchunk_t) * CHAR_BIT)
21072  #define FS_BITS_PER_BLOCK(b)   (FS_BITMAP_CHUNKS(b) * FS_BITCHUNK_BITS)
21073
21074  /* Derived sizes pertaining to the V1 file system. */
21075  #define V1_ZONE_NUM_SIZE            usizeof (zone1_t)  /* # bytes in V1 zone  */
21076  #define V1_INODE_SIZE               usizeof (d1_inode)  /* bytes in V1 dsk ino */
21077
21078  /* # zones/indir block */
21079  #define V1_INDIRECTS (STATIC_BLOCK_SIZE/V1_ZONE_NUM_SIZE)
```

```
21080
21081    /* # V1 dsk inodes/blk */
21082    #define V1_INODES_PER_BLOCK (STATIC_BLOCK_SIZE/V1_INODE_SIZE)
21083
21084    /* Derived sizes pertaining to the V2 file system. */
21085    #define V2_ZONE_NUM_SIZE          usizeof (zone_t)  /* # bytes in V2 zone  */
21086    #define V2_INODE_SIZE             usizeof (d2_inode)  /* bytes in V2 dsk ino */
21087    #define V2_INDIRECTS(b)   ((b)/V2_ZONE_NUM_SIZE)  /* # zones/indir block */
21088    #define V2_INODES_PER_BLOCK(b) ((b)/V2_INODE_SIZE)/* # V2 dsk inodes/blk */
```

```
+++++++++++++++++++++++++++++++++++++++++++++++++++++++++++++++++++++++++++++
                         servers/fs/type.h
+++++++++++++++++++++++++++++++++++++++++++++++++++++++++++++++++++++++++++++
```

```
21100    /* Declaration of the V1 inode as it is on the disk (not in core). */
21101    typedef struct {                  /* V1.x disk inode */
21102      mode_t d1_mode;                 /* file type, protection, etc. */
21103      uid_t d1_uid;                   /* user id of the file's owner */
21104      off_t d1_size;                  /* current file size in bytes */
21105      time_t d1_mtime;                /* when was file data last changed */
21106      u8_t d1_gid;                    /* group number */
21107      u8_t d1_nlinks;                 /* how many links to this file */
21108      u16_t d1_zone[V1_NR_TZONES];    /* block nums for direct, ind, and dbl ind */
21109    } d1_inode;
21110
21111    /* Declaration of the V2 inode as it is on the disk (not in core). */
21112    typedef struct {                  /* V2.x disk inode */
21113      mode_t d2_mode;                 /* file type, protection, etc. */
21114      u16_t d2_nlinks;                /* how many links to this file. HACK! */
21115      uid_t d2_uid;                   /* user id of the file's owner. */
21116      u16_t d2_gid;                   /* group number HACK! */
21117      off_t d2_size;                  /* current file size in bytes */
21118      time_t d2_atime;                /* when was file data last accessed */
21119      time_t d2_mtime;                /* when was file data last changed */
21120      time_t d2_ctime;                /* when was inode data last changed */
21121      zone_t d2_zone[V2_NR_TZONES]; /* block nums for direct, ind, and dbl ind */
21122    } d2_inode;
```

```
+++++++++++++++++++++++++++++++++++++++++++++++++++++++++++++++++++++++++++++
                         servers/fs/proto.h
+++++++++++++++++++++++++++++++++++++++++++++++++++++++++++++++++++++++++++++
```

```
21200    /* Function prototypes. */
21201
21202    #include "timers.h"
21203
21204    /* Structs used in prototypes must be declared as such first. */
21205    struct buf;
21206    struct filp;
21207    struct inode;
21208    struct super_block;
21209
21210    /* cache.c */
21211    _PROTOTYPE( zone_t alloc_zone, (Dev_t dev, zone_t z)              );
21212    _PROTOTYPE( void flushall, (Dev_t dev)                           );
21213    _PROTOTYPE( void free_zone, (Dev_t dev, zone_t numb)             );
21214    _PROTOTYPE( struct buf *get_block, (Dev_t dev, block_t block,int only_search));
```

```
21215   _PROTOTYPE( void invalidate, (Dev_t device)                           );
21216   _PROTOTYPE( void put_block, (struct buf *bp, int block_type)          );
21217   _PROTOTYPE( void rw_block, (struct buf *bp, int rw_flag)              );
21218   _PROTOTYPE( void rw_scattered, (Dev_t dev,
21219                           struct buf **bufq, int bufqsize, int rw_flag)  );
21220
21221   /* device.c */
21222   _PROTOTYPE( int dev_open, (Dev_t dev, int proc, int flags)            );
21223   _PROTOTYPE( void dev_close, (Dev_t dev)                               );
21224   _PROTOTYPE( int dev_io, (int op, Dev_t dev, int proc, void *buf,
21225                           off_t pos, int bytes, int flags)              );
21226   _PROTOTYPE( int gen_opcl, (int op, Dev_t dev, int proc, int flags)    );
21227   _PROTOTYPE( void gen_io, (int task_nr, message *mess_ptr)             );
21228   _PROTOTYPE( int no_dev, (int op, Dev_t dev, int proc, int flags)      );
21229   _PROTOTYPE( int tty_opcl, (int op, Dev_t dev, int proc, int flags)    );
21230   _PROTOTYPE( int ctty_opcl, (int op, Dev_t dev, int proc, int flags)   );
21231   _PROTOTYPE( int clone_opcl, (int op, Dev_t dev, int proc, int flags)  );
21232   _PROTOTYPE( void ctty_io, (int task_nr, message *mess_ptr)            );
21233   _PROTOTYPE( int do_ioctl, (void)                                      );
21234   _PROTOTYPE( int do_setsid, (void)                                     );
21235   _PROTOTYPE( void dev_status, (message *)                              );
21236
21237   /* dmp.c */
21238   _PROTOTYPE( int do_fkey_pressed, (void)                               );
21239
21240   /* dmap.c */
21241   _PROTOTYPE( int do_devctl, (void)                                     );
21242   _PROTOTYPE( void build_dmap, (void)                                   );
21243   _PROTOTYPE( int map_driver, (int major, int proc_nr, int dev_style)  );
21244
21245   /* filedes.c */
21246   _PROTOTYPE( struct filp *find_filp, (struct inode *rip, mode_t bits)  );
21247   _PROTOTYPE( int get_fd, (int start, mode_t bits, int *k, struct filp **fpt) );
21248   _PROTOTYPE( struct filp *get_filp, (int fild)                         );
21249
21250   /* inode.c */
21251   _PROTOTYPE( struct inode *alloc_inode, (dev_t dev, mode_t bits)       );
21252   _PROTOTYPE( void dup_inode, (struct inode *ip)                        );
21253   _PROTOTYPE( void free_inode, (Dev_t dev, Ino_t numb)                  );
21254   _PROTOTYPE( struct inode *get_inode, (Dev_t dev, int numb)            );
21255   _PROTOTYPE( void put_inode, (struct inode *rip)                       );
21256   _PROTOTYPE( void update_times, (struct inode *rip)                    );
21257   _PROTOTYPE( void rw_inode, (struct inode *rip, int rw_flag)           );
21258   _PROTOTYPE( void wipe_inode, (struct inode *rip)                      );
21259
21260   /* link.c */
21261   _PROTOTYPE( int do_link, (void)                                       );
21262   _PROTOTYPE( int do_unlink, (void)                                     );
21263   _PROTOTYPE( int do_rename, (void)                                     );
21264   _PROTOTYPE( void truncate, (struct inode *rip)                        );
21265
21266   /* lock.c */
21267   _PROTOTYPE( int lock_op, (struct filp *f, int req)                    );
21268   _PROTOTYPE( void lock_revive, (void)                                  );
21269
21270   /* main.c */
21271   _PROTOTYPE( int main, (void)                                          );
21272   _PROTOTYPE( void reply, (int whom, int result)                        );
21273
21274   /* misc.c */
```

```
21275   _PROTOTYPE( int do_dup, (void)                                        );
21276   _PROTOTYPE( int do_exit, (void)                                       );
21277   _PROTOTYPE( int do_fcntl, (void)                                      );
21278   _PROTOTYPE( int do_fork, (void)                                       );
21279   _PROTOTYPE( int do_exec, (void)                                       );
21280   _PROTOTYPE( int do_revive, (void)                                     );
21281   _PROTOTYPE( int do_set, (void)                                        );
21282   _PROTOTYPE( int do_sync, (void)                                       );
21283   _PROTOTYPE( int do_fsync, (void)                                      );
21284   _PROTOTYPE( int do_reboot, (void)                                     );
21285   _PROTOTYPE( int do_svrctl, (void)                                     );
21286   _PROTOTYPE( int do_getsysinfo, (void)                                 );
21287
21288   /* mount.c */
21289   _PROTOTYPE( int do_mount, (void)                                      );
21290   _PROTOTYPE( int do_umount, (void)                                     );
21291   _PROTOTYPE( int unmount, (Dev_t dev)                                  );
21292
21293   /* open.c */
21294   _PROTOTYPE( int do_close, (void)                                      );
21295   _PROTOTYPE( int do_creat, (void)                                      );
21296   _PROTOTYPE( int do_lseek, (void)                                      );
21297   _PROTOTYPE( int do_mknod, (void)                                      );
21298   _PROTOTYPE( int do_mkdir, (void)                                      );
21299   _PROTOTYPE( int do_open, (void)                                       );
21300
21301   /* path.c */
21302   _PROTOTYPE( struct inode *advance,(struct inode *dirp, char string[NAME_MAX]));
21303   _PROTOTYPE( int search_dir, (struct inode *ldir_ptr,
21304                       char string [NAME_MAX], ino_t *numb, int flag)  );
21305   _PROTOTYPE( struct inode *eat_path, (char *path)                     );
21306   _PROTOTYPE( struct inode *last_dir, (char *path, char string [NAME_MAX]));
21307
21308   /* pipe.c */
21309   _PROTOTYPE( int do_pipe, (void)                                       );
21310   _PROTOTYPE( int do_unpause, (void)                                    );
21311   _PROTOTYPE( int pipe_check, (struct inode *rip, int rw_flag,
21312           int oflags, int bytes, off_t position, int *canwrite, int notouch));
21313   _PROTOTYPE( void release, (struct inode *ip, int call_nr, int count)  );
21314   _PROTOTYPE( void revive, (int proc_nr, int bytes)                     );
21315   _PROTOTYPE( void suspend, (int task)                                  );
21316   _PROTOTYPE( int select_request_pipe, (struct filp *f, int *ops, int bl) );
21317   _PROTOTYPE( int select_cancel_pipe, (struct filp *f)                  );
21318   _PROTOTYPE( int select_match_pipe, (struct filp *f)                   );
21319
21320   /* protect.c */
21321   _PROTOTYPE( int do_access, (void)                                     );
21322   _PROTOTYPE( int do_chmod, (void)                                      );
21323   _PROTOTYPE( int do_chown, (void)                                      );
21324   _PROTOTYPE( int do_umask, (void)                                      );
21325   _PROTOTYPE( int forbidden, (struct inode *rip, mode_t access_desired) );
21326   _PROTOTYPE( int read_only, (struct inode *ip)                         );
21327
21328   /* read.c */
21329   _PROTOTYPE( int do_read, (void)                                       );
21330   _PROTOTYPE( struct buf *rahead, (struct inode *rip, block_t baseblock,
21331                       off_t position, unsigned bytes_ahead)            );
21332   _PROTOTYPE( void read_ahead, (void)                                   );
21333   _PROTOTYPE( block_t read_map, (struct inode *rip, off_t position)     );
21334   _PROTOTYPE( int read_write, (int rw_flag)                             );
```

```
21335 _PROTOTYPE( zone_t rd_indir, (struct buf *bp, int index)              );
21336
21337 /* stadir.c */
21338 _PROTOTYPE( int do_chdir, (void)                                       );
21339 _PROTOTYPE( int do_fchdir, (void)                                      );
21340 _PROTOTYPE( int do_chroot, (void)                                      );
21341 _PROTOTYPE( int do_fstat, (void)                                       );
21342 _PROTOTYPE( int do_stat, (void)                                        );
21343 _PROTOTYPE( int do_fstatfs, (void)                                     );
21344
21345 /* super.c */
21346 _PROTOTYPE( bit_t alloc_bit, (struct super_block *sp, int map, bit_t origin));
21347 _PROTOTYPE( void free_bit, (struct super_block *sp, int map,
21348                                            bit_t bit_returned)         );
21349 _PROTOTYPE( struct super_block *get_super, (Dev_t dev)                 );
21350 _PROTOTYPE( int mounted, (struct inode *rip)                           );
21351 _PROTOTYPE( int read_super, (struct super_block *sp)                   );
21352 _PROTOTYPE( int get_block_size, (dev_t dev)                            );
21353
21354 /* time.c */
21355 _PROTOTYPE( int do_stime, (void)                                       );
21356 _PROTOTYPE( int do_utime, (void)                                       );
21357
21358 /* utility.c */
21359 _PROTOTYPE( time_t clock_time, (void)                                  );
21360 _PROTOTYPE( unsigned conv2, (int norm, int w)                          );
21361 _PROTOTYPE( long conv4, (int norm, long x)                             );
21362 _PROTOTYPE( int fetch_name, (char *path, int len, int flag)            );
21363 _PROTOTYPE( int no_sys, (void)                                         );
21364 _PROTOTYPE( void panic, (char *who, char *mess, int num)               );
21365
21366 /* write.c */
21367 _PROTOTYPE( void clear_zone, (struct inode *rip, off_t pos, int flag)  );
21368 _PROTOTYPE( int do_write, (void)                                       );
21369 _PROTOTYPE( struct buf *new_block, (struct inode *rip, off_t position) );
21370 _PROTOTYPE( void zero_block, (struct buf *bp)                          );
21371
21372 /* select.c */
21373 _PROTOTYPE( int do_select, (void)                                      );
21374 _PROTOTYPE( int select_callback, (struct filp *, int ops)              );
21375 _PROTOTYPE( void select_forget, (int fproc)                            );
21376 _PROTOTYPE( void select_timeout_check, (timer_t *)                     );
21377 _PROTOTYPE( void init_select, (void)                                   );
21378 _PROTOTYPE( int select_notified, (int major, int minor, int ops)       );
21379
21380 /* timers.c */
21381 _PROTOTYPE( void fs_set_timer, (timer_t *tp, int delta, tmr_func_t watchdog, int arg));
21382 _PROTOTYPE( void fs_expire_timers, (clock_t now)                       );
21383 _PROTOTYPE( void fs_cancel_timer, (timer_t *tp)                        );
21384 _PROTOTYPE( void fs_init_timer, (timer_t *tp)                          );
21385
21386 /* cdprobe.c */
21387 _PROTOTYPE( int cdprobe, (void)                                        );
```

```
++++++++++++++++++++++++++++++++++++++++++++++++++++++++++++++++++++++++++++
                            servers/fs/glo.h
++++++++++++++++++++++++++++++++++++++++++++++++++++++++++++++++++++++++++++

21400   /* EXTERN should be extern except for the table file */
21401   #ifdef _TABLE
21402   #undef EXTERN
21403   #define EXTERN
21404   #endif
21405
21406   /* File System global variables */
21407   EXTERN struct fproc *fp;          /* pointer to caller's fproc struct */
21408   EXTERN int super_user;            /* 1 if caller is super_user, else 0 */
21409   EXTERN int susp_count;            /* number of procs suspended on pipe */
21410   EXTERN int nr_locks;              /* number of locks currently in place */
21411   EXTERN int reviving;              /* number of pipe processes to be revived */
21412   EXTERN off_t rdahedpos;           /* position to read ahead */
21413   EXTERN struct inode *rdahed_inode;     /* pointer to inode to read ahead */
21414   EXTERN Dev_t root_dev;            /* device number of the root device */
21415   EXTERN time_t boottime;           /* time in seconds at system boot */
21416
21417   /* The parameters of the call are kept here. */
21418   EXTERN message m_in;              /* the input message itself */
21419   EXTERN message m_out;             /* the output message used for reply */
21420   EXTERN int who;                   /* caller's proc number */
21421   EXTERN int call_nr;               /* system call number */
21422   EXTERN char user_path[PATH_MAX];/* storage for user path name */
21423
21424   /* The following variables are used for returning results to the caller. */
21425   EXTERN int err_code;              /* temporary storage for error number */
21426   EXTERN int rdwt_err;              /* status of last disk i/o request */
21427
21428   /* Data initialized elsewhere. */
21429   extern _PROTOTYPE (int (*call_vec[]), (void) ); /* sys call table */
21430   extern char dot1[2];     /* dot1 (&dot1[0]) and dot2 (&dot2[0]) have a special */
21431   extern char dot2[3];     /* meaning to search_dir: no access permission check. */



++++++++++++++++++++++++++++++++++++++++++++++++++++++++++++++++++++++++++++
                            servers/fs/fproc.h
++++++++++++++++++++++++++++++++++++++++++++++++++++++++++++++++++++++++++++

21500   /* This is the per-process information.  A slot is reserved for each potential
21501    * process. Thus NR_PROCS must be the same as in the kernel. It is not
21502    * possible or even necessary to tell when a slot is free here.
21503    */
21504   EXTERN struct fproc {
21505     mode_t fp_umask;               /* mask set by umask system call */
21506     struct inode *fp_workdir;      /* pointer to working directory's inode */
21507     struct inode *fp_rootdir;      /* pointer to current root dir (see chroot) */
21508     struct filp *fp_filp[OPEN_MAX];/* the file descriptor table */
21509     uid_t fp_realuid;              /* real user id */
21510     uid_t fp_effuid;               /* effective user id */
21511     gid_t fp_realgid;              /* real group id */
21512     gid_t fp_effgid;               /* effective group id */
21513     dev_t fp_tty;                  /* major/minor of controlling tty */
21514     int fp_fd;                     /* place to save fd if rd/wr can't finish */
```

```
21515     char *fp_buffer;                  /* place to save buffer if rd/wr can't finish*/
21516     int  fp_nbytes;                   /* place to save bytes if rd/wr can't finish */
21517     int  fp_cum_io_partial;           /* partial byte count if rd/wr can't finish */
21518     char fp_suspended;                /* set to indicate process hanging */
21519     char fp_revived;                  /* set to indicate process being revived */
21520     char fp_task;                     /* which task is proc suspended on */
21521     char fp_sesldr;                   /* true if proc is a session leader */
21522     pid_t fp_pid;                     /* process id */
21523     long fp_cloexec;                  /* bit map for POSIX Table 6-2 FD_CLOEXEC */
21524 } fproc[NR_PROCS];
21525
21526 /* Field values. */
21527 #define NOT_SUSPENDED      0      /* process is not suspended on pipe or task */
21528 #define SUSPENDED          1      /* process is suspended on pipe or task */
21529 #define NOT_REVIVING       0      /* process is not being revived */
21530 #define REVIVING           1      /* process is being revived from suspension */
21531 #define PID_FREE           0      /* process slot free */
21532
21533 /* Check is process number is acceptable - includes system processes. */
21534 #define isokprocnr(n)   ((unsigned)((n)+NR_TASKS) < NR_PROCS + NR_TASKS)
21535
```

```
++++++++++++++++++++++++++++++++++++++++++++++++++++++++++++++++++++++++++++++++++
                              servers/fs/buf.h
++++++++++++++++++++++++++++++++++++++++++++++++++++++++++++++++++++++++++++++++++
```

```
21600 /* Buffer (block) cache.  To acquire a block, a routine calls get_block(),
21601  * telling which block it wants.  The block is then regarded as "in use"
21602  * and has its 'b_count' field incremented.  All the blocks that are not
21603  * in use are chained together in an LRU list, with 'front' pointing
21604  * to the least recently used block, and 'rear' to the most recently used
21605  * block.  A reverse chain, using the field b_prev is also maintained.
21606  * Usage for LRU is measured by the time the put_block() is done.  The second
21607  * parameter to put_block() can violate the LRU order and put a block on the
21608  * front of the list, if it will probably not be needed soon.  If a block
21609  * is modified, the modifying routine must set b_dirt to DIRTY, so the block
21610  * will eventually be rewritten to the disk.
21611  */
21612
21613 #include <sys/dir.h>                    /* need struct direct */
21614 #include <dirent.h>
21615
21616 EXTERN struct buf {
21617   /* Data portion of the buffer. */
21618   union {
21619     char b__data[MAX_BLOCK_SIZE];                    /* ordinary user data */
21620 /* directory block */
21621     struct direct b__dir[NR_DIR_ENTRIES(MAX_BLOCK_SIZE)];
21622 /* V1 indirect block */
21623     zone1_t b__v1_ind[V1_INDIRECTS];
21624 /* V2 indirect block */
21625     zone_t  b__v2_ind[V2_INDIRECTS(MAX_BLOCK_SIZE)];
21626 /* V1 inode block */
21627     d1_inode b__v1_ino[V1_INODES_PER_BLOCK];
21628 /* V2 inode block */
21629     d2_inode b__v2_ino[V2_INODES_PER_BLOCK(MAX_BLOCK_SIZE)];
```

```
21630    /* bit map block */
21631        bitchunk_t b__bitmap[FS_BITMAP_CHUNKS(MAX_BLOCK_SIZE)];
21632      } b;
21633
21634    /* Header portion of the buffer. */
21635    struct buf *b_next;           /* used to link all free bufs in a chain */
21636    struct buf *b_prev;           /* used to link all free bufs the other way */
21637    struct buf *b_hash;           /* used to link bufs on hash chains */
21638    block_t b_blocknr;            /* block number of its (minor) device */
21639    dev_t b_dev;                  /* major | minor device where block resides */
21640    char b_dirt;                  /* CLEAN or DIRTY */
21641    char b_count;                 /* number of users of this buffer */
21642    } buf[NR_BUFS];
21643
21644    /* A block is free if b_dev == NO_DEV. */
21645
21646    #define NIL_BUF ((struct buf *) 0)        /* indicates absence of a buffer */
21647
21648    /* These defs make it possible to use to bp->b_data instead of bp->b.b__data */
21649    #define b_data     b.b__data
21650    #define b_dir      b.b__dir
21651    #define b_v1_ind   b.b__v1_ind
21652    #define b_v2_ind   b.b__v2_ind
21653    #define b_v1_ino   b.b__v1_ino
21654    #define b_v2_ino   b.b__v2_ino
21655    #define b_bitmap   b.b__bitmap
21656
21657    EXTERN struct buf *buf_hash[NR_BUF_HASH];        /* the buffer hash table */
21658
21659    EXTERN struct buf *front;       /* points to least recently used free block */
21660    EXTERN struct buf *rear;        /* points to most recently used free block */
21661    EXTERN int bufs_in_use;         /* # bufs currently in use (not on free list)*/
21662
21663    /* When a block is released, the type of usage is passed to put_block(). */
21664    #define WRITE_IMMED   0100 /* block should be written to disk now */
21665    #define ONE_SHOT      0200 /* set if block not likely to be needed soon */
21666
21667    #define INODE_BLOCK        0                        /* inode block */
21668    #define DIRECTORY_BLOCK    1                        /* directory block */
21669    #define INDIRECT_BLOCK     2                        /* pointer block */
21670    #define MAP_BLOCK          3                        /* bit map */
21671    #define FULL_DATA_BLOCK    5                        /* data, fully used */
21672    #define PARTIAL_DATA_BLOCK 6                        /* data, partly used*/
21673
21674    #define HASH_MASK (NR_BUF_HASH - 1)      /* mask for hashing block numbers */
```

++
                          servers/fs/file.h
++

```
21700    /* This is the filp table.  It is an intermediary between file descriptors and
21701     * inodes.  A slot is free if filp_count == 0.
21702     */
21703
21704    EXTERN struct filp {
21705      mode_t filp_mode;             /* RW bits, telling how file is opened */
21706      int filp_flags;               /* flags from open and fcntl */
21707      int filp_count;               /* how many file descriptors share this slot?*/
21708      struct inode *filp_ino;       /* pointer to the inode */
21709      off_t filp_pos;               /* file position */
```

```
21710
21711        /* the following fields are for select() and are owned by the generic
21712         * select() code (i.e., fd-type-specific select() code can't touch these).
21713         */
21714        int filp_selectors;              /* select()ing processes blocking on this fd */
21715        int filp_select_ops;             /* interested in these SEL_* operations */
21716
21717        /* following are for fd-type-specific select() */
21718        int filp_pipe_select_ops;
21719   } filp[NR_FILPS];
21720
21721   #define FILP_CLOSED      0        /* filp_mode: associated device closed */
21722
21723   #define NIL_FILP (struct filp *) 0        /* indicates absence of a filp slot */
```

```
++++++++++++++++++++++++++++++++++++++++++++++++++++++++++++++++++++++++++++++
                                servers/fs/lock.h
++++++++++++++++++++++++++++++++++++++++++++++++++++++++++++++++++++++++++++++
```

```
21800   /* This is the file locking table.  Like the filp table, it points to the
21801    * inode table, however, in this case to achieve advisory locking.
21802    */
21803   EXTERN struct file_lock {
21804     short lock_type;               /* F_RDLOCK or F_WRLOCK; 0 means unused slot */
21805     pid_t lock_pid;                /* pid of the process holding the lock */
21806     struct inode *lock_inode;      /* pointer to the inode locked */
21807     off_t lock_first;              /* offset of first byte locked */
21808     off_t lock_last;               /* offset of last byte locked */
21809   } file_lock[NR_LOCKS];
```

```
++++++++++++++++++++++++++++++++++++++++++++++++++++++++++++++++++++++++++++++
                                servers/fs/inode.h
++++++++++++++++++++++++++++++++++++++++++++++++++++++++++++++++++++++++++++++
```

```
21900   /* Inode table.  This table holds inodes that are currently in use.  In some
21901    * cases they have been opened by an open() or creat() system call, in other
21902    * cases the file system itself needs the inode for one reason or another,
21903    * such as to search a directory for a path name.
21904    * The first part of the struct holds fields that are present on the
21905    * disk; the second part holds fields not present on the disk.
21906    * The disk inode part is also declared in "type.h" as 'd1_inode' for V1
21907    * file systems and 'd2_inode' for V2 file systems.
21908    */
21909
21910   EXTERN struct inode {
21911     mode_t i_mode;                 /* file type, protection, etc. */
21912     nlink_t i_nlinks;              /* how many links to this file */
21913     uid_t i_uid;                   /* user id of the file's owner */
21914     gid_t i_gid;                   /* group number */
21915     off_t i_size;                  /* current file size in bytes */
21916     time_t i_atime;                /* time of last access (V2 only) */
21917     time_t i_mtime;                /* when was file data last changed */
21918     time_t i_ctime;                /* when was inode itself changed (V2 only)*/
21919     zone_t i_zone[V2_NR_TZONES];   /* zone numbers for direct, ind, and dbl ind */
21920
21921     /* The following items are not present on the disk. */
21922     dev_t i_dev;                   /* which device is the inode on */
21923     ino_t i_num;                   /* inode number on its (minor) device */
21924     int i_count;                   /* # times inode used; 0 means slot is free */
```

```
21925        int i_ndzones;              /* # direct zones (Vx_NR_DZONES) */
21926        int i_nindirs;              /* # indirect zones per indirect block */
21927        struct super_block *i_sp;   /* pointer to super block for inode's device */
21928        char i_dirt;                /* CLEAN or DIRTY */
21929        char i_pipe;                /* set to I_PIPE if pipe */
21930        char i_mount;               /* this bit is set if file mounted on */
21931        char i_seek;                /* set on LSEEK, cleared on READ/WRITE */
21932        char i_update;              /* the ATIME, CTIME, and MTIME bits are here */
21933    } inode[NR_INODES];
21934
21935    #define NIL_INODE (struct inode *) 0    /* indicates absence of inode slot */
21936
21937    /* Field values.  Note that CLEAN and DIRTY are defined in "const.h" */
21938    #define NO_PIPE             0   /* i_pipe is NO_PIPE if inode is not a pipe */
21939    #define I_PIPE              1   /* i_pipe is I_PIPE if inode is a pipe */
21940    #define NO_MOUNT            0   /* i_mount is NO_MOUNT if file not mounted on*/
21941    #define I_MOUNT             1   /* i_mount is I_MOUNT if file mounted on */
21942    #define NO_SEEK             0   /* i_seek = NO_SEEK if last op was not SEEK */
21943    #define ISEEK               1   /* i_seek = ISEEK if last op was SEEK */


++++++++++++++++++++++++++++++++++++++++++++++++++++++++++++++++++++++++++++++++
                              servers/fs/param.h
++++++++++++++++++++++++++++++++++++++++++++++++++++++++++++++++++++++++++++++++

22000    /* The following names are synonyms for the variables in the input message. */
22001    #define acc_time       m2_l1
22002    #define addr           m1_i3
22003    #define buffer         m1_p1
22004    #define child          m1_i2
22005    #define co_mode        m1_i1
22006    #define eff_grp_id     m1_i3
22007    #define eff_user_id    m1_i3
22008    #define erki           m1_p1
22009    #define fd             m1_i1
22010    #define fd2            m1_i2
22011    #define ioflags        m1_i3
22012    #define group          m1_i3
22013    #define real_grp_id    m1_i2
22014    #define ls_fd          m2_i1
22015    #define mk_mode        m1_i2
22016    #define mk_z0          m1_i3
22017    #define mode           m3_i2
22018    #define c_mode         m1_i3
22019    #define c_name         m1_p1
22020    #define name           m3_p1
22021    #define name1          m1_p1
22022    #define name2          m1_p2
22023    #define name_length    m3_i1
22024    #define name1_length   m1_i1
22025    #define name2_length   m1_i2
22026    #define nbytes         m1_i2
22027    #define owner          m1_i2
22028    #define parent         m1_i1
22029    #define pathname       m3_ca1
22030    #define pid            m1_i3
22031    #define pro            m1_i1
22032    #define ctl_req        m4_l1
22033    #define driver_nr      m4_l2
22034    #define dev_nr         m4_l3
```

```
22035   #define dev_style        m4_l4
22036   #define rd_only          m1_i3
22037   #define real_user_id     m1_i2
22038   #define request          m1_i2
22039   #define sig              m1_i2
22040   #define slot1            m1_i1
22041   #define tp               m2_l1
22042   #define utime_actime     m2_l1
22043   #define utime_modtime    m2_l2
22044   #define utime_file       m2_p1
22045   #define utime_length     m2_i1
22046   #define utime_strlen     m2_i2
22047   #define whence           m2_i2
22048   #define svrctl_req       m2_i1
22049   #define svrctl_argp      m2_p1
22050   #define pm_stime         m1_i1
22051   #define info_what        m1_i1
22052   #define info_where       m1_p1
22053
22054   /* The following names are synonyms for the variables in the output message. */
22055   #define reply_type       m_type
22056   #define reply_l1         m2_l1
22057   #define reply_i1         m1_i1
22058   #define reply_i2         m1_i2
22059   #define reply_t1         m4_l1
22060   #define reply_t2         m4_l2
22061   #define reply_t3         m4_l3
22062   #define reply_t4         m4_l4
22063   #define reply_t5         m4_l5
```

```
++++++++++++++++++++++++++++++++++++++++++++++++++++++++++++++++++++++++++++++++
                              servers/fs/super.h
++++++++++++++++++++++++++++++++++++++++++++++++++++++++++++++++++++++++++++++++
```

```
22100   /* Super block table.  The root file system and every mounted file system
22101    * has an entry here.  The entry holds information about the sizes of the bit
22102    * maps and inodes.  The s_ninodes field gives the number of inodes available
22103    * for files and directories, including the root directory.  Inode 0 is
22104    * on the disk, but not used.  Thus s_ninodes = 4 means that 5 bits will be
22105    * used in the bit map, bit 0, which is always 1 and not used, and bits 1-4
22106    * for files and directories.  The disk layout is:
22107    *
22108    *     Item          # blocks
22109    *     boot block     1
22110    *     super block    1      (offset 1kB)
22111    *     inode map      s_imap_blocks
22112    *     zone map       s_zmap_blocks
22113    *     inodes         (s_ninodes + 'inodes per block' - 1)/'inodes per block'
22114    *     unused         whatever is needed to fill out the current zone
22115    *     data zones     (s_zones - s_firstdatazone) << s_log_zone_size
22116    *
22117    * A super_block slot is free if s_dev == NO_DEV.
22118    */
22119
22120   EXTERN struct super_block {
22121     ino_t s_ninodes;                 /* # usable inodes on the minor device */
22122     zone1_t  s_nzones;               /* total device size, including bit maps etc */
22123     short s_imap_blocks;             /* # of blocks used by inode bit map */
22124     short s_zmap_blocks;             /* # of blocks used by zone bit map */
```

```
22125        zone1_t s_firstdatazone;        /* number of first data zone */
22126        short s_log_zone_size;          /* log2 of blocks/zone */
22127        short s_pad;                    /* try to avoid compiler-dependent padding */
22128        off_t s_max_size;               /* maximum file size on this device */
22129        zone_t s_zones;                 /* number of zones (replaces s_nzones in V2) */
22130        short s_magic;                  /* magic number to recognize super-blocks */
22131
22132        /* The following items are valid on disk only for V3 and above */
22133
22134        /* The block size in bytes. Minimum MIN_BLOCK SIZE. SECTOR_SIZE
22135         * multiple. If V1 or V2 filesystem, this should be
22136         * initialised to STATIC_BLOCK_SIZE. Maximum MAX_BLOCK_SIZE.
22137         */
22138        short s_pad2;                   /* try to avoid compiler-dependent padding */
22139        unsigned short s_block_size;    /* block size in bytes. */
22140        char s_disk_version;            /* filesystem format sub-version */
22141
22142        /* The following items are only used when the super_block is in memory. */
22143        struct inode *s_isup;           /* inode for root dir of mounted file sys */
22144        struct inode *s_imount;         /* inode mounted on */
22145        unsigned s_inodes_per_block;    /* precalculated from magic number */
22146        dev_t s_dev;                    /* whose super block is this? */
22147        int s_rd_only;                  /* set to 1 iff file sys mounted read only */
22148        int s_native;                   /* set to 1 iff not byte swapped file system */
22149        int s_version;                  /* file system version, zero means bad magic */
22150        int s_ndzones;                  /* # direct zones in an inode */
22151        int s_nindirs;                  /* # indirect zones per indirect block */
22152        bit_t s_isearch;                /* inodes below this bit number are in use */
22153        bit_t s_zsearch;                /* all zones below this bit number are in use*/
22154 } super_block[NR_SUPERS];
22155
22156 #define NIL_SUPER (struct super_block *) 0
22157 #define IMAP              0             /* operating on the inode bit map */
22158 #define ZMAP              1             /* operating on the zone bit map */
```

```
++++++++++++++++++++++++++++++++++++++++++++++++++++++++++++++++++++++++++++++
                           servers/fs/table.c
++++++++++++++++++++++++++++++++++++++++++++++++++++++++++++++++++++++++++++++

22200 /* This file contains the table used to map system call numbers onto the
22201  * routines that perform them.
22202  */
22203
22204 #define _TABLE
22205
22206 #include "fs.h"
22207 #include <minix/callnr.h>
22208 #include <minix/com.h>
22209 #include "buf.h"
22210 #include "file.h"
22211 #include "fproc.h"
22212 #include "inode.h"
22213 #include "lock.h"
22214 #include "super.h"
22215
22216 PUBLIC _PROTOTYPE (int (*call_vec[]), (void) ) = {
22217        no_sys,          /*  0 = unused  */
22218        do_exit,         /*  1 = exit    */
22219        do_fork,         /*  2 = fork    */
```

```
22220        do_read,        /*  3 = read    */
22221        do_write,       /*  4 = write   */
22222        do_open,        /*  5 = open    */
22223        do_close,       /*  6 = close   */
22224        no_sys,         /*  7 = wait    */
22225        do_creat,       /*  8 = creat   */
22226        do_link,        /*  9 = link    */
22227        do_unlink,      /* 10 = unlink  */
22228        no_sys,         /* 11 = waitpid */
22229        do_chdir,       /* 12 = chdir   */
22230        no_sys,         /* 13 = time    */
22231        do_mknod,       /* 14 = mknod   */
22232        do_chmod,       /* 15 = chmod   */
22233        do_chown,       /* 16 = chown   */
22234        no_sys,         /* 17 = break   */
22235        do_stat,        /* 18 = stat    */
22236        do_lseek,       /* 19 = lseek   */
22237        no_sys,         /* 20 = getpid  */
22238        do_mount,       /* 21 = mount   */
22239        do_umount,      /* 22 = umount  */
22240        do_set,         /* 23 = setuid  */
22241        no_sys,         /* 24 = getuid  */
22242        do_stime,       /* 25 = stime   */
22243        no_sys,         /* 26 = ptrace  */
22244        no_sys,         /* 27 = alarm   */
22245        do_fstat,       /* 28 = fstat   */
22246        no_sys,         /* 29 = pause   */
22247        do_utime,       /* 30 = utime   */
22248        no_sys,         /* 31 = (stty)  */
22249        no_sys,         /* 32 = (gtty)  */
22250        do_access,      /* 33 = access  */
22251        no_sys,         /* 34 = (nice)  */
22252        no_sys,         /* 35 = (ftime) */
22253        do_sync,        /* 36 = sync    */
22254        no_sys,         /* 37 = kill    */
22255        do_rename,      /* 38 = rename  */
22256        do_mkdir,       /* 39 = mkdir   */
22257        do_unlink,      /* 40 = rmdir   */
22258        do_dup,         /* 41 = dup     */
22259        do_pipe,        /* 42 = pipe    */
22260        no_sys,         /* 43 = times   */
22261        no_sys,         /* 44 = (prof)  */
22262        no_sys,         /* 45 = unused  */
22263        do_set,         /* 46 = setgid  */
22264        no_sys,         /* 47 = getgid  */
22265        no_sys,         /* 48 = (signal)*/
22266        no_sys,         /* 49 = unused  */
22267        no_sys,         /* 50 = unused  */
22268        no_sys,         /* 51 = (acct)  */
22269        no_sys,         /* 52 = (phys)  */
22270        no_sys,         /* 53 = (lock)  */
22271        do_ioctl,       /* 54 = ioctl   */
22272        do_fcntl,       /* 55 = fcntl   */
22273        no_sys,         /* 56 = (mpx)   */
22274        no_sys,         /* 57 = unused  */
22275        no_sys,         /* 58 = unused  */
22276        do_exec,        /* 59 = execve  */
22277        do_umask,       /* 60 = umask   */
22278        do_chroot,      /* 61 = chroot  */
22279        do_setsid,      /* 62 = setsid  */
```

```
22280          no_sys,           /* 63 = getpgrp */
22281
22282          no_sys,           /* 64 = KSIG: signals originating in the kernel */
22283          do_unpause,       /* 65 = UNPAUSE */
22284          no_sys,           /* 66 = unused  */
22285          do_revive,        /* 67 = REVIVE  */
22286          no_sys,           /* 68 = TASK_REPLY       */
22287          no_sys,           /* 69 = unused */
22288          no_sys,           /* 70 = unused */
22289          no_sys,           /* 71 = si */
22290          no_sys,           /* 72 = sigsuspend */
22291          no_sys,           /* 73 = sigpending */
22292          no_sys,           /* 74 = sigprocmask */
22293          no_sys,           /* 75 = sigreturn */
22294          do_reboot,        /* 76 = reboot */
22295          do_svrctl,        /* 77 = svrctl */
22296
22297          no_sys,           /* 78 = unused */
22298          do_getsysinfo,    /* 79 = getsysinfo */
22299          no_sys,           /* 80 = unused */
22300          do_devctl,        /* 81 = devctl */
22301          do_fstatfs,       /* 82 = fstatfs */
22302          no_sys,           /* 83 = memalloc */
22303          no_sys,           /* 84 = memfree */
22304          do_select,        /* 85 = select */
22305          do_fchdir,        /* 86 = fchdir */
22306          do_fsync,         /* 87 = fsync */
22307          no_sys,           /* 88 = getpriority */
22308          no_sys,           /* 89 = setpriority */
22309          no_sys,           /* 90 = gettimeofday */
22310  };
22311  /* This should not fail with "array size is negative": */
22312  extern int dummy[sizeof(call_vec) == NCALLS * sizeof(call_vec[0]) ? 1 : -1];
22313


++++++++++++++++++++++++++++++++++++++++++++++++++++++++++++++++++++++++++++++
                            servers/fs/cache.c
++++++++++++++++++++++++++++++++++++++++++++++++++++++++++++++++++++++++++++++

22400  /* The file system maintains a buffer cache to reduce the number of disk
22401   * accesses needed.  Whenever a read or write to the disk is done, a check is
22402   * first made to see if the block is in the cache.  This file manages the
22403   * cache.
22404   *
22405   * The entry points into this file are:
22406   *   get_block:   request to fetch a block for reading or writing from cache
22407   *   put_block:   return a block previously requested with get_block
22408   *   alloc_zone:  allocate a new zone (to increase the length of a file)
22409   *   free_zone:   release a zone (when a file is removed)
22410   *   rw_block:    read or write a block from the disk itself
22411   *   invalidate:  remove all the cache blocks on some device
22412   */
22413
22414  #include "fs.h"
22415  #include <minix/com.h>
22416  #include "buf.h"
22417  #include "file.h"
22418  #include "fproc.h"
22419  #include "super.h"
```

```
22420
22421  FORWARD _PROTOTYPE( void rm_lru, (struct buf *bp) );
22422
22423  /*===========================================================================*
22424   *                              get_block                                    *
22425   *===========================================================================*/
22426  PUBLIC struct buf *get_block(dev, block, only_search)
22427  register dev_t dev;             /* on which device is the block? */
22428  register block_t block;         /* which block is wanted? */
22429  int only_search;                /* if NO_READ, don't read, else act normal */
22430  {
22431  /* Check to see if the requested block is in the block cache.  If so, return
22432   * a pointer to it.  If not, evict some other block and fetch it (unless
22433   * 'only_search' is 1).  All the blocks in the cache that are not in use
22434   * are linked together in a chain, with 'front' pointing to the least recently
22435   * used block and 'rear' to the most recently used block.  If 'only_search' is
22436   * 1, the block being requested will be overwritten in its entirety, so it is
22437   * only necessary to see if it is in the cache; if it is not, any free buffer
22438   * will do.  It is not necessary to actually read the block in from disk.
22439   * If 'only_search' is PREFETCH, the block need not be read from the disk,
22440   * and the device is not to be marked on the block, so callers can tell if
22441   * the block returned is valid.
22442   * In addition to the LRU chain, there is also a hash chain to link together
22443   * blocks whose block numbers end with the same bit strings, for fast lookup.
22444   */
22445
22446    int b;
22447    register struct buf *bp, *prev_ptr;
22448
22449    /* Search the hash chain for (dev, block). Do_read() can use
22450     * get_block(NO_DEV ...) to get an unnamed block to fill with zeros when
22451     * someone wants to read from a hole in a file, in which case this search
22452     * is skipped
22453     */
22454    if (dev != NO_DEV) {
22455          b = (int) block & HASH_MASK;
22456          bp = buf_hash[b];
22457          while (bp != NIL_BUF) {
22458                  if (bp->b_blocknr == block && bp->b_dev == dev) {
22459                          /* Block needed has been found. */
22460                          if (bp->b_count == 0) rm_lru(bp);
22461                          bp->b_count++;  /* record that block is in use */
22462
22463                          return(bp);
22464                  } else {
22465                          /* This block is not the one sought. */
22466                          bp = bp->b_hash; /* move to next block on hash chain */
22467                  }
22468          }
22469    }
22470
22471    /* Desired block is not on available chain.  Take oldest block ('front'). */
22472    if ((bp = front) == NIL_BUF) panic(__FILE__,"all buffers in use", NR_BUFS);
22473    rm_lru(bp);
22474
22475    /* Remove the block that was just taken from its hash chain. */
22476    b = (int) bp->b_blocknr & HASH_MASK;
22477    prev_ptr = buf_hash[b];
22478    if (prev_ptr == bp) {
22479          buf_hash[b] = bp->b_hash;
```

```
22480        } else {
22481               /* The block just taken is not on the front of its hash chain. */
22482               while (prev_ptr->b_hash != NIL_BUF)
22483                       if (prev_ptr->b_hash == bp) {
22484                               prev_ptr->b_hash = bp->b_hash;  /* found it */
22485                               break;
22486                       } else {
22487                               prev_ptr = prev_ptr->b_hash;     /* keep looking */
22488                       }
22489        }
22490
22491        /* If the block taken is dirty, make it clean by writing it to the disk.
22492         * Avoid hysteresis by flushing all other dirty blocks for the same device.
22493         */
22494        if (bp->b_dev != NO_DEV) {
22495               if (bp->b_dirt == DIRTY) flushall(bp->b_dev);
22496        }
22497
22498        /* Fill in block's parameters and add it to the hash chain where it goes. */
22499        bp->b_dev = dev;                /* fill in device number */
22500        bp->b_blocknr = block;          /* fill in block number */
22501        bp->b_count++;                  /* record that block is being used */
22502        b = (int) bp->b_blocknr & HASH_MASK;
22503        bp->b_hash = buf_hash[b];
22504        buf_hash[b] = bp;               /* add to hash list */
22505
22506        /* Go get the requested block unless searching or prefetching. */
22507        if (dev != NO_DEV) {
22508               if (only_search == PREFETCH) bp->b_dev = NO_DEV;
22509               else
22510               if (only_search == NORMAL) {
22511                       rw_block(bp, READING);
22512               }
22513        }
22514        return(bp);                     /* return the newly acquired block */
22515 }

22517 /*===========================================================================*
22518  *                              put_block                                    *
22519  *===========================================================================*/
22520 PUBLIC void put_block(bp, block_type)
22521 register struct buf *bp;        /* pointer to the buffer to be released */
22522 int block_type;                 /* INODE_BLOCK, DIRECTORY_BLOCK, or whatever */
22523 {
22524 /* Return a block to the list of available blocks.   Depending on 'block_type'
22525  * it may be put on the front or rear of the LRU chain.  Blocks that are
22526  * expected to be needed again shortly (e.g., partially full data blocks)
22527  * go on the rear; blocks that are unlikely to be needed again shortly
22528  * (e.g., full data blocks) go on the front.  Blocks whose loss can hurt
22529  * the integrity of the file system (e.g., inode blocks) are written to
22530  * disk immediately if they are dirty.
22531  */
22532    if (bp == NIL_BUF) return;   /* it is easier to check here than in caller */
22533
22534    bp->b_count--;               /* there is one use fewer now */
22535    if (bp->b_count != 0) return; /* block is still in use */
22536
22537    bufs_in_use--;               /* one fewer block buffers in use */
22538
22539    /* Put this block back on the LRU chain.  If the ONE_SHOT bit is set in
```

```
22540        * 'block_type', the block is not likely to be needed again shortly, so put
22541        * it on the front of the LRU chain where it will be the first one to be
22542        * taken when a free buffer is needed later.
22543        */
22544       if (bp->b_dev == DEV_RAM || block_type & ONE_SHOT) {
22545               /* Block probably won't be needed quickly. Put it on front of chain.
22546                * It will be the next block to be evicted from the cache.
22547                */
22548               bp->b_prev = NIL_BUF;
22549               bp->b_next = front;
22550               if (front == NIL_BUF)
22551                       rear = bp;        /* LRU chain was empty */
22552               else
22553                       front->b_prev = bp;
22554               front = bp;
22555       } else {
22556               /* Block probably will be needed quickly.  Put it on rear of chain.
22557                * It will not be evicted from the cache for a long time.
22558                */
22559               bp->b_prev = rear;
22560               bp->b_next = NIL_BUF;
22561               if (rear == NIL_BUF)
22562                       front = bp;
22563               else
22564                       rear->b_next = bp;
22565               rear = bp;
22566       }
22567
22568       /* Some blocks are so important (e.g., inodes, indirect blocks) that they
22569        * should be written to the disk immediately to avoid messing up the file
22570        * system in the event of a crash.
22571        */
22572       if ((block_type & WRITE_IMMED) && bp->b_dirt==DIRTY && bp->b_dev != NO_DEV) {
22573               rw_block(bp, WRITING);
22574       }
22575   }


22577   /*===========================================================================*
22578    *                              alloc_zone                                   *
22579    *===========================================================================*/
22580   PUBLIC zone_t alloc_zone(dev, z)
22581   dev_t dev;                           /* device where zone wanted */
22582   zone_t z;                            /* try to allocate new zone near this one */
22583   {
22584   /* Allocate a new zone on the indicated device and return its number. */
22585
22586     int major, minor;
22587     bit_t b, bit;
22588     struct super_block *sp;
22589
22590     /* Note that the routine alloc_bit() returns 1 for the lowest possible
22591      * zone, which corresponds to sp->s_firstdatazone.  To convert a value
22592      * between the bit number, 'b', used by alloc_bit() and the zone number, 'z',
22593      * stored in the inode, use the formula:
22594      *     z = b + sp->s_firstdatazone - 1
22595      * Alloc_bit() never returns 0, since this is used for NO_BIT (failure).
22596      */
22597     sp = get_super(dev);
22598
22599     /* If z is 0, skip initial part of the map known to be fully in use. */
```

```
22600      if (z == sp->s_firstdatazone) {
22601            bit = sp->s_zsearch;
22602      } else {
22603            bit = (bit_t) z - (sp->s_firstdatazone - 1);
22604      }
22605      b = alloc_bit(sp, ZMAP, bit);
22606      if (b == NO_BIT) {
22607            err_code = ENOSPC;
22608            major = (int) (sp->s_dev >> MAJOR) & BYTE;
22609            minor = (int) (sp->s_dev >> MINOR) & BYTE;
22610            printf("No space on %sdevice %d/%d\n",
22611                   sp->s_dev == root_dev ? "root " : "", major, minor);
22612            return(NO_ZONE);
22613      }
22614      if (z == sp->s_firstdatazone) sp->s_zsearch = b;      /* for next time */
22615      return(sp->s_firstdatazone - 1 + (zone_t) b);
22616 }


22618 /*===========================================================================*
22619  *                              free_zone                                    *
22620  *===========================================================================*/
22621 PUBLIC void free_zone(dev, numb)
22622 dev_t dev;                            /* device where zone located */
22623 zone_t numb;                          /* zone to be returned */
22624 {
22625 /* Return a zone. */
22626
22627   register struct super_block *sp;
22628   bit_t bit;
22629
22630   /* Locate the appropriate super_block and return bit. */
22631   sp = get_super(dev);
22632   if (numb < sp->s_firstdatazone || numb >= sp->s_zones) return;
22633   bit = (bit_t) (numb - (sp->s_firstdatazone - 1));
22634   free_bit(sp, ZMAP, bit);
22635   if (bit < sp->s_zsearch) sp->s_zsearch = bit;
22636 }


22638 /*===========================================================================*
22639  *                              rw_block                                     *
22640  *===========================================================================*/
22641 PUBLIC void rw_block(bp, rw_flag)
22642 register struct buf *bp;          /* buffer pointer */
22643 int rw_flag;                      /* READING or WRITING */
22644 {
22645 /* Read or write a disk block. This is the only routine in which actual disk
22646  * I/O is invoked. If an error occurs, a message is printed here, but the error
22647  * is not reported to the caller.  If the error occurred while purging a block
22648  * from the cache, it is not clear what the caller could do about it anyway.
22649  */
22650
22651   int r, op;
22652   off_t pos;
22653   dev_t dev;
22654   int block_size;
22655
22656   block_size = get_block_size(bp->b_dev);
22657
22658   if ( (dev = bp->b_dev) != NO_DEV) {
22659         pos = (off_t) bp->b_blocknr * block_size;
```

```
22660                op = (rw_flag == READING ? DEV_READ : DEV_WRITE);
22661                r = dev_io(op, dev, FS_PROC_NR, bp->b_data, pos, block_size, 0);
22662                if (r != block_size) {
22663                    if (r >= 0) r = END_OF_FILE;
22664                    if (r != END_OF_FILE)
22665                        printf("Unrecoverable disk error on device %d/%d, block %ld\n",
22666                              (dev>>MAJOR)&BYTE, (dev>>MINOR)&BYTE, bp->b_blocknr);
22667                    bp->b_dev = NO_DEV;      /* invalidate block */
22668
22669                    /* Report read errors to interested parties. */
22670                    if (rw_flag == READING) rdwt_err = r;
22671                }
22672        }
22673
22674      bp->b_dirt = CLEAN;
22675  }
22676
22677  /*===========================================================================*
22678   *                              invalidate                                   *
22679   *===========================================================================*/
22680  PUBLIC void invalidate(device)
22681  dev_t device;                          /* device whose blocks are to be purged */
22682  {
22683  /* Remove all the blocks belonging to some device from the cache. */
22684
22685    register struct buf *bp;
22686
22687    for (bp = &buf[0]; bp < &buf[NR_BUFS]; bp++)
22688          if (bp->b_dev == device) bp->b_dev = NO_DEV;
22689  }
22690
22691  /*===========================================================================*
22692   *                              flushall                                     *
22693   *===========================================================================*/
22694  PUBLIC void flushall(dev)
22695  dev_t dev;                     /* device to flush */
22696  {
22697  /* Flush all dirty blocks for one device. */
22698
22699    register struct buf *bp;
22700    static struct buf *dirty[NR_BUFS];     /* static so it isn't on stack */
22701    int ndirty;
22702
22703    for (bp = &buf[0], ndirty = 0; bp < &buf[NR_BUFS]; bp++)
22704          if (bp->b_dirt == DIRTY && bp->b_dev == dev) dirty[ndirty++] = bp;
22705    rw_scattered(dev, dirty, ndirty, WRITING);
22706  }
22707
22708  /*===========================================================================*
22709   *                              rw_scattered                                 *
22710   *===========================================================================*/
22711  PUBLIC void rw_scattered(dev, bufq, bufqsize, rw_flag)
22712  dev_t dev;                             /* major-minor device number */
22713  struct buf **bufq;                     /* pointer to array of buffers */
22714  int bufqsize;                          /* number of buffers */
22715  int rw_flag;                           /* READING or WRITING */
22716  {
22717  /* Read or write scattered data from a device. */
22718
22719    register struct buf *bp;
```

```
22720          int gap;
22721          register int i;
22722          register iovec_t *iop;
22723          static iovec_t iovec[NR_IOREQS];   /* static so it isn't on stack */
22724          int j, r;
22725          int block_size;
22726
22727          block_size = get_block_size(dev);
22728
22729          /* (Shell) sort buffers on b_blocknr. */
22730          gap = 1;
22731          do
22732                  gap = 3 * gap + 1;
22733          while (gap <= bufqsize);
22734          while (gap != 1) {
22735                  gap /= 3;
22736                  for (j = gap; j < bufqsize; j++) {
22737                          for (i = j - gap;
22738                                  i >= 0 && bufq[i]->b_blocknr > bufq[i + gap]->b_blocknr;
22739                                  i -= gap) {
22740                                  bp = bufq[i];
22741                                  bufq[i] = bufq[i + gap];
22742                                  bufq[i + gap] = bp;
22743                          }
22744                  }
22745          }
22746
22747          /* Set up I/O vector and do I/O.  The result of dev_io is OK if everything
22748           * went fine, otherwise the error code for the first failed transfer.
22749           */
22750          while (bufqsize > 0) {
22751                  for (j = 0, iop = iovec; j < NR_IOREQS && j < bufqsize; j++, iop++) {
22752                          bp = bufq[j];
22753                          if (bp->b_blocknr != bufq[0]->b_blocknr + j) break;
22754                          iop->iov_addr = (vir_bytes) bp->b_data;
22755                          iop->iov_size = block_size;
22756                  }
22757                  r = dev_io(rw_flag == WRITING ? DEV_SCATTER : DEV_GATHER,
22758                          dev, FS_PROC_NR, iovec,
22759                          (off_t) bufq[0]->b_blocknr * block_size, j, 0);
22760
22761                  /* Harvest the results.  Dev_io reports the first error it may have
22762                   * encountered, but we only care if it's the first block that failed.
22763                   */
22764                  for (i = 0, iop = iovec; i < j; i++, iop++) {
22765                          bp = bufq[i];
22766                          if (iop->iov_size != 0) {
22767                                  /* Transfer failed. An error? Do we care? */
22768                                  if (r != OK && i == 0) {
22769                                          printf(
22770                                  "fs: I/O error on device %d/%d, block %lu\n",
22771                                                  (dev>>MAJOR)&BYTE, (dev>>MINOR)&BYTE,
22772                                                  bp->b_blocknr);
22773                                          bp->b_dev = NO_DEV;      /* invalidate block */
22774                                  }
22775                                  break;
22776                          }
22777                          if (rw_flag == READING) {
22778                                  bp->b_dev = dev;         /* validate block */
22779                                  put_block(bp, PARTIAL_DATA_BLOCK);
```

```
22780                   } else {
22781                           bp->b_dirt = CLEAN;
22782                   }
22783           }
22784           bufq += i;
22785           bufqsize -= i;
22786           if (rw_flag == READING) {
22787                   /* Don't bother reading more than the device is willing to
22788                    * give at this time.  Don't forget to release those extras.
22789                    */
22790                   while (bufqsize > 0) {
22791                           put_block(*bufq++, PARTIAL_DATA_BLOCK);
22792                           bufqsize--;
22793                   }
22794           }
22795           if (rw_flag == WRITING && i == 0) {
22796                   /* We're not making progress, this means we might keep
22797                    * looping. Buffers remain dirty if un-written. Buffers are
22798                    * lost if invalidate()d or LRU-removed while dirty. This
22799                    * is better than keeping unwritable blocks around forever..
22800                    */
22801                   break;
22802           }
22803     }
22804   }

22806   /*===========================================================================*
22807    *                              rm_lru                                        *
22808    *===========================================================================*/
22809   PRIVATE void rm_lru(bp)
22810   struct buf *bp;
22811   {
22812   /* Remove a block from its LRU chain. */
22813     struct buf *next_ptr, *prev_ptr;
22814
22815     bufs_in_use++;
22816     next_ptr = bp->b_next;          /* successor on LRU chain */
22817     prev_ptr = bp->b_prev;          /* predecessor on LRU chain */
22818     if (prev_ptr != NIL_BUF)
22819           prev_ptr->b_next = next_ptr;
22820     else
22821           front = next_ptr;         /* this block was at front of chain */
22822
22823     if (next_ptr != NIL_BUF)
22824           next_ptr->b_prev = prev_ptr;
22825     else
22826           rear = prev_ptr;          /* this block was at rear of chain */
22827   }
```

```
++++++++++++++++++++++++++++++++++++++++++++++++++++++++++++++++++++++++++++
                        servers/fs/inode.c
++++++++++++++++++++++++++++++++++++++++++++++++++++++++++++++++++++++++++++

22900   /* This file manages the inode table.  There are procedures to allocate and
22901    * deallocate inodes, acquire, erase, and release them, and read and write
22902    * them from the disk.
22903    *
22904    * The entry points into this file are
```

```
22905    *     get_inode:    search inode table for a given inode; if not there,
22906    *                   read it
22907    *     put_inode:    indicate that an inode is no longer needed in memory
22908    *     alloc_inode:  allocate a new, unused inode
22909    *     wipe_inode:   erase some fields of a newly allocated inode
22910    *     free_inode:   mark an inode as available for a new file
22911    *     update_times: update atime, ctime, and mtime
22912    *     rw_inode:     read a disk block and extract an inode, or corresp. write
22913    *     old_icopy:    copy to/from in-core inode struct and disk inode (V1.x)
22914    *     new_icopy:    copy to/from in-core inode struct and disk inode (V2.x)
22915    *     dup_inode:    indicate that someone else is using an inode table entry
22916    */
22917
22918    #include "fs.h"
22919    #include "buf.h"
22920    #include "file.h"
22921    #include "fproc.h"
22922    #include "inode.h"
22923    #include "super.h"
22924
22925    FORWARD _PROTOTYPE( void old_icopy, (struct inode *rip, d1_inode *dip,
22926                                        int direction, int norm));
22927    FORWARD _PROTOTYPE( void new_icopy, (struct inode *rip, d2_inode *dip,
22928                                        int direction, int norm));
22929
22930    /*===========================================================================*
22931     *                              get_inode                                     *
22932     *===========================================================================*/
22933    PUBLIC struct inode *get_inode(dev, numb)
22934    dev_t dev;                        /* device on which inode resides */
22935    int numb;                         /* inode number (ANSI: may not be unshort) */
22936    {
22937    /* Find a slot in the inode table, load the specified inode into it, and
22938     * return a pointer to the slot.  If 'dev' == NO_DEV, just return a free slot.
22939     */
22940
22941      register struct inode *rip, *xp;
22942
22943      /* Search the inode table both for (dev, numb) and a free slot. */
22944      xp = NIL_INODE;
22945      for (rip = &inode[0]; rip < &inode[NR_INODES]; rip++) {
22946            if (rip->i_count > 0) { /* only check used slots for (dev, numb) */
22947                    if (rip->i_dev == dev && rip->i_num == numb) {
22948                            /* This is the inode that we are looking for. */
22949                            rip->i_count++;
22950                            return(rip);     /* (dev, numb) found */
22951                    }
22952            } else {
22953                    xp = rip;        /* remember this free slot for later */
22954            }
22955      }
22956
22957      /* Inode we want is not currently in use.  Did we find a free slot? */
22958      if (xp == NIL_INODE) {          /* inode table completely full */
22959            err_code = ENFILE;
22960            return(NIL_INODE);
22961      }
22962
22963      /* A free inode slot has been located.  Load the inode into it. */
22964      xp->i_dev = dev;
```

```
22965    xp->i_num = numb;
22966    xp->i_count = 1;
22967    if (dev != NO_DEV) rw_inode(xp, READING);      /* get inode from disk */
22968    xp->i_update = 0;              /* all the times are initially up-to-date */
22969
22970    return(xp);
22971  }

22973  /*===========================================================================*
22974   *                              put_inode                                    *
22975   *===========================================================================*/
22976  PUBLIC void put_inode(rip)
22977  register struct inode *rip;      /* pointer to inode to be released */
22978  {
22979  /* The caller is no longer using this inode.  If no one else is using it either
22980   * write it back to the disk immediately.  If it has no links, truncate it and
22981   * return it to the pool of available inodes.
22982   */
22983
22984    if (rip == NIL_INODE) return; /* checking here is easier than in caller */
22985    if (--rip->i_count == 0) {    /* i_count == 0 means no one is using it now */
22986          if (rip->i_nlinks == 0) {
22987                  /* i_nlinks == 0 means free the inode. */
22988                  truncate(rip);  /* return all the disk blocks */
22989                  rip->i_mode = I_NOT_ALLOC;      /* clear I_TYPE field */
22990                  rip->i_dirt = DIRTY;
22991                  free_inode(rip->i_dev, rip->i_num);
22992          } else {
22993                  if (rip->i_pipe == I_PIPE) truncate(rip);
22994          }
22995          rip->i_pipe = NO_PIPE;  /* should always be cleared */
22996          if (rip->i_dirt == DIRTY) rw_inode(rip, WRITING);
22997    }
22998  }

23000  /*===========================================================================*
23001   *                              alloc_inode                                  *
23002   *===========================================================================*/
23003  PUBLIC struct inode *alloc_inode(dev_t dev, mode_t bits)
23004  {
23005  /* Allocate a free inode on 'dev', and return a pointer to it. */
23006
23007    register struct inode *rip;
23008    register struct super_block *sp;
23009    int major, minor, inumb;
23010    bit_t b;
23011
23012    sp = get_super(dev);   /* get pointer to super_block */
23013    if (sp->s_rd_only) {   /* can't allocate an inode on a read only device. */
23014          err_code = EROFS;
23015          return(NIL_INODE);
23016    }
23017
23018    /* Acquire an inode from the bit map. */
23019    b = alloc_bit(sp, IMAP, sp->s_isearch);
23020    if (b == NO_BIT) {
23021          err_code = ENFILE;
23022          major = (int) (sp->s_dev >> MAJOR) & BYTE;
23023          minor = (int) (sp->s_dev >> MINOR) & BYTE;
23024          printf("Out of i-nodes on %sdevice %d/%d\n",
```

```
23025                           sp->s_dev == root_dev ? "root " : "", major, minor);
23026               return(NIL_INODE);
23027       }
23028       sp->s_isearch = b;                   /* next time start here */
23029       inumb = (int) b;                     /* be careful not to pass unshort as param */
23030
23031       /* Try to acquire a slot in the inode table. */
23032       if ((rip = get_inode(NO_DEV, inumb)) == NIL_INODE) {
23033               /* No inode table slots available.  Free the inode just allocated. */
23034               free_bit(sp, IMAP, b);
23035       } else {
23036               /* An inode slot is available. Put the inode just allocated into it. */
23037               rip->i_mode = bits;          /* set up RWX bits */
23038               rip->i_nlinks = 0;           /* initial no links */
23039               rip->i_uid = fp->fp_effuid;  /* file's uid is owner's */
23040               rip->i_gid = fp->fp_effgid;  /* ditto group id */
23041               rip->i_dev = dev;            /* mark which device it is on */
23042               rip->i_ndzones = sp->s_ndzones; /* number of direct zones */
23043               rip->i_nindirs = sp->s_nindirs; /* number of indirect zones per blk*/
23044               rip->i_sp = sp;              /* pointer to super block */
23045
23046               /* Fields not cleared already are cleared in wipe_inode().  They have
23047                * been put there because truncate() needs to clear the same fields if
23048                * the file happens to be open while being truncated.  It saves space
23049                * not to repeat the code twice.
23050                */
23051               wipe_inode(rip);
23052       }
23053
23054       return(rip);
23055   }

23057   /*===========================================================================*
23058    *                              wipe_inode                                   *
23059    *===========================================================================*/
23060   PUBLIC void wipe_inode(rip)
23061   register struct inode *rip;      /* the inode to be erased */
23062   {
23063   /* Erase some fields in the inode.  This function is called from alloc_inode()
23064    * when a new inode is to be allocated, and from truncate(), when an existing
23065    * inode is to be truncated.
23066    */
23067
23068       register int i;
23069
23070       rip->i_size = 0;
23071       rip->i_update = ATIME | CTIME | MTIME;        /* update all times later */
23072       rip->i_dirt = DIRTY;
23073       for (i = 0; i < V2_NR_TZONES; i++) rip->i_zone[i] = NO_ZONE;
23074   }

23076   /*===========================================================================*
23077    *                              free_inode                                   *
23078    *===========================================================================*/
23079   PUBLIC void free_inode(dev, inumb)
23080   dev_t dev;                       /* on which device is the inode */
23081   ino_t inumb;                     /* number of inode to be freed */
23082   {
23083   /* Return an inode to the pool of unallocated inodes. */
23084
```

```
23085     register struct super_block *sp;
23086     bit_t b;
23087
23088     /* Locate the appropriate super_block. */
23089     sp = get_super(dev);
23090     if (inumb <= 0 || inumb > sp->s_ninodes) return;
23091     b = inumb;
23092     free_bit(sp, IMAP, b);
23093     if (b < sp->s_isearch) sp->s_isearch = b;
23094   }

23096   /*===========================================================================*
23097    *                              update_times                                 *
23098    *===========================================================================*/
23099   PUBLIC void update_times(rip)
23100   register struct inode *rip;      /* pointer to inode to be read/written */
23101   {
23102   /* Various system calls are required by the standard to update atime, ctime,
23103    * or mtime.  Since updating a time requires sending a message to the clock
23104    * task--an expensive business--the times are marked for update by setting
23105    * bits in i_update.  When a stat, fstat, or sync is done, or an inode is
23106    * released, update_times() may be called to actually fill in the times.
23107    */
23108
23109     time_t cur_time;
23110     struct super_block *sp;
23111
23112     sp = rip->i_sp;                 /* get pointer to super block. */
23113     if (sp->s_rd_only) return;     /* no updates for read-only file systems */
23114
23115     cur_time = clock_time();
23116     if (rip->i_update & ATIME) rip->i_atime = cur_time;
23117     if (rip->i_update & CTIME) rip->i_ctime = cur_time;
23118     if (rip->i_update & MTIME) rip->i_mtime = cur_time;
23119     rip->i_update = 0;             /* they are all up-to-date now */
23120   }

23122   /*===========================================================================*
23123    *                              rw_inode                                     *
23124    *===========================================================================*/
23125   PUBLIC void rw_inode(rip, rw_flag)
23126   register struct inode *rip;      /* pointer to inode to be read/written */
23127   int rw_flag;                     /* READING or WRITING */
23128   {
23129   /* An entry in the inode table is to be copied to or from the disk. */
23130
23131     register struct buf *bp;
23132     register struct super_block *sp;
23133     d1_inode *dip;
23134     d2_inode *dip2;
23135     block_t b, offset;
23136
23137     /* Get the block where the inode resides. */
23138     sp = get_super(rip->i_dev);    /* get pointer to super block */
23139     rip->i_sp = sp;                /* inode must contain super block pointer */
23140     offset = sp->s_imap_blocks + sp->s_zmap_blocks + 2;
23141     b = (block_t) (rip->i_num - 1)/sp->s_inodes_per_block + offset;
23142     bp = get_block(rip->i_dev, b, NORMAL);
23143     dip  = bp->b_v1_ino + (rip->i_num - 1) % V1_INODES_PER_BLOCK;
23144     dip2 = bp->b_v2_ino + (rip->i_num - 1) %
```

```
23145                    V2_INODES_PER_BLOCK(sp->s_block_size);
23146
23147        /* Do the read or write. */
23148        if (rw_flag == WRITING) {
23149                if (rip->i_update) update_times(rip);   /* times need updating */
23150                if (sp->s_rd_only == FALSE) bp->b_dirt = DIRTY;
23151        }
23152
23153        /* Copy the inode from the disk block to the in-core table or vice versa.
23154         * If the fourth parameter below is FALSE, the bytes are swapped.
23155         */
23156        if (sp->s_version == V1)
23157                old_icopy(rip, dip,  rw_flag, sp->s_native);
23158        else
23159                new_icopy(rip, dip2, rw_flag, sp->s_native);
23160
23161        put_block(bp, INODE_BLOCK);
23162        rip->i_dirt = CLEAN;
23163  }
23164
23165  /*===========================================================================*
23166   *                              old_icopy                                     *
23167   *===========================================================================*/
23168  PRIVATE void old_icopy(rip, dip, direction, norm)
23169  register struct inode *rip;      /* pointer to the in-core inode struct */
23170  register d1_inode *dip;          /* pointer to the d1_inode inode struct */
23171  int direction;                   /* READING (from disk) or WRITING (to disk) */
23172  int norm;                        /* TRUE = do not swap bytes; FALSE = swap */
23173
23174  {
23175  /* The V1.x IBM disk, the V1.x 68000 disk, and the V2 disk (same for IBM and
23176   * 68000) all have different inode layouts.  When an inode is read or written
23177   * this routine handles the conversions so that the information in the inode
23178   * table is independent of the disk structure from which the inode came.
23179   * The old_icopy routine copies to and from V1 disks.
23180   */
23181
23182    int i;
23183
23184    if (direction == READING) {
23185          /* Copy V1.x inode to the in-core table, swapping bytes if need be. */
23186          rip->i_mode    = conv2(norm, (int) dip->d1_mode);
23187          rip->i_uid     = conv2(norm, (int) dip->d1_uid );
23188          rip->i_size    = conv4(norm,       dip->d1_size);
23189          rip->i_mtime   = conv4(norm,       dip->d1_mtime);
23190          rip->i_atime   = rip->i_mtime;
23191          rip->i_ctime   = rip->i_mtime;
23192          rip->i_nlinks  = dip->d1_nlinks;                  /* 1 char */
23193          rip->i_gid     = dip->d1_gid;                     /* 1 char */
23194          rip->i_ndzones = V1_NR_DZONES;
23195          rip->i_nindirs = V1_INDIRECTS;
23196          for (i = 0; i < V1_NR_TZONES; i++)
23197                  rip->i_zone[i] = conv2(norm, (int) dip->d1_zone[i]);
23198    } else {
23199          /* Copying V1.x inode to disk from the in-core table. */
23200          dip->d1_mode   = conv2(norm, (int) rip->i_mode);
23201          dip->d1_uid    = conv2(norm, (int) rip->i_uid );
23202          dip->d1_size   = conv4(norm,       rip->i_size);
23203          dip->d1_mtime  = conv4(norm,       rip->i_mtime);
23204          dip->d1_nlinks = rip->i_nlinks;                  /* 1 char */
```

```
23205              dip->d1_gid   = rip->i_gid;                  /* 1 char */
23206         for (i = 0; i < V1_NR_TZONES; i++)
23207              dip->d1_zone[i] = conv2(norm, (int) rip->i_zone[i]);
23208     }
23209 }

23211 /*===========================================================================*
23212  *                            new_icopy                                     *
23213  *===========================================================================*/
23214 PRIVATE void new_icopy(rip, dip, direction, norm)
23215 register struct inode *rip;    /* pointer to the in-core inode struct */
23216 register d2_inode *dip; /* pointer to the d2_inode struct */
23217 int direction;                  /* READING (from disk) or WRITING (to disk) */
23218 int norm;                       /* TRUE = do not swap bytes; FALSE = swap */
23219
23220 {
23221 /* Same as old_icopy, but to/from V2 disk layout. */
23222
23223   int i;
23224
23225   if (direction == READING) {
23226         /* Copy V2.x inode to the in-core table, swapping bytes if need be. */
23227         rip->i_mode   = conv2(norm,dip->d2_mode);
23228         rip->i_uid    = conv2(norm,dip->d2_uid);
23229         rip->i_nlinks = conv2(norm,dip->d2_nlinks);
23230         rip->i_gid    = conv2(norm,dip->d2_gid);
23231         rip->i_size   = conv4(norm,dip->d2_size);
23232         rip->i_atime  = conv4(norm,dip->d2_atime);
23233         rip->i_ctime  = conv4(norm,dip->d2_ctime);
23234         rip->i_mtime  = conv4(norm,dip->d2_mtime);
23235         rip->i_ndzones = V2_NR_DZONES;
23236         rip->i_nindirs = V2_INDIRECTS(rip->i_sp->s_block_size);
23237         for (i = 0; i < V2_NR_TZONES; i++)
23238              rip->i_zone[i] = conv4(norm, (long) dip->d2_zone[i]);
23239   } else {
23240         /* Copying V2.x inode to disk from the in-core table. */
23241         dip->d2_mode   = conv2(norm,rip->i_mode);
23242         dip->d2_uid    = conv2(norm,rip->i_uid);
23243         dip->d2_nlinks = conv2(norm,rip->i_nlinks);
23244         dip->d2_gid    = conv2(norm,rip->i_gid);
23245         dip->d2_size   = conv4(norm,rip->i_size);
23246         dip->d2_atime  = conv4(norm,rip->i_atime);
23247         dip->d2_ctime  = conv4(norm,rip->i_ctime);
23248         dip->d2_mtime  = conv4(norm,rip->i_mtime);
23249         for (i = 0; i < V2_NR_TZONES; i++)
23250              dip->d2_zone[i] = conv4(norm, (long) rip->i_zone[i]);
23251   }
23252 }

23254 /*===========================================================================*
23255  *                            dup_inode                                     *
23256  *===========================================================================*/
23257 PUBLIC void dup_inode(ip)
23258 struct inode *ip;                /* The inode to be duplicated. */
23259 {
23260 /* This routine is a simplified form of get_inode() for the case where
23261  * the inode pointer is already known.
23262  */
23263
23264   ip->i_count++;
```

```
23265    }




++++++++++++++++++++++++++++++++++++++++++++++++++++++++++++++++++++++++++
                              servers/fs/super.c
++++++++++++++++++++++++++++++++++++++++++++++++++++++++++++++++++++++++++
23300    /* This file manages the super block table and the related data structures,
23301     * namely, the bit maps that keep track of which zones and which inodes are
23302     * allocated and which are free.  When a new inode or zone is needed, the
23303     * appropriate bit map is searched for a free entry.
23304     *
23305     * The entry points into this file are
23306     *   alloc_bit:      somebody wants to allocate a zone or inode; find one
23307     *   free_bit:       indicate that a zone or inode is available for allocation
23308     *   get_super:      search the 'superblock' table for a device
23309     *   mounted:        tells if file inode is on mounted (or ROOT) file system
23310     *   read_super:     read a superblock
23311     */
23312
23313    #include "fs.h"
23314    #include <string.h>
23315    #include <minix/com.h>
23316    #include "buf.h"
23317    #include "inode.h"
23318    #include "super.h"
23319    #include "const.h"
23320
23321    /*===========================================================================*
23322     *                              alloc_bit                                     *
23323     *===========================================================================*/
23324    PUBLIC bit_t alloc_bit(sp, map, origin)
23325    struct super_block *sp;           /* the filesystem to allocate from */
23326    int map;                          /* IMAP (inode map) or ZMAP (zone map) */
23327    bit_t origin;                     /* number of bit to start searching at */
23328    {
23329    /* Allocate a bit from a bit map and return its bit number. */
23330
23331      block_t start_block;            /* first bit block */
23332      bit_t map_bits;                 /* how many bits are there in the bit map? */
23333      unsigned bit_blocks;            /* how many blocks are there in the bit map? */
23334      unsigned block, word, bcount;
23335      struct buf *bp;
23336      bitchunk_t *wptr, *wlim, k;
23337      bit_t i, b;
23338
23339      if (sp->s_rd_only)
23340            panic(__FILE__,"can't allocate bit on read-only filesys.", NO_NUM);
23341
23342      if (map == IMAP) {
23343            start_block = START_BLOCK;
23344            map_bits = sp->s_ninodes + 1;
23345            bit_blocks = sp->s_imap_blocks;
23346      } else {
23347            start_block = START_BLOCK + sp->s_imap_blocks;
23348            map_bits = sp->s_zones - (sp->s_firstdatazone - 1);
23349            bit_blocks = sp->s_zmap_blocks;
```

```
23350    }
23351
23352    /* Figure out where to start the bit search (depends on 'origin'). */
23353    if (origin >= map_bits) origin = 0;    /* for robustness */
23354
23355    /* Locate the starting place. */
23356    block = origin / FS_BITS_PER_BLOCK(sp->s_block_size);
23357    word = (origin % FS_BITS_PER_BLOCK(sp->s_block_size)) / FS_BITCHUNK_BITS;
23358
23359    /* Iterate over all blocks plus one, because we start in the middle. */
23360    bcount = bit_blocks + 1;
23361    do {
23362            bp = get_block(sp->s_dev, start_block + block, NORMAL);
23363            wlim = &bp->b_bitmap[FS_BITMAP_CHUNKS(sp->s_block_size)];
23364
23365            /* Iterate over the words in block. */
23366            for (wptr = &bp->b_bitmap[word]; wptr < wlim; wptr++) {
23367
23368                    /* Does this word contain a free bit? */
23369                    if (*wptr == (bitchunk_t) ~0) continue;
23370
23371                    /* Find and allocate the free bit. */
23372                    k = conv2(sp->s_native, (int) *wptr);
23373                    for (i = 0; (k & (1 << i)) != 0; ++i) {}
23374
23375                    /* Bit number from the start of the bit map. */
23376                    b = ((bit_t) block * FS_BITS_PER_BLOCK(sp->s_block_size))
23377                        + (wptr - &bp->b_bitmap[0]) * FS_BITCHUNK_BITS
23378                        + i;
23379
23380                    /* Don't allocate bits beyond the end of the map. */
23381                    if (b >= map_bits) break;
23382
23383                    /* Allocate and return bit number. */
23384                    k |= 1 << i;
23385                    *wptr = conv2(sp->s_native, (int) k);
23386                    bp->b_dirt = DIRTY;
23387                    put_block(bp, MAP_BLOCK);
23388                    return(b);
23389            }
23390            put_block(bp, MAP_BLOCK);
23391            if (++block >= bit_blocks) block = 0;    /* last block, wrap around */
23392            word = 0;
23393    } while (--bcount > 0);
23394    return(NO_BIT);                      /* no bit could be allocated */
23395  }

23397  /*===========================================================================*
23398   *                              free_bit                                     *
23399   *===========================================================================*/
23400  PUBLIC void free_bit(sp, map, bit_returned)
23401  struct super_block *sp;          /* the filesystem to operate on */
23402  int map;                         /* IMAP (inode map) or ZMAP (zone map) */
23403  bit_t bit_returned;              /* number of bit to insert into the map */
23404  {
23405  /* Return a zone or inode by turning off its bitmap bit. */
23406
23407    unsigned block, word, bit;
23408    struct buf *bp;
23409    bitchunk_t k, mask;
```

```
23410        block_t start_block;
23411
23412        if (sp->s_rd_only)
23413              panic(__FILE__,"can't free bit on read-only filesys.", NO_NUM);
23414
23415        if (map == IMAP) {
23416              start_block = START_BLOCK;
23417        } else {
23418              start_block = START_BLOCK + sp->s_imap_blocks;
23419        }
23420        block = bit_returned / FS_BITS_PER_BLOCK(sp->s_block_size);
23421        word = (bit_returned % FS_BITS_PER_BLOCK(sp->s_block_size))
23422                    / FS_BITCHUNK_BITS;
23423
23424        bit = bit_returned % FS_BITCHUNK_BITS;
23425        mask = 1 << bit;
23426
23427        bp = get_block(sp->s_dev, start_block + block, NORMAL);
23428
23429        k = conv2(sp->s_native, (int) bp->b_bitmap[word]);
23430        if (!(k & mask)) {
23431              panic(__FILE__,map == IMAP ? "tried to free unused inode" :
23432                    "tried to free unused block", NO_NUM);
23433        }
23434
23435        k &= ~mask;
23436        bp->b_bitmap[word] = conv2(sp->s_native, (int) k);
23437        bp->b_dirt = DIRTY;
23438
23439        put_block(bp, MAP_BLOCK);
23440  }

23442  /*===========================================================================*
23443   *                            get_super                                      *
23444   *===========================================================================*/
23445  PUBLIC struct super_block *get_super(dev)
23446  dev_t dev;                       /* device number whose super_block is sought */
23447  {
23448  /* Search the superblock table for this device.  It is supposed to be there. */
23449
23450     register struct super_block *sp;
23451
23452     if (dev == NO_DEV)
23453           panic(__FILE__,"request for super_block of NO_DEV", NO_NUM);
23454
23455     for (sp = &super_block[0]; sp < &super_block[NR_SUPERS]; sp++)
23456           if (sp->s_dev == dev) return(sp);
23457
23458     /* Search failed.  Something wrong. */
23459     panic(__FILE__,"can't find superblock for device (in decimal)", (int) dev);
23460
23461     return(NIL_SUPER);                /* to keep the compiler and lint quiet */
23462  }

23464  /*===========================================================================*
23465   *                            get_block_size                                 *
23466   *===========================================================================*/
23467  PUBLIC int get_block_size(dev_t dev)
23468  {
23469  /* Search the superblock table for this device. */
```

```
23470
23471      register struct super_block *sp;
23472
23473      if (dev == NO_DEV)
23474            panic(__FILE__,"request for block size of NO_DEV", NO_NUM);
23475
23476      for (sp = &super_block[0]; sp < &super_block[NR_SUPERS]; sp++) {
23477            if (sp->s_dev == dev) {
23478                    return(sp->s_block_size);
23479            }
23480      }
23481
23482      /* no mounted filesystem? use this block size then. */
23483      return MIN_BLOCK_SIZE;
23484  }

23486  /*===========================================================================*
23487   *                              mounted                                       *
23488   *===========================================================================*/
23489  PUBLIC int mounted(rip)
23490  register struct inode *rip;      /* pointer to inode */
23491  {
23492  /* Report on whether the given inode is on a mounted (or ROOT) file system. */
23493
23494      register struct super_block *sp;
23495      register dev_t dev;
23496
23497      dev = (dev_t) rip->i_zone[0];
23498      if (dev == root_dev) return(TRUE);     /* inode is on root file system */
23499
23500      for (sp = &super_block[0]; sp < &super_block[NR_SUPERS]; sp++)
23501            if (sp->s_dev == dev) return(TRUE);
23502
23503      return(FALSE);
23504  }

23506  /*===========================================================================*
23507   *                              read_super                                    *
23508   *===========================================================================*/
23509  PUBLIC int read_super(sp)
23510  register struct super_block *sp; /* pointer to a superblock */
23511  {
23512  /* Read a superblock. */
23513      dev_t dev;
23514      int magic;
23515      int version, native, r;
23516      static char sbbuf[MIN_BLOCK_SIZE];
23517
23518      dev = sp->s_dev;                 /* save device (will be overwritten by copy) */
23519      if (dev == NO_DEV)
23520            panic(__FILE__,"request for super_block of NO_DEV", NO_NUM);
23521      r = dev_io(DEV_READ, dev, FS_PROC_NR,
23522            sbbuf, SUPER_BLOCK_BYTES, MIN_BLOCK_SIZE, 0);
23523      if (r != MIN_BLOCK_SIZE) {
23524            return EINVAL;
23525      }
23526      memcpy(sp, sbbuf, sizeof(*sp));
23527      sp->s_dev = NO_DEV;             /* restore later */
23528      magic = sp->s_magic;            /* determines file system type */
23529
```

```
23530    /* Get file system version and type. */
23531    if (magic == SUPER_MAGIC || magic == conv2(BYTE_SWAP, SUPER_MAGIC)) {
23532          version = V1;
23533          native  = (magic == SUPER_MAGIC);
23534    } else if (magic == SUPER_V2 || magic == conv2(BYTE_SWAP, SUPER_V2)) {
23535          version = V2;
23536          native  = (magic == SUPER_V2);
23537    } else if (magic == SUPER_V3) {
23538          version = V3;
23539          native = 1;
23540    } else {
23541          return(EINVAL);
23542    }
23543
23544    /* If the super block has the wrong byte order, swap the fields; the magic
23545     * number doesn't need conversion. */
23546    sp->s_ninodes =        conv4(native, sp->s_ninodes);
23547    sp->s_nzones =         conv2(native, (int) sp->s_nzones);
23548    sp->s_imap_blocks =    conv2(native, (int) sp->s_imap_blocks);
23549    sp->s_zmap_blocks =    conv2(native, (int) sp->s_zmap_blocks);
23550    sp->s_firstdatazone = conv2(native, (int) sp->s_firstdatazone);
23551    sp->s_log_zone_size = conv2(native, (int) sp->s_log_zone_size);
23552    sp->s_max_size =       conv4(native, sp->s_max_size);
23553    sp->s_zones =          conv4(native, sp->s_zones);
23554
23555    /* In V1, the device size was kept in a short, s_nzones, which limited
23556     * devices to 32K zones.  For V2, it was decided to keep the size as a
23557     * long.  However, just changing s_nzones to a long would not work, since
23558     * then the position of s_magic in the super block would not be the same
23559     * in V1 and V2 file systems, and there would be no way to tell whether
23560     * a newly mounted file system was V1 or V2.  The solution was to introduce
23561     * a new variable, s_zones, and copy the size there.
23562     *
23563     * Calculate some other numbers that depend on the version here too, to
23564     * hide some of the differences.
23565     */
23566    if (version == V1) {
23567          sp->s_block_size = STATIC_BLOCK_SIZE;
23568          sp->s_zones = sp->s_nzones;     /* only V1 needs this copy */
23569          sp->s_inodes_per_block = V1_INODES_PER_BLOCK;
23570          sp->s_ndzones = V1_NR_DZONES;
23571          sp->s_nindirs = V1_INDIRECTS;
23572    } else {
23573          if (version == V2)
23574                  sp->s_block_size = STATIC_BLOCK_SIZE;
23575          if (sp->s_block_size < MIN_BLOCK_SIZE)
23576                  return EINVAL;
23577          sp->s_inodes_per_block = V2_INODES_PER_BLOCK(sp->s_block_size);
23578          sp->s_ndzones = V2_NR_DZONES;
23579          sp->s_nindirs = V2_INDIRECTS(sp->s_block_size);
23580    }
23581
23582    if (sp->s_block_size < MIN_BLOCK_SIZE) {
23583          return EINVAL;
23584    }
23585    if (sp->s_block_size > MAX_BLOCK_SIZE) {
23586          printf("Filesystem block size is %d kB; maximum filesystem\n"
23587          "block size is %d kB. This limit can be increased by recompiling.\n",
23588          sp->s_block_size/1024, MAX_BLOCK_SIZE/1024);
23589          return EINVAL;
```

```
23590      }
23591      if ((sp->s_block_size % 512) != 0) {
23592            return EINVAL;
23593      }
23594      if (SUPER_SIZE > sp->s_block_size) {
23595            return EINVAL;
23596      }
23597      if ((sp->s_block_size % V2_INODE_SIZE) != 0 ||
23598         (sp->s_block_size % V1_INODE_SIZE) != 0) {
23599            return EINVAL;
23600      }
23601
23602      sp->s_isearch = 0;              /* inode searches initially start at 0 */
23603      sp->s_zsearch = 0;              /* zone searches initially start at 0 */
23604      sp->s_version = version;
23605      sp->s_native  = native;
23606
23607      /* Make a few basic checks to see if super block looks reasonable. */
23608      if (sp->s_imap_blocks < 1 || sp->s_zmap_blocks < 1
23609                                    || sp->s_ninodes < 1 || sp->s_zones < 1
23610                                    || (unsigned) sp->s_log_zone_size > 4) {
23611            printf("not enough imap or zone map blocks, \n");
23612            printf("or not enough inodes, or not enough zones, "
23613                         "or zone size too large\n");
23614            return(EINVAL);
23615      }
23616      sp->s_dev = dev;               /* restore device number */
23617      return(OK);
23618   }



+++++++++++++++++++++++++++++++++++++++++++++++++++++++++++++++++++++++++++++++
                           servers/fs/filedes.c
+++++++++++++++++++++++++++++++++++++++++++++++++++++++++++++++++++++++++++++++

23700   /* This file contains the procedures that manipulate file descriptors.
23701    *
23702    * The entry points into this file are
23703    *   get_fd:    look for free file descriptor and free filp slots
23704    *   get_filp:  look up the filp entry for a given file descriptor
23705    *   find_filp: find a filp slot that points to a given inode
23706    */
23707
23708   #include "fs.h"
23709   #include "file.h"
23710   #include "fproc.h"
23711   #include "inode.h"
23712
23713   /*===========================================================================*
23714    *                             get_fd                                        *
23715    *===========================================================================*/
23716   PUBLIC int get_fd(int start, mode_t bits, int *k, struct filp **fpt)
23717   {
23718   /* Look for a free file descriptor and a free filp slot.  Fill in the mode word
23719    * in the latter, but don't claim either one yet, since the open() or creat()
23720    * may yet fail.
23721    */
23722
23723     register struct filp *f;
23724     register int i;
```

```
23725
23726        *k = -1;                            /* we need a way to tell if file desc found */
23727
23728        /* Search the fproc fp_filp table for a free file descriptor. */
23729        for (i = start; i < OPEN_MAX; i++) {
23730                if (fp->fp_filp[i] == NIL_FILP) {
23731                        /* A file descriptor has been located. */
23732                        *k = i;
23733                        break;
23734                }
23735        }
23736
23737        /* Check to see if a file descriptor has been found. */
23738        if (*k < 0) return(EMFILE);    /* this is why we initialized k to -1 */
23739
23740        /* Now that a file descriptor has been found, look for a free filp slot. */
23741        for (f = &filp[0]; f < &filp[NR_FILPS]; f++) {
23742                if (f->filp_count == 0) {
23743                        f->filp_mode = bits;
23744                        f->filp_pos = 0L;
23745                        f->filp_selectors = 0;
23746                        f->filp_select_ops = 0;
23747                        f->filp_pipe_select_ops = 0;
23748                        f->filp_flags = 0;
23749                        *fpt = f;
23750                        return(OK);
23751                }
23752        }
23753
23754        /* If control passes here, the filp table must be full.  Report that back. */
23755        return(ENFILE);
23756 }
23757
23758 /*===========================================================================*
23759  *                              get_filp                                     *
23760  *===========================================================================*/
23761 PUBLIC struct filp *get_filp(fild)
23762 int fild;                              /* file descriptor */
23763 {
23764 /* See if 'fild' refers to a valid file descr.  If so, return its filp ptr. */
23765
23766   err_code = EBADF;
23767   if (fild < 0 || fild >= OPEN_MAX ) return(NIL_FILP);
23768   return(fp->fp_filp[fild]);    /* may also be NIL_FILP */
23769 }
23770
23771 /*===========================================================================*
23772  *                              find_filp                                    *
23773  *===========================================================================*/
23774 PUBLIC struct filp *find_filp(register struct inode *rip, mode_t bits)
23775 {
23776 /* Find a filp slot that refers to the inode 'rip' in a way as described
23777  * by the mode bit 'bits'. Used for determining whether somebody is still
23778  * interested in either end of a pipe.  Also used when opening a FIFO to
23779  * find partners to share a filp field with (to shared the file position).
23780  * Like 'get_fd' it performs its job by linear search through the filp table.
23781  */
23782
23783   register struct filp *f;
23784
```

```
23785        for (f = &filp[0]; f < &filp[NR_FILPS]; f++) {
23786              if (f->filp_count != 0 && f->filp_ino == rip && (f->filp_mode & bits)){
23787                    return(f);
23788              }
23789        }
23790
23791        /* If control passes here, the filp wasn't there.  Report that back. */
23792        return(NIL_FILP);
23793  }



++++++++++++++++++++++++++++++++++++++++++++++++++++++++++++++++++++++++++++++++
                              servers/fs/lock.c
++++++++++++++++++++++++++++++++++++++++++++++++++++++++++++++++++++++++++++++++

23800  /* This file handles advisory file locking as required by POSIX.
23801   *
23802   * The entry points into this file are
23803   *   lock_op:    perform locking operations for FCNTL system call
23804   *   lock_revive: revive processes when a lock is released
23805   */
23806
23807  #include "fs.h"
23808  #include <minix/com.h>
23809  #include <fcntl.h>
23810  #include <unistd.h>
23811  #include "file.h"
23812  #include "fproc.h"
23813  #include "inode.h"
23814  #include "lock.h"
23815  #include "param.h"
23816
23817  /*===========================================================================*
23818   *                              lock_op                                      *
23819   *===========================================================================*/
23820  PUBLIC int lock_op(f, req)
23821  struct filp *f;
23822  int req;                              /* either F_SETLK or F_SETLKW */
23823  {
23824  /* Perform the advisory locking required by POSIX. */
23825
23826      int r, ltype, i, conflict = 0, unlocking = 0;
23827      mode_t mo;
23828      off_t first, last;
23829      struct flock flock;
23830      vir_bytes user_flock;
23831      struct file_lock *flp, *flp2, *empty;
23832
23833      /* Fetch the flock structure from user space. */
23834      user_flock = (vir_bytes) m_in.name1;
23835      r = sys_datacopy(who, (vir_bytes) user_flock,
23836          FS_PROC_NR, (vir_bytes) &flock, (phys_bytes) sizeof(flock));
23837      if (r != OK) return(EINVAL);
23838
23839      /* Make some error checks. */
23840      ltype = flock.l_type;
23841      mo = f->filp_mode;
23842      if (ltype != F_UNLCK && ltype != F_RDLCK && ltype != F_WRLCK) return(EINVAL);
23843      if (req == F_GETLK && ltype == F_UNLCK) return(EINVAL);
23844      if ( (f->filp_ino->i_mode & I_TYPE) != I_REGULAR) return(EINVAL);
```

```
23845        if (req != F_GETLK && ltype == F_RDLCK && (mo & R_BIT) == 0) return(EBADF);
23846        if (req != F_GETLK && ltype == F_WRLCK && (mo & W_BIT) == 0) return(EBADF);
23847
23848        /* Compute the first and last bytes in the lock region. */
23849        switch (flock.l_whence) {
23850              case SEEK_SET:  first = 0; break;
23851              case SEEK_CUR:  first = f->filp_pos; break;
23852              case SEEK_END:  first = f->filp_ino->i_size; break;
23853              default:        return(EINVAL);
23854        }
23855        /* Check for overflow. */
23856        if (((long)flock.l_start > 0) && ((first + flock.l_start) < first))
23857              return(EINVAL);
23858        if (((long)flock.l_start < 0) && ((first + flock.l_start) > first))
23859              return(EINVAL);
23860        first = first + flock.l_start;
23861        last = first + flock.l_len - 1;
23862        if (flock.l_len == 0) last = MAX_FILE_POS;
23863        if (last < first) return(EINVAL);
23864
23865        /* Check if this region conflicts with any existing lock. */
23866        empty = (struct file_lock *) 0;
23867        for (flp = &file_lock[0]; flp < & file_lock[NR_LOCKS]; flp++) {
23868              if (flp->lock_type == 0) {
23869                    if (empty == (struct file_lock *) 0) empty = flp;
23870                    continue;        /* 0 means unused slot */
23871              }
23872              if (flp->lock_inode != f->filp_ino) continue;   /* different file */
23873              if (last < flp->lock_first) continue;   /* new one is in front */
23874              if (first > flp->lock_last) continue;   /* new one is afterwards */
23875              if (ltype == F_RDLCK && flp->lock_type == F_RDLCK) continue;
23876              if (ltype != F_UNLCK && flp->lock_pid == fp->fp_pid) continue;
23877
23878              /* There might be a conflict.  Process it. */
23879              conflict = 1;
23880              if (req == F_GETLK) break;
23881
23882              /* If we are trying to set a lock, it just failed. */
23883              if (ltype == F_RDLCK || ltype == F_WRLCK) {
23884                    if (req == F_SETLK) {
23885                          /* For F_SETLK, just report back failure. */
23886                          return(EAGAIN);
23887                    } else {
23888                          /* For F_SETLKW, suspend the process. */
23889                          suspend(XLOCK);
23890                          return(SUSPEND);
23891                    }
23892              }
23893
23894              /* We are clearing a lock and we found something that overlaps. */
23895              unlocking = 1;
23896              if (first <= flp->lock_first && last >= flp->lock_last) {
23897                    flp->lock_type = 0;      /* mark slot as unused */
23898                    nr_locks--;              /* number of locks is now 1 less */
23899                    continue;
23900              }
23901
23902              /* Part of a locked region has been unlocked. */
23903              if (first <= flp->lock_first) {
23904                    flp->lock_first = last + 1;
```

```
23905                          continue;
23906                  }
23907
23908              if (last >= flp->lock_last) {
23909                      flp->lock_last = first - 1;
23910                      continue;
23911              }
23912
23913              /* Bad luck. A lock has been split in two by unlocking the middle. */
23914              if (nr_locks == NR_LOCKS) return(ENOLCK);
23915              for (i = 0; i < NR_LOCKS; i++)
23916                      if (file_lock[i].lock_type == 0) break;
23917              flp2 = &file_lock[i];
23918              flp2->lock_type = flp->lock_type;
23919              flp2->lock_pid = flp->lock_pid;
23920              flp2->lock_inode = flp->lock_inode;
23921              flp2->lock_first = last + 1;
23922              flp2->lock_last = flp->lock_last;
23923              flp->lock_last = first - 1;
23924              nr_locks++;
23925      }
23926      if (unlocking) lock_revive();
23927
23928      if (req == F_GETLK) {
23929              if (conflict) {
23930                      /* GETLK and conflict. Report on the conflicting lock. */
23931                      flock.l_type = flp->lock_type;
23932                      flock.l_whence = SEEK_SET;
23933                      flock.l_start = flp->lock_first;
23934                      flock.l_len = flp->lock_last - flp->lock_first + 1;
23935                      flock.l_pid = flp->lock_pid;
23936
23937              } else {
23938                      /* It is GETLK and there is no conflict. */
23939                      flock.l_type = F_UNLCK;
23940              }
23941
23942              /* Copy the flock structure back to the caller. */
23943              r = sys_datacopy(FS_PROC_NR, (vir_bytes) &flock,
23944                      who, (vir_bytes) user_flock, (phys_bytes) sizeof(flock));
23945              return(r);
23946      }
23947
23948      if (ltype == F_UNLCK) return(OK);      /* unlocked a region with no locks */
23949
23950      /* There is no conflict.  If space exists, store new lock in the table. */
23951      if (empty == (struct file_lock *) 0) return(ENOLCK);  /* table full */
23952      empty->lock_type = ltype;
23953      empty->lock_pid = fp->fp_pid;
23954      empty->lock_inode = f->filp_ino;
23955      empty->lock_first = first;
23956      empty->lock_last = last;
23957      nr_locks++;
23958      return(OK);
23959  }
```

```
23961   /*===========================================================================*
23962    *                              lock_revive                                  *
23963    *===========================================================================*/
23964   PUBLIC void lock_revive()
23965   {
23966   /* Go find all the processes that are waiting for any kind of lock and
23967    * revive them all.  The ones that are still blocked will block again when
23968    * they run.  The others will complete.  This strategy is a space-time
23969    * tradeoff.  Figuring out exactly which ones to unblock now would take
23970    * extra code, and the only thing it would win would be some performance in
23971    * extremely rare circumstances (namely, that somebody actually used
23972    * locking).
23973    */
23974
23975     int task;
23976     struct fproc *fptr;
23977
23978     for (fptr = &fproc[INIT_PROC_NR + 1]; fptr < &fproc[NR_PROCS]; fptr++){
23979           task = -fptr->fp_task;
23980           if (fptr->fp_suspended == SUSPENDED && task == XLOCK) {
23981                   revive( (int) (fptr - fproc), 0);
23982           }
23983     }
23984   }
```

```
++++++++++++++++++++++++++++++++++++++++++++++++++++++++++++++++++++++++++++++
                            servers/fs/main.c
++++++++++++++++++++++++++++++++++++++++++++++++++++++++++++++++++++++++++++++

24000   /* This file contains the main program of the File System.  It consists of
24001    * a loop that gets messages requesting work, carries out the work, and sends
24002    * replies.
24003    *
24004    * The entry points into this file are:
24005    *   main:    main program of the File System
24006    *   reply:   send a reply to a process after the requested work is done
24007    *
24008    */
24009
24010   struct super_block;            /* proto.h needs to know this */
24011
24012   #include "fs.h"
24013   #include <fcntl.h>
24014   #include <string.h>
24015   #include <stdio.h>
24016   #include <signal.h>
24017   #include <stdlib.h>
24018   #include <sys/ioc_memory.h>
24019   #include <sys/svrctl.h>
24020   #include <minix/callnr.h>
24021   #include <minix/com.h>
24022   #include <minix/keymap.h>
24023   #include <minix/const.h>
24024   #include "buf.h"
24025   #include "file.h"
24026   #include "fproc.h"
24027   #include "inode.h"
24028   #include "param.h"
24029   #include "super.h"
```

```
24030
24031  FORWARD _PROTOTYPE( void fs_init, (void)                          );
24032  FORWARD _PROTOTYPE( int igetenv, (char *var, int optional)        );
24033  FORWARD _PROTOTYPE( void get_work, (void)                         );
24034  FORWARD _PROTOTYPE( void load_ram, (void)                         );
24035  FORWARD _PROTOTYPE( void load_super, (Dev_t super_dev)            );
24036
24037  /*===========================================================================*
24038   *                              main                                         *
24039   *===========================================================================*/
24040  PUBLIC int main()
24041  {
24042  /* This is the main program of the file system.  The main loop consists of
24043   * three major activities: getting new work, processing the work, and sending
24044   * the reply.  This loop never terminates as long as the file system runs.
24045   */
24046   sigset_t sigset;
24047   int error;
24048
24049   fs_init();
24050
24051   /* This is the main loop that gets work, processes it, and sends replies. */
24052   while (TRUE) {
24053          get_work();                     /* sets who and call_nr */
24054
24055          fp = &fproc[who];       /* pointer to proc table struct */
24056          super_user = (fp->fp_effuid == SU_UID ? TRUE : FALSE);   /* su? */
24057
24058          /* Check for special control messages first. */
24059          if (call_nr == SYS_SIG) {
24060                  sigset = m_in.NOTIFY_ARG;
24061                  if (sigismember(&sigset, SIGKSTOP)) {
24062                          do_sync();
24063                          sys_exit(0);            /* never returns */
24064                  }
24065          } else if (call_nr == SYN_ALARM) {
24066                  /* Not a user request; system has expired one of our timers,
24067                   * currently only in use for select(). Check it.
24068                   */
24069                  fs_expire_timers(m_in.NOTIFY_TIMESTAMP);
24070          } else if ((call_nr & NOTIFY_MESSAGE)) {
24071                  /* Device notifies us of an event. */
24072                  dev_status(&m_in);
24073          } else {
24074                  /* Call the internal function that does the work. */
24075                  if (call_nr < 0 || call_nr >= NCALLS) {
24076                   error = ENOSYS;
24077                   printf("FS,warning illegal %d system call by %d\n",call_nr,who);
24078                  } else if (fp->fp_pid == PID_FREE) {
24079                   error = ENOSYS;
24080                   printf("FS, bad process, who = %d, call_nr = %d, slot1 = %d\n",
24081                                  who, call_nr, m_in.slot1);
24082                  } else {
24083                          error = (*call_vec[call_nr])();
24084                  }
24085
24086                  /* Copy the results back to the user and send reply. */
24087                  if (error != SUSPEND) { reply(who, error); }
24088                  if (rdahed_inode != NIL_INODE) {
24089                          read_ahead(); /* do block read ahead */
```

```
24090                    }
24091               }
24092        }
24093     return(OK);                              /* shouldn't come here */
24094  }

24096  /*===========================================================================*
24097   *                            get_work                                       *
24098   *===========================================================================*/
24099  PRIVATE void get_work()
24100  {
24101     /* Normally wait for new input.  However, if 'reviving' is
24102      * nonzero, a suspended process must be awakened.
24103      */
24104     register struct fproc *rp;
24105
24106     if (reviving != 0) {
24107           /* Revive a suspended process. */
24108           for (rp = &fproc[0]; rp < &fproc[NR_PROCS]; rp++)
24109                   if (rp->fp_revived == REVIVING) {
24110                           who = (int)(rp - fproc);
24111                           call_nr = rp->fp_fd & BYTE;
24112                           m_in.fd = (rp->fp_fd >>8) & BYTE;
24113                           m_in.buffer = rp->fp_buffer;
24114                           m_in.nbytes = rp->fp_nbytes;
24115                           rp->fp_suspended = NOT_SUSPENDED; /*no longer hanging*/
24116                           rp->fp_revived = NOT_REVIVING;
24117                           reviving--;
24118                           return;
24119                   }
24120           panic(__FILE__,"get_work couldn't revive anyone", NO_NUM);
24121     }
24122
24123     /* Normal case.  No one to revive. */
24124     if (receive(ANY, &m_in) != OK) panic(__FILE__,"fs receive error", NO_NUM);
24125     who = m_in.m_source;
24126     call_nr = m_in.m_type;
24127  }

24129  /*===========================================================================*
24130   *                            buf_pool                                       *
24131   *===========================================================================*/
24132  PRIVATE void buf_pool(void)
24133  {
24134  /* Initialize the buffer pool. */
24135
24136     register struct buf *bp;
24137
24138     bufs_in_use = 0;
24139     front = &buf[0];
24140     rear = &buf[NR_BUFS - 1];
24141
24142     for (bp = &buf[0]; bp < &buf[NR_BUFS]; bp++) {
24143           bp->b_blocknr = NO_BLOCK;
24144           bp->b_dev = NO_DEV;
24145           bp->b_next = bp + 1;
24146           bp->b_prev = bp - 1;
24147     }
24148     buf[0].b_prev = NIL_BUF;
24149     buf[NR_BUFS - 1].b_next = NIL_BUF;
```

```
24150
24151        for (bp = &buf[0]; bp < &buf[NR_BUFS]; bp++) bp->b_hash = bp->b_next;
24152        buf_hash[0] = front;
24153
24154   }

24156   /*===========================================================================*
24157    *                               reply                                       *
24158    *===========================================================================*/
24159   PUBLIC void reply(whom, result)
24160   int whom;                         /* process to reply to */
24161   int result;                       /* result of the call (usually OK or error #) */
24162   {
24163   /* Send a reply to a user process. It may fail (if the process has just
24164    * been killed by a signal), so don't check the return code.  If the send
24165    * fails, just ignore it.
24166    */
24167     int s;
24168     m_out.reply_type = result;
24169     s = send(whom, &m_out);
24170     if (s != OK) printf("FS: couldn't send reply %d: %d\n", result, s);
24171   }

24173   /*===========================================================================*
24174    *                               fs_init                                     *
24175    *===========================================================================*/
24176   PRIVATE void fs_init()
24177   {
24178   /* Initialize global variables, tables, etc. */
24179     register struct inode *rip;
24180     register struct fproc *rfp;
24181     message mess;
24182     int s;
24183
24184     /* Initialize the process table with help of the process manager messages.
24185      * Expect one message for each system process with its slot number and pid.
24186      * When no more processes follow, the magic process number NONE is sent.
24187      * Then, stop and synchronize with the PM.
24188      */
24189     do {
24190           if (OK != (s=receive(PM_PROC_NR, &mess)))
24191                 panic(__FILE__,"FS couldn't receive from PM", s);
24192           if (NONE == mess.PR_PROC_NR) break;
24193
24194           rfp = &fproc[mess.PR_PROC_NR];
24195           rfp->fp_pid = mess.PR_PID;
24196           rfp->fp_realuid = (uid_t) SYS_UID;
24197           rfp->fp_effuid = (uid_t) SYS_UID;
24198           rfp->fp_realgid = (gid_t) SYS_GID;
24199           rfp->fp_effgid = (gid_t) SYS_GID;
24200           rfp->fp_umask = ~0;
24201
24202     } while (TRUE);                      /* continue until process NONE */
24203     mess.m_type = OK;                    /* tell PM that we succeeded */
24204     s=send(PM_PROC_NR, &mess);           /* send synchronization message */
24205
24206     /* All process table entries have been set. Continue with FS initialization.
24207      * Certain relations must hold for the file system to work at all. Some
24208      * extra block_size requirements are checked at super-block-read-in time.
24209      */
```

```
24210      if (OPEN_MAX > 127) panic(__FILE__,"OPEN_MAX > 127", NO_NUM);
24211      if (NR_BUFS < 6) panic(__FILE__,"NR_BUFS < 6", NO_NUM);
24212      if (V1_INODE_SIZE != 32) panic(__FILE__,"V1 inode size != 32", NO_NUM);
24213      if (V2_INODE_SIZE != 64) panic(__FILE__,"V2 inode size != 64", NO_NUM);
24214      if (OPEN_MAX > 8 * sizeof(long))
24215            panic(__FILE__,"Too few bits in fp_cloexec", NO_NUM);
24216
24217      /* The following initializations are needed to let dev_opcl succeed .*/
24218      fp = (struct fproc *) NULL;
24219      who = FS_PROC_NR;
24220
24221      buf_pool();                      /* initialize buffer pool */
24222      build_dmap();                    /* build device table and map boot driver */
24223      load_ram();                      /* init RAM disk, load if it is root */
24224      load_super(root_dev);            /* load super block for root device */
24225      init_select();                   /* init select() structures */
24226
24227      /* The root device can now be accessed; set process directories. */
24228      for (rfp=&fproc[0]; rfp < &fproc[NR_PROCS]; rfp++) {
24229            if (rfp->fp_pid != PID_FREE) {
24230                    rip = get_inode(root_dev, ROOT_INODE);
24231                    dup_inode(rip);
24232                    rfp->fp_rootdir = rip;
24233                    rfp->fp_workdir = rip;
24234            }
24235      }
24236  }

24238  /*===========================================================================*
24239   *                              igetenv                                      *
24240   *===========================================================================*/
24241  PRIVATE int igetenv(key, optional)
24242  char *key;
24243  int optional;
24244  {
24245  /* Ask kernel for an integer valued boot environment variable. */
24246    char value[64];
24247    int i;
24248
24249    if ((i = env_get_param(key, value, sizeof(value))) != OK) {
24250        if (!optional)
24251          printf("FS: Warning, couldn't get monitor param: %d\n", i);
24252        return 0;
24253    }
24254    return(atoi(value));
24255  }

24257  /*===========================================================================*
24258   *                              load_ram                                     *
24259   *===========================================================================*/
24260  PRIVATE void load_ram(void)
24261  {
24262  /* Allocate a RAM disk with size given in the boot parameters. If a RAM disk
24263   * image is given, the copy the entire image device block-by-block to a RAM
24264   * disk with the same size as the image.
24265   * If the root device is not set, the RAM disk will be used as root instead.
24266   */
24267    register struct buf *bp, *bp1;
24268    u32_t lcount, ram_size_kb;
24269    zone_t zones;
```

```
24270    struct super_block *sp, *dsp;
24271    block_t b;
24272    Dev_t image_dev;
24273    static char sbbuf[MIN_BLOCK_SIZE];
24274    int block_size_image, block_size_ram, ramfs_block_size;
24275    int s;
24276
24277    /* Get some boot environment variables. */
24278    root_dev = igetenv("rootdev", 0);
24279    image_dev = igetenv("ramimagedev", 0);
24280    ram_size_kb = igetenv("ramsize", 0);
24281
24282    /* Open the root device. */
24283    if (dev_open(root_dev, FS_PROC_NR, R_BIT|W_BIT) != OK)
24284        panic(__FILE__,"Cannot open root device",NO_NUM);
24285
24286    /* If we must initialize a ram disk, get details from the image device. */
24287    if (root_dev == DEV_RAM) {
24288        u32_t fsmax, probedev;
24289
24290        /* If we are running from CD, see if we can find it. */
24291        if (igetenv("cdproberoot", 1) && (probedev=cdprobe()) != NO_DEV) {
24292            char devnum[10];
24293            struct sysgetenv env;
24294
24295            /* If so, this is our new RAM image device. */
24296            image_dev = probedev;
24297
24298            /* Tell PM about it, so userland can find out about it
24299             * with sysenv interface.
24300             */
24301            env.key = "cdproberoot";
24302            env.keylen = strlen(env.key);
24303            sprintf(devnum, "%d", (int) probedev);
24304            env.val = devnum;
24305            env.vallen = strlen(devnum);
24306            svrctl(MMSETPARAM, &env);
24307        }
24308
24309        /* Open image device for RAM root. */
24310        if (dev_open(image_dev, FS_PROC_NR, R_BIT) != OK)
24311            panic(__FILE__,"Cannot open RAM image device", NO_NUM);
24312
24313        /* Get size of RAM disk image from the super block. */
24314        sp = &super_block[0];
24315        sp->s_dev = image_dev;
24316        if (read_super(sp) != OK)
24317            panic(__FILE__,"Bad RAM disk image FS", NO_NUM);
24318
24319        lcount = sp->s_zones << sp->s_log_zone_size;    /* # blks on root dev*/
24320
24321        /* Stretch the RAM disk file system to the boot parameters size, but
24322         * no further than the last zone bit map block allows.
24323         */
24324        if (ram_size_kb*1024 < lcount*sp->s_block_size)
24325            ram_size_kb = lcount*sp->s_block_size/1024;
24326        fsmax = (u32_t) sp->s_zmap_blocks * CHAR_BIT * sp->s_block_size;
24327        fsmax = (fsmax + (sp->s_firstdatazone-1)) << sp->s_log_zone_size;
24328        if (ram_size_kb*1024 > fsmax*sp->s_block_size)
24329            ram_size_kb = fsmax*sp->s_block_size/1024;
```

```
24330    }
24331
24332    /* Tell RAM driver how big the RAM disk must be. */
24333    m_out.m_type = DEV_IOCTL;
24334    m_out.PROC_NR = FS_PROC_NR;
24335    m_out.DEVICE = RAM_DEV;
24336    m_out.REQUEST = MIOCRAMSIZE;                    /* I/O control to use */
24337    m_out.POSITION = (ram_size_kb * 1024);         /* request in bytes */
24338    if ((s=sendrec(MEM_PROC_NR, &m_out)) != OK)
24339            panic("FS","sendrec from MEM failed", s);
24340    else if (m_out.REP_STATUS != OK) {
24341            /* Report and continue, unless RAM disk is required as root FS. */
24342            if (root_dev != DEV_RAM) {
24343                    report("FS","can't set RAM disk size", m_out.REP_STATUS);
24344                    return;
24345            } else {
24346                    panic(__FILE__,"can't set RAM disk size", m_out.REP_STATUS);
24347            }
24348    }
24349
24350    /* See if we must load the RAM disk image, otherwise return. */
24351    if (root_dev != DEV_RAM)
24352            return;
24353
24354    /* Copy the blocks one at a time from the image to the RAM disk. */
24355    printf("Loading RAM disk onto /dev/ram:\33[23CLoaded:     0 KB");
24356
24357    inode[0].i_mode = I_BLOCK_SPECIAL;     /* temp inode for rahead() */
24358    inode[0].i_size = LONG_MAX;
24359    inode[0].i_dev = image_dev;
24360    inode[0].i_zone[0] = image_dev;
24361
24362    block_size_ram = get_block_size(DEV_RAM);
24363    block_size_image = get_block_size(image_dev);
24364
24365    /* RAM block size has to be a multiple of the root image block
24366     * size to make copying easier.
24367     */
24368    if (block_size_image % block_size_ram) {
24369            printf("\nram block size: %d image block size: %d\n",
24370                    block_size_ram, block_size_image);
24371            panic(__FILE__, "ram disk block size must be a multiple of "
24372                    "the image disk block size", NO_NUM);
24373    }
24374
24375    /* Loading blocks from image device. */
24376    for (b = 0; b < (block_t) lcount; b++) {
24377            int rb, factor;
24378            bp = rahead(&inode[0], b, (off_t)block_size_image * b, block_size_image);
24379            factor = block_size_image/block_size_ram;
24380            for(rb = 0; rb < factor; rb++) {
24381                    bp1 = get_block(root_dev, b * factor + rb, NO_READ);
24382                    memcpy(bp1->b_data, bp->b_data + rb * block_size_ram,
24383                            (size_t) block_size_ram);
24384                    bp1->b_dirt = DIRTY;
24385                    put_block(bp1, FULL_DATA_BLOCK);
24386            }
24387            put_block(bp, FULL_DATA_BLOCK);
24388            if (b % 11 == 0)
24389            printf("\b\b\b\b\b\b\b%6ld KB", ((long) b * block_size_image)/1024L);
```

```
24390      }
24391
24392      /* Commit changes to RAM so dev_io will see it. */
24393      do_sync();
24394
24395      printf("\rRAM disk of %u KB loaded onto /dev/ram.", (unsigned) ram_size_kb);
24396      if (root_dev == DEV_RAM) printf(" Using RAM disk as root FS.");
24397      printf(" \n");
24398
24399      /* Invalidate and close the image device. */
24400      invalidate(image_dev);
24401      dev_close(image_dev);
24402
24403      /* Resize the RAM disk root file system. */
24404      if (dev_io(DEV_READ, root_dev, FS_PROC_NR,
24405          sbbuf, SUPER_BLOCK_BYTES, MIN_BLOCK_SIZE, 0) != MIN_BLOCK_SIZE) {
24406          printf("WARNING: ramdisk read for resizing failed\n");
24407      }
24408      dsp = (struct super_block *) sbbuf;
24409      if (dsp->s_magic == SUPER_V3)
24410          ramfs_block_size = dsp->s_block_size;
24411      else
24412          ramfs_block_size = STATIC_BLOCK_SIZE;
24413      zones = (ram_size_kb * 1024 / ramfs_block_size) >> sp->s_log_zone_size;
24414
24415      dsp->s_nzones = conv2(sp->s_native, (u16_t) zones);
24416      dsp->s_zones = conv4(sp->s_native, zones);
24417      if (dev_io(DEV_WRITE, root_dev, FS_PROC_NR,
24418          sbbuf, SUPER_BLOCK_BYTES, MIN_BLOCK_SIZE, 0) != MIN_BLOCK_SIZE) {
24419          printf("WARNING: ramdisk write for resizing failed\n");
24420      }
24421  }

24423  /*===========================================================================*
24424   *                              load_super                                    *
24425   *===========================================================================*/
24426  PRIVATE void load_super(super_dev)
24427  dev_t super_dev;                          /* place to get superblock from */
24428  {
24429      int bad;
24430      register struct super_block *sp;
24431      register struct inode *rip;
24432
24433      /* Initialize the super_block table. */
24434      for (sp = &super_block[0]; sp < &super_block[NR_SUPERS]; sp++)
24435          sp->s_dev = NO_DEV;
24436
24437      /* Read in super_block for the root file system. */
24438      sp = &super_block[0];
24439      sp->s_dev = super_dev;
24440
24441      /* Check super_block for consistency. */
24442      bad = (read_super(sp) != OK);
24443      if (!bad) {
24444          rip = get_inode(super_dev, ROOT_INODE); /* inode for root dir */
24445          if ( (rip->i_mode & I_TYPE) != I_DIRECTORY || rip->i_nlinks < 3) bad++;
24446      }
24447      if (bad) panic(__FILE__,"Invalid root file system", NO_NUM);
24448
24449      sp->s_imount = rip;
```

```
24450      dup_inode(rip);
24451      sp->s_isup = rip;
24452      sp->s_rd_only = 0;
24453      return;
24454  }
```

```
++++++++++++++++++++++++++++++++++++++++++++++++++++++++++++++++++++++++++++
                           servers/fs/open.c
++++++++++++++++++++++++++++++++++++++++++++++++++++++++++++++++++++++++++++
```

```
24500  /* This file contains the procedures for creating, opening, closing, and
24501   * seeking on files.
24502   *
24503   * The entry points into this file are
24504   *   do_creat:   perform the CREAT system call
24505   *   do_open:    perform the OPEN system call
24506   *   do_mknod:   perform the MKNOD system call
24507   *   do_mkdir:   perform the MKDIR system call
24508   *   do_close:   perform the CLOSE system call
24509   *   do_lseek:   perform the LSEEK system call
24510   */
24511
24512  #include "fs.h"
24513  #include <sys/stat.h>
24514  #include <fcntl.h>
24515  #include <minix/callnr.h>
24516  #include <minix/com.h>
24517  #include "buf.h"
24518  #include "file.h"
24519  #include "fproc.h"
24520  #include "inode.h"
24521  #include "lock.h"
24522  #include "param.h"
24523  #include "super.h"
24524
24525  #define offset m2_l1
24526
24527  PRIVATE char mode_map[] = {R_BIT, W_BIT, R_BIT|W_BIT, 0};
24528
24529  FORWARD _PROTOTYPE( int common_open, (int oflags, mode_t omode)          );
24530  FORWARD _PROTOTYPE( int pipe_open, (struct inode *rip,mode_t bits,int oflags));
24531  FORWARD _PROTOTYPE( struct inode *new_node, (char *path, mode_t bits,
24532                                                 zone_t z0)          );
24533
24534  /*===========================================================================*
24535   *                              do_creat                                      *
24536   *===========================================================================*/
24537  PUBLIC int do_creat()
24538  {
24539  /* Perform the creat(name, mode) system call. */
24540      int r;
24541
24542      if (fetch_name(m_in.name, m_in.name_length, M3) != OK) return(err_code);
24543      r = common_open(O_WRONLY | O_CREAT | O_TRUNC, (mode_t) m_in.mode);
24544      return(r);
24545  }
```

```
24547  /*===========================================================================*
24548   *                              do_open                                      *
24549   *===========================================================================*/
24550  PUBLIC int do_open()
24551  {
24552  /* Perform the open(name, flags,...) system call. */
24553
24554    int create_mode = 0;            /* is really mode_t but this gives problems */
24555    int r;
24556
24557    /* If O_CREAT is set, open has three parameters, otherwise two. */
24558    if (m_in.mode & O_CREAT) {
24559          create_mode = m_in.c_mode;
24560          r = fetch_name(m_in.c_name, m_in.name1_length, M1);
24561    } else {
24562          r = fetch_name(m_in.name, m_in.name_length, M3);
24563    }
24564
24565    if (r != OK) return(err_code); /* name was bad */
24566    r = common_open(m_in.mode, create_mode);
24567    return(r);
24568  }

24570  /*===========================================================================*
24571   *                              common_open                                  *
24572   *===========================================================================*/
24573  PRIVATE int common_open(register int oflags, mode_t omode)
24574  {
24575  /* Common code from do_creat and do_open. */
24576
24577    register struct inode *rip;
24578    int r, b, exist = TRUE;
24579    dev_t dev;
24580    mode_t bits;
24581    off_t pos;
24582    struct filp *fil_ptr, *filp2;
24583
24584    /* Remap the bottom two bits of oflags. */
24585    bits = (mode_t) mode_map[oflags & O_ACCMODE];
24586
24587    /* See if file descriptor and filp slots are available. */
24588    if ( (r = get_fd(0, bits, &m_in.fd, &fil_ptr)) != OK) return(r);
24589
24590    /* If O_CREATE is set, try to make the file. */
24591    if (oflags & O_CREAT) {
24592          /* Create a new inode by calling new_node(). */
24593          omode = I_REGULAR | (omode & ALL_MODES & fp->fp_umask);
24594          rip = new_node(user_path, omode, NO_ZONE);
24595          r = err_code;
24596          if (r == OK) exist = FALSE;        /* we just created the file */
24597          else if (r != EEXIST) return(r); /* other error */
24598          else exist = !(oflags & O_EXCL); /* file exists, if the O_EXCL
24599                                              flag is set this is an error */
24600    } else {
24601          /* Scan path name. */
24602          if ( (rip = eat_path(user_path)) == NIL_INODE) return(err_code);
24603    }
24604
24605    /* Claim the file descriptor and filp slot and fill them in. */
24606    fp->fp_filp[m_in.fd] = fil_ptr;
```

```
24607        fil_ptr->filp_count = 1;
24608        fil_ptr->filp_ino = rip;
24609        fil_ptr->filp_flags = oflags;
24610
24611        /* Only do the normal open code if we didn't just create the file. */
24612        if (exist) {
24613                /* Check protections. */
24614                if ((r = forbidden(rip, bits)) == OK) {
24615                        /* Opening reg. files directories and special files differ. */
24616                        switch (rip->i_mode & I_TYPE) {
24617                            case I_REGULAR:
24618                                /* Truncate regular file if O_TRUNC. */
24619                                if (oflags & O_TRUNC) {
24620                                        if ((r = forbidden(rip, W_BIT)) !=OK) break;
24621                                        truncate(rip);
24622                                        wipe_inode(rip);
24623                                        /* Send the inode from the inode cache to the
24624                                         * block cache, so it gets written on the next
24625                                         * cache flush.
24626                                         */
24627                                        rw_inode(rip, WRITING);
24628                                }
24629                                break;
24630
24631                            case I_DIRECTORY:
24632                                /* Directories may be read but not written. */
24633                                r = (bits & W_BIT ? EISDIR : OK);
24634                                break;
24635
24636                            case I_CHAR_SPECIAL:
24637                            case I_BLOCK_SPECIAL:
24638                                /* Invoke the driver for special processing. */
24639                                dev = (dev_t) rip->i_zone[0];
24640                                r = dev_open(dev, who, bits | (oflags & ~O_ACCMODE));
24641                                break;
24642
24643                            case I_NAMED_PIPE:
24644                                oflags |= O_APPEND;        /* force append mode */
24645                                fil_ptr->filp_flags = oflags;
24646                                r = pipe_open(rip, bits, oflags);
24647                                if (r != ENXIO) {
24648                                        /* See if someone else is doing a rd or wt on
24649                                         * the FIFO.  If so, use its filp entry so the
24650                                         * file position will be automatically shared.
24651                                         */
24652                                        b = (bits & R_BIT ? R_BIT : W_BIT);
24653                                        fil_ptr->filp_count = 0; /* don't find self */
24654                                        if ((filp2 = find_filp(rip, b)) != NIL_FILP) {
24655                                                /* Co-reader or writer found. Use it.*/
24656                                                fp->fp_filp[m_in.fd] = filp2;
24657                                                filp2->filp_count++;
24658                                                filp2->filp_ino = rip;
24659                                                filp2->filp_flags = oflags;
24660
24661                                                /* i_count was incremented incorrectly
24662                                                 * by eatpath above, not knowing that
24663                                                 * we were going to use an existing
24664                                                 * filp entry.  Correct this error.
24665                                                 */
24666                                                rip->i_count--;
```

```
24667                                            } else {
24668                                                    /* Nobody else found.  Restore filp. */
24669                                                    fil_ptr->filp_count = 1;
24670                                                    if (b == R_BIT)
24671                                                            pos = rip->i_zone[V2_NR_DZONES+0];
24672                                                    else
24673                                                            pos = rip->i_zone[V2_NR_DZONES+1];
24674                                                    fil_ptr->filp_pos = pos;
24675                                            }
24676                                    }
24677                                    break;
24678                            }
24679                    }
24680            }
24681
24682      /* If error, release inode. */
24683      if (r != OK) {
24684            if (r == SUSPEND) return(r);                  /* Oops, just suspended */
24685            fp->fp_filp[m_in.fd] = NIL_FILP;
24686            fil_ptr->filp_count= 0;
24687            put_inode(rip);
24688            return(r);
24689      }
24690
24691      return(m_in.fd);
24692 }

24694 /*===========================================================================*
24695  *                              new_node                                     *
24696  *===========================================================================*/
24697 PRIVATE struct inode *new_node(char *path, mode_t bits, zone_t z0)
24698 {
24699 /* New_node() is called by common_open(), do_mknod(), and do_mkdir().
24700  * In all cases it allocates a new inode, makes a directory entry for it on
24701  * the path 'path', and initializes it.  It returns a pointer to the inode if
24702  * it can do this; otherwise it returns NIL_INODE.  It always sets 'err_code'
24703  * to an appropriate value (OK or an error code).
24704  */
24705
24706      register struct inode *rlast_dir_ptr, *rip;
24707      register int r;
24708      char string[NAME_MAX];
24709
24710      /* See if the path can be opened down to the last directory. */
24711      if ((rlast_dir_ptr = last_dir(path, string)) == NIL_INODE) return(NIL_INODE);
24712
24713      /* The final directory is accessible. Get final component of the path. */
24714      rip = advance(rlast_dir_ptr, string);
24715      if ( rip == NIL_INODE && err_code == ENOENT) {
24716            /* Last path component does not exist.  Make new directory entry. */
24717            if ( (rip = alloc_inode(rlast_dir_ptr->i_dev, bits)) == NIL_INODE) {
24718                    /* Can't creat new inode: out of inodes. */
24719                    put_inode(rlast_dir_ptr);
24720                    return(NIL_INODE);
24721            }
24722
24723            /* Force inode to the disk before making directory entry to make
24724             * the system more robust in the face of a crash: an inode with
24725             * no directory entry is much better than the opposite.
24726             */
```

```
24727                rip->i_nlinks++;
24728                rip->i_zone[0] = z0;             /* major/minor device numbers */
24729                rw_inode(rip, WRITING);          /* force inode to disk now */
24730
24731                /* New inode acquired.  Try to make directory entry. */
24732                if ((r = search_dir(rlast_dir_ptr, string, &rip->i_num,ENTER)) != OK) {
24733                        put_inode(rlast_dir_ptr);
24734                        rip->i_nlinks--;        /* pity, have to free disk inode */
24735                        rip->i_dirt = DIRTY;    /* dirty inodes are written out */
24736                        put_inode(rip); /* this call frees the inode */
24737                        err_code = r;
24738                        return(NIL_INODE);
24739                }
24740
24741        } else {
24742                /* Either last component exists, or there is some problem. */
24743                if (rip != NIL_INODE)
24744                        r = EEXIST;
24745                else
24746                        r = err_code;
24747        }
24748
24749        /* Return the directory inode and exit. */
24750        put_inode(rlast_dir_ptr);
24751        err_code = r;
24752        return(rip);
24753 }

24755 /*===========================================================================*
24756  *                              pipe_open                                     *
24757  *===========================================================================*/
24758 PRIVATE int pipe_open(register struct inode *rip, register mode_t bits,
24759           register int oflags)
24760 {
24761 /*   This function is called from common_open. It checks if
24762  *   there is at least one reader/writer pair for the pipe, if not
24763  *   it suspends the caller, otherwise it revives all other blocked
24764  *   processes hanging on the pipe.
24765  */
24766
24767   rip->i_pipe = I_PIPE;
24768   if (find_filp(rip, bits & W_BIT ? R_BIT : W_BIT) == NIL_FILP) {
24769        if (oflags & O_NONBLOCK) {
24770                if (bits & W_BIT) return(ENXIO);
24771        } else {
24772                suspend(XPOPEN);            /* suspend caller */
24773                return(SUSPEND);
24774        }
24775   } else if (susp_count > 0) {/* revive blocked processes */
24776        release(rip, OPEN, susp_count);
24777        release(rip, CREAT, susp_count);
24778   }
24779   return(OK);
24780 }

24782 /*===========================================================================*
24783  *                              do_mknod                                      *
24784  *===========================================================================*/
24785 PUBLIC int do_mknod()
24786 {
```

```
24787  /* Perform the mknod(name, mode, addr) system call. */
24788
24789    register mode_t bits, mode_bits;
24790    struct inode *ip;
24791
24792    /* Only the super_user may make nodes other than fifos. */
24793    mode_bits = (mode_t) m_in.mk_mode;              /* mode of the inode */
24794    if (!super_user && ((mode_bits & I_TYPE) != I_NAMED_PIPE)) return(EPERM);
24795    if (fetch_name(m_in.name1, m_in.name1_length, M1) != OK) return(err_code);
24796    bits = (mode_bits & I_TYPE) | (mode_bits & ALL_MODES & fp->fp_umask);
24797    ip = new_node(user_path, bits, (zone_t) m_in.mk_z0);
24798    put_inode(ip);
24799    return(err_code);
24800  }

24802  /*===========================================================================*
24803   *                              do_mkdir                                      *
24804   *===========================================================================*/
24805  PUBLIC int do_mkdir()
24806  {
24807  /* Perform the mkdir(name, mode) system call. */
24808
24809    int r1, r2;                    /* status codes */
24810    ino_t dot, dotdot;             /* inode numbers for . and .. */
24811    mode_t bits;                   /* mode bits for the new inode */
24812    char string[NAME_MAX];         /* last component of the new dir's path name */
24813    register struct inode *rip, *ldirp;
24814
24815    /* Check to see if it is possible to make another link in the parent dir. */
24816    if (fetch_name(m_in.name1, m_in.name1_length, M1) != OK) return(err_code);
24817    ldirp = last_dir(user_path, string);   /* pointer to new dir's parent */
24818    if (ldirp == NIL_INODE) return(err_code);
24819    if (ldirp->i_nlinks >= (ldirp->i_sp->s_version == V1 ?
24820          CHAR_MAX : SHRT_MAX)) {
24821          put_inode(ldirp);        /* return parent */
24822          return(EMLINK);
24823    }
24824
24825    /* Next make the inode. If that fails, return error code. */
24826    bits = I_DIRECTORY | (m_in.mode & RWX_MODES & fp->fp_umask);
24827    rip = new_node(user_path, bits, (zone_t) 0);
24828    if (rip == NIL_INODE || err_code == EEXIST) {
24829          put_inode(rip);               /* can't make dir: it already exists */
24830          put_inode(ldirp);             /* return parent too */
24831          return(err_code);
24832    }
24833
24834    /* Get the inode numbers for . and .. to enter in the directory. */
24835    dotdot = ldirp->i_num;         /* parent's inode number */
24836    dot = rip->i_num;              /* inode number of the new dir itself */
24837
24838    /* Now make dir entries for . and .. unless the disk is completely full. */
24839    /* Use dot1 and dot2, so the mode of the directory isn't important. */
24840    rip->i_mode = bits;    /* set mode */
24841    r1 = search_dir(rip, dot1, &dot, ENTER);        /* enter . in the new dir */
24842    r2 = search_dir(rip, dot2, &dotdot, ENTER);   /* enter .. in the new dir */
24843
24844    /* If both . and .. were successfully entered, increment the link counts. */
24845    if (r1 == OK && r2 == OK) {
24846          /* Normal case.  It was possible to enter . and .. in the new dir. */
```

```
24847              rip->i_nlinks++;         /* this accounts for . */
24848              ldirp->i_nlinks++;       /* this accounts for .. */
24849              ldirp->i_dirt = DIRTY;   /* mark parent's inode as dirty */
24850      } else {
24851              /* It was not possible to enter . or .. probably disk was full. */
24852              (void) search_dir(ldirp, string, (ino_t *) 0, DELETE);
24853              rip->i_nlinks--;         /* undo the increment done in new_node() */
24854      }
24855      rip->i_dirt = DIRTY;             /* either way, i_nlinks has changed */
24856
24857      put_inode(ldirp);                /* return the inode of the parent dir */
24858      put_inode(rip);                  /* return the inode of the newly made dir */
24859      return(err_code);                /* new_node() always sets 'err_code' */
24860  }

24862  /*===========================================================================*
24863   *                              do_close                                      *
24864   *===========================================================================*/
24865  PUBLIC int do_close()
24866  {
24867  /* Perform the close(fd) system call. */
24868
24869      register struct filp *rfilp;
24870      register struct inode *rip;
24871      struct file_lock *flp;
24872      int rw, mode_word, lock_count;
24873      dev_t dev;
24874
24875      /* First locate the inode that belongs to the file descriptor. */
24876      if ( (rfilp = get_filp(m_in.fd)) == NIL_FILP) return(err_code);
24877      rip = rfilp->filp_ino;           /* 'rip' points to the inode */
24878
24879      if (rfilp->filp_count - 1 == 0 && rfilp->filp_mode != FILP_CLOSED) {
24880              /* Check to see if the file is special. */
24881              mode_word = rip->i_mode & I_TYPE;
24882              if (mode_word == I_CHAR_SPECIAL || mode_word == I_BLOCK_SPECIAL) {
24883                      dev = (dev_t) rip->i_zone[0];
24884                      if (mode_word == I_BLOCK_SPECIAL)  {
24885                              /* Invalidate cache entries unless special is mounted
24886                               * or ROOT
24887                               */
24888                              if (!mounted(rip)) {
24889                                      (void) do_sync();       /* purge cache */
24890                                      invalidate(dev);
24891                              }
24892                      }
24893                      /* Do any special processing on device close. */
24894                      dev_close(dev);
24895              }
24896      }
24897
24898      /* If the inode being closed is a pipe, release everyone hanging on it. */
24899      if (rip->i_pipe == I_PIPE) {
24900              rw = (rfilp->filp_mode & R_BIT ? WRITE : READ);
24901              release(rip, rw, NR_PROCS);
24902      }
24903
24904      /* If a write has been done, the inode is already marked as DIRTY. */
24905      if (--rfilp->filp_count == 0) {
24906              if (rip->i_pipe == I_PIPE && rip->i_count > 1) {
```

```
24907                        /* Save the file position in the i-node in case needed later.
24908                         * The read and write positions are saved separately.  The
24909                         * last 3 zones in the i-node are not used for (named) pipes.
24910                         */
24911                        if (rfilp->filp_mode == R_BIT)
24912                                rip->i_zone[V2_NR_DZONES+0] = (zone_t) rfilp->filp_pos;
24913                        else
24914                                rip->i_zone[V2_NR_DZONES+1] = (zone_t) rfilp->filp_pos;
24915                }
24916                put_inode(rip);
24917        }
24918
24919        fp->fp_cloexec &= ~(1L << m_in.fd);   /* turn off close-on-exec bit */
24920        fp->fp_filp[m_in.fd] = NIL_FILP;
24921
24922        /* Check to see if the file is locked.  If so, release all locks. */
24923        if (nr_locks == 0) return(OK);
24924        lock_count = nr_locks;          /* save count of locks */
24925        for (flp = &file_lock[0]; flp < &file_lock[NR_LOCKS]; flp++) {
24926                if (flp->lock_type == 0) continue;        /* slot not in use */
24927                if (flp->lock_inode == rip && flp->lock_pid == fp->fp_pid) {
24928                        flp->lock_type = 0;
24929                        nr_locks--;
24930                }
24931        }
24932        if (nr_locks < lock_count) lock_revive();      /* lock released */
24933        return(OK);
24934 }

24936 /*===========================================================================*
24937  *                              do_lseek                                     *
24938  *===========================================================================*/
24939 PUBLIC int do_lseek()
24940 {
24941 /* Perform the lseek(ls_fd, offset, whence) system call. */
24942
24943    register struct filp *rfilp;
24944    register off_t pos;
24945
24946    /* Check to see if the file descriptor is valid. */
24947    if ( (rfilp = get_filp(m_in.ls_fd)) == NIL_FILP) return(err_code);
24948
24949    /* No lseek on pipes. */
24950    if (rfilp->filp_ino->i_pipe == I_PIPE) return(ESPIPE);
24951
24952    /* The value of 'whence' determines the start position to use. */
24953    switch(m_in.whence) {
24954        case 0: pos = 0;          break;
24955        case 1: pos = rfilp->filp_pos;  break;
24956        case 2: pos = rfilp->filp_ino->i_size;  break;
24957        default: return(EINVAL);
24958    }
24959
24960    /* Check for overflow. */
24961    if (((long)m_in.offset > 0) && ((long)(pos + m_in.offset) < (long)pos))
24962            return(EINVAL);
24963    if (((long)m_in.offset < 0) && ((long)(pos + m_in.offset) > (long)pos))
24964            return(EINVAL);
24965    pos = pos + m_in.offset;
24966
```

```
24967        if (pos != rfilp->filp_pos)
24968                rfilp->filp_ino->i_seek = ISEEK;        /* inhibit read ahead */
24969        rfilp->filp_pos = pos;
24970        m_out.reply_l1 = pos;           /* insert the long into the output message */
24971        return(OK);
24972   }
```

```
++++++++++++++++++++++++++++++++++++++++++++++++++++++++++++++++++++++++++++++
                              servers/fs/read.c
++++++++++++++++++++++++++++++++++++++++++++++++++++++++++++++++++++++++++++++
```

```
25000   /* This file contains the heart of the mechanism used to read (and write)
25001    * files.  Read and write requests are split up into chunks that do not cross
25002    * block boundaries.  Each chunk is then processed in turn.  Reads on special
25003    * files are also detected and handled.
25004    *
25005    * The entry points into this file are
25006    *   do_read:    perform the READ system call by calling read_write
25007    *   read_write: actually do the work of READ and WRITE
25008    *   read_map:   given an inode and file position, look up its zone number
25009    *   rd_indir:   read an entry in an indirect block
25010    *   read_ahead: manage the block read ahead business
25011    */
25012
25013   #include "fs.h"
25014   #include <fcntl.h>
25015   #include <minix/com.h>
25016   #include "buf.h"
25017   #include "file.h"
25018   #include "fproc.h"
25019   #include "inode.h"
25020   #include "param.h"
25021   #include "super.h"
25022
25023   FORWARD _PROTOTYPE( int rw_chunk, (struct inode *rip, off_t position,
25024           unsigned off, int chunk, unsigned left, int rw_flag,
25025           char *buff, int seg, int usr, int block_size, int *completed));
25026
25027   /*===========================================================================*
25028    *                              do_read                                       *
25029    *===========================================================================*/
25030   PUBLIC int do_read()
25031   {
25032     return(read_write(READING));
25033   }
25034
25035   /*===========================================================================*
25036    *                              read_write                                    *
25037    *===========================================================================*/
25038   PUBLIC int read_write(rw_flag)
25039   int rw_flag;                      /* READING or WRITING */
25040   {
25041   /* Perform read(fd, buffer, nbytes) or write(fd, buffer, nbytes) call. */
25042
25043     register struct inode *rip;
25044     register struct filp *f;
```

```
25045    off_t bytes_left, f_size, position;
25046    unsigned int off, cum_io;
25047    int op, oflags, r, chunk, usr, seg, block_spec, char_spec;
25048    int regular, partial_pipe = 0, partial_cnt = 0;
25049    mode_t mode_word;
25050    struct filp *wf;
25051    int block_size;
25052    int completed, r2 = OK;
25053    phys_bytes p;
25054
25055    /* left unfinished rw_chunk()s from previous call! this can't happen.
25056     * it means something has gone wrong we can't repair now.
25057     */
25058    if (bufs_in_use < 0) {
25059         panic(__FILE__,"start - bufs_in_use negative", bufs_in_use);
25060    }
25061
25062    /* MM loads segments by putting funny things in upper 10 bits of 'fd'. */
25063    if (who == PM_PROC_NR && (m_in.fd & (~BYTE)) ) {
25064         usr = m_in.fd >> 7;
25065         seg = (m_in.fd >> 5) & 03;
25066         m_in.fd &= 037;          /* get rid of user and segment bits */
25067    } else {
25068         usr = who;               /* normal case */
25069         seg = D;
25070    }
25071
25072    /* If the file descriptor is valid, get the inode, size and mode. */
25073    if (m_in.nbytes < 0) return(EINVAL);
25074    if ((f = get_filp(m_in.fd)) == NIL_FILP) return(err_code);
25075    if (((f->filp_mode) & (rw_flag == READING ? R_BIT : W_BIT)) == 0) {
25076         return(f->filp_mode == FILP_CLOSED ? EIO : EBADF);
25077    }
25078    if (m_in.nbytes == 0)
25079         return(0);      /* so char special files need not check for 0*/
25080
25081    /* check if user process has the memory it needs.
25082     * if not, copying will fail later.
25083     * do this after 0-check above because umap doesn't want to map 0 bytes.
25084     */
25085    if ((r = sys_umap(usr, seg, (vir_bytes) m_in.buffer, m_in.nbytes, &p)) != OK)
25086         return r;
25087    position = f->filp_pos;
25088    oflags = f->filp_flags;
25089    rip = f->filp_ino;
25090    f_size = rip->i_size;
25091    r = OK;
25092    if (rip->i_pipe == I_PIPE) {
25093         /* fp->fp_cum_io_partial is only nonzero when doing partial writes */
25094         cum_io = fp->fp_cum_io_partial;
25095    } else {
25096         cum_io = 0;
25097    }
25098    op = (rw_flag == READING ? DEV_READ : DEV_WRITE);
25099    mode_word = rip->i_mode & I_TYPE;
25100    regular = mode_word == I_REGULAR || mode_word == I_NAMED_PIPE;
25101
25102    if ((char_spec = (mode_word == I_CHAR_SPECIAL ? 1 : 0))) {
25103         if (rip->i_zone[0] == NO_DEV)
25104              panic(__FILE__,"read_write tries to read from "
```

```
25105                            "character device NO_DEV", NO_NUM);
25106              block_size = get_block_size(rip->i_zone[0]);
25107        }
25108        if ((block_spec = (mode_word == I_BLOCK_SPECIAL ? 1 : 0))) {
25109              f_size = ULONG_MAX;
25110              if (rip->i_zone[0] == NO_DEV)
25111                    panic(__FILE__,"read_write tries to read from "
25112                    " block device NO_DEV", NO_NUM);
25113              block_size = get_block_size(rip->i_zone[0]);
25114        }
25115
25116        if (!char_spec && !block_spec)
25117              block_size = rip->i_sp->s_block_size;
25118
25119        rdwt_err = OK;                    /* set to EIO if disk error occurs */
25120
25121        /* Check for character special files. */
25122        if (char_spec) {
25123              dev_t dev;
25124              dev = (dev_t) rip->i_zone[0];
25125              r = dev_io(op, dev, usr, m_in.buffer, position, m_in.nbytes, oflags);
25126              if (r >= 0) {
25127                    cum_io = r;
25128                    position += r;
25129                    r = OK;
25130              }
25131        } else {
25132              if (rw_flag == WRITING && block_spec == 0) {
25133                    /* Check in advance to see if file will grow too big. */
25134                    if (position > rip->i_sp->s_max_size - m_in.nbytes)
25135                          return(EFBIG);
25136
25137                    /* Check for O_APPEND flag. */
25138                    if (oflags & O_APPEND) position = f_size;
25139
25140                    /* Clear the zone containing present EOF if hole about
25141                     * to be created.  This is necessary because all unwritten
25142                     * blocks prior to the EOF must read as zeros.
25143                     */
25144                    if (position > f_size) clear_zone(rip, f_size, 0);
25145              }
25146
25147              /* Pipes are a little different.  Check. */
25148              if (rip->i_pipe == I_PIPE) {
25149                    r = pipe_check(rip, rw_flag, oflags,
25150                          m_in.nbytes, position, &partial_cnt, 0);
25151                    if (r <= 0) return(r);
25152              }
25153
25154              if (partial_cnt > 0) partial_pipe = 1;
25155
25156              /* Split the transfer into chunks that don't span two blocks. */
25157              while (m_in.nbytes != 0) {
25158
25159                    off = (unsigned int) (position % block_size);/* offset in blk*/
25160                    if (partial_pipe) {  /* pipes only */
25161                          chunk = MIN(partial_cnt, block_size - off);
25162                    } else
25163                          chunk = MIN(m_in.nbytes, block_size - off);
25164                    if (chunk < 0) chunk = block_size - off;
```

```
25165
25166                        if (rw_flag == READING) {
25167                                bytes_left = f_size - position;
25168                                if (position >= f_size) break;   /* we are beyond EOF */
25169                                if (chunk > bytes_left) chunk = (int) bytes_left;
25170                        }
25171
25172                        /* Read or write 'chunk' bytes. */
25173                        r = rw_chunk(rip, position, off, chunk, (unsigned) m_in.nbytes,
25174                                        rw_flag, m_in.buffer, seg, usr, block_size, &completed);
25175
25176                        if (r != OK) break;       /* EOF reached */
25177                        if (rdwt_err < 0) break;
25178
25179                        /* Update counters and pointers. */
25180                        m_in.buffer += chunk;     /* user buffer address */
25181                        m_in.nbytes -= chunk;     /* bytes yet to be read */
25182                        cum_io += chunk;          /* bytes read so far */
25183                        position += chunk;        /* position within the file */
25184
25185                        if (partial_pipe) {
25186                                partial_cnt -= chunk;
25187                                if (partial_cnt <= 0)  break;
25188                        }
25189            }
25190     }
25191
25192     /* On write, update file size and access time. */
25193     if (rw_flag == WRITING) {
25194            if (regular || mode_word == I_DIRECTORY) {
25195                    if (position > f_size) rip->i_size = position;
25196            }
25197     } else {
25198            if (rip->i_pipe == I_PIPE) {
25199                    if ( position >= rip->i_size) {
25200                            /* Reset pipe pointers. */
25201                            rip->i_size = 0;         /* no data left */
25202                            position = 0;            /* reset reader(s) */
25203                            wf = find_filp(rip, W_BIT);
25204                            if (wf != NIL_FILP) wf->filp_pos = 0;
25205                    }
25206            }
25207     }
25208     f->filp_pos = position;
25209
25210     /* Check to see if read-ahead is called for, and if so, set it up. */
25211     if (rw_flag == READING && rip->i_seek == NO_SEEK && position % block_size== 0
25212                && (regular || mode_word == I_DIRECTORY)) {
25213            rdahed_inode = rip;
25214            rdahedpos = position;
25215     }
25216     rip->i_seek = NO_SEEK;
25217
25218     if (rdwt_err != OK) r = rdwt_err;       /* check for disk error */
25219     if (rdwt_err == END_OF_FILE) r = OK;
25220
25221     /* if user-space copying failed, read/write failed. */
25222     if (r == OK && r2 != OK) {
25223            r = r2;
25224     }
```

```
25225      if (r == OK) {
25226              if (rw_flag == READING) rip->i_update |= ATIME;
25227              if (rw_flag == WRITING) rip->i_update |= CTIME | MTIME;
25228              rip->i_dirt = DIRTY;              /* inode is thus now dirty */
25229              if (partial_pipe) {
25230                      partial_pipe = 0;
25231                              /* partial write on pipe with */
25232                      /* O_NONBLOCK, return write count */
25233                      if (!(oflags & O_NONBLOCK)) {
25234                              fp->fp_cum_io_partial = cum_io;
25235                              suspend(XPIPE);    /* partial write on pipe with */
25236                              return(SUSPEND);   /* nbyte > PIPE_SIZE - non-atomic */
25237                      }
25238              }
25239              fp->fp_cum_io_partial = 0;
25240              return(cum_io);
25241      }
25242      if (bufs_in_use < 0) {
25243              panic(__FILE__,"end - bufs_in_use negative", bufs_in_use);
25244      }
25245      return(r);
25246  }

25248  /*===========================================================================*
25249   *                              rw_chunk                                     *
25250   *===========================================================================*/
25251  PRIVATE int rw_chunk(rip, position, off, chunk, left, rw_flag, buff,
25252    seg, usr, block_size, completed)
25253  register struct inode *rip;     /* pointer to inode for file to be rd/wr */
25254  off_t position;                 /* position within file to read or write */
25255  unsigned off;                   /* off within the current block */
25256  int chunk;                      /* number of bytes to read or write */
25257  unsigned left;                  /* max number of bytes wanted after position */
25258  int rw_flag;                    /* READING or WRITING */
25259  char *buff;                     /* virtual address of the user buffer */
25260  int seg;                        /* T or D segment in user space */
25261  int usr;                        /* which user process */
25262  int block_size;                 /* block size of FS operating on */
25263  int *completed;                 /* number of bytes copied */
25264  {
25265  /* Read or write (part of) a block. */
25266
25267    register struct buf *bp;
25268    register int r = OK;
25269    int n, block_spec;
25270    block_t b;
25271    dev_t dev;
25272
25273    *completed = 0;
25274
25275    block_spec = (rip->i_mode & I_TYPE) == I_BLOCK_SPECIAL;
25276    if (block_spec) {
25277            b = position/block_size;
25278            dev = (dev_t) rip->i_zone[0];
25279    } else {
25280            b = read_map(rip, position);
25281            dev = rip->i_dev;
25282    }
25283
25284    if (!block_spec && b == NO_BLOCK) {
```

```
25285              if (rw_flag == READING) {
25286                      /* Reading from a nonexistent block.  Must read as all zeros.*/
25287                      bp = get_block(NO_DEV, NO_BLOCK, NORMAL);    /* get a buffer */
25288                      zero_block(bp);
25289              } else {
25290                      /* Writing to a nonexistent block. Create and enter in inode.*/
25291                      if ((bp= new_block(rip, position)) == NIL_BUF)return(err_code);
25292              }
25293      } else if (rw_flag == READING) {
25294              /* Read and read ahead if convenient. */
25295              bp = rahead(rip, b, position, left);
25296      } else {
25297              /* Normally an existing block to be partially overwritten is first read
25298               * in.  However, a full block need not be read in.  If it is already in
25299               * the cache, acquire it, otherwise just acquire a free buffer.
25300               */
25301              n = (chunk == block_size ? NO_READ : NORMAL);
25302              if (!block_spec && off == 0 && position >= rip->i_size) n = NO_READ;
25303              bp = get_block(dev, b, n);
25304      }
25305
25306      /* In all cases, bp now points to a valid buffer. */
25307      if (bp == NIL_BUF) {
25308              panic(__FILE__,"bp not valid in rw_chunk, this can't happen", NO_NUM);
25309      }
25310      if (rw_flag == WRITING && chunk != block_size && !block_spec &&
25311                                      position >= rip->i_size && off == 0) {
25312              zero_block(bp);
25313      }
25314
25315      if (rw_flag == READING) {
25316              /* Copy a chunk from the block buffer to user space. */
25317              r = sys_vircopy(FS_PROC_NR, D, (phys_bytes) (bp->b_data+off),
25318                              usr, seg, (phys_bytes) buff,
25319                              (phys_bytes) chunk);
25320      } else {
25321              /* Copy a chunk from user space to the block buffer. */
25322              r = sys_vircopy(usr, seg, (phys_bytes) buff,
25323                              FS_PROC_NR, D, (phys_bytes) (bp->b_data+off),
25324                              (phys_bytes) chunk);
25325              bp->b_dirt = DIRTY;
25326      }
25327      n = (off + chunk == block_size ? FULL_DATA_BLOCK : PARTIAL_DATA_BLOCK);
25328      put_block(bp, n);
25329
25330      return(r);
25331 }


25334 /*===========================================================================*
25335  *                              read_map                                     *
25336  *===========================================================================*/
25337 PUBLIC block_t read_map(rip, position)
25338 register struct inode *rip;       /* ptr to inode to map from */
25339 off_t position;                   /* position in file whose blk wanted */
25340 {
25341 /* Given an inode and a position within the corresponding file, locate the
25342  * block (not zone) number in which that position is to be found and return it.
25343  */
25344
```

```
25345     register struct buf *bp;
25346     register zone_t z;
25347     int scale, boff, dzones, nr_indirects, index, zind, ex;
25348     block_t b;
25349     long excess, zone, block_pos;
25350
25351     scale = rip->i_sp->s_log_zone_size;    /* for block-zone conversion */
25352     block_pos = position/rip->i_sp->s_block_size; /* relative blk # in file */
25353     zone = block_pos >> scale;      /* position's zone */
25354     boff = (int) (block_pos - (zone << scale) ); /* relative blk # within zone */
25355     dzones = rip->i_ndzones;
25356     nr_indirects = rip->i_nindirs;
25357
25358     /* Is 'position' to be found in the inode itself? */
25359     if (zone < dzones) {
25360          zind = (int) zone;       /* index should be an int */
25361          z = rip->i_zone[zind];
25362          if (z == NO_ZONE) return(NO_BLOCK);
25363          b = ((block_t) z << scale) + boff;
25364          return(b);
25365     }
25366
25367     /* It is not in the inode, so it must be single or double indirect. */
25368     excess = zone - dzones;         /* first Vx_NR_DZONES don't count */
25369
25370     if (excess < nr_indirects) {
25371          /* 'position' can be located via the single indirect block. */
25372          z = rip->i_zone[dzones];
25373     } else {
25374          /* 'position' can be located via the double indirect block. */
25375          if ( (z = rip->i_zone[dzones+1]) == NO_ZONE) return(NO_BLOCK);
25376          excess -= nr_indirects;               /* single indir doesn't count*/
25377          b = (block_t) z << scale;
25378          bp = get_block(rip->i_dev, b, NORMAL);  /* get double indirect block */
25379          index = (int) (excess/nr_indirects);
25380          z = rd_indir(bp, index);              /* z= zone for single*/
25381          put_block(bp, INDIRECT_BLOCK);        /* release double ind block */
25382          excess = excess % nr_indirects;       /* index into single ind blk */
25383     }
25384
25385     /* 'z' is zone num for single indirect block; 'excess' is index into it. */
25386     if (z == NO_ZONE) return(NO_BLOCK);
25387     b = (block_t) z << scale;                 /* b is blk # for single ind */
25388     bp = get_block(rip->i_dev, b, NORMAL);    /* get single indirect block */
25389     ex = (int) excess;                        /* need an integer */
25390     z = rd_indir(bp, ex);                     /* get block pointed to */
25391     put_block(bp, INDIRECT_BLOCK);            /* release single indir blk */
25392     if (z == NO_ZONE) return(NO_BLOCK);
25393     b = ((block_t) z << scale) + boff;
25394     return(b);
25395  }
25396
25397  /*===========================================================================*
25398   *                              rd_indir                                     *
25399   *===========================================================================*/
25400  PUBLIC zone_t rd_indir(bp, index)
25401  struct buf *bp;                    /* pointer to indirect block */
25402  int index;                         /* index into *bp */
25403  {
25404  /* Given a pointer to an indirect block, read one entry.  The reason for
```

```
25405   * making a separate routine out of this is that there are four cases:
25406   * V1 (IBM and 68000), and V2 (IBM and 68000).
25407   */
25408
25409    struct super_block *sp;
25410    zone_t zone;                        /* V2 zones are longs (shorts in V1) */
25411
25412    sp = get_super(bp->b_dev);     /* need super block to find file sys type */
25413
25414    /* read a zone from an indirect block */
25415    if (sp->s_version == V1)
25416          zone = (zone_t) conv2(sp->s_native, (int)  bp->b_v1_ind[index]);
25417    else
25418          zone = (zone_t) conv4(sp->s_native, (long) bp->b_v2_ind[index]);
25419
25420    if (zone != NO_ZONE &&
25421               (zone < (zone_t) sp->s_firstdatazone || zone >= sp->s_zones)) {
25422          printf("Illegal zone number %ld in indirect block, index %d\n",
25423                (long) zone, index);
25424          panic(__FILE__,"check file system", NO_NUM);
25425    }
25426    return(zone);
25427  }

25429  /*===========================================================================*
25430   *                              read_ahead                                   *
25431   *===========================================================================*/
25432  PUBLIC void read_ahead()
25433  {
25434  /* Read a block into the cache before it is needed. */
25435    int block_size;
25436    register struct inode *rip;
25437    struct buf *bp;
25438    block_t b;
25439
25440    rip = rdahed_inode;             /* pointer to inode to read ahead from */
25441    block_size = get_block_size(rip->i_dev);
25442    rdahed_inode = NIL_INODE;       /* turn off read ahead */
25443    if ( (b = read_map(rip, rdahedpos)) == NO_BLOCK) return;     /* at EOF */
25444    bp = rahead(rip, b, rdahedpos, block_size);
25445    put_block(bp, PARTIAL_DATA_BLOCK);
25446  }

25448  /*===========================================================================*
25449   *                              rahead                                       *
25450   *===========================================================================*/
25451  PUBLIC struct buf *rahead(rip, baseblock, position, bytes_ahead)
25452  register struct inode *rip;     /* pointer to inode for file to be read */
25453  block_t baseblock;             /* block at current position */
25454  off_t position;                /* position within file */
25455  unsigned bytes_ahead;          /* bytes beyond position for immediate use */
25456  {
25457  /* Fetch a block from the cache or the device.  If a physical read is
25458   * required, prefetch as many more blocks as convenient into the cache.
25459   * This usually covers bytes_ahead and is at least BLOCKS_MINIMUM.
25460   * The device driver may decide it knows better and stop reading at a
25461   * cylinder boundary (or after an error).  Rw_scattered() puts an optional
25462   * flag on all reads to allow this.
25463   */
25464    int block_size;
```

```
25465    /* Minimum number of blocks to prefetch. */
25466    # define BLOCKS_MINIMUM          (NR_BUFS < 50 ? 18 : 32)
25467      int block_spec, scale, read_q_size;
25468      unsigned int blocks_ahead, fragment;
25469      block_t block, blocks_left;
25470      off_t ind1_pos;
25471      dev_t dev;
25472      struct buf *bp;
25473      static struct buf *read_q[NR_BUFS];
25474
25475      block_spec = (rip->i_mode & I_TYPE) == I_BLOCK_SPECIAL;
25476      if (block_spec) {
25477            dev = (dev_t) rip->i_zone[0];
25478      } else {
25479            dev = rip->i_dev;
25480      }
25481      block_size = get_block_size(dev);
25482
25483      block = baseblock;
25484      bp = get_block(dev, block, PREFETCH);
25485      if (bp->b_dev != NO_DEV) return(bp);
25486
25487      /* The best guess for the number of blocks to prefetch:  A lot.
25488       * It is impossible to tell what the device looks like, so we don't even
25489       * try to guess the geometry, but leave it to the driver.
25490       *
25491       * The floppy driver can read a full track with no rotational delay, and it
25492       * avoids reading partial tracks if it can, so handing it enough buffers to
25493       * read two tracks is perfect.  (Two, because some diskette types have
25494       * an odd number of sectors per track, so a block may span tracks.)
25495       *
25496       * The disk drivers don't try to be smart.  With todays disks it is
25497       * impossible to tell what the real geometry looks like, so it is best to
25498       * read as much as you can.  With luck the caching on the drive allows
25499       * for a little time to start the next read.
25500       *
25501       * The current solution below is a bit of a hack, it just reads blocks from
25502       * the current file position hoping that more of the file can be found.  A
25503       * better solution must look at the already available zone pointers and
25504       * indirect blocks (but don't call read_map!).
25505       */
25506
25507      fragment = position % block_size;
25508      position -= fragment;
25509      bytes_ahead += fragment;
25510
25511      blocks_ahead = (bytes_ahead + block_size - 1) / block_size;
25512
25513      if (block_spec && rip->i_size == 0) {
25514            blocks_left = NR_IOREQS;
25515      } else {
25516            blocks_left = (rip->i_size - position + block_size - 1) / block_size;
25517
25518            /* Go for the first indirect block if we are in its neighborhood. */
25519            if (!block_spec) {
25520                  scale = rip->i_sp->s_log_zone_size;
25521                  ind1_pos = (off_t) rip->i_ndzones * (block_size << scale);
25522                  if (position <= ind1_pos && rip->i_size > ind1_pos) {
25523                        blocks_ahead++;
25524                        blocks_left++;
```

```
25525                         }
25526                 }
25527         }
25528
25529         /* No more than the maximum request. */
25530         if (blocks_ahead > NR_IOREQS) blocks_ahead = NR_IOREQS;
25531
25532         /* Read at least the minimum number of blocks, but not after a seek. */
25533         if (blocks_ahead < BLOCKS_MINIMUM && rip->i_seek == NO_SEEK)
25534                 blocks_ahead = BLOCKS_MINIMUM;
25535
25536         /* Can't go past end of file. */
25537         if (blocks_ahead > blocks_left) blocks_ahead = blocks_left;
25538
25539         read_q_size = 0;
25540
25541         /* Acquire block buffers. */
25542         for (;;) {
25543                 read_q[read_q_size++] = bp;
25544
25545                 if (--blocks_ahead == 0) break;
25546
25547                 /* Don't trash the cache, leave 4 free. */
25548                 if (bufs_in_use >= NR_BUFS - 4) break;
25549
25550                 block++;
25551
25552                 bp = get_block(dev, block, PREFETCH);
25553                 if (bp->b_dev != NO_DEV) {
25554                         /* Oops, block already in the cache, get out. */
25555                         put_block(bp, FULL_DATA_BLOCK);
25556                         break;
25557                 }
25558         }
25559         rw_scattered(dev, read_q, read_q_size, READING);
25560         return(get_block(dev, baseblock, NORMAL));
25561  }
```

```
+++++++++++++++++++++++++++++++++++++++++++++++++++++++++++++++++++++++++++++++++++
                              servers/fs/write.c
+++++++++++++++++++++++++++++++++++++++++++++++++++++++++++++++++++++++++++++++++++
```

```
25600   /* This file is the counterpart of "read.c".  It contains the code for writing
25601    * insofar as this is not contained in read_write().
25602    *
25603    * The entry points into this file are
25604    *   do_write:     call read_write to perform the WRITE system call
25605    *   clear_zone:   erase a zone in the middle of a file
25606    *   new_block:    acquire a new block
25607    */
25608
25609   #include "fs.h"
25610   #include <string.h>
25611   #include "buf.h"
25612   #include "file.h"
25613   #include "fproc.h"
25614   #include "inode.h"
```

```
25615   #include "super.h"
25616
25617   FORWARD _PROTOTYPE( int write_map, (struct inode *rip, off_t position,
25618                          zone_t new_zone)                              );
25619
25620   FORWARD _PROTOTYPE( void wr_indir, (struct buf *bp, int index, zone_t zone) );
25621
25622   /*===========================================================================*
25623    *                              do_write                                      *
25624    *===========================================================================*/
25625   PUBLIC int do_write()
25626   {
25627   /* Perform the write(fd, buffer, nbytes) system call. */
25628
25629     return(read_write(WRITING));
25630   }
25631
25632   /*===========================================================================*
25633    *                              write_map                                     *
25634    *===========================================================================*/
25635   PRIVATE int write_map(rip, position, new_zone)
25636   register struct inode *rip;      /* pointer to inode to be changed */
25637   off_t position;                  /* file address to be mapped */
25638   zone_t new_zone;                 /* zone # to be inserted */
25639   {
25640   /* Write a new zone into an inode. */
25641     int scale, ind_ex, new_ind, new_dbl, zones, nr_indirects, single, zindex, ex;
25642     zone_t z, z1;
25643     register block_t b;
25644     long excess, zone;
25645     struct buf *bp;
25646
25647     rip->i_dirt = DIRTY;            /* inode will be changed */
25648     bp = NIL_BUF;
25649     scale = rip->i_sp->s_log_zone_size;          /* for zone-block conversion */
25650           /* relative zone # to insert */
25651     zone = (position/rip->i_sp->s_block_size) >> scale;
25652     zones = rip->i_ndzones;        /* # direct zones in the inode */
25653     nr_indirects = rip->i_nindirs;/* # indirect zones per indirect block */
25654
25655     /* Is 'position' to be found in the inode itself? */
25656     if (zone < zones) {
25657           zindex = (int) zone;     /* we need an integer here */
25658           rip->i_zone[zindex] = new_zone;
25659           return(OK);
25660     }
25661
25662     /* It is not in the inode, so it must be single or double indirect. */
25663     excess = zone - zones;         /* first Vx_NR_DZONES don't count */
25664     new_ind = FALSE;
25665     new_dbl = FALSE;
25666
25667     if (excess < nr_indirects) {
25668           /* 'position' can be located via the single indirect block. */
25669           z1 = rip->i_zone[zones];         /* single indirect zone */
25670           single = TRUE;
25671     } else {
25672           /* 'position' can be located via the double indirect block. */
25673           if ( (z = rip->i_zone[zones+1]) == NO_ZONE) {
25674                 /* Create the double indirect block. */
```

```
25675                    if ( (z = alloc_zone(rip->i_dev, rip->i_zone[0])) == NO_ZONE)
25676                            return(err_code);
25677                    rip->i_zone[zones+1] = z;
25678                    new_dbl = TRUE; /* set flag for later */
25679            }
25680
25681            /* Either way, 'z' is zone number for double indirect block. */
25682            excess -= nr_indirects; /* single indirect doesn't count */
25683            ind_ex = (int) (excess / nr_indirects);
25684            excess = excess % nr_indirects;
25685            if (ind_ex >= nr_indirects) return(EFBIG);
25686            b = (block_t) z << scale;
25687            bp = get_block(rip->i_dev, b, (new_dbl ? NO_READ : NORMAL));
25688            if (new_dbl) zero_block(bp);
25689            z1 = rd_indir(bp, ind_ex);
25690            single = FALSE;
25691      }
25692
25693      /* z1 is now single indirect zone; 'excess' is index. */
25694      if (z1 == NO_ZONE) {
25695            /* Create indirect block and store zone # in inode or dbl indir blk. */
25696            z1 = alloc_zone(rip->i_dev, rip->i_zone[0]);
25697            if (single)
25698                    rip->i_zone[zones] = z1;          /* update inode */
25699            else
25700                    wr_indir(bp, ind_ex, z1);          /* update dbl indir */
25701
25702            new_ind = TRUE;
25703            if (bp != NIL_BUF) bp->b_dirt = DIRTY;  /* if double ind, it is dirty*/
25704            if (z1 == NO_ZONE) {
25705                    put_block(bp, INDIRECT_BLOCK);  /* release dbl indirect blk */
25706                    return(err_code);          /* couldn't create single ind */
25707            }
25708      }
25709      put_block(bp, INDIRECT_BLOCK);          /* release double indirect blk */
25710
25711      /* z1 is indirect block's zone number. */
25712      b = (block_t) z1 << scale;
25713      bp = get_block(rip->i_dev, b, (new_ind ? NO_READ : NORMAL) );
25714      if (new_ind) zero_block(bp);
25715      ex = (int) excess;                       /* we need an int here */
25716      wr_indir(bp, ex, new_zone);
25717      bp->b_dirt = DIRTY;
25718      put_block(bp, INDIRECT_BLOCK);
25719
25720      return(OK);
25721 }
25722
25723 /*===========================================================================*
25724  *                              wr_indir                                     *
25725  *===========================================================================*/
25726 PRIVATE void wr_indir(bp, index, zone)
25727 struct buf *bp;                          /* pointer to indirect block */
25728 int index;                               /* index into *bp */
25729 zone_t zone;                             /* zone to write */
25730 {
25731 /* Given a pointer to an indirect block, write one entry. */
25732
25733      struct super_block *sp;
25734
```

```
25735       sp = get_super(bp->b_dev);      /* need super block to find file sys type */
25736
25737       /* write a zone into an indirect block */
25738       if (sp->s_version == V1)
25739               bp->b_v1_ind[index] = (zone1_t) conv2(sp->s_native, (int)  zone);
25740       else
25741               bp->b_v2_ind[index] = (zone_t)  conv4(sp->s_native, (long) zone);
25742  }
25743
25744  /*===========================================================================*
25745   *                              clear_zone                                    *
25746   *===========================================================================*/
25747  PUBLIC void clear_zone(rip, pos, flag)
25748  register struct inode *rip;     /* inode to clear */
25749  off_t pos;                      /* points to block to clear */
25750  int flag;                       /* 0 if called by read_write, 1 by new_block */
25751  {
25752  /* Zero a zone, possibly starting in the middle.  The parameter 'pos' gives
25753   * a byte in the first block to be zeroed.  Clearzone() is called from
25754   * read_write and new_block().
25755   */
25756
25757    register struct buf *bp;
25758    register block_t b, blo, bhi;
25759    register off_t next;
25760    register int scale;
25761    register zone_t zone_size;
25762
25763    /* If the block size and zone size are the same, clear_zone() not needed. */
25764    scale = rip->i_sp->s_log_zone_size;
25765    if (scale == 0) return;
25766
25767    zone_size = (zone_t) rip->i_sp->s_block_size << scale;
25768    if (flag == 1) pos = (pos/zone_size) * zone_size;
25769    next = pos + rip->i_sp->s_block_size - 1;
25770
25771    /* If 'pos' is in the last block of a zone, do not clear the zone. */
25772    if (next/zone_size != pos/zone_size) return;
25773    if ( (blo = read_map(rip, next)) == NO_BLOCK) return;
25774    bhi = (  ((blo>>scale)+1) << scale)    - 1;
25775
25776    /* Clear all the blocks between 'blo' and 'bhi'. */
25777    for (b = blo; b <= bhi; b++) {
25778            bp = get_block(rip->i_dev, b, NO_READ);
25779            zero_block(bp);
25780            put_block(bp, FULL_DATA_BLOCK);
25781    }
25782  }
25783
25784  /*===========================================================================*
25785   *                              new_block                                     *
25786   *===========================================================================*/
25787  PUBLIC struct buf *new_block(rip, position)
25788  register struct inode *rip;     /* pointer to inode */
25789  off_t position;                 /* file pointer */
25790  {
25791  /* Acquire a new block and return a pointer to it.  Doing so may require
25792   * allocating a complete zone, and then returning the initial block.
25793   * On the other hand, the current zone may still have some unused blocks.
25794   */
```

```
25795
25796    register struct buf *bp;
25797    block_t b, base_block;
25798    zone_t z;
25799    zone_t zone_size;
25800    int scale, r;
25801    struct super_block *sp;
25802
25803    /* Is another block available in the current zone? */
25804    if ( (b = read_map(rip, position)) == NO_BLOCK) {
25805            /* Choose first zone if possible. */
25806            /* Lose if the file is nonempty but the first zone number is NO_ZONE
25807             * corresponding to a zone full of zeros.  It would be better to
25808             * search near the last real zone.
25809             */
25810            if (rip->i_zone[0] == NO_ZONE) {
25811                    sp = rip->i_sp;
25812                    z = sp->s_firstdatazone;
25813            } else {
25814                    z = rip->i_zone[0];      /* hunt near first zone */
25815            }
25816            if ( (z = alloc_zone(rip->i_dev, z)) == NO_ZONE) return(NIL_BUF);
25817            if ( (r = write_map(rip, position, z)) != OK) {
25818                    free_zone(rip->i_dev, z);
25819                    err_code = r;
25820                    return(NIL_BUF);
25821            }
25822
25823            /* If we are not writing at EOF, clear the zone, just to be safe. */
25824            if ( position != rip->i_size) clear_zone(rip, position, 1);
25825            scale = rip->i_sp->s_log_zone_size;
25826            base_block = (block_t) z << scale;
25827            zone_size = (zone_t) rip->i_sp->s_block_size << scale;
25828            b = base_block + (block_t)((position % zone_size)/rip->i_sp->s_block_size);
25829    }
25830
25831    bp = get_block(rip->i_dev, b, NO_READ);
25832    zero_block(bp);
25833    return(bp);
25834 }

25836 /*===========================================================================*
25837  *                              zero_block                                   *
25838  *===========================================================================*/
25839 PUBLIC void zero_block(bp)
25840 register struct buf *bp;          /* pointer to buffer to zero */
25841 {
25842 /* Zero a block. */
25843   memset(bp->b_data, 0, MAX_BLOCK_SIZE);
25844   bp->b_dirt = DIRTY;
25845 }
```

```
++++++++++++++++++++++++++++++++++++++++++++++++++++++++++++++++++++++++++
                              servers/fs/pipe.c
++++++++++++++++++++++++++++++++++++++++++++++++++++++++++++++++++++++++++
25900   /* This file deals with the suspension and revival of processes.  A process can
25901    * be suspended because it wants to read or write from a pipe and can't, or
25902    * because it wants to read or write from a special file and can't.  When a
25903    * process can't continue it is suspended, and revived later when it is able
25904    * to continue.
25905    *
25906    * The entry points into this file are
25907    *   do_pipe:      perform the PIPE system call
25908    *   pipe_check:   check to see that a read or write on a pipe is feasible now
25909    *   suspend:      suspend a process that cannot do a requested read or write
25910    *   release:      check to see if a suspended process can be released and do
25911    *                 it
25912    *   revive:       mark a suspended process as able to run again
25913    *   do_unpause:   a signal has been sent to a process; see if it suspended
25914    */
25915
25916   #include "fs.h"
25917   #include <fcntl.h>
25918   #include <signal.h>
25919   #include <minix/callnr.h>
25920   #include <minix/com.h>
25921   #include <sys/select.h>
25922   #include <sys/time.h>
25923   #include "file.h"
25924   #include "fproc.h"
25925   #include "inode.h"
25926   #include "param.h"
25927   #include "super.h"
25928   #include "select.h"
25929
25930   /*===========================================================================*
25931    *                              do_pipe                                       *
25932    *===========================================================================*/
25933   PUBLIC int do_pipe()
25934   {
25935   /* Perform the pipe(fil_des) system call. */
25936
25937     register struct fproc *rfp;
25938     register struct inode *rip;
25939     int r;
25940     struct filp *fil_ptr0, *fil_ptr1;
25941     int fil_des[2];              /* reply goes here */
25942
25943     /* Acquire two file descriptors. */
25944     rfp = fp;
25945     if ( (r = get_fd(0, R_BIT, &fil_des[0], &fil_ptr0)) != OK) return(r);
25946     rfp->fp_filp[fil_des[0]] = fil_ptr0;
25947     fil_ptr0->filp_count = 1;
25948     if ( (r = get_fd(0, W_BIT, &fil_des[1], &fil_ptr1)) != OK) {
25949           rfp->fp_filp[fil_des[0]] = NIL_FILP;
25950           fil_ptr0->filp_count = 0;
25951           return(r);
25952     }
25953     rfp->fp_filp[fil_des[1]] = fil_ptr1;
25954     fil_ptr1->filp_count = 1;
```

```
25955
25956    /* Make the inode on the pipe device. */
25957    if ( (rip = alloc_inode(root_dev, I_REGULAR) ) == NIL_INODE) {
25958          rfp->fp_filp[fil_des[0]] = NIL_FILP;
25959          fil_ptr0->filp_count = 0;
25960          rfp->fp_filp[fil_des[1]] = NIL_FILP;
25961          fil_ptr1->filp_count = 0;
25962          return(err_code);
25963    }
25964
25965    if (read_only(rip) != OK)
25966          panic(__FILE__,"pipe device is read only", NO_NUM);
25967
25968    rip->i_pipe = I_PIPE;
25969    rip->i_mode &= ~I_REGULAR;
25970    rip->i_mode |= I_NAMED_PIPE;   /* pipes and FIFOs have this bit set */
25971    fil_ptr0->filp_ino = rip;
25972    fil_ptr0->filp_flags = O_RDONLY;
25973    dup_inode(rip);                /* for double usage */
25974    fil_ptr1->filp_ino = rip;
25975    fil_ptr1->filp_flags = O_WRONLY;
25976    rw_inode(rip, WRITING);        /* mark inode as allocated */
25977    m_out.reply_i1 = fil_des[0];
25978    m_out.reply_i2 = fil_des[1];
25979    rip->i_update = ATIME | CTIME | MTIME;
25980    return(OK);
25981 }
25982
25983 /*===========================================================================*
25984  *                              pipe_check                                   *
25985  *===========================================================================*/
25986 PUBLIC int pipe_check(rip, rw_flag, oflags, bytes, position, canwrite, notouch)
25987 register struct inode *rip;    /* the inode of the pipe */
25988 int rw_flag;                   /* READING or WRITING */
25989 int oflags;                    /* flags set by open or fcntl */
25990 register int bytes;            /* bytes to be read or written (all chunks) */
25991 register off_t position;       /* current file position */
25992 int *canwrite;                 /* return: number of bytes we can write */
25993 int notouch;                   /* check only */
25994 {
25995 /* Pipes are a little different.  If a process reads from an empty pipe for
25996  * which a writer still exists, suspend the reader.  If the pipe is empty
25997  * and there is no writer, return 0 bytes.  If a process is writing to a
25998  * pipe and no one is reading from it, give a broken pipe error.
25999  */
26000
26001    /* If reading, check for empty pipe. */
26002    if (rw_flag == READING) {
26003          if (position >= rip->i_size) {
26004                /* Process is reading from an empty pipe. */
26005                int r = 0;
26006                if (find_filp(rip, W_BIT) != NIL_FILP) {
26007                      /* Writer exists */
26008                      if (oflags & O_NONBLOCK) {
26009                            r = EAGAIN;
26010                      } else {
26011                            if (!notouch)
26012                                  suspend(XPIPE); /* block reader */
26013                            r = SUSPEND;
26014                      }
```

```
26015                              /* If need be, activate sleeping writers. */
26016                              if (susp_count > 0 && !notouch)
26017                                      release(rip, WRITE, susp_count);
26018                      }
26019                      return(r);
26020              }
26021      } else {
26022              /* Process is writing to a pipe. */
26023              if (find_filp(rip, R_BIT) == NIL_FILP) {
26024                      /* Tell kernel to generate a SIGPIPE signal. */
26025                      if (!notouch)
26026                              sys_kill((int)(fp - fproc), SIGPIPE);
26027                      return(EPIPE);
26028              }
26029
26030              if (position + bytes > PIPE_SIZE(rip->i_sp->s_block_size)) {
26031                      if ((oflags & O_NONBLOCK)
26032                       && bytes < PIPE_SIZE(rip->i_sp->s_block_size))
26033                              return(EAGAIN);
26034                      else if ((oflags & O_NONBLOCK)
26035                       && bytes > PIPE_SIZE(rip->i_sp->s_block_size)) {
26036                      if ( (*canwrite = (PIPE_SIZE(rip->i_sp->s_block_size)
26037                              - position)) > 0)  {
26038                                      /* Do a partial write. Need to wakeup reader */
26039                                      if (!notouch)
26040                                              release(rip, READ, susp_count);
26041                                      return(1);
26042                              } else {
26043                                      return(EAGAIN);
26044                              }
26045                      }
26046                      if (bytes > PIPE_SIZE(rip->i_sp->s_block_size)) {
26047                              if ((*canwrite = PIPE_SIZE(rip->i_sp->s_block_size)
26048                                      - position) > 0) {
26049                                      /* Do a partial write. Need to wakeup reader
26050                                       * since we'll suspend ourself in read_write()
26051                                       */
26052                                      release(rip, READ, susp_count);
26053                                      return(1);
26054                              }
26055                      }
26056                      if (!notouch)
26057                              suspend(XPIPE); /* stop writer -- pipe full */
26058                      return(SUSPEND);
26059              }
26060
26061              /* Writing to an empty pipe.  Search for suspended reader. */
26062              if (position == 0 && !notouch)
26063                      release(rip, READ, susp_count);
26064      }
26065
26066      *canwrite = 0;
26067      return(1);
26068  }
26069
26070  /*===========================================================================*
26071   *                              suspend                                      *
26072   *===========================================================================*/
26073  PUBLIC void suspend(task)
26074  int task;                          /* who is proc waiting for? (PIPE = pipe) */
```

```
26075  {
26076  /* Take measures to suspend the processing of the present system call.
26077   * Store the parameters to be used upon resuming in the process table.
26078   * (Actually they are not used when a process is waiting for an I/O device,
26079   * but they are needed for pipes, and it is not worth making the distinction.)
26080   * The SUSPEND pseudo error should be returned after calling suspend().
26081   */
26082
26083    if (task == XPIPE || task == XPOPEN) susp_count++;/* #procs susp'ed on pipe*/
26084    fp->fp_suspended = SUSPENDED;
26085    fp->fp_fd = m_in.fd << 8 | call_nr;
26086    fp->fp_task = -task;
26087    if (task == XLOCK) {
26088        fp->fp_buffer = (char *) m_in.name1;    /* third arg to fcntl() */
26089        fp->fp_nbytes = m_in.request;           /* second arg to fcntl() */
26090    } else {
26091        fp->fp_buffer = m_in.buffer;            /* for reads and writes */
26092        fp->fp_nbytes = m_in.nbytes;
26093    }
26094  }

26096  /*===========================================================================*
26097   *                              release                                      *
26098   *===========================================================================*/
26099  PUBLIC void release(ip, call_nr, count)
26100  register struct inode *ip;      /* inode of pipe */
26101  int call_nr;                    /* READ, WRITE, OPEN or CREAT */
26102  int count;                      /* max number of processes to release */
26103  {
26104  /* Check to see if any process is hanging on the pipe whose inode is in 'ip'.
26105   * If one is, and it was trying to perform the call indicated by 'call_nr',
26106   * release it.
26107   */
26108
26109    register struct fproc *rp;
26110    struct filp *f;
26111
26112    /* Trying to perform the call also includes SELECTing on it with that
26113     * operation.
26114     */
26115    if (call_nr == READ || call_nr == WRITE) {
26116        int op;
26117        if (call_nr == READ)
26118            op = SEL_RD;
26119        else
26120            op = SEL_WR;
26121        for(f = &filp[0]; f < &filp[NR_FILPS]; f++) {
26122            if (f->filp_count < 1 || !(f->filp_pipe_select_ops & op) ||
26123                f->filp_ino != ip)
26124                    continue;
26125            select_callback(f, op);
26126            f->filp_pipe_select_ops &= ~op;
26127        }
26128    }
26129
26130    /* Search the proc table. */
26131    for (rp = &fproc[0]; rp < &fproc[NR_PROCS]; rp++) {
26132        if (rp->fp_suspended == SUSPENDED &&
26133                    rp->fp_revived == NOT_REVIVING &&
26134                    (rp->fp_fd & BYTE) == call_nr &&
```

```
26135                              rp->fp_filp[rp->fp_fd>>8]->filp_ino == ip) {
26136                       revive((int)(rp - fproc), 0);
26137                       susp_count--;    /* keep track of who is suspended */
26138                       if (--count == 0) return;
26139               }
26140       }
26141   }

26143   /*===========================================================================*
26144    *                               revive                                      *
26145    *===========================================================================*/
26146   PUBLIC void revive(proc_nr, returned)
26147   int proc_nr;                        /* process to revive */
26148   int returned;                       /* if hanging on task, how many bytes read */
26149   {
26150   /* Revive a previously blocked process. When a process hangs on tty, this
26151    * is the way it is eventually released.
26152    */
26153
26154     register struct fproc *rfp;
26155     register int task;
26156
26157     if (proc_nr < 0 || proc_nr >= NR_PROCS)
26158           panic(__FILE__,"revive err", proc_nr);
26159     rfp = &fproc[proc_nr];
26160     if (rfp->fp_suspended == NOT_SUSPENDED || rfp->fp_revived == REVIVING)return;
26161
26162     /* The 'reviving' flag only applies to pipes.  Processes waiting for TTY get
26163      * a message right away.  The revival process is different for TTY and pipes.
26164      * For select and TTY revival, the work is already done, for pipes it is not:
26165      *  the proc must be restarted so it can try again.
26166      */
26167     task = -rfp->fp_task;
26168     if (task == XPIPE || task == XLOCK) {
26169           /* Revive a process suspended on a pipe or lock. */
26170           rfp->fp_revived = REVIVING;
26171           reviving++;                  /* process was waiting on pipe or lock */
26172     } else {
26173           rfp->fp_suspended = NOT_SUSPENDED;
26174           if (task == XPOPEN) /* process blocked in open or create */
26175                   reply(proc_nr, rfp->fp_fd>>8);
26176           else if (task == XSELECT) {
26177                   reply(proc_nr, returned);
26178           } else {
26179                   /* Revive a process suspended on TTY or other device. */
26180                   rfp->fp_nbytes = returned;        /*pretend it wants only what there is*/
26181                   reply(proc_nr, returned);         /* unblock the process */
26182           }
26183     }
26184   }

26186   /*===========================================================================*
26187    *                               do_unpause                                  *
26188    *===========================================================================*/
26189   PUBLIC int do_unpause()
26190   {
26191   /* A signal has been sent to a user who is paused on the file system.
26192    * Abort the system call with the EINTR error message.
26193    */
26194
```

```
26195          register struct fproc *rfp;
26196          int proc_nr, task, fild;
26197          struct filp *f;
26198          dev_t dev;
26199          message mess;
26200
26201          if (who > PM_PROC_NR) return(EPERM);
26202          proc_nr = m_in.pro;
26203          if (proc_nr < 0 || proc_nr >= NR_PROCS)
26204                  panic(__FILE__,"unpause err 1", proc_nr);
26205          rfp = &fproc[proc_nr];
26206          if (rfp->fp_suspended == NOT_SUSPENDED) return(OK);
26207          task = -rfp->fp_task;
26208
26209          switch (task) {
26210              case XPIPE:              /* process trying to read or write a pipe */
26211                      break;
26212
26213              case XLOCK:              /* process trying to set a lock with FCNTL */
26214                      break;
26215
26216              case XSELECT:            /* process blocking on select() */
26217                      select_forget(proc_nr);
26218                      break;
26219
26220              case XPOPEN:             /* process trying to open a fifo */
26221                      break;
26222
26223              default:                 /* process trying to do device I/O (e.g. tty)*/
26224                      fild = (rfp->fp_fd >> 8) & BYTE;/* extract file descriptor */
26225                      if (fild < 0 || fild >= OPEN_MAX)
26226                              panic(__FILE__,"unpause err 2",NO_NUM);
26227                      f = rfp->fp_filp[fild];
26228                      dev = (dev_t) f->filp_ino->i_zone[0];   /* device hung on */
26229                      mess.TTY_LINE = (dev >> MINOR) & BYTE;
26230                      mess.PROC_NR = proc_nr;
26231
26232                      /* Tell kernel R or W. Mode is from current call, not open. */
26233                      mess.COUNT = (rfp->fp_fd & BYTE) == READ ? R_BIT : W_BIT;
26234                      mess.m_type = CANCEL;
26235                      fp = rfp;           /* hack - ctty_io uses fp */
26236                      (*dmap[(dev >> MAJOR) & BYTE].dmap_io)(task, &mess);
26237          }
26238
26239          rfp->fp_suspended = NOT_SUSPENDED;
26240          reply(proc_nr, EINTR);          /* signal interrupted call */
26241          return(OK);
26242  }

26244  /*===========================================================================*
26245   *                              select_request_pipe                          *
26246   *===========================================================================*/
26247  PUBLIC int select_request_pipe(struct filp *f, int *ops, int block)
26248  {
26249          int orig_ops, r = 0, err, canwrite;
26250          orig_ops = *ops;
26251          if ((*ops & SEL_RD)) {
26252                  if ((err = pipe_check(f->filp_ino, READING, 0,
26253                          1, f->filp_pos, &canwrite, 1)) != SUSPEND)
26254                          r |= SEL_RD;
```

```
26255                        if (err < 0 && err != SUSPEND && (*ops & SEL_ERR))
26256                                r |= SEL_ERR;
26257                }
26258                if ((*ops & SEL_WR)) {
26259                        if ((err = pipe_check(f->filp_ino, WRITING, 0,
26260                                1, f->filp_pos, &canwrite, 1)) != SUSPEND)
26261                                r |= SEL_WR;
26262                        if (err < 0 && err != SUSPEND && (*ops & SEL_ERR))
26263                                r |= SEL_ERR;
26264                }
26265
26266                *ops = r;
26267
26268                if (!r && block) {
26269                        f->filp_pipe_select_ops |= orig_ops;
26270                }
26271
26272                return SEL_OK;
26273        }
26274
26275        /*===========================================================================*
26276         *                              select_match_pipe                            *
26277         *===========================================================================*/
26278        PUBLIC int select_match_pipe(struct filp *f)
26279        {
26280                /* recognize either pipe or named pipe (FIFO) */
26281                if (f && f->filp_ino && (f->filp_ino->i_mode & I_NAMED_PIPE))
26282                        return 1;
26283                return 0;
26284        }
```

```
++++++++++++++++++++++++++++++++++++++++++++++++++++++++++++++++++++++++++++++
                              servers/fs/path.c
++++++++++++++++++++++++++++++++++++++++++++++++++++++++++++++++++++++++++++++

26300   /* This file contains the procedures that look up path names in the directory
26301    * system and determine the inode number that goes with a given path name.
26302    *
26303    *   The entry points into this file are
26304    *   eat_path:    the 'main' routine of the path-to-inode conversion mechanism
26305    *   last_dir:    find the final directory on a given path
26306    *   advance:     parse one component of a path name
26307    *   search_dir: search a directory for a string and return its inode number
26308    */
26309
26310   #include "fs.h"
26311   #include <string.h>
26312   #include <minix/callnr.h>
26313   #include "buf.h"
26314   #include "file.h"
26315   #include "fproc.h"
26316   #include "inode.h"
26317   #include "super.h"
26318
26319   PUBLIC char dot1[2] = ".";        /* used for search_dir to bypass the access */
```

```
26320  PUBLIC char dot2[3] = "..";      /* permissions for . and ..              */
26321
26322  FORWARD _PROTOTYPE( char *get_name, (char *old_name, char string [NAME_MAX]) );
26323
26324  /*===========================================================================*
26325   *                              eat_path                                     *
26326   *===========================================================================*/
26327  PUBLIC struct inode *eat_path(path)
26328  char *path;                      /* the path name to be parsed */
26329  {
26330  /* Parse the path 'path' and put its inode in the inode table. If not possible,
26331   * return NIL_INODE as function value and an error code in 'err_code'.
26332   */
26333
26334    register struct inode *ldip, *rip;
26335    char string[NAME_MAX];         /* hold 1 path component name here */
26336
26337    /* First open the path down to the final directory. */
26338    if ( (ldip = last_dir(path, string)) == NIL_INODE) {
26339        return(NIL_INODE);         /* we couldn't open final directory */
26340        }
26341
26342    /* The path consisting only of "/" is a special case, check for it. */
26343    if (string[0] == '\0') return(ldip);
26344
26345    /* Get final component of the path. */
26346    rip = advance(ldip, string);
26347    put_inode(ldip);
26348    return(rip);
26349  }

26351  /*===========================================================================*
26352   *                              last_dir                                     *
26353   *===========================================================================*/
26354  PUBLIC struct inode *last_dir(path, string)
26355  char *path;                      /* the path name to be parsed */
26356  char string[NAME_MAX];           /* the final component is returned here */
26357  {
26358  /* Given a path, 'path', located in the fs address space, parse it as
26359   * far as the last directory, fetch the inode for the last directory into
26360   * the inode table, and return a pointer to the inode.  In
26361   * addition, return the final component of the path in 'string'.
26362   * If the last directory can't be opened, return NIL_INODE and
26363   * the reason for failure in 'err_code'.
26364   */
26365
26366    register struct inode *rip;
26367    register char *new_name;
26368    register struct inode *new_ip;
26369
26370    /* Is the path absolute or relative?  Initialize 'rip' accordingly. */
26371    rip = (*path == '/' ? fp->fp_rootdir : fp->fp_workdir);
26372
26373    /* If dir has been removed or path is empty, return ENOENT. */
26374    if (rip->i_nlinks == 0 || *path == '\0') {
26375        err_code = ENOENT;
26376        return(NIL_INODE);
26377    }
26378
26379    dup_inode(rip);                  /* inode will be returned with put_inode */
```

```
26380
26381          /* Scan the path component by component. */
26382          while (TRUE) {
26383                  /* Extract one component. */
26384                  if ( (new_name = get_name(path, string)) == (char*) 0) {
26385                          put_inode(rip); /* bad path in user space */
26386                          return(NIL_INODE);
26387                  }
26388                  if (*new_name == '\0') {
26389                          if ( (rip->i_mode & I_TYPE) == I_DIRECTORY) {
26390                                  return(rip);      /* normal exit */
26391                          } else {
26392                                  /* last file of path prefix is not a directory */
26393                                  put_inode(rip);
26394                                  err_code = ENOTDIR;
26395                                  return(NIL_INODE);
26396                          }
26397                  }
26398
26399                  /* There is more path.  Keep parsing. */
26400                  new_ip = advance(rip, string);
26401                  put_inode(rip);             /* rip either obsolete or irrelevant */
26402                  if (new_ip == NIL_INODE) return(NIL_INODE);
26403
26404                  /* The call to advance() succeeded.  Fetch next component. */
26405                  path = new_name;
26406                  rip = new_ip;
26407          }
26408  }

26410  /*===========================================================================*
26411   *                              get_name                                     *
26412   *===========================================================================*/
26413  PRIVATE char *get_name(old_name, string)
26414  char *old_name;                     /* path name to parse */
26415  char string[NAME_MAX];              /* component extracted from 'old_name' */
26416  {
26417  /* Given a pointer to a path name in fs space, 'old_name', copy the next
26418   * component to 'string' and pad with zeros.  A pointer to that part of
26419   * the name as yet unparsed is returned.  Roughly speaking,
26420   * 'get_name' = 'old_name' - 'string'.
26421   *
26422   * This routine follows the standard convention that /usr/ast, /usr//ast,
26423   * //usr///ast and /usr/ast/ are all equivalent.
26424   */
26425
26426    register int c;
26427    register char *np, *rnp;
26428
26429    np = string;                        /* 'np' points to current position */
26430    rnp = old_name;                     /* 'rnp' points to unparsed string */
26431    while ( (c = *rnp) == '/') rnp++;   /* skip leading slashes */
26432
26433    /* Copy the unparsed path, 'old_name', to the array, 'string'. */
26434    while ( rnp < &old_name[PATH_MAX]  &&  c != '/'   &&  c != '\0') {
26435          if (np < &string[NAME_MAX]) *np++ = c;
26436          c = *++rnp;                   /* advance to next character */
26437    }
26438
26439    /* To make /usr/ast/ equivalent to /usr/ast, skip trailing slashes. */
```

```
26440          while (c == '/' && rnp < &old_name[PATH_MAX]) c = *++rnp;
26441
26442          if (np < &string[NAME_MAX]) *np = '\0';          /* Terminate string */
26443
26444          if (rnp >= &old_name[PATH_MAX]) {
26445                  err_code = ENAMETOOLONG;
26446                  return((char *) 0);
26447          }
26448          return(rnp);
26449  }

26451  /*===========================================================================*
26452   *                              advance                                      *
26453   *===========================================================================*/
26454  PUBLIC struct inode *advance(dirp, string)
26455  struct inode *dirp;                    /* inode for directory to be searched */
26456  char string[NAME_MAX];                 /* component name to look for */
26457  {
26458  /* Given a directory and a component of a path, look up the component in
26459   * the directory, find the inode, open it, and return a pointer to its inode
26460   * slot.  If it can't be done, return NIL_INODE.
26461   */
26462
26463          register struct inode *rip;
26464          struct inode *rip2;
26465          register struct super_block *sp;
26466          int r, inumb;
26467          dev_t mnt_dev;
26468          ino_t numb;
26469
26470          /* If 'string' is empty, yield same inode straight away. */
26471          if (string[0] == '\0') { return(get_inode(dirp->i_dev, (int) dirp->i_num)); }
26472
26473          /* Check for NIL_INODE. */
26474          if (dirp == NIL_INODE) { return(NIL_INODE); }
26475
26476          /* If 'string' is not present in the directory, signal error. */
26477          if ( (r = search_dir(dirp, string, &numb, LOOK_UP)) != OK) {
26478                  err_code = r;
26479                  return(NIL_INODE);
26480          }
26481
26482          /* Don't go beyond the current root directory, unless the string is dot2. */
26483          if (dirp == fp->fp_rootdir && strcmp(string, "..") == 0 && string != dot2)
26484                          return(get_inode(dirp->i_dev, (int) dirp->i_num));
26485
26486          /* The component has been found in the directory.  Get inode. */
26487          if ( (rip = get_inode(dirp->i_dev, (int) numb)) == NIL_INODE)  {
26488                  return(NIL_INODE);
26489                  }
26490
26491          if (rip->i_num == ROOT_INODE)
26492                  if (dirp->i_num == ROOT_INODE) {
26493                          if (string[1] == '.') {
26494                                  for (sp = &super_block[1]; sp < &super_block[NR_SUPERS]; sp++){
26495                                          if (sp->s_dev == rip->i_dev) {
26496                                                  /* Release the root inode.  Replace by the
26497                                                   * inode mounted on.
26498                                                   */
26499                                                  put_inode(rip);
```

```
26500                                mnt_dev = sp->s_imount->i_dev;
26501                                inumb = (int) sp->s_imount->i_num;
26502                                rip2 = get_inode(mnt_dev, inumb);
26503                                rip = advance(rip2, string);
26504                                put_inode(rip2);
26505                                break;
26506                        }
26507                    }
26508                }
26509            }
26510      if (rip == NIL_INODE) return(NIL_INODE);
26511
26512      /* See if the inode is mounted on.  If so, switch to root directory of the
26513       * mounted file system.  The super_block provides the linkage between the
26514       * inode mounted on and the root directory of the mounted file system.
26515       */
26516      while (rip != NIL_INODE && rip->i_mount == I_MOUNT) {
26517            /* The inode is indeed mounted on. */
26518            for (sp = &super_block[0]; sp < &super_block[NR_SUPERS]; sp++) {
26519                    if (sp->s_imount == rip) {
26520                            /* Release the inode mounted on.  Replace by the
26521                             * inode of the root inode of the mounted device.
26522                             */
26523                            put_inode(rip);
26524                            rip = get_inode(sp->s_dev, ROOT_INODE);
26525                            break;
26526                    }
26527            }
26528      }
26529      return(rip);              /* return pointer to inode's component */
26530 }

26532 /*===========================================================================*
26533  *                              search_dir                                   *
26534  *===========================================================================*/
26535 PUBLIC int search_dir(ldir_ptr, string, numb, flag)
26536 register struct inode *ldir_ptr; /* ptr to inode for dir to search */
26537 char string[NAME_MAX];           /* component to search for */
26538 ino_t *numb;                     /* pointer to inode number */
26539 int flag;                        /* LOOK_UP, ENTER, DELETE or IS_EMPTY */
26540 {
26541 /* This function searches the directory whose inode is pointed to by 'ldip':
26542  * if (flag == ENTER)  enter 'string' in the directory with inode # '*numb';
26543  * if (flag == DELETE) delete 'string' from the directory;
26544  * if (flag == LOOK_UP) search for 'string' and return inode # in 'numb';
26545  * if (flag == IS_EMPTY) return OK if only . and .. in dir else ENOTEMPTY;
26546  *
26547  *    if 'string' is dot1 or dot2, no access permissions are checked.
26548  */
26549
26550   register struct direct *dp = NULL;
26551   register struct buf *bp = NULL;
26552   int i, r, e_hit, t, match;
26553   mode_t bits;
26554   off_t pos;
26555   unsigned new_slots, old_slots;
26556   block_t b;
26557   struct super_block *sp;
26558   int extended = 0;
26559
```

```
26560   /* If 'ldir_ptr' is not a pointer to a dir inode, error. */
26561   if ( (ldir_ptr->i_mode & I_TYPE) != I_DIRECTORY) return(ENOTDIR);
26562
26563   r = OK;
26564
26565   if (flag != IS_EMPTY) {
26566         bits = (flag == LOOK_UP ? X_BIT : W_BIT | X_BIT);
26567
26568         if (string == dot1 || string == dot2) {
26569               if (flag != LOOK_UP) r = read_only(ldir_ptr);
26570                               /* only a writable device is required. */
26571         }
26572         else r = forbidden(ldir_ptr, bits); /* check access permissions */
26573   }
26574   if (r != OK) return(r);
26575
26576   /* Step through the directory one block at a time. */
26577   old_slots = (unsigned) (ldir_ptr->i_size/DIR_ENTRY_SIZE);
26578   new_slots = 0;
26579   e_hit = FALSE;
26580   match = 0;                    /* set when a string match occurs */
26581
26582   for (pos = 0; pos < ldir_ptr->i_size; pos += ldir_ptr->i_sp->s_block_size) {
26583         b = read_map(ldir_ptr, pos);   /* get block number */
26584
26585         /* Since directories don't have holes, 'b' cannot be NO_BLOCK. */
26586         bp = get_block(ldir_ptr->i_dev, b, NORMAL);     /* get a dir block */
26587
26588         if (bp == NO_BLOCK)
26589               panic(__FILE__,"get_block returned NO_BLOCK", NO_NUM);
26590
26591         /* Search a directory block. */
26592         for (dp = &bp->b_dir[0];
26593               dp < &bp->b_dir[NR_DIR_ENTRIES(ldir_ptr->i_sp->s_block_size)];
26594               dp++) {
26595               if (++new_slots > old_slots) { /* not found, but room left */
26596                     if (flag == ENTER) e_hit = TRUE;
26597                     break;
26598               }
26599
26600               /* Match occurs if string found. */
26601               if (flag != ENTER && dp->d_ino != 0) {
26602                     if (flag == IS_EMPTY) {
26603                           /* If this test succeeds, dir is not empty. */
26604                           if (strcmp(dp->d_name, "." ) != 0 &&
26605                                 strcmp(dp->d_name, "..") != 0) match = 1;
26606                     } else {
26607                           if (strncmp(dp->d_name, string, NAME_MAX) == 0) {
26608                                 match = 1;
26609                           }
26610                     }
26611               }
26612
26613               if (match) {
26614                     /* LOOK_UP or DELETE found what it wanted. */
26615                     r = OK;
26616                     if (flag == IS_EMPTY) r = ENOTEMPTY;
26617                     else if (flag == DELETE) {
26618                           /* Save d_ino for recovery. */
26619                           t = NAME_MAX - sizeof(ino_t);
```

```
26620                              *((ino_t *) &dp->d_name[t]) = dp->d_ino;
26621                              dp->d_ino = 0;  /* erase entry */
26622                              bp->b_dirt = DIRTY;
26623                              ldir_ptr->i_update |= CTIME | MTIME;
26624                              ldir_ptr->i_dirt = DIRTY;
26625                      } else {
26626                              sp = ldir_ptr->i_sp;    /* 'flag' is LOOK_UP */
26627                              *numb = conv4(sp->s_native, (int) dp->d_ino);
26628                      }
26629                      put_block(bp, DIRECTORY_BLOCK);
26630                      return(r);
26631              }
26632
26633              /* Check for free slot for the benefit of ENTER. */
26634              if (flag == ENTER && dp->d_ino == 0) {
26635                      e_hit = TRUE;   /* we found a free slot */
26636                      break;
26637              }
26638          }
26639
26640          /* The whole block has been searched or ENTER has a free slot. */
26641          if (e_hit) break;          /* e_hit set if ENTER can be performed now */
26642          put_block(bp, DIRECTORY_BLOCK); /* otherwise, continue searching dir */
26643      }
26644
26645      /* The whole directory has now been searched. */
26646      if (flag != ENTER) {
26647          return(flag == IS_EMPTY ? OK : ENOENT);
26648      }
26649
26650      /* This call is for ENTER.  If no free slot has been found so far, try to
26651       * extend directory.
26652       */
26653      if (e_hit == FALSE) { /* directory is full and no room left in last block */
26654          new_slots++;               /* increase directory size by 1 entry */
26655          if (new_slots == 0) return(EFBIG); /* dir size limited by slot count */
26656          if ( (bp = new_block(ldir_ptr, ldir_ptr->i_size)) == NIL_BUF)
26657                  return(err_code);
26658          dp = &bp->b_dir[0];
26659          extended = 1;
26660      }
26661
26662      /* 'bp' now points to a directory block with space. 'dp' points to slot. */
26663      (void) memset(dp->d_name, 0, (size_t) NAME_MAX); /* clear entry */
26664      for (i = 0; string[i] && i < NAME_MAX; i++) dp->d_name[i] = string[i];
26665      sp = ldir_ptr->i_sp;
26666      dp->d_ino = conv4(sp->s_native, (int) *numb);
26667      bp->b_dirt = DIRTY;
26668      put_block(bp, DIRECTORY_BLOCK);
26669      ldir_ptr->i_update |= CTIME | MTIME;  /* mark mtime for update later */
26670      ldir_ptr->i_dirt = DIRTY;
26671      if (new_slots > old_slots) {
26672          ldir_ptr->i_size = (off_t) new_slots * DIR_ENTRY_SIZE;
26673          /* Send the change to disk if the directory is extended. */
26674          if (extended) rw_inode(ldir_ptr, WRITING);
26675      }
26676      return(OK);
26677  }
```

```
+++++++++++++++++++++++++++++++++++++++++++++++++++++++++++++++++++++++++++++
                              servers/fs/mount.c
+++++++++++++++++++++++++++++++++++++++++++++++++++++++++++++++++++++++++++++
26700   /* This file performs the MOUNT and UMOUNT system calls.
26701    *
26702    * The entry points into this file are
26703    *   do_mount:  perform the MOUNT system call
26704    *   do_umount: perform the UMOUNT system call
26705    */
26706
26707   #include "fs.h"
26708   #include <fcntl.h>
26709   #include <minix/com.h>
26710   #include <sys/stat.h>
26711   #include "buf.h"
26712   #include "file.h"
26713   #include "fproc.h"
26714   #include "inode.h"
26715   #include "param.h"
26716   #include "super.h"
26717
26718   FORWARD _PROTOTYPE( dev_t name_to_dev, (char *path)                );
26719
26720   /*===========================================================================*
26721    *                              do_mount                                     *
26722    *===========================================================================*/
26723   PUBLIC int do_mount()
26724   {
26725   /* Perform the mount(name, mfile, rd_only) system call. */
26726
26727     register struct inode *rip, *root_ip;
26728     struct super_block *xp, *sp;
26729     dev_t dev;
26730     mode_t bits;
26731     int rdir, mdir;                 /* TRUE iff {root|mount} file is dir */
26732     int r, found;
26733
26734     /* Only the super-user may do MOUNT. */
26735     if (!super_user) return(EPERM);
26736
26737     /* If 'name' is not for a block special file, return error. */
26738     if (fetch_name(m_in.name1, m_in.name1_length, M1) != OK) return(err_code);
26739     if ( (dev = name_to_dev(user_path)) == NO_DEV) return(err_code);
26740
26741     /* Scan super block table to see if dev already mounted & find a free slot.*/
26742     sp = NIL_SUPER;
26743     found = FALSE;
26744     for (xp = &super_block[0]; xp < &super_block[NR_SUPERS]; xp++) {
26745           if (xp->s_dev == dev) found = TRUE;     /* is it mounted already? */
26746           if (xp->s_dev == NO_DEV) sp = xp;       /* record free slot */
26747     }
26748     if (found) return(EBUSY);       /* already mounted */
26749     if (sp == NIL_SUPER) return(ENFILE);  /* no super block available */
26750
26751     /* Open the device the file system lives on. */
26752     if (dev_open(dev, who, m_in.rd_only ? R_BIT : (R_BIT|W_BIT)) != OK)
26753           return(EINVAL);
26754
```

```
26755        /* Make the cache forget about blocks it has open on the filesystem */
26756        (void) do_sync();
26757        invalidate(dev);
26758
26759        /* Fill in the super block. */
26760        sp->s_dev = dev;                    /* read_super() needs to know which dev */
26761        r = read_super(sp);
26762
26763        /* Is it recognized as a Minix filesystem? */
26764        if (r != OK) {
26765                dev_close(dev);
26766                sp->s_dev = NO_DEV;
26767                return(r);
26768        }
26769
26770        /* Now get the inode of the file to be mounted on. */
26771        if (fetch_name(m_in.name2, m_in.name2_length, M1) != OK) {
26772                dev_close(dev);
26773                sp->s_dev = NO_DEV;
26774                return(err_code);
26775        }
26776        if ( (rip = eat_path(user_path)) == NIL_INODE) {
26777                dev_close(dev);
26778                sp->s_dev = NO_DEV;
26779                return(err_code);
26780        }
26781
26782        /* It may not be busy. */
26783        r = OK;
26784        if (rip->i_count > 1) r = EBUSY;
26785
26786        /* It may not be special. */
26787        bits = rip->i_mode & I_TYPE;
26788        if (bits == I_BLOCK_SPECIAL || bits == I_CHAR_SPECIAL) r = ENOTDIR;
26789
26790        /* Get the root inode of the mounted file system. */
26791        root_ip = NIL_INODE;               /* if 'r' not OK, make sure this is defined */
26792        if (r == OK) {
26793                if ( (root_ip = get_inode(dev, ROOT_INODE)) == NIL_INODE) r = err_code;
26794        }
26795        if (root_ip != NIL_INODE && root_ip->i_mode == 0) {
26796                r = EINVAL;
26797        }
26798
26799        /* File types of 'rip' and 'root_ip' may not conflict. */
26800        if (r == OK) {
26801                mdir = ((rip->i_mode & I_TYPE) == I_DIRECTORY);  /* TRUE iff dir */
26802                rdir = ((root_ip->i_mode & I_TYPE) == I_DIRECTORY);
26803                if (!mdir && rdir) r = EISDIR;
26804        }
26805
26806        /* If error, return the super block and both inodes; release the maps. */
26807        if (r != OK) {
26808                put_inode(rip);
26809                put_inode(root_ip);
26810                (void) do_sync();
26811                invalidate(dev);
26812                dev_close(dev);
26813                sp->s_dev = NO_DEV;
26814                return(r);
```

```
26815    }
26816
26817    /* Nothing else can go wrong.  Perform the mount. */
26818    rip->i_mount = I_MOUNT;          /* this bit says the inode is mounted on */
26819    sp->s_imount = rip;
26820    sp->s_isup = root_ip;
26821    sp->s_rd_only = m_in.rd_only;
26822    return(OK);
26823  }

26825  /*===========================================================================*
26826   *                              do_umount                                     *
26827   *===========================================================================*/
26828  PUBLIC int do_umount()
26829  {
26830  /* Perform the umount(name) system call. */
26831    dev_t dev;
26832
26833    /* Only the super-user may do UMOUNT. */
26834    if (!super_user) return(EPERM);
26835
26836    /* If 'name' is not for a block special file, return error. */
26837    if (fetch_name(m_in.name, m_in.name_length, M3) != OK) return(err_code);
26838    if ( (dev = name_to_dev(user_path)) == NO_DEV) return(err_code);
26839
26840    return(unmount(dev));
26841  }

26843  /*===========================================================================*
26844   *                               unmount                                      *
26845   *===========================================================================*/
26846  PUBLIC int unmount(dev)
26847  Dev_t dev;
26848  {
26849  /* Unmount a file system by device number. */
26850    register struct inode *rip;
26851    struct super_block *sp, *sp1;
26852    int count;
26853
26854    /* See if the mounted device is busy.  Only 1 inode using it should be
26855     * open -- the root inode -- and that inode only 1 time.
26856     */
26857    count = 0;
26858    for (rip = &inode[0]; rip< &inode[NR_INODES]; rip++)
26859          if (rip->i_count > 0 && rip->i_dev == dev) count += rip->i_count;
26860    if (count > 1) return(EBUSY); /* can't umount a busy file system */
26861
26862    /* Find the super block. */
26863    sp = NIL_SUPER;
26864    for (sp1 = &super_block[0]; sp1 < &super_block[NR_SUPERS]; sp1++) {
26865          if (sp1->s_dev == dev) {
26866                sp = sp1;
26867                break;
26868          }
26869    }
26870
26871    /* Sync the disk, and invalidate cache. */
26872    (void) do_sync();                 /* force any cached blocks out of memory */
26873    invalidate(dev);                  /* invalidate cache entries for this dev */
26874    if (sp == NIL_SUPER) {
```

```
26875                    return(EINVAL);
26876      }
26877
26878      /* Close the device the file system lives on. */
26879      dev_close(dev);
26880
26881      /* Finish off the unmount. */
26882      sp->s_imount->i_mount = NO_MOUNT;        /* inode returns to normal */
26883      put_inode(sp->s_imount);          /* release the inode mounted on */
26884      put_inode(sp->s_isup);            /* release the root inode of the mounted fs */
26885      sp->s_imount = NIL_INODE;
26886      sp->s_dev = NO_DEV;
26887      return(OK);
26888   }


26890   /*===========================================================================*
26891    *                              name_to_dev                                  *
26892    *===========================================================================*/
26893   PRIVATE dev_t name_to_dev(path)
26894   char *path;                        /* pointer to path name */
26895   {
26896   /* Convert the block special file 'path' to a device number.  If 'path'
26897    * is not a block special file, return error code in 'err_code'.
26898    */
26899
26900      register struct inode *rip;
26901      register dev_t dev;
26902
26903      /* If 'path' can't be opened, give up immediately. */
26904      if ( (rip = eat_path(path)) == NIL_INODE) return(NO_DEV);
26905
26906      /* If 'path' is not a block special file, return error. */
26907      if ( (rip->i_mode & I_TYPE) != I_BLOCK_SPECIAL) {
26908            err_code = ENOTBLK;
26909            put_inode(rip);
26910            return(NO_DEV);
26911      }
26912
26913      /* Extract the device number. */
26914      dev = (dev_t) rip->i_zone[0];
26915      put_inode(rip);
26916      return(dev);
26917   }
```

```
++++++++++++++++++++++++++++++++++++++++++++++++++++++++++++++++++++++++++++++
                              servers/fs/link.c
++++++++++++++++++++++++++++++++++++++++++++++++++++++++++++++++++++++++++++++

27000   /* This file handles the LINK and UNLINK system calls.  It also deals with
27001    * deallocating the storage used by a file when the last UNLINK is done to a
27002    * file and the blocks must be returned to the free block pool.
27003    *
27004    * The entry points into this file are
27005    *   do_link:    perform the LINK system call
27006    *   do_unlink:  perform the UNLINK and RMDIR system calls
27007    *   do_rename:  perform the RENAME system call
27008    *   truncate:   release all the blocks associated with an inode
27009    */
```

```
27010
27011   #include "fs.h"
27012   #include <sys/stat.h>
27013   #include <string.h>
27014   #include <minix/com.h>
27015   #include <minix/callnr.h>
27016   #include "buf.h"
27017   #include "file.h"
27018   #include "fproc.h"
27019   #include "inode.h"
27020   #include "param.h"
27021   #include "super.h"
27022
27023   #define SAME 1000
27024
27025   FORWARD _PROTOTYPE( int remove_dir, (struct inode *rldirp, struct inode *rip,
27026                           char dir_name[NAME_MAX])                          );
27027
27028   FORWARD _PROTOTYPE( int unlink_file, (struct inode *dirp, struct inode *rip,
27029                           char file_name[NAME_MAX])                         );
27030
27031   /*===========================================================================*
27032    *                              do_link                                       *
27033    *===========================================================================*/
27034   PUBLIC int do_link()
27035   {
27036   /* Perform the link(name1, name2) system call. */
27037
27038     register struct inode *ip, *rip;
27039     register int r;
27040     char string[NAME_MAX];
27041     struct inode *new_ip;
27042
27043     /* See if 'name' (file to be linked) exists. */
27044     if (fetch_name(m_in.name1, m_in.name1_length, M1) != OK) return(err_code);
27045     if ( (rip = eat_path(user_path)) == NIL_INODE) return(err_code);
27046
27047     /* Check to see if the file has maximum number of links already. */
27048     r = OK;
27049     if (rip->i_nlinks >= (rip->i_sp->s_version == V1 ? CHAR_MAX : SHRT_MAX))
27050           r = EMLINK;
27051
27052     /* Only super_user may link to directories. */
27053     if (r == OK)
27054           if ( (rip->i_mode & I_TYPE) == I_DIRECTORY && !super_user) r = EPERM;
27055
27056     /* If error with 'name', return the inode. */
27057     if (r != OK) {
27058           put_inode(rip);
27059           return(r);
27060     }
27061
27062     /* Does the final directory of 'name2' exist? */
27063     if (fetch_name(m_in.name2, m_in.name2_length, M1) != OK) {
27064           put_inode(rip);
27065           return(err_code);
27066     }
27067     if ( (ip = last_dir(user_path, string)) == NIL_INODE) r = err_code;
27068
27069     /* If 'name2' exists in full (even if no space) set 'r' to error. */
```

```
27070        if (r == OK) {
27071                if ( (new_ip = advance(ip, string)) == NIL_INODE) {
27072                        r = err_code;
27073                        if (r == ENOENT) r = OK;
27074                } else {
27075                        put_inode(new_ip);
27076                        r = EEXIST;
27077                }
27078        }
27079
27080        /* Check for links across devices. */
27081        if (r == OK)
27082                if (rip->i_dev != ip->i_dev) r = EXDEV;
27083
27084        /* Try to link. */
27085        if (r == OK)
27086                r = search_dir(ip, string, &rip->i_num, ENTER);
27087
27088        /* If success, register the linking. */
27089        if (r == OK) {
27090                rip->i_nlinks++;
27091                rip->i_update |= CTIME;
27092                rip->i_dirt = DIRTY;
27093        }
27094
27095        /* Done.  Release both inodes. */
27096        put_inode(rip);
27097        put_inode(ip);
27098        return(r);
27099 }

27101 /*===========================================================================*
27102  *                              do_unlink                                    *
27103  *===========================================================================*/
27104 PUBLIC int do_unlink()
27105 {
27106 /* Perform the unlink(name) or rmdir(name) system call. The code for these two
27107  * is almost the same.  They differ only in some condition testing.  Unlink()
27108  * may be used by the superuser to do dangerous things; rmdir() may not.
27109  */
27110
27111    register struct inode *rip;
27112    struct inode *rldirp;
27113    int r;
27114    char string[NAME_MAX];
27115
27116    /* Get the last directory in the path. */
27117    if (fetch_name(m_in.name, m_in.name_length, M3) != OK) return(err_code);
27118    if ( (rldirp = last_dir(user_path, string)) == NIL_INODE)
27119            return(err_code);
27120
27121    /* The last directory exists.  Does the file also exist? */
27122    r = OK;
27123    if ( (rip = advance(rldirp, string)) == NIL_INODE) r = err_code;
27124
27125    /* If error, return inode. */
27126    if (r != OK) {
27127            put_inode(rldirp);
27128            return(r);
27129    }
```

```
27130
27131          /* Do not remove a mount point. */
27132          if (rip->i_num == ROOT_INODE) {
27133                  put_inode(rldirp);
27134                  put_inode(rip);
27135                  return(EBUSY);
27136          }
27137
27138          /* Now test if the call is allowed, separately for unlink() and rmdir(). */
27139          if (call_nr == UNLINK) {
27140                  /* Only the su may unlink directories, but the su can unlink any dir.*/
27141                  if ( (rip->i_mode & I_TYPE) == I_DIRECTORY && !super_user) r = EPERM;
27142
27143                  /* Don't unlink a file if it is the root of a mounted file system. */
27144                  if (rip->i_num == ROOT_INODE) r = EBUSY;
27145
27146                  /* Actually try to unlink the file; fails if parent is mode 0 etc. */
27147                  if (r == OK) r = unlink_file(rldirp, rip, string);
27148
27149          } else {
27150                  r = remove_dir(rldirp, rip, string); /* call is RMDIR */
27151          }
27152
27153          /* If unlink was possible, it has been done, otherwise it has not. */
27154          put_inode(rip);
27155          put_inode(rldirp);
27156          return(r);
27157  }
27158
27159  /*===========================================================================*
27160   *                              do_rename                                     *
27161   *===========================================================================*/
27162  PUBLIC int do_rename()
27163  {
27164  /* Perform the rename(name1, name2) system call. */
27165
27166          struct inode *old_dirp, *old_ip;     /* ptrs to old dir, file inodes */
27167          struct inode *new_dirp, *new_ip;     /* ptrs to new dir, file inodes */
27168          struct inode *new_superdirp, *next_new_superdirp;
27169          int r = OK;                          /* error flag; initially no error */
27170          int odir, ndir;                      /* TRUE iff {old|new} file is dir */
27171          int same_pdir;                       /* TRUE iff parent dirs are the same */
27172          char old_name[NAME_MAX], new_name[NAME_MAX];
27173          ino_t numb;
27174          int r1;
27175
27176          /* See if 'name1' (existing file) exists.  Get dir and file inodes. */
27177          if (fetch_name(m_in.name1, m_in.name1_length, M1) != OK) return(err_code);
27178          if ( (old_dirp = last_dir(user_path, old_name))==NIL_INODE) return(err_code);
27179
27180          if ( (old_ip = advance(old_dirp, old_name)) == NIL_INODE) r = err_code;
27181
27182          /* See if 'name2' (new name) exists.  Get dir and file inodes. */
27183          if (fetch_name(m_in.name2, m_in.name2_length, M1) != OK) r = err_code;
27184          if ( (new_dirp = last_dir(user_path, new_name)) == NIL_INODE) r = err_code;
27185          new_ip = advance(new_dirp, new_name); /* not required to exist */
27186
27187          if (old_ip != NIL_INODE)
27188                  odir = ((old_ip->i_mode & I_TYPE) == I_DIRECTORY);  /* TRUE iff dir */
27189
```

```
27190        /* If it is ok, check for a variety of possible errors. */
27191        if (r == OK) {
27192                same_pdir = (old_dirp == new_dirp);
27193
27194                /* The old inode must not be a superdirectory of the new last dir. */
27195                if (odir && !same_pdir) {
27196                        dup_inode(new_superdirp = new_dirp);
27197                        while (TRUE) {            /* may hang in a file system loop */
27198                                if (new_superdirp == old_ip) {
27199                                        r = EINVAL;
27200                                        break;
27201                                }
27202                                next_new_superdirp = advance(new_superdirp, dot2);
27203                                put_inode(new_superdirp);
27204                                if (next_new_superdirp == new_superdirp)
27205                                        break;  /* back at system root directory */
27206                                new_superdirp = next_new_superdirp;
27207                                if (new_superdirp == NIL_INODE) {
27208                                        /* Missing ".." entry.  Assume the worst. */
27209                                        r = EINVAL;
27210                                        break;
27211                                }
27212                        }
27213                        put_inode(new_superdirp);
27214                }
27215
27216                /* The old or new name must not be . or .. */
27217                if (strcmp(old_name, ".")==0 || strcmp(old_name, "..")==0 ||
27218                    strcmp(new_name, ".")==0 || strcmp(new_name, "..")==0) r = EINVAL;
27219
27220                /* Both parent directories must be on the same device. */
27221                if (old_dirp->i_dev != new_dirp->i_dev) r = EXDEV;
27222
27223                /* Parent dirs must be writable, searchable and on a writable device */
27224                if ((r1 = forbidden(old_dirp, W_BIT | X_BIT)) != OK ||
27225                    (r1 = forbidden(new_dirp, W_BIT | X_BIT)) != OK) r = r1;
27226
27227                /* Some tests apply only if the new path exists. */
27228                if (new_ip == NIL_INODE) {
27229                        /* don't rename a file with a file system mounted on it. */
27230                        if (old_ip->i_dev != old_dirp->i_dev) r = EXDEV;
27231                        if (odir && new_dirp->i_nlinks >=
27232                            (new_dirp->i_sp->s_version == V1 ? CHAR_MAX : SHRT_MAX) &&
27233                            !same_pdir && r == OK) r = EMLINK;
27234                } else {
27235                        if (old_ip == new_ip) r = SAME; /* old=new */
27236
27237                        /* has the old file or new file a file system mounted on it? */
27238                        if (old_ip->i_dev != new_ip->i_dev) r = EXDEV;
27239
27240                        ndir = ((new_ip->i_mode & I_TYPE) == I_DIRECTORY); /* dir ? */
27241                        if (odir == TRUE && ndir == FALSE) r = ENOTDIR;
27242                        if (odir == FALSE && ndir == TRUE) r = EISDIR;
27243                }
27244        }
27245
27246        /* If a process has another root directory than the system root, we might
27247         * "accidently" be moving it's working directory to a place where it's
27248         * root directory isn't a super directory of it anymore. This can make
27249         * the function chroot useless. If chroot will be used often we should
```

```
27250          * probably check for it here.
27251          */
27252
27253         /* The rename will probably work. Only two things can go wrong now:
27254          * 1. being unable to remove the new file. (when new file already exists)
27255          * 2. being unable to make the new directory entry. (new file doesn't exists)
27256          *    [directory has to grow by one block and cannot because the disk
27257          *     is completely full].
27258          */
27259         if (r == OK) {
27260               if (new_ip != NIL_INODE) {
27261                       /* There is already an entry for 'new'. Try to remove it. */
27262                     if (odir)
27263                             r = remove_dir(new_dirp, new_ip, new_name);
27264                     else
27265                             r = unlink_file(new_dirp, new_ip, new_name);
27266               }
27267               /* if r is OK, the rename will succeed, while there is now an
27268                * unused entry in the new parent directory.
27269                */
27270         }
27271
27272         if (r == OK) {
27273               /* If the new name will be in the same parent directory as the old one,
27274                * first remove the old name to free an entry for the new name,
27275                * otherwise first try to create the new name entry to make sure
27276                * the rename will succeed.
27277                */
27278               numb = old_ip->i_num;            /* inode number of old file */
27279
27280               if (same_pdir) {
27281                     r = search_dir(old_dirp, old_name, (ino_t *) 0, DELETE);
27282                                                 /* shouldn't go wrong. */
27283                     if (r==OK) (void) search_dir(old_dirp, new_name, &numb, ENTER);
27284               } else {
27285                     r = search_dir(new_dirp, new_name, &numb, ENTER);
27286                     if (r == OK)
27287                         (void) search_dir(old_dirp, old_name, (ino_t *) 0, DELETE);
27288               }
27289         }
27290         /* If r is OK, the ctime and mtime of old_dirp and new_dirp have been marked
27291          * for update in search_dir.
27292          */
27293
27294         if (r == OK && odir && !same_pdir) {
27295               /* Update the .. entry in the directory (still points to old_dirp). */
27296               numb = new_dirp->i_num;
27297               (void) unlink_file(old_ip, NIL_INODE, dot2);
27298               if (search_dir(old_ip, dot2, &numb, ENTER) == OK) {
27299                       /* New link created. */
27300                       new_dirp->i_nlinks++;
27301                       new_dirp->i_dirt = DIRTY;
27302               }
27303         }
27304
27305         /* Release the inodes. */
27306         put_inode(old_dirp);
27307         put_inode(old_ip);
27308         put_inode(new_dirp);
27309         put_inode(new_ip);
```

```
27310        return(r == SAME ? OK : r);
27311    }
27312
27313    /*===========================================================================*
27314     *                              truncate                                     *
27315     *===========================================================================*/
27316    PUBLIC void truncate(rip)
27317    register struct inode *rip;       /* pointer to inode to be truncated */
27318    {
27319    /* Remove all the zones from the inode 'rip' and mark it dirty. */
27320
27321        register block_t b;
27322        zone_t z, zone_size, z1;
27323        off_t position;
27324        int i, scale, file_type, waspipe, single, nr_indirects;
27325        struct buf *bp;
27326        dev_t dev;
27327
27328        file_type = rip->i_mode & I_TYPE;       /* check to see if file is special */
27329        if (file_type == I_CHAR_SPECIAL || file_type == I_BLOCK_SPECIAL) return;
27330        dev = rip->i_dev;                       /* device on which inode resides */
27331        scale = rip->i_sp->s_log_zone_size;
27332        zone_size = (zone_t) rip->i_sp->s_block_size << scale;
27333        nr_indirects = rip->i_nindirs;
27334
27335        /* Pipes can shrink, so adjust size to make sure all zones are removed. */
27336        waspipe = rip->i_pipe == I_PIPE;        /* TRUE is this was a pipe */
27337        if (waspipe) rip->i_size = PIPE_SIZE(rip->i_sp->s_block_size);
27338
27339        /* Step through the file a zone at a time, finding and freeing the zones. */
27340        for (position = 0; position < rip->i_size; position += zone_size) {
27341            if ( (b = read_map(rip, position)) != NO_BLOCK) {
27342                z = (zone_t) b >> scale;
27343                free_zone(dev, z);
27344            }
27345        }
27346
27347        /* All the data zones have been freed.  Now free the indirect zones. */
27348        rip->i_dirt = DIRTY;
27349        if (waspipe) {
27350            wipe_inode(rip);            /* clear out inode for pipes */
27351            return;                     /* indirect slots contain file positions */
27352        }
27353        single = rip->i_ndzones;
27354        free_zone(dev, rip->i_zone[single]);  /* single indirect zone */
27355        if ( (z = rip->i_zone[single+1]) != NO_ZONE) {
27356            /* Free all the single indirect zones pointed to by the double. */
27357            b = (block_t) z << scale;
27358            bp = get_block(dev, b, NORMAL); /* get double indirect zone */
27359            for (i = 0; i < nr_indirects; i++) {
27360                z1 = rd_indir(bp, i);
27361                free_zone(dev, z1);
27362            }
27363
27364            /* Now free the double indirect zone itself. */
27365            put_block(bp, INDIRECT_BLOCK);
27366            free_zone(dev, z);
27367        }
27368
27369        /* Leave zone numbers for de(1) to recover file after an unlink(2).  */
```

```
27370  }

27372  /*===========================================================================*
27373   *                            remove_dir                                     *
27374   *===========================================================================*/
27375  PRIVATE int remove_dir(rldirp, rip, dir_name)
27376  struct inode *rldirp;                   /* parent directory */
27377  struct inode *rip;                      /* directory to be removed */
27378  char dir_name[NAME_MAX];                /* name of directory to be removed */
27379  {
27380    /* A directory file has to be removed. Five conditions have to met:
27381     *      - The file must be a directory
27382     *      - The directory must be empty (except for . and ..)
27383     *      - The final component of the path must not be . or ..
27384     *      - The directory must not be the root of a mounted file system
27385     *      - The directory must not be anybody's root/working directory
27386     */
27387
27388    int r;
27389    register struct fproc *rfp;
27390
27391    /* search_dir checks that rip is a directory too. */
27392    if ((r = search_dir(rip, "", (ino_t *) 0, IS_EMPTY)) != OK) return r;
27393
27394    if (strcmp(dir_name, ".") == 0 || strcmp(dir_name, "..") == 0)return(EINVAL);
27395    if (rip->i_num == ROOT_INODE) return(EBUSY); /* can't remove 'root' */
27396
27397    for (rfp = &fproc[INIT_PROC_NR + 1]; rfp < &fproc[NR_PROCS]; rfp++)
27398         if (rfp->fp_workdir == rip || rfp->fp_rootdir == rip) return(EBUSY);
27399                              /* can't remove anybody's working dir */
27400
27401    /* Actually try to unlink the file; fails if parent is mode 0 etc. */
27402    if ((r = unlink_file(rldirp, rip, dir_name)) != OK) return r;
27403
27404    /* Unlink . and .. from the dir. The super user can link and unlink any dir,
27405     * so don't make too many assumptions about them.
27406     */
27407    (void) unlink_file(rip, NIL_INODE, dot1);
27408    (void) unlink_file(rip, NIL_INODE, dot2);
27409    return(OK);
27410  }

27412  /*===========================================================================*
27413   *                            unlink_file                                    *
27414   *===========================================================================*/
27415  PRIVATE int unlink_file(dirp, rip, file_name)
27416  struct inode *dirp;             /* parent directory of file */
27417  struct inode *rip;             /* inode of file, may be NIL_INODE too. */
27418  char file_name[NAME_MAX];      /* name of file to be removed */
27419  {
27420  /* Unlink 'file_name'; rip must be the inode of 'file_name' or NIL_INODE. */
27421
27422    ino_t numb;                   /* inode number */
27423    int   r;
27424
27425    /* If rip is not NIL_INODE, it is used to get faster access to the inode. */
27426    if (rip == NIL_INODE) {
27427         /* Search for file in directory and try to get its inode. */
27428         err_code = search_dir(dirp, file_name, &numb, LOOK_UP);
27429         if (err_code == OK) rip = get_inode(dirp->i_dev, (int) numb);
```

```
27430              if (err_code != OK || rip == NIL_INODE) return(err_code);
27431    } else {
27432         dup_inode(rip);              /* inode will be returned with put_inode */
27433    }
27434
27435    r = search_dir(dirp, file_name, (ino_t *) 0, DELETE);
27436
27437    if (r == OK) {
27438         rip->i_nlinks--;             /* entry deleted from parent's dir */
27439         rip->i_update |= CTIME;
27440         rip->i_dirt = DIRTY;
27441    }
27442
27443    put_inode(rip);
27444    return(r);
27445 }
```

```
++++++++++++++++++++++++++++++++++++++++++++++++++++++++++++++++++++++++++++++++
                            servers/fs/stadir.c
++++++++++++++++++++++++++++++++++++++++++++++++++++++++++++++++++++++++++++++++

27500    /* This file contains the code for performing four system calls relating to
27501     * status and directories.
27502     *
27503     * The entry points into this file are
27504     *   do_chdir:   perform the CHDIR system call
27505     *   do_chroot:  perform the CHROOT system call
27506     *   do_stat:    perform the STAT system call
27507     *   do_fstat:   perform the FSTAT system call
27508     *   do_fstatfs: perform the FSTATFS system call
27509     */
27510
27511    #include "fs.h"
27512    #include <sys/stat.h>
27513    #include <sys/statfs.h>
27514    #include <minix/com.h>
27515    #include "file.h"
27516    #include "fproc.h"
27517    #include "inode.h"
27518    #include "param.h"
27519    #include "super.h"
27520
27521    FORWARD _PROTOTYPE( int change, (struct inode **iip, char *name_ptr, int len));
27522    FORWARD _PROTOTYPE( int change_into, (struct inode **iip, struct inode *ip));
27523    FORWARD _PROTOTYPE( int stat_inode, (struct inode *rip, struct filp *fil_ptr,
27524                        char *user_addr)                          );
27525
27526    /*===========================================================================*
27527     *                              do_fchdir                                     *
27528     *===========================================================================*/
27529    PUBLIC int do_fchdir()
27530    {
27531         /* Change directory on already-opened fd. */
27532         struct filp *rfilp;
27533
27534         /* Is the file descriptor valid? */
```

```
27535            if ( (rfilp = get_filp(m_in.fd)) == NIL_FILP) return(err_code);
27536            return change_into(&fp->fp_workdir, rfilp->filp_ino);
27537    }

27539    /*===========================================================================*
27540     *                              do_chdir                                      *
27541     *===========================================================================*/
27542    PUBLIC int do_chdir()
27543    {
27544    /* Change directory.  This function is  also called by MM to simulate a chdir
27545     * in order to do EXEC, etc.  It also changes the root directory, the uids and
27546     * gids, and the umask.
27547     */

27549      int r;
27550      register struct fproc *rfp;

27552      if (who == PM_PROC_NR) {
27553            rfp = &fproc[m_in.slot1];
27554            put_inode(fp->fp_rootdir);
27555            dup_inode(fp->fp_rootdir = rfp->fp_rootdir);
27556            put_inode(fp->fp_workdir);
27557            dup_inode(fp->fp_workdir = rfp->fp_workdir);

27559            /* MM uses access() to check permissions.  To make this work, pretend
27560             * that the user's real ids are the same as the user's effective ids.
27561             * FS calls other than access() do not use the real ids, so are not
27562             * affected.
27563             */
27564            fp->fp_realuid =
27565            fp->fp_effuid = rfp->fp_effuid;
27566            fp->fp_realgid =
27567            fp->fp_effgid = rfp->fp_effgid;
27568            fp->fp_umask = rfp->fp_umask;
27569            return(OK);
27570      }

27572      /* Perform the chdir(name) system call. */
27573      r = change(&fp->fp_workdir, m_in.name, m_in.name_length);
27574      return(r);
27575    }

27577    /*===========================================================================*
27578     *                              do_chroot                                     *
27579     *===========================================================================*/
27580    PUBLIC int do_chroot()
27581    {
27582    /* Perform the chroot(name) system call. */

27584      register int r;

27586      if (!super_user) return(EPERM);        /* only su may chroot() */
27587      r = change(&fp->fp_rootdir, m_in.name, m_in.name_length);
27588      return(r);
27589    }
```

```
27591   /*===========================================================================*
27592    *                              change                                        *
27593    *===========================================================================*/
27594   PRIVATE int change(iip, name_ptr, len)
27595   struct inode **iip;              /* pointer to the inode pointer for the dir */
27596   char *name_ptr;                  /* pointer to the directory name to change to */
27597   int len;                         /* length of the directory name string */
27598   {
27599   /* Do the actual work for chdir() and chroot(). */
27600     struct inode *rip;
27601
27602     /* Try to open the new directory. */
27603     if (fetch_name(name_ptr, len, M3) != OK) return(err_code);
27604     if ( (rip = eat_path(user_path)) == NIL_INODE) return(err_code);
27605     return change_into(iip, rip);
27606   }

27608   /*===========================================================================*
27609    *                              change_into                                   *
27610    *===========================================================================*/
27611   PRIVATE int change_into(iip, rip)
27612   struct inode **iip;              /* pointer to the inode pointer for the dir */
27613   struct inode *rip;               /* this is what the inode has to become */
27614   {
27615     register int r;
27616
27617     /* It must be a directory and also be searchable. */
27618     if ( (rip->i_mode & I_TYPE) != I_DIRECTORY)
27619           r = ENOTDIR;
27620     else
27621           r = forbidden(rip, X_BIT);        /* check if dir is searchable */
27622
27623     /* If error, return inode. */
27624     if (r != OK) {
27625           put_inode(rip);
27626           return(r);
27627     }
27628
27629     /* Everything is OK.  Make the change. */
27630     put_inode(*iip);                 /* release the old directory */
27631     *iip = rip;                      /* acquire the new one */
27632     return(OK);
27633   }

27635   /*===========================================================================*
27636    *                              do_stat                                       *
27637    *===========================================================================*/
27638   PUBLIC int do_stat()
27639   {
27640   /* Perform the stat(name, buf) system call. */
27641
27642     register struct inode *rip;
27643     register int r;
27644
27645     /* Both stat() and fstat() use the same routine to do the real work.  That
27646      * routine expects an inode, so acquire it temporarily.
27647      */
27648     if (fetch_name(m_in.name1, m_in.name1_length, M1) != OK) return(err_code);
27649     if ( (rip = eat_path(user_path)) == NIL_INODE) return(err_code);
27650     r = stat_inode(rip, NIL_FILP, m_in.name2);    /* actually do the work.*/
```

```
27651      put_inode(rip);                    /* release the inode */
27652      return(r);
27653  }

27655  /*===========================================================================*
27656   *                              do_fstat                                     *
27657   *===========================================================================*/
27658  PUBLIC int do_fstat()
27659  {
27660  /* Perform the fstat(fd, buf) system call. */
27661
27662    register struct filp *rfilp;
27663
27664    /* Is the file descriptor valid? */
27665    if ( (rfilp = get_filp(m_in.fd)) == NIL_FILP) return(err_code);
27666
27667    return(stat_inode(rfilp->filp_ino, rfilp, m_in.buffer));
27668  }

27670  /*===========================================================================*
27671   *                              stat_inode                                   *
27672   *===========================================================================*/
27673  PRIVATE int stat_inode(rip, fil_ptr, user_addr)
27674  register struct inode *rip;    /* pointer to inode to stat */
27675  struct filp *fil_ptr;          /* filp pointer, supplied by 'fstat' */
27676  char *user_addr;               /* user space address where stat buf goes */
27677  {
27678  /* Common code for stat and fstat system calls. */
27679
27680    struct stat statbuf;
27681    mode_t mo;
27682    int r, s;
27683
27684    /* Update the atime, ctime, and mtime fields in the inode, if need be. */
27685    if (rip->i_update) update_times(rip);
27686
27687    /* Fill in the statbuf struct. */
27688    mo = rip->i_mode & I_TYPE;
27689
27690    /* true iff special */
27691    s = (mo == I_CHAR_SPECIAL || mo == I_BLOCK_SPECIAL);
27692
27693    statbuf.st_dev = rip->i_dev;
27694    statbuf.st_ino = rip->i_num;
27695    statbuf.st_mode = rip->i_mode;
27696    statbuf.st_nlink = rip->i_nlinks;
27697    statbuf.st_uid = rip->i_uid;
27698    statbuf.st_gid = rip->i_gid;
27699    statbuf.st_rdev = (dev_t) (s ? rip->i_zone[0] : NO_DEV);
27700    statbuf.st_size = rip->i_size;
27701
27702    if (rip->i_pipe == I_PIPE) {
27703        statbuf.st_mode &= ~I_REGULAR;  /* wipe out I_REGULAR bit for pipes */
27704        if (fil_ptr != NIL_FILP && fil_ptr->filp_mode & R_BIT)
27705            statbuf.st_size -= fil_ptr->filp_pos;
27706    }
27707
27708    statbuf.st_atime = rip->i_atime;
27709    statbuf.st_mtime = rip->i_mtime;
27710    statbuf.st_ctime = rip->i_ctime;
```

```
27711
27712      /* Copy the struct to user space. */
27713      r = sys_datacopy(FS_PROC_NR, (vir_bytes) &statbuf,
27714                  who, (vir_bytes) user_addr, (phys_bytes) sizeof(statbuf));
27715      return(r);
27716   }

27718   /*===========================================================================*
27719    *                              do_fstatfs                                   *
27720    *===========================================================================*/
27721   PUBLIC int do_fstatfs()
27722   {
27723      /* Perform the fstatfs(fd, buf) system call. */
27724      struct statfs st;
27725      register struct filp *rfilp;
27726      int r;
27727
27728      /* Is the file descriptor valid? */
27729      if ( (rfilp = get_filp(m_in.fd)) == NIL_FILP) return(err_code);
27730
27731      st.f_bsize = rfilp->filp_ino->i_sp->s_block_size;
27732
27733      r = sys_datacopy(FS_PROC_NR, (vir_bytes) &st,
27734                  who, (vir_bytes) m_in.buffer, (phys_bytes) sizeof(st));
27735
27736       return(r);
27737   }
```

```
+++++++++++++++++++++++++++++++++++++++++++++++++++++++++++++++++++++++++++++++
                              servers/fs/protect.c
+++++++++++++++++++++++++++++++++++++++++++++++++++++++++++++++++++++++++++++++

27800   /* This file deals with protection in the file system.  It contains the code
27801    * for four system calls that relate to protection.
27802    *
27803    * The entry points into this file are
27804    *   do_chmod:  perform the CHMOD system call
27805    *   do_chown:  perform the CHOWN system call
27806    *   do_umask:  perform the UMASK system call
27807    *   do_access: perform the ACCESS system call
27808    *   forbidden: check to see if a given access is allowed on a given inode
27809    */
27810
27811   #include "fs.h"
27812   #include <unistd.h>
27813   #include <minix/callnr.h>
27814   #include "buf.h"
27815   #include "file.h"
27816   #include "fproc.h"
27817   #include "inode.h"
27818   #include "param.h"
27819   #include "super.h"
27820
```

```
27821  /*===========================================================================*
27822   *                              do_chmod                                     *
27823   *===========================================================================*/
27824  PUBLIC int do_chmod()
27825  {
27826  /* Perform the chmod(name, mode) system call. */
27827
27828    register struct inode *rip;
27829    register int r;
27830
27831    /* Temporarily open the file. */
27832    if (fetch_name(m_in.name, m_in.name_length, M3) != OK) return(err_code);
27833    if ( (rip = eat_path(user_path)) == NIL_INODE) return(err_code);
27834
27835    /* Only the owner or the super_user may change the mode of a file.
27836     * No one may change the mode of a file on a read-only file system.
27837     */
27838    if (rip->i_uid != fp->fp_effuid && !super_user)
27839          r = EPERM;
27840    else
27841          r = read_only(rip);
27842
27843    /* If error, return inode. */
27844    if (r != OK)  {
27845          put_inode(rip);
27846          return(r);
27847    }
27848
27849    /* Now make the change. Clear setgid bit if file is not in caller's grp */
27850    rip->i_mode = (rip->i_mode & ~ALL_MODES) | (m_in.mode & ALL_MODES);
27851    if (!super_user && rip->i_gid != fp->fp_effgid)rip->i_mode &= ~I_SET_GID_BIT;
27852    rip->i_update |= CTIME;
27853    rip->i_dirt = DIRTY;
27854
27855    put_inode(rip);
27856    return(OK);
27857  }

27859  /*===========================================================================*
27860   *                              do_chown                                     *
27861   *===========================================================================*/
27862  PUBLIC int do_chown()
27863  {
27864  /* Perform the chown(name, owner, group) system call. */
27865
27866    register struct inode *rip;
27867    register int r;
27868
27869    /* Temporarily open the file. */
27870    if (fetch_name(m_in.name1, m_in.name1_length, M1) != OK) return(err_code);
27871    if ( (rip = eat_path(user_path)) == NIL_INODE) return(err_code);
27872
27873    /* Not permitted to change the owner of a file on a read-only file sys. */
27874    r = read_only(rip);
27875    if (r == OK) {
27876          /* FS is R/W.  Whether call is allowed depends on ownership, etc. */
27877          if (super_user) {
27878                /* The super user can do anything. */
27879                rip->i_uid = m_in.owner;       /* others later */
27880          } else {
```

```
27881                              /* Regular users can only change groups of their own files. */
27882                              if (rip->i_uid != fp->fp_effuid) r = EPERM;
27883                              if (rip->i_uid != m_in.owner) r = EPERM;    /* no giving away */
27884                              if (fp->fp_effgid != m_in.group) r = EPERM;
27885                      }
27886              }
27887      if (r == OK) {
27888              rip->i_gid = m_in.group;
27889              rip->i_mode &= ~(I_SET_UID_BIT | I_SET_GID_BIT);
27890              rip->i_update |= CTIME;
27891              rip->i_dirt = DIRTY;
27892      }
27893
27894      put_inode(rip);
27895      return(r);
27896  }

27898  /*===========================================================================*
27899   *                              do_umask                                      *
27900   *===========================================================================*/
27901  PUBLIC int do_umask()
27902  {
27903  /* Perform the umask(co_mode) system call. */
27904      register mode_t r;
27905
27906      r = ~fp->fp_umask;              /* set 'r' to complement of old mask */
27907      fp->fp_umask = ~(m_in.co_mode & RWX_MODES);
27908      return(r);                      /* return complement of old mask */
27909  }

27911  /*===========================================================================*
27912   *                              do_access                                     *
27913   *===========================================================================*/
27914  PUBLIC int do_access()
27915  {
27916  /* Perform the access(name, mode) system call. */
27917
27918      struct inode *rip;
27919      register int r;
27920
27921      /* First check to see if the mode is correct. */
27922      if ( (m_in.mode & ~(R_OK | W_OK | X_OK)) != 0 && m_in.mode != F_OK)
27923              return(EINVAL);
27924
27925      /* Temporarily open the file whose access is to be checked. */
27926      if (fetch_name(m_in.name, m_in.name_length, M3) != OK) return(err_code);
27927      if ( (rip = eat_path(user_path)) == NIL_INODE) return(err_code);
27928
27929      /* Now check the permissions. */
27930      r = forbidden(rip, (mode_t) m_in.mode);
27931      put_inode(rip);
27932      return(r);
27933  }

27935  /*===========================================================================*
27936   *                              forbidden                                     *
27937   *===========================================================================*/
27938  PUBLIC int forbidden(register struct inode *rip, mode_t access_desired)
27939  {
27940  /* Given a pointer to an inode, 'rip', and the access desired, determine
```

```
27941    * if the access is allowed, and if not why not.  The routine looks up the
27942    * caller's uid in the 'fproc' table.  If access is allowed, OK is returned
27943    * if it is forbidden, EACCES is returned.
27944    */
27945
27946     register struct inode *old_rip = rip;
27947     register struct super_block *sp;
27948     register mode_t bits, perm_bits;
27949     int r, shift, test_uid, test_gid, type;
27950
27951     if (rip->i_mount == I_MOUNT)   /* The inode is mounted on. */
27952          for (sp = &super_block[1]; sp < &super_block[NR_SUPERS]; sp++)
27953                  if (sp->s_imount == rip) {
27954                          rip = get_inode(sp->s_dev, ROOT_INODE);
27955                          break;
27956                  } /* if */
27957
27958     /* Isolate the relevant rwx bits from the mode. */
27959     bits = rip->i_mode;
27960     test_uid = (call_nr == ACCESS ? fp->fp_realuid : fp->fp_effuid);
27961     test_gid = (call_nr == ACCESS ? fp->fp_realgid : fp->fp_effgid);
27962     if (test_uid == SU_UID) {
27963          /* Grant read and write permission.  Grant search permission for
27964           * directories.  Grant execute permission (for non-directories) if
27965           * and only if one of the 'X' bits is set.
27966           */
27967          if ( (bits & I_TYPE) == I_DIRECTORY ||
27968              bits & ((X_BIT << 6) | (X_BIT << 3) | X_BIT))
27969                  perm_bits = R_BIT | W_BIT | X_BIT;
27970          else
27971                  perm_bits = R_BIT | W_BIT;
27972     } else {
27973          if (test_uid == rip->i_uid) shift = 6;          /* owner */
27974          else if (test_gid == rip->i_gid ) shift = 3;    /* group */
27975          else shift = 0;                                 /* other */
27976          perm_bits = (bits >> shift) & (R_BIT | W_BIT | X_BIT);
27977     }
27978
27979     /* If access desired is not a subset of what is allowed, it is refused. */
27980     r = OK;
27981     if ((perm_bits | access_desired) != perm_bits) r = EACCES;
27982
27983     /* Check to see if someone is trying to write on a file system that is
27984      * mounted read-only.
27985      */
27986     type = rip->i_mode & I_TYPE;
27987     if (r == OK)
27988          if (access_desired & W_BIT)
27989                  r = read_only(rip);
27990
27991     if (rip != old_rip) put_inode(rip);
27992
27993     return(r);
27994  }

27996  /*===========================================================================*
27997   *                              read_only                                    *
27998   *===========================================================================*/
27999  PUBLIC int read_only(ip)
28000  struct inode *ip;               /* ptr to inode whose file sys is to be cked */
```

```
28001    {
28002    /* Check to see if the file system on which the inode 'ip' resides is mounted
28003     * read only.  If so, return EROFS, else return OK.
28004     */
28005
28006      register struct super_block *sp;
28007
28008      sp = ip->i_sp;
28009      return(sp->s_rd_only ? EROFS : OK);
28010    }
```

```
++++++++++++++++++++++++++++++++++++++++++++++++++++++++++++++++++++++++++++++++
                              servers/fs/dmap.c
++++++++++++++++++++++++++++++++++++++++++++++++++++++++++++++++++++++++++++++++
```

```
28100    /* This file contains the table with device <-> driver mappings. It also
28101     * contains some routines to dynamically add and/ or remove device drivers
28102     * or change mappings.
28103     */
28104
28105    #include "fs.h"
28106    #include "fproc.h"
28107    #include <string.h>
28108    #include <stdlib.h>
28109    #include <ctype.h>
28110    #include <unistd.h>
28111    #include <minix/com.h>
28112    #include "param.h"
28113
28114    /* Some devices may or may not be there in the next table. */
28115    #define DT(enable, opcl, io, driver, flags) \
28116      { (enable?(opcl):no_dev), (enable?(io):0), \
28117            (enable?(driver):0), (flags) },
28118    #define NC(x) (NR_CTRLRS >= (x))
28119
28120    /* The order of the entries here determines the mapping between major device
28121     * numbers and tasks.  The first entry (major device 0) is not used.  The
28122     * next entry is major device 1, etc.  Character and block devices can be
28123     * intermixed at random.  The ordering determines the device numbers in /dev/.
28124     * Note that FS knows the device number of /dev/ram/ to load the RAM disk.
28125     * Also note that the major device numbers used in /dev/ are NOT the same as
28126     * the process numbers of the device drivers.
28127     */
28128    /*
28129      Driver enabled     Open/Cls  I/O     Driver #      Flags Device  File
28130      --------------     --------  ------  -----------   ----- ------  ----
28131    */
28132    struct dmap dmap[NR_DEVICES];                          /* actual map */
28133    PRIVATE struct dmap init_dmap[] = {
28134      DT(1, no_dev,    0,      0,            0)          /* 0 = not used   */
28135      DT(1, gen_opcl,  gen_io, MEM_PROC_NR,  0)          /* 1 = /dev/mem   */
28136      DT(0, no_dev,    0,      0,            DMAP_MUTABLE) /* 2 = /dev/fd0   */
28137      DT(0, no_dev,    0,      0,            DMAP_MUTABLE) /* 3 = /dev/c0    */
28138      DT(1, tty_opcl,  gen_io, TTY_PROC_NR,  0)          /* 4 = /dev/tty00 */
28139      DT(1, ctty_opcl, ctty_io, TTY_PROC_NR, 0)          /* 5 = /dev/tty   */
28140      DT(0, no_dev,    0,      NONE,         DMAP_MUTABLE) /* 6 = /dev/lp    */
28141      DT(1, no_dev,    0,      0,            DMAP_MUTABLE) /* 7 = /dev/ip    */
28142      DT(0, no_dev,    0,      NONE,         DMAP_MUTABLE) /* 8 = /dev/c1    */
28143      DT(0, 0,         0,      0,            DMAP_MUTABLE) /* 9 = not used   */
28144      DT(0, no_dev,    0,      0,            DMAP_MUTABLE) /*10 = /dev/c2    */
```

```
28145    DT(0, 0,        0,       0,        DMAP_MUTABLE)   /*11 = not used  */
28146    DT(0, no_dev,   0,       NONE,     DMAP_MUTABLE)   /*12 = /dev/c3   */
28147    DT(0, no_dev,   0,       NONE,     DMAP_MUTABLE)   /*13 = /dev/audio */
28148    DT(0, no_dev,   0,       NONE,     DMAP_MUTABLE)   /*14 = /dev/mixer */
28149    DT(1, gen_opcl, gen_io,  LOG_PROC_NR, 0)           /*15 = /dev/klog  */
28150    DT(0, no_dev,   0,       NONE,     DMAP_MUTABLE)   /*16 = /dev/random*/
28151    DT(0, no_dev,   0,       NONE,     DMAP_MUTABLE)   /*17 = /dev/cmos  */
28152  };
28153
28154  /*===========================================================================*
28155   *                              do_devctl                                    *
28156   *===========================================================================*/
28157  PUBLIC int do_devctl()
28158  {
28159    int result;
28160
28161    switch(m_in.ctl_req) {
28162    case DEV_MAP:
28163        /* Try to update device mapping. */
28164        result = map_driver(m_in.dev_nr, m_in.driver_nr, m_in.dev_style);
28165        break;
28166    case DEV_UNMAP:
28167        result = ENOSYS;
28168        break;
28169    default:
28170        result = EINVAL;
28171    }
28172    return(result);
28173  }
28174
28175  /*===========================================================================*
28176   *                              map_driver                                   *
28177   *===========================================================================*/
28178  PUBLIC int map_driver(major, proc_nr, style)
28179  int major;                        /* major number of the device */
28180  int proc_nr;                      /* process number of the driver */
28181  int style;                        /* style of the device */
28182  {
28183  /* Set a new device driver mapping in the dmap table. Given that correct
28184   * arguments are given, this only works if the entry is mutable and the
28185   * current driver is not busy.
28186   * Normal error codes are returned so that this function can be used from
28187   * a system call that tries to dynamically install a new driver.
28188   */
28189    struct dmap *dp;
28190
28191    /* Get pointer to device entry in the dmap table. */
28192    if (major >= NR_DEVICES) return(ENODEV);
28193    dp = &dmap[major];
28194
28195    /* See if updating the entry is allowed. */
28196    if (! (dp->dmap_flags & DMAP_MUTABLE))  return(EPERM);
28197    if (dp->dmap_flags & DMAP_BUSY)  return(EBUSY);
28198
28199    /* Check process number of new driver. */
28200    if (! isokprocnr(proc_nr))  return(EINVAL);
28201
28202    /* Try to update the entry. */
28203    switch (style) {
28204    case STYLE_DEV:       dp->dmap_opcl = gen_opcl;        break;
```

```
28205        case STYLE_TTY:          dp->dmap_opcl = tty_opcl;        break;
28206        case STYLE_CLONE:        dp->dmap_opcl = clone_opcl;      break;
28207        default:                 return(EINVAL);
28208        }
28209        dp->dmap_io = gen_io;
28210        dp->dmap_driver = proc_nr;
28211        return(OK);
28212  }

28214  /*===========================================================================*
28215   *                              build_dmap                                   *
28216   *===========================================================================*/
28217  PUBLIC void build_dmap()
28218  {
28219  /* Initialize the table with all device <-> driver mappings. Then, map
28220   * the boot driver to a controller and update the dmap table to that
28221   * selection. The boot driver and the controller it handles are set at
28222   * the boot monitor.
28223   */
28224        char driver[16];
28225        char *controller = "c##";
28226        int nr, major = -1;
28227        int i,s;
28228        struct dmap *dp;
28229
28230        /* Build table with device <-> driver mappings. */
28231        for (i=0; i<NR_DEVICES; i++) {
28232            dp = &dmap[i];
28233            if (i < sizeof(init_dmap)/sizeof(struct dmap) &&
28234                    init_dmap[i].dmap_opcl != no_dev) {        /* a preset driver */
28235                dp->dmap_opcl = init_dmap[i].dmap_opcl;
28236                dp->dmap_io = init_dmap[i].dmap_io;
28237                dp->dmap_driver = init_dmap[i].dmap_driver;
28238                dp->dmap_flags = init_dmap[i].dmap_flags;
28239            } else {                                        /* no default */
28240                dp->dmap_opcl = no_dev;
28241                dp->dmap_io = 0;
28242                dp->dmap_driver = 0;
28243                dp->dmap_flags = DMAP_MUTABLE;
28244            }
28245        }
28246
28247        /* Get settings of 'controller' and 'driver' at the boot monitor. */
28248        if ((s = env_get_param("label", driver, sizeof(driver))) != OK)
28249            panic(__FILE__,"couldn't get boot monitor parameter 'driver'", s);
28250        if ((s = env_get_param("controller", controller, sizeof(controller))) != OK)
28251            panic(__FILE__,"couldn't get boot monitor parameter 'controller'", s);
28252
28253        /* Determine major number to map driver onto. */
28254        if (controller[0] == 'f' && controller[1] == 'd') {
28255            major = FLOPPY_MAJOR;
28256        }
28257        else if (controller[0] == 'c' && isdigit(controller[1])) {
28258            if ((nr = (unsigned) atoi(&controller[1])) > NR_CTRLRS)
28259                panic(__FILE__,"monitor 'controller' maximum 'c#' is", NR_CTRLRS);
28260            major = CTRLR(nr);
28261        }
28262        else {
28263            panic(__FILE__,"monitor 'controller' syntax is 'c#' of 'fd'", NO_NUM);
28264        }
```

```
28265
28266     /* Now try to set the actual mapping and report to the user. */
28267     if ((s=map_driver(major, DRVR_PROC_NR, STYLE_DEV)) != OK)
28268         panic(__FILE__,"map_driver failed",s);
28269     printf("Boot medium driver: %s driver mapped onto controller %s.\n",
28270         driver, controller);
28271 }
```

```
++++++++++++++++++++++++++++++++++++++++++++++++++++++++++++++++++++++++++++++++
                            servers/fs/device.c
++++++++++++++++++++++++++++++++++++++++++++++++++++++++++++++++++++++++++++++++
```

```
28300     /* When a needed block is not in the cache, it must be fetched from the disk.
28301      * Special character files also require I/O.  The routines for these are here.
28302      *
28303      * The entry points in this file are:
28304      *   dev_open:   FS opens a device
28305      *   dev_close:  FS closes a device
28306      *   dev_io:     FS does a read or write on a device
28307      *   dev_status: FS processes callback request alert
28308      *   gen_opcl:   generic call to a task to perform an open/close
28309      *   gen_io:     generic call to a task to perform an I/O operation
28310      *   no_dev:     open/close processing for devices that don't exist
28311      *   tty_opcl:   perform tty-specific processing for open/close
28312      *   ctty_opcl:  perform controlling-tty-specific processing for open/close
28313      *   ctty_io:    perform controlling-tty-specific processing for I/O
28314      *   do_ioctl:   perform the IOCTL system call
28315      *   do_setsid:  perform the SETSID system call (FS side)
28316      */
28317
28318     #include "fs.h"
28319     #include <fcntl.h>
28320     #include <minix/callnr.h>
28321     #include <minix/com.h>
28322     #include "file.h"
28323     #include "fproc.h"
28324     #include "inode.h"
28325     #include "param.h"
28326
28327     #define ELEMENTS(a) (sizeof(a)/sizeof((a)[0]))
28328
28329     extern int dmap_size;
28330
28331     /*===========================================================================*
28332      *                              dev_open                                     *
28333      *===========================================================================*/
28334     PUBLIC int dev_open(dev, proc, flags)
28335     dev_t dev;                      /* device to open */
28336     int proc;                       /* process to open for */
28337     int flags;                      /* mode bits and flags */
28338     {
28339       int major, r;
28340       struct dmap *dp;
28341
28342       /* Determine the major device number call the device class specific
28343        * open/close routine.  (This is the only routine that must check the
28344        * device number for being in range.  All others can trust this check.)
```

```
28345       */
28346     major = (dev >> MAJOR) & BYTE;
28347     if (major >= NR_DEVICES) major = 0;
28348     dp = &dmap[major];
28349     r = (*dp->dmap_opcl)(DEV_OPEN, dev, proc, flags);
28350     if (r == SUSPEND) panic(__FILE__,"suspend on open from", dp->dmap_driver);
28351     return(r);
28352   }

28354   /*===========================================================================*
28355    *                              dev_close                                    *
28356    *===========================================================================*/
28357   PUBLIC void dev_close(dev)
28358   dev_t dev;                    /* device to close */
28359   {
28360     (void) (*dmap[(dev >> MAJOR) & BYTE].dmap_opcl)(DEV_CLOSE, dev, 0, 0);
28361   }

28363   /*===========================================================================*
28364    *                              dev_status                                   *
28365    *===========================================================================*/
28366   PUBLIC void dev_status(message *m)
28367   {
28368           message st;
28369           int d, get_more = 1;
28370
28371           for(d = 0; d < NR_DEVICES; d++)
28372                   if (dmap[d].dmap_driver == m->m_source)
28373                           break;
28374
28375           if (d >= NR_DEVICES)
28376                   return;
28377
28378           do {
28379                   int r;
28380                   st.m_type = DEV_STATUS;
28381                   if ((r=sendrec(m->m_source, &st)) != OK)
28382                           panic(__FILE__,"couldn't sendrec for DEV_STATUS", r);
28383
28384                   switch(st.m_type) {
28385                       case DEV_REVIVE:
28386                               revive(st.REP_PROC_NR, st.REP_STATUS);
28387                               break;
28388                       case DEV_IO_READY:
28389                               select_notified(d, st.DEV_MINOR, st.DEV_SEL_OPS);
28390                               break;
28391                       default:
28392                        printf("FS: unrecognized rep %d to DEV_STATUS\n",st.m_type);
28393                               /* Fall through. */
28394                       case DEV_NO_STATUS:
28395                               get_more = 0;
28396                               break;
28397                   }
28398           } while(get_more);
28399
28400           return;
28401   }
```

```
28403   /*===========================================================================*
28404    *                              dev_io                                       *
28405    *===========================================================================*/
28406   PUBLIC int dev_io(op, dev, proc, buf, pos, bytes, flags)
28407   int op;                          /* DEV_READ, DEV_WRITE, DEV_IOCTL, etc. */
28408   dev_t dev;                       /* major-minor device number */
28409   int proc;                        /* in whose address space is buf? */
28410   void *buf;                       /* virtual address of the buffer */
28411   off_t pos;                       /* byte position */
28412   int bytes;                       /* how many bytes to transfer */
28413   int flags;                       /* special flags, like O_NONBLOCK */
28414   {
28415   /* Read or write from a device.  The parameter 'dev' tells which one. */
28416     struct dmap *dp;
28417     message dev_mess;
28418
28419     /* Determine task dmap. */
28420     dp = &dmap[(dev >> MAJOR) & BYTE];
28421
28422     /* Set up the message passed to task. */
28423     dev_mess.m_type    = op;
28424     dev_mess.DEVICE    = (dev >> MINOR) & BYTE;
28425     dev_mess.POSITION  = pos;
28426     dev_mess.PROC_NR   = proc;
28427     dev_mess.ADDRESS   = buf;
28428     dev_mess.COUNT     = bytes;
28429     dev_mess.TTY_FLAGS = flags;
28430
28431     /* Call the task. */
28432     (*dp->dmap_io)(dp->dmap_driver, &dev_mess);
28433
28434     /* Task has completed.  See if call completed. */
28435     if (dev_mess.REP_STATUS == SUSPEND) {
28436           if (flags & O_NONBLOCK) {
28437                   /* Not supposed to block. */
28438                   dev_mess.m_type = CANCEL;
28439                   dev_mess.PROC_NR = proc;
28440                   dev_mess.DEVICE = (dev >> MINOR) & BYTE;
28441                   (*dp->dmap_io)(dp->dmap_driver, &dev_mess);
28442                   if (dev_mess.REP_STATUS == EINTR) dev_mess.REP_STATUS = EAGAIN;
28443           } else {
28444                   /* Suspend user. */
28445                   suspend(dp->dmap_driver);
28446                   return(SUSPEND);
28447           }
28448     }
28449     return(dev_mess.REP_STATUS);
28450   }

28452   /*===========================================================================*
28453    *                              gen_opcl                                     *
28454    *===========================================================================*/
28455   PUBLIC int gen_opcl(op, dev, proc, flags)
28456   int op;                          /* operation, DEV_OPEN or DEV_CLOSE */
28457   dev_t dev;                       /* device to open or close */
28458   int proc;                        /* process to open/close for */
28459   int flags;                       /* mode bits and flags */
28460   {
28461   /* Called from the dmap struct in table.c on opens & closes of special files.*/
28462     struct dmap *dp;
```

```
28463        message dev_mess;
28464
28465        /* Determine task dmap. */
28466        dp = &dmap[(dev >> MAJOR) & BYTE];
28467
28468        dev_mess.m_type   = op;
28469        dev_mess.DEVICE   = (dev >> MINOR) & BYTE;
28470        dev_mess.PROC_NR  = proc;
28471        dev_mess.COUNT    = flags;
28472
28473        /* Call the task. */
28474        (*dp->dmap_io)(dp->dmap_driver, &dev_mess);
28475
28476        return(dev_mess.REP_STATUS);
28477  }
28478
28479  /*===========================================================================*
28480   *                              tty_opcl                                      *
28481   *===========================================================================*/
28482  PUBLIC int tty_opcl(op, dev, proc, flags)
28483  int op;                        /* operation, DEV_OPEN or DEV_CLOSE */
28484  dev_t dev;                     /* device to open or close */
28485  int proc;                      /* process to open/close for */
28486  int flags;                     /* mode bits and flags */
28487  {
28488  /* This procedure is called from the dmap struct on tty open/close. */
28489
28490        int r;
28491        register struct fproc *rfp;
28492
28493        /* Add O_NOCTTY to the flags if this process is not a session leader, or
28494         * if it already has a controlling tty, or if it is someone elses
28495         * controlling tty.
28496         */
28497        if (!fp->fp_sesldr || fp->fp_tty != 0) {
28498              flags |= O_NOCTTY;
28499        } else {
28500              for (rfp = &fproc[0]; rfp < &fproc[NR_PROCS]; rfp++) {
28501                    if (rfp->fp_tty == dev) flags |= O_NOCTTY;
28502              }
28503        }
28504
28505        r = gen_opcl(op, dev, proc, flags);
28506
28507        /* Did this call make the tty the controlling tty? */
28508        if (r == 1) {
28509              fp->fp_tty = dev;
28510              r = OK;
28511        }
28512        return(r);
28513  }
28514
28515  /*===========================================================================*
28516   *                              ctty_opcl                                     *
28517   *===========================================================================*/
28518  PUBLIC int ctty_opcl(op, dev, proc, flags)
28519  int op;                        /* operation, DEV_OPEN or DEV_CLOSE */
28520  dev_t dev;                     /* device to open or close */
28521  int proc;                      /* process to open/close for */
28522  int flags;                     /* mode bits and flags */
```

```
28523  {
28524  /* This procedure is called from the dmap struct in table.c on opening/closing
28525   * /dev/tty, the magic device that translates to the controlling tty.
28526   */
28527
28528    return(fp->fp_tty == 0 ? ENXIO : OK);
28529  }

28531  /*===========================================================================*
28532   *                              do_setsid                                    *
28533   *===========================================================================*/
28534  PUBLIC int do_setsid()
28535  {
28536  /* Perform the FS side of the SETSID call, i.e. get rid of the controlling
28537   * terminal of a process, and make the process a session leader.
28538   */
28539    register struct fproc *rfp;
28540
28541    /* Only MM may do the SETSID call directly. */
28542    if (who != PM_PROC_NR) return(ENOSYS);
28543
28544    /* Make the process a session leader with no controlling tty. */
28545    rfp = &fproc[m_in.slot1];
28546    rfp->fp_sesldr = TRUE;
28547    rfp->fp_tty = 0;
28548    return(OK);
28549  }

28551  /*===========================================================================*
28552   *                              do_ioctl                                     *
28553   *===========================================================================*/
28554  PUBLIC int do_ioctl()
28555  {
28556  /* Perform the ioctl(ls_fd, request, argx) system call (uses m2 fmt). */
28557
28558    struct filp *f;
28559    register struct inode *rip;
28560    dev_t dev;
28561
28562    if ( (f = get_filp(m_in.ls_fd)) == NIL_FILP) return(err_code);
28563    rip = f->filp_ino;              /* get inode pointer */
28564    if ( (rip->i_mode & I_TYPE) != I_CHAR_SPECIAL
28565          && (rip->i_mode & I_TYPE) != I_BLOCK_SPECIAL) return(ENOTTY);
28566    dev = (dev_t) rip->i_zone[0];
28567
28568    return(dev_io(DEV_IOCTL, dev, who, m_in.ADDRESS, 0L,
28569          m_in.REQUEST, f->filp_flags));
28570  }

28572  /*===========================================================================*
28573   *                              gen_io                                       *
28574   *===========================================================================*/
28575  PUBLIC void gen_io(task_nr, mess_ptr)
28576  int task_nr;                    /* which task to call */
28577  message *mess_ptr;              /* pointer to message for task */
28578  {
28579  /* All file system I/O ultimately comes down to I/O on major/minor device
28580   * pairs.  These lead to calls on the following routines via the dmap table.
28581   */
28582
```

```
28583          int r, proc_nr;
28584          message local_m;
28585
28586          proc_nr = mess_ptr->PROC_NR;
28587          if (! isokprocnr(proc_nr)) {
28588              printf("FS: warning, got illegal process number (%d) from %d\n",
28589                  mess_ptr->PROC_NR, mess_ptr->m_source);
28590              return;
28591          }
28592
28593          while ((r = sendrec(task_nr, mess_ptr)) == ELOCKED) {
28594                  /* sendrec() failed to avoid deadlock. The task 'task_nr' is
28595                   * trying to send a REVIVE message for an earlier request.
28596                   * Handle it and go try again.
28597                   */
28598                  if ((r = receive(task_nr, &local_m)) != OK) {
28599                          break;
28600                  }
28601
28602                  /* If we're trying to send a cancel message to a task which has just
28603                   * sent a completion reply, ignore the reply and abort the cancel
28604                   * request. The caller will do the revive for the process.
28605                   */
28606                  if (mess_ptr->m_type == CANCEL && local_m.REP_PROC_NR == proc_nr) {
28607                          return;
28608                  }
28609
28610                  /* Otherwise it should be a REVIVE. */
28611                  if (local_m.m_type != REVIVE) {
28612                          printf(
28613                          "fs: strange device reply from %d, type = %d, proc = %d (1)\n",
28614                                  local_m.m_source,
28615                                  local_m.m_type, local_m.REP_PROC_NR);
28616                          continue;
28617                  }
28618
28619                  revive(local_m.REP_PROC_NR, local_m.REP_STATUS);
28620          }
28621
28622          /* The message received may be a reply to this call, or a REVIVE for some
28623           * other process.
28624           */
28625          for (;;) {
28626                  if (r != OK) {
28627                          if (r == EDEADDST) return;        /* give up */
28628                          else panic(__FILE__,"call_task: can't send/receive", r);
28629                  }
28630
28631                  /* Did the process we did the sendrec() for get a result? */
28632                  if (mess_ptr->REP_PROC_NR == proc_nr) {
28633                          break;
28634                  } else if (mess_ptr->m_type == REVIVE) {
28635                          /* Otherwise it should be a REVIVE. */
28636                          revive(mess_ptr->REP_PROC_NR, mess_ptr->REP_STATUS);
28637                  } else {
28638                          printf(
28639                          "fs: strange device reply from %d, type = %d, proc = %d (2)\n",
28640                                  mess_ptr->m_source,
28641                                  mess_ptr->m_type, mess_ptr->REP_PROC_NR);
28642                          return;
```

```
28643            }
28644
28645            r = receive(task_nr, mess_ptr);
28646     }
28647 }

28649 /*===========================================================================*
28650  *                              ctty_io                                      *
28651  *===========================================================================*/
28652 PUBLIC void ctty_io(task_nr, mess_ptr)
28653 int task_nr;                        /* not used - for compatibility with dmap_t */
28654 message *mess_ptr;                  /* pointer to message for task */
28655 {
28656 /* This routine is only called for one device, namely /dev/tty.  Its job
28657  * is to change the message to use the controlling terminal, instead of the
28658  * major/minor pair for /dev/tty itself.
28659  */
28660
28661   struct dmap *dp;
28662
28663   if (fp->fp_tty == 0) {
28664        /* No controlling tty present anymore, return an I/O error. */
28665        mess_ptr->REP_STATUS = EIO;
28666   } else {
28667        /* Substitute the controlling terminal device. */
28668        dp = &dmap[(fp->fp_tty >> MAJOR) & BYTE];
28669        mess_ptr->DEVICE = (fp->fp_tty >> MINOR) & BYTE;
28670        (*dp->dmap_io)(dp->dmap_driver, mess_ptr);
28671   }
28672 }

28674 /*===========================================================================*
28675  *                              no_dev                                       *
28676  *===========================================================================*/
28677 PUBLIC int no_dev(op, dev, proc, flags)
28678 int op;                             /* operation, DEV_OPEN or DEV_CLOSE */
28679 dev_t dev;                          /* device to open or close */
28680 int proc;                           /* process to open/close for */
28681 int flags;                          /* mode bits and flags */
28682 {
28683 /* Called when opening a nonexistent device. */
28684
28685   return(ENODEV);
28686 }

28688 /*===========================================================================*
28689  *                              clone_opcl                                   *
28690  *===========================================================================*/
28691 PUBLIC int clone_opcl(op, dev, proc, flags)
28692 int op;                             /* operation, DEV_OPEN or DEV_CLOSE */
28693 dev_t dev;                          /* device to open or close */
28694 int proc;                           /* process to open/close for */
28695 int flags;                          /* mode bits and flags */
28696 {
28697 /* Some devices need special processing upon open.  Such a device is "cloned",
28698  * i.e. on a succesful open it is replaced by a new device with a new unique
28699  * minor device number.  This new device number identifies a new object (such
28700  * as a new network connection) that has been allocated within a task.
28701  */
28702   struct dmap *dp;
```

```
28703      int minor;
28704      message dev_mess;
28705
28706      /* Determine task dmap. */
28707      dp = &dmap[(dev >> MAJOR) & BYTE];
28708      minor = (dev >> MINOR) & BYTE;
28709
28710      dev_mess.m_type   = op;
28711      dev_mess.DEVICE   = minor;
28712      dev_mess.PROC_NR  = proc;
28713      dev_mess.COUNT    = flags;
28714
28715      /* Call the task. */
28716      (*dp->dmap_io)(dp->dmap_driver, &dev_mess);
28717
28718      if (op == DEV_OPEN && dev_mess.REP_STATUS >= 0) {
28719          if (dev_mess.REP_STATUS != minor) {
28720              /* A new minor device number has been returned.  Create a
28721               * temporary device file to hold it.
28722               */
28723              struct inode *ip;
28724
28725              /* Device number of the new device. */
28726              dev = (dev & ~(BYTE << MINOR)) | (dev_mess.REP_STATUS << MINOR);
28727
28728              ip = alloc_inode(root_dev, ALL_MODES | I_CHAR_SPECIAL);
28729              if (ip == NIL_INODE) {
28730                  /* Oops, that didn't work.  Undo open. */
28731                  (void) clone_opcl(DEV_CLOSE, dev, proc, 0);
28732                  return(err_code);
28733              }
28734              ip->i_zone[0] = dev;
28735
28736              put_inode(fp->fp_filp[m_in.fd]->filp_ino);
28737              fp->fp_filp[m_in.fd]->filp_ino = ip;
28738          }
28739          dev_mess.REP_STATUS = OK;
28740      }
28741      return(dev_mess.REP_STATUS);
28742  }
```

```
+++++++++++++++++++++++++++++++++++++++++++++++++++++++++++++++++++++++++++++
                           servers/fs/time.c
+++++++++++++++++++++++++++++++++++++++++++++++++++++++++++++++++++++++++++++

28800  /* This file takes care of those system calls that deal with time.
28801   *
28802   * The entry points into this file are
28803   *   do_utime:        perform the UTIME system call
28804   *   do_stime:        PM informs FS about STIME system call
28805   */
28806
28807  #include "fs.h"
28808  #include <minix/callnr.h>
28809  #include <minix/com.h>
```

```
28810  #include "file.h"
28811  #include "fproc.h"
28812  #include "inode.h"
28813  #include "param.h"
28814
28815  /*===========================================================================*
28816   *                              do_utime                                      *
28817   *===========================================================================*/
28818  PUBLIC int do_utime()
28819  {
28820  /* Perform the utime(name, timep) system call. */
28821
28822    register struct inode *rip;
28823    register int len, r;
28824
28825    /* Adjust for case of 'timep' being NULL;
28826     * utime_strlen then holds the actual size: strlen(name)+1.
28827     */
28828    len = m_in.utime_length;
28829    if (len == 0) len = m_in.utime_strlen;
28830
28831    /* Temporarily open the file. */
28832    if (fetch_name(m_in.utime_file, len, M1) != OK) return(err_code);
28833    if ( (rip = eat_path(user_path)) == NIL_INODE) return(err_code);
28834
28835    /* Only the owner of a file or the super_user can change its time. */
28836    r = OK;
28837    if (rip->i_uid != fp->fp_effuid && !super_user) r = EPERM;
28838    if (m_in.utime_length == 0 && r != OK) r = forbidden(rip, W_BIT);
28839    if (read_only(rip) != OK) r = EROFS;  /* not even su can touch if R/O */
28840    if (r == OK) {
28841        if (m_in.utime_length == 0) {
28842                rip->i_atime = clock_time();
28843                rip->i_mtime = rip->i_atime;
28844        } else {
28845                rip->i_atime = m_in.utime_actime;
28846                rip->i_mtime = m_in.utime_modtime;
28847        }
28848        rip->i_update = CTIME;  /* discard any stale ATIME and MTIME flags */
28849        rip->i_dirt = DIRTY;
28850    }
28851
28852    put_inode(rip);
28853    return(r);
28854  }
28855
28856  /*===========================================================================*
28857   *                              do_stime                                      *
28858   *===========================================================================*/
28859  PUBLIC int do_stime()
28860  {
28861  /* Perform the stime(tp) system call. */
28862    boottime = (long) m_in.pm_stime;
28863    return(OK);
28864  }
```

APPENDIX C

INDEX TO FILES

C

INDEX TO FILES

INDEX

ABOUT THE AUTHORS

Andrew S. Tanenbaum has an S.B. degree from M.I.T. and a Ph.D. from the University of California at Berkeley. He is currently a Professor of Computer Science at the Vrije Universiteit in Amsterdam, The Netherlands, where he heads the Computer Systems Group. Until stepping down in Jan. 2005, for 12 years he had been Dean of the Advanced School for Computing and Imaging, an inter-university graduate school doing research on advanced parallel, distributed, and imaging systems.

In the past, he has done research on compilers, operating systems, networking, and local-area distributed systems. His current research focuses primarily on computer security, especially in operating systems, networks, and large wide-area distributed systems. Together, all these research projects have led to over 100 refereed papers in journals and conference proceedings and five books.

Prof. Tanenbaum has also produced a considerable volume of software. He was the principal architect of the Amsterdam Compiler Kit, a widely-used toolkit for writing portable compilers, as well as of MINIX, a small UNIX clone. This system provided the inspiration and base on which Linux was developed. Together with his Ph.D. students and programmers, he helped design the Amoeba distributed operating system, a high-performance microkernel-based local-area distributed operating system. After that he was one of the designers of Globe, a wide-area distributed system intended to handle a billion users. All of this software is now available for free via the Internet.

His Ph.D. students have gone on to greater glory after getting their degrees. He is very proud of them. In this respect he resembles a mother hen.

Prof. Tanenbaum is a Fellow of the ACM, a Fellow of the the IEEE, and a member of the Royal Netherlands Academy of Arts and Sciences. He is also winner of the 1994 ACM Karl V. Karlstrom Outstanding Educator Award, winner of the 1997 ACM/SIGCSE Award for Outstanding Contributions to Computer Science Education, and winner of the 2002 Texty award for excellence in textbooks. In 2004 he was named as one of the five new Academy Professors by the Royal Academy. His home page on the World Wide Web can be found at URL *http://www.cs.vu.nl/~ast/* .

Albert S. Woodhull has an S.B. degree from M.I.T. and a Ph.D. from the University of Washington. He entered M.I.T. intending to become an electrical engineer, but he emerged as a biologist. He considers himself a scientist with an appreciation of engineering. For more than 20 years he was a faculty member in the School of Natural Science of Hampshire College in Amherst, Massachusetts. He has been a visiting faculty member at several other colleges and universities. As a biologist using electronic instrumentation, he started working with microcomputers when they became readily available. His instrumentation courses for science students evolved into courses in computer interfacing and real-time programming.

Dr. Woodhull has always had strong interests in teaching and in the role of science and technology in development. Before entering graduate school he taught high school science for two years in Nigeria. He also spent several sabbaticals teaching computer science in Nicaragua, at the Universidad Nacional de Ingenieria and the Universidad Nacional Autonoma de Nicaragua

He is interested in computers as electronic systems, and in interactions of computers with other electronic systems. He particularly enjoys teaching in the areas of computer architecture, assembly language programming, operating systems, and computer communications. He has worked as a consultant in the development of electronic instrumentation and related software, and as a computer system administrator.

He has many nonacademic interests, including various outdoor sports, amateur radio, and reading. He enjoys travelling and trying to make himself understood in languages other than his native English. He is a user and advocate of MINIX. He operates a Web server that runs MINIX and provides support for MINIX users. His personal home page is located there. You can find it at URL *http://minix1.hampshire.edu/asw/* .

Modern Operating Systems, 2nd edition

This comprehensive text covers the principles of modern operating systems in great detail and illustrates them with numerous real world examples. The first six chapters cover the basic concepts, starting with an introduction to the subject, then moving on to processes and threads, deadlocks, memory management, input/output, and file systems. The next six chapters cover advanced material, starting with multimedia operating systems. Other topics covered at length include multiple processor systems and security. Then come two long examples: first UNIX/Linux, then Windows 2000. After that comes a unique chapter on how to design an operating system, based on the author's long experience in the field.

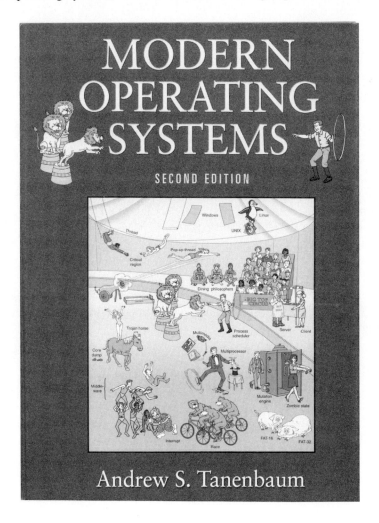

Computer Networks, 4th edition

This widely read classic, now in its fourth edition, provides the ideal introduction to today's and tomorrow's networks. It explains in detail how modern networks are structured. Starting with the physical layer and working up to the application layer, the book covers a vast number of important topics, including wireless communication, fiber optics, data link protocols, Ethernet, routing algorithms, network performance, security, DNS, electronic mail, The World Wide Web, Internet radio, voice over IP, and video on demand. The book has especially thorough coverage of TCP/IP and the Internet.

BY ANDREW S. TANENBAUM AND MAARTEN VAN STEEN

Distributed Systems Principles and Paradigms
Distributed systems are increasingly common nowadays, and this book covers both the principles and paradigms of modern distributed systems. In the first part, it covers the principles of communication, processes, naming, synchronization, consistency and replication, fault tolerance, and security in detail. Then in the second part, it goes into different paradigms used to build distributed systems, including object-based systems, distributed file systems, document-based systems, and coordination-based systems.

ABOUT THE MINIX 3 CD

SYSTEM REQUIREMENTS

Below is a list of Minimum System Requirements to install the software supplied on this CD.

HARDWARE

MINIX 3 OS requires the following hardware:

- PC with a Pentium or compatible processor
- 16 Mb or more of RAM
- 200 Mb of free disk space
- IDE CD-ROM driver
- IDE hard disk

NOT SUPPORTED: Serial ATA, USB, and SCSI disks are not supported. For alternative configurations, visit http://www.minix3.org

SOFTWARE

MINIX 3 OS is an operating system. If you wish to retain your existing operating system and data (recommended) and create a dual-boot machine, you will need to partition your hard drive. You may use one of the following:

- Partition Magic (http://www.powerquest.com/partitionmagic) or
- The Partition Resizer (http://www.zeleps.com) or
- Follow the instructions at http://www.minix3.org/partitions.html

INSTALLATION

Installation can be completed without a live internet connection, but some advanced documentation is only available online at http://www.minix3.org. Complete installation instructions are supplied on the CD in Adobe Acrobat PDF format.

PRODUCT SUPPORT

For further technical information about the MINIX software on this CD, visit the official MINIX website at http://www.minix3.org